KODANSHA
ENCYCLOPEDIA OF
JAPAN

Distributors
JAPAN: KODANSHA LTD., Tokyo.
OVERSEAS: KODANSHA INTERNATIONAL LTD., Tokyo.
  U.S.A., Mexico, Central America, and South America: KODANSHA INTERNATIONAL/USA LTD.
    through HARPER & ROW, PUBLISHERS, INC., New York.
  Canada: FITZHENRY & WHITESIDE LTD., Ontario.
  U.K., Europe, the Middle East, and Africa: INTERNATIONAL BOOK DISTRIBUTORS LTD.,
    Hemel Hempstead, Herts., England.
  Australia and New Zealand: HARPER & ROW (AUSTRALASIA) PTY. LTD., Artarmon, N.S.W.
  Asia: TOPPAN COMPANY (S) PTE. LTD., Singapore.

Published by Kodansha Ltd., 12-21, Otowa 2-chome, Bunkyo-ku, Tokyo 112 and Kodansha
International/USA Ltd., 10 East 53rd Street, New York, New York 10022.
Copyright © 1983 by Kodansha Ltd.
All rights reserved.
Printed in Japan.
First edition, 1983.

LCC 83-80778
ISBN 0-87011-627-4 (Volume 7)
ISBN 0-87011-620-7 (Set)
ISBN 4-06-144537-5 (0) (in Japan)

Library of Congress Cataloging in Publication Data
Main entry under title:

Kodansha encyclopedia of Japan.

  Includes index.
  1. Japan—Dictionaries and encyclopedias. I. Title:
Encyclopedia of Japan.
DS805.K633 1983   952'.003'21   83-80778
ISBN 0-87011-620-7 (U.S.)

KODANSHA
ENCYCLOPEDIA OF
JAPAN

7

KODANSHA

S

sake

A brewed alcoholic beverage made from fermented rice, known also in English as "sake." The Japanese term is also applied generically to all alcoholic beverages. The formal name for refined *sake*, the kind most commonly drunk in Japan, is *seishu*; it is often referred to as *nihonshu* (Japanese *sake*) to distinguish it from Western liquors (*yōshu*). The other alcoholic beverage traditionally produced in Japan is a distilled spirit called *shōchū*. Malted rice *(kōji)* is used as the fermenting agent in both refined *sake* and *shōchū*.

Refined Sake—— There are about 3,000 manufacturers of refined *sake* in Japan. The chief producing districts are Kyōto and Hyōgo prefectures. National brands are also manufactured in other prefectures, including Akita and Hiroshima, but the number of such brands is small. *Jizake* (local brands) are numerous and produced across the country. In recent years, the rising price of rice has reduced the profit margins of *sake* producers.

In order to manufacture *sake*, a yeast is first made from rice, malted rice, and water and placed in a vat. Additional amounts of these three ingredients are then added to the yeast, and the mixture is left to ferment for 20 days. The mixture is pressed, filtrated, and blended, and then pasteurized, bottled, and stored. The drained solids of the mixture, called *sakekasu* (dregs), are used in cooking and the preparation of *tsukemono* (PICKLES).

The alcohol content of crude *sake* is about 40 proof, and of *sake* on the market, about 32 proof. A good quality *sake* will have a subtle blend of the so-called five flavors (sweetness, sourness, pungency, bitterness, and astringency) and a mellow fragrance. Old *sake* will have a mellow and soft taste. However, *sake* is rarely stored for more than a year. *Sake* is classified by a national inspection agency as special, first, and second grade. There are also carbonated, sweet, dry, hard, and aged types of *sake*. Unrefined *sake* is called *nigori-zake*.

Sake is usually served before a meal and may also be used in cooking (a sweet *sake*, *mirin*, is made especially for cooking). The traditional and most common way of drinking *sake* is to heat it to 50°C (122°F) in a *tokkuri* (a small, earthenware bottle) and then pour it into a *sakazuki* (small cup). A special type of *sake* is brewed for drinking cold or on ice. It is still a popular Japanese custom to drink *sake* while appreciating the beauty of nature, especially the moon, flowers, and newly fallen snow.

The manufacture of *sake* with rice as its main ingredient is ancient in origin, coming some time after the introduction of wet rice cultivation to Japan around 300 BC. The first written record of *sake* in Japan dates to the 3rd century AD, and the first reference to the manufacture of *sake*, to the 8th century. In ancient Japan, *sake* was manufactured primarily by the imperial court or by large temples and shrines. The upper classes would drink their *sake* after it had been filtered through a cloth, but the general public would drink unfiltered *sake*. At that time, *sake* was closely associated with religious agricultural ceremonies.

From the end of the 12th century the general populace also began to manufacture *sake*. It was traded as a commodity sometime after, and began to be taxed in the 14th century. By the beginning of the 16th century, the present process of manufacturing *sake* had nearly been perfected. Nada (in Hyōgo Prefecture), the chief producing district, enjoyed its greatest prosperity in the beginning of the 19th century. Although laws against drinking or manufacturing *sake* were promulgated from time to time, none of them had much effect.

Shōchū—— *Shōchū* is classified into two types, A *(kō)* and B *(otsu)*. The B-type is the standard *shōchū* and is generally made from grain. Principal production centers are Kagoshima and Miyazaki prefectures in Kyūshū. The *shōchū* of Okinawa Prefecture is called *awamori* (millet brandy). Until the 1960s, the demand for *shōchū* was concentrated in the Kyūshū area, but since then consumption has spread throughout the country.

A-type *shōchū* uses molasses as its main ingredient, while B-type uses rice, sweet potatoes, barley, rye, buckwheat, corn, or raw sugar. Both use malted rice for fermentation. A-type *shōchū* is fermented and then distilled using a patent still. B-type is fermented and then distilled with a pot still. The former has a plain taste, while the taste of the latter depends on its basic ingredient. The alcohol content varies from 40 to 80 proof, depending on the type and where it is produced; most are about 40 to 50 proof. *Shōchū* is generally drunk with hot or cold water, or it may be heated and drunk undiluted. *Shōchū* did not originate in Japan, but is assumed to have been introduced from the Ryūkyū Islands (present-day Okinawa). *Awamori* appeared in the Ryūkyūs in the 15th century, and the first historical mention of *shōchū* in Japan was in the 16th century. At present *shōchū* is used only as an alcoholic drink, but through the end of the Edo period (1600–1868) it had an important medical use as a disinfectant.

Current Drinking Patterns—— Until about 1950, refined *sake* was the primary alcoholic beverage of the Japanese. Consumption of beer and whiskey grew rapidly during the 1960s, and Western wines became popular in the 1970s. Changing tastes can be attributed to increases in disposable income and Westernization, especially of eating habits. See also BREWING; FOOD AND EATING.

📖——Katō Benzaburō, *Nihon no sake no rekishi* (1977). Sakaguchi Kin'ichirō, *Nihon no sake* (1964). Sugama Seinosuke, *Minaosareru daisan no sake* (1975). *Miyano Nobuyuki*

sake → salmons

Sakhalin

An elongated island north of Hokkaidō, separated from the continent by a narrow strait; traditionally called Karafuto in Japanese. Originally inhabited by AINU and Gilyaks (a Paleosiberian people), Sakhalin was attacked by the Mongols in the 13th century and came under Chinese suzerainty in the 15th century. Early Chinese associations with the island led the 19th-century cartographer TAKAHASHI KAGEYASU to suggest that its Japanese name derived from *karabito* (Chinese person).

The Japanese probably knew about Sakhalin from the 13th century, but the first documented contact occurred in 1635 when the *daimyō* of Matsumae (in what is now Hokkaidō) is said to have sent a surveying mission there. The Dutch navigator de Vries sighted the island in 1643, and the Cossack Poyarkov learned of *Saghalien ura anga hata* (land at the mouth of the Amur River) from Tungusic natives on the lower Amur in 1644. Both Russians and Japanese visited Sakhalin periodically during the 18th century, and the daimyō of Matsumae established a trading post on the southern tip in 1790. Between 1787 and 1805, English (Broughton), French (Jean François La Pérouse) and Russian (Adam J. von Krusenstern) explorers charted Sakhalin's coasts, and the shogunal surveyor MAMIYA RINZŌ discovered in 1809 that it was an island. Mamiya's clarification of Sakhalin's relationship to the Amur River estuary, publicized in Europe by the Bavarian naturalist Philipp Franz von SIEBOLD and confirmed by a tsarist naval expedition in 1849, contributed to Russia's growing appreciation of the area's strategic importance.

In 1855, the Treaty of Shimoda provided for Sakhalin's joint occupation by Russia and Japan, a formula which led to escalating friction during the 1860s and early 1870s when both countries sent settlers and garrisons to the island. Attempts by the Tokugawa shogunate and, after 1868, by the Meiji government to partition or buy the island failed. In 1874 Japan's leaders were persuaded by KURODA KIYOTAKA, deputy director of the Hokkaidō Colonization Office (KAITAKUSHI), to give up Sakhalin in order to consolidate the northern frontier and avoid a confrontation with Russia. Accordingly, in the Treaty of St. Petersburg signed 7 May 1875, Japan exchanged its rights in Sakhalin for the central and northern Kuril Islands. Japan retained important commercial and fishing privileges.

In the final stages of the RUSSO-JAPANESE WAR (1904–05), Japanese forces seized all of Sakhalin, but the Treaty of PORTSMOUTH of 5 September 1905 entitled Japan to keep only that portion south of the 50th parallel, corresponding to less than half of the island. Called Karafuto (in this case, southern Sakhalin), Japan's new colony was valued at first for its rich fisheries. Thereafter, capital investment promoted the development of coal and timber industries, in which Mitsubishi Mining and Ōji Paper companies played prominent roles. During the 1930s, Karafuto supplied 70 percent of Japan's pulp. In 1942, with a population of 448,000 Japanese settlers and 80,000 Korean laborers (mostly miners), Karafuto ceased to be a colony and was made an integral part of the homeland.

Although legally Russian (later Soviet) territory, northern Sakhalin after 1905 saw significant Japanese involvement. The discovery of oil deposits prompted Japanese requests for investment in 1916. In retaliation for the massacre of about 700 Japanese soldiers and civilians at Nikolaevsk (a town on the lower Amur) in the spring of 1920, Japan occupied northern Sakhalin (see NIKOLAEVSK INCIDENT). Forces were withdrawn in 1925 when Japan and the Soviet Union established diplomatic relations, but Japan retained oil and coal concessions in northern Sakhalin until 1944.

Soviet forces invaded Karafuto both by sea and across the 50th parallel on 11 August 1945, a few days before the conclusion of World War II. About 30,000 Japanese were evacuated to Hokkaidō in August, and 87,000 managed to escape during the next four months. Most of the remaining 300,000 were repatriated between 1947 and 1949, but a few were held in the USSR until 1959. Of the 41,000 Koreans who remain on Sakhalin, about 3,000 still seek repatriation to Japan or South Korea.

Southern Sakhalin was formally incorporated into the Russian Soviet Federated Socialist Republic of the USSR in 1947 as part of a newly created Sakhalin Oblast which also included northern Sakhalin and the Kuril Islands. The Japanese government is not demanding the return of southern Sakhalin but is withholding complete recognition of Soviet sovereignty there pending a resolution of Tōkyō's irredentist claims to the southern Kuril Islands.

—— John J. Stephan, *Sakhalin: A History* (1971).

John J. STEPHAN

Sakhalin-Kuril Islands Exchange Treaty → St. Petersburg, Treaty of

sakimori

Soldiers in ancient Japan charged with the defense of Kyūshū. The chronicle *Nihon shoki* (720) states that *sakimori* were first sent to Kyūshū in 562 after the fall of the Japanese enclave of KAYA on the Korean peninsula. In fact, however, it was not until the imperial edict of 645 proclaiming the TAIKA REFORM that the term was first used. Under the provisions for national defense in the newly instituted RITSURYŌ SYSTEM of administration, soldiers were conscripted from all over the country and sent to Kyūshū on a three-year rotational basis. After 730, however, only those from the eastern provinces of Honshū were sent.

There was a special office (Sakimori no Tsukasa) in DAZAIFU, the government headquarters in northern Kyūshū, to handle matters related to *sakimori*. Besides performing military duties, *sakimori* were expected to grow their own food. During their term of service, they were exempted from corvée labor and a produce tax (see SO, YŌ, AND CHŌ), but, since they had to bear the costs of armor and of food and travel as far as the port of Naniwa (now Ōsaka), many of the poorer peasants ran away or otherwise evaded service. Because of famine, epidemics, and general social distress, it became increasingly difficult to recruit conscripts. In 795 it was decided to abolish the *sakimori* system altogether and to entrust the defense of Kyūshū to local militia. Recruitment, nevertheless, seems to have continued well into the 10th century.

The 8th-century poetry anthology MAN'YŌSHŪ includes about 100 poems by *sakimori* (SAKIMORI UTA). Although many of them reflect the pride and exultation of being summoned by the emperor to defend the country, many others express the grief and sorrow of parting with loved ones.

Kitamura Bunji

sakimori uta

(Poems of the Frontier Guards). Poems by young peasants from eastern Japan who were sent for military guard duty on the southern island of Kyūshū and offshore islands in the 7th and 8th centuries. In Japan, the *sakimori* were established in Kyūshū—Tsukushi as it was then known—after the failure of a Japanese imperialist venture in Korea and the withdrawal of the defeated forces in 663 created a fear of retaliatory action by the Koreans. At any one time the guards constituted a force of 3,000 men. At first recruited from all over the country, after 730 they were recruited from the 10 easternmost provinces of Honshū. They were sent in annual contingents of 1,000, each required to serve three years. The conscripts were responsible for their own food and maintenance as far as the staging area at the port of Naniwa southwest of the capital, and many fell victim to starvation and disease on the long journey from home. At Naniwa they reported to officials of the Board of War, who superintended the sea voyage to the military headquarters at Dazaifu in northwestern Kyūshū. This journey also took its toll. At home, the wives, children, and parents of the absent men suffered great hardship and privation from the loss of their strongest male worker and head of the household. The *sakimori* system was modified in time and was eventually abandoned, partly because of the misery it caused, partly because the Korean crisis abated, but more important, perhaps, because the eastern conscripts were needed locally to deal with uprisings by Ainu tribesmen to the north.

All extant poems of the frontier guards are preserved in the MAN'YŌSHŪ (ca 759), the first great anthology of Japanese vernacular poetry: a group of 5 in Book 14, and a series of 93 in Book 20. It is believed that the former may have been gathered by TAKAHASHI NO MUSHIMARO, an important poet and probably one of the compilers of the *Man'yōshū*, who is believed to have been an official in the eastern province of Mutsu; the latter poems are thought to have been selected from a considerable stock of material by ŌTOMO NO YAKAMOCHI, another important poet and perhaps the principal compiler of the anthology, who was at Naniwa in 755 as an official of the Ministry of Military Affairs. The 5 examples in Book 14 are identified as "Poems of Frontier Guards," but the authors and places of origin are not indicated. They are among a large group of so-called "Poems of the East" (Azuma *uta*)—poems whose provincial origin is attested by their strong folk flavor and many dialect words. The poems in Book 20 bear no generic designation, but the authors' names, provinces, and districts of origin are carefully recorded. Except for one *chōka* ("long poem"), all of the poems of the frontier guards are consistently regular 31-syllable *tanka* ("short poem")—a suspicious circumstance suggesting either that influences of the sophisticated court literary culture penetrated even the rural areas of the east at that early date, or else, more likely, that the poems were revised and metrically regularized by court poets, Yakamochi chief among them. Yakamochi and others may also have composed an indefinite number themselves in the guise of frontier guards. Such a pose had venerable precedents, for Chinese literati had long composed poems representing the feelings of men drafted for corvée labor or sent to guard the frontiers, and the sorrows and sufferings of their loved ones. However, the fact that they may be a kind of literary genre and that some may be fictitious does not detract from their strong emotional impact. Thematically, they fall into two main types: declarations of fealty to the sovereign, and willingness to die in his service; and laments at parting, expressions of tenderness and concern about the fate of those left behind, and dread of the loneliness to come. Sometimes the two types are combined. The poems resemble one another in technique, diction, and imagery—an indication of extensive use of traditional materials from the rich store of folk song and poetry of the eastern regions and of certain popular customs such as the exchange of impromptu but conventional verses at courtship rituals. Some were more successful than others, for a note in the *Man'yōshū* states that Yakamochi made his selection of 93 poems from a total of 166, rejecting nearly half as of inferior quality. In addition to the group of the mid-750s or thereabouts, a few labeled "poems by frontier guards of long ago" may in fact be considerably older. As a whole, the poems are among the most moving that survive from Japan's early literary period.

—— Robert H. Brower and Earl Miner, *Japanese Court Poetry* (1961). Ian H. Levy, *The Ten Thousand Leaves* (1981–). Nippon Gakujutsu Shinkōkai, *The Man'yōshū: One Thousand Poems* (1940, repr 1965).

Robert H. BROWER

Sakisaka Itsurō (1897–   )

Marxist economist and theoretician. Born in Fukuoka Prefecture, he graduated from the economics department of Tōkyō University. After studying Marxist theories in Germany from 1922 to 1925, he returned to Japan and joined the faculty of Kyūshū University, but he was dismissed from the university in 1928 during a government crackdown on leftists (see MARCH 15TH INCIDENT). In the same year he joined *Rōnō*, a scholarly Marxist periodical under the editorship of YAMAKAWA HITOSHI, and became a leading spokesman for the RŌNŌHA group of Marxist theoreticians during their ideological debates with the rival KŌZAHA group (see also NIHON SHIHON SHUGI RONSŌ). He was imprisoned from 1937 through 1939 as a result of the POPULAR FRONT INCIDENT, but returned to Kyūshū University in 1945. In 1947 he published the journal *Zenshin*, which was influential in the left wing of the JAPAN SOCIALIST PARTY (JSP), and in 1951, together with ŌUCHI HYŌE and Yamakawa, he established the Shakai Shugi Kyōkai (Socialist Association). Sakisaka also organized classes for workers and provided ideological guidance during the MIIKE STRIKE of 1959–60. After his retirement from Kyūshū University in 1960, he was active in the Shakai Shugi Kyōkai and exerted strong ideological influence on the JSP and on SŌHYŌ (General Council of Trade Unions of Japan). He was the editor of the 27-volume *Marukusu–Engerusu zenshū* (1928–35, Complete Works of Marx and Engels). His other works include *Shihonron* (1946–56), a translation of *Das Kapital; Marukusu den* (1962, Biography of Marx); and *Keizaigaku hōhō ron* (1950, The Methodology of Economics).   SUGIHARA Shirō

Sakishima Islands

(Sakishima Shotō). Group of islands southwest of the main island of Okinawa; made up of the MIYAKO ISLANDS and YAEYAMA ISLANDS and administratively a part of Okinawa Prefecture. The principal products of the Sakishima Islands are sugarcane and pineapple. Part of the Iriomote National Park. Area: 811 sq km (313 sq mi).

Sakoku → National Seclusion

Saku

City in eastern Nagano Prefecture, central Honshū, on the river Chikumagawa. Saku is noted for its rice and for its electronics industry; it is also known for carp hatcheries. It is part of the Myōgi–Arafune–Saku Kōgen Quasi-National Park. Pop: 57,361.

saku

(stockades or palisades; also pronounced *ki*). Fortresses in frontier regions that were built at the command of the imperial court. They first appeared in the middle of the 7th century, but most of them were constructed in northeastern Honshū between the 8th and 10th centuries, both for defense against the aboriginal EZO tribesmen and for administration of the surrounding countryside. Similar fortifications are thought to have been built along the southwestern frontiers in Kyūshū. Among the most famous palisades are TAGAJŌ (in what is now Miyagi Prefecture), IZAWAJŌ (Iwate Prefecture), and AKITAJŌ (Akita Prefecture). Recent archaeological excavations at these sites have uncovered much material and indicate that the palisades had strongly built wooden walls and towers, with buildings inside the enclosures. Other remains include records concerning government administration, such as earthenware inscribed with ink and wooden writing tablets (MOKKAN). These findings have led many scholars to regard the *saku* not merely as military establishments, but also as provincial administrative centers (KOKUFU). See also NUTARI NO KI; IWAFUNE NO KI.   KITAMURA Bunji

Saku Basin

(Saku Bonchi). In eastern Nagano Prefecture, central Honshū. Situated along the upper reaches of the river Shinanogawa, this triangular-shaped basin consists of the flood plain of the river Chikumagawa in the south and uplands covered with mud flows and volcanic ash from the volcano Asamayama in the north. Apples and highland vegetables are cultivated on the uplands and rice is grown in the lowlands. The basin is a center for carp breeding. Industries have recently moved into this area. The major cities are Komoro and Saku. Area: approximately 300 sq km (116 sq mi).

Sakuma Dam

A gravity dam located on the middle reaches of the river TENRYŪGAWA, central western Shizuoka Prefecture, central Honshū. One of Japan's largest dams. Completed in 1956, it created Lake Sakuma, now a popular tourist attraction. The dam is utilized for electric power generation with a maximum output of 350,000 kilowatts. Height of embankment: 155.5 m (510 ft); storage capacity: 200 million cu m (7,060 million cu ft).

Sakuma Kanae (1888–1970)

Linguist and psychologist. Born in Chiba Prefecture and graduated from Tōkyō University. He was a professor at Kyūshū and Tōyō universities and a member of the JAPAN ACADEMY. Besides the introduction into Japan of Gestalt psychology he is noted for his research on the grammar of modern spoken Japanese and for a study of Japanese phonetics based on the Tōkyō dialect. His chief works are *Nihon onseigaku* (1929), a study of the phonetics of Japanese; *Gendai nihongo no hyōgen to gohō* (1936), an investigation of contemporary expression and usage; and *Nihongo no gengo riron* (1959), a theoretical study of the Japanese language.
                    UWANO Zendō

Sakuma Shōzan (1811–1864)

Also called Sakuma Zōzan. A progressive *samurai* intellectual of the latter part of the Edo period (1600–1868). Born in Matsushiro, the castle town of the Matsushiro domain (now Nagano Prefecture), Shōzan studied Chinese learning under his father, a scholar-administrator of the domain and SATŌ ISSAI, a professor at Shōheikō (the Confucian school of the Tokugawa shogunate) in Edo (now Tōkyō). Shōzan, like other intellectuals of his time, was keenly awakened to the danger from the West as illustrated by China's humiliation in the Opium War (1839–42). From 1842 onward he devoted all his thoughts and activities to studying the West and exploring how Japan could safeguard its security and independence from Western encroachment. He studied under many scholars of WESTERN LEARNING (Yōgaku), many of whom he was to surpass in a few years—EGAWA TARŌZAEMON, Shimosone Kinzaburō (1806–74), Kurokawa Ryōan (1817–90), Tsuboi Shindō (1795–1848), and others. So rapid was his progress in learning Western-style gunnery and military tactics and even applied science that he soon became one of the best-informed men on the West in Japan. In 1850 he opened his own private school of Western gunnery in Edo, and his fame spread. Among those who flocked to the school were some of the most illustrious figures of Japan in the second half of the 19th century: YOSHIDA SHŌIN, SAKAMOTO RYŌMA, NAKAOKA SHINTARŌ, HASHIMOTO SANAI, KATŌ HIROYUKI, and NISHIMURA SHIGEKI. As Shōzan immersed himself in the technical knowledge of the West during the 1840s, he conducted a series of experiments. Relying on the Dutch translation of a French encyclopedia by M. Noel Chomel, he produced glass in 1844. Following other Dutch books he later cast Western-style bronze cannon. In Matsushiro he encouraged the eating of pork, a relatively new dietary habit, and even raised some hogs. He also introduced the large-scale cultivation of potatoes, and tried unsuccessfully to mine copper and lead. At age 42 he married Katsu Junko, Katsu Kaishū's 16-year-old sister.

By the time Commodore Matthew Calbraith PERRY's American ships entered Edo Bay (now Tōkyō Bay) in mid-1853, Shōzan had come to believe that studying Western-language books was not enough, for it was tantamount to "scratching an itchy foot through one's shoe." He maintained that the most effective way of knowing the enemy, the Western "barbarian," was to send the talented to the enemy's lands to observe conditions there. This belief led him to encourage his disciple Yoshida Shōin to try to go abroad by stowing away on board a Western vessel in violation of Japan's NATIONAL SECLUSION policy. When Shōin's second attempt failed in 1854, Shōzan's connivance was discovered. This disclosure brought about an eight-year-long domiciliary confinement at Matsushiro. During the early part of his confinement he wrote his famous work, *Seikenroku* (Reflections on My Errors). Much of the work, written in Chinese *(kambun)*, consists of a criticism of the general ignorance of Western science on the part of Confucian scholars and the ineptness of the shogunate in dealing with Perry. In this respect the *Seikenroku* concerned itself more with others' errors than with Shōzan's own.

In June 1864 he was made an adviser to the shogunate on defense matters and went to Kyōto, then the hotbed of *sonnō jōi* (Revere the Emperor, Expel the Barbarians) advocates. In sending Shōzan to Kyōto, the shogunate appears to have intended not only to have him serve as an adviser but also to win the *sonnō jōi* faction over to the MOVEMENT FOR UNION OF COURT AND SHOGUNATE. Unfortunately, before he could exercise any influence on the defense policy of the shogunate, he was assassinated by *sonnō jōi* adherents in August 1864.

Although Shōzan was a creative and diligent scholar, all his life he remained exceedingly proud, uncompromising, and even immodest. The more he learned about the West, the more highly he thought of himself. The reputation he enjoyed as a scholar of Western learning, together with the Confucian emphasis on men of talent, made him think that he was entitled to communicate his views on national defense to the shogunate. But since Shōzan was only a rear vassal *(baishin)* of the shōgun, there were virtually no officially approved channels through which he could transmit his recommendations directly to the proper authorities. The conflict between the unlimited confidence in his solutions and the limited influence of a person of his status was partly resolved by his conviction that later generations would see the wisdom of his views.

Shōzan is best remembered for his motto "Eastern ethics and Western technique." After studying Western technology and science and comparing it with Neo-Confucianism (SHUSHIGAKU), he concluded that they were the two indispensable aspects of the total sum of human knowledge, and that of the two the spiritual aspect, Eastern ethics, was the more exalted. The motto thus foreshadowed the transformation of modern Japan since the mid-19th century, for the outstanding feature of that transformation has been the blending of the old and new, of the East and West.

📖 —— Sakuma Shōzan, *Zōtei Shōzan zenshū,* 5 vols (Shinano Kyōikukai, 1934–35). Richard T. Chang, *From Prejudice to Tolerance: A Study of the Japanese Image of the West, 1826–1864* (1970), part 2. Miyamoto Chū, *Sakuma Shōzan* (rev ed, 1940). Ōhira Kimata, *Sakuma Shōzan* (1959).
Richard T. CHANG

Sakunami Hot Spring

(Sakunami Onsen). Located near the upper reaches of the river Hirosegawa west of the city of Sendai, central western Miyagi Prefecture, northern Honshū. An alkaline, saline, gypsum spring; water temperature is approximately 60°C (140°F). The area is noted for its autumn foliage. There is skiing in winter.

Sakura

City in northern Chiba Prefecture, central Honshū; south of IMBANUMA marsh. It prospered during the Edo period (1600–1868) as the castle town of Sakura Castle, built by DOI TOSHIKATSU. With many thriving industries, it is rapidly becoming a satellite city of Tōkyō. The area around Imbanuma, part of a prefectural park, has facilities for hiking and fishing. Pop: 101,180.

sakura → cherry, flowering

Sakurada Ichirō (1904–)

Chemist. Noted for his work involving the viscosity of high polymers and X-ray analyses of their structures. He was also a part of the three-man team that succeeded in the first Japanese production of synthetic fibers in 1938. Born in Kyōto Prefecture, he graduated from Kyōto University in 1926. He became professor there in 1935 and dean of engineering in 1965. He retired in 1967 to become professor at Dōshisha University.

Sakurada Jisuke

The name of a succession of major dramatists in the KABUKI theater. Jisuke I (1734–1806) wrote over 120 *jidai-mono* (historical plays) and *sewa-mono* (domestic plays) and more than 100 *shosagoto* (dance pieces). Although his full-length works are no longer performed, his shorter *shosagoto* pieces, such as *Oshiegusa Yoshiwara suzume* (1768, Birds of Yoshiwara) and *Modorikago iro ni aikata* (1788, A Returning Palanquin), are still frequently presented.

His disciple, Jisuke II (1768–1829), excelled in the *shosagoto*. Jisuke III (1802–77), a pupil of Jisuke II, achieved some prominence but was soon overshadowed by Kawatake MOKUAMI, who became the dominant kabuki playwright after the mid-1850s. Jisuke IV

(dates unknown), who had once worked under Jisuke III, abandoned his 30-year playwriting career to become a journalist.
📖 —— Aubrey S. Halford and Giovanna M. Halford, *The Kabuki Handbook* (1956). Kawatake Shigetoshi, *Kabuki sakusha no kenkyū* (1940).
Ted T. TAKAYA

Sakuradamongai Incident

The assassination of the shogunal great elder *(tairō)* II NAOSUKE outside the Sakurada Gate of Edo Castle on 24 March 1860 by a group of 18 antiforeign, antishogunate activists from the Mito domain (now part of Ibaraki Prefecture) and the Satsuma domain (now Kagoshima Prefecture). Ii had earned the hatred of the SONNŌ JŌI (Revere the Emperor, Expel the Barbarians) activists when he signed the ANSEI COMMERCIAL TREATIES without imperial sanction. His ruthless suppression of political dissent following the 1858 shogunal succession dispute (see ANSEI PURGE) further alienated him from the progressive *daimyō,* who sought rapprochement between the court and the Tokugawa shogunate (see MOVEMENT FOR UNION OF COURT AND SHOGUNATE). In their notice to the shogunate, the assassins claimed that they had punished Ii for capitulating to the Western powers and defying the imperial will. The murder of the great elder in broad daylight thoroughly discredited Tokugawa absolutism and set the stage for further antishogunate activities and the eventual overthrow of the shogunate in 1867–68. Of the 18 assassins, 1 was killed in the fray, 4 committed suicide, having been seriously wounded, 11 were eventually captured and executed, and only 2 survived. See also MEIJI RESTORATION.

Sakuradamon Incident

(Sakuradamon Jiken). A political assassination attempt on Emperor HIROHITO on 8 January 1932. As the emperor was on his way back to the palace after attending the New Year's military review a hand grenade was thrown at the procession near the Sakuradamon gate of the palace, causing minor damage to one of the carriages. Prime Minister INUKAI TSUYOSHI took responsibility for the incident and immediately submitted his resignation, but the request was not accepted by the emperor. The suspect, a Korean, was executed after he was convicted in a secret trial.

Sakurada Takeshi (1904–)

Businessman. Born in Hiroshima Prefecture and a graduate of Tōkyō University. Sakurada joined NISSHIN SPINNING CO, LTD, in 1926, becoming president in 1945 and chairman in 1964. He helped create NIKKEIREN (Japan Federation of Employers' Associations) and served as its executive director and permanent executive secretary, leading the federation in many conflicts with labor unions. Sakurada served as chairman of the federation from 1974 to 1979. A leader in the business-industrial community, he was counted among the "big four" of the business world during the premiership of IKEDA HAYATO and continued to wield strong influence in later years.
TANAKA Yōnosuke

Sakurai

City in northern Nara Prefecture, central Honshū. One of the market towns and POST-STATION TOWNS during the Edo period (1600–1868). After the opening of a railway line in the late 19th century, it became a distribution center for lumber from nearby mountains. Attractions include Ōmiwa Shrine and the temple Hasedera. Pop: 56,441.

Sakurajima

Volcanic island connected to the Ōsumi Peninsula on the Kyūshū mainland, Kagoshima Bay, central Kagoshima Prefecture, southern Kyūshū. An active stratovolcano composed of the peaks Kitadake, Nakadake, and Minamidake. The highest is Kitadake with an altitude of 1,117 m (3,664 ft). As a result of a large eruption in 1914, the island became fused with the Ōsumi Peninsula. Even today smoke is sometimes spewed out to a height of more than 3,000 meters (9,840 ft). Sakurajima forms part of the Kirishima–Yaku National Park, and the hardened lava flows are a tourist attraction. It is the site of numerous hot springs as well. The special product of the island is Sakurajima *daikon* (a large, fat, white radish). Area: 77 sq km (30 sq mi).

Sakurakai

(Cherry Blossom Society). Secret society established by young army officers with the object of total national reform; organized in September 1930 by Lt. Col. HASHIMOTO KINGORŌ, then chief of the Russian Section of the Army General Staff. The society called for the reorganization of the state on more totalitarian, militaristic lines, and it claimed that to achieve its purpose it would resort to military force, even a coup d'etat if necessary. The criteria for membership were that the applicant must hold the rank of lieutenant colonel or lower and that he be an enthusiastic advocate of reorganizing the state. The Sakurakai began with a membership of about 10, mostly field-grade officers from the General Staff and the Army Ministry. Later, company-grade officers attached to regiments joined the society, and by February 1931 membership totaled more than 50. Not all of the members were fervent advocates of revolutionary tactics. Nevertheless, twice in 1931 (see MARCH INCIDENT; OCTOBER INCIDENT) Sakurakai members in concert with ultranationalist civilian elements tried to topple the government and set up a military cabinet. With the arrest of 12 members, including Hashimoto, after the October Incident, the Sakurakai was dissolved, and the movement by army officers to reorganize the state became fragmented.

AWAYA Kentarō

sakurasō → primroses

Sakura Sōgorō (mid-17th century)

Also known as Sakura Sōgo. Farmer and folk hero of the early part of the Edo period (1600–1868). Real name Kiuchi Sōgorō. As a village headman (SHŌYA) in the Sakura domain in Shimōsa Province (now part of Chiba Prefecture), Sōgorō is said to have petitioned the *daimyō* of Sakura to reduce the extremely heavy taxes from which the peasants of the region were suffering. Unsuccessful in his plea, legend has it that Sōgorō went alone to Edo (now Tōkyō) and presented a direct appeal (JIKISO) to the shōgun, an action usually punishable by death. It is said that his request was granted, but that he and his family were executed nonetheless. Although historical evidence points to the existence of such a person—a 1652 village register lists a farmer named Sōgo, and the gazetteer *Sakura fudoki* (1722) records the execution of a certain Sōgorō—it is difficult to separate fact from the fictional accounts of Sōgorō in popular literature, of which the *kabuki* play *Sakura gimin den* by MOKUAMI is particularly well known. See also HYAKUSHŌ IKKI.

sakushiki

(cultivators' rights). Rights of cultivation and livelihood, held by farmers (*sakunin*) over land rented from the proprietary lords (RYŌSHU) of estates (SHŌEN) in the Kamakura (1185–1333) and Muromachi (1333–1568) periods. Also called *sakuteshiki, sakushoshiki, sakuninshiki, sakushushiki,* and *hyakushōshiki.* Cultivators' rights were subordinate to *myōshushiki* (rights of the landholder, or MYŌSHU), which in turn were subordinate to *ryōshushiki* (rights of the proprietary lord). There were three kinds of tenure: (1) indefinite, so long as the holder paid annual rent and labor service; (2) revocable at the proprietary lord's discretion; and (3) limited to the term of one year. The first was the most common. Like other *shiki* (rights over the land), *sakushiki* were separable from the duties they entailed. A holder of *sakushiki* was responsible for rent and labor service from the land, but he could let it out to others. He could also let out or sell his rights at a profit. The growing number of such transactions during the Muromachi period indicates that many holders of *sakushiki* were not directly engaged in farming but were in effect small proprietors. In such cases, the actual cultivators were said to hold *shita sakushiki* or *shita-byakushōshiki* (subordinate cultivators' rights). *Sakushiki,* together with the *shōen* system, were officially abolished at the time of the nationwide land survey (KENCHI) ordered by the national unifier Toyotomi Hideyoshi in the 1580s.

KOYANAGI Shun'ichirō

salamanders

(*sanshōuo*). In Japanese, *sanshōuo* is the general name for amphibians of the order Urodela, family Salamandridae, with the exception of newts (IMORI). Some 13 species are found in Japan; most common are the Hakone *sanshōuo* (*Onychodactylus japonicus*) and ka-

sumi *sanshōuo* (*Hynobius nebulosus*), which hide under rocks and fallen trees in forests by day—except during the breeding season when they swarm about stagnant pools—and move about at night to prey on insects and earthworms. The *ō sanshōuo* (*Megalobatrachus japonicus*), a giant species native to Japan, is usually 60-70 centimeters long (24-28 in) but sometimes reaches a length of more than 120 centimeters (47 in). It is the world's largest amphibian. Inhabiting streams or rivers in mountainous areas of Honshū southward from Gifu Prefecture and in northern Kyūshū, it digs holes 2-3 meters (7-10 ft) deep in riverbanks, hiding by day and coming out at night to prowl for food.

IMAIZUMI Yoshiharu

salmons

(*sake; masu*). The Japanese terms *sake* and *masu* are the common names for various species of anadromous fish of the family Salmonidae. *Sake* refers chiefly to fish of the genus *Oncorhynchus,* and *masu* to certain, usually sea-running, fish of the genera *Oncorhynchus, Salmo,* and *Salvelinus.*

Sake refers specifically to the dog salmon (*Oncorhynchus keta*), the most important Japanese salmon. This fish, which grows to a length of about one meter (39 in), is distributed in the northern Pacific Ocean and adjoining seas, as well as the rivers emptying into them. The southernmost rivers that it ascends in Japan are the river Tonegawa on the Pacific Ocean side of Honshū and the Nakagawa on the Sea of Japan side of Kyūshū. Salted *sake* is highly favored by the Japanese, *shiozake* being the term for fully salted fish, and *aramaki* for lightly salted. The roe is also considered a delicacy; *sujiko* is the term for the whole roe and *ikura* for the loose salmon eggs or caviar.

The word *masu* is often translated into English as "trout"; however the only trout of any importance in Japan is the rainbow trout or *nijimasu* (*Salmo gairdneri*), which was introduced from the United States in 1877 as a sport fish. More importantly, *masu* is the general commercial name for such fish as the Karafuto *masu* or *sepparimasu* (pink salmon; *Oncorhynchus gorbuscha*). The word *masu* formerly conveyed an image of comparatively low-grade fish since the salted and dried Karafuto *masu* was, particularly before World War II, the cheapest of Japanese salmons. However, when canned the Karafuto *masu* is not inferior to the highly favored *sake* or dog salmon.

ABE Tokiharu

The first mention in Japanese records of *sake* occurs in the collection of government regulations Engi Shiki (completed in 927), which relates that the fish was caught in the rivers of Shinano and Echigo provinces (now Nagano and part of Niigata prefectures) and brought to the imperial court. Mention also appears in the history of the Kamakura shogunate (1192–1333), *Azuma kagami,* among records for the year 1190, and it is thought that salmon was by this time eaten by a large portion of the common people. In the Edo period (1600–1868) salmon was the subject of *haiku* by Matsuo BASHŌ, Yosa BUSON, and Kobayashi ISSA, and up to the time of World War II it was a staple fish. Today it is very expensive; nevertheless, the custom persists of giving year-end gifts of lightly salted salmon (*aramaki*).

In the 8th century an annual tribute of *masu* was offered to the emperor by a representative of Dazaifu, the government headquarters in Kyūshū, apparently a formal expression of the region's fidelity to the emperor patterned after a Chinese practice. Today various *masu,* including rainbow trout, are raised by fish-farming in ponds throughout Japan and *masu* are now often considered freshwater fish.

SAITŌ Shōji

Salvation Army

(Kyūseigun). Japanese branch of the international Christian evangelical and charitable organization. Carries out missionary work among the poor as well as various welfare programs for the less fortunate. Headquartered in Tōkyō. The Salvation Army was first organized in Japan under Colonel Edward Wright in 1895, about 30 years after its founding in London. Although it did not receive much public support at first, as more Japanese joined the organization, the Salvation Army in Japan became better adjusted to native conditions and its activities received more recognition.

Among the founding Japanese members, YAMAMURO GUMPEI was prominent for his work as a missionary, social worker, and author and was promoted to the rank of commander of the Salvation Army in Japan in 1926. The organization's early campaigns included a drive against prostitution in 1900 and an annual year-end fund-raising campaign. Suffering a hard blow during World War II, it made a remarkable comeback after the war under the leadership of Commander Uemura Masuzō (1885–1969). It now operates various welfare facilities, including low-cost dormitories for day laborers and students, nurseries for working mothers, sanatoriums, and job training centers for the handicapped. The members and baptized followers of the Salvation Army in Japan totaled 9,793 in 1980. See also CHRISTIANITY; PROTESTANT MISSIONARIES. *Hiroki* SHIOJI

Sambesan

Double volcano, in the Hakusan Volcanic Zone, central Shimane Prefecture, western Honshū; composed of granite-based quartz amphibole and biotite andesite. In the central cone is Muronouchi Pond. Sambe Hot Spring is in the foothills. Part of Daisen-Oki National Park. The highest peak is Osambe (1,126 m; 3,693 ft).

Sambetsu Kaigi

(abbreviation of Zen Nihon Sangyōbetsu Rōdō Kumiai Kaigi; Congress of Industrial Labor Unions of Japan). Sambetsu Kaigi was organized in August 1946 on the model of the Congress of Industrial Organizations (CIO) in the United States. Initially it had 21 affiliated unions with a total membership of 1,630,000. It comprised 44 percent of the organized labor force at that time and was the largest national labor organization. It had strong ties with the JAPAN COMMUNIST PARTY, and, following the policies of the World Federation of Trade Unions (WFTU), it led political struggles such as the GENERAL STRIKE of 1947, often confronting the Occupation authorities. Divisions within Sambetsu Kaigi led to the formation of Sambetsu Minshuka Dōmei (Democratic Congress of Industrial Organizations) in 1948, and in 1950, of SŌHYŌ (General Council of Trade Unions of Japan). At the same time the organization came under outside attack through the RED PURGE of the Occupation authorities. Because of these events, Sambetsu Kaigi quickly lost both influence and membership; when it finally disbanded in 1958, its membership had dwindled to less than 10,000. *KURITA Ken*

Sambō Hombu → Army General Staff Office

Sambugyō

(the Three Commissioners). A term of the Edo period (1600–1868). Sambugyō refers to the three most important administrative offices of the Tokugawa shogunate (1603–1867): the EDO MACHI BUGYŌ, who were in charge of the Edo (now Tōkyō) commoner populace; the KANJŌ BUGYŌ, who handled shogunal finances and rural lands; and the JISHA BUGYŌ, who oversaw all religious establishments. See also BUGYŌ. *Conrad* TOTMAN

Samguk sagi

(History of the Three Kingdoms; J: *Sangoku shiki*). The oldest extant history of the KOREAN THREE KINGDOMS PERIOD. It was compiled about 1145 under the supervision of the KORYŌ-dynasty scholar Kim Pu-sik (1075–1151). The work resembles a Chinese dynastic history in its organization, with coverage extending from the legendary origins of the three kingdoms to Silla's demise in 935. The *Samguk sagi* is of considerable value to historians of ancient Korean history and also contains information on the relationship between the Japanese and Korean languages.
C. Kenneth QUINONES

Samguk yusa

(Memorabilia of the Three Kingdoms; J: *Sangoku iji*). A medieval Korean work written in Chinese by the KORYŌ-dynasty Buddhist monk Iryŏn (1206–89). Compiled sometime around 1285, it contains Buddhist lore and other anecdotal materials concerning the KOREAN THREE KINGDOMS PERIOD. Historians of ancient Korea have found it of considerable interest, because its Buddhist perspective of life complements the Confucian orientation of the SAMGUK SAGI.
C. Kenneth QUINONES

Samil Independence Movement

(San'ichi Dokuritsu Undō). Also known as the March First (Samil) Movement after the day in 1919 when the Koreans launched their

Samma

most determined attempt to gain independence from Japan (see KOREA, ANNEXATION OF). United States President Woodrow Wilson's call for national self-determination at the Paris Peace Conference had inspired Koreans to plan a peaceful expression of nationalistic sentiment, but the sudden death of King KOJONG (r 1864–1907) in January 1919 provided the immediate catalyst for the movement.

March first, two days before the date set for the monarch's funeral, was selected because Seoul would be filled with mourners. That morning posters appeared, claiming that the king had been assassinated by poisoning and explaining the principle of self-determination. Students gathered in Seoul's Pagoda Park to read a declaration of independence, while most of its signatories met in a restaurant to await arrest; people filled the streets chanting *manse* (J: *banzai*), the movement's rallying cry. Similar noisy but nonviolent demonstrations occurred throughout Korea on that day.

The Japanese government responded with brutal force, fanning Korean emotions into a rage that was not subdued until the end of April. By then officials estimated 500,000 Koreans had participated in more than 1,000 separate incidents, resulting in at least 553 Koreans killed, 1,409 seriously injured, and 26,713 imprisoned, many of whom were severely tortured. Nine Japanese died and 186 were injured during the same two-month period. Order was not fully imposed, however, until the spring of 1920.

The movement failed to restore Korea's independence, but it did force the Japanese to reform their colonial administration. Admiral SAITŌ MAKOTO replaced General Hasegawa Yoshimichi (1850–1924), and less oppressive policies were inaugurated. Japanese government-general officials were barred from wearing their military uniforms and swords. The number of schools for Koreans was increased, some taxes were reduced, and Koreans were allowed to establish their own newspapers. The despised gendarmerie was reorganized as a civilian police force that proved less intimidating in appearance but far more effective in its surveillance activities. These measures stabilized the situation, at least until the KWANGJU STUDENT RESISTANCE MOVEMENT of 1929. See also KOREA AND JAPAN: Japanese colonial control of Korea; PAK YŎL; SIN'GANHOE.
━━━ Frank Baldwin, "Participatory Anti-Imperialism: The 1919 Independence Movement," *Journal of Korean Studies* 1 (1979). Chong-sik Lee, *The Politics of Korean Nationalism* (1965).
C. Kenneth QUINONES

samma

(saury). *Cololabis saira*. A littoral and pelagic migratory fish of the class Osteichthyes, order Atheriniformes, family Scombresocidae. It reaches 40 centimeters (16 in) in length and is distributed in the temperate and subarctic zones of the northern Pacific Ocean and adjoining waters. Unlike the fish of the same family living in the Atlantic Ocean, the *samma* has short upper and lower jaws. The annual haul in Japan ranges from 200,000 to 600,000 metric tons (220,000–660,000 short tons). It is used for food by broiling with salt and canning, and as bait for tuna. *ABE Tokiharu*

There are several combinations of Chinese characters that can be used to write the word *samma*. An interesting fact is that they invariably contain elements of metal or a sword in them, as best exemplified by the combination, "autumn-sword-fish," suggesting the shape and the color of the fish as well as the best season to eat it. The fish is used as a symbol of a man's loneliness in the poem "Samma no uta" (Song of a Saury) by SATŌ HARUO (1892–1964).

SAITŌ Shōji

Samp'o Incident

(J: Sampo no Ran). A 1510 uprising by Japanese merchants and residents in three southeastern Korean ports (*samp'o*). Regulated trade between Japan and Korea had been established in 1426 at Naeip'o (now Chep'o, in Ungch'ŏn district), Pusanp'o (now Pusan, in Tongnae district), and Yŏmp'o (in Ulsan district). A 1443 trade agreement between Korea and the *daimyō* of Tsushima limited the number of Japanese ships calling at each port to 50 per year, but the population of Japanese traders increased steadily. Korean government attempts to limit the trade led to the 1510 uprising, after which the Japanese were expelled and the ports closed. Relations were renewed with a trade agreement in 1512, but only Naeip'o was reopened and trade ships were limited to 25 per year. Pusanp'o was reopened in 1521; except for periodic disruptions in Korean-Japanese relations, it remained the center of intercourse until the KANGHWA Treaty of 1876. See also KOREA AND JAPAN: premodern relations; WAEGWAN.

C. Kenneth QUINONES

Sampo no Ran → Samp'o Incident

samurai

(literally, "one who serves"). Also known as *bushi* ("military gentry"). Term designating the warrior elite of premodern Japan that emerged in the provinces from at least the early 10th century and became the real ruling class of the country from the late 12th century (the beginning of the medieval age) until Japan's entry into the modern period with the Meiji Restoration of 1868. The official, privileged status of the *samurai* class was dissolved in the mid-1870s, but former samurai were by then firmly established as leaders in government and other sectors of a modernizing Japan.

Origins of the Samurai——The earliest historical evidence of the existence of a military elite in the provinces of Japan dates from the late 930s, when there were disturbances among warring clans in the Kantō region. Although the Kantō, in east-central Honshū, has traditionally been regarded as the birthplace of the samurai, it is quite possible that the fighting tradition of this class goes back to a much earlier time—perhaps to the protohistorical tomb period of the 4th to 7th centuries (see KOFUN PERIOD)—in the Kantō as well as other regions of Japan. At any rate, samurai proliferated in the provinces during the remainder of the Heian period (794–1185) to the point that, by the late 12th century, they became the dominant ruling elite in both central and provincial affairs throughout the country.

The most fundamental reason for the rise of the samurai class was the failure of the central government in Kyōto, controlled by courtiers in the service of the emperor, to maintain adequate administration of the provinces. As early as 792, two years before the transfer of the capital to Heiankyō (now the city of Kyōto), the court had abandoned its policy of countrywide conscription of peasants and had made district-level officials responsible for keeping peace in the provinces through the organization of local militia (KONDEI). With the passage of time, the Heian court paid increasingly less attention to the general administration of provincial affairs. It became common, for example, for courtiers appointed as provincial governors to remain in the capital and to leave the actual management of their respective provinces to lesser officials, most of whom were natives of the provinces in which they served. Under such conditions, it was inevitable that a military class should grow and thrive in the provinces. And from about mid-Heian times on, samurai became active not only as the lesser officials in de facto charge of provincial governments but also as functionaries in the SHŌEN or private estates of courtiers and religious institutions.

Organization of the Samurai——Modern studies of the growth of the samurai class focus primarily on samurai organization into BUSHIDAN or warrior bands. The first *bushidan* were little more than family organizations, that is, military units recruited by chieftains almost entirely from among their kinsmen. In addition, these *bushidan* were maintained only so long as necessary to complete specific military campaigns. When battles ended, members quickly

dispersed to return to the management of their farming lands. By the 11th century, however, *bushidan* had developed into more permanent, feudal-like entities structured on lord-vassal ties between and among fighting men who were not necessarily related by blood. Such ties, moreover, tended to be perpetuated generationally in the families of both lords and vassals and were even conceived of in fictive kinship terms. Vassals, for example, were typically designated as KENIN (housemen) or *ienoko* (children of the house; see IENOKO AND RŌTŌ), and lords were looked upon as fathers.

Leaders of the Samurai Class——Leadership of the samurai class, as it evolved in the provinces of ancient Japan, came to be assumed chiefly by men who were descended from the imperial family. Since emperors were polygamous, they often produced large numbers of offspring. It became the practice from early Heian times on to deprive surplus members of the imperial family of royal status and to give them the surnames of either Taira or Minamoto (see TAIRA FAMILY; MINAMOTO FAMILY). Some of these imperial kinsmen remained in Kyōto as courtiers, but others accepted appointments to the provinces and eventually settled there. Thus, for example, branches of the Taira began appearing in the Kantō from about 900 on, and in the 10th and 11th centuries the Minamoto established spheres of influence and a great fighting reputation both in Kantō and the northern provinces of Honshū.

The northern provinces of Mutsu (now Aomori, Iwate, Miyagi and Fukushima prefectures) and Dewa (now Akita and Yamagata prefectures) had been the scene in the early Heian period of the final defeat of the EZO tribesmen, who had until then maintained an existence separate from the historically evolving Japanese state. Even in later centuries there remained a frontier atmosphere in Mutsu-Dewa, and when, in the mid-11th century, the ABE FAMILY of Mutsu was seen as flouting Kyōto authority, the court commissioned a Minamoto chieftain to deal with it. This led to two conflicts, known as the EARLIER NINE YEARS' WAR and the LATER THREE YEARS' WAR, which actually spanned nearly half a century (1051–87). During the course of the fighting the Minamoto defeated first the Abe and later the Kiyohara of Dewa. By the late 11th century, the Minamoto were recognized as the most powerful samurai clan in an area extending from the Kantō to Mutsu-Dewa.

The great hero of the latter phase of the Minamoto fighting in the north was MINAMOTO NO YOSHIIE (1039–1106), who became known as Hachiman Tarō (first-born son of the War God, Hachiman) and was from this time revered as the most illustrious forebear of the Seiwa Genji, the leading branch of samurai Minamoto, which traced its ancestry back to Emperor Seiwa (850–881). So great was Yoshiie's renown that warriors in the Kantō region and elsewhere began to commend their lands directly to him and indeed to regard him as a potential hegemon (*tōryō*) of all samurai in the land.

Struggle between Taira and Minamoto——Elements in Kyōto feared the rise of Minamoto no Yoshiie as an independent powerholder in the provinces. One response to this fear was the bestowal of favor upon Taira clansmen, especially by retired emperors, who became influential in Kyōto politics from the late 11th century on (see INSEI). By the mid-12th century, the Ise branch of the Taira had risen to particular prominence in the service of successive retired emperors. The Minamoto, while less powerful than they had been under Yoshiie, were also conspicuous in court affairs, most notably in the service of the FUJIWARA FAMILY, who had for centuries functioned as regents (*sesshō* and *kampaku*) to the throne (see REGENCY GOVERNMENT).

In the mid-12th century two armed clashes occurred in Kyōto, ostensibly caused by succession disputes within both the imperial and Fujiwara families. In retrospect it is far more significant that these conflicts ushered in an age of samurai dominance that was to last until modern times. In the HŌGEN DISTURBANCE of 1156 there were Taira and Minamoto on both sides of the fighting, but in the HEIJI DISTURBANCE (1160) the Taira stood solidly on one side opposed to the Minamoto on the other. A Taira victory enabled this leading samurai clan to enter a period, from 1160 until the early 1180s, during which it became the new aristocracy at court.

Again, in retrospect, it is clear that the Taira were doomed to failure because they behaved like courtiers in Kyōto politics instead of seeking—in accord with their warrior heritage—to establish a new network for the administration and control of the provincial samurai class. In 1180 various Minamoto chieftains rose in the provinces to precipitate a war (TAIRA–MINAMOTO WAR) that led to the crushing defeat of the Taira in 1185.

The Medieval Age——The main victor in the Taira-Minamoto War was MINAMOTO NO YORITOMO, who in 1192 established the first true WARRIOR GOVERNMENT in Japanese history, the KAMA-KURA SHOGUNATE (1192–1333). The choice of Kamakura in the eastern provinces as the site of the shogunate reflected the fact that the source of Yoritomo's power was the territorial hegemony he had established over the Kantō during the course of the Taira-Minamoto War. In 1192 Yoritomo received from the court appointment as *seii tai shōgun* or "barbarian-subduing generalissimo," the principal title that in ensuing centuries symbolized military overlordship of Japan (see SHŌGUN).

The founding of the Kamakura shogunate marked the beginning of the medieval age of Japanese history, which lasted until the late 16th century. The affairs of this age were mainly the affairs of the samurai class. There was frequent warfare, as samurai chieftains at all levels—local, regional, and national—competed for control over land and men. The Kamakura shogunate, overthrown in 1333, was succeeded by the MUROMACHI SHOGUNATE (1338–1573). It was during this period that Japanese society most clearly came to resemble the feudal society of medieval Europe. Peasants were bound as serfs to the land and paid harvest rent to samurai, who held superior proprietary rights in the form of fiefs (CHIGYŌ). The samurai themselves were organized into lord-vassal hierarchies, and the values that governed their behavior were military and feudal: honor, loyalty, and manly demeanor; duty and self-effacing service for the good of the collective unit, whether family or military. See also FEUDALISM.

The last century of the Muromachi period, beginning with the ŌNIN WAR (1467–77), was a time of civil strife known as the SEN-GOKU PERIOD. The authority of the Muromachi shogunate extended scarcely beyond Kyōto and its environs, and fighting raged from one end of the country to the other. Gradually, during the first half of the 16th century, a new class of samurai hegemons called DAIMYŌ arose and established territorial domains throughout Japan; and from about mid-century a competition began among the leading daimyō to unify the entire country. Unification was finally achieved by three successive leaders, ODA NOBUNAGA (1534–82), TOYOTOMI HIDEYOSHI (1537–98), and TOKUGAWA IEYASU (1543–1616).

There was a marked expansion in the scale and scope of samurai warfare during the 16th century. To protect their domains and advance their interests in general, daimyō needed ever larger and more permanently organized armies. In addition to the traditional samurai cavalrymen, infantry (ASHIGARU) recruited from among the peasantry became a standard part of such armies. After the arrival in 1543 of the Portuguese as the first Europeans to visit Japan, Western-style rifles and later cannon were used by those daimyō able to obtain them (see FIREARMS, INTRODUCTION OF).

One of the most significant social developments of the age of unification was a greater separation of and distinction between the samurai and peasant classes. Samurai were increasingly obliged to leave the countryside and to take up residence in castle towns and cities in the permanent service of their daimyō lords. Peasants, on the other hand, were forbidden to leave their farms; and, in a series of decrees issued during the final process of unification toward the close of the 16th century, they were also deprived of the right to possess weapons (see SWORD HUNT).

The Tokugawa Shogunate —— The TOKUGAWA SHOGUNATE (1603–1867), founded by Ieyasu at Edo (now Tōkyō), brought peace that lasted until the late 19th century, the beginning of the modern age in Japan. However welcome this peace may have been after generations of warfare, it posed certain fundamental problems of identity for the ruling samurai class. Some samurai, at both the shogunate and daimyō domainal levels, were employed in government. But many more became idle stipendiaries. With no wars to fight and often with no regular, meaningful employment, the samurai as a class became in good part anomalous, although no one openly challenged their right by birth to constitute a ruling class.

In response to these problems of the samurai during the peaceful Edo period (1600–1868), intellectuals formulated the code of BU-SHIDŌ or the "Way of the warrior." *Bushidō* romanticized the Japanese warrior tradition of former ages and enjoined samurai to maintain military preparedness; it also called upon samurai to cultivate their mental faculties in order to serve the intellectual and moral needs of Tokugawa society.

A fundamental policy of the Tokugawa shogunate that contributed to its longevity as a government was the NATIONAL SECLUSION policy, whereby from the late 1630s Japanese relations with the outside world were reduced to little more than a limited trade with the Dutch and the Chinese at Nagasaki. It was the expansion once again of contacts with the West in the 19th century that eventually led to

the downfall of the shogunate. The visit to Japan in 1853 of a squadron of ships commanded by Commodore Matthew PERRY of the United States brought the Tokugawa seclusion to an end. During the next decade and a half, owing to its inability to deal effectively with the rapid increase in foreign relations, the shogunate was increasingly criticized and attacked, especially by samurai opponents within those domains, including Satsuma (now Kagoshima Prefecture) and Chōshū (now Yamaguchi Prefecture), that had never been permitted to participate directly in central government affairs. Ultimately there arose in the mid-1860s an imperial-loyalist movement, led by lower-level samurai from Satsuma, Chōshū, and a few other key domains, which branded the shogunate an unworthy government and even charged the Tokugawa shōgun with being a usurper of imperial authority.

Dissolution of the Samurai Class —— Few of the samurai who participated in the overthrow of the Tokugawa shogunate and the MEIJI RESTORATION of 1868 can have imagined the momentous changes they were helping to bring about. All but the principal leaders of these samurai presumably thought that they could recreate an ideal from the past whereby they would be true and direct subjects of the emperor. They can scarcely have conceived that entry into the modern age, which the Restoration unmistakably marked, would result in the inevitable demise of their class. Yet the new leaders in the Meiji period (1868–1912), most of whom were themselves samurai, realized with increasing conviction that there was no place for privileged samurai status in a new Japan. For one thing, the Meiji government could ill afford to continue payment of the hereditary samurai stipends; for another, continuance of the samurai's elite warrior status was incompatible with the building of a modern conscript army.

Dissolution of the samurai class was carried out between 1873 and 1876 in a series of measures collectively called CHITSUROKU SHOBUN against a background of power struggle within the Meiji oligarchy. Some samurai leaders who had been excluded from the government around 1873 to 1874 undertook armed rebellions, the last of which—the great SATSUMA REBELLION—was put down in 1877; others founded Western-style political parties and launched a movement for representative government (see FREEDOM AND PEOPLE'S RIGHTS MOVEMENT). Thus both major camps in the struggle for power in mid- and late-Meiji times—the entrenched Meiji oligarchy and the opposition political parties—had emerged from the former samurai class. There could be no more striking evidence of the vitality with which at least a portion of this centuries-old warrior elite was able to lead Japan into the mainstream of the modern world. See also SHIZOKU.

🐟 ——John W. Hall, *Government and Local Power in Japan* (1966). Itō Tasaburō, *Nihon hōken seido shi* (1951). Ivan Morris, *The Nobility of Failure* (1975). H. Paul Varley, *The Samurai* (1970).

H. Paul VARLEY

Samurai-dokoro

(Board of Retainers). Office of the Kamakura (1192–1333) and Muromachi (1338–1573) shogunates. Originally an office in the residences of imperial princes and high-ranking nobles, the Samurai-dokoro was established in 1180 by MINAMOTO NO YORITOMO as a formal bureau to control the activities of his vassals (GOKENIN). Together with the KUMONJO (Public Documents Office, later called MANDOKORO or Administrative Board) and the MONCHŪJO (Board of Inquiry), it was one of the central organs of Yoritomo's government. WADA YOSHIMORI served as its first administrative director (*bettō*), but after the downfall of the Wada family in 1213, the post was held concurrently by the HŌJŌ FAMILY regent. The duties of the Samurai-dokoro were gradually extended to include supervision of the police authority (KENDAN) of the estate stewards (JITŌ) appointed by the shogunate.

The office was retained by the Muromachi shogunate, with members of the YAMANA FAMILY, AKAMATSU FAMILY, Isshiki family, and KYŌGOKU FAMILY acting in rotation as its director (now called *shoshi*). During this period the Samurai-dokoro was also responsible for guarding Kyōto and its environs and overseeing property owned by the shogunate and religious institutions. This enabled the *shoshi*, who usually served concurrently as the administrator (*shugoshoku*) of Yamashiro Province (now part of Kyōto Prefecture), to wield great influence over the city's politics. The office was abolished sometime during the Bummei era (1469–87). The *Samurai-dokoro sata hen*, compiled late in the Muromachi period, spells out the functions of the office and contains examples of its actual rulings.

Sanada Yukimura (1567–1615)

(more properly Sanada Nobushige). Warrior of the Azuchi-Momoyama period (1568–1600) and the early part of the Edo period (1600–1868); son of Sanada Masayuki (1545–1609), the lord of Ueda in Shinano (now Nagano Prefecture). In 1585, when his father was involved in a conflict with the future shōgun TOKUGAWA IEYASU, Yukimura sought the backing of UESUGI KAGEKATSU, the *daimyō* of Echigo (now part of Niigata Prefecture), and was granted a fief by him. By 1587, however, he had switched his allegiance to the national unifier TOYOTOMI HIDEYOSHI, whom he served in the ODAWARA CAMPAIGN of 1590 and at the Kyūshū headquarters of Hideyoshi's invasion of Korea in 1592 (see INVASIONS OF KOREA IN 1592 AND 1597). In the great conflict which led to the Battle of SEKIGAHARA in 1600, Yukimura initially joined Ieyasu's expedition against Uesugi Kagekatsu but then adhered to the "Western Army" of ISHIDA MITSUNARI; his brother Nobuyuki (1566–1658) remained loyal to the Tokugawa, supposedly according to a plan to preserve the Sanada family whatever the outcome. Although Masayuki's and Yukimura's resistance in Shinano prevented the forces under Ieyasu's son TOKUGAWA HIDETADA from participating in the Battle of Sekigahara, their lives were spared after the Tokugawa victory, and they were permitted to withdraw to a hermitage at Mt. Kōya (Kōyasan), where Masayuki died. Yukimura survived to heed the call to arms once again in the Ōsaka campaigns of 1614–15 (see ŌSAKA CASTLE, SIEGES OF); one of the stalwarts of TOYOTOMI HIDEYORI's party, he fell in battle after inflicting terrible damage on Tokugawa troops on 2–3 June 1615 (Keichō 20.5.6–7), the eve and the day of Ōsaka Castle's fall.

George ELISON

Sanage

Ceramic production area in Aichi Prefecture near the present-day city of Nagoya that began making SUE WARE during the late 5th century. From the late 8th century, Sanage became the largest ceramic production site in Japan by developing the first intentionally ash-glazed ceramic in Japan. These new wares were produced until the end of the 12th century.

Although a few ancient Sanage kilns were discovered in the late 19th century, it was not until 1954, during the construction of an irrigation system, that the true size of the site was realized. Archaeological excavations, which began the following year, are still continuing. These investigations have revealed that the kilns are scattered throughout a roughly rectangular area of about 110 square kilometers (68.4 sq mi) east of Nagoya. The kiln site is named after Mt. Sanage (Sanageyama), which is located in the extreme northeast of this area, and consists of a total of 438 Kofun (ca 300–710), Nara (710–794), and Heian (794–1185) period kilns, and about 800 medieval (13th to 16th centuries) kilns.

Until the late 8th century, the *sue* wares produced here were very similar in shape to those made elsewhere in central Japan, although they had a slightly lighter-colored gray body owing to the scant iron content of the clay in the Sanage area.

As well as those forms commonly associated with the *sue* wares of the Nara period, Sanage also produced inkstones of various shapes, censers with perforated lids, votive miniature horses and pagodas, spittoons, elegant vases, and architectural items such as decorated roofend tiles and the flamelike ornaments found on the spires of pagodas called *suien*. A great deal of pottery from this area has been found on the sites of excavated temples and the residences of the nobility, showing that production was geared to the demands of the priesthood and ruling classes.

Sanage, however, is more famous for the green ash-glazed stonewares known as *shiki* (or more recently, as *shirashi*), which were produced from about the mid-8th century. Numerous vase and bottle forms were made, the most notable in the Sanage repertoire being multispouted bottles (*tashihei*), long-necked bottles (*suibyō*), and some long-necked bottles with spouts (*jōhei*). Sets of drinking cups and jugs and a range of plates and stemmed serving dishes were also produced. In general, the body of this ware is light buff, which shows off the rich transparent green ash glaze to good advantage. Methods of decoration include incising, perforation, and underglaze painting in iron salts, the painted motif showing up as darker passages of green.

As a result of military strife and the decline of courtly patronage from the late 11th century, the area went into decline. Many potters returned to the fields, although some kilns continued to produce the primitive *yamachawan*. These kilns made small, unglazed bowls well into the 14th century. Potters from Sanage migrated to the Seto area, where vessels bearing incised decoration and an applied ash glaze were made in the subsequent era, Seto in effect carrying on something of the Sanage tradition, which had developed over some five centuries. See CERAMICS: ash-glazed wares.

■——Narasaki Shōichi, *Sanageyō*, vol 31 of *Tōki zenshū* (Heibonsha, 1966). Narasaki Shōichi, *Shirashi*, vol 6 of *Nihon tōji zenshū* (Chūō Kōron Sha, 1976).

Richard MELLOTT *and Brian* HICKMAN

Sanda

City in southeastern Hyōgo Prefecture, western Honshū. Sanda developed as a castle town during the Edo period (1600–1868). It is known for its rice and cattle. The city is fast becoming a residential suburb of Ōsaka and Kōbe. Of interest are the temples Konshinji and Eitakuji. Pop: 36,529.

Sandai Jiken Kempaku Movement

(Movement to Memorialize Three Important Items). An antigovernment political movement led by members of the FREEDOM AND PEOPLE'S RIGHTS MOVEMENT in 1887. In 1886, Foreign Minister INOUE KAORU submitted a program for revision of the so-called Unequal Treaties, which had been imposed on Japan in the 1850s (see UNEQUAL TREATIES, REVISION OF). Among other things, he proposed that extraterritoriality be gradually eliminated and that in the transitional period a mixed court of foreign and Japanese judges be established to try cases involving foreigners. He also pressed for a policy of rapid Westernization as a means to convince the foreign powers that Japan deserved equal treatment. In June 1887 Inoue's program was inadvertently made public. Gustave Emile BOISSONADE DE FONTARABIE, adviser to the Japanese Home Ministry, and TANI KANJŌ, minister of agriculture and commerce, submitted memorials denouncing Inoue's plans as too accommodating to Westerners. Their statements were also leaked to the press, causing a political crisis that forced Inoue to resign. ITAGAKI TAISUKE, the leader of the People's Rights Movement, took advantage of this turn of events and submitted a memorial to the emperor, advocating an end to the unequal treaty system. In September 1887 HOSHI TŌRU, another popular-rights activist, addressed a mass political rally in Tōkyō and called for treaty revision, reduction of the land tax, and freedom of speech and public assembly. A month later KATAOKA KENKICHI forwarded a petition to the GENRŌIN (Chamber of Elders, a protosenatorial body) requesting approval of these three demands. Mass demonstrations were held to put pressure on the government. The government, however, suppressed this political agitation by issuing the PEACE PRESERVATION LAW OF 1887 (Hoan Jōrei) on 25 December. Between 26 and 28 December some 570 of the more prominent members of the political opposition were expelled from Tōkyō. Despite these repressive measures, however, the popular-rights activists continued to agitate for the establishment of a parliamentary system. See also DAIDŌ DANKETSU MOVEMENT.

Sanetaka Kō ki

Diary, in some 60 chapters, of the latter part of the Muromachi period (1333–1568) courtier SANJŌNISHI SANETAKA. Sanetaka served three emperors, GO-HANAZONO (r 1428–64), Go-Tsuchimikado (1442–1500; r 1464–1500), and Go-Kashiwabara (1464–1526; r 1500–1526), as a high official. He was also a noted scholar, poet, and compiler of court ceremonial. His diary covers the years 1474–1536 and is a basic source for the study of late Muromachi history. Besides information concerning his own family, it is rich in details of courtier culture and its penetration into the provinces, and the social and political upheavals of the day.

G. Cameron HURST III

San Felipe Incident

(*San Feripe gō* Jiken). The confiscation of the Spanish galleon *San Felipe* by the hegemon TOYOTOMI HIDEYOSHI in December 1596, inaugurating his persecution of Catholic missionaries to Japan. Bound from Manila to Acapulco, the *San Felipe* was dismasted in a typhoon and stranded at Urado, Tosa Province (now Kōchi Prefecture), on 7 December 1596 (Keichō 1.10.19). At this time Hideyoshi was in great financial straits owing to his military expeditions in Korea and a disastrous earthquake that had devastated the region around Kyōto. He ordered the confiscation of the rich cargo of the *San Felipe* and in February 1597 executed most of the Spanish Franciscan missionary friars then in Japan, together with a few Japanese Jesuit lay brothers, on the grounds that they were subversive disturbers of the public peace. Many of the Spanish survivors considered that Hideyoshi had been provoked to take these steps by the intrigues of the Portuguese Jesuit missionaries in Japan. Whatever the truth of these allegations, Hideyoshi made it quite clear to the governor of the Philippines, when the latter protested against the execution of the friars, that he could no more tolerate the propagation of Christianity in Japan than would the king of Spain and Portugal allow Shintō or Buddhist missionaries in his realms.

🔖 C. R. Boxer, *The Christian Century in Japan, 1549–1650* (1951, repr 1974). Michael Cooper, *Rodrigues the Interpreter: An Early Jesuit in Japan and China* (1974). Matsuda Kiichi, "San Feripe gō jiken no saikentō," *Seisen joshi daigaku kiyō* 14 (1966).

C. R. BOXER

San Francisco Peace Treaty

The name commonly given to the treaty of peace signed by Japan and 48 other nations at San Francisco on 8 September 1951 and formally implemented on 28 April 1952 (its formal name in English is Treaty of Peace with Japan). Essentially a document that restored full sovereignty to Japan and ended the Allied OCCUPATION of Japan, the treaty by itself presents little to historians. The intricate negotiations leading up to the signing and the supplementary agreements that became part of the negotiating process, on the other hand, are fascinating examples of cold-war diplomacy, the effects of which have remained one of the central issues in Japan's debate over its proper place in the world.

Negotiations for a postwar peace settlement became a public issue at least as early as 17 March 1947, when General Douglas MACARTHUR, the supreme commander of the Allied Occupation forces, held a news conference to urge the quick conclusion of a peace treaty with Japan. In MacArthur's view, the first two years of the Occupation had successfully demilitarized Japan, implemented the structural reforms necessary for democracy, and provided what he called the "spiritual revolution" essential to Japan's future welfare. What was necessary now, he thought, was for Japan to regain a spirit of independence so that its economy could grow without excessive reliance on American aid. MacArthur stressed that a prolonged occupation would only create resentments that might undo what had so painstakingly been accomplished.

MacArthur's comments helped to set off a fierce debate about the kind of treaty that should be written. On the one hand, the British Commonwealth countries, China, and many of the Southeast Asian nations that had suffered most at the hands of the Japanese, argued that the treaty should be tough, complete with provisions for reparations and demilitarization under close international supervision. Great Britain also worried about a flood of cheap Japanese exports that would have serious economic consequences for the British position in Asia. Advocates of a tough treaty claimed that the Treaty of Versailles (1919) had helped to cause World War II by not sufficiently demonstrating to the German people that they had been thoroughly defeated in World War I. This position was apparently held by Hugh Borton (b 1903) and other prominent officials in the US State Department, and it was reflected in several of the draft treaties produced by the Borton group in the year after MacArthur's press conference.

Advocates of a softer peace treaty held just the opposite view of Versailles. Claiming that the harsh *Diktat* of 1919 had both spawned the resentments that brought Adolf Hitler to power and imposed unreasonable reparations demands that eventually destroyed Europe's economy, this group put primary emphasis upon a treaty that the ruling Japanese government could regard without humiliation. Advocates of this view rapidly gained influence in the United States, both because the Occupation was generally popular in Japan—suggesting that further structural reforms were unnecessary—and because the cold war with Russia and the Marshall Plan in Europe had stretched American capabilities to the utmost. Secretary of State Dean Acheson was the most prominent member of this group, believing, as he later put it in his memoirs, that it was "obvious beyond doubt" that "Western Europe and the United States could not contain the Soviet Union and suppress Germany and Japan at the same time."

Who should participate in the negotiation process was also a thorny question. As the dominant power in the Occupation, the United States naturally wished to ensure that its policies would prevail in any treaty that was signed. Countering this wish were not only Russian demands for a radically different kind of negotiating process, but also calls by the British Commonwealth countries and the other members of the 13-nation FAR EASTERN COMMISSION for honest and adequate consultation. The victory of the communists on the mainland of China and the establishment of a separate Chinese nationalist regime on Taiwan in 1949 added a third, particularly emotional, point of contention over who should be invited to participate. This issue divided the noncommunist powers, as both Great Britain and India recognized the People's Republic of China and believed that this government, not the American-backed Nationalists, should represent China.

The question of Japan's defense was a third major concern throughout the treaty negotiations. Many US Defense Department officials, upset by the riots and the general strength of the Left in Japan, apparently believed that it would be impossible to maintain American military bases in Japan unless the United States had enough control over the Japanese government to ensure that domestic insurrection could be put down. Others accepted the logic of Acheson's and MacArthur's idea that a prolonged occupation would actually decrease the likelihood of friendly relations, but thought that discussions of peace would be "premature" until the Korean War, which had broken out on 25 June 1950, was ended. Of the four parties involved in the negotiating process, Acheson later recalled that the Pentagon offered the "most stubborn and protracted opposition" precisely because its wishes could not be ignored.

In an effort to resolve these problems, the United States began its "piecemeal peace" program of restoring as much national sovereignty to the Japanese government as possible, and at the same time hinted that it would conclude peace with the Japanese whether or not the other Allies agreed. Also important was the appointment by President Harry S. Truman and Secretary Acheson of John Foster DULLES as foreign policy adviser to the US secretary of state. The foremost Republican foreign policy expert outside of the government, Dulles was expected to bring badly needed bipartisan support to this exceedingly complex issue.

Dulles embarked upon a series of bilateral negotiations designed to complete the treaty. British Commonwealth objections were met by including some British suggestions in the final text, by making the United Kingdom cosponsor of the actual peace conference, and by appointing the Australian ambassador to the United States, P.C. Spender, as vice-president of the conference. Moreover, the signing of the ANZUS treaty of defense between Australia, New Zealand, and the United States, tended to dispel fears of revived Japanese militarism. Intense Philippine objections were met by the promise of American aid and by the Philippine defense pact signed on 31 August 1951. Disputes over China were settled by inviting neither Chinese government to the conference and by asking Japan to negotiate the problem of Chinese relations separately. This decision plus the continued presence of American troops in Japan caused India to withdraw from the formal San Francisco Peace Conference held between 4 and 8 September 1951; nevertheless, 51 other Allied nations and Japan carried forward the negotiations for peace.

At the conference itself, the United States and Britain quickly moved certain rules of procedure to govern the scope of the debate. When these passed handily, Acheson, acting now in his capacity as president of the peace conference, ruled communist protests on the substance of the treaty out of order and proceeded to call for a vote. Although often described as a skillful outmaneuvering of the communist side, the failure of attempts to change the draft appears in hindsight to have been due primarily to the overwhelming preponderance of American power in Japan. The Soviet Union, Poland, and Czechoslovakia, the only communist countries represented, had little hope of influencing the outcome and soon walked out without signing a treaty. Peace with the Soviet Union and the fate of various northern territories such as the HABOMAI ISLANDS would continue to be major problems for Japanese diplomacy throughout the postwar period.

The treaty was reasonably generous in its terms. As promised in various wartime statements, Japan was deprived of all of its territories seized since 1895, including Taiwan, Korea, southern Sakhalin, and subsidiary islands. American trusteeship of the RYŪKYŪ ISLANDS including OKINAWA was permitted indefinitely, though a 1972 treaty later returned these American-held islands to Japan. Japan was not permitted to pardon war criminals convicted by the

International Military Tribunal for the Far East, except upon majority approval by the 11 participating nations; the last such approval was requested and granted in 1958. Japan renounced all claims to property in its former colonies and occupied territories and agreed to pay reparations for war damage, but, in a major victory for the "soft peace" advocates, it was clearly stated in the treaty that Japan's fragile economic position would have to be respected. Other clauses promised Japan various technical rights, suggested support for United Nations membership, and generally granted sovereignty immediately upon ratification of the treaty by the United States and a majority of 11 other major non-communist nations. Japan and 48 other nations signed this document at San Francisco on 8 September 1951.

Ensuring US ratification then became the principal task for the American and Japanese negotiators. Warned by Dulles, then visiting Japan as a special envoy, that any dealings with the People's Republic of China would jeopardize Senate approval of the treaty, the Japanese prime minister YOSHIDA SHIGERU, in a 24 December 1951 letter to Dulles, promised to deal only with the Nationalists. Accordingly, on 28 April 1952, a peace treaty was signed with Nationalist China. In another letter to Dulles, on 7 February 1951, Yoshida promised cooperation with the powerful Pacific Fisheries Conference as a means of defusing Western opposition. Most important of all, the United States Japan Security Treaty (see UNITED STATES–JAPAN SECURITY TREATIES), signed two hours after the peace treaty, assured the continued presence of American forces and military bases in Japan. By 26 October 1951, the upper house of the Japanese Diet had approved the peace treaty by a vote of 174 to 45, and the security treaty by a vote of 147 to 76, while the lower house approved the peace treaty by a vote of 307 to 47 and the security treaty by a vote of 284 to 71. On 20 March 1952 the US Senate ratified the peace treaty by a vote of 60 to 10 and the security treaty by 58 to 9. The peace treaty went into effect on 28 April 1952, after the necessary majority of the other major ratifying powers had been achieved.

In the legal sense, the San Francisco Peace Treaty of 1951 is a document that ended the state of war between Japan and most of the Allied powers. It is notable chiefly for its relatively generous terms with regard to reparations, "war guilt," and the like, at least as these terms pertain to the four main islands of Japan. In a larger sense, however, the San Francisco Peace Treaty is an example of the way in which the Dulles–Acheson coalition replaced the Occupation of Japan with a network of US security alliances extending beyond Japan to the other nations of South and East Asia. Nominally the end of a state of war, the treaty and its accompanying entanglements actually set the stage for a new relationship between Japan and the United States that would become a major source of political contention in Japan.   *Peter* FROST

sangaku → **sarugaku**

Sangatsu Jiken → **March Incident**

Sanger, Margaret (1883–1966)

Leader of the birth control movement in the United States. Born in Corning, New York. In June 1921 an article by Sanger appeared in the Japanese magazine *Kaizō,* and in March 1922 at the invitation of the publisher she arrived in Japan to give a series of lectures. Although closely watched by police, who confiscated most of her pamphlets and contraceptives, she was able to give eight lectures in Tōkyō and Yokohama. However, in deference to official opposition she did not speak, as planned, in Kyōto, Ōsaka, and Kōbe and left Japan early in April. Sanger's activities aroused much interest, and she is considered the initiator of the birth control movement in Japan. Her tract, *Family Limitation,* in which she discusses specific means of preventing pregnancy, was translated and privately published by YAMAMOTO SENJI. In 1954 she again went to Tōkyō to attend the founding ceremony of the Nihon Kazoku Keikaku Remmei (Family Planning Federation of Japan). See also FAMILY PLANNING.

sangi

(councillor). 1. An extrastatutory post (RYŌGE NO KAN), that is, one not prescribed by the TAIHŌ CODE (701) and YŌRŌ CODE (effective 757) as part of the RITSURYŌ SYSTEM of government. Created in

729. Chosen from among officials of the fourth rank and above (see COURT RANKS), the *sangi,* who numbered eight from the 9th century onward, worked with the grand minister of state *(dajō daijin)* and other members of the policy-making section of the Grand Council of State (DAJŌKAN), the nation's highest deliberative body.

2. A post in the Meiji Dajōkan, as the early Meiji government (i.e., that of 1868–85) was called. The post was established in August 1869, and the first to hold it were ŌKUBO TOSHIMICHI and others from the domains that had led the movement that resulted in the Meiji Restoration. Until 1871 the role of the *sangi* (their number varied, but there were usually around 10) was to assist the ministers of the left and right *(sadaijin* and *udaijin)* and the great counselors *(dainagon).* Under the third Meiji Dajōkan system (i.e., after the reorganization of 13 September 1871), the *sangi,* together with the newly reestablished grand minister of state *(dajō daijin)* and the ministers of the left and the right, formed the Seiin, the central deliberative body of the new government. Except for one brief period it was customary for the *sangi* to serve concurrently as heads of the ministries. The post ceased to exist when the Dajōkan was replaced by the cabinet system in 1885.

Sangoku jidai → **Korean Three Kingdoms period**

Sangoku Kanshō → **Tripartite Intervention**

Sangyō gisho

The three commentaries on Buddhist sutras by Prince SHŌTOKU (574–622), under whose patronage Buddhism became fully established in Japan. The three commentaries are *Shōmangyō gisho* (on the *Śrīmālādevī-siṃhanāda-sūtra*), *Yuimagyō gisho* (on the *Vimala-kīrti-nirdeśa-sūtra*), and *Hokke gisho* (on the LOTUS SUTRA), all probably composed between 609 and 615. Although these are the oldest Japanese Buddhist commentaries, they show a remarkable grasp of Buddhist philosophy and manifest deep religious feeling. Some recent scholars have argued that these commentaries may not be by Prince Shōtoku.   *Robert* RHODES

San'ichigo Jiken → **March 15th Incident**

San'in Coast National Park

(San'in Kaigan Kokuritsu Kōen). A long, narrow park, situated in western Honshū, in Kyōto, Hyōgo, and Tottori prefectures, stretching some 77 km (48 mi) along the Sea of Japan coast. The park is characterized by numerous small bays and islets, strangely shaped rock formations, and gentle hills. Kinosaki Hot Spring, in the eastern end of the park, near the town of KINOSAKI, is a popular resort facing the sea and surrounded by low hills. The coasts around Kasumi, in the center of the park, and at Uradome, in the west are noted for their rock islands and caves. At the western tip of the park are the TOTTORI SAND DUNES, the largest in Japan. Notable among the plant and animal life are the black pine *(kuromatsu),* the Japanese martin *(iwatsubame),* and the black-tailed gull *(umineko).* Area: 90 sq km (34.7 sq mi).

Sanja Festival

(Sanja Matsuri). Annual festival of the Asakusa Shrine (also known as Sanja Myōjin) in Taitō Ward, Tōkyō. One of the major festivals of Edo (now Tōkyō) along with the KANDA FESTIVAL and the SANNŌ FESTIVAL. High points of the festival include the parading of about 100 portable shrines (MIKOSHI), the dance called *binzasara no mai,* and *tekomai,* a dance perfomed by *geisha.* In the Edo period (1600–1868) the festival was held in the third lunar month, but since the Meiji period (1868–1912) it has been held on the Saturday and Sunday nearest to 17–18 May.   *Ōtō Tokihiko*

sanjo

A medieval type of "base people" (*semmin;* see RYŌMIN). The term, literally meaning "scattered places," originated late in the Heian period (794–1185) and was used in contradistinction to *honjo,* the main residence and managerial headquarters of an aristocratic SHŌEN (landed estate) proprietor, to denote such scattered possessions as suburban villas, pasturage, and timberland; in the Kamakura period (1185–1333) it came to mean the nonagricultural portions of a *shōen*. The service population grouped together in such places, originally called *sanjo zōshiki* or *sanjo meshitsugi*, by extension also became known as *sanjo*. Their provenance was among people who sought to escape various exactions by subordinating themselves to powerful individuals or institutions, for whom they performed miscellaneous specialized services in exchange for protection. As early as 1072, *sanjo zōshiki* exempt from public duties are mentioned in official documents, along with analogous groups such as JINNIN.

Sanjo included fishermen and boatmen, sweepers, gardeners, dike builders, charcoal burners, metal casters and swordsmiths, entertainers (*shomoji*) and soothsayers (*ommyōji*); they engaged in farming only as a secondary occupation. They were set apart from and increasingly ostracized by farmers; especially as the sense of solidarity and exclusiveness grew among members of agricultural communities in the Muromachi period (1333–1568), *sanjo* became objects of discrimination, being considered "base" along with such other groups as KAWARAMONO ("riverbed dwellers"). *Kawaramono*, however, were subject to no particular master, whereas *sanjo* were; accordingly, *sanjo* enjoyed certain privileges and a marginally higher social status. In 1428, for instance, *sanjo* (equated in the contemporary source with *shomoji*) replaced *kawaramono* (identified as *eta* and "unclean") as the sweepers of the Imperial Palace grounds in Kyōto.

In response to discrimination, *sanjo* formed their own communities, variously labeled *sanjo mura*, *shomoji mura*, and *kotsujiki chō* ("beggar settlements"). An early instance is the *sanjo* community associated with the Shingon temple TŌJI in Kyōto, mentioned from 1317; by 1394 it had grown to occupy a fairly extensive area along Kujō Avenue. Members of this community by 1489 had formed a guild (ZA) under the protection of the aristocratic Sanjō and Sanjōnishi families and secured monopolistic privileges in the production and distribution of indigo. Other *sanjo* communities in the Kyōto vicinity developed the strength to engage in conflicts, involving up to 2,000 people, with their social "betters," for example with retainers of the KONOE FAMILY in 1527, the Yamashina family in 1549, and the Fushimi family the following year. Although *sanjo* thereby managed to better their social position in the Sengoku period (1467–1568), these and similar settlements are regarded by some historians as the antecedents of the *hisabetsu buraku* ("communities that suffer discrimination"; see BURAKUMIN) of the Edo (1600–1868) and modern periods.

George ELISON

Sanjō

City in central Niigata Prefecture, central Honshū. Located on the river Shinanogawa, Sanjō developed as one of the POST-STATION TOWNS on the highway Hokuriku Kaidō during the Edo period (1600–1868). Its ironware industry dates from the early 18th century and is especially known for its carpenter's tools, scissors, and knives. Of note are the temples Honjōji, founded in the 13th century, and a branch of Kyōto's Higashi Honganji. Pop: 85,276.

Sanjō, Emperor (976–1017)

The 67th sovereign (*tennō*) in the traditional count (which includes several nonhistorical emperors); reigned 1011–16. Second son of Emperor Reizei (950–1011; r 967–969); his mother was a sister of FUJIWARA NO MICHINAGA. Chafing under the domination of Michinaga, who was then at the height of his career (a daughter of Michinaga was also one of Sanjō's consorts) and suffering from an eye ailment, Sanjō relinquished the throne after an ineffectual and uneventful reign of five years.

Sanjōnishi Sanetaka (1455–1537)

Courtier, poet, and polymath of the Sengoku period (1467–1568). The son of the *naidaijin* (inner minister) Sanjōnishi (Fujiwara) Kin'yasu (d 1460), Sanetaka was himself appointed to that high court post in 1506. His reputation, however, does not rest on his service to the powerless imperial court or his close association with leading figures of the increasingly impotent MUROMACHI SHOGUNATE. Rather, it is based on his maintenance and transmission of the highest cultural standards in an age that he himself described as "unspeakable" and a time of "war, contention, and brute force."

Sanetaka studied with some of the period's leading literary figures, including SŌGI, whom he assisted in compiling the *renga* (linked-verse; see RENGA AND HAIKAI) collection SHINSEN TSUKUBASHŪ and by whom he was initiated into the secret traditions (see KOKIN DENJU) of the KOKINSHŪ poetry anthology. He was himself a highly accomplished WAKA and *renga* poet; the author of at least one NŌ play, *Sagoromo*; an authority on classical Japanese literature, notably the TALE OF GENJI; a student of Chinese history; an expert on etiquette and ceremonial matters (YŪSOKU KOJITSU); a renowned calligrapher; and a master of SHŌGI (Japanese chess). Among his notable works are the poetry collections *Setsugyokushū* and *Chōsetsushū*; the diary of his poetic activities, *Saishōshō*; the book of poetic theory, *Eika taigaishō*; the study of the *Tale of Genji*, *Genji monogatari sairyūshō*; and the treatise on ceremonial matters, *Shōzokushō*. His diary, SANETAKA KŌ KI, which with some interruptions covers the years 1474–1536, is an indispensable source for the history of politics, society, art, and culture in his age.

George ELISON

Sanjō Sanetomi (1837–1891)

Court noble and political leader at the time of the MEIJI RESTORATION of 1868. Born in Kyōto to one of the GOSEKKE, the five main branches of the Fujiwara family whose members were entitled to be appointed imperial regent. Under the influence of his father, Sanetsumu (1802–59), who had met shogunate censure in the ANSEI PURGE, Sanjō became a supporter of the SONNŌ JŌI (Revere the Emperor, Expel the Barbarians) movement. In 1863 he was appointed to the newly created post of *kokuji goyō-gakari* (commissioner of state affairs) at the imperial court, where he played a leading role among the nobles eager to overthrow the Tokugawa shogunate (1603–1867) and restore political power to the emperor. He established contacts with *samurai* from Chōshū (now Yamaguchi Prefecture), the domain most active in the imperial cause. When the COUP D'ETAT OF 30 SEPTEMBER 1863 brought to power Aizu (now part of Fukushima Prefecture) and Satsuma (now Kagoshima Prefecture), the two domains favoring reconciliation between the shogunate and the court, Sanjō and six other nobles fled to Chōshū (see SHICHIKYŌ OCHI). He returned to Kyōto after the last Tokugawa shōgun, TOKUGAWA YOSHINOBU, returned government powers to the emperor (see TAISEI HŌKAN) in November 1867. Named to the Gijō (Office of Administration; see SANSHOKU) in the following year, together with the nobleman IWAKURA TOMOMI he became a central figure in the new government. In 1869 he was appointed *udaijin* (minister of the right), and two years later he became *dajō daijin* (grand minister of state). He remained in the post until 1885, when the cabinet system was introduced. Although Sanjō occupied high posts, he was by nature a timid man, and in crises such as the debate over invading Korea (see SEIKANRON), he was easily intimidated by Iwakura and others.

Sanjūrokkasen

(The Thirty-Six Poetic Geniuses). A listing of outstanding Japanese poets from the time of the poetry anthology *Man'yōshū* (759) to the end of the 10th century, based on a no longer extant anthology known as the *Sanjūrokunin sen* (Selection of Thirty-Six Poets), which was compiled in the early 11th century by the influential poet and critic FUJIWARA NO KINTŌ and inspired by the earlier group of the Six Poetic Geniuses (ROKKASEN). The chief importance of the list is that it led in the mid-11th century to the making or remaking of personal poetry collections (SHIKASHŪ) for all of the 36 poets, thus helping to preserve their work.

Kintō chose about 150 poems, 3 to 5 of the finest poems of each poet, probably with the intention of comparing them in an imaginary poetry contest. The sumptuous 12th-century Nishi Honganji version of the anthology of the type known as the Anthologies of the Thirty-Six Poets (Sanjūrokunin Kashū) comprises the vastly expanded complete collections of the works of each poet.

These poets were a favored topic with artists, and paintings of the 36 as a group (KASEN-E) were probably first produced in the 12th century, but the earliest extant examples date from the 13th century and were inspired by a new interest in realistic portraiture. These early portraits generally took the form of horizontal handscrolls in which each seated poet was paired with one of his or her poems to represent an ideal integration of painting, poetry, and calligraphy. Kintō's set of 36 remained the most popular, but subsequent generations assembled their own favorites and illustrated them not only in scrolls but in albums, plaques, and screens.

Sanjūsangendō

The present structure, dating from 1266, is a reconstruction of the original built in 1164. Rengeōin, Kyōto. National Treasure.

Not all the poets are now considered first-rate, but the complete list in alphabetical order is as follows: ARIWARA NO NARIHIRA, Bishop HENJŌ, Fujiwara no Asatada, Fujiwara no Atsutada, FUJIWARA NO KANESUKE, Fujiwara no Kiyotada, Fujiwara no Motozane, Fujiwara no Muneyuki, Fujiwara no Nakafumi, Fujiwara no Okikaze, Fujiwara no Takamitsu, Fujiwara no Toshiyuki, ISE, KAKINOMOTO NO HITOMARO, KI NO TOMONORI, KI NO TSURAYUKI, Kiyohara no Motosuke, Kodai no Kimi, Mibu no Tadami, MIBU NO TADAMINE, Minamoto no Kintada, Minamoto no Saneakira, Minamoto no Shigeyuki, MINAMOTO NO SHITAGAU, Nakatsukasa, Ōnakatomi no Yorimoto, ŌNAKATOMI NO YOSHINOBU, ONO NO KOMACHI, ŌSHIKŌCHI NO MITSUNE, ŌTOMO NO YAKAMOCHI, Saigū no Nyōgo, Sakanoue no Korenori, Sarumaru no Daibu (Sarumaru Dayū), the priest SOSEI, Taira no Kanemori, YAMABE NO AKAHITO. *Phillip T. HARRIES and Julia MEECH-PEKARIK*

Sanjūsangendō

The main hall (hondō), and only building, of the Rengeōin, a small Buddhist temple affiliated with the Myōhōin, a TENDAI SECT temple located in Higashiyama Ward, Kyōto. The Sanjūsangendō is so named because the inner sanctum is made up of 33 (sanjūsan) bays (ken) separated by evenly spaced pillars. It houses numerous valuable pieces of Buddhist sculpture dating from the Kamakura period (1185–1333) and is itself a representative example of Kamakura Buddhist architecture.

The Sanjūsangendō has a rather complex history. In 1130 the retired emperor TOBA converted the temple Hōjūji into his imperial residence, and then in 1132, he had built on the same site a *sentai kannondō* (hall for a thousand images of KANNON), which became known as Tokuchōjuin. Later, the retired emperor GO-SHIRAKAWA moved his residence near the Tokuchōjuin and had the warrior ruler TAIRA NO KIYOMORI construct another temple, the Rengeōin on its west side (1164); the *hondō* (main hall) of the Rengeōin was a *sentai kannondō* which became known as the Sanjūsangendō. In 1185 an earthquake destroyed the Tokuchōjuin, and the structure was never rebuilt. The Rengeōin was also destroyed by fire in 1249. By 1266 its *hondō* had been reconstructed by the retired emperor GO-TOBA; it is this structure that is presently known as Rengeōin or Sanjūsangendō.

Among the statuary housed in the temple sanctum are 1,001 "Thousand-armed Kannon" (Senju Kannon) statues carved by the Kamakura master sculptor TANKEI (1173–1256), Kōen (b 1207), and others; there are also carvings of the wind and thunder gods and of the 28 followers of Kannon. The numerous carvings of Kannon were executed in the belief that the people of this degenerate latter age of Buddha's law (*mappō;* see ESCHATOLOGY) could be saved only through innumerable pious acts of devotion. The *nandaimon* (south main gate) and the adjoining *tsuijibei* (*tsuiji* fence) were both erected by the hegemon Toyotomi Hideyoshi in the late 16th century and have been designated Important Cultural Properties.

During the Edo period (1600–1868) the Sanjūsangendō was famous as a site for archery contests known as *tōshiya*. Matches were held under the overhanging eaves of the narrow outer passageway. Competing archers tested their skill by shooting from one end at targets set at the opposite end of the passageway, a distance of some 120 meters (394 ft), and seeing how many hits they could score in a fixed period of time. *Tōshiya* contests became so popular for a time that another Sanjūsangendō was built in Edo (now Tōkyō) for similar competitions, but it was destroyed in 1833 and never rebuilt.

Hoyu ISHIDA

sanka

(literally, "mountain cave"). Term referring to a type of people who formerly maintained a migratory way of life in the mountains of Japan. Typically traveling in family units and living in tents pitched along mountain streams, they made their living by selling the fish they caught or the winnows, baskets, and brooms they produced. They moved south in the winter and north in the summer. Nothing definite is known about their origins. Their number diminished drastically during and after World War II. *Sanka* are one type of *yamabito* ("mountain people"), a broad term covering all those who make their living in the mountains. Such people have always been treated as strange and different by the rest of Japanese society, where settled pursuit of agriculture represents the traditional ideal.

SAKURADA Katsunori

Sankan → sekisho

sankechi

(literally, "three press-dyes"). Three resist-dyeing techniques of *kyōkechi, rōkechi* and *kōkechi;* also referred to as Tempyō *no sankechi* (*sankechi* of the Tempyō era [729–749]). Along with the introduction of Buddhism and Chinese culture to Japan in the 6th century, continental dyeing techniques were imported and flourished in Japan. Numerous samples of all three resist-dyeing techniques are preserved at both the temple HŌRYŪJI and the SHŌSŌIN repository in Nara.

The details of *kyōkechi*, a block-resist technique, remain a mystery of the Nara period (710–794). It is thought to have been accomplished by folding silk gauze (*ra*), clamping it between two boards cut through with a design, pressing firmly and immersing in dye; if several colors were desired, the sections were dyed by pouring dye into the openings in the boards.

In *rōkechi*, a technique similar to batik, the cloth was stamped with wax (*rō*) or other resin by means of a printing block, then dyed. Multicolored pieces of cloth were made by repeating these steps; also, by using blocks, a large design could be printed over the entire piece of fabric. Both *kyōkechi* and *rōkechi* were used with silk and thus produced high quality goods (see also WAX-RESIST DYEING).

Kōkechi is single color TIE-DYEING, including white-spotted or dapple tie-dyeing, stitched tie-dyeing, folded or pressed tie-dyeing. Almost all the methods used now derive from this ancient technique, but *kōkechi* alone has survived to the present. All these methods were primarily used by craftsmen affiliated with the court, temples, and shrines, and their products were used in temple or shrine ceremonies or as clothing for members of the court.

HIROI Nobuko

Sankeien

Garden in Naka Ward, Yokohama, Kanagawa Prefecture; built by Hara Tomitarō, a wealthy businessman, and opened to the public in 1906. It consists of several ponds and many varieties of flowering tree, including apricot and cherry trees, as well as azaleas and wisteria. A number of historic buildings have been brought here; these include an old farmhouse from Gifu Prefecture, and a tea ceremony house built by the shōgun TOKUGAWA IEMITSU.

Sankei shimbun

A large national daily newspaper. It was first launched in Ōsaka in 1933 by Maeda Hisakichi as a financial trade paper under the banner *Nihon kōgyō shimbun*. During World War II when many newspapers were forced to merge, the *Nihon kōgyō* absorbed many smaller papers. In 1942 the name was changed to *Sangyō keizai shimbun*. The paper began putting out an edition in Tōkyō in 1950, and the business news format was dropped in favor of more general news coverage. In 1955 it merged with the JIJI SHIMPŌ to form the *Sankei jiji*. This enterprise did not prosper, and in 1958 it took the name *Sankei shimbun* and businessman MIZUNO SHIGEO became company president. The *Sankei* underwent rapid modernization of management. In 1967 it joined with FUJI TELECASTING CO, LTD, NIPPON CULTURAL BROADCASTING, INC, and NIPPON BROADCASTING SYSTEM, INC, in forming the Fuji–Sankei group, a large newspaper and radio and television concern. The *Sankei* generally tends to be politically conservative and maintains an anticommunist stand. Its main offices are in Tōkyō and Ōsaka with regional offices in Kyūshū and Hokkaidō where it cooperates with various local papers. It maintains 11 overseas news bureaus and has special contractual agreements with the Associated Press (AP) and the *Chicago Daily News.* In addition to its daily, it also publishes two other papers, *Sankei supōtsu* and *Fuji-Sankei ribingu;* a weekly magazine, *Shūkan sankei;* and books. In 1980 its capital funds totaled ¥2 billion (US $9.1 million). Circulation: 1.97 million (1980).

Sanki Engineering Co, Ltd

(Sanki Kōgyō). Company engaged mainly in the installation of equipment for air conditioning, water supply, drainage, electricity, and other systems in construction projects. A member of the MITSUI group, it supplies equipment to the mining and chemical industries, and is involved in producing labor-saving transportation and environmental protection equipment. It is active in introducing foreign technology. Plans for the future include increased operations to develop resource and energy conservation equipment. Sales for the fiscal year ending March 1982 totaled ¥117.2 billion (US $486 million) and the company was capitalized at ¥4 billion (US $16.6 million). Its head office is in Tōkyō.

sankin kōtai

(alternate attendance). A rule of the TOKUGAWA SHOGUNATE formalized in 1635, whereby *daimyō* were required to reside in alternate years at Edo (now Tōkyō) in attendance on the shōgun.

The *sankin kōtai* system was a device of the Tokugawa shogunate, the government of Japan from 1603 to 1867, to maintain control over the more than 260 daimyō or territorial lords who were the virtually autonomous feudal rulers of four-fifths of the country. The term *sankin,* which meant "reporting to one's lord to render service," referred to the obligation of the daimyō as feudatories of the shōgun to attend him at his capital in Edo, dividing their time equally between the capital and their domains. This service—actually a polite form of hostageship—was performed in alternating groups so that when one group of daimyō reported to the capital, its counterpart was made to *kōtai* or "rotate" back to the provinces. To perform this *sankin* obligation, the daimyō had to maintain *yashiki* or residential estates in Edo, where their wives and children were permanently detained by the shogunate.

The *sankin kōtai* system was based on customs and practices observed by Japanese vassals and their suzerains since early feudal times. These precedents were utilized by the 16th-century unifiers of feudal Japan, ODA NOBUNAGA, TOYOTOMI HIDEYOSHI, and TOKUGAWA IEYASU, to strengthen their power over the daimyō who had submitted to them. It remained for Ieyasu's immediate successors to shape these practices into a comprehensive system of feudal control. After an initial period of more or less informal enforcement, the *sankin kōtai* was regularized and made a compulsory system between 1635 and 1642 under the third shōgun, TOKUGAWA IEMITSU.

Under the compulsory *sankin kōtai* system, the typical daimyō traveled to the capital every other year, returning to his domain after a year's service. (Hereditary vassals of the Tokugawa usually rotated every six months.) He made each journey during a specified month of the year in accordance with a fixed schedule laid down by the shogunate. He normally traveled with a retinue of 150 to 300, sometimes many more (see DAIMYŌ PROCESSIONS), over a designated route, using the main highways, which were all under shogunal control (see GOKAIDŌ). He was received at the capital as a guest of the shōgun, with whom he exchanged customary gifts on his arrival and departure and on numerous other ceremonial occasions. He sometimes contributed guards to man the gates of the shogunal palace and temples, but his main duties were to serve in attendance at the shōgun's court. Normally, he maintained at least three *yashiki* in Edo, to house himself, his family, and a large number of retainers and servants. He paid for his journeys, the staffing and upkeep of his Edo establishments, and other *sankin* expenses by selling tax rice from his domain in Ōsaka or Edo. About 70 to 80 percent of his total income was consumed by *sankin*-related expenditures. This steady financial drain, together with frequent emergency outlays, kept him chronically in debt to the moneylenders and merchants of the city.

The acute financial distress of the daimyō and the erosion of feudal power caused by the *sankin kōtai* system led to frequent questioning of its merits and to various reform proposals. However, except for an eight-year suspension between 1722 and 1730 for emergency reasons, the system remained in operation without significant change for over 200 years until it was finally terminated in 1862.

During its long life the *sankin kōtai* system had a pervasive influence on the political, economic, and social development of the Japanese nation and contributed significantly to preparing the ground for the modern state that emerged after the collapse of the Tokugawa regime. The effectiveness of the *sankin kōtai* system in concentrating power in the hands of the shogunate helped ease the transition after 1868 from feudal rule to the more centralized administration of the new Meiji government. By fostering the growth of Edo and Ōsaka into populous cities and centers of commerce involving the whole country, it helped create a national economy. Moreover, by expanding contacts and providing the means for the exchange of ideas and information among leadership elements and intellectuals from all parts of Japan, it promoted the cultural and ideological unification of the country, thus helping the new Japan of the Meiji Restoration (1868) to cope more effectively and successfully with the challenges of modern nationhood.

◼ ——Toshio G. Tsukahira, *Feudal Control in Tokugawa Japan: The Sankin Kōtai System* (1966). *Toshio G. TSUKAHIRA*

sankōsha gogengyō

(the three public corporations and five government enterprises). General term for Japan's three most important public corporations (*kōsha*) and five important government enterprises (*gengyō*). The three public corporations are the JAPANESE NATIONAL RAILWAYS, NIPPON TELEGRAPH AND TELEPHONE PUBLIC CORPORATION, and the JAPAN TOBACCO AND SALT PUBLIC CORPORATION. All these are run independently of the state, although the state funds and has ultimate authority over them. The five government enterprises, on the other hand, are run by government agencies. They are the postal services (Ministry of Posts and Telecommunications), the national forests (Ministry of Agriculture, Forestry, and Fisheries), the Alcohol Monopoly Enterprise Bureau (Ministry of International Trade and Industry), the Printing Bureau, and the Mint Bureau (the last two under the Ministry of Finance). These eight organizations are distinguished from other public corporations and government enterprises because their employees are treated by law as government employees, so that although they do have the right to collective bargaining, they do not have the right to strike, a fact which has been a source of discontent and agitation over the years. See PUBLIC CORPORATIONS.

Sankō Steamship Co, Ltd

(Sankō Kisen). One of Japan's leading maritime transport companies. Established in 1934, it opposed the government's policy of consolidating the shipping industry in 1964 and followed an independent course, growing into one of the world's largest tanker operators. During Japan's high economic growth period, the company concentrated on operation of middle-sized tankers, and as a result it encountered less difficulties than those companies operating larger vessels following the OIL CRISIS OF 1973. It also is engaged in the buying and selling of securities and ships, and has companies incorporated in Hong Kong, Singapore, Amsterdam, and New York. It owns 45 ships totaling 7,183,000 deadweight tons. Sales for the fiscal year ending March 1982 totaled ¥312.4 billion (US $1.3 billion), and the company was capitalized at ¥40.4 billion (US $167.8 million). Corporate headquarters are located in Ōsaka.

Sankyō Aluminium Industry Co, Ltd

(Sankyō Aruminiumu Kōgyō). Manufacturer of aluminum sash and kitchenwares. Established in 1960, it was originally engaged in the production of aluminum kitchen products, but with the initiation of aluminum sash production in 1960, it won a nationwide market and is now the third largest sash maker in Japan. Sales for the fiscal year ending May 1982 totaled ¥158.1 billion (US $667 million), and the company was capitalized at ¥3.9 billion (US $16.5 million) in the same year. Corporate headquarters are located in the city of Takaoka, Toyama Prefecture.

Sankyō Co, Ltd

Manufacturer of pharmaceuticals, agricultural chemicals, food additives, and chemical products. Sankyō was established in 1899 to market the digestive medicine Taka-Diastase invented by TAKAMINE JŌKICHI. It also developed numerous pharmaceuticals, including the vitamin B_1 supplement Oryzanin first extracted by SUZUKI UMETARŌ. It has technical and business tie-ups with companies in the United States and Europe and joint venture companies in India and Taiwan. Sales for the fiscal year ending March 1982 totaled ¥205 billion (US $851 million), and the company was capitalized at ¥10 billion (US $42 million) in the same year. Corporate headquarters are located in Tōkyō.

Sankyō Seikō Co, Ltd

Trader in fabrics, fashion apparel, interior decorating materials, and electrical and industrial machinery; also a leading importer and licensed producer of famous American and European brands of fashion apparel. Established in 1938, it is now attempting to expand its garment manufacturing operations overseas and establish technical tie-ups with leading foreign companies. It has three overseas subsidiaries and is participating in two joint overseas ventures. Sales for the fiscal year ending September 1981 totaled ¥107.9 billion (US $469 million), and the company was capitalized at ¥3 billion (US $13 million). Corporate headquarters are located in Kōbe.

Sankyū, Inc

(Sankyū Un'yu Kikō). Company engaged in the shipment of material chiefly among the various steel mills of the NIPPON STEEL CORPORATION; the unloading of imported iron ore and other steelmaking materials; and the shipment, installation, and maintenance of plants. It was established in 1917. In parallel with the increase in steel plants exported by Nippon Steel, the company's volume of overseas projects has risen in recent years. It has joint companies which act as distribution bases in Hong Kong, Singapore, and Rio de Janeiro. Annual revenue at the end of March 1982 was ¥137.9 billion (US $572.9 million), of which 40 percent was from Nippon Steel; the company was capitalized at ¥10.1 billion (US $42 million). Corporate headquarters are located in Tōkyō.

Sannō Festival

(Sannō Matsuri). Major Shintō festival of the HIE SHRINE (popularly called Sannōsama) in Tōkyō; celebrated in recent times in odd numbered years over several days around 10–16 June. During the Edo period (1600–1868) the deity Sannō Gongen, associated with the shrine, was designated a tutelary deity of the Tokugawa family, and Hie Shrine was granted shogunal patronage. The extravagant Sannō Festival was held every other year, alternating with the KANDA FESTIVAL. The Sannō, Kanda and Nezu festivals were considered the three great *matsuri* of Edo. Neighborhood groups carried portable shrines (MIKOSHI) and paraded floats (DASHI) of their own design into Edo Castle. The festival lost much of its grandeur early in this century.

Sannō Festival refers as well to the annual festival of the original Hie Shrine (Hiyoshi Taisha) in the city of Ōtsu, Shiga Prefecture. Though not as well known, the Ōtsu festival has a much longer history than the one in Tōkyō. Also called Hie Matsuri, it is held from 12 April to 15 April; the highlight is a flotilla of *mikoshi* on Lake Biwa on 14 April.   INOKUCHI Shōji

Sannō Ichijitsu Shintō

A syncretic Buddhist-Shintō school that sought to harmonize the teachings of the Buddhist TENDAI SECT with the cult of the Hie Shrine on Mt. Hiei (Hieizan). When the monk Saichō (767–822) established the Enryakuji, the chief temple of the Tendai sect on Mt. Hiei, he is said to have chosen Ōyamakui no Kami, a deity of the Hie Shrine who presides over Mt. Hiei, to protect the temple. This deity was soon renamed Sannō (Mountain King) after the Chinese deity of this name who guarded Mt. Tiantai (T'ien-t'ai) in China, where Saichō had studied.

Although Saichō is traditionally regarded as the founder of Sannō Shintō, the school in fact arose in the 13th century under the influence of RYŌBU SHINTŌ. Based on the prevailing belief that Shintō deities were Japanese manifestations of Buddhist divinities (see HONJI SUIJAKU), Sannō Shintō held that the deities of the Hie

and Ise shrines corresponded, respectively, to the Buddhas Shaka (Skt: Śākyamuni) and Dainichi (Skt: Mahāvairocana). Just as Shaka, who preached the Lotus Sutra (Skt: *Saddharmapuṇḍarīka-sūtra*; J: Hokkekyō), and Dainichi, who is the central deity of ESOTERIC BUDDHISM (mikkyō), were ultimately identical in the view of Japanese Tendai, so too were the deities Sannō Gongen of the Hie Shrine and AMATERASU ŌMIKAMI of the Ise Shrine.

According to Sannō Shintō, the exoteric Buddha Shaka and the esoteric Buddha Dainichi transformed themselves in the various Buddhist lands into countless Buddhas and bodhisattvas in order to respond to the individual needs of mankind; in Japan, however, these two Buddhas became Sannō and Amaterasu, who in turn manifested themselves as the myriad Shintō deities of the Japanese islands. Since the Tendai sect regarded the Lotus Sutra as the only scripture relevant for Japan, it especially encouraged the worship of the deity Sannō, whom it regarded as the Japanese incarnation of Shaka, the Buddha of the Lotus Sutra.

Sannō Shintō was further developed by the Tendai monk Tenkai (1536–1643), who was a close adviser to the first Tokugawa shōgun, Ieyasu (1543–1616). Building on the earlier ideas of Sannō Shintō, Tenkai taught a doctrine known as Sannō Ichijitsu Shintō (Shintō That Reveals the One Truth of Sannō), which maintained that Amaterasu, while being the Shintō counterpart of Dainichi, is the ultimate source from which all Buddhist and Shintō deities spring. His ideas regarding Ichijitsu Shintō were formally accepted by the shogunate and were reflected in the decision to inter Ieyasu at Nikkō, where an elaborate Shintō-Buddhist mausoleum complex was erected. After the collapse of the shogunate in 1867, Sannō Ichijitsu Shintō virtually disappeared as a religious movement. See also ICHIJITSU SHINTŌ KI.   Stanley WEINSTEIN

Sano

City in southwestern Tochigi Prefecture, central Honshū. Sano developed in the Edo period (1600–1868) as one of the POST-STATION TOWNS on the highway to NIKKŌ and as a producer of cotton textiles and cast ironware. Principal industries are textiles and clothing, although the precision instrument, automobile parts, and plastic industries have been promoted in recent years. Pop: 78,351.

Sano Manabu (1892–1953)

Economist; social activist. Born in Ōita Prefecture. As a student at Tōkyō University, Sano became interested in the socialist movement and helped to found the study group SHINJINKAI. He received an appointment at Waseda University as a lecturer in economics in 1920. In 1922 he joined the newly established Japan Communist Party (JCP). Sano escaped the mass arrests of communists in the wake of the great Tōkyō Earthquake (1923) and fled to the Soviet Union. He returned to Japan in 1925 and helped to revive the JCP, serving as Central Committee chairman and also as a Comintern Committee member. In 1928 he again went to the Soviet Union just before another roundup of communists (see MARCH 15TH INCIDENT); there he attended the sixth Comintern meeting. On his return home Sano was arrested by Japanese authorities in Shanghai and sentenced by the Tōkyō District Court to life imprisonment. In June 1933, together with Nabeyama Sadachika (1901–79), he repudiated communism from his prison cell; his act inspired a series of recantations by fellow communists (see TENKŌ). His prison term was reduced to 15 years, and he was released in 1943. After World War II, he returned to Waseda University. He also founded a research center, the Nihon Seiji Keizai Kenkyūjo, for the study of socialist principles that might be applicable to a nation under an emperor.

Sano no Chigami no Otome (fl early 8th century)

("The Maiden Sano no Chigami"). A palace attendant of low rank, she served in the Bureau of the High Priestess of the Great Shrine at Ise. In violation of the strict taboo against the presence of men in the palace of the priestess, she had a clandestine affair with Nakatomi no Yakamori. The lovers were discovered, and Yakamori was exiled in 738 or thereabouts to the province of Echizen (now part of Fukui Prefecture). Book 15 of the MAN'YŌSHŪ (ca 759), the first great anthology of Japanese vernacular poetry, contains a series of 63 love poems exchanged between Chigami and Yakamori on the miseries of their separation. Of these, 23 poems are by Chigami. Running to hyperbole and stylish mannerisms, her poems nonetheless show technical skill and polish, and some convey a tone of passionate intensity which became a distinctive strain in women's poetry of the 9th century and later.

■ ——Ian H. Levy, *The Ten Thousand Leaves* (1981–). Nippon Gakujutsu Shinkōkai, tr, *The Man'yōshū: One Thousand Poems* (1940, repr 1965).   Robert H. BROWER

Sano Tsunetami (1822–1902)

Politician who founded the Red Cross in Japan. Born in the Saga domain (now part of Saga Prefecture), Sano studied WESTERN LEARNING, as Western-style science was then called, under Hirose Mototaka, OGATA KŌAN, ITŌ GEMBOKU, and others. He participated in the first naval training program held by the Tokugawa shogunate at Nagasaki and played a leading role in introducing Western science and in founding a naval force in his domain. In 1867 Sano inspected the military systems of various European countries; after the Meiji Restoration (1868), he took part in establishing the Japanese navy. In 1877, he established a relief organization called the Hakuaisha to treat soldiers who had been wounded in the SATSUMA REBELLION. This organization became the JAPANESE RED CROSS SOCIETY in 1887, and Sano served as its first president. He also served in the GENRŌIN, a protosenatorial body, and as minister of finance (*ōkurakyō*), privy councillor, and minister of agriculture and commerce.   SŌDA Hajime

Sanoyasu Dockyard Co, Ltd

(Sanoyasu Dokku). Medium-sized shipbuilding company producing ships in the 25,000–100,000 ton class. It also accepts orders for ship repairs as well as construction of bridges and steel structures. It was established in 1940 in Ōsaka and grew rapidly after World War II by increasing exports. In 1974 it expanded with the building of the Mizushima Shipyard in Okayama Prefecture. It is affiliated with SUMITOMO HEAVY INDUSTRIES, LTD. Sales for the fiscal year ending March 1982 totaled ¥39.6 billion (US $164.5 million), most of which derived from exports; the company was capitalized at ¥1.4 billion (US $5.8 million) in the same year. Corporate headquarters are located in Ōsaka.

Sanraku → Kanō Sanraku

Sanriku Coast

(Sanriku Kaigan). Coastal area. Extends from Samekaku in the city of Hachinohe, Aomori Prefecture, to KINKAZAN off the Oshika Peninsula in Miyagi Prefecture, northern Honshū. It is noted for its narrow beaches, terraced shores, and heavily indented coastline. Much of it is included in the RIKUCHŪ COAST NATIONAL PARK. The area is known for its earthquakes (and resultant tidal waves) whose epicenters are usually located off the coast. Length: 600 km (373 mi).

Sanrizuka

District in the southeastern part of the city of Narita, northern Chiba Prefecture, central Honshū. Until recently, a farm owned by the imperial family to produce dairy goods for its own use was located here. Now Sanrizuka is the site of the New Tōkyō International Airport.

Sanron school

(School of the Three Treatises). Buddhist school which employed three philosophical treatises as its basic texts: the *Chūron* (Skt: *Mādhyamika-śāstra* or Treatise of the Middle Way), the *Jūnimonron* (Skt: *Dvādaśamukha-śāstra* or Treatise of the Twelve Gates), both by the Indian Buddhist monk-philosopher Nāgārjuna (ca AD 150–ca AD 250), and the *Hyakuron* (Skt: *Śata-śāstra* or One Hundred Treatises) by Āryadeva (fl 3rd century), Nāgārjuna's disciple. The central theme of these treatises is EMPTINESS (J: *kū*) and the relativity of various philosophical positions taken by various Buddhist sutras. The school taught that the true path lies in the middle way. These treatises were first introduced into China by Kumārajīva (344–413), the famous Central Asian translator of Buddhist texts. The monk Jizang (Chi-tsang, 549–623) summarized and systematized the doc-

trine, and a school centered on its study developed under his guidance. Ekan (K: Ekwan) of the Korean kingdom of KOGURYŎ brought the school to Japan in 625. It was the first of the so-called "Six Schools of the Southern Capital" (Nanto Rokushū, see NARA BUDDHISM) to reach Japanese soil. Outstanding disciples such as Fukuryō and Chizō, Chizō's disciple Dōji (d 744), and others, many of whom studied in Tang (T'ang) China, propounded the doctrine. The school had its centers at the temples GANGŌJI and DAIANJI and at a subtemple of TŌDAIJI. The school continued until the Edo period (1600–1868).   MATSUNAMI Yoshihiro

Sanshimpō

("Three New Laws"). Laws defining the first comprehensive system for local administration devised by the Meiji government; drawn up as a result of the second meeting (July 1878) of the ASSEMBLY OF PREFECTURAL GOVERNORS and promulgated on 22 July 1878. The Three Laws regulated, respectively, prefectural administrative organization (Gun-ku-chō-son Hensei Hō), elected metropolitan and prefectural assemblies (Fukenkai Kisoku), and local taxation (Chihōzei Kisoku). The first measure replaced the large and small districts (*daiku, shōku*) with new administrative units: districts (*gun*), towns (*chō*), and villages (*son*). The second measure stipulated that the franchise for local assemblies would be limited to males paying ¥5 or more in land taxes; it further stipulated that the powers of the assemblies would be limited to discussing tax and budgetary matters and that the prefectural governor would have the right to initiate all bills and to veto the assembly's decisions. The third measure laid down rules for the collection of taxes on the prefectural level; it also ensured that the central government would have a say in allocating these revenues. As a departure from the completely autocratic centralization that had previously existed, the Sanshimpō were at the time considered a victory for the FREEDOM AND PEOPLE'S RIGHTS MOVEMENT. Although often revised, they remained in force until the implementation of a new local autonomy system in 1888 and 1890.

Sanshoku

(Three Offices). The first administrative organs of the Meiji government; established 3 January 1868 (Keiō 3.12.9). They were the Office of the President (Sōsai), the Office of Administration (Gijō), and the Office of Councillors (San'yo). On 10 February 1868 (Keiō 4.1.17) seven departments were created to oversee public worship, internal affairs, foreign affairs, the armed forces, the budget, penal laws, and general organization; the governmental structure was now known as Sanshoku Shichika (Three Offices and Seven Departments). On 25 February the General Administrative Bureau (Sōsaikyoku) was added to the seven existing departments, which were renamed bureaus, and the administrative system became known as Sanshoku Hachikyoku (Three Offices and Eight Bureaus). All of these organs were abolished on 11 June, when the SEITAISHO ("Constitution of 1868") established the DAJŌKAN (Grand Council of State) as the highest organ of government.

The division of responsibilities within the Sanshoku system was as follows. The president, who was the highest official, had control over all matters of government policy. The first president appointed was Prince ARISUGAWA NO MIYA TARUHITO. Under the Eight Bureaus system the Office of the President was strengthened with the establishment of the General Administrative Bureau, which had overall control of the other seven bureaus, and the president became the chief administrative officer, his position resembling closely that of the later prime minister. The *gijō* or officials in the Office of Administration were appointed from the ranks of the imperial family, the court nobles, and the former *daimyō*. (Originally there were 10 such officials, but their numbers were later increased.) They consulted as a body on affairs of state. Under the Sanshoku-Shichika system the *gijō*, together with the *san'yo* or councillors, supervised the work of each department. Under the Sanshoku–Hachikyoku system, a *gijō* was appointed to head each of the bureaus. When the Sanshoku system was replaced by the Dajōkan system, the *gijō* were appointed members of the Giseikan, the legislative department of the Dajōkan. Councillors or *san'yo* were usually chosen from lower-ranking nobles who had supported the overthrow of the Tokugawa shogunate and representatives of the powerful domains of Satsuma and Chōshū (now Kagoshima and Yamaguchi prefectures, respectively). They assisted the administrative officers of each government

Sansuiga

Detail of the winter painting from a pair entitled *Autumn and Winter Landscapes* by Sesshū Tōyō (1420–1506). Thought to have been painted in Sesshū's later years. Hanging scroll. Ink on paper. 46.4 × 29.4 cm. Late 15th century. Tōkyō National Museum. National Treasure.

bureau. When the Dajōkan replaced the Sanshoku, the councillors too were appointed to the Giseikan.

At an earlier period the term Sanshoku was collectively applied to the offices of the grand minister of state *(dajō daijin)*, the ministers of the left and right *(sadaijin* and *udaijin)*, and the councillors *(sangi)*, the three highest posts in the Dajōkan as originally instituted under the RITSURYŌ SYSTEM in the early 8th century.

sanshōuo → salamanders

sanshu no jingi → imperial regalia

Sansom, George Bailey (1883–1965)

Diplomat, historian, and doyen of Japanese studies in the West. Born in Kent, England, in 1883, Sir George Sansom was educated in France and entered the British consular service at the age of 19. He was sent to the Far East in 1904 and, as a student interpreter at Nagasaki, began a career of service in Japan that was to last, with only a few periods of interruption, to the eve of World War II nearly 40 years later.

Sansom's years in Japan were filled with intense activity both as a career diplomat who moved easily in Japanese society and the highest levels of government and as a scholar who had established himself by the late 1920s and early 1930s as the leading Western student of Japanese language, culture, and history. In 1928 he published *An Historical Grammar of Japanese* and in 1931, *Japan: A Short Cultural History*. It was the latter book, still widely used as a classroom text, that first brought fame to Sansom as a scholar and writer. Wonderfully graceful in style, it remains one of the classics of the Western literature on Japan.

Sansom was knighted in 1935 and served on the FAR EASTERN COMMISSION in Washington after World War II. In 1947 he accepted an offer to become the first director of the East Asian Institute at Columbia University and played a major role in the American academic world's response to the enormous demand in the postwar period for scholarly training in and study of Japan. Sansom remained at Columbia until 1954, and it was during his Columbia years that he wrote *The Western World and Japan* (1951), his study of the interaction of Japan and the West from the mid-16th until the late 19th centuries.

An appointment to Stanford University gave Sansom the leisure time and financial support necessary to undertake the major scholarly work of his life, the three-volume *A History of Japan,* published between 1958 and 1963. Whereas the earlier *Short Cultural History* dealt primarily with the cultural and artistic heritage of Japan, *A History of Japan,* which extends to the end of the Edo period in 1868, is concerned more with institutional, social, and political developments. Failing in health, Sansom completed the final volume of *A History of Japan* in his 80th year, only two years before his death.

H. Paul VARLEY

Sansui Electric Co, Ltd

(Sansui Denki). Specialized maker of audio products. Sansui was founded in 1947 as a manufacturer of audio transformers, but later began to manufacture general audio equipment. Beginning in the 1960s it directed its efforts toward the export market and established sales firms in the United States in 1966 and in the United Kingdom and West Germany in 1980. Sales for the fiscal year ending October 1981 totaled ¥50.9 billion (US $220 million), and the export ratio was 60 percent, and the company was capitalized at ¥1.2 billion (US $5.2 million) in the same year. Corporate headquarters are located in Tōkyō.

sansuiga

(landscape painting). One of three broad categories of Far Eastern art, the other two being *jimbutsuga* (figure painting) and *kachōga* (BIRD-AND-FLOWER PAINTING). By the 5th century, scholar-painters in China had laid the foundations for landscape as a subject for expressing philosophical principles as well as for interpreting natural beauty, but realization of this idea in painting was a phenomenon of the Song (Sung) dynasty (960–1279). During this time, the basic compositional types were established and techniques were developed for handling trees, structuring mountains, and suggesting rock textures. Solutions devised by celebrated Song artists were used as models for subsequent painters. The style associated with Dong Yuan (Tung Yüan) and Juran (Chü-jan) in the 10th century became the basis for the so-called Southern school of Chinese literati painters (see NANGA), traceable through the Four Great Masters of the Yuan (Yüan) period (1279–1368) to the Wu school of the Ming dynasty (1368–1644). Distinguished by rounded rock forms textured by long, fibrous strokes drawn with a center-tipped brush, this style contrasts markedly with what 16th-century critics called the Northern school. This manner, characterized by the technique of faceting angular rocks with slashing strokes made with the side of the brush, was immediately linked with Xia Gui (Hsia Kuei), Ma Yuan (Ma Yüan), and the court artists active in Hangzhou (Hangchow) during the 13th century, finding its successors in the Zhe (Che) school of the Ming.

In Heian-period Japan (794–1185), trees and hills and lakes were painted as settings for Buddhist narrative and as independent evocations of seasonal themes *(shiki-e)* or places famous in literature *(meisho-e)*. Landscapes with the philosophical significance of Chinese *sansuiga,* however, were not painted in Japan until the 15th century. The importation of Song and Yuan culture that accompanied the development of Zen Buddhism brought scores of Chinese paintings. Early Japanese landscapists, such as the 15th-century Shōkokuji priest-painter SHŪBUN, used motifs from the paintings of Chinese priests or academic court artists to create evocative, idealized landscapes. With increased knowledge of Chinese styles, Shūbun's follower SESSHŪ TŌYŌ magnified the forces of nature into a style of dynamic grandeur. In the 16th century the demand for wall paintings to decorate residential architecture brought about a uniquely Japanese transformation of landscape painting on large-scale surfaces, notably in the creative synthesis achieved by KANŌ MOTONOBU.

Chinese Northern school paintings provided the techniques developed by Muromachi-period (1333–1568) landscapists, and artists of the professional schools that formed during the 16th century continued to paint *sansuiga* according to these established modes. In the 18th century, heightened awareness of the Chinese Southern school tradition generated a revitalization of landscape painting in the hands of *nanga* artists. Painters such as IKE NO TAIGA and Yosa BUSON consulted new models and achieved new transformations. Increasing interest in sketching from nature among such masters as TANI BUNCHŌ, MARUYAMA ŌKYO, and HOKUSAI lead away from conceptual *sansuiga* to realistic scenic views referred to as *fūkeiga*.

Carolyn WHEELWRIGHT

Santō Kyōden (1761–1816)

A leading writer of popular fiction (GESAKU) in late 18th-century Edo (now Tōkyō). He was also an illustrator, *ukiyo-e* artist, poet, antiquarian, and shopkeeper. As an artist he used the name Kitao Masanobu. His work was most prolific and brilliant in the realms of the KIBYŌSHI and the SHAREBON, but he also wrote KOKKEIBON, *hanashibon*, GŌKAN, and YOMIHON, all genres of Edo popular fiction.

Born Iwase Samuru, son of a pawnbroker, Kyōden lived in Edo all his life. He was educated at home and at a nearby village school (TERAKOYA). At 29 he married Okiku, from the Yoshiwara pleasure quarter, but she died less than four years later. In 1800 Kyōden remarried, again choosing his wife from among the Yoshiwara courtesans. The second wife, Yuri, lived until 1818. There were no children. Kyōden's younger brother Kyōzan (1769?–1858) was also a writer of *gesaku*, and one of the chroniclers of Kyōden's life. He had two younger sisters, Kinu and Yone. Yone (1771–1788) wrote KYŌKA (a genre of comic verse) and *kibyōshi* under the name Kurotobi Shikibu.

Kyōden lived in the Ginza district of Edo and from the age of 33 ran a tobacco shop near Ginza Itchōme. This he carried on with the verve of a passionate amateur, delighting in the creation of advertisements and packaging for the goods he sold. He scarcely traveled out of Edo, though in 1795 he spent three months touring west of Edo in the regions of Uraga, Mishima, and Numazu. He died of heart disease, after attending a literary party. The rumor that his death was precipitated by an argument about literature bears witness to the common description of Kyōden as a man of irascible temper. Takizawa BAKIN (1767–1848), Kyōden's former pupil and arch rival in literature, was his most eloquent critic.

It was in the *kibyōshi* that Kyōden made his earliest contributions to popular fiction. In about 1775 he went to study *ukiyo-e* under KITAO SHIGEMASA (1739–1820), and in the subsequent years he wrote and illustrated some 130 *kibyōshi*. This period lasted from about 1780 to about 1806. Kyōden was fined for his illustrations of Ishibe Kinkō's *Kokubyaku mizukagami* (1789), whose sharp satire, thinly veiled in historical dress, incurred the wrath of the authorities. His most famous *kibyōshi*, *Edo umare uwaki no kabayaki*, was one of six which were published in 1785. Its blundering hero, Enjirō, was drawn with a comical triangular nose, known thereafter as the "Kyōden nose." Kyōden's *kibyōshi* are light, humorous, and thoroughly urbane. He was still writing *kibyōshi* in 1808, but from 1809 to 1816 he deserted them entirely for the comparatively pallid *gōkan*.

In 1785 Kyōden began to write *sharebon*, and during the following five years he wrote many successful works in the genre. The finest of these is *Tsūgen sōmagaki* (1787), which exemplifies his technical mastery and the realism and warm humanity with which he is able to portray the manners of the pleasure quarters.

It was in his role as author of *sharebon* that Kyōden came to grief in 1791. In the previous year the shogunate had issued edicts severely restricting the publication of fictional writings, which had frequently been used as a vehicle of satire. But in 1791, possibly at the urging of his publisher Tsutaya Jūzaburō (1750–97), Kyōden produced three lively *sharebon*: *Shōgi kinuburui*, *Nishiki no ura*, and *Shikake bunko*. Though each was clearly marked *kyōkun yomihon* ("didactic reading matter"), the authorities were not deceived, and Kyōden was obliged to spend 50 days in manacles as punishment. Tsutaya was heavily fined, but in fact the three *sharebon* were immensely popular. The notoriety of trial and punishment further increased Kyōden's fame, yet his activities gradually changed direction during the last decade of the century. This new course had already been signaled by the publication in the spring of 1790 of Kyōden's first work in the manner of a *yomihon*, *Tsūzoku Daiseiden* (A Popular Biography of Confucius).

From 1799 a new spurt of creativity was under way. From then until 1813 Kyōden published 10 *yomihon*, many of which were extremely well received, most notably *Sakurahime zenden akebonozōshi* (1805) and *Mukashi-gatari inazuma-byōshi* (1806). Kyōden's *yomihon* owe much to the popular theater, as well as to the long Chinese novels which they also claimed as models. In the *yomihon* Kyōden was soon outstripped by Bakin, in whose hands the genre reached maturity.

Kyōden was an active member of *kyōka* circles and was clearly a vigorous participant in literary debate. Toward the end of his life he became interested in the manners and customs of the early Edo period and wrote such miscellanies as *Kinsei kiseki kō* (1804) and *Kottōshū* (1814–15).

📖 ——Works by Santō Kyōden: *Kyōden kessaku shū* (1928). *Edo umare uwaki no kabayaki*, *Tsūgen sōmagaki*, and other works, in *Kibyōshi sharebon shū: Nihon koten bungaku taikei*, vol 59 (Iwanami Shoten, 1958). Works about Santō Kyōden: Koike Tōgorō, *Santō Kyōden no kenkyū* (1935). Koike Tōgorō, *Santō Kyōden* (1961). Peter F. Kornicki, "*Nishiki no Ura*: An Instance of Censorship and the Structure of a *Sharebon*," *Monumenta Nipponica* 32.2 (1977).   Jane DEVITT

Santō Mondai → Shandong (Shantung) Question

Sanuki Folk Arts Museum

(Sanuki Mingeikan). Located in RITSURIN PARK at Takamatsu, Kagawa Prefecture. The museum, established in 1965, houses a large and varied group of regional handicrafts. Among the objects are many kinds of household items and a particularly distinguished group of ceramics. There is also a special collection of roof tiles displayed in a separate building. The complex of buildings, in a contemporary style that harmonizes well with the FOLK CRAFTS displayed, is set at the edge of the park.   *Laurance ROBERTS*

Sanuki Mountains

(Sanuki Sammyaku). Also called Asan Mountains. Mountain range forming the border between Kagawa and Tokushima prefectures, northern Shikoku. Running east to west, it consists of peaks in the 1,000 m (3,280 ft) range including the highest peak, Ryūōzan (1,057 m; 3,467 ft). The gently sloping northern side has numerous dams and lakes. Villages are mainly concentrated on the steep southern side, with its well-developed terraces.

Sanuki no Suke no nikki

(The Diary of Lady Sanuki). An account of a brief period in the life of Fujiwara no Nagako, who, under the official title Lady Sanuki, was lady-in-waiting to Emperor Horikawa and later to his son and successor, Emperor TOBA. She was probably born in 1079, the same year as Horikawa, and is occasionally referred to as his foster sister. Nominally she was one of his personal attendants, having entered court service around 1099, but the relationship seems to have been a deep and complex one, having the character both of a love affair and of a simple brother-sister intimacy.

The diary itself is divided into two volumes and seems to have originally had a middle volume which is now lost. Volume 1 describes in a vivid but factual style the last illness of Horikawa, which began in the sixth month of 1107 and ended in his death one month later, and it concludes with the shock and prostration of Lady Sanuki and other attendants of the emperor immediately following his death. Volume 2 begins with her unexpected recall to court service to attend the boy emperor Toba in the autumn of 1107 and ends with the last night of 1108. Lady Sanuki describes her experiences and feelings during this period with great personal lyricism and includes many recollections of the dead Horikawa, reminders of whom greet her wherever she looks in the palace. It is this section, showing a very human emperor and the deep devotion of Lady Sanuki, that gives the work much of its charm and value.

Phillip T. HARRIES

Sanuki Plain

(Sanuki Heiya). Located in northern Kagawa Prefecture, Shikoku. Consisting of alluvial fans, as well as flood plains and deltas, of the rivers Gōtōgawa, Dokigawa, and Saitagawa, it is bounded by the fault scarps of the Sanuki Mountains in the south and the Inland Sea in the north. The area is a rice-producing region, where low precipitation is offset by some 18,600 ponds, among which the most famous is Mannō Pond. The area is now a focus of industrial development. The major city is Takamatsu. Area: approximately 410 sq km (154 sq mi).

Sanwa Bank, Ltd

(Sanwa Ginkō). One of Japan's leading city banks, ranking fifth among all city banks in the volume of its deposits. It was established in 1933 through the merger of Kōnoike Bank, Yamaguchi Bank, and Sanjūshi Bank. The merger was a countermeasure taken by the three Ōsaka-based banks against ZAIBATSU-affiliated banks, which were expanding their influence in the wake of the financial panic of

1927, when a great number of smaller banks failed. Sanwa grew rapidly, with spinning and trading companies in the Ōsaka area as its main clients. The ZAIBATSU DISSOLUTION program of the post-World War II years did not affect it as drastically as it did the *zaibatsu*-affiliated banks, and Sanwa Bank expanded its network of branches throughout the country, rapidly increasing deposits. Because its principal clients are individuals and small- and medium-sized enterprises, it was the first to initiate a network service in which a client is able to withdraw or deposit money from ordinary deposits at any branch of the bank. The bank was also the first to start consumer financing, individual loans which could be used for any purpose, and a management consulting service. The bank's first overseas branch, opened in San Francisco, was followed by the opening of branches in London, New York, Hong Kong, and other centers of international finance. In 1972 the Golden State Sanwa Bank was established in San Francisco, followed by the establishment of various types of financial and securities companies in London and Southeast Asia. At the end of March 1982, the bank's total deposits were ¥14.5 trillion (US $60.2 billion) and capitalization stood at ¥111.4 billion (US $462.8 million). In fiscal 1981 its funds were composed of time deposits (51 percent), ordinary deposits (8 percent), current deposits (8 percent), and others (33 percent). Its assets in the same year consisted of loans (52 percent), negotiable securities (10 percent), cash and deposits (18 percent), and others (20 percent). The bank's headquarters are located in Ōsaka.

San'yō Electric Co, Ltd

(San'yō Denki). Manufacturer and distributor of household appliances, consumer electronics, and commercial electrical products. Ranks second, behind MATSUSHITA ELECTRIC INDUSTRIAL CO, LTD, in sales of household appliances. The late Iue Toshio established the San'yō Electric Works (San'yō Denki Seisakusho) in 1947 to manufacture bicycle lamps, and the operation gave birth to San'yō Electric Co, Ltd, in 1950. San'yō made its entry into the electric products field by being the first in Japan to begin production and sale of radios in plastic casings. In 1953 San'yō was the first to sell whirlpool-type washing machines in Japan, helping to create Japan's household appliance boom. With the later addition of television sets, refrigerators, and air conditioners, San'yō emerged as an all-round electrical appliance maker. The production of videotape recorders (VTRs) has increased rapidly in response to strong domestic and overseas demand.

San'yō has 28 factories in 19 countries whose production value amounted to ¥188.7 billion (US $892 million) in 1978. The company stresses the importance of developing information processing and energy-related technologies. It has developed and put into operation a solar-energy air conditioning and hot water supply system, and has taken the initiative in developing photovoltaic cells. In the high technology field, San'yō has been working on VLSI (very large-scale integration), having already developed a voice recognition mechanism. Sales for the fiscal year ending November 1981 totaled ¥761.4 billion (US $3.4 billion), of which consumer electronics constituted 45 percent, electrical household products 37 percent, commercial electrical equipment 13 percent, and other products 5 percent. In that year the export ratio was 40 percent and the company's capitalization stood at ¥47.3 billion (US $211 million). The head office is located in Moriguchi, Ōsaka Prefecture.

San'yō–Kokusaku Pulp Co, Ltd

A company engaged in the manufacture of paper, pulp, construction materials, and chemical products, San'yō–Kokusaku was established in 1970 through the merger of the San'yō Pulp Co and the Kokusaku Pulp Co. It is the largest producer of printing and writing paper in Japan. It has concluded tie-ups with two American firms, Scott Paper and the Mead Corporation, as well as with companies in Australia and New Zealand; it is expanding its operations in international markets from the making of pulp to the manufacture of finished products. It is also striving to acquire a stable supply of raw materials and reduce its manufacturing costs. Sales for the fiscal year ending March 1982 totaled ¥246.5 billion (US $1 billion), of which paper accounted for 50 percent; construction materials 11 percent; pulp 15 percent; and chemical products, lumber, and other products 24 percent; and the company was capitalized at ¥14.1 billion (US $58.6 million). Corporate headquarters are located in Tōkyō.

San'yūtei Enchō (1839–1900)

Professional RAKUGO storyteller; noted for his masterful presentation of tales of human compassion (*ninjō-banashi*) drawn from everyday life. Real name Izubuchi Jirokichi. Born in Edo (now Tōkyō), he was apprenticed early to master storyteller San'yūtei Enshō II (1806–62), and took the name Koenta. In 1855 he changed his name to Enchō and began making regular stage appearances. He gradually gained popularity and by age 21 was a leading *rakugo* performer. Possessed of a truly creative capacity, he wrote his own monologues and excelled in the presentation of stories accompanied by music or told before painted scenes. It is said that no one was more skillful in the recitation of *ninjō-banashi* and tales of the supernatural. He is also noted for the publication of stenographic records of his performances and for the fact that KABUKI plays were written based on his tales. His works are collected in the eight-volume *Enchō zenshū* (Kadokawa Shoten, 1976). Kojima Masajirō published an informative biography entitled *Sanyūtei Enchō* in 1978.

ORITA Kōji

Sanze Isshin no Hō

(Law of Three Generations or a Lifetime). A law designed to encourage cultivation of wasteland; enacted in 723. Under the land distribution system (HANDEN SHŪJU SYSTEM) of the Chinese-inspired RITSURYŌ SYSTEM of administration established in the late 7th century, all land belonged to the state, and individuals were only granted the right to use a prescribed amount of land during their productive years. Arable land was limited, however, and a need soon arose to expand the available tillage. The Sanze Isshin no Hō provided incentives to open new land. It granted private ownership for three generations (*sanze*) to the families of those who reclaimed land by constructing new irrigation systems, and for one generation (*isshin*) to those who reclaimed land by extending existing systems. But cultivators were loath to work their land when the term drew to a close, and in 743 a new law, the KONDEN EISEI SHIZAI HŌ, was enacted, granting the land in perpetuity. Under both laws, wealthy provincial magnates and temples—those with the means to open new land—were able to amass large tracts of land legally. This practice led to the breakdown of the system of public ownership and control of land and the development of the landed-estate (SHŌEN) system of private landholding.

Sanzen'in

Temple of the Enryakuji branch of the TENDAI SECT of Buddhism; located in the Ōhara district, Sakyō Ward, Kyōto. During the Enryaku era (782–806), SAICHŌ, the founder of the Tendai sect, built a Buddhist hall in the Tōtō section of Mt. Hiei (see HIEIZAN); in 860 the monk Shōun reconstructed the hall at the behest of the Emperor Seiwa (r 858–876) as a *chokuganji,* a temple at which prayers were offered for the peace of the country and the health of the emperor. A statue of the Buddha of healing, Yakushi (Skt: Bhaiṣajyaguru), made by Saichō, was installed in a building named Sanzen'in En'yūbō, and Saichō was designated its official founder. In 1086 a new temple in the Kajii district of the village of Sakamoto (now in the city of Ōtsu), was dedicated, and the main sanctuary of Sanzen'in was transferred there. Nine golden images of the Buddha Amida (Skt: Amitābha; see AMIDA) were installed in the new temple, and it was from this time on that the worship of Amida at Sanzen'in became central to its religious practices. When Prince Saiun (1104–62), the second son of Emperor Horikawa (r 1087–1107), became the chief priest of the temple in 1130, Sanzen'in officially became a *monzeki* temple (a temple whose chief priest was or had been an imperial prince). Thereafter, as one of the three Tendai *monzeki* temples (the other two being Shōren'in and Myōhōin), Sanzen'in frequently had as its chief priest a member of the imperial family. The temple was later moved several more times; it was after the ŌNIN WAR (1467–77) that it was established at its present site.

The main hall (*kondō*) of Sanzen'in is called Ōjō Gokurakuin; it has been designated an Important Cultural Property. According to legend, the hall was built in 985 by GENSHIN, a Tendai Pure Land priest; it is more likely that it was built around 1148. The interior of the hall is done in a style typical of the early part of the Heian period (794–1185) during which the FUJIWARA FAMILY dominated Japan. The hall houses an image of Amida flanked by two bodhisattva images, one Avalokiteśvara (KANNON) and the other Mahāsthāmaprāpta (J: Seishi). The hall is used for meditation on Amida by devotees seeking to be born into the Pure Land. The ceiling of the hall above the image is quite unusual; it is shaped like a ship's bottom, and is the oldest design of its kind.

The services hall (shinden) is located north of the Ōjō Gokurakuin. It was reconstructed in 1926. In the sanctum of the hall there is an image of the Buddha Yakushi; in the west hall there are images of Guze Kannon and Fudō Myōō (see MYŌŌ). The temple garden is known as the Rurikōtei. It is spacious and is known for its beautiful autumn foliage.

The guest hall (kyakuden) was built during the Tenshō era (1573–92). On the doors and fusuma (paper sliding doors) are a number of fine paintings by TAKEUCHI SEIHŌ and others. The Shūhekien to the side of the guest hall is a small garden with a pond famous for its maple and cherry trees.

To the north of these buildings, across a river, is the Shōrin'in subdivision of Sanzen'in. It was founded by the priest Jakugen in 1013. The main hall, Shōko no Amidadō, was burned in 1736 and rebuilt in 1778. To the east of the Ōjō Gokurakuin is the Raigōin subdivision of Sanzen'in. The main hall of Raigōin was built in 1109 at the behest of Emperor TOBA by RYŌNIN, the founder of the YŪZŪ NEMBUTSU SECT. Raigōin is well known as the birthplace of Tendai chanting and singing in praise of Buddha.   Hoyu ISHIDA

sanzonzō

(images of Buddhist trinities). Sculptural or pictorial representations of Buddhist trinities or triads in which a large central image of the Buddha is flanked by two smaller, attendant bodhisattvas. The earliest extant examples are in Buddhist cave-temples in China and date from the 6th century; from China the convention spread to Japan. The earliest surviving sanzonzō in Japan is a bronze sculptural group attributed to KURATSUKURI NO TORI in the 7th-century Nara temple HŌRYŪJI. It shows the Buddha Shaka (Skt: Śākyamuni) attended by the bodhisattvas Monju (Skt: Mañjuśrī) and Fugen (Skt: Samantabhadra). Other examples of Buddhist trinities include AMIDA (Skt: Amitābha) flanked by KANNON (Skt: Avalokiteśvara) and Seishi (Skt: Mahāsthāma-prāpta), and Yakushi (Skt: Bhaiṣajyaguru) flanked by Nikkō (Skt: Sūryaprabha) and Gakkō (Skt: Candraprabha).

saotome

Name for the women who traditionally transplanted seedlings into the flooded paddies at rice-planting time. They were originally young women of a farmer's household, and it is thought that their participation in the task was vital, serving as a sort of ritual honoring the god of the paddy fields (TA NO KAMI) to ensure a good harvest. In modern times the word is also used as an epithet for women or girls from other villages hired to help with rice transplanting.
                                                    NOGUCHI Takenori

Sapporo

Capital of Hokkaidō. Located in the southwestern part of ISHIKARI PLAIN in western Hokkaidō. The city is laid out in a checkerboard pattern on the alluvial fan of the river Toyohiragawa. It was the administrative center of Hokkaidō after the establishment of a colonial office (KAITAKUSHI) in 1869. Since World War II its commercial and industrial significance has increased. Major industries include food processing, printing, machinery repair and maintenance, and construction. The Toyoha mines in the western section produce lead and zinc. Sapporo is also known for its beer. Other products include onions and watermelons. It was host to the Winter Olympic Games in 1972 (see SAPPORO WINTER OLYMPIC GAMES). Attractions include the forests of Maruyama and Moiwayama; the campus of Hokkaidō University, in which there is a statue of the American educator William Smith CLARK; Hokkaidō University Botanical Gardens; Nakanoshima Park; Maruyama Zoological Gardens; and JŌZANKEI HOT SPRING, part of Shikotsu-Tōya National Park. Area: 4,118 sq km (1,590 sq mi); pop: 1,401,758.

Sapporo Breweries, Ltd

(Sapporo Bīru). Company engaged in the production of beer and soft drinks as well as the import and sale of alcoholic beverages. It is the second largest brewer in Japan after the KIRIN BREWERY CO, LTD. Its predecessor was the Sapporo Brewing Co, Ltd, established in 1876; the star trademark adopted at that time remains the symbol of the current company. In 1906 it absorbed two brewing companies

Sapporo

Ōdōri, a broad tree-lined street running through downtown Sapporo, the capital of Hokkaidō.

and changed its name to the Dai Nippon Brewery Co, Ltd, which controlled approximately 70 percent of Japan's domestic beer market before World War II. The Dai Nippon Brewery split into two independent companies in 1949, one of which, Nippon Breweries, Ltd, became Sapporo Breweries, Ltd, in 1964. It presently owns and operates 18 breweries, five soft drink plants, two hop farms, and a research laboratory. Sapporo beer is exported to Hong Kong, Singapore, Australia, the United States, France, West Germany, and other countries. Sales for fiscal year ending December 1981 totaled ¥330.5 billion (US $1.5 billion), and the company was capitalized at ¥14.2 billion (US $64.9 million) in the same year. Corporate headquarters are located in Tōkyō.

Sapporo Winter Olympic Games

Held in Sapporo, Hokkaidō, 3–13 February 1972. The 11th Winter Olympics and the first to take place in Asia. The 1972 winter games included skiing, skating, ice hockey, bobsledding, luge (small sled) racing, and the biathlon (cross-country skiing combined with rifle-shooting). The competitors totaled 1,641 athletes from 35 countries. KASAYA YUKIO took first place in the 70 meter ski-jump event, becoming the first Japanese to receive a gold medal in a Winter Olympics, and the silver and bronze medals in that same event were also won by Japanese.   TAKEDA Fumio

sararīman

("salaried man"). Term referring to a broad grouping of salaried white-collar workers, in contrast to self-employed and manual, or blue-collar, workers. However, the monthly wage system in Japan is widely used among the blue-collar working class as well, so that different occupational groups cannot be strictly classified on the basis of how and when they are paid. Generally speaking, the sararī-man category includes managers, salaried professionals, office workers, and sales personnel employed in government agencies and private business firms.

The growth of large business enterprises following World War I was accompanied by increased demand for better job placement from employees with middle or high school educations, a demand which resulted in their frequently being placed in administrative or managerial positions. Since blue-collar workers were at the time generally paid according to a daily wage system, the term sararīman was created to distinguish white-collar employees from those engaged in manual labor. With the continued development of big business and the rapid expansion of government bureaucracies, these white-collar workers held very secure positions in work and society, and were soon regarded as a "new middle class." Their status, however, has meaning only in the context of a large bureaucratic organization. Since the white-collar worker loses his status outside this organization, upward movement or promotion (shōshin) is paramount to his career and in many cases becomes the white-collar worker's sole purpose in life. The range of promotion possibilities extends as far up as company president or chairman of the board of directors. Loyalty to the firm or agency is required, and it is expected that the sararīman will continue working at the same company until he reaches the mandatory retirement age. Status and promotion within a firm or government office are strongly influenced by the employee's academic background. Since there are differences even among workers with the same level of education based on the prestige of the school from which they graduated, school cliques are easily formed.

White-collar workers are generally prudent. They rarely, if ever, participate in social activities not sponsored by the company or in political affairs. Members of this group tend to identify strongly with the institutions for which they work, and are likely to adhere to conservative values in most matters. The *sarariīman* is said to be highly susceptible to the trends of the times, preferring to conform rather than take the risk of opposition, which would presumably threaten his job security. With the increased education of the blue-collar worker and the advancement of automation, however, many of what were once special characteristics of the white-collar worker are gradually disappearing. See LABOR.

📖——Ezra Vogel, *Japan's New Middle Class* (1963).

KURITA Ken

sarasa

(calico or batik). Cotton calico, or *sarasa,* was first imported from India to Japan by Spanish, Portuguese, and Dutch merchants in the late 16th and early 17th centuries. It became popular among the high-ranking *samurai* and rich merchants, who used it to make tobacco pouches, *obi,* and purses. In the latter part of the Edo period (1600–1868), when cotton became more accessible in Japan, local *sarasa* began to be produced. At first, domestic *sarasa* imitated Indian and Indonesian cottons in motif and color, but eventually a Japanese-style *sarasa,* called *wasarasa* (or *wazarasa*), appeared.

Japanese *sarasa* may be hand-painted, stenciled, or block printed; composite methods are sometimes used. Patterns are often exotic, including tropical flowers, plants, birds, beasts, or figures, with designs generally filling the whole surface of the fabric. There are several different kinds of Japanese *sarasa,* their names reflecting their place of origin: Amakusa *sarasa* (Amakusa Islands in Kumamoto Prefecture), Nabeshima *sarasa* (former name of Saga Prefecture), Kyō *sarasa* (Kyōto Prefecture) and Edo *sarasa* (Tōkyō). Only after World War II was the technique applied to SILK. Today, *sarasa* silk KIMONO are valued for their high artistic quality.

📖——Motoyoshi Harusaburō et al, *Nihon no senshoku: Sarasa* (1976).

Yasuko YABE

Sarashina nikki

(Sarashina Diary). The confessional memoirs in prose and poetry written by a woman of the Heian period (794–1185) shortly after the year 1059. Like many works of classical Japanese literature, the *Sarashina nikki* was originally anonymous and untitled. Poems from it have been included in other collections with authorship indicated, making it possible to deduce that the author was a lady known by the name of SUGAWARA NO TAKASUE NO MUSUME (Daughter of Sugawara no Takasue; b 1008). Although other works—the HAMAMATSU CHŪNAGON MONOGATARI and the YORU NO NEZAME—are also believed to be hers, the *Sarashina nikki* is the only work that can be attributed to her with a degree of certainty.

Unlike other diaries by court ladies of the Heian period, which were usually kept for shorter periods of time (e.g., one year), the *Sarashina nikki* covers almost the entire lifespan of the author, starting at the age of 12 and ending in her early fifties (much of it written long after the fact). Most details about her life are known only through the *Sarashina nikki.* Her ancestors and relatives included such important men and women of letters as SUGAWARA NO MICHIZANE, NŌIN, and "Michitsuna's Mother" (author of the KAGERŌ NIKKI). She spent most of her childhood in a province near what is now Tōkyō, where her father served as vice-governor. In 1020 she went with her family to the capital (now Kyōto), where she remained except for pilgrimages. Around the age of 31, she became a lady-in-waiting to an imperial princess. She soon left to marry Tachibana no Toshimichi, governor of Shinano Province (now Nagano Prefecture), and had three children. The last poem of the *Sarashina nikki* strongly suggests that after the death of her husband she became a nun and spent her last days in a nunnery in the vicinity of the capital. The date of her death is unknown.

Rather than a diary with regular daily entries, the *Sarashina nikki* is a later record of the main emotional events and poetic correspondences in the author's life. Such happy events as marriage and childbirths are ignored in favor of more tragic events such as the deaths of her nurse, the daughters of Fujiwara no Yukinari, her cat, her sister, and her husband—the last in 1058.

Other diaries of this period are based on central themes, like specific court functions or love affairs. Likewise, the *Sarashina nikki* seems to develop around a central theme—the author's passion for romantic tales, evidenced by this quotation from the beginning: "Yet even shut away in the provinces I somehow came to hear that the world contains things known as Tales, and from that moment my greatest desire was to read them for myself." Her passion for fantastic tales is also mentioned at the end: "If only I had not given myself over to Tales and poems since my young days but had spent my time in religious devotions, I should have been spared this misery."

From beginning to end, with only minor deviations, the *Sarashina nikki* records the author's infatuation with romanticism, which prevented her from becoming aware of the realities of life. Her passion stood not only between herself and reality but also between her and religion. In a number of dreams she is told to abandon her passion. First she ignored the prophetic qualities of her dreams but later, especially during her numerous pilgrimages, she tried to rid herself of her romantic interest. It was only at her husband's death that she finally overcame what seems to have been her life's major obstacle.

The attention given to about a dozen dreams stems from the religious and therapeutic value attached to dreams. As seen from the viewpoint of a spiritual and emotional development from a passion for a fantastic, unreal world of fiction to an awareness of the sad realities of both human existence and religion, the *Sarashina nikki* belongs to a category of literature to which the TOWAZUGATARI also belongs—a confession. From the point of view of style and form the *Sarashina nikki* includes elements of diary, tale *(monogatari),* and travel literature. It is a classic of Japanese literature, with its beautiful passages in prose and poetry. The most celebrated is an account of a three-month journey from what is now Chiba Prefecture to the capital, which includes unforgettable tales and poems about places and human encounters. Also of interest, especially to the literary historian, is the fact that the *Sarashina nikki* mentions the *Genji monogatari* (TALE OF GENJI) at a time (1021) when it may have been still unfinished.

📖——*Sarashina nikki,* tr with an introduction by Ivan Morris as *As I Crossed a Bridge of Dreams* (1971).   Herbert E. PLUTSCHOW

sardines

(iwashi). In Japanese, *iwashi* is the general term for several species of small fish of the class Osteichthyes, order Clupeiformes, but refers particularly to the *maiwashi (Sardinops melanosticta)* of the family Clupeidae; others are the round herring, *urume iwashi (Etrumeus micropus),* also of the family Clupeidae, and the anchovy, *katakuchi iwashi (Engraulis japonica)* of the family Engraulidae.

Maiwashi attain 20 centimeters (8 in) in length and resemble the Pacific sardine *(Sardinops caerulea)* of the west coast of North America, but they have fewer vertebrae and more gill-rakers. Over the years there has been remarkable variation in their abundance; the annual haul exceeds 1 million metric tons (1.1 million short tons) in some years in Japan, but falls below 10,000 metric tons (11,000 short tons) in other years. Sardines are used as food, broiled with salt or perserved by salting and drying and then broiled or deep fried. The quantity consumed as fresh food, however, is smaller than the quantity used for extracting oil, processing, and as fish feed.

ABE Tokiharu

In the Engi Shiki (905–927; tr *Procedures of the Engi Era,* 1970–72), there appears a record of dried sardines presented to the imperial court as a tribute; in the medieval period (13th to 16th century) dried sardines were used as rations for warriors. The fish has long been in demand as a source of protein and as fertilizer. It was once believed that the head of a sardine pierced with a twig of *hiiragi* (a tree resembling holly) and attached to the front door at the beginning of spring served to ward off evil spirits, and this custom is still practiced in some places today.   SAITŌ Shōji

Saris, John (1580?–1643)

Captain of the first English voyage to Japan in 1613. Saris, who had been chief factor of the trading post maintained at Bantam in Java by the company of "Governors and Merchants of London Trading into the East Indies" (founded in 1600), was sent to Japan with credentials from King James I and instructions to establish a trading factory. With the help of William ADAMS, the English pilot of a Dutch ship who had arrived in Japan in 1600 and become TOKUGAWA IEYASU's adviser on foreign affairs, Saris obtained audiences with Ieyasu, who had retired in Sumpu (now the city of Shizuoka), and the shōgun TOKUGAWA HIDETADA in Edo (now Tōkyō). He was promised extensive trading privileges for the English; however, in spite of official encouragement to settle at Uraga (now Yokosuka), a harbor convenient to Edo, Saris chose Hirado in Kyūshū as the site of the English factory. In December 1613 Saris departed for England, never again to "tempt fortune in the East." Richard COCKS was left in charge at Hirado, where the English were in the shadow of the better-established Dutch, who undersold them from the start. Since the English also failed to gain entry into China, the most profitable source of goods for Japan, their trading venture proved unsuccessful, and the Hirado factory was abandoned in 1623. Saris's journal, as edited by Ernest M. SATOW in *The Voyage of Captain John Saris to Japan, 1613* (1900), is an important historical source.

George ELISON

Sarobetsu Plain

(Sarobetsu Gen'ya). Located in northern Hokkaidō. Consisting of the flood plains of the rivers Teshiogawa and Sarobetsugawa and bordering the Sea of Japan, it has numerous lakes inland and high sand dunes along the coast. With its cold climate and vast peat bogs, it consists of largely undeveloped pastureland. The plain, a part of the Rishiri–Rebun–Sarobetsu National Park, is renowned for its wild flowers. Area: approximately 150 sq km (58 sq mi).

Saroma, Lake

(Saromako). Lagoon on the coast of the Sea of Okhotsk, northeastern Hokkaidō. Located within Abashiri Quasi-National Park, it is the largest lake in Hokkaidō and the third largest in Japan. A large sandbar separates it from the Sea of Okhotsk. Scallop, oyster, and seaweed cultures flourish, as do prawns and flatfish. Area: 151.7 sq km (58.6 sq mi); circumference: 72 km (45 mi); depth: 20 m (66 ft).

sarugaku

Also called *sangaku*. A genre of performing art in ancient Japan which developed into a dramatic form known as the precursor of the classical NŌ drama. Also an old name for Nō. The word *sarugaku* is written with two Chinese characters that mean, literally, "monkey music." However, it is believed to be a phonetic corruption of the alternate term *sangaku*, which was originally the name of a type of Chinese popular performing art (Ch: *sanyue* or *san-yüeh*) that had been imported to Japan. (The pronunciation *sarugaku* may have resulted from confusion with the name of certain pantomimic dancers, *sarume no kimi*, or "monkey maidens"; however, there is also the possibility that it is related to "Sarugaku," the name of a piece in the classical *bugaku* [see GAGAKU] dance repertory.) The pronunciations *sarugaku* and *sangaku* were used interchangeably through the 10th century, after which the latter became obsolete. After the 11th century, the word *sarugaku* denotes a specific type of theatrical.

Sangaku (or *sarugaku*), the Chinese repertory of variety arts (acrobatics, juggling, conjuring, pantomime, and so forth) had reached Japan by the 8th century. The court enjoyed combined programs as banquet entertainment, and some numbers developed into *bugaku* pieces. At temples and shrines *sarugaku* intermingled with other traditions. It absorbed new elements such as the dances of another type of performing art known as DENGAKU and gradually changed in character until, in the 11th century, dramatic sketches of a comic nature had become the most important part, while acrobatics and other elements dropped out of the repertory. By the late 12th century, the term *sarugaku* had come to encompass humorous dialogues based on word play (*tōben*), improvised comical party dances (*rambu*), short plays involving several actors, and musical arrangements based on the courtesan tradition. During the 13th century there was a general development toward standardization of words, gestures, musical arrangement, and program combinations. The tradition emerging from this process formed the basis on which outstanding *sarugaku* players of the 14th century created Nō and the comic genre called KYŌGEN.

After its introduction into Japan the *sangaku* tradition was maintained by officially sponsored households called *sangakko* until sponsorship was ended in 782. Afterwards the tradition was transmitted more spontaneously by *sangaku* specialists within the Imperial Bodyguard (Konoefu), by semiprofessional performers in the service of religious institutions, and by itinerant professionals.

From the 10th century, famous *sarugaku* players and their troupes appeared regularly at religious festivals, which by that time had begun to be visited in great numbers by spectators. At first their performances were a kind of side-show, but later they came to act in place of the religious or communal functionaries in charge of ritual dances, and so forth. As the great temples and shrines proceeded to invite and even sponsor free *sarugaku* troupes, the necessity to define areas of interest and to settle ruinous competition in the 13th century brought about the adoption of the guild (*za*) system. The results were economic security, hierarchic stability, and artistic continuity. All present-day Nō schools can be traced back to old *sarugaku* guilds.

—— Hagen Blau, *Sarugaku und Shushi, Beiträge zur Ausbildung dramatischer Elemente im weltlichen und religiösen Volkstheater der Heian-Zeit unter besonderer Berücksichtigung seiner sozialen Grundlagen* (1966), contains translation of *Shin sarugakuki* by Fujiwara no Akihira (11th century). Geinōshi Kenkyūkai, ed, *Dengaku, sarugaku,* in *Nihon shomin bunka shiryō shūsei,* vol 2 (1974), contains *sarugaku* texts. Ogata Kamekichi, *Sangaku genryū kō* (1954). Patrick Geoffrey O'Neill, *Early Nō Drama* (1958).

Gerhild ENDRESS

Sarugawa

River in southern Hokkaidō, originating in the northern Hidaka Mountains and emptying into the Pacific Ocean. The areas along the upper reaches are heavily forested. The town of Hiratori, a center of Ainu culture, is located in the river basin. Length: 104 km (65 mi); area of drainage basin: 1,350 sq km (521 sq mi).

Sarukani kassen

(The Battle between the Monkey and the Crab). Folktale. A sly monkey exchanges his persimmon seed for a crab's rice ball. The crab plants the seed, which grows into a large tree and bears fruit. The monkey climbs the tree and takes the ripe fruit for himself but throws green fruit at the crab and kills it. The crab is eventually avenged by its children, aided by such other characters as wasps, chestnuts, and a walking mortar.

SUCHI Tokuhei

Sarusawa Pond

(Sarusawa no Ike). Artificial pond in the eastern part of the city of Nara, Nara Prefecture, central Honshū. Situated immediately south of the temple Kōfukuji and within Nara Park. The image of the five-story pagoda of Kōfukuji reflected in the pond's water makes it a famous tourist attraction. Width: 100 m (328 ft); length: 70 m (230 ft); circumference: 360 m (1,180 ft).

sasa → bamboo

Sasagawanagare

Prefectural park on the Sea of Japan coast, Niigata Prefecture, northern Honshū. Noted for its oddly shaped rocks and cliffs, it is some 10 km (6 mi) in length.

Sasago Pass

(Sasago Tōge). Located on the eastern fringe of the Kōfu Basin, central Yamanashi Prefecture, central Honshū. Formerly a pass of the highway Kōshū Kaidō, it lost its transportational importance with the completion of the Sasago Tunnel of the Japanese National Railways' Chūō Main Line in 1903, and also with the completion of the New Sasago Tunnel Route No. 20 in 1958. Altitude: 1,096 m (3,595 ft).

Sasaki Kōzō (1900–   )

Politician and leader of the JAPAN SOCIALIST PARTY. A graduate of Nihon University, he was active in the agricultural labor union movement before World War II. Following the war he joined the Japan Socialist Party and was elected to the House of Representatives in 1948. He later served as vice-director and director-general of the party and, between 1965 and 1967, as party chairman. He was a major leader and ideologist of the party's left wing.

Sasaki Nobutsuna (1872–1963)

Scholar and WAKA poet. Born in Mie Prefecture, the son of a KOKU-GAKU (National Learning) scholar. Sasaki graduated in 1888 from Tōkyō University, where he majored in Japanese. Sasaki published commentaries on the Japanese classics as well as his own waka, new-style poetry, marches, and songs. His first collection of waka, Omoigusa, appeared in 1903. After he was appointed lecturer at Tōkyō University in 1905, Sasaki spent much of his time writing commentaries on the poetic anthology MAN'YŌSHŪ (ca 759) and histories of waka. His extensive studies of the Japanese classics focused on detailed textual analysis. In 1912 he published Shingetsu, his second and most important collection of waka, and in 1917 he received the Japan Academy Prize. He retired from Tōkyō University in 1931 and was awarded the Order of Culture in 1937. He wrote several autobiographies, including Sakka hachijūninen (1959).

James R. MORITA

Sasaki Ryōsaku (1915–   )

Chairman of the DEMOCRATIC SOCIALIST PARTY. Born in Hyōgo Prefecture. Graduate of Kyōto University. He was elected to the House of Councillors in 1947 after working as a labor leader, serving as secretary-general of the All-Japan Electric Industry Workers' Union and as chairman of the Central Joint Struggle Committee. He was elected to the House of Representatives in 1955, and in 1960 he left the Japan Socialist Party to help form the Democratic Socialist Party. He was appointed to the posts of party secretary-general and chairman of the party's Diet Policy Committee and became vice-chairman of the party in 1975. Following Chairman KASUGA IKKŌ's retirement in 1977, Sasaki succeeded to the post of chairman.

Sasaki Sōichi (1878–1965)

Legal scholar. Born in Tottori Prefecture, he became a lecturer at Kyōto University after his graduation there in 1903 and studied administrative law in Germany and France from 1909 to 1912. He became a professor at the university in 1913, but in 1933 he resigned in protest against an infringement of academic freedom, the dismissal of his colleague TAKIKAWA YUKITOKI (see KYŌTO UNIVERSITY INCIDENT); he then became president of Ritsumeikan University. Immediately after World War II, Sasaki and KONOE FUMIMARO were assigned by the lord keeper of the privy seal (naidaijin) to suggest possible revisions of the Meiji Constitution of 1889. His interpretations of constitutional and administrative law were characterized by meticulous logic and thorough objectivity. Sasaki was awarded the Bunka Kunshō (Order of Culture) in 1952. His writings include Nihon gyōseihō ron (1924, Japanese Administrative Law), Nihon kempō yōron (1933, Essentials of the Japanese Constitution), and Nihonkoku kempō ron (1949, The Japanese Constitution).

SATŌ Kōji

Sasaki Takaoki (1878–1966)

Medical scientist. Born in Tōkyō. Graduate of Tōkyō University. After serving as professor of internal medicine at Kyōto University, he became director of the Kyōundō Hospital. Sasaki is noted for his cancer research, using rats in which he induced liver cancer by the oral administration of an azo dye (in collaboration with YOSHIDA TOMIZŌ). He received the Japan Academy Prize in 1924 and 1936 and the Order of Culture in 1940.

SŌDA Hajime

Sasaki Takatsuna (?–1214)

Warrior of the Kamakura period (1185–1333). Grandson of Minamoto no Tameyoshi (1096–1156) on his mother's side. His family was destroyed in the HEIJI DISTURBANCE of 1159–60, but because he was a small child he was spared and allowed to live with an aunt in Kyōto. In 1180 Sasaki joined MINAMOTO NO YORITOMO, who had raised troops in eastern Japan against the rule of the TAIRA FAMILY, and he saved Yoritomo's life in the Battle of Ishibashiyama. He helped MINAMOTO NO YOSHITSUNE in the final destruction of the Taira, and for his services he was made military governor (shugo) of Nagato Province (now part of Yamaguchi Prefecture). It is said that

he relinquished his title and possessions to his son in 1195 and became a Shingon priest at Mt. Kōya (Kōyosan). The story of his race across the river Ujigawa with Kajiwara Kagesue (1162–1200) to be the first to engage in battle with the enemy in 1184 is a popular subject in war tales and paintings.

Sasaki Takauji (1306–1373)

General of the early Muromachi period (1333–1568); better known by his religious name, Sasaki Dōyo. Born in Ōmi Province (now Shiga Prefecture) to a famous warrior family. After serving HŌJŌ TAKATOKI, the last regent with any power under the Kamakura shogunate, Sasaki helped ASHIKAGA TAKAUJI to overturn the short-lived KEMMU RESTORATION (1333–36) and to establish the Muromachi shogunate. He also participated in the compilation of the KEMMU SHIKIMOKU, the fundamental administrative code of the shogunate enacted in 1336. At various times he served as military governor (SHUGO) of six provinces, including Ōmi, and also held important posts in the shogunate's central administration, becoming chief officer of the Administrative Board (MANDOKORO) in 1354. Sasaki was noted as a waka and renga (linked-verse) poet and also as a patron of local Ōmi sarugaku (a primitive form of Nō); he figures in the great 14th-century war tale TAIHEIKI as the quintessential military aristocrat and the model of extravagance and luxury (basara).

Sasaki Takayuki (1830–1910)

Politician. Born into a samurai family in the Tosa domain (now Kōchi Prefecture). With fellow activists SAKAMOTO RYŌMA and GOTŌ SHŌJIRŌ, Sasaki participated in the imperial restoration movement in Tosa. Sasaki joined the ministry of justice after the Meiji Restoration (1868) and traveled to Europe with the IWAKURA MISSION in 1871 to study judicial systems. In the controversy over a possible invasion of Korea (see SEIKANRON), unlike many from Tosa who resigned from their posts in disagreement over official policy, Sasaki remained in the government. He was also instrumental in keeping former samurai of Tosa from joining the SATSUMA REBELLION of 1877. Sasaki later served on the Privy Council and as tutor to the crown prince (later Emperor TAISHŌ) but always remained outside the mainstream of politics.

Sasaki Toyoju (1853–1901)

Feminist and social activist. Born in the Sendai domain (now part of Miyagi Prefecture), the daughter of a Confucian scholar; original name, Hoshi Toyoshi. She studied the Chinese classics and then attended the predecessor of the Ferris Girls' School in Yokohama. With YAJIMA KAJIKO and others, she helped found, in 1886, the KYŌFŪKAI (Japan's branch of the Women's Christian Temperance Union). She also organized, in 1889, the Fujin Hakuhyō Kurabu (Women's Ballot Club) to study political questions, and she contributed to the magazine JOGAKU ZASSHI.

Sasamegoto

(Murmured Conversations). A Muromachi-period (1333–1568) poetic treatise on renga (linked verse; see RENGA AND HAIKAI) written by the poet-priest SHINKEI in 1463 or, by some accounts, 1461. A profound expression of the principles of renga as a serious art equal to WAKA, the treatise is also a seminal work of medieval aesthetics in its integration of religious ideas into a poetic theory. Central to the attitude of Sasamegoto is the primary importance it attaches to the nature and spirit (kokoro) of the poet, over and above the diction and technique of the verse (kotoba). Consequently, it sees the poet's training as essentially spiritual and akin to Buddhist shugyō (see ASCETICISM), the ascetic discipline for attaining enlightenment through liberation from worldly illusions and cultivation of the sense of mutability. Such an enlightened spirit manifests itself in a verse having a "chill and meager" (hie-yase) or "withered" (see SABI), suggesting at once a material deprivation and an inner purity and power. The ideal renga poet, moreover, when linking his own verse to the preceding one, does not resort to superficial wordplay and imagistic associations. Rather, he strives by a kind of mystic contemplation to enter the inner world of the preceding verse in order to re-create it in a different form. Shinkei equates the distinction between these two methods of linking to that between doctrinal

Buddhism, transmitted through words, and the direct perception of ZEN. *Sasamegoto* had a profound influence on the spiritual orientation of later poets such as SŌGI and, indirectly, BASHŌ. It was instrumental, too, in the emergence of *sabi* as the central aesthetic idea of the tea ceremony, an art that was closely allied to *renga* at its inception.

Esperanza RAMIREZ-CHRISTENSEN

sasara

A folk music instrument; the name is onomatopoeic. The two most common types are: (1) those in which a bamboo whisk is scraped along a serrated length of wood or bamboo; (2) those in which small, flat pieces of wood are connected by string at one end and shaken. Both types are frequently used in DENGAKU performances.

MIYAMOTO Mizuo

Sasayama

Town in eastern Hyōgo Prefecture, western Honshū. A former castle town on the highway San'in Urakaidō, Sasayama was a military outpost during World War II. Principal industries are agriculture and commerce. Pop: 22,663.

Sasebo

City in northern Nagasaki Prefecture, Kyūshū. It has been a naval base since 1886 and suffered great damage during World War II. It was rebuilt and modernized after it was taken over by the US Navy and the Japanese Maritime Self Defense Force during the Korean War. Its principal industry is shipbuilding. It is the gateway to Saikai National Park. Pop: 251,188.

Sasebo Heavy Industries Co, Ltd

(Sasebo Jūkōgyō). Company engaged in shipbuilding, ship repairing, and the manufacture of boilers and diesel engines for ships. It was established in 1946, when it took over the shipbuilding facilities of the former naval arsenal in the city of Sasebo. It specializes in building large tankers and supertankers. In 1960 it completed what was then the world's largest tanker, the *Nisshō maru*. The company experienced severe difficulties in the wake of the OIL CRISIS OF 1973, and is currently being rehabilitated under the aegis of the Kurushima Dockyard group. It received the contract for the repair work on the atomic-powered ship MUTSU. It has a sales company in Hong Kong. Sales for the fiscal year ending March 1982 totaled ¥84.9 billion (US $352.7 million), with an export ratio of 72 percent. The company was capitalized at ¥8.4 billion (US $34.9 million) in the same year. Corporate headquarters are located in Tōkyō.

sashiko

Garments made of one or more layers of INDIGO-dyed hemp or cotton fabric and quilted in various patterns for the purpose of mending, reinforcement, warmth, or decoration. Also, a style of weaving in imitation of this stitching.

Originally, very simple running stitches were made in straight lines in order to reinforce areas of work garments, cloths, and rags that were apt to wear. Later, as the decorative element became increasingly important, the stitches became more elaborate, each region of Japan developing distinct designs: *sashiko* stitching in Shōnai (the western coast of Yamagata Prefecture) and San'in (the Sea of Japan coasts of Kyōto, Hyōgo, Tottori, and Shimane prefectures); *kogin* stitching in Tsugaru (the western half of Aomori Prefecture); and *hishizashi* stitching in Nambu (north of Morioka, Iwate Prefecture and the eastern half of Aomori Prefecture). The AINU of Hokkaidō are noted for their *sashiko* stitching in curvilinear designs.

Reinforcement stitches on peasants' and fishermen's work garments were commonly seen until recent times in rural areas throughout Japan, and intricate *sashiko* firemen's garments were common in urban areas as well. Although since the Meiji period (1868–1912) mass-produced fabrics have become more accessible and the need to recycle fabrics has virtually disappeared, the decorative use of *sashiko* and *kogin* was revived under the influence of the *mingei* (FOLK CRAFTS) movement led by YANAGI MUNEYOSHI. *Sashiko* stitching for reinforcement can still be seen on garments worn in the martial arts.

Techniques —— *Sashiko* stitching runs in all directions over the fabric, attaching two layers of fabric so that the front and reverse

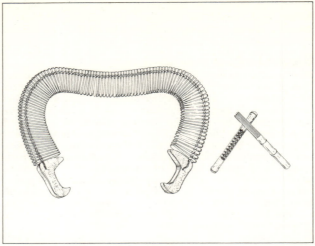

Sasara —— The two most common types

sides show the same patterns. The simplest pattern consists of parallel running stitches that create dots over the entire garment *(tsuzurezashi)*. Straight and curved stitches are combined to make traditional designs such as persimmon flowers, measuring-boxes, hemp leaves, lozenges, tortoise shells, waves, and so on.

Kogin stitching runs only parallel to the weft, from selvage to selvage, creating designs in dark blue and white tones reversed on the front and back of the fabric. About 50 commonly used basic motifs from nature and daily life (plum blossoms, bamboo joints, etc) are repeated in horizontal, vertical, diagonal, or juxtaposed composition.

Hishizashi stitches also run parallel to the weft of the fabric, creating varieties of lozenges *(hishi)*. Traditionally, white or black thread was stitched on pale-blue *(asagi)* hemp fabric; colored woolen yarns were added to the stitching as they became available in the market. *Hishizashi* has a uniquely colorful and gay appearance compared to the subdued and elegant *kogin*. See also EMBROIDERY.

▧ —— Ema Mieko, "Nichijō seikatsu no irui," *Nihon minzokugaku taikei*, vol 6 (1958). Yoshida Eiko, *Sashiko* (1977).

Junco Sato POLLACK

sashimi

Also called *tsukuri*. Fresh seafood fillets cut into bite-sized pieces and eaten raw with soy sauce and *wasabi* (Japanese horseradish). The texture and translucent quality of raw fish are especially esteemed by the Japanese. At traditional restaurants it is usually included as one of the courses; at home it is served as an accompaniment to *sake* or as a side dish with rice.

Surrounded by the sea, Japan has been blessed with an abundance of seafood, and it is thought that seafood has been eaten both cooked and raw since primitive times. In the ancient past fish was cut into shreds and seasoned with salt and vinegar. Later, thick slices were served with a sauce of mustard vinegar, ginger vinegar, or *tadesu* (vinegar sauce with ground *tade* or smartweed leaves). It was only from late in the Edo period (1600–1868), when soy sauce became popular, that *sashimi* was served in its present style.

Almost any fish can be used for *sashimi*, but most common are red-meat fish like tuna and bonito, white-meat fish like sea bream, flounder, and sea bass, or freshwater fish like carp and *ayu* (sweetfish). In addition, shrimp, squid, abalone, and ark shell are often used. These are sliced, diced, or shredded. Professional chefs use a long, thin, single-edged knife especially made for slicing *sashimi*.

Sashimi is served either on a flat plate or in a shallow bowl on a bed of finely shredded *daikon* (Japanese radish), garnished with aromatic green *shiso* (beefsteak plant; *Perilla frutescens* var. *crispa*) leaves or buds, or with edible chrysanthemum flowers, and with the essential *wasabi*. Freshly grated ginger or lemon slices can also be used. Soy sauce is served separately in a small saucer. To eat *sashimi* one dips it into soy sauce in which *wasabi* has been dissolved, or places a small amount of *wasabi* on it and then dips it into the soy sauce. The garnishes are also edible and provide a refreshing contrast.

Tsuji Shizuo

sata

A word used chiefly in premodern times with a wide range of meanings (judgment, proceedings, report, incident), and important during the Kamakura (1185–1333) through the Edo (1600–1868) periods as a legal and administrative term referring to trials, decisions, and other governmental actions. The original meaning of *sata* was the sifting of gold, rice, or other valuable matter from sand; it was extended to the distinguishing of good from evil, right from wrong. In the sense of the correct and discriminating handling of affairs, *sata* was used as a generic term for governmental decisions, imperial decrees (such as RINJI and SENJI), trials, lawsuits, and examinations. Such activities as the management of fiefs, landholdings, levies, tax contributions, and even public gatherings and amusements came to be referred to as *sata*. In the medieval period (13th–16th centuries) *sata* was used chiefly to refer to decisions and proceedings of an official nature. More extended meanings such as "report" and "rumor" came in the Edo period. *Koyanagi Shun'ichirō*

Sata Ineko (1904–   )

Novelist and leftist social critic. Born in Nagasaki; daughter of Takayanagi Yuki, the 14-year-old daughter of a Saga postmaster, and Tajima Masabumi, the 18-year-old son of the Miike Mines Hospital director. Having formalized their marriage, her parents entered her in the family register in 1910 as their foster child, under the name Ine. The following year, her mother died of tuberculosis. Because of medical expenses and her father's dissipation, the family became steadily poorer. When Ine was 11, she went with her father to Tōkyō to stay with his younger brother Sata Hidezane (whose surname she adopted in 1946). Ine, then in fifth grade, quit school to work at a caramel factory during the winter of 1915–16. Between 1916 and 1924, she worked in restaurants, a knitting mill, and then the Western goods section of Tōkyō's Maruzen Bookstore. She also read avidly in Western and Japanese literature.

Her first marriage was in 1924 to a Keiō University student named Kobori Kaizō, the son of a wealthy family; the following year she attempted suicide and was taken home to Hyōgo Prefecture. She never returned to the Kobori family. In 1926 she moved back to Tōkyō and worked at a café, where she met the writers and leftist social critics producing the literary magazine *Roba* (1926–28, Donkey), among them NAKANO SHIGEHARU, who encouraged her to write. She married a member of this group, KUBOKAWA TSURUJIRŌ.

Her first short story, the autobiographical "Kyarameru kōba kara" (1928, From the Caramel Factory), was published in the magazine *Puroretaria geijutsu* (Proletarian Arts). After this story's success, she became an active participant in the PROLETARIAN LITERATURE MOVEMENT and with the novelist MIYAMOTO YURIKO she worked with the women's committee of the Proletarian Authors' Association (1929–31); she also edited the proletarian women's bulletin *Hataraku fujin* (1932–33, Working Women) and maintained contact with such underground activists as KOBAYASHI TAKIJI and MIYAMOTO KENJI. She joined the outlawed JAPAN COMMUNIST PARTY in 1932.

While caring for her two children, she suffered poverty and political oppression: Kubokawa and Nakano were arrested in 1932 and she was imprisoned for two months in 1935. She wrote about these experiences in her novel *Kurenai* (1936, Scarlet). Her estrangement from the leftist movement (see TENKŌ) around this time led to a growing rift with her husband until they were divorced in 1945.

In 1940–43 she traveled in Korea, China, and Southeast Asia with HAYASHI FUMIKO and other authors, in trips organized by the newspaper *Asahi shimbun* and the military authorities for the purpose of comforting soldiers at the front. After the war, her leftist associates criticized her for such activities, and although she rejoined the Communist Party in 1946, she was expelled in 1951, the same year as the military trial of her son Kenzō. Her party membership, restored in 1955, was finally revoked in 1964. During this period she wrote candidly on the theme of wartime collaboration and her disillusionment with the Communist Party in such works as *Sozō* (1966, Plastic Sculpture).

Despite her changing relationship with the Communist Party she continued to be active politically, campaigning in connection with the MATSUKAWA INCIDENT and the Sanrizuka airport struggle (see NEW TŌKYŌ INTERNATIONAL AIRPORT). However, after *Sozō* her works have dealt mainly with the complex impact of historical events on essentially apolitical people.

Her other works include *Suashi no musume* (1940, Barefoot Girl); *Watakushi no Tōkyō chizu* (1946–48, My Tōkyō Map); *Kikai no naka no seishun* (1954, Youth among Machines); *Onna no yado* (1963, Women's Lodgings); *Omoki nagare ni* (1968–69, On the Heavy Tide); *Juei* (1970–72, Tree Shade); and "Toki ni tatsu" (1975; tr "Standing Still in Time," 1977).

🖪 ——Sata Ineko, *Sata Ineko zenshū*, 18 vols (Kōdansha, 1977–79). Itagaki Naoko, *Fujin sakka hyōden* (1954). Miyamoto Yuriko, *Fujin to bungaku* (1947). G. T. Shea, *Leftwing Literature in Japan* (1964). *Kyōko Iriye SELDEN*

Satake family

Warrior family of medieval Japan. A branch of the Seiwa line of the MINAMOTO FAMILY, the Satake took its name from the village of Satake in the province of Hitachi (now Ibaraki Prefecture), where its founder Minamoto no Yoshimitsu (1045–1127) established himself early in the 12th century. Originally powerful enough to oppose MINAMOTO NO YORITOMO, the head of the Seiwa Minamoto line, the Satake finally joined his rebellion against the Taira in 1180 and developed into a major power in the northern Kantō region. After the fall of the Kamakura shogunate in 1333, the Satake supported the ASHIKAGA FAMILY. During the Sengoku period (1467–1568), under the leadership of Satake Yoshishige, the family extended its rule to most of Hitachi and Shimotsuke provinces (the latter now Tochigi Prefecture). They were important supporters of the national unifier TOYOTOMI HIDEYOSHI, who confirmed them in their landholdings, assessed at 545,800 *koku* (see KOKUDAKA). The family moved its base to Mito Castle. Still owing allegiance to the Toyotomi in the Battle of SEKIGAHARA in 1600, the Satake were shifted by the victorious TOKUGAWA IEYASU to a smaller fief farther north in the Akita domain (now Akita Prefecture). The Satake continued for 14 generations during the Edo period (1600–1868). After the Meiji Restoration in 1868 Satake Yoshitaka was made a marquis for his services during the Boshin Civil War that accompanied the overthrow of the Tokugawa shogunate. *G. Cameron HURST III*

Satake Shozan (1748–1785)

Daimyō of the Akita domain (now part of Akita Prefecture) and founder of the AKITA SCHOOL of Western-style painting. Also called Satake Yoshiatsu. Born in Edo (now Tōkyō), Shozan became daimyō of Akita in 1758. In 1773 he invited HIRAGA GENNAI to Akita to give advice on local copper production. While there, Gennai introduced his theories of Western art to Shozan and Shozan's retainer ODANO NAOTAKE. In 1778, with the assistance of Naotake, Shozan composed three essays entitled, respectively, "Gahō kōryō" (Art of Painting), "Gato rikai" (Understanding Painting and Composition), and "Tanseibu" (Red and Blue, a technical discussion of pigments). In "Gato rikai," Shozan included diagrams illustrating linear perspective, an intricate spiral staircase, and methods of drawing figures modeled on the Dutch painting manual *Groot Schilderboek* (1712), written by Gerard de Lairesse. These essays were collected in one of three sketchbooks and constituted the first theoretical works on Western-style painting written in Japan. These sketchbooks by Shozan provide superb examples of his fine-line technique. Subjects include nature studies of flowers, grasses, birds, insects, and water creatures. *Cal FRENCH*

Sata mirensho

(Book for Those Unversed in Lawsuits). Manual of legal terminology and litigation procedures of the Kamakura shogunate (1192–1333). Although its authorship is unclear, the manual is thought to have been completed around 1323. The *Sata mirensho* consists of three parts: an explanation of legal terms and clerical procedures for initiating lawsuits in the shogunal courts, an explanation of the rank system of court nobles in Kyōto, and examples of documentary forms necessary for lawsuits. Written in a plain style, the manual was intended for those who were unfamiliar with the complicated legal procedures of the shogunate.

Satamisaki

Cape on southern Ōsumi Peninsula, Kagoshima Prefecture; southernmost point of Kyūshū. Known for its rocky coastline, reefs, and a large lighthouse and for its mild climate and subtropical plants such as the sago palm. Part of Kirishima–Yaku National Park.

Satchō Dōmei → Satsuma–Chōshū Alliance

satellites, artificial → space technology

satodairi

(literally, "rustic" imperial palace). A provisional imperial residence outside the imperial palace complex in Kyōto. During the Heian period (794–1185) emperors frequently moved to temporary quarters when fires damaged or destroyed the palace or when inauspicious events occurred. They usually took up residence in the mansions of maternal relatives, staying from one day to as long as a year. The first *satodairi* was designated in 976, when Emperor En'yū (959–991; r 969–984), after a fire, moved to the Horikawa mansion of imperial regent *(kampaku)* FUJIWARA NO KANEMICHI for nearly a year. Beginning in the reign (1073–87) of Emperor SHIRAKAWA, the main palace was no longer inhabited at all, being reserved for ceremonial purposes, and some 30 different places served as provisional palaces thereafter, some of them specially built for the purpose. From the period of the Northern and Southern Courts (1336–92) until the end of the Edo period (1600–1868), the Higashi no Tōin Tsuchimikado mansion (now called the Kyōto *gosho*, or Imperial Palace) was used. *G. Cameron* HURST III

Satō Eisaku (1901–1975)

Prime minister from 9 November 1964 to 6 July 1972, Satō set the record for the longest continuous tenure in Japan. Recipient of the Nobel Peace Prize in 1974, he counted among his diplomatic accomplishments the normalization of relations with South Korea (1965) and the reversion of Okinawa from the United States to Japanese administration (1972).

Satō was born in Yamaguchi Prefecture, the third son of Satō Hidesuke and younger brother of another postwar premier, KISHI NOBUSUKE. Upon graduation from Tōkyō University in 1924, Satō joined the Ministry of Railways (later the Ministry of Transport). Aside from holding a number of administrative positions, his experiences included a study tour to the United States from August 1934 to April 1936 and two tours in Japanese-occupied China in 1938 and 1939 to help with railway construction. At the end of World War II he was appointed director of the Ōsaka District Railway Bureau, and in 1947 he reached the position of vice-minister of transportation.

In 1948 Satō was named director of the Cabinet Secretariat by Prime Minister YOSHIDA SHIGERU. He won a seat in the House of Representatives as a member of the Democratic Liberal Party (Minshu Jiyūtō) in 1949. Under Yoshida, Satō served as minister of posts and telecommunications and as minister of construction. In 1953 he was chosen by Yoshida to be secretary-general of the LIBERAL PARTY. His political career suffered a serious setback in 1954 when he was accused of accepting bribes from a shipbuilders' association (see SHIPBUILDING SCANDAL OF 1954). He was indicted for violation of the Political Fund Control Law, but was released in 1956, before completion of his trial, in a general amnesty following Japan's entry into the United Nations; he reemerged in politics as finance minister in Kishi's cabinet in 1958. In the IKEDA HAYATO cabinet he was minister of international trade and industry and the minister in charge of the Tōkyō Olympics. In 1964 he unsuccessfully challenged Ikeda for the presidency of the LIBERAL DEMOCRATIC PARTY (Jiyū Minshutō). A few months later, Ikeda fell ill with terminal cancer and named Satō to succeed him.

As prime minister, Satō continued Ikeda's policy of high economic growth, making Japan the world's third largest economic power. His rapprochement with South Korea began with a commitment of $800 million to build up that country's economy. Through two visits to Southeast Asian countries in 1967, Satō demonstrated Japan's desire to maintain close economic and political ties with that region. He called his approach to the United States a new era of cooperation, but revaluation of the yen, disputes over textile exports, and President Nixon's sudden announcement of his visit to the People's Republic of China showed the strains between the United States and Japan. In 1970 the United States–Japan Security Treaty of 1960 (see UNITED STATES–JAPAN SECURITY TREATIES) could have been renegotiated or abrogated, but Satō chose to extend them automatically, thus avoiding a recurrence of the antitreaty demonstrations of 1960.

Satō signed the nuclear nonproliferation treaty in 1970 but did not push for its ratification. His three nonnuclear principles (HI-KAKU SANGENSOKU), subsequently cited as one of the reasons for his nomination for the Nobel Peace Prize, were nonmanufacturing, nonpossession, and nonintroduction into Japan of nuclear weapons.

Satō was a consummate politician, able to bind together divergent factions within his own party. His tenure of office was generally marked by steady cooperation and goodwill between the United States and Japan. But once that stability was challenged by the "NIXON SHOCKS," Satō's political fortunes also waned.

📖 ——Okamoto Fumio, *Satō seiken* (1974). Satō Hiroko, *Saishō fujin hiroku* (1974). *David J.* LU

satogo

Child reared by foster parents *(satooya)*. This practice has taken special forms in Japanese history. From shortly before the Edo period (1600–1868) into the 19th century some aristocratic families in Kyōto and merchant families in Ōsaka, Kyōto, and Edo (now Tōkyō) sent their children to live as *satogo* for several years with peasant families in the surrounding countryside. This arrangement, it was thought, would help the children grow up strong and healthy. Some scholars believe that it is related to the practice whereby natural parents would temporarily leave their offspring, born perhaps in an inauspicious year (YAKUDOSHI), with others to thwart evil influences which might otherwise plague the child or themselves.

In other ranks of society an illegitimate, orphaned, or poor child was sent to live with another family as its *satogo*. In return for providing bed and board the foster parents secured extra labor and could often expect (except from the very poor), child support from the natural parents. Since 1948 *satogo* have been cared for under a foster family program established in accord with the Child Welfare Law (Jidō Fukushi Hō). *Noguchi Takenori*

Satō Hachirō (1903–1973)

The son of the author SATŌ KŌROKU. Born in Tōkyō. As a youth Satō was a delinquent student, changing schools eight times and failing three times before finally quitting middle school. At the age of 16, he began to compose poetry, and in 1926 his first collection of poems, *Tsumeiro no ame* (Fingernail-Colored Rain) was published. Writing about life among the lower classes who lived in the SHITAMACHI area of Tōkyō, he achieved popularity as a lyric poet. He also tried popular song writing and composed a number of well-known songs such as "Reijin no uta" (1930, Song of the Beauty), and "Anata to yobeba" (1935, When I Call You). In the period just after the end of World War II, his songs "Ringo no uta" (The Apple Song) and "Nagasaki no kane" (The Bell of Nagasaki) were extremely popular; they are often referred to in discussions of conditions in the immediate postwar period. Beginning with the NHK radio program "Hanashi no izumi" (1946–64), he also was very active as a television and radio personality. His postwar poetry includes the popular "Chiisai aki mitsuketa" (1954, I Found a Small Autumn) and the best-selling collection of poems entitled *Okāsan* (1961–63, Mother, 3 vols). *Itasaka Tsuyoshi*

Satō Haruo (1892–1964)

Poet and novelist. Born in 1892 in Shingū, Wakayama Prefecture, the eldest son of a doctor. From his early youth, Haruo's only ambition was to become a writer, and he devoted his school years to writing traditional WAKA poetry and modern verse. Upon graduation from school in 1910, Haruo entered Keiō University to study literature under NAGAI KAFŪ.

Haruo began his literary career publishing poetry in various literary journals, but after leaving Keiō in 1913 he concentrated on writing fiction. Later, he was befriended by writers AKUTAGAWA RYŪNOSUKE and TANIZAKI JUN'ICHIRŌ and was helped by the latter in publishing his early works. He gained serious recognition as a writer in 1919 with his first full-length novel *Den'en no yūutsu* (Pastoral Melancholy), and thereafter produced a steady flow of fiction, poetry, and personal essays, as well as drama and translations of Chinese poetry, until his death in 1964.

Haruo served on the selection committees of several literary prizes, including the Akutagawa Prize (see LITERARY PRIZES), and was instrumental in launching the careers of many young writers of his day. In 1948 he was elected a member of the Japan Art Academy, and in 1960 he received the Order of Culture, the highest decoration awarded by the Japanese government for advancement of the arts and sciences.

Poetry —— Haruo's early poems are recognizable by their statements of protest. In works such as *Gusha no shi* (1911, Death of a Fool), on the subject of a young socialist implicated in the alleged plot to assassinate Emperor MEIJI (see HIGH TREASON INCIDENT OF 1910), he voiced his strong concern for social and political justice. After he left Keiō, his poetry took on a more lyrical, personal note, and his concerns were more toward resolving emotional problems born out of romantic entanglements and justifying the choice of a way of life. His first collection, *Junjō shishū* (1921, Poems of Innocence), contains the best examples of his lyrical poems from this period.

Haruo's poetry is characteristically elaborate and rich in language. He often employed the 5–7 syllabic count of traditional versification but was equally effective writing in the style of modern verse. The language and modes of expression of his poems were often classical, but his themes and concerns were those of a modern man attempting to come to terms with ennui and the complexities of existence. His translations of classical Chinese poetry are best represented in the collection *Shajinshū* (1929, Wagon Dust).

Fiction —— Haruo's most acclaimed works in fiction are *Den'en no yūutsu* and its companion novel *Tokai no yūutsu* (1922, Urban Melancholy). The former is in the style of an expanded prose poem and traces the troubled mind of its poet through the recurring symbol of the ailing rose; the latter portrays the hero's progress in the city following his return from the country. These works are two of the finest examples of the "artist novel" in the modern period and are significant in that they evidence a clear shift from the elaborate poetic language and personal descriptions of the earlier novel to the spare, objective narration of its sequel, a style that characterizes his later works.

Haruo experimented with the stream-of-consciousness technique as early as 1914 with the short story "Arukinagara" (While Walking), and was one of the first Japanese writers to introduce Freudian psychoanalysis in fiction, with the highly acclaimed mystery *Kōseiki* (1929, A Chronicle of Rebirth). His love of fantasy and cosmopolitan characters and settings is most clearly witnessed in "Supein inu no ie" (1917; tr "The House of a Spanish Dog," 1961). In *Kono mittsu no mono* (1925–26, These Three Things), a serialized novel, Haruo attempted to weave into fiction the story of the love triangle that involved himself, Tanizaki Jun'ichirō, and the latter's first wife.

Akiko mandara (1954, Akiko Mandala), an artistic rendering of the life of YOSANO AKIKO, Japan's foremost woman poet of the early 1900s, won Haruo the Yomiuri Literary Prize in 1955 and represented his best effort in the vein of biography and historical fiction, to which he turned later in his career.

—— *Satō Haruo zenshū*, 12 vols (Kōdansha, 1966–70). Nakamura Mitsuo, *Satō Haruo ron* (1962).   James T. KENNEY

Satō Issai (1772–1859)

Confucian scholar of the late Edo period (1600–1868). Born the son of a high-ranking retainer of the Iwamura domain (now part of Gifu Prefecture), Satō became an attendant to the *daimyō's* son, Matsudaira Taira, who later was adopted by the Hayashi family, official Confucian scholars to the shogunate, and took the name HAYASHI JUSSAI. Satō went to Ōsaka in 1791 to study with Nakai Chikuzan (1730–1804), and then to Kyōto to study with Minagawa Kien (1734–1807). In 1793 he went to Edo (now Tōkyō) to study with Jussai. In 1805 he was appointed principal teacher of the SHŌHEIKŌ, the shogunal school for Confucian studies, of which Jussai was the head. Following Jussai's death in 1841, Satō was made professor at the Shōheikō and was frequently called upon to give advice to the shogunate. He is said to have had 3,000 students, including several daimyō and prominent scholars such as Ōhashi Totsuan (1816–62), SAKUMA SHŌZAN, and WATANABE KAZAN. As an official shogunate scholar Satō was obliged to teach the Zhu Xi (Chu Hsi) school of Confucianism (see SHUSHIGAKU), although his personal leanings were toward the more intuitive, less intellectually oriented Wang Yangming school (YŌMEIGAKU). Of his works, the best known is his collection of essays on scholarship and life, *Genshi shiroku*.

Satō Kōgyō Co, Ltd

A company engaged in civil engineering, construction, and real estate. Established in 1931, it is one of the largest companies in its field in Japan and a leader in tunneling shield projects. It has affiliates in Singapore, Malaysia, and Saudi Arabia, and plans to expand its operations further in Southeast Asia and the Middle East. Sales for the fiscal year ending September 1981 totaled ¥279.5 billion (US $1.2 billion), and the company was capitalized at ¥11.1 billion (US $48.3 million) in the same year. Corporate headquarters are located in Tōkyō.

Satō Kōroku (1874–1949)

Novelist. Born in Aomori Prefecture. A middle-school dropout, he began his career as a popular storyteller before turning to writing the juvenile fiction for which he is best known. He also participated in the modern HAIKU movement led by MASAOKA SHIKI. He is the father of the poet SATŌ HACHIRŌ and the writer Satō Aiko (b 1923). His principal works include the play *Kyōenroku* (1906) and the novels *Aa gyokuhai ni hana ukete* (1927–28) and *Eiyū kōshinkyoku* (1936).

Satomi Ton (1888–1983)

Novelist. Real name Yamauchi Hideo. Born into the Arishima family in Kanagawa Prefecture, legally adopted by his mother's family, Yamauchi. After withdrawing from Tōkyō University, he began his long career as a fiction writer, joining the literary coterie known as the SHIRAKABA SCHOOL in 1910 with his brothers ARISHIMA TAKEO and Arishima Ikuma (1882–1974). From the 1920s he remained independent of any literary school or political ideology. He was a consummate craftsman, attaining in his novels a storyteller's fluency as well as refinement of expression in both narrative and dialogue. In 1959 he received the Order of Culture. His principal novels include *Tajō busshin* (1922–23) and *Gokuraku tombo* (1961).

Satomura Jōha (1524–1602)

Also known as Satomura Shōha. Poet of *renga* (see RENGA AND HAIKAI), or linked verse; foremost *renga* master of the late 16th century. His surname was originally Matsumura, but he changed it to Satomura on the death of his teacher, Satomura Shōkyū, in 1552. According to some sources, the year of his birth was 1527.

At the age of 12, Jōha became a novice at the Kōfukuji monastery in Nara, and he began his study of linked verse shortly afterward. Becoming a full-fledged priest in 1545, he took the name Jōha and accompanied the *renga* master Shūkei (d 1544) to Kyōto. There he participated in numerous linked-verse gatherings and also received instruction in classical literature, studying classical poetry and the TALE OF GENJI *(Genji monogatari)* under prominent members of the old court nobility. On Shūkei's death, Jōha became a disciple of Shōkyū, and when this master died he took charge of the education and upbringing of Shōkyū's young son and heir Shōshitsu (1541–1603). From this time on, Jōha was the foremost *renga* master of the day. Amid the unsettled political strife and warfare of the late 16th century, it was dangerous to be prominent, and Jōha came under suspicion more than once for verses that, taken as allegory, could have had treasonable implications. At one point he was placed under house arrest for suspected involvement in TOYOTOMI HIDETSUGU's plot against his adoptive father TOYOTOMI HIDEYOSHI. However, Jōha's political acumen and fearlessness enabled him to steer a safe, if perilous, course through the troubled waters of the age.

Jōha was the author of several handbooks and critical treatises on linked verse which had a wide influence. The most important of his works is *Renga shihō shō* (1585, Treasures of Linked Verse). His critical views and ideals were important and original in his time. In particular, he advocated the treatment of a composite *renga* poem of 50 or 100 stanzas as an integrated literary structure, thus calling attention away from the contemporary overemphasis upon the techniques of linking stanza to stanza to the detriment of the total effect of the whole.

—— Earl Miner, *Japanese Linked Poetry* (1979).

Robert H. BROWER

Satō Naokata (1650–1719)

Neo-Confucian scholar of the early part of the Edo period (1600–1868). Born in Fukuyama (now part of Hiroshima Prefecture). He studied with YAMAZAKI ANSAI in Kyōto, and, together with ASAMI KEISAI and Miyake Shōsai (1662–1741), was regarded as one of Ansai's three outstanding disciples. Both Naokata and Keisai were expelled, however, for opposing Ansai's attempts to reconcile Shintō teachings with the metaphysics of Neo-Confucianism (SHU-

SHIGAKU). Naokata served as Confucian lecturer and adviser to his native Fukuyama as well as other domains. He strongly advocated pure Neo-Confucianism throughout his life. Naokata is remembered for criticizing the deeds of the masterless *samurai* who avenged the death of their lord in the FORTY-SEVEN RŌNIN INCIDENT.

Satō Naotake (1882–1971)

Diplomat and politician. Born in Ōsaka; graduate of Tōkyō Kōtō Shōgyō Gakkō (now Hitotsubashi University). Satō entered the Ministry of Foreign Affairs in 1905 and, after holding consular posts in Russia, Manchuria, Switzerland, and France, was named minister to Poland in 1923. After representing Japan at several international conferences, including the first disarmament conference held by the League of Nations in Geneva in 1932, he became successively ambassador to Belgium and to France. In 1937 he became foreign minister in the HAYASHI SENJŪRŌ cabinet, accepting the post on condition that he be allowed to pursue a policy that would avert war, treat China as an equal, avoid military confrontation with the Soviet Union, and promote closer ties with Great Britain. The Hayashi cabinet lasted barely four months, however, and under the new foreign minister, HIROTA KŌKI, Japan's foreign policy took a decidedly aggressive turn. In 1942 Satō was named ambassador to the Soviet Union. As Japan's war situation rapidly deteriorated, Satō, under instructions from Foreign Minister TŌGŌ SHIGENORI, tried in vain to have Russia act as an intermediary with the Allies, and he personally sent a cable to Tōkyō urging the government to accept the terms of surrender as articulated in the POTSDAM DECLARATION. (The Russians not only equivocated but themselves declared war on Japan on 8 August 1945.) Satō was elected to the House of Councillors in the first postwar election (1947). He served as president of the House from 1954 to 1958 and withdrew from politics in 1965. He published his memoirs as *Kaiko hachijūnen* (1963, Looking Back over Eighty Years).

Satō Nempuku (1898–)

HAIKU poet. Born Satō Kenjirō in Niigata Prefecture, he settled in a Japanese agricultural colony at Aliança, Brazil, and worked as a farmer. A *haiku* poet of the coterie associated with the magazine HOTOTOGISU, Satō took up the teaching of *haiku* in Brazil as his mission and for over 50 years has worked to enrich the cultural life of Brazil's Japanese immigrants.　　　　*Saitō Hiroshi*

Satō–Nixon Communiqué

A joint communiqué issued on 21 November 1969 by Prime Minister SATŌ EISAKU of Japan and President Richard Nixon of the United States, following three days of talks in Washington. The communiqué stated that they had reviewed relations between their two countries in light of the international situation and had agreed to speed up consultations "with a view to accomplishing the reversion in 1972" of OKINAWA to the administrative control of Japan. Okinawa, the major island of the Nansei Shotō group (see RYŪKYŪ ISLANDS), had been seized by US forces after a bloody World War II battle, and article 3 of the 1951 SAN FRANCISCO PEACE TREATY provided that those islands south of 29° north latitude would be under the sole administering authority of the United States, with the possibility of a future United Nations trusteeship left open.

The 1969 communiqué, which had been carefully drafted by the two governments over a period of months, embodied various related understandings: Japan recognized the security of South Korea as "essential" and that of Taiwan as "a most important factor" for its own security; the United States–Japan Security Treaty (see UNITED STATES–JAPAN SECURITY TREATIES) would be applied "without modification" to Okinawa; and the United States would carry out the reversion "in a manner consistent with the policy of the Japanese government" in regard to nuclear weapons, meaning that the United States would withdraw its nuclear weapons stored on Okinawa. The reversion treaty was signed on 17 June 1971 and administrative control was turned over to Japan on 15 May 1972.

The statement also stressed the need for Japan and the United States to take steps to strengthen the world economic system, to promote free and balanced trade, to contribute to the economic development of Asia, and to control inflation. The communiqué did not refer to US limitations on the import of Japanese textiles, although the two leaders had briefly discussed this thorny issue and agreed to work for a mutually satisfactory solution.

The Satō–Nixon agreement on Okinawa was the culmination of many years of discussion between the two governments and settled the last of the major issues between them arising from World War II. It served to strengthen ties between the two peoples and also had the effect of increasing the electoral popularity of Prime Minister Satō and his LIBERAL DEMOCRATIC PARTY.　　*Richard B. FINN*

Satō Nobuhiro (1769–1850)

Agronomist of the late Edo period (1600–1868). Born into a family of scholars in Dewa Province (now Akita Prefecture). As a child he traveled with his father, going as far as what is now Hokkaidō, and was deeply moved by the desperate conditions of the peasants who were then suffering from the TEMMEI FAMINE. After his father's death, he went to Edo (now Tōkyō) to study with the Rangaku (see WESTERN LEARNING) scholar Udagawa Genzui (1755–97). After a brief service with the Tsuyama domain (now part of Okayama Prefecture), he traveled around the country, acquiring practical knowledge about agriculture. He settled down for a while in Kazusa (now part of Chiba Prefecture) to write, but spent most of his life traveling. He became interested in Shintō and entered the school of the KOKUGAKU (National Learning) scholar HIRATA ATSUTANE. About the same time he also became friends with TAKANO CHŌEI and WATANABE KAZAN and narrowly escaped punishment in the shogunate arrest of Rangaku scholars (BANSHA NO GOKU). Satō's fame gradually spread, and he was invited by several *daimyō* to advise on agricultural techniques, the economy, and maritime defense. It was in response to senior councillor MIZUNO TADAKUNI's request that he wrote his *Fukkohō gaigen*, in which he proposed unifying Japan under a single ruler and placing all land, production, commerce, and transportation under direct government control.

satori

(awakening; enlightenment). The heart of the Buddhist faith, the concept of *satori* (Ch: *wu*) achieved prominence particularly in the Zen tradition. The term *satori*, as used by Daisetz SUZUKI in the meaning "sudden enlightenment," has passed into English usage. Because all men are considered to be already Buddhas, and because enlightenment must be total, the radical Zen tradition has insisted on "sudden, not gradual, enlightenment." By mere recognition of one's a priori enlightenment one awakens suddenly to one's innate Buddhahood. The experience has been compared to that of a "sudden falling out of the bottom of a wooden bathtub." Though self-validating, the *satori* experience traditionally requires the seal of approval from one's master. See ZEN.　　*Whalen LAI*

Satō Satarō (1909–)

WAKA poet. Born in Miyagi Prefecture. When he was very young Satō worked for the publishing firm Iwanami in Tōkyō. In 1926 he joined the *waka* poets' society associated with the magazine ARARAGI, and in 1940 he published *Hodō*, his first collection of *waka*. His third collection, *Kichō* (1952), won the Yomiuri Literary Prize. His works, based mostly on ordinary daily events, are not particularly innovative or exciting, but they are well wrought and poetically intense. Satō was a principal editor of the collected works of his mentor, SAITŌ MOKICHI. He has published studies of Saitō Mokichi as well as numerous critiques of *waka*.　　*James R. MORITA*

Satō Takeo (1899–1972)

Architect. Born in Nagoya. Graduated from Waseda University where he became an assistant professor and, later, professor. He collaborated with Satō Kōichi (1878–1941) on the design of Waseda's (modern Gothic) Ōkuma Auditorium (1927). A pioneer in the field of architectural acoustics in Japan, Satō designed many public halls and auditoriums. His buildings include Kōfu City Hall (1960), Okayama Civic Hall (1963), Kōtō Public Hall and Auditorium (1965), and Ōtsu City Hall (1967).　　*WATANABE Hiroshi*

Satō Tatsuo (1904–1974)

Government official. Born in Fukuoka Prefecture. After graduating from Tōkyō University in 1928, Satō joined the Home Ministry and later moved to the Cabinet Legislative Bureau (Hōseikyoku). As chief of the bureau's Second Department after World War II, he helped prepare the draft of the 1947 CONSTITUTION. His book *Nihonkoku kempō seiritsu shi*, 2 vols (1962, 1964, History of the Creation of the Japanese Constitution) is an instructive account of the Japanese negotiations with OCCUPATION authorities over the postwar political structure of Japan. As president of the NATIONAL PERSONNEL AUTHORITY from 1962 until his death, Satō was instrumental in improving the salaries of civil servants. Although a specialist in law, he distinguished himself also as a poet, essayist, and botanist.   *Itō Masami*

Satow, Ernest Mason (1843–1929)

English diplomat, linguist, and scholar; active on the British diplomatic staff in Japan from 1862 to 1882 during the final years of the Tokugawa shogunate and the beginning of the Meiji government. Knowing well the leaders of the Meiji Restoration of 1868 and having command of Japanese and Chinese, he became minister plenipotentiary to Japan (1895–1900) and to China (1900–1906), his last diplomatic post. Before and after retirement he wrote learned articles about Japan and on diplomacy.

Ernest Satow was born in London; his mother was English, his father a Swedish merchant who had emigrated to England. At 18 Satow received his BA from London University. Passing first in a competitive aptitude examination for interpreters, he chose Japan to begin his career. Satow reached Yokohama in 1862, four years after the ANSEI COMMERCIAL TREATIES had opened Japan to Western trade. It was a difficult time: the Tokugawa shogunate was losing its authority, and the domains of Chōshū (now Yamaguchi Prefecture) and Satsuma (now Kagoshima Prefecture) wanted to restore the emperor to power, to end the shōgun's monopoly of foreign trade, and to share in the government. From either side no foreigner was safe. Satow learned Japanese quickly. He was an invaluable help to the ministers, Sir Rutherford ALCOCK and, after June 1865, Sir Harry PARKES, in understanding the civil conflict. He was present at the allied victories at Kagoshima (1863) and at Shimonoseki (1864) and won the respect of the defeated *daimyō* (see KAGOSHIMA BOMBARDMENT; SHIMONOSEKI BOMBARDMENT). He attended Parkes when the allied force finally received imperial ratification of the Ansei treaties. Although he knew the retainers of many daimyō, he sided with those of Chōshū and Satsuma.

Satow became secretary to the embassy in 1868 after the restoration of imperial rule. He was with Parkes when he presented his credentials to the emperor. He was sympathetic to the leaders of that difficult period—IWAKURA TOMOMI, ITŌ HIROBUMI, INOUE KAORU, ŌKUMA SHIGENOBU, and others—when Japan emerged from feudalism to the beginnings of a modern centralized state. In 1883 Satow left Japan for successful diplomatic assignments in Siam, Uruguay, and Morocco. He was knighted in 1895 and appointed minister plenipotentiary to Japan.

Since Britain wanted to draw closer to Japan to check Russia's schemes for acquiring an ice-free port, Satow was the ideal choice for the post. He knew the Meiji government, its leaders, and the languages of Japan, China, and continental Europe. His return coincided with Japan's becoming a factor in Far Eastern politics. The peace terms after Japan's victory over China in the SINO-JAPANESE WAR OF 1894–1895 would have upset the balance of power in Asia. Russia, Germany, and France forced Japan to return to China the Liaodong (Liaotung) peninsula, including Port Arthur (see TRIPARTITE INTERVENTION). England was sympathetic but unwilling to give help. Japan began an immense armament program.

Satow's dispatches are outstanding for their acute perceptiveness and conscientiousness. He kept Britain abreast of Japan's armaments; he told Japan that Britain's interest in Korea was secondary; and he advised Japan to avoid confrontation with Russia until Japan could stand alone. Russia's fortification of Port Arthur intensified Japan's war preparations. Satow thought Japan would not fight before 1903. But he left Japan for home leave without recommending an alliance with Britain because of Lord Salisbury's probable disapproval.

Satow became minister to China in October 1900, near the end of the BOXER REBELLION, after the besieged legations in Beijing (Peking) had been relieved by an international force. With a knowledge of commerce and finance as well as diplomacy, he persuaded the Chinese government to submit and pay the indemnities. And believing in the independence of China, he reconciled the competing claims of the various allies with firmness and suavity, showing understanding of East and West. He received credit for the accord

signed between China and the Western powers at Beijing in 1901. Satow was not previously consulted about the conclusion of the ANGLO-JAPANESE ALLIANCE in 1902, which he opposed. He was withdrawn from China in 1906.

Appointments to the Privy Council and to a six-year term in the Court of Arbitration at The Hague quickly followed. Nevertheless, in late 1907 Satow retired to Ottery St. Mary in Devonshire, England. There for 22 years he continued his writing on legal subjects and lectured at Cambridge. Among his varied publications are: numerous articles on Japan for the *Transactions of the Asiatic Society of Japan* (1872–99); *An English-Japanese Dictionary of the Spoken Language*, with Masakata Ishibashi (1878); *The Jesuit Mission Press in Japan, 1591–1610* (1888), a compendium of findings in eight libraries of England and Europe; *A Guide to Diplomatic Practice*, 2 vols (1917); and *A Diplomat in Japan* (1921; repr 1968).

■——B. M. Allen, *The Rt. Hon. Sir Ernest Mason Satow: A Memoir* (1933). George Alexander Lensen, *Korea and Manchuria between Russia and Japan: Observations of Sir Ernest Satow* (1966). Ian H. Nish, *The Anglo-Japanese Alliance* (1966). Shōwa Joshi Daigaku, ed, *Kindai bungaku kenkyū sōsho*, vol 31 (1969).
                                             Grace Fox

Satsuei Sensō → Kagoshima Bombardment

satsuki → azaleas

Satsuma and Chōshū oligarchs → hambatsu

Satsuma–Chōshū Alliance

(Satchō Dōmei). A military coalition formed in 1866 against the Tokugawa shogunate by the powerful Satsuma (now Kagoshima Prefecture) and Chōshū (now Yamaguchi Prefecture) domains. In the early 1860s Satsuma tended to take a moderate position toward the failing Tokugawa shogunate, while Chōshū acted as the center of the movement to overthrow the shogunate. By 1865, however, Satsuma leaders, particularly SAIGŌ TAKAMORI and ŌKUBO TOSHIMICHI, had come to agree with Chōshū that the shogunate must be removed by force, and in August 1865, through the good offices of SAKAMOTO RYŌMA from Tosa (now Kōchi Prefecture), Satsuma agreed to buy Western arms for Chōshū. Then in March 1866 Sakamoto brought together Saigō and Ōkubo of Satsuma and KIDO TAKAYOSHI of Chōshū and persuaded them to form a secret military pact between their two domains. The alliance was a major factor in the failure of the second of the CHŌSHŪ EXPEDITIONS in 1866 and the eventual fall of the Tokugawa shogunate in 1867–68. The two domains continued to dominate the new imperial government (see HAMBATSU). See also MEIJI RESTORATION.

Satsuma Peninsula

(Satsuma Hantō). Located in western Kagoshima Prefecture, southern Kyūshū. Occupying the western half of the prefecture, it is composed of low-lying volcanic hills and plateaus. The principal agricultural products are sweet potatoes, tea, tobacco, and dairy products. Makurazaki, Yamagawa, and Kushikino are bases for deep-sea fishing. The peninsula is part of Kirishima–Yaku National Park.

Satsuma Province

(Satsuma no Kuni). One of the 11 provinces of the Saikaidō (Western Sea Circuit) in Kyūshū; established under the KOKUGUN SYSTEM in 646, it comprised what is now the western half of Kagoshima Prefecture. From the middle of the Heian period (794–1185) onward, many landed estates (SHŌEN) in Satsuma were owned by the Fujiwara regent families (see GOSEKKE) and by temples and shrines of the capital region. The SHIMAZU FAMILY, who held the post of steward (*gesu* or *geshi*) on the estates of the KONOE FAMILY (one of the Gosekke), gradually expanded their power and from the 12th through 16th centuries acted as military governors (SHUGO) of Satsuma. The Shimazu later took over the governorships of neighboring provinces, and by the Sengoku period (1467–1568) they controlled most of Kyūshū, but their defeat by the national unifier TOYOTOMI HIDEYOSHI in 1587 resulted in a great diminution of their domain. Because of its geographical position, Satsuma served as the point of entry for foreign goods such as the harquebus in 1543 (see FIREARMS, INTRODUCTION OF) and the sweet potato in the 17th century; it was at Kagoshima that Francis XAVIER landed in 1549. Under the Tokugawa shogunate (1603–1867) the Satsuma domain was further reduced, but the Shimazu remained powerful and eventually played a leading role in the MEIJI RESTORATION of 1868. With the establishment of the PREFECTURAL SYSTEM in 1871, Satsuma was combined with Ōsumi Province to form KAGOSHIMA PREFECTURE.

Satsuma Rebellion

(Seinan Sensō or Seinan no Eki; Southwestern Campaign). The last major armed uprising to protest the reforms of the new Meiji government. Fought by the former *samurai* of the Satsuma domain (now Kagoshima Prefecture) under the leadership of SAIGŌ TAKAMORI, the rebellion lasted from 29 January 1877 to 24 September 1877. The outcome proved the effectiveness of the government's new conscript army in modern warfare.

Ironically, the Meiji government owed its existence to these veterans from Satsuma, who had led the way for the MEIJI RESTORATION in 1868 and provided security during its early years. Their sacrifices and services resulted in the disestablishment of the samurai class and hence the abolition of their social privileges, the drastic reduction of their former income, and the denigration of their traditional way of life. Thus they were infuriated when their hero, Saigō Takamori, was politically discredited in October 1873 in the debate on whether to wage war on Korea (see SEIKANRON), and they left their posts in the army and police force en masse to return to Kagoshima with Saigō. Saigō, in turn, provided for them by placing them in the local government and putting them in charge of a network of military-oriented "private" schools (the network was called the Shigakkō) that Saigō and his friends had established and funded. These Shigakkō officials, who represented the conservative elements of the former Satsuma leadership (the progressive members having stayed in Tōkyō with ŌKUBO TOSHIMICHI), soon came to dominate the government in Kagoshima.

The central government, fearing a possible revolt in Kagoshima, sent a naval unit to remove munitions stored there. Shigakkō youths anticipated them however, and attacked the army munitions depot and naval yard, seizing the arms and ammunition. Saigō, who had been in semiretirement, was astounded by the precipitate action of his followers, but since the situation was beyond repair, he resigned himself to leading a force to Tōkyō to demand an explanation for the government harassment. The expeditionary force of about 40,000 was hastily organized, poorly equipped, and ill-financed. Saigō devised no particular strategy except to march directly toward Tōkyō, hoping to enlist support along the way.

Arriving at Kumamoto on 22 February, the Satsuma army was challenged by the local garrison commanded by General TANI KANJŌ. The battle at Kumamoto lasted 50 days, but in the end the arrival of government reinforcements turned the tide and forced Saigō's retreat. For the next few months the Satsuma forces fought their way through the mountains of southern Kyūshū and arrived in Kagoshima with about 400 troops. The rebellion came to an end with a last charge by Saigō and his men, followed by Saigō's suicide.

📖 ——Tamamuro Taijō, *Seinan sensō* (1958).　　Robert K. SAKAI

Satsuma ware

(satsuma-yaki). Ceramic ware for the TEA CEREMONY and general use made at kiln sites in Kagoshima Prefecture (formerly the Satsuma domain) in southern Kyūshū. Production includes Naeshirogawa ware (Naeshirogawa, 1604–present), Tateno ware (Kagoshima, 1601–1871), Ryūmonji ware (Kajiki, 1598–present), Nishimochida ware (Kajiki, 1663–1763) and Hirasa ware (Sendai, 1768–ca 1915).

The Korean potter Kim Hae (1570–1621; J: Kin Kai, later known as Hoshiyama Chūji), who studied in Seto for five years, founded several of the earliest Tateno kilns; the Korean potter Pak P'yŏng-ŭi (J: Boku Heii, later called Kiyoemon; 1560–1629) was responsible for the founding and operation of the earliest Naeshirogawa kilns. Kawahara Hōkō (1727–98) invented "sharkskin" ware and after studying with the Kinkōzan family in Kyōto, introduced *nishikide* (brocade ware) to Satsuma. So-called black Satsuma, with dull, somber black or warm, reddish brown ash glazes, was made at the Naeshirogawa and Ryūmonji kilns from their start, but true black Satsuma with a lustrous black glaze was rare before the Meiji period

(1868–1912), when black glazes using manganese were introduced. White wares, first made in 1602, were initially reserved for *daimyō* use.

Satsuma products based on Sawankhalok ware from Thailand were made in the 17th and 18th centuries; sharkskin ware, which is grayish, light sepia, or yellowish and has a fine granular surface, and three-color ware were made only at Ryūmonji starting in the late 18th century. Symmetrically decorated black, yellow, and green Hirasa tortoiseshell ware was first made in the 18th century but perfected in 1869. So-called scorpion ware, unique to the Nishimochida kiln, has either a white background with fine reticulated lines of black glaze that looks as if it were cracked during drying or a black background with white lines.

The Satsuma brocade ware, familiar in the West, was introduced in the late 18th century with techniques imported from Hizen Province (now Saga and Nagasaki prefectures) and Kyōto and refined in the Bunsei era (1818–30). First for daimyō use but later for export and made at the Naeshirogawa and Tateno kilns, it is a polychrome pottery with a white crackle base and primarily red, blue, and gold decoration. Increasingly ornate and minute in design, by the Meiji period it had lost its original simplicity and charm, but was manufactured and exported to the West in vast quantities not only from Kagoshima but also from Kyōto, Tōkyō, and Yokohama.

Frederick BAEKELAND

Satsumon culture

(Satsumon *bunka*). An iron-tool-using culture that flourished in Hokkaidō and the northern Tōhoku region between the 8th and 12th centuries (some scholars assign its farthest limit to a later period). Satsumon culture developed from the influence of KOFUN culture (ca 300–710) on the so-called Continuing Jōmon culture (vestiges of the earlier JŌMON CULTURE which survived in the far north for many centuries after its demise in central and southern Japan) and is distinguished by the following traits: the exterior of Satsumon pottery was finished by wood-scraping (hence the term *satsumon*, or "scraped design"), as was HAJI WARE; modified versions of Kofun-period mounded tombs were built for some burials; spindle whorls were used in making cloth; iron swords and other iron implements such as axes and spades were in use; and interior hearths were constructed against one wall of the square PIT HOUSES. The relationship of the Satsumon culture to the contemporary but more northern OKHOTSK CULTURE and to the succeeding AINU culture is unclear.

KITAMURA Bunji

Satsunan Islands

(Satsunan Shotō). Group of islands, extending from southern Kagoshima Prefecture, Kyūshū, to Okinawa. They form the northern half of the RYŪKYŪ ISLANDS and are administratively a part of Kagoshima Prefecture. The group is composed, from north to south, of Kuchinomishima, the Ōsumi Islands, the TOKARA ISLANDS, and the AMAMI ISLANDS. The principal activities are the cultivation of sugarcane, bananas, and pineapples.

Sawada Miki (1901–1980)

Social worker. Founder and director of the ELIZABETH SAUNDERS HOME for racially mixed orphans in Japan after World War II. Born in Tōkyō, she was a granddaughter of Iwasaki Yatarō, founder of the MITSUBISHI industrial empire. In 1922 she married Sawada Renzō, a diplomat and administrator in the Japanese Foreign Ministry. Disturbed by widespread hostility toward orphans born of Japanese women and Occupation soldiers, she founded a home for them in 1948 and named it after Elizabeth Saunders, an impoverished British national and longtime resident of Japan who contributed $170, her life savings, toward its establishment. Continuing as director until her death, Sawada made 18 fund-raising trips to the United States, gaining a number of supporters, including the novelist Pearl Buck and the jazz singer and dancer Josephine Baker. In 1966 she received the Prime Minister's Award from the Japanese government and in 1970 an honorary Doctor of Laws degree from the University of Bridgeport.

Nathan O. STRONG

Sawada Shōjirō (1892–1929)

Actor; founder of the SHINKOKUGEKI (New National Theater) troupe. Born in Ōtsu, Shiga Prefecture, Sawada graduated in English literature from Waseda University. While at Waseda he became one of TSUBOUCHI SHŌYŌ's first acting students and took minor roles in the professor's Bungei Kyōkai SHINGEKI (new theater) performances.

Upon the demise of the Bungei Kyōkai, Sawada joined MATSUI SUMAKO and SHIMAMURA HŌGETSU's Geijutsuza troupe in 1913 as Matsui's leading man. He left within a year to play leads in several landmark *shingeki* productions of foreign works, including Chekhov's *The Cherry Orchard* and Maeterlinck's *Monna Vanna*. In 1917, he established the Shinkokugeki troupe.

Sawada first experimented with *shingeki* plays as well as with SHIMPA standards but found neither approach to modern theater satisfactory for his troupe. Excited by the success of popular novels that focused on Edo-period (1600–1868) sword fighters and recalling the swashbuckling action of rural barnstorming troupes, Sawada steered Shinkokugeki and his house dramatist Yukitomo Rifū (1877–1959) into melodramatic period plays with spectacular action. With Sawada in the title roles of such Yukitomo plays as *Tsukigata Hampeita* and *Kunisada Chūji*, Shinkokugeki came to prominence in Ōsaka in 1919 and two years later in Tōkyō.

The troupe made film versions of several of its sword fighting plays in the early 1920s that strongly influenced the early development of the *jidaigeki* (period drama) motion picture. Although specializing in costume drama, Sawada mixed his stage repertoire with plays in contemporary domestic settings as well as with a few adaptations of modern European works.

Despite the mien of a meek intellectual off stage, Sawada had a commanding stage presence. With this he created the definitive characterization of the nihilistic sword fighter which became the model for heroes in many period films and plays. Sawada's hagiographic portrayals of historical figures such as Ii Naosuke, Saigō Takamori, and Hara Takashi were also highly praised. When he died in midcareer from complications arising from an ear infection in 1929, his funeral in Tōkyō was the largest ever held for an actor. Over 100,000 people, including the prime minister, attended.

Sawada's orientation for the Shinkokugeki came from his conviction that the *shingeki* movement was too self-conscious, too intellectual, and too Westernized to be a valid Japanese form. He sought to fill the wide gap between *shingeki* and traditional KABUKI. During the 1920s when the theatrical world was full of cosmopolitan experiment, Sawada's famous command to his troupe was "Half a step forward!" He advised his actors that they stand in the middle "with art on the right and the public on the left."

——Higuchi Jūichi, *Sawada Shōjirō* (1948). J. L. ANDERSON

Sawamura Sōjūrō

One of the most prestigious names among the KABUKI acting families. Sōjūrō I (1685–1756) began his career in the Kyōto-Ōsaka area but later achieved distinction in Edo (now Tōkyō), where he was reputed to be the equal of Ichikawa Danjūrō II (1688–1758; see ICHIKAWA DANJŪRŌ), the outstanding performer of the area. An actor of extraordinary versatility, Sōjūrō I excelled in both *jidai mono* (historical plays) and *sewa mono* (domestic plays). Sōjūrō II (1713–70) was recognized for his portrayal of villains taken from an earlier period of Japanese history. His son, Sōjūrō III (1753–1801), was a gifted actor whose skill ranged over both *jidai mono* and *sewa mono;* he was particularly noted for his portrayal of romantic leads. The playwright Namiki Gohei I (1747–1808; see NAMIKI GOHEI) wrote many of the works in which Sōjūrō III starred. Sōjūrō V (1802–53) specialized in the gentle, romantic roles found in the *sewa mono* but was equally known for the broad scope of his accomplished acting; in addition, he performed brilliantly as an ONNAGATA (female impersonator).

In recent times, Sōjūrō VII (1875–1949) was regarded as the last great kabuki actor who retained the distinctive acting style of the *wagotoshi* (performers of male romantic leads) associated with the Edo tradition. Sōjūrō VIII (1908–75), the son of Sōjūrō VII, specialized in *onnagata* roles. His son, Sawamura Tosshō V (b 1933), who became Sōjūrō IX in 1976, is also an *onnagata.* Ted T. TAKAYA

Sawa Nobuyoshi (1836–1873)

Court noble who during the 1860s advocated a radical program of loyalty to the emperor and expulsion of foreigners (SONNŌ JŌI). In 1858 he denounced the ANSEI COMMERCIAL TREATIES, which the Tokugawa shogunate had concluded with Western nations, and with the support of other courtiers persuaded the emperor to withhold his

sanction from the treaties. In 1863 Sawa was closely associated with the *sonnō jōi* activists who dominated Kyōto politics and was one of the seven court nobles who fled from Kyōto (see SHICHIKYŌ OCHI) to Chōshū (now Yamaguchi Prefecture) when troops from the Satsuma (now Kagoshima Prefecture) and Aizu (now part of Fukushima Prefecture) domains reestablished shogunate control over the court in the COUP D'ETAT OF 30 SEPTEMBER 1863. Later in that year Sawa was the nominal leader of an uprising (the IKUNO DISTURBANCE) in which imperial activists attempted to use peasant unrest to attack the shogunate. The uprising was quickly suppressed, and Sawa returned to exile to Chōshū. After the MEIJI RESTORATION of 1868 Sawa held several posts in the new national government. In 1869 he was appointed minister of foreign affairs. He was designated minister to Russia in 1873 but died before he could take up his duties.

Sawara

City in northeastern Chiba Prefecture, central Honshū. Located on the river Tonegawa, Sawara developed as a river port for goods transported to Edo (now Tōkyō) during the Edo period (1600–1868). It was known for its rice, soy sauce, and vegetables but is being rapidly industrialized with the development of the Kashima Coastal Industrial Region and the opening of the New Tōkyō International Airport. It is part of Suigō-Tsukuba Quasi-National Park. Historic attractions include KATORI SHRINE and the home of the cartographer-geographer, INŌ TADATAKA. Pop: 49,199.

Sawayanagi Masatarō (1865–1927)

Educator. Born in Nagano Prefecture. Graduate of Tōkyō University. Sawayanagi served as vice-minister of education, first president of Tōhoku University, and president of Kyōto University. He devoted his energies to putting new educational theories into practice, founding in 1917 Seijō Elementary School, one of the early experimental schools of its day, and later adding the middle school and high school. One of the leaders of progressive education in Japan (see SHIN KYŌIKU UNDŌ), he maintained that pedagogical research must be based on actual teaching experience and be useful in solving actual teaching problems. SUGIYAMA Akio

Sayama

City in southern Saitama Prefecture, central Honshū. The site of the imperial Japanese army's Air Force Academy, which was taken over by the US Army after World War II to become the Johnson Military Base. It was returned to Japan in 1963 and is now a base for the Japanese Air Self Defense Force. Local products are tea and burdock. Industrial complexes have been established since 1965. Pop: 124,025.

Sayama, Lake

(Sayamako). Also called Yamaguchi Reservoir. Artificial reservoir in southern Saitama Prefecture, central Honshū. Constructed in 1934, it is fed by water from the Hamura Dam on the river Tamagawa. One of the main sources of water for Tōkyō. Located in a hilly and wooded area within Sayama Prefectural Natural Park, it is a popular recreation area, with the UNESCO Village situated next to the lake. Area: 1.6 sq km (0.6 sq mi); circumference: 20 km (12 mi); storage capacity: 19.5 million cu m (688.4 million cu ft).

Sayo no Nakayama

Mountain pass located east of the city of Kakegawa, Shizuoka Prefecture, central Honshū. Formerly a pass of the old highway Tōkaidō. National Route No. 1 runs through a tunnel under the pass. A place name often mentioned in classical *waka* poetry (see UTA MAKURA). Altitude: 200 m (656 ft).

sazanka

(sasanqua). *Camellia sasanqua.* An evergreen tree of the tea family (Theaceae) native to mountainous areas of western Honshū, Shikoku, and Kyūshū; also cultivated as an ornamental and for hedges. Although it can be found in China, it is generally known abroad as a Japanese plant. It reaches about 7–10 meters (23–33 ft) in height and has many branches, the younger ones covered with hairs. Its leaves

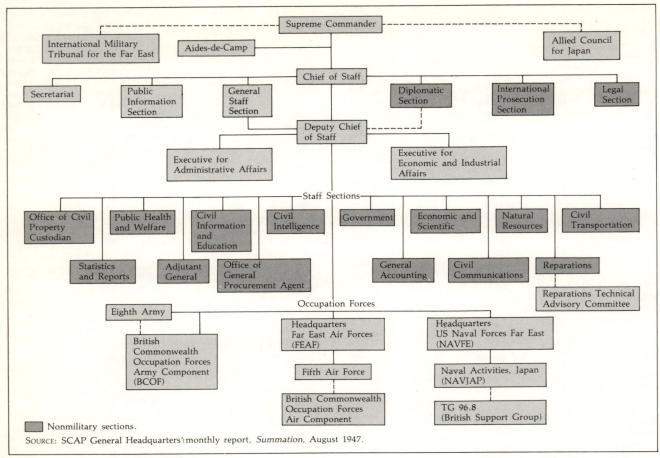

```
                                    ┌──────────────────┐
                                    │ Supreme Commander │
                                    └──────────────────┘
```

| International Military Tribunal for the Far East | Aides-de-Camp | | Allied Council for Japan |

Chief of Staff

| Secretariat | Public Information Section | General Staff Section | Diplomatic Section | International Prosecution Section | Legal Section |

Deputy Chief of Staff

| Executive for Administrative Affairs | Executive for Economic and Industrial Affairs |

Staff Sections

| Office of Civil Property Custodian | Public Health and Welfare | Civil Information and Education | Civil Intelligence | Government | Economic and Scientific | Natural Resources | Civil Transportation |

| Statistics and Reports | Adjutant General | Office of General Procurement Agent | General Accounting | Civil Communications | Reparations |

Reparations Technical Advisory Committee

Occupation Forces

| Eighth Army | Headquarters Far East Air Forces (FEAF) | Headquarters US Naval Forces Far East (NAVFE) |

| British Commonwealth Occupation Forces Army Component (BCOF) | Fifth Air Force | Naval Activities, Japan (NAVJAP) |

| British Commonwealth Occupation Forces Air Component | TG 96.8 (British Support Group) |

▓ Nonmilitary sections.

Source: SCAP General Headquarters' monthly report, *Summation*, August 1947.

SCAP —— Organization of GHQ-SCAP, August 1947

Sazanka

widely used for the handles of farming and carpentry tools as well as other implements. The oil pressed from its seed has been used, like camellia oil, for cooking and hair grooming.   *Matsuda Osamu*

SCAP

(Supreme Commander for the Allied Powers). A term used to refer both to the chief executive of the Allied OCCUPATION of Japan and, especially as an acronym, to his General Headquarters (GHQ) in Tōkyō. GHQ-SCAP was part of the combined US Headquarters which carried out both Allied responsibilities for the Occupation of Japan as GHQ–SCAP and US military responsibilities throughout the Far East as General Headquarters, Far East Command (GHQ–FEC; see FAR EAST COMMAND). General Douglas MACARTHUR and his successor, General Matthew B. RIDGWAY, both served as supreme commander for the Allied powers and as commander-in-chief, United States Far East Command.

The supreme commander served as the sole executive authority for the Allied powers in Japan and was subject to the policy-making authority of the FAR EASTERN COMMISSION in Washington. GHQ–SCAP consisted of the basic military staff sections and, by August 1947, of 17 additional nonmilitary sections, such as the Government Section, the Economic and Scientific Section, the Diplomatic Section, the International Prosecution Section, and the Public Health and Welfare Section (see organization chart of GHQ–SCAP). The Occupation authorities did not institute direct military government. Each SCAP section was responsible for direct contact with the Japanese government on matters within its jurisdiction. This contact was maintained initially through the Central Liaison Office, and later with the concerned agencies of the Japanese government. United States military government teams were set up throughout Japan under the control of the US Eighth Army, based in Yokohama, to oversee the implementation of SCAP orders and to maintain contact with local Japanese officials. The BRITISH COMMONWEALTH OCCUPATION FORCE in 1947 occupied the Chūgoku region and the island of Shikoku under the operational control of the commanding gen-

are alternate and elliptical, with finely serrated edges and pointed tips. Toward the end of autumn, it bears five-petaled flowers. In the wild form the flowers are white, while in the cultivated varieties they may be red, pink, or parti-colored. Double-flowered varieties have also been developed. Unlike the camellia, the *sazanka*'s flower petals do not form a cylinder but are attached to each other at the base.

Like the other Japanese CAMELLIAS, this tree was not cultivated as an ornamental until the Edo period (1600–1868). It was introduced to Europe by the German naturalist Engelbert KAEMPFER in a book published in 1712. Export of *sazanka* to the United States and other countries has increased considerably since the end of World War II. Its wood is noted for its hardness and fine grain, so it is eral of the US Eighth Army, initially General Robert L. EICHEL-BERGER, and later, General Walton Walker.

GHQ–FEC exercised unified command over all US forces in the Far East and included among its missions support of the Occupation forces in Japan. A number of its staff sections, such as G-1, G-2, G-3, and G-4, performed functions for GHQ–SCAP as well.

SCAP administration was generally considered efficient, fair, and economical of manpower, although some observers believed that certain elements, notably the Government Section, had disproportionate influence and that military government teams in the field had inadequate contact with policy-forming sections of SCAP.

📖 ——General Headquarters, SCAP and FEC, *Selected Data on the Occupation of Japan* (February–June 1950).   Richard B. FINN

scarecrows → kakashi

school administration

Administration in the elementary, middle, and high schools in Japan is the responsibility of the principal (*kōchō*) and vice-principal (*kyōtō*), supported by heads of departments and other members of both the teaching and nonteaching staff. The school administration is organized into such groups as the faculty council, composed of the principals and faculty, various committees of teachers, and office personnel.

The principal has overall responsibility for school management and administration and must supervise the faculty as well as the nonfaculty staff of the school. Opinion is divided as to whether his authority over the faculty extends to control of teaching content and methods or is limited to guidance and advice on such matters. Principals of public schools are selected by the prefectural superintendent of schools through examinations and appointed by the prefectural board of education. As an aide to the principal, the vice-principal acts on his behalf and has the right of proxy. Selection is made through examination and appointment by the prefectural superintendent of schools. Department heads function primarily in the role of adviser and coordinator in their particular fields. Selection is made by either the principal or the area superintendent of schools. See also EDUCATION: school system administration and finance.   TAKANO Keiichi

school administration and finance → education

school architecture

In Japan school construction first began on a wide scale with the establishment of the modern education system (see EDUCATION: modern education) in 1872. In the beginning most school buildings were designed and constructed in a Western or "pseudo-Western" style using traditional Japanese materials and building techniques. A mode of architecture reminiscent of the American colonial style was used in many early schools. A typical example from this early period is Kaichi Elementary School in Nagano Prefecture, which was built in 1876. Thereafter school architecture tended toward a mixture of Japanese and Western styles accompanied by the use of new materials for outer walls such as a combination of tile and plaster. After 1900, the increased rate of school attendance and the need for rapid construction of additional classroom space brought about the standardization of school construction. The typical Japanese school was either a one- or two-story wooden structure with a one-sided corridor running along the outer north side; the size of the classrooms was gradually standardized at 4×5 *ken* (7.3 × 9.1 m; 24 × 30 ft).

A number of reinforced concrete buildings were built about 1920, and (after the great Tōkyō Earthquake of 1923 demonstrated their resistance to fire and their durability compared to wooden buildings) reinforced concrete rapidly came to be used in the construction of new schools, particularly in big cities. Schools designed by the Tōkyō Metropolitan Bureau of Architecture, with a functional design utilizing plain concrete walls and large windows, became popular. The Yotsuya Daigo Elementary School in Tōkyō, constructed in 1934, is a good example of this type of building. Most of these reinforced concrete structures were three-story buildings; their structural characteristics, such as the one-sided corridor on the north, were similar to those of earlier buildings.

Because of the shortage of lumber during World War II, the size of classrooms in wooden school buildings was restricted to about 5.5 × 10 meters (18 × 33 ft). The loss of school buildings by fire during the war together with the baby boom after the war forced school authorities to put as many as 75 students in one classroom and to hold classes outside or in corridors. One of the main concerns of Japanese educators in the immediate postwar period was to amend the shortage of classrooms.

As part of the restoration process after the war, the construction of fire-resistant, reinforced concrete schools was actively promoted in the big cities. New standards were established to ensure uniform classrooms measuring approximately 7 × 9 meters (23 × 30 ft). This type of school building had much larger windows and a pleasanter atmosphere than the older school buildings. However, the fundamental structural characteristics of these new schools exhibited no significant change, as the one-sided corridor system was still used. This type of plan was well suited to prewar educational methods, which centered on the simultaneous instruction of a large group of students and were little altered in spite of curriculum changes made in accordance with the 6-3 educational system that was implemented in 1947. Even today the majority of school buildings are constructed following this type of old structural arrangement. There are several reasons for this: first, though there have been changes in the educational curriculum and in teaching methods, there has been no corresponding change in the fundamental class unit management system; second, the construction of schools is subsidized in part by national government funding, so that building design tends toward the conservative. As a whole, the Japanese centralized system of educational administration, in comparison with that of the United States or England, has been conservative and conformist regarding education and school construction and has discouraged innovation.

In the last few decades, though, a few so-called new-style schools have been designed and constructed. The first new-style schools, built in the mid-1950s, were designed according to plans based on a careful consideration of function. This type of school building shunned the one-sided corridor system and employed instead a battery or cluster arrangement of classrooms. Miyamae Elementary School in Tōkyō, which was built in 1955, is one of the earliest examples of this type of school; it was constructed by the Ministry of Education as a model school and utilized a steel frame construction.

A second group of new-style schools includes a series of structures built in the 1960s with a better spatial solution through the creation of greater organic space by means of such devices as higher ceilings and floor-level variation and the utilization of rich coloring. Shichinohe Elementary School in Aomori Prefecture, built in 1968, is an example of this type.

Around 1970 a third group of new-style schools began to be built with the aim of facilitating individualized education. Katō Gakuen Elementary School, built in 1972, is a good example of this type of school; it employed an open classroom plan common in the United States. Most new public schools in Japan, however, have only partially incorporated open space into traditional classroom plans because nongraded or individualized small-group instruction is rare.

In recent years there has been some experimentation in school design aimed at multipurpose buildings which can accommodate various social and community programs and exercise facilities. But, in comparison with community school programs in England and the United States, these experiments have been limited at best.

In the late 1970s a systematic program of school construction referred to as the GSK system (Gakkō Shisetsu Kensetsu Shisutemu) and patterned after the CLASP system (Consortium of Local Authorities Special Program) of England and the SCSD system (School Construction Systems Development Project) of the United States was instituted.

The construction of public schools, which by far outnumber private schools, is administered by local governments. Construction costs are split about evenly between national and local government funding. Financing generally depends partly on financing by the national government and partly on the sale of bonds. In cases where spending exceeds financing, the local government has to pay the difference in cost. Designs are drawn up either by the construction department of the local government or by a private architectural design firm. Large local governments frequently request that designs meet standardized specifications. Low fees and design control by the Ministry of Education generally discourage first-rate innovative architects from engaging in school construction design so that Japanese schools tend to be conservative in design.

FUNAKOSHI Tōru

School curriculum —— Table 1

Standard Curriculum for Elementary Schools, 1980
(based on school hours per year)[1]

| | | | | Grade | | | |
		1	2	3	4	5	6
Subjects	Japanese language	272	280	280	280	210	210
	Social studies	68	70	105	105	105	105
	Arithmetic	136	175	175	175	175	175
	Science	68	70	105	105	105	105
	Music	68	70	70	70	70	70
	Arts and crafts	68	70	70	70	70	70
	Physical education	102	105	105	105	105	105
	Homemaking	—	—	—	—	70	70
Moral education[2]		34	35	35	35	35	35
Extracurricular activities[3]		34	35	35	70	70	70
Total		850	910	980	1,015	1,015	1,015

[1] One school hour is a class period of 45 minutes.
[2] Private elementary schools may substitute religious education for a portion of the school hours required for moral education.
[3] In Japan "extracurricular" activities include not only after-school activities but also such activities as class assemblies, field trips, library-use training, traffic safety training, and guidance, for which time is designated within the school curriculum.

School curriculum —— Table 2

Standard Curriculum for Middle Schools, 1980
(based on school hours per year)[1]

| | | Grade | | |
		7	8	9
Required subjects	Japanese language	175	140	140
	Social studies	140	140	105
	Mathematics	105	140	140
	Science	105	105	140
	Music	70	70	35
	Fine arts	70	70	35
	Health and physical education	105	105	105
	Industrial arts or homemaking	70	70	105
Elective subjects	Foreign languages[2] or other special subject	105	105	105
	Other subjects[3]	—	—	35
Moral education		35	35	35
Extracurricular activities[4]		70	70	70
Total		1,050	1,050	1,050

[1] One school hour is a class period of 50 minutes.
[2] Nearly all middle school students study English.
[3] Students are required to take one of the following subjects: music, fine arts, health and physical education, industrial arts, or homemaking.
[4] In Japan "extracurricular" activities include not only after-school activities but also activities for which time has been designated within the school curriculum.

school course guidelines

(gakushū shidō yōryō). Basic outlines stating the aim of each subject taught in Japanese schools and the aims and contents of teaching in each grade. Issued by the minister of education. These guidelines are drawn up separately for elementary schools, middle schools, high schools, and schools for the blind, deaf, and handicapped. School course guidelines were drawn up for the first time in 1947 by the Ministry of Education and patterned after American models. At first they were part of a reaction to the prewar method of standardized, textbook-centered education; they emphasized the importance of relating knowledge to the student's life experiences. During the 1950s, however, there was a reexamination of postwar trends in education, and in 1958 extensive revisions were made in the guidelines. The result was that they became a mechanism for the standardization of curricula with the force of law, spelling out as they did the content as well as the objectives of each course.

The guidelines were revised in 1968 and again in 1977–78. The objectives of the latter revision were (1) to emphasize basic subjects; (2) to reduce the number of classroom hours and allow schools discretion in utilizing the free time thus provided; and (3) to allow a more flexible application of the guidelines by reducing their legal binding power. The main purpose of the revisions was to give each school greater discretion in organizing its own curriculum without abandoning national standards. TAKAKUWA Yasuo

school curriculum

The courses and extracurricular activities offered by Japanese schools are prescribed by the SCHOOL EDUCATION LAW OF 1947, while standards for the curriculum, goals for each course and grade level, and course content are set by SCHOOL COURSE GUIDELINES. These guidelines are drawn up by the MINISTRY OF EDUCATION and indicate minimum requirements for elementary, middle, and high schools and schools for the blind, the deaf, and the handicapped.

Within these guidelines, each school draws up its own curriculum. At the elementary school level, the aim is to provide a uniform, basic education for every child as a future citizen. Middle schools have the additional purpose of providing basic vocational and technical education according to the students' needs and aptitudes. Both required and elective courses are offered. At the high school level, an emphasis is placed on elective courses that are appropriate to the students' abilities, aptitudes, and future course of study. Both elementary and middle school curricula include one hour of MORAL EDUCATION per week, and additional guidance is provided in all

educational activities. Religious education is not included in the public school curriculum. Great importance is attached to extracurricular activities. Curriculum standards are reviewed by the Curriculum Council (Kyōiku Katei Shingikai) of the Ministry of Education and are usually revised every ten years. TAKAKUWA Yasuo

The Structure of Education —— In elementary school the courses given are Japanese language, social studies, arithmetic, science, music, arts and crafts, physical education, and homemaking. In middle school, Japanese language, social studies, mathematics, and science are required subjects; music, fine arts, health and physical education, and industrial arts or homemaking are partly required and partly elective. Foreign language is an elective, but nearly all middle school students study English; other languages (generally French or German) are offered at only a few schools. In high school, Japanese language, social studies, mathematics, science, health and physical education, fine arts, and home economics (for girls) are common required courses. English language is an elective taken by the majority of students; far fewer students take French or German, although the number of high schools offering these languages is substantially greater than the number of middle schools that do so. In addition to these there are subjects for students in specialized vocational courses. Moral education is required in elementary and middle schools, and extracurricular activities are required in all grades. The contents of the principal courses are as follows:

Japanese language. Traditionally, greater importance was attached to the teaching of reading and writing than to the spoken language. The pre-World War II emphasis on the appreciation of works of literature has been replaced by a focus on explanation and criticism. In middle and high schools the reading and appreciation of CLASSICAL JAPANESE (kobun) and KAMBUN (classical Chinese) are included. By the time the students complete their compulsory elementary and middle school education they are expected to have learned the 1,945 characters that constitute the JŌYŌ KANJI. Pupils are taught composition from the first year of elementary school using the KANA syllabary and Chinese characters, and from the third year of elementary school they are taught calligraphy, using a brush.

Social studies. Social studies were included in the curriculum after World War II in order to teach democracy and pacifism, but the subject is now divided into geography, history, and civics. In elementary school, students learn about their community, their nation, and Japanese history in a combined course. In middle school they study geography and history concurrently in the first and second years; in the third year they study civics (politics, economics, and society). In high school, a course on modern society is required,

School curriculum —— Table 3

Standard High School Curriculum, 1983

Subject area	Course	Standard number of credits[1]
Japanese language	*Japanese language I	4
	Japanese language II	4
	Japanese expression	2
	Modern Japanese	3
	Classics	4
Social studies	*Modern society	4
	Japanese history	4
	World history	4
	Geography	4
	Ethics	2
	Political science and economics	2
Mathematics	*Mathematics I	4
	Mathematics II	3
	Algebra and geometry	3
	Basic analysis	3
	Differentiation and integration	3
	Probability and statistics	3
Science	*Science I	4
	Science II	2
	Physics	4
	Chemistry	4
	Biology	4
	Earth science	4
Physical education and health	*Physical education	7~11
	*Health	2
Music and arts	*Music I	2
	Music II	2
	Music III	2
	*Fine arts I	2
	Fine arts II	2
	Fine arts III	2
	*Handicraft I	2
	Handicraft II	2
	Handicraft III	2
	*Calligraphy I	2
	Calligraphy II	2
	Calligraphy III	2
Foreign language[2]	English I	4
	English II	5
	English II-A	3
	English II-B	3
	English II-C	3
Home economics	*General homemaking	4

[1] One credit consists of 35 unit hours; one unit hour is 50 minutes. A minimum of 80 credits is required to graduate.

[2] French or German may be substituted for English.

NOTE: Required subjects are marked with asterisks. The following exceptions should be noted, however. Students are required to take one art or music course; they have the option of selecting Music I, Fine arts I, Handicrafts I, or Calligraphy I. Only girls are required to take home economics. Boys, except those following vocational courses, are required to take 11 credits of physical education. Boys following vocational courses and all girls are required to take between 7 and 9 credits of physical education.

Science. In elementary school students learn about living things and their environment, matter and energy, the earth and the universe, all of which aim at familiarizing children with the world around them. In middle school science comprises physics, chemistry, biology, and earth science. In high school comprehensive, basic science is a required course; physics, chemistry, biology, and earth science are electives.

Music and art. In elementary, middle, and high school, students study singing, instrumental music, composing, and music appreciation. Elementary school students are taught to appreciate and express themselves through drawing, sculpture, design, and handicrafts. In middle school training in artistic expression and the appreciation of outstanding works of art is stressed. In high school, a minimum of three credits must be chosen from among music, painting and drawing, sculpture, graphic design, calligraphy, crafts, and product design; in reality, however, since each course carries two credits, students take a minimum of four credits in arts.

Health and physical education. In physical education students may take calisthenics, gymnastics, track and field, swimming, various kinds of ball games, *kendō, sumō, jūdō,* and dancing. In health classes they study the functions and development of the body and mind, the prevention of accidents and illness, and aspects of the conduct and environment of daily life that are necessary for the maintenance and improvement of good health. Health education is also carried on through school events which teach students about public health.

Home economics. Students acquire basic knowledge and skill relating to food, clothing, shelter, and child care. In elementary school these classes are conducted coeducationally in the fifth and sixth grades. In middle school industrial arts and home economics are required of all students; girls generally take classes in diet, clothing, shelter, and child care, while boys generally take industrial arts. In some schools, however, these courses of study overlap. In high school, basic instruction relating to food, clothing, shelter, and child care from the standpoint of household management is required for girls, while vocational training in home economics is an elective. Boys are offered industrial arts as an elective; theoretically they can instead elect to take home economics, although very few do so.

Foreign language. English is taught in middle and high school, and German and French are offered in some middle and high schools. See FOREIGN LANGUAGE TRAINING IN THE SCHOOLS.

Extracurricular activities. Additional student activities include class assemblies, club activities, ceremonies, athletic meets, school plays and concerts, excursions and field trips, and educational guidance relating to student life, such as traffic safety guidance and training in the use of the school library.

HANAMURA Masaru, HIBI Yutaka,
MIYAWAKI Osamu, NAKAJIMA Kenzō,
and ŌMORI Kazuko

History —— Before the Meiji Restoration (1868), subject matter differed according to the social class to which the students belonged. For example, the children of *samurai* studied the Chinese classics and were trained in martial arts, while children of commoners were taught reading, writing, and the use of the abacus.

At the beginning of the Meiji period (1868–1912), when the modern educational system was established, American and some European curricula were introduced into Japan. The contributions of Marion McCarrell SCOTT, David MURRAY, and other foreigners were outstanding. However, after the 1880s a reaction against excessive Westernization set in and the government took control over curricula, which took on a nationalistic quality. SHŪSHIN (courses instilling patriotism) was particularly stressed.

The first regular curriculum was set up in 1886 by the government. Under COMPULSORY EDUCATION (initially four years of elementary school), required subjects were *shūshin*, reading and writing, composition, penmanship, arithmetic, and physical education. Drawing and singing were sometimes included. After the Sino-Japanese War of 1894–95, the school system was rapidly consolidated and the curriculum was provided with more up-to-date subject matter. The subjects taught under the compulsory education of that time (six years after 1907) were *shūshin*, Japanese language, arithmetic, physical education, Japanese history, geography, science, drawing, singing, and sewing for girls.

In the more progressive political climate at the turn of the century, progressive educational ideas were introduced from Europe and the United States (see SHIN KYŌIKU UNDŌ). In the vanguard were elementary schools affiliated with normal schools and privately

while Japanese history, world history, geography, ethics, and political science and economics are electives. Prewar education in history was centered on the emperor system, and mythology was taught as historical fact. Today the student is encouraged to develop independent judgment of the past and present. The initial focus of geography education is on one's own community and then gradually expands to cover a larger sphere. In middle and high school students begin with a view of the world as a whole and then study Japan and their own city. The role of social studies is becoming increasingly important today from the viewpoint of international understanding and education.

Mathematics. In elementary school mathematics is composed of four areas: numbers and calculation, quantity and measurement, graphs, and quantity relationships. In middle school students learn numbers and formulas, functions, graphs, probability, and statistics. In high school they study general mathematics, algebra, geometry, basic analysis, differentiation and integration, and probability and statistics.

established schools. The experiments of Kinoshita Takeji, SAWAYA-NAGI MASATARŌ, Noguchi Entarō, and others are notable. Kinoshita reasoned that a curriculum should take shape as children follow their own interests and synthesize their learning experiences. Sawayanagi carried on experiments which were bold for the time, such as abolishing *shūshin* in the lower grades, discontinuing arithmetic in the first grade, and teaching science and English. However, their new empirical approach was limited to only a few schools and was later suppressed by the government.

In 1941 elementary schools were reorganized as KOKUMIN GAKKŌ (national people's schools), and the curriculum was drastically revised to meet the objective of training loyal subjects of the emperor.

After the Japanese defeat in 1945, the Occupation authorities suspended the teaching of *shūshin*, Japanese history, and geography, all of which had exhibited militaristic tendencies. In accordance with the recommendations of the UNITED STATES EDUCATION MISSIONS TO JAPAN, a new curriculum was developed. The educational system was decentralized and revised to accord with regional differences and individual needs. Further, social studies was established as a new subject and a new emphasis was placed on educating students as responsible members of society (see EDUCATIONAL REFORMS OF 1947).

In the 1950s, criticism arose in certain quarters about the decline in basic knowledge and the deterioration of morality. A 1958 curriculum revision strengthened government control, and a new emphasis was placed on factual content. In 1977 central control was somewhat relaxed and the schools were given freer rein. See also EDUCATION: modern education. ——*Takakuwa Yasuo*

School Education Law of 1947

(Gakkō Kyōiku Hō). The basic law providing for the framework and organization of the Japanese school system. Passed in 1947 together with the Fundamental Law of Education (see EDUCATION, FUNDAMENTAL LAW OF), which outlines the ultimate objectives of education. Before World War II different types of schools (i.e., kindergartens, elementary, middle, and higher schools, and special schools, etc) were governed by separate ordinances called SCHOOL ORDERS. The present law applies to the entire school system. It is based on the principles of simplifying the school system and providing equal educational opportunities for all. After stating general guidelines for the establishment and organization of schools, the law sets forth rules on the purpose, curriculum, and duration of study for schools at each level. ——*Sagara Iichi*

school libraries

From the time compulsory education was instituted in Japan in the early part of the Meiji period (1868–1912) until the end of World War II, teaching and the school curricula centered primarily on textbooks, teacher-pupil contact in the classroom, and verbal instruction. Schools generally ignored written materials other than those textbooks adopted for use by the Ministry of Education. School libraries were seen as places where students could read books unrelated to their courses of study, not as an integral source of educational material. With the exception of some private schools which put particular emphasis on developing the student's individual potential or on inculcating a nationalist outlook, school and classroom libraries generally had meager holdings.

After World War II, textbooks came to be regarded as merely one aspect of the entire educational process. The use of other kinds of educational material both printed and audiovisual was stressed. In 1948 the Ministry of Education put out a *School Library Handbook* as a guide to establishing and managing school libraries. The following year it published a position paper setting standards for school libraries. These steps marked the first time since the establishment of the modern school system that the central government had taken the lead in improving school libraries. This was due in part to the efforts of Japanese educators but perhaps more to the advice and counsel of American education specialists who visited Japan early in the postwar era.

In 1950 the Japan School Library Association was founded by a group of interested teachers and school librarians to promote and conduct studies on school libraries. The association, supported by growing public interest, was able to push through the School Library Law (Gakkō Toshokan Hō) in 1953. This law defined the purposes and functions of a school library. The government also decided to

train and appoint teacher-librarians and to fund public school libraries. In 1968 the minister of education issued a directive that schools incorporate libraries as an integral part of the curricula for elementary, middle, and senior high schools and that students be provided with instruction in the use of library resources.

School libraries have thus become academically, administratively, and financially a fixed part of the Japanese educational system. Problems remain, however. There are not enough trained library personnel; school librarians are employed in 90 percent of the high schools but in only 30 percent of the elementary schools. There is insufficient funding to acquire enough books to meet student demands. According to a 1979 survey, libraries had 7.3 books per student on the elementary level, 9.6 on the junior high school level, and 15.3 on the senior high school level. School libraries have not been as fully utilized as anticipated. The typical school library is merely a collection of books without secondary resources that could truly make it a media center. ——*Fukagawa Tsuneyoshi*

school lunch program

Program to provide lunches in elementary and middle schools, special-education schools, and high-school evening courses. While the students' parents pay for the cost of the food, preparation facilities and operational costs are paid for by the local government bodies that established the schools. School meal programs before World War II were mainly welfare programs for needy children, but during the postwar food shortage the Allied Occupation started a nationwide school lunch program. With the School Lunch Law of 1954 the practice was established on a permanent basis. By 1978, 99.4 percent of elementary schools and 82.2 percent of middle schools had lunch programs. ——*Takakuwa Yasuo*

school orders

(gakkōrei). A general term for government education ordinances issued from 1886, when the Education Order of 1879 was repealed, until the enactment of the SCHOOL EDUCATION LAW OF 1947; separate ordinances were issued according to the type of school. In 1886 the first minister of education, MORI ARINORI, issued the following ordinances: the Imperial University Order, the Normal School Order, the Middle School Order, and the Elementary School Order. Other orders followed in rapid succession: the Higher School Order (1894), the second Middle School Order (1899), the Girls' Higher School Order (1899), and the Vocational School Order (1899). The Professional School Order of 1903 was meant to increase opportunities in higher education. To consolidate elementary schools throughout the nation the second (1890) and third (1900) elementary school orders were enacted. The Teacher Education Order (1897) was established for the training of teachers.

After World War I the University Order and second Higher School Order were passed to augment the higher education system. These were followed by the Blind, Deaf, and Dumb Schools Order (1923), Kindergarten Order (1925), and Youth Order (1935; see SEINEN GAKKŌ).

The proliferation of school orders made for difficulty in coordinating different school levels and lines of authority and responsibility; after World War II a single composite law, the School Education Law (Gakkō Kyōiku Hō) of 1947, superseded the school orders. ——*Satō Hideo*

schools for Japanese children abroad

This article deals with school facilities provided for children of Japanese nationals living temporarily in foreign countries and not with Japanese students attending foreign schools, colleges, and universities, for which see STUDY ABROAD. These latter students, known since the Meiji period (1868–1912) as *ryūgakusei*, are those who actively seek a foreign educational environment or who have been sent by their employers to gain training or skills overseas. The Japanese term *kaigai shijo kyōiku* (overseas education of children) refers to the training of the "accidental" or "involuntary" sojourners who are to return to elementary or secondary schools in Japan. These are children of Japanese businessmen, bureaucrats, and others who are posted overseas on assignments from their ministry, firm, or university.

As of 1979 there were about 23,000 Japanese children of "compulsory education age" (6–14 years) living overseas, approximately double the number of 10 years before. The overseas and return education of these children has become a public issue in Japan due principally to the functions and nature of the Japanese educational system. Entrance into a prestigious university has long been considered the key to future success and, inevitably, entrance into the best secondary schools became an important step. Secondary education thus has emphasized the acquisition of examination skills and socialization to the patterns of Japanese institutions. In recent years this pattern has extended down to elementary school, and it is felt that without a Japanese education at all levels a person cannot be successful in Japan. Some parents feel this so strongly that they prefer to leave school-age children in Japan rather than interrupt their education. Therefore, 19 percent of school-age children of overseas-assigned parents remain in Japan.

The increasing number of children with overseas educational experiences has led to the development of special facilities in Japan and overseas. Japanese overseas educational facilities were first established in Manchuria by companies around 1897. By 1905, about 50 such schools were recognized or supervised by the Japanese government. Postwar overseas education began in Bangkok, Thailand, where in 1956 the first school was begun. Wives of the Japanese Embassy staff served as teachers. Beginning in the early 1960s, schools were established in various cities throughout the world. These schools developed out of informal Japanese-language classes that had been set up by concerned parents.

Pressure from parents and Japanese organizations to "protect" Japanese children from the effects of absence from their home schools has recently led to the establishment of Japanese schools wherever there are Japanese communities of sufficient size. These schools are of two types: part-time supplementary schools (hoshūkō) which meet afternoons and/or weekends and which concentrate on language and mathematical skills, and full-time Japanese schools (nihonjin gakkō) which replicate the curriculum of schools in Japan.

As of 1978, there were 69 part-time and 49 full-time Japanese schools overseas. The former tend to be located in "advanced" nations where it is felt that the local school system is adequate for the academic needs of Japanese children, and the latter, in less developed countries where it is felt that attending local schools would produce greater handicaps on returning to Japan. However, full-time schools have also been established in New York, Paris, London, Sydney, and other major cities. This would seem to indicate that it is not the educational curriculum alone which determines the acceptability of a school, but that there are other needs which are felt by Japanese parents and the home educational system.

These needs are emphasized in the programs of the Foundation for Japanese Overseas Education (Kaigai Shijo Kyōiku Shinkō Zaidan), which was established in 1970 by the ministries of education and foreign affairs and a group of corporations with large numbers of overseas employees. This foundation, staffed by former teachers and retired ministry officials, is attempting to upgrade and develop centralized control of the overseas schools to ensure that their students will be able to move smoothly into Japanese schools. It also provides correspondence courses, counselling services, tutoring, and school placement services for returnees.

The difficulty in the reassimilation of returnees is also seen in the increasing numbers of special programs and schools for them in Japan. There are three types of returnee classes and schools. The first is special schools, for returnees only, formed with the object of providing an intensive "re-entry" education before they enter ordinary schools. These schools are used by families whose children have been most dislocated or who have forgotten their language or other "Japanese" skills. The next type of school is actually a section of a public school or a school attached to a university where there are special counselors for returnees, remedial language classes, and individual tutoring, but where in many cases the children spend at least part of their school day in classes with ordinary children. The third type of returnee education is "international": classes or sections in private schools also attended by foreign students, from which children continue to foreign or international universities.

Facilities for the children of overseas Japanese were established to fill an urgent need but have not entirely met the demand either for consistently high quality education overseas or for an easy readjustment to the Japanese school system. Part of the reason for the failure is the ambivalence toward "international" or "different" experiences exhibited by the educational system in its treatment of returnee children in Japan. As greater numbers of Japanese live overseas and the returnee population in Japanese schools grows, the educational system will be forced either to organize and make coherent a separate high quality "international" stream of education or to change the strongly conservative and conformist nature of its pro-

grams and the "narrow gate" of the examinations in order to admit those who have had different educational experiences. If Japanese educational administrators do not face squarely the complexity of the issue of "internationalization" and the implications it bears for the socialization of Japanese children, overseas and returnee classes will continue as patchwork attempts to limit rather than broaden educational experiences.

Merry I. WHITE

school system → education

school textbooks

(kyōkasho). In Japan all schools are obliged to use government-approved textbooks as main teaching materials. Except for a few compiled by the Ministry of Education, most of the textbooks currently used in primary and secondary schools are written or compiled by private publishers under authorization of the minister of education. Textbooks are required to conform to government-issued SCHOOL COURSE GUIDELINES, but the publishers are given a certain amount of leeway in the style of presentation and choice of illustrations. Today, it usually takes about four years to compile and publish a new textbook.

The purpose of the official authorization of textbooks is the standardization of education. Objectivity and neutrality, both political and religious, are given serious consideration. Authorization is given only after the manuscript is checked and evaluated by textbook specialists at the Ministry of Education and other examiners appointed by the minister of education. Before final approval, the examiners' reports are reviewed by the Textbook Authorization and Research Council, which is an advisory organ of the Ministry of Education. The examiners are appointed by the minister of education from among university professors and teachers of elementary schools, middle schools, and high schools. Recently, the textbook authorization system was brought into question by the author of a textbook who brought suit against the government, charging that the authorization process was both illegal and unconstitutional (see IENAGA TEXTBOOK REVIEW CASE).

During the premodern period, Chinese and Japanese classics, as well as Buddhist scriptures were often used as textbooks. The first books written specifically as textbooks were the ŌRAIMONO that appeared late in the Heian period (794–1185). These books drew their sources from letters and essays of noted people and served as copybooks and readers. In the Edo period (1600–1868), the ōraimono were used extensively in the TERAKOYA (village schools).

At the beginning of the Meiji period (1868–1912) translations of European and American textbooks came to be widely used, and the compilation of nationwide textbooks for elementary schools was started by the National Normal School in Tōkyō. In the beginning there were no restrictions on compilation, publication, and use of textbooks. However, with the textbook authorization system coming into effect in 1886, the responsibility for control was placed in the hands of the central government. In 1903 it was decided that only textbooks compiled by the Ministry of Education could be used in elementary schools. In 1943 this system of textbook compilation by the state was enlarged to cover textbooks for middle schools and normal schools. Since the start of the new education system after World War II, the present system of textbook authorization has been in effect.

In Japan textbooks are selected and adopted for a district or city as one unit. This system was put into law in 1963 when the free distribution of textbooks for compulsory education was established. The choice of textbooks to be used in each school district is the responsibility of the local board of education; in the case of private schools the responsibility lies with the principal of each school. There are periodic textbook exhibitions held by the authorities to provide teachers with the opportunity to view new textbooks under consideration. Once adopted by a school, the same textbook is required by law to be used for three consecutive years. The total expenditure resulting from the free distribution of textbooks is borne by the state.

TAKAKUWA Yasuo

Science and Technology Agency

(Kagaku Gijutsu Chō). Agency of the national government responsible for the formulation, coordination, and implementation of many programs and research in science and technology. Established in 1956, it plays a major role in the formulation of government policies toward science and technology, budgets funds for some government-associated programs and research and assists in the formulation of budgets of other government offices in the areas of science and technology, and coordinates joint research and development programs being conducted by various government bureaus.

The agency supervises numerous research institutes and organizations, including the Japan ATOMIC ENERGY RESEARCH INSTITUTE, the NATIONAL AEROSPACE LABORATORY, the NATIONAL SPACE DEVELOPMENT AGENCY OF JAPAN, and the Japan Information Center for Science and Technology. Its Atomic Energy Bureau forms and implements policies and programs for the peaceful uses of atomic energy, and its Nuclear Safety Bureau regulates and enforces safety standards of the nuclear power industry.

While the agency has promoted some important programs concerning industrial technology, it has put a greater emphasis on the development of scientific research. In the 1970s it spent much of its funds on two projects, the promotion of atomic energy and of programs concerning outer space.

The agency is administratively attached to the Prime Minister's Office and is headed by a director-general who is a cabinet member and appointed by the prime minister.　　*Daniel A.* METRAUX

Science and Technology, Council for

(Kagaku Gijutsu Kaigi). Organ established within the Prime Minister's Office in 1959. It advises the prime minister concerning basic and comprehensive policies to be adopted on matters of science and technology. The prime minister serves as council chairman. The council is made up of 10 members: the minister of finance, the minister of education, the director-general of the Economic Planning Agency, the director-general of the Science and Technology Agency, the president of the Science Council of Japan, and 5 other members appointed by the prime minister for three-year terms.

Science Council of Japan

(Nihon Gakujutsu Kaigi; JSC). Organization to represent Japanese scientists both domestically and abroad. Established in 1949. Its purpose is to improve and develop the level of scientific research and to communicate its findings to the governmental and industrial spheres, as well as to the public.

Though the Science Council is a government agency, it operates autonomously and its main functions are to act as a deliberative body and as a communications or liaison arm for matters pertaining to science. As a deliberative body, the JSC answers inquiries from the government on important scientific matters; it also has the right to offer advice on these matters. As a research liaison agency, the JSC represents Japan in such international organizations as the International Council of Scientific Unions, sends representatives to international conferences, hosts conferences, joins in international cooperative undertakings, and takes a central role in international scientific exchange.

The JSC is composed of 210 representatives, with 30 in each of its 7 departments. The tenure of office is three years. Members are elected by scientists who have specific qualifications and who are registered as voting members after authorization by the election administration committee. In 1978 the number of voting members was 202,641.　　WATANABE Tadashi

science fiction

Before World War II science fiction was regarded in Japan as merely a variant form of detective fiction and was read mainly by young boys. However, since World War II it has established itself as a popular literary genre for adult readers as well. Novels commonly referred to today as science fiction include not only those based on scientific facts and imagination but also those that can be termed new, speculative fiction.

Edo Period (1600–1868) —— As early as the Edo period, the Japanese public demonstrated a preference for free-spirited, fantastic adventure stories. In the latter half of this era, various adaptations for Japanese readers of two well-known 16th-century Chinese romantic tales, *Xiyou ji* (*Hsi-yu chi;* Journey to the West; tr *Monkey,* 1942) and *Shuihu zhuan* (*Shui-hu chuan;* Water Margin; tr *All Men Are Brothers,* 1933), were very popular with the reading public. The year 1774 marked the publication of *Wasobei ikoku monogatari,* a Japanese novel similar in many respects to *Gulliver's Travels.* Toward the end of the period, the growing concern within the edu-

cated class about the expansion of Western influence in Asia led to attempts to enlighten the public through fiction about the possibly dire consequences of a new international age. One such book, *Saisei kaishin hen,* written by the Confucian scholar Iwagaki Kesshū (1808–73), depicted a war in the future.

Meiji Period (1868–1912) to World War II —— With the opening of Japan to the West, new information concerning the social systems of the United States and Europe, scientific technology, and the current international situation started pouring into Japan. Western literature was also introduced to Japan in this period. In 1878 Jules Verne's *Around the World in Eighty Days* was translated into Japanese; it was followed by translations of the works of H. G. Wells and Arthur Conan Doyle. Oshikawa Shunrō (1876–1914), a leading writer of science fiction for children, later added political touches about Japan's expansion on the Asian continent to his adaptations of Verne's books. In the 1930s, works by Japanese science fiction writers like Unno Jūza (1897–1949), Kigi Takatarō (1897–1969), and OGURI MUSHITARŌ appeared; they were much influenced by the progenitors of America's first science fiction boom, writers like Hugo Gernsback and Edmond Hamilton. Their works, however, were initially treated as nothing more than a variation of detective fiction, to be read only by young boys. In the 1940s translations of such Western authors as Villiers L'Isle-Adam, Selma Lagerlöf, Karel Čapek, Aldous Huxley, Guillaume Apollinaire, Comte de Lautréamont, and Franz Kafka were popular in Japan. These exerted considerable influence on ABE KŌBŌ, the foremost writer in the first period of science fiction writing in Japan after World War II.

Post–World War II —— Tezuka Osamu (b 1926) started doing outstanding work in comics for children during the late 1940s, and the science fiction film *Godzilla* was a hit in the mid-1950s. However, it was during the 1960s that Japanese science fiction found its place as light reading material second in popularity only to mystery fiction. In 1960 the Japanese *SF magajin* (published in association with the American magazine *Fantasy & Science Fiction*) started publication, introducing British and American science fiction writers to Japan. The works of these authors had an overwhelming influence in fostering new Japanese science fiction authors and readers. In 1970, the year the international exposition was held in Japan, science fiction writers from England, the United States, Canada, and the Soviet Union were invited to a World Symposium of Science Fiction Authors in Japan to establish more interchange between international members of the science fiction world. The year 1975 saw the start of another science fiction magazine, *Kisō tengai.*

Today over one hundred original and translated science fiction works are published annually. The translation of science fiction has been much more active in Japan than in the United States and Europe; in addition to British and American works, those from Russia and Eastern Europe are often translated into Japanese. Through television and comics, Japanese science fiction has thus become extremely popular, primarily among teenagers, although since 1965 the range has broadened to include older readers. Despite the notable foreign influence on Japanese science fiction, it has developed its own distinctive style with material gathered from Japanese life and literature from ancient times to the present, especially the tradition of fantasy. At the same time, Japanese science fiction strives to maintain a high standard in the treatment of universal human themes.

Leading contemporary science fiction writers in Japan include HOSHI SHIN'ICHI, known for the brevity and wit of his 800-plus short stories; KOMATSU SAKYŌ, who utilizes his broad scientific knowledge in his tales about the future which contain elements of social criticism; Tsutsui Yasutaka, popular among the young for his trenchant satire and experimentation with new styles; and Mitsuse Ryū, who continues to write grand tales about outer space against a background of Eastern nihilism. Other science fiction writers include Hammura Ryō, Mayumura Taku, Toyoda Aritsune, Hirai Kazumasa, Ishikawa Kyōji, and Kōsai Tadashi. Four young authors born since World War II are Yamada Masaki, Kambe Musashi, Yokota Jun'ya, and Hori Akira; women science fiction writers include Nakajima Azusa, Yamao Yūko, and Arai Motoko. Among translators and critics are Yano Tetsu (who has introduced American science fiction in addition to writing his own stories), Fukami Jun (active in introducing Soviet and East European science fiction), Asakura Hisashi, Itō Norio, Fukamachi Mariko, and Obi Fusa. An organization of Japanese science fiction authors, the Nihon SF Sakka Kurabu (Japan SF Authors Club), was organized in 1963.

Some representative works in Japanese science fiction since 1969 are Hoshi Shin'ichi's "Bokko chan" (1958; tr "Bokko," 1978) and

"Ōi dete koi" (1958; tr "Hey, Come Out," 1978), both of which are included in a collection of his stories translated into English as *The Spiteful Planet and Other Stories* (1978); Komatsu Sakyō's *Hateshinaki nagare no hate ni* (1965) and *Nihon chimbotsu* (1974; tr *Japan Sinks*, 1976); Tsutsui Yasutaka's *Afurika no bakudan* (1968) and *Dassō to tsuiseki no samba* (1971); Mitsuse Ryū's *Tasogare ni kaeru* (1961) and *Hyakuoku no hiru to sen'oku no yoru* (1965–66); Hammura Ryō's *Musubinoyama hiroku* (1972) and *Yōseiden* (1975–76); Mayumura Taku's *Shōmetsu no kōrin* (1976–78); Toyoda Aritsune's *Mongoru no zankō* (1967); Hirai Kazumasa's *Saibōgu burūsu* (1971) and *Jinrō tenshi* (1978–79); Aramaki Yoshio's *Shinseidai* (1976–77); and Kōsai Tadashi's *Honda ga rēsu ni kamubakku suru toki* (1976).

KOMATSU Sakyō

scientific thought, premodern

This article explores some of the thought patterns, beliefs, and attitudes that underlay the largely Chinese-influenced science of premodern Japan. For a general history of science in Japan, see NATURAL SCIENCES. See also such individual articles as WASAN (on traditional Japanese mathematics) and the sections on history of medicine and traditional medicine in MEDICINE.

Until the 6th century AD, the Japanese did not have a system of writing, and there are thus no written records to indicate what level they had reached before then in knowledge of nature and in simple numerical processes. The transformation of ancient Japanese society from migratory tribal life to settled agrarian communities, which began in the 3rd century BC, was precipitated by the introduction from Korea of irrigated farming and bronze and iron. Eventually, regional states were formed, and by sometime in the Yamato period (ca AD 300–710) these had been brought together into Japan's first unified state. More advanced crafts were then introduced from Korea and China. Throughout these centuries there was a gradual accumulation of practical knowledge of weather, farming, fishing, simple architecture (with rudimentary skills in numerical calculation and measurement), and a limited materia medica (mostly roots, barks, and grasses) for some symptoms of sickness. By the 6th century there had developed a typical folkloric sense of closeness to nature, related to early SHINTŌ beliefs. MYTHOLOGY abounded, but there was not yet an explicit cosmology defining the structure and extent of the universe.

Following the TAIKA REFORM of 645 an effort was begun to reshape both Japanese state and society according to the model of Tang (T'ang) China. Under this ambitious program, diplomatic envoys and students sent to China became the pipeline for the continuing introduction of Chinese administrative structures, literature, religion (Buddhism), crafts, and science. Although the term "science" in its modern sense does not strictly apply to what was borrowed from China at this time, the knowledge of astrology, calendrical astronomy, mathematics, and medicine introduced under the reform program had gone through over a millennium of development in China. As the Chinese government maintained institutes for the study and use of these kinds of knowledge, the reformist Japanese government also founded similar but smaller institutes of learning. The program of adoption was sustained until the end of the 9th century, but since teachers and students alike had first to master Chinese writing and calculation methods, the Japanese were, even after two centuries, still far behind their Chinese mentors.

Two characteristics of the imported knowledge may be noted by reference to astrology and calendrical astronomy. The first is that astronomy was studied in China, and thus in Korea and Japan, for calendrical purposes (until the modern era, there was in all East Asia no observational astronomy independent of the astrological and calendrical arts). Production and promulgation of the civil calendar, moreover, were among the principal tasks of the Chinese emperor, whose title *tianzi (t'ien-tzu)* meant literally "Heaven's son." Astronomy, like other sciences, was therefore an official function of government. Official sponsorship has remained a prominent feature of Japanese scholarship from the Taika Reform to the present day, though independent and private scholarship in time evolved in Japan, as it had much earlier in China.

The second characteristic is that the Chinese believed that the emperor conducted the affairs of state under the Mandate of Heaven. This did not mean simply that the emperor's mandate was subject to a capricious "will of Heaven." Rather, the political world was supposed to be kept in accord with the natural order, and this order was to be discerned through observation of natural, and especially celestial, phenomena. These phenomena were recognized as including both regularities (predictable phenomena that it fit a pattern) and irregularities (unpredictable phenomena that did not).

The Japanese, with a supposedly unbroken imperial line, had less reason to be concerned with the "mandate" notion. It was not the regularities of mathematical astronomy expressed as eternal truths but the irregularities of unforeseeable omens, interpreted by astrologers, that attracted more attention in Japan. Historical analogy, not tightly constructed logical reasoning, was favored. The adopted astrology did not lack abstract theoretical arguments, but such was far less important to the Japanese than to the Chinese.

While there was considerable overlap in the subject matter of Eastern and Western knowledge of nature, there were enormous differences in style and often methods. The conviction that eternal patterns underlie the flux of nature is so central to the Western tradition that it might seem no science is possible without them. Chinese science, however, while assuming that regularities were there for the finding, considered the ultimate texture of reality much too subtle to be fully measured or comprehended by empirical investigation or logical codification. The Japanese paid even less attention to the general, while showing a keen interest in the particular and evanescent.

The two characteristics noted above apply on the whole to the Japanese reception of Chinese medicine and mathematics. In medical theory, man was viewed as the microcosm of the natural order, and health was to be maintained—or, in the event of illness, restored—by therapies for bringing bodily functions into harmony with cosmic phases. Therapy relied mainly on drugs (mineral, vegetable, and animal), but included auxiliary methods such as massage, acupuncture, and incantations. The physical organs were of little interest because the human body was understood as a complex of functional systems that were defined in terms of vitality or energy, especially by use of yin-yang concepts and, somewhat later, the five cyclical phases. Conceptual complexities appear to have commanded less attention than the practical needs to procure, classify, and apply the many drugs required in Chinese medicine. As for mathematics, even though it involved much less theory it seems to have been too rational to win the attention gained by the other sciences.

The trends outlined above became pronounced between the 10th and the 15th centuries when Japan lost interest in further adoption from China. During these five centuries travel to China by the Japanese was prohibited, except for a few Buddhist priests granted special permission, and Chinese merchant vessels visiting Japan were subject to strict regulations. Japanese culture evolved along more indigenous lines, notably in literature and religion.

Neither the imperial court nobility who ruled during the earlier part of this period nor the warriors who ruled later were particularly interested in the sciences. Official sponsorship was retained but largely neglected and each of the disciplines was made the hereditary province of some noble family. These families did little more than preserve their inherited knowledge. The calendrical system last adopted from China in 862 remained unrevised until 1684, by which time there was two days' discord with the tropical year. Mathematical ability declined drastically; revival would come only after the rise of a fairly large merchant class with more practical needs. Government-sponsored medicine remained in the service of the imperial and noble households, and medical care for the masses was extended mainly by Buddhist priest-practitioners. As might be expected, there was no noteworthy development in scientific thought. This period of relative seclusion from China was marked, rather, by the popularity of divination and various other superstitious practices.

Western influences reached Japan for the first time in the middle of the 16th century by way of European traders and Catholic missions. Both groups served to stimulate new interest in scientific matters, especially in technical areas such as navigation and gunnery but also in cosmology and surgery. However, a new policy of NATIONAL SECLUSION imposed by the Tokugawa shogunate (1603–1867) had driven all Westerners from Japan by 1639, and although carefully controlled contact with the Dutch was maintained residual European influences were insufficient to stimulate a revival of scientific effort in Japan.

The needed stimulus came, rather, from renewed contact with China following the reopening of trade relations in the 15th century. Buddhist priests had in the interim become the most learned class. During the 16th century a number of Buddhist priest-practitioners began devoting themselves entirely to medical study, teaching, and practice in order to catch up with the now more advanced Chinese theories and methods. Through them and their disciples, the 13th-century Chinese synthesis of natural knowledge and Confucianism—which had become intricately allied with Chinese medicine—entered the Japanese intellectual scene. From early in the 17th century many books were printed in virtually every scholarly field as part of an intellectual renaissance in which the entire spectrum of Chinese learning and science came to be understood critically and comprehensively. Achievements made in the 17th century and subsequently were, of course, greatly advanced over the introductory efforts of the 7th to 9th centuries. But certain thought patterns established in the earlier period naturally appeared in the later activities as well.

The East Asian tradition, as explained above, not only had frames in which regularities could be comprehended but also a great many others in which irregularities were classified. Sorting exceptional phenomena into proper frames was as satisfying for the Japanese scholar as integrating them into a unified frame was for the Platonist or Aristotelian (the Chinese preference was intermediate).

This attitude may be seen in SHIBUKAWA SHUNKAI (1639–1715), who made the first independent calendrical revision (1684) and was therefore made the first official astronomer to the Tokugawa shōgun (a revival of "official sponsorship"). In the preface to an early treatise, *Shunjū jutsureki* (discussions on the calendar reflected in the Chinese Confucian classic *Spring and Autumn Annals*), he stated, "Astronomers have rigidly maintained that when Confucius dated the events in his annals of the Spring and Autumn era he made conventional use of the current calendar, with little care paid to its astronomical meaning; and that hence the dates are not very reliable. Their error is due to their commitment to mathematical astronomy, so that they do not admit that extraordinary events happen in the heavens. . . . Extraordinary phenomena do in fact take place in the heavens. We should not therefore doubt the authenticity of [Confucius's] sacred writing-brush."

In his own work in mathematical astronomy Shibukawa was thoroughly empirical, but he believed that a professional astronomer should be fully competent in both major branches of celestial studies—omen-oriented astrology and exact calendrical science. It was no less important to furnish the means by which astrological portents could be classified. He was convinced that the heavens could not be fully comprehended through mathematical regularity. The heavens were of such depth that the tools of no single discipline could plumb them.

Once admitting, as Shibukawa did, that regular motion was too limited an assumption, one could easily admit such notions as that astronomical parameters might vary from century to century. In the official calendar of the 13th century and earlier, the discrepancy between ancient records in the *Spring and Autumn Annals* and recent observations was explained by a secular variation in tropical year-length. Shibukawa revived this variation in the Japanese calendar, and ASADA GŌRYŪ (1734–99) extended it to other basic parameters to account for Western as well as Eastern observations then available to him.

OGYŪ SORAI (1666–1728), the influential Japanese Confucian philosopher, commented on the variation of astronomical parameters: "The sky and the earth, the sun and the moon are living bodies. According to Chinese calendrics, the length of the tropical year was greater in the past and will decrease in the future. As for me, I cannot comprehend events a million years ahead." Since the heavens were thought to be imbued with vital force, the length of the year could change freely, and constancy was not to be expected in the heavens. Indeed, only a dead universe could be governed solely by law and regularity, and the study of such a cosmos would be of no interest to the natural philosopher. It was precisely the vital aspects of nature that interested Ogyū; he remained agnostic toward physical cosmology. "All scholarship should finally converge in historical studies," said Ogyū. Because he was a Confucian philosopher, "history" meant human history; nature was judged in the light of social and ethical norms. This moralistic, anthropocentric, and often anthropomorphic view of nature was common among Confucian thinkers throughout East Asia. Many of them were unable to imagine that mathematical astronomy could make any greater contribution than providing an accurate calendar.

Medicine, perhaps due to its alliance with Confucian thought, also had a strong vitalistic bias. Until modern times, for instance, the Japanese did not locate thought processes in the head. The cognitive and imaginative functions of the brain were unknown, and their anatomical substratum undemonstrated. Learned treatises of the Chinese and Japanese medical traditions lacked terminology not only for the brain but also for mental processes. Conventional

Chinese discourse was not much concerned with what we would consider epistemology. Vocabular for mental operations was rudimentary and, to a considerable extent, borrowed from Indian Buddhism. As already noted, Chinese and Japanese medicine were concerned primarily with functions and only secondarily with tissues and organs. The sites of functions to which most attention was paid were two groups in the thorax: a set of six *fu* (J: *fu*) that were thought to ferment food, separate extracted energy from waste, and excrete the latter; and five *zang* (*tsang*; J: *zō*) that were thought to store the refined energy. These functional operations, or "spheres," were identified with the physical viscera, but the physiological nature of the latter was of such minor importance that little was known about them, and they had no abiding role in medical discourse. Occasional simple drawings of the human body ignored both the interior of the head and the nervous tissues, neither of which were assigned specific functions (at least in the Chinese medical writings most influential in Japan).

As knowledge was not thought of as localized and stored, there was no reason to investigate the physiological basis of cognition. The need to explore relations between the mind and the brain did not exist for East Asians because they assumed neither a mind-matter dualism nor a dualism between self and the outer world. All nature was seen as an encompassing functional system in which functional patterns (*li*; J: *ri*) of individual things participate.

Traditional East Asian theories of bodily function and pathology are closer to the European humoralist tradition than to that of the solidist. Health was related to the balance of energy (*qi* or *ch'ij* J: *ki*), which was not considered a ponderable fluid, as were the humors, nor like inorganic gas, but something more like the stoic pneuma of the West. In medical theory its vital or energetic aspect—in a purely qualitative sense—was preponderant in discussions of the causes of disease. As refined energy, it was responsible for all vital functions.

In this vitalistic context of physiology and pathology, East Asian medicine had no use for precise anatomy. For the latter to be accepted, its utility would have to be proved, and proof would have to appeal to a different conception of nature and of the human body. The 17th-century intellectual renaissance yielded a mastery of Chinese medicine, which in the 18th century led some Japanese to feel that Chinese medicine was overburdened by speculative theory that was quite useless in therapeutic practice. Opposition to received theories came mainly from the *koihō* or classicist school. Some of its adherents thought that certain tumors and internal swelling resulted from stagnation or congealing of *qi* in the body. If *qi* was involved in the physical processes of the body, then the body itself might merit more attention. A first step toward a more materialistic, solidist orientation appeared, then, in the criticism of traditional Chinese anatomical charts advanced by YAMAWAKI TŌYŌ (1704–62), who probably had access to a Western anatomical chart. He could not read the legends on the latter, but his own experience in making dissections very likely convinced him that the Western schema was a great deal more accurate than the Chinese.

Objections to dissections were raised, of course, by those loyal to traditional physiology. Sano Yasusada (fl 1760) in his "refutation" of Yamawaki's anatomical chart said, "What the *zang* truly signify is not a matter of morphology; they are containers in which vital energy with various functions is stored. Lacking that energy, the *zang* become no more than emptied containers." Nothing could be learned, he claimed, by dissecting a cadaver since it lacks this vital energy.

Adherents of the *koihō* school were prepared, however, to take a more materialistic line than their predecessors had. As dissections were performed with increased frequency, functional analysis gradually lost its importance, and the physical organs could be studied for their own sake. Soon the traditional charts were recognized as crude and inaccurate representations of the physical organs. In the latter part of the 18th century, SUGITA GEMPAKU (1733–1817) and others undertook the study of anatomy because it seemed the most tangible, and therefore most readily comprehensible, part of Western medicine (called "Dutch medicine" since access during the national seclusion period was limited to contacts with the Dutch traders in Nagasaki, the only Westerners allowed to trade with Japan at the time). Following this breakthrough, it became unmistakably clear that to understand Western medicine fully it was necessary to extend study to physics, biology, and chemistry, and the consequence was to open the way to the world of modern science. The Copernican influence in Japan was minor by comparison, as Japanese cosmology had not been defined by religious authority. The

Screen and wall painting —— Blossoming Cherry Trees

Detail of one of a set of four painted panels at the temple Chishakuin in Kyōto. Part of an 11-panel group entitled *Cherries and Maples*. Colors and gold leaf on paper. Each panel 172.4 × 139.4 cm. Late 16th century. National Treasure.

impact of anatomical studies had challenged not only traditional medicine but natural philosophy as well, and the long-range effect was bound to be revolutionary.

In the latter half of the 19th century, Japanese scholars embarked upon gaining mastery of modern science. Thenceforth there was nothing specifically distinguishable as "Japanese science" or "Japanese scientific thought," since Japanese scientists became participants and partners in the pursuit and use of modern science with all its benefits and risks. Scientific thought in Japan was greatly conditioned, however, by the fact that the scientific disciplines now introduced were already highly institutionalized in university, industry, and military organizations. The longstanding orientation toward the extraordinary gave way to the general, as a rule, but preference for the exceptional remained faintly reflected in the word coined for science, *kagaku*, which means a specific discipline. And "official sponsorship" was fully reflected in the fact that the Japanese government was the primary initial agent in the systematic introduction of modern science.

📖 ——Shigeru Nakayama, *A History of Japanese Astronomy: Chinese Background and Western Impact* (1969). Shigeru Nakayama, *Characteristics of Scientific Development in Japan* (1977). Shigeru Nakayama, "Japanese Scientific Thought," in *Dictionary of Scientific Biography*, vol 15 (1978). Shigeru Nakayama, David Swain, and E. Yagi, ed, *Science and Society in Modern Japan* (1974). E. Smith and Y. Mikami, *A History of Japanese Mathematics* (1914). M. Sugimoto and David Swain, *Science and Culture in Traditional Japan, 600–1854* (1978). Shigeru NAKAYAMA and David L. SWAIN

Scott, Marion McCarrell (1843–1922)

American educator who contributed to the establishment of a modern educational system in Meiji-period (1868–1912) Japan, working as a textbook editor, compiler of teachers' manuals, and adviser on teaching methods. Scott came to Japan in 1871 and taught at the Daigaku Nankō (now Tōkyō University). From 1872 to 1874 he worked at Tōkyō Normal School (Tōkyō Shihan Gakkō; later Tōkyō University of Education). At the latter he introduced American methods in elementary education into the training of elementary-school teachers, using imported educational equipment and texts. These methods were widely spread in Japan by his former students. He left Japan in 1881. TAKAKUWA Yasuo

screen and wall painting

(*shōbyōga*; also pronounced *shōhekiga*). Paintings executed on screens or walls of traditional Japanese-style buildings; one of the major formats in the history of Japanese painting. Among other terms, *shōhekiga* has been used most frequently as the generic term for wall and screen painting; strictly speaking, however, *shōhekiga* should refer only to paintings executed on walls or doors. Paintings on free-standing, folding screens are known as *byōbu-e*. The term

shōbyōga, an abbreviation of *shōhekiga* and *byōbu-e*, covers both wall and screen painting.

Shōhekiga —— *Shōhekiga* can be subdivided into two major formats: paintings on doors and paintings on walls. *Shō*, which literally means "to block or hinder," refers to paintings on doors. These can be wooden doors on hinges, such as those on the Tamamushi Shrine (a miniature sanctuary) at the temple HŌRYŪJI, or those at the Phoenix Hall at the BYŌDŌIN. More commonly, however, the paintings are on sliding panels constructed of paper or silk stretched over a light wooden frame. These are known today as *fusuma*, though before the medieval period they were called *fusumashōji*.

Heki literally means "wall." This refers to all forms of wall painting, though in its broadest sense it can also include paintings on pillars or ceilings. The earliest wall paintings in Japan date to the protohistoric Kofun period (ca 300–710). A number of tomb sites have been excavated in Kyūshū, such as Idera and Takehara, which are decorated with primitive figure paintings or geometric designs executed directly on the stone walls (see ORNAMENTED TOMBS). Later wall paintings were done on a variety of surfaces including stone, wood, and plaster. Like paintings on doors, the artist often painted first on silk or paper, which was then pasted on the walls.

Byōbu-e —— Unlike *shōhekiga*, *byōbu-e* ("screen pictures") are not permanent architectural fixtures. They are free-standing, portable folding screens. Since there are no architectural requirements dictating their size or form, more variety is possible. Screens range in size from about 1 to 1.8 meters (3 to 6 ft) high, and from about 1 to 5.5 meters (3 to 18 ft) wide. They can have two, three, four, six, or eight panels. Most commonly, however, screens have been arranged in pairs, each screen with six panels and measuring approximately 1.5 meters (5 ft) high by 3.7 meters (12 ft) wide. The reason for the popularity of this particular arrangement is unknown, but it has been the prevailing one since as early as the Nara period (710–794).

Early screens were rather awkward and heavy. Panels were linked together at the corners with silken or leather cords. The holes for these cords were reinforced by wooden washers shaped like Japanese coins. This type of construction was known as *zenigata* ("coin-shaped") construction. The screens were heavy, since it was necessary to reinforce the panels with relatively thick wooden frames to protect them from damage when they were moved. Usually the panels were covered with silken brocade that separated the panels compositionally. It was not until the 14th century that this method of construction was significantly improved. In the new method, layers of strong paper were stretched over light wooden frames. These panels were then linked with overlapping and interlocking strips of paper pasted between panels. When the screen was unfolded, a single, unbroken surface with no intrusive borders resulted. The screens constructed in this way were both lighter and stronger. With few modifications, this method of construction is still used.

In addition to the standard folding screens, there are also freestanding, single-panel screens called *tsuitate*. These screens, constructed entirely of wood, are supported on low wooden feet. The format was particularly popular in China, where the screens were often placed in doorways to protect against demons, the common belief being that demons were only able to travel in straight lines. In Japan, *tsuitate* are mentioned frequently in early records, but they do not seem to have been as popular as *byōbu*. In later periods, the format was employed infrequently.

Early Shōbyōga —— The earliest Japanese *shōbyōga* were the Kofun-period wall paintings. These paintings had little impact on later Japanese art. The majority of later wall and screen paintings can be traced to Chinese prototypes that were introduced to Japan sporadically throughout its history, beginning in the late 6th and the 7th centuries (see ASUKA CULTURE; HAKUHŌ CULTURE).

Surviving examples of Japanese wall paintings in Buddhist temples date from the last 50 years of this period, but records suggest that such paintings were done in the early part as well. A number of important temples were constructed during the period, including the Shitennōji (ca 593) and Hōryūji (ca 607). Unfortunately, the original buildings of both temples were destroyed by fires, and any wall paintings decorating the buildings were lost. Both temples were rebuilt.

The earliest extant Buddhist paintings decorate the Tamamushi Shrine at Hōryūji. This shrine is undated, but stylistically it can be dated to the latter half of the 7th century. Another early shrine containing wall paintings, known as the Tachibana Shrine, is also at Hōryūji. It is considerably less well preserved, but stylistically, at least, some of the paintings appear to date from the late 7th century. The Tachibana Shrine also contains the earliest example of a folding screen in Japan: a small model of a threefold screen in bronze standing behind the Amida triad. This type of triptych arrangement was popular in China, particularly for Buddhist subjects. Stylistically the screen seems to date from the end of the 7th century.

Byōbu were introduced to Japan slightly earlier than this screen. The earliest reference is in the 8th-century chronicle NIHON SHOKI, which mentions a screen presented to Emperor Temmu in 686 by a Korean envoy. In China, folding screens can be traced to a much earlier period and were in use as early as the 3rd century BC.

In Japan, screen painting was well established by the Nara period. The *Tōdaiji kemmotsu chō*, a record of objects donated from Emperor Shōmu's collection to the temple Tōdaiji in 756 (see SHŌSOIN), includes 100 screens in its inventory. These works, carefully cataloged by subject, include a wide range of secular as well as Buddhist subjects. Thus, by the mid-8th century, *byōbu* were a common furnishing, at least at court.

The earliest references to *fusuma-e* (*fusuma* paintings) also occur in this period. Two sliding doors are mentioned in the Shōsoin records from 762, although this format was not fully developed until the Heian period (794–1185).

Wall painting continued to develop in the Nara period. Among the most important examples of Buddhist wall painting anywhere were those preserved on the walls of the main hall at Hōryūji, which had been reconstructed sometime after 670. Although a fire in 1949 nearly obliterated these paintings, the works had been hand-copied and photographed before the fire, so it is still possible to study them.

In the Heian period, native Japanese subject matter began to develop. Though wall painting continued to be devoted almost exclusively to Buddhist subjects, screen painting, that is, *fusuma-e* and *byōbu-e,* which was used more commonly as decoration in the homes of aristocrats and at court, generally had secular subjects. In the later part of this period, these secular subjects were often designated as YAMATO-E (Japanese-style painting), as distinguished from *kara-e* (Chinese-style painting).

In Japanese homes and palaces the preference was for formats that combined the functional and the decorative. Rarely have Japanese used paintings for purely aesthetic purposes. Indeed, the word *byōbu* literally means "barrier against the wind": screens served a useful function as protection against cold drafts and, in addition, they were used as backdrops in religious and court ceremonies and very often as room partitions in large interiors. The word *fusuma* literally means "blocking" or "separating," referring to their function as doors for rooms or storage areas.

Almost no examples of screen painting have survived from the Heian period. There are no *fusuma-e* extant from that period, and only one example of *byōbu-e* survives. This screen, the *Senzui byōbu* from the temple Tōji in Kyōto, was used in religious ceremonies and is not typical of the secular screen painting that flourished during the Heian period. Fortunately, a number of important sources providing information on early secular screen painting are

available. There are literary references, such as court diaries, narratives, and poetry anthologies, and pictorial sources, particularly the large number of late-Heian-period and Kamakura-period (1185–1333) handscrolls that include scenes of room interiors.

The literary sources describe the kinds of subjects and formats used in painting at the time. A number of 10th-century poetry anthologies are particularly useful, among them the KOKINSHŪ, the SHŪI WAKASHŪ, and the collected poems of KI NO TSURAYUKI. The poems in these works date from the late 9th and early 10th centuries, and many of them were specifically composed to accompany screen paintings. The largest number of these were for *byōbu*. In the *Shūi wakashū*, for example, 129 poems were composed for paintings, 119 for *byōbu*, and only 3 for *fusuma*. In other records, though references to *fusuma-e* are not uncommon, they are far outnumbered by references to *byōbu-e*.

Illustrated handscrolls (EMAKIMONO) give an even clearer picture of screen painting during the Heian and Kamakura periods. Interior scenes in these works often include detailed depictions of screens in which both the subject and the style of the painting can be seen. The paintings were colorful, with soft green hills in the background. However, the most common subject was landscape in four seasons. However, genre scenes depicting aristocrats and commoners at famous sites in and around Kyōto, or participating in seasonal celebrations and ceremonies, were also common. Among the most important of these handscrolls are GENJI MONOGATARI EMAKI, *Nenchū gyōji emaki, Matsuzaki tenjin engi, Hōnen shōnin eden,* and *Taima mandara engi*.

Medieval Shōbyōga —— The tradition of Buddhist paintings for walls and secular *yamato-e* painting for screens continued into the Kamakura period. However, in the mid-Kamakura period, under the influence of renewed contacts with China, monochrome ink painting inspired by paintings of the Song (Sung) dynasty (960–1279) began to gradually supplant *yamato-e* for screens. Unfortunately, no examples of this type of screen painting have survived from the Kamakura period, though it is possible to reconstruct them to some extent with literary and pictorial sources.

In the Muromachi period (1333–1568), Buddhist painting declined, and with it wall painting. The most important subject for secular screens was still landscape, though Chinese literary themes and paintings of flowers and birds were also popular. In the 15th century, the basic compositional formula was established for screens representing landscape in four seasons. The compositions unfolded from right to left in three parts: spring landscape at the right, summer and fall in the center, and winter at the left. The paintings were subdued and detailed, with few bright colors.

The earliest extant example of *shōbyōga* from this period is the famous *Catching a Catfish with a Gourd* by JOSETSU. This painting, now mounted as a hanging scroll, was originally a single-panel screen or *tsuitate*. Screen paintings were executed by all of the major ink painters after Josetsu, beginning with SHŪBUN and SESSHŪ TŌYŌ, and culminating in the late 15th and early 16th centuries with SESSON SHŪKEI, SŌAMI, KANŌ MASANOBU, and his son KANŌ MOTONOBU. In these works two lines of development can be discerned. The screens by Shūbun and Sōami continue the tradition of pure Song dynasty Chinese ink painting. Sesshū, however, under the influence of Ming-dynasty (1368–1644) painters, developed a style of painting that was more decorative. This style was further developed by Masanobu and Motonobu and culminated in the subsequent Momoyama decorative style.

The Azuchi-Momoyama period (1568–1600) is referred to as the golden age of screen painting. This is true both literally and figuratively. During this period screens with backgrounds sprinkled with gold dust or covered with wafer-thin gold leaf became prominent. Gilt screens had been known in the Muromachi period also, and mid-15th century records indicate that Japan was exporting screens of this type to both China and Korea. Still, it was not until the Azuchi-Momoyama period that such lavishly decorated screens became truly fashionable. This is largely attributable to the rise of military warlords who required castle decorations that reflected their wealth and power. In addition, the gilt screens served to brighten otherwise gloomy castle interiors.

These screens were often brightly colored and the compositions boldly simplified, with stronger and more immediate appeal than the naturalistic Muromachi-period treatments. The major artists of the period, KANŌ EITOKU, KANŌ SANRAKU, Tosa Mitsuyoshi, UNKOKU TŌGAN, HASEGAWA TŌHAKU, and KAIHŌ YŪSHŌ, all painted a wide range of subject matter. In addition to landscapes, a large repertoire of narrative and genre subjects was developed in this period.

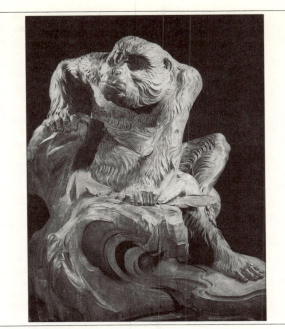

Modern sculpture

The Aging Monkey (Rōen) by Takamura Kōun. Wood. Height with base 106 cm. 1893. Tōkyō National Museum.

Screens illustrated tales from classical Japanese literature, such as the TALE OF GENJI, and genre scenes, such as *rakuchū rakugai* (scenes of Kyōto and its environs).

Edo-Period Shōbyōga —— For the most part, painters of the Edo period (1600–1868) continued the tradition of *shōbyōga* developed by the Azuchi-Momoyama-period artists. The wide range of subject matter was more fully explored by the various Edo-period schools. The KANŌ SCHOOL, which had dominated Azuchi-Momoyama-period screen painting, continued to be extremely influential. These painters were patronized by the Tokugawa shōguns as the official school of painting. The subject matter tended to be conservative, Chinese-inspired scenes, and few of the individual artists, with the exception of KANŌ TAN'YŪ, were outstanding.

In the same conservative vein, the TOSA SCHOOL continued the *yamato-e* tradition. Among the more interesting examples of their work are a large number of anonymous paintings illustrating scenes from everyday life. These were produced in shops by *machi eshi* (town painters) for the growing class of wealthy merchants.

The most creative and innovative of the Edo-period schools were the RIMPA, BUNJINGA, and NAGASAKI schools. Artists in each of these schools painted screens. However, screen painting was of less importance in the Nagasaki-realist and *bunjinga* schools. Screen paintings were almost always commissioned, and *bunjinga* artists, though professionals, tried to avoid such overt patronage and the loss of artistic freedom which it implied. As for the Nagasaki-realist school, their avowed desire was to paint directly from nature, and smaller formats were more convenient.

It was the Rimpa school that brought decorative screen painting to new heights of accomplishment. Artists such as Tawaraya SŌTA-TSU and KŌRIN painted subjects derived largely from classical literature. Their patrons were highly cultured aristocrats and merchants thoroughly versed in the literary subject. Thus, it was unnecessary and even undesirable to present detailed illustrations: bold, simplified compositions where a few motifs could convey a range of subtly different nuances were preferred. The end result can be admired for its extremely modern aesthetic, but for the educated Japanese its literary allusion would also have been readily apparent and an integral part of their appreciation of the work.

After the 18th century, no wall or screen painting of real importance is found. Screen paintings of genre subjects favored by the UKIYO-E school, such as those of courtesans, the gay quarters of Edo (now Tōkyō), KABUKI theater, and festivals, were executed in large numbers, for a time, to satisfy a growing middle-class demand. These were often done on smaller sixfold screens, since they were for private homes. However, most of the major schools of Edo-period painting were in decline, and with their decline, *shōbyōga* declined as well.

—— Elise Grilli, *The Art of the Japanese Screen* (1970). Miyeko Murase, *Byōbu: Japanese Screens from New York Collections* (1971).

M. YOCHUM

scrolls → emakimono

sculpture, modern

The notion of sculpture *(chōkoku)* as an independent genre of the plastic arts did not emerge in Japan until the Meiji period (1868–1912), when an imported European ideology of art began to affect traditional aesthetics. Before the Meiji period, sculpture was referred to as *horimono* (carved and engraved objects) and existed only in didactic and decorative forms; BUDDHIST SCULPTURE, for example, possessed a long iconographic history, and crafts such as metal and ivory carving, dolls, and NETSUKE exemplified sculpture as a decorative art. With the advent of new ideas about art among Meiji intellectuals, sculpture was freed from the constraints of religious or decorative function. The word *chōkoku* came into use as part of the transition, replacing the broader term *horimono* and denoting a specific form of art in the round.

Sculpture of the Meiji and Taishō (1912–1926) Periods —— In 1876 the Meiji government opened the Kōbu Bijutsu Gakkō (Technical Fine Arts School) and invited the Italian bronze sculptor Vincenzo RAGUSA (1841–1928) to head its department of Western-style sculpture. A neoclassicist who was nevertheless influenced by the Italian baroque tradition, Ragusa taught academic realism and introduced current European techniques of modeling in clay preparatory to bronze casting. Before returning to Italy in 1882, Ragusa executed a number of works sympathetically depicting Japanese people, among them *Musume no kyōzō* (Bust of a Young Girl) and *Nihon no daiku* (Japanese Carpenter). Prominent among Ragusa's students was Ōkuma Ujihiro (1856–1934), who traveled to Europe for study in 1888. In 1893 Ōkuma completed the portrait *Ōmura Masujirō*, which is noted as a pioneering work in Japanese Western-style bronze sculpture.

The Kōbu Bijutsu Gakkō was closed in 1882, and Western-style sculpture entered a temporary period of decline. This was due in part to a resurgence of interest in conservative Japanese-style sculpture; also, many Western-style sculptors were abroad. In 1887 the Tōkyō Chōkōkai (Tōkyō Sculptors Association) was formed to encourage traditionalist currents in sculpture. Among its members were TAKAMURA KŌUN (1852–1934), a member of an old Edo family of *busshi* (Buddhist sculptors), and Ishikawa Kōmei (1852–1913) and Takeuchi Kyūichi (1857–1916), both from established families of ivory carvers.

In 1889 the Tōkyō Bijutsu Gakkō (now Tōkyō University of Fine Arts and Music) was opened, but it did not contain a department or even courses in Western-style sculpture, offering only training in traditional wood carving. Both Takamura and Takeuchi taught there, emphasizing small-scale works with a strong decorative content. Takamura's finely worked *Rōen* (The Aging Monkey) won a prize and international acclaim at the Chicago World Exposition of 1893.

Renewed interest in Western-style sculpture gained momentum as artists returned from study abroad. By 1898 the Bijutsu Gakkō contained a course in Western-style clay modeling, and in 1899 a full department of Western-style sculpture was established. Naganuma Moriyoshi (1857–1942), back from a long stay in Italy, was instrumental in the reintroduction of academicism at this time. His bronze *Rōfu* (Head of an Aging Laborer, 1898) won the gold prize at the Paris World Exposition of 1900.

With the institution in 1907 of the government-sponsored BUNTEN painting and sculpture competition, Western-style sculptors gained official recognition with the added advantage of a public arena for their works. They exhibited alongside their more conservative Japanese-style counterparts and were judged by representatives from both camps, such as Takamura Kōun and Ōkuma Ujihiro. Shinkai Taketarō (1868–1927), who had returned from Germany in 1902, entered *Yuami* (Bather, 1907) and was much praised for his classical realism. Other Western-style sculptors represented in the first Bunten were Kitamura Shikai (1871–1927), Yamazaki Chōun (1867–1954), Tatehata Taimu (1880–1942), and ASAKURA FUMIO (1883–1964).

Among the predominantly neoclassicist Western-style sculptors showing in the first Bunten was a small group of artists inclined to newer trends in European sculpture, which had developed away from academicism toward the romantic realism epitomized by the sculptor Auguste Rodin (1840–1917). Most influential of this group was OGIWARA MORIE (1879–1910), who had spent several years studying academic painting in New York and then Paris. In 1904 he saw Rodin's *Le Penseur* (The Thinker, 1880) in Paris and was moved to cast aside not only the neoclassicist approach but painting as well. Ogiwara became a sculptor in the manner of Rodin, seeking to express through sculpture the inner rhythms of living form. His *Onna* (Woman) of 1910 exemplifies this paradoxical concern. Ogiwara met an untimely death shortly after completing this work, but his influence among sculptors remained significant.

By the early years of the Taishō period (1912–26), Rodin's works, which enjoyed an enthusiastic following among Japanese artists, had been widely publicized in the literary journal *Shirakaba* (see SHIRAKABA SCHOOL). Takamura Kōun's eldest son TAKAMURA KŌTARŌ (1883–1956), a Western-style sculptor who equaled Ogiwara in influence and also was recognized as an outstanding poet, translated Rodin's views on art as *Rodan no kotoba* (1915–20). This book became a pillar of the aesthetics of modern Japanese sculpture.

Rodin's style displaced that of neoclassicism, and most Western-style sculptors were attracted to it as an avenue of greater individual expression. Fujikawa Yūzō (1882–1935) sought out Rodin in Paris to become his student and eventually his assistant. Although personally close to Rodin, Fujikawa did not blindly imitate him; his *Burondo* (Blonde, ca 1910) is a well-tempered interpretation of Rodin's style. More strongly affected by Rodin were the works of Nakahara Teijirō (1888–1921) and Tobari Kōgan (1882–1927). Both originally were painters who, like their friend Ogiwara, turned to sculpture as the medium most conducive to expressing Rodin's romantic notion of art. Tobari's *Ashigei* (Juggler, 1914) captures the pathos of a Japanese juggler's life while delineating the stark vitality of her motions.

While Western ideals and Rodin's stylistic influence were dominant, they were not all encompassing. A number of sculptors continued to work in wood in the more conservative vein of Takamura Kōun, among them HIRAGUSHI DENCHŪ (1872–1979), Satō Chōzan (1888–1963), and Shinkai Takezō (1897–1968). Hiragushi's prolific career spanned the Meiji, Taishō, and most of the Shōwa (1926–) periods; he was 107 at the time of his death in 1979 and had witnessed the full course of development of modern Japanese sculpture. Recognized at an early age by the art critic OKAKURA KAKUZŌ (1862–1913), a traditionalist who nevertheless sought a common ground for Western and Japanese modes in art, Hiragushi was for many years an active member of the JAPAN FINE ARTS ACADEMY (Nihon Bijutsuin).

By the end of the Taishō period, conceptually and stylistically Japanese sculpture consisted of two streams, European and traditional. Although occasionally these merged into a successful hybrid, as in the works of Hiragushi, the general trend was parallel development. Within Western-style sculpture, neoclassicism had given way to romanticism, which became the stylistic paradigm for most sculpture until the mid-1920s.

Sculpture of the Shōwa Period —— Since the 1920s the Japanese art world has been inundated by successive waves of stylistic influence from abroad. The wide variety of formal styles among modern Japanese sculptors derives from the eclectic character of the art world as a whole. While it is difficult to delineate with any confidence specific Shōwa-period schools or stylistic currents, two general trends are apparent. First, as an outgrowth of the Taishō-period concern with the art and philosophy of Rodin, modern sculptors have explored the possibilities of individual expression to an increasingly pronounced degree. Second, the majority of sculptors have achieved a level of interpretation in their work that has given the form and content of Japanese sculpture an international as opposed to a derivative or provincial character.

During the 1920s and 1930s sculptors who had studied for some time in Europe returned to Japan and laid the ground for new formal and conceptual directions. For example, Shimizu Takashi (1897–1981), Kinouchi Yoshi (1892–1977), and Yasuda Ryūmon (1891–1965), all of whom had worked under Émile Antoine Bourdelle (1861–1929) at his studio in Paris, introduced a monumental, almost architectural style much influenced by archaic Greek sculpture. Yamamoto Toyoichi (b 1899) studied under Aristide Maillol (1861–1944), whose energetically depicted figures of women are based on classical Greek and Roman sculpture, and he brought this distinctive style to Japan. Other sculptors active in introducing new trends during this period were Kikuchi Kazuo (b 1908), who had

Modern sculpture

Woman (Onna), the last work of Ogiwara Morie. Bronze. Height 98.5 cm. 1910. National Museum of Modern Art, Tōkyō.

studied under the Maillol-influenced Charles Despiau (1874–1946); Yanagihara Yoshitatsu (b 1910), a pupil of Emmanuel Auricoste; the expressionist sculptor Hongō Shin (1905–80); Satō Chūryō (b 1912), whose work reflects the influence of contemporary Italian sculpture; Funakoshi Yasutake (b 1912), skilled in the working of marble; and Yodoi Toshio (b 1911), who was much influenced by Alberto Giacometti (1901–66).

After World War II, Japanese sculptors began to participate actively in the international art world, sending works to exhibitions such as the São Paulo International Biennial, the Venice International Biennial, and the Antwerp International Sculpture Biennial. Formal and conceptual trends describing the European and American art scenes soon surfaced in Japan as well. Outdoor sculpture was taken up with enthusiasm during the 1950s and 1960s, and the first generation of Japanese abstract sculptors also became active, among them Kasagi Sueo (1901–67), HORIUCHI MASAKAZU (b 1911), Mukai Ryōkichi (b 1918), Tatehata Kakuzō (b 1919), and Tsuji Shindō (1910–81).

A concern with the phenomenological aspects of the object in space, and with its physical properties as related to its form or content, emerged among Japanese sculptors of the 1970s, again in response to developments abroad. Sculptors who have addressed themselves to this issue include Kiyomizu Kyūbei (b 1922), Iida Yoshikuni (b 1923), Tada Minami (b 1924), Tsuchitani Takeshi (b 1926), Yuhara Kazuo (b 1930), Inoue Bukichi (b 1930), and Yasuda Haruhiko (b 1930). A related trend was the notion of sculpture in relation to urban space, which also involved the introduction of new methods and materials.

Other notable figures currently active in sculpture include Sumikawa Kiichi (b 1931) and Eguchi Shū (b 1932), who work in wood, and Nagare Masayuki (b 1923), Hayami Shirō (b 1927), and Kimura Kentarō (b 1928), who work in stone. Wakabayashi Isamu (b 1936), who uses iron as his basic medium, has greatly stimulated the field, and Muraoka Saburō (b 1928), Yamaguchi Katsuhiro (b 1928), Miyawaki Aiko (b 1929), and Shinoda Morio (b 1931) have brought an invigorating experimental approach to modern sculpture. A number of sculptors have taken up residence abroad, among them Toyofusa Tomonari (b 1925) and Azuma Kenjirō (b 1926) in Milan and Mizui Yasuo (b 1925) in Paris, where they have achieved recognition as significant members of the world art community.

■ ——Hijikata Teiichi, *Kindai chōkoku to gendai chōkoku* (1978). Miki Tamon, *Chōkoku,* vol 13 of *Genshoku gendai Nihon no bijutsu* (1978). Sakai Tadayasu, *Chōkoku no niwa: Gendai chōkoku no sekai* (1982).   SAKAI Tadayasu

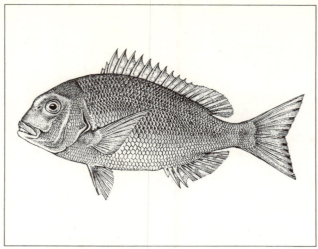

Sea bream —— Madai

sculpture, premodern → Buddhist sculpture

sea bream

(tai). The term *tai* is used both as a general name for saltwater fish of the class Osteichthyes, order Perciformes, family Sparidae, and to refer specifically to the *madai (Pagrus major),* an especially popular species in Japan. Of the approximately 120 species of the fish of the family Sparidae known worldwide, 11 species are found in Japan; these resemble the sea bream of the United Kingdom and the porgy of the United States. The *madai* is native to Japan and its vicinity; it excels in beauty of shape and color and grows to over 80 centimeters (32 in) in length. It is used for ordinary meals and for festive banquets and as gifts. Over 200 species of fish which are not of the family Sparidae, but with slightly flattened bodies, are given names suffixed with *-tai,* which indicates the popularity of the *tai* itself. It is caught by angling or with a net; it is eaten raw, broiled with salt, or in soups.   ABE Tokiharu

Bones of the *madai* and other *tai* have been found in archaeological sites from the Jōmon period (ca 10,000 BC–ca 300 BC), and the *tai* is referred to as *akame* in early chronicles such as the *Kojiki* (712) and *Nihon shoki* (720). Poems praising the taste of *tai* are found in the *Man'yōshū* (completed in the latter half of the 8th century), while the ENGI SHIKI (905–927; tr *Procedures of the Engi Era,* 1970–72) records that dried *tai, tai* pickled with salt, steamed-and-mashed *tai,* and fresh *tai* were presented to the court as offerings. It was only with the development of the fishing industry in the early modern period that the common people came to eat *tai.* The Tokugawa shogunate used large quantities of *tai* for rituals and feasts. The fact that the *tai* was regarded as a celebratory fish is thought to be due not only to its beauty of form and color but also because *tai* suggests the word *medetai,* "auspicious."   SAITŌ Shōji

sea cucumbers

(namako). Members of the phylum Echinodermata, class Holothuroidea. Species are numerous. The *manamako (Stichopus japonicus),* distributed in shallow seas, spawns in April through June (July through August in Hokkaidō) and aestivates when the water temperature rises. It is eaten raw dipped in vinegar and soy sauce; the salt-pickled internal organs *(konowata)* are relished as a side dish for *sake.* The *kinko (Cucumaria frondosa japonica)* found in northern Japan, and *baika namako (Thelenota ananas),* found in southern Japan, including Okinawa, are used in Chinese cooking. There are various stories connected with the sea cucumber, traditionally valued for its nutritive value, in Japanese folklore, one of which appears in the *Kojiki* (712). It has even been seen as a fit subject for *haiku.*
HABE Tadashige and SAITŌ Shōji

seagulls → gulls

seals

(inshō; imban; hankō; in). Official or private seals or stamps engraved with the name of the office, institution, or individual to which each belongs; the impressions of these seals are used to endorse documents of all kinds.

The Japanese attach relatively little importance to signatures as marks of personal identification. On most occasions that would call for a signature in the West, Japanese custom requires the impression of a person's seal, called *inshō* or *hanko.* No legal document is valid, no contract is binding without the required seals affixed to it. Moreover, seals are indispensable in many day-to-day activities: without a seal it is difficult to rent a house, buy a car, withdraw money from the bank, or send and receive certain kinds of mail.

The oldest seal found to date in Japan, discovered in 1784 in Kyūshū, is made of gold and is thought to have been presented to the ruler of the state of Na of Wa (Japan) in AD 57 by Emperor Guangwu (Kuang-wu) of the latter Han dynasty (AD 25–222; see KAN NO WA NO NA NO KOKUŌ NO IN). But seals were formally introduced in 701 when, in imitation of Chinese practice, the TAIHŌ CODE established the first system regulating their manufacture and use. Four types were authorized: the imperial seal; the seal of the Dajōkan, or Grand Council of State; seals of the various government departments and bureaus; and seals for each province. Some of the great religious establishments also possessed seals, but because the temples and shrines were official organs of the state these, too, were cast and issued by the central government. Impressions were stamped in vermilion ink in various parts of all official documents; each sheet of paper on which words were written carried the seal of the issuing authority.

Official use of seals as symbols of the emperor or of the government was always strictly controlled and had a twofold purpose: seals furnished documents with dignity and authority and at the same time guaranteed their authenticity.

The government seals were seldom used after the FUJIWARA FAMILY created the regency and took effective control of the government in the 10th century (see REGENCY GOVERNMENT). The precedent set by the Fujiwara was followed through the late 16th century: seals were replaced by KAŌ, or monograms, of the persons responsible for a document. The powerless imperial court continued to use seals, but they appear on no documents issued by the Kamakura (1192–1333) or Muromachi (1338–1573) shogunates.

Outside the realm of government affairs, seals acquired new significance and wider use, especially with the rise of Zen Buddhism in the 12th and 13th centuries. Chinese monks visiting Japan and Japanese monks returning after study in China brought with them seals of the type favored by the Chinese literati, and use of seals by individuals spread for the first time.

It was not long before personal seals were also adopted by high-ranking military leaders—the patrons of Zen Buddhism—though they were used only to sign art works or as library seals, and were never used on official documents. A major change followed the ŌNIN WAR (1467–77), when powerful independent *daimyō* began to set their personal seals to documents issued within their domains. As well as being practical and convenient, seals provided a needed symbol of authority. By the time Japan was reunified in the late 16th century, there were few daimyō who did not possess and use personal seals.

The seals of the military aristocrats, like those of the Zen monks, varied considerably in size, shape, material, and the words they bore. Seals were not always carved with a person's actual name; sometimes maxims or even pictures were selected to express the ideals of the owner. ODA NOBUNAGA, for example, chose a phrase to express his dream of a peaceful, united Japan, while TOKUGAWA IEYASU favored mottoes with Confucian moral overtones. Although the inscriptions were normally written in *tensho* (ancient Chinese "seal characters"), for a short time in the 16th century some Christian daimyō used seals carved with Roman letters.

It was customary to have more than one seal and to distinguish between their uses. Depending on the nature and content of the document, either vermilion or black ink, the latter an innovation of the Zen clergy, was used.

At the beginning of the 17th century, personal seals were used only by daimyō and a few of their ranking retainers; their use was determined by the relative social positions of the sender and the recipient of a document. It was not until the reign of the third Tokugawa shōgun, Iemitsu (1623–51), that personal seals were adopted by the general populace. This development stemmed from the growth of urban centers and the greatly expanding economy. The frequency and scale of business transactions, including the borrowing and lending of money, necessitated the keeping of careful records, and it became established practice to set one's seal to documents of any contractual relationship to which one was a party. Before long, each family had its own seal.

Universal use of seals led to widespread counterfeiting. To correct this, the government in 1694 ordered the registration of all personal seals with the proper local government administrators. This was the beginning of the system of registration of *jitsuin* ("true seals").

In 1871, after the MEIJI RESTORATION, the government revived and expanded the 8th-century Taihō system of government seals. It created a seal of state and revised the old imperial seal. Use of the imperial seal was discontinued after World War II, but seals are still used by all central and local government agencies. In the same year a nationwide system for the registration and certification of private seals was established, one which remains in effect today.

Individuals must register their *jitsuin* with the head of their local government unit, which keeps an impression on permanent file. Only *jitsuin* may be used on legal documents. For this reason everyone possesses other seals for daily use. When *jitsuin* are used, they are normally affixed below one's signature, and in addition, proof must be furnished in the form of a certificate from the local government that the seal used is in fact the legally registered *jitsuin*.

When the modern system of private seals developed, illiteracy was widespread, and seals provided an indispensable proof of identity. But there are now some who argue that personal seals are relics of the past that have outlived their original purpose and are unsuited to a modern industrial society with the highest literacy rate in the world.

■———Aida Nirō, *Sengoku daimyō no inshō* (1976). Igi Hisaichi, *Zōtei Nihon komonjo gaku* (1976). Ishii Ryōsuke, *Han* (1964). Jichishō Shinkōka, ed, *Inkan tōroku shōmei no jitsumu* (1976). Kiuchi Takeo, ed, *Nihon no koin* (1949). Kuroita Katsumi, "Waga kuni no inshō ni tsuite," *Kyoshin bunshū* 5 (1941). Nakamura Naokatsu, *Nihon komonjo gaku* 3 (1977). Ogino Minahiko, *Inshō* (1966).

Noboru HIRAGA

Sea of Japan

(Nihonkai). One of the three marginal seas around Japan (see EAST CHINA SEA; OKHOTSK SEA). It is situated between the Asian continent and the Japanese archipelago and connected to adjacent seas by the straits of Mamiya, Sōya, Tsugaru, Kammon, and Tsushima. It is the smallest of the three marginal seas (1,008,000 sq km; 389,000 sq mi) and the deepest (maximum depth: 3,712 m; 12,175 ft; average depth: 1,350 m; 4,428 ft). The Sea of Japan has few islands, but it provides good fishing grounds for cuttlefish, mackerel, cod, herring, salmon, walleye pollack, and king crab. In the winter cold air from high pressure areas over Siberia picks up moisture from the Sea of Japan, hits the mountain ridges of the main island, Honshū, and causes heavy snowfall, particularly in the Hokuriku region of west central Honshū.

Sea of Japan, Battle of → Tsushima, Battle of

sea urchins

(uni). Shellfish of the phylum Echinodermata, class Echinoidea. Species commonly found in Japan include the dark purple *murasaki uni (Anthocidaris crassispina)*, the red *aka uni (Pseudocentrotus depressus)*, and the grayish green *bafun uni (Hemicentrotus pulcherrimus)*, all of which live on coastal reefs washed by warm currents. The first two species spawn in June and July and the third in early spring. The *kita murasaki uni (Strongylocentrotus nudus)* and *ezo bafun uni (S. intermedius)* are distributed on the coasts of northern Japan and spawn in autumn. These two species are gathered for food. Other Japanese species include the *gangaze* (needle-spined sea urchin; *Diadema setosum*) in southern Japan, the *futozao uni* (slate-pencil sea urchin; *Heterocentrotus mamillatus*) with thick spines, found on coral reefs of the Okinawa and Ogasawara islands, and the thin-shelled *okame bumbuku (Echinocardium cordatum)*, found on muddy bay bottoms.

HABE Tadashige

Sea urchin remains are reported to have been unearthed from archaeological sites of the Jōmon period (ca 10,000 BC–ca 300 BC), indicating that sea urchins were already part of the Japanese diet in

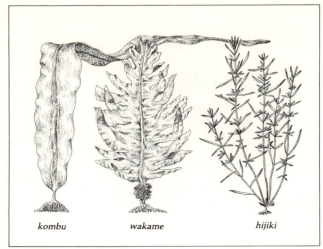

kombu   *wakame*   *hijiki*

Seaweed

prehistoric days. In the Nara period (710–794) the sea urchin was ranked among the "delicacies of all lands and seas," but it was only in the Edo period (1600–1868) that improvements in the nation's distribution system made it commonly accessible. The Shimonoseki area joined Fukui and Kagoshima prefectures as a center of sea urchin production after the Meiji period (1868–1912). Nowadays it is used mainly in *sushi* and other fancy cuisine, commanding high prices. Much of the supply has to be imported because of contamination of Japanese reefs.

SAITŌ Shōji

seaweed

(sōrui). Stretching from north to south and surrounded by both cold and warm currents, Japan is favored with a rich variety (almost 1,200 kinds) and abundance of seaweed. The cold water region around Hokkaidō to the north is especially rich in *kombu* (genus *Laminaria*), which grows to a length of 10 meters (33 ft). *Wakame* (genus *Undaria*), *hijiki* (genus *Hizikia*), *hondawara* (genus *Sargassum*), *arame* (genus *Eisenia*), and *kajime* (genus *Ecklonia*) are found in warmer water from Honshū to Kyūshū. Red algae such as *amanori* (genus *Porphyra*), *tsunomata* (genus *Chondrus*), and *tengusa* (genus *Gelidium*) are also found in large quantities. In waters south of the southernmost tip of Kyūshū there are *kasanori* (genus *Acetabularia*), *iwazuta* (genus *Caulerpa*), *kirinsai* (genus *Eucheuma*), *makuri* (genus *Digenea*), and other smaller warm-water seaweeds.

Surrounded by the sea, the Japanese have always relied heavily on seaweed. The 8th-century *Man'yōshū* anthology contains more than 90 poems which mention seaweeds. The Japanese more than any other people make use of it in their diet. *Asakusanori* (genus *Porphyra*), *kombu*, *aonori* (genus *Enteromorpha*) and *tsunomata* are used in the manufacture of starch. Certain kinds of brown algae are used to make alginic acid, and *makuri* in the formulation of insecticides. *Kanten* or vegetable gelatin is obtained from *tengusa*.

KAZAKI Hideo

seaweed cultivation

The major seaweeds cultivated in Japan are NORI (laver; *Porphyra*), *hitoegusa (Monostroma), wakame (Undaria pinnatifida)*, and *kombu* (kelp; *Laminaria japonica*). Of these the most important is *nori*.

The history of Japanese *nori* cultivation goes back about 300 years. However, recent advances in technology for such procedures as artificial seeding, low-temperature storage of *nori* nets, and floating cultivation, along with the raising of highly productive cultured strains, have contributed to large production gains.

Japan's total annual production in one season (October through April), from approximately 640 square kilometers (250 sq mi) of cultivating beds, is about 7 billion sheets (20 million kg or 44 million lbs, dry weight). Representative of the principal cultivated varieties are *susabi nori (Porphyra yezoensis)* and *asakusa nori (P. tenera)*; of these *narawa-susabi nori (P. yezoensis* form. *narawaensis)* and *ōba-asakusa nori (P. tenera var. tamatsuensis)*, selected for their high-yield characteristics, are widely cultivated today. In addition to the older method of cultivation, in which the *nori* net is spread over a

Seaweed cultivation

Nets being stretched between poles for the older and still most widely used method of *nori* cultivation, in which the netting is exposed at low tide, as here. Artificially cultivated spores will be spread on the netting and left to grow. A small bay along the Pacific coast in Mie Prefecture.

supporting fence and exposed for drying at low tide, the floating-fence method, which does not allow the *nori* to dry, has become widespread. This has resulted in the utilization of offshore areas with depths of 20–50 meters (65–165 ft) in addition to traditional shoreline cultivation. The main production areas include Ise Bay, Mikawa Bay, the Inland Sea, Tōkyō Bay, and Shiogama Bay, all on the Pacific coast. There are only a few cultivation sites on the Sea of Japan coast.

Hitoegusa, mainly *hirohano hitoegusa (Monostroma latissima)*, is cultivated by a method similar to that of *nori* and has an annual yield of 150 million sheets (56,000 kg or 120,000 lbs, dry weight). *Wakame* is cultivated by using hanging-curtain *(noren)*, floating-raft, or rope-type cultivation rigs, yielding annually about 100 million kilograms (220 million lbs). *Kombu* is cultivated using the same method as *wakame*.

◼ —A. Miura, "*Porphyra* Cultivation in Japan," in J. Tokida and H. Hirose, eds, *Advance of Phycology in Japan* (1975). Ueda Saburō, *Shimpen nori yōshoku dokuhon* (1973). ARUGA Yūshō

Sebald, William Joseph (1901–)

American diplomat. Headed the Diplomatic Section of SCAP (headquarters for the Allied Occupation of Japan) from 1947 to 1952 and, as General Douglas MACARTHUR's deputy and US member, served as chairman of the ALLIED COUNCIL FOR JAPAN from 1947 to 1951. He won a reputation as a well-informed and reliable expert on Japan. Born 5 November 1901 in Baltimore, Maryland, he graduated from the US Naval Academy in 1922 and from the University of Maryland Law School in 1933. After serving as naval language officer in Japan, he resigned from the navy and entered law practice in Japan. After naval service in World War II, he entered the Foreign Service, went to Japan in 1946, and later became US political adviser to General MacArthur, with the rank of ambassador. He thereafter served as ambassador to Burma (1952–54), deputy-assistant secretary of state (1954–57), and ambassador to Australia (1957–61). He is the author of a number of books, including *With MacArthur in Japan* (1965), and several studies of Japanese laws and legal procedures. He was decorated with the Order of the Rising Sun, First Class. Richard B. FINN

SECOM Co, Ltd

(Nihon Keibi Hoshō). Japan's leading security company. Founded in 1962, it engages in comprehensive security work: research and development, manufacture, installation, maintenance, computerized monitoring, guard service, armored car service, training and education, and consulting. It was the first company in Japan to establish a total security system using both men and machines, and has expanded from fire and burglary prevention to energy conservation and overall building security. It maintains a joint venture company in Australia and a licensee in Taiwan. Sales for the fiscal year ending November 1981 totaled ¥50.6 billion (US $226.2 million), and

the company was capitalized at ¥2.7 billion (US $12.1 million). Corporate headquarters are located in Tōkyō.

secondary industries

An industrial sector that comprises manufacturing, mining, and construction including public works. Manufacturing played a vital role in the development of the modern Japanese economy. During the 1880s, manufacturing produced about 10 percent of net national income; in the 1970s it accounted for over 30 percent. Manufacturing suffered great damage during World War II but recovered rapidly; with large-scale investment in equipment, the sector came to be centered on heavy and chemical industries. Particularly between 1955 and 1970, the period of rapid economic growth, Japan's industrial structure changed considerably. This change was reflected in the percentage of the national product contributed by each of the sectors. Production in the PRIMARY INDUSTRIES (agriculture, forestry, and fishing) fell from 24.3 percent in 1955 to 8.4 percent in 1970, while that of the secondary industries rose from 28.5 percent to 37.6 percent, and that of TERTIARY INDUSTRIES (service) from 47.2 percent to 54.3 percent. A similar change took place in the structure of employment: employment in the primary sector declined from 41.1 percent in 1955 to 19.3 percent in 1970; employment in the secondary sector, meanwhile, rose from 23.4 percent to 34.0 percent, and in the tertiary sector from 35.5 percent to 46.6 percent (see also table at PRIMARY INDUSTRIES).

The average economic growth rate between 1951 and 1970 was approximately 14 percent. The manufacturing industries that supported this rapid growth were the chemical, petroleum, steel, and heavy machinery industries. The growth rate among these heavy and chemical industries was considerably higher than that of the secondary industries as a whole. The principal manufacturing industries are foodstuffs, textiles, lumber, chemicals, ceramics, metals, and machinery. In the decade after 1935, the main manufacturing industries were foodstuffs, textiles, and machinery; their composite value added rates were, respectively, 15.1 percent, 21.3 percent, and 21.8 percent. In the decade after 1955, the main manufacturing industry was chemicals, followed by machinery and metals, while the textile industry declined in importance. In 1970, when the period of rapid growth ended, the composite value added rate for the machinery industry registered a remarkable 33.7 percent, while that of the metal and chemical industries was 16 percent. The foodstuff and textile industries, on the other hand, had fallen to 7.8 percent.

The volume of exports and imports of industrial products has also changed dramatically in the approximately 100 years since Japanese industrialization began. During the early years of the Meiji period (1868–1912), industrial products constituted 91 percent of total imports and 58 percent of total exports. By the end of the Meiji period, exports had exceeded imports. With the substitution of domestically produced industrial products, the country's reliance on imports declined steadily until, just prior to the outbreak of World War II, imports of industrial products had fallen to the 40 percent level. After the war, industrial products fell below 30 percent of total imports. See also INDUSTRIAL STRUCTURE. KATŌ Hiroshi

Second United Front

The name for the cooperation between the Chinese Guomindang (Kuomintang) Party and the Chinese Communist Party in the late 1930s that suspended civil war in a common cause against Japanese aggression. So called to distinguish it from an earlier, abortive united front (1924–27).

As Japanese pressure in North China intensified after Japan's takeover of Manchuria in 1931 (see MANCHURIAN INCIDENT), the Communist Party, which had already declared war on Japan in 1932, called for a united front against Japan in the AUGUST FIRST DECLARATION of 1935. During 1936 the communists made concrete proposals for an agreement and had initiated negotiations with the Guomindang by October of that year. The Guomindang under CHIANG KAI-SHEK, however, continued to follow a policy of appeasement toward Japan and of suppression toward the communists despite increasing pressure from patriotic Guomindang members and rising popular demand for a united resistance to Japan. Disagreement with Chiang's Japan policy sparked armed revolts from forces nominally under Guomindang control, in Fusian (Fukien) and in North China, where the XI'AN (SIAN) INCIDENT of December 1936 finally compelled Chiang to accept the principle of a united front with the communists.

The final agreement between the Guomindang and the Communist Party was not concluded until 22 September 1937, two months after the outbreak of the SINO-JAPANESE WAR OF 1937–1945. The United Front brought an end to the civil war, some liberalization of the Guomindang government's internal policies, and an easing of the blockade of the area governed by the communists (see YAN'AN [YENAN] GOVERNMENT). The Communist Party agreed to cease anti-Guomindang propaganda and to rename its soviet government as a regional government within Guomindang jurisdiction and its Red Army as the Nationalist Revolutionary Army, a part of the Guomindang forces. It also agreed to moderate class struggle, granting democratic rights to all citizens within its jurisdiction and halting confiscation of landlords' land, and to affirm the legacy of SUN YAT-SEN.

Despite its significance for the cessation of civil war and for resistance to Japan, the Second United Front was never firm. Tensions rose between the rival parties in 1940, amid rumors of a compromise peace between the Guomindang and Japan, and by January 1941, when Guomindang forces wiped out a section of the communist army (the so-called New Fourth Army Incident), the United Front had collapsed. After Japan's surrender in 1945 and the failure of American attempts at mediation between the Chinese parties, the civil war resumed, ending with the communist victory in 1949.

——Stuart Schram, *Mao Tse-tung* (1967). Lyman P. Van Slyke, *Enemies and Friends: The United Front in Chinese Communist History* (1967).

Sect Shintō

(Kyōha Shintō or Shintō Jūsampa). A designation originally applied to the 13 independent Shintō sects accorded recognition by the Japanese government between 1876 and 1908. Before World War II the term "Sect Shintō" was usually contrasted with "SHRINE SHINTŌ," the latter referring to that aspect of Shintō associated with the public shrines, which all had some degree of official status. The 13 Shintō sects, on the other hand, were regarded by the government as private religious organizations in much the same manner as were the Buddhist and Christian denominations. As independent religious bodies, the Shintō sects, along with Buddhism and Christianity, came under the jurisdiction of the Ministry of Education, whereas the public shrines, which, technically, were not treated as religious institutions, were administered by the Home Ministry.

The 13 traditional Shintō sects are of relatively recent origin, having for the most part been founded in the 18th and 19th centuries by charismatic teachers. Unlike Shrine Shintō, however, each of the traditional Shintō sects generally has its own unique set of scriptures, either composed or revealed by its founder. These sects were not permitted to maintain shrines but rather conducted their religious services at houses of worship *(kyōkaisho)* or lecture halls *(fukyōsho)*. They were not allowed to copy the shrine architectural styles for their places of worship, nor were they permitted to use the *torii,* the traditional gateway that stands at the approach to a shrine.

The 13 traditional Shintō sects may be classified in five groups: (1) Pure Shintō (three sects), which emphasize Shintō themes found either in the KOJIKI (712, Records of Ancient Matters) or in RESTORATION SHINTŌ; (2) Confucian (two sects), which stress Confucian ethical principles; (3) Purification (two sects), which encourage the practice of MISOGI (purification rite) and asceticism; (4) Mountain (three sects), which are organized around the traditional worship of sacred mountains such as FUJI and ONTAKE; and (5) Faith Healing (three sects: KUROZUMIKYŌ, TENRIKYŌ, KONKŌKYŌ), which seek to effect cures through Shintō rituals. When government controls over religion were removed after 1945, the number of Shintō sects proliferated. By 1979 there were 82 sects, with a total of 5.6 million followers, claiming to stand in the lineage of Sect Shintō; in addition there were 48 other sects, with 2 million adherents, that described themselves as belonging to the "New Sect Shintō" (Shin Kyōha Shintō). See also SECT SHINTŌ, ASSOCIATION OF.

Stanley WEINSTEIN

Sect Shintō, Association of

(Kyōha Shintō Rengōkai). One of the five constituent groups that make up the membership of the Nihon Shūkyō Remmei (JAPAN FEDERATION OF RELIGIONS), which was established in 1946. The Kyōha Shintō Rengōkai is basically a liaison organization that represents and speaks on behalf of SECT SHINTŌ. It is supported by 11 Shintō sects, among which the directorship of the association rotates

annually. Of the 13 officially recognized Shintō sects before 1945, the Shinshūkyō, Shintō Taiseiha, and TENRIKYŌ are not currently members. The ŌMOTO is the only Shintō sect not recognized before 1945 to have membership in the association. *Stanley* WEINSTEIN

Securities Exchange Law

(Shōken Torihiki Hō). A law enacted in 1948 for the purpose of protecting investors by ensuring that securities are issued and traded fairly. Modeled after the US Securities Act of 1933 and Securities Exchange Act of 1934, the law regulates both the market in which securities are issued and the market in which they are traded. Under this law, securities are defined narrowly; the only domestic securities covered are stocks, convertible bonds, and unsecured bonds, and there are no provisions to cover such transactions as investment contracts. Foreign government bonds are subject to its disclosure requirements.

The Securities Exchange Law provides that issuers of securities must register with the MINISTRY OF FINANCE before making any public offering. Sales of securities must be accompanied by a prospectus. An obligation to file annual financial disclosure statements is imposed on all issuers of listed securities, certain over-the-counter securities, and publicly offered securities. These types of security are also subject to regulations on tender offers made outside an exchange. Brokers and securities exchanges must be licensed by the government.

When this law was enacted, the Securities Exchange Commission was placed in charge of its execution. This commission was abolished in 1952, however, and at present the minister of finance has the duty of executing the law, with the actual administration being performed by the Securities Bureau of the Ministry of Finance. A person who makes an untrue statement or otherwise commits an unlawful act in connection with the issuance or trading of protected securities is civilly liable. The procedures to be followed when a company issues stock or bonds are regulated by the COMMERCIAL CODE and other laws which fall under the jurisdiction of the minister of justice. *Tatsuta Misao*

Sefuri Mountains

(Sefuri Sanchi). Also called Seburi Mountains. Mountain range in Saga and Fukuoka prefectures, northern Kyūshū, running east to west along the northern edge of the Saga Plain. The range includes numerous low-lying peaks under 1,000 m (3,280 ft). The highest peak is Sefurisan (1,055 m; 3,460 ft).

Segawa Jokō

The name of a succession of important playwrights in the KABUKI theater. Jokō I (1739–94), an *onnagata* (female-impersonator) in the Ōsaka kabuki theater, later became a leading playwright for the Edo (now Tōkyō) stage.

At the height of his career, Jokō II (1757–1833), a pupil of Jokō I, was regarded as second only to the great Tsuruya Namboku IV (1755–1829; see TSURUYA NAMBOKU) in ability. Among his *shosagoto* (dance) pieces, *Kashima odori* (1813, Kashima Dance), *Hyōtan namazu* (1828, Catfish Angling), *Kakubei* (1828), and *Sanja matsuri* (1832, Sanja Festival) are still popular items in today's kabuki repertory.

Jokō III (1806–81) was an apprentice of Tsuruya Namboku V (1796–1852). During his brief role as the favorite dramatist of actor Ichikawa Kodanji IV (1812–66), Jokō III created *Konoshita Soga megumi no masagoji* (Thief Goemon Gets Boiled Alive), *Higashiyama sakura sōshi* (Sakura Sōgo)—both presented in 1851—and *Yo wa nasake ukina no yokogushi* (1853, Carved up Yosa), but after breaking with Kodanji he gradually sank into obscurity.

Both Jokō IV (1857–1938) and Jokō V (1888–1957) wrote for the kabuki theater in the period after the Meiji Restoration (1868).

——Kawatake Shigetoshi, *Kabuki sakusha no kenkyū* (1940). A. C. Scott, *Gen'yadana: a Japanese Kabuki Play* (1953), a translation of a celebrated act from *Yo wa nasake ukina no yokogushi.*

Ted T. Takaya

segregation of Japanese schoolchildren in the United States

Refers to a regulation passed by the San Francisco Board of Education on 11 October 1906 by which children of Japanese descent were to attend special segregated schools. By 1900 there were about 24,000 Japanese immigrants on the American mainland. Most of them lived on the West Coast and made up 1 percent of the population of California. After Japan's success in the Russo-Japanese War of 1904–05, however, Californians became increasingly exclusionist and xenophobic. A strong anti-Japanese movement emerged, led by Mayor James D. Phelan of San Francisco. Claiming that the San Francisco Earthquake of 1906 had resulted in overcrowding in schools and that an existing law gave the school board power to segregate the schools under certain circumstances, the San Francisco Board of Education ordered school children of Japanese descent to attend an Oriental public school. The Japanese government registered an official protest. President Theodore Roosevelt, who considered the act an affront to the Japanese, threatened to sue the board. At the same time he tried to persuade the Japanese government to sign a treaty preventing Japanese from emigrating to the United States. When this move failed, he informed the board that he would not go to court against it, provided that it rescind the order in return for an executive action excluding Japanese laborers from the United States. The board agreed. In 1907 President Roosevelt persuaded the Japanese government not to issue passports to laborers who intended to go to the mainland of the United States. This action, which came to be known as the GENTLEMEN'S AGREEMENT, was formalized the next year.

seibo

The custom of giving year-end gifts, and the gifts themselves, presented as an expression of appreciation for favors received in the past year. The Chinese characters for *seibo* mean "year end." Those in a socially superior position, such as a marriage mediator (*nakōdo*), a family physician, or a teacher of traditional arts such as flower arrangement or tea ceremony, are typical recipients of *seibo*, as well as of midyear CHŪGEN gifts. Gifts are presented by those in inferior positions and are usually considered to be from family to family, or business to business. According to a survey made in 1969, the average number of *seibo* that sample families in Kyōto received was 6.1, although 14 percent did not receive any at all. While most families receive only a handful, some, in the socially superior positions mentioned above, receive a disproportionate number. A considerable portion of the population (30 percent in the above survey) dislikes the custom of *seibo*, probably because it is obligatory, but of all calendrically determined gift-giving occasions, *seibo* is by far the most important. In recent years it has been greatly encouraged by commercialism and payment of the year-end bonus, an amount as much as three to four months' salary, which cannot help but encourage further spending. Traditionally, *seibo* were personally delivered, but today people often will have the stores deliver or send the gifts through the mail, a practice gaining wider acceptance. See also GIFT GIVING.

Harumi BEFU

Seibu Department Stores, Ltd

(Seibu Hyakkaten). Major department store company with its principal store in Ikebukuro, Tōkyō, and nine branch stores in the Kantō (Tōkyō–Yokohama) region. It ranks fourth among Japan's department store chains in sales volume. It is also the leading member of the Seibu distribution group, which includes a total of approximately 100 companies. Its predecessor was the Musashino Department Store, opened in Ikebukuro in 1940 by the Musashino Tetsudō (now the SEIBU RAILWAY CO, LTD). It took its current name in 1949, and in 1956 it established Seibu Store, Ltd (now SEIYŪ STORES, LTD), a chain of supermarkets. It expanded rapidly as the population increased in areas along the Seibu Railway lines; it also invested heavily in tie-ups with provincial department stores. During the 1970s it established new shopping centers with various specialty stores located in a single building in the Kantō and Kinki (Kyōto–Ōsaka) regions through its subsidiary, Parco Co, Ltd. It has six overseas subsidiaries and is affiliated with approximately 45 foreign companies. Other members of its group include such major companies as Seibu Department Stores, Kansai, Ltd, and the Seibu Credit Co, Ltd (formerly Midoriya Department Stores, Ltd). Annual sales for 1981 totaled ¥550 billion (US $2.5 billion), of which clothing accounted for 40 percent, foodstuffs 18 percent, household goods 36 percent, and other merchandise 6 percent; the company was capitalized at ¥2 billion (US $9 million) in the same year. Corporate headquarters are located in Tōkyō.

Seibu Railway Co, Ltd

(Seibu Tetsudō). Private railway company based in the northwestern part of the Tōkyō metropolitan area and engaged in transportation, tourism, real estate, and leisure enterprises. It is the nucleus of the Seibu Railway group; together with the Seibu distribution group (centered on SEIBU DEPARTMENT STORES, LTD, and the supermarket chain SEIYŪ STORES, LTD) and approximately 100 other companies, it constitutes the Seibu group. The predecessor of Seibu Railway was the Musashino Tetsudō, a railway company established in 1912, which started operations in 1915 on a 43.8-kilometer (27.2 mi) route between Ikebukuro and Hannō using steam locomotives. It gradually developed by electrifying its lines, laying double tracks, extending its routes, and absorbing other railway firms, and took on its current name in 1946. After World War II it recovered quickly from wartime destruction, and in response to the growth in population within its service area, it constructed new lines, laid more double tracks, and increased its quantity of rolling stock. In 1982 the company had two trunk lines and 10 branch lines totaling 178.2 kilometers (110.6 mi) in length, and transported an average of approximately 1,520,000 passengers daily. Total sales for the fiscal year ending in March 1982 were ¥92.2 billion (US $383 million), of which railway operations accounted for 51 percent, tourism 27 percent, and real estate 22 percent; the company was capitalized at ¥14.4 billion (US $59.8 million) in the same year. Corporate headquarters are located in Tōkyō.

Seichō no le

(House of Growth). A contemporary religious sect founded in Kōbe in 1930 by TANIGUCHI MASAHARU, when he first began publishing the journal, *Seichō no ie*, which gave counsel to people who suffered from ill health and other problems. In 1934 he moved the headquarters of the sect to Tōkyō and began disseminating his teachings throughout the country. Taniguchi emphasized what he called man's filial relationship with the divine through each individual's effort to realize "the truth of life." One who returns to this truth, he maintained, will be free of misfortunes. He claimed to have integrated in his teachings the doctrines of Shintō, Buddhism, Christianity, and other religions. His teachings supported emperor worship and the militarist regime which was heading the nation toward World War II, and the group grew rapidly. The sect upholds the Shintō-oriented spirituality of the pre–World War II period. It claimed about 3 million adherents in 1977. See also NEW RELIGIONS.

Kenneth J. DALE

Seidan

(Discourses on Government). A four-volume work by the Confucian scholar OGYŪ SORAI. Completed sometime between 1716 and 1728, it was originally written as a memorial to the shōgun TOKUGAWA YOSHIMUNE. Sorai discusses in detail the political and economic problems facing the Tokugawa shogunate and recommends, among other things, that *samurai* be relocated to the countryside in order to alleviate their financial hardship, that men of talent be promoted, and that the administrative structure of the shogunate be reorganized.

seidō

(literally, "western hall"). Status title of monks in Zen monasteries. *Seidō* originally referred to the western hall of a monastery or to the monks who lived there. Gradually it came to designate a monk who, upon retirement from the abbacy of one monastery, took up residence in the western hall of another. (The title *tōdō*, by contrast, designated an abbot who retired to the eastern hall of his own monastery.) In the early part of the Muromachi period (1333–1568), when the shogunate strictly ranked all Zen establishments, *seidō* came to designate a monk who had served as abbot in any of about 200 monasteries of the third rank or above; it was from this class of monks that the abbots of the 10 highest-ranking Zen monasteries (GOZAN) were chosen. During the Edo period (1600–1868) the Gozan system decayed, and the rank of *seidō* became simply a mark of respect. At present it refers to a senior monk who supervises novices learning monastic discipline in preparation for holy orders.

seii tai shōgun → shōgun

seiji shōsetsu

("political novel"). A term that refers specifically to a rather large, heterogeneous group of novels written mainly during the 1880s in connection with the FREEDOM AND PEOPLE'S RIGHTS MOVEMENT (Jiyū Minken Undō).

Seiji Shōsetsu and the Rehabilitation of the Novel —— During the first years of the Meiji period (1868–1912), fiction had been thought of as at best irrelevant and at worst actually detrimental to the march of progress, but from the late 1870s, fiction in the tradition of the Edo period (1600–1868) began to be reinstated, and the works of European novelists (Jules Verne and Edward Bulwer-Lytton) appeared in translation for the first time.

It was against this background that certain journalists belonging to the democratic movement first tried their hand at writing fiction to get across to uneducated people the basic ideas of "freedom" and "people's rights." For their models they turned to the Edo period and to Chinese popular fiction; sometimes they translated or adapted European novels such as those of Alexandre Dumas père. A number of them, like Komuro Angaidō (1852–85), Miyazaki Muryū (1853–89), and Sakazaki Shiran (1853–1913), who had originally been political activists, became rather popular authors; their subject matter ranged from the Restoration movement at the end of the Edo period to the French Revolution and the Russian "nihilists."

A more sophisticated use of politically oriented fiction can be observed in YANO RYŪKEI (1850–1931), who in 1883–84 published his *Keikoku bidan* (A Noble Tale of Statesmanship). This rather learned book, set in ancient Greece and written in a ponderous style, was directed at the educated reader. It seemed, therefore, that fiction was beginning to be socially acceptable.

Seiji Shōsetsu and the New Literature —— To those new writers who, like TSUBOUCHI SHŌYŌ (1859–1935), were striving, from about 1885 onwards, to make a completely fresh start, the *seiji shōsetsu* presented itself as just another offshoot of a fundamentally unchanged literary tradition. They, however, wanted the novel to serve only its own aims, which should be confined to the description of human emotions and manners. These convictions were doubtless colored by the defeat of the radical wing of the people's rights movement in 1884 and 1885. It was in this situation that literary realism came to be associated with political gradualism and even complete withdrawal into private life.

Some writers tried to adjust to this situation. SUEHIRO TETCHŌ (1849–96) in his *Setchūbai* (1886, Plum Blossoms in the Snow) sought to combine the political message with elements of the new concept, the novel of manners. Others, like TŌKAI SANSHI (1852–1922) remained quite unaffected by literary developments. From 1885 onwards he published his voluminous *Kajin no kigū* (1885–97, Chance Meetings with Beautiful Women), an imaginative romance about the battles being fought for freedom in contemporary Asia, Africa, and Europe.

The *seiji shōsetsu* reached the height of its popularity in the late 1880s (now following established European precedents such as the novels of Disraeli), although its historical importance was already in decline. During the 1890s it gradually merged with the novel of manners, set in the world of politicians, and the popular adventure novel, with its nationalistic overtones.

The Significance of Seiji Shōsetsu —— In general, the *seiji shōsetsu* mirrored the basic weakness of the people's rights movement it had served: an inability to reconcile ambitious concepts of state and nation with the actual subtleties of human thought and feeling. Accordingly, there was no future for it in modern literature, whose first commandment read: individuality. However, by showing that fiction could be employed not merely to entertain but to disseminate new ideas capable of influencing the emerging middle class, the *seiji shōsetsu* took a significant step toward establishing the novel at the center of modern literature.

It might also be added that the Japanese *seiji shōsetsu* exercised some influence on the Chinese novel—as in the case of the writings of LIANG QICHAO (Liang Ch'i-ch'ao; 1873–1929)—which is the first instance ever of Japanese influence on Chinese literature.

📖 ——Collections of *seiji shōsetsu*: *Meiji seiji shōsetsu shū*, vols 5 and 6 of *Meiji bungaku zenshū* (Chikuma Shobō, 1966, 1967). *Meiji seiji shōsetsu shū*, vol 2 of *Nihon kindai bungaku taikei* (Kadokawa Shoten, 1974), contains a bibliography. Works on *seiji shōsetsu*: Horace Z. Feldman, "The Meiji Political Novel: A Brief Survey," *Far Eastern Quarterly* 9.3 (May 1950). Iwamoto Yoshio, "Suehiro Tetchō—A Meiji Political Novelist," in E. Skrzypczak, ed, *Japan's Modern Century* (1968). Yanagida Izumi, *Seiji shōsetsu kenkyū*, 3 vols (new edition, 1967–68).
Wolfgang SCHAMONI

Seikadō Bunko

(Seikadō Library). A major repository of East Asian culture, containing nearly 200,000 volumes and some 5,000 art objects. Located in Setagaya Ward, Tōkyō, this private collection was founded in 1892 by Iwasaki Yanosuke (1851–1908), a son of the founder of the MITSUBISHI financial combine. Since Yanosuke's death it has been supported by successive generations of the Iwasaki family. At present it is a private foundation; its invaluable book collection is open to scholars and selections of its priceless art collection are on display three times a year.

Concerned about the Westernization of East Asian culture and the reported loss of its cultural heritage to foreign collectors, Iwasaki Yanosuke sought with the help of his teacher SHIGENO YASUTSUGU to preserve in Japan as many East Asian cultural objects as possible. Major progress was made in 1907 with his acquisition of 45,000 volumes, about 200 of them printed in the Chinese Song (Sung) dynasty (960–1279), from a son of the noted bibliophile Lu Xinyuan (Lu Hsin-yüan; 1834–94). In 1924 the collection was moved to its present site, an imposing Victorian edifice on top of a forested hillside; MOROHASHI TETSUJI became its director and commenced the compilation of its book catalog. The collection and building survived World War II unscathed. In 1948, after the death of Yanosuke's son IWASAKI KOYATA, the library was made an affiliate of the NATIONAL DIET LIBRARY, along with the TŌYŌ BUNKO (Oriental Library). In 1970 the library reverted to its private status, and in 1977 a museum was set up in an adjoining building.
Theodore F. WELCH

Seikanron

The argument (*ron*) over whether Japan should "conquer Korea" (*seikan*), an issue that divided, indeed split asunder, the Japanese government in 1873. The new Meiji government, shortly after its establishment in 1868, sought to notify Korea officially of the "restoration" (*ishin*) of the emperor to power in Japan and to reorganize relations with Korea generally. Korea, however, had long been a Confucian dependent state of China and regarded the Japanese overture as an attempt by Japan to arrogate China's rank in the Confucian hierarchy. Accordingly, the Koreans responded negatively and, the Japanese thought, insultingly. Negotiations at Pusan between Korean local officials, who had since the early part of the Edo period (1600–1868) dealt with Japanese traders from the island of Tsushima, and Japanese government representatives, first under the *daimyō* of Tsushima and then under Yoshioka Kōki, a foreign ministry official, proved fruitless, and the idea of "punishing" Korea began to be discussed in Japan. However, many key members of the Meiji government were absent from Japan on the IWAKURA MISSION to Western countries (1871–73), and it had been agreed that no large projects would be undertaken until their return.

Meanwhile, the caretaker government at home, which included SAIGŌ TAKAMORI, a leading *samurai* from the former domain of Satsuma (now Kagoshima Prefecture), ITAGAKI TAISUKE, and Foreign Minister SOEJIMA TANEOMI, decided to pursue the Korean issue independently. Soejima went to Beijing (Peking) in March 1873 and came away with the impression that China claimed no authority and had no interest "concerning war or peace for Korea." In August Saigō obtained approval from the Grand Council of State (Dajōkan) to go to Korea and provoke war (and thus force the Koreans to establish relations with Japan), but when the president of the council, SANJŌ SANETOMI, who was somewhat ambivalent on the matter, sought the young Emperor Meiji's final approval, he brought back to the council the imperial "decision" that the emperor wished to be informed of Saigō's appointment "after the return of Iwakura."

IWAKURA TOMOMI returned in September, well informed on international politics and sensitive to the weakness of Japan. When he learned of Saigō's plans, he became determined to counter them. He immediately moved to have ŌKUBO TOSHIMICHI, Saigō's fellow native of Satsuma, who had been a member of the mission to the West and had become equally cautious about Japan's position, appointed to the Grand Council of State. In subsequent meetings during October he maneuvered Ōkubo into taking the lead in the argument against Saigō, which, in a setting of samurai honor, became so intense that Sanjō suffered a breakdown. Iwakura, who as a court noble ranked next to Sanjō, then assumed the council presidency. Although threatened with death by Kirino Toshiaki (1838–77), a supporter of Saigō, he announced that he would not permit the emperor to approve the appointment of Saigō to Korea and accepted the resignations of all the prowar councillors.

Saigō left Tōkyō in a fury and returned to Satsuma. As prowar and other samurai dissidents gathered there, he gradually emerged as the leader of the antigovernment movement that was to culminate in the SATSUMA REBELLION of 1877. The rebellion was crushed by the government's new conscript army, which was being developed by YAMAGATA ARITOMO, and Saigō committed suicide. A year later Ōkubo was assassinated in Tōkyō by followers of Saigō. But Iwakura, his protégé ITŌ HIROBUMI, and others of the "antiwar" faction of 1873 continued to guide the destinies of the Meiji state and to chart its course toward modernization.

At the height of the great October quarrel about conquering Korea, Ōkubo had laid down his "Reasons for Opposing the Korean Expedition." These included: the need to establish the new government on a firm base, the need to avoid enormous expense and foreign loans, the need to stimulate industries and foreign trade in order to avoid giving Russia or Britain an excuse to interfere in Japan's foreign affairs, and the need to give first priority to revising Japan's Unequal Treaties (see UNEQUAL TREATIES, REVISION OF). "The Korean business would come after that."

There have been various interpretations of the Seikanron, the prevalent one during the World War II era being that it was the first bold advocacy of Japanese aggression and that even the "peace advocates" who blocked it were only concerned with the timing of the conquest of Korea and merely preferred a later date. Although the remarks of some of the peace advocates, such as KIDO TAKAYOSHI, Yamagata Aritomo, and even Ōkubo himself, would seem to support this idea, it should be pointed out that the gulf between them and Saigō was really very wide. In contrast to Saigō and the war party, they and their colleagues who remained in the government had become thoroughly impressed with Japan's smallness in the wider world of international politics and were determined to conduct foreign policy in a cautious and pragmatic, rather than an adventurous, way.

🔳——Hilary Conroy, *The Japanese Seizure of Korea, 1868–1910* (1960). Key-Hiuk Kim, *The Last Phase of the East Asian World Order: Korea, Japan, and the Chinese Empire, 1860–1882* (1980). Marlene Mayo, "The Korean Crisis of 1873 and Early Meiji Foreign Policy," *Journal of Asian Studies* 31.4 (1972). Tabohashi Kiyoshi, *Kindai Nissen kankei no kenkyū*, 2 vols (1940).   Hilary CONROY

Seikatsu Tsuzurikata Undō

(literally, "Life Composition Movement"). An educational movement for free, realistic self-expression in writing, conducted in primary schools during the early part of the Shōwa period (1926–). The movement also sought to use the writing of compositions to guide the development of perception, thinking, and feeling and to provide students with a good understanding of reality.

From the beginning of the Meiji period (1868–1912), education in Japan was standardized under the direction of the state. *Tsuzurikata* (composition) was used for ideological indoctrination and was restricted to certain sentence patterns. In the second decade of the 20th century, ASHIDA ENOSUKE, a primary school teacher, began to promote a method of teaching composition that placed more emphasis on free expression by the students. In 1918, the writer SUZUKI MIEKICHI, through his children's literary magazine *Akai tori* (Red Bird), began to advocate the principle, "Ari no mama ni kaku" (To write about things as they are), encouraging free expression. His magazine also published children's compositions.

The Seikatsu Tsuzurikata Undō developed from these beginnings in the early part of the Shōwa period. It was a time of great suffering as a consequence of the financial panic of 1929 and students were encouraged to write realistic accounts of their lives. The 1929 publication of *Tsuzurikata seikatsu*, edited by the popular educator Sasaoka Tadayoshi (1897–1937), helped to spread the movement throughout the nation. This teaching method was practiced principally by young teachers in rural primary schools, and the movement reached its peak in 1934. With the beginning of World War II in 1941, the movement was suppressed by state authorities who considered it leftist. In the wartime KOKUMIN GAKKŌ (people's schools), composition was once more used for inculcating nationalism, but the democratization of education after the war revived the spirit of the movement.   SUGIYAMA Akio

Seiken igen

(Last Words of Loyalists). A two-volume work on the concept of loyalty and duty by the Confucian scholar ASAMI KEISAI (1652–1712). The work is divided into eight chapters, each containing a short biography and pertinent sayings and writings of eight exemplars of loyalty from Chinese history, for example, Qu Yuan (Ch'ü Yüan), Tao Qian (T'ao Ch'ien), and Zhu Geliang (Chu Ko-liang). *Seiken igen* had a great influence on antishogunate thinkers and activists of the latter part of the Edo period (1600–1868). Its date of completion is unknown, but *Seiken igen kōgi*, a collection of lectures by Asami on the *Seiken igen*, is dated Genroku 2 (1689).

Seikōkai

(Anglican-Episcopal Church). The foundations of this church in Japan were laid by missionaries from the Protestant Episcopal Church in the United States (from 1859), the Church Missionary Society of England (from 1869), and the Society for the Propagation of the Gospel of England (from 1873). These three groups were united in 1887 to form the Nihon Seikōkai; the Missionary Society of the Church of England in Canada joined the organization in 1888. The church consists of 10 dioceses with 275 churches and claimed 55,000 members in 1978. It runs Rikkyō (St. Paul's) University in Tōkyō and Momoyama Gakuin University in Ōsaka, among others, as well as hospitals and other institutions.

🔳——Charles W. Iglehart, *A Century of Protestant Christianity in Japan* (1959).
                                                Kenneth J. DALE

Seikyōsha

(Society for Political Education). Cultural and political association established in 1888; it opposed the government's acceptance of the Unequal Treaties imposed by the Western powers and its advocacy of the Westernization of Japanese culture (see UNEQUAL TREATIES, REVISION OF). The founders, including SUGIURA SHIGETAKE, MIYAKE SETSUREI, and SHIGA SHIGETAKA, were mostly graduates of the Sapporo Agricultural College (now part of Hokkaidō University) and Tōkyō University. NAITŌ KONAN and TAOKA REIUN later joined the association. In their magazine, NIHONJIN, these early members advocated not a narrow nationalism but a pluralistic world culture in which Japanese culture would play an active role. However, they failed to reach a common understanding of Japanese culture. The Seikyōsha was reorganized in 1923, and Miyake withdrew from active management; under the leadership of Ioki Ryōzō (1870–1937) it espoused a militaristic PAN-ASIANISM consonant with Japan's nationalism. It was dissolved in February 1945.

🔳——Kenneth B. Pyle, *The New Generation in Meiji Japan* (1969).

Seikyō yōroku

(Essentials of the Sacred Teachings). Work by YAMAGA SOKŌ (1622–85), the Confucian scholar and founder of the Yamaga school of military science. Excerpted from *Yamaga gorui*, a collection of lectures set down by his disciples, the *Seikyō yōroku* was published in 1665. Sokō criticizes the contending schools of Confucianism, particularly the officially supported Zhu Xi (Chu Hsi) school of Neo-Confucianism (SHUSHIGAKU), as being too theoretical and impractical; he then explains his own position, the KOGAKU school, which called for a return to the *Analects* and the *Mencius* to discover Confucian truths. The work immediately earned the opprobrium of the shogunate, and Sokō was banished temporarily from Edo (now Tōkyō) to Akō (Hyōgo Prefecture).

Seimikyoku

Two government institutes established in Ōsaka and Kyōto during the early years of the Meiji period (1868–1912) as educational and research facilities in the natural sciences. The word *seimi* is a phonetic rendering of *chemie*, the Dutch word for chemistry. The Ōsaka Seimikyoku, established in 1868, was considered the most advanced facility for Western scientific learning in the Kyōto–Ōsaka–Kōbe area. The Dutch chemist K. W. Gratama (1831–88) taught there for a time. It later developed into the Third Higher School. The Kyōto Seimikyoku was founded in 1870 with the WESTERN LEARNING scholar Akashi Hiroakira (1839–1910) as director. The German scholar Gottfried WAGENER also lectured there. It closed in

1881. The Seimikyoku grew out of the emphasis on scientific education (particularly chemistry) existing at the end of Tokugawa shogunal rule. The bureaus contributed to scientific and technological education as well as to the development of industry during the early years of the Meiji period. *Etō Kyōji*

Seinan Sensō → Satsuma Rebellion

seinen gakkō

(youth schools). Secondary educational facilities for working boys and girls that were operated between 1935 and the educational reforms of 1947. Classes were conducted at night for young people who did not attend either middle or high school, concentrating on vocational and military training. All students were taught Japanese history and ethics (SHŪSHIN); in addition, boys were given military training, and girls were taught home economics. In 1939, all boys between the ages of 12 and 19 who were not enrolled in another educational facility were required to attend the youth schools. Many private institutions were also established, and by 1945 there were 15,000 youth schools with a total enrollment of 2.6 million students. *KURAUCHI Shirō*

Seiryōki

Chronicle of the life of Doi Kiyoyoshi (Doi Seiryō; 1546–1629), lord of Ōmori Castle in Iyo Province (now Ehime Prefecture). It is ascribed to Doi Mizunari and is thought to have been completed in the Kan'ei (1624–43) or the Empō (1673–81) era. Various editions contain 30, 33, or 36 volumes *(kan)*. Belonging to the genre known as GUNKI MONOGATARI (military tales), the work focuses on Kiyoyoshi's military exploits. The seventh volume, however, consists of questions and answers between Kiyoyoshi and his retainer Matsuura Sōan on agricultural policy; it sheds considerable light on the agricultural technology of the time and is generally considered the earliest Japanese treatise on the subject.

seishō

(literally, "political merchants"). Merchants and financiers who made use of their close connections with the early Meiji government to found commercial empires. Some, such as the MITSUI and SUMITOMO families, had already built up their financial base during the Edo period (1600–1868); they consolidated their position after the Meiji Restoration of 1868 by extending financial support to the new government. Others, such as IWASAKI YATARŌ, YASUDA ZENJIRŌ, and ASANO SŌICHIRŌ, started from modest beginnings, but took advantage of the upheaval accompanying the Restoration to realize enormous profits. Still others, like SHIBUSAWA EIICHI and GODAI TOMOATSU, used their government positions to increase their fortunes. In all cases, however, they received government patronage, either through grants of monopolies, direct subsidies, easy financial terms, or purchase of government enterprises at nominal prices. Mitsui and MITSUBISHI were particularly skillful in forming alliances with political parties from the late Meiji period on. It was common knowledge that Mitsui contributed regularly to the political party RIKKEN SEIYŪKAI and that Mitsubishi gave financial backing to a rival party, the RIKKEN MINSEITŌ.

Sei Shōnagon (fl late 10th century)

One of the best known of the brilliant women writers of the Heian period (794–1185); author of *Makura no sōshi* (The Pillow Book).

Two superlative prose works distinguish Japanese literature of the period around the year 1000. One is *Genji monogatari* (see TALE OF GENJI), the best known and undoubtedly the greatest of the early court novels, a masterpiece whose thematic power, psychological insight, and stylistic refinement have brought it admiration not only in Japan but throughout the world. The other is *Makura no sōshi*, a much different and altogether less ambitious work, a slender volume of short eye-witness narratives, casual essays, impressions, reflections, lists, and imagined scenes. The unstructured informality of such a book has had an enduring appeal to Japanese authors and readers. *Makura no sōshi* and similar works constitute a genre known as ZUIHITSU, a term meaning "to follow the brush," implying a total absence of premeditated direction. As the first *zuihitsu*, *Makura no sōshi* occupies an important position in Japanese literary history.

The Author —— Like the *Tale of Genji*, and indeed like much of the best literature of the Heian period, *The Pillow Book* was written by a woman. Sei Shōnagon is the name by which she is known, but this is merely the nickname given her during her service at the imperial court in the 990s. She was a Kiyohara, and Sei is the Sino-Japanese reading of the first character used in writing this family name. Shōnagon means "lesser counselor," a typical court-lady's cognomen, but no one knows why she was called that and not something else. Her father was Motosuke (908–990), a noted scholar and poet of some repute. As one of the Five Gentlemen of the Pear Chamber (Nashitsubo no Gonin), Motosuke had participated in the compilation of the second imperial WAKA (classical poetry) anthology, the *Gosenshū*, in 951. Shōnagon's great-grandfather Fukayabu was also a poet of distinction. Her mother is unknown, but on the paternal side at least, Shōnagon came of a literary and scholarly lineage.

As with most women writers of the period, it is only the middle part of Sei Shōnagon's life about which much is known. She emerges with startling brilliance in her own writings, but she does not deal with her childhood, and her late years are recorded more in legend than in fact. No one knows when she was born, or when or under what circumstances she died. Even in her maturity the course of her career comes across more in scintillating flashes than in plain connected narrative. In one degree or another the same might be said of her contemporaries the poet IZUMI SHIKIBU and the novelist MURASAKI SHIKIBU: these creative spirits blazed like meteors across the void, and no one knows for sure where or when they fell to rest. The pattern speaks both of the nature of genius and of the society which cherished it but did not sufficiently regard the women who were its vessels to record their births and deaths.

Speculation centers on 965 as the year of Sei Shōnagon's birth. At some time in the early 990s she became a lady-in-waiting at the court of Sadako (976–1001; see FUJIWARA NO TEISHI), the consort of the young emperor ICHIJŌ (980–1011; r 986–1011). This may have been as early as 990 or as late as 993. She presumably remained in service until Sadako's death, and although her subsequent fate is obscure, she was known to Murasaki Shikibu, the author of the *Tale of Genji*, who writes of her in her own diary of 1008–1010 in such a way as to lead one to believe that Shōnagon was still a well-known character at court. Murasaki, who was not known for her generosity to female rivals such as Izumi Shikibu and Sei Shōnagon, has the following to say of Sei Shōnagon:

> Sei Shōnagon: the very picture of conceit and arrogance. When one looks carefully at the compositions in Chinese script which she pretentiously scatters about, their inadequacies are legion. Anyone who takes such pleasure in making herself different from others will inevitably fall in their regard, and her fortunes will go from bad to worse. Once addicted to a life of glamor she will proceed to give displays of her fine feelings even on the dreariest and most ridiculous occasions, and in her efforts not to miss out on anything exciting she will as a matter of course become notorious for her triviality. What good can come to such an inanity in the end?

These disparaging remarks are the earliest and only contemporary allusion to Shōnagon's literary activities, other than the comments we find in *The Pillow Book* itself.

The Work —— Those activities have a spontaneous joyousness about them that, whatever Murasaki may have thought, makes *The Pillow Book* a pleasure to read. One feels that Sei Shōnagon was a born writer, an irrepressible spirit who spontaneously and effortlessly recorded her impressions of the world about her and jotted down whatever stray thoughts passed through her mind. The list— of things liked or disliked, or simply of interesting names, or natural phenomena such as various types of precipitation, or birds, or mountains—is one of the basic and recurrent motifs of her thought, and the noun clause, the unfinished sentence, a typical mode of expression. Her book begins with a passage on the four seasons, the time of day most appropriate to each, and a few selected images. In the process she paints a series of deft vignettes, capturing the mood of each scene and season in a manner which has been much admired and practiced in Japanese literature over the centuries.

It has been theorized, and is plausible, that Sei Shōnagon began her book by recording the categories of things in which she happened to take a passing interest. The more extended accounts of events she participated in or witnessed, which make up the largest part of the text, could have been the next stage in her writing, after she had become accustomed to making frequent entries. Often a category leads directly into an anecdote. Internal evidence indicates that some of these anecdotes were written after the lapse of at least a few years. The book also retells stories of a traditional nature that have nothing to do with the author. A fourth type of content in *The Pillow Book* is composed of what are apparently imagined scenes such as a lover writing his next-morning letter to his mistress, or a householder raising a fuss about late-night visitors. It is these passages which are the most intriguing of all, hinting as they do at an interest on the part of the author in experimenting with her own fiction, and it is tempting to speculate that they may have been the last stratum of *The Pillow Book* to develop. There are four textual lineages of *Pillow Book* manuscripts, two of which are described as *zassanteki* or "miscellaneous," and two as *ruisanteki* or "classified." The classified texts segregate the various types of entries, but in the miscellaneous texts, on which the standard modern editions are based, all four strata are intermingled, so that the reader is obliged to skip nimbly about among lists of Sei Shōnagon's pet peeves, scenes of court life, and flights of her creative imagination.

At the end of those texts of *Makura no sōshi* which follow the miscellaneous arrangement can be found Shōnagon's explanation of how she started to write, and a hint as to the meaning of the title by which her book is known. One day in 994 Empress Sadako's brother, FUJIWARA NO KORECHIKA (973–1010), brought to court a large supply of paper. The empress asked her ladies what she should do with it, and Shōnagon replied that it would be just right for a "pillow" (*makura ni koso wa haberame*). Readers have long speculated over what precisely Shōnagon meant by this term, but it seems quite plausible that she had in mind just the sort of notebook for jottings that *The Pillow Book* actually is. She may also have been alluding to a line by the Tang (T'ang) poet Bo Juyi (Po Chü-i, 772–846), a favorite in Heian Japan, in which he described himself as snoozing through an autumn day, his head pillowed on a book. Shōnagon goes on to tell how a gentleman visitor discovered part of her manuscript lying on a mat beside her, made off with it, and began passing it around the court. She assures us that she was most upset about the accidental notoriety.

The Author's Personality —— *The Pillow Book* reveals the tastes and prejudices of a lady who was aristocratic to her fingertips, and the picture the author gives of her own vivacious personality is one of the major attractions of the book. To her the royalty she serves, and especially the empress Sadako, are above reproach. She constantly emphasizes how awed and thrilled she feels to be allowed to bask in their presence. By the same token she is merciless in her ridicule of those whom she considers her inferiors, especially if they exhibit an eccentricity which offends or amuses her in any way. Taira no Narimasa, the hapless steward whose gates were too narrow for Shōnagon's carriage, is one such butt of her humor. Another is Fujiwara no Nobutsune, a braggart whose deplorable calligraphy earned him the author's courtly scorn. Takashina no Akinobu is also raked over the coals for his countrified ways, and Minamoto no Masahiro is treated as a complete buffoon. Her sharp eye notices and her sensibilities are revolted by the uncouth habits of carpenters and mendicant nuns, but she appears at her most heartless when she laughs at an illiterate old man whose house has burned down. On the other hand, she tells a touching if embellished story about a pet dog named Okinamaro who was beaten and driven from the palace for chasing the emperor's cat. The account is both affecting and amusing. Shōnagon's natural bent is to be amused, and her anecdotes sparkle always on the verge of laughter. The laughter while often unkind is frequently directed at herself. She shows herself aware of her own foibles and shortcomings, temperamental and physical, and her honesty in this regard helps make palatable her satire on the men and women around her. She confesses that she is no beauty and lets us see the frivolous, opinionated, and aggressively competitive sides of her character. This competitiveness is displayed particularly toward the men of her courtly world. Empress Sadako and other imperial ladies were her idols, and she gives us lustrous descriptions of their splendor and charm, but the women who were her colleagues at court seem to have engaged her interest less than the men. She cultivated the reputation of a wit, and male recognition was the warranty of her success. Her knowledge of the Chinese classics, a male domain, seems to have been a particular point of pride. Her relations with courtiers such as Fujiwara no Tadanobu (967–1035) and FUJIWARA NO YUKINARI (972–1027) combined intellectual and social camaraderie with a tingle of sexual excitement that provides a certain breathlessness to her anecdotes. To stump such men with a literary allusion was her greatest triumph, and to tease and banter with them her daily pleasure. She gives an attractive picture of a woman thoroughly at ease among men.

The world of Sei Shōnagon, that is, the world of the Heian court, was one that prized the art of love. Love was a yearning expressed in poetry, and the amatory literature of the period relies heavily on implication, convention, and metaphor. The classical love tradition is not only delicate and indirect but basically tragic: love affairs end unhappily in Heian poetry and fiction. Sei Shōnagon, however, was a comic artist, and her vision of love is realistic and satirical. Besides, she was a woman of the court, where opportunities for female autonomy and an adventurous amorality were greatest. The game of love in its lighter ranges went on before her eyes. Some of her best passages depict lovers' trysts and partings. She tells of the soft, insistent nocturnal tapping of one finger on a partition somewhere in the sleeping quarters of the palace. She shows us a man who has spent a night of love in one lady's cubicle stopping by another's to chaff with her (she too has just said goodbye to her lover and is still lying in bed) on his way back to his room. She gives a sketch of a shivering lady who has imprudently quarreled herself out of a warm bed on a cold night. And she warns that departing lovers make a poor impression when they don their trousers and buckle their belts in too businesslike a fashion. Wary of the standard ploys, skeptical of motivation, she declines to be impressed by an inattentive lover who struggles through a downpour to his ill-chosen tryst. Above all, Shōnagon wants it to be known that she is nobody's fool.

Private Life and Career —— The author is curiously offhand and laconic about her own love life. It seems likely that she had a liaison with Fujiwara no Tadanobu and perhaps had at one time been married to Tachibana no Norimitsu (b 965). That Norimitsu and she had a special relationship is indicated by the fact that they were referred to at court as "elder brother" and "younger sister"; on the other hand, she treats him as a bit of a fool and says that they parted on bad terms. Nevertheless, there is a tradition that she was the mother of his son Norinaga (982–1034). Shōnagon's married life with Norimitsu, if she had one, must have taken place before she entered court service, and it is conjectured that its failure may have been one reason for the latter. There is also a tradition that she later married Fujiwara no Muneyo, and that she had a daughter by him called Koma no Myōbu. Still another man mentioned as a possible husband or lover is Fujiwara no Sanekata (d 998). All these men were minor court officials and provincial governors.

Marriage institutions among the Heian aristocracy were casual to a degree, especially as regards divorce, and *Makura no sōshi* in any case is by no means an autobiography. As far as we can judge from her writings, Shōnagon's interests centered on her career at court, and her domestic arrangements were of secondary concern. Empress Sadako died in childbirth early in 1001. By that time her court was already in eclipse, the center of power and literary activity having shifted to the entourage of Sadako's cousin and rival Akiko (988–1074; Shōshi), the daughter of her uncle FUJIWARA NO MICHINAGA (966–1028). Sadako's father Michitaka, Michinaga's elder brother, died in 995, and Michinaga soon maneuvered Sadako's brother Korechika out of the succession to the Fujiwara regency which dominated Heian politics. Very little of this is apparent from *The Pillow Book*. Like other women writers of the time, Shōnagon refers only obliquely to male power struggles. But by 1001 Shōnagon had certainly lost her patron, and one cannot help wondering about her subsequent career. As mentioned above, Murasaki Shikibu, who served in Akiko's court, discusses Sei Shōnagon in her diary of 1008–1010, and a few entries in *The Pillow Book* date from after Sadako's death. It has been suggested that Shōnagon may have stayed on to care for Sadako's daughter Shūshi (997–1049), or even that she may have entered Akiko's service. Tradition has it that she ended her days old and impoverished, thus bearing out the implications of Murasaki's sour prediction. But similar legends surround the latter days of other famous women such as the 9th-century poetess ONO NO KOMACHI, and it seems safe to discern here the hand of the moralistic storyteller. The only Shōnagon we can know is the one who painted so brightly the splendors of her small world, and when she is no longer part of that world she ceases to exist.

Shōnagon's Literary Significance —— Sei Shōnagon's contribution to Japanese literature is unique. It should be mentioned that in addition to *The Pillow Book* she left a small collection of her poems, the *Sei Shōnagon shū*. As for *Makura no sōshi*, it established a new literary genre (*zuihitsu*). In addition, it is a work of considerable historical value in that it gives a detailed account of events and customs at the Heian court. But more important, it provided a vehicle for the revelation of a brilliant author's vivacious personality and style. Opinionated and abrasive she certainly was, but at the same time possessed of a rare sensitivity to the colors of the passing scene, and of a talent for rendering her impressions with sharp economy. She tosses off in passing a few lines on the sheer beauty of icicles gleaming in the moonlight, or the innocent charm of a child eating strawberries, and the images stick in the mind. Her views of the world, like her commentaries on life, are quick, direct, and unpremeditated. She was an original, an author whose unquenchable verve created its own unstructured expression and who shines with unapologetic cheerfulness in a dominantly sad and wistful tradition.

■ ——Works by Sei Shōnagon: Ikeda Kikan and Kishigami Shinji, ed, *Makura no sōshi*, in *Nihon koten bungaku taikei*, vol 19 (Iwanami Shoten, 1958). *Makura no sōshi*, tr Arthur Waley as *The Pillow-Book of Sei Shōnagon* (1928). *Makura no sōshi*, tr André Beaujard as *Les notes de chevet de Séi Shōnagon, Dame d'Honneur au Palais de Kyōto* (1934). *Makura no sōshi*, tr Ivan Morris as *The Pillow-Book of Sei Shōnagon*, 2 vols (1967). Matsuo Satoshi and Nagai Kazuko, ed, *Makura no sōshi*, in *Nihon koten bungaku zenshū*, vol 11 (Shōgakukan, 1974). Tanaka Jūtarō, ed, *Makura no sōshi*, 4 vols, in *Nihon koten hyōshaku zenchūshaku sōsho* (Kadokawa Shoten, 1972–). Works about Sei Shōnagon: André Beaujard, *Séi Shōnagon, son temps et son oeuvre* (1934). Ikeda Kikan, ed, *Zenkō makura no sōshi* (1956). Kaneko Motoomi, ed, *Makura no sōshi hyōshaku* (1927). Kishigami Shinji, *Sei Shōnagon*, in *Jimbutsu sōsho*, vol 86 (Yoshikawa Kōbunkan, 1962). Mekada Sakuo, *Makura no sōshi ron* (1975). Mark Morris, "Sei Shōnagon's Poetic Catalogues," *Harvard Journal of Asiatic Studies* 40.1 (June 1980). Tanaka Jūtarō, *Makura no sōshi hombun no kenkyū* (1960). Yūseidō Henshūbu, ed, *Makura no sōshi kōza*, 4 vols (1975–76).

Edwin A. CRANSTON

Seitai no Eki → Taiwan Expedition of 1874

Seitaisho

Also known as the "Constitution of 1868" or the "Organic Act." The first "constitution" of the Meiji government; issued on 11 June 1868. It was drafted by junior councillors FUKUOKA TAKACHIKA and SOEJIMA TANEOMI as the fulfillment of the pledge contained in the emperor's CHARTER OATH, promulgated earlier in the same year, regarding the establishment of representative government. In drafting the Seitaisho, besides consulting RYŌ NO GIGE and other Japanese works, the authors drew on a history of the United States by Elijah C. Bridgeman (translated into Japanese from the Chinese), Fukuzawa Yukichi's SEIYŌ JIJŌ, and the constitution of the United States. The final result represented an intermingling of Western political concepts, notably the separation of powers, with ancient Chinese and Japanese concepts of government. Under the Seitaisho all authority was vested in the DAJŌKAN (Grand Council of State), within which were seven administrative departments. It also provided for a bicameral deliberative assembly (Giseikan), but this was virtually ignored from the outset and eventually abandoned. The Dajōkan, however, remained the central executive organ of government until the cabinet system was adopted in 1885.

■ ——W. W. McLaren, ed, "Japanese Government Documents," *Transactions of the Asiatic Society of Japan* 42 (May 1914).

Wayne C. McWILLIAMS

Seitōsha

(Bluestocking Society). An organization, lasting from 1911 to 1916, that marked the beginning of the Japanese feminist movement. There had been earlier women's groups like the KYŌFŪKAI (Woman's Christian Temperance Union, founded in 1893) and women pioneers like KISHIDA TOSHIKO and FUKUDA HIDEKO, who propagated women's suffrage and political activities, but the Seitōsha was the first to arouse nationwide interest, being identified with the "new women," who, since the turn of the century, had begun penetrating the world of men by becoming teachers, nurses, officials, or artists. As in other countries, progress in education led to self-affirmation on the part of daughters of well-to-do families. The Seitōsha, too, was of bourgeois origin; most of its members had received a high school education and some had attended what is now JAPAN WOMEN'S UNIVERSITY. Seitōsha members shared the spiritual unrest and the consequent interest in Western individualism with the generation born after 1880. They started as a group of women interested in

literature, but in their quest for self-realization, they necessarily became involved in the feminist movement.

The Seitōsha started by publishing the literary magazine *Seitō* ("Bluestocking") in September 1911. The idea of a magazine by and for women only, as well as this name, was inspired by the literary critic IKUTA CHŌKŌ, who proposed the plan to HIRATSUKA RAICHŌ, one of his pupils in a literary study group called the Keishū Bungaku Kai (Association of Women Writers). Together with Yasumochi Yoshiko and three other women, who knew each other from school days, Raichō founded the group and its magazine, with her mother contributing the money she had set aside for her daughter's wedding.

In the first numbers, established women writers and poets like YOSANO AKIKO, Hasegawa Shigure, Okada Yachiyo, Mori Shige, and TAMURA TOSHIKO were represented. Though the *Seitō* never achieved a literary reputation of its own, it was significant for the publication of works such as Yosano Akiko's poem "Sozorogoto" (Chat), which prophesied women's awakening, and Raichō's prose-poem manifesto "Genshi josei wa taiyō de atta" (In the Beginning Woman Was the Sun), in which Raichō proclaimed the revelation of women's talent and self-consciousness. As many as several hundred women entered the Seitōsha and took part in its activities; at the lecture meeting on feminism in February 1913, members of the Seitōsha lectured as well as prominent male writers like Ikuta Chōkō, IWANO HŌMEI, and BABA KOCHŌ.

It was not these activities that brought the Seitōsha its reputation of being an association of "new women," but rumors of their allegedly scandalous way of life. For example, there were reports that members of the Seitōsha were drinking in public "five-colored alcohol" (a Western-style cocktail), and a scandal was precipitated by Otake Kōkichi (later known as Tomimoto Kazue), a gifted painter with lesbian tendencies. Otake was forced to resign from the Seitōsha in October 1912, but the misunderstandings she caused resulted in the Seitōsha becoming even more articulate on women's problems.

The *Seitō* in the first phase up to December 1912 was dominated by literary contributions that more or less consciously illustrated women's problems in marriage and society, and from 1913 it also contained essays and translations that treated the feminist movement generally or specific issues related to it. By 1914 the movement began to decline not only because public criticism forced a number of women to retreat, but also because many members had married and were occupied with children. In November 1914 Raichō, faced with family and financial hardships, thought of giving up the publication of the *Seitō* altogether. However, ITŌ NOE, already under the influence of the anarchist ŌSUGI SAKAE, decided to continue it on her own. She took over editorship of the *Seitō* in January 1915 and dealt with issues like prostitution, abortion, and chastity but had to discontinue publication in February 1916.

■ ——*Seitō* (September 1911–February 1916, repr 1968–70). Nancy Andrew, "The Seitōsha: An Early Japanese Women's Organization, 1911–1916," *Papers on Japan* 6 (1972). Hiratsuka Raichō, *Watakushi no aruita michi* (1956). Hiratsuka Raichō, *Genshi josei wa taiyō de atta*, 3 vols (1971–72). Margret Neuss, "Die Seitōsha—Der Ausgangspunkt der japanischen Frauenbewegung in seinen zeitgeschichtlichen und sozialen Bedingungen," *Oriens Extremus*, vol 18 nos. 1 and 2 (1971).

Margret NEUSS

Seiwa Genji → Minamoto family

Seiyō jijō

(Conditions in the West). Book by FUKUZAWA YUKICHI, the preeminent scholar of the MEIJI ENLIGHTENMENT movement. Made up of three volumes (published in 1866, 1868, and 1870), the work is based on the knowledge Fukuzawa acquired on three separate trips abroad (1860–67) and on his extensive translations of Western authors, among them the American educator Francis Wayland (1796–1865) and the British jurist Sir William Blackstone (1723–80).

Volume 1 discusses in detail a number of Western institutions: schools, newspapers, libraries, government bonds, orphanages, museums, steamships, telegraphs—in short, those aspects of modern Western life that Fukuzawa hoped Japan would emulate. It then gives capsule sketches of the history, government, military systems, and finances of the United States, the Netherlands, and Britain. Volume 2 contains translations of excerpts on governments and economics from a popular British series, *Chamber's Educational Course*.

Volume 3 presents general material by Blackstone on human rights and by Wayland on taxes and then supplies historical and other data on Russia and France. Throughout his work Fukuzawa sought to explain Western political systems, and, particularly, the concepts of liberty and rights. The work exerted a powerful influence on the Japanese public of the time. As Fukuzawa claimed in the preface to the collected edition of his works (1897), *Seiyō jijō* was widely regarded as the principal handbook for acquiring knowledge about Western society. Volume 1 alone sold 150,000 copies, not to mention pirated editions. FUKUOKA TAKACHIKA (1835–1919), one of the drafters of the CHARTER OATH and of the SEITAISHO, the Meiji government's protoconstitution, later wrote that in formulating ideas for a new political structure after the Restoration, he and his colleagues relied almost exclusively on the *Seiyō jijō*. Similar statements were made by other statesmen of the time, and even after the new government was established, the leaders continued to draw upon it as an encyclopedic reference.

Teruko CRAIG

Seiyū Hontō

(True Seiyū Party). Conservative political party formed in January 1924 by TOKONAMI TAKEJIRŌ and other RIKKEN SEIYŪKAI members who were unhappy with the TAKAHASHI KOREKIYO faction's dominance of the Seiyūkai. They left that party to support the KIYOURA KEIGO cabinet, which was then under heavy criticism from the Seiyūkai and other parties for consisting almost exclusively of peers. Closely allied with the bureaucratic elite, the Seiyū Hontō advocated national harmony and opposed expansion of the electoral franchise. Initially the largest party in the Diet, with 149 seats, it won only 109 seats in the 1924 election. In 1926 it retained only 87 seats, for 22 members returned to the Seiyūkai when TANAKA GIICHI replaced Takahashi as the Seiyūkai's president. In June 1927 it joined the relatively progressive KENSEIKAI to form the RIKKEN MINSEITŌ. See also POLITICAL PARTIES.

Seiyūkai → Rikken Seiyūkai

Seiyū Stores, Ltd

One of the three largest chain store companies in Japan, Seiyū Stores became independent of SEIBU DEPARTMENT STORES, LTD, in 1956, and is currently a leading member of the Seibu distribution group. Its stores serve as branches of the Seibu Department Stores, catering primarily to clients in the suburbs of Tōkyō. Seiyū has expanded its network rapidly in the western part of Tōkyō and created a small revolution in the retailing business through its mass-sales system and drastic cutdowns on costs. Since the 1960s it has emerged as the top-ranking chain store company in the Tōkyō metropolitan area. It has business tie-ups in the United States with Sears Roebuck & Co, Jewel Associates, Inc, and Allstate Insurance Co, and purchasing offices in Chicago, Hong Kong, Beijing (Peking), London, and Paris. As of December 1981 Seiyū had 226 stores, 73 of which were operated by subsidiaries. Sales for the fiscal year ending February 1982 totaled ¥607.1 billion (US $2.6 billion), and the company was capitalized at ¥6.5 billion (US $27.6 million). Corporate headquarters are located in Tōkyō.

seizonken

(right to live). The responsibility of the state to protect citizens from poverty and destitution and the responsibility to develop policies to guarantee the welfare of the people. These rights are generally called social rights of the type guaranteed by international agreements on human rights. The CONSTITUTION of Japan regards highly the doctrine of the free state and emphasizes guarantees of freedom, but it also guarantees several social rights and corrects abuses that arise from the exercise of freedom. The *seizonken* guaranteed by article 25 is the core of these rights. The first section of that article provides: "All persons shall have the right to maintain the minimum standards of wholesome and cultured living."

The legal nature of this right is the subject of some theoretical dispute, but it is commonly thought that this clause does not give citizens the right to claim relief by lawsuit, when laws and resources provided by the state do not provide these minimum standards. The Supreme Court stated in the Asahi case, a 1967 decision regarding a suit over the reduction of welfare assistance, that even if the protection of one's livelihood is markedly low, one cannot sue to recover the difference on constitutional grounds. Instead, scholarly opinion considers the *seizonken* to be a "program provision" that directs government policy. The constitution provides: "In all spheres of life, the state shall use its endeavors for the promotion and extension of social welfare and security, and public health" (art. 25, sec. 2). The state bears the responsibility of enacting legislation to this end, such as the LIVELIHOOD PROTECTION LAW (Seikatsu Hogo Hō), the CHILD WELFARE LAW (Jidō Fukushi Hō), the Social Welfare Activities Law (Shakai Fukushi Jigyō Hō; see SOCIAL WELFARE), and the National Pension Law (Kokumin Nenkin Hō; see PENSIONS).

ITŌ Masami

seizure

(*sashiosae*). Compulsory procedure provided by civil courts to prevent persons from disposing of their assets or the legal rights to such assets by physical or legal means. Seizures under the Code of Civil Procedure (see CIVIL PROCEDURE, CODE OF) are most typically a part of compulsory civil enforcement proceeding. As the first step in obtaining satisfactions of monetary claims under private law, the code forbids the debtor from disposing of his or her assets or from exercising his or her legal rights regarding such assets and requires such assets to be preserved. For seizure to be permitted, there must be a judgment for payment, a provisional order for payment, an instrument of execution, or some other proof of debt authorizing the seizure.

In general, all the property of the debtor at the time of the seizure may be levied upon, but there are some exceptions: things that cannot be transferred because of their intrinsic nature (personal rights) or because of legal prohibitions (opium, counterfeit money) and things that are exempted from seizure for various other reasons (necessaries for daily living of the debtor and his family). Personal property in the debtor's possession may be seized by the marshal and placed under his control, and the debtor's claims against third parties may be seized by a court order of seizure. Seizure in the case of the compulsory sale of real property, ships, or other similar assets is effected by the decision of the court to commence the compulsory sale by auction, and the seizure for compulsory sequestration of real property is effected by the court's decision to start compulsory sequestration proceedings.

Through these seizure orders, debtors are forbidden to dispose of the things seized. If a debtor does transfer to a third party something that has been seized, the validity of the transfer may not be asserted by the debtor against his creditor. With respect to the debtor's relationship with the third party, however, the transfer is valid. Seizure does not give the creditor who has applied for the seizure any new rights.

Seizures under ADMINISTRATIVE LAW occur in cases of delinquencies in the payment of national or local taxes. The Tax Administration Agency carries out the seizure according to procedures that are simpler than those under the Code of Civil Procedure described above.

Seizure under the Code of Criminal Procedure is a form of confiscation. The term refers to two separate kinds of proceeding: The first is a decision by the court, and the enforcement thereof, to take possession by force of material evidence or other objects that the court has determined should be seized. The second is a judicial decision permitting criminal investigation agencies to take possession by force of such objects, and the acts of seizure based on such a decision. In the former case a writ of seizure is required, unless the hearing to determine whether the seizure is to be permitted is conducted in open court.

MATSUURA Kaoru

Seji kembunroku

(Record of Personal Observations of Society). Collection of essays completed in about 1816 by an unidentified writer using the pen name Buyō Inshi. The author addresses a wide variety of subjects, ranging from class and occupational groups such as *samurai*, merchants, priests, fortune-tellers, and physicians to crop production, *kabuki* plays, and contemporary mores. His sharp and candid remarks, written in a tone of high moralistic disapproval, make the book an important source for social conditions at a time when the merchant class was in the ascendant.

Sekai

(World). A general monthly magazine (*sōgō zasshi*) published by IWANAMI SHOTEN PUBLISHERS since 1946. It strives to be a forum where intellectuals can express their views on current national and international political and social topics of interest and thus be an outlet for the long-range exposition and clarification of major trends of thought. It is characterized by strong ideological tendencies and by having among its contributors both foreign and Japanese scholars and thinkers of international repute. The magazine is noted for its sharp criticism of the status quo. Many of its articles, serial novels, and short fiction stories have stirred controversy and sensation among postwar critical and literary circles. Circulation: 120,000 (1978).

Sekai fujin

(Women of the World). First socialist women's journal in Japan; published from January 1907 to August 1909 (39 issues) by FUKUDA HIDEKO, aided by Kanagawa Matsuko. It espoused socialism and women's independence from the traditional family system and carried articles on political issues in Japan and women's movements abroad. Its contributors included such major leftists as KŌTOKU SHŪSUI, SAKAI TOSHIHIKO, and especially ISHIKAWA SANSHIRŌ.

Sekai Heiwa Apīru Shichinin Iinkai → Committee of Seven to Appeal for World Peace

Sekai Kyūsei Kyō

(The Religion for the Salvation of the World). One of Japan's NEW RELIGIONS, founded in 1935 by OKADA MOKICHI (1882–1955). Also called Sekai Meshiya Kyō. The religion claimed 796,998 followers in 1977. Sekai Kyūsei Kyō's central teachings, formulated by its founder, are that the world is rapidly approaching the day of final judgment, that after this judgment a paradise will be built on earth, that people must prepare for the judgment by purifying themselves if they wish to participate in the creation of the earthly paradise, and that Okada was a Messiah sent by God to lead men in the building of paradise. Okada rejected all medicines as well as fertilizers and other agricultural chemicals as sources of poison and evil.

The group grew rapidly between the end of World War II and Okada's death. During that period he proselytized actively and legitimized his teachings by claiming to have received divine revelation. Followers are drawn primarily to the faith-healing powers of jōrei (purification of the spirit), which, Okada taught, can be set in motion by any believer. According to Okada, jōrei is a process that dissipates clouds on the soul, which are the sources of the world's sufferings.

Okada's elaborate cosmology and system of beliefs were strongly influenced by his years as a follower of the ŌMOTO religion, an intense attraction to Christianity, and a fading interest in Buddhism. His ideas on medicine reflect his own painful experiences with disease, general physical weakness, and fruitless medical treatments. His early aspiration to become a painter led to an emphasis on the spiritually uplifting value of art, and the group's HAKONE MUSEUM OF ART and MOA MUSEUM OF ART in Atami contain some of Japan's greatest art treasures. Both museums symbolize the belief that beauty, because it has purifying qualities, is one of the main attributes of paradise on earth.

After Okada's death, the group received a great deal of adverse publicity when several followers who had refused medical treatment died in 1957 and 1958. He was succeeded as leader by his wife and then by his daughter Okada Itsuki (b 1927). A growing tendency under her leadership to compromise the strict proscription on medicine and fertilizers led to several schisms, and the original sect reportedly lost many members in the 1960s and early 1970s.

Patricia MURRAY

Seki

City in southern Gifu Prefecture, central Honshū. Seki has been known for its swordsmiths, such as Seki no Magoroku, since the 12th century. The city produces about 90 percent of all the safety razor blades in Japan, as well as fine-quality scissors and knives. Pop: 59,192.

Seki

Town in northern Mie Prefecture, central Honshū. Suzuka no Seki, an important barrier station (SEKISHO), was established here in the 7th century to guard the capital region against encroachment from eastern Japan. During the Edo period (1600–1868) it prospered as a POST-STATION TOWN on the highway Tōkaidō. Forestry, rice and tea cultivation, and dairy farming are active. Pop: 7,092.

Sekigahara

Town in southwestern Gifu Prefecture, central Honshū. Fuwa no Seki, one of three important barrier stations (SEKISHO), was situated here in the 7th century, but it is with the Battle of Sekigahara (1600), in which TOKUGAWA IEYASU won control of all Japan, that the place is most closely associated. It retained its strategic importance as one of the POST-STATION TOWNS on the highway Tōkaidō for the next 300 years and is still a transportation center. Pop: 10,483.

Sekigahara, Battle of

(Sekigahara no Tatakai). The decisive battle in the rise of TOKUGAWA IEYASU to the shogunate; it took place in 1600 at Sekigahara in Mino Province (now Gifu Prefecture). Ieyasu's forces destroyed some of his most vigorous rivals, and after the battle he trimmed the domains of others, thereby reducing sharply the possibility of another hostile coalition that might threaten his hegemony.

After the death of TOYOTOMI HIDEYOSHI in 1598 the principal daimyō soon fell to quarreling, and during the summer of 1600 two armies mobilized for war. One, composed mostly of daimyō forces from the western part of Japan, was led by ISHIDA MITSUNARI. The other, composed mostly of eastern warriors, was led by Ieyasu.

Pro-Ieyasu armies led by DATE MASAMUNE and Ieyasu's second son, Yūki Hideyasu (1574–1607), remained in the Kantō region to check the move of pro-Ishida daimyō, notably Uesugi Kagekatsu of Aizu (now part of Fukushima Prefecture). While Ieyasu's third son, TOKUGAWA HIDETADA, led an army against Sanada Masayuki (1545–1609) and his son SANADA YUKIMURA at Ueda in Shinano Province (now Nagano Prefecture), Ieyasu led his own army westward via the Tōkaidō road. The principal armies deployed in a rather narrow valley just west of the village of Sekigahara. Ieyasu's forces were composed of units led by his fourth son, MATSUDAIRA TADAYOSHI, major vassals like Honda Tadakatsu (1548–1610) and II NAOMASA, and about 15 daimyō, including YAMANOUCHI KAZUTOYO, IKEDA TERUMASA, KURODA NAGAMASA, and TŌDŌ TAKATORA. Ishida was supported by forces of the great MŌRI, SHIMAZU, and Ukita families in addition to troops commanded by KONISHI YUKINAGA, ANKOKUJI EKEI, KOBAYAKAWA HIDEAKI, and Wakizaka Yasuharu (1554–1626).

The two armies deployed their forces during the rainy night of 20 October (Keichō 5.9.14), and the fighting commenced at about eight the following morning. Of the total forces available on both sides, somewhat over half, or about 110,000 men, were actually committed to battle. The morning's combat was indecisive, but in the afternoon the forces of Kobayakawa, Wakizaka, and three other daimyō went over to the eastern army. Their surprise assault thoroughly confused the western army and led to its utter rout by four in the afternoon.

In the following days Ieyasu overran Mitsunari's castle at Sawayama (adjacent to Hikone) and then went on to Ōsaka. Seizing the chance presented by his dramatic victory, he quickly issued a series of orders punishing his enemies and rewarding his supporters. The resulting balance of power rested heavily in Ieyasu's favor and underlay the effectiveness of subsequent moves to solidify his control of the realm.

Conrad TOTMAN

Sekigunha → Red Army faction

Seki Hironao (1852–1935)

Founder of the advertising agency HAKUHŌDŌ, INC. Born in Toyama Prefecture. Seki was a local government employee when, on the advice of a friend who had seen such operations in the United States, he started an advertising agency in 1895. He first inserted advertisements in newspapers that specialized in education and gradually extended his business to include advertisements in all kinds of publications. Hakuhōdō is now the second largest advertising agency in Japan, after DENTSŪ, INC. Seki donated his highly valued collection of newspapers and magazines of the Meiji period (1868–1912) to Tōkyō University.

KAWAKAMI Hiroshi

Sekirankai

(Red Wave Society). Women's socialist group founded in April 1921 with some 40 members, including YAMAKAWA KIKUE, ITŌ NOE, Kutsumi Fusako (1890–1980), and Sakai (later Kondō) Magara (1903–80). An auxiliary of the NIHON SHAKAI SHUGI DŌMEI (Japan Socialist League), it was composed largely of the women relatives of active male leftists. Calling for the abolition of capitalism, which it saw as the cause of women's oppression, the group worked specifically for equal wages, mothers' welfare, and the abolition of prostitution. It also sponsored lectures and cooperated with men's socialist groups. The Sekirankai met with police violence while participating in Japan's second May Day rally in 1921 and again while distributing pacifist leaflets during the fall of that year in an area where military maneuvers were being held. Facing suppression, in March 1922 the group was reorganized, without its anarchist faction, as the Yōkakai (Eighth Day Association), taking its name from 8 March, the date of International Women's Day. Many women university students joined its ranks, but it disbanded in June 1923.

sekirei → wagtails

sekisen

(literally, "barrier money"). Tolls, originally collected in the form of rice as stipends for the guards at barrier stations (SEKISHO) or for the upkeep of temples. The practice of collecting tolls began in the Heian period (794–1185), when many barrier stations came into the hands of the local aristocracy and owners of private landed estates (SHŌEN). It was not until the Muromachi period (1333–1568), however, that the collection of sekisen reached significant proportions. Unable to raise sufficient taxes on their lands, the imperial court, the shogunate, aristocrats, and shōen proprietors came to depend on sekisen, now paid in coins, as a major source of income. For example, along the 50 kilometers (31 mi) of the river Yodogawa between Kyōto and Ōsaka, there were more than 600 toll gates. The collection of tolls not only discouraged travel but also disrupted the circulation of goods, resulting in higher prices. To encourage the development of a national economy, the hegemons ODA NOBUNAGA and TOYOTOMI HIDEYOSHI abolished barrier stations and tolls in the late 16th century. They were revived in the Edo period (1600–1868), and sekisen was collected by the shogunate and the daimyō.

sekisho

(barrier stations). Government installations at strategic points along traffic routes, where travelers were stopped for inspection from ancient times through the early modern period. The system of barrier stations was established under the TAIKA REFORM of 645, with primary emphasis on those in the Kinai region, or home provinces, near the capital. The barrier stations at Suzuka in Ise Province (now part of Mie Prefecture), Fuwa in Mino Province (now part of Gifu Prefecture), and Arachi in Echizen Province (now part of Fukui Prefecture)—the so-called Sankan or Three Barriers—were considered particularly important, officials from the central government being sent to oversee the closing of these barriers in case of an emperor's abdication or death, a rebellion, or other national emergency. The Sankan fell into disuse in the middle of the Heian period (794–1185) with the disintegration of the RITSURYŌ SYSTEM of government. As lands became increasingly absorbed into private landed estates (SHŌEN), proprietary lords (ryōshu) set up and maintained private barrier stations within their estates. Known variously as kawate or tsuryō, these stations levied tolls (SEKISEN) in one form or another. During the Muromachi period (1333–1568) there was a conspicuous proliferation of barrier stations as the shogunate and regional lords sought additional sources of revenue. These sekisho tended to impede the flow of traffic and goods, and they were abolished in the late 16th century by the national unifiers ODA NOBUNAGA and TOYOTOMI HIDEYOSHI. Sekisho were revived under the Tokugawa shogunate (1603–1867), more than 50 being established at Hakone, Imagire, Kobotoke, Usui, and other points on the main roads (GOKAIDŌ) leading to the shogunal capital at Edo (now Tōkyō). Especially stringent inspections were made for "incoming weapons and outgoing women" (irideppō deonna), i.e., contraband weapons and distaff members of daimyō families required to reside in Edo (see SANKIN KŌTAI). Sekisho were abolished by the Meiji government on 2 March 1869.   WATANABE Ichirō

Sekisui Chemical Co, Ltd

(Sekisui Kagaku Kōgyō). Chemical company which ranks first in Japan in the production and processing of synthetic resins and unit prefabricated homes. Sekisui Chemical was established in 1947 by seven former employees of the Nippon Chisso Fertilizer Co. In the following year it began production of plastic goods with Japan's first automatic injection molding machine. In 1949 it constructed a new plant in Ōsaka and started to manufacture a wide variety of industrial components and consumer goods made of vinyl-related resins, growing into a major enterprise. In the latter half of the 1950s it began production of such home construction materials as vinyl chloride pipes, roofing materials, and vinyl boards. It also created a nationwide network of production subsidiaries (such as Sekisui Resin and Sekisui Kaseihin Industries) and sales firms totaling 50 companies to form the Sekisui group. In 1960 it established SEKISUI HOUSE, LTD, and in 1971 started mass production of unit prefabricated homes called Haim. Sekisui Chemical has close relations with ASAHI CHEMICAL INDUSTRY CO, LTD, another offspring of the Nippon Chisso Fertilizer Co. It has more than 20 affiliates and joint venture companies throughout the world, supervised by an affiliate in Hong Kong. Sales for the fiscal year ending March 1982 totaled ¥297.6 billion (US $1.2 billion), of which houses accounted for 37 percent, pipe-making machinery 18 percent, wrapping and packing materials 13 percent, chemical products 12 percent, housing materials 10 percent, plastic goods 9 percent, and others 1 percent; the export ratio was 2 percent. The company was capitalized at ¥14.4 billion (US $59.8 million) in the same year. Corporate headquarters are located in Ōsaka.

Sekisui House, Ltd

(Sekisui Hausu). Maker of houses, condominiums, dormitories, offices, and other buildings; a leading member of the Sekisui group. Its main product is steel-frame houses, and it ranks first among Japan's manufacturers of prefabricated buildings. Founded as a subsidiary of SEKISUI CHEMICAL CO, LTD, in 1960, it now has 4 plants and 50 subsidiary and affiliated companies, including 2 overseas subsidiaries, Sekisui Deutschland Bau GmbH of West Germany and Sekisui Systeembouw NV of the Netherlands. It has no sales agents on the domestic market, unlike most other companies in the field; it prefers to deal directly with home buyers. Sales have increased rapidly in recent years and are expected to continue growing. After-tax profits have also shown rapid growth. Sales for the fiscal year ending January 1982 totaled ¥433.9 billion (US $1.9 billion), with housing construction accounting for 77 percent and real estate 23 percent; the company was capitalized at ¥14.2 billion (US $63.2 million) in the same year. Corporate headquarters are located in Ōsaka.

Seki Takakazu (1642–1708)

Mathematician. Seki is considered the greatest figure in premodern Japanese mathematics. His antecedents are unknown, although it is certain that he worked in the office in charge of clothing and furnishings for the Tokugawa shōgun. He is generally believed to have been self-made and self-educated. He developed a method for approximating the roots of a higher-order algebraic equation quite similar to the well-known "Newton's method," and it is now generally recognized that Seki's formulation of the theory of determinants preceded that of the German mathematician Gottfried Leibnitz, considered the originator of this theory. Seki is sometimes credited with discovering some of the fundamental concepts of calculus. His algebraic techniques were later developed and expanded by his pupil TAKEBE KATAHIRO.

sekkan seiji → regency government

sekke shōgun

(shōguns from the regents' house). Refers to the courtiers Fujiwara (or Kujō) Yoritsune (1218–56) and Fujiwara (or Kujō) Yoritsugu (1239–56), the fourth and fifth shōguns of the Kamakura shogunate. Japan's three warrior governments—the Kamakura (1192–1333), Muromachi (1338–1573), and Tokugawa (1603–1867) shogunates—were each normally headed by a member of the leading warrior house. The system began with MINAMOTO NO YORITOMO's acquisition of the title SHŌGUN from the emperor in 1192. His Kamakura

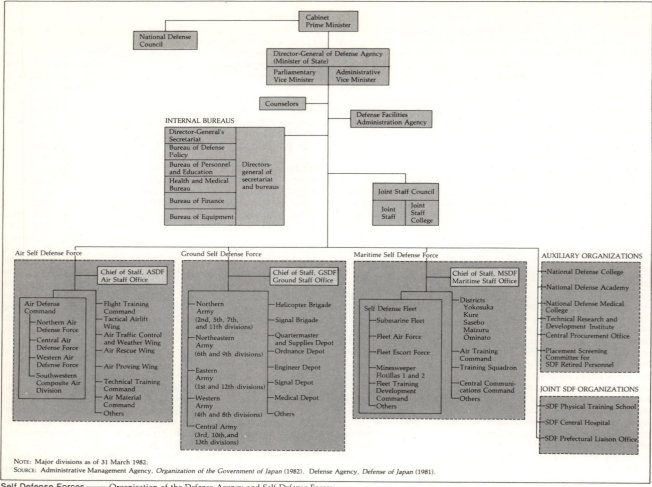

NOTE: Major divisions as of 31 March 1982.
SOURCE: Administrative Management Agency, *Organization of the Government of Japan* (1982). Defense Agency, *Defense of Japan* (1981).

Self Defense Forces —— Organization of the Defense Agency and Self Defense Forces

shogunate faced a succession crisis, however, when MINAMOTO NO YORIIE and MINAMOTO NO SANETOMO, his sons and successors, were assassinated in 1204 and 1219, respectively. Their maternal relatives, the HŌJŌ FAMILY, took control of the shogunate but lacked sufficient status to assume the title of shōgun. Consequently, they arranged with the court to appoint a scion of the KUJŌ FAMILY, one of the five Fujiwara regents' houses (GOSEKKE), as nominal shōgun to legitimate their control. Yoritsune, distantly related to Yoritomo, was made shōgun in 1226 and was succeeded by his son Yoritsugu in 1244. In 1252, however, the shogunal regent (shikken) HŌJŌ TO-KIYORI sent Yoritsugu back to Kyōto, and the imperial prince MU-NETAKA was installed in his place.　　　*G. Cameron Hurst III*

sekku

(seasonal festival). A term that originally applied to offerings *(ku)* of food made on certain days traditionally recognized as marking changes in the seasons *(sechi)*, it came to refer to the actual days. *Sekku* are also referred to as *monobi* or *mombi*, that is, the days on which people dress in formal *kimono* bearing the family crest *(mon)*.

In ancient times, the Japanese court, in imitation of China, observed several *sekku* as part of a larger set calendar of annual events *(nenchū gyōji)*; this calendar resulted from an integration of Japanese notions of seasonal division with the Chinese calendrical system, in which certain days were set aside to mark seasonal changes. In the Edo period (1600–1868) the Tokugawa shogunate prescribed the following days as *sekku*: 7 January (Jinjitsu no Sekku), commonly referred to as Nanakusa no Sekku (Seven Herb Festival); 3 March (Jōshi no Sekku; see DOLL FESTIVAL), commonly known as Momo no Sekku (Peach Festival); 5 May (Tango no Sekku; see CHILDREN'S

DAY), commonly called Shōbu no Sekku (Iris Festival); 7 July (TANA-BATA FESTIVAL), and 9 September (Chōyō no Sekku), commonly known as Kiku no Sekku (CHRYSANTHEMUM FESTIVAL). These have been informally observed by families up to the present.

On the days of *sekku* it is customary to prepare special foods. For example on 7 January, people eat *nanakusa-gayu* ("seven herb gruel"); on 3 March *hishimochi*, a three-layered diamond-shaped rice cake; and on 5 May, *chimaki*, steamed rice wrapped in bamboo leaves.　　　*Inokuchi Shōji*

Self Defense Forces

(Jieitai; abbreviated SDF). Armed organizations responsible for the ground, sea, and air defense of Japan. The term "self-defense" is used in the official title because the 1947 CONSTITUTION prohibits the nation from possessing military forces. Members of the SDF who are expected to bear arms are designated "self-defense personnel," or *jieikan* (they are also referred to as the *seifukugumi* or "uniformed corps"), to distinguish them from civilian personnel of the SDF, who are called *bunkan*.

Historical Development —— When Japan surrendered to the Allied nations in August 1945, its army and navy and their attendant air forces were dismantled according to the Allied OCCUPATION's policies of eradicating Japanese militarism and establishing a peaceful and democratic society. However, increased tension between East and West culminated in the outbreak of the Korean War in June 1950, and American forces occupying Japan were dispatched to the Korean peninsula. General Douglas MACARTHUR, commander of the Occupation forces, ordered the establishment of a NATIONAL

Self Defense Forces

		Number of Personnel (in thousands)		
	Actual 1954	Actual 1980	Authorized 1980	Actual/Authorized 1980 (%)
GSDF personnel	130.0	154.3	180.0	86
MSDF personnel	15.8	40.5	42.3	96
ASDF personnel	6.3	43.6	45.5	96
Civilian employees	12.4	27.3	27.7	99
Total	164.5	265.7	295.5	90

NOTE: Figures do not include members of the Joint Staff Council and the Defense Facilities Administration Agency.
SOURCE: Defense Agency, unpublished figures.

POLICE RESERVE of 75,000 men to strengthen Japan's capacity to maintain public order. From its inception, this force was recognized as possessing greater firepower and mobility than the police. In 1952 its name was changed to the NATIONAL SAFETY FORCES and, together with the Maritime Guard, it was administered by the newly established Safety Agency.

With the passage of the Self Defense Forces Law in 1954, the Safety Agency became the DEFENSE AGENCY (Bōeichō), and the existing forces were reorganized as the Self Defense Forces, with three services, the Ground Self Defense Force, the Maritime Self Defense Force, and the Air Self Defense Force (known as the Rikujō, Kaijō, and Kōkū Jieitai, respectively).

Organization and Command —— Supreme command and supervisory responsibilities rest with the prime minister, who represents the cabinet. The director-general of the Defense Agency, a member of the cabinet, receives his orders from the prime minister and is responsible for the SDF's execution of its duties. The director-general is assisted by the civilian personnel serving in the agency's offices, by SDF personnel who serve on the command staffs of the various bureaus of the ground, maritime, and air self defense forces, and by the JOINT STAFF COUNCIL. The chiefs of staff of the three forces carry out within their commands the orders of the director-general and supervise the activities of their respective branches. In the event of war, integrated units would be formed among the three forces, and the chairman of the Joint Staff Council would assume command, but in peacetime the chairman's powers are limited to the formulation and coordination of overall defense planning. Hence the principle of civilian control of the military is in operation much as it is in the United States, except that in Japan there are no civilian officials appointed over each of the three services. The chairman of the Joint Staff Council does not have as much power as his American counterpart, the chairman of the Joint Chiefs of Staff.

Duties and Operations —— Article 3 of the Self Defense Forces Law states: "The chief function of the SDF is to preserve the peace and independence of our country and to defend against direct and indirect aggression threatening the security of the nation. When the need arises, the SDF will also be employed to preserve public order." Five courses of action that may be taken to fulfill these functions are delineated.

1. Mobilization of defense forces: when attack from abroad occurs or is threatened, mobilization occurs at the order of the prime minister after he has obtained permission from the Diet, though in an emergency permission may be sought after the command has been given (art. 76 of the SDF Law).

2. Mobilization for the preservation of public order: in the face of indirect aggression or other sudden disturbances that are beyond the capacity of the ordinary police to handle, mobilization may occur at the command of the prime minister but consent must be sought from the Diet within 20 days of the order. If a prefectural governor considers a situation a grave threat to the public order, the prime minister may order mobilization, but the governor must subsequently make full reports to his prefectural assembly (arts. 78 and 81).

3. Police action at sea: in order to protect life and property at sea, or in special circumstances to preserve the peace, mobilization can be ordered by the director-general after receiving the permission of the prime minister (art. 82).

4. Disaster relief: in order to protect life and property in the event of a natural or other kind of disaster, mobilization can be ordered at the request of a prefectural governor, or, in emergencies, on the initiative of the director-general and lesser officials designated by him (art. 83).

5. Response to encroachments on Japanese airspace: when a foreign aircraft enters Japanese airspace in violation of international law or flight regulations and action is required to force the plane to land or to leave, it can be taken at the order of the director-general (art. 84).

Personnel —— The SDF employs a system of voluntary enlistment of young people between the ages of 18 and 25. The term of service is two or three years but it may be extended. Because of a long period of eased international tensions and a high level of economic growth in Japan, the SDF has had difficulty in recruiting personnel and in meeting authorized force limits. However, in recent years the slower rate of economic growth has led to an increase in the number of applicants. Moreover, in 1974, in order to supplement its personnel deficit, the SDF initiated the recruitment of women. They have shown a relatively high rate of enlistment and the scale of the program continues to expand annually; an unofficial figure for 1980 showed roughly 3,000 women in the SDF.

A reserve corps of SDF personnel made up of volunteers who had resigned from active duty was formed in 1970. Figures for 1980 were 37,900 Ground Self Defense Force reserves and 580 Maritime Self Defense Force reserves.

Retirement age is fixed at 50 for those from the rank of sergeant to lieutenant colonel, while that for colonels is 53, major generals and rear admirals 55, and lieutenant generals and vice admirals 58. These are relatively young in comparison with the ages in the United States, where 60 is the retirement age for the ranks from lieutenant to brigadier general and rear admiral. Deferment of retirement beyond present limits is now under study.

The actual strength of the SDF in 1954 and authorized and actual strengths in 1980 are given in the table.

Defense Budget —— Referred to as "defense-related expenses" in the national budget, appropriations in 1980 totaled approximately ¥2.23 trillion (US $10 billion). This total equaled approximately 0.9 percent of the estimated gross national product (GNP). Since the inception of the SDF, its share of the GNP has actually decreased and since 1960 has remained at a level below 1 percent. Calls to expand the SDF's portion of both the GNP and the national budget were growing more insistent in the early 1980s, but counterarguments noting that actual appropriations have continued to climb in real terms are also strong.

SDF expenses are divided between the Defense Agency and the Defense Facilities Administration Agency, with the Defense Agency sustaining nearly 90 percent. In 1980 the breakdown for the three services was Ground SDF 40 percent, Maritime SDF 23 percent, Air SDF 23 percent, and internal bureaus and auxiliary organs about 3 percent. Expenditures were divided approximately as follows: personnel expenses 49 percent, armaments 21 percent, maintenance 14 percent, military bases 10 percent, and research and development 1 percent.

Because of Japan's painful experience during World War II, when the huge quantity of war bonds issued to cover military expenses resulted in tremendous inflation, the raising of defense funds through the issuance of government bonds is forbidden. This severely restricts the expansion of military spending, and, together with the November 1976 Outline of the National Defense Program, which set a limit of 1 percent of the GNP as a maximum total expenditure for the SDF, serves as a powerful check on rapid expansion of Japan's SDF.

Units and Their Deployment —— The Ground Self Defense Force is divided into 13 divisions, which are grouped into five regional armies: the Northern Army, headquartered in Sapporo, Hokkaidō; the Northeastern Army, headquartered in Sendai, Miyagi Prefecture; the Eastern Army, headquartered in Ichigaya in Tōkyō; the Central Army, headquartered in Itami, Hyōgo Prefecture; and the Western Army, headquartered in Kumamoto, Kumamoto Prefecture. The greatest emphasis has been placed on the defense of Hokkaidō.

The Maritime Self Defense Force has its Self Defense Fleet general headquarters at Yokosuka, Kanagawa Prefecture; it is responsible for the deployment of the Fleet Escort Force, the Fleet Air Force, the submarine and minesweeper flotillas, and ship assignments for five regional districts (Yokosuka, Kure, Sasebo, Maizuru, and Ōminato). The Fleet Escort Force is further divided into four escort flotillas. The Maritime Self Defense Force regards antisubmarine warfare as its most important mission.

The Air Self Defense Force has three regional air defense forces, each with its own command headquarters: the Northern Air Defense Force, stationed in Misawa, Aomori Prefecture; the Central Air Defense Force, stationed in Iruma, Saitama Prefecture; and the Western Air Defense Force, stationed in Kasuga, Fukuoka Prefecture. There is also a Southwestern Composite Air Division, stationed in Naha, Okinawa Prefecture, making a total of four air zones. All fighter aircraft and Nike surface-to-air missiles posted in each air zone, as well as 28 radar sites throughout the country, are under the unified direction of the Air Defense Command in Fuchū, Tōkyō. Operational emphasis is placed on the swift identification of aircraft encroaching on Japanese airspace and on a quick response to a possible consolidated air attack.

In an effort to facilitate recruitment activities, there is an SDF liaison office in each prefecture, headed by either a major general or colonel class officer, or a civilian equivalent. This system has proven quite effective.

Defense Buildup —— The SDF has developed three defense plans since the first one in 1958. These have all been conceived on the assumption that, despite considerable tensions in international relations, the general stability in the military and political balance between the United States and the Soviet Union has made the large-scale invasion of Japan only a remote possibility. In the fourth defense plan, completed by the government in 1976 and accepted by the NATIONAL DEFENSE COUNCIL and the cabinet as the basic guideline for the 10 years beyond 1977, the concept of a standard defense force was central. According to this concept, barring great changes in international conditions, Japan was equipped to respond on its own to a limited surprise attack and should therefore concentrate on improving the quality and support structures of its defense forces.

Education and Training —— Guidelines established in 1961 emphasize the moral training and education of SDF personnel, i.e., the inculcation of awareness of mission, sense of responsibility, fulfillment of duties, observance of regulations, and esprit de corps. Middle school and high school graduates, as well as some SDF personnel who have come up from lower ranks, undergo noncommissioned officer training, which includes general education and technical and tactical training. Officers are selected from among the graduates of the NATIONAL DEFENSE ACADEMY (Bōei Daigakkō) and graduates of ordinary universities who have passed a qualifying examination, together with noncommissioned officers who have received high scores in a selective examination. They study at the officer candidate schools of each service. Officers who are candidates for higher-level commands and staff positions undergo further training in the classroom and on command and staff assignments. They may also be selected to study at the NATIONAL DEFENSE COLLEGE (Bōei Kenshūsho).

Arms and Equipment —— At the time of the SDF's formation, arms and equipment were furnished mainly by the United States. However, special procurements of war matériel by the US upon the outbreak of the Korean War contributed to the revival of the Japanese defense industry. Following the 1958 plans for defense buildup, a structure was created for domestic production. Since 1967, 90 percent of equipment procurements have been made within Japan. Japanese arms manufacturing capability, in both sophistication and quality, approaches that of other sectors. Small arms, ammunition, and artillery for the Ground Self Defense Force, as well as armored fighting vehicles including the excellent Type-74 medium tank, are produced. The Maritime Self Defense Force is equipped with destroyers, submarines, minesweepers, and antisubmarine craft such as the domestically produced Haruna, and operates US-designed ASW aircraft, including the newly introduced P3C. The Air Self Defense Force is largely equipped with US aircraft types manufactured under license in Japan, with combat planes of the F4EJ type in service and F15 fighters entering service. Japan has produced its own fighter plane, the F1, and training planes such as the T33 and T2. Stocks of ammunition and replacement parts are, however, very low, reflecting budgetary constraints. See also DEFENSE INDUSTRY.

The Constitution and the SDF —— Since its inception the SDF has faced the charge that its existence is in violation of article 9 of the constitution. To this, the government has responded that although the constitution forbids war as a means of resolving international disputes, it does not negate the right of self defense (see NATIONAL DEFENSE). Although criticism continues, the SDF has won general acceptance from the Japanese public, and the voices for its abolition are less evident than those calling for its strengthening.

■ ——Asagumo Shimbunsha, ed, *Bōei nenkan* (1978). Bōeichō, ed, *Nihon no bōei* (1978, 1979). Fujii Haruo, *Sensō keikaku—Jieitai tatakaeba* (1978). Inagaki Osamu, *Jieitai no sensō keikaku* (1978). Inoki Masamichi, *Kuni o mamoru* (1973). Kaihara Osamu, *Watakushi no kokubō hakusho* (1975). Ishikawa Kanshi, Nakamura Ryūhei, and Uchida Kazuomi, *Jieitai tatakawaba—bōei shutsudō* (1976).

Mutsu Gorō

self-defense, national right of

(jieiken). The concept of international law used to justify the creation of Japan's SELF DEFENSE FORCES (SDF), in apparent violation of article 9 of the 1947 constitution, which prohibits the establishment of land, sea, or air forces or other war potential. Article 51 of the Charter of the United Nations recognizes "the inherent right of individual or collective self-defense" for all its members. The peace treaty between Japan and the Allied nations signed in San Francisco in September 1951 states that the Allied powers, Japan's former enemies, recognize that Japan "as a sovereign nation possesses the inherent right of individual or collective self-defense" as referred to in article 51, even though they had earlier adopted the policy of complete disarmament and demilitarization of Japan.

The Japanese government with some public support has taken the view that the right of self-defense, because it is "inherent," justifies the creation of the SDF. In addition, it is argued that because article 9 does not prohibit military forces for purposes of defense, the SDF are therefore not unconstitutional. Those who oppose the SDF do not recognize the right of self-defense and therefore argue that the SDF are unconstitutional. See also RENUNCIATION OF WAR; CONSTITUTION, DISPUTE OVER REVISION OF.

John M. Maki

self-employment

(jieigyō). General term which refers to the work of farmers, small retailers and manufacturers, and independent craftspeople. In most countries the number of persons employed in these areas decreased sharply after industrialization. In Japan, however, these traditional areas of employment were preserved, existing side by side with, and in fact being utilized by, the modernizing sectors of the economy. The self-employed in early modern Japan did not constitute a particular social and economic class; instead they were often part-time farmer and part-time factory worker or part-time merchant and part-time factory worker.

After World War II there was rapid economic growth accompanied by the advancement of industrial technology and modern management; with these developments came a steady rise in the level of wages. As a result, the proportion of self-employed persons declined as more workers became full-time wage earners. In 1977 the self-employed accounted for slightly more than 14 percent of all nonagricultural workers. The income of self-employed workers ranges widely, but most are making relatively low earnings, below the level of most workers employed in corporate enterprises.

Kurita Ken

self-help

(jiryoku kyūsai). In Japanese law, the preservation or realization of one's rights through the use of one's own means, without resort to official organs or resources. An example of self-help is the use of force by a property owner against another who, without authority, is occupying or in possession of such property, in order to expel such a person or recover the property. In modern nations, the basic premise is that to preserve or realize one's rights, one must obtain a judgment from a court of the nation and obtain a compulsory execution based on that judgment, which is accomplished through official organs. A private individual's realization of his rights by his own force is impermissible because it disrupts the social order.

The manifestation of this principle in the realm of property is the right of possession (SEN'YŪ). Even an unauthorized possessor has a possessory right protected by law. Therefore, if the owner should, by force, seize the thing possessed, the possessor may obtain its return. In order to assert his right of ownership, the owner would have no legal recourse but to realize this right by instituting a separate action after the possessor had recovered the object by his own action.

Academic theory recognizes an exception to this, however, when a thief takes another person's property. In such a case one may achieve recovery by force. This is based on the possessory right but may also be said to be an exceptional case in which self-help is permissible. If self-help is allowed, such action loses its illegal character and does not give rise to penalties or awards of compensation for damages in torts. Thus, self-help is recognized in emergency situations, where, unless force is used to protect one's rights, those rights will become extremely difficult to realize, or where the disadvantage suffered would be very great. There are not, however, many decisions in Japan based on the principle of self-help.

It has been pointed out that in those countries (including Japan) whose legal system derives from the continental legal system, in which authority is concentrated in the state, self-help is not recognized in principle. In England and America, however, where a self-regulated society is highly valued, self-help is recognized. In Japan, there are no statutory provisions regarding instances in which self-help is recognized. However, there have been proposals to give self-help broader recognition.

KATŌ Ichirō

sembakoki

("thousand-tooth thresher"). A threshing implement used by farmers in less developed areas as late as the 1940s. It had about 20 flat, pointed iron tines (1.5 cm by 40 cm or 0.6 in by 16 in) attached to a crossbar frame. Rice stalks drawn through the tines were stripped of their ripe grains. It is said that the tool was invented by an Ōsaka carpenter and came into general use around 1700. The *sembakoki* was also called *gokedaoshi* ("widow-killer"), because it was much more efficient than the primitive threshing tools used by poor widows, who were consequently put out of work.

Sembon Matsubara

Pine grove in the city of Numazu, Shizuoka Prefecture, central Honshū. Located west of the mouth of the river Kanōgawa, it extends to the river Fujikawa, constituting part of a great belt of wooded area that is protection against wind and tidal waves. Devastated during the Sengoku period (1467–1568), it was later replanted. There are memorial plaques for the men of letters WAKAYAMA BOKUSUI and INOUE YASUSHI here. The area also offers good swimming resorts.

semburi

Swertia japonica. A biennial herb of the gentian family (Gentianaceae) which grows wild in sunny fields and hills throughout Japan. Its dark purple stem grows straight up to a height of 25–30 centimeters (10–12 in). Its leaves, which grow in opposite pairs along its branches, are thin, linear, entire, and often purplish green. In autumn many white flowers with purple stripes bloom in clusters atop the branches and in the leaf axils. The corolla is deeply split into five sections.

Semburi has been used as a stomach medicine from ancient times to the present. The entire plant is collected when in blossom, then dried in the shade and boiled down. It has a bitter taste which supposedly survives a thousand immersions in boiling water, hence its name *semburi* (from *sen*, one thousand, and *furi*, decoctions).

Two similar species not usable as medicine are *murasaki semburi* (*S. pseudochinensis*) and *inusemburi* (*S. diluta* var. *tosaensis*). The former grows throughout the warm areas of East Asia; larger than *semburi*, it has wide, dark purplish leaves which open flat. The latter differs from *semburi* in that it has oblanceolate leaves, a slimmer flower nectary, and an almost total lack of a bitter taste.

MATSUDA Osamu

sembutsu → Buddha tiles

Semenov, Grigorii Mikhailovich (1890–1946)

Cossack leader and Japanese protégé in Siberia and Manchuria from 1918 until 1945. Born in the Trans-Baikal region of eastern Siberia, he joined the Russian army in 1908 and rose to the rank of captain by 1917. Commissioned by the Provisional Government after the March Revolution to recruit a detachment in Trans-Baikalia for service on the European front, he instead took advantage of chaotic conditions attending the Russian Civil War and Allied Intervention (see SIBERIAN INTERVENTION) to become a virtually independent warlord. Styling himself a White (anti-Bolshevik) leader, Semenov won Japanese patronage, but his indiscriminate savagery and his insubordination to the acknowledged White leader Admiral Kolchak antagonized the British and Americans. As the anti-Bolshevik cause foundered in 1920, he retired to Dalny (J: Dairen; Ch: Dalian or Talien). For the next 20 years, under Japanese guidance, he wielded influence among Russian and Cossack communities throughout Manchuria and China. Captured in Dairen by Soviet paratroopers on 22 August 1945, he was flown to Moscow, tried as a counterrevolutionary, and executed by hanging on 30 August 1946.

📖 ———Ataman Semenov, *O sebe* (About Myself; 1938).

John J. STEPHAN

semi → cicadas

Semimaru

Legendary blind lute player and poet, the subject of several premodern works of poetry, fiction, and drama. His name first appeared in the imperial WAKA anthology GOSEN WAKASHŪ (ca 955–966), where authorship of a single poem is attributed to Semimaru. The headnote asserts that it was composed "on seeing the passersby when living in a hut at Ausaka Barrier." Throughout history Semimaru has been associated with Ausaka (now Ōsakayama), a slope about five miles east of the center of modern Kyōto, along the natural route through a narrow pass in the mountain range separating Kyōto from the Lake Biwa area. From 646 on, Ausaka was the site of a government-controlled checkpoint, Ausaka Barrier (Ausaka no Seki; pronounced Ōsaka no Seki); even when the barrier was no longer strictly maintained, Ausaka remained a natural stopping point for travelers and a place where roadside entertainments were offered.

In addition to the *Gosen wakashū* poem, his most famous work, Semimaru is credited with three other poems in imperial anthologies, while three anonymous poems in the KOKINSHŪ (905) are ascribed informally to him as well. These seven Semimaru poems show striking thematic similarity, all evoking an atmosphere of impermanence, uncertainty, homelessness, and suffering. The *Gosen wakashū* poem, concerning travelers meeting and parting at Ausaka Barrier, was included by FUJIWARA NO SADAIE (also known as Teika) in HYAKUNIN ISSHU (ca 1235–41), his selection of single poems by 100 poets.

The most important prose work concerning Semimaru is a story in the KONJAKU MONOGATARI (12th century). Here, Semimaru is called a former servant of Prince Atsuzane, the eighth son of Emperor Uda (r 887–897). Semimaru, now blind and living in a hut by the Ausaka Barrier, was renowned for his skill as a lutenist. Minamoto no Hiromasa, a courtier interested in hearing Semimaru perform, traveled every night for three years to the Ausaka Barrier. Finally, on the last night of the third year, when Hiromasa revealed his presence, he learned from Semimaru three secret melodies for the lute. The story ends with the statement that Semimaru was the first BIWA HŌSHI, or blind "lute priest."

The Semimaru legend reaches its peak of pathos with the NŌ play *Semimaru*, generally ascribed to the major Nō playwright ZEAMI Motokiyo. Here Semimaru is described as the fourth son of Emperor Daigo (r 897–930). Because Semimaru's congenital blindness is interpreted as the result of evil conduct in a previous incarnation, the emperor orders his son abandoned at Ausaka. A courtier escorts Semimaru to his place of exile, symbolically shaves his head, dresses him as a beggar-priest, and leaves him with a single possession from his life as prince, his lute. There Semimaru's mad sister Sakagami finds him by chance, having heard his music, remains briefly with him, and leaves him again to his terrible loneliness.

The last major work concerning Semimaru is the puppet drama *Semimaru* (ca 1688), an early work of the great playwright CHIKAMATSU MONZAEMON. The third act is closely modeled on the Nō version, but the complex plot also features love affairs, the curses of Semimaru's jealous wife, swashbuckling battles, and a happy ending for Semimaru with the restoration of his sight and the promise of a prosperous future for his descendants.

— Kawamata Keiichi, ed, *Chikamatsu Monzaemon shū*, Nihon bungaku sōsho, series 2, vol 11 (1928). Susan Matisoff, *The Legend of Semimaru, Blind Musician of Japan* (1978). Muroki Yatarō, *Katarimono no kenkyū* (1970). Sanari Kentarō, ed, *Yōkyoku taikan*, vol 3 (rev ed, 1964). Tashiro Keiichirō, "Yōkyoku *Semimaru* ni tsuite," *Hikaku bungaku kenkyū* (March 1973 and September 1973).
Susan MATISOFF

semmin

("lowborn" or outcasts). Generally hereditary groups classified below free commoners (RYŌMIN) in premodern Japan. Under the RITSURYŌ SYSTEM established in the late 7th century, there were five levels in this lowest class of society, as there were in the Chinese model for the system. The *gosen* ("five *semmin*") as these levels were called, were, in descending order, the *ryōko*, guards of the imperial tombs, the *kanko*, government menials, the *kenin*, servants of aristocratic families, the *kunuhi* (or *kannuhi*), slaves of government officials, and the *shinuhi*, slaves of aristocratic families. The *kunuhi* and *shinuhi*, who were in the NUHI, or slave category, could actually be bought and sold, and they were not allowed to establish families of their own. In the Nara period (710–794), 10 percent of the population was *semmin*, but in the early 10th century the *semmin* system was abolished. Nevertheless, succeeding periods of Japanese history continued to have their own lowborn or outcast strata at the bottom of society. The GENIN of the medieval period (13th to 16th centuries) suffered harsh social discrimination, as did the *eta* and HININ of the Edo period (1600–1868). In 1871 the outcast system was abolished by law.

semmon gakkō

(professional school). A type of higher education institution in the pre–World War II education system. Established by the Professional School Order of 1903. Graduation from middle school or girl's higher school was required for entrance, and the course of study was three years or more. Some professional schools were affiliated with universities and some were independent. Many gave instruction in the fields of medicine, law, economics, and commerce; those that gave training in agriculture, technology, and business were called *jitsugyō semmon gakkō* (technical colleges).

In 1935 there were 177 *semmon gakkō*, of which 52 were national, 11 were other public schools, and 114 were private. Almost all the national and other public schools were vocational schools offering a single course of study. Throughout the prewar period all institutions of higher education for women were professional schools. In contrast to the universities which tried to create an intellectual elite, the professional schools worked to produce a pool of trained personnel.

In the prewar period the bulk of students in institutions of higher learning were in the professional schools: in 1905, 81 percent of the total number of higher education graduates were from these schools and in 1935, 65 percent. After World War II the professional school system was abolished under the new system and most of the schools became four-year universities.
AMANO Ikuo

semmyō

(literally, "to proclaim a decree"). The generic name for ancient imperial decrees composed in Japanese, as distinguished from those in Chinese. Before the Nara period (710–794) all imperial proclamations *(mikotonori)* were written in Japanese, and only in the 8th century, when the Chinese-influenced RITSURYŌ SYSTEM of government was consolidated, were most of the decrees and statements of the emperor written in KAMBUN (classical Chinese). Imperial edicts in the Chinese language were called *shō* (or *shōsho*) and *choku* (or *chokusho*). The term *semmyō* for edicts in Japanese has been used since the Heian period (794–1185).

Semmyō were drawn up in the Ministry of Central Imperial Affairs (Nakatsukasashō) and read aloud on the emperor's behalf by a special herald *(semmyōshi)*, usually a minister of high rank. The audience was composed of nobles and functionaries of the state, who received these edicts on such occasions as accessions to the throne, nominations of successors to the throne, deaths in the imperial family, changes of the era names (NENGŌ), diplomatic missions, the commendation or reprimand of high officials and nobles, revelations of subversive activities, and so forth. In tone, *semmyō* are similar to the ancient Japanese ritual prayers (NORITO), since their mode of conception is Shintoistic and based on the idea of the emperor's divinity. But in contrast to *norito*, *semmyō* contain elements of Buddhist and Confucian thought.

The texts of the *semmyō* followed a fixed formula *(semmyōtai)* prescribed in chapter 21 of the TAIHŌ CODE (702). *Semmyō* were written in Chinese characters but were intended to be read in Japanese. That is, the word order corresponded to Japanese syntax, and semantically used characters were followed by smaller characters used phonetically to mark Japanese grammatical morphemes. This writing system, known as *semmyōgaki*, was obviously influenced by the old Korean Idu script. It can be considered a forerunner of the mixed Sino-Japanese writing system *(wakan konkōbun)* of medieval and modern Japanese.

Semmyō are preserved in all the RIKKOKUSHI (Six National Histories) except the first one, *Nihon shoki* (720), in which all imperial edicts are given in Chinese—presumably a subsequent translation from the original Japanese. The largest number of extant *semmyō* are included in the *Shoku nihongi* (797), the second of the Rikkokushi, in which there are 62 *semmyō*, ranging from the edict proclaiming Emperor MOMMU's accession to the throne in 697 to Emperor KAMMU's pardon of General Ki no Kosami in 789. The latest *semmyō* are preserved in the *Nihon sandai jitsuroku* (901), the last of the Rikkokushi. These last examples contain a great number of Sinicisms and stereotyped repetition of traditional forms. See also DIPLOMATICS.

— Aida Jirō, *Nihon no komonjo*, 2 vols (1954). Kaneko Takeo, *Shoku nihongi semmyō kō* (1941). H. Zachert, *Die kaiserlichen Erlasse des Shoku-Nihongi* (1950).
Bruno H. LEWIN

sempai-kōhai

(senior-junior). An informal relationship ubiquitous in Japanese organizations, schools, and associations, in which older, experienced members offer friendship, assistance, and advice to inexperienced members, who reciprocate with gratitude, respect, and, often, personal loyalty. The relationship usually involves males only.

The *sempai-kōhai* tie is determined by the date of entrance into a particular organization. The *sempai*, perhaps a graduate of the same school or a senior in the work-group, acts as a friend and patron, disciplining and teaching the neophyte appropriate conduct. If they are both students, the *sempai* sometimes tutors his junior, as well as drilling him in skills, as would happen in an athletic club. *Sempai-kōhai* ties sometimes provide mechanisms for conflict resolution, as the *sempai* becomes an intermediary in the transmission of warnings, complaints, and other information from senior managers to younger workers. In addition, the *sempai* is the newcomer's social guide, introducing him to bars, women, and suitable social manners for the group. Over time a member of a company or other large organization will have had several *sempai* and many of his own *kōhai*.

In return for this friendship and assistance, the *kōhai* may address the *sempai* in honorific language. In fact, he may continue to do so for the rest of his life, as the ties may outlast their participation in the same organization. He is expected to show gratitude and enthusiasm for the senior's leadership; later he may be in the position to perform personal favors for the *sempai* or his family.

Sempai-kōhai ties permeate Japanese society. HABATSU, BATSU, and other personal networks function to some extent in *sempai-kōhai* terms, and *sempai-kōhai* alliances often smooth the way toward a quick, satisfactory resolution of a problem. Successful careers have often been promoted by these long-term relationships, which can also result in help for younger members of the family.

The *sempai-kōhai* relationship as described above represents an ideal type, varying according to area, age, and the size and nature of the organization. It can also have its negative aspects, as when the *sempai* exploits his *kōhai*. Again, in other contexts, such as in the prewar Imperial Japanese Army, *dōki* (same graduating class) ties sometimes took precedence over *sempai-kōhai* ties.
Thomas P. ROHLEN

Sendai

Downtown Sendai, the capital of Miyagi Prefecture, northern Honshū. The river in the left foreground is the Hirosegawa.

Senaga Kamejirō (1907–)

Politician and leader of social movements in Okinawa. Vice-chairman of the JAPAN COMMUNIST PARTY (JCP). Born in Okinawa, Senaga became interested in Marxism-Leninism while a student at the Seventh Higher School in Kagoshima. He was expelled for his leftist activities and thereafter worked in various factories. He again came into conflict with the authorities for taking part in a strike and was jailed for three years. After his release in 1935, he saw military service in China and returned to Okinawa in 1940. Under United States military rule after World War II, Senaga was active as a leader and later chairman of the Okinawa People's Party (Okinawa Jimmintō). He was especially involved in its campaign against the maintenance of US military bases in Okinawa. In 1956 he was elected mayor of the city of Naha but was removed from office by the American military government. Later he became active in the movement for Okinawan reversion to Japan. In 1970, under a new provision allowing Okinawan participation in Japanese national elections, he was elected to the lower house of the Diet as a candidate of the Okinawa People's Party; in 1973, a year after reversion, his party merged with the JCP. See also OKINAWA: military bases and the land issue.
Harada Katsumasa

Senchakushū

(*Senchaku hongan nembutsu shū*, 1198, The Selection of the *Nembutsu* of the Original Vow). Also known as *Senjakushū*. A treatise by HŌNEN (1133–1212), the founder of the JŌDO SECT, detailing the principles of his Pure Land Buddhist faith. The work is arranged in 16 chapters, each quoting the scriptural basis for a point of Hōnen's doctrine together with his explanations and his replies to hypothetical questions and criticisms. It identifies the *Dai muryōju kyō* (Larger *Sukhāvatīvyūha-sūtra*), the *Kammuryōju kyō* (*Amitāyurdhyāna-sūtra),* and the *Amidakyō* (Smaller *Sukhāvatīvyūha-sūtra*) as the threefold scripture of the "Pure Land school," and Bodhiruci (fl ca 500 AD), Tanluan (T'an-luan, 476–542), Daochuo (Tao-ch'o, 562–645), and Shandao (Shan-tao, 613–681) as its major patriarchs. On the basis of the teachings of these scriptures and patriarchs, Hōnen maintains the following points in support of faith in the Buddha AMIDA alone and in NEMBUTSU, or salvation through the recitation of Amida's name: (1) there are two paths to liberation from the bondage of life, suffering, and death (Skt: *saṃsāra*), either through strenuous efforts of saintly beings or through reliance on the vows of Amida Buddha to save all sentient beings in his Pure Land; (2) because of the decadence of the age (J: *mappō*), only the second of these is feasible; (3) invoking *nembutsu* is by itself totally sufficient to achieve rebirth into the Pure Land; and (4) this is so because *nembutsu* is the practice expressly selected by Amida as the vehicle of enlightenment.

The *Senchakushū* set down the doctrinal basis for an independent Pure Land Buddhist movement. It gave to what had been an amorphous piety and marginal monastic cult a firm grounding in the continental Buddhist tradition and a clear set of doctrines consistent with the Mahāyāna ideal of universal salvation. It brought Pure Land Buddhism to the forefront of Japanese religious life.
Allan A. Andrews

Sendai

Capital of Miyagi Prefecture, northern Honshū. It is the largest city in northeastern Japan and the political, economic, and cultural center of the region. The town developed around Sendai Castle (also called Aoba Castle), built by DATE MASAMUNE in 1601. Although destroyed by Allied bombing during World War II, it has been completely rebuilt. Industries include manufacture of silk, wood products, rubber, foodstuffs, and steel. There are also petrochemical and printing plants. Rice and vegetables are cultivated in the surrounding area. Educational centers include Tōhoku University, museums, and an observatory. The former site of the castle, the Ōsaki Hachiman Shrine, and the Tanabata Festival, held in August, draw visitors. Pop: 664,799.

Sendai

City in Kagoshima Prefecture, Kyūshū. During the Nara period (710–794) it was the seat of a provincial capital (*kokufu*) and temple (KOKUBUNJI). Industries include paper, of which it is the leading manufacturer in the prefecture, lacquer ware, and foodstuffs. Rice is its principal agricultural product. A city planning project, which included the construction of a river port, was under way in the early 1980s. Pop: 65,642.

Sendai Bay

(Sendai Wan). Inlet of the Pacific Ocean, on the southeastern coast of Miyagi Prefecture, northern Honshū. Extends from the Oshika Peninsula to Unoozaki, a cape in northeastern Fukushima Prefecture. Facing the Sendai Plain, it serves as an ocean port area for the Sendai Industrial Zone.

Sendaigawa

River in northern Kagoshima Prefecture, Kyūshū, flowing west to enter the East China Sea at the city of Sendai. It is the second largest river in Kyūshū. The Tsuruta Dam, located on the middle reaches, is used for flood prevention and electric power generation. Numerous hot springs are located along the river. The water is used for irrigation. Length: 137 km (85 mi); area of drainage basin: 1,600 sq km (618 sq mi).

Sendai Plain

(Sendai Heiya). Located in central Miyagi Prefecture, northern Honshū. Bordering the Pacific Ocean, the northern part consists of the flood plain of the river Kitakamigawa, where marshes abound, and the southern part of the flood plain of the rivers Natorigawa and Abukumagawa. High-quality rice is cultivated. The major cities are Sendai and Ishinomaki, and the area is now a focus of industrial development. Area: approximately 1,000 sq km (386 sq mi).

Sengai Gibon (1750–1837)

Zen painter and calligrapher whose works are animated by a warm, satiric, and often self-mocking humor. Born in Mino (now Gifu Prefecture), Sengai became a Rinzai-sect monk at the age of 11. (Gibon was his Buddhist priest name.) After 50 years as a monk, he retired in 1811 from the position of 123rd abbot of Shōfukuji in Hakata (now the city of Fukuoka), the oldest Zen temple in Japan. Sengai devoted his final 26 years to teaching, painting, and calligraphy. Sengai wrote that his ink-play should not be considered serious art; nevertheless, there was a steady stream of people who visited him and requested his brushwork, and he willingly painted for all who asked. His works treat a wide variety of themes, from traditional Buddhist figures such as Daruma (Skt: Bodhidharma) and Kannon (Skt: Avalokiteśvara) to landscapes, flowers, plants, and animals. Sengai frequently added inscriptions to his works in free, unassuming calligraphy, often containing puns and jokes. One of his most famous works is *Circle, Triangle, and Square*. The painting, outwardly so simple, employs different tones of ink, rapid and decisive brushwork, overlapping of forms, and strength of composition. Nevertheless, its ultimate "meaning" cannot be translated into words; perhaps this is why in his old age Sengai, like many other Zen masters, took up the brush. The Idemitsu Art Gallery in Tōkyō owns the largest collection of his works.
Stephen Addiss

Sengen Shrine

(Sengen Jinja; formerly Fujisan Hongū Sengen Jinja). Shintō shrine in the city of Fujinomiya, Shizuoka Prefecture, dedicated to the goddess Konohana no Sakuyahime no Mikoto and two other deities. The Sengen Jinja is the central shrine of a cult that venerates the volcano Mt. Fuji (Fujisan) as a sacred mountain (see MOUNTAINS, WORSHIP OF). Based primarily in the prefectures in the vicinity of Mt. Fuji, the cult has more than 1,300 shrines, most of which bear the name Sengen (or Asama) Jinja, including well-known shrines such as the Sengen Jinja (Shingū) in the city of Shizuoka and the Sengen (Asama) Jinja in Ichinomiya, Yamanashi Prefecture. Although Mt. Fuji was originally venerated only by inhabitants of the region, belief in the mountain as a benefactor gradually spread throughout much of eastern Japan after the 17th century as a result of proselytizing by itinerant priests (OSHI). One of these oshi, Hasegawa Kakugyō (1541–1646), established regional Fuji associations designed to promote pilgrimages to the mountain. Fuji associations (Fujikō; see KŌ) were popular in Edo (now Tōkyō) and surrounding areas throughout the Edo period (1600–1868) and were eventually organized into SECT SHINTŌ groups, such as Maruyamakyō, Fusō-kyō, and Jikkōkyō. The present building of the Sengen Shrine was restored by the first Tokugawa shōgun, TOKUGAWA IEYASU, and is known for the two-story Sengen style architecture of the main hall (honden). The major annual festival is held on 4 November; YABU-SAME (archery on horseback) is held 4–6 May.

Stanley WEINSTEIN

Sengoku daimyō

General term for powerful local lords who, during the Sengoku or Warring States period (1467–1568), displaced the military governors (SHUGO DAIMYŌ) appointed by the Muromachi shogunate (1338–1573) in the mid-14th century. Sengoku daimyō by the 1540s had gained considerable independent control of the lands they held. As they increased in military strength, they began to fight among themselves for regional hegemony, but in the 1570s and 1580s they were subjugated by the hegemons ODA NOBUNAGA and TOYOTOMI HIDE-YOSHI. Sengoku daimyō rose to power from positions such as important vassals of shugo daimyō (the UESUGI FAMILY and the ODA FAMILY), local proprietors (the MŌRI FAMILY and the TOKUGAWA FAMILY), and the ranks of masterless samurai (the Later Hōjō [see HŌJŌ FAMILY] and the Saitō), or had themselves been shugo daimyō (the TAKEDA FAMILY, the IMAGAWA FAMILY, the ŌUCHI FAMILY, and the SHIMAZU FAMILY). As they grew, they recruited as their housemen powerful provincial warrior-landowners (KOKUJIN) and through them increased their military capacities and their control over the peasantry. In their effort to establish their domains as independent political and economic entities, they laid down house laws (KAKUN; BUNKOKUHŌ), built castles, made cadastral surveys, and encouraged the development of commerce and industry. They developed new rice lands to increase revenue, built irrigation systems, and erected post stations along major thoroughfares. However, unlike the daimyō of the Edo period (1600–1868), the Sengoku daimyō were obliged to leave their more powerful retainers in possession of private fiefs. They did not draw samurai away from the villages and garrison them in their castle towns and thus were unable to set up a fully centralized power structure. On the national level the first to attempt establishment of such a centralized administrative system were Oda Nobunaga and Toyotomi Hideyoshi, and by submitting to them, the Sengoku daimyō prepared the way for the emergence of the Edo-period kinsei daimyō (see DAIMYŌ).

John W. HALL

Sengokuhara

Highland north of the lake ASHINOKO, near the town of Hakone, southwestern Kanagawa Prefecture, central Honshū. It was formed from an old volcanic crater of HAKONEYAMA. Until recently a wild and desolate area covered with grasses and clusters of marsh plants, it now has golf courses and ice skating rinks as well as a few modern hotels. Average elevation: 700 m (2,296 ft).

Sengoku period

Also known as the Warring States period. The years from 1467, the beginning of the ŌNIN WAR (1467–77), until 1568, when ODA NO-BUNAGA entered Kyōto to assert national hegemony. The Sengoku period is also dated by some historians from 1490, when Hosokawa

Masamoto (1430–73), the KANREI or shogunal deputy, took over the actual power of the MUROMACHI SHOGUNATE; or alternately from 1491, when HŌJŌ SŌUN conquered Izu Province (now part of Shizuoka Prefecture) and began to rise to control over the Kantō region.

The term GEKOKUJŌ (the overturning of those on top by those below) is most often used to characterize this period. As a result of weakening shogunal leadership, local shugodai (deputy military governors) and KOKUJIN (local military proprietors) established military and political control over provinces that had hitherto been ruled by the great SHUGO (military governor) houses. The imperial court, the Ashikaga shōgun, the shugo based in Kyōto, and temples found themselves powerless against this new group of local rulers, called Sengoku daimyō by historians. These regional leaders waged constant war to defend or enlarge their domains, and it was not until the 1560s that Nobunaga defeated his competitors and emerged as a potential national unifer.

Despite political instability there was remarkable economic growth during the Sengoku period. The Sengoku daimyō worked to enrich their domains and build up their armies. They carried out flood control and land reclamation projects; rice harvests increased substantially, as did the production of raw materials for handicraft industries. The mining industry witnessed the most conspicuous growth, with many new mines opened for the production of gold, silver, copper, and iron. This in turn furthered the development of smiths and foundries. The cotton industry also had its beginnings in this period. Before that time all cotton yarn and cloth had been imported, but cultivation of cotton started in Mikawa Province (now part of Aichi Prefecture) around this time, leading to the production of domestic yarn and cloth, with cotton cloth becoming the principal fabric of the premodern period. Paralleling the development of local industries, commerce also expanded. Numerous stores were established in towns and along heavily traveled roads, boat transportation flourished, and the daimyō were able to trade with provinces far from their own.

The increase in trade over a wide area resulted in the formation of commercial cities, where commodities were collected and distributed. Representative cities were Sakai, Hyōgo (now Kōbe), Kuwana, and Hakata. With the end of the Ōnin War, Kyōto, once a battlefield, revived as the industrial and commercial center of the nation. Powerful merchants managed the affairs of these cities and towns and attained a degree of political autonomy, defending them in cooperation with the ordinary citizenry. Christian missionaries in Sakai at the time were struck with the similarities between Sakai and the free cities of medieval Europe. During the later Sengoku period, CASTLE TOWNS grew up around the castles of influential daimyō and served as political and commercial centers.

Another paradoxical development during the century of civil war was the nationwide diffusion of culture, formerly the prerogative of the nobility and clergy in Kyōto and Nara. A major role in this process was played by Zen priests and rengashi (linked-verse poets) who were invited to the provinces by the Sengoku daimyō. The Zen priests taught Confucianism, classical Chinese poetry (kanshi), and INK PAINTING and were also influential in the publication of various books. The rengashi taught RENGA AND HAIKAI and the Japanese classics. Under the patronage of the wealthy merchants of Sakai and Kyōto, who were themselves outstanding practitioners, the traditional arts, the TEA CEREMONY, NŌ, and various types of music flourished. Books aimed at the general public, like OTOGI-ZŌSHI (collections of moralistic stories) and the KANGINSHŪ (a collection of popular songs), were published. The SETSUYŌSHŪ, a dictionary for everyday use compiled by Zen priests, was also published. Christianity was introduced to Japan by Francis XAVIER in 1549. He and his fellow missionaries also brought with them European, or namban ("southern barbarian"), culture.

Although some scholars see the Sengoku period as marking a transitional period between the medieval and premodern ages in light of various emergent trends, the most commonly held view is that it represents the final stage of Japan's middle ages.

Suzuki Ryōichi

Sen Hime (1597–1666)

Daughter of the shōgun TOKUGAWA HIDETADA (r 1605–23) and wife of TOYOTOMI HIDEYORI, son of the national unifier TOYOTOMI HIDEYOSHI; her mother, Tatsu Hime, and Hideyori's mother, YODO-GIMI, were sisters. Sen Hime was wedded to Hideyori on 4 September 1603 (Keichō 8.7.28), a half year after her grandfather TOKUGAWA IEYASU became shōgun; the union between the two children accorded with the dead Hideyoshi's wishes but was evidently a political design on the part of the Tokugawa to paper over the growing differences between the two families. That design was doomed to failure, since the Toyotomi party refused to countenance Hideyori's submission to the Tokugawa. The conflict was resolved in favor of the Tokugawa in the Ōsaka campaigns of 1614–15 (see ŌSAKA CASTLE, SIEGES OF); as Ōsaka Castle was about to fall on 3 June 1615 (Keichō 20.5.7), Sen Hime was sent to her father to plead for her husband's life, but her intercession failed, and Hideyori committed suicide. The next year Sen Hime was remarried to Honda Heihachirō Tadatoki, son of the *daimyō* of Kuwana (later of Himeji), and after his death in 1626 lived out the rest of her life in Edo (now Tōkyō) as a widow. The famous story of her attempted abduction by Sakazaki Naomori (d 1616), who is said to have claimed Sen Hime's hand as her rescuer from the flames of Ōsaka Castle and interrupted her bridal procession to Honda's residence, has some historical basis. Less credible is the legend of Sen Hime as an insatiable, man-devouring young widow; this story of dissolute living in high places, apparently current already in Sen Hime's lifetime, was made popular in song, moralistic KŌDAN tales, and *kabuki* plays such as *Yoshida goten maneku furisode* (1891; The Beckoning Kimono Sleeve) by Takeshiba Kenji.

George ELISON

seniority system

(*nenkō joretsu; nenkō* system). System of employment in Japan in which an employee's rank, salary, and qualifications within a firm are based on the length of service in the company. In this system, wage increases and promotions are tightly regulated by one's school background, sex, and type of work.

The practice can be traced to a period of serious labor shortages during World War I when the Yokosuka Naval Shipyard adopted it as a means of securing enough technical and skilled workers. The system has won wide acceptance, especially among Japan's big businesses, and, together with the compulsory RETIREMENT system, has led to the uniquely Japanese system of lifetime employment.

The seniority system has several important features. Workers, upon hire, are expected to stay with the company until their retirement. Identification with their company is exceptionally strong: employees are regularly recruited from among young people graduating from school, and hiring of midcareer workers from the open labor market is rare. Starting wages are determined by educational background, age, sex, and type of job, while wage increases are primarily governed by age and length of service; retirement pay is based on length of employment, position, and wage level at the time of retirement. Seniority is also an important factor in promotions; white-collar workers with a university education generally advance at the same speed as their colleagues of similar educational background, age, and length of service. The speed of promotions is slower for clerical workers with high school backgrounds, and the highest positions they can attain are generally limited. Demotions are rare. In some recent cases, however, position assignments have been based on competence, although wages continue to be determined on the basis of seniority. Reassignments of job duties within a position level are very common.

The seniority system enables employees to benefit from stability of employment: the longer they work at a single company, even at comparatively low wages, the greater their overall remuneration. It makes it extremely difficult for workers to shift from one employer to another, although this is not necessarily true with blue-collar workers, whose turnover has shown a sharp increase since 1970. The seniority system also is a mixed blessing to employers. They can benefit from strong worker loyalty and stability and the resultant ease with which they can formulate personnel plans. They suffer, however, from the necessity of carrying along surplus workers, difficulty in assigning employees to appropriate tasks, and growing inflexibility within their organizations.

In the 1970s, with the steady increase in numbers of employees in higher age brackets, the pyramidal personnel structure, long the basis of the seniority system, started to crumble as Japanese corporations began to suffer from skyrocketing labor costs. A growing number of corporations started reviewing the seniority system in the late 1970s, and some have even stopped giving pay raises to workers in their forties or older. Faced with a variety of difficult problems, including lower economic growth, intensifying competition, and internationalized activities, Japanese corporations have been forced to place more emphasis on their employees' talents and abilities. Japan's seniority system has thus been placed at an important crossroads. See also EMPLOYMENT SYSTEM, MODERN; WAGE SYSTEM.

YAMADA Makiko

Seni Pramot (1905–)

Also known as M. R. Seni Pramoj. Thai politician, lawyer, and poet. While serving as the Thai ambassador to the United States in 1942, he was informed by Prime Minister PHIBUL SONGKHRAM that Thailand had declared war against the United States. Rather than formally transmit this message, Seni asked the US government for support in organizing military units for the anti-Japanese FREE THAI MOVEMENT. Under Seni's leadership, those units were stationed at the US Army Air Force base at Yunnan, China, in 1943. Cooperating with units of the Free Thai Movement in England, Seni's units provided intelligence services for the Allied forces until the end of the war. Seni was appointed prime minister in September 1945. He concluded peace treaties with Great Britain and China in early 1946. See also THAILAND AND JAPAN.

ICHIKAWA Kenjirō

senji

A form of imperial edict used during the Heian period (794–1185); developed after the establishment of the KURŌDO–DOKORO (Bureau of Archivists or Chamberlains' Office) in 810. It was less complicated to draft and issue than the *shō* (or *shōsho*) and *choku* (or *chokusho*), earlier forms of imperial edict. An imperial handmaid (*naishi*) conveyed the orders of the sovereign to an official in the Kurōdo–dokoro, who in turn relayed them to the ranking noble on duty at the court that day. The noble then had it drafted and issued as an edict either through the secretary (*geki*) or the Controlling Board (Benkan). Edicts issued through the Benkan were termed *kansenji*. Several different types of *senji* were employed, depending on which official issued it to which clerk, or on the contents of the edict.

G. Cameron HURST III

Senjinkun

(Instructions for the Battlefield). Military code issued to soldiers on 8 January 1941 in the name of TŌJŌ HIDEKI, then army minister. As the SINO-JAPANESE WAR OF 1937–1945 dragged on and military morale and discipline sagged, it was decided that in addition to the IMPERIAL RESCRIPT TO SOLDIERS AND SAILORS (1882) and several other exhortative codes, a new set of instructions would be issued. The drafting of the code was led by Imamura Hitoshi (1886–1968), chief of the Army Headquarters Education Administration, who was assisted by writers like YOSHIKAWA EIJI.

The code was phrased as a series of injunctions concerning the Japanese empire, the imperial armed forces, military regulations, esprit de corps, combat readiness, faith in ultimate victory, veneration of Shintō deities, filial piety, sense of responsibility, attitudes toward life and death, and so on. The concept of Japan's unique national polity (KOKUTAI) was stressed throughout. More specifically, the code enjoined absolute obedience to orders and forbade retreat ("A soldier must never abandon the field to the enemy, even at the risk of his life") or surrender ("A soldier must never suffer the disgrace of being captured alive"). All soldiers on active duty were given copies of the Senjinkun; the instructions were also frequently read aloud by commanding officers. As Japan's military position deteriorated in World War II, prohibitions against retreat and surrender were increasingly emphasized. This sometimes led to suicide missions and the annihilation of whole battalions. Toward the end of the war, copies of the Senjinkun were distributed among the civilian population, including schoolchildren, to prepare them for the expected Allied invasion.

📖 ——Hashikawa Bunzō, ed, *Shōwa shisō shū*, vol 2 (1978).

AWAYA Kentarō

Senjōgahara

Highland. In the mountain Nantaisan's western foothills, northwestern Tochigi Prefecture, central Honshū; transitional from a dry swampland to a grassy highland. Popular with campers, hikers, and trout fishers; it is known for its alpine flora and autumn foliage. Part of Nikkō National Park. Average elevation: 1,400 m (4,592 ft); area: approximately 10 sq km (3.9 sq mi).

Senjōgatake

Also known as Senjōdake. Mountain on the border between Nagano and Yamanashi prefectures, central Honshū; in the northern part of the Akaishi Mountains. Composed of Paleozoic strata. A cirque stretches east and north from the summit. Height: 3,033 m (9,948 ft).

Senjōsan

Hill on the northern slope of DAISEN, western Tottori Prefecture, western Honshū. Surrounded on the east, north and west by 30–50 m (98–164 ft) vertical cliffs of the kind called *byōbuiwa* ("folding-screen rock"). It is known for its historical sites associated with the KEMMU RESTORATION, during which Emperor GO-DAIGO was restored to the throne (1333). Height: 616 m (2,020 ft).

Senjuji

Head temple of the Takada branch of the JŌDO SHIN SECT of Buddhism, located in the city of Tsu, Mie Prefecture. Although tradition claims that the temple was established by SHINRAN, the founder of the Jōdo Shin sect, in 1225, in all probability Senjuji was built by Shinran's disciple Shimbutsu (1209–58) and the latter's followers in the Kantō region. Originally situated in the Takada district (now part of Ninomiya Machi) of Shimotsuke Province (now Tochigi Prefecture), Senjuji was moved to its present site in 1465 by the 10th abbot, Shin'e (1434–1512). In 1477 it was designated a *chokuganji*, or temple commissioned by the imperial family to offer regular prayers for its well-being as well as for the prosperity of the empire. In 1574 Senjuji was given the status of *monzekidera*, or temple whose chief abbot was from the imperial family or aristocracy. Among its many treasures are handwritten manuscripts by Shinran. A powerful group of devotees in the early history of the Jōdo Shin sect, the Takada branch today claims about 290,000 followers.

Stanley WEINSTEIN

Senju Woolen Mill

(Senju Seijūsho). Japan's first woolen mill; one of a number of model factories established by the Meiji government in order to introduce a modern industrial system to Japan. Set up in the Senju district of Tōkyō, it began operation in 1879. Built by German technicians with machinery imported from Germany, it was designed to serve as a model for private enterprise and to meet the growing demand for military uniforms and other woolens. Administration of the mill was transferred from the Home Ministry to the Ministry of Agriculture and Commerce in 1881 and to the Army Ministry in 1888. Unique among state enterprises, it was the only government factory to introduce a completely new branch of industry and, in view of the slow growth of the private woolen industry compared to silk reeling and cotton spinning, the only one in the textile field to retain its importance for several decades. It remained the major producer of woolen textiles until after the turn of the century. See GOVERNMENT-OPERATED FACTORIES, MEIJI PERIOD.

Senkaku (1203–?)

Also known as Sengaku. Scholar and monk of the TENDAI SECT of Buddhism in the early part of the Kamakura period (1185–1333); born in Hitachi Province (now Ibaraki Prefecture). Senkaku devoted himself to the study of the 8th century poetry anthology MAN'YŌSHŪ. His bibliographical research, textual criticism, and annotations laid the foundation for future studies of the *Man'yōshū*. His main work, the *Man'yōshū chūshaku*, also known as *Sengakushō*, was completed in 1269. He died sometime after 1272.

Senkaku Islands

(Senkaku Shotō). Group of islands 160 km (99.4 mi) north of the YAEYAMA ISLANDS, western Okinawa Prefecture, including Uotsurishima (area: 4.3 sq km or 1.7 sq mi), Kōbisho (also called Kubashima), Kita Koshima, Minami Koshima, and Sekibisho. These islands are uninhabited, but the seas surrounding them are rich fishing grounds for bonito, and recently undersea oilfields have been discovered. Since the late 1960s Taiwan and the People's Republic of China have claimed the islands as Chinese, although the United States returned them to Japan with the reversion of Okinawa in 1971.

Senkaku Islands, dispute over → territory of Japan

Senke Motomaro (1888–1948)

Poet. His poetry, known for its optimistic and humanistic tone, reflects the philosophy of the SHIRAKABA SCHOOL, to which he was attracted in his youth and remained faithful until his death. He wrote prolifically, in some years publishing 30 to 40 poems each month. As he said, his poems were often too "artless." But from such artlessness came his best poems: those that describe daily occurrences without forced emotionalism. Notable among his books are *Jibun wa mita* (1918, I Saw), whose opening poem, "Kuruma no oto" (The Noise of the Carts), is frequently anthologized, and *Mukashi no ie* (1929, House of Long Ago), a long autobiographical narrative poem which attempts to describe his aristocratic upbringing.

Hiroaki SATŌ

Senki

(Battle Flag). A major leftist literary journal published from May 1928 to December 1931; from its inception until September 1930, it was the organ of the Zen Nihon Musansha Geijutsu Remmei (All Japan Federation of Proletarian Arts), better known by the acronym NAPF from its Esperanto name, Nippona Artista Proleta Federacio (see LITERARY GROUPS). *Senki* was opposed by the leftist journal BUNGEI SENSEN, the organ of another faction of the PROLETARIAN LITERATURE MOVEMENT. It was managed and edited principally by TSUBOI SHIGEJI and Yamada Seizaburō (b 1896). Contributors included KURAHARA KOREHITO, NAKANO SHIGEHARU, KOBAYASHI TAKIJI, TOKUNAGA SUNAO, and SATA INEKO. Not only did its circulation exceed 20,000 by 1930, but NAPF's distribution system—which formed *Senki* study groups at factories, farms, and schools—gave it an even larger audience. *Senki* eventually separated from NAPF and shifted from literature to propaganda in an attempt to gain political advantage from its popularity.

Theodore W. GOOSSEN

senkyo kanshō

("election interference"). Obstruction by the government of the election campaigns of opposition candidates. Three instances are particularly well known. The first took place in February 1892, following the dissolution of the Diet by the MATSUKATA MASAYOSHI cabinet, which had been forced to accept drastic budget cuts demanded by the opposition parties, the JIYŪTŌ and RIKKEN KAISHINTŌ. Throughout the campaign, the government assigned Home Minister SHINAGAWA YAJIRŌ to use every possible measure against the opposition parties. There was even bloodshed in some areas; the official report listed 25 dead and 388 wounded. The antigovernment parties, however, emerged from the election with a majority of 163 seats.

The second instance took place after ŌKUMA SHIGENOBU dissolved the Diet when his plans for military expansion were blocked by the RIKKEN SEIYŪKAI, the majority party. In the March 1915 campaign Home Minister ŌURA KANETAKE flagrantly bought votes for candidates of the RIKKEN DŌSHIKAI and other progovernment parties. He also brought considerable pressure to bear on prefectural governors to assure government victories in their districts. As a result, the Dōshikai won with a resounding majority.

The third case occurred soon after the formation of the TANAKA GIICHI cabinet in 1927. Tanaka dissolved the Diet when the RIKKEN MINSEITŌ, newly formed through a merger of the KENSEIKAI and the SEIYŪ HONTŌ, attained a majority in the House of Representatives. Although the election of February 1928 was the first one held after the passage of the Universal Manhood Suffrage Law, the government did not hesitate to interfere through the agency of Home Minister SUZUKI KISABURŌ. The government party (Seiyūkai) was returned with a majority of one seat, but Suzuki was severely criticized and forced to resign soon after.

Sennan

City in southwestern Ōsaka Prefecture, central Honshū, on Ōsaka Bay. Long known for its Izumi cotton cloth, it is still a textile center. Asbestos products are also manufactured. Principal agricultural products are rice and onions. Pop: 53,325.

sennimbari

("thousand-stitch" cloths). A strip of white cloth embellished with 1,000 stitches (French knots) sewn with red thread by 1,000 women. Red was traditionally an auspicious color, and these *sennimbari,* which were worn as sashes, were given to soldiers to ward off bullets and ensure a safe return. The custom of making *sennimbari* originated during the Sino-Japanese War of 1894–95 and continued through World War II. HARADA Katsumasa

sennin

(immortal one; Ch: *xianren* or *hsien-jen*). Persons manifesting the ideals of religious Taoism, who were imagined to have attained supernatural powers, especially immortality, by means of ascetic exercises practiced in remote mountain regions. *Sennin* were similar to the Hindu *ṛṣi* (holy man), Vedic seers who lived in mountain forests, possessed psychic powers, and were able to levitate. In China, adepts were believed to preserve a youthful appearance indefinitely by drinking elixirs containing such ingredients as powdered cinnamon, mica, deer horn, and cinnabar, and allegedly could levitate, ride clouds, and make the winds blow. The concept of the *xianren* was introduced to Japan along with Taoism, and the earliest references to Japanese *sennin* appear in Nara-period (710–794) legends concerning Ōtomo no Sennin, Azumi no Sennin, and Kume no Sennin. In the NIHON RYŌIKI (ca 822), EN NO GYŌJA (fl late 7th century), regarded as the founder of the Buddhist ascetic cult SHUGENDŌ, is referred to as a *sennin.* The term was adopted by Buddhists and occasionally used as a designation for the Buddha, because of his mastery over life and death, but more often for religious figures of great accomplishment who belonged to heterodox faiths. INOKUCHI Shōji

Sen no Rikyū (1522–1591)

Tea master of the Azuchi-Momoyama period (1568–1600); founder of the Sen school of TEA CEREMONY. His grandfather, Tanaka Sen'ami, is said to have been one of the *dōbōshū* (special retainers to the Muromachi shogunate who practiced the tea ceremony and other arts) in the service of the shōgun ASHIKAGA YOSHIMASA. Rikyū's father, Yohei, moved to Sakai in Izumi Province (now part of Ōsaka Prefecture); tradition has it that Yohei took the character *sen* of his father's name as his family name. The family apparently became wholesale fish dealers and eventually joined the ranks of the EGŌSHŪ, a group of wealthy merchants who formed a virtually autonomous city government.

Rikyū was born in Sakai and first studied tea ceremony under Kitamuki Dōchin (1504–62) of the Nōami school and later under Takeno Jōō (1502–55) of the school founded by Murata Shukō (or Jukō, 1422–1502). He also studied Zen under the master Shōrei Shūkin at the temple DAITOKUJI in Kyōto. From 1570 to 1573, with IMAI SŌKYŪ and TSUDA SŌGYŪ, Rikyū served as *sadō* (tea-ceremony officiant) for the military hegemon ODA NOBUNAGA. He went on to perform the same duties for the national unifier TOYOTOMI HIDEYOSHI, from whom he received extensive landholdings. In 1585 Sen no Rikyū officiated at the sumptuous tea ceremony that Hideyoshi held for Emperor Ōgimachi (1517–93; r 1557–86) in the Imperial Palace. With Tsuda Sōgyū, he also officiated at Hideyoshi's magnificent outdoor tea ceremony held at the KITANO SHRINE in 1587.

In 1591 Rikyū suddenly fell afoul of Hideyoshi and was forced to commit suicide. Several reasons have been suggested for this: that he placed a life-sized statue of himself in the Kimmōkaku, a structural addition to the main gate of the Daitokuji that he and his family donated, that he refused to give his daughter to Hideyoshi, or that he demanded exorbitant prices for his tea utensils. He died on 21 April 1591 (Tenshō 19.2.28).

Sen no Rikyū imposed his unerring taste on the tea ceremony, introducing implements such as flower holders fashioned from bamboo, rough black teabowls known as RAKU WARE, and the *Amida no kama,* a type of iron kettle. He preferred to use simple objects close at hand and to emphasize the ordinary, everyday aspect of the tea ceremony. In one of his poems he reminds his disciples that "the tea ceremony is nothing more than boiling water, steeping tea, and drinking it." He was also responsible for reducing the size of the teahouse (chashitsu). The trend had begun in the Muromachi period (1333–1568), when the so-called *shoin*-style teahouse was simplified to produce a rustic effect (see SHOIN-ZUKURI). Sen no Rikyū reduced the size to only two TATAMI mats, or even one and a half, in

his pursuit of the ideal of *yoriai,* the special communion among participants in the tea ceremony. KUWATA Tadachika

Sen'oku Hakkokan

A large collection of Chinese bronze vessels, Chinese and Japanese mirrors, and a few Chinese bronze Buddhist figures, brought together by Sumitomo Kichizaemon VII before his death in 1926. Located in Kyōto, it is housed in a building erected in 1970. The quality and variety of the more than 500 pieces make this one of the great Oriental bronze collections of the world. Laurance ROBERTS

senryōbako

("thousand-*ryō* box"). An Edo period (1600–1868) cash box made of wood and reinforced with external iron fittings. When an account was settled, sums of 50 or 100 RYŌ would be wrapped in paper, sealed, and deposited in the box. One box would hold about 1,000 *ryō* in KOBAN coins, a considerable sum in those days. A 2,000-*ryō* box appeared in the late Edo period. INAGAKI Shisei

senryū → zappai and senryū

Sensuijima

Small island in the central Inland Sea, 300 m (984 ft) east of Tomonoura, in the city of Fukuyama, southeastern Hiroshima Prefecture. Sea-eroded caves, oddly shaped rocks, and other natural sights attract tourists. It is known for net fishing of sea bream and good bathing beaches. Area: 0.9 sq km (0.4 sq mi).

sentai butsu

(literally, "thousand Buddhas"). Groups of 1,000 small images of the Buddha. The idea of making sets of 1,000 images of AMIDA or 1,000 images of KANNON began in India, spread to China, and eventually came to Japan, where it became very popular by the Heian period (794–1185). Although they were originally meant to portray the 1,000 Buddhas of each of the three *kalpas* (past, present, and future), it was popularly believed that the multiplication of images enhanced the power of the Buddha. These icons were carved or cast and sometimes painted; some groups occupied an entire temple wall or, in miniature, the halo (J: *kōhai*) of a larger figure. The mural paintings in the Caves of the Thousand Buddhas (6th–8th centuries) at Dunhuang (Tun-huang) in northwest China are particularly famous. Two notable Japanese examples of *sentai butsu* are the copperplate relief sculpture (see OSHIDASHIBUTSU) inside the Tamamushi Shrine of the temple HŌRYŪJI in Nara and the larger-scale images in the SANJŪSANGENDŌ in Kyōto.

Sentsūzan

Mountain on the border between Tottori and Shimane prefectures, western Honshū. It is the setting for legends mentioned in the 8th-century records KOJIKI and the *Izumo no Kuni fudoki.* It has an excellent mountain climbing trail. Hinokami Hot Spring is in the foothills. Sentsūzan is part of Hiba-Dōgo-Taishaku Quasi-National Park. Height: 1,142 m (3,746 ft).

sen'yū

(possession). Legal term referring to a person's intentional holding of property for his own purposes. The Civil Code classifies the right of possession, the substance of which is occupancy, as one kind of *bukken,* or real right (Civil Code, art. 180).

The right to sue for possession. In order to maintain social order it is necessary to guarantee the state of affairs in which a person is actually in control of property. Therefore, one cannot be permitted to take away possession of property from someone holding that property without following certain procedures, even if the person desiring possession is the rightful owner. Thus, if a possessor's right of possession is, or is in danger of, being interfered with, the Civil Code recognizes the right of the holder of the possessory rights to demand the removal of the disturbance. This is known as the right to sue for possession *(sen'yū soken).* The suit to establish possession, the suit to maintain possession, and the suit to recover possession are the three kinds of established suits. The owner of the property has no legal recourse against the party in possession other than the right to sue for his property on the basis of ownership.

Possession and acquisition by prescription. A person who, with the intent of owning a certain piece of property, possesses that property for a long period of time, can acquire ownership of that property. Usually, when there has been 20 years of possession, the right of acquisition by prescription is recognized. However, one who possesses in good faith, without negligence, may acquire ownership through 10 years of possession of the property. In such cases, an intent to own must be demonstrated. The Civil Code recognizes acquisitive prescription out of respect for an actual state of continued possession and to preserve the stability of business relations.

Immediate acquisition. A person who purchases movable property from a possessor who he believes has ownership of the property can acquire ownership even though the person in possession is not actually the owner of the property. This is called immediate acquisition *(sokuji shutoku)*. Immediate aquisition is designed to further business stability by protecting the person who takes possession in good faith without negligence. Immediate acquisition is not recognized, however, if the movables are stolen goods or lost articles.

The relationship between owner and possessor. A possessor in good faith can acquire the fruits of the possessed property. Also, he can demand from the owner reimbursement for expenditures made for the benefit of the possessed property. If the possessor destroys or damages the possessed property, he is liable to the owner for compensation for damages. *KAWAI Takeshi*

Senzai wakashū

(Collection of a Thousand Years; the full title is usually abbreviated to *Senzaishū*). The seventh and one of the greatest of the imperial anthologies *(chokusenshū)* of classical Japanese poetry (WAKA); ordered in 1183 by ex-Emperor GO-SHIRAKAWA (1127–92; r 1155–58); completed in 1187 or 1188, with a few later additions. Compiled by FUJIWARA NO TOSHINARI (Shunzei, 1114–1204), who also wrote the Japanese preface; 20 books; 1,285 poems.

Compilation —— The years during which Shunzei was engaged in the project were perhaps the most cataclysmic Japan had ever known, since the entire country was embroiled in the struggles of the Taira and Minamoto clans for military and political supremacy (see TAIRA–MINAMOTO WAR). Meanwhile, Shunzei remained in Kyōto working on the *Senzaishū* with a detachment from worldly events befitting the priestly state that he had assumed several years previously. It is not surprising that the troubled times should have caused delays and difficulties and that the anthology should have taken as long as five years to complete.

The final text officially presented to the ex-emperor, probably in 1188, consisted of 20 manuscript scrolls in Shunzei's own hand.

Composition and Structure —— The compiler's avowed purpose was to provide a selection of superior poetry of the previous 200 years, both recent poems and older ones, that had missed inclusion in the previous three imperial anthologies. In order to reestablish a link with old traditions and to afford himself sufficient scope, he returned to the 20-book format of the first four imperial anthologies, beginning with the KOKINSHŪ (ca 905, Collection of Ancient and Modern Times), which had been abridged to 10 books in the two collections preceding his own. The overall structure also recalls the *Kokinshū*, with nature poems dominating the first 10 books and love poems dominating the last 10 books. The most striking innovation is that the last two books are devoted to religious poems—an expression, no doubt, of Shunzei's personal interests and the increasingly religious cast of the age.

Major Poets —— There are 383 individuals represented in the anthology. A wide range of people is represented—not only nobles, courtiers, officials, and ladies of the court, but also a great many priests, nuns, and even a courtesan. Shunzei strikes a balance between older and newer poets, men and women, and poetic conservatives and innovators. The range reflects his tolerant attitude and catholic tastes, albeit governed by high standards and lofty aesthetic ideals.

By numbers of poems included, the most prominent poets are: MINAMOTO NO TOSHIYORI (1055?–1129), 52 poems; Shunzei, 36 poems (most of them added by Go-Shirakawa's command); FUJIWARA NO MOTOTOSHI (ca 1056–1142?), 26 poems; ex-Emperor SUTOKU (1119–64; r 1123–42), 23 poems; priest SHUN'E (Toshiyori's son and heir, 1113–ca 1190?), 22 poems; and Lady IZUMI SHIKIBU (fl ca 1000), 21 poems.

Poetic Styles —— A neoclassicist, Shunzei turned from the frivolities and excesses of the 11th century "Fujiwara style," advocating

instead a return to the standards of decorum, elegance, dignity, and refinement embodied in the *Kokinshū*. In the *Senzaishū* he created an admirable and representative precursor of the great SHIN KOKINSHŪ (some 73 *Senzaishū* poets are also represented there), and its new poetry of high artistic commitment.

■ —— Robert H. Brower and Earl Miner, *Japanese Court Poetry* (1961). *Robert H. BROWER*

Seoul, Treaty of

(Kanjō Jōyaku). An agreement between Japan and Korea signed 9 January 1885. The treaty restored diplomatic relations disrupted by the KAPSIN POLITICAL COUP of 1884. Korea agreed to apologize to Japan and pay a ¥110,000 indemnity for harm done to Japanese citizens and their property, to provide a new site and buildings for Japan's legation, and to build quarters and provide maintenance for Japan's legation guard in accordance with the 1882 Treaty of CHEMULP'O. This paved the way for the TIANJIN (TIENTSIN) CONVENTION between China and Japan. See also KOREA AND JAPAN: early modern relations. *C. Kenneth QUINONES*

Seppuku

(Foreign release title: *Harakiri*). A 1962 film directed by KOBAYASHI MASAKI on the cruelty of the warrior code of ethics (BUSHIDŌ), starring NAKADAI TATSUYA and MIKUNI RENTARŌ. A young masterless *samurai* (RŌNIN) of a provincial family whose training has been as a teacher of Confucianism visits the Edo (now Tōkyō) headquarters of a prosperous warrior household to petition for money in order to feed his starving family. He asks permission to disembowel himself by committing HARAKIRI (more formally known as *seppuku*) in the garden of the mansion unless he is taken in and employed or sent away with a sum of money. This type of ultimatum became somewhat common in the decades following the Tokugawa consolidation of power in the early 17th century, when many hereditary samurai were unemployed. Suicide was thought to be an honorable form of death for a warrior who had lost his livelihood, but was potentially embarrassing for a domain which was not generous to the petitioner. The practice thus became corrupted by men who had no intention of killing themselves. Domainal officers call the young man's bluff, forcing him to commit *harakiri* with the only sword he now carries, one of bamboo. He had previously pawned his blade, the symbol of his class standing.

A short time later, another, somewhat older, man arrives at the same household and makes the same request. He, too, is ordered to make good his threat and carry out the act. He reveals that he is the young man's father-in-law and succeeds in slaying many of a large band of swordsmen set upon him by those responsible for the young man's unjust and unnecessary death before also disemboweling himself.

This film is an explicit criticism of the warrior code of ethics and an implicit criticism of the rigid rules derived from that code by which contemporary Japanese society seemingly operates. The tight symmetrical compositions, photographed often at sharp angles in stark black and white, heighten the conflicts. The effect is a slow revelation of a world which at first seems precisely ordered but which is in actuality severely out of balance. *David OWENS*

seppuku → harakiri

sericulture

The raising of silkworms for the production of raw silk. The climate of Japan is suitable for the raising of both the mulberry (J: *kuwa*) and the silkworm *(kaiko),* which feeds on mulberry leaves, and sericulture has been practiced there since ancient times. The Japanese preference for silk fabrics has also supported its growth. Silkworms were traditionally reared inside a family dwelling, but today, it is most common for them to be reared in a specially built silkworm house. The traditional method of picked leaf rearing involved much labor, but the development of the automatic leaf feeder and other such technology has greatly lessened the work involved. Research in an attempt to develop an artificial diet is also in progress. Harvested about four times a year from May through October, cocoons are either reeled (and the fabric woven) by agricultural cooperative associations or sold to manufacturers of silk fabrics through reelers acting as factors.

Sesshū Tōyō —— Haboku Landscape

Detail of a painting in Sesshū's *haboku* or "broken ink" technique in which the splashes of ink in the foreground, approaching abstraction but suggestive of cliffs, trees, and dwellings, is set off against the misty mountains that loom in the background. Ink on paper. 147.9 × 32.7 cm. 1495. Tōkyō National Museum. National Treasure.

Sericulture is said to have started more than 5,000 years ago in China and to have been introduced to Japan via the Korean peninsula. The earliest mention of sericulture in Japan is found in a 3rd-century Chinese history, the WEI ZHI *(Wei chih)*. The 8th-century Japanese chronicle NIHON SHOKI contains the earliest descriptions of ancient Japanese sericulture. According to this work, the government encouraged sericulture and collected silk as taxes as early as the 5th century. Sericulture has remained one of the important industries of Japan. During the Meiji period (1868–1912) the government regarded the export of raw silk as a mainstay of its economy. As a result, in the 1900s Japan came to lead the world in silk production and export.

In the past, nearly all exported raw silk went to the United States. However, with the outbreak of World War II this market was lost. Silk trade with the United States was resumed in 1946 but did not regain its former volume. Today, Japan is second in the world in terms of total production after the People's Republic of China; however, Japanese demand for silk fabrics has grown in recent years, and it must import silk from China and Korea. See also SILK.

NIKI Isao

Serizawa Keisuke (1895–   )

Textile designer, illustrator, and painter. Born in the city of Shizuoka. He adapted an Okinawan method of stencil dyeing called *bingata-zome* ("red-pattern dyeing"; see OKINAWAN TEXTILES) and infused it with a modern sense of design and bold color. In 1956, the Japanese government designated him one of their LIVING NATIONAL TREASURES for preserving this indigenous craft and developing it into a recognized art.

Barbara F. SMITH

Serizawa Kōjirō (1897–   )

Novelist. Born in Shizuoka Prefecture. After graduating from Tōkyō University, he worked for the Ministry of Agriculture and Commerce. He resigned from the ministry in 1925 and went to France to study economics at the University of Paris until 1929. Serizawa's recuperation from tuberculosis in a Swiss sanatorium became the basis of his short story "Burujoa" (1930), which began his career as an author. This short story was followed by *Asu o oute* (1931) and *Isu o sagasu* (1932), novels depicting the internal turmoil of Japanese intellectuals in the midst of the PROLETARIAN LITERATURE MOVEMENT. In 1931 Serizawa became a lecturer in economics at Chūō

University, but the school authorities viewed his literary pursuits as detrimental to his scholarship, and as a result the following year he left the university to pursue his writing career. After World War II, he wrote about Japan's wartime experiences and of the young men who had died in battle. Serizawa's works are colored by a deep religious outlook and show a closer relationship to the logical structure of the European novel than to the looser, confessional mode of Japanese autobiographical fiction. Many of his works have been translated into French, including *Pari ni shisu* (1942; tr *J'irai mourir à Paris*, 1954) and *Pari fujin* (1955; tr *Madame Aida*, 1958). He was chairman of the Japan P.E.N. Club from 1965 to 1974 and received an award from the French Academy in 1957. Other works include *Ningen no ummei* (1962–68) and *Hitotsu no sekai* (1952–53; tr *One World*, 1954).

📖 —— Serizawa Kōjirō, *Serizawa Kōjirō sakuhinshū*, 16 vols (Shinchōsha, 1974–75).

serow → kamoshika

sesshō

Imperial regent for a minor emperor as opposed to KAMPAKU, regent for an adult emperor. A *sesshō* was originally a member of the imperial family appointed as regent when the emperor was either a child or a woman. Prince SHŌTOKU, for example, acted as *sesshō* (593–622) for the empress SUIKO. The first person outside the imperial family to be appointed to this extrastatutory office was FUJIWARA NO YOSHIFUSA, who took the title in 866, after having placed his own grandson, the child emperor Seiwa (850–881; r 858–876) on the throne (he had ruled as de facto regent since 858). For the next two centuries, Yoshifusa's descendants held exclusive control over both the office of *sesshō* and of *kampaku*, the latter created in 887 (see REGENCY GOVERNMENT). With the establishment of the INSEI system of rule by successive retired emperors in the 11th century, the office of *sesshō* lost its political significance, although it remained an important post until the Meiji Restoration (1868). Under the IMPERIAL HOUSEHOLD LAW, enacted at the same time as the 1889 Meiji Constitution, it was stipulated that only a member of the imperial family could be appointed *sesshō*. The present emperor Hirohito acted as regent for his ailing father Emperor TAISHŌ, from 1921 to 1926.

Under the 1947 Imperial Household Law a *sesshō* can be appointed when the emperor is less than 18 years of age, when the emperor cannot conduct his official duties due to mental or physical disorder, or when he has been seriously injured. In these cases, the *sesshō* is to be appointed after an imperial household conference and is to conduct state affairs in the name of the emperor. A designated order was also established for the appointment of the *sesshō* from among members of the imperial family. See also EMPEROR.

Sesshū Tōyō (1420–1506)

Major ink painter active during the second half of the 15th century. Born into the Oda family in Bitchū Province (now part of Okayama Prefecture), he went to Kyōto in his early years, becoming a monk at the temple SHŌKOKUJI. There he acted as attendant to the priest Shunrin Shūtō (fl 1430–65) and studied painting with the monk-painter SHŪBUN. The name Sessō Tōyō is thought by some to be Sesshū's early name, but this theory is far from established. Around 1462 he was given the art name Sesshū. He moved to the Unkokuan studio in Yamaguchi (in what is now Yamaguchi Prefecture) in 1464, a region then under the control of the ŌUCHI FAMILY. That move was indicative of the tendency of artistic talents in the late 15th century, a time of civil disturbance, to move away from the confines of the metropolitan cultural centers—from Kyōto and the Zen monasteries.

In 1467 Sesshū traveled to China with a trade mission dispatched by the Ōuchi family. This trip, which lasted until 1469, took him from Ningbo (Ningpo) to Beijing (Peking), giving him many opportunities to see not only some famous Chinese scenery, but also many Chinese paintings, including those by Ming dynasty (1368–1644) painters still unknown in Japan. Sesshū also visited the famous monastery of Tiantongshan (T'ien-t'ung-shan) in Siming (Ssu-ming), where he attained the rank of *shuso* or primate. While in China Sesshū did a wall painting in the building of the Board of Rites in Beijing and made many village sketches, some of which survive today through later copies. He returned to Japan in 1469. By 1476 he had opened a studio in Bungo Province (now part of Ōita Prefecture), which he named the Tenkai Togarō. Most of the works attributed to Sesshū surviving today are believed to have been painted after his return from China.

Sesshū learned both from contemporary Ming-dynasty paintings and from Song (Sung; 960–1279) and Yuan (Yüan; 1279–1368) models. His knowledge of works by Song masters such as Li Tang (Li T'ang; fl late 12th century), Xia Gui (Hsia Kuei; fl ca 1195–1224), Muqi (Mu-ch'i, J: MOKKEI; fl 13th century), Mi Younen (Mi Yu-jen; 1086–1165), and Yujian (Yü-chien; mid-13th century?) is evident from sketches he made, some of which are known only through later copies.

Sesshū's style is remarkable in its clear departure from the lyrical mode associated with his teacher, Shūbun. Dynamic brushwork and structured composition dominate Sesshū's works. *Autumn and Winter Landscapes,* a pair of hanging scrolls (Tōkyō National Museum); *Landscape of the Four Seasons* in horizontal handscroll format (1486; Mōri Foundation, Hōfu, Yamaguchi Prefecture); and *Landscape* (ca 1505; Ōhara Collection, Okayama), are representative of his architectonic compositions. His best-known work, *Haboku Landscape* (1495; Tōkyō National Museum), is done in the manner of Yujian and was given to his follower Josui SŌEN, according to the attached colophon written by Sesshū himself, which describes his artistic relationship to JOSETSU, Shūbun, and to contemporary Ming painters such as Li Zai (Li Tsai) and Zhang Yousheng (Chang Yusheng). Another well-known work by Sesshū done in a different manner is a landscape sketch of *Amanohashidate* (ca 1501; Kyōto National Museum), a scenic spot on the Sea of Japan coast that he presumably visited on a trip he took around Honshū.

Sesshū also painted portraits and other figure subjects. *Portrait of Masuda Kanetaka* (1479; formerly Masuda Collection) and *Huike (Hui-k'o) Severing His Arm* (1496; Sainenji, Aichi Prefecture) are noteworthy examples. His versatility extended to the genre of BIRD-AND-FLOWER PAINTING; numerous sets of screens of this subject are attributed to him, some of them gracing Western collections. The most reliable attribution is a pair of screens in the Kosaka Collection in Tōkyō.

In his lifetime Sesshū's disciples included Josui Sōen, SHŪGETSU TŌKAN, and Tōshun. Later followers of his style included SESSON SHŪKEI. Sesshū's prestige was so great that in the 16th century the artist UNKOKU TŌGAN, who had taken his professional name from Sesshū's studio in Yamaguchi, and HASEGAWA TŌHAKU became embroiled in a legal dispute over the right to claim artistic descent from Sesshū. Tōgan won and in the Edo period (1600–1868) the UNKOKU SCHOOL painters maintained their claim to stylistic descent from Sesshū.

📖 ——Tanaka Ichimatsu and Nakamura Tanio, *Sesshū, Sesson,* vol 7 of *Suiboku bijutsu taikei* (Kōdansha, 1973). Ichimatsu Tanaka, *Japanese Ink Painting: From Shūbun to Sesshū* (1972), tr Bruce Darling. Kumagai Nobuo, *Sesshū Tōyō,* vol 4 of *Nihon bijutsu sōsho* (1954). Yoshiaki SHIMIZU

Sesson Shūkei (ca 1504–ca 1589)

Ink painter whose career spanned a half-century following the deaths of the luminaries SESSHŪ TŌYŌ, SHŌKEI, and SŌAMI. Sesson was born in Hitachi (now Ibaraki Prefecture), remote from the major centers of Japanese INK PAINTING. In the 1540s he worked in Aizu (now Fukushima Prefecture) under the patronage of Ashina Moriuji (1521–80). In the 1550s he worked in close association with the Zen Buddhist temple Sōunji in Odawara, under the patronage of the powerful HŌJŌ FAMILY. He retired in 1573. Sesson's known corpus of over 60 paintings, few of which are dated, includes a rich variety of subjects and formats. His figure and animal subjects, especially Taoist immortals and dragons among clouds, have a turbulent vivacity, and even landscape forms in his later paintings seem mutable and vital.

Sesson's unique contribution to Japanese painting was his radical departure in his maturity from dependence on both Chinese and Japanese prototypes. His treatise on painting, *Setsumon teishi* (1542), sets forth the theories embodied in his later work: the importance of observing nature and of copying master paintings in order to achieve the ability to simplify nature. Considerable attention is given to the use of ink, especially the suggestive use of light and dark tonalities, an outstanding feature of his work. Sesson was perhaps the first Japanese painter to view painting as the creation of a world of forms embodying its own expressive principles, bound neither to model paintings nor to nature.

Sesson Shūkei

A pair of hanging scrolls on the motif of a hawk in a pine tree. The work shows the close observance of nature and suggestive use of light and dark ink tonalities characteristic of Sesson. Ink on paper. 126.9 × 53.6 cm. Mid-16th century. Tōkyō National Museum.

📖 ——Nakamura Tanio, "Sesson to Kantō suibokuga," in *Nihon no bijutsu* no. 63 (August 1971). Yoshiaki Shimizu and Carolyn Wheelwright, ed, *Japanese Ink Paintings from American Collections: the Muromachi Period* (1976). Ann YONEMURA

Sesson Yūbai (1290–1346)

Zen monk of the Rinzai sect, poet; with KOKAN SHIREN one of the two great figures in early GOZAN LITERATURE (Chinese learning in medieval Japanese Zen monasteries). Born in Echigo Province (now Niigata Prefecture). As a young boy Sesson became a disciple of ISSAN ICHINEI. In 1307 he went to China with Issan's recommendation and was well received but was jailed in 1310 as part of Emperor Wu Zong's (Wu Tsung) attempt to avenge himself upon the Japanese for his grandfather Khubilai's humiliation in the abortive MONGOL INVASIONS OF JAPAN. Released after 3 years, Sesson had yet to endure 13 years of exile in remote parts of China. Ultimately honored by the Yuan (Yüan) court, he was nevertheless refused permission to return home until 1329. Sesson's remarkable strength of character was matched by his severe demeanor. Though persuaded to assume abbacies for brief periods, he preferred seclusion. In poetry, too, he went his own way, preferring the freer *gushih* (ku-shih) form to the more popular *lushi* (lü-shih) form. His poems are collected in the anthology *Mingashū.* Marian URY

Setagawa

River in Shiga Prefecture, central Honshū. It originates at the southern edge of Lake Biwa (its source) and flows into Kyōto Prefecture, where its name becomes UJIGAWA. It is thus the upper part of a longer river with three names, the lower reaches being called YODOGAWA. The latter empties into Ōsaka Bay. Tourist attractions include the Karahashi bridge at Seta and the temple ISHIYAMADERA. Length: 15 km (9 mi).

Setagaya Ward

(Setagaya Ku). One of the 23 wards of Tōkyō. On the Musashino Plateau. Bordered on the southwest by the river Tamagawa. A residential area, it is Tōkyō's largest ward with an area of 58.8 sq km (22.7 sq mi). From the middle of the Meiji period (1868–1912), army installations were constructed in various parts of the ward. After the

Tōkyō Earthquake of 1923, private railway companies began various land development projects. Among the numerous recreational facilities are the Komazawa Olympic Park Sports Grounds and Baji Kōen, a horse-riding park. Pop: 796,821.

Setchūgakuha

A school of Confucianism during the middle of the Edo period (1600–1868); it was a composite of theories of the three major schools of Confucianism, SHUSHIGAKU, KOGAKU, and YŌMEIGAKU. Advocates of the Setchūgakuha in the latter part of the 18th century included the scholars Inoue Kinga (1732–84), Katayama Kenzan (1730–82), and HOSOI HEISHŪ.

Seto

City in northern Aichi Prefecture, central Honshū, 18 km (11 mi) northeast of Nagoya. Its ceramics industry (the Japanese word for ceramic ware is *setomono*), dating from the 13th century, is the largest in the country owing largely to the good-quality clay found in the nearby foothills of Sanageyama. Pop: 120,775.

Seto Naikai → Inland Sea

Setō Shōji (1891–   )

Electrical engineer. Born in Wakayama Prefecture, he graduated from Tōkyō University in 1915. After studying abroad, he became professor at Tōkyō University, and began his work on anodized aluminum at its Institute of Physical and Chemical Research. He was active in Japan's independent electron microscope development project during World War II and for this work received the Order of Culture in 1973.

Setouchi

General term denoting the southern part of the Chūgoku region facing the Inland Sea, the northern part of the Shikoku region, and the islands dotting the Inland Sea. Favored by blue skies and a mild climate even in winter, it has placid seas and beautiful coastal scenery. Setouchi was an important route for travel to and from the Asian continent from ancient times, and developed into one of the more culturally advanced districts of Japan. Cities and industries grew rapidly after World War II, but one result has been a considerable increase in the pollution of the Inland Sea in recent years.

Setouchi Harumi (1922–   )

Novelist. Born in Tokushima Prefecture. Graduate of Tōkyō Christian Women's University. Setouchi started to write actively in the late 1950s, establishing her name with a biography of the pioneer feminist author TAMURA TOSHIKO, which was awarded the first Tamura Toshiko Prize in 1960. She continued to write biographies of contemporary political and literary feminists and also published semiautobiographical novels. In 1973 she became a Buddhist nun but continued to publish novels. Setouchi's principal works include *Natsu no owari* (1962), a novel, and *Kanoko ryōran* (serialized 1962–64; published in book form 1971), a biography of the contemporary woman writer OKAMOTO KANOKO.

Seto ware

(seto-yaki). Predominant glazed ceramic ware in Japan from the 12th century to the end of the 15th century. The remains of the Seto kilns are scattered around the present-day city of Seto, just northeast of Nagoya in Aichi Prefecture.

In the 12th century, ash-glazing technology spread from the SANAGE kilns east of Nagoya to the western part of present-day Seto, where a group of kilns called the Higashiyama group was established. Here, ash-glazed bottles, bowls, dishes, and jars with four small handles on their shoulders, similar to those produced at Sanage, were made.

New kilns were built slightly to the east, in what is now the central part of Seto, during the 13th century. About 80 kilns from this period have been excavated. Tall jars with narrow necks, dishes, and jars with four handles were made in large quantities. The four-handled jars were of two distinct types, one with a slightly everted mouth rim and a rounded shoulder modeled on Chinese

Northern Song (Northern Sung; 960–1126) jars, and the other with a rolled mouth rim modeled after the white porcelain jars of the Southern Song (Southern Sung; 1127–1279). Stamped surface decorations were used during the first half of the century, while incised and combed designs appeared during the second half. Also during the later half of the century numerous other shapes came to be made, such as covered boxes, ewers, and bottles for general household use, as well as nesting bowls, flower vases, and Buddhist ritual incense burners.

The 14th century was the most prosperous for the Seto kilns. An area in the southeastern part of Seto called Akazu, with over 60 kilns identified thus far, appears to have been the major center of that time. New shapes included small jars, candlesticks, water droppers, and lion-dogs *(komainu),* among others. Decorative techniques included stamped, carved, applied, and combed patterns. A finer, more even ash glaze of light green color came to be made with an improvement in the kiln structure and the addition of more feldspar in the glaze.

Production of iron-glazed wares began during this century at Seto, inspired by imported Chinese wares. Teabowls and tea caddies were the earliest of the iron-glazed wares, although numerous other shapes were also made. The first iron glaze at Seto was thin, uneven, and nearly transparent, quite unlike the smooth, opaque, brownish black glaze *(temmoku)* on the Chinese pieces. It was not until the 15th century that the Seto potters achieved a beautiful dark iron-brown glaze.

Most Seto products during the 15th and the first half of the 16th centuries were for household use, rather than for Buddhist altars. Fine TEA-CEREMONY utensils were made in large numbers. The ash-glazed wares of this period have a deep green color. Imported Chinese Yuan (Yüan; 1279–1368) and Ming (1368–1644) porcelains inspired several new bowl and dish shapes. But by the mid-16th century, Mino area kilns seem to have taken over from Seto as the major production center (see MINO WARE). Seto went into rapid decline, although limited production has continued up to the present. *Richard L.* MELLOTT

Setsubun

A traditional ceremony to dispel demons, now observed on the third or fourth of February. The practice of scattering beans *(mamemaki)* to drive away demons is one of a number of magical rites performed to ward off evil (see MAYOKE).

The term *setsubun* originally referred to the eve of the first day of any of the 24 divisions of the solar year known as *setsu*. Later it came to be applied more specifically to the last day of the *setsu* called *daikan* ("great cold"), which corresponded to the eve of Risshun ("the first day of spring"), the New Year's Day of the ancient solar calendar and the traditional beginning of spring (see CALENDAR, DATES, AND TIME).

Since Risshun and the traditional celebration of the New Year fell at about the same time, Setsubun became associated with those rites of purification and EXORCISM of evil deemed essential to preparing oneself for the coming year and the spring planting season. In many places in Japan the observance of Setsubun includes rites associated with Koshōgatsu ("Little New Year's"; see NEW YEAR) such as *toshiura,* auguries for forecasting the year's crop; and *narikizeme,* spells for a plentiful fruit harvest.

The association of Setsubun with the bean-scattering ceremony is said to date from the Muromachi period (1333–1568). This rite is linked to the observance of *tsuina* (Ch: *zhuinuo* or *chui-no*), a Chinese ceremony for driving off devils dating from the Zho (Chou) dynasty (1027 BC–256 BC). In China on New Year's Eve men dressed in bear skins and masks and pretended to drive away devils with sharp weapons. Adopted in Japan, by the mid-9th century the rite of *tsuina* was incorporated into the cycle of annual events observed by the imperial court, and from the Muromachi period it came to be enacted at Setsubun.

On Setsubun beans (usually soybeans) are roasted and placed in a small wooden box *(masu)* of the type used for measuring. The beans are scattered inside and outside the house or building to the common chant of *oni wa soto, fuku wa uchi* ("Out with demons! In with good luck!"). It is customary for family members to eat the same number of beans as their age. In recent years it has become common practice at famous temples and shrines for well-known personalities born under the Chinese zodiacal sign for that year (see JIKKAN JŪNISHI) to be invited to throw out beans as a means of soliciting visitors. *INOKUCHI Shōji*

SOURCE: *Butsuzō zui*, an 18th-century work first published during the Meiji period (1868–1912). From the copy in the possession of Komazawa University. Daikokuten is often represented as wearing a black cap and carrying a mallet.

The Seven Deities of Good Fortune

setsuwa bungaku

("tale" or "anecdotal literature"). Though coined as an equivalent of the Western folktale, fairy tale, or *märchen,* as distinct from *densetsu* (legend) or *shinwa* (myth), the word *setsuwa* now has a very general meaning. Not only are individual items of legend and myth as well as fairy tales termed *setsuwa,* but so too are the episodes about Chinese history interpolated in the Kamakura-period (1185–1333) war tales, or anecdotes about ordinary life, including the everyday life of courtiers of the Heian period (794–1185). In practice, "*setsuwa* literature" is a blanket term used to refer to a number of collections of short tales or anecdotes compiled between 800 and 1300 AD. The category excludes the more literary and lyrical genre of *uta monogatari* (poem tales). These collections do not contain fairy tales or myths. They feature the unusual or the remarkable and make much of the supernatural; but their stories purport to recount incidents that actually happened, or were thought to have happened, in real life.

Many collections deal exclusively with Buddhism, Buddhist miracles, and pious Buddhist figures. The earliest Japanese Buddhist collection, NIHON RYŌIKI, sought to emulate Chinese models by recounting Japanese examples of miraculous retribution for sin or reward for faith. Most Buddhist collections before the early 12th century were written in Chinese; several contained *ōjōden* (tales of persons who achieved rebirth in Amida's Paradise), and one contained tales about the Lotus Sutra. Later collections in Japanese include one possibly compiled by SAIGYŌ (*Senjūshō*), one attributed to KAMO NO CHŌMEI (*Hosshinshū*, about the awakening of faith), and two by Mujū Ichien (see SHASEKISHŪ).

Secular collections, found from the 12th century on, vary widely in subject matter. Some are specialized—e.g., *Kyōkunshō* has tales about music, *Kara monogatari,* tales about China—but others have a range of subjects. Some collections record baldly, in the Chinese style of men's diaries, anecdotes connected with famous figures like ŌE NO MASAFUSA (*Gōdanshō*) or Fujiwara no Tadazane (*Chūgaishō, Fuke godan*). Two noteworthy collections of the mid-13th century are JIKKUNSHŌ, containing groups of stories illustrating Confucian precepts, and *Kokon chomonjū,* a large collection of anecdotes intended as subjects for pictures, dealing with matters as varied as religion, literature and the arts, love, archery, horsemanship, gambling, and so forth.

None of the above works is of major importance in Japanese literature, but one *setsuwa* collection stands out: the vast *Konjaku monogatari shū* (also known as the KONJAKU MONOGATARI; compiled by about 1120). About two-thirds of its more than 1,000 tales

are Buddhist, including stories of India and China as well as Japan; the remainder are secular stories of Japan. *Konjaku* is important not only for its size and the range of its contents but also for its quality, first brought to the attention of the modern reading public by AKUTAGAWA RYŪNOSUKE, for whom it was the "human comedy" of the prefeudal period, full of the forcefulness and freshness of life in the raw. Claims that the compiler of *Konjaku* was a brilliant short-story writer, however, ignore the fact that much of it is stereotyped and repetitive. Above all, we do not know how it was compiled, by whom (one person or more than one), for what purpose (though it was possibly connected with preaching), and from what sources. Some of it is obviously derived from written sources, some from oral transmission. Complicating the mystery of the *Konjaku* is the pattern of its correspondences not only in story content but also in wording with items in UJI SHŪI MONOGATARI and the recently discovered *Kohon setsuwashū* (ca 1130). For various reasons these works cannot be thought to have copied the *Konjaku.* It is not known how the correspondences arose—through borrowing from some common source or from slight variations in the course of oral transmission. We have no knowledge of what sort of storytellers might have had reason to preserve the wording of texts that were not sacred and thus not appropriate for use in preaching.

Whatever the part played by oral transmission, however, it would be misleading to speak of these collections as "oral literature." Despite its great difference from the more artistic products of Heian court literature, *setsuwa* literature is not "folk literature." We know that these tales interested, and often were compiled by, aristocrats; they do not reflect only the life and beliefs of the lower, uncultured strata of society. The religion and superstition they embody were that of the aristocracy as well, and we are given very human and sometimes amusing sidelights on the life of court nobles as well as of the common people.

——Bernard Frank, *Histoires qui sont maintenant du passé* (1968). D. E. Mills, *A Collection of Tales from Uji* (1970). Marian Ury, *Tales of Times Now Past* (1979).   *Douglas E.* MILLS

Setsuyōshū

Mid-15th century Japanese-language dictionary. Also known as *Setchōshū*. Editor unknown. Essentially a lexicon of the spoken language of the Muromachi period (1333–1568), it also contains some material of a more encyclopedic nature. The words are entered in *kana* (the Japanese phonetic syllabary) together with their corresponding Chinese characters. In some cases there are more detailed definitions and explanations of etymology. Words are grouped by first syllable in *iroha* order (the old order of the *kana* syllabary; see IROHA POEM) and within these groups by subject. The dictionary, which was convenient and easy to use, went through many revisions and enlargements, the last of which appeared in the late 19th century. The word *setsuyōshū* became a general term for concise, easy-to-use dictionaries in *iroha* order, especially in the Edo period (1600–1868).

Uwano Zendō

Settsu

City in central Ōsaka Prefecture; contiguous with the city of Ōsaka. Formerly a rice-producing area, Settsu is now a suburb of Ōsaka, with many industrial plants, transport companies, and warehouses. Pop: 80,686.

Seven Deities of Good Fortune

(Shichifukujin). The seven gods who are are said to bring wealth and long life. The group usually consists of EBISU, DAIKOKUTEN, Bishamonten (Skt: Vaiśravaṇa), Benzaiten (Skt: Sarasvatī), Jurōjin (Fukurokuju), Hotei, and Kichijōten (Skt: Śrīmāhādevī) or Shōjō. The grouping includes gods and sages of Indian, Chinese, and Japanese origin. Specifically, Ebisu, Daitokuten, and Bishamonten are considered gods of fortune; Ebisu is also venerated as the fishing deity and Daitokuten in folk religion is identified with the mythic figure ŌKUNINUSHI NO MIKOTO. Benzaiten is the deity of water and music, and Fukurokuju and Jurōjin are deities of long life. Hotei (Ch: Budai or Putai) is thought to be an eccentric Zen priest who was believed to be an incarnation of the bodhisattva Maitreya. The number of the deities is thought to be related to the common use of the number seven in such Buddhist expressions as "the seven misfortunes and the seven blessings." The Seven Deities of Good Fortune came to be widely worshiped in the 16th and 17th centuries, particularly among the merchant classes. Even today it is quite common to make a New Year's pilgrimage to a series of shrines and temples associated with these deities. Particularly popular is the custom of placing a picture of the seven gods, aboard a treasure ship, by one's pillow on the night of 1 January to guarantee that the first dream of the year will be a lucky one.

Ōtō Tokihiko

Seven Samurai

(Shichinin no samurai). A 1954 film directed by KUROSAWA AKIRA that has been called Kurosawa's best picture and one of the finest Japanese films ever made. It is an epic—well over three hours long in the uncut version—about a farm village menaced by bandits during the 15th-century period of civil wars. The village elders ask an unemployed *samurai*, Kambei (played by SHIMURA TAKASHI) to help them. He gathers together six other disaffiliate warriors and these seven samurai undertake to protect the village and defeat the bandits. This they eventually do, though four of them are killed in the resulting battles. Peace restored, the remaining three gaze at the farmers, now busily planting their spring rice, and the leader, Kambei, says the famous closing lines of the film: "And again we lose. They, the farmers, they are the real winners."

A heroic film, it affirms action in a good cause and yet at the same time questions it. It is this quality that makes the picture a modern epic. Kurosawa's most spectacular film—as well as his longest and his most expensive—its scenario (written by HASHIMOTO SHINOBU, Oguni Hideo, and Kurosawa himself) is prefectly balanced and its realization is incisive to a degree unusual even in Kurosawa's art. In the full version of the picture, the editing is revealed as masterful. Kurosawa himself has said that it is the editing of which he is proudest. In any event this picture is his own favorite among all the films he has made.

Donald Richie

Seventeen-Article Constitution

(Jūshichijō no Kempō). Principles of government said to have been promulgated by Prince SHŌTOKU in 604; often described as Japan's first written law, but actually a collection of precepts for officials. Although the word *kempō* has traditionally been translated as "constitution," in this instance it has neither the connotation nor the binding power of the modern sense of the term. The Seventeen-Article Constitution is rather a set of moral injunctions based on Confucian and Buddhist doctrines. The purpose of the articles was to exhort government officials to work in harmony for the good of the central government. To this end, the divine origin of the emper-

or's authority and the role of officials as the emperor's loyal servants are strongly emphasized. Both in content and in format, this "constitution" strongly influenced codes established by various authorities in later ages, most notably the KEMMU SHIKIMOKU of 1336 and the 17-Article Code written by Asakura Toshikage in the latter half of the 15th century (see ASAKURA TOSHIKAGE, 17-ARTICLE CODE OF).

Michiko Y. Aoki

sexagenary cycle → jikkan jūnishi

sex education

Sex education is not taught as an independent subject in Japanese public schools, although there is now little debate over the necessity of providing guidance about sex to students. This is conducted in the context of other classroom studies and is incorporated into curriculum guidelines; private counseling is also provided to students experiencing difficulties with sexual matters. Before the late 1960s, sex education had been limited to education in sexual morality and the prevention of venereal disease for teenage boys and girls. Education now includes lessons in sexual growth and the physical and psychological characteristics of boys and girls, as well as discussion of the social and personal facets of sex and love. However, since sex education is not taught in a systematized fashion, content and teaching methods have lagged in development.

Sex education is incorporated into the curriculum in the following subject areas: health and physical education, science, social studies, and home economics; guidance is also provided in homerooms, in student activity clubs, and by student counselors. The first sex-related item in the national curriculum guidelines is in the fifth grade of elementary school, when children are taught about the physical changes that accompany puberty. In middle school, students are taught further about the hormonal system and physical development. In the high school curriculum, education in family living is included in discussions of mother-child welfare and care for the aged, while the sexual organs are studied in science classes.

Matsui Hideji

sex in Japanese folk culture

In traditional Japanese society, particularly among farming and fishing folk, sex was not considered as something to be hidden, whether the relations were within or outside the family. In plays and dances at village festivals, the depiction of sexual activities and symbols was common; furthermore, men and women were permitted to engage in promiscuous sex on festival days. Such aspects of commoner life are rarely discussed in written sources. However, the great number of ethnographical studies by folklorists and cultural anthropologists during the last century attest to the accuracy of the above picture.

The American ethnologist John Fee EMBREE conducted fieldwork in the village of Sue, Kumamoto Prefecture, in 1935–36. In 1939 he published *Suye Mura: A Japanese Village*, a pioneer work in the ethnography of Japanese agricultural life. Embree discovered in Sue a surprising number of patterns of cooperation, particularly of communal labor for rice planting, harvesting, roof thatching, road and bridge repairs, and so on. Such cooperative endeavor was invariably accompanied by erotic banter or songs. At the conclusion of the task there was always a banquet at which participants took turns singing and dancing, usually erotically. Such occasions were important in strengthening village solidarity and reaffirming membership in the social unit. However, as Embree noted, mechanization and other modern changes have reduced the necessity for such communal labor, thus also eliminating the banquets. Embree's Sue was by no means exceptional: throughout traditional Japan there were numerous opportunities for erotic expression, both in public and private.

Sex in Japanese Folk Song ——— Many of Japan's folk songs have erotic verses, although these verses are rarely heard in public performances today. Here are a few examples.

1. Sample verses of "Sōran-bushi" (a Hokkaidō fishing song):
   a) Tonight I sleep on a damask pillow (i.e., with a prostitute),
      Tomorrow on board ship, pillowed by the waves.
   b) After sex, no matter what I eat,
      It doesn't taste as good as a vagina.
   c) A 30-year-old woman and a temple bell—
      The more you sock it to them, the more they moan.
   d) Took a wife at 88,
      The sun comes up and he still hasn't done the job.

e) Now it seems to be there, now it doesn't—
   The bone in a penis.
2. Sample verses of "Akita ondo" (a song from Akita Prefecture):
   a) My sister and the guy next door/Got it on in the squash field;/They didn't have any paper to wipe with,/So they used squash leaves,/And they were sore for three days!
   b) After our neighbor's wife had a difficult birth,/she swore off sex for the rest of her life;/But not three days had passed/When she found a huge mushroom:/"Wow! With one like this, I'd do it 'til I die!"

Such verses exist in countless number throughout Japan; at banquets they were accompanied by exaggeratedly erotic dances. Also, especially in the snowy areas of northern Japan, there are the erotic tales and legends known as *enshōtan*. Children were not prevented from hearing these songs and tales.

Religious Observances with Sexual Themes —— Among the many festivals dealing with sex, a typical example is a pair of festivals held jointly on 15 March in Aichi Prefecture: the Henoko Matsuri (Penis Festival) at Tagata Shrine in the city of Komaki and the Ososo Matsuri (Vagina Festival) at Ōagata Shrine in the city of Inuyama. At the former, a large banner with a penis drawn on it leads the procession; following behind is a MIKOSHI (portable shrine) containing a magnificent scarlet phallus, which childless women rush to touch while praying for pregnancy. The festival is said to be efficacious in assuring good crops, curing sterility and impotence, and guaranteeing business success and propagation of descendants. The shrine talisman (*omamori*) resembles a penis, and people whose prayers for pregnancy have borne fruit generally offer a large phallus to the shrine. At Ōagata Shrine, the object of worship is a clam representing the vagina; its beneficence includes marital harmony, finding a spouse, conception, the curing of sexual diseases, and abundant crops. The worship of such deities is widespread in Japan (see KONSEI) and takes many forms. The roadside DŌSOJIN are also frequently erotic in nature, sometimes representing a god and goddess in sexual union. Again, these phenomena are not hidden from public view—quite the opposite.

This seemingly liberated approach to sex is not surprising in a basically agricultural society. As Mircea Eliade observes in his classic *Traité d'histoire des religions* (1948), the connection between agricultural abundance and human impregnation is easily made via the concept of increase. Hence the display of sexual symbols, or in some cases the actual practice of intercourse, on sacred occasions is clearly the expression of a prayer for a bountiful harvest—a so-called "rite of increase." The connection is obvious in Japan, where such festivals traditionally took place just before the onset of rice cultivation or at thanksgiving rites just after harvest. Today, however, the religious underpinnings of these observances have withered away, and they survive simply as local entertainment.

—— Ishikawa Hiroyoshi and Noguchi Takenori, *Sei* (1974).
                                          NOGUCHI Takenori

seyakuin

(medical dispensaries). Charitable institutions to provide medical care for the poor. Prince SHŌTOKU is said to have built such a facility at the temple SHITENNŌJI in Ōsaka, but the first historically confirmed institution is that established in 723 at the temple KŌFUKUJI. It was operated in conjunction with the HIDEN'IN, a refuge for the destitute and orphaned that was in the same compound. Similar facilities were built in Kyōto during the Heian period (794–1185), under the patronage of the FUJIWARA FAMILY. In the following centuries, such institutions survived at a few temples, though on a smaller scale. The *seyakuin* in Kyōto was revived under TOYOTOMI HIDEYOSHI, and during the Edo period (1600–1868) the Yōjōsho, the shogunate hospital in Edo (now Tōkyō), and similar institutions sponsored by religious organizations were referred to as *seyakuin*.

shaga → irises

Shakai Minshu Rengō → United Social Democratic Party

Shakai Minshutō

(Social Democratic Party). Japan's first socialist party, formed on 18 May 1901 by ABE ISOO, KATAYAMA SEN, KŌTOKU SHŪSUI, KINO-

SHITA NAOE, and other members of the Shakai Shugi Kyōkai (see SHAKAI SHUGI KENKYŪKAI). Two days later it announced its goals in several newspapers: total disarmament, abolition of the class system, and public ownership of land, capital, and the transportation system. The initial steps it advocated included government financing of compulsory education, the right of labor to organize, universal manhood suffrage and eligibility for election, abolition of the House of Peers, and reduction of armaments. The same day the government proscribed the party. See also POLITICAL PARTIES.

Shakai Minshūtō

(Socialist People's Party). A proletarian political party formed in December 1926 by the right wing of the RŌDŌ NŌMINTŌ (Labor-Farmer Party). The first chairman was ABE ISOO and the secretary-general KATAYAMA TETSU. It advocated anticommunist socialism and parliamentarianism and drew its main support from the SŌDŌMEI (Japan Federation of Labor) and the Nippon Kaiin Kumiai (Japan Seamen's Union). When the Japanese military occupied Manchuria in the MANCHURIAN INCIDENT of 1931, the party announced its policy of supporting Japanese expansionism abroad, accelerating its rightist leanings. It was split by internal dissension in April 1932, and in July of the same year it merged with the Zenkoku Rōnō Taishūtō (National Labor-Farmer Masses Party) to form the SHAKAI TAISHŪTŌ (Socialist Masses Party).

Shakai Shimin Rengō → United Social Democratic Party

Shakai Shugi Kenkyūkai

(Society for the Study of Socialism). The first Japanese socialist study group; founded in October 1898 mainly by Christian socialists to study the principles of socialism and their applicability in Japan. Its head was Murai Tomoyoshi (1861–1944), and its principal members included KATAYAMA SEN, KŌTOKU SHŪSUI, and ABE ISOO. In January 1900 it was reorganized as the Shakai Shugi Kyōkai, the members of which formed in 1901 Japan's first socialist party, the SHAKAI MINSHŪTŌ. See also POLITICAL PARTIES.

Shakai Taishūtō

(Socialist Masses Party). Moderate-leftist political party formed in July 1932 through a merger of the Zenkoku Rōnō Taishūtō (National Labor-Farmer Masses Party) and the SHAKAI MINSHŪTŌ, with ABE ISOO as chairman. Opposed to capitalism, communism, and fascism at home and abroad, it attempted in the polarized political world of the 1930s to occupy a middle position and was inevitably riven with contradictions. At home it favored extensive economic relief for the impoverished countryside but criticized the rising military budget only as inflationary. Abroad, it supported Japanese aggression in Manchuria but opposed Japan's withdrawal from the League of Nations; it advocated international cooperation, as in a proposed Japan-Russia mutal nonaggression pact, but in 1937 declared the invasion of China a "holy war." The only "leftist" party legally allowed to operate in the 1930s, it increasingly espoused the nationalistic and militaristic policies of ASŌ HISASHI, the leader of its dominant faction. In 1934 it publicly shed its "class character" for more nationalistic garb and in 1937 purged those of its members who had been involved in the POPULAR FRONT INCIDENT. The long-festering dispute between the party's main faction and the more leftist faction composed of former Shakai Minshūtō members came to a head in February 1940, when the party, led by the Asō faction, supported the expulsion from the Diet of Saitō Takao (1870–1949), a RIKKEN MINSEITŌ representative, for publicly criticizing the military. In July of that year the party was dissolved. See also POLITICAL PARTIES.

Shakaitō

(literally, "Rickshaw Party," a play on its homophone "Shakaitō," meaning "Socialist Party"). A political association of rickshawmen, established in December 1882 in Tōkyō by the JIYŪTŌ (Liberal Party) politician OKUMIYA TAKEYUKI and the rickshawman "boss" Miura Kamekichi to oppose use of the newly introduced horse-drawn streetcar (see HORSECARS). Members wore hats emblazoned with the word *jiyū* (liberty), attended meetings twice a month, and

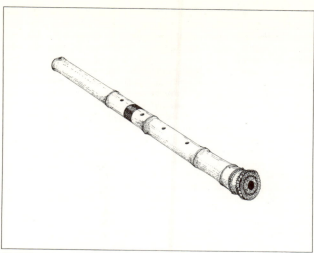

Shakuhachi

paid dues of three *sen* a month. The organization soon degenerated into a strong-arm force for the Jiyūtō; in 1884, after the Nagoya Incident in which Okumiya and Miura were imprisoned for striking a policeman, the party was dissolved.

Shakkintō → Kommintō

Shakotan Peninsula

(Shakotan Hantō). Located in the northern part of Oshima Peninsula, western Hokkaidō. It juts into the Sea of Japan and has a hilly terrain with little level land. Stretches of sea cliffs extend along the coast. The fishing ports of Yoichi, Iwanai, and Furubira, which once flourished as bases for herring fishing, are found here. The population is small, and consequently industrial growth is retarded. The peninsula is part of Niseko Shakotan–Otaru Coast Quasi-National Park.

Shaku Chōkū → Orikuchi Shinobu

shakuhachi

A vertical bamboo flute with a notched mouthpiece and five finger holes. It takes its name from the standard length of the instrument in traditional measuring units, one *shaku*, eight *(hachi) sun,* or 54.5 centimeters (21.46 inches). The unique repertoire of spiritually oriented solo *shakuhachi* pieces which has been transmitted to the present descends primarily from the Edo period (1600–1868), when the instrument was widely played by mendicant Zen priests called *komusō* (a word written with Chinese characters meaning literally "priests of nothingness"). From the latter 19th century, the *shakuhachi* became prominent in classical ensemble music with the string instruments KOTO and SHAMISEN, and in folk music; in the 20th century it has also become active in modern music.

The *shakuhachi* is made from *madake* bamboo (*Phyllostachys bambusoides*). The bamboo is severed near the root, which becomes the bell of the instrument, and a notched mouthpiece with an inserted blowing edge of steer or water buffalo horn is fashioned at the top, generally the seventh node. Four finger holes are placed equidistant on the front face, with an upper thumb hole on the rear face, and the inner bore is lacquered. The instrument is played with the lower lip nearly covering the opening at the blowing end and the airstream directed toward the notch.

History —— The *shakuhachi,* imported from China with other imperial court instruments, first appeared in Japan in the latter part of the 7th century. This early *shakuhachi,* with six finger holes in the Chinese manner, was a regular member of the Japanese court orchestra (GAGAKU) until the end of the 9th century. Occasional historical references to the *shakuhachi* continue to appear throughout the Kamakura (1185–1333) and Muromachi (1333–1568) periods, but when and how the six-hole form gave way to the five-hole instrument is unclear.

In the early 16th century, the *shakuhachi* began its association with mendicancy in the hands of wandering beggars called *komosō* (a word written with Chinese characters meaning "straw-mat priests"). The *komosō* are generally known to have played the HITOYOGIRI, a smaller vertical flute with only one node along its length, but the real distinction between the *hitoyogiri* and the *shakuhachi* did not become clearly defined until the 17th century. It was at this time that the more spiritual-sounding term *komusō* became prevalent in referring to the players and that the *shakuhachi* began to prosper in a decidedly religious role under the protection of the Tokugawa authorities. The shorter, thinner *hitoyogiri,* unable to successfully adapt to the evolving musical style of the period, declined and finally disappeared.

The *komusō* comprised a sect of Zen Buddhism called the Fuke sect, the theoretical basis of which was the playing of *shakuhachi* as a spiritual discipline; they claimed legitimacy by tracing their origins to the 9th-century Chinese priest Fuke (Ch: Puhua or P'u-hua). The legendary history of the sect relates that Fuke's chanting inspired the creation of the piece entitled *Kyotaku* or *Kyorei* (Empty or False Bell), the source of *shakuhachi* meditation practice, and that the 13th-century Japanese priest Shinchi Kakushin (also known as Hōtō Kokushi, 1207–98) learned *Kyorei* in China and brought it to Japan. The Fuke sect was granted official recognition by the government in the 17th century and licensed *komusō* were given the exclusive right to play the *shakuhachi.* Although the sect served as a refuge for large numbers of RŌNIN (masterless *samurai*) and many *komusō* were clearly not spiritually inclined, the Zen practice of *shakuhachi* playing was maintained throughout the Edo period and even after the abolition of the Fuke sect by the new Meiji government in 1871.

With the demise of the Fuke sect and the prohibition of *komusō* activity, many performers encouraged the development of the *shakuhachi* as a secular musical instrument while others strove to revitalize the Zen tradition, and a number of schools developed. Today, the Myōan, Kinko, and Tozan schools are best known. The Myōan represents the original Zen ideals of the Fuke sect; the Kinko descends from the 18th century but developed in later years with stylistic influence from *koto* and *shamisen* music; and the Tozan, founded in 1896, signals a new departure under the influence of Western music. Other schools include the Chikuho, Ueda, Seien, and Wadatsumidō.

The Music —— The *shakuhachi* repertoire consists of several categories of pieces: *honkyoku* ("original pieces"), spiritually based solo pieces deriving from the Fuke sect tradition; *gaikyoku* ("outside pieces"), pieces adapted in the 19th century from the *koto* and *shamisen* repertoires and played in ensemble with those instruments; *shinkyoku* ("new pieces"), modern music of the early 20th century composed in Japan after the influx of 19th-century European music; and *gendai-mono* ("contemporary pieces"), music of the postwar era by composers who draw upon both the international avant-garde style and Japanese tradition. In addition, the *shakuhachi* is used in folk music. However, it is the solo *honkyoku* repertoire, found today in a large number of stylistic variations, that is most characteristic of the *shakuhachi.* The *honkyoku* repertoire ranges from profoundly spiritual pieces, such as *Kyorei* (Empty Bell) and *Kokū* (Empty Sky), to those of a more poetic, even programmatic, quality, such as *Shika no tōne* (The Distant Call of the Deer). Music notation, in a form specific to each school, presents an outline of the melodic and rhythmic structure, but the manner of executing each phrase and the complex use of ornaments must be learned directly from a qualified teacher.

As a music based on meditation, breath is the primary element in *honkyoku.* The performance practice may focus on the cyclical breathing pattern of sitting Zen meditation, on the development of each individual sound from nothingness to fullness and return, or on the sound of breath and air itself. Phrases are long and full; in the absence of a regular rhythmic pulse, rhythm is defined by the breathing pattern, and attention is drawn to each individual tone and its subtle variations in pitch, quality, and dynamics. Weak tones, called *meri,* played with a small blowing angle and partially covered finger holes, contrast with strong tones, called *kari,* played with a wide blowing angle on fully open or closed holes. Melodic structure centers around a series of fourths (D, G, and C on an instrument of standard length). Much of the music approximates the *miyako-bushi* scale of *koto* and *shamisen* music, utilizing the minor second as an important intermediate tone within the tetrachord. See also MUSIC, TRADITIONAL.

📖 ——Kamisangō Hiroyasu, "Shakuhachigaku ryakushi," pamphlet included with *Suizen* (Columbia Record KX7001–3, 1974). Kurihara Kōta, *Shakuhachishi kō* (1918). Gen'ichi Tsuge, "The History of Kyotaku," *Asian Music* 8.2 (1977). Elliot Weisgarber, "The Honkyoku of the Kinko-Ryū," *Ethnomusicology* (September 1968).
Ralph SAMUELSON

shakunage → rhododendrons

Shaku nihongi

The oldest extant commentary on the chronicle NIHON SHOKI (or *Nihongi;* 720); compiled by Urabe Kanekata (late 13th–early 14th centuries), a Shintō priest. Lectures and discussions on the *Nihon shoki* were frequently conducted at the imperial court during the Heian period (794–1185), but over time the records were dispersed. Kanekata, whose father Kanefumi had lectured at court, devoted his life to collecting these materials; his efforts culminated in the 28-volume *Shaku nihongi.* The work is valued also for its inclusion of historical materials that have not survived elsewhere, including the *Kōnin shiki* (810–824, Private Records of the Kōnin Era) and fragments of the FUDOKI.
Michiko Y. AOKI

Shaku Sōen (1859–1919)

Monk of the RINZAI SECT of Zen Buddhism. Born in Takahama, Wakasa Province (now part of Fukui Prefecture). After studying at the temple MYŌSHINJI in Kyōto and ENGAKUJI in Kamakura, he entered Keiō University. Upon graduation from Keiō in 1889, he traveled extensively in Ceylon and India. In 1892 he became the abbot general of Engakuji and its dependent abbeys. In 1905–06 he lectured in the United States and held the first Zen meditation (*zazen*) session there. The seed thus planted was cultivated by D.T. SUZUKI, who went to the United States at Sōen's recommendation. Another disciple, Ōzuma Chikudō, wrote a book on Zen in German while studying in Germany, promoting an interest in Zen in Europe. Sōen died at Engakuji. His writings are collected in forty volumes.
📖 ——*Nihon shūkyō jiten* (1956–57). Soyen Shaku, *Zen for Americans* (1906, repr 1974).
Paul SHEPHERD

shakuyaku → peonies

shamanism

The shaman is a particular kind of religious specialist, of whom the prototype is found in Siberia. His significant characteristics are as follows: (1) In early life he is sickly and neurotic. (2) These symptoms disappear when he receives his "call" to the religious life. A supernatural figure, later to become his guardian spirit, appears to him in a vision and commands him to become a shaman. His soul is then snatched from his body and carried off to heaven and the underworld, where he undergoes terrifying experiences of a markedly initiatory kind. (3) As a result of his call, he undergoes a period of rigorous ascetic training, usually involving solitude and fasting. (4) From this retreat he emerges gifted with special powers which enable him to serve his community in a variety of ways. He can at will pass into a state of trance in which he can communicate with spiritual beings. He is thereby gifted with the powers of healing, exorcism, and prophesy and can act for his community as medicine man, oracular mouthpiece, and sometimes guide to the afterlife. (5) He is assisted in his various tasks by certain spirits, conferred on him by his guardian. (6) He is capable of rousing within himself a particular kind of interior heat which renders him impervious to heat and cold, burning coals and arctic ice alike.

Examples of religious specialists conforming more or less to this prototype can be found in many parts of the world. In Japan it was only during the last 50 years that shamanic elements were recognized as present in the folk religion, and only in the last 30 that these have been described and analyzed. Two broad cultural streams are believed to have contributed to the fusion found in Japan: a northern stream from an Altaic or Tungusic source on the Asian continent, which spread through Korea and the Ryūkyū Islands as well as Japan; and a southern stream believed to have spread northward from Polynesia or Melanesia.

Evidence from the early chronicles indicates the use of shamanic practices in the Yamato court of the 6th and 7th centuries, particularly those involving an oracular medium. Because of the sinicizing reforms of the mid-7th century, however, these practices were abandoned in the court and central government and relegated to the level of folk religion, where they have survived in an increasingly fragmented condition.

Today two principal shamanic practitioners may be distinguished: (1) the MIKO or medium, usually a woman, whose trance enables a spiritual being, *kami* or ancestral spirit, to possess her body and speak through her mouth; (2) the *gyōja* or YAMABUSHI, an ascetic, usually a man with Buddhist affiliation whose powers include healing, exorcism, out-of-the-body travel, and the summoning of *kami* from their own world into the body of the medium.

These two figures with their complementary powers may have originally coexisted in one person and split apart into their respective active and passive roles only when Buddhism took over the active masculine side of the shamanic complex. Both figures, until recent times, apparently exhibited the distinctively shamanic characteristics of the visionary call, initiatory ordeals, rigorous training, and subsequent powers. It is clear from their common and complementary functions that they are meaningfully treated together.

The medium today is found operating alone and in conjunction with the ascetic. Alone, she is represented in rather degenerate form by the blind *itako* of the Tōhoku area. These women are not true shamans insofar as they rarely experience the call and interior initiation. Blind from birth, they are apprenticed to a teacher and undergo a rigorous training culminating in an initiatory marriage with a god (*kamizukeshiki*) in which can be discerned the remnants of a genuine shamanic ritual and practice. Thereafter they act as professional mouthpieces for *kami* or ancestral spirits. The gathering of *itako* at the mountain OSOREZAN in Aomori Prefecture, during the 20–24 July, is celebrated.

In conjunction with the ascetic, the medium used to be employed at village rituals where an oracle was sought (*takusen matsuri*) to pronounce on the future prospects of the village—harvest, fires, sickness, etc. The ascetic called the *kami* into the medium's body, questioned him, elicited oracular responses, and finally dispatched him back to his own world. Such rituals are now almost extinct, though survivals may still be seen practiced among certain *kō* or pilgrim clubs.

The ascetic's services as a healer and exorcist are still widely in demand. Here the shamanic prototype is more clearly preserved, many *gyōja* and *yamabushi* still experiencing the characteristic visionary call to the sacred life, initiatory ordeals, and regime of austerities before practicing their gifts. The ascetic training includes fasting, bathing in cold water, and the recitation of a sacred text. The distinctive ascetic training of the *yamabushi* includes a retreat into a holy mountain and austerities with a symbolic correspondence to the shaman's out-of-the-body journey to other realms of the cosmos. The distinctively shamanic accomplishment of the visionary, out-of-the-body trance is now rare in Japan, though modern instances such as that of Deguchi Onisaburō still occasionally occur.

The fully professional ascetic is sought largely for his powers of healing and exorcism. His shamanic "mastery of fire" may be seen demonstrated at certain seasonal rituals involving a fire-walking (*hiwatari*).

Interesting modern examples of the shaman in Japan may be found among the founders of *shinkō shūkyō*, religious sects newly arisen during the last hundred years (see NEW RELIGIONS). Most of the successful sects are recognized to have arisen at the inspiration of a man or woman exhibiting shamanistic traits. Notable examples are NAKAYAMA MIKI, the foundress of Tenrikyō, DEGUCHI NAO and Deguchi Onisaburō, the founders of the ŌMOTO sect, and KITAMURA SAYO, the foundress of Tenshō Kōtai Jingū Kyō.
📖 ——Carmen Blacker, *The Catalpa Bow: A Study of Shamanistic Practices in Japan* (1975). H. Byron Earhart, *A Religious Study of the Mount Haguro Sect of Shugendo* (1970). Ichiro Hori, *Folk Religion in Japan* (1968). Hori Ichirō, *Nihon no shamanizumu* (1971). Miyake Hitoshi, *Shugendō girei no kenkyū* (1971). Nakayama Tarō, *Nihon fujoshi* (1969). Sakurai Tokutarō, *Nihon no shamanizumu* (1974).
Carmen BLACKER

shamisen

A three-stringed plucked lute that was originally associated with the urban world of the pleasure quarters and theaters of the Edo period (1600–1868) and later became a concert instrument as well. It is called *samisen* in the Kyōto–Ōsaka area and *sangen* when used in classical chamber music. It developed from an instrument appar-

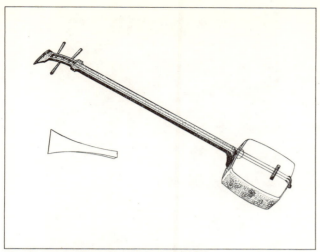

Shamisen——Shamisen with plectrum (bachi)

ently imported from the Ryūkyū Islands in the mid-16th century, and may be of mainland Chinese origin. Both the Okinawan (*san-shin* or *jamisen*) and the Chinese (*sanxian* or *san-hsien*) forms are still used today, but they differ greatly from the instrument used in Japan.

Shamisen come in many different sizes, varying from 1.1 to 1.4 meters (3.6 to 4.6 feet) in length according to the sound ideals of the various kinds of music played on them. They are generally distinguished by the thickness of their unfretted fingerboard, but other differences are found in string gauges, bridge weights, body sizes, and the design and size of their plectrums *(bachi)*. The wooden parts of the *shamisen* are made of red sandalwood, mulberry, or quince, and the heads which cover the front and back of the body are cat or dog skin. Pegs and plectrums are ivory, wood, or plastic. Strings are twisted silk or nylon. Three basic tunings are *honchōshi* (a fourth and a fifth), *niagari* (a fifth and a fourth), and *sansagari* (two fourths). The fundamental pitch is set by the singer (often between A and middle C). Thus *shamisen* notation indicates intervals (MA) rather than specific pitches.

William P. MALM

Shandong (Shantung) Question

(Santō Mondai). Controversy over Japanese control of China's Shandong Province from the Paris Peace Conference of 1919 to the WASHINGTON CONFERENCE of 1921–22. Shandong, in northeastern China, jutting out into the Yellow Sea south of Manchuria, early attracted the attention of foreign powers. Germany in particular, seeking a foothold for its Asian naval and economic expansion, was interested in the provincial port of Qingdao (Tsingtao) on Jiaozhou (Kiaochow) Bay. When two German missionaries were murdered in the area in 1896, the German navy took the opportunity to seize and occupy the harbor. This became the basis of the establishment, in the following year, of a German sphere of influence that covered Qingdao and its environs. Germany also obtained a concession to build a railway linking the city with the provincial capital of Jinan (Tsinan), 400 kilometers (250 mi) in the interior.

There matters stood, with Germany administering the leasehold, building the provincial railway, and otherwise treating the sphere as part of its empire—not very profitable, but of symbolic importance to national prestige. When war broke out in Europe in August 1914, however, Japan, which was allied with Germany's principal enemy, Great Britain, considered it, as the oligarch YAMAGATA ARITOMO said, "an opportunity of a thousand years" and proceeded to dislodge the Germans from their stronghold. In fact, as early as 1911, when the Republican revolution took place in China, several Japanese in the army and in the Ministry of Foreign Affairs had expressed a desire to extend Japanese influence from Manchuria southward to the Shandong peninsula. World War I thus provided them with an opportune moment. Despite Britain's misgivings, the Japanese declared war on Germany and invaded Qingdao in early September 1914. By 7 November Japanese troops had established control over the entire leasehold as well as the Jinan-Qingdao railway. Almost immediately afterward, the Japanese government de-

manded that China recognize the transfer of German rights in Shandong to Japan. This was one of the TWENTY-ONE DEMANDS.

The Chinese had no intention of granting the Japanese demands, least of all that regarding Shandong. They viewed any Japanese-German agreement on the future of the region as invalid. Although other parts of the Twenty-One Demands were equally odious from the Chinese point of view, Shandong became a symbol of China's nationalistic resistance to Japanese imperialism, and the Shandong question was born.

It was not, however, to be simply a bilateral dispute. From the beginning the United States was interested, partly because its merchants complained of being denied equal opportunities in the province under Japanese control and partly because the United States had emerged as a champion of Chinese territorial integrity. Even more important was the wartime orientation of President Woodrow Wilson's foreign policy, which stressed such themes as "peace without victory" and the emancipation of weaker countries from the bondage established by the strong. The Chinese thus appealed to the United States to intercede on their behalf. Unfortunately, all the United States would or could do at that time was to issue a declaration that America would not recognize any agreement concerning China that violated the OPEN DOOR POLICY or the integrity of that country. Undeterred, the Japanese made their stay permanent by entering into secret agreements with Britain, France, and Russia in which these nations pledged to support Japanese claims for Shandong at the peace settlement.

Shandong proved to be a major difficulty during the Paris Peace Conference. Japanese determination to hold onto its gains by maintaining a military presence and expanding the German leasehold came to be seen as the selfish act of an imperialist, out of keeping with a conference that, it was hoped, would put an end to war and to all injustices. But the Japanese were adamant, mainly because the government of HARA TAKASHI could not give up Shandong without risking fierce domestic opposition. In the end they had their way. Infuriated, the Chinese delegates refused to sign the peace treaty. In China, university students, merchants, and intellectuals began an extensive boycott of Japanese goods; this developed into the MAY FOURTH MOVEMENT of 1919.

Japan's victory proved to be short-lived. Hara and his colleagues, including Army Minister TANAKA GIICHI, soon realized that it would be unwise to antagonize the United States or to turn the Chinese permanently against Japan. American capital and technology, and China's market, were more important than a single leasehold. During the Washington Conference (1921–22), therefore, the Japanese delegates met with the Chinese and worked out an arrangement whereby all Japanese forces would be evacuated from the area, in return for which China would indemnify Japan for the cost of improving and maintaining the railway. The Shandong Question appeared to have been settled. Within a few years, however, Japanese troops would be back to obstruct the path of the Chinese Nationalists' northern expedition. So long as Japan controlled southern Manchuria and Korea, the Shandong Peninsula was fated to be a thorn in Chinese-Japanese relations.

——Russell Fifield, *Woodrow Wilson and the Far East: Diplomacy of the Shantung Question* (1952). John Schrecker, *Imperialism and Chinese Nationalism: Germany in Shantung* (1971).

Akira IRIYE

Shanghai Incident

(Shanhai Jiken). Military confrontation between Chinese and Japanese troops in Shanghai from 28 January to 5 May 1932. It marked the first clash between the two nations in China proper following the MANCHURIAN INCIDENT of 18 September 1931.

By January 1932 the GUANDONG (KWANTUNG) ARMY, the Japanese field army in Manchuria, had successfully completed its operations in southern Manchuria and extended its control to the city of Jinzhou (Chinchow) at the border between Manchuria and Inner Mongolia. The Chinese central government under CHIANG KAI-SHEK, however, had chosen not to engage the Japanese in direct combat, and no war had been declared between the two countries. Japan's opposition had thus been confined to the forces of the Three Northeast Provinces (Manchuria) under ZHANG XUELIANG (Chang Hsüeh-liang). The League of Nations had convened an emergency meeting of its council to discuss the crisis, and the United States, although not a member of the League, had shown a serious interest in settling the dispute in the framework of international cooperation. Before they could act, however, a series of quick military victories had placed the Guandong Army in virtually complete control of Manchuria, and in the meantime the cabinet of WAKATSUKI REIJIRŌ had been replaced by a cabinet under INUKAI TSUYOSHI, who was more inclined to accept the military faits accomplis in Manchuria. China was able to retaliate only with a patriotic boycott of Japanese goods.

In Shanghai on 18 January 1932 a small group of Japanese Buddhist monks and their disciples were attacked by a Chinese mob while begging for alms, and one of the Japanese died six days later. The incident, which had actually been fomented by a handful of Japanese officers, generated tension between the city's Japanese community and its vast Chinese population. Sporadic clashes took place, and both sides held rallies and counter-rallies. On 28 January China's 19th Route Army skirmished with Japanese marines. Because its troops were greatly outnumbered (1,000 men against 35,000), Japan dispatched additional forces, army as well as marine. The two sides engaged in extensive fighting throughout February, and finally, on 3 March, the Chinese forces withdrew.

It was not immediately clear why the Japanese should have provoked such an incident, far from Manchuria, in the key urban center of China where Western enterprises abounded and where the Western powers might become involved. Certainly neither the Japanese supreme command nor the Guandong Army was ready to extend hostilities from Manchuria to China proper; nor did they want another diplomatic crisis. Thus on 5 May they signed a truce agreement that provided for a demilitarized zone around the international settlement, an end to the boycott, and the evacuation of Japanese forces. For its instigators, however, the incident was not a needless diversion. They used it successfully to weaken Japan's civilian leadership and so assure little domestic resistance when the Guandong Army set up the puppet regime of MANCHUKUO in March 1932.

Such machinations cost Japan dearly in the long run. By involving the international community of Shanghai in its war against China, it turned the Manchurian Incident into an international crisis. The British government abandoned its equivocal stand and sought cooperation from the United States to check further Japanese expansion. Although little came of this cooperation—the effort was to tarnish United States–British relations for years—Japan's disregard for foreign rights and interests only undermined whatever good will it could still expect from other nations. How to prevent Japan from threatening the security and stability of East Asia would become the principal Asian issue for China and the Western powers. Ten days after the signing of the Shanghai truce agreement, Prime Minister Inukai and members of his government were assassinated by right-wing ultranationalists (see MAY 15TH INCIDENT), an act that put an end to party politics in prewar Japan and brought the military to the fore.

📖——Hata Ikuhiko, *Gun fashizumu undō shi* (1962). Ōuchi Tsutomu, *Fashizumu e no michi* (1967). Christopher Thorne, *The Limits of Foreign Policy* (1973).   Akira IRIYE

Shanghai International Settlement

Formed in 1863 by the merger of the British and American settlements north of the old walled city of Shanghai, the Shanghai International Settlement was a product of the treaty port system whereby foreign merchants, under the principle of extraterritoriality, governed areas leased in perpetuity and controlled local tax and police systems. Shanghai was opened to foreign residence and commerce by the Treaty of Nanjing (Nanking), which concluded the Opium War (1839–42), and it soon had British, French, and American settlements. Linked by the Yangzi (Yangtze) River to the Chinese countryside, Shanghai was central to Britain's sphere of interest in China. After the signing of the Treaty of SHIMONOSEKI (1895) which provided the right for foreign establishment of manufacturing, Shanghai became the most important manufacturing as well as commercial and financial center in China. The settlement also provided a sanctuary for Chinese dissidents. At the same time, ruled by foreigners through the Shanghai Municipal Council, it was a symbol of foreign exploitation and as such became the site of radical and nationalistic movements.

In the 1920s there was an increase in union organizing and strikes in Shanghai, culminating in the 1925 MAY 30TH INCIDENT. Although sparked by the killing of a Chinese worker by a Japanese textile mill foreman, it was primarily directed against the British, and it resulted in the inclusion of some Chinese representatives on the Shanghai Municipal Council. Between January and February of 1932, following a Chinese boycott in reaction to Japan's seizure of

Sharaku

One of Sharaku's half-length portraits of *kabuki* actors. This particular print shows the male actor Sanogawa Ichimatsu III playing a female role in 1794. Full-color woodblock print. 36.8 × 25.0 cm. Tōkyō National Museum.

Manchuria (1931), an undeclared war broke out between Japanese and Chinese just outside the settlement. Patriotic sentiment emerged again in Shanghai in 1936 with the growth of the NATIONAL SALVATION ASSOCIATION in response to Japan's aggressive action in North China.

📖——E. M. Hinder, *Life and Labour in Shanghai* (1944). Rhodes Murphy, *Shanghai, Key to Modern China* (1953).

Sharaku (active mid-1794–early 1795)

Also known as Tōshūsai Sharaku. UKIYO-E artist who specialized in portraits of KABUKI actors. A relatively obscure artist in his own day, Sharaku was first discovered in the Meiji period (1868–1912) by Westerners; thereafter, his work received increased attention. His known oeuvre consists of 145 color woodblock prints, a group of 8 block copies of drawings for an illustrated book, and a group of 10 drawings of wrestlers, only one of which survives. The woodblock prints were all published in Edo (now Tōkyō) by Tsutaya Jūzaburō. There is some extrinsic evidence of paintings of actors by Sharaku, but few actual paintings with Sharaku signatures are known.

Prints——Sharaku's earliest and most important work is a series of 28 large half-length portraits of 30 kabuki actors printed with dark mica backgrounds which reflect a metallic sheen like a mirror. The actors are portrayed in roles they acted in plays at the three major Edo kabuki theaters in the fifth month of 1794. The prints are uniform in size and seem to have been originally conceived and issued together as a set, including the portraits of several minor actors. Although other *ukiyo-e* artists had issued sets of half-length and large-head portraits of actors and had worked with white mica ground, nothing of comparable scale to the Sharaku set had ever been attempted.

The color of the mica background on prints in this series varies on different impressions from a lustrous silver to a rather dark black. The signature, censorship seal, and publisher's mark were engraved on a separate block and were stamped over the opaque mica, and their position often varies from impression to impression. The paper on which the images are printed varies from heavy absorbent sheets to rough thin sheets with defects and imperfections. Certain impressions are printed with gray, others with black outlines. The color schemes of the prints are usually simple, but some have traces of contemporary hand-coloring on the faces, many have lacquer on the wigs, and a few are printed with embossing, surface polishing, and gold. Other impressions lack these niceties and show noticeable signs of colors clogging and keyblock wear. There are also differences in color from impression to impression.

The second group of Sharaku prints is a series of seven large sheets with full-length portraits of pairs of actors in plays performed in the summer, the seventh and eighth months of 1794. Most of these prints have a light mica ground, often with a glossy pinkish cast. It seems likely that an eighth print, the portrait of the theater director Miyako Dennai kneeling before the audience in formal costume and reading a prologue, was published at the same time since it also has a light, pinkish mica background. The print may have served as a frontispiece since the paper in Dennai's hand bears a printed inscription: "We shall now submit to your approval a second series of hitherto unpublished portraits." Fewer prints in this group than in the first have survived.

Sharaku also designed 30 panel prints depicting full-length portraits of actors in the summer plays, against plain gray or yellow backgrounds. Many of these panels were designed in groups forming larger compositions of two or more figures. These, like all of Sharaku's panel prints, are now rare. Some of the prints bear the handwriting of the writer SHIKITEI SAMBA, others the seal of the scholar and poet ŌTA NAMPO (also called Ōta Shokusanjin), and still others the date seals of a man who collected only actor portraits by KATSUKAWA SHUN'EI and Sharaku in 1793 and 1794.

Sharaku produced 60 portraits of actors in plays performed in the 11th and 12th months of 1794, including 47 panel prints, 11 large heads in medium format with yellow backgrounds, and 2 prints in medium format designed as a memorial for a deceased actor. In addition, he designed 4 portraits of wrestlers: 1 in medium format, and 3 in large, the latter forming a triptych. Prints from this group are uneven in quality: some of the large heads and panel portraits are outstanding, others are uninteresting and dull, particularly those with architectural backgrounds. All these prints are rare. Several seem to require companion prints to form larger compositions, and it is likely that several companion designs have not survived.

Sharaku's last prints were 10 full-length panel portraits of actors in plays performed in the first month of 1795, 2 portraits of wrestlers, 2 pictures of warriors, and a picture of Ebisu, one of the Seven Deities of Good Fortune. Four of these 5 last prints are in medium format, one is large. All prints in this group are relatively awkward and uninteresting.

Drawings —— Eight block copies for an unpublished book of actors' portraits may have been drawn by Sharaku or by a professional draftsman from Sharaku's designs at the end of 1794. The illustrations are for tableaux of an imaginary performance of the play *Go taiheiki shiraishi-banashi*, with a cast of leading actors of all the three major Edo kabuki theaters.

Sharaku's last recorded works seem to have been a series of 10 drawings, apparently for an unpublished series of full-length woodblock portraits of pairs of *sumō* wrestlers. Nine of these drawings were destroyed in the Tōkyō earthquake of 1923 and are known only by photographs. The 10th is drawn with a sure, lively, spontaneous line, quite different from the block copies, and may very well be the only surviving direct work from the artist's hand.

Identity —— Over the years various hypotheses have been put forward concerning Sharaku's identity and the course of his career. In the 1800s or early 1810s, one of the compilers of *Ukiyo-e ruikō* (Notes on the Schools of Ukiyo-e Artists) wrote of Sharaku that he drew actor portraits, that to achieve an extreme of truthfulness or accuracy he drew in an unusual manner, but that he did not maintain his popularity with the general public for long and stopped after one or two years. Around 1820, Shikitei Samba added that Sharaku used the secondary name Tōshūsai, lived in the Hatchōbori district of Edo, and was active for slightly more than half a year. It is possible, but not proven, that Sharaku was a NŌ actor in the troupe of the lord of the Awa domain (now Tokushima Prefecture and part of Hyōgo Prefecture) in Shikoku. On the other hand, some modern writers have tried unpersuasively to identify him with HOKUSAI, Chōki, various other artists, and the publisher Tsutaya.

Sharaku produced a larger number of prints during the nine months of his productivity than any other artist, with the possible exception of UTAMARO. Sharaku's respect for each actor's personal features was not shared by any other Edo artist; it was, however, a mark of the Ōsaka style of Suifutei (fl ca 1782) and Ryūkōsai (fl 1772–1816). Perhaps the most plausible explanation of Sharaku's sudden large output and subsequent eclipse, and the noticeable difference in the quality of his first and last published work, is that Sharaku's prints were designed and published for two different au-

diences: the large heads and full-length portraits with mica backgrounds were designed for a private group or individual who underwrote the cost of publication, while the prints without mica backgrounds were commercial productions aimed at the general public.

A private commission would explain how a successful publisher like Tsutaya could entrust a commercially unknown artist with the designs of the largest, most ambitious, and most costly venture of his entire publishing career. It would also explain the number of minor actors in the set of large heads, and the choice of a group of plays performed during the fifth month, since this was the publisher's slack season, and the best engravers and printers would not be engaged with other work.

Influence —— Sharaku's influence on his contemporaries has been exaggerated. His contemporaries Shun'ei and UTAGAWA TOYO-KUNI, and later UTAGAWA KUNIMASA, may all have found license in Sharaku's work for their own exaggerations in pose and expression, and the example of Sharaku's large heads may have been a factor in the popularity of similar portraits of actors during the rest of the decade, but none of these artists were much affected by his vision or style of portraiture. Sharaku's prestige continued, however, and UTAGAWA KUNISADA staked his claim to preeminence among actor portraitists of the mid-1810s with a Sharaku-like series of seven half-length portraits of actors with mica backgrounds. Sharaku's greatest influence was not on contemporary artists, but on collectors and writers of his own and later periods who have been deeply moved by the power and dignity of his work.

📖 ——Harold Henderson and Louis V. Ledoux, *The Surviving Works of Sharaku* (1939). Jūzō Suzuki, *Sharaku* (1968).

Roger KEYES

sharebon

(literally, "witty book"). A genre of Edo-period (1600–1868) popular fiction (GESAKU) that flowered in the 1770s and 1780s. It is concerned exclusively with life in the pleasure quarters, mainly in the capital of Edo (now Tōkyō). The prototypes of the genre that began to appear in the 1750s were mock-learned guidebooks to the pleasure quarters, at first written in Chinese. The structural and stylistic pattern of most subsequent *sharebon* was fixed in about 1770 by the pseudonymous author of *Yūshi hōgen* (Playboy's Dialect).

The central protagonist of standard *sharebon* is the *tsū* or *tōrimono*: the sophisticated man-about-town, well informed about the pleasure quarters, fashions, and similar subjects. The *sharebon* usually opens with the *tōrimono* on his way to the quarter and describes the main stages of his entertainment there, lasting from late afternoon till dawn, without, however, dwelling on more intimate scenes. The narrative—if one can call it that—unfolds in a loose succession of dialogue sketches, written in colloquial language that even records peculiarities of dialect and personal speech idiosyncrasies. Besides the *tōrimono* and the denizens of the pleasure quarter, the stock figures in *sharebon* are the *hankatsū* (pseudo-*tōrimono*), the *yabo* (a yokel or boorish fellow whose role as an object of ridicule was usually played by a country *samurai*), and the *musuko* (a young man, wealthy but inexperienced, sometimes taken as an example of the authentic *tōrimono*, with others who postured as *tōrimono* in turn being unmasked as *hankatsū*). The main interest of the author lies in enumerating the minute details of the customs of the quarter, its fashions, argot, and so on, thus establishing his own credentials as a *tōrimono*. This demonstration of mastery of arcane detail which only the insider could know was called *ugachi* (literally, "piercing").

Sharebon production reached a peak in the 1770s and 1780s. Notable writers in the genre were ŌTA NAMPO (alias Yamanote no Bakabito; 1749–1823), Hōraisanjin Kikyō (dates unknown), Tanishi Kingyo (dates unknown), and SANTŌ KYŌDEN (1761–1816), the most versatile author of the time who not only published all kinds of popular fiction but was also an important UKIYO-E artist. Kyōden (who was of merchant-class origin, whereas most other writers were samurai) published a total of 18 *sharebon*, mastering brilliantly the whole range of the genre, from brothel guide to elaborate comedy and realistic love story. Beneath the hard *ugachi* exterior of Kyōden's world, there are signs of a more discriminating attitude toward his subject matter. Occasionally he transcends the stereotyped *tōrimono* approach and gives the reader a glimpse of "the other side of the brocade" (the title of one of his last *sharebon*: *Nishiki no ura*, 1791), of what life in the pleasure quarters meant, not to the guests who were entertained there but to the courtesans who entertained them. There were likewise *sharebon* writers who were turning their attention to the pleasure quarters in the countryside, exploring the provincial brothel through the eyes of the cultivated townsman. In such cases the element of comedy became dominant and the sophisticated *tōrimono* attitude was toned down.

When, in the course of the 1780s, as a consequence of the almost manic obsession with *ugachi*, the original humor of the *sharebon* was beginning to wear thin and the more sordid side of life in the pleasure quarters was being meticulously recorded, Morishima Chūryō (also known as Manzōtei; 1754–1808), disciple of HIRAGA GENNAI (1728–80), appealed to his contemporaries to restore to *sharebon* its original gaiety. He set an example with his *Inaka shibai* (1787, Village Theater), which ignored the pleasure quarters altogether, depicting rustic scenes from a village theater performance instead. Thus he pioneered the way for the KOKKEIBON writers who emerged after the turn of the century as the literary heirs of the comic aspects of *sharebon*.

During the KANSEI REFORMS (1787–93), which were introduced to reinforce the crumbling structure of feudalism, Santō Kyōden (among other writers) was severely punished on charges of obscenity and gave up *sharebon* writing altogether. At about the same time the fundamental change in popular fiction effected by the growth of the reading public dictated a new course to the *sharebon* writers. Increasingly they turned away from the small separate world of the pleasure quarters to life outside; they dropped the detached *ugachi* attitude to and description of the affairs of courtesans and their clients, and began to discover "true love." This eventually resulted in the sketch-like style of the *sharebon* being displaced by more complex narrative structures. In the course of time the shift in emphasis was to lead to the rise of an entirely new genre, the NINJŌBON. Thus, although the dialogue technique is common to both genres, *ninjōbon* and *kokkeibon* carried on two distinct aspects of the *sharebon*.

From the literary-historical point of view the main achievement of *sharebon* was perhaps to have established a new form of fiction, based on the exact recording of actual dialogue, which was capable of registering the subtle shifts of the human psyche. It is a consequence of the inherent limitations of the framework in which the feudal age pictured man and life that this technique could never be exploited to the full extent of its possibilities.

📖 ——Collections of *sharebon*: *Sharebon taikei*, 12 vols (Rikugōkan, 1930–32). Mizuno Minoru, ed, *Kibyōshi sharebon shū*, vol 59 of *Nihon koten bungaku taikei* (Iwanami Shoten, 1958). *Sharebon taisei*, 29 vols (Chūō Kōron Sha, 1978–). *Sharebon kokkeibon ninjōbon*, vol 47 of *Nihon koten bungaku zenshū* (Shōgakukan, 1971). Works on *sharebon*: James T. Araki, "Sharebon: Books for Men of Mode," *Monumenta Nipponica* 29.1-2 (1969). Peter F. Kornicki, "Nishiki no Ura: An Instance of Censorship and the Structure of a Sharebon," *Monumenta Nipponica* 32.2 (1977). Mizuno Minoru, *Edo shōsetsu ronsō* (1974). Mizuno Minoru, *Kibyōshi sharebon no sekai* (1976). Nakamura Yukihiko, *Kinsei shōsetsu shi no kenkyū* (1961).   Wolfgang SCHAMONI

Sharp Corporation

Electronic equipment maker producing television sets, refrigerators, air conditioning equipment and other household electric appliances; copying machines, cash registers, and other business machines; acoustic equipment; and electronic components. Together with CASIO COMPUTER CO, LTD, it is one of Japan's leading makers of electronic desk-top calculators. Sharp traces its origins to 1912, when Hayakawa Tokuji started a metal processing company in Tōkyō. In 1915 he invented and marketed a mechanical pencil called Ever Sharp. After the great TOKYŌ EARTHQUAKE OF 1923, he went to Ōsaka and studied production of radio sets. He succeeded in the mass production of a small-size crystal radio set called the Sharp Radio in 1925 and established a joint-stock company 10 years later. In 1953 the corporation started selling television sets simultaneously with the commencement of television broadcasting in Japan. It then moved into the fields of refrigerators and washing machines. In 1964 it pioneered the development of an all-transistor desk-top calculator and followed this with the development of integrated circuit (IC) technology. The company took its current name in 1970. In the 1970s, it concentrated its efforts on the development and mass production of semiconductors as well as the development of electronic equipment for industrial use. At the same time it actively engaged in overseas operations, with a total of eight production companies in 7 countries and sales companies in 11 countries. It has adopted a policy of relegating management duties to the overseas production

companies, providing assistance only on technological and manufacturing processes. In 1979 it started production of color television sets in Tennessee through a subsidiary company. Sales for the fiscal year ending March 1982 were ¥580 billion ($2.4 billion), of which industrial equipment constituted 33 percent, household electrical appliances 32 percent, electronic equipment 19 percent, and acoustic equipment 16 percent. The export ratio was 51 percent and the company was capitalized at ¥33.7 billion (US $140 million) in the same year. Corporate headquarters are located in Ōsaka.

Shasekishū

(Collection of Sand and Pebbles). A collection of didactic tales composed by the Buddhist monk Mujū Ichien (1226–1312) between 1279 and 1283; a minor but unique literary and religious classic. Like similar collections of legends and anecdotes (see SETSUWA BUNGAKU), the *Shasekishū* reveals a lack of sustained narrative and character development, but as a record of the practical and sometimes earthy aspects of ordinary life in the Kamakura period (1185–1333), it complements the better-known classics of court and military society. Its special charm is a refreshing sense of humor, and the collection is unique in that it duplicates few of the anecdotes appearing in earlier collections, recounting events that the author purports to have either witnessed himself, or had on good authority. It is also a valuable document on the popular Buddhism of its time and is sometimes classified as a vernacular tract or *kana hōgo*.

The hybrid nature and intent of the work is stated in its preface: "Through the wanton sport of specious words and profane talk *(kyōgen kigyo)* I wish to bring others into the marvelous Way of the Buddha's Teaching; and with unpretentious examples taken from the common ordinary affairs of life I should like to illustrate the profound significance of this splendid doctrine . . . Those who search for gold extract it from sand; those who take pleasure in jewels gather pebbles and polish them. So I call this book *Collection of Sand and Pebbles.*"

The *Shasekishū* consists of 134 anecdotes divided among 10 books, each illustrating one or two themes, and each subdivided into chapters ranging from a few lines to a few pages. Characteristically, the initial anecdote, or exemplum, is followed by a religious discourse which it illuminates. The sequence of tale and discourse is loosely connected, and the storyteller occasionally forgets that he is a moralist.

The 10 chapters of Book I argue the identity of Shintō and Buddhist deities, influencing the *Shintōshū* (ca 1358–61), a late *setsuwa* collection centering on the HONJI SUIJAKU doctrine. Other *Shasekishū* themes include the dangers of attachment to mundane matters, karmic retribution, and poetry as a means of religious realization— each supported with anecdotes and extensive citations from Buddhist sources and the Chinese classics. The work was popular among the clergy of the Muromachi period (1333–1568) and left its impression on the SASAMEGOTO, a theoretical work on linked verse *(renga; see RENGA AND HAIKAI)* by SHINKEI (1406–75). The KYŌGEN farce *Busu* also owes its inspiration to the *Shasekishū*.

The Author——Mujū Ichien was born in Kamakura soon after it had become the seat of the military government. He took the tonsure in 1243 at the age of 17, possibly because of his limited secular prospects thanks to his kinship to the ill-fated villain of the MINAMOTO NO YOSHITSUNE legend, Kajiwara Kagetoki. The Heian-period (794–1185) spirit of religious tolerance and accommodation is conspicuous in his life and writings, in contrast to the zealous parochialism of his times. Standard biographies identify Mujū as a ZEN monk of the RINZAI SECT by virtue of his having become, in 1261, a disciple of ENNI (1202–80), founder of the temple Tōfukuji; but the bias of Mujū's writings is toward the eclecticism of the TENDAI SECT, encompassing Shintō, Shingon, Zen, and Pure Land doctrines. In 1263, with the support of HŌJŌ TOKIYORI (1227–63), Mujū rebuilt a rural temple in what is now the city of Nagoya, renaming it Chōboji, which today maintains writings and artifacts ascribed to him. Here he remained for the next half century, except for occasional trips to the ISE SHRINE, Kyōto, and Mt. Kōya (KŌYASAN). Mujū presumably died at the Chōboji, although some biographies opt for the Rengeji in Kuwana (now the city of Kuwana, Mie Prefecture), which he visited in his later years.

Mujū's other works include a second collection of Buddhist *setsuwa*, the *Zōtanshū* (Collection of Casual Digressions), completed in 1305; *Shōzaishū* (Collection of Sacred Assets), a doctrinal work composed in 1299; and *Tsuma kagami* (Mirror for Women), a Buddhist tract written in 1300 and an instructive contrast to the 18th century Confucian ONNA DAIGAKU (The Great Learning for Women).

▰ ——Robert E. Morrell, "Tales from the Collection of Sand and Pebbles," *Literature East and West* 14.2 (1970). Robert E. Morrell, "Mujū Ichien's Shintō-Buddhist Syncretism; *Shasekishū*, Book 1," *Monumenta Nipponica* 28.4 (1973). Robert E. Morrell, "Mirror for Women: Mujū Ichien's *Tsuma Kagami*," *Monumenta Nipponica* 35.1 (1980). Hartmut O. Rotermund, "La conception des kami japonais à l'époque de Kamakura: Notes sur le premier chapitre du 'Sasekishū,'" *Revue de l'Histoire des Religions* 182.1 (1972). Hartmut O. Rotermund, *Collection de sable et de pierres: Shasekishū par Ichien Mujū* (Gallimard, 1979). Watanabe Tsunaya, ed, *Shasekishū*, in *Nihon koten bungaku taikei*, vol 85 (Iwanami Shoten, 1966). Yamada Shōzen and Miki Sumito, ed, *Zōtanshū* (Miyai Shoten, 1973).

Robert E. MORRELL

shasō

Granaries established by village organizations and domainal governments during the Edo period (1600–1868) as a precaution against famines. In contrast to the charitable granaries (*gisō*) administered by the central government, the *shasō* received their grain in the form of voluntary contributions according to each participant's income and status, and the contributors themselves administered its storage and distribution. Based on long-established systems in China and Korea, the idea was introduced into Japan by YAMAZAKI ANSAI. The first *shasō* was established in 1655 by HOSHINA MASAYUKI in the Aizu domain (now part of Fukushima Prefecture), and other domains quickly followed suit. Most of the *shasō* were abolished at the time of the Meiji Restoration (1868).

Shaw, Glenn William (1886–1961)

American educator, writer, translator, and government official, active in Japan from 1916 to 1940 and from 1949 to 1957. He promoted Western understanding of Japan before World War II by translating the works of important modern Japanese writers into English. After the war he contributed to Japanese-American reconciliation through his knowledge of modern Japan and his friendship with its leading writers. Born in Los Angeles, Shaw graduated from Colorado College (1910) and taught English in Hawaii, Japan, China, and India; between 1916 and 1940 he taught chiefly in the Ōsaka area. While at the Ōsaka School of Foreign Languages, he wrote and produced radio broadcasts for the Ōsaka Mainichi Newspaper Company and regularly contributed a column to the newspaper *Ōsaka asahi shimbun*.

Shaw's knowledge of Japanese led to civilian service with the US Navy from 1940 to 1949, organizing Japanese-language instruction and serving as director of the Navy Language School in Boulder, Colorado, and then as dean of the Navy Intelligence School in Washington, DC. He returned to Japan in 1949 as a State Department historian to supervise the microfilming of Japanese Ministry of Foreign Affairs documents. He served with the American Embassy in Tōkyō as a United States Information Agency cultural officer from 1952 until his retirement in 1957. He was awarded the American Presidential Certificate of Merit (1947), an Honorary Doctorate of Literature from Colorado College (1954), and three Japanese imperial orders.

His published works include *Ōsaka Sketches* (1929), *Japanese Scrap-Book* (1932), and *Living in Japan* (1936). Among his translations are KURATA HYAKUZŌ's *Shukke to sono deshi* (tr *The Priest and His Disciples*, 1922); FUTABATEI SHIMEI's *Heibon* (tr *Mediocrity*, 1927); KIKUCHI KAN's *Tojuro no koi* (tr *Tojuro's Love*, 1925). He also published a translation of a collection of stories by AKUTAGAWA RYŪNOSUKE entitled *Tales Grotesque and Curious* (1930).

Dallas FINN

shellfish

This article deals with shellfish in the sense of mollusks, which is the sense of the Japanese word *kai*, i.e., invertebrate animals with univalve or bivalve shells which belong to the phylum Mollusca. For crustaceans, see SHRIMPS, PRAWNS, AND LOBSTERS; CRABS; HORSESHOE CRAB.

About 6,000 species of marine shellfish are found in Japan. On the Pacific coast are warm water shellfish such as the *takaragai* (cowrie; genus *Cypraea*) and *imogai* (cone shell; genus *Conus*); they decrease in number toward the north. Coldwater shellfish such as the

ezobai (whelk; genus *Buccinum*) and *ezobora* (neptune whelk; genus *Neptunea*) decrease toward the south until the molluscan fauna show major changes at the Bōsō Peninsula. A similar distribution is seen on the Sea of Japan coast, but there is no distinct boundary between these two elements. In the Inland Sea and large bays, there are shellfish different from those mentioned above. These are the remains of species distributed in Japan when it was still connected with the continent; they have, however, gradually been disappearing. For example, the *haigai* (*Tegillarca granosa*), now distributed widely from Southeast Asia to the Korean peninsula, was once distributed up to northern Honshū; although it is one of the important species found in SHELL MOUNDS on the coast of Tōkyō Bay, it is now found only in the Inland Sea and Ariake Sea.

As for freshwater shellfish, about 90 species are found in Japan, many of which are similar to those of the Asian continent, especially central south China. In particular Lake Biwa, which belongs to the Miocene epoch of the Tertiary period, abounds in endemic species such as the *ikechōgai* (*Hyriopsis schlegelii*), *setashijimi* (*Corbicula sandai*) and *nagatanishi* (*Heterogen longispira*). The *kawa shinjugai* (freshwater pearl mussel; *Margaritifera laevis*), a northern species now found widely throughout Honshū, is considered a relic of an interglacial epoch.

Important Species ——The most important Japanese species of shellfish is the *okina ebisugai* (slit shell; family Pleurotomariidae). These flourished from the Paleozoic era through the Jurassic period of the Mesozoic era and declined later, with only 12 species surviving in the West Indies, the western Pacific and South Africa. Five of these species are found in Japan. Among these, the *beniokina ebisugai* (Hirase's slit shell; *Mikadotrochus hirasei*) and *okina ebisugai* (*M. beyrichii*) had already been described, with illustrations, in Japan in 1775 and 1843, respectively, that is, before the slit shells were discovered in the West Indies. The *ōitokakegai* (precious wentletrap; *Epitonium scalare*) and *chimakibora* (miracle shell; *Thatcheria mirabilis*) are famous for their beautiful shapes. The bivalves, *shōjōgai* (thorny oyster; *Spondylus regius*) and *tsukihigai* (sun and moon shell; *Amusium japonicum*) are also representative species.

The important edible mollusks are, among the snails: ABALONES (*awabi*), found among reefs, the *sazae* (spiny turban shell; *Turbo cornutus*), with big spines on the shell, the *bai* (ivory shell; *Babylonia japonica*), found in shallow seas, the *ezobai* (*Buccinum middendorfi*) and *ezobora* (*Neptunea polycostata*), distributed in northern Japan. Among the bivalves: the *asari* (Japanese little neck; *Ruditapes philippinarum*), the *hamaguri* (*Meretrix lusoria*), *bakagai* (*Mactra chinensis*) and *ubagai* (*Spisula sybillae*). The *magaki* (Japanese oyster; *Crassostrea gigas*), which lives in bays with a low salt content, is actively cultured, and the seedlings are exported to the United States and Canada. This is a species close to the American oyster (*C. virginica*) and Portuguese oyster (*C. angulata*). The *itabogaki* (*Ostrea denselamellosa*) is a species close to the European oyster (*O. edulis*) but is not cultured in Japan. The *hotategai* (Ezo giant scallop; *Patinopecten yessoensis*) is distributed in the shallow seas of northern Japan and is actively cultured. The blue mussel (*Mytilus edulis*), introduced from Europe, is established in Japan though not cultured for eating. The *igai* (*M. coruscus*), a native species close to the blue mussel, is also harvested.

The *akoyagai* (*Pinctada fucata martensii*) is used for pearl culture. The *ikechōgai*, a freshwater mussel living in Lake Biwa, is also used as mother shell for pearl culture.

Among other mollusks, a phylum which includes OCTOPUSES and SQUID AND CUTTLEFISH, about 700 species of terrestrial snails are found in Japan, resembling those in central and south China. These have mostly developed into endemic genera and species. As in the countries of Southeast Asia, the Afurika *maimai* (giant snail; *Achatina fulica*) has recently invaded Okinawa and Ogasawara and damaged agricultural crops. Species of mollusk introduced to Japan from North America are the land snail *kohakugai* (*Zonitoides arboreus*) and the bivalved shellfish *shimamenō funegai* (onyx slipper shell; *Crepidula onyx*).

HABE Tadashige

Shell mounds attest the importance shellfish had in the life of the ancient Japanese. It was Edward Sylvester MORSE who first took notice of Japanese shell mounds during his visit to Japan to study shellfish in 1877. The full-scale research initiated by Morse of the ŌMORI SHELL MOUNDS, which he had noticed from a train window, was the beginning of Japanese archaeology. The number of shell mounds found throughout Japan totals about 2,000, with the greater part on the Pacific coast. About 500 species of shellfish, both freshwater and marine, have been found in these mounds.

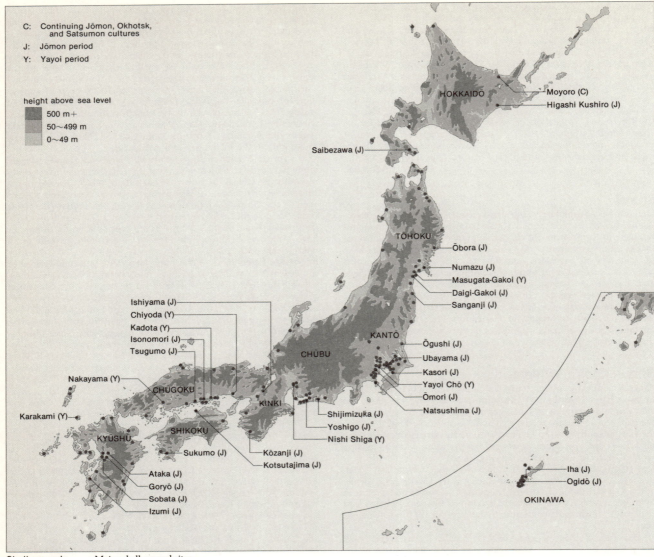

Shell mounds ———— Major shell mound sites

In literature shellfish make their first appearance in the *Kojiki* (completed in 712) and *Nihon shoki* (completed in 720). These are the *akagai (Scapharca broughtonii)* and *hamaguri,* which were to occupy important positions in both Japanese food and technical arts in subsequent periods. There appears a detailed description of the *mategai (Solen strictus)* in the *Honzō wamyō* (completed in 918), a dictionary of natural history from the Heian period (794–1185), while instances of the use of the *igai* for the payment of tax in kind to the court are described in the Engi Shiki (completed in 927, Procedures of the Engi Era). It is also known that the technique of sending preserved *igai* to distant places had already been developed by that time. Nobles of the Heian period no doubt relished *hamaguri* and *igai* brought from the provinces.

In addition to the use of shells in fashioning various implements and artistic handicrafts, nobles of the court in Kyōto played a game called KAI-AWASE. The *kai oke* (shell pot) used to keep the shells for *kai-awase* was usually hexagonal, wooden, lacquered, or sprinkled with gold and silver powder and came to be a part of the bridal trousseau in the Edo period (1600–1868). From the Kamakura period (1185–1333) through the Muromachi period (1333–1568) people used to write one or several characters of a Buddhist sutra on shells picked up from the beach and bury them in SUTRA MOUNDS *(kyō-zuka),* a medieval custom known as the *kaigarakyō* offering.

Hamaguri and *akagai* were appreciated above all others for their taste among the common people of Edo and Ōsaka in early modern times. As sea transport developed, the *hotategai* and *itayagai (Pecten albicans)* were brought to cities from afar. The shellfish came to

be considered a propitious object and indispensable at banquets. The *miyairigai (Oncomelania nosophora)* and *hime monoaragai (Bakerlymnaea viridis),* however, are noxious as they may host parasites. Nowadays shellfish from the seas surrounding Japan are sometimes dangerous to eat because of contaminated seawater.

—— Kanai Shiun, *Gyokai to geijutsu* (1933). Kinoshita Kenjirō, *Zoku bimi gushin* (1937). SAITŌ Shōji

shell mounds

(kaizuka). Heaps of shells or kitchen middens left by shellfood eaters, dating from the Jōmon (ca 10,000 BC–ca 300 BC) and, to a lesser extent, Yayoi (ca 300 BC–ca AD 300) and Kofun (ca 300–710) periods (see HISTORY OF JAPAN: prehistory). Besides shells, these mounds usually contain other plant and animal food remains, discarded cultural materials, especially pottery, and even burials, and thus serve as valuable repositories of information for ARCHAEOLOGY. About 2,000 shell mounds are known from Hokkaidō (see MOYORO SHELL MOUND) to Okinawa Prefecture (see IHA SHELL MOUND; OGIDŌ SHELL MOUND). Most are found along the eastern coast of Japan where warm water and natural sandy inlets and beaches provided good conditions for shellfish breeding; nearly half of the known total are concentrated in the Kantō region alone.

Shell mounds take on a variety of shapes and sizes, depending on factors such as their location and length of deposition. Shells may be loosely scattered over a small area or be packed several meters deep on sloped terrain. They may fill abandoned PIT HOUSES or be concentrated around village sites in crescent, horseshoe-shaped or circular deposits. Investigations of growth rings on discarded clam shells suggest that they were collected only during certain seasons, possibly implying that the shell mound sites were also seasonally utilized although over several centuries. Shell mounds of the Earliest and Early Jōmon periods (ca 7500 BC–ca 3500 BC) are only of modest dimensions, but in Middle and especially Late Jōmon times (ca 3500 BC–ca 1000 BC), they increased greatly in size (see KASORI SHELL MOUNDS). Dependence on shellfish decreased after the beginning of wet rice agriculture in the Early Yayoi period (ca 300 BC–ca 100 BC); however, sporadic disposal of shells in midden form has continued in peripheral areas until modern times.

Skeletal remains of the Jōmon people seldom survive in Japan's acidic soil, but those that were buried in the shell mounds have been preserved by the calcium content of the shells. Up to 340 skeletons in both extended and flexed burials (see PREHISTORIC BURIALS) have been excavated from the Late Jōmon shell mound of Yoshigo in Aichi Prefecture, showing increases over earlier Jōmon middens as evidence of a growing population. The conditions of the skeletons provide information about social customs and changes in physical characteristics through time (see JŌMON CULTURE).

The diet of Jōmon peoples is attested to by a variety of shells, fish and animal bones, and seeds also preserved in the shell mounds. Several hundred species of both freshwater and marine shellfish have been recovered, including from least to most common: abalone and snail shells, oysters and scallops, and several kinds of clams. Over 30 different species of fish have been identified; salmon, trout, and dolphin are characteristic elements of northern lifeways, and the offshore varieties of perch, sea bass, mullet, gilthead, snapper, dragonet, and sea bream indicate the development of offshore fishing. Occasional whale bones and turtle shells indicate utilization but not regular exploitation. Fishing gear including hooks, harpoons (with detachable heads in the Late Jōmon period), weights, spearheads, and dugout canoes up to six meters (20 feet) in length have been unearthed.

Additional land food included gourds, chestnuts, walnuts, acorns, and hazelnuts; edible fowl such as geese, pheasants, white cranes, and kites; and the meat of Japanese deer, wild boar, brown bear, Siberian mountain lion, monkey, flying squirrel, rabbit, TANUKI ("racoon dog"), and badger. Deer bones are usually those of older male deer, but other animals were hunted without regard to age or sex. In addition to the meat, the bones, skins, furs, and fat of all these animals were used in a variety of ways.

Bones of small dogs, the ancestors of the modern *shibainu* are frequently found in shell mounds of Middle Jōmon age and later. From occasional special burials, it is surmised that the dogs were kept as watchdogs and household pets, although they too may have served as sources of food along with a kind of cat of a more northern species than the surviving Iriomote wildcat and a horse the size of the Tokara pony.

In addition to providing information on the life of ancient peoples in Japan, shell mounds can also be used to reconstruct the prehistoric environment. Since specific shell species are known to prefer certain habitats, their presence in the shell mounds indicates those habitat conditions prevailing near the site when the shells were collected. For example, ark shells (*haigai*), razor shells (*agemaki*), and jackknife clams (*ōnogai*) proliferate in muddy conditions. Most clams, especially common orient clams (*hamaguri*), Japanese littlenecks (*asari*), and surf clams (*shiofuki*) prefer sandy beaches. Limpets (*kasagai*), top shells (*kubogai*), and turbans (*ishidatami*), on the other hand, thrive on rocky coasts. From the presence of such shells in shell mounds, prehistoric coastal environments, fluctuations in water temperature and changes from marine to fresh water can be recognized. Moreover, the geographical distribution of shell mounds when matched with their contents can be used to locate prehistoric shorelines. See also MUKŌGAOKA SHELL MOUND; ŌMORI SHELL MOUNDS.

—— Esaka Teruya, *Jōmon doki to kaizuka*, in *Kodaishi hakkutsu*, vol 2 (Kōdansha, 1973). Kiyono Kenji, *Nihon kaizuka no kenkyū* (1969). Sakazume Nakao, *Nihon kaizuka chimei hyō* (1959). Sakazume Nakao, "Kaizuka," in Nihon Kōkogaku Kyōkai, ed, *Nihon kōkogaku jiten* (1962). J. Edward KIDDER, JR.

Shell Sekiyu Co, Ltd

(Shell Oil). Japanese-incorporated company of the Royal Dutch Shell group, wholly owned by the Shell Petroleum Co of London. Established in 1900 as the Rising Sun Petroleum Co to import and sell oil products, it now imports crude oil and petroleum products and distributes them to 1,200 dealers as well as to about 4,800 service stations. Annual sales totaled ¥1,425 billion (US $6.5 billion) in the fiscal year ending in December 1981, and it was capitalized at ¥6.9 billion (US $31.5 million). Corporate headquarters are located in Tōkyō.

Shen Nanpin (Shen Nan-p'in) (fl mid-18th century)

(J: Chin Nampin or Shin Nampin). Chinese practitioner of BIRD-AND-FLOWER PAINTING. Real name Shen Quan (Shen Ch'üan; J: Chin Sen or Shin Sen). Born in Zhejiang (Chekiang) Province. In 1731, he traveled to Japan where he remained for approximately two years. Despite the brevity of his visit, his influence was considerable and brought about the flourishing of colorful and realistic painting of birds and flowers (*kachōga*) in Japan. Among his disciples who formed the Nampin school within the so-called NAGASAKI SCHOOL of painting was KUMASHIRO YŪHI.

Shen Weijing (Shen Wei-ching) (?–1597)

(J: Shin Ikei). Envoy of the Ming dynasty (1368–1644) of China who was sent to Korea and Japan at the time of TOYOTOMI HIDEYOSHI's first invasion of Korea in 1592 (see INVASIONS OF KOREA IN 1592 AND 1597). Hideyoshi's forces initially encountered little resistance from the Koreans, but when the Ming dynasty came to the aid of its tributary state, the Japanese decided to hold truce talks with the Chinese. Shen was sent to meet with the Japanese general KONISHI YUKINAGA, who was encamped at Seoul, but no agreement could be reached, since China insisted that Japan admit vassalage to the Ming. In 1596 Shen was dispatched to Japan to negotiate directly with Hideyoshi. The mission ended in failure, and as a result Shen was put to death on his return to China and Hideyoshi launched a second invasion in 1597.

shiatsu

(literally, "finger pressure"; often referred to as acupressure). Curative and preventive therapy consisting of pressing specific points and areas of the body with the fingers, palms, elbows, knees, or feet. The *shiatsu* therapist is expected to have empathy with the patient's state of body and mind and to awaken and stimulate the natural healing powers of the patient.

The difference between *shiatsu* and other therapeutic manipulations legally authorized in Japan (traditional AMMA massage and other Western massages) is that they consist of deliberate, rhythmical, active hand manipulations while *shiatsu* uses simple, natural pressure. In contrast to massage, which stimulates the sympathetic nerves and promotes the flow of blood in the circulatory system, *shiatsu* employs a uniform, stable, and continuous pressure and induces the parasympathetic nerves to stimulate the internal organs. *Shiatsu* relaxes the muscles, reduces the stress that suppresses the activity of the internal organs, and produces a restful state.

To treat disease, the *shiatsu* practitioner stimulates specific points (called *tsubo* or *keiketsu*) in the body and thereby regulates the flow of energy or life force (*ki*) in the meridians (*keiraku*) throughout the body. According to the philosophy of traditional Chinese and Japanese medicine, this meridian system is a fundamental, life-sustaining mechanism present in some form even in the most primitive life forms, and *shiatsu* aims at stimulating the innate healing powers of the patient by restoring the harmony of the organism that has been disturbed by disease. It has proven to be effective in healing many diseases, especially functional diseases, stress-induced diseases, and kinetic disorders.

At the beginning of the 20th century, many therapeutic manipulations developed out of traditional *amma* massage, a branch of Chinese medicine that had tended to degenerate into nothing more than a means of relaxation. In 1955 these, together with Western manual therapies (chiropractic, osteopathic, etc), came to be included by law under the term *shiatsu*. MASUNAGA Shizuto

Shiba family

One of the three warrior families that monopolized the powerful post of KANREI (shogunal deputy) during the Muromachi period (1333–1568), the other two being the HATAKEYAMA FAMILY and the HOSOKAWA FAMILY. A branch of the ASHIKAGA FAMILY, the Shiba were based in Mutsu, in the far north of Honshū, but were also hereditary successors to the governorship of the more centrally located province of Owari (now part of Aichi Prefecture). Shiba Taka-tsune (1305–67) sided with ASHIKAGA TAKAUJI when he rebelled against Emperor GO-DAIGO in 1335, and he was appointed military governor (SHUGO) of Echizen and Wakasa (now Fukui Prefecture) soon after Takauji established his shogunate in Kyōto. One of Takatsune's sons, Yoshimasa (1350–1410), greatly extended the family's power when he was appointed *kanrei* for three separate terms by the Ashikaga shōguns. He was also given the governorships of Echizen, Shinano (now Nagano Prefecture), and several other provinces. His son Yoshishige (1371–1418) and grandson Yoshiatsu also served as *kanrei*. In the mid-1400s, however, the Shiba family fell into a bitter succession dispute; this was to become entangled with similar disputes in other great families and was one cause of the ŌNIN WAR (1467–77). After the war the family fortunes continued to decline. Shiba lands were taken over piecemeal by the IMAGAWA FAMILY and the ASAKURA FAMILY, and the stronghold of the family in Owari was finally destroyed by ODA NOBUNAGA in 1561. The CHIKUBASHŌ, a set of moral rules for samurai, was written by Shiba Yoshimasa.

Shiba Kōkan (1747?–1818)

Artist, innovator, and pioneer in the Westernization of Japan who achieved revolutionary advances in Western-style oil painting and created the first copperplate etchings in the country. According to some sources, the year of his birth was 1738. He studied geography, etched copperplate maps of the world, and wrote texts to accompany them. He also turned his attention to astronomy and introduced the theories of Copernicus to a society imbued with an antithetical, Confucian world order. Opposed to the generally conservative position of the Tokugawa government, Kōkan sought to establish an ideal social order, which to him was synonymous with his notions of European social and cultural mores. Though never actively involved in politics, he regarded himself as the chief prophet of Western culture in Japan and his work as crucial for Japan's modernization.

Kōkan was born in Edo (now Tōkyō). His early training was in the KANŌ SCHOOL style of painting, but at the age of 15 he switched allegiance to become the student of Sō Shiseki (1712–86), a master of Chinese-style BIRD-AND-FLOWER PAINTING. At age 23 he turned to making woodblock prints, forging the designs and signature of the master Suzuki HARUNOBU (Kōkan eventually changed his signature to Harushige). He created his first Western-style oil paintings around 1780 and in 1783 made his first copperplate etching on the basis of techniques learned from a Dutch encyclopedia.

In 1788 Kōkan embarked on a historic journey to Nagasaki, traveling on foot from Edo and keeping a diary, which he later published. He was a prolific writer; some of his major works include *Chikyū zenzu ryakusetsu* (1793, Explanation of the Complete Map of the World), *Saiyū ryodan* (1794, Account of a Western Journey), *Oranda tensetsu* (1796, Explanation of Dutch Astronomy), *Seiyōga dan* (1799, Discussion of Western Painting), *Oranda tsūhaku* (1805, Dutch Navigation), *Kopperu temmon zukai* (1808, Illustrated Explanation of Copernican Astronomy), *Shumparō hikki* (1811, Notes by Shumparō), *Mugon Dōjin hikki* (1814, Notes by Mugon Dōjin), *Saiyū nikki* (1815, Diary of a Western Journey), and *Tenchi ridan* (1816, Discussion of Astronomy and Geography).

In old age Kōkan turned away from scientific inquiry and Western-style painting; his late writings express an outlook increasingly influenced by the teachings of the ancient Chinese sages. He embraced a kind of Taoism, declaring that all his youthful ambitions, strivings, and successes had been vain. He became a disciple of ZEN Buddhism and retired to a monastery. From there in 1813, according to one anecdote, he sent notice of his "death" to his friends, many of whom sent offerings of money and gifts in honor of the "deceased." The five years that he lived after his published death were a period of paradox, since Kōkan was unable to reconcile the conflicting goals of worldly success and nonstriving spirituality. His only desire, he wrote, was to "leave behind paintings that can be seen by posterity so that my fame will live on." Today he is recognized not only as an artist, but as one of the important pioneers behind Japan's eventual emergence as a modern nation.

━━ Calvin L. French, *Shiba Kōkan* (1974). Calvin L. French, *Through Closed Doors: Western Influence on Japanese Art* (1977). Hosono Masanobu, *Shiba Kōkan* (1974).   Cal FRENCH

Shibano Ritsuzan (1736–1807)

Confucian scholar of the Edo period (1600–1868); he is thought to have formulated senior councillor MATSUDAIRA SADANOBU's 1790 edict, the so-called Kansei Igaku no Kin, making the knowledge of Zhu Xi (Chu Hsi) Confucianism (SHUSHIGAKU) as taught by the Hayashi family a prerequisite for entering the shogunate administration (see also KANSEI REFORMS). Shibano was born in Sanuki Province (now Kagawa Prefecture), and after studying at SHŌHEIKŌ, the shogunal academy for Confucian studies headed by the Hayashi family, he held a post as tutor in the Tokushima domain (now Tokushima Prefecture). In 1788 he was named official Confucian scholar to the shogunate and was appointed to the staff at Shōheikō.

Shiba Ryōtarō (1923–   )

Novelist. Born in Ōsaka. Graduate of Ōsaka Gaigo Gakkō (now Ōsaka University of Foreign Studies) where he studied Mongolian. Working as a newspaper reporter, he started writing popular historical novels in the mid-1950s. He received the Naoki Prize for *Fukurō no shiro* (1959). His works, which are primarily entertaining, often depict the lives and behavior of people in turbulent times of history, such as the Meiji Restoration, and provide a new interpretation of those times. Principal works include *Ryōma ga yuku* (1962–66), *Yo ni sumu hibi* (1969–70), and *Saka no ue no kumo* (1969–72).

Shibata

City in northern Niigata Prefecture, central Honshū. A castle town from the 15th century through the Edo period (1600–1868), it is now the center of the surrounding rice-growing area. Local products include *sake* (rice wine) and pears. There is an emerging plastics and machine industry. Pop: 76,210.

Shibata Katsuie (1522?–1583)

One of the principal captains of the hegemon ODA NOBUNAGA. Shibata supported Nobunaga's younger brother Nobuyuki in the struggle between the two but later betrayed Nobuyuki (killed in 1557) and passed into Nobunaga's service. He distinguished himself in a series of Nobunaga's major campaigns: in Ise (now part of Mie Prefecture) in 1569; in Ōmi (now Shiga Prefecture) from 1570 to the destruction of the *daimyō* ASAI NAGAMASA and ASAKURA YOSHIKAGE in 1573; and against armed confederations (IKKŌ IKKI) of the Buddhist JŌDO SHIN SECT on the Ōsaka, Ise Nagashima, and Echizen fronts between 1570 and 1575. After the subjugation of Echizen (now part of Fukui Prefecture) in 1575, he was invested with that province, and governed it under a set of "regulations" (*okite*) and the supervision of three inspectors (*metsuke*) imposed by Nobunaga. His policies in Echizen, namely the separation of the peasant from the *samurai* status (*heinō bunri*), a SWORD HUNT, a land survey (KENCHI), and a prototypal religious inquisition, illustrate important features of the Nobunaga regime's approach to provincial governance; these policies were later expanded, systematized, and applied nationwide by Nobunaga's successors in the unification of Japan, TOYOTOMI HIDEYOSHI and TOKUGAWA IEYASU. The conquest of the regional domain of the Ikkō sect in Kaga and Noto (now Ishikawa Prefecture) in 1580 was Shibata's last major accomplishment on Nobunaga's behalf. In the contest for the succession to Nobunaga after his death in 1582, Shibata proved no match for his long-time rival Hideyoshi. Defeated by Hideyoshi in the Battle of SHIZUGATAKE on 11 June 1583 (Tenshō 11.4.21), Shibata committed suicide three days later.   George ELISON

Shibata Keita (1877–1949)

Plant physiologist and biochemist. Born in Tōkyō. His father, Shibata Shōkei (1850–1910), was a famous pharmacologist. A graduate of Tōkyō University, he later taught there. He studied in Germany under the plant physiologist Wilhelm Pfeffer (1845–1920). In addition to his research on the distribution of flavonoid compounds in the plant world, he also carried out successful research in such fields as respiration and metabolism. He also trained many outstanding scientists.   SUZUKI Zenji

Shibata Kyūō (1783–1839)

Propagator and scholar of SHINGAKU, a commoner-oriented school of ethics of the Edo period (1600–1868). In his twenties he became a professional teller of heroic tales (KŌDAN), an art in which he gained modest fame. He began the study of Shingaku under Satta Tokuken (1778–1836) in his late thirties and dedicated the rest of his life to its cause, traveling and lecturing despite the loss of his sight at age 44.

His simple and persuasive style appealed to farmers, *samurai,* and nobility alike. His *Kyūō dōwa* (1835), a collection of moral tales, is considered a masterpiece among Shingaku writings.

Shibata Renzaburō (1917–1978)

Novelist. Born in Okayama Prefecture. Graduate of Keiō University. Shibata received the Naoki Prize in 1951 for his short story "Iesu no sue." He established himself with his period novel *Nemuri Kyōshirō burai hikae,* serialized from 1956 to 1958 in the weekly magazine *Shūkan shinchō,* in which he created a new hero, Nemuri Kyōshirō, a tough and unemotional swordsman. The novel was so successful that he followed it with many sequels, all written in a fast-paced, action-oriented style. Together with GOMI YASUSUKE's novels in a similar vein, it created the so-called *kengō* (strong swordsman) fiction boom in the late 1950s. Other works include *Akai kagebōshi* (1960).

Shibata Shō (1935–)

Novelist. Born in Tōkyō. A graduate of Tōkyō University, where he majored in German literature. As a graduate student he specialized in Goethe. After winning the Japan Goethe Society Award in 1961, he traveled to Germany and eventually became a teacher of German literature at Tōkyō University. In 1964 his *Saredo warera ga hibi* won the Akutagawa Prize and triggered a "Shibata Shō boom" among Japanese youth, who were attracted by his sentimental, introverted, nostalgic style and basic positivism. From 1970 to 1973 he participated in the publication of the coterie magazine *Ningen to shite* along with TAKAHASHI KAZUMI, ODA MAKOTO, KAIKŌ KEN, and Matsugi Nobuhiko. *Tsugumichi* WATANABE

Shiba Tatto (6th century)

Early promoter of BUDDHISM in Japan. A record by the Enryakuji monk Zenshin quoted in the 12th-century history *Fusō ryakki* says that Shiba Tatto was Chinese and that he immigrated to Japan in 522, soon thereafter establishing a hermitage containing a Buddhist image at Sakatahara in Takechi no Kōri (now the Asuka region in Nara Prefecture). His actual date of arrival, however, is more likely to have been 582. The chronicle NIHON SHOKI (720) says that in 584 Shiba Tatto, at the request of SOGA NO UMAKO, took part in a search for people already practicing Buddhism in Japan and that his 12-year-old daughter Shima became a nun in the same year. His son Kuratsukuri no Tasuna produced Buddhist images for Japan's oldest large temple, the Sakatadera, and Tasuna's son KURATSUKURI NO TORI is known for having made the bronze image of the Buddha at the temple ASUKADERA in 606 and the bronze Shaka triad of the temple HŌRYŪJI in 623. The names of Shiba Tatto and his descendants are often prefixed by the clan designation *kuratsukuri,* indicating some relationship to a hereditary group of saddlemakers, and *suguri* or *obito,* titles usually held by immigrants who came from or via Korea. See also KIKAJIN. *William R.* CARTER

Shibata Zeshin (1807–1891)

Outstanding lacquer artist of the 19th century, noted for the originality and elegance of his designs. In his youth, Zeshin studied lacquer for eight years with Koma Kansai II (1767–1835). He went on to acquire training as a painter in the naturalistic style of the Shijō school (see MARUYAMA–SHIJŌ SCHOOL), working with Suzuki Nanrei (1775–1844) and Okamoto Toyohiko (1773–1845) in Kyōto. Although he established a name for himself as a painter in 1841 with the dramatic depiction of a female demon commissioned as a votive plaque for Ōji Inari Shrine in Tōkyō, his subject matter is generally restricted to pleasant and uncontroversial bird-and-flower or genre themes. In his old age, during the 1870s and 1880s, Zeshin added the unusual technique of lacquer painting *(urushi-e)* to his repertoire. These works, probably inspired by the popularity of Western oil painting in the Meiji period (1868–1912), won numerous prizes at international expositions in Europe and America and illustrate his skill as both painter and lacquer artist. The finest examples are painted with utmost delicacy, focusing on one small corner of nature. Between 1886 and 1889 he assisted in the lacquer decoration of the Imperial Palace in Tōkyō. Zeshin's lacquer ware is characterized by a preference for somber colors such as black, brown, and green, and by subtle textural contrasts. He especially delighted in imitating natural materials as well as aged and weathered surfaces.

———— Gōke Tadaomi, *Shibata Zeshin,* no. 93 of *Nihon no bijutsu* (February 1974). *Julia* MEECH-PEKARIK

Shiberia Shuppei → Siberian Intervention

Shibetsu

City in north central Hokkaidō, on the river Teshiogawa. It was developed from 1899 by colonizing militia (TONDENHEI) from Honshū. Principal products are rice, potatoes, beans, beet sugar, asparagus, coal, and lumber. Pop: 28,970.

shibori → tie-dyeing

Shibue Chūsai (1805–1858)

Physician and philologist. Although he served as physician to the Tsugaru family of the Hirosaki domain (now part of Aomori Prefecture), Chūsai was born and spent most of his life in Edo (now Tōkyō). In 1844 he was appointed professor at the Tokugawa shogunate school of Chinese medicine, the Seijukan, where he remained until his death. As a scholar of Confucianism, Chūsai is known as a major figure in the Kōshōgaku (Textual Criticism) school. He continued the tradition of philological studies begun by his teachers Ichino Meian (1765–1826) and Kariya Ekisai (1775–1835) and, with his friend Mori Kien (1807–85), wrote a comprehensive bibliography of classical Chinese texts, *Keiseki hōko shi,* that is still highly regarded by modern scholars. In the area of medical studies, he was a leading member of the staff responsible for the Seijukan-sponsored publication of *Ishimpō,* the rediscovered medical book from the Heian period (794–1185). He also wrote commentaries on the classics of Chinese medicine. Both Chūsai and his teacher of medicine, Isawa Ranken (1777–1829), were made famous through Chūsai's biography (1916) by MORI ŌGAI. *Yoshiyuki* NAKAI

Shibugaki

(Sour Persimmons). A collection of Kamakura-period (1185–1333) writings; compiler and date unknown, but it is believed to have been compiled in either the 15th or 16th century. It contains four items. The first is an account of the life of the Buddhist holy man MYŌE and includes the anecdote about his refusal to accept an estate *(shōen)* from HŌJŌ YASUTOKI, the regent of the Kamakura shogunate. The second is a letter from the holy man MONGAKU to the shōgun MINAMOTO NO YORITOMO, advising him on the principles of governance. The third is also a letter, dated 13 February 1192 (Kenkyū 2. intercalary 12.28), in which Yoritomo sends his condolences to the warrior Sasaki Sadatsuna (1142–1205), who has lost a son. The last, another letter, contains advice from Hōjō Yasutoki to his son Tokiuji (1203–30) on the proper attitudes of a warrior.

shibui

An adjective designating a subtle, unobtrusive, and deeply moving beauty, cherished by artists and connoisseurs since the Muromachi period (1333–1568). The term is applied to color, design, taste, and voice as well as to human behavior in general. Originating in medieval aesthetic sensibility, it is related to and sometimes overlaps such concepts as WABI, SABI, and *iki* (see IKI AND SUI). Its noun form is *shibusa* or *shibumi.*

The word *shibui* literally means "astringent," commonly referring to the acid flavor of an unripe persimmon. Its antonym is *amai* (sweet). In its early usage, *shibui* (*shibushi* in classical Japanese) therefore had pejorative connotations. Yet, as medieval artists cultivated a taste for simple, unostentatious beauty, it gradually took on a positive meaning. The use of *shibui* in the new favorable sense became widespread when urban commoners of the Edo period (1600–1868), who prided themselves on their refined taste, asserted their preference for a quietly appealing ambiance. The subdued voice of a master singer, the disciplined performance of a seasoned actor, or the simple pattern designed by an expert ceramic artist had a beauty of understatement, and as such was praised as *shibui.* Colorful beauty was for the unsophisticated, but *shibui* was for connoisseurs who were not to be misled by the dazzling surface; it was to be appreciated by those who were satiated by all other types of beauty.

The penchant for *shibui* still survives in Japan, forming part of the basic aesthetic taste and manifesting itself in architecture, interior design, ceramic art, and other arts. The term is even applied to baseball: a player is said to be *shibui* when he makes no spectacular plays on the field but contributes to the team in an unobtrusive way. The concept has been known to the West since around 1960, when the American magazine *House Beautiful* published two special issues on *shibui*.

📖——*House Beautiful* 102 (August and September 1960). Kuki Shūzō, *"Iki" no kōzō* (1930).

Makoto UEDA

Shibukawa

City in central Gumma Prefecture, central Honshū. Near the confluence of the rivers Tonegawa and Agatsumagawa, it developed as a POST-STATION TOWN and market town on the Mikuni Kaidō highway. It is primarily an industrial city with chemical, lumber, electrical appliance, and cement block industries. Attractions include the nearby volcano HARUNASAN, Lake Haruna, and the Ikaho Hot Spring. Pop: 47,034.

Shibukawa Shunkai (1639–1715)

Astronomer and scholar of calendrical science. Also known as Shibukawa Harumi and Yasui Santetsu, the later being also the name of his father. He began astronomical and calendrical studies at an early age. After making observations over a period of years, he discovered errors in the Xuanming (Hsüan-ming) calendar (J: Semmyō-reki), a calendar of Chinese origin in use in Japan for more than 800 years. He succeeded in having his own calendar, the Jōkyōreki, which was based on a calendar of the Yuan dynasty (1279–1368), officially adopted by the Tokugawa shogunate in 1684 and entered the Bureau of Astronomy the same year. (This calendar was used until 1754.) In 1699 he released an "Astronomical Formations Chart," which included several new constellations not found in the traditional Chinese star chart. See also CALENDAR, DATES, AND TIME.

OHARA Satoru

Shibusawa Eiichi (1840–1931)

Entrepreneur and business leader during the Meiji (1868–1912) and Taishō (1912–26) periods. Born in the village of Chiaraijima in what is now Saitama Prefecture. Shibusawa's family, small farmers, had owned no more than two acres of land for generations, but his father became the richest man in the village by dealing in indigo. Influenced by Confucianism, he gave Shibusawa a better education than was usual for a man of his social class.

Shibusawa's impressionable years were dominated by the turmoil following the advent of Commodore Matthew PERRY in 1853. He attributed the decay of the Tokugawa shogunate (1603–1867) to a lack of social mobility in Tokugawa society. In 1863 he left his home, ostensibly to save Japan (he joined an abortive plot to expel foreigners from Yokohama), but actually with the dream of becoming a person of importance.

In 1864 Shibusawa was enlisted as a *samurai* by the Hitotsubashi domain, a branch family of the Tokugawa. In 1867 he became an aide-de-camp to the shōgun's younger brother TOKUGAWA AKITAKE, who led the Japanese delegation to the Paris International Exposition. There, Shibusawa was so impressed by Western civilization that he went back to Japan with hopes of transplanting the world of factories, banks, and the corporate form of business to his own country. But upon his return in 1868, he found himself a member of a deposed regime. Nevertheless, because of his supposed knowledge of the West, he obtained the financial support of the new Meiji government for the founding of a trading company, the Shōhō Kaisho, one of Japan's first joint-stock companies, and in 1869 he was appointed as a ranking official in the Ministry of Finance. As a protégé of ŌKUMA SHIGENOBU and INOUE KAORU, leaders in the new government, he played a key role in the establishment of the government-operated TOMIOKA SILK-REELING MILL in 1872 and in the introduction of a modern banking system the same year.

Shibusawa resigned from the Ministry of Finance in 1873 (he was assistant to the vice-minister at the time), following the rejection of his proposal to trim the budget. Even before this he had secured the presidencies of the Dai-Ichi Bank (now DAI-ICHI KANGYŌ BANK, LTD) and the ŌJI PAPER CO, LTD, both of which he had persuaded the MITSUI and other merchant houses to found in corporate form.

He and his bank were consulted and emulated when other national and private banks mushroomed during the years 1877 to 1880.

In 1882 Shibusawa organized the ŌSAKA SPINNING MILL by soliciting capital from leading businessmen and former *daimyō*. The new company, with 10,500 spindles, was unique in that it made profits in the first year of its operation, while many smaller mills were plagued with technical and financial difficulties. Companies modeled on the Ōsaka company and several other enterprises promoted by Shibusawa, including railway companies, proliferated from 1886 to 1890. During this period of rapid industrialization, Shibusawa was involved in organizing over 36 enterprises, including the Tōkyō Chemical Fertilizer Company, the first of its kind in Japan.

During a second period of rapid industrialization from 1895 to 1897, Shibusawa was involved in founding more than 23 enterprises. He was associated with more than 300 enterprises during his lifetime. Most of these were organized in corporate form, since Shibusawa firmly believed that this form would most benefit Japan.

Like many other men of the Meiji period, Shibusawa had a meteoric rise, but he remained a decent human being, believing business and ethics should go hand in hand. Influenced by the Christian concept of charity, he engaged in philanthropic work, founding schools and homes for the aged. He was apprehensive about the deterioration in Japanese–American relations after the Russo-Japanese War of 1904–05 and, regarding himself as a friend of the United States, attempted to improve the situation by organizing and heading a committee on Japanese-American relations as well as a goodwill mission to the United States. At the same time, unlike others who deserted Confucianism after the Meiji Restoration of 1868, Shibusawa continued to tailor his life according to Confucian teachings and remained to the end a true Confucian gentleman.

📖——Tsuchiya Takao, *Shibusawa Eiichi den* (1955).

Kee Il CHOI

Shibusawa Keizō (1896–1963)

Businessman; grandson of the entrepreneur SHIBUSAWA EIICHI. Born in Tōkyō, he graduated from Tōkyō University. After working for the Yokohama Specie Bank (now Bank of Tōkyō) and the Dai-Ichi Bank, he assumed the presidency of the Bank of Japan in 1944. Shibusawa served as minister of finance in the SHIDEHARA KIJŪRŌ cabinet (1945–1946). As a result of the OCCUPATION PURGE he was barred from public office. After the removal of restrictions, he was active as a leader in the business world, becoming president of KOKUSAI DENSHIN DENWA CO, LTD, and chairman of NIPPON CULTURAL BROADCASTING, INC. Shibusawa was deeply interested in Japanese folk culture; in 1921 he established in his home the Attic Museum, which later became the Nihon Jōmin Bunka Kenkyūjo (Japanese Folk Culture Research Institute), and supported the research of young ethnology students. As president of the Japanese Society of Ethnology (Nihon Minzokugaku Kyōkai) and the Anthropological Society of Japan (Nihon Jinruigaku Kai), he worked to bring together the various disciplines related to Japanese folk studies.

ITŌ Mikiharu

Shibushi Bay

(Shibushi Wan). Formerly called Ariake Wan (Ariake Bay; not to be confused with Ariake Sea). Inlet of the Pacific Ocean on the northeastern coast of the Ōsumi Peninsula, Kagoshima and Miyazaki prefectures, Kyūshū. Extends from the cape TOIMISAKI to the cape Hizaki. In recent years there has been much debate over plans for the industrial development of the area, which is a good fishing ground.

Shibuya Tengai (1906–)

Comic actor and playwright. Born in Kyōto. Real name Shibutani Kazuo. He succeeded his father Shibuya Tengai I, also a comic actor, who died at the age of 37. He formed the Shōchiku Kateigeki theater in 1928, and reacting against earlier comedy in the all-male *kabuki* tradition, he cast Naniwa Chieko and other actresses in plays of his own writing. He and Naniwa Chieko were married in 1930 and divorced in 1950. In 1948 he created the Shōchiku Shinkigeki (Shōchiku New Comedy). The nonsensical humor of his plays was well-received by the youth of the postwar generation. A great comic star, he has also appeared in movies. His disciple Fujiyama Kambi became a star in his own right.

ITASAKA Tsuyoshi

Shibuya Ward

(Shibuya Ku). One of the 23 wards of Tōkyō. On the Musashino Plateau. Primarily a residential area, Shibuya has many colleges, department stores and parks, but little industry. The commercial and amusement area near Shibuya Station has become one of the major centers of Tōkyō with many department stores, movie houses, and restaurants. Shibuya Station is one of Tōkyō's major transportation centers, being served by the Yamanote Line of the Japanese National Railways, private railways, subways, and bus lines. Located in Shibuya are the Meiji Shrine, the Yoyogi Sports Center, the NHK Broadcasting Center, the University of the Sacred Heart, Tōkai University, Kokugakuin University, Jissen Women's University, Aoyama Gakuin University, the Gotō Planetarium, and several embassies. Pop: 246,958.

shichi

A kind of material collateral for loans. The usage and definition of this term have varied throughout history. In ancient times, it referred to pawning, in which the possession of the object offered as collateral is transferred to the creditor, and to mortgaging, in which the possession of the object is not transferred to the creditor.

Under the RITSURYŌ SYSTEM of government, enacted in the late 7th century, in the event of nonfulfillment of a debt, the security object was to be sold off to settle the account. In actual practice, this procedure was followed when movable property was used for security, but when the security was in the form of real estate, the rights of possession belonged to the creditor as unredeemed property. It was common at this time for wealthy individuals like nobles and priests to take crops or land from farmers as collateral for loans.

In the Kamakura (1185–1333) and Muromachi (1333–1568) periods, *shichi* continued to refer to pawned security and mortgaged security, but the terms *irejichi* (pawned security) and *kenjichi* (mortgaged security) came to be used to differentiate the two. When movable property was used as collateral, loans were generally of the *irejichi* type and the collateral was transferable to the creditor in case the borrower failed to repay the loan. Pawnshops called *dosō* and *kuramoto* handled these transactions. In cases where real estate was used as collateral, *kenjichi* usually entailed revertible possession, but with *irejichi* the creditor did not have the right to foreclose the property. Instead of using real estate as *kenjichi*, there were cases in which the title deeds to the property were used as *irejichi*. Using a hostage (HITOJICHI) for collateral was also practiced in both the *irejichi* and *kenjichi* forms.

In the Edo period (1600–1868), the word *shichi* was in its broad sense still used to include nonpossessory (mortgaged) security, but in practice was more commonly used to mean possessory (pawned) security, and it is in this sense that the term is used today: For nonpossessory security, the term *kakiire* was used. Movable security continued to be handled by pawnshops in the Edo period. *Shichibōkō* (collateral labor), in which human beings were used as security, was also practiced. The use of houses as collateral was called *iejichi* and was widespread in urban areas. Pledges of farm fields were generally revertible and thus were used by large landlords as a means of expanding their holdings. The shogunate imposed strict conditions on the use of farmlands as collateral, and in cases where these conditions were not fully met, the loan was regarded as of the *kakiire* type, and the creditor was deprived of legal protection through *honkuji* (main suit), a type of formal litigation.

In the early part of the Meiji period (1868–1912) the use of human beings as collateral was prohibited, but the term *shichiire* (pawnage) remained in use until the enactment in 1898 of Japan's first modern civil code.　　　　　　　　　　*KOYANAGI Shun'ichirō*

shichibukin tsumitate

(literally, "seven-tenths of the cash reserves"). Emergency reserve fund established in 1791 by the senior councillor (*rōjū*) MATSUDAIRA SADANOBU as a part of the KANSEI REFORMS. After analyzing the municipal expenditures of Edo (now Tōkyō) for the years 1785–89, Sadanobu reduced the city's annual expenses by 10 percent, of which one-tenth was allocated for unbudgeted outlays and two-tenths was refunded to the merchant and landlord taxpayers of Edo. The remaining seven-tenths, called *shichibukin tsumitate*, was annually deposited at the Edo Office for Town Affairs (Edo Machikaisho) for use in emergencies. Approximately half of the capital was spent

on rice, which was kept in storehouses (SHASŌ). The cash reserve, when not required for emergency relief, was lent to the poor at low interest. So well did this arrangement function under government managers and rich townsmen that by 1828 the fund had accumulated 462,400 *ryō* in savings, 280,000 *ryō* in loans, and 467,178 *koku* of rice (1 *koku* = about 180 liters or 5 US bushels; see KOKUDAKA). During the TEMPŌ FAMINE (1833–36) these reserves were used to feed the people of Edo. After the Meiji Restoration of 1868, the accumulated *shichibukin tsumitate*, amounting to 1.43 million *ryō*, was used for new public buildings and social welfare projects under the supervision of SHIBUSAWA EIICHI.

Shichifukujin → Seven Deities of Good Fortune

shichigenkin

Also known as *kin* (Ch: *qin* or *ch'in*). A seven-string musical instrument of the zither type, made of hollowed wood; approximately 110 centimeters (43 in) long and 20 centimeters (8 in) wide.

Broadly speaking, it is a kind of KOTO (the same written character is used for *kin* and *koto*), though, unlike the more common and slightly larger type of *koto*, the *kin* does not utilize movable bridges for each string. Instead, the strings are stopped by the fingers of the left hand and plucked in various ways by the fingers of the right hand.

For two thousand years in China, the *shichigenkin* has been considered the instrument of the sage, poet, and scholar. It was first imported into Japan during the Nara period (710–794). In the TALE OF GENJI, written in the beginning of the 11th century, the *shichigenkin* is mentioned as going out of fashion. However, the instrument was revived in Japan in the early part of the Edo period (1600–1868) by the immigrant Chinese monk of the Sōtō Zen sect Shin'etsu (Ch: Hsin-yüeh or Xinyue; 1639–96), who came to Japan in 1677. Shin'etsu, who was also accomplished in the arts of painting, calligraphy, seal-carving, and poetry, taught the *shichigenkin* to many Japanese pupils, and the instrument remained popular among literati until the end of the Edo period. One of its most famous practitioners was URAGAMI GYOKUDŌ (1745–1820), now known primarily as a painter, who composed new Japanese music for the *shichigenkin*; most other musicans were content to play Chinese compositions. The popularity of the *shichigenkin* did not outlive the taste for Chinese culture in Japan, and declined during the Meiji period (1868–1912).　　　　　　　　　*Stephen ADDISS*

Shichigosan

("Seven-Five-Three" Festival). The custom, observed on 15 November, of taking five-year-old boys and seven- or three-year-old girls to the local Shintō shrine to pray for their safe and healthy future. It was originally connected with the belief that children of certain ages were especially prone to bad luck and hence in need of divine protection. Even today, in some areas, seven, five, and three are considered "bad-luck years." *Shichigosan* is thought to have evolved from ancient rites of passage. A newborn infant was thought of as unformed flesh that gradually took shape as an adult only after a series of ritual observances; at the age of seven the child was finally recognized as a social entity. In many parts of Japan, the child is received as a member of the shrine parish (*ujiko*) when he is seven. *Himo otoshi*, the custom of replacing a cloth band (*himo*) with an OBI after the child turns three or four, and *hakamagi*, the custom of giving a pleated, divided skirt (*hakama*) to a five- or six-year-old boy, are also, in a sense, rites of passage. *Shichigosan*, as it is known today in urban areas, can be traced back to the Edo period (1600–1868), but it is only since the Meiji period (1868–1912) that the various ages have been standardized as seven, five, and three. More recently, parents have tended to take their children to large and prestigious shrines, rather than to the local one. It is customary after the visit to buy *chitose-ame* ("thousand-year candy"), sold at the shrine, to distribute to relatives.　　　　　　　　　　*INOKUCHI Shōji*

Shichihakase Jiken

(Seven Professors Incident). Incident surrounding a written statement by seven professors, most of them members of the law faculty of Tōkyō University, in June 1903, eight months before the outbreak of the RUSSO-JAPANESE WAR (1904–05). Critical of what they regarded as the pusillanimous foreign policy of the government toward Russia, TOMII MASAAKI, Tomizu Hirondo (1861–1935), and five other professors urged Prime Minister KATSURA TARŌ to declare war immediately, while Japan still enjoyed military superiority. Their statement, which was published in the newspaper *Tōkyō nichinichi shimbun* (its editorial condemned the professors' views), influenced public opinion in favor of war. After the war the professors took an equally aggressive stand against the Treaty of PORTSMOUTH, calling not only for rejection of its terms but for the annexation of Karafuto (Sakhalin) and part of the Siberian coast as well. When the government dismissed Tomizu from his post at Tōkyō University, the law faculty sent a formal protest to the Ministry of Education, charging it with infringement of academic freedom. The government retaliated by dismissing the president of the university, whereupon the entire faculty threatened to resign. Ultimately the minister of education, Kubota Yuzuru (1847–1936), was compelled to resign, and Tomizu was reinstated.

Shichikyō Ochi

The flight of seven court nobles from Kyōto to the Chōshū domain (now Yamaguchi Prefecture) in the fall of 1863. These nobles, of whom SANJŌ SANETOMI was the most famous, supported the Chōshū-led antiforeign, antishogunate activists who dominated Kyōto in 1862 and 1863. When the extremists were driven out of Kyōto in the COUP D'ETAT OF 30 SEPTEMBER 1863, the nobles followed them to the Chōshū port of Mitajiri, which subsequently became a gathering place for loyalists from throughout Japan. In 1864 Chōshū requested the pardon of the seven nobles and permission to return to Kyōto. Denial of this and other requests contributed to mounting tensions that culminated in an unsuccessful countercoup by Chōshū in the summer of 1864 (see HAMAGURI GOMON INCIDENT). The nobles remained in exile until the MEIJI RESTORATION (1868).

Shichinin no samurai → Seven Samurai

Shichirigahama

Coastal area southwest of the city of Kamakura, Kanagawa Prefecture, central Honshū. Located on Sagami Bay, it is famous as a vacation and health resort with numerous villas and hospitals and for its views of Mt. Fuji (FUJISAN) and ENOSHIMA. Land development and housing projects have increased rapidly in recent years. Length: 4 km (2.5 mi).

shichiya

("seventh night"). A celebration on the seventh day after the birth of a child. Still widely observed in Japan, it traditionally includes giving the child a name, which is written on paper and posted, and inviting relatives. The impurity *(imi)* resulting from childbirth is usually considered to end after 21 days, with each 7-day period marking a stage. In some areas, the emergence of the mother from the birthing room is observed with a ceremony. It is considered safe to take the infant out of the house on this day, and in some places it is presented to whatever Shintō gods may be enshrined in the house.

INOKUCHI Shōji

Shidehara Kijūrō (1872–1951)

Twice minister of foreign affairs (1924–27; 1929–31) and once prime minister (October 1945–April 1946); the so-called Shidehara diplomacy of the 1920s was distinguished by its advocacy of international cooperation among the imperialist nations and a "conciliatory" attitude toward China.

Shidehara was born in Ōsaka in 1872 to a wealthy landlord family. He attended the Third Higher School in Kyōto, and Tōkyō University, graduating in law in 1895. After passing the foreign service examination in 1896 he served in Korea, Tōkyō, the United States, and Europe. In 1903 he married Iwasaki Masako, daughter of the head of MITSUBISHI. In 1915 he returned home to become vice-minister for foreign affairs under ISHII KIKUJIRŌ in the ŌKUMA SHIGENOBU cabinet. He retained this position under five different ministers until 1919.

In 1919 Shidehara was named ambassador to the United States. His most prominent service there was as one of Japan's delegates to the WASHINGTON CONFERENCE in 1921–22. Although the main focus of the conference was on naval limitation, Shidehara concentrated on issues concerning China. His negotiations led to the return of Shandong (Shantung) Province and a reduction in Sino-Japanese tensions (see SHANDONG [SHANTUNG] QUESTION).

After a brief period of inactivity because of illness, in 1924 he accepted the post of minister of foreign affairs in the KATŌ TAKAAKI cabinet. Shidehara was an admirer of Britain and the United States, and as foreign minister he wished to retain friendly ties with the West while continuing the cooperative policy toward China that the imperialistic powers had followed before World War I. "Shidehara diplomacy" came to be associated with an attitude toward China that was distinguished by its supposed differences from the "Tanaka diplomacy" pursued by Prime Minister (and Minister of Foreign Affairs) TANAKA GIICHI in 1927–29. Whereas Tanaka's policy was described at the time as "positive" and featured military intervention, Shidehara's ostensibly stood for nonintervention in the Chinese republican revolution and for the pursuit of Japanese economic expansion.

In his initial Diet speech as foreign minister, Shidehara pledged a policy of international cooperation in accordance with the Covenant of the League of Nations and the recently signed treaties in Washington. He also promised to respect the just and reasonable aspirations of China. In 1929, after two Tanaka years, Shidehara reaffirmed a nonintervention policy and stressed that the objectives of Japan's China policy would be mutual prosperity and coexistence. This is subject to various interpretations, but clearly he did not intend to preside over the liquidation of Japanese interests on the continent. In fact, Shidehara frequently indicated that, although Japan would give all possible assistance to the Chinese in their national struggle, the nation would also protect its own legitimate rights and interests. He avoided the hints about using force so common in the Tanaka administration.

The first test of Shidehara's policy came in the autumn of 1924 with a conflict in North China known as the Feng-Zhi (Feng-Chih) War. Japanese military authorities generally favored intervention in order to prevent hostilities from reaching Manchuria. Shidehara managed to resist these pleas, confining Japan's official reaction to a note of caution to the warring parties. Other incidents provoked a similar response from Shidehara, although the Japanese field army in Manchuria sometimes took unilateral action.

Another example of the Shidehara line is provided by the Beijing (Peking) Customs Conference, which opened in October 1925. Japan surprised the delegates of the other treaty powers by announcing immediate approval in principle of the Chinese demand for tariff autonomy. Developments in China forced suspension of this conference in March 1926 before any agreements were reached, but Shidehara continued to point to the customs conference as an instance of Japan's conciliatory China policy. Later, however, Japan decidedly lagged behind the other powers in granting tariff autonomy in 1930, during Shidehara's second term as foreign minister.

One of the last affairs of the first Shidehara period, the celebrated NANJING (NANKING) INCIDENT of March 1927, tested as never before the durability of conciliation. When Chinese Nationalist troops entered Nanjing, some of them began to attack foreign consulates and settlements, provoking retaliatory bombardment from American and British gunboats. Shidehara refused to allow Japan to participate in an ultimatum that foreign officials prepared to send to Chiang Kai-shek. In each of the above cases Shidehara was severely criticized in Japan for weakness, and reaction against the nonintervention policy played a major role in the collapse of the WAKATSUKI REIJIRŌ cabinet in April 1927.

In the second Shidehara period the hands-off policy was renewed with difficulty in a changed situation. China was seemingly united under the Nanjing government of Chiang Kai-shek, but the Tanaka administration had intervened several times in the past two years. Now, moreover, there were other preoccupations such as the LONDON NAVAL CONFERENCES. Shidehara's and the Ministry of Foreign Affairs' approval of the London treaty in April 1930 precipitated a major political crisis in Japan. The policy of compromise was again criticized strongly, but it conformed to Shidehara's pro-Anglo-Saxon views of international cooperation.

In November 1930 Prime Minister HAMAGUCHI OSACHI was shot and seriously wounded by an assassin. Shidehara assumed the post of interim premier until March 1931 and represented the government's views in the Diet. That Shidehara was not a gifted parliamentary politician is revealed in his "verbal lapse" in February in which he appeared to bring the name of the emperor into the controversy occasioned by the London Naval Treaty (see TŌSUIKEN). Shidehara was heckled so fiercely that the Diet had to be recessed twice.

Shidehara's final crisis was the MANCHURIAN INCIDENT, which erupted in September 1931. Although he had been attempting to settle some minor incidents that had occurred earlier in Manchuria, he and the cabinet were powerless to stop the occupation of Manchuria by the Japanese GUANDONG (KWANTUNG) ARMY. This brought to an end the cabinet and Shidehara's career as foreign minister. Though a member of the House of Peers, from 1931 to 1945 Shidehara was in semiretirement. For this reason, and because of his pro-American reputation, Shidehara was selected, at 73, as the second postwar prime minister in October 1945 to succeed HIGASHI-KUNI NARUHIKO. In the postwar period Shidehara was conspicuous for his efforts to preserve the emperor system and other prewar features of the Japanese polity. Nonetheless, Shidehara himself suggested that he was the author of the famous article 9 of the 1947 constitution, which outlawed war and vowed that Japan would never maintain armed forces (see RENUNCIATION OF WAR). Others, including General Douglas MACARTHUR, the commander of the Occupation forces, have also claimed that the idea was Shidehara's. Constitutional revision was indeed achieved during the Shidehara administration, but his role remains subject to controversy. Certainly, as prime minister Shidehara was more interested in preserving the emperor system (which seemed in jeopardy) than in anything else. The antiwar article and the suggestion that the emperor disclaim divinity—also attributed to Shidehara—were probably advanced in order to ease external criticism of the emperor system and make it more palatable to Occupation authorities (see EMPEROR, RENUNCIATION OF DIVINITY BY).

The first postwar general election was held in April 1946. Shidehara was nominally the head of the Nihon Shimpotō (Japan Progressive Party), which was defeated, and his cabinet resigned, effective in May. He was later elected twice to the House of Representatives and became speaker of the house in 1949. He died on 10 March 1951.

In Japanese history Shidehara is better remembered for his internationalist foreign policy of the 1920s than as prime minister. He was representative of a certain interwar type, liberal perhaps in a contemporary Japanese context, but conservative and traditionalist in the world of the 20th century. As an individual Shidehara impressed people as single-minded, consistent, and unimaginative. His memoirs reveal a certain sentimentality that his acquaintances rarely recalled. As a politician he lacked flexibility, and his pro-Western views made his loyalty seem questionable in the eyes of some of his nationalistic countrymen.

——Shidehara Kijūrō, *Gaikō gojūnen* (1951). Nobuya Bamba, *Japanese Diplomacy in a Dilemma: New Light on Japan's China Policy, 1924–1929* (1972). Sidney D. Brown, "Shidehara Kijūrō: The Diplomacy of the Yen," in Richard D. Burns and Edward M. Bennett, ed, *Diplomats in Crisis: United States-Chinese-Japanese Relations, 1919–1941* (1974). Imai Seiichi, "Seitō seiji to Shidehara gaikō," *Rekishigaku kenkyū* 219 (1958). Akira Iriye, *After Imperialism: The Search for a New Order in the Far East, 1921–1931* (1965). Nezu Masashi, "Shidehara gaikō no saihyōka," in *Hihan Nihon gendai shi* (1958). Shidehara Heiwa Zaidan, *Shidehara Kijūrō* (1955). Tabata Shinobu, "Kempō kyūjō no hatsuansha, Shidehara Kijūrō," in Tabata Shinobu, *Teikōken* (1965). Ujita Naoyoshi, *Shidehara Kijūrō* (1958). Usui Katsumi, "Shidehara gaikō oboegaki," *Nihon rekishi* 126 (1958).   Daniel B. RAMSDELL

shiden

1. (private fields). Rice lands assigned by the government for private use under the RITSURYŌ SYSTEM of administration initiated in the late 7th century. Under this system, all land belonged to the central government, to be distributed as it chose. The produce of "public fields" (KŌDEN) went directly to the government. The remaining lands (*shiden*) included the fields (KUBUNDEN) that the government distributed to cultivators under the HANDEN SHŪJU SYSTEM of allotment as well as fields awarded to individuals on the basis of court rank or government service (*iden* and *shikiden*, respectively). These lands were not actually owned by their holders, who merely received the right of usufruct. Most of them were obliged to pay taxes during their tenure, which was either their lifetime, as in the case of *kubunden* and *iden*, or for the duration of their official appointment, as in the case of *shikiden*. From the mid-8th century onward, the term *shiden* was applied more narrowly to lands officially recognized as the permanent private property of those who had originally developed them (see KONDEN EISAI SHIZAI HŌ).

2. (bestowed fields). Rice lands granted by the emperor during

the Nara (710–794) and Heian (794–1185) periods in recognition of extraordinary service to the state.

Shidō Bunan (1603–1676)

Also known as Shidō Munan. Zen monk of the RINZAI SECT. Bunan succeeded to the family business of keeping an officially appointed inn (*honjin*) at Sekigahara, Mino Province (now part of Gifu Prefecture), but sometime around 1654 (or 1649?) he became a disciple of Gudō Tōshoku (1579–1661), the celebrated Zen master and sometime abbot of the temple MYŌSHINJI in Kyōto. He eventually became a monk in Edo (now Tōkyō). Bunan gained renown as a great spiritual master; until his death he resided in a hermitage at Koishikawa, Edo. His disciple Dōkyō Etan (also known as Shōju Rōjin; 1642–1721), a great eremitic of Shinano Province (now Nagano Prefecture), handed down his simple yet rigorous discipline for spiritual life to HAKUIN, whose lineage eventually formed the whole of the Rinzai tradition. These three great masters were largely responsible for the immense popularization of Zen during the Edo period (1600–1868). Bunan's instruction is collected in his *Kana hōgo* (first published in 1671).
——Kōda Rentarō, ed, *Shidō Munan zenji shū* (1940, 1956).
TSUCHIDA Tomoaki

Shie Incident

(Shie Jiken; literally, "Purple Robe Incident"). Intervention in 1627 by the Tokugawa shogunate in what was the traditional prerogative of the imperial court, the conferral of *shie*, the purple robes that symbolized the highest order of priesthood. The court had been receiving payment amounting to a considerable proportion of its income in return for granting this honor. In an attempt to demonstrate its power over the imperial court in 1613, the Tokugawa shogunate issued regulations stating that imperial conferral of *shie* required shogunal approval. When Emperor GO-MIZUNOO bestowed *shie* on priests of the temples Daitokuji and Myōshinji in 1627, the shogunate pronounced the *shie* invalid and confiscated them. Emperor Go-Mizunoo abdicated in protest in 1629, and others, including TAKUAN SŌHŌ, a Daitokuji priest who vehemently objected to the shogunate's move, were exiled.

Shiga Kiyoshi (1870–1957)

Bacteriologist. Born in the Sendai domain (now Miyagi Prefecture). Original surname Satō. He graduated from the Faculty of Medicine of Tōkyō University in 1896. While working at the Institute for Infectious Diseases under KITAZATO SHIBASABURŌ, Shiga discovered the bacillus causing dysentery (*Shigella dysenteriae*) in 1897, when he was only 27. He later twice visited Germany to study serology, immunology, and tuberculosis with Paul Ehrlich. After his return to Japan, he participated in the establishment of the Kitazato Institute. He was appointed professor at Keiō Gijuku (now Keiō University) in 1920 and later served as professor (1925) and president (1929–31) of Keijō University in Seoul, Korea. He was awarded the Order of Culture in 1944.   TANAKA Akira

Shiga Kōgen

Highland in northeastern Nagano Prefecture, central Honshū. Surrounded by towering mountains, it is noted for its numerous lakes and ponds, dense white birch forests, and alpine flora. The site of many hot spring resorts, including Kumanoyu and Hoppo. A popular year-round resort area, it attracts numerous sightseers, hikers, campers, anglers, and skiers. A major attraction of Jōshin'etsu Kōgen National Park. Average elevation: 1,600 m (5,248 ft); area: approximately 400 sq km (154 sq mi).

Shiga Naoya (1883–1971)

Novelist; short-story writer. Born in Miyagi Prefecture; attended Gakushūin (the Peers' School) and Tōkyō University. Shiga has widely been considered by critics the perfecter of the *watakushi shōsetsu*, or the "personal novel" (see I-NOVEL). Although several of the short stories which established his reputation—"Kamisori" (1910; tr "The Razor," 1979), "Seibei to hyōtan" (1913; tr "Seibei and Gourds," 1979), "Manazuru" (1920; tr "Manazuru," 1979)—are clearly not autobiographical, such ventures into longer fiction as *Ōtsu Junkichi* (1912), *Wakai* (1917, Reconciliation), and *An'ya kōro*

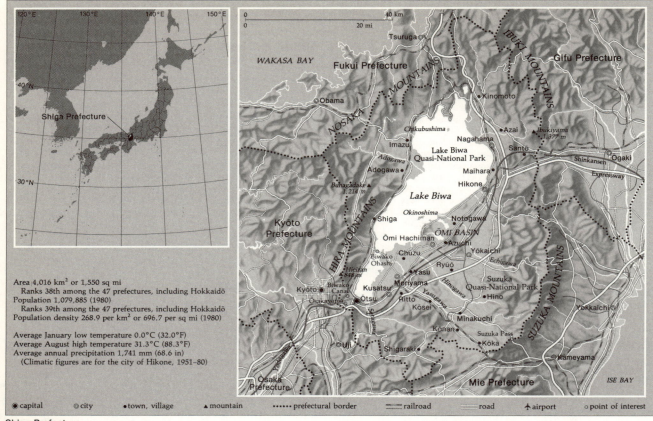

Area 4,016 km² or 1,550 sq mi
  Ranks 38th among the 47 prefectures, including Hokkaidō
Population 1,079,885 (1980)
  Ranks 39th among the 47 prefectures, including Hokkaidō
Population density 268.9 per km² or 696.7 per sq mi (1980)

Average January low temperature 0.0°C (32.0°F)
Average August high temperature 31.3°C (88.3°F)
Average annual precipitation 1,741 mm (68.6 in)
  (Climatic figures are for the city of Hikone, 1951–80)

● capital   ◎ city   • town, village   ▲ mountain   ••••• prefectural border   ▭ railroad   ▭ road   ✈ airport   ∘ point of interest

Shiga Prefecture

(1921–37; tr *A Dark Night's Passing*, 1976) certainly are, to one extent or another, rooted in the events of his own life.

What seems most intense in Shiga's life and most germane to his works as a whole can only be reconstructed partially from some of his more or less openly confessional early stories: "Sobo no tame ni" (1912; tr "For Grandmother," 1979), "Haha no shi to atarashii haha" (1912, Mother's Death and a New Mother), and others; and from the quasi-autobiographical works beginning with *Ōtsu Junkichi*, which are generally called a "trilogy." The psychological profile of his protean fictional alter ego as a child and young man is characterized by obsessive involvement in emotional tangles with family and a few friends, and by remarkably satisfying, if transitory, retreats into the realms of nature and art, usually in the form of spare works of visual art. Whether "true" or not, it is around such manifestations of the universal "family romance," and the slow process of finding some measure of self-love and love for a few others, that Shiga chose to construct most of his narratives.

The relatively wide and devoted audience that Shiga's works won in the first half of this century suggests that for many of his readers, these works in some fashion transcended the obvious limitations in the mere outlines of their plots. This they no doubt do partly because of Shiga's tightly controlled style.

An'ya kōro recapitulates the central themes of Shiga's earlier works, developing them in a more detached fashion, and in various ways represents the summation of his craft. The "long night" of the title stands for the protracted passage of the still-adolescent hero (though he is roughly 30 at the outset) through a sequence of disturbing and often "regressive" experiences into a hard-won truce with destructive forces within himself; an almost mystical embracing of nature, including the constant imminence of death; and an unsentimental acceptance of a few fellow human beings. The reemergence of childhood passions that dominate the novel's first part recalls such earlier works as "Haha no shi," *Wakai*, and others. The spare, lyrical descriptions of nature and folk life that occur throughout the second part are reminiscent of several lyrical sketches, for example, the much admired "Takibi" (1920; tr "Night Fires," 1979). The combination of private moralism and noninstitutional religious faith in the concluding chapters brings to mind similar qualities in "Dekigoto" (1913, An Accident), "Han no hanzai" (1913; tr "Han's Crime," 1955), and "Kinosaki nite" (1917; tr "At Kinosaki," 1979).

Shiga suffered the fate of many authors of personal fiction in his apparent failure to find something new to say once he had reached the final telling of his own experience, or something subjectively close to it, which he did in *An'ya kōro*. The last three-and-a-half decades of his long life were spent in the enjoyment of a reputedly happy domestic life and in an often half-hearted performance of the role allotted to him by various journalists and literary entrepreneurs, that of *bungaku no kamisama*, or patron saint of literature. Having spent his youth in a remarkably idle, or at least in conventional terms unproductive, life (he was a poor scholar and dropped out of the university quickly), Shiga appeared in fact not to suffer greatly in his premature retirement.

Largely on account of his youthful association with the SHIRA-KABA SCHOOL and his brief infatuation with the Christian movement of UCHIMURA KANZŌ, Shiga has figured prominently in the annals of standard intellectual and social histories of modern Japan. Yet his was surely a deeply intuitive and nonintellectual sensibility, and with it he created, at his best, lucid, mythopoeic works that transcend both his times and the narrow personal circumstances on which he often drew.

📖 ——Shiga Naoya, *Shiga Naoya zenshū*, 14 vols (Iwanami Shoten, 1973). Shiga Naoya, *An'ya kōro* (1936), tr Edwin McClellan as *A Dark Night's Passing* (1976). Francis Mathy, *Shiga Naoya* (1974). Nakamura Mitsuo, *Shiga Naoya ron* (1966). William Sibley, *The Shiga Hero* (1979). Yasuoka Shōtarō, *Shiga Naoya shiron* (1968).

William F. SIBLEY

Shiga Prefecture

(Shiga Ken). Located in central Honshū and bordered by Kyōto, Mie, Gifu, and Fukui prefectures. The prefecture takes the form of a basin surrounded by mountains on all sides. Lake BIWA, in central Shiga, is the largest lake in Japan. The climate is moderate, with heavy snowfall in the northern half.

Known as Ōmi Province after the TAIKA REFORM of 645–646, the area was important from early on. The city of ŌTSU served briefly as the imperial capital in the 7th century (see ŌTSU NO MIYA). Various warlords gained dominance through the feudal period, and its proximity to the capital of Kyōto made it the site of several major battles. In the late 16th century, the national unifier ODA NOBUNAGA established his base at AZUCHI CASTLE near the eastern shore of Lake Biwa. Under the Tokugawa shogunate, the area was divided among the Ii family of Hikone and several lesser domains. The merchants of Ōmi were noted for their entrepreneurial skills during the Edo period (1600–1868). The present name and boundaries were established in 1881.

Agriculture is still a major occupation, with rice as the main crop. Lake Biwa provides an abundant supply of freshwater fish. Major industries, centered in the southern portion on the fringe of the Kyōto–Ōsaka metropolitan area, include textiles, electrical products, transportation equipment, and chemicals.

The main tourist attraction is the Lake Biwa area, which has been made into a quasi-national park. It includes the temple ENRYAKUJI on Mt. Hiei (HIEIZAN), the HIE SHRINE, and the temples ISHIYAMA-DERA and MIIDERA in Ōtsu. The city of Hikone on the lake's eastern shore retains the atmosphere of an old castle town. The Suzuka Mountains have been designated as a quasi-national park. Area: 4,016 sq km (1,150 sq mi); pop: 1,079,885; capital: Ōtsu. Other major cities include Hikone, Nagahama, Kusatsu, and Ōmi Hachiman.

Shigaraki

Town in southern Shiga Prefecture, central Honshū, on the river Daidogawa. With plentiful supplies of good-quality clay and feldspar, it has long been known for its SHIGARAKI WARE. The prefectural ceramics experimental institute is located here. Shigaraki was the site of SHIGARAKI NO MIYA, an imperial palace built by the emperor Shōmu in the 8th century. Pop: 13,511.

Shigaraki no Miya

(Shigaraki Palace; also known as Kōka no Miya). One of the imperial residences in the Nara period (710–794); located in what is now the town of Shigaraki in the Kōka district of Shiga Prefecture. In 741, following the Rebellion of FUJIWARA NO HIROTSUGU, Emperor SHŌMU moved his capital from HEIJŌKYŌ (Nara) to KUNI NO MIYA (in the present Sōraku district of Kyōto Prefecture). In the following year he built a separate residence at Shigaraki 30 kilometers to the northeast, with the aim of eventually moving the capital there. He changed his plans, however, and moved instead to NANIWAKYŌ. In February 745 (Tempyō 17.1) Shōmu suddenly moved the capital again, this time to Shigaraki; but the inaccessibility of the place and the prevalence of earthquakes and forest fires persuaded him to return to Heijōkyō barely four months later. According to the chronicle Shoku nihongi (797; see RIKKOKUSHI), the palace at Shigaraki had an audience hall and several government offices, but the only archaeological remains in the area are those of a later temple.

KITAMURA Bunji

Shigaraki ware

(shigaraki-yaki). The stonewares produced by several villages in the Shigaraki valley in southern Shiga Prefecture. Tiles for the Shigaraki Palace, built for Emperor SHŌMU (r 724–749) between 742 and 745, were made in the area. Nevertheless, the ceramic tradition in Shigaraki is said to have begun in the Kamakura period (1185–1333), when pottery was produced here for purely local domestic use, wide- and narrow-mouthed jars and mortar bowls being most common.

The larger vessels were coil built; smaller items were thrown on the wheel from the 16th century onward. Pieces were fired in simple kilns dug into the hillside, referred to as tunnel kilns (anagama). The Korean-type climbing kilns (noborigama) were introduced during the late 16th century. Intentionally glazed wares appeared in the 16th century, although streaks of natural ash glaze are frequently found on the shoulders of larger vessels. The range of hardness found in the traditional wares is said to have resulted from the location of the pieces in the kiln during firing. Large seed jars placed just inside the firemouth tend to be hardest. In contrast, mortar bowls, which are usually placed at the back of the chamber, may be quite soft. A temperature range of 600° C (1,112°F) at the rear to 1,300° C (2,372°F) near the front of the kiln has been given as the probable temperature range of the kiln.

From the beginning of the 16th century, Shigaraki ware caught the attention of the followers of the Way of tea. Humble domestic pots were given sophisticated new names and were highly prized as TEA CEREMONY wares. In 1632 the TOKUGAWA SHOGUNATE desig-

nated Shigaraki as suppliers of official tea storage jars to the Uji tea producers for presentation to the shogunate.

Since the late 19th century, Shigaraki has shifted to the production of various wares, including molded planters, braziers, and other miscellaneous garden furniture, along with large ceramic tanuki, or raccoon dogs, holding sake jugs. Traditional teabowls and water jars are still being made by atelier potters and these retain much of the rustic charm and quality of the wares of earlier times.

The body fabric of traditional wares is generally reddish brown and coarse grained; Shigaraki pottery can be identified by the white specks and grains of feldspar and quartz that melt during firing and protrude from the surface.

▬——Louise Cort, Shigaraki: Potters' Valley (1979).

Brian HICKMAN

Shiga Shigetaka (1863–1927)

Geographer and proponent of enlightened nationalism at a time when Westernization was rampant; also known as Shiga Jūkō. Born in the Mikawa domain (now part of Aichi Prefecture); educated at Sapporo Agricultural College (now Hokkaidō University). On a trip through the South Pacific islands in 1886, Shiga was struck by what he thought were the principles of social Darwinism at work in Western colonialism. On his return to Japan he published Nan'yō jiji (1887, Conditions in the South Seas), in which he appealed to his readers to be aware of both the strength and the vulnerability of Japan as an island country and stressed the need to strengthen the country through commerce and industry. The following year, with MIYAKE SETSUREI, he founded the SEIKYŌSHA (Society for Political Education). In articles for its journal, Nihonjin (The Japanese), he expounded his notion of kokusui hozon (preservation of the national essence) in the face of indiscriminate modernization. Shiga developed his ideas further in his "Nihon fūkei ron" (1894, The Landscape of Japan), a cultural-geographical treatise that was also a lively description of the geological factors underlying the unique variety in Japanese landscape. Thus he reawakened an aesthetic sensibility and appreciation of the physical environment that was to become an important aspect of Japanese nationalism. Shiga continued his activities as a critic, and as a member of the lower house of the Diet from 1902 to 1904 he participated briefly in politics. He devoted the last two decades of his life to geographical studies, exploring the Poronaj River in Sakhalin and traveling through the Middle East. His Sekai sansui zusetsu (1911, Illustrated Geography of the World) and his lectures at Waseda University helped to popularize geographical studies.

▬——Shiga Shigetaka, Shiga Shigetaka zenshū, 8 vols (Shiga Shigetaka Kankōkai, 1927). Iwai Tadakuma, "Shiga Shigetaka ron," Ritsumeikan bungaku 12 (1960). Kenneth Pyle, The New Generation in Meiji Japan (1969).

Margret NEUSS

Shiga Yoshio (1901–   )

Politician. Born in Fukuoka Prefecture. While still a student at Tōkyō University he joined the leftist study group SHINJINKAI and became a member of the newly formed Japan Communist Party (JCP). Upon graduating in 1926, together with TOKUDA KYŪICHI and others he reestablished the JCP, which had been dissolved the year before. Following the mass arrest of communists in 1928 (see MARCH 15TH INCIDENT) he was imprisoned for 18 years. Unlike many of his colleagues, Shiga steadfastly refused to recant (see TENKŌ). Upon his release after World War II he helped to form the postwar JCP and became editor-in-chief of the party organ, AKAHATA (Red Flag). He was elected to the Diet in 1946 but was debarred from office in the so-called RED PURGE by American Occupation authorities in 1950. Following Cominform criticism of party tactics that same year, he went underground. Shiga resumed public activity in 1955 and was elected to the Central Committee of the JCP. In 1964, however, Shiga, who had always looked to the Soviet Union for guidance, was expelled from the party for supporting ratification of the 1963 Nuclear Test Ban Treaty.

Shigemitsu Mamoru (1887–1957)

Career diplomat who served three times as foreign minister during and after World War II. Convicted as a war criminal in 1948, he returned to prominence as a party politician after the Allied Occupation.

Shigemitsu was born in Ōita Prefecture in 1887, graduated from Tōkyō University in 1911, and entered the Ministry of Foreign Affairs the same year. He served mostly in Europe in the early years and was a member of Japan's delegation at the Paris Peace Conference in 1919. In 1928 he was appointed consul-general in Shanghai, and when Japan's minister to China died in 1930, he became acting head of the delegation at a very delicate time in Sino-Japanese relations. He was made minister to China in August 1931, after which he was involved in negotiations with the new Guomindang (Kuomintang; Nationalist Party) government when the MANCHURIAN INCIDENT occurred in September. After negotiating a settlement of the SHANGHAI INCIDENT in 1932, Shigemitsu was seriously injured in April when a Korean threw a bomb into a crowd of Japanese officials.

In 1933 Shigemitsu was named vice-minister of foreign affairs, a post he retained until 1936 in the SAITŌ MAKOTO and OKADA KEISUKE cabinets. In these years he was associated with a group in the Ministry of Foreign Affairs known as the Asia faction. Led by ARITA HACHIRŌ, it stood in opposition to the Europe–America faction and to a more radical renovationist clique. Shigemitsu's faction favored the aggressive foreign policy toward China that Japan pursued during the mid-1930s. The policy involved threats of military force and was given formal expression in the so-called AMŌ STATEMENT of April 1934.

Shigemitsu was appointed ambassador to the USSR in 1936 and to Britain in 1938. When the European war broke out in 1939, he opposed Japan's alliance with Germany. Upon his return to Japan in 1941 he cautioned against war with the United States. He served again in China as ambassador to the puppet regime of WANG JING-WEI (Wang Ching-wei) from December 1941 until April 1943, at which time he returned home to serve in the reorganized TŌJŌ HIDEKI cabinet.

As foreign minister until April 1945, Shigemitsu became a leading member of the group seeking to achieve an early peace. He tried unsuccessfully to institute a policy that would return China to the Chinese. He also favored making concessions to the Soviet Union and made other peace overtures in 1944 and 1945. Although he was no longer in the government when the end of the war drew near, he returned to Tōkyō in August to urge acceptance of the conditions of surrender of the Potsdam Declaration. As foreign minister in the HIGASHIKUNI NARUHIKO cabinet he represented the Japanese government at the official surrender ceremony on the USS *Missouri* on 2 September.

On 29 April 1946 Shigemitsu was indicted as one of 28 major war criminals by the International Military Tribunal for the Far East (see WAR CRIMES TRIALS). He was not on the original list prepared by Americans but was added at the suggestion of the Soviet Union. His inclusion was controversial, but he was nevertheless found guilty of waging aggressive war and failure to prevent war crimes. He was sentenced to seven years, the lightest of any of the original defendants still alive. He was released from Sugamo Prison on 21 November 1950 after serving four years and seven months.

Shigemitsu promptly returned to politics and government service. He joined the newly formed Nihon Kaishintō (Japan Reform Party) in June 1952 and became its president. Although he openly aspired to the premiership, he was not an effective party leader. In 1954 the Kaishintō merged with the Nihon Jiyūtō (Japan Liberal Party) to form the NIHON MINSHUTŌ (Japan Democratic Party), and Shigemitsu became vice-president under HATOYAMA ICHIRŌ. When the new party, with the help of the Japan Socialist Party, forced out the YOSHIDA SHIGERU cabinet in December 1954, Shigemitsu became foreign minister and deputy premier in the Hatoyama cabinet. He retained these positions throughout the Hatoyama years until December 1956.

Shigemitsu differed with Hatoyama over the handling of negotiations with the Soviet Union for the normalization of relations. The foreign minister favored a cautious policy without major concessions, but he suddenly accepted the Russian position while he was in Moscow in August 1956. He apparently did this in order to improve his own standing in Japanese domestic politics. His position was rejected by Tōkyō, and Shigemitsu was called home. Shortly thereafter, Hatoyama himself went to Russia and came back with the normalization agreement, paving the way for Japan's membership in the United Nations. When Hatoyama resigned, as promised, in December 1956 and ISHIBASHI TANZAN replaced him, Shigemitsu left the cabinet. He died on 26 January 1957.

◼ ——Works by Shigemitsu Mamoru: *Shōwa no dōran* (1952). *Gaikō kaisō roku (1953)*. *Sugamo nikki* (1953). *Zoku Sugamo nikki* (1953). Works about Shigemitsu Mamoru: Robert J. C. Butow, *Japan's Decision to Surrender* (1954). Alvin D. Coox, "Shigemitsu

Mamoru: The Diplomacy of Crisis," in Richard D. Burns and Edward M. Bennett, ed, *Diplomats in Crisis: United States-Chinese-Japanese Relations, 1919–1941* (1974). Toshikazu Kase, *Journey to the "Missouri"* (1950). Usui Katsumi, "The Role of the Foreign Ministry," in Dorothy Borg and Shumpei Okamoto, ed, *Pearl Harbor as History: Japanese-American Relations, 1931–1941* (1973).

Daniel B. RAMSDELL

Shigeno Yasutsugu (1827–1910)

Historian. Born in the Satsuma domain (now Kagoshima Prefecture), he studied at the Shōheikō, the shogunate academy in Edo (now Tōkyō), returning to teach at the domainal school in Satsuma. He joined the Ministry of Education after the Meiji Restoration (1868) and was put in charge of the collection and compilation of historical records at the Office of Historiography (Shūshikyoku). When the office was absorbed by Tōkyō University in 1888, Shigeno was appointed professor of history. As an editor he insisted on separating apocryphal matter from the historical record, and he was adamantly opposed to the moralistic use of history. Both Shigeno and his colleague KUME KUNITAKE came under fire from Shintō nationalists and were forced to resign from the university—Kume in 1892 and Shigeno in 1893.

shigi kempō

(private draft constitutions). Various constitutional drafts prepared by government officials, political groups, or private individuals before the promulgation of Japan's first CONSTITUTION in 1889. The first such draft was composed in 1867 by NISHI AMANE, a scholar and Tokugawa shogunate retainer who had returned from three years of study in the Netherlands. Nishi proposed a division of power between the Tokugawa shogunate, the imperial court, and the feudal domains in a last-ditch effort to preserve the shogunate's political authority. A second draft constitution, one that closely followed the Prussian model, was written in 1872, four years after the Meiji Restoration, by the diplomat AOKI SHŪZŌ.

In 1876 the Meiji government began to consider seriously the question of framing a constitution. In response the GENRŌIN, the government's legislative body, presented a draft constitution (Nihon Kokken An) in 1878. This draft, which clearly established controls limiting the power of the emperor, was rejected by the government as unsuitable to the traditional Japanese pattern of government. While the government was at work preparing a constitution to be granted by the emperor, forces outside the government, particularly the FREEDOM AND PEOPLE'S RIGHTS MOVEMENT, campaigned on behalf of a constitution drawn up by the people themselves. Between 1879 and 1881, more than 40 drafts were composed by private individuals or groups. The most radical draft was by UEKI EMORI, an intellectual leader of the people's rights movement. His 1881 draft (Tōyō Dai Nihonkoku Kokken An) placed sovereignty in the hands of the people and provided for unconditional guarantees of civil rights, including the right of citizens to resist an oppressive government. These private drafts were published in newspapers and widely discussed. Most of them took the British or American constitutions as models. After the POLITICAL CRISIS OF 1881, however, the government firmly decided to follow the Prussian example in preparing a constitution to be granted to the people in 1889. Thereafter the production of private constitutional drafts fell off considerably and the people's rights movement concentrated on the formation of political parties in preparation for the new parliamentary system that the government had promised would be instituted by 1890.

Shigisan

Hill in northwestern Nara Prefecture, central Honshū, in the southern part of the Ikoma Mountains. On the slopes is Shigisanji, a temple of the Kōyasan Shingon sect of Buddhism. The temple, also known as Chōgo Sonshigi or the Bishamonten (Skt: Vaiśravaṇa) of Shigi, possesses the SHIGISAN ENGI EMAKI, a famous set of picture scrolls. A temple town *(monzen machi)* flourishes near the temple. Height: 437 m (1,433 ft).

Shigisan engi emaki

(The Legends of Mt. Shigi). A set of three narrative handscrolls, dated circa 1156–80, preserved at Chōgo Sonshiji, Mt. Shigi (Shigisan), Nara Prefecture, a mountain monastery restored in the late 9th century by the monk Myōren (see SHIGISANJI). The scrolls are re-

Shigisan engi emaki —— The Flying Granary (Scroll I)

Detail. Ink and colors on paper. Height of scroll 31.5 cm. Ca 1156–80. Chōgo Sonshiji, Nara. National Treasure.

markable in many respects, not least in their subject matter, which departs from the formula for illustrated scrolls of Buddhist legends, which usually depict the legendary origins of temples and sects. The *Shigisan* scrolls illustrate three miracles attributed to Myōren, who lived most of his adult life in retreat at Mt. Shigi.

Scroll I (31.5 x 872.2 cm; about 12.4 x 343.6 in), popularly titled *The Flying Granary,* is the shortest of the three. It tells of Myōren's rice bowl, which daily flew from Mt. Shigi to be filled at a rich landlord's estate; after having been locked inside the granary, the bowl carried storehouse and contents to the sequestered monk. Scroll II (31.5 x 1,273.0 cm; about 12.4 x 501.6 in), *The Exorcism of the Engi Emperor,* narrates the miraculous cure of the emperor Daigo (r 897–930) through the mediation of Myōren's prayers and the consequent divine intercession of the boy-form Buddhist guardian spirit Ken no Gohō. Scroll III (31.5 x 1,416.0 cm; about 12.4 x 557.9 in), *The Story of the Nun,* tells of Myōren's elder sister's search for her brother, and of their reunion after her prayers to the Great Buddha at the temple Tōdaiji, Nara, resulted in a dream wherein his whereabouts were revealed. Scrolls II and III contain brief opening and central passages of text, which correspond in substance to stories preserved in two collections of ancient legends, the *Kohon setsuwashū* (ca 1130), and the UJI SHŪI MONOGATARI (ca 1220). The same sources recount the tale of the flying granary, and presumably Scroll I originally included a complete text.

The *Shigisan engi emaki* is the earliest surviving example of the continuous narrative method of illustration. Executed in flexible ink lines and light color washes on paper, each scroll unfolds the plot in an unbroken sequence of events, with the leading characters repeatedly shown before changing architectural and landscape backdrops. The hallmark of the style is the brushwork that affords life and substance to highly individualized figure types and to the settings they inhabit. Color is secondary, serving to reinforce the descriptive intent of the linework, without obscuring its lively rhythms. In the caricature-like treatment of the figures, the calligraphic brushwork, the landscape treatment, the focus on a telling narration of events, and the subject matter, drawn from provincial lore rather than from court literature, the *Shigisan engi emaki* is an invaluable stylistic milestone in the history of Japanese painting. See also EMAKIMONO.
📖 ——Miya Tsugio et al, *Shigisan engi,* vol 2 of *Nihon emakimono zenshū* (Kadokawa Shoten, 1958). Kasai Masaaki, *Shigisan engi emaki no kenkyū* (1971). Gail Capitol WEIGL

Shigisanji

A SHINGON SECT temple located on the eastern slope of the mountain Shigisan in the town of Heguri, Nara Prefecture; properly called Chōgo Sonshiji. The chief deity enshrined is Vaiśravaṇa (J: Bishamonten). The temple is said to have been originally founded by Prince SHŌTOKU (574–622), but the priest Myōren, who donated the statue of Vaiśravaṇa during the Kampyō era (889–898), is considered to have made it famous. During the Sengoku period (1467–1568) a local military ruler, Matsunaga Hisahide (1510–77), constructed a castle on the mountain and repaired various temple buildings. However, after Hisahide revolted against ODA NOBUNAGA, the entire complex was laid to waste (1577) by Nobunaga's troops. The temple

was reconstructed by TOYOTOMI HIDEYORI in 1602. Among the possessions of the temple are three 12th-century picture scrolls, the SHIGISAN ENGI EMAKI, depicting three of the miraculous deeds of the priest Myōren. Followers of the Shigisan Shingon sect number more than 500,000 (1980).

Shihō Kenshūjo → Legal Training and Research Institute

Shihōshō

(Ministry of Justice). Government ministry charged with administration of the judicial system in the pre–World War II period. Established on 24 August 1871, it replaced the Gyōbushō (Ministry of Punishments) and the Danjōdai (Board of Censors), which had been set up in 1869 during the early phase of the Meiji government. According to the CONSTITUTION of 1889 the courts were to function as an independent judiciary, but the Shihōshō, with its wide-ranging authority over judicial matters, retained control of the appointment of judges. In 1947 the ministry was abolished by the OCCUPATION authorities; thereafter administration of the courts and appointment of court personnel were transferred to the SUPREME COURT. Other administrative functions were taken over in 1948 by the Hōmuchō (Justice Bureau), which became the Hōmufu (Justice Office) in 1949, and finally by the Hōmushō (MINISTRY OF JUSTICE) in 1952. See also JUDICIAL SYSTEM.

Shiiba

Village in northwestern Miyazaki Prefecture, Kyūshū. Located in a remote, sparsely inhabited mountainous area, Shiiba relies on lumbering and farming. In 1960, Japan's first arched dam was built here by the Kyūshū Electric Power Co on the river Mimikawa. Shiiba is also known as the refuge of the warriors of the Taira family who were defeated in the TAIRA–MINAMOTO WAR in the 12th century. Pop: 5,478.

Shiina Rinzō (1911–1973)

Novelist. Real name Ōtsubo Noboru; born in Sosa village (in the city of Himeji, Hyōgo Prefecture). Three days after his birth his mother, Misu, attempted suicide; consequently she and her son were sent by police to join her husband, who had been working in Ōsaka. The family lived in various Ōsaka tenement houses until the autumn of 1920, when Misu returned to Sosa with her three children. She managed a poor but stable household. Shiina attended the local primary school and was at the head of his class. A young anarchist painter, Fukumoto Kumaichi, became Shiina's friend and mentor, introducing him to the ideas of Kropotkin and the Japanese anarchist ŌSUGI SAKAE. Shiina entered the Himeji Middle School in 1924, but in his third year the family experienced an acute economic crisis when his father stopped sending money from Ōsaka. Shiina left school and went to Ōsaka to ask his father for money. When the father refused, Shiina, unable to return home empty-handed, became a vagrant in the streets of Ōsaka.

Between the ages of 15 and 17, Shiina supported himself from day-to-day, working in cheap restaurants and shops, and for a period, joining a gang of delinquents. He completed his middle-school education taking correspondence courses at night, avidly reading Darwin, Marx, and texts in the natural sciences. In 1928 his mother again attempted suicide. A policeman involved in the case found Shiina a job as a railroad conductor. There Shiina helped organize a new labor union, which developed an affiliation with Zenkyō, a national federation of left-wing labor unions. He later became head of a Communist Party cell of railroad employees.

Shiina was arrested during the mass roundup of communists in the Kyōto-Ōsaka area in August 1931 and was imprisoned until April 1933. Reading Nietzsche in prison led him to question and finally turn away from the Communist Party. After being released from prison, he returned to Himeji, only to discover that his mother had died during his absence. He moved to Tōkyō and married Sogaya Sumiko in 1934; initially the two supported themselves by running a street stall. In 1938 Shiina became an office worker in a Tōkyō steel company. Inspired by his reading of Dostoevsky, Kierkegaard, and Nietzsche, he began to write fiction, publishing in 1939 his first short story, ''Ie'' (The House), in the little magazine *Sōsaku.*

During the war years he twice evaded the draft by feigning illness. In 1949 he resigned from the company to concentrate on writing.

Shiina's debut in the literary world came with the publication in 1947 of his novella *Shin'ya no shuen* (tr *Midnight Banquet,* 1970). Its protagonist, a starving ex-communist and street peddler, seeks to endure in the face of life's meaninglessness and the certainty of death, rejecting all ideology. Shiina was seen as an *après-guerre (sengoha)* writer, and also as an "existentialist" because of similarities between his work and Sartre's, which was published in Japan shortly after Shiina completed the manuscript of *Shin'ya no shuen.* The theme of life in despair, perceived with grim humor by the narrator, unifies Shiina's other early short stories including "Omoki nagare no naka ni" (1947; tr "In the Sluggish Stream," 1974) and "Fukao Masaharu no shuki" (1948, The Diary of Fukao Masaharu). Shiina's long novel *Eien naru joshō* (1948, Eternal Prologue), depicting a man dying of tuberculosis, asks whether the state of "freedom" is possible as long as death is inevitable. In December 1950, when many were predicting Shiina's despair would lead to suicide, he converted to Christianity and was baptized.

Although troubled by a serious heart ailment in the last two decades of his life, Shiina maintained a prolific output of fiction, drama, translations, and essays on literature and Christian existentialism. His fictional works after 1950 express a Christian existentialist vision and comic sense of the absurd. *Akai kodokusha* (1951, Lone Red) depicts a man unable to resolve the conflict between his communist sympathies and existentialist philosophy. *Jiyū no kanata de* (1953–54, This Side of Freedom) is a reexamination of Shiina's youthful communist period from a Christian perspective and contains valuable biographical data. His novel *Utsukushii onna* (1955, A Beautiful Woman), an allegorical tale depicting the role of Christian faith in sustaining banal, day-to-day existence, was awarded an Agency for Cultural Affairs Prize for the Arts in 1955.

📖 ——Shiina Rinzō, *Shiina Rinzō zenshū,* 22 vols (Tōjusha, 1970–78). Shiina Rinzō, *Ai no shōgen* (1955), tr Sydney Gifford as *The Flowers Are Fallen* (1961). Shiina Rinzō, *The Go-between and Other Stories,* tr Noah S. Brannen (1970). Okaniwa Noboru, *Shiina Rinzō ron* (1972). Sasaki Keiichi, *Shiina Rinzō no bungaku* (1968). Sasaki Keiichi, *Shiina Rinzō kenkyū* (1974). Yoshimura Yoshio, *Shiina Rinzō ron* (1955).   Brett DE BARY

Shijōnawate

City in northeastern Ōsaka Prefecture; 13 km (8 mi) northeast of Ōsaka, of which it is a suburb. A former farming area, it has several small factories. Of interest are Shijōnawate Shrine and the hill Iimoriyama, both associated with Kusunoki Masatsura (d 1348), a tragic military hero of the period of the Northern and Southern Courts. Pop: 50,582.

Shijō school → Maruyama-Shijō school

Shijūhattai Butsu

("The 48 Buddhas"). A collection of small 7th- and 8th-century gilt bronze Buddhist images, averaging 30 centimeters (11.8 in) in height. Actually 59 in number, they were presented to the Meiji emperor in 1878 by the temple HŌRYŪJI in Nara and were transferred to the Tōkyō National Museum in 1947. It is thought that these images, which vary in style and execution, were presented to Hōryūji as individual votive offerings by members of the nobility at different times during the 7th and 8th centuries. Some of the images are inscribed with the dates 651 and 666. In the Heian period (794–1185), more than 40 images were transferred from the temple Tachibanadera in Nara to Hōryūji, where the collection already numbered over 100 images. Although only about half of the original collection has survived, it is the largest extant in Japan. In the Edo period (1600–1868), the collection became associated with the so-called 48 Blessings of the Buddha Amida (*shijūhachigan,* see AMIDA), and it began to be popularly known as "The 48 Buddhas." See also HŌRYŪJI, TREASURES OF.

shijuku

(private school). Educational facility of the Edo period (1600–1868) that used the teacher's own home as the classroom and based the curriculum on the particular learning of the teacher. They were neither protected nor interfered with by shogunal or domainal au-

Shijūhattai Butsu

One of the Shijūhattai Butsu ("48 Buddhas") in the Hōryūji Treasure House at the Tōkyō National Museum. This small gilt bronze image of the Buddha Amida with attendants Kannon (right) and Seishi (left) is one of the oldest such representations in Japan. Height of Amida 28.4 cm. Late 7th century.

thorities. Standards were higher than those at the TERAKOYA (village schools). Pupils came from all parts of the country and from all social classes.

Representative *shijuku* were the Tōju Shoin of NAKAE TŌJU, the Kōshūdō of MATSUNAGA SEKIGO, the KOGIDŌ of ITŌ JINSAI, the Kōyō Sekiyo Sonsha (also called Renjuku) of KAN SAZAN, and the Kangien of HIROSE TANSŌ. The above were all under the direction of Confucian scholars, but National Learning (KOKUGAKU) was also represented in such schools as the Suzuya of MOTOORI NORINAGA and the Ibukinoya of his disciple HIRATA ATSUTANE. There were also institutions such as the Tekijuku of OGATA KŌAN, known for its curricula in WESTERN LEARNING, and the Shōka Sonjuku, founded by YOSHIDA SHŌIN, the proimperial ideologue. See also EDUCATION: Edo-period education.   ETŌ Kyōji

Shikanoshima

Island at the mouth of Hakata Bay, Fukuoka Prefecture, northern Kyūshū. There are gardens and rice fields on the western slopes of the island and quick-growing fruits and vegetables are also cultivated. The scene of fighting between Japanese and Mongolian forces during the MONGOL INVASIONS OF JAPAN, the island is also known as the site where a historic gold seal (see KAN NO WA NO NA NO KOKUŌ NO IN) was discovered. It is part of the Genkai Quasi-National Park. Area: 5.8 sq km (2.2 sq mi); circumference: about 11 km (6.8 mi).

shikashū

Personal poetry collections as distinguished from the IMPERIAL ANTHOLOGIES (*chokusen wakashū* or *chokusenshū*). The collected poems of individual poets in the WAKA tradition of Japanese classical poetry, compiled from the late 9th to the early 19th century. Many *shikashū* have been lost, but extant collections number several hundred. It is extremely rare for a poet to have more than one *shikashū,* and in most cases this one collection comprises the bulk of a poet's surviving work, even though it may contain only a fraction of the thousands of poems a court poet would have composed in his lifetime. Many *shikashū* also contain poems by persons other than the main poet, since basic material was often drawn from poetic exchanges in which both the poem sent and the poem received are included. *Shikashū* occur in various forms, some consisting of fewer than 50 poems, others of more than 1,000: some are arranged according to the formal categories of the imperial anthologies, with very little in the way of prose headnotes (see KOTOBAGAKI); others are random collections with no discernible sense of order; still others are arranged more or less in chronological order with long prose headnotes so that they may be read as diaries or autobiographies.

The traditional term for *shikashū* is *ie no shū* (house collections), and early examples often exhibit a strong sense of family pride. *Shikashū* constituted the basic material for the first imperial anthology, the KOKINSHŪ (ca 905), and the creation of *shikashū* was in turn stimulated by the compilation of imperial anthologies. From the 10th century onward *shikashū* were compiled in great numbers, often in response to the commands of members of the imperial family or powerful noblemen, but increasingly from a purely creative and artistic urge. Some *shikashū* were compiled by the poets themselves, while others were compiled posthumously by close relatives. *Shikashū* have been particularly susceptible to alteration and frequently present textual problems, but they constitute an extremely rich source of material for the study of Japanese poetry.

——Phillip T. Harries, "Personal Poetry Collections," *Monumenta Nipponica* 35.3 (1980).   Phillip T. HARRIES

Shikatsube Magao (1753–1829)

KYŌKA poet and KIBYŌSHI writer of the late Edo period. Also known as Koikawa Sukimachi. Born in Edo (now Tōkyō). Shikatsube was a merchant but gave up his business for writing. He studied with KOIKAWA HARUMACHI and Yomo no Akara (also known as ŌTA NAMPO) and became a leading *kyōka* poet after the retirement of his teachers from the literary scene following the KANSEI REFORMS of 1787–93. As his pen name suggests (*shikatsube magao* may be loosely translated as "sanctimonious straight-face"), he advocated a restrained, genteel *kyōka* and was opposed to the more earthy, humorous school of ISHIKAWA MASAMOCHI. His best-known collection of verse is *Ashiogishū* (1815, Collection of Reeds), also known as *Rotekishū*.

Shika wakashū

(Collection of Verbal Flowers; the full title is usually shortened to *Shikashū*). The sixth imperial anthology (*chokusenshū*) of classical Japanese poetry (WAKA), ordered in 1144 by ex-Emperor Sutoku (1119–64; r 1123–42). Compiled by FUJIWARA NO AKISUKE (also called Rokujō no Akisuke; 1090–1155), the first draft was probably completed in 1151; the second, official draft was accepted in 1152 or 1153, and consisted of 10 books, 411 poems.

Akisuke was the head of the most prominent family of court poets of the day, the Rokujō branch of the Fujiwara, and was well established as an outstanding poet and the most authoritative poetic judge of the mid-12th century. A conservative poet by training and inclination, Akisuke nevertheless attempted in his choices to steer a middle course between the conservative and the innovative. However, he tended to favor older poets over more recent ones, among the latter giving preference to members of his own family and their close associates from the imperial family on down, so that his conservative tastes manifested themselves despite his intentions.

Consisting of 10 books, the collection is, with 411 poems, the shortest of the imperial anthologies. In conformity with precedent, it falls into two halves, the first dominated by nature poems arranged by season, and the second by poems on love and miscellaneous topics. Between the two halves are a book each of celebration and of parting, and unlike the KIN'YŌ WAKASHŪ (the fifth imperial anthology, compiled some 24 years before), there is no special category of linked poems. In general the structure is as conservative within its small scope as is the general tone of the collection. Even so, Akisuke recognized new trends along with the old, giving considerable space to descriptive nature poetry, which had become increasingly accepted and appreciated from the late 11th century.

The anthology's 411 poems are distributed among some 192 individuals, most of whom are allotted a single poem each, the policy appearing to have been to avoid choosing many poems by any one person. Major poets by number of items included are SONE NO YOSHITADA, 17 poems; Lady IZUMI SHIKIBU, 16; ŌE NO MASAFUSA, 14; and MINAMOTO NO TOSHIYORI, 11.

The *Shikashū* was violently attacked by disaffected contemporaries, suffering more abuse than any previous imperial anthology. This attack was symptomatic of the deepening divisions between innovators and conservatives and between rival poetic schools,

which had made the appearance of each imperial anthology since the *Go shūishū* (1086, Later Collection of Gleanings) an occasion for acrimony and polemic, and which were not to be overcome until the late 12th century.

——Robert H. Brower and Earl Miner, *Japanese Court Poetry* (1961).   Robert H. BROWER

Shiki

City in southern Saitama Prefecture, central Honshū. It prospered in the Edo period (1600–1868) as a river port on the river Shingashi-gawa and as a distribution center for local produce. It is now primarily a residential town for commuters to Tōkyō. Pop: 50,926.

Shikibō, Ltd

(Shikishima Bōseki). Company engaged in the manufacture and sale of cotton and synthetic fibers and textiles, as well as secondary textile products and interior decorating materials. Shikibō was established in 1892. It is one of the nine largest companies in its field in Japan, and was the first Japanese manufacturer to develop technology on the mixed weaving of polyester and cotton. Shikibō's products are well known abroad under the brand name Mermaid. It has established joint ventures in Thailand, Indonesia, and Kenya with local capital participation. Sales for the fiscal year ending April 1982 totaled ¥65.2 billion (US $266.3 million), and the company was capitalized at ¥4.5 billion (US $18.4 million) in the same year. Its corporate headquarters are in Ōsaka

Shikidō ōkagami

(The Great Mirror of the Erotic Way). A 17th-century study of prostitution in Japan by Hatakeyama Kizan (d 1704). It is a scholarly and encyclopedic work that describes the history, customs, and day-to-day operations of the so-called pleasure districts of the Edo period (1600–1868). Published in 1678, the *Shikidō ōkagami* is today essentially a curiosity, of interest largely to social historians and other specialists. In Edo Japan, however, it functioned practically as a book of etiquette and guide to the licensed quarters, which had their own customs and standards of behavior for both the women and their patrons. These licensed districts were also the focus of the popular literary culture of the period, and the home of the fashionable restaurants and theaters.

Kizan describes, often in meticulous detail, the various aspects of life in the many such districts throughout Japan that had been officially set aside for the purpose of prostitution. He begins the 18-chapter study with a chapter explaining the special terminology used in the pleasure quarters. Several chapters are devoted to clothing and etiquette, two to the music and musical instruments of the quarter, and two more provide guidance for potential visitors, including hours of operation, prices, maps, and a brief history of each district. There are also chapters devoted to proper epistolary form, crests, anecdotes, and brief biographies of prostitutes who had achieved prominence in their calling. One of the more interesting, if bizarre, chapters is a discussion of *shinjū*, i.e., the self-injurious acts that prostitutes resorted to in order to demonstrate their love, whether real or feigned. These included vows written in blood, tattooing, cutting off of one's hair, and the amputation of a finger. (The word *shinjū* can also refer to love suicide, but does not have that sense here; see SUICIDE).

The *Shikidō ōkagami* ends with a cautionary essay enumerating the types of behavior by habitués of the pleasure quarters that Kizan considered impermissible and to constitute grounds for disowning a son. The dominant constraint was the essentially Confucian doctrine of moderation. Kizan was intent on describing, even idealizing, institutionalized prostitution in Japan. He was not concerned with sexual matters as such. Thus, in spite of its suggestive title, *The Great Mirror of the Erotic Way* is not a sex manual, nor is it even remotely erotic. Kizan's attention to detail is relentless: "Nails should be cut straight across. They look vulgar rounded off. The same is true of toenails."

The influence of the *Shikidō ōkagami* was not restricted to the visitors to the pleasure quarters. It was also exploited as a source book by the writers of the day. The novelist Ihara SAIKAKU (1642–93) was well acquainted with the *Shikidō ōkagami* and cognizant of Kizan's unique expertise. It has even been suggested that Kizan, who devoted over 30 years to his research of the quarters, was the prototype for the profligate hero of Saikaku's *Kōshoku ichi-dai otoko* (1682; tr *The Life of an Amorous Man*, 1964).

Little is known of Kizan's life. He was born in Kyōto either in 1626 or 1628 and apparently orphaned at an early age. Kizan studied *haiku* under the poet MATSUNAGA TEITOKU (1571–1653) and paleography under Kohitsu Ryōsa (1582–1662). He is also known as Fujimoto Kizan.

📖 ——Fujimoto Kizan, *Kampon shikidō ōkagami*, ed Noma Kō-shin (1961). Donald Keene, "Fujimoto Kizan and *The Great Mirror of Love*," in *Landscapes and Portraits* (1971).

Lawrence W. ROGERS

shikikin → deposit money

shikimi

Illicium religiosum or *I. anisatum*. An evergreen tree of the family Magnoliaceae that grows wild in the warm areas of Kyūshū, Shikoku, and central and western Honshū. It is also cultivated in cemeteries and Buddhist temple grounds as an offering flower. It reaches about 3–5 meters (10–16 ft) in height and develops numerous branches. The leaves are alternate, oblong, 6–8 centimeters (2.4–3.1 in) long, and fragrant. Around April the plant opens light yellow flowers in the axils in the upper part of the branches. Each flower has a total of 12 petals and sepals of nearly the same shape and color. After flowering it bears star-shaped fruits (follicles) which split open when ripe in autumn and scatter yellow seeds. Although the seeds are poisonous, the fresh branches have long been used as offerings on the household Buddhist altars (*butsudan*), and incense powder is made from the leaves. The *shikimi* is also known abroad and was exported to Europe in 1790.

MATSUDA Osamu

shikimoku

1. Compilations of laws and regulations issued by warrior governments and regional warlords from the 13th through the 16th centuries. They took the form of collections of precepts to govern the behavior of *samurai* retainers or "housemen" (GOKENIN). The best-known examples include the Kamakura shogunate's GOSEIBAI SHIKIMOKU of 1232, the Muromachi shogunate's KEMMU SHIKIMOKU of 1336, and the Rokkaku family's YOSHIHARU SHIKIMOKU of 1567. See also BUKEHŌ; BUNKOKUHŌ. A *shikimoku* governing the court aristocracy was maintained by the Records Office (Kirokusho) at the imperial court in Kyōto.

2. In literature, lists of rules for composing RENGA AND HAIKAI verse. Such rules for *renga* were compiled by NIJŌ YOSHIMOTO and for *haikai* by MATSUNAGA TEITOKU.

shikinaisha

(*shikinai* shrines). Also called *shikisha* or *kansha*. The Shintō shrines listed in the "register of deities" (*jimmyōchō*) in books 9 and 10 of the ENGI SHIKI (Procedures of the Engi Era) of 927. A total of 2,861 shrines throughout Japan, enshrining 3,132 deities (*kami*), are listed. These were divided into major shrines (*taisha*) and minor shrines (*shōsha*), which in turn were classified into those directly supported by offerings for important ritual occasions from the Jingikan (Office of Shintō Worship) of the central government and those which received them from provincial governments. Shrines not in this official system were called *shikige* or *shikigai*. The *shikinai* shrines have for the most part survived, at least in name, and are now the object of detailed study as to origins, history, traditions, buildings, priestly family, and adherents. See also SHRINES.

📖 ——Shikinaisha Kenkyūkai, *Shikinaisha chōsa hōkoku*, 25 vols (1976).

Felicia G. BOCK

Shiki no Miko (?–716)

(Prince Shiki). Imperial prince, poet of the early literary period (late 7th–early 8th centuries). His exact identity is uncertain because the two half-brothers, emperors TENJI (626–672) and TEMMU (d 686), each had a son known as Prince Shiki. However, authorities agree that the poet by that name represented in the MAN'YŌSHŪ (ca 759, Collection for Ten Thousand Generations or Collection of Ten Thousand Leaves), the first great anthology of Japanese vernacular poetry, is probably the son of Emperor Tenji.

Although Prince Shiki's extant works consist of a mere six 31-syllable *tanka* ("short poem") in the *Man'yōshū*, he is nonetheless regarded as one of the finest poets of the age. His innovative verse evinces the beginnings of a courtly elegance combined with dignity and simplicity of expression. Such touches are perhaps indicative of his closeness, as a member of the highest court circles, to the most up-to-date literary influences from China.

📖 ——Ian H. Levy, *The Ten Thousand Leaves* (1981). Nippon Gakujutsu Shinkōkai, *The Man'yōshū: One Thousand Poems* (1940, repr 1965).

Robert H. BROWER

Shikishi, Princess (?–1201)

(Shikishi Naishinnō). Also known as Shokushi Naishinnō (Princess Shokushi). Poet, Shintō high priestess. Daughter of Emperor GO-SHIRAKAWA (1127–92; r 1155–58). Shikishi was appointed high priestess of the Kamo Shrine in Kyōto in 1159 at about the age of nine—a post that she occupied for 11 years, resigning because of illness in 1169. Little is known about her life immediately thereafter. However, from the fact that the famous poets Fujiwara no Shunzei (FUJIWARA NO TOSHINARI) and his son Fujiwara no Teika (FUJIWARA NO SADAIE) made visits to her residence, it is surmised that she was actively interested in poetry. Shunzei included nine of her poems in the seventh imperial anthology, SENZAI WAKASHŪ, which he completed in 1188. In 1197 Shunzei presented the princess his treatise *Korai fūtei shō* (Notes on Poetic Style through the Ages), which he had written at her request.

Shikishi had been a helpless and unhappy bystander during the troubled times that followed the HEIJI DISTURBANCE of 1160, but in 1197 she was suspected of being actively involved in a plot against the government, and she took Buddhist orders to escape punishment. Thereafter she lived a lonely, retired life. In 1200 she was appointed foster mother to the future emperor Juntoku (1197–1242; r 1210–21), and in 1200 she composed her Hundred-Poem Sequence of the Shōji Era at the invitation of ex-Emperor GO-TOBA (1180–1239; r 1183–98). By then she was already seriously ill, and died the following spring.

As a poet, Shikishi numbers among the foremost figures of an extraordinarily talented age. She accepted the aesthetic ideals of "mystery and depth" (*yūgen*) and "ethereal charm" (*yōen*) advocated by Shunzei and Teika, and some of her most memorable poems are suffused with the romantic evocativeness so prized by them. At the same time, many of Shikishi's poems display a fervent passion, written as they are in the conventional pose of the passionate woman—a convention dating back to the poetry of ONO NO KOMACHI in the 9th century. One hundred sixty-four of Shikishi's poems are found in imperial anthologies, including the unusually large number of 49 poems—more than for any other woman poet—in the great anthology of her time, the SHIN KOKINSHŪ (1205). Her personal collection contains some 360 poems.

📖 ——Robert H. Brower and Earl Miner, *Japanese Court Poetry* (1961). Satō Hiroaki, *Poems of Princess Shikishi* (1973).

Robert H. BROWER

Shikitei Samba (1776–1822)

Early 19th century GESAKU fiction writer. One of the earliest Japanese writers to earn a living from fiction, Samba is best known for his KOKKEIBON ("funny books"), a kind of humorous fiction, principally *Ukiyoburo* (1809–13, The Bathhouse of the Floating World), but was author as well of a large number of best-selling stories in the GŌKAN ("bound volume") format, a form of lavishly illustrated fiction popular from the early 19th century onward, and many works in other genres of fiction. He was born Kikuchi Taisuke, the son of a master woodblock carver of Edo (now Tōkyō), and so from his childhood knew intimately the world of commercial printing and publishing. As a youth he was an apprentice in a major Edo publishing house, and both his first wife, who died soon after their marriage, and his second, who survived him, were daughters of publishers.

Samba published his first work, a KIBYŌSHI ("yellow cover"), a variety of illustrated fiction popular in the late 18th century, heavily indebted in its style and content to the works of SANTŌ KYŌDEN, at the age of 17 or 18. Probably in part because he was an insider in the publishing trade, this and most of his other early works, while of no great distinction, were illustrated by some of the best-known artists of the day, primarily UTAGAWA TOYOKUNI and his students, and consequently enjoyed good sales. His first real success, however, came in 1799 with a *kibyōshi* entitled *Kyan taiheiki mukō hachimaki,* which treated satirically a battle that had recently taken place between two neighborhood fire brigades in Edo. One of these brigades, offended by Samba's satiric attack, stormed his house and that of the book's publisher. The firefighters were jailed, but Samba and his publisher were also punished for their role in the incident. While he was punished for contributing to a breach of the peace and not for violating the strict censorship laws of the day, Samba never again wrote in a satiric vein about contemporary events. The notoriety of the *Kyan taiheiki* incident, however, ensured his subsequent popularity.

In 1806 Samba published a 10-volume *kibyōshi*-style story entitled *Ikazuchi Tarō gōaku monogatari,* which Samba himself as well as many of his contemporaries regarded as the first example of a book published in the *gōkan* format. Prior to this time, each volume of a multivolume *kibyōshi* had been separately bound with its own cover. The 10 volumes of this work, however, were bound in 2 larger volumes of 5 each. The new format encouraged the development of longer, more complicated stories and soon displaced the *kibyōshi* as the dominant form of illustrated fiction. Samba went on to write over 70 *gōkan,* many of them extremely popular. Most were typical of the *gōkan* in this period: adventure-packed stories of vengeance, banditry, or feuds within or between military clans, virtually all set in a vague medieval past. Many were similar to or explicitly based on popular KABUKI or puppet plays (see JŌRURI) of the time, and a great number were embellished with *nigao-e,* illustrations in the likeness of popular kabuki actors.

Samba wrote several SHAREBON, a genre of late 18th century *gesaku* fiction that deals exclusively with the pleasure quarters, of which *Tatsumi fugen* (1798) and its sequels interest scholars as examples of a trend in the genre away from the narrow focus of the early *sharebon* toward the greater, almost novelistic complexity of the later NINJŌBON romances. Other notable works include *Kusazōshi kojitsuke nendaiki* (1802), an illustrated history of popular fiction, and *Chūshingura henchikiron* (1812), a satiric attack on the solemn homage then accorded the great puppet play *Kanadehon chūshingura* (1748, The Treasury of Loyal Retainers).

The works for which Samba is best remembered are his *kokkeibon,* of which *Ukiyoburo* and its sequel *Ukiyodoko* (1813–14, The Barbershop of the Floating World) have enjoyed the most enduring popularity. *Ukiyoburo,* his longest comic work, is a plotless collection of vignettes of the activities in a public bathhouse in Edo, loosely organized chronologically from dawn to dusk and divided into four books, two dealing with the men's bath and two with the women's. The vignettes consist almost entirely of conversations among various typical bathhouse patrons—generally, middle-class commoners—written with great fidelity to the dialects and speech habits of Edo. The humor of *Ukiyoburo,* more subtle than the slapstick comedy of JIPPENSHA IKKU's *Tōkaidōchū hizakurige* (1802–22; tr *Shank's Mare,* 1960) derives from Samba's unique genius for writing dialogue, through which he was able to capture with uncanny accuracy the quirks and obsessions of the broad range of different kinds of people who patronize the bathhouse. While his characters remain anonymous types, they are not stereotypes but rather distinct personalities given universality by Samba's cynical and ironic but essentially kindhearted vision of everyday human experience and behavior. *Ukiyodoko* similarly treats the patrons and atmosphere of the barbershop, another typical Edo gathering place, but the work is on the whole less successful than *Ukiyoburo,* perhaps because of its all-male cast; the most perceptive and original parts of *Ukiyoburo* are those dealing with the women's bath.

Samba considered himself to be a literary disciple of HIRAGA GENNAI, but while he clearly copied Gennai's style in his comic essays and the narrative portions of *Ukiyoburo* and similar works, his humor is both less bitterly cynical and less intellectual than that of his model. Probably the strongest influence in Samba's *kokkeibon* is that of RAKUGO and other humorous storytelling forms. *Ukiyoburo* and *Ukiyodoko,* as well as some of his less well-known *kokkeibon* like *Namaei katagi* (1806, Portraits of Drunks) and *Kokon hyaku baka* (1814, A Hundred Fools, Ancient and Modern), show clear and sometimes explicit links with *rakugo* stories and storytellers.

In spite of the frankly commercial nature of much of his writing, Samba saw himself as a guardian of the old gentleman-amateur tradition in *gesaku* fiction, and lamented the disappearance of the playful spirit that animated the works of Gennai, KOIKAWA HARUMACHI, and others of his predecessors. Though his poetry was undistinguished, he participated enthusiastically in comic verse

(KYŌKA) parties and competitions, and in other ways as well seems to have tried to live up to a previous generation's ideal of the pleasure-seeking, cynical, sometimes almost bohemian but always sophisticated writer. His work is often marred by a haste and repetitiousness born of economic necessity, but at his best Samba shows a gift for characterization and a sensitivity to the contradictions and ironies of human nature rare among his contemporaries.

——Margarete Donath-Wiegand, *Zur literarhistorischen Stellung des Ukiyoburo von Shikitei Samba* (1963).

Robert W. LEUTNER

shikken

(shogunal regent). A title of the KAMAKURA SHOGUNATE (1192–1333). It was first assumed in 1203 by HŌJŌ TOKIMASA, who had been gathering the reins of government since the death of MINAMOTO NO YORITOMO, his son-in-law and the founder of the shogunate. As regent for the shōgun MINAMOTO NO SANETOMO and as head of the MANDOKORO (Administrative Board), he became the the de facto ruler in 1203, affixing his seal to all documents issued by the shogunate. An even firmer footing was gained by his son, and successor as *shikken,* Hōjō Yoshitoki. In 1213 Yoshitoki became simultaneously head of the SAMURAI-DOKORO (Board of Retainers) after crushing the Wada family, who had previously dominated that position. Thereafter the title was held by successive members of the HŌJŌ FAMILY. The post of assistant regent (RENSHO, or cosigner) was established by HŌJŌ YASUTOKI in 1224, and the creation of the HYŌJŌSHŪ (Council of State) in 1226 allowed for further collegial sharing of power. In time, however, particularly after the MONGOL INVASIONS OF JAPAN in 1274 and 1281, effective political power shifted to the TOKUSŌ, the patrimonial head of the main branch of the Hōjō family.

Shikoku Electric Power Co, Ltd

(Shikoku Denryoku). A supplier of electric power to the four prefectures on the island of Shikoku, the Shikoku Electric Power Co was established in 1951. Although its generating capacity is sizable, the company has concluded contracts with companies in Europe, the United States, and Australia for the refining and enrichment of uranium in an effort to diversify its fuel sources and end its excessive reliance on petroleum. Its nuclear generating plant at Ikata in Ehime Prefecture began operations in 1977. In the fiscal year that ended March 1982 the company sold 16.3 billion kilowatt hours worth ¥382.1 billion (US $1.6 billion) and was capitalized at ¥103.2 billion (US $428.7 million).

Shikoku karst

(Shikoku *karusuto*). Japan's highest limestone plateau. It overlaps Ehime and Kōchi prefectures, Shikoku, and serves as a natural park for both prefectures. It is noted for its karst topography, with numerous dolines and limestone caves. Elevation: 1,400 m (4,592 ft); width: 25 km (16 mi).

Shikoku Mountains

(Shikoku Sanchi). Series of mountain ranges extending east to west about 180 km (112 mi), from the Kii Channel to the Bungo Channel, central Shikoku. Included are the Tsurugi, Ishizuchi, and other mountain ranges. The highest peak is ISHIZUCHISAN (1,982 m; 6,501 ft). The mountains are noted for their rugged and wild terrain. The now abandoned Besshi Copper Mine was located here. There is heavy precipitation, and large areas are covered with forests. Lumbering and the cultivation of *mitsumata* and *kōzo* trees for making *washi* (Japanese paper) are carried on. Tourist attractions include the Shikoku Karst Prefectural Natural Park and gorges such as ŌBOKE and IYADANI.

Shikoku region

(Shikoku *chihō*). Region consisting of Shikoku, the smallest of Japan's four main islands, and numerous surrounding islands. Shikoku lies to the south of western Honshū across the INLAND SEA and across the Bungo Channel from northeastern Kyūshū. It consists of Kagawa, Tokushima, Ehime, and Kōchi prefectures. It has a dissected topography with high mountains and steep slopes, which severely limit agriculture, habitation, and communication. The climate is subtropical with short mild winters and long hot summers. Northern Shikoku has an "Inland Sea-type" climate with many fair days, and southern Shikoku has an "Omote Nihon-type" (the Pacific coast) climate with heavy rainfall in summer and frequent typhoons.

Northern Shikoku developed early, partly because the Inland Sea was the main traffic artery in ancient times, but southern Shikoku (Kōchi Prefecture) developed later. At present much of the island is a thinly populated agricultural region with few natural resources and little large-scale industry. Arable land in basins, valleys, and along the coast allows the production of rice, vegetables, and citrus fruit; extensive livestock raising and coastal fishing are also carried out. Industrial products include synthetic fibers, furniture, petrochemicals, ships, and machinery. The planned Honshū–Shikoku Bridge is expected to change the economy of the island by bringing in many new industries. Extensive land reclamation in Kagawa and Tokushima prefectures should provide more room for industrial expansion. Two national parks, Inland Sea and Ashizuri-Uwakai, and three quasi-national parks are located in Shikoku as well as a famous pilgrimage route to 88 temples. Takamatsu and Matsuyama are the largest cities. Area: 18,792 sq km (7,254 sq mi); pop: 4,163,-177.

Shikotan

Island approximately 75 km (47 mi) northeast of the Nemuro Peninsula, eastern Hokkaidō. The island is hilly, averaging 300 m (984 ft) in elevation, with little level ground. It is surrounded by sea cliffs. Shakotan, on the northeastern coast of the island, is an excellent natural port. The principal activity is fishing; marine products include cod, crab, and kelp. The island is currently under the administration of the Soviet Union (see TERRITORY OF JAPAN). Area: 255 sq km (98.4 sq mi).

Shikotsu, Lake

(Shikotsuko). Caldera lake in the city of Chitose, southwestern Ishikari Plain, southwestern Hokkaidō. Japan's northernmost ice-free lake and second deepest lake after Lake Tazawa in Akita Prefecture. Located within Shikotsu-Tōya National Park, it attracts numerous anglers, fishing for *himemasu* (*Oncorhynchus nerka* var. *adonis*) between June and August. Area: 77.3 sq km (29.8 sq mi); circumference: 40 km (25 mi); depth: 360 m (1,181 ft); transparency: 18 m (59 ft); altitude: 248 m (813 ft).

Shikotsu–Tōya National Park

(Shikotsu-Tōya Kokuritsu Kōen). Situated in southwest Hokkaidō, 10 km (6 mi) southwest of the city of SAPPORO. The chief features of this mountainous region are active volcanoes, numerous hot spring resorts, and three large caldera lakes. In the east lies Lake SHIKOTSU, the largest lake in the park and the second deepest lake in Japan (360 m; 1,181 ft), ringed by high cliffs and active volcanoes such as Eniwadake (1,320 m; 4,330 ft) and TARUMAEZAN (1,042 m; 3,418 ft). To the southwest lies the circular Lake TŌYA, on whose southern shore are two active volcanoes: USUZAN (727 m; 2,385 ft), noted for its frequent eruptions, the last one in 1977; and SHŌWA SHINZAN (408 m; 1,338 ft), formed in the 20th century. North of Lake Tōya, the volcano YŌTEIZAN (1,893 m; 6,209 ft) is distinguished by the dense forests that cover its lower slopes and the lava fields on its upper slopes, where numerous species of alpine plant flourish. At the southern edge of the park is Lake KUTTARA, with Noboribetsu Hot Spring nearby. JŌZANKEI HOT SPRING is found in the north of the park, near Shiraito Falls. Typical trees of the area are the Yeddo spruce (*ezomatsu*), Sakhalin fir (*todomatsu*), silver birch, and Japanese oak (*nara*). Area: 986.6 sq km (380.8 sq mi).

shikunshi

("the four gentlemen"; Ch: *si junzi* or *ssu chün-tzu*). A Chinese painting subject. The combination of blossoming plum, orchid, chrysanthemum, and bamboo as a painting subject alludes to the purity and nobility of the Confucian gentleman. In China, each of these four plants has a long literary history of association with virtue, and one by one became scholar-painter subjects during the Song (Sung; 960–1279) and Yuan (Yüan; 1279–1368) dynasties. Their union as *The Four Gentlemen* was established by the early 15th century and figures prominently in the 17th-century Chinese codification of scholar-painting, *The Mustard Seed Garden Manual* (J: *Kaishien gaden*; Ch: *Jieziyuan huazhuan* or *Chieh-tzu-yüan hua-*

chuan). In Japan, *shikunshi* was a favored subject of literati painting (BUNJINGA).

Carolyn WHEELWRIGHT

Shimabara

City in Nagasaki Prefecture, Kyūshū. During the Edo period (1600–1868) Shimabara was a castle town of the Matsudaira family and the site of the SHIMABARA UPRISING (1637–38), a rebellion by Christians and peasants. In 1792 the nearby volcano Mayuyama erupted, creating the scenic islands called Tsukumoshima. Principal products are mandarin oranges, tobacco, and tea. Rainbow trout hatcheries are located here. The remains of Shimabara Castle, built by Matsukura Shigemasa (d 1631) in 1618; the site of Hara Castle, the base of the Christian rebels; old warrior houses; Christian graves; and Shimabara Hot Spring draw tourists. Pop: 46,637.

Shimabara Peninsula

(Shimabara Hantō). Located in Nagasaki Prefecture, western Kyūshū and separating the Ariake Sea from Tachibana Bay. As the center of Christianity when it was first introduced to Japan in the 16th century, it has many historical sites associated with this era. Site of Unzendake and other peaks in Unzen–Amakusa National Park. The Shimabara and Unzen hot springs are bases for sightseeing.

Shimabara Uprising

(Shimabara no Ran). Peasant uprising (IKKI) that broke out on 11 December 1637 (Kan'ei 14.10.25); it occasioned the last great mobilization of the armed forces of the Tokugawa shogunate (1603–1867) until the conflicts leading to the Meiji Restoration of 1868. The uprising began in the notoriously overtaxed Shimabara domain (now part of Nagasaki Prefecture) of the *daimyō* Matsukura Katsuie (d 1638) and immediately spread to the Amakusa Islands (now part of Kumamoto Prefecture), a part of the domain of the daimyō of Karatsu, Terazawa Kataka (1609–47). Both areas had been Christianized before the general persecution of the faith began in February 1614: Shimabara under ARIMA HARUNOBU after his baptism in 1580, Amakusa since the 1570s under several lords (see CHRISTIAN DAIMYŌ), most notably KONISHI YUKINAGA. Hence the shogunate viewed the rebellion as Christian-inspired. This view was a critical factor in its final decision to cut off all contact with Catholic lands (see NATIONAL SECLUSION), but it was not an accurate analysis. Not orthodox Christianity but social chiliasm inspired the rebels: the peasants, led by Amakusa Shirō (also known as Masuda Shirō Tokisada; Christian name, Jerônimo; 1622?–38), entertained millenarian hopes for a better world.

Amakusa Shirō's father, Masuda Jimbyōe Yoshitsugu (d 1638), had been a *samurai* in the service of Konishi Yukinaga. When Yukinaga, one of the principal opponents of TOKUGAWA IEYASU's claims to national hegemony, was executed after defeat in the Battle of SEKIGAHARA in 1600, large numbers of former Konishi vassals were deprived of their privileges and became masterless samurai (*rōnin*). When chronic poverty, recurrent famine, extortionate taxation, and religious persecution in the traditionally Christian Shimabara–Amakusa region combined to create the conditions for a peasant rebellion, discontented *rōnin* joined the peasants' ranks, and the messianic youth Amakusa Shirō emerged as their leader. A Japanese counterpart of miracle-working European leaders of peasant uprisings, Shirō was proclaimed by his followers to be "an angel from Heaven"; in documents attributed to the rebels he is called "Heavenly Child," "Heavenly Master," and "the Good Lord." Thus, although the insurgents' battle standard declared "Praised be the Most Holy Sacrament," their ideology was chiliastic rather than purely Christian. (That flag, which is frequently used in illustrations, may be a forgery, however; and it is doubtful that all the documents ascribed to the rebels in Edo-period sources are authentic.)

After initial successes, the rebels were put under siege in Hara Castle on the Shimabara Peninsula by a huge army levied from the shogunate's feudatories in northern Kyūshū. Amakusa Shirō was killed when the castle fell on 12 April 1638 (Kan'ei 15.2.28). Women and children were not spared. Altogether 37,000 of the rebels are said to have perished in the slaughter. See also CHRISTIANITY.

George ELISON

Shimada

City in central Shizuoka Prefecture, central Honshū. In the Edo period (1600–1868) it was a crossing point for the river Ōigawa and a prosperous POST-STATION TOWN on the highway Tōkaidō. Now a distribution center for lumber, it also produces foodstuffs and machinery. Tea and mandarin oranges are cultivated on the plateau Makinohara. Pop: 70,705.

Shimada Saburō (1852–1923)

Politician and journalist. Born in Edo (now Tōkyō), he studied at Daigaku Nankō, the predecessor of Tōkyō University. In 1873 he became a reporter for the newspaper *Yokohama mainichi shimbun*, the first Japanese daily, and a champion of the FREEDOM AND PEOPLE'S RIGHTS MOVEMENT. In 1875 Shimada entered government service under the sponsorship of MUTSU MUNEMITSU, but he resigned at the time of the POLITICAL CRISIS OF 1881, when ŌKUMA SHIGENOBU was ousted from the government. He joined in the founding of the RIKKEN KAISHINTŌ (Constitutional Reform Party) and at the same time resumed his journalistic career with the *Yokohama mainichi*, of which he eventually became manager. Although he was elected to 14 successive terms in the Diet, beginning with the first election in 1890, and was known as a gifted orator, Shimada was excluded from key positions in the Kenseitō and the Kensei Hontō (successors to the Kaishintō Party) because of his outspoken condemnation of political corruption, particularly in connection with the SIEMENS INCIDENT and the ASHIO COPPER MINE INCIDENT.

Shimadzu Corporation

(Shimazu Seisakusho). Manufacturer of precision measuring, medical, aviation, and industrial instruments. Shimadzu Corporation was established in 1875. It exports its products throughout the world, centering on medical and analytical instruments. It has overseas offices in Egypt, Singapore, and Argentina and three foreign subsidiaries (two in the United States and one in West Germany), as well as over 100 overseas sales agencies. Annual sales totaled ¥106.7 billion (US $443.3 million) in the fiscal year ending in March 1982, of which exports constituted 17 percent; the company was capitalized at ¥10.9 billion (US $45.3 million) in the same year. Corporate headquarters are located in Kyōto.

Shima Hot Spring

(Shima Onsen). Located in the northern part of the town of Nakanojō, northwestern Gumma Prefecture, central Honshū. A voluminous weak saline hot spring; water temperature 70°C (158°F). Located within Jōshin'etsu Kōgen National Park, this spa is situated along the scenic river Shimagawa and is a noted summer and health resort.

Shimai Sōshitsu (1539?–1615)

Merchant and tea connoisseur of the Azuchi-Momoyama period (1568–1600) and the early part of the Edo period (1600–1868). The Shimai family were *sake* brewers and pawnbrokers in the port city of Hakata (now Fukuoka; see HAKATA MERCHANTS); in addition, Sōshitsu engaged in trade with Tsushima and Korea. Through commerce and the tea ceremony, Sōshitsu had by the 1570s established ties with his counterparts in SAKAI, Japan's other major trading city, and with powerful *daimyō* such as ŌTOMO SŌRIN; between 1580 and 1582 he visited the Kyōto-Ōsaka area in order to expand his contacts in the related worlds of politics, mercantile affairs, and the connoisseurship of tea; by 1583 he had come to the notice of the national unifier TOYOTOMI HIDEYOSHI. Upon Hideyoshi's conquest of Kyūshū in 1587, Sōshitsu together with KAMIYA SŌTAN was assigned responsibilities in the reconstruction of Hakata, which had suffered severely in the wars of the previous two decades. Sōshitsu participated in the negotiations that preceded Hideyoshi's invasions of Korea, traveling to that country in 1589 and 1592 as the associate of Sō Yoshitomo (1568–1615), the daimyō of Tsushima, and KONISHI YUKINAGA; the three supposedly opposed Hideyoshi's aggressive aims, but Sōshitsu assumed a quartermaster's role in Hakata once the invasion was launched. As one of Hakata's most influential citizens, Sōshitsu assisted Kobayakawa Takakage (1533–97), KOBAYAKAWA HIDEAKI, ISHIDA MITSUNARI, and KURODA NAGAMASA in their successive administration of the area but is said to have refused elevation to *samurai* status. The testamentary injunctions he addressed to

his adopted son Tokuzaemon on 8 February 1610 (Keichō 15.1.15) constitute a remarkable exposition of the merchant values of the period.

George ELISON

Shimaji Mokurai (1838–1911)

Buddhist priest and reformer of the JŌDO SHIN SECT; an advocate of freedom of religion and the separation of religion and government in the Meiji period (1868–1912). Born in Suō Province (now part of Yamaguchi Prefecture), after taking his priestly vows he went to the temple Nishi Honganji in Kyōto, where he was active in the sect reform movement. This movement was brought about by the internal confusion among sect adherents that resulted from efforts by the Meiji government to make SHINTŌ the state religion. In 1872 Shimaji traveled to Europe to observe cultural and religious institutions there, becoming one of the first Japanese Buddhist priests to go to Europe. After side trips to Greece, Egypt, Jerusalem, and India, he returned to Japan in 1873. Impressed by the separation of religion and state he observed in Europe, Shimaji submitted a number of written petitions to the government calling for the dissolution of the Daikyōin (Office of Religion, established in 1872), through which the Meiji government attempted to spread Shintō as the national creed. His efforts were instrumental in securing abolition of this office in 1875 and promoting a government religious policy more tolerant toward Buddhism. Despite his espousal of freedom of religion, Shimaji was critical of Christianity. Besides being an ardent spokesman for Buddhists in Japan, he was also the founder of an early weekly news magazine, the *Shimbun zasshi*, and editor of the *Nihonjin*, a national magazine. He helped found a school for women and the Japanese Red Cross.

Robert RHODES

Shimaki Akahiko (1876–1926)

WAKA poet. Real name Kubota Toshihiko. Born in Nagano Prefecture. Graduate of Nagano Normal School (now part of Shinshū University). A career elementary school teacher, he started composing *waka*, inspired by the modern *waka* reformer MASAOKA SHIKI, who promoted a realistic description of nature. In 1908 he became a contributor to ARARAGI, a magazine published by an influential coterie of *waka* poets who adopted Shiki's style, and in 1914 he became its editor. He combined a crisp style, reminiscent of the school of Japanese naturalism, with a moralizing tone, which he advocated as a principal element in *waka*. His major collections are *Taikyoshū* (1924) and *Shiinshū* (1926).

Shimaki Kensaku (1903–1945)

Novelist. Real name Asakura Kikuo. Born in Hokkaidō to a poor family, he supported himself from a young age and managed to enter Tōhoku University. Inspired by the so-called proletarian movement of the 1920s, however, he left school in 1926 and participated in labor and farmers' union movements. Shimaki joined the Communist Party, probably in 1927, and was arrested in the mass arrests of 15 March 1928 (see MARCH 15TH INCIDENT). He developed tuberculosis in prison and was released in 1932 after promising to forsake communism. After his forced withdrawal from political activities, he began to write while living in Tōkyō with his mother and older brother, who owned a second-hand bookstore. His novels evoke his painful struggles of conscience in abandoning his political commitments. His principal works are *Saiken* (1935), *Seikatsu no tankyū* (1937–38), and "Akagaeru" (published posthumously in 1946).

Shimamura Hōgetsu (1871–1918)

Literary critic, novelist, playwright. Real name Shimamura Takitarō. Born in Shimane Prefecture. Graduate of Tōkyō Semmon Gakkō (now Waseda University) where he was a student of TSUBOUCHI SHŌYŌ, the respected novelist and pioneer of the modern theater movement. In 1902 he went to study aesthetics and psychology in England and Germany. Returning to Japan in 1905, he became a professor of English and European literature at Waseda, emerging as a leading critic by giving support and constructive analysis to writers of the naturalist school. A founding member, together with Shōyō, of the Bungei Kyōkai (Association of Literary Arts; 1905–13), he also participated actively in the modern theater movement, introducing a number of modern European plays, including Ibsen's *A Doll's House*. After the Bungei Kyōkai was dissolved due to disagreement

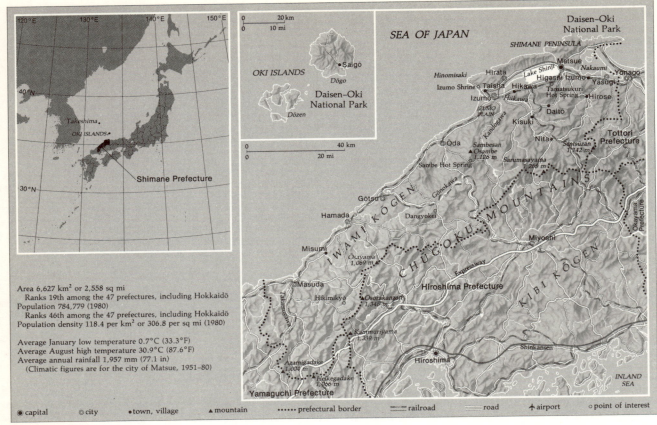

Area 6,627 km² or 2,558 sq mi
   Ranks 19th among the 47 prefectures, including Hokkaidō
Population 784,779 (1980)
   Ranks 46th among the 47 prefectures, including Hokkaidō
Population density 118.4 per km² or 306.8 per sq mi (1980)

Average January low temperature 0.7°C (33.3°F)
Average August high temperature 30.9°C (87.6°F)
Average annual rainfall 1,957 mm (77.1 in)
   (Climatic figures are for the city of Matsue, 1951–80)

Shimane Prefecture

among members, Hōgetsu founded an independent theater group, the Geijutsuza, with Matsui Sumako (1886–1919), the star actress in *A Doll's House* who was also his lover. Hōgetsu's major contribution as a dramatist was the popularization of modern-day Western issues such as greater freedom for women. His name is best remembered in association with Sumako, who played Katusha in his dramatization of Tolstoy's *Resurrection*. She committed suicide shortly after his death. His principal works include *Ran'unshū* (1906), a collection of stories, and *Kindai bungei no kenkyū* (1909), a collection of literary essays.

Shimanaka Incident

(Shimanaka Jiken). The planned murder in 1960 of Shimanaka Hōji (b 1923), president of the publishing firm Chūō Kōron Sha. After the short story "Fūryū mutan" (An Elegant Fantasy) by FUKAZAWA SHICHIRŌ appeared in the December 1960 issue of the magazine CHŪŌ KŌRON, rightist groups and the Imperial Household Agency filed protests with the magazine, citing as blasphemous the scene in which the imperial family are executed. Shimanaka, the publisher, was considering how to respond to these protests when a young right-wing terrorist broke into his house and in his absence stabbed his maid to death and seriously wounded his wife. The magazine published a statement in its March 1961 issue and in newspapers apologizing for having offended the dignity of the imperial house. Some felt that this was an unfortunate surrender to right-wing intimidation.
                                                            HARADA Katsumasa

Shimanaka Yūsaku (1887–1949)

Editor, publisher, and president of CHŪŌ KŌRON SHA, INC. Born in Nara Prefecture. After graduating from Waseda University, Shimanaka entered Chūō Kōron Sha, Inc, the publisher of *Chūō kōron,* a leading journal for intellectuals. He worked as an editor under TAKITA CHOIN. In 1916 he brought out FUJIN KŌRON, a magazine for educated women. Named president of the company in 1928, the following year he started publishing books as well. Some of his most successful publishing ventures were translations of Western works such as *Im Westen Nichts Neues* (tr as *Seibu sensen ijō nashi*)

by Erich Maria Remarque and the complete works of Shakespeare and the translation of the *Genji monogatari* (see TALE OF GENJI) into modern Japanese by TANIZAKI JUN'ICHIRŌ. As a result of military repression, in 1944 he dissolved his company. It resumed publication in 1945.
                                                            ARASE Yutaka

Shimane Peninsula

(Shimane Hantō). Located in northeastern Shimane Prefecture, western Honshū. It runs parallel with the Chūgoku Mountains and is separated from them by Lake Shinji. The Shimane Peninsula is composed chiefly of mountains. The northern coast, a heavily indented coastline, forms part of the Daisen–Oki National Park. Tourist attractions include the Miho Shrine, Izumo Shrine, and Hinomisaki Shrine, all of which are associated with ancient myths. Length: east to west about 65 km (40 mi); greatest width: 18 km (11 mi).

Shimane Prefecture

(Shimane Ken). Located in western Honshū and bounded on the north by the Sea of Japan, on the east by Tottori Prefecture, on the south by Hiroshima Prefecture, and on the west by Yamaguchi Prefecture. The terrain is largely mountainous, with the main level areas situated near the coast in the northeast. The small Oki Islands, located north of the city of MATSUE in the Sea of Japan, are administratively a part of the prefecture. The climate is relatively mild, with many overcast days.

The area was divided into the provinces of Izumo, Iwami, and Oki after the TAIKA REFORM of 645. The Izumo region is mentioned in the mythic cycles of the *Kojiki* (712), Japan's first chronicle, and the IZUMO SHRINE remains one of the most important centers of the Shintō religion. The area came under the control of a succession of warrior families from the latter part of the Heian period (794–1185) to the Edo period (1600–1868) and was incorporated into the modern prefectural system in 1881.

Agriculture, especially rice production, remains the main occupation. Fishing is also important. Industry is limited to textiles, farming tools, and woodworking, as well as molybdenum mining.

Attractions include the city of Matsue with its restored castle, Izumo Shrine, and the Oki Islands. The mountain SAMBESAN and Shimane Peninsula are part of the DAISEN–OKI NATIONAL PARK. Area: 6,627 sq km (2,558 sq mi); pop: 784,779; capital: Matsue. Other major cities include HAMADA, IZUMO, and MASUDA.

Shimantogawa

River in southwestern Kōchi Prefecture, Shikoku, originating in the western Shikoku Mountains and flowing through the Nakamura Plain into Tosa Bay. It is the second largest river in Shikoku. The river basin is mountainous. The area about the upper reaches produces pulp trees, shiitake (a species of mushroom), and charcoal. Sweetfish (ayu) is a local specialty. The volume of water is abundant, but the river's hydroelectric potential is undeveloped. Length: 85 km (115.5 mi); area of drainage basin: 2,270 sq km (876 sq mi).

Shimao Toshio (1917–)

Author. Born in Yokohama. Shimao was drafted immediately after graduating from Kyūshū University, and in the final days of World War II, was the commander of a naval suicide-mission unit. He began publishing soon after the war, writing about war and love in an abstract, often surrealistic, style. Several of his works, among them Shima no hate (1948, Island's End) and Shuppatsu wa tsui ni otozurezu (1962, Orders for Departure Never Came) are based on his wartime experiences. Perhaps his best-known work is Shi no toge (1960, Thorns of Death), an account of the author's reaction to his wife's mental illness and an exploration of the conflict between moral responsibility and the human need for love.

Shima Peninsula

(Shima Hantō). Located in southeastern Mie Prefecture, central Honshū. With Atsumi Peninsula it encloses Ise Bay. The southern part has heavily indented coasts with an abrasion platform called Sakishima. Pearl culture flourishes in Ago and Matoya bays; women divers fish for shellfish off the eastern coast. With a mild climate, it has numerous tourist attractions, particularly near the city of Toba and Sakishima. The entire peninsula is designated as Ise–Shima National Park.

Shimazaki Tōson (1872–1943)

Poet and novelist; most famous Japanese proponent of NATURALISM. Born in Magome in Nagano Prefecture. The Shimazaki family, though of the farmer class, had for generations been one of the leading families of the region, and the male heirs, including Tōson's father Masaki, were in the Edo period (1600–1868) the hereditary headmen of Magome.

Tōson (literary name; his given name was Haruki) was Masaki's fourth son. In 1881 he was sent away to Tōkyō for schooling; in 1887 he entered Meiji Gakuin, a college with Protestant Christian affiliations, and graduated from there in 1891. Soon afterward he became one of the coterie that began the famous literary journal Bungakukai (1893–98, World of Literature). In 1896 he left Tōkyō for Sendai to teach; while there he put together his first collection of verse, Wakanashū (1897, Collection of Young Herbs), which immediately established him as a leading "new style" poet. The poetry of Wakanashū is highly romantic in spirit, possibly too flamboyantly emotional for our taste today. But to the young readers of his time it seemed remarkably new, with its flowing cadences, its fresh imagery, and explicit emotionalism.

The publication in 1906 of his first novel Hakai (tr The Broken Commandment, 1974)—after he had returned to Tōkyō—began Tōson's distinguished career as a novelist. The novel is still considered a landmark of modern Japanese realism. The hero, a BURAKUMIN schoolteacher who keeps his outcast origin a secret until he divulges it toward the end of the novel to save his self-respect, is drawn with great insight and force, and remains to this day one of the memorable characters in modern Japanese fiction. The bigotry of the community, the hero's shame and guilt, his moral confusion about keeping his burakumin origin a secret (before dying his father had admonished him never to divulge it)—these are depicted by Tōson with a psychological and social realism unprecedented in modern Japan.

His next novel, Haru (1908, Spring), was a totally different kind of work. Weakly plotted, much less explicit in language than Hakai,

it is a lyrical and often too sentimental autobiographical account of his youthful days with the Bungakukai group. He was never again to write a novel like Hakai. For whatever reason, he eschewed the fictionality of that early distinguished work and continued after Haru to write autobiographical novels—the only exception being his last completed work, Yoake mae (1929–35, Before the Dawn), a novel about his father's life before and after the Meiji Restoration of 1868.

Ie (1910–11; tr The Family, 1976), however, is a work of distinction. It is deemed by many to be the "classic" Japanese naturalistic novel. Understated in tone (though sometimes theatrically so), conscientious in its maintenance of objectivity, it is a slow-moving and very carefully detailed account of the decline of two provincial families with whom the author is closely related. So reticent does the author become in his stance of objectivity that the reader is constantly in danger of missing the significance suggested by the gestures and silences of the characters or the subtle presence of the surroundings. Yet Ie is indeed a persuasive novel, if closely read, and deserves its admirers.

Shinsei (1918–19, New Life), a more explicitly emotional work, describes the author's seduction of one of his nieces, her pregnancy, and his ignominious flight from confrontation with his relations by exiling himself to France for a while. Understandably it caused a sensation when it was published, and was attacked by some critics and fellow writers, perhaps unjustly, for its alleged hypocrisy (in the author's presentation of himself and his motives). But there is no gainsaying the courage and determination of Tōson in deciding to write such a confessional novel, and there are readers who are moved by the power of what they see as his real search for redemption and "rebirth" (hence the title).

Yoake mae, the most ambitious of Tōson's novels in scope, is a very large historical novel in which the author tries both to describe the Meiji Restoration from the point of view of a provincial loyalist—his own father—and to describe the tragedy of this man, who dies in bitter disillusionment. There is genuine grandeur in Tōson's conception, some of which is indeed realized in the novel. But it is a very uneven work, often marred by the author's typical commitment to description of the mundane and his penchant for heavy understatement.

All in all, however, Tōson's reputation as a novelist will survive; for, at least in Hakai and Ie, he wrote two masterpieces in their respective genres.

▬▬ ——Works by Tōson: Wakanashū (1897). Hakai (1906), tr Kenneth Strong as The Broken Commandment (1974). Haru (1908). Ie (1910–11), tr Cecilia Segawa Seigle as The Family (1976). Shinsei (1918–19). Yoake mae (1929–35). Works about Tōson: Edwin McClellan, Two Japanese Novelists: Sōseki and Tōson (1969). Janet A. Walker, The Japanese Novel of the Meiji Period and the Ideal of Individualism (1980). Edwin McCLELLAN

Shimazono Junjirō (1877–1937)

Scientist and specialist in internal medicine. Born in Wakayama Prefecture; graduate of the Faculty of Medicine of Tōkyō University. Shimazono proved that a shortage of vitamin B_1 was the cause of beriberi by analyzing meals served in factories and school dormitories where the disease was prevalent. He also observed that symptoms similar to those of beriberi developed when meals lacking in vitamin B_1 were served to healthy persons. Shimazono taught at both Kyōto and Tōkyō universities. He received the Japan Academy Prize in 1926 for his study on vitamin B_1 deficiency, carried out in cooperation with OGATA TOMOSABURŌ. SŌDA Hajime

Shimazu family

Provincial leaders and later daimyō in southern Kyūshū from the 12th century to 1868. In 1197 Shimazu Tadahisa (1179–1227), a vassal of MINAMOTO NO YORITOMO, was appointed military governor (shugo) of Ōsumi and Satsuma provinces (now Kagoshima Prefecture) under the Kamakura shogunate (1192–1333). His descendants consolidated their control over the area, and under Shimazu Yoshihisa (1533–1611) the family came to control almost all of Kyūshū. When Yoshihisa was defeated by the forces of the national unifier TOYOTOMI HIDEYOSHI in 1587, however, the Shimazu holdings were reduced to the original two provinces. Moreover, Yoshihisa's brother SHIMAZU YOSHIHIRO fought on the losing side in the Battle of SEKIGAHARA (1600), and the family barely escaped confiscation of their lands by the victorious TOKUGAWA IEYASU. Nonetheless, under the Tokugawa shogunate (1603–1867) the heads of the Shimazu family served as daimyō of the important TOZAMA ("outside vassal") domain of Satsuma, with their seat at Kagoshima. Yoshihiro's son Iehisa (1578–1638) conquered Okinawa in 1609 and established his family's firm control of the island's lucrative entrepôt trade. In the 19th century several able Shimazu leaders appeared in succession. SHIMAZU NARIAKIRA strengthened his domain's financial and military position by introducing Western techniques during the period of the TEMPŌ REFORMS, and his half-brother SHIMAZU HISAMITSU was prominent in the MOVEMENT FOR UNION OF COURT AND SHOGUNATE and participated in the MEIJI RESTORATION (1868). See also SATSUMA PROVINCE.

Shimazu Genzō (1869–1951)

Inventor and industrialist. Born in Kyōto. He took over the family company, Shimazu Seisakusho, Ltd, after his father's death in 1895, and developed the small firm into a large enterprise (see SHIMADZU CORPORATION). Among his accomplishments was the introduction of mass-production techniques in the manufacture of lead-acid storage batteries. In 1896 he was successful in taking the first X-ray photographs in Japan, and in 1928 he developed the Shimazu-type induction generator. In 1930 he was formally recognized by the government as one of Japan's 10 leading inventors.

Shimazu Hisamitsu (1817–1887)

De facto ruler of the Satsuma domain (now Kagoshima Prefecture) in the years immediately preceding the MEIJI RESTORATION of 1868. The third son of Shimazu Narioki, in 1851 he lost out to his elder half brother SHIMAZU NARIAKIRA in a brief struggle for succession as daimyō. When Nariakira died in 1858, Hisamitsu's son Tadayoshi succeeded, but Hisamitsu himself held actual power.

After the assassination of the shogunate great elder (tairō) II NAOSUKE in 1860, Hisamitsu sought to bring Satsuma into national politics by promoting a policy of reconciliation between the imperial court and the Tokugawa shogunate (see MOVEMENT FOR UNION OF COURT AND SHOGUNATE). In 1862 he led a force of over 1,000 men to Kyōto, where his arrival was awaited with great eagerness by antiforeign, proimperial activists who expected Hisamitsu to lend his support to their cause. But Hisamitsu ordered activist Satsuma samurai to return to their domain, urged the court to take steps to control radical elements, and sent troops to suppress die-hard Satsuma samurai who were holding out at an inn outside Kyōto (see TERADAYA INCIDENT).

In order to push forward his plans for shogunate reform, Hisamitsu and his troops went to Edo (now Tōkyō), where he succeeded in having TOKUGAWA YOSHINOBU appointed as shogunal regent (kōkenshoku). On his way back to Kyōto, he and his entourage encountered a group of Englishmen. Members of his retinue attacked the group, killing one, when they thought the foreigners had failed to show sufficient respect for their lord (see RICHARDSON AFFAIR). In Kyōto he found that extremists from the rival domain of Chōshū (now Yamaguchi Prefecture) had taken over the city, and he withdrew to Satsuma in late 1862.

Hisamitsu returned to Kyōto following the expulsion of the Chōshū extremists in the COUP D'ETAT OF 30 SEPTEMBER 1863. He was a central figure in a newly formed council of daimyō, but the council was suspended when it became clear that the shōgun was still unwilling to relinquish his monopoly over national policy making. Thereafter Hisamitsu's influence declined, and men like ŌKUBO TOSHIMICHI and SAIGŌ TAKAMORI, who saw no alternative to overthrowing the Tokugawa regime by force, came to dominate Satsuma affairs. Hisamitsu served briefly in the Meiji government but, largely ignored for his extreme conservatism, resigned in 1876 and returned to Satsuma.

Shimazu Nariakira (1809–1858)

Daimyō of the Satsuma domain (now Kagoshima Prefecture); his Westernization program enabled Satsuma to assume a principal role in the MEIJI RESTORATION of 1868. The eldest son of Shimazu Narioki, Nariakira studied Dutch as a youth and gained a reputation for his progressive views. In 1851 he succeeded his father as daimyō with the support of ŌKUBO TOSHIMICHI, SAIGŌ TAKAMORI, and other reform-minded retainers of low rank. On their advice Nariakira initiated a series of modernizing reforms. He built a refinery for the manufacture of munitions and ordered construction of a reverberatory furnace (HANSHARO), completed in 1856, to make heavy artillery and machinery. In addition, he established the Shūseikan, a Western-style factory that produced gunpowder, glass, ceramics, and chemicals and carried out experiments in photography and telegraphy. He also built several naval vessels. Convinced that a sweeping reform of the Tokugawa shogunate was necessary to meet the threat of the West, in 1853 he urged the shogunate to employ men of talent regardless of rank and to pursue a policy of Westernization. He also called for a national league of powerful domains to supplant the autocratic rule of the Tokugawa family; to that end he supported TOKUGAWA YOSHINOBU of the Hitotsubashi branch in the 1858 shogunal succession dispute. His hopes were dashed by the appointment of II NAOSUKE as tairō (great elder) in 1858.

Shimazu Yasujirō (1897–1945)

Film director, chiefly remembered for his pioneering work in creating the shomingeki, or dramas of ordinary people. He is also credited with having created a "neo-realist" movement in Japan 10 years before the term came into use to describe a kind of postwar Italian cinema. Another of his affinities was with the jumbungaku (pure literature) movement of the 1930s. Few of his films have been seen outside Japan, but his influence on several other prominent directors was profound.

Shimazu originally trained as an actor for the fledgling Japanese cinema but soon turned his attention to script writing. He was an assistant director at SHŌCHIKU CO, LTD, for some of its pioneering silent films, such as MURATA MINORU's Rojō no reikon (Souls on the Road, 1921). He then advanced to directing his own comedies, which were distinguished by their depth and underlying seriousness. His comedies evolved naturally into a broader range of films about ordinary salaried men and working people that grew into an entire genre, the shomingeki. One of his most notable films is a blend of the shomingeki with the jumbungaku movement: Okoto to Sasuke (Okoto and Sasuke, 1935) was the first and best of numerous adaptations of TANIZAKI JUN'ICHIRŌ's novel of a young apprentice who becomes a slave to the desires of a blind musician. Shimazu was also a great teacher of film. Several of the assistants he trained—GOSHO HEINOSUKE, TOYODA SHIRŌ, and YOSHIMURA KŌZABURŌ—went on to become prominent in their own right.   David OWENS

Shimazu Yoshihiro (1535–1619)

Daimyō of the Azuchi-Momoyama period (1568–1600). Yoshihiro's father, Takahisa (1514–71), had consolidated the SHIMAZU FAMILY's control over Satsuma and Ōsumi (now Kagoshima Prefecture), the southernmost provinces of Kyūshū, and Yoshihiro's early career was spent in assisting his elder brother Yoshihisa (1533–1611) in the contest for the rest of the island against the Itō family, RYŪZŌJI FAMILY, and ŌTOMO FAMILY. The Shimazu largely attained their goals; their very success, however, in 1587 drew the massive intervention of the national unifier TOYOTOMI HIDEYOSHI into Kyūshū. Defeated and forced to submit to Hideyoshi, the Shimazu were left with their original two provinces; Yoshihisa retired from affairs and Yoshihiro became the lord of Ōsumi and the head of his house. In 1592 he participated in the first of Hideyoshi's invasions of Korea; after his return in 1595, he was on the basis of a cadastral survey (KENCHI) confirmed in a domain assessed at 560,000 koku (see KOKUDAKA) that covered Satsuma, Ōsumi, and a part of Hyūga (now Miyazaki Prefecture). Perhaps Yoshihiro's most noteworthy measure as daimyō was the prohibition of the JŌDO SHIN SECT, issued in 1597 as he embarked on Hideyoshi's second invasion of Korea; during the Edo period (1600–1868), this Buddhist sect would remain as severely proscribed as Christianity in the Shimazu domain. Although in 1592 some of his samurai had revolted against service in Korea (the rebellion of Umekita Kunikane), and Yoshihiro's forces were therefore late in joining the first invasion, he emerged as one of the Japanese heroes of the second invasion, his victory at Sach'ŏn (J: Shisen) permitting the orderly withdrawal of Japanese forces from the peninsula after Hideyoshi's death in 1598. Yoshihiro fought against the future shōgun TOKUGAWA IEYASU at Sekigahara in 1600 (see SEKIGAHARA, BATTLE OF); his breakthrough to safety through the enemy's camp as the battle was lost is famous. The Shimazu once again reached an accommodation with the victor; Yoshihiro passed on the family headship to his son Iehisa (1578–1638) and lived out the rest of his life in retirement.   George ELISON

Shimizu

View of Mt. Fuji (Fujisan) from Miho no Matsubara.

Shimbunshi Hō → Press Law of 1909

Shimbunshi Jōrei → Press Ordinance of 1875

shimbun shōsetsu

Novels serialized in newspapers. In general, a newspaper serial runs from about 100 to 300 installments, each consisting of several hundred words accompanied by an illustration. The *shimbun shōsetsu* does not differ from other novels, except that since it appears in a daily newspaper its contents tend to stress timeliness and a very Japanese concern for the season. It had a profound influence on the structure and style of the modern Japanese novel, characterized by brief encapsulated episodes and numerous climaxes and tension points.

The genre was most important in Japan from the 1890s to the 1950s. From about 1906 to 1918, in particular, many works now considered masterpieces of modern Japanese literature were first published as newspaper serials. In recent years, however, newspaper serials have commanded a smaller readership.

Growth and Development——The number and readership of newspapers in Japan grew rapidly after 1871, when the first modern daily, the *Yokohama mainichi shimbun*, appeared. There were two categories of early modern newspapers: *ōshimbun*, which emphasized political issues; and *koshimbun*, which centered on crimes, missing persons, advice, and entertaining reading. Most editors and writers for the *koshimbun* were authors of the traditional popular literary genre known as GESAKU, and their articles tended to be anecdotal, didactic, or humorous, rather than straightforward news.

It was from such *koshimbun* articles that newspaper serials originally developed. The first serialized story was *Iwata Yasohachi no hanashi* (1875), which appeared in the newspaper *Hiragana eiri shimbun*. Written by a staff member, Maeda Kōsetsu (1841–1916), it told the story of a sailor who commits a crime of passion. It was close to nonfiction in its style and relied heavily on the format of the KUSAZŌSHI stories of the latter part of the Edo period (1600–1868). Other examples of *koshimbun* fiction include Kubota Hikosaku's (1846–98) *Torioi Omatsu no den* (1877–78), published in the *Kanayomi shimbun*, and KANAGAKI ROBUN's *Dokufu Takahashi Oden no hanashi* (1879; published in book form the same year as *Takahashi Oden yasha monogatari*), published in the same paper. Because of the popularity of these stories, the *ōshimbun* also began to publish—in keeping with their dignity—political novels as well as translations of foreign novels by authors such as Alexandre Dumas the elder. It was also at about this time that the distinction between *ōshimbun* and *koshimbun* gradually began to disappear.

Once they realized the commercial potential of serialized fiction, newspapers eagerly sought to develop the genre and introduce new talent. Among the popular new writers enlisted were OZAKI KŌYŌ (1890, *Kyara makura*; published in the *Yomiuri shimbun*) and KŌDA ROHAN (1891–92, *Gojū no tō*; in *Kokkai*). The great popularity of Kōyō's *Konjiki yasha* (1897–1902), published in the *Yomiuri*, firmly established the newspaper serial as a genre; it was reported that readers could hardly wait for their morning newspapers, impatient to find out the fate of Kōyō's hapless heroine Omiya. Other notable novels serialized in this period include IZUMI KYŌKA's *Teriha kyōgen* (1896), published in the *Yomiuri*, and TOKUTOMI ROKA's *Hototogisu* (1898–99), which appeared in the *Kokumin shimbun*.

The Golden Age——The years from 1907, when NATSUME SŌSEKI resigned from Tōkyō University and became literary editor of the *Asahi shimbun*, to 1918 constituted the golden age of newspaper fiction. Most of the classics of modern literature written at that time were first published as newspaper serials, including FUTABATEI SHIMEI's *Heibon* (1907), all of Sōseki's novels from *Gubijinsō* (1907) through *Meian* (1916; tr *Light and Darkness*, 1971), SHIMAZAKI TŌSON's *Haru* (1908) and *Shinsei* (1918–19), NAGAI KAFŪ's *Reishō* (1909–10), NAGATSUKA TAKASHI's *Tsuchi* (1910), and TOKUDA SHŪSEI's *Kabi* (1911), all of which were published in the *Tōkyō asahi*. Its rival, the *Tōkyō nichinichi shimbun* (now the *Mainichi shimbun*) serialized MORI ŌGAI's *Shibue Chūsai* (1916), while the *Ōsaka mainichi shimbun* published AKUTAGAWA RYŪNOSUKE's "Gesaku zammai" (1917; tr "Absorbed in Letters," 1964) and "Jigokuhen" (1918; tr "Hell Screen," 1948), ARISHIMA TAKEO's *Umareizuru nayami* (1918; tr *The Agony of Coming into the World*, 1955), and TANIZAKI JUN'ICHIRŌ's *Haha o kouru ki* (1919). The *Yomiuri* published Kōda Rohan's *Sora utsu nami* (1903–05), Tōson's *Ie* (1910; tr *The Family*, 1976), Shūsei's *Ashiato* (1910), and SHIGA NAOYA's "Seibei to hyōtan" (1913; tr "Seibei and Gourds," 1979). Some of these works were the first successes for their authors, and many are remembered as their masterpieces.

Newspapers actively sought out writers and provided them with economic security; no sooner did the *Asahi* sign an exclusive contract with Sōseki than its major rival, the *Mainichi*, signed on Ōgai, while the *Yomiuri* was for a time the stronghold of the Japanese naturalist school. It was, in short, a honeymoon period between newspapers and writers.

Popularization——In the years following World War I, newspaper circulation climbed rapidly, but the increase in the number of readers brought with it a decline in the quality of newspaper fiction, and the popular novel known as the *taishū shōsetsu* came to be the mainstay of newspaper serials. Representative popular novels dealing with contemporary life include KIKUCHI KAN's *Shinju fujin* (1920; published in the *Tōkyō nichinichi* and *Ōsaka mainichi*) and *Daini no seppun* (1925; in the *Asahi*), and YOSHIYA NOBUKO's *Otto no teisō* (1936–37; in the *Tōkyō nichinichi*). Popular novels with a historical setting included OSARAGI JIRŌ's *Akō rōshi* (1927–28; in the *Tōkyō nichinichi*), SHIRAI KYŌJI's *Fuji ni tatsu kage* (1924–27; in the *Hōchi shimbun*), and YOSHIKAWA EIJI's *Miyamoto Musashi* (1935–39; in the *Tōkyō asahi*; tr *Musashi*, 1981). Some works of high literary quality continued to be published, including Tanizaki's *Chijin no ai* (1924–25; in the *Ōsaka asahi*), Kafū's *Bokutō kidan* (1937; in the *Tōkyō asahi*; tr *A Strange Tale from East of the River*, 1958), and the first part of YOKOMITSU RIICHI's *Ryoshū* (1937; in the *Tōkyō nichinichi*). During World War II, Shishi Bunroku's *Kaigun* (1942; in the *Tōkyō asahi*) met with the approval of the authorities, but other novels such as Tokuda Shūsei's *Shukuzu* (1941; in the *Miyako shimbun*) were forced to suspend publication, and in general the war years were a dark period for newspaper fiction.

Postwar Period——In the decade immediately following Japan's defeat, it seemed that the golden age of newspaper fiction had been revived. Nurtured by a new vigor in journalistic activity, notable newspaper serials appeared in rapid succession, including ISHIZAKA YŌJIRŌ's *Aoi sammyaku* (1947; in the *Asahi*) and Shishi Bunroku's *Jiyū gakkō* (1950; in the *Asahi*), both of which depicted contemporary manners and mores, and historical novels such as MURAKAMI GENZŌ's *Sasaki Kojirō* (1949–50; in the *Asahi*) and YAMAMOTO SHŪGORŌ's *Momi no ki wa nokotta* (1954–56; in the *Nihon keizai shimbun*). Other popular authors were FUNAHASHI SEIICHI, HAYASHI FUSAO, HINO ASHIHEI, YAMAOKA SŌHACHI, and Osaragi Jirō. Writers generally identified with "pure" (as opposed to popular) literature, including KAWABATA YASUNARI (1950–51, *Maihime*; in the *Asahi*) and Tanizaki (1949–50, *Shōshō Shigemoto no haha*; in the *Mainichi*; partial tr *The Mother of Captain Shigemoto*, 1956) also applied their talents to newspaper serials. However, with the spread of television starting in the early 1950s and the growth of new weekly magazines, newspaper fiction began to lose much of its audience. Even so, the form remains popular, and such writers as ISHIKAWA TATSUZŌ, INOUE YASUSHI, MATSUMOTO SEICHŌ, ENDŌ SHŪSAKU, ARIYOSHI SAWAKO, SHIBA RYŌTARŌ, MINAKAMI TSUTOMU, and TANABE SEIKO retain large followings.

——Takagi Takeo, *Shimbun shōsetsu shi: Meiji hen* (1974). Takagi Takeo, *Shimbun shōsetsu shi: Taishō hen* (1976).

ASAI Kiyoshi

shimbutsu bunri → Shintō and Buddhism, separation of

shimbutsu shūgō → syncretism

Shimizu

City in central Shizuoka Prefecture, central Honshū. On Suruga Bay, it developed as a POST-STATION TOWN on the highway Tōkaidō during the Edo period (1600–1868). The port of Shimizu is a base for deep-sea fishing. Principal industries are shipbuilding and canned goods production; main agricultural products are mandarin oranges, strawberries, and tea. Many tourists visit the scenic hills of NIHONDAIRA as well as MIHO NO MATSUBARA, a famed pine grove on the beach of the Miho spit. Pop: 241,578. See photo on previous page.

Shimizu Construction Co, Ltd

(Shimizu Kensetsu). One of Japan's leading construction firms, Shimizu traces its history back to 1804. In 1868 it built one of Japan's first Western-style buildings, the Tsukiji Hotel, and it went on to construct many of Japan's major modern buildings. It is now active in the construction of high-rise buildings, atomic power facilities, and other energy installations, as well as local development projects. It has 7 subsidiaries overseas and 11 overseas offices. Future plans call for the firm's development into an engineering and construction company of international scale, utilizing its high level of technology. Sales for the fiscal year ending March 1982 totaled ¥777 billion (US $3.2 billion), of which construction accounted for 75 percent, public works projects 24 percent, and real estate 1 percent; overseas construction projects accounted for 6 percent of this total. The company was capitalized at ¥34 billion (US $141.2 million) in the same year. Corporate headquarters are located in Tōkyō.

Shimizu Hamaomi (1776–1824)

KOKUGAKU (National Learning) scholar and WAKA poet of the late Edo period. Born in Edo (now Tōkyō). A practicing physician, he produced exegetic and philological studies of the literary classics. His main works include the *waka* collection *Sazanaminoyashū*, written in an elegant yet fresh style, often employing classical themes, and published posthumously in 1829 by his son Mitsufusa, and *Gorin ruiyō*, a glossary of the poetry of the Heian period (794–1185).

Shimizu Muneharu (?–1582)

A vassal of the MŌRI FAMILY, lords of several provinces in western Honshū, who is famous for the dramatic circumstances of his suicide. Muneharu was the holder of Takamatsu Castle in Bitchū (now part of the city of Okayama), a powerful fortress situated in swampy terrain. In the early summer of 1582 it was besieged by TOYOTOMI HIDEYOSHI, who was waging a campaign against the Mōri on behalf of the hegemon ODA NOBUNAGA. It was the rainy season, and by diverting the waters of the river Ashimorigawa, Hideyoshi flooded the castle. With the surroundings "transformed into a lake," according to a contemporary account, the Mōri attempt to relieve Takamatsu Castle was frustrated; moreover, it was known that Nobunaga himself was preparing to join the campaign and had ordered several generals, including AKECHI MITSUHIDE, to move strong forces to this front. Hence the Mōri were prepared to sign an armistice whose conditions were the surrender of Takamatsu and Muneharu's suicide; the garrison would be spared in exchange for the castellan's death. This agreement was jeopardized when, late on the evening of 22 June 1582 (Tenshō 10.6.3), word reached Hideyoshi that Mitsuhide had assassinated Nobunaga in Kyōto the previous day (see HONNŌJI INCIDENT). This momentous news was, however, successfully kept from the Mōri, and the next morning Shimizu Muneharu committed *seppuku* (HARAKIRI) in a small boat on the waters surrounding the fortress. With the armistice concluded, Hideyoshi rushed to the Kyōto area; he eliminated Mitsuhide at the Battle of YAMAZAKI nine days after Muneharu's suicide, and thereupon began his career as national unifier.

George ELISON

Shimmei Masamichi (1898–)

Sociologist. Born in Taiwan. After graduating from Tōkyō University, he taught at various universities, including Kansei Gakuin University, Tōhoku University, and Chūō University. Shimmei developed a theoretical system integrating what he called general sociology, historical sociology, and practical sociology. He also contributed to the advancement of Japanese sociology through his critical introductions to Japan of American sociology, schematic studies of the development of various social theories, and the compilation of a dictionary of the social sciences, *Shakaigaku jiten* (1944). Among Shimmei's many works are *Shakai honshitsu ron* (1942, The Essence of Society), *Shakaigaku shi gaisetsu* (1954, An Outline History of Sociology), and *Shimmei Masamichi chosakushū* (The Collected Works of Shimmei Masamichi), 11 vols (Seishin Shobō, 1976–).

HASUMI Otohiko

Shimmi Masaoki (1822–1869)

Official of the Tokugawa shogunate. Appointed as commissioner of foreign affairs (GAIKOKU BUGYŌ) in 1859, the following year he was chosen as one of the leaders of the delegation to Washington, DC, to exchange ratifications of the United States–Japan Treaty of Amity and Commerce (see UNITED STATES, MISSION OF 1860 TO). Returning to Japan, he found the country swept by antiforeign sentiment, and although promoted to the important position of *sobashū* (chamberlain), he was obliged to retire in 1864.

Shimminato

City in northern Toyama Prefecture, central Honshū. Located at the mouth of the river Shōgawa, it first developed as a river port. The opening of an aluminum plant in 1968 has led to rapid industrialization. Fishing is also important. Pop: 43,094.

Shimmura Izuru (1876–1967)

Philologist. Born in Yamaguchi Prefecture, Shimmura graduated from Tōkyō University. After studying in Europe he taught at Kyōto University and in 1956 was awarded the Order of Culture. Continuing in the tradition of UEDA KAZUTOSHI he introduced Western linguistic methods to Japan and devoted himself to the establishment of the scientific study of language and of the Japanese language in particular. He is also known for his research on the introduction into Japan of NAMBAN or Western culture by Europeans in the 16th and 17th centuries. Among his works are: *Tōhō gengo shi sōkō* (1927), essays on the history of oriental languages; *Tōa gogen shi* (1930), an etymological study of East Asian languages; *Kōjien* (1955), a Japanese language dictionary; and *Namban kōki* (1925), a study of Namban culture. His complete works were published in 15 volumes in 1971–73.

UWANO Zendō

Shimobe

Town in southwestern Yamanashi Prefecture, central Honshū. It is primarily known for its hot springs, which were patronized by the 16th-century warlord TAKEDA SHINGEN. FUJI FIVE LAKES and the temple MINOBUSAN are within easy reach. A Takeda Shingen festival is held every May at Kumano Shrine here. Pop: 7,719.

Shimoda

City in eastern Shizuoka prefecture, central Honshū, on the Izu Peninsula. In the Edo period (1600–1868) Shimoda was a prosperous port of call for ships transporting goods between Edo (now Tōkyō) and Ōsaka. At the conclusion of the KANAGAWA TREATY with the United States in 1854 it became an open port. In 1856 the first American consulate general was opened with Townsend HARRIS as its head. The port is a base for fishing off the Izu Peninsula; shipbuilding and marine food processing industries, as well as abalone and shrimp farming, are active. Attractions are the temple Ryōsenji, where the Kanagawa Treaty was signed; the temple Gyokusenji, where Harris lived; Shimoda Hot Spring; and the Black Ship Festival in May. Pop: 31,007.

Shimodate

City in western Ibaraki Prefecture, central Honshū. At one time known for its *tabi* (cotton socks worn with *kimono*), Shimodate now has electrical appliance and confectionery plants. Pop: 61,325.

Shimoda Utako (1854–1936)

Educator. Original name, Hirao Seki. Born into a *samurai* family of the Iwamura domain (now Gifu Prefecture), she began seven years of court service in 1873; she was given the name Utako by the empress in recognition of her poetic talents. She left the court to marry Shimoda Takeo but was widowed in 1884. Encouraged by friends such as the oligarch ITŌ HIROBUMI, she began during her husband's long illness to teach the Japanese and Chinese classics in her home to the wives and daughters of the elite; from 1881 to 1885, she ran a private school for about 50 such students, known as the Tōyō Gakkō (or Tōyō Jojuku). Then she turned her attention to helping to establish in 1885 an official school for female relatives of the peerage (called Kazoku Jogakkō; from 1896, Gakushūin Jogakubu). From 1893 to 1895 she toured Europe and the United States to observe methods of educating women. As a woman often in the public eye, she was the subject of various attacks in the media; for example, she was charged with using her influence at court to further the schemes of a Shintō soothsayer named Iino Kichisaburō (1867–1944), who was dubbed "Japan's Rasputin."

In 1898, to promote educational and charitable activities for women throughout Japan, Utako and other women from the elite formed the Teikoku Fujin Kyōkai (Imperial Women's Society), which published the magazine *Nihon fujin* (Japanese Women). The next year, after leaving her position as superintendent at the Peers' School for Girls, she was able to put into practice her ideas on education for those at other social levels by founding the Jissen Girls' School (now Jissen Women's University) and, for training in practical skills, the Joshi Kōgei Gakkō (Women's Crafts School). She also opened in 1904 a school for Chinese women in Japan. Furthermore, she helped to form the patriotic women's society AIKOKU FUJINKAI in 1901 and later served as its president (1920–31). She published WAKA poems, a diary titled *Hana fubuki* (Snowstorm of Flowers), and many works advocating improved women's education for the sake of Japan's future.

Shimokita Peninsula

(Shimokita Hantō). Located in northeastern Aomori Prefecture, northern Honshū, projecting north into the Tsugaru Strait, and embracing Mutsu Bay to the southwest. This desolate mountain region includes OSOREZAN, a volcanic group, and numerous hot springs. ŌMAZAKI, a cape at the northern tip of the peninsula, is the northernmost point of Honshū. Fishing, forestry, and sightseeing are the main industries; Mutsu is the major city. Much of the peninsula is included in Shimokita Peninsula Quasi-National Park.

Shimokōbe Chōryū (1624–1686)

Also known as Shimokōbe Nagaru. WAKA poet and classical scholar of the early part of the Edo period (1600–1868). Son of a *samurai*; born in Yamato Province (now Nara Prefecture). He is known particularly for his extensive research on the poetic anthology MAN'YŌ-SHŪ (ca 759), culminating in the *Man'yōshū kanken* (ca 1661) which contributed many insights and influenced *Man'yōshū* scholarship of the later Edo period. Influenced by KINOSHITA CHŌSHŌSHI, he sought to free *waka* poetry from the constrictive formulas and secret traditions that were prevalent at this time, and so in compiling the anthology *Rin'yō ruijinshū* (1670) included a number of poems by commoners. KEICHŪ, a close friend of his, carried on the tradition of scholarship that Chōryū had pioneered and also compiled the *Bankashū* (1686), a posthumous anthology of Chōryū's poetry.

Shimomoto Kenkichi (1897–1957)

Leader of the Japanese immigrant community in Brazil. Born in Kōchi Prefecture, Shimomoto emigrated to Brazil at the age of 16. He helped establish the Cotia Cooperative Society, one of Brazil's first agricultural cooperative societies, and, as its managing director, continued to guide immigrant farmers until his death. Sincere and active, Shimomoto helped reorient the Japanese community during the difficult years following World War II. *Saitō Hiroshi*

Shimomura Kanzan (1873–1930)

An eclectic Japanese-style painter. Born in Wakayama Prefecture to a family of NŌ artists. When his father moved to Tōkyō in 1881,

Kanzan studied with KANŌ HŌGAI and, from 1886, with HASHIMOTO GAHŌ. He attended the Tōkyō Bijutsu Gakkō (now Tōkyō University of Fine Arts and Music), where he became a faculty member in 1894. When OKAKURA KAKUZŌ resigned its directorship in 1898 and founded the JAPAN FINE ARTS ACADEMY (Nihon Bijutsuin), Kanzan joined him; he also resumed teaching at the Tōkyō Bijutsu Gakkō from 1901 to 1908. From 1903 to 1905 he studied in England. In 1914 he helped to form the reorganized Japan Fine Arts Academy, and in 1917 was appointed an artist for the imperial household *(teishitsu gigeiin)*. He was both a judge and an exhibitor at the BUNTEN and Inten exhibitions. He was a student of early Buddhist iconographic painting and TOSA SCHOOL narrative handscrolls. Blending such traditional influences with elements from the KANŌ SCHOOL and from RIMPA-style painting with a dash of Western realism, he evolved a distinctive style for his traditional subject matter. Among his best-known paintings are *Autumn in the Forest* (1907), *Interference by Demons* (1910), *The White Fox* (1914), and *Portrait of Tenshin* (1922). See also NIHONGA.

Frederick BAEKELAND

Shimonaka Yasaburō (1878–1961)

Founder of the publishing house Heibonsha (see HEIBONSHA, LTD, PUBLISHERS); educator and political activist. Born in Hyōgo Prefecture. Largely self-educated, having had only a few years of elementary school, Shimonaka earned a teaching certificate and taught at Saitama Normal School. He founded Heibonsha in 1914, which published an inexpensive series of books of popular fiction and fine arts in the 1920s and a multivolume dictionary and encyclopedia in the 1930s. A social reformer, he also acted as a leader in various education, labor, and women's movements, and founded Japan's first teachers' union, the Keimeikai, in 1919. Shimonaka gradually adopted a nationalist stance, however, and in the 1930s, founded and served in several rightist organizations. After World War II he was purged by OCCUPATION authorities for his prewar and wartime activities. Returning to Heibonsha in 1951, he published in succession several encyclopedias, thereby establishing Heibonsha as one of Japan's foremost publishers of reference works. His political interests took a new turn, and during the last decade of his life he participated actively in the World Federation Movement and served on the COMMITTEE OF SEVEN TO APPEAL FOR WORLD PEACE. *FUKUDA Kizō*

Shimonita

Town in southwestern Gumma Prefecture, central Honshū. It is known for its Welsh onions and *konnyaku* (a common ingredient in Japanese cooking). Charcoal and silk industries are also active. Shimonita is the gateway to the Myōgi–Arafune–Saku Kōgen Quasi-National Park. Pop: 15,228.

Shimonoseki

City in southwestern Yamaguchi Prefecture, western Honshū, on the Kammon Strait. It was the seat of the provincial capital *(kokufu)* of Nagato Province in the ancient past. The Battle of DANNOURA, in which the Taira were destroyed by the Minamoto, was fought in the sea near here in 1185. The city was bombarded by foreign battleships during the closing days of the Tokugawa shogunate (see SHIMONOSEKI BOMBARDMENT). Today it is the largest commercial city in the prefecture as well as one of the biggest deep-sea fishing bases in the country. Principal industries include processing of marine products, shipbuilding, and manufacture of fishing tackle. There are large metal and chemical plants. Shimonoseki is served by several railway lines and is connected to Kyūshū by two undersea rail tunnels and a highway tunnel (the Kammon Tunnels) and the 1,068 m (3,503 ft) Kammon Bridge (a highway bridge). Tourist attractions include the Sumiyoshi Shrine, Akama Shrine, Hinoyama Park, and the Shimonoseki Aquarium. Pop: 268,964. See photo on the following page.

Shimonoseki Bombardment

(Shikoku Kantai Shimonoseki Hōgeki Jiken; also known as Bakan Sensō). Naval expedition of September 1864 against the Chōshū domain (now Yamaguchi Prefecture) by the joint forces of Britain, France, the Netherlands, and the United States in retaliation for Chōshū's attacks on Western ships passing through the Shimonoseki Strait.

The ANSEI COMMERCIAL TREATIES signed in 1858 by the Tokugawa shogunate opened Japan to trade with Western nations. Antiforeign, antishogunate activists, who were eager to see the treaties abrogated, persuaded the imperial court to issue an edict setting 25 June 1863 (Bunkyū 3.5.10) as the date for "expelling the barbarians" (see SONNŌ JŌI). On that day Chōshū shore batteries fired on an American ship passing through the Shimonoseki Strait, at the western end of the Inland Sea, and similarly attacked other Western ships in the following month. Sir Rutherford ALCOCK, the British minister, rallied British, French, Dutch, and American forces to launch a punitive mission against Chōshū. Between 5 and 8 September 1864 (Genji 1.8.5-8) 17 Western ships bombarded the Shimonoseki emplacements, and a landing party seized and destroyed Chōshū's weapons and fortifications. A truce was reached on 14 September; its terms exacted from the shogunate an immense indemnity of 3 million Mexican dollars.

This incident, closely following the defeat of Chōshū activists in a takeover attempt in Kyōto on 20 August (see HAMAGURI GOMON INCIDENT), discredited the antishogunate, anti-Western faction in Chōshū. Moreover, the shogunate's inability to pay the indemnity was used as a bargaining tool by the new British minister, Sir Harry PARKES, who secured further trade concessions in return for deferral of payment.

Shimonoseki ——— Kammon Bridge

Japan's longest suspension bridge and the ninth longest suspension bridge in the world at the time of its construction in 1973, the Kammon Bridge over the Kammon Strait links Honshū and Kyūshū. Looking from Shimonoseki on the Honshū side toward the city of Kita Kyūshū in Kyūshū.

Shimonoseki, Treaty of

(Shimonoseki Jōyaku). Treaty concluding the SINO-JAPANESE WAR OF 1894–1895, signed at Shimonoseki, Yamaguchi Prefecture, on 17 April 1895 and ratified by the two countries in the following month. The treaty was a product of Japanese territorial ambitions on the Asian continent, Chinese efforts to thwart them, and Western pressures. Although the immediate cause of the war had been the Korean question (see KOREA AND JAPAN: early modern relations), the Japanese government was interested in more than simply detaching Korea from Chinese influence. With each victory on land or sea, the Japanese armed forces, political parties, press, and intellectuals felt justified in insisting on more and more spoils of war. In part this reflected the feeling that here was a real opportunity for the nation to augment its wealth and power. Japan would be doing only what other countries had done in times of war. The army, in particular, was interested in obtaining territory in southern Manchuria in order to prevent another power, specifically Russia, from interfering in Korean politics. The navy, for its part, had its eyes on the island of Taiwan as a base for future operations.

Perhaps even more important than these specific aims was the psychology of peacemaking. The war, together with the recently signed treaty in which Britain had relinquished its privileges of extraterritoriality in Japan (see ANGLO-JAPANESE COMMERCIAL TREATY OF 1894), persuaded the Japanese that their long quest for great-power status had finally been attained. Henceforth Japan would be regarded as an equal of the great Western powers and as such could now obtain the same rights in China that the latter had conceded to Western countries. Having freed itself from the unequal treaties with Britain, Japan would now impose one upon China. Furthermore, great-power status meant economic development and expansion. The Japanese would make use of their military successes to promote industrialization at home and expansion abroad. A large indemnity payment from China would provide the capital needed to develop heavy industry. The peace settlement would also enable Japanese to go abroad in large numbers. Expansion, as many publicists noted, need not be limited to colonial activities; it could involve commercial and agricultural enterprises as well. The Japanese, in any event, should be provided an outlet for their energies and resources, not only on the Asian continent but also in the South Seas.

The terms of peace that the Japanese plenipotentiary ITŌ HIROBUMI presented to his Chinese counterpart LI HONGZHANG (Li Hung-chang) at Shimonoseki reflected all these strands of thinking. Japan demanded that China recognize Korea as an independent country, cede the Liaodong (Liaotung) Peninsula, Taiwan, and the Pescadores Islands, pay an indemnity of 200 million taels over seven years (the indemnity was paid in Europe in British money), and sign a commercial treaty similar to those the Chinese government had concluded with Western powers. These demands were more than the Chinese were willing to yield. At first they had thought that the guarantee of Korean independence would be enough. They were also hopeful that the Western powers would persuade Japan to moderate its terms. No such intercession was forthcoming, however,

during the peace conference, and in the end Li had no choice but to give in. Originally, he had sought to draw the Japanese into talks on a Chinese-Japanese entente against the greedy Western countries. He had recognized the need to stabilize relations between the two countries and advised his government to end the war quickly.

A few days after the treaty was signed, Germany, France, and Russia intervened to force Japan to give up the Liaodong Peninsula (see TRIPARTITE INTERVENTION); but they did not object to the rest of the peace terms and even concurred with Japan's demand that China increase the indemnity by 30 million taels as compensation. Although the Japanese were incensed at the intervention, there is little doubt that the treaty marked the beginning of Japanese imperialistic expansion at the expense of China. Japan would now exploit China for strategic, political, and economic ends. Not surprisingly, Chinese public opinion turned strongly against the government for having consented to such a humiliating agreement. At the same time it is interesting that some of the Chinese who most bitterly denounced the treaty would soon find much to emulate in Japan's development since the Meiji Restoration (1868). They would return to Japan as a source of inspiration and support, and in Japan a pan-Asianist movement would emerge, stressing the theme of Asian solidarity.

—— Hilary Conroy, *Japan's Seizure of Korea* (1963). Ian Nish, *The Anglo-Japanese Alliance* (1966). Tabohashi Kiyoshi, *Nisshin sen'eki gaikō shi no kenkyū* (1951). Akira IRIYE

Shimose Masachika (1859–1911)

Developer of Shimose gunpowder, the powerful explosive that gave the Japanese Imperial Navy an important edge against the Russian fleets during the RUSSO-JAPANESE WAR. Born in what is now Hiroshima Prefecture, he graduated from Tōkyō University's College of Engineering in 1884. He became a navy technician in 1887 and a year later developed his superior gunpowder, using picric acid as its main ingredient. He was one of Japan's earliest doctors of engineering.

Shimo Suwa

Town in central Nagano Prefecture, central Honshū, on Lake Suwa. In the Edo period (1600–1868) it developed as a POST-STATION TOWN at the junction of several important highways. It was also known for its hot spring. From the Meiji period (1868–1912) silk reeling flourished, but this has been replaced since World War II by precision-instrument, knitting, and *miso* (bean paste) industries. The hot spring, Suwa Grand Shrine, Lake Suwa, and the Kirigamine highland are major attractions. Pop: 26,575.

shimotsuke

Spiraea japonica. A deciduous shrub of the rose family (Rosaceae) which grows wild in mountainous regions throughout Japan and is also cultivated as an ornamental. Its distribution extends to Korea and China. The stems grow in bundles and reach about 1 meter (3 ft) high. The leaves are alternate and oblong to broadly lanceolate, with serrated margins. Around June small pink aromatic flowers of five petals develop in clusters (corymbs) at the ends of the branches. Similar species found in Japan include *iwashimotsuke (S. nipponica)* with white flowers, *maruba shimotsuke (S. betulifolia)* with round leaves and white flowers, *yukiyanagi (S. thunbergii)* with numerous small, almost stalkless white flowers on thin twigs, and *kodemari (S. cantoniensis)* with ball-like clusters (umbels) of white flowers.

MATSUDA Osamu

Shimotsuma

City in western Ibaraki Prefecture, central Honshū, on the river Kinugawa. Shimotsuma developed as a castle town and river port. Its mainstay has been agriculture, with rice as the chief product. Vegetable and fruit cultivation has begun in recent years and industrialization is also proceeding. Pop: 30,731.

Shimoyama Incident

(Shimoyama Jiken). A controversial criminal incident of the Allied OCCUPATION period. On the morning of 6 July 1949 the dismembered body of Shimoyama Sadanori (1900–1949), then president of the Japanese National Railways (JNR), was found alongside some railway tracks in Adachi Ward in northern Tōkyō. He had been run over by a train.

Shimoyama had been at the center of national controversy during the spring of 1949. Japan was beginning to implement the so-called DODGE LINE—the policies of radical economic retrenchment, balanced budgets, and promotion of exports that had been recommended for the economic rehabilitation of Japan by Joseph M. Dodge, an American banker and the chief economic consultant to the Supreme Commander for the Allied Powers (SCAP). As president of the JNR, which was the country's largest economic enterprise and one of the chief causes of the inflationary drain from the national treasury, Shimoyama was under orders from the government and from SCAP to fire some 97,000 national railway employees during July. Only two days before his death, he had approved dismissal notices for 37,000 workers. SCAP and the Japanese government were also pressing Shimoyama to proceed promptly with the layoffs because the National Railway Workers' Union (NRWU) was dominated by the Japan Communist Party. The Occupation authorities and the government of Prime Minister YOSHIDA SHIGERU intended to use the firings to break the hold of the Communist Party over the NRWU, and communist workers were prominent among those being dismissed.

A furious controversy developed concerning the autopsy of Shimoyama's corpse. Two professors of forensic medicine at Tōkyō University Medical School, who actually conducted the autopsy, concluded that Shimoyama had been dead when his body was hit by the train. They believed that Shimoyama had been murdered and then placed on the tracks. This view was attacked by a professor of Keiō University Medical School, who argued that Shimoyama had committed suicide by placing himself on the tracks. The police and the public prosecutors were divided over the murder versus the suicide theory of Shimoyama's death, and the matter was carried to the House of Representatives of the Diet, where it was debated. The police at first accepted the murder theory, but they subsequently reversed their view and endorsed the conclusion that Shimoyama had committed suicide.

The dispute over Shimoyama's death was always more political than medical, and the controversy continued well into the 1960s. During the Occupation period conservative opinion generally held that Shimoyama had been murdered, probably by NRWU communists in retaliation for their having been fired. Leftist groups sought instead to show that he had committed suicide out of remorse over his responsibility for dismissing so many workers. Twenty years later the positions had become reversed. Left-wing writers on the case came to argue that Shimoyama was murdered, not by communists but by agents of SCAP for the alleged motives of discrediting the unions and bringing in a tougher JNR president, while conservatives accepted the police view that he had, in fact, committed suicide, having been driven to the breaking point by the rigid economies of the Dodge line.

The main writer on the incident to hold that Shimoyama was probably murdered by the Americans has been the novelist MATSU-

MOTO SEICHŌ. The authorities do not regard the Shimoyama case as unsolved, having declared it to be a suicide, but in 1968 a group of prominent professors and intellectuals, including NAMBARA SHIGERU, former president of Tōkyō University, formed the Association to Study the Shimoyama Case, in order to continue the investigation. The latest development in the controversy has been the publication in 1976 of a book by Satō Hajime, one of the defendants in another celebrated Occupation case, the MATSUKAWA INCIDENT. Satō began his 12-year study of the evidence convinced that Shimoyama had been murdered, but the conclusion reached in the book is that his death was the result of suicide.

The significance of the incident lies in the belief of the press and public during 1949 that Shimoyama, a high-ranking public official, had been murdered by communist railroad workers. Together with the Matsukawa Incident and the MITAKA INCIDENT, both of which also occurred during the summer of 1949, the Shimoyama case was a factor in turning public opinion against the Communist Party and in favor of the policies of economic recovery and alliance with the United States advocated by the Liberal Party (Jiyūtō). These three incidents marked the turning point in the Occupation of Japan from an emphasis on "democratization" to an emphasis on economic growth.

——Chalmers Johnson, *Conspiracy at Matsukawa* (1972). Matsumoto Seichō, *Nihon no kuroi kiri* (1962). Shimoyama Jiken Kenkyūkai, ed, *Shiryō Shimoyama jiken* (1969). Chalmers JOHNSON

Shimozawa Kan (1892–1968)

Novelist. Real name Umetani Matsutarō. Born in Hokkaidō. Graduate of Meiji University. After working as a newspaper reporter in Tōkyō, he turned to writing popular historical novels about the latter part of the Edo period (1600–1868). He was drawn to that age because of his family's Edo heritage, and his grandfather's loyalty to the shōgun during the time of the Meiji Restoration (1868). His works are faithful to historical detail and known for their fine descriptions of people and life in old Edo (now Tōkyō). His principal novels include *Shinsengumi shimatsuki* (1928), *Kunisada Chūji* (1932–33), and *Oyakodaka* (1955–56).

shimpa

The first modern Japanese theatrical movement and tradition. *Shimpa* means "new school," in opposition to KABUKI, the old school of theater.

Shimpa is distinct from the subsequent form of modern theater known as SHINGEKI (new theater). The latter closely resembles the modern theater as found in most Western countries, whereas *shimpa* is an intermediate form descended from the kabuki tradition.

In 1888, radical agitator Sudō Sadanori (1867–1907) assembled a few amateurs and began to stage crude plays as vehicles for his political tirades, which had been suppressed by the police. Sudō's moderate success attracted another FREEDOM AND PEOPLE'S RIGHTS MOVEMENT agitator, KAWAKAMI OTOJIRŌ. Kawakami organized a would-be professional troupe in early 1891 and traveled throughout the country performing political plays.

As Kawakami's political activism abated, he turned to melodrama. During the Sino-Japanese War of 1894–95, he staged spectacular patriotic dramas that reproduced battle scenes on stage. By outgrossing all other theatrical attractions, Kawakami established the commercial viability of "modern" drama, although these early productions of his—despite their contemporary settings and crude theatrical realism—relied heavily on traditional acting style and staging techniques.

One of Kawakami's earliest associates, Ii Yōhō (1871–1932), organized a rival troupe, Saibikan, in 1891 in association with kabuki playwright Yoda Gakkai (1833–1909). This group used actresses and thereby ended the two-and-a-half-century-old ban on mixed casts of men and women; the practice was later adopted by Kawakami's and other troupes. The Saibikan and its successors sought to create a realistic style for plays based on Japanese history.

In 1905 Ii, Takata Minoru (1871–1916), KITAMURA ROKURŌ, Kawai Takeo (1877–1942), and other leading new school actors joined forces. They drew extensively on adaptations of best-selling melodramatic novels such as OZAKI KŌYŌ's *Konjiki yasha* (1897–1902; tr *The Golden Demon*, 1905), Kikuchi Yūhō's *Ono ga tsumi* (1899–1900, My Sin), and TOKUTOMI ROKA's *Hototogisu* (1898–99; tr *Namiko*, 1904) to create a basic *shimpa* repertoire. Because *shimpa* actors were at last equal in skill to their kabuki counterparts and because their vehicles were "modern" in a so-called age of modernization, *shimpa* was able to dominate the Japanese theater during the first decade of the 20th century. This "Golden Age of Shimpa" (also known as the "Hongōza Era" after the Tōkyō theater where most of the plays were staged) set the essential *shimpa* form: women's roles shared by ONNAGATA (female impersonators) and a few actresses; an acting style with realist pretensions which stressed virtuoso performance; stories set in a contemporary milieu; and plots dominated by melodramatic action and pathos.

During the following decade, *shimpa* became the stylistic basis for the earliest Japanese motion pictures with contemporary settings. Several *shimpa* troupes also developed a highly popular mixed medium called "chained drama" in which action scenes on film were alternated with dialogue scenes on stage. Although other theatrical activities overshadowed *shimpa* after the early 1910s, the popularity of its female impersonators and the nostalgic appeal of its turn-of-the-century stories kept the form alive.

Shimpa underwent major reform after the success of Seto Eiichi's (1892–1934) *Futasujimichi* (Two Paths) in 1931. With the appearance of this and other new plays by writers who could fully exploit what *shimpa* had to offer, the primary focus shifted from melodrama to slice-of-life stories set in the world of the GEISHA and other feminine subcultures. The principal creator of the new repertoire was KAWAGUCHI MATSUTARŌ with his *Fūryū Fukagawa uta* (1935, Song of the Elegant Fukagawa), *Meiji ichidai onna* (1935, Life of a Meiji Era Woman), and *Tsuruhachi Tsurujirō* (1934, Tsuruhachi and Tsurujirō). Yagi Ryūichirō (1906–65), TANIZAKI JUN'ICHIRŌ, IZUMI KYŌKA, and other major novelist-playwrights also wrote finely crafted vehicles for female impersonators Kitamura Rokurō and HANAYAGI SHŌTARŌ and for *shimpa* actresses, principally MIZUTANI YAEKO.

Since the 1949 consolidation of *shimpa* production into the one troupe that is active today, there have been many successful seasons built around the old and new works of Kawaguchi. HŌJŌ HIDEJI also provided such widely acclaimed additions to the repertoire as *Okami* (1952, Madame) and *Kottai-san* (1955, Courtesan). With the deaths of its irreplaceable female impersonator stars, *shimpa* productions are now dominated by strong actresses. Mizutani Yaeko, the former head of the troupe, was for many years regarded as the leading stage actress of Japan. *Shimpa* continues to face shrinking audiences but remains dedicated more to preservation than to change. The troupe remains true to its traditions as a showcase for virtuosity, nostalgia, sentiment, and gynecocracy.
—— Hōjō Hideji, *Shimpa gunzō* (1976). Yanagi Eijirō, *Shimpa no rokujūnen* (1948).   J. L. ANDERSON

shimpan

(related houses or collateral *daimyō*). In *samurai* society the kinsmen of a lord were variously identified as *ichimon*, *ichizoku*, or *kamon*. The Tokugawa shogunate (1603–1867) designated the 20-or-so *kamon* lineages that were descended by birth or adoption from TOKUGAWA IEYASU (and were of *daimyō* status and hence held domains, or HAN) as *shimpan*, literally "related *(shin)* domains *(han)*." These *shimpan* lineages mostly derived from Ieyasu through the GOSANKE *daimyō* of the Mito (now part of Ibaraki Prefecture), Owari (now part of Aichi Prefecture), and Kii domains (now Wakayama Prefecture) and Ieyasu's descendants living in Echizen Province (now part of Fukui Prefecture); see list under TOKUGAWA FAMILY. *Shimpan* domains ranged in size from mighty Owari with an assessed income of 619,000 *koku* (see KOKUDAKA) to such inconsequential domains of 10,000 *koku* as Yada and Itoigawa. See also GOSANKYŌ.   *Conrad* TOTMAN

Shimpeitai Incident

("Divine Soldiers" Incident). Conspiracy by rightist civilians and military officers to establish by force a nationalist-military regime; uncovered in July 1933. Suzuki Zen'ichi of the ultranationalist Dai Nippon Seisantō (Great Japan Production Party), together with members of the Aikoku Kinrōtō (Patriotic Labor Party), and Commander Yamaguchi Saburō of the navy (brother of the ultranationalist INOUE NISSHŌ), planned to organize several thousand "divine soldiers" *(shimpei)*, bomb by air the prime minister's residence and the Diet building, take over the headquarters of the liberal parties as well as the Metropolitan Police headquarters, attack a bank and an industrialists' club, and assassinate prominent politicians. They

hoped that martial law would then be declared and a military government set up. An advance party assembled at the Meiji Shrine Hall on 10 July. Their arrest (the police had been particularly watchful since the MAY 15TH INCIDENT of the previous year) led to the discovery of the plot. The trials of the conspirators did not begin until November 1937. They were given mild sentences, not on charges of conspiracy to raise an insurrection but for having planned to commit arson and homicide. They were all released in March 1941. The arrest of the principal figures, however, led to a temporary cessation of extremist political activity.

Shimpotō

(Progressive Party). Political party established in March 1896 through a merger of the RIKKEN KAISHINTŌ, the Rikken Kakushintō, and several minor Diet parties; it sought to counterbalance the temporary alliance between the oligarch ITŌ HIROBUMI and the rival party JIYŪTŌ. Under the leadership of ŌKUMA SHIGENOBU it formed one alliance after another to compel the government to correct its inflationary fiscal policy, create a cabinet system responsible to the Diet, expand the freedoms of press, speech, and assembly, and strengthen Japan's international position. On receiving assurances that these demands would be met, Ōkuma joined the second MATSUKATA MASAYOSHI cabinet in September 1896. In November 1897 he resigned after a disagreement with Matsukata over land-tax increases and other administrative and fiscal measures. In June 1898 the Shimpotō allied with the Jiyūtō to create the KENSEITŌ. See also POLITICAL PARTIES.

Shimura Takashi (1905–1982)

Film actor. Real name Shimazaki Shōji. Born in Hyōgo Prefecture. Not a handsome man or a big star, Shimura has, along with MIFUNE TOSHIRŌ, appeared in leading roles in films directed by KUROSAWA AKIRA. A latecomer to motion pictures, he began making films at age 30. He appeared in a succession of Kurosawa pictures; *Waga seishun ni kui nashi* (1946, No Regrets for Our Youth), *Yoidore tenshi* (1948, Drunken Angel), and *Norainu* (1949, Stray Dog). His calm, unaffected performances gave meaningful expression to the Kurosawa theme of humanism and were highly acclaimed. Shimura gave a particularly distinguished performance in *Yoidore tenshi* as a doctor who has but a short time to live. He has appeared in all the major Kurosawa films: RASHŌMON (1950), IKIRU (1952), *Shichinin no samurai* (1954, SEVEN SAMURAI), *Kumonosujō* (1957, Throne of Blood), *Kakushi toride no san'akunin* (1958, The Hidden Fortress), *Yōjimbō* (1961) and *Tsubaki Sanjūrō* (1962, Sanjuro). These pictures were much praised when shown overseas and brought Shimura international popularity.   ITASAKA Tsuyoshi

Shinagawa Refractories Co, Ltd

(Shinagawa Shirorenga). Ceramic company engaged in the production of refractories and in engineering projects. The leading manufacturer of refractories in Japan, it traces its origins back to 1875, when Nishimura Katsuzō became the first to produce refractories domestically. The present company was established in 1903 and has consistently been a pioneer in its field. After World War II it expanded its operations to match the rapid development of Japan's steel industry. It is now active in exporting plants and technologies for the manufacture of refractories. Sales for the fiscal year ending March 1982 totaled ¥79.5 billion (US $330.3 million), and the company was capitalized at ¥3.3 billion (US $13.7 million) in the same year. Corporate headquarters are located in Tōkyō.

Shinagawa Ward

(Shinagawa Ku). One of the 23 wards of Tōkyō. During the Edo period (1600–1868), Shinagawa was a POST-STATION TOWN on the highway TŌKAIDŌ. After the Meiji Restoration (1868), it underwent rapid industrialization. Today, eastern Shinagawa, built on alluvial and reclaimed land along Tōkyō Bay, is an industrial area with numerous electronics and machine factories; part of the Keihin Industrial Zone. Western Shinagawa Ward is a residential district. The ward is a vital transportation center of the Japanese National Railways and major highways. Racetracks and auto-racing grounds are located on the reclaimed land of Katsushima. Pop: 346,236.

Shinagawa Yajirō (1843–1900)

Politician. Born in the Chōshū province (now Yamaguchi Prefecture). Like many other leaders of the MEIJI RESTORATION (1868), he had studied under YOSHIDA SHŌIN, the ideologue of the SONNŌ JŌI (Revere the Emperor, Expel the Barbarians) movement. Together with KIDO TAKAYOSHI, a fellow *samurai* from Chōshū, he was instrumental in bringing about the SATSUMA–CHŌSHŪ ALLIANCE. After the Restoration, he was sent by the government in 1870 to England and Germany to study local government, agricultural policy, and cooperatives. He returned six years later and in 1882 was appointed vice minister *(tayū)* of agriculture and commerce. He helped found the Dai Nihon Nōkai (Great Japan Agricultural Association) and set up the Kyōdō Un'yu Kaisha, a transportation company, to compete with the Mitsubishi Shipping Line of IWASAKI YATARŌ. In 1891 Shinagawa became home minister in the first MATSUKATA MASAYOSHI cabinet, but he incurred criticism from all quarters for masterminding a massive interference in the Diet election of the following year and was forced to resign (see SENKYO KANSHŌ). In the same year, together with SAIGŌ TSUGUMICHI, he founded the KOKUMIN KYŌKAI, an organization to support government policies.

Shinanogawa

River in Nagano and Niigata prefectures, central Honshū; originating in the mountain Kobushigatake in the Kantō Mountains, and flowing through the Saku, Ueda, Nagano, Iiyama, and Tōkamachi basins and across the Niigata Plain to enter the Sea of Japan at the city of Niigata. It is the longest river in Japan and has approximately 280 tributaries. Called CHIKUMAGAWA in Nagano Prefecture, it joins with its largest tributary, Saigawa, at Kawanakajima in the Nagano Basin. The port of Niigata, at the river's mouth, was important in the premodern period as a stopping place for ships plying the Sea of Japan. River transportation networks, with the port as a base, have been developed since antiquity. The lower reaches were the site of frequent floods before the digging, completed in 1923, of the Shin Shinanogawa (New Shinanogawa), which carries most of the river's volume to the sea from a point some 50 km (31 mi) upstream of the river's mouth. Numerous electric power plants are located on the main river and its tributaries. The water is utilized for irrigation, industry, and drinking. Length: 367 km (228 mi); area of drainage basin: 12,050 sq km (4,651 sq mi).

Shinchō

(New Currents). A large-scale literary monthly devoted to quality literature. This old and respected journal has reported on literary events and trends and introduced new writers while publishing many of the outstanding works of the modern era. It has been published since May 1904 by the SHINCHŌSHA COMPANY. It was launched by Satō Giryō (1878–1951), founder of the magazine *Shinsei* (July 1896–August 1903). Many of *Shinchō*'s original staff had previously worked on *Shinsei,* which had occupied a dominant position in the literary world of its day. *Shinchō* rapidly became Japan's premier literary magazine, helping to establish Shinchōsha as a major publishing house. In the fall of 1908 Nakamura Murao (1886–1949) took over as editor, and through such innovations as special issues on various literary topics and sponsorship of round-table discussions he defined the particular character of the magazine. Nakamura's willingness to accept work from all schools made *Shinchō* the "public organ" of the literary world. In content it tended toward aestheticism, and when the so-called proletarian literature was enjoying its great popularity in the late 1920s and early 1930s, *Shinchō* emphasized works by the more aesthetically-minded SHINKANKAKU SCHOOL (School of New Sensibilities) and later the SHINKŌ GEIJUTSU HA ("New Art school") writers. It was also notable for its active interest in introducing foreign literature, carrying translations of such works as Camus's *The Stranger* and Kafka's "Metamorphosis." Contributors of original works included such well-known writers as ARISHIMA TAKEO, AKUTAGAWA RYŪNOSUKE, KIKUCHI KAN, ITŌ SEI, and MISHIMA YUKIO, to list but a few. Among more recent contributors are ŌE KENZABURŌ, INOUE MITSUHARU, YASUOKA SHŌTARŌ, and KURAHASHI YUMIKO. *Theodore W.* GOOSSEN

Shinchō Kō ki

(Chronicle of Nobunaga; also known as *Nobunaga Kō ki*). An account of the career of the hegemon ODA NOBUNAGA by Ōta Gyūichi (1527–after 1610). The work, completed around 1610, consists of an introduction and 15 parts. The introduction is a summary of Nobunaga's career up to the eve of his emergence into national prominence in 1568. Part I treats his embrace of the cause of ASHIKAGA YOSHIAKI and his entry into Kyōto to install Yoshiaki as shōgun in late 1568; each of the subsequent 14 parts gives a detailed chronological account of the events of a single year, concluding with 1582 and Nobunaga's assassination in the HONNŌJI INCIDENT. Although uncritical and sometimes inaccurate, the work is remarkable for its comprehensiveness. The author, who was the foremost chronicler of his age, had served Nobunaga before entering the employ of his successor to the national hegemony, TOYOTOMI HIDEYOSHI; he had direct experience of many of the events he described, and some of the materials he presents are unavailable elsewhere. The *Shinchō Kō ki* is his finest work; it is the single most important source for a study of Nobunaga's policies and campaigns, and its wealth of detail makes it indispensable also for broader studies of the Azuchi-Momoyama period (1568–1600). *George* ELISON

Shinchōsha Company

(Shinchōsha). Publishing company. Active in all fields of publishing, particularly of Japanese literary works and foreign literature in Japanese translation. In 1896, Satō Giryō founded Shinseisha (the forerunner of Shinchōsha) with *Shinsei,* a magazine which published unsolicited manuscripts from its readers. In 1904, he brought out the monthly magazine *Shinchō,* and at the same time changed the company name to Shinchōsha. In the 1920s, the age of the inexpensive books called *empon* ("one-yen books"), the company successfully marketed its World Literature Series (Sekai Bungaku Zenshū). In 1956 it launched a weekly magazine, *Shūkan shinchō,* the first weekly magazine to be brought out by a major Japanese publishing house. The magazine *Shinchō* has become an important institution of the Japanese literary world, introducing many new writers to the literary public. KOBAYASHI *Kazuhiro*

shinden

(literally, "Shintō fields"). Also called *mitoshiro* or *mitoshiroda.* Land owned by Shintō shrines under the RITSURYŌ SYSTEM of government, which was instituted in the late 7th century. Although private ownership of land was in principle abolished under this system, shrines and temples, as well as certain noble families, were allowed to retain some of their holdings. *Shinden* were cultivated by peasants in the area; being exempt from taxes, they provided a major source of income for the shrines. By the middle of the Heian period (794–1185) *shinden,* like other private holdings, had increased greatly in size through commendation and reclamation, and they developed into private landed estates (SHŌEN).

shinden kaihatsu

(development of new fields). The opening of new lands to cultivation and the conversion of dry fields to paddy during the Edo period (1600–1868). Also called *shinkai.* Before the Edo period *shinden* was called *konden.* The Edo period was one of the most active periods of land reclamation in Japanese history. New farmland producing an estimated 1.3 million *koku* (1 *koku* = about 180 liters or 5 US bushels; see KOKUDAKA) of rice was brought under cultivation during this time. Most of this growth occurred before the 18th century, but another major increase in reclaimed land is evident from 1830 to 1871, following the TEMPŌ REFORMS.

There were three major categories of reclamation. *Shinden* referred to reclamation of new land for use as paddy. Reclamation of land for dry-field crops such as wheat, barley, cotton, and tobacco was called *hatakebiraki.* Dry fields converted to paddy were called *hatakenaoshi shinkai.*

The Tokugawa shogunate and the *daimyō* encouraged land reclamation in order to increase the base for their major source of revenue, the annual land tax (NENGU). In recognition of the fact that newly reclaimed land was not as fertile as older, well-prepared fields *(honden),* and in order to stimulate reclamation, domains granted various forms of tax relief to cultivators of reclaimed land. Before the shogunate and daimyō standardized their tax-exemption policies, the extent and duration of the tax relief were subject to negotiation between domain authorities and would-be reclaimers. When two parties wished to reclaim the same land, they competed for official permission by offering to pay more taxes than their rival.

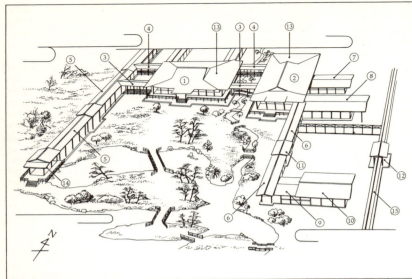

① shinden
(main dwelling)

② tainoya
(annex)

③ sukiwatadono
(open corridor)

④ wataridono
(corridor)

⑤ sukirō
(open corridor)

⑥ chūmonrō
(covered entrance arcade)

⑦ futamunerō
(2-bay wide, or double, corridor)

⑧ saburairō
(warrior's office)

⑨ kurumayadori
(ox-carriage house)

⑩ zuishinjo
(guardhouse)

⑪ chūmon
(inner gate)

⑫ yotsuashimon
(four-footed gate)

⑬ nurigome
(sleeping chamber)

⑭ tsuridono
(open pavilion)

⑮ dobei
(earthen wall)

Tōsanjō Palace, built by the powerful Fujiwara family and regarded as the most distinguished aristocratic residence of Heian times (794–1185). Of asymmetrical design without the traditional western pavilion, it occupied a double plot measuring 240 meters from north to south.

Shinden-zukuri —— Reconstruction drawing of Tōsanjō Palace, Kyōto

Once a daimyo's tax exemption policies for reclaimed land became uniform, they usually included a period of complete tax exemption, ranging from 2 or 3 to 10 years, and occasionally an additional period of partial tax relief before the land was subject to the full tax rate *(kuwashita nenki)*. In many cases, however, taxes on reclaimed land never reached the full rate applied to neighboring older fields.

Daimyō often financed reclamation projects. Their support was particularly important in large-scale endeavors that employed technological advances derived from castle construction and mining. Such projects often created whole new villages in the flood plains and deltas of major rivers. The domains provided materials and management and also paid for landless peasants (MIZUNOMI-BYAKUSHŌ) to settle the new villages as full-fledged independent peasants (HOMBYAKUSHŌ). Most large-scale, officially financed reclamation occurred in the 17th century.

Townsmen also financed land reclamation projects, particularly in the 18th and 19th centuries. By the 18th century the limits of paddy reclamation had been reached in many regions, and dry-field reclamation became more common. Since only marginal land remained, reclamation costs were relatively high. Nonetheless, merchants possessing the necessary capital were often able to profit from reclamation by planting commercial crops such as cotton or tobacco. Some merchants reclaimed land only to sell it to peasants. Temples and shrines also sponsored some reclamation.

Reclamation projects undertaken by individual peasants or as cooperative village endeavors were generally on a small scale. Villagers terraced hillsides, drained marshlands, cleared small mountain valleys, or gradually extended existing fields into bordering uncultivated land.

The reclamation of agricultural land sometimes had adverse effects on parts of a village community. For example, when communal land that supplied grass for fertilizer was reclaimed, peasants were forced to purchase fertilizer elsewhere. Some irrigation resources were badly strained and watersheds were occasionally destroyed, leading to increased flooding. However, the benefits of reclamation far outweighed these losses and contributed greatly to the rise in agricultural productivity during the Edo period.

——Kikuchi Toshio, *Shinden kaihatsu* (rev ed, 1977).

Philip BROWN

shinden-zukuri

A style of domestic architecture used mainly in the palatial mansions of the aristocracy and also in private residences of high-ranking Buddhist clerics and warriors. It was perfected in the Heian period (794–1185) and continued to influence Japanese residential architecture until the mid-15th century. The name is derived from its central feature, the *shinden,* master quarters or main hall. *Shinden-zukuri,* along with SHOIN-ZUKURI, a later form of domestic architecture, is one of the two major styles in the history of Japanese residential architecture.

History —— The *shinden* style is considered to be the result of the naturalization or Japanization as it were of Nara-period (710–794) aristocratic dwellings, which were patterned after ornate Chinese architectural models, especially Buddhist temple architecture. The style was perfected in its distinctively Japanese expression around the 10th century. No authentic examples or remains of the *shinden*-style residence are extant, all having been destroyed over the centuries by wars, or fires and other natural disasters. We can, however, ascertain the general design features of the *shinden* mansion of that time by means of paintings such as the *Nenchū gyōji emaki,* a multivolume illustrated scroll painting depicting scenes from the cycle of annual events, which dates from the 12th century (the earliest extant version is a 17th century copy). There are also numerous reproductions and scale models. *Shinden-zukuri* continued as an upper-class residential style well into the medieval period. The early Ashikaga shōguns, in particular, who led lives modeled after the aristocracy *(kuge),* preserved its use, and the *shinden* survived until the Muromachi period (1333–1568) as the central feature of the public part of their residences. Under the shōgun ASHIKAGA YOSHIMASA, however, residential architectural styles underwent a radical change. *Shinden-zukuri* was eventually discontinued in favor of the *shoin* style which became more and more popular with the ruling warrior class.

Sites for the *shinden* conformed naturally to the grid pattern layout of the capital of Heiankyō (now Kyōto). The standard size lot as prescribed by law measured one *chō,* or block, square (approximately 120 meters to a side) and was enclosed by small streets. There were also larger residences which measured twice or four times this size. Tōsanjō Palace, for example, the residence of the powerful Fujiwara family and a representative example of *shinden*-style architecture, occupied a parcel of property two blocks in length along its north-south axis. There were also smaller houses with lots that were a subdivision of the standard block.

Design and Composition —— The typical *shinden* mansion was originally arranged in a right-left pattern of symmetry. This may have derived in part from its Chinese models, but a more direct influence was probably the Imperial Palace, which was considered the paradigm for *shinden*-style architecture and which was itself symmetrical in ground plan design. The palace was destroyed by fire a number of times in the Heian period, and the emperor usually sought temporary quarters in aristocratic residences. The *shinden-zukuri,* therefore, was designed to fulfill a palatial function. This probably accounts for the basic symmetry of the *shinden* style and explains why the arrangement lasted so long. In the course of the Heian period, however, *shinden-zukuri* gradually lost its symmetry, reflecting changes in design preference on the part of the aristocracy.

The *shinden* or main hall was constructed in the center of the lot; it faced south and was slightly more wide than deep. The sloping roof was semigabled and covered with cypress bark. There was an extension of the roof on the south side that covered the steps up to the *shinden* from an elaborate landscape garden. To the east, west, and north there were attached pavilions or annexes *(tainoya).* When necessary additional pavilions could be added to the northeast and northwest. The eastern or western pavilion was often left out, destroying the right-left symmetry, or simpler buildings called *tainodai* were erected instead of a *tainoya* annex. The pavilions had gabled roofs with ridges oriented in a north-south direction, and to the south they had a pent roof one bay deep.

Each pavilion was connected to the *shinden* or to another pavilion by various types of covered and open passageways. The *sukiwatadono* was an open-style passage connecting the main building with an annex and had a floor like an arched-bridge under which flowed a brook. Another type of passageway was the *futamunerō,* a passageway two bays wide which could be used as a room when necessary. The *chūmonrō,* a covered entrance arcade, extended south from the eastern and western pavilions and embraced the south garden. In the center of this entrance arcade there was a *chūmon* (inner gate), which functioned both as a passageway into the south garden and as a side entrance for entering the residence. A *tsuridono,* a small open pavilion used for musical entertainment, was built at the tip of the *chūmonrō* out over an artifical pond. The *izumidono,* a small building similar to the *tsuridono,* was erected where there was a spring of water.

Topographically, Kyōto is higher in altitude to the north and east, so that water flows from the northeast to the southwest. Water could thus be drawn into the compound and directed in a narrow stream under the *sukiwatadono* into a man-made lake in the south garden. Since it was used as a place for holding ceremonies, the south garden was laid out on a broad area of level ground. There was usually a pond with an island and bridges.

Auxiliary buildings were located outside the *chūmonrō.* These included the ox-carriage house, guardhouse, and office. North of the main hall stood the building where food was prepared. No special space or facilities were provided for the bath or toilet, since portable facilities were used. An earthen wall surrounded the compound and there were gates to the east, west, and north but not to the south.

Details of the Main Hall —— The main hall was composed of an inner building and an outer building, with at times a further outer building. There were doors on either side, and the main hall was enclosed by latticed wall panels that swung open upward (*shitomido*). Usually these latticed panels came in vertically stacked pairs; the top panel could be raised parallel to the floor and the bottom panel could be removed. Except for a small room called a *nurigome* (originally a sleeping room but normally used for storage) within the inner building, there were few partitions in the main hall. The floor was boarded, and woven rush mats and cushions were used for sitting and sleeping. Folding screens or curtains were used to divide the large single room into sections as circumstances required. Blinds were hung on the inner side of the latticed wall panels. The interior of the other buildings was very much like that of the main hall.

Itō Nobuo

Shindō Kaneto (1912–)

Scenarist and film director. Born in Hiroshima. The son of a farmer, from a family of rich landlords who suffered bankruptcy, he frequently depicts rural Japanese and their problems. Shindō entered the film world in 1934 as an assistant art director and eventually worked with renowned director MIZOGUCHI KENJI in this capacity. (He would later make a fine documentary on the life of Mizoguchi.) Shindō has also been a scriptwriter, providing screenplays for directors as diverse as Mizoguchi, KINOSHITA KEISUKE, ICHIKAWA KON, and YOSHIMURA KŌZABURŌ. Two of his best-known scripts are *Yoru no tsuzumi* (1958, Night Drum) for IMAI TADASHI, and the remake of *Robō no ishi* (1960, A Pebble by the Wayside) for Hisamatsu Seiji.

In 1950 Shindō formed his own company, Kindai Eiga Kyōkai, and made his first film, *Aisai monogatari* (1951, The Story of a Beloved Wife). This much-admired film was autobiographical in character, focusing on a scenario writer who tries to convince a noted director (a thinly disguised characterization of Mizoguchi Kenji) to accept his work. Throughout his struggle his wife encourages him. She dies at the end of the film, always to be remembered and cherished by a husband grateful for her unstinting support. Shindō also made several so-called *rumpen-mono* in the 1950s, films concerned with the oppressed lives of the "lumpen proletariat." These include *Shukuzu* (1953, Epitome), which exposes the sordid life of a GEISHA, and *Dobu* (1954, Gutter), which excoriates the social maltreatment of the mentally retarded.

In 1952 Shindō was invited by the Japan Teachers' Union to produce a film about the atomic bomb. The result was *Gembaku no*

ko (1952, Children of the Atom Bomb), which concerns a teacher who returns to Hiroshima to track down each of her former pupils who had been caught in the attack. Using real orphans and actual victims, the film is extremely moving, as is the montage sequence in which Shindō reconstructs the five minutes prior to the detonation. The film is not sentimental, but the Japan Teachers' Union thought differently. Contending that Shindō had reduced the story to a tearjerker and destroyed its political orientation by being insufficiently critical of the United States military, they commissioned Sekigawa Hideo to make *Hiroshima* (1953), a film which portrays American tourists buying souvenir bones of A-bomb victims and makes little distinction between the United States government and Americans per se.

Shindō's best-known film is a much acclaimed semidocumentary, HADAKA NO SHIMA (1960, Naked Island; shown abroad as *The Island*), the story of an impoverished rural couple living with their children on a barren island in the Inland Sea. Not a word of dialogue is spoken throughout the film, as their very existence precludes either the energy or the indulgent luxury of conversation.

During the mid-1960s, after years of making films centered on social observation, Shindō began to emphasize the role of erotic feelings in our lives, an interest that attracted harsh criticism. The first in this group was *Onibaba* (1963, Hags), a period film *(jidaigeki)* which studies two women during wartime left to survive as they will. This they do by killing dying *samurai* and stripping their bodies of armor, which they sell for rice. Another film in this group, *Kuroneko* (1968, Black Cat), is brilliant in its treatment of the conflict between Oedipal and upwardly mobile social drives.

At their best Shindō's films achieve a subtle interplay between the sexual or emotive and social dimensions of experience. His radical perception declines to isolate sexual life, locating it always in the context of the mores and demands of a specific social class. Shindō's diverse and large body of work includes such thrillers as *Kagerō* (1969, Heat Wave Island) and an adaptation of NATSUME SŌSEKI's novel, *Kokoro* (1973, The Heart), for which he also wrote the script.

■ ——Joseph L. Anderson and Donald Richie, *The Japanese Film: Art and Industry* (1960). Joan Mellen, *Voices from the Japanese Cinema* (1975). Joan Mellen, *The Waves at Genji's Door: Japan through Its Cinema* (1976). Donald Richie, *Japanese Cinema: Film Style and National Character* (1971). Arne Svensson, *Screen Series: Japan* (1971). Richard N. Tucker, *Japan: Film Image* (1973).

Joan MELLEN

Shin–Etsu Chemical Co, Ltd

(Shin'etsu Kagaku Kōgyō). Chemical company manufacturing synthetic resins and electronic materials. Known for its technologies for the production of silicone resins and polyvinyl chloride. It was established in 1926 in Nagano Prefecture by the Kosaka family for the production of nitrolime and carbides. After World War II it began the manufacture of plastics, and in recent years it has placed emphasis on the production of silicone resins for use in semiconductors. It has joint venture companies in Portugal, Peru, Nicaragua, and the United States. Sales for the fiscal year ending May 1982 totaled ¥149.8 billion (US $632 million), with an export ratio of 9 percent. The company was capitalized at ¥13.3 billion (US $56 million) in the same year. Corporate headquarters are located in Tōkyō.

Shin Fujin Kyōkai

(New Woman's Association). Japan's first national women's rights group (1920–22), led by HIRATSUKA RAICHŌ, ICHIKAWA FUSAE, and OKU MUMEO. The group advocated equal opportunity for men and women, with protection of mothers' and children's interests, and published a magazine, *Josei dōmei* (Women's League). Its major achievement, mainly under Oku's leadership, was persuading the Diet to revoke article 5 of the 1886 Public Order and Police Law, which forbade women to attend political meetings.

Shingaku

(literally, "Heart Learning"). The teachings of ISHIDA BAIGAN and his school. The term Shingaku (Ch: Xinue or Hsin-hsüeh) was originally used to refer to a school of Chinese philosophy developed by Lu Xiangshan (Lu Hsiang-shan; 1139–92) and Wang Yangming (1472–1529; see YŌMEIGAKU). Also Japanese Confucian scholars of the early part of the Edo period (1600–1868), such as NAKAE TŌJU, called their scholarly activities Shingaku. It was not, however, until the emergence of the Sekimon Shingaku movement, founded by

Ishida Baigan, that the term became popular. Shingaku syncretized the teachings of SHINTŌ, CONFUCIANISM, and BUDDHISM into doctrines aimed at the moral edification of the common people and well suited to the growing merchant class.

In 1729 Ishida Baigan began a series of public lectures on Shingaku in Kyōto. Among his followers, TESHIMA TOAN and NAKA-ZAWA DŌNI were instrumental in introducing it in the Kansai and Kantō regions. Fuse Shōō (1725–85), Uekawa Kisui (1748–1817), Kamada Issō (1721–1804), Kamada Ryūō (1754–1821), and SHIBATA KYŪŌ contributed to its nationwide popularization. Later, there were Shingaku followers even among the high-ranking *daimyō* and *samurai*.

Ishida Baigan's teachings were based primarily on the Zhu Xi (Chu Hsi) school of Confucianism (see SHUSHIGAKU) but were eclectic, containing elements of Shintō and Buddhism as well. Baigan did not regard learning as a matter of intellectual, conceptual understanding. Rather, he considered the first task of learning to be the subjective investigation of human nature through personal experience and reflection. His studies convinced him of the universality of morality and led to the practical application of this belief to the problems of contemporary society. He insisted that the merchant—who was assigned the lowest rank in the traditional division of society into four classes (see SHI-NŌ-KŌ-SHŌ)—should be equal to the samurai, farmer, or craftsman when it came to moral practices. He proposed the establishment of a merchant ethic, emphasizing the importance of the merchant's role in society (see CHŌNINDŌ). Baigan's followers later expanded Shingaku into a broad philosophy of life envisioning the integration of all classes in a harmonious world. Because of these features Shingaku may be considered an example of modern humanistic thought.

Shingaku followers not only believed in the study of human nature but also involved themselves deeply in the propagation of their beliefs. Two means of propagation were the *dōwa*, an informal lecture that addressed concrete problems regarding family, employment, religion, and personal relationships; and *sein*, a type of poster, occasionally illustrated, which conveyed in verse a simple moral lesson. Followers also contributed significantly to mass education by publishing Shingaku tracts and holding special talk sessions for children. Involving themselves actively in TERAKOYA (village schools), they were enthusiastic supporters of academic and moral education. Their social activities, however, extended to larger social problems as well, including relief activities in times of famine and efforts to liberate people from superstition.

◾——Robert N. Bellah, *Tokugawa Religion* (1957). Ronald P. Dore, *Education in Tokugawa Japan* (1965). Ishikawa Ken, *Sekimon shingaku shi no kenkyū* (1938). Herbert Passin, *Society and Education in Japan* (1965). Shibata Minoru, ed, *Sekimon shingaku*, in *Nihon shisō taikei*, vol 42 (Iwanami Shoten, 1971). IMAI Jun

Shingei → Geiami

Shingeki

(New Drama). Theater magazine published since April 1954 by Hakusuisha. Founded as a successor to an earlier coterie organ of a drama group headed by KISHIDA KUNIO, *Shingeki* has stayed abreast of and influenced current developments in modern theater by recruiting young playwrights to help write and staff the journal. Among its members, TANAKA CHIKAO, KINOSHITA JUNJI, MISHIMA YUKIO, and FUKUDA TSUNEARI have played central roles. It has published several special collections of original one-act plays, as well as criticism and essays on modern European theater. *Shingeki* continues to be a positive force in the world of drama.

Theodore W. GOOSSEN

shingeki

(literally, "new theater"). A form of theater roughly comparable to that found in most Western countries in the 20th century. Both in terms of dramaturgy and performance, the new theater of Japan stands in opposition to such traditional Japanese theater as KABUKI and NŌ, where dancing and a musical form of declamation play an important part. Plays written in the modern style use a conversational form of dialogue and show the same tendencies toward psychological realism as do the Western dramas written from the time of Ibsen onwards. Actors are trained for the new theater in methods almost wholly different from those appropriate to kabuki actors, for

example, and with the exception of a few isolated instances, performers from one theatrical form do not appear in the other, just as in Western theater opera singers seldom appear in spoken drama.

The leaders of the new theater movement, which began at the turn of the century, developed this new art form out of a self-conscious desire to create a drama (and the means to perform it correctly) responsive to the rapid changes in the economy, the politics, and the psychology of Japanese life. For these men, kabuki was too traditional in its mentality and too stylized in its methods of performance to serve as a proper vehicle for contemporary concerns. The new theater was an experiment, carried on by intellectuals, and the general seriousness of the movement for actors, dramatists, and audiences alike remains very much in evidence even today. The new theater has always served as much as a means to instruct as to entertain. In each generation, the intellectual avant-garde has taken an interest in contemporary Western drama, so that the various European aesthetic movements such as symbolism, expressionism, and the Theater of the Absurd have been repeated in Japan. Western dramas are widely performed in translation, along with plays by Japanese authors.

The impetus for this movement to create a modern Japanese drama can be said to have begun in earnest with the introduction of translations of Henrik Ibsen's plays in Japan. In 1901, *An Enemy of the People* and *A Doll's House* were published; by 1906, various young writers formed a society to study the Norwegian dramatist's works and thoughts. The most influential of these enthusiasts was OSANAI KAORU (1881–1928), who decided to find some means to actually mount Ibsen on the stage. Inspired by the example of Antoine, whose famed Théâtre Libre had brought serious plays before the French public at the end of the 19th century, Osanai formed in 1909 his own company, which he called the Jiyū Gekijō (Free Theater), named after its Parisian counterpart, mounting as his first effort a translation of Ibsen's *John Gabriel Borkman*. The experiment was a notable success, and Osanai's company continued, on a somewhat sporadic basis, to produce both Western and new Japanese plays until 1919. Osanai's greatest difficulties came in his choice of performers. The only professionals available to him were kabuki actors, whose training was quite inadequate for modern drama; even worse, he had no actresses, since men in kabuki played both male and female roles. Thus Ibsen's heroines were played by female impersonators.

Another important figure in the movement, the eminent critic, novelist, and translator of Shakespeare, TSUBOUCHI SHŌYŌ (1859–1935), realized the necessity for training actors and actresses capable of performing this new kind of drama in an accomplished fashion. He decided to train amateurs, both men and women, to understand and interpret these new texts. His group, the Bungei Kyōkai (Literary Society), began its efforts in 1906. Shōyō and his colleagues worked slowly and carefully. In 1910, they presented public performances of Shakespeare's *Hamlet* in Shōyō's own translation, and the year following, the group produced Ibsen's *A Doll's House*.

The next impetus for the development of the new theater movement came in 1924. In the great Tōkyō Earthquake of the previous year, most theaters were destroyed and any efforts toward renewed activity seemed at a standstill. Osanai, however, with the financial help of a wealthy colleague and disciple, Hijikata Yoshi (1898–1959), was able to construct in the Tsukiji district of downtown Tōkyō an excellent small theater equipped with the most modern stage machinery available. Osanai's Tsukiji Shōgekijō (Tsukiji Little Theater) became the training ground for those interested in any aspect of the modern theater. His company presented a wide variety of modern plays (mostly European, to the chagrin of the Japanese playwrights), until Osanai's death in 1928. Many actors, directors, and designers still active in Japan today began their work with Osanai, and the importance of the troupe in the development of the modern Japanese theater cannot be overestimated. Indeed, the very concept of the theatrical troupe as the chief organizational means to propagate modern drama gained real currency through the work and influence of Osanai. In no Western nation did the idea of a theater company play such a role. In Europe, Shaw, Ibsen, Pirandello, and their contemporaries remained more powerful influences than their interpreters. In the Japanese case, however, theatrical companies, rather than dramatists, became the focal point of the modern theater movement.

Osanai's company also brought politics into the theater, chiefly through the activities of Hijikata, who served as one of Osanai's directors. Excited by the postrevolutionary Soviet theater he saw in Moscow on a trip through Russia, Hijikata brought to the theater a

Marxist influence that was already becoming widespread in many other areas of Japanese artistic and intellectual life at the time.

With the death of Osanai in 1928, actors, directors, writers, and audiences alike lost their greatest patron. The original Tsukiji company split in two, certain of Osanai's influential actors and directors expressing a strong interest in developing a militant proletarian, political theater. In the eyes of the general public, the new theater movement seemed to be moving far to the left. By the early 1930s, however, the government began to take steps to restrain the activities of the politically active companies, and by the outbreak of World War II, most of them were closed down, and many important figures were imprisoned. Some of these men and women, such as the director Senda Koreya (b 1904), emerged in postwar years to play a significant role in the postwar phases of the movement.

The prewar political theater produced some playwrights of considerable merit, notably KUBO SAKAE (1901–58), who studied drama in Germany after World War I and whose work bears some traces of his interest in expressionism. KINOSHITA JUNJI (b 1914), the leading playwright of the postwar period, was an admirer of Kubo and shows in his own work the same degree of political commitment. Kinoshita has written many plays on political subjects, in particular the moving *Ottō to yobareru nihonjin* (1962, A Japanese Called Otto), which deals with the Sorge spy ring active in Tōkyō just before World War II. Kinoshita also developed a new form of folk play, mixing elements from earlier, simpler Japanese dramatic forms with the kind of psychological sophistication possible in modern drama. His most successful experiment along these lines is his 1949 *Yūzuru* (Twilight Crane), which has been translated and performed around the world.

Other actors, directors, and playwrights in prewar years sought a new theater more closely allied to literary and aesthetic ideals. Chief among these was the playwright KISHIDA KUNIO (1890–1954), who studied with the celebrated Paris director Jacques Copeau in 1921 and 1922 and witnessed many productions of European classics and contemporary drama by Copeau's Vieux Colombier troupe. In his own dramas, Kishida tried to create a theater devoted to psychological insights, written in a thoroughly contemporary language. Kishida managed to free himself from both the older traditions of stage rhetoric (often redolent of kabuki histrionics) and from Marxist polemics. He encouraged younger playwrights as well, and at least two of his disciples, MORIMOTO KAORU (1912–46) and KATŌ MICHIO (1918–53), earned important reputations as well. The finest of the playwrights who worked with Kishida is doubtless TANAKA CHIKAO (b 1905), whose ability to write poetic dialogue was stimulated by his contact with the older writer. Tanaka's most highly regarded play, *Maria no kubi* (1959, The Head of the Madonna), is a mystical and religious treatment of the bombing of Nagasaki, in which this lurid subject matter is treated with unusual restraint and compassion.

Along with his activities as a playwright, Kishida also helped foster the development of several theater companies, notably the Bungakuza (Literary Theater), which began its productions in 1938. This company, which continues to occupy an important position in the Japanese modern theater today, was permitted by government authorities to continue to mount productions during the war years. With the closing of the other companies, however, the new theater movement came to a temporary halt. Nevertheless, much had been gained in the three decades of experimentation since Osanai's introduction of Ibsen. A number of gifted, highly professional actors, directors, and writers were now available. Many had traveled abroad and had come to realize the necessity for lifting the standards of performance. In the early postwar years, a new flowering of talent brought the new theater to a gratifying level of accomplishment.

In the postwar period, theater troupes continued to provide the focus for actors and dramatists alike. Such a system can provide certain advantages for the Japanese playwright, in that he can compose his texts with certain performers in mind. Actors and directors in the troupes often work in other media (films, popular theater, and, more recently, television) so as to earn funds to subsidize the work of the troupe, thereby showing a loyalty to their profession unusual outside Japan. The theater troupes have also undertaken to expand their work to the provincial cities outside Tōkyō. Through touring productions, often sponsored by labor unions and other similar organizations, the new theater has come to attract a wide national audience, although it remains to date more a white-collar and intellectual group than the audience of "worker-spectators" sought for by the more active leftist groups.

Along with the Bungakuza, which continues to produce Japanese and foreign plays of literary merit, a number of troupes active in postwar Japan have produced modern theater of high quality. Chief among them are the Haiyūza (Actor's Theater) led by Senda Koreya, and Mingei (The People's Theater), which often produces drama of a leftist, political nature. Other newer companies, such as Kumo, founded in 1963, stage avant-garde productions, and there are many smaller experimental groups as well.

Because of the rising prestige and ever greater performing skill of these theater companies, a number of prominent contemporary novelists have written for the stage in recent years. ABE KŌBŌ (b 1924) and MISHIMA YUKIO (1925–70), both well-known writers, have composed highly successful plays. Among younger writers, YAMAZAKI MASAKAZU (b 1934) has brought metaphysical speculation and contemporary psychological theory to his dramas. Others, such as YASHIRO SEIICHI (b 1927) and Betsuyaku Minoru (b 1937), have mirrored the most contemporary of social and philosophical concerns in their plays, which find a wide audience and an even wider readership in printed form.

At the present time, the Japanese new theater movement has achieved real stability. Strong political attitudes taken by some of the troupes in former years are now considerably tempered by a thoroughgoing professionalism and an ever increasing regard for the sensibilities and expectations of a wide audience. In many ways, *shingeki* has reached a satisfying maturity. Now Japanese dramas of intellectual and theatrical merit are well performed and well attended. For an art form with a history of roughly 70 years, these are considerable accomplishments. See also LITERATURE: modern drama.

——Akiba Tarō, *Nihon shingeki shi*, 3 vols (1955–56). Matsumoto Kappei, *Nihon shakai shugi engeki shi* (1975). J. Thomas Rimer, *Toward a Modern Japanese Theater* (1974). Tanaka Chikao, ed, *Gekibungaku*, in *Kindai bungaku kanshō kōza*, vol 22 (Kadokawa Shoten, 1959).   J. T. RIMER

Shingen Kahō

Collective name for two codes established in the mid-16th century by the TAKEDA FAMILY, *daimyō* of Kai (Kōshū) Province (now Yamanashi Prefecture). The first is the Kōshū Hatto no Shidai (Legal Articles of Kōshū), a domainal legal code (BUNKOKUHŌ) of 57 articles enacted by TAKEDA SHINGEN in 1547 and 1554. It comprises various regulations concerning the administration of the Takeda domains and shows clearly the influence of the IMAGAWA KANA MOKUROKU. The second is the Takeda Nobushige Kakun (Household Precepts of Takeda Nobushige), a collection of household precepts (KAKUN) or house regulations *(kahō)* in 99 articles drawn up by Shingen's brother in 1558. It sets forth moral admonitions and norms of behavior for the Takeda family and its retainers, quoting liberally from the Chinese Confucian classics. The two codes were combined under the title Shingen Kahō by an unknown editor of the Edo period (1600–1868).

Shingon sect

Major Buddhist sect. A branch of Mahāyāna Buddhism, founded by KŪKAI in the beginning of the 9th century. It is also referred to as the Shingon-darani (Skt: *mantra-dhāranī*) sect, Mandara (MANDALA) sect, Yuga (Yoga) sect, Dainichi (Mahāvairocana) sect, and generally as Mikkyō (ESOTERIC BUDDHISM). The basic doctrines and patterns of practice were established by Kūkai, who synthesized Indo-Chinese esoteric Buddhism on the basis of Mādhyamika, Yogācāra, and Huayan (Hua-yen; J: Kegon) thought. No significant innovations in the teachings have been made since Kūkai; therefore, the essential tenets of Shingon Buddhism are found in the writings of Kūkai. In the area of praxis—MANTRA recitation, *mudrā* (J: INZŌ) formation, mandala drawing, the use of varieties of images for meditation, consecration rites (*kanjō*; Skt: *abhiṣeka*)—many key elements of the Indian esoteric Buddhism which Kūkai found in Tang (T'ang, 618–907) China are preserved. Consequently, among the major sects of Japanese Buddhism, the Shingon sect maintains the closest affinity with Hinduism and with the Lamaist Buddhism of Tibet and the Himalayan countries.

In contradistinction to the common belief that the Buddhist teachings are derived from the historical Buddha Śākyamuni, Shingon takes the stand that its basic sutras, the *Mahāvairocana-sūtra* (J: *Dainichikyō*) and the *Vajraśekhara-sūtra (Kongōchō-gyō)*, were expounded by the Mahāvairocana Buddha (J: Dainichi), the Dharmakāya (Body of Dharma), the Ultimate Reality. Śākyamuni is interpreted as one of many manifestations of Mahāvairocana. According to Kūkai's *Transmission of Dharma (Fuhōden)*, Vajrasattva received the teachings directly from Mahāvairocana and sealed the sutras in an iron *stupa* (tower) in South India; 800 years after Śākyamuni's demise, Nāgārjuna (J: Ryūju or Ryūmyō) opened the iron stupa and revealed the sutras to the world. Represented by these two sutras, esoteric Buddhism flourished in 7th-century India at Nālanda, the Buddhist university located near Buddh Gaya.

At the behest of Dharmagupta, rector of the university, the first missionary of Indian esoteric Buddhism, Śubhakarasimha (637–735)—though nearly 80 at the time—traveled to Tang China by way of Central Asia, arriving in the capital of Chang'an (Ch'ang-an) in 716. Well received by Emperor Xuanzong (Hsüan-tsung; r 712–756) and by the court, Śubhakarasimha translated the *Mahāvairocana-sūtra* from Sanskrit into Chinese with the help of Yixing (I-hsing; 683–727), thereby laying the foundation of esoteric Buddhism in China. The second esoteric Buddhist master, Vajrabodhi (671–741), also from Nālanda, arrived in Canton by sea in 720 and undertook the translation of the *Vajraśekhara-sūtra* under the patronage of the imperial household. Amoghavajra (Ch: Bukong; Pu-k'ung; 705–774) became the chosen disciple of Vajrabodhi. Well versed in Sanskrit and Chinese, Amoghavajra is regarded as one of the four great translators of Buddhist texts in China. The successor of Amoghavajra was the first native Chinese master of esoteric Buddhism, Huiguo (Hui-kuo; 746–805), under whom Kūkai studied.

The interval between the transmission of esoteric Buddhism from India to China and its introduction from China to Japan was less than a century. Chinese esoteric Buddhism remained more or less in the stage of translation with little systematization. The final task of systematizing the teachings and practices of esoteric Buddhism fell upon Huiguo's disciple, Kūkai.

In the process of systematizing the newly imported religion in Japan, Kūkai advanced his own answers to the perennial and central questions of Buddhism: who is the Buddha? what is enlightenment? how can one attain it? Kūkai interpreted the Buddha as the Dharmakāya Mahāvairocana who revealed the *Mahāvairocana* and *Vajraśekhara* sutras. To attain enlightenment meant to realize the "glorious mind, the most secret and sacred" (J: *himitsu shōgon shin*). He taught that man is intrinsically capable—through the grace (*kaji*; Skt: *adhiṣṭhāna*) of Mahāvairocana and through his own practice of *yoga-samādhi*—of participating here and now in the Real, of becoming Mahāvairocana (J: *sokushin jōbutsu*).

Kūkai's identification of Mahāvairocana with the Dharmakāya was a great leap in Buddhist speculation, for hitherto the Dharmakāya had been regarded as formless, imageless, voiceless, and totally transcendent. By defining Mahāvairocana as the Dharmakāya, Kūkai identified Mahāvairocana with the eternal Dharma, the uncreated, imperishable, beginningless and endless Ultimate Reality. It is the realization of this Dharma that made Gautama Siddhārta the Enlightened One, that likewise makes all sentient beings endowed with intrinsic enlightenment into Buddhas. The sun is the source of light and warmth, the source of life. Similarly, Mahāvairocana is the Great Luminous One at the center of the esoteric Buddhist mandala, surrounded by multitudes of Buddhas, bodhisattvas, and spiritual powers; He is at once the source of enlightenment and the unity underlying all varieties of existence in the universe. To attain enlightenment means to realize Mahāvairocana, the implication being that Mahāvairocana is originally within man himself. Hence, Kūkai called Mahāvairocana the "enlightened mind" (Skt: *bodhicitta*), a synonym for Suchness, or the element of "original enlightenment" (J: HONGAKU) within all sentient beings. Speaking of this immanence of the Dharmakāya, Kūkai says: "Where is the Dharmakāya? It is not far away; it is in our body. The source of wisdom? In our mind; indeed, it is close to us." The motto of the Shingon sect is, "attaining enlightenment in this very existence."

From the theme of attaining enlightenment in this very existence, Kūkai developed the idea of the "preaching of the Dharmakāya (J: *hosshin seppō*)." He insisted that esoteric Buddhism had been preached by the Dharmakāya Mahāvairocana, while all other Buddhist teachings were preached by the Nirmāṇakāya Buddha Śākyamuni, a temporal incarnation of the timeless Dharmakāya Mahāvairocana. At first Kūkai employed the word "preaching" in conformance with its traditional usage in the Buddhist canon; but as the years went by, he came to interpret Dharmakāya preaching in a more fully symbolic sense.

Kūkai speculated on the nature and value of the *mantra* (J: *shingon*), the shortest verbal form of the "preaching of the Dharmakāya." He reasoned that the sutras of esoteric Buddhism, such as the *Mahāvairocana* and the *Vajraśekhara* sutras, are records of the preaching of the Dharmakāya Buddha and exist because of his compassion and wisdom. Therefore, it is the mantras, conveying as they do the essential meaning of these sutras, that are most thoroughly impregnated with the preacher's spirit, compassion, wisdom, and saving power.

At the same time that he linked the nature and value of the mantra to the preaching of the Dharmakāya Buddha, Kūkai expanded the meaning of the word "preaching" to include all phenomena, interpreting it as the acts of communication of the Dharmakāya Mahāvairocana. Oral preaching is only one means of communication; nonoral preaching may be pursued by means of, for example, silence, gesture (Skt: *mudrā*), color, or form. Kūkai's speculation along this line culminated in his work, *The Meanings of Sound, Word, and Reality (Shōji jissō gi)*, in which he asserted that the Dharmakāya Mahāvairocana is reality (J: *jissō*) and that he reveals himself through all objects of sense and thought. In other words, all things in the universe reveal the presence of Mahāvairocana. All phenomena point to the underlying reality, Mahāvairocana, and at the same time are the expressions of that Reality.

In *Attaining Enlightenment in This Very Existence (Sokushin jōbutsu gi)*, Kūkai explains his conception of Mahāvairocana as the Body of Six Great Elements, consisting of the three constituents: the Six Great Elements, the Four Mandalas, and the Three Mysteries. These three correspond respectively to the essence (J: *tai*), the attributes (*sō*), and the functions (*yū*) of the Dharmakāya Mahāvairocana. The Six Great Elements are earth, water, fire, wind, space, and consciousness. The adjective "Great" signifies the universality of each element. The first five stand for all material elements and the last, for the spiritual element; that is, the body and the mind of Mahāvairocana. These Six Great Elements create all Buddhas, all sentient beings, and all material worlds. There is no creator other than the Six Great Elements, which are at once the creating and the created. Mahāvairocana, consisting of the Six Great Elements and abiding in a state of cosmic harmony, is one without a second and the totality of all existences and activities in the universe. Thus all the diverse manifestations of the phenomenal world are identical in their constituents; all are in a state of constant transformation; no absolute difference exists between man and nature; body and mind are nondual.

The Four Mandalas (four types of mandala) are the *mahā-maṇḍala*, *samaya-maṇḍala*, *dharma-maṇḍala*, and *karma-maṇḍala*. These represent Mahāvairocana seen from four different perspectives. The *mahā-maṇḍala* is the great (*mahā*) circle, the universe, Mahāvairocana seen in his physical extension. The *samaya-maṇḍala* is the same circle seen from the viewpoint of the omnipresence of Mahāvairocana's "intention" (*samaya*). The *dharma-maṇḍala* is the same circle viewed as the sphere where the revelation of the truth (*dharma*) takes place, namely, Mahāvairocana's field of communication. Finally, the *karma-maṇḍala* is the same circle seen from the viewpoint of his action (*karma*). The Four Mandalas stand for Mahāvairocana's extension, intention, communication, and action. His extension is the totality of the five great elements; his intention is affinity—love and compassion; his communication is the revelation of himself as the "preaching of the Dharmakāya"; and his action, all activities in the universe.

The Three Mysteries are the suprarational activities of the body, speech, and mind of Mahāvairocana. The mystery of the activities of body is manifested universally through the forms or patterns of phenomena; the mystery of the activities of mind, through aesthetic and ecstatic experiences of *yoga-samādhi*. Kūkai interprets the Three Mysteries as the expression of the compassion of Mahāvairocana toward sentient beings. He holds that faith comes through the grace (J: *kaji*) of the Buddha: it is not acquired by the individual but given. Because of Kūkai's emphasis on the grace of the Three Mysteries, the Shingon sect has also been identified as the religion of the "Three Mysteries and Grace" (*sammitsu kaji*).

The basic principle of the practice of Shingon meditation is to integrate the microcosmic activities of body, speech, and mind of the individual existence into the macrocosmic activities of body, speech, and mind, the contents of the *yoga-samādhi* of Mahāvairocana. This is done through symbolic acts of the body (the pose of sitting in meditation and the use of hand gestures, *mudrā*); of speech (the recitation of mantras, the symbols of the essence of speech of Mahāvairocana); and of mind (practices involving thinking, feeling, imagining, visualizing, listening, and of ceasing the activities of the mind). This is called the practice of "entering self into self so that the self enters into self" (J: *nyūga ganyū*).

There exist a variety of methods of meditation, just as there are many manifestations of Mahāvairocana shown in the paintings of the Diamond Realm (KONGŌKAI) and Womb Realm (TAIZŌKAI) mandalas. Among these methods are the meditations on the Diamond Realm, on the Womb Realm, on the Moon (symbol of enlightened mind), on the letter *A* (Mahāvairocana), and on Acala (J: Fudō). All can be regarded as the practice of the *samādhi* of Mahāvairocana, since the object invoked in each meditation is none other than a manifestation of Mahāvairocana. Some are extremely simple, consisting of only a single mantra and one *mudrā*. Thus, despite the complexity of its teachings and its somewhat secretive approach, its readily accessible practice of mantra recitation and the popularity of its founder Kūkai have earned Shingon Buddhism the support of people in all walks of life.

The Sanskrit title Mahāvairocana (J: Dainichi) means "Great Sun." The great sun goddess (AMATERASU ŌMIKAMI) is the central figure in the Shintō pantheon, and the obvious parallel had curious ramifications in the relationship between esoteric Buddhism and Shintō. With the development of RYŌBU SHINTŌ in the medieval period, Amaterasu came to be widely recognized as an avatar of Dainichi. Esoteric Buddhism—developed in India and embracing indiscriminately within its mandalas a plethora of native Hindu deities—provided the ground for the fusion of Buddhism and Shintō; Shingon Buddhism was, in fact, instrumental in forming SHUGENDŌ, supplying its theories and patterns of practice. Even today, the headquarters of Shugendō (Tōzan branch) is a Shingon temple, DAIGOJI in Kyōto.

There are two major divisions in the Shingon sect: Old *(kogi)* and New Shingon *(shingi)*. Toward the end of the Heian period, KAKUBAN (1095–1143), an ardent follower of Kūkai, established on Mt. Kōya (Kōyasan) an institute for the transmission of dharma (the Dai Dembōin), which came into conflict with the mountain's time-honored headquarters, Kongōbuji. One hundred and forty years later, the doctrine of the "preaching of the Dharmakāya" led Raiyu (1226–1304), a descendant in Kakuban's line, to advocate a new theory which held that the esoteric Buddhist sutras were preached by the Body of Grace of Mahāvairocana *(kajishin seppō)*. A fierce controversy broke out, with the traditionalists maintaining that these sutras were preached by the Body of Mahāvairocana's Intrinsic State (Honjishin Seppō). Raiyu left Mt. Kōya and established, about 25 kilometers (15.5 mi) northwest of Mt. Kōya, the temple Negoroji, the headquarters of the New Shingon. Following the destruction of the Negoroji by the warlord Toyotomi Hideyoshi in 1585, two new centers were created by the followers of Kakuban: one at the temple HASEDERA, also called Chōkokuji (Buzan branch); another at the CHISHAKUIN (Chizan branch). The Old Shingon sect includes the following subsects: the TŌJI, Daigo, Daikakuji, Omuro (see NINNAJI), Sennyūji, Yamashina, and ZENTSŪJI subsects. In 1980 the Shingon sect consisted of 47 subsects, 12,237 temples, and approximately 12 million followers.

◼——Yoshito S. Hakeda, *Kūkai: Major Works, Translated, with an Account of His Life and a Study of His Thought* (1972). Mikkyō Bunka Kenkyūjo, ed, *Kōbōdaishi zenshū*, 8 vols (3rd ed, 1967). Pierre Rambach, *The Secret Message of Tantric Buddhism* (1979). Tajima Ryūjun, *Les deux grands mandalas et la doctrine de l'ésotérisme Shingon* (1959).   Yoshito S. HAKEDA

Shingū

City in southeastern Wakayama Prefecture, central Honshū. It originally developed as a shrine town around the Hayatama Shrine (see KUMANO SANZAN SHRINES) and in the Edo period (1600–1868) became a castle town of the Mizuno family. Lumber and paper industries flourish. It is the gateway to the Yoshino–Kumano National Park and to the scenic gorge DOROKYŌ. Pop: 39,992.

Shinji, Lake

(Shinjiko). In northeastern Shimane Prefecture, western Honshū. Part of the Shinji Trough, the area between the Chūgoku Mountains and the Shimane Peninsula. The river Hiigawa flows into the lake while the Ōhashigawa flows out of the lake into the lagoon called Nakaumi. Lake Shinji is connected with the Sea of Japan by the man-made river Sadagawa. Catches include pond smelt, icefish, corbicula, eel, perch, prawn, and carp. The city of Matsue is located on its eastern shore. One of the centers of tourism in the San'in region, with main attractions being Matsue Hot Spring, Tamatsukuri Hot Spring, and the IZUMO SHRINE. Area: 79.7 sq km (30.8 sq mi); circumference: 45 km (28 mi); depth: 6 m (20 ft).

Shinjinkai

(New Man Society). Political organization founded on 7 December 1918 by a group of students of the Faculty of Law at Tōkyō University. Espousing political democracy and social reform, the Shinjinkai continued until its dissolution in 1929 to be the largest and most influential group in a flourishing left-wing student movement in Japan.

For the first three years, the members of the Shinjinkai sought to proselytize democracy and reform through a wide variety of activities. Most notable was its publication of an intellectual journal, which passed through several titles: *Demokurashī* (Democracy; 8 issues), *Senku* (The Pioneer; 7 issues), *Dōhō* (Comrade; 8 issues), and *Narōdo* (Russian: *Narod*, The People; 9 issues). The magazine was discontinued in April 1922 following a decision to reorganize the Shinjinkai as a purely campus group; the growing alumni membership was reorganized as the Shakai Shisōsha (Social Thought Society). The early Shinjinkai members also devoted themselves to agitation and organization of the growing labor movement. They were particularly active among a group of workers at celluloid factories in east Tōkyō and helped to organize a union that became popularly known as the "Shinjin Celluloid Workers Union."

A new phase of activity under a more radical generation of students began in mid-1922. By this time, the early Shinjinkai emphasis on "liberal democracy" had shifted in the direction of orthodox Marxism–Leninism. Although only a minority of the membership of the Shinjinkai ever joined the underground JAPAN COMMUNIST PARTY, most considered themselves Marxists and devoted much time to the reading and discussion of Marxist literature.

The Shinjinkai of the mid-1920s devoted far more attention than before to campus-based organization and agitation. In efforts to mobilize the "student masses," the Shinjinkai came to have a preponderant influence in the university newspaper *(Teikoku daigaku shimbun)*, the student government (Gakuyūkai), the debating club, and the university-affiliated settlement project in the slums of east Tōkyō. Shinjinkai members were also prominent in the leadership of the Gakuren (Gakusei Shakai Kagaku Rengōkai; Student Federation of Social Science), a national left-wing student federation, and saw to the establishment of Shinjinkai chapters at other universities. At the same time, many continued to be active in a wide variety of off-campus activities, participating in every area of the socialist and communist movements of the 1920s. After graduation, they commonly moved into positions of leadership on the left.

Opposition to the Shinjinkai began to mount after about 1926, both from an increasingly active right-wing campus group called the Shichiseisha (Seven Lives Society) and from the university authorities. The confrontation with the Shichiseisha reached a climax in the winter of 1927–28, resulting in the dissolution of the Gakuyūkai, a clear defeat for the Shinjinkai. Official university pressure culminated in the forced dissolution of the Shinjinkai as a legal association on 17 April 1928, in the wake of the public revelation that many current and former Shinjinkai members had been among those arrested in the government's mass round-up of suspected communists on 15 March (see MARCH 15TH INCIDENT).

The Shinjinkai survived as an underground group for another year and a half, active both on and off campus and increasingly harassed by both police and educational officials. In mid-1929 preparations were made to reorganize the Shinjinkai as a branch of the communist youth movement, in accord with a resolution of the Fifth Congress of the Young Communist International (Moscow, August 1928). The Shinjinkai was formally dissolved on 23 November 1929, and its activities were carried on in ever greater secrecy and under mounting surveillance for another five years as the Tōkyō University branch of the Japanese Communist Youth League.

The Shinjinkai at its peak in the late 1920s had about 40 members in each graduating class of Tōkyō University, chiefly from the faculties of law, economics, and letters. Of a total membership of four to five hundred over its 11-year history, over 350 have been positively identified. Many Shinjinkai members went on to prominent careers in politics, including ASŌ HISASHI, NOSAKA SANZŌ, and SHIGA YOSHIO; in academic life, including Rōyama Masamichi (1895–1980), HATTORI SHISŌ, and Kajinishi Mitsuhaya (1906–64); and in literature, including KAMEI KATSUICHIRŌ, HAYASHI FUSAO, and NAKANO SHIGEHARU. A few members later shifted their views markedly to the right, but the majority continued to support the progressive causes of their student days. See also STUDENT MOVEMENTS.

📖 ——Kikukawa Tadao, *Gakusei shakai undō shi* (1955). Henry D. Smith II, *Japan's First Student Radicals* (1972).

Henry D. Smith II

Shin Jiyū Kurabu → New Liberal Club

Shinjō

City in northern Yamagata Prefecture, northern Honshū. It developed as a castle town of the Tozawa domain during the Edo period (1600–1868). Before and during World War II, horses for military use were bred here. With the completion of the Masuzawa Dam, large tracts of rice fields have been created. The lumber industry is also active. Visitors are drawn to the Shinjō Hot Spring and the boat rides down the river Mogamigawa. Pop: 42,911.

Shinjō Basin

(Shinjō Bonchi). In northern Yamagata Prefecture, central Honshū. Flanked on the east by the Ōu Mountains and on the west by the Dewa and Asahi mountains, it consists of alluvial fans covered with volcanic ash and the flood plain of the river Mogamigawa. It is a rich rice-producing area. Thick Japanese cedar forests grow in the hilly northern part. The major city is Shinjō. Area: approximately 200 sq km (77.2 sq mi).

shinjū → suicide

Shinjuku Gyoen National Garden

(Shinjuku Gyoen Kokuritsu Kōen). Park and landscape garden in Shinjuku and Shibuya wards, Tōkyō. Famous for its cherry blossoms in April and chrysanthemums in November. Occupies the site of the Naitō *daimyō's* mansion, which was turned over to the imperial household in 1872; designed in 1906 in the manner of a European park. Became a public park after World War II. Area: 58.5 hectares (144.5 acres).

Shinjuku Ward

(Shinjuku Ku). One of the 23 wards of Tōkyō. On the Musashino Plateau. During the Edo period (1600–1868), Shinjuku was one of the POST-STATION TOWNS on the Kōshū Kaidō (Kōshū Highway). A small farming village in the Meiji period (1868–1912), it developed rapidly during the Taishō period (1912–26). Today it is one of the major business and entertainment centers of Tōkyō (see URBAN SUBCENTERS). Large department stores, restaurants, theaters, and shops surround Shinjuku Station, a center for many national and private railways and bus routes. This area is known as a center for young people. Eastern Shinjuku Ward is principally a commercial and residential area, and central Shinjuku Ward is composed mainly of housing complexes. In northern Shinjuku Ward, on the river Edogawa, are numerous dyeing and printing plants. Points of interest include the Shinjuku Gyoen National Garden, the Outer Gardens of the Meiji Shrine, and the National Sports Stadium. Pop: 343,749.

Shinkankaku school

(Shinkankaku Ha). Modernist literary group of the mid-1920s. Its name is often translated as Neo-Impressionist school, but School of New Sensibilities would be closer to its actual meaning. Among the 19 young writers who were members of the group at one time or another during the three or four years of its existence were YOKOMITSU RIICHI, KAWABATA YASUNARI, KATAOKA TEPPEI, NAKAGAWA YOICHI, KON TŌKŌ, KISHIDA KUNIO, Ishihama Kinsaku (1899–1968), Sasaki Mosaku (1894–1966), and Jūichiya Gisaburō (1897–1937). These writers published the coterie magazine *Bungei jidai* (Literary Age) from October 1924 to May 1927; however, many of the works most often cited as examples of the Shinkankaku style were actually printed in other periodicals. The word *shinkankaku* (new sensibilities) was applied to the group by the critic Chiba Kameo (1878–1935) in a sympathetic review of the first issue of their magazine, and they quickly adopted it as their name.

The Shinkankaku writers, who saw it as their mission to provide an art-centered alternative to the drab confessional fiction of the so-called Japanese NATURALISM on the one hand and the politically oriented writings of the Japanese PROLETARIAN LITERATURE MOVEMENT on the other, were strongly attracted to such post–World War I European artistic movements as futurism, cubism, expressionism, and dadaism. Specific influences that have been seen in the work of the group as a whole include the fiction of Paul Morand (b 1888), particularly his *Ouvert la nuit* (1922), the expressionist plays of Georg Kaiser (1878–1945), and the expressionist film *The Cabinet of Doctor Caligari* (1919).

However, it was Yokomitsu Riichi who made the Shinkankaku movement his own, and it was he who really developed the writing style that is associated with it, a highly polished style marked by careful attention to rhythm and imagery, by conscious use of symbolism, and by ways of looking at and describing things that were startling to the Japanese readers of his day. (He himself later wrote that his activities at this time amounted to a "war of utter rebellion against the Japanese language.") The passage most often cited as an example of the Shinkankaku style is the opening of Yokomitsu's short story "Atama narabi ni hara" (Head and Belly), published in the first issue of *Bungei jidai:* "It was high noon. The crowded special-express train was hurtling down the track at full speed. The small stations along the way were ignored like stones." This unremarkable passage from an otherwise forgotten story is so often quoted because its third sentence, which in effect personifies the stations, startled and angered contemporary Japanese critics. A better example of the kind of effects Yokomitsu employed in the works of this period is found later in the same story, when a crowd of people waiting on a railway platform are seen from above, their movements being described in terms of changing abstract patterns. This kind of reduction of human activity to a moving abstraction, which occurs often in Yokomitsu's Shinkankaku works, is reminiscent of what was already being done in the European cinema of that time. Other cinematic effects often used by Yokomitsu include the description of scenes, and sometimes of entire actions, as mirrored in glass or some other reflecting object.

Aside from Yokomitsu, the other writers of the group who managed to write in the Shinkankaku style included Kataoka Teppei (who was, along with Yokomitsu, a leading theoretician of the movement), Nakagawa Yoichi, and Kon Tōkō. Kawabata Yasunari and some of the others incorporated it in their writing to some extent. However, the efforts of most were rather contrived, and few other than Yokomitsu and Kawabata produced anything of lasting value. By the time that *Bungei jidai* ceased publication, many writers had begun to drift away to other movements and styles better suited to their individual talents. Yokomitsu himself continued to write in this style for another few years, but by the time he completed *Shanhai* (Shanghai), his only full-length Shinkankaku-style novel, in 1931, he had already begun to explore a completely different approach to fiction. As a group of writers, the Shinkankaku school had ceased to exist by 1928.

Some important works produced by writers while members of the group are Yokomitsu's *Shanhai* (1928–31), "Naporeon to tamushi" (1926, Napoleon's Ringworm), and "Haru wa basha ni notte" (1926, Spring in a Surrey); some of the short short stories Kawabata later published as the collection called *Tanagokoro no shōsetsu* (Stories for the Palm of the Hand); Kataoka's "Tsuna no ue no shōjo" (1927); and Kon's "Yaseta hanayome" (1925).

Alan CAMPBELL

Shinkansen

(New Trunk Line). A high-speed passenger railroad system operated by the JAPANESE NATIONAL RAILWAYS (JNR). Often called the "bullet train" because of its shape and speed. The first section of the line to be completed is also called the Tōkaidō Shinkansen because it was a new trunk line on the route of the TŌKAIDŌ between Tōkyō and Ōsaka. The line has since been extended south to Hakata in Kyūshū, for a route length of 1,069 kilometers (664 mi). The train has a maximum speed of 210 kilometers per hour (130 mph), and the minimum trip time between Tōkyō and Hakata is 6 hours and 40 minutes. In 1981, 255 trains were scheduled per day, each with a uniform 16 cars. Between the inauguration of service on the line in 1964 and early 1981, the Shinkansen carried 1.6 billion passengers and traveled 600 million route kilometers (373 million miles, or the equivalent of 15,000 trips around the earth) without a fatal accident.

The success of the Shinkansen revolutionized thinking about modern railroads. One railroad expert said the line was "a savior of the declining railroad industry"; the project has stimulated many other countries to take on the new construction or rehabilitation of railroads as national projects.

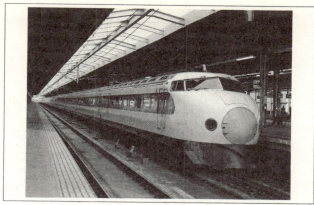

Shinkansen

A Shinkansen train at Shin Ōsaka Station, terminus of the first section of the high-speed line, on which service from Tōkyō began in 1964. This line was extended to Hakata (Fukuoka), with service beginning in 1975. In 1983 two new sections of the system began operations: the Tōhoku Shinkansen to Morioka and the Jōetsu Shinkansen to Niigata.

Shinkansen

The Shinkansen central control room at Tōkyō Station. Lighted numbers on the large display board indicate the position of Shinkansen trains.

Development of the Line—— The railroad that serves the 500 kilometer (311 mi) corridor between Tōkyō and Ōsaka has always been considered the main artery of Japan. Located on the Pacific coast of central Honshū, this zone is the industrial and socioeconomic nucleus of Japan; almost half the population and two-thirds of the nation's industry are concentrated there on only 16 percent of the total land area.

Over the years, improvements and innovations on the Tōkaidō line that serves this district were given priority over other lines in an effort to meet steadily increasing demand. Nevertheless, by 1961 the double-track line reached its transport capacity with 26,000 route kilometers (16,150 mi) of traffic per day. Because of the significance of the line, it became imperative to increase the capacity.

The JNR had established an investigative committee in 1956 to explore alternative solutions to the problem. The committee reported in 1957 that the system should be expanded from a double-track line to a four-track line, either by adding a second narrow-gauge (1,067 mm or 41.6 in) double-track line next to the existing line or by building an independent standard-gauge (1,435 mm or 56.5 in) double-track line. The committee recommended a public investigation of these options.

A second national committee decided in 1958 that a high-speed railroad should be constructed on a separate double track. They set goals of an estimated construction cost of ¥194.8 billion (US $541 million), a construction period of five years, and a three-hour travel time between Tōkyō and Ōsaka. Ground was broken for the epoch-making project in April 1959, with a proposed completion date of mid-1964, in time for the fall opening of the Tōkyō Olympics.

Systematic research and development on a high-speed train had begun earlier, and by 1957 (the 50th anniversary of the founding of the JNR) the Railway Technical Research Institute of the JNR was ready to proclaim the feasibility of a three-hour trip between Tōkyō and Ōsaka, despite the fact that actual operation of a train for long periods of time at the required speed of 210 kilometers per hour was unprecedented. Approximately 30 kilometers (18.6 mi) of the proposed line was completed by 1962 for test purposes. Two sets of prototype trains were tested on the track over the next two years to examine the new technologies and to identify the optimum design in cases where there were several options.

The construction of the entire line was completed on schedule in July 1964. The total construction cost was ¥380 billion (US $1.1 billion), double the original estimate. Service was begun on 1 October 1964, with initial daily service of 60 trains with 12 cars each. The Shinkansen was enthusiastically received by the public, and some trains were at full capacity within months. Expedited production of equipment enabled an increase in service to 110 trains per day in November 1965, and service has increased steadily since then.

The Shinkansen reduced the trip time between Tōkyō and Ōsaka from 6 hours and 30 minutes to 3 hours and 10 minutes. A business trip between the two cities was no longer an overnight journey, a fact that altered business activities. Demand for domestic airline service over this route also dropped considerably. The Tōkyō Olympics, which opened 10 days after the inauguration of service on the new line, brought international attention to the Shinkansen, as did the world exposition held in Ōsaka in 1970.

The line's popularity and the rapid growth in traffic demand brought about calls for improved transportation west of Ōsaka. The westward extension of the Shinkansen, a 160.9 kilometer (100 mi) stretch between Ōsaka and Okayama, was completed and opened for service in March 1972. This extension took five years to complete at a cost of ¥224 billion (US $739 million). The line was further extended to Hakata in Kyūshū through the Kammon undersea tunnel in March 1975. The construction period for this stretch of 392.8 kilometers (244 mi) was also five years, and the cost was ¥720 billion (US $2.4 billion). The completed line for revenue service thus reached 1,069 kilometers (664 mi).

The Shinkansen earned one-third of the total JNR passenger revenue in 1979, with a ratio of operating costs to revenue of 57 percent: operating costs of ¥399.1 billion (US $1.8 billion) and revenues of ¥698.9 billion (US $3.2 billion). In 1971 the construction of two new lines was begun from Tōkyō north to Niigata (270 km; 168 mi) and northeast to Morioka (465 km; 289 mi); both lines were completed in 1982.

Technical Aspects—— What makes the Shinkansen different from all other JNR lines is its high-speed service. All the mechanisms on the line are geared to providing this service with the utmost safety. They are designed, manufactured, operated, and maintained in order to be integrated into a well-balanced system. The engineering design is considered as a total system, which includes software elements such as train scheduling and dispatching.

The gauge is the standard 1,435 millimeters (56.5 in), which differs from the narrow gauge common in Japan. Minimum radius of a curve is 4,000 meters (13,120 ft) between Ōsaka and Hakata and 2,500 meters (8,200 ft) between Tōkyō and Ōsaka, except for some locations where sharper curves are dictated by topography. For these locations, speed restrictions are established. The maximum gradient is 1.5 percent between Ōsaka and Hakata and 2 percent between Tōkyō and Ōsaka, again with some exceptions for short stretches.

The track is a conventional ballasted track either on embankment or viaduct between Tōkyō and Ōsaka, using 60 kilogram per meter (121 lb per yd) welded rail on prestressed concrete ties. This track structure, however, requires a great deal of time and labor to maintain track geometry for high-speed and high-density operation. Consequently, slab track was adopted at the time of the westward extension beyond Okayama. Instead of ballast and ties, concrete slabs (5 × 2.3 × 0.19 m or 16.4 × 7.5 × 0.6 ft) are laid over a viaduct and welded rails are fastened directly onto the slabs. As predicted, the slab track is maintenance-free and also contributes to the quality of the ride.

The Shinkansen uses multiple-unit (MU) electric cars, which were selected over locomotive-hauled coaches for a number of reasons: the even distribution of axle load results in less strain on track structure; dynamic brakes can be applied to all axles; the turnaround operation is simpler; and the failure of one or two units does not interrupt the operation of the entire train. Braking was especially important, since dynamic brakes (where the motor is used for the braking function) were required to bring the train down from high speeds.

Shinkansen trains have two consists, the super express Hikari ("Light") and the limited express Kodama ("Echo"), both with 16 cars. The Hikari seats 1,342 passengers and is composed of 2 first-class cars, 12 regular-class cars, 1 dining car, and 1 buffet car with seats, while the Kodama seats 1,483 passengers with two kinds of make-up (one with 1 first-class car, 1 buffet car, 1 shop car, and 13 regular-class cars and the other with 2 first-class cars, 1 buffet car, and 13 regular-class cars).

The car body is streamlined. Cars are air-conditioned and are airtight to prevent ear discomfort caused by pressure changes when the train enters tunnels. Windows have double glass panels that do not open, but ventilation is possible.

Motor and Power Source —— The Shinkansen has a DC series traction motor installed on each single-wheel axle; each car has two trucks with two axles each, for a total of 4 motors per car, or 64 motors for each train. The 25,000-volt AC electrical current is carried by catenary (trolley wire) and collected by pantograph (a trolley carried on a collapsible frame) attached to the cars. The current is stepped down by transformer and then rectified by silicone rectifier into a pulsating current that drives the motor. The output of each motor is 185 kilowatts.

Since there is a traction motor on each axle, dynamic brakes can be applied to all axles at once. The brake is a generative one (the motor becomes a generator driven by the momentum of the wheels and thus exerts a drag on the train) that functions in the speed range between 210 kilometers per hour and 30 kilometers per hour. Below 30 kilometers per hour, a pneumatic brake automatically takes over. When an electric brake fails, a pneumatic brake of equal capacity works automatically, utilizing friction between a brake shoe and a doughnut-shaped disk attached to the side of the wheel.

The traction power required to operate such a high-speed train is so great that the only feasible system is AC electrification, which can provide high-voltage power; hence the decision to adopt 25,000 volt, 60 hertz AC electrification. For a distance of 150 kilometers (93 mi) west of Tōkyō, the commercial power frequency is 50 hertz; this is converted to 60 hertz by frequency converters installed at two locations.

It is difficult to match voltage and phase in the electrical current provided by separate substations, which are located about every 50 kilometers (31 mi) along the route. In order to avoid a mixed contact with currents of different phase, dead-section phase breaks are usually provided between substations; the Shinkansen adopted a special phase break system that switches power automatically from one substation to another as the train proceeds so that the train can go through the switchover with its propulsion power on.

In congested areas, the abatement of electromagnetic interference (EMI) is a concern. Booster transformers were utilized for this purpose between Tōkyō and Ōsaka, and autotransformers were used on the westward extension to Hakata. Both systems abate EMI by preventing the return current from flowing into the ground.

Good contact is maintained between the catenary and the pantograph by keeping the height of the catenary as uniform as possible, and the tension in the wire is increased to allow multiple pantographs to collect power effectively. This type of catenary is called the heavy compound catenary.

Operation and Maintenance —— Automatic Train Control (ATC) is used by the Shinkansen to prevent collision by maintaining a safe distance between trains. The permissible train speed is automatically indicated in the cab according to the distance between trains, the proximity of the next station stop, and the condition of the track (both temporary and permanent). These speed limits are 210, 160, 110, 70, 30, and 0 kilometers per hour. The handling of the throttle is left to the engine operator, but the brake operates automatically if the train exceeds the permissible speed. Deceleration and acceleration are left to the discretion of the operator within the speed limits, and the operator also brings the train to a stop at the proper position in the station after receiving the 30 kilometer per hour signal.

During the height of operation, approximately 100 trains are on the track between Tōkyō and Hakata at one time. The trains are monitored and controlled from the Shinkansen central control room at Tōkyō Station through a system called Centralized Traffic Control (CTC). At each station, the selection of route between the main track for a passing train and the submain track with platform for a stopping train is done automatically by computer-aided traffic control (COMTRAC). The computer is also capable of a primitive stage of conflict resolution; for example, when trains are running behind

Shinkansen

Operating Costs and Revenues, 1964–1980 (in millions of US dollars)		
	Revenues	Expenses
1964	53.9	75.6
1965	152.8	188.3
1966	247.8	202.2
1967	305.0	208.9
1968	352.8	215.8
1969	456.7	238.1
1970	579.4	253.1
1971	571.5	260.3
1972	829.1	412.7
1973	1,070.3	497.8
1974	1,116.9	579.4
1975	1,610.2	997.3
1976	1,843.5	1,115.2
1977	2,293.8	1,379.8
1978	3,101.1	1,778.7
1979	3,189.3	1,821.2
1980	3,214.3	1,898.7

NOTE: Converted into US dollars for the reader's convenience according to the rates shown in the table at YEN.
SOURCE: Japanese National Railways, *Shinkansen* (annual): 1982.

schedule, COMTRAC suggests a change in overtaking sequence that is implemented after being affirmed by a dispatcher. The general control room is equipped with a large display board, switch control panels, and COMTRAC terminals. The position and identification of all trains, the scheduled route, and the route condition are all displayed on the board. Turnout points at all stations can be remotely controlled by the switch control panels.

Electric power supply to the trains is also monitored and controlled from the same room by electric power dispatchers. A Centralized Substation Control (CSC) display board and control panels monitor and control 36 substations, 35 sectioning posts, and three frequency-changing substations. In case of an accident or other problem, the dispatcher acts promptly to secure alternative power to restore the failure.

The casualty-free record of Shinkansen operation is ascribed to careful maintenance. Soon after operation began, concern shifted from whether it was possible to build such a high-speed train to whether it was possible to keep it running. Much of the technology of maintenance and operation is software, which is more difficult than hardware because it requires more trial and error experimentation, practice, measurement, analysis, and modification.

Periodic inspections of Shinkansen equipment are conducted in order to keep the cars in top condition and to minimize out-of-service time. Cars are inspected every 48 hours and given a thorough inspection after 30 days or a 30,000 kilometer (18,636 mi) run. Trucks are overhauled after 12 months or 300,000 kilometers (186,360 mi), and a general overhaul is conducted after 30 months or 900,000 kilometers (559,080 mi). The ATC system is inspected after 3 months or 60,000 kilometers (37,272 mi) of operation.

As a rule, preventive maintenance is performed only on failout components, those parts that can result in accidents if they fail (the brake system, ATC system, and truck components, for example). Failsafe components (those that do not impair safety when they fail, such as the traction motor) are not disassembled or inspected until the general overhaul; they are repaired as they fail. Consumable parts and materials are replaced or replenished periodically. All components and subsystems are standardized and interchangeable.

A special inspection and maintenance system is used to keep the track in a condition suitable for high-speed operation. A general inspection train inspects the track, electrification, communication, and signal systems. It makes a scheduled run every 10 days on the entire route at the same speed as the regular trains. It consists of seven cars, built much the same way as the regular cars with a special three-truck configuration in order to conduct track geometry measurements. It employs the latest onboard measurement devices and produces charts of 23 parameters. The entire inspection system is computerized and the data are used to plan track maintenance and to inspect repair work done by contractors. Maintenance work is performed between midnight and 6 AM while the railroad is shut down.

📖 ——Japanese National Railways, *Facts and Figures* (annual). Kōyūsha, ed, *Shinkansen no unten to shingō* (1977). Nihon Tetsudō Unten Kyōkai, ed, *Shōkai Shinkansen* (1975). Ohm-sha, ed, *The Shinkansen* (1980).   ŌTSUKA Shigeru

Shinkei (1406–1475)

Poet of WAKA and linked verse; Buddhist priest. Shinkei embarked upon the priestly life at a very young age, taking the name Shin'e, which he changed to Shinkei in 1451. He rose quite high in the Buddhist hierarchy, becoming resident priest of the temple Jūjūshin In in the Kiyomizu district of Kyōto and attaining the rank of acting archbishop (*gon daisōzu*). Thus, although surrounded in later life by poetically inclined men of common origins, Shinkei's ecclesiastical rank entitled him to the deference accorded to members of the nobility.

Shinkei became a poetic disciple of the *waka* poet-priest SHŌTE-TSU around 1430, and remained so until Shōtetsu's death in 1459. He also studied *renga* (linked verse; see RENGA AND HAIKAI), and in his 40s and 50s became widely known in and around the capital as a poet of both genres. In 1467, when Kyōto became the battlefield of the destructive ŌNIN WAR, Shinkei left the area and traveled about making sojourns in various provinces, where he was welcomed on all sides by provincial warriors and wealthy commoners eager to learn the arts of classical poetry and linked verse. From 1471 he settled into a hermitage in the mountains of Sagami Province (now Kanagawa Prefecture). Among the disciples of his later years was the young Kensai (1452–1510), a foremost *renga* poet of his generation.

It is for his contributions to linked verse that Shinkei is most famous, being regarded as the most important *renga* poet and critic before the great SŌGI. In the practice of *renga* he revitalized the techniques of linking, calling for a return to the "distantly related verses" (*soku*) derived by the earlier master GUSAI from the practice of the innovating Kyōgoku–Reizei classical poets of the late 13th and early 14th centuries. The most important of his numerous critical writings, *Sasamegoto* (1463, Murmured Conversations), *Hitorigoto* (1468, Talking to Myself), and *Oi no kurigoto* (1471, An Old Man's Repetitive Talk), are based upon the thesis that *waka* and linked verse are products of the same artistic sensibility, and that devotion to poetry is of equal value to religious devotion, leading just as surely to the same end. For his aesthetic ideals he reached back in the poetic tradition by way of his teacher Shōtetsu to the great FUJI-WARA NO TOSHINARI (Fujiwara no Shunzei) and FUJIWARA NO SADAIE (Fujiwara no Teika), redefining their ideals of *sabi* ("loneliness"), *yūgen* ("mystery and depth"), and *yōen* ("ethereal beauty") into the more reticent evocativeness of *hie* ("coolness") and *yase* ("slenderness"). These aesthetic concepts were bequeathed to Kensai and Sōgi, and through them to the great 17th-century *haikai* poet BASHŌ.

📖 ——Earl Miner, *An Introduction to Japanese Court Poetry* (1968). Earl Miner, *Japanese Linked Poetry* (1979). Wolfram Naumann, *Shinkei in seiner Bedeutung für die japanische Kettendichtung* (1967).   Robert H. BROWER

Shinkiron

(literally, "On Prudence in Acting"). Treatise by the WESTERN LEARNING scholar WATANABE KAZAN, written in 1838. In 1825 the Tokugawa shogunate, in accordance with its 200-year-old NATIONAL SECLUSION policy, issued an ordinance calling on coastal domains to repel any foreign vessel that might enter Japanese waters. When in 1837 the American ship *Morrison* was driven off by artillery (see MORRISON INCIDENT), Kazan was moved to criticism of shogunate policy. In *Shinkiron* he wrote of world conditions in general and predicted that, isolated as it was from the rest of the world, Japan would soon become "prey to ravenous wolves." Unlike a similar book by Watanabe's associate TAKANO CHŌEI, which was copied and widely circulated, Kazan's work remained in manuscript form. He was nevertheless arrested and imprisoned during the BAN-SHA NO GOKU suppression of Western Learning scholars; and although his prison sentence was commuted to domiciliary confinement for life, Kazan eventually committed suicide lest he cause embarrassment to the *daimyō* of his domain.

Shinkō Geijutsu Ha

("New Art school"). A loose coalition of writers sharing a common interest in art for its own sake and a dislike for Marxist notions of art who came together in the late 1920s. They formed a kind of club that competed with the PROLETARIAN LITERATURE MOVEMENT, which then dominated the literary scene. Proclaiming the superiority of art over politics, the Shinkō Geijutsu Ha drew adherents from various proart factions. Its two principal spokesmen were Ryūtanji Yū (b 1901) and Kuno Toyohiko (1896–1971). Other early participants included Nakamura Murao (1886–1949), Katō Takeo (1888–1956), Yoshiyuki Eisuke (1906–40), and KAMURA ISOTA. Nakamura functioned as the group's unofficial sponsor, working behind the scenes as editor of the literary magazine *Shinchō* (New Currents), whose parent company, Shinchōsha, published anthologies of the group's short stories and individual novels. Such later well-known writers as KAWABATA YASUNARI, FUNAHASHI SEIICHI, KOBAYASHI HIDEO, IBUSE MASUJI, ABE TOMOJI, and others were also associated with the group early in their careers. A very short-lived association, the Shinkō Geijutsu school did not espouse any one particular style or ideology but rather reflected an avant-garde approach to literature typical of the late 1920s, ranging from dadaism and exoticism to modernism and urbanism.

The Shinkō Geijutsu Ha was in part an outgrowth of the negative reaction to the proletarian literary movement, which had despite continuous internal division greatly influenced the Japanese literary establishment (BUNDAN) in the early 1920s. Antipathy toward proletarian literature, however, still ran deep in many circles, as was evidenced in 1928 when Nakamura Murao published a book of critical essays titled *Dare da? Hanazono o arasu mono wa!* (Who's Messing Up the Garden!), an anticommunist declaration attacking the proletarian faction. The following year Tsunekawa Hiroshi (1906–1973) published his *Geijutsu ha sengen* (Art School Declaration), emphasizing the "urgency of artistic expression" as opposed to the proletarian faction's "urgency of reality." This became, so to speak, the informal manifesto of the "art first" faction that was formally established as the Shinkō Geijutsu Ha Kurabu (New Art School Club) in April 1930, a regrouping of an earlier club centered around Nakamura.

Members of the group included writers who regularly contributed to various leading literary journals. Ryūtanji Yū was perhaps typical: he first attracted attention with his novel *Hōrō jidai* (1928, Years of Wandering), a still very readable novel about life in Japan in the 1920s. His writing is characterized by an unconventional style and a penchant for the erotic and grotesque. Ryūtanji's most representative work is *Machi no nansensu* (1930, Street Nonsense), a best seller in its day. Together with Abe Tomoji's *Koi to Afurika* (1930, Love and Africa) and Yoshiyuki Eisuke's *Onna hyakkaten* (1930, Women's Department Store), it represents the best of the Shinkō Geijutsu Ha's literary output.

During 1931 and 1932 the Shinkō Geijutsu Ha split into several smaller factions and finally disappeared. Its rapid demise was due in part to its increasing tendency toward commercialization and journalism, to the differing literary concerns of its members, and to the growing enforcement of militarist controls after 1931.

The literature of the Shinkō Geijutsu Ha has received rather negative treatment from literary critics, who characterize it as *ero guro nansensu bungaku*, or literature of the erotic, grotesque, and nonsensical. Though it cast no lasting influence over literary circles of its day, it did contribute indirectly to the flowering of postwar literature in the late 1940s and early 1950s.

📖 ——Naruse Masakatsu, *Shōwa bungaku jūyonkō* (1966). Odagiri Susumu, *Shōwa bungaku no seiritsu* (1965). Takami Jun, *Shōwa bungaku seisuishi* (1952–57).   KOMATA Yūsuke

Shin kokinshū

(New Collection of Ancient and Modern Times; the full title is *Shin kokin wakashū*; often cited by court poets as simply *Shin kokin*). The eighth, and with the KOKINSHŪ, one of the two greatest of the 21 imperial anthologies (*chokusenshū*) of classical Japanese poetry (WAKA); ordered in 1201 by the retired emperor GO-TOBA (1180–1239; r 1183–98); officially completed in 1205, but underwent numerous later revisions. Compiled by Fujiwara no Teika (FUJI-WARA NO SADAIE), Fujiwara no Ariie, FUJIWARA NO IETAKA, the priest JAKUREN, Minamoto no Michitomo, and ASUKAI MASATSUNE. Japanese preface by FUJIWARA NO YOSHITSUNE; Chinese preface by Hino no Chikatsune. Twenty books; 1,981 poems in the common text (based on pre-1210 version, but including 3 poems previously deleted).

Compilation—— Although largely compiled by the committee of high-ranking courtiers listed above, the *Shin kokinshū* was a very personal project of Go-Toba, who maintained a lively interest in its compilation and exercised active editorial control, calling for extensive revisions of earlier drafts and retaining veto power over the grouping of poems in books and the ordering of them into sequences. Such revisions, called *kiritsugi*, were carried on by the committee with many arguments and disagreements and led to strong differences and strained relations, in particular between the ex-sovereign and Fujiwara no Teika, who strenuously disapproved of many of his exalted patron's choices. Although the official completion of the committee's work was celebrated by a banquet in the third month of 1205, Go-Toba caused extensive changes to be made thereafter. Again, many years later, when he was sent into exile in the Oki Islands following his unsuccessful attempt to overthrow the shogunate in the JŌKYŪ DISTURBANCE of 1221, he took a copy of the anthology and made extensive new revisions. The resulting version, known as the "Oki text" (Okibon), has not survived independently, but it can be largely reconstructed from annotations in copies of earlier versions of the anthology. In general, therefore, owing to the long process of refinement carried out either personally by Go-Toba or at his behest, the textual history of the *Shin kokinshū* is unusually complicated, and it is impossible to fix an exact date for its completion.

Literary Status—— The talented and artistically inclined Go-Toba had as his deliberate intention to make his reign as ex-emperor as brilliant culturally as the golden ages of emperors DAIGO and Murakami in the Engi (901–923) and Tenryaku (947–957) eras, the so-called ENGI TENRYAKU NO CHI. Go-Toba was determined to produce an anthology of poetry which would be a worthy successor in the great tradition of the *Kokinshū*, but which would also demonstrate the great revival of Japanese poetry that had taken place over the past three generations and the emergence of brilliant new poetic styles and modes expressive of the altered tastes and interests of the age. In this connection, the title chosen for the anthology was significant: "New Collection of Ancient and Modern Times" echoed the title of the first anthology and invited comparison with it; it announced the hope of Go-Toba and his committee of compilers of recapturing the standard of poetic excellence that, it was held, had gradually deteriorated over most of the intervening three centuries. The *Shin kokinshū* was to contain some of the best poetry of the past while providing the coveted means of publishing the finest work of the compilers' own day. Within the anthology, the arrangement of poems by poetic topics, the progression of the seasons and the like, and the nature of the poems themselves offer a kind of running metaphor as individual poems and groups of poems echo comparable segments of the *Kokinshū*, sometimes emphasizing differences of treatment stemming from altered poetic styles, sometimes suggesting continuity and the persistence of the grand tradition over the centuries of the high court culture.

Major Poets—— The retired sovereign's ambitions for the *Shin kokinshū* could hardly have led to such important results were it not that the so-called "Age of the *Shin kokinshū*"—the generation of Go-Toba and of such younger innovative poets as Teika, Ietaka, Ariie, and Jakuren, together with the immediately preceding generation of Fujiwara no Shunzei (FUJIWARA NO TOSHINARI) and the priest SAIGYŌ—was a brilliant poetic age, a period when the court was graced by at least a score of the finest of Japan's classical poets. Although poetic skill and quality were but two of several criteria governing the decisions to include few or many poems by a given individual in the *Shin kokinshū*, the poets represented by the highest number of poems are in fact among the foremost talents of this and the previous age. The most prominent poets in terms of the number of their poems selected are, for the age of the *Shin kokinshū*: Priest Saigyō, 94; Archbishop JIEN, 92; Fujiwara no Yoshitsune, 79; Fujiwara no Shunzei, 72; Princess SHIKISHI, 49; Fujiwara no Teika, 46; Fujiwara no Ietaka, 43; Jakuren, 35; ex-Emperor Go-Toba, 34; and FUJIWARA NO TOSHINARI NO MUSUME (Toshinari's daughter), 29. Of poets of earlier periods, those with the largest numbers of poems are: KI NO TSURAYUKI, 34; Lady IZUMI SHIKIBU, 25; KAKINOMOTO NO HITOMARO, 23, of which several are false attributions; MINAMOTO NO TSUNENOBU, 19; and SUGAWARA NO MICHIZANE and SONE NO YOSHITADA, 16 each.

Structure—— Like the *Kokinshū*, whose structure provided the basic pattern for subsequent imperial anthologies, the *Shin kokinshū* consists of 20 books in the following order: Books 1–6, The Seasons (1–2, Spring; 3, Summer; 4–5, Autumn; 6, Winter); Book 7, Felicitations; Book 8, Laments; Book 9, Partings; Book 10, Travel; Books 11–15, Love; Books 16–18, Miscellaneous; Book 19, Shintō Poems; Book 20, Buddhist Poems. Great care was taken in the ordering and integration of the poems in accordance with the principles of association and progression. Thus, within the first 6 books, the poems follow a sequence portraying the natural advance of the seasons from beginning to end; the 5 books of love poems dramatize the development of a courtly love affair from the lover's first approaches to his eventual abandonment of the woman to loneliness and despair. Within such larger progressions, there are numerous subprogressions which also serve to bind the individual poems into larger units. For example, some subsequences may show a geographical progression from mountains to plains to the sea; others reflect a natural cycle of time from dawn to daylight to twilight to night. Still other subgroups are contrived to play off a set of older poems on a given poetic topic against a set by more recent poets; others may consist of sets of poems on a progression of topics selected from a common source, such as the record of a poetry contest or the like. In addition to such considerations, mostly having to do with the principle of progression, care was also usually taken to provide a smooth transition from poem to poem by varying kinds of association—each poem being harmoniously related to the preceding one by some common image or images, by contrasting or related images, or even by the more complex device of common allusion to an older poem. The principles of association and progression, already seen at work in the structure of the *Kokinshū*, had been followed with varying degrees of fidelity and success in all six of the imperial anthologies that succeeded it, but never before (or since) were they applied with equal skill and subtlety to create such a stunning aesthetic effect as in the *Shin kokinshū*. Much of the credit for this unusual attention to the ordering of poems is due to Go-Toba, who insisted upon numerous revisions in order to achieve the desired effect.

Poetic Styles—— Containing poems from all periods of Japanese poetry, the *Shin kokinshū* displays a great variety of poetic styles and modes. The typical poetry of the "Age of the *Shin kokinshū*," however, is unequaled for its rich, romantic evocativeness and subtle nuances of tone. The most distinctive feature of the new poetry of the age is its tonal depth—a depth achieved partly by frequent allusion to older poetry, and partly by employing natural images as symbols of tone and feeling. Such poetry is preeminently neoclassical, exploring and exploiting the resources of what was by now a classical poetic tradition of three-and-a-half centuries. Tradition had endowed the images of nature—the moon, cherry blossoms, autumn foliage, snow—with tonal associations of beauty, fragility, loneliness, and so on, which could be used by the poets as universal symbols of mind and feeling. Thus, the great nature poetry of the age is a poetry of descriptive symbolism, dominated by Fujiwara no Shunzei's ideal of *yūgen* (mystery and depth), and Fujiwara no Teika's ideals of *yōen* (ethereal beauty) and *ushin* (conviction of feeling).

Despite the subtle shadings of tone for which the poetry of the age is so remarkable, there is undeniably a dominant or overarching feeling of sadness and melancholy *(sabi)*, even on such disparate subjects as nature and love. The poetry of loneliness represented an aesthetic ideal rather than a prevailingly pessimistic spirit of the age, but there were other ideals as well. Another important style, expressive of an ideal favored particularly by Go-Toba, sought an elevated and lofty tone (called *taketakashi* or *tōshiroshi*), conveyed typically by a refreshing simplicity of declaration or description. Such poems often presented a large natural panorama surveyed from a distant vantage point.

Influence on Later Literature—— The *Shin kokinshū* and its poetry had a profound influence upon later poets and other literary genres, from linked verse (RENGA AND HAIKAI) to the Nō drama. The great Nō playwright ZEAMI (1363–1443) sought aesthetic ideals and effects borrowed and adapted from Fujiwara no Shunzei's *yūgen* and Fujiwara no Teika's *yōen*. The foremost *haikai* poet, BASHŌ (1644–94), looked back both to the great father and son and to Saigyō for inspiration and poetic precedent. And although less highly esteemed in the later 19th century and early 20th, chiefly owing to the influence of the poet and critic MASAOKA SHIKI (1867–1902), the *Shin kokinshū* has come into favor again in recent decades. At the present time, it is one of the most studied and written about of Japan's classical literary works, and contemporary poets have come to appreciate its triumphs of tone and technique and the unique beauty of its poems.

——Ariyoshi Tamotsu, *Shin kokin wakashū no kenkyū: Dempon to kōsei* (1968). Robert H. Brower and Earl Miner, *Japanese Court Poetry* (1961). Fujihira Haruo, *Shin kokin kafū no keisei*

(1969). Gotō Shigeo, *Shin kokin wakashū no kisoteki kenkyū* (1968). Kazamaki Keijirō, *Shin kokin jidai* (1932). Kojima Yoshio, *Shin kokin wakashū no kenkyū* (1944–46). Konishi Jin'ichi, "Association and Progression: Principles of Integration in Anthologies and Sequences of Japanese Court Poetry," *Harvard Journal of Asiatic Studies* 21 (1958). Kubota Jun, *Shin kokin kajin no kenkyū* (1973). Kubota Jun, *Shin kokin wakashū zenhyōshaku* (1976–77). Kubota Utsubo, *Kampon shin kokin wakashū* (1964–65).

Robert H. BROWER

Shinkokugeki

Modern drama troupe founded in 1917 by actor-manager SAWADA SHŌJIRŌ and named Shinkokugeki (New National Theater) in accordance with the SHINGEKI (new theater) principles of Sawada's mentor TSUBOUCHI SHŌYŌ. Dissatisfied with the overintellectual *shingeki* movement, Sawada sought to create with the Shinkokugeki troupe a popular, indigenous, contemporary theatrical form.

After a number of early Shinkokugeki failures, Sawada's small group of actors and actresses found increasing success with swashbuckling period plays in minor theaters around Ōsaka. Riding a contemporary current boom in novels about swordfighters, Sawada staged and starred in period plays dominated by athletic, realistic action. Yukitomo Rifū (1877–1959), the troupe's first important playwright, created the initial core of the Shinkokugeki repertoire with works about famous swordsmen, *Kunisada Chūji* (1919) and *Tsukigata Hampeita* (1919).

During the early 1920s the troupe's appearances in silent film versions of several of their hit plays became an important base on which pioneer motion picture directors like KINUGASA TEINOSUKE built the *jidaigeki* (period drama) film tradition of Japan. The most popular Shinkokugeki sword plays of this decade were Yukitomo's adaptation of NAKAZATO KAIZAN's novel *Daibosatsu Tōge* (1913–41; tr *Dai-Bosatsu Toge: Great Boddhisattva Pass*, 1929); Nukada Mutsutomi's Japanization of Rostand's *Cyrano de Bergerac* titled *Shirano Benjūrō*; and several works derived from the familiar KABUKI play *Kanadehon chūshingura* (1748, The Treasury of Loyal Retainers; tr *Chūshingura*, 1971).

Sawada varied his bills with plays out of the *shingeki* tradition such as Shakespeare's *Coriolanus* and SATŌ KŌROKU's *Kirisuto* (1928, Christ) as well as with the troupe's interpretations of SHIMPA standards such as the adaptation of OZAKI KŌYŌ's *Konjiki yasha* (1897–1902; tr *The Golden Demon*, 1905). All of this made Shinkokugeki the dominant theatrical troupe of the 1920s.

Following the sudden death of Sawada in 1929, the troupe lost momentum for several years. Two new stars, Shimada Shōgo (b 1905) and Tatsumi Ryūtarō (b 1905), emerged from the rank and file to share the founder's principal roles. Under the leadership of these two men, the reorganized troupe continued to develop playwrights like popular novelist HASEGAWA SHIN, who wrote many Shinkokugeki standard plays including *Seki no Yatappe* (1929, Yatappe at the Barrier), *Mabuta no haha* (1930, Mother in My Dreams), and *Kutsukake Tokijirō* (1928). Although the troupe continued to emphasize its hallmark sword-action plays, Shinkokugeki in the mid-1930s also developed a strong line of local color, slice-of-life plays in modern settings.

When the postwar American Occupation prohibited swordplays because of their "feudal content," Shinkokugeki increased its production of plays about contemporary low life. *Ōshō* (1947, Chess Master), by the troupe's playwright HŌJŌ HIDEJI, was the major achievement of this period. The troupe eventually revived its sword-fighting spectaculars and returned to a balanced mixed repertoire.

During the 1950s, Shinkokugeki became active in film, radio, and eventually television. When changes in the economy of the theatrical world made it increasingly difficult to maintain the company strength of 150 members, the troupe reorganized in 1954 to allow its actors opportunities to pursue independent careers. After six decades of uninterrupted activity, Shinkokugeki continues as a historic force in popular theater with several month-long performances every year.

▰ ——Shinkokugeki, ed, *Shinkokugeki gojūnen* (1967).

J. L. ANDERSON

Shinkokushi

(New National History). Official court history compiled in the mid-10th century by Fujiwara no Saneyori (900–970) and/or Ōe no Asatsuna (886–957) at the command of Emperor Murakami (r 946–967).

It was a continuation of the *Nihon sandai jitsuroku* (901; see RIKKOKUSHI) and is also known as *Shoku sandai jitsuroku*. The work is lost, and little is known of its contents; but it was presumably modeled on its predecessor and probably recorded the reigns of the emperors UDA (r 887–897), DAIGO (r 897–930), and Suzaku (r 930–946).

Shin Kyōiku Undō

(New Education Movement). Early 20th century educational movement emphasizing the individuality and initiative of the student in opposition to the standardized education of the state-controlled school system as it had existed since the early Meiji period (1868–1912). The principles and methods espoused by the Japanese movement were those of the European and American progressive education movement that arose in the late 19th and early 20th centuries.

The need for such a movement in Japan was suggested by TANIMOTO TOMERI, who spent three years (1900–1903) in Europe and the United States studying new educational theories. These ideas were first put into practice in Japan in the early Taishō period (1912–26) by OIKAWA HEIJI; he adopted group education methods based on the German *Gruppenunterricht* at the elementary school attached to Akashi Women's Normal School. The Japanese movement continued to develop during this period and was centered in the elementary schools attached to normal schools and at private elementary schools. Private schools such as SAWAYANAGI MASATARŌ's Seijō Elementary School, HANI MOTOKO's Jiyū Gakuen, Akai Yonekichi's Myōjō Gakuen, and OBARA KUNIYOSHI's Tamagawa Gakuen made "new education" a basic tenet of their teaching philosophy. The movement, however, suffered under the conservative educational policies of the militarists in the 1930s and had lost much of its vitality by the time World War II began. Many of the movement's central ideas were revived during the postwar educational reform.

SUGIYAMA Akio

Shinkyō Kyōdōtai

(literally, "State of Mind Community"). Small cooperative community in Kasama, Haibara Chō, Nara Prefecture. It operates the Shinkyō Nōsan, a factory producing *fusuma* (sliding doors), as well as the Shinkyō Sōen (established 1966), a facility for the mentally retarded. In 1936 Ozaki Masutarō (b 1900), a proselytizer for the religious group TENRIKYŌ, went through a religious crisis and smashed the Shintō altar in the local Tenrikyō office where he lived. Among other reasons, he cited the continued illness of his daughter despite the claims of the Tenrikyō religion to cure sickness. Ozaki persuaded several neighbors to smash their altars as well, and they soon found themselves ostracized (see MURAHACHIBU) by the villagers of Kasama. In order to survive, Ozaki and four families formed an agricultural cooperative. During World War II, some 40 members emigrated to Manchuria. Reunited as a group in 1946, they decided to make *tatami* mats to supplement their income; in 1968 they changed to the production of *fusuma*. Membership at present is composed of 17 or 18 families, a total of about 60 people, and there are some 120 residents of the facility for the retarded. The community seeks a way of life in which all its members may live in complete harmony and equality. Each member works according to his abilities and receives daily necessities; he is also free to help himself from a communal cash box. All members bathe communally every day after work; great ritual significance is attached to this activity as a transition between the periods of work and rest. The commune has no legal status and is held together simply by devotion and loyalty to Ozaki. A memoir of the founding of the community by Sugihara Yoshie (b 1907), one of Ozaki's closest followers has been translated with an afterword by David Plath as *Sensei and His People: The Building of a Japanese Commune* (1969). Another book by Sugihara about the community is *Ai no aru mura: Shinkyō Kyōdōtai no Kiroku* (1978).

Shin Nampin → Shen Nanpin (Shen Nan-p'in)

Shin Nan'yō

City in southern Yamaguchi Prefecture, western Honshū, on the Inland Sea. Formerly a fishing and farming area, more recently it has seen the construction of petrochemical and steel plants on reclaimed land. Rice and tea are grown in the surrounding areas. Pop: 34,367.

Shin Nihon bungaku

(New Japanese Literature). Literary organ founded immediately after World War II by the Shin Nihon Bungaku Kai (New Japanese Literature Society), an organization of veterans of the prewar PROLETARIAN LITERATURE MOVEMENT who were still committed to the leftist cause. The society was founded in December 1945 and a preliminary issue, including articles by members MIYAMOTO YURIKO, TOKUNAGA SUNAO, and NAKANO SHIGEHARU, appeared the next month; regular publication started in March 1946. FUJIMORI SEIKICHI, Akita Ujaku (1883–1962), Eguchi Kiyoshi (1887–1975), KURAHARA KOREHITO, KUBOKAWA TSURUJIRŌ, and TSUBOI SHIGEJI were also among the nine original members, and later arrivals included ODAGIRI HIDEO and NOMA HIROSHI. In 1947 it engaged in a debate with the KINDAI BUNGAKU coterie about politics and literature. Over the years it has published original works and essays by such writers as SATA INEKO, KAIKŌ KEN, FUJIEDA SHIZUO, and KUROI SENJI. Despite recurring factionalism and a succession of disputes with the Japan Communist Party, *Shin Nihon bungaku* has survived until the present day. — *Theodore W. Goossen*

Shin Nihon Shūkyō Dantai Rengōkai → Union of New Religious Organizations of Japan

Shinoda Masahiro (1931–   )

Film director; the only politically and aesthetically conservative filmmaker to emerge from the so-called Shōchiku New Wave (Nūberu Bāgu; i.e., *nouvelle vague*) at the Shōchiku motion picture company (see SHŌCHIKU CO, LTD) in the early 1960s. Shinoda's films are distinguished by an innovative use of traditional dramatic forms, abrupt cutting, and a studied prettiness.

Shinoda was born in 1931 in Gifu Prefecture, where his prominent family had a long tradition of involvement in the arts. Shinoda went to Waseda University, where he studied theater history and probably would have remained a perennial graduate student had his mother not died. The cessation of the living allowance she had provided forced him to seek employment.

In 1953, he took the Shōchiku employment exam, and was one of the 8 out of 2,000 candidates to be accepted by the studio as an assistant director. Shinoda excelled in this capacity under almost all of Shōchiku's established directors, including OZU YASUJIRŌ. But at the end of the 1950s Shōchiku was losing its mainstay female audience to television, and the company was in serious financial difficulties. The success of the *nouvelle vague* in France inspired a similar gamble on the youngest and most iconoclastic of the assistant directors, ŌSHIMA NAGISA. The critical acclaim for his first two leftist-flavored, nihilistic films raised hopes for the garnering of a youth audience. Shinoda and another colleague, Yoshida Yoshishige (b 1933), were next in line for the company-created New Wave. Shinoda seized upon the New Wave opportunity to bring new life into the established scripts and music of the Shōchiku film. Although his earliest works are little melodramas that embarrass him to this day—"my diaper period" is the way he refers to everything before his 1962 *Namida o shishi no tategami ni* (Tears on the Lion's Mane)—he was able to introduce new writers and composers during the brief moment of freedom the New Wave provided. He claims poet-playwright-filmmaker TERAYAMA SHŪJI and composer TAKEMITSU TŌRU, who has done almost all Japanese film scores of distinction since 1960, as his personal discoveries.

Shaken by Japan's defeat in the Pacific War, when he was still a high school student, Shinoda has set out to analyze the Japanese character and aesthetics. For example, in his *Kawaita hana* (1963, Pale Flower), he explores ceremonial behavior, focusing on gangster organizations, because "the gang is the only place where the Japanese ceremonial structure can be fully sustained." Other favorite Shinoda themes include what he sees as the masochistic and suicidal tendencies in the Japanese, particularly in the context of erotic love. For Shinoda, love is always heightened by the risk of disaster, and that risk becomes a certainty as soon as jealousy emerges.

One of the outstanding aspects of Shinoda's films is his innovative use of traditional forms. *Shinjū ten no Amijima* (1969, Love Suicide at Amijima or Double Suicide) is based on a popular 1720 *bunraku* puppet play. Many traditional devices have been kept in the film, including a narrator and the presence of stagehands, who direct the actors at times, making the latter appear more puppetlike. Admiring his predecessor, MIZOGUCHI KENJI, Shinoda has selected

Shinran —— Portrait

Shinran in his later years. Detail. Ink on paper. 71.8 × 32.9 cm. Mid-13th century. Nishi Honganji, Kyōto. National Treasure.

similar subjects to film: traditional theater, e.g., *Buraikan* (1970, The Scandalous Adventures of Buraikan), which is a celebration of KABUKI; the literature of IZUMI KYŌKA, e.g., *Yashagaike* (1979, The Demon Pond); and male-female relationships in different historical eras. His individuality as a director lies in the consistency of his theme of sexual and political sadomasochism in every walk of Japanese life at every point in history. In recent years his style has tended toward a peculiar mannerism; for example, in the use of kabuki actor Bandō Tamasaburō to play a sweet country bride in *Yashagaike*.

📖 —— Audie Bock, *Japanese Film Directors* (1978).

Audie Bock

shi-nō-kō-shō

(warrior-farmer-artisan-merchant). The four classes into which the Japanese people were divided during the Edo period (1600–1868). This system of occupational class distinction originated in ancient China. In Japan it was officially established in the mid-17th century, although in fact a four-tier social hierarchy had been in existence since the late 16th century, when a series of decrees issued by the national unifier TOYOTOMI HIDEYOSHI forbade *samurai* to engage in farming or trade and peasants from leaving the land for other pursuits. The distinction between warrior and farmer was sharpened by Hideyoshi's SWORD HUNT of 1588, when all weapons were confiscated from the peasantry. Besides the four main categories, there existed small outcaste groups, HININ and *eta* (see BURAKUMIN). For all practical purposes, however, Japanese society was divided into samurai and nonsamurai. Artisans and merchants were often collectively called "townsmen" (CHŌNIN). The four-class system was abolished in 1869, a year after the Meiji Restoration; at that time, of a population of 30,090,000, the samurai class constituted 6.4 percent, the lower three classes 90.62 percent, outcastes 1.73 percent, and others (court nobles, monks and nuns) 1.25 percent. The Meiji government established three new categories: *kazoku* (nobility; see PEERAGE), SHIZOKU (former samurai), and HEIMIN (commoners). The Meiji system was itself abolished at the end of World War II.

Shino ware → Mino ware

Shinran (1173–1263)

Founder of the JŌDO SHIN SECT of PURE LAND BUDDHISM, a sect based on the principle of birth into the Pure Land (attainment of enlightenment) through faith *(shinjin)* alone.

Although details concerning his life are sparse, there are five generally recognized periods in his career. Shinran entered the monastic life at about the age of eight in 1181 and served as a *dōsō* (menial monk) at the temple ENRYAKUJI on Mt. Hiei (Hieizan) outside of Kyōto until 1201, when he became a disciple of HŌNEN, the founder of the JŌDO SECT. After a period of study under Hōnen, Shinran, with his master and several other disciples, was sent into exile by the government in 1207. In 1212 he received a pardon, and in about 1214 he migrated to the Kantō region, settling in Inada in Hitachi Province (now Ibaraki Prefecture). Around 1235 he returned to Kyōto, where he remained until his death.

The letters of Shinran's wife, Eshin Ni, provide clear evidence that Shinran was a *dōsō* on Mt. Hiei. *Dōsō* were low-ranking monks who served mainly in the Hall of Continuous Nembutsu (Jō-gyō Zammaidō), where they performed NEMBUTSU (recitations of the name of the Buddha AMIDA [Skt: Amitābha]) in services sponsored by the nobility on behalf of their departed kin. The letters also record that Shinran became anxious about his birth into the Pure Land and sought relief by undertaking 100 days of intense meditation in the temple Rokkakudō in Kyōto. On the 95th day he had a dream of Prince SHŌTOKU that led him to Hōnen, with whom he studied another 100 days, finally becoming his disciple. Hōnen, convinced of the difficulty of attaining enlightenment through one's self-power in an age of degeneracy (*mappō*; see ESCHATOLOGY), was then proclaiming the practice of *nembutsu* as the sole means of birth into the Pure Land. Shinran later dated this event in his work KYŌ-GYŌSHINSHŌ: "But I, Gutoku (Ignorant Bald Head) Shinran, in the first year of Kennin (1201), abandoned the difficult practices and took refuge in the Primal Vow."

The years of intimate association with Hōnen, during which he was permitted to copy the master's major work, the *Senchaku hongan nembutsu shū* (Treatise on the Selection of the Nembutsu of the Primal Vow; see SENCHAKUSHŪ), and his portrait, were very brief. As Hōnen's *nembutsu* group became popular and influential among the people, criticism and opposition by the monks of Mt. Hiei and Kōfukuji in Nara, as well as alleged indiscretions by his disciples, led to the abolition of the community by the government, the exile of major followers, and the execution of two members. Hōnen was banished to Shikoku, while Shinran was exiled to Echigo Province (now Niigata Prefecture) and given the secular name Fujii Zenshin. In the *Kyōgyōshinshō* Shinran later denounced the injustice of the government in this affair, especially the exile of his master, Hōnen, who was over 70 years old at the time.

Shinran's life during the four-year period of exile is very obscure, though it is clear that he married and began to raise a family of seven or eight children. Shinran was the first Buddhist priest to be publicly married; thereafter the practice became fairly common. The necessity of living in the harsh environment of Echigo as a religious layman laid the basis for his distinctive interpretations of Buddhist doctrine.

Shinran did not return to Kyōto after his pardon at the end of 1211, for his master died at the beginning of the following year. Instead, he migrated with his family to the Kantō region. In the course of his ministry in the eastern provinces, he gathered a body of followers, of whom 74 are known. As leaders, they must have represented a much larger group of believers. A major development in this phase of his life was the compilation of his monumental work, *Kyōgyōshinshō*. Interspersed with interpretive comments, it is an anthology drawing from sutras and commentaries in order to make clear the true teaching (*kyō*), living (*gyō*), faith (*shin*), and realizing (*shō*) of the Pure Land school. Its central purpose was, perhaps, to provide a fuller exposition of Hōnen's doctrines. However, an important feature of the work is the insertion of a section on faith within the traditional Buddhist outline of teaching, living, and realizing. Shinran made faith, conferred by Amida Buddha, the precondition for attainment of birth into the Pure Land, rather than an individual's practice. In later years Shinran revised and copied the text for his disciples. Its themes were further popularized in WASAN (poems or hymns in the Japanese language).

After his return to Kyōto around 1235, Shinran devoted himself to literary efforts, which extended to about 1260. From his vantage point in Kyōto, he counseled or assisted his disciples through a variety of writings. He copied Pure Land texts or made commentaries on them; he also composed many *wasan* and continued to refine the *Kyōgyōshinshō*. A major part of his writings during this period was the correspondence he carried on with distant disciples. His letters, of which 43 survive, give insight into Shinran's personality and attitudes, his relations with his disciples, and the problems and disputes that beset the early Jōdo Shin community.

The most tragic incident of this period was Shinran's decision in 1256 to disown his eldest son Zenran (1210–92) who had assumed authority over the Kantō disciples. In some instances Zenran divided congregations, drawing believers to himself and creating confusion among the followers of Shinran. Whatever the true nature of the situation, Shinran had to sever relations with his son in order to demonstrate his good faith with his leading disciples.

After a period of turbulence caused by disputes and suits against Pure Land teaching, the fellowship became more tranquil, and Shinran communicated some of his deepest insights in such works as *Jinen hōni shō* (Treatise on the Ultimate Truth of Things). He died in 1263 in Kyōto, tended by his brother Jin'yu, a Tendai priest, and his daughter Kakushin Ni (1224–83). His ashes were interred in the Ōtani area, west of Higashiyama in Kyōto; the site became a devotional center, and later the location of the temple HONGANJI.

The central thesis of Shinran's teaching developed from his deep awareness of human imperfection as manifested in profound and persistent egoism and the ineradicability of passion. He came to the conclusion that the possibility of birth in the Pure Land and attainment of enlightenment arise solely from the working and fulfillment of the Vows of Amida, particularly the 18th Vow of the Larger *Sukhāvatī-vyūha-sūtra* (one of the triple Pure Land sutras) in which Amida declares his intention to lead all sentient beings who recite his name to enlightenment and birth in the Pure Land. The working of the Vow arouses faith and creates confidence that one is embraced by Amida's compassion. While traditional Buddhist schools understood faith as an inward spiritual movement through which people aspired to enlightenment, Shinran stressed that the root source of that faith was Amida's compassion manifested sincerely and truly in the mind of the person. Faith is, therefore, not a human act but transcendental reality coming to realization in the person.

In his later years Shinran's conception of Amida deepened and became more absolute. He viewed Amida as the Eternal (*kuon jitsujō*) Buddha with neither beginning nor end in contrast to a Buddha who has a beginning though no end. His attitude may have been shaped by the important teaching of original enlightenment (HONGAKU) in Tendai thought, as well as by his own evolving religious awareness. In addition, he employed the term *jinen hōni* (dharma as is), which refers to the highest and genuine level of reality which is beyond human conception. From this perspective he constantly contrasted the natural and spontaneous fulfillment of the Vow with the deliberations and calculations of individual self-assertion (*hakarai*).

As a result of Shinran's strong denial that enlightenment required any efforts on the part of the person for its attainment, he affirmed that the assurance of enlightenment arises in the moment of awakening faith. Although he advocated the recitation of the *nembutsu*, Shinran regarded it as an outward manifestation of this inward realization. As a response to the awareness of Amida's compassion, its purpose was to express gratitude rather than to gain merit or achieve purification as a condition for birth in the Pure Land.

Shinran set aside the traditional belief that, as evidence that they had the required virtue for birth, Amida would welcome devotees who lay on their deathbeds into the Pure Land. Rather, the moment of faith was for him simultaneously the moment one attains assurance of birth and entry into the assembly of the truly assured (*shōjōju*). According to Shinran, believers are thus "equal to *tathāgata*" (enlightened ones; see NYORAI) and to Maitreya Buddha (see MIROKU). The causes which make it certain that we will attain final Buddhahood have been established as surely as they have been for Buddhas as well as for Maitreya, who, though still a bodhisattva, is already a Buddha. Shinran's reinterpretation of key Pure Land teachings transformed the focus of religious interest and concern. The followers of the Jōdo Shin sect could develop their lives in this world, knowing that their final destiny was assured and all the dark fears of this world dispelled through the light of Amida's absolute compassionate embrace.

■ ——Alfred Bloom, *Shinran's Gospel of Pure Grace* (1965). Alfred Bloom, *The Life of Shinran Shonin: The Journey to Self-acceptance* (1968). Futaba Kenkō, *Shinran no kenkyū* (1963). Kikumura Norihiko, *Shinran: His Life and Thought* (1972). *Kyōgyōshinshō*, Ryūkoku Translation Series V (1966). Daigan and Alicia Matsunaga, *Foundation of Japanese Buddhism, 2* (1976). Matsuno Junkō, *Shinran* (1960). Nishi Honganji, Kyōgaku Shinkō Iinkai, ed, *Rekishi no naka no Shinran* (1973). Ohtani Yoshiko, *Eshin-ni, the Wife of Shinran shonin* (1970). *Shinshū shōgyō zensho*, 5 vols (1953). Daisetz T. Suzuki, *Shin Buddhism* (1970). Ueda Yoshifumi, ed, *The Letters of Shinran* (1978). Yamamoto Kōshō, *Kyōgyōshinshō* (nd).
Alfred BLOOM

Shinritsu Kōryō

The first national code of criminal law in modern Japan; promulgated by the Dajōkan (Grand Council of State) in 1870, soon after the MEIJI RESTORATION. Consisting of 192 statutes, it was based mainly on the criminal codes of the Ming (1368–1644) and Qing (Ch'ing; 1644–1912) dynasties of China and showed virtually no influence from Western legal traditions. Together with its amendment and supplement, the KAITEI RITSUREI (1873), it remained in force until 1882, when it was replaced by the new Criminal Code (Keihō).

Shinron

(New Discourse). Two-volume work completed in 1825 by AIZAWA SEISHISAI, a scholar of the MITO SCHOOL of historical studies. Writing in response to the increase in the number of foreign ships frequenting Japanese waters in defiance of the NATIONAL SECLUSION policy, the author discussed world conditions and his belief in Japan's innate superiority as manifested by its unique national polity (kokutai). He argued that Western nations were subverting people with Christianity and attempting to conquer the world through trade and military power. He argued further that to counter this, the Japanese should carry out political reforms, build up their military, and under imperial leadership properly venerate the Shintō gods and act as one. Although Seishisai presented the work to the daimyō of Mito (now part of Ibaraki Prefecture), it could not be published because of its extremist views; copies were secretly made and circulated by his disciples. Shinron provided an ideological framework for the SONNŌ JŌI (Revere the Emperor, Expel the Barbarians) movement that was to gather force in later years and culminate in the Meiji Restoration of 1868.

Shinsambetsu

(official name Zenkoku Sangyōbetsu Rōdō Kumiai Rengō; National Federation of Industrial Labor Organizations). An independent group of industrial labor unions organized in 1949, when it seceded from the SAMBETSU KAIGI (Congress of Industrial Labor Unions of Japan). It then took the name Shinsambetsu, meaning "new Sambetsu." Shinsambetsu joined SŌHYŌ (General Council of Trade Unions of Japan) in 1950, when the latter was formed. Because Sōhyō had become increasingly leftist, Shinsambetsu separated from it in 1952. The federation, though relatively small, has pursued an independent course as a neutral organization in the Japanese labor movement, in which Sōhyō and its rival, DŌMEI (Japanese Confederation of Labor), play dominant roles. It has little influence in wage bargaining but has attracted attention as a potential catalyst for the unification of the Japanese labor movement. Total membership stood at 61,000 in 1978. KURITA Ken

Shinseisakuza

Theater company of approximately 130 members. Founded in 1950, Shinseisakuza has been led since then by Mayama Miho (b 1922), daughter of MAYAMA SEIKA. From its inception the company has specialized in touring throughout Japan, performing before audiences which have no other opportunities to watch theater. Its early productions consisted mainly of plays by Mayama Miho. In 1960 the "Shinseisakuza Festival," a program of folk dances, songs, and short sketches, was added to the repertoire. Regular productions of plays by Mayama Seika began in 1972. Shinseisakuza has toured extensively abroad since 1963, to Indonesia, Brazil, and China. The company is now divided into four groups, of which the first produces plays by Mayama Seika; the second, "Festival"; and the third and fourth, plays by Mayama Miho. Although Shinseisakuza frequently appears in large theaters in the big cities, its main effort is still directed toward theatrically deprived rural areas.
Brian POWELL

Shinsengumi

Small, elite group of swordsmen commissioned by the Tokugawa shogunate in 1863 as a special police unit to counter antishogunate activities in Kyōto. Called at first the Rōshigumi (most of its members were RŌNIN), the group was organized in Edo (now Tōkyō) in 1863 and sent to Kyōto to guard the shogun, who was visiting that city. However, Kiyokawa Hachirō (1830–63), one of its leaders, and his faction were recalled to Edo for expressing proimperial sentiments. The approximately 20 remaining members reorganized under Serizawa Kamo (d 1863) and took the name Shinsengumi. Serizawa was murdered in an internal struggle, and KONDŌ ISAMI

and Hijikata Toshizō (1835–69) emerged as the new leaders. With headquarters at Mibu in Kyōto, the Shinsengumi acted under orders from the KYŌTO SHUGOSHOKU, the commissioner newly appointed to keep peace in the city. The group was involved in the famous massacre of imperial-loyalist activists at the Ikedaya inn in 1864 (IKEDAYA INCIDENT) and in the defense of the Imperial Palace in the HAMAGURI GOMON INCIDENT. Even after the Meiji Restoration (1868) the Shinsengumi remained loyal to the shōgun, fighting against the imperial forces in the BOSHIN CIVIL WAR.

Shinsen jikyō

A Chinese-Japanese character dictionary compiled by the Buddhist monk Shōjū (dates unknown) in the late 9th or early 10th century. It contains more than 20,000 Chinese characters (KANJI) arranged by radical with the Japanese approximation of the Chinese pronunciation (see ON READINGS). It also includes the Japanese pronunciation (see KUN READINGS) of some 3,000 words (character or character compounds), being the oldest existing Japanese dictionary to provide such information. It draws on numerous other documents for its sources. The Shinsen jikyō is an important resource work for the study of Chinese characters as well as for research into the phonology and vocabulary of Japanese in ancient times and the study of ancient documents. See also DICTIONARIES.
Uwano Zendō

Shinsen shōjiroku

(Newly Compiled Record of Surnames). A genealogy of important noble families of the early part of the Heian period (794–1185). The compilation was begun at the order of Emperor KAMMU in 799 by a committee led by his son Prince Manda (788–830); it was completed in the reign of Emperor SAGA and presented to the throne in 815. The work, in 30 sections, lists 1,177 (originally 1,182) families (UJI) living in the capital and the five surrounding provinces. They are grouped in categories including kōbetsu (offshoots of the imperial line, descended from AMATERASU ŌMIKAMI), shimbetsu (those claiming descent from other deities), bambetsu (those of foreign origin), and so forth. It is a valuable source for the study of ancient Japanese history.
G. Cameron HURST III

Shinsen tsukubashū

The second important anthology of renga (linked verse; see RENGA AND HAIKAI) following the pioneering TSUKUBASHŪ (1356); it marked the high point of renga's development in the Muromachi period (1333–1568). Compiled in 1495 by SŌGI and INAWASHIRO KENSAI, it came about through the recommendation and support of the daimyō Ōuchi Masahiro, then a powerful official in the capital, and, submitted to Emperor Go-Tsuchimikado, was designated an "honorary imperial anthology" (jun chokusenshū). It includes some 2,000 verses composed roughly between 1429 and 1495 by some 241 poets of the nobility, the clergy, and the warrior class. Fully one-fourth of the verses are by SHINKEI and others of the so-called Renga Shichiken (Seven Sages of Renga), the poet-monks who dominated the art from the mid-15th century on. This, coupled with the deliberate omission of haikai no renga (comic renga; a precursor of HAIKU), which was becoming increasingly popular at the time, clearly indicates Sōgi's desire to make the anthology representative of the orthodox renga style.

Shinshichō

(New Currents of Thought). Literary magazine whose publication extended through 18 series, with lapses, from 1907 to 1970; the first four series are generally regarded as most important. Series one Shinshichō (October 1907–March 1908) was founded by OSANAI KAORU, a man of many literary talents. Its aim was the introduction of modern drama and new literary trends from abroad. Accordingly, it published translations of criticism on and works by Western playwrights and writers such as Ibsen, Strindberg, Stendahl, Hardy, and Chekhov. It also introduced original essays, stories, and poems by writers like MASAMUNE HAKUCHŌ, OGURI FŪYŌ, KAMBARA ARIAKE, and IWANO HŌMEI. Series one Shinshichō was a precursor of the SHINGEKI ("new theater") movement and was opposed to the so-called Japanese NATURALISM.

Series two Shinshichō (September 1910–March 1911) was also edited by Osanai. Most of its collaborators were literature students at Tōkyō University and included WATSUJI TETSURŌ and TANIZAKI JUN'ICHIRŌ. It continued to emphasize criticism and drama and was, along with MITA BUNGAKU, founded that same year, one of the leading literary journals of the period. Tanizaki was the most prominent novelist associated with series two.

Series three *Shinshichō* (February–September 1914) was revived by a group of Tōkyō University graduates, including KUME MASAO, AKUTAGAWA RYŪNOSUKE, and YAMAMOTO YŪZŌ, who were joined by KIKUCHI KAN, then a Kyōto University student. They proclaimed individual expression as the guiding principle of the magazine, which was split between a tendency toward symbolism and realism. One of the group, Sangū Makoto (1892–1967), contributed a series of critical essays on writers ranging from Maeterlinck to Rimbaud to James and the impressionist and cubist schools of painting. Kume and Yamamoto were interested in realistic social drama, thus continuing *Shinshichō's* emphasis on theater.

Series four (February 1916–March 1917) was comprised mostly of members of the series three group. The major format change was the dropping of foreign works in translation and a concentration on original works by coterie members. The writings of this group were highly crafted and generally emphasized intellect over emotion; they were collectively referred to as the intellectual or neorealist school. Series five through eighteen, published intermittently between 1918 and 1970, continued *Shinshichō* as a college coterie magazine.

Theodore W. GOOSSEN

Shinshiro

City in eastern Aichi Prefecture, central Honshū, on the river Toyogawa. It prospered in the Edo period (1600–1868) as a river port and as a market town on the highway Ina Kaidō. Still the center of local commerce, it has many lumber mills and rubber plants. Pop: 34,558.

shinsho → paperback books

Shinshōji

Major temple of the Chizan branch (see CHISHAKUIN) of the SHINGON SECT of Buddhism, located in the city of Narita, Chiba Prefecture. Popularly known as Naritasan or Narita Fudō, Shinshōji was built to house an image of the ferocious Buddhist divinity Fudō Myōō (Skt: Acalanātha; see MYŌŌ), who is believed to suppress evil and vanquish the enemies of its devotees. According to tradition, the image which reputedly was carved by KŪKAI, the founder of the Shingon sect, was brought from JINGOJI in the Takao district of Kyōto to Narita in the hope that it would prove efficacious in helping to crush the rebellion of TAIRA NO MASAKADO. Shinshōji was built shortly after the latter's defeat and death in 940. Enjoying enormous popularity since the Edo period (1600–1868), the temple is thronged with pilgrims throughout the year, as it has become the center of the worship of Fudō, uniting many branch temples elsewhere.

Stanley WEINSTEIN

Shinshōsetsu

(New Fiction). Literary magazine of the late Meiji and Taishō periods (roughly 1889 to 1926) which sought to present new forms of the novel. Founded by AEBA KŌSON, Sudō Nansui (1857–1920), and Morita Shiken (1861–97), the original *Shinshōsetsu* appeared briefly from January 1889 to June 1890. In addition to original works of fiction, it carried plays, translations, and essays. The second series of *Shinshōsetsu* was published from July 1896 to November 1926. It was created to compete with BUNGEI KURABU, a periodical largely devoted to fiction. The editorship of *Shinshōsetsu* passed through several hands, including KŌDA ROHAN and ISHIBASHI NINGETSU in the early period and SUZUKI MIEKICHI, AKUTAGAWA RYŪNOSUKE, and KIKUCHI KAN later on. Devoted to the novel, it sought to encourage new writers; single issues were sometimes given up to the publication of a long work in its entirety. Writers whose works appeared in *Shinshōsetsu* included HIROTSU RYŪRŌ, IZUMI KYŌKA, SHIMAZAKI TŌSON, NATSUME SŌSEKI, TAYAMA KATAI, IWANO HŌMEI, and NAGAI KAFŪ.

Shinsui Kyōyo Rei

(Order for the Provision of Fuel and Water). Decree issued in 1842 by the Tokugawa shogunate ordering that foreign ships be provided with food, water, and other necessities, on condition that they leave Japan immediately. In the face of mounting pressure from Western powers to open its ports to trade, and especially after the news of China's defeat in the Opium War (1839–42), the shogunate recognized that it could no longer enforce its earlier order to repel foreign ships (GAIKOKUSEN UCHIHARAI REI). It therefore issued the Shinsui Kyōyo Rei as a compromise measure, hoping to retain the more essential features of its NATIONAL SECLUSION policy.

Shin Taisei Undō → New Order Movement

Shintō

Japan's indigenous religion. The word Shintō is written with two Chinese characters; the first, *shin* (Ch: *shen*), is also used to write the native Japanese term *kami* ("numinous entity" or "divinity"); the second, *tō* (Ch: *dao* or *tao*), is also used to write the native word *michi* ("way"). Shintō is a rich and complex system of religious practices, ideas, and institutions which slowly emerged at the dawn of Japanese history, crystallized as a religious system during the Nara (710–794) and Heian (794–1185) periods, and subsequently was in a constant and dynamic interaction with the other religious and philosophical systems of Asia: Buddhism, Taoism, and Confucianism. This interaction, which developed at all levels and gave birth to syncretic schools as well as to various cults for most of Japanese history, caused in the Edo period (1600–1868) a reaction which ultimately led to a revival of Shintō as the "Ancient Way," from which all foreign influences would supposedly be absent. This expurgated system was developed into a state religion at the end of the 19th century; however, in 1945 this status was abolished and Shintō was considered again as a religion among others.

Shintō may be looked at as a multiheaded phenomenon: appearing at times as a loosely structured set of practices, creeds, and attitudes rooted in local communities, it is also a strictly defined and organized religion at the level of the state. These two basic aspects are however not entirely separate and are responsible for, or reflect, much of the Japanese national character as it is expressed in sociopolitical structures, psychological attitudes, and aesthetic criteria.

ORIGINS AND FORMATIVE PERIOD

Archaeology for the Jōmon period (ca 10,000 BC–ca 300 BC) has yielded only scant information concerning the religious practices of the people who inhabited the archipelago at the time. Earthen statuettes (*dogū;* see JŌMON FIGURINES) found in sites in western Japan show exaggerated sex signs which seem to suggest the existence of fertility cults, but their relationship to burial customs is not understood. These statuettes represent animals as well and may have been used in connection with hunting. (Many animals were considered to be "messengers" of divinities in later periods.) The "rope" designs on the earliest vases do not provide any clue to their ritual use. In the latter part of the Jōmon period, drums and masks were made, which seems to point to shamanistic practices. Rites of passage were performed on both sexes, as the sawing or removal of front teeth indicates. Corpses were sometimes buried in jars in the fetal position.

The Yayoi period (ca 300 BC–ca AD 300), during which important population movements occurred and contacts with the continent intensified, left numerous artifacts showing that religious life was becoming more complex. Wetland agriculture necessitated well-organized and stable communities, and agricultural rites—which later played such an important role in Shintō—were developed. By that time the original horizontal perspective on the universe coexisted with the newer, shamanistic vertical perspective in which this world was capped by a Heaven where divinities reside, and covered a dark realm to which the dead went. One can still see signs of the horizontal perspective in a number of religious festivals, in which the divinities do not descend from above but come from beyond the horizon. Wooden statuettes representing anthropomorphic figures were recently found in Shiga Prefecture; this is important because divine entities in Shintō are anthropomorphic only in a few cases. Metal implements, such as weapons and mirrors, were deposited in burial sites, no doubt as emblems of political legitimacy. Cups and jars for food offerings have been found, which is significant if one considers the later stipulation of Shintō to the effect that the primary way of worship consists in offering food. Furthermore, the presence of such implements in burial sites seems to suggest a new vision of an afterlife. The exact use of certain bronze bell-shaped ritual objects called DŌTAKU remains yet to be determined. Oracular bones show the increasing importance of divination. Rites of passage were still practiced, though the removal of teeth was to disappear during the following historical period.

The Kofun period (ca 300–710) was marked by heavy influences from the continent. It was a time of dramatic changes which led to the emergence of Japan as a nation. Future research may provide us with crucial information concerning the exact nature of the relationships between Japan and Korea, which seem to have had an impact on the development of Shintō practices. The 100 or so Japanese "kingdoms" mentioned in the Chinese Wei Chronicles (WEI ZHI [Wei chih]) were gradually unified as relationships of clientage and allegiance were formed around the emerging powerful Yamato clan, which was to become the imperial lineage. The rulers of clans, which were based on territorial ties and not necessarily on blood ties, were buried in large stone chambers covered by earthen mounds (KOFUN) of varying size. The emblems of legitimacy found in these funeral mounds include swords, curved stones (magatama), and mirrors, suggestive of the myth of the three IMPERIAL REGALIA. It was during this period that the first and foremost shrines of the main Shintō tradition were created: ISE SHRINE and IZUMO SHRINE. As Japanese society became set in its major forms with the appearance of clans (uji)—each worshiping its own tutelary divinity (UJIGAMI)—and corporate groups (BE), rituals and thought connected with this organization were created and helped stabilize the entire system. The introduction of Confucianism and of yin-yang philosophy played an important part in this process and the two were to remain fundamental elements of Shintō throughout Japanese history. Religious activity was on the one hand grounded in each community and was concerned with agriculture and seasonal acts of worship, while on the other hand it was central to the ritual and political life of the leading clans both in and out of the Yamato area. It is safe to assume that by the 5th century Japanese religion already exhibited two of its major characteristics: a local character with its own legends and myths, and a supralocal character developed around those groups responsible for the unification of the country. The introduction of Chinese civilization and of Buddhism helped to promote the supralocal character as central to the establishment of a distinct Japanese identity, and helped to crystallize those elements of religious practice that were in the making; at the same time the position of the clans which accepted the new religion was reinforced. This position of authority had to be grounded in some sort of legitimacy, based on mythical, ritual, and religious coherence; this essential search for legitimacy and coherence on the part of the ruling class led to the compilation of the KOJIKI (712) and of the NIHON SHOKI or Nihongi (720). In these books, Japan expressed a mythical vision of its origins and of its history. On the one hand, the distinction between myth and history is not clear, thereby leaving the impression that history is a myth in the making. On the other hand, the structure of the pantheon is connected to the structure of society: the position of leading clans in regard to the imperial family being the result of relationships that occurred "in illo tempore" between their respective ancestors. These books fixed once and for all the legitimacy of the imperial lineage and established the myths that are central to Shintō in its relationship to the state. Thus the Japanese nation turned to the Kojiki and the Nihon shoki in times of international and national crises. The composition of these books was already a syncretic endeavor, since Confucianism and the yin-yang theories are essential components not only of the philosophy backing the imperial institution, but also of all rituals connected to the imperial family and to the welfare of the state. The Office of Shintō Worship (Jingikan) created in the system of codes (RITSURYŌ SYSTEM) after the Taika Reform (645) was responsible for this amalgamation of native tendencies and foreign rituals which can be seen in the annual cycle of ceremonies (nenchū gyōji), in funeral customs (more emphasis on ancestor worship), and in the development of the technique of divination, as can be inferred from the establishment of a Bureau of Yin and Yang (Ommyōryō), which was closely linked to political decisions. Several clans specialized in these areas of religious duties; the Nakatomi (part of which became the Fujiwara), the Imbe, and the Urabe were concerned with Shintō, while the Abe and Kamo clans emphasized yin-yang theories.

Thus, continental influences helped form the main Shintō tradition at its beginning and had originally little impact on the provinces: it is only with Buddhism that the "Way of yin and yang" (OMMYŌDŌ) spread to the people, while Confucianism became a major ingredient of popular Shintō only during the Edo period. The major Shintō rituals surrounding the imperial family and its satellite clans were set in writing and codified only at the end of the 9th century (in the Jōgan Gishiki) and in the 10th century (in the ENGI SHIKI). By

that time, Shintō had achieved its status as a coherent religious system, with its myths, rituals, priestly families and specialists, and shrines. One can infer the organization of Shintō from the formation of the "Twenty-Two Shrines" (Nijūnisha) which were supported economically by the imperial family until the middle of the Muromachi period (1333–1568), and by the government from 1868 to 1945. These shrines were subdivided into three groups: the top seven (the Ise, IWASHIMIZU HACHIMAN, KAMO, Matsunoo, Hirano, FUSHIMI INARI, and KASUGA shrines) were directly related to the imperial family, with the exception of Fushimi Inari, which was dedicated to the divinities of rice and was an object of popular worship. The middle seven (the Ōharano, ŌMIWA, ISONOKAMI, Ōyamato, HIROSE, TATSUTA and SUMIYOSHI shrines), with one exception (Ōharano), were also ancient shrines of historical and mythical importance. The lower eight (the HIE, Umenomiya, Yoshida, HIROTA, Gion [YASAKA], KITANO, Niunokawakami, and Kibune shrines) were connected with Buddhism, major clans, popular worship, or rain-making rituals. These shrines, which are still of importance today, are all located in or near the ancient capitals of Nara and Kyōto. The Procedures of the Engi Era (Engi Shiki) note 3,132 shrines in the country at the time. Each of them was given rank and status according to its historical, economic, or popular fame.

The recognition of Buddhism around 538 and its swift development thereafter among the upper strata of society not only caused, as stated above, a systematization of Shintō; but, in addition, Buddhism and Shintō were to communicate at all levels. It is obvious from texts such as the NIHON RYŌIKI (ca 822) that Buddhism spread to the popular level very quickly and was confronted with the presence of divine figures which were firmly entrenched in communities and intricately connected to everyday life: their dislocation was out of the question. The only solution left was coexistence and interaction. As one would expect, this union occurred at the level of local shrines and temples within their particular contexts, long before any abstract theories of syncretism were known. Already at the beginning of the 8th century, Buddhist temples were built on or next to the location of Shintō shrines: they were called jingūji, literally, "shrine-temple." For instance, the Kehi Jingūji at the KEHI SHRINE in the province of Echizen (now part of Fukui Prefecture) in 715; in 717 the Wakasahiko Jingūji, also in Echizen; in 725 the Mirokuji of the USA HACHIMAN SHRINE. A Buddhist monk named Mangan built a jingūji in Kashima in 749–756 and in Tado in 763. This last one was erected after the following oracle was revealed to Mangan: "I am the Kami of Tado. For a long time now I have accumulated negative karma, and (fell into) the Way of the Kami as a retribution. I presently wish to discard this body of kami, and take refuge in the Three Treasures" (i.e., the Buddha, the Buddhist Law, and the Buddhist Community). This reaction to Buddhism, its elevated philosophy, its rituals and its awesome power typifies some of the early contacts: the kami were considered (by monks) as lower beings which needed to be saved from endless transmigration, a feat that only Buddhism could accomplish. This explains why Buddhist sutras were offered, read, and commented upon by monks in front of Shintō shrines. One instance of this kind occurred in 741, when the Lotus Sutra and others were offered by the court to the Usa Hachiman Shrine. In 743, upon ordering the construction of the huge statue of the Buddha at the TŌDAIJI in Nara, Emperor SHŌMU sent Tachibana no Moroe to the Grand Shrine of Ise, in order to enquire the will of the sun goddess Amaterasu Ōmikami. The divine response was positive, for Amaterasu herself revealed that she and the cosmic Buddha (Vairocana or Mahāvairocana; see DAINICHI) were two aspects of one single reality. These oracles were astute political statements: they satisfied everyone. In 745, the Usa Hachiman Shrine sent funds for the completion of the Tōdaiji, and became protector of several Buddhist temples. Such services among others earned Hachiman the title of "bodhisattva" in 783. In 861, another Hachiman shrine was built south of the new capital of Kyōto, at Iwashimizu (see IWASHIMIZU HACHIMAN SHRINE). This shrine-temple complex became a major cultic center of syncretism during the 12th and 13th centuries, and was part of a large constellation of Hachiman shrines in Japan.

Crucial developments in these interactions occurred during the Heian period, after SAICHŌ (767–822) brought back the Tendai sect from China, and KŪKAI (774–835) introduced the Shingon sect. Tendai was heavily permeated by Shingon doctrines after Saichō died, and the two sects represented ESOTERIC BUDDHISM (mikkyō), which allowed a systematic relationship with Shintō and established ritual and philosophical systems for that relationship during the entire medieval period (roughly 13th–16th centuries). There were several reasons for this: first, esoteric Buddhism had a tendency to build all-encompassing systems of thought and practice; second, it had a great inclination to use magical formulas (Skt: *dhāraṇī*) and gestures (Skt: *mūdra*), themselves present in Buddhism as the result of syncretism in India; and third, it had a short but powerful history of acknowledging foreign systems through the use of its own theory of emanation, in which all beings—both animate and inanimate—were seen as parts of the Body of Essence of the Buddha. In these systems, everything was seen as a Buddha, or as a Buddha-to-be: the message was life-affirming and universal, and it recognized form as a path to the absolute, if not an outright identity between the two.

In many ways, these tenets were in harmony with basic Shintō attitudes: the Shintō dialectic between nature and culture was close to that proposed by esoteric Buddhism, as can be readily seen in the level of communication which occurred between the two in the realm of aesthetics. Furthermore, the rituals esoteric Buddhism used to exorcise evil spirits were quickly adopted by the magic-hungry aristocrats and shamans alike; two examples illustrate this point: the emergence of the syncretic school of mountain ascetics (SHUGENDŌ), and the development of the Kitano cult, which is associated with a category of religious phenomena called "angry spirits" (*onryō*). Forced into unjust exile at Dazaifu in Kyūshū by Fujiwara jealousy and rivalry, the minister SUGAWARA NO MICHIZANE died there in 903. It was a common understanding at the time that the spirits of people who had died for unjust reasons remained in this world to torment their enemies and cause pestilences, earthquakes, droughts, floods, and fires: the sense of guilt on the part of the perpetrators took a cosmic dimension because it was believed that any human wrongdoing caused a destruction of the ideally harmonious balance of nature. These angry spirits had then to be pacified, and magic was central to this process. Michizane's spirit was propitiated with offerings and posthumous titles and, finally, worshiped as a *kami*. By the 12th century, he was considered to be an incarnation of the Buddhist divinity of compassion, Avalokiteśvara (J: Kannon); he had been fully exorcised, pacified, and civilized. Worshiped by commoners as well as by the intelligentsia, he became—under Zen influence—a patron of poetry and of culture in general. Today, some 3,500 or so shrines are dedicated to him. Shintō-Buddhist syncretism was central to the development of such cults and was so pervasive that treating Shintō separately from Buddhism in the medieval period leads to gross misinterpretations of Japanese religiosity.

THE MEDIEVAL PERIOD AND SYNCRETIC SYSTEMS

Of several pivotal theories of amalgamation introduced by Buddhism, the HONJI SUIJAKU theory ("original prototype and local manifestation") played a key role in the evolution of Shintō-Buddhist relationships. At its core lies the notion that Shintō divinities are manifestations of members of the Buddhist pantheon, so that the relations—while retaining the appearance of power relationships—are described in the Buddhist terms of non-twoness. Consequently, worshiping a *kami* amounted to worshiping a Buddha in its *kami* form, as was done by Buddhist monks residing in shrine-temples (they were called *shasō*: shrine monks) and by the people. This enhanced the status of the autochthonous divinities, by interpreting their connection to the Buddhas and bodhisattvas in terms of parent/child unions rather than the original savior/sinner context. The crucial point is that these systematic associations were always established at the level of particular shrines and temples and not at an abstract, national level. In other words, Shintō-Buddhist syncretism remained grounded in each particular religious community, thereby retaining original Shintō characteristics. This is why studies of these systems of communication between cultures must be made *in situ* before any general conclusions may be drawn: the syncretism found at the Hie shrines is characteristically different from that found at the Kasuga shrines, Kumano shrines, Hachiman shrines, and so on. As each shrine-temple complex devised its own system of rituals and practices surrounding the associations in the pantheon—and these associations were themselves based on oracles, visions, revelations and other religious phenomena—the systems were put in writing and painting in a semimythical, semilegendary form; these texts are called *engi-mono*, many of which are today famed painted scrolls (EMAKIMONO). While these were for publicity purposes and for popular consumption, mythical, historical, and philosophical treatises of importance were composed by scholarly monks and priests: during the period from the 13th to the 19th centuries a vast religious literature dealt with the nature of Shintō-Buddhist relationships. Its major categories are: treatises based on Buddhist schools, especially the Tendai and Shingon sects; treatises based on shrine traditions, with a distinction made between popular shrines and aristocracy-owned shrines; and finally, treatises written by Shintō priests. The first category could be called Buddhist Shintō: Tendai created its SANNŌ ICHIJITSU SHINTŌ, while Shingon created its RYŌBU SHINTŌ. The second category is representative of popular syncretism and of the major cults originating in major classical shrines: Kumano, Hachiman, Kasuga, and so on. The third category represents a reaction within the main tradition of Shintō: Watarai Shintō at Ise Shrine, and Yuiitsu Shintō at Yoshida Shrine; this last trend was to survive during the Edo period and to mix with Neo-Confucianism.

Sannō Ichijitsu Shintō——"Sannō" literally means "Mountain King" and designates a unit of three groups of divinities worshiped at the Hie Shrine on the eastern slope of Mt. Hiei (Hiezan) near Kyōto. These three groups were associated with the Buddhist divinities worshiped in the three groups of temples located on top of Mt. Hiei. The economic, political, and religious fate of the Hie shrines was closely connected to that of the Buddhist school. The first major treatise of syncretism was composed around 1223; called *Yōtenki* (Notes on Heavenly Luminaries), it describes the specific nature of this shrine in its connection to each of these temples, their history, and their myths. This Shintō-Buddhist complex grew to extraordinary proportions during the medieval period, as more texts were written and as it became a pilgrimage center. Due to the esotericization of Tendai, most of these texts were kept secret and were only transmitted orally. Much of this oral transmission can be found in a book entitled *Keiran jūyō shū* (Compilations of Leaves Gathered in Stormy Streams), which was composed before 1347; a close analysis of its contents reveals nearly equal amounts of Shintō, esoteric Buddhism, Tendai doctrine, Taoism and *yin-yang* theory. This form of Buddhist Shintō became politically important after TOKUGAWA IEYASU (1543–1616), the unifier of Japan and founder of the Tokugawa shogunate, was buried in 1617 according to its rituals. The great mausoleum at NIKKŌ, where Ieyasu is enshrined as a Shintō-Buddhist divinity under the name of "The Great Avatar Illuminating the East" (Tōshō Daigongen), is representative of Sannō syncretism as it was devised by the monk Tenkai (1536–1643).

Ryōbu Shintō——This school is the only Buddhist syncretic system in which a direct connection with the great tradition of Shintō at Ise was attempted. *Ryōbu* designates the two main mandalas which, in Shingon Buddhism, are graphic and ritual representations of the universe seen in its twofold aspect of noumenon/phenomenon (see MANDALA). Because the central Buddha of Shingon was called Dainichi (Great Sun), early associations with Amaterasu Ōmikami, the solar deity worshiped at Ise as the ancestress of the imperial lineage, had been accepted. Several apocryphal texts had been secretly transmitted from the middle of the Heian period on, but the *Tenchi reiki ki* (Notes on the Numinous Energy of Heaven and Earth) is the fundamental treatise on the subject; it was probably composed during the latter half of the Kamakura period (1185–1333), even though the tradition long attributed it to Kūkai. Also a complex syncretism between Shintō, Buddhism, and *yin-yang* theory, its main point resides in the connection of the two mandalas with the Outer and Inner Shrines of Ise. As usual with syncretic phenomena in Japan, numerous associations of a philosophical, ritual, phonetic, graphic, and numerologic nature were proposed in order to indicate the essential identity of Shintō and Buddhism. Ryōbu Shintō declined as the main Shintō tradition reacted, first with its own brand of syncretism, and then with an outright rejection of Buddhism.

Indeed, syncretisms that took the side of Buddhist doctrines were not all there was to the Japanese religious tradition or, for that matter, to Shintō. During the Heian period, "pure" Shintō scholarship focusing on the great tradition, i.e., Ise, the *Kojiki* and *Nihongi*, had slowly developed, but its impact was limited to a number of priestly families. After the beginning of the 13th century however, the situation had clearly changed: first, there was a need to react against the Pure Land schools (see PURE LAND BUDDHISM) and their emphasis on sole reliance on the Buddha; second, political and economic power had slipped away from the imperial lineage and from the aristocracy; third, Japan had been threatened by Mongol invasions; and finally, a major dispute between two branches of the imperial family erupted in 1336, leading to the split between the NORTHERN AND SOUTHERN COURTS. The economic losses of the Ise shrines and all the above reasons forced the priestly families out of their splendid isolation. Few priests were ready to admit that Shintō was nothing more than Buddhism in disguise.

Watarai Shintō——In spite of its role in the history of Shintō, Watarai Shintō (also called Ise Shintō or Gekū Shintō) has not been studied by Western scholars. Watarai is the name of the priestly family charged with the administration of the Outer Shrine (Gekū) of Ise. By the end of the 13th century, scholarly priests had composed five texts which they attributed to distant imperial and divine figures; they are known as the *Shintō gobusho* (The Five Books of Shintō). Regarded as revealed and sacred scriptures, they could be read only by priests over 60 years of age, and deal with mythology, history, ritual, and fundamental attitudes and practices such as purification and ethics. Buddhism, though mentioned, is pushed into the background; the emphasis is on symbolical explanations of rituals, myths, and architectural details in which one can recognize extremely early aspects of the native cult as well as Chinese influences. It was Watarai Ieyuki (1256–1351) who finally established in 1320 a compendium of Shintō knowledge, the *Ruijū jingi hongen,* which can be seen as the great "summa" of medieval Shintō, and in which the level of scholarship is astounding. Marking the revival of Shintō, this text was read by the supporters of the Southern Court and influenced KITABATAKE CHIKAFUSA (1293–1354) as he composed his *Tōkahiden* and *Gengenshū.* An important characteristic of Watarai Shintō is the emphasis on a primordial divinity which preceded the birth of the cosmos and was responsible for it. Naturally, that divinity is the one worshiped at the Outer Shrine, together with other divinities which the Watarai family considered to be of the same substance with different names. Though this sounds like competition with the Inner Shrine, it nevertheless represents a trend which was to develop in Shintō's search for an ultimate cosmic agent. In this respect, Chinese influence is evident. As time passed, Watarai Shintō leaned more toward Confucianism; representative of this direction was Deguchi Nobuyoshi (1615–90), who taught YAMAZAKI ANSAI.

Yuiitsu Shintō —— This school of Shintō (also called Yoshida Shintō) marked the reversal of the *honji suijaku* doctrine while it heralded a national reorganization of the religion. Though it was based on the scholarship of several generations of the Yoshida family (formerly Urabe), it was essentially the creation of Yoshida Kanetomo (1435–1511).

The four tutelary and ancestral divinities of the Fujiwara family, which had come to be worshiped at the Kasuga Shrine of Nara in the middle of the 8th century, were invoked in new shrines whenever the capital was moved to new sites: the Ōharano Shrine was built in Nagaoka in 784, and when the capital was moved to Kyōto, the Yoshida Shrine was built in 859 on the hill Kaguraoka, northeast of the city. The Urabe family, which specialized in divination, was charged with its administration. In 1081 the Yoshida Shrine had become one of the Twenty-Two Shrines supported by the imperial family; in the course of time, the Urabe split into different branches which took control of several important shrines in Kyōto: Hirano, Umenomiya, and Awata. The branch staying at Yoshida took that name in 1375. Many scholars were born in that family; they composed commentaries on the *Kojiki* and *Nihongi,* and gave lectures on them at the court. YOSHIDA KENKŌ, the famed author of the *Tsurezuregusa,* was born in 1283; his older brother, Jihen, was trained as a Tendai monk but turned to Shintō toward the end of his life and wrote several important treatises of syncretism; linked to the Watarai family, he also supported the Southern Court. Gradually, the Yoshida family created its own teachings, which it transmitted orally between its members; the *Kojiki* and the *Nihongi* came to be regarded as sacred texts in 1398, when they were placed on altars and became the object of chanted recitation like sutras in Buddhism. Yoshida Kanetomo inherited these traditions and practices at a time of major social and political upheavals: the shrines were burnt to the ground during the Ōnin War in 1468; their reconstruction, the return to imperial authority, and the supremacy of Shintō became Kanetomo's obsession.

The school that he created was extremely syncretic, but with the difference that Shintō was regarded as the origin of all things—Confucianism, Taoism, and Buddhism included. In the major scripture of the school, the *Yuiitsu shintō myōbō yōshū,* he established a distinction between exoteric and esoteric Shintō; the exoteric teachings *(kenrokyō)* are based on the *Kojiki* and the *Nihongi,* while the esoteric teachings *(on'nyūkyō)* are based on scriptures which he claimed had been revealed by various divinities in mythical times and transmitted in his family. He built in 1484 a shrine called Daigengū (Palace of the Great Origin), in which all architectural elements are based on his interpretation and syncretic use of Shintō, Taoist, and Buddhist symbolism. In the shrine a central pillar, grounded in earth, covered with 3,132 stones representing the divinities named in the Engi Shiki, stands for the unity of Shintō which he

Shintō

A *shimenawa* above the entrance to the worship hall *(haiden)* at the Izumo Shrine in Shimane Prefecture. One of many found at the shrine, the *shimenawa*—a common ritual object in Shintō—serves to denote a sacred space.

was looking for. By the beginning of the 16th century, Kanetomo had established himself as the foremost figure in Shintō. Even though he considered Buddhism to be a mere manifestation of his religion, it is clear that esoteric Buddhism pervades his system of philosophy, his symbolism, and his complicated rituals, which we know today from written sources only. In 1598, when Toyotomi Hideyoshi died, the Yoshida school was charged with the funeral rites and the deification of the great warrior at the Toyokuni Shrine. A few years later, when Tokugawa Ieyasu died, Yoshida, playing the same role, built a mausoleum at Mt. Kunō (Kunozan) on the outskirts of the city of Shizuoka, but the Tendai monk Tenkai was able to wrest the responsibility away and built the better known mausoleum at Nikkō according to the Sannō tradition. However, the Yoshida school became quite powerful during the Edo period, supervising the initiation and nomination of Shintō priests in much of the country. It played a major role in the history of Shintō institutions, doctrines, practices, and ethics. The Meiji Restoration in 1868 marked its end.

THE EDO PERIOD

The Watarai and Yoshida schools of Shintō, however syncretic and bizarre they may have been, rekindled a formidable interest in the native tradition. The Edo period (1600–1868) saw a dramatic shift of Shintō away from Buddhism and its rapprochement with Neo-Confucianism, while the movement called National Learning (KOKUGAKU) used its high level of scholarship in the disciplines of history, philology, and thought to redefine the Japanese identity.

Early in the 17th century the thinker HAYASHI RAZAN (1583–1657), who became the Confucian adviser to four shōguns, founded the first school that tried to harmonize Shintō and Neo-Confucianism. Among many other works, he composed the *Honchō jinja kō* (Reflections on the Shrines of this Nation) and the *Shintō denju* (Shintō Transmission), in which he emphasized the union between Shintō and the Imperial Way, the immanence of the absolute as *kami* within the heart-mind of human beings, ethical behavior as the mark of the divine, and the conduct of government as the manifestation of divine virtue. Razan violently criticized Kanetomo's system as well as all Buddhist interference, and expressed a fundamental nostalgia for pre-Buddhist times. Two other proponents of the union between Neo-Confucianism and Shintō were YOSHIKAWA KORETARI and Yamazaki Ansai.

Yoshikawa Koretari (1616–94) was born in a warrior family but raised in that of a merchant. While living as a recluse in Kamakura, he became fascinated with Shintō, went to Kyōto and after much insistence became a disciple of Hagiwara Kaneyori, then the great master of Yoshida Shintō. Koretari was so brilliant and so devoted that he was initiated at the highest level and became the de facto head of the school in 1657. Moving back east, he looked for support among the new rulers, and received it from several *daimyō,* but especially from Hoshina Masayuki, the shōgun Tokugawa Iemitsu's younger brother. He ultimately became the adviser on Shintō to the shogunate, a position filled thereafter by his descendants. His main achievements consisted of completing the secret transmissions of Yoshida, in effecting a more dramatic inclination toward Neo-Confucianism, and in refining some theological and ethical elements. He firmly set up the divinity Kuninotokotachi no Mikoto as the central figure of the Shintō pantheon, identifying it with the primordial chaos preceding the appearance of Heaven and Earth, of yin and yang, and of the Five Elements. Within the context of a microcosm/macrocosm relationship between nature and humanity, he proposed a concrete path of inner and outer purification to allow communication between the divine and man. This communication was made possible by a fundamental attitude of "tsutsushimi" (reverence and humility) on the part of the worshiper as he attempted to return to the absolute before the appearance of thought.

Suika Shintō —— The school called Suika Shintō was founded by Yamazaki Ansai (1619–82). Trained as a Zen monk, he "defected" to Neo-Confucianism and became a passionate proponent of Shintō. His influence on Edo-period intelligentsia cannot be neglected. Spending most of his adult life commuting between Kyōto and Edo (now Tōkyō), he befriended Masayuki, who had protected Koretari, and received from Koretari himself the initiation name (reishagō) Shidemasu (more commonly pronounced Suika). Ansai forcefully insisted on a scholarly approach to Neo-Confucianism; he compared Neo-Confucianism with what he saw as the main philosophical and ethical aspects of Shintō and found many similarities, though he never advocated a syncretism of the two. That Neo-Confucianism and Shintō were so "similar" was to him a matter of endless fascination. It is in this light that he proposed Neo-Confucian interpretations of Japanese mythology, which led him to state that the Heavenly Way and the Human Way were identical in foundation and nature. This identity could be realized by adequate understanding of the mythical and religious nature of government. Ansai most emphatically supported loyalty as a quintessential characteristic of Shintō. Advocating emperor worship, he stated: "The divine is the force that resides in the heart-mind. It is symbolized by the jewel (tama); its radiance is symbolized by the mirror, and its awesome virtue is symbolized by the sword."

Suika Shintō was developed after Ansai's death by Tamaki Masahide (1672?–1736). Because there were no rituals, its institutional evolution was slow, and it was forced to enter in contact with the Tachibana branch of Shintō. An important proponent of the doctrine was Yoshimi Yukikazu (1673–1761), who belonged to the priestly family in charge of the Tokugawa mausoleum in Nagoya. Yukikazu was a conscientious and systematic critic of the Watarai and Yoshida branches, which placed him in a contradictory position since his criticism necessarily touched all those aspects of Suika Shintō that originated in these schools. But Yukikazu held firm and proposed his own brand of "purified" Shintō. A brief movement of return to the form originally developed by Ansai was initiated by Atobe Yoshiaki (1659–1729), but it failed to inject the vigor necessary to compete with the enormous institutional power of Yoshida. Matsuoka Yūen (1701–83) was expelled from the school by Masayuki and joined Yoshida. Ansai's Shintō opened the way to the scholars of the National Learning, and in this sense is important. But scholarly Shintō was not all there was at the time; many "free" thinkers who could not receive the highest levels of secret transmissions proposed their own interpretations at the popular level and marked the beginning of the revival of a popular Shintō without Buddhist overtones. Religious figures like Sawata Gennai, KUMAZAWA BANZAN, ISHIDA BAIGAN, and the popular street-corner preacher Masuho Nokoguchi (1656–1742) belong to this category and were precursors of Kamo no Norikiyo (1798–1861), Inoue Masakane (1790–1849), and the others who were responsible for the appearance of Sect Shintō.

Restoration Shintō (Fukko Shintō) —— This important movement is represented by thinkers like KEICHŪ (1640–1701), KAMO NO MABUCHI (1697–1769), MOTOORI NORINAGA (1730–1801), HIRATA ATSUTANE (1776–1843), and many others. Surrounded by the nationalist mood of the times and in the midst of a global fascination with mythology, these scholars proposed a return to the sources of Japanese identity through a proper and rigorous philological study of language, and consequently of all ancient texts of mythology, poetry, and literature. Ironically, it was a Shingon monk, Keichū, who laid the foundations for this enterprise with his writings on the Man'yōshū and several other classics; it should be noted that esoteric Buddhism, ever since its introduction by Kūkai, had expressed a central concern for language. But if all schools of syncretism had presented themselves as comparative games in which linguistic associations played a central role, they had strayed away from scientific etymo-

logical or philological studies. By contrast, the studies appearing out of the National Learning movement were exact. Let us note that one of the last Buddhist brands of syncretism was proposed by Jiun (1718–1804), who wrote one of the largest existing studies on Sanskrit. Kamo no Mabuchi looked for the Ancient Way through a study, in this order, of poetry, literature, and mythology. He suggested to Norinaga that he should accomplish a study of the Kojiki, on which that great scholar spent 30 years of his life. Norinaga was opposed to Neo-Confucianism, Chinese culture, and Buddhism, and spent his life focusing on what he considered to be essentially Japanese. One may suggest that in the midst of these scholarly endeavors and speculations concerning the relationships between nature and culture, a central quest for answers concerning the nature of history, of politics, and of the human situation was taking place. Japan was then closed to the rest of the world, but knew of its existence and was frantically searching for a viable identity to present. Though Norinaga was not interested in politics, his work was interpreted differently by his successors. The international threat was compounded toward the end of the Edo period by national unrest which was evidenced in popular religion by sudden mass pilgrimages to Ise (OKAGE MAIRI) and by movements such as "EEJANAIKA."

It is in this context that Hirata Atsutane proposed a return to imperial rule and to Shintō as the sole Way. A man of wide learning and many writings, Atsutane spread the views of the movement to the masses, laying the foundations for the religious aspects of the Meiji Restoration, in which his adopted son Kanetane (1799–1880) played a major role.

THE MEIJI PERIOD AND AFTER

The 19th century was thus a crucial turning point in Shintō history: on one hand a number of religious movements emerged to form Sect Shintō, which is varied and where syncretic tendencies can be found; on the other hand, the expurgated Ancient Way became the state religion, giving to the Meiji Restoration of 1868 all appearances of a return to the Age of the Gods. Indeed, the system of national shrines was reinstated, as well as the classical Office of Shintō Worship (Jingikan). Shrines were supported by the government, Shintō became an orthodoxy taught in schools, and the union of church and state took on an increasingly nationalistic coloration. Buddhism was briefly attacked but quickly reacted with its own brand of scholarship. After the defeat in World War II, State Shintō was disestablished. Distinctions were drawn between State Shintō, Shrine Shintō (which represents the bulk of Shintō traditions at the regional and local levels), and Sect Shintō as the "NEW RELIGIONS" which had sprung up at the end of the 19th century. Shrine Shintō and the 13 branches of Sect Shintō came to be regarded as legal religious bodies which are independent from the state.

The religious picture of today's Japan is complex; statistics fail to suggest the numerous layers of interactions that have emerged, floated, disappeared, and reemerged throughout the centuries; syncretic tendencies and a popular nonchalance concerning religious phenomena in general make it impossible for the uninitiated to come up with a clear image. There is no doubt that the identification of the great tradition of Shintō with nationalism has hurt the tradition considerably, even though in many ways Shintō's essence belongs only to the local shrines which have little to do with the great tradition. But where political questions are secondary, economic and social problems have taken their toll: the increasing mobility of society, the movement away from the villages and into the big cities, industrialization, and fundamental social changes are now confronting Shintō with what may be its biggest challenge yet.

RITUAL DIMENSIONS AND THOUGHT

A historical overview as brief as the one above, while useful, fails to describe Shintō's essential character which is to be found in its ritual dimensions. Distinctions may be drawn between the great and the little traditions, provided one recognizes the extraordinary importance of the so-called little tradition in Japan as well as the existence of some profound connections between the two.

Shintō practices are inscribed within the context of sacred space and sacred time. Sacred space is that of the manifestation of the divine where shrines are located. Sacred time is the period when major rituals are performed. The most ancient known form of sacred space, still to be seen in some shrines, is a rectangular area covered with pebbles, surrounded by stones, and marked off by a rope linking four corner-pillars; in the middle of this area is either a stone (iwasaka or iwakura), or a pillar, or tree (himorogi). This ritually purified place where divinities are called upon and invoked *(kanjō)* may be located in the midst of a sacred grove *(kami no mori)* which is quite often the sign of the presence of a shrine. The shrine itself is sacred of course, but what gives it much of its character is its location within a landscape which has been chosen for its natural beauty or for its strategic situation, such as the junction of rivers. A typical shrine *(jinja)* would be located near a source of a river at the foot of a mountain; surrounded by a fence *(tamagaki)*, its entrance is marked by a wooden gate *(torii)* of simple style, on which a rope *(shimenawa)* symbolizing purity has been affixed. The shrine stands as a pivot between the mountainous area—which represents death and renewal, and is therefore forbidden ground in a sense—and the plains, which are associated with life and activity through the cultivation of crops. Humans dwell in the village built around the shrine, where they worship the divinities in a seasonal cycle. Calling on them in spring and inviting their presence in the plains to oversee the growth process, they show their gratitude in autumn, offering the first fruit of the harvest and then sending the divinities back to the mountains to regenerate.

Sacred time in Shintō is that of the origins described in the books of mythology as well as the time at which these origins are commemorated on a regular and fixed basis. Each shrine has thus its own dates for rituals and ceremonies which are performed by the priests or by a rotating group of members of the community, on a cyclical and yearly basis *(nenchū gyōji)*. Each word uttered in the presence of the divine, each gesture and movement (such as standing, sitting, moving, taking and holding utensils), and each ceremony (such as opening and closing the doors of a shrine, calling on the divinities, offering food, expressing the community's wishes, purification) are prescribed in ritual codes, which were legal edicts between the early part of the Meiji period and 1945, and which are today set for all shrines in books such as the *Saishi kitei*, published by the National Organization of Shrines (Jinja Honchō).

Of all rituals, perhaps those concerning food offerings and purification stand out as most representative of Shintō. Food offerings *(shinsen; mike* in ancient times) are the core of each ceremony and festival *(matsuri)*; products from the sea, from the rivers, plains and mountains are prepared in the shrine's kitchen *(shinsen-dokoro)* on a special fire *(kiribi)*. Certain foods are the object of taboo *(imi)* at certain times, and most products have names that are used only within the context of Shintō. Categories may be established according to the mode of preparation or to the mode of offering: food is either cooked *(jukusen)* or raw *(seisen,* or *marumono)*, or comes from live animals *(ikenie)* such as birds or fish. Sometimes, it is prescribed that food have no fish taste, in which case it is called *sosen*. In offering, a distinction is made between food that is supposed to be ingested by the divinities *(kyōō shinsen)* and food that is to be viewed by them *(kyōkan shinsen)*. Modes of offering include placing on a table, hanging, dispersing, putting into the earth or throwing into water. Each major shrine has its own complex style of offering and of preparation. As anthropology has demonstrated, food systems are a central aspect of culture and of religious behavior; therefore, food systems represent one of the areas of Shintō that deserve and need to be studied. Much of the essence and practices of Japanese cuisine are grounded in Shintō, in which types of food are as strictly regulated according to taste, season, and color as they are arranged. Careful attention is given to the number of dishes, the number of tables, the number of food elements in each dish, as well as to the order of gestures that accompany the offering; rice always comes first and water last. Special attention is given to rice wine *(sake; miki* in Shintō); it is offered at most ceremonies, and is ingested by all participants as a sign of participation with the divine. For instance, a *matsuri* would traditionally close with a *naorai*, a meeting in which, originally, mistakes in ritual order were corrected. However, as time passed, this meeting was interpreted as the end of the enforcement of taboos and various interdictions, and turned into a banquet where the food which has been offered is shared by the community. At the level of the little tradition, one could mention the last night of the year at the Yasaka Shrine in Kyōto, at which time shrinegoers receive from the priests a slowly burning cord which has been lit at the sacred fire of the shrine; keeping the cord incandescent by spinning it in their hands, they walk back home and prepare the first food of the year over this purifying fire. At the level of the great tradition, it should be remembered that much of the enthronement ceremony of the emperor consists essentially of food preparation and partaking (see DAIJŌSAI).

The other great ritual aspect of Shintō, the centrality of which is impossible to emphasize enough, is purification. It is grounded in mythology, where it takes two forms: *misogiharae,* purification from contact with spoiling elements *(kegare)* such as disease or death, and *harae,* the purpose of which is to restore proper relationships after wrongdoing, through the offering of compensation. The first one originated in the myth in which the deity Izanagi no Mikoto, after having followed his consort Izanami no Mikoto to the Land of Darkness (Yomi no Kuni; the nether world) and seen her in a state of decomposition, returns to the world and "washes off" in a stream. As he does so, the purification of his left eye results in the appearance of the solar divinity Amaterasu Ōmikami, the purification of his right eye results in the appearance of the lunar divinity Tsukiyomi no Mikoto, the purification of his nose causes the appearance of Susanoo no Mikoto, while the purification of the rest of his body causes the appearance of many other divinities (see MYTHOLOGY). The central point is that important parts of the cosmos are seen as the result of purification, and that consequently this act is charged with important connotations. The second form of purification concerns Susanoo no Mikoto, who after having rampaged through the palace of his sister Amaterasu, tries to wash away his offenses and redeem himself by cutting his beard and nails and by making various offerings as symbols of repentance and sincerity. Perhaps one could already see in these examples the origins of later distinctions between "outer purification" and "inner purification."

As Shintō developed during the classical period, private and public rites of purification were devised and performed on a semiannual basis and, in times of natural calamities as well as before ceremonies, they were preceded by the observance of interdictions *(monoimi,* or *kessai)*, the duration and depth of which varied with the importance of the occasion. There were thus minor observances *(maimi)* and major observances *(araimi)* which concerned death, disease, menstruation, sexual activity, wounds, food types and food preparation, clothing, and cleanliness. These observances were followed by the priestly figures and some of the public figures involved in the ceremonies; as time passed, there was a popularization of these practices and a greater emphasis on lustration. Then any ceremony could take its course, purification having allowed access to and contact with the divine, as well as having established a general character of renewal. Of the nearly endless list of utensils used in ceremonies, a great many have no other function than to symbolize purity, such as the folded paper strips *(shide)* which are affixed to ropes, gates, sacred trees, and so on; or materials such as bamboo, hemp, and ramie, and elements or natural products such as fire, water, salt, and rice.

As stated above, purification is related to processes of creation reported in the myths, and therefore to notions of renewal which are central to Shintō's philosophy of time, insufficiently characterized as cyclical. The insistence in Shintō on periodic renewal, return to the origins and identification with the divine through purification, should be connected to an equal insistence on the consequences, which are the ability to establish a sacred present *(nakaima)* and the sacralization of government; history viewed as a myth in the making is directly related to the renewed experience of the origins and to the awesome power and efficacy of purification. The complete rebuilding *(sengūsai)* of the Ise shrines on an adjacent site every 20 years is a perfect example of fundamental attitudes concerning ritual, concerning purification, concerning the austere simplicity—if not outright stylization—inherent in modes of renewal, and concerning history.

What has been hereto mentioned as "divinity" is the general term *kami,* the etymology of which is unclear. The Shintō pantheon—which is structured only at the level of the great tradition or in terms of political and/or economic status—consists of what the tradition calls *yaoyorozu no kami,* literally, "eight-hundred myriads of divinities." Therefore, the presence of the *kami* is overwhelming and pervades all aspects of life, not only because natural elements (wind, sun, moon, water, mountains, trees, etc) *per se* are *kami,* but also because specialized *kami* overlook and patronize human activities and dwell in man-made objects as well. Certain *kami* are divinized ancestors, or great figures of the past; the emperor has been regarded as divine. Each *kami* is endowed with a characteristic efficient force called *tama,* which is sometimes regarded under the categories of *aramitama* (coarse or violent aspect) and *nigimitama* (refined or peaceful aspect), and which is in fact the object of ritual activity. *Tama,* as the force which supports life and appears under purification, dwells in human beings as well, where it is called *tamashii;* disease or death were regarded as a sudden weakening of that force, which was then ritually reactivated *(tamafuri)* or recalled *(tamashizume)* in ceremonies such as the *chinkonsai* for the imperial family in classical times. The *tama* of a *kami* is called upon at the outset of a ceremony and invited to listen to the praise of the community and to its wishes; then it is offered food, praised again, and finally sent back. The "landing-site" of the *kami* is the *himorogi* or *iwasaka* described earlier; usually, a *kami* resides in a "support" (*shintai*; literally, "*kami* body") which can be a natural object (stone, root, branch), or a man-made object (mirror, sword) which is always hidden and placed in the main shrine. Sometimes an entire mountain is sacred and is regarded as the *kami* itself, in which case it is called *kannabiyama* or *shintaizan*. It should be noted that the *tama* of a *kami* is virtually inexhaustible, so that any *kami* can be invoked and enshrined in many different locations as a "fragment" (*bunshin*) which is no less efficient than the divinity worshiped at the original shrine.

It has been noted earlier that in the medieval period there was speculation about the establishment of some ultimate *kami* at the head of the pantheon. At the same time a process of interiorization took place whereby the emphasis was put on the heart-mind as the true abode of the divine, and where ritual was seen as a projection of inner processes. There may very well have been Buddhist influences over this process, but it is quite possible to regard it as a natural shift of emphasis from the object of the ritual to the subject performing it. These speculations, which were linked to purification and ethics, opened the door for Shintō's gradual transformation into a secular, but sacred, way of life. If any notion of individuality is to be found in Shintō, it should be in this area, for in general Shintō appears to be a communal phenomenon. Festivals and rites of passage are essentially participatory in character, due to the early aspects of union between religion and politics at the communal level and of union within the social structure of the clans. Some divinities like Inari (rice-fertility) may be worshiped by all and anyone; some divinities may be worshiped for personal reasons, such as Kitano Tenjin by students preparing for exams; some are worshiped for common protection, such as Atago which protects homes against fire; some are worshiped every morning on the family altar (*kamidana*). It is possible to suggest that Shintō's many facets could be approached from the angle of the nation, of the community, of the clan, of the family, and of the individual. As the unification of the country progressed during the medieval period, transcommunal phenomena like pilgrimages made their appearance; an individual may well be associated with his or her community's shrine, but this does not preclude participation in religious ceremonies at other shrines, or the expression of respect for other divinities. By the end of the medieval period for instance, it was believed that the visit to a thousand shrines was more efficient than countless visits to the same one, so pilgrims went on "Thousand Shrine Visits" (*senja mairi*). These were forbidden by the government during the Tempō era (1831–45). (The mass pilgrimages to Ise were mentioned earlier.) Visits to famous temples and shrines were part of Edo's cultural life, as in some sense they still are today. The shrines are extremely beautiful architectural creations set in remarkable landscapes and, at the time of religious festivals, the intense joyful activity, theatrical presentations, *sumō* wrestling bouts, dances, music, shops set up on the roads leading to the shrines, priests and priestesses selling protections (*ofuda*) and amulets (*omamori*), colorful processions with highly decorated floats, all continue to make Shintō a celebration of life in the cities as well as in the countryside.

A discussion of Shintō would be incomplete without a few comments on literature and arts. Japanese scholarship has not established a category of "Shintō literature," perhaps because sometimes the distinction between "Japanese" and "Shintō" is obscure. However, if one allows for the existence of the category "religious literature," then it is possible to focus on those works that tend toward Shintō. From this perspective—and putting mythology aside—at least three subcategories are obvious: poetry, Shintō-Buddhist literature, and doctrinal or technical scriptures. The category of poetry must be recognized by students of Shintō, since the great Shintō scholars of the Edo period have turned toward poetry—especially that of the *Kojiki*, *Nihongi*, and *Man'yōshū*—in order to define the essence of Japanese culture and identity. It is in poems that one will find the most direct expressions of Japanese attitudes concerning life and death, for instance. The form itself is related to Shintō, for one offers poems to the divinities, asks for support and inspiration from the divinities, while the divinities themselves speak "poetically," in both form and substance. It ought to be remembered as well that "pure" Japanese language is the language of Shintō as well as that of poetry, though some exception must be made for the medieval period, during which classical Chinese was used to some extent. There

is evidence to suggest that poetry was seen in religious circles as potent magical formulas, whose function was to pacify the heart; a chapter of the *Shasekishū* (1283) proposes that the WAKA form of poetry is really what esoteric Buddhism calls "*dhāraṇī*" (magical formula). Some Shintō priests were great poets, like Ōnakatomi no Yoshinobu (921–991); a syncretic divinity (SUGAWARA NO MICHIZANE, deified as Kitano Tenjin) was the patron saint of poets. The second subcategory, "Shintō-Buddhist literature," would contain all SETSUWA BUNGAKU (didactic and popular literary works dealing with extraordinary events) involving Shintō, such as the *Ujishūi monogatari*, the *Kokon chomonjū*, the *Shasekishū*, the *Shintōshū*, the *Fusōryakki*, and so on; or works presenting the myths and legends which are at the origins of shrine-temples (*jisha engi*); or various genres of popular tales. It should be noted that theater was linked to shrines as well, both in origin and content; Zeami's connection with the Kasuga Shrine (NŌ theater), and Izumo no Okuni's connection with the Izumo Shrine (KABUKI theater), for instance. It is generally agreed that theater began in religious ritual, in the dances (KAGURA) and songs offered to the divinities. It took Japanese theater a long time to free itself from the limits of the sacred in particular and of religion in general. The third subcategory of "doctrinal and technical scriptures" might not, technically speaking, belong to the category of religious literature, but, in imitation of Buddhism, it may be included, because of the literary quality of several works, especially those dealing with the relationships between the different religions.

It may be said that "Shintō literature" does not exist today, and that the relationships between Shintō and other modes of thought are nearly nonexistent; interactions with the West take place mainly at the secular level. Shintō has become a crystallized tradition.

In the domain of the fine arts, the same categories could be proposed, though with some modifications, and there again the discussion hinges on the interpretation of relationships between religion and aesthetics—which we cannot address here—before the appearance of sweeping secularization movements.

It is appropriate to follow the tradition and include in the category of Shintō arts the artifacts found in archaeological sites: stones (*tama*, *magatama*), mirrors, swords, earthenware statuettes (*dogū*) and other ritual implements; these constitute what are usually called "shrine treasures" (*shahō*). Whereas most of these artifacts have been revered for their function, quality, and antiquity, their production and offering to the divinities seem to have ceased quite early in history. Mirrors and swords, however, are exceptions in that they have been used as religious offerings throughout history. It has been suggested that wooden sculptures representing anthropomorphic divinities owed their appearance to the introduction of Buddhism, or, perhaps, to Chinese influence in general. In any case, a number of such statues which have been preserved are of extreme beauty, characterized by august simplicity (those in Matsunoo Shrine and Kumano Hayatama Shrine), or by stern but refined elegance (Tamayori Hime of the Yoshino Mikumari Shrine). Divinities have been represented in painting mainly within the context of Shintō-Buddhist syncretism. The Buddhist deities were painted in Chinese style and according to the canons of iconography, while their Shintō counterparts were represented in the indigenous *yamato-e* style, on a background which was also in the *yamato-e* style, creating a harmony particular to syncretism. Such depictions were called "mandala," and the inner organization they denote is that of Shintō-Buddhist relationships, or Indian and Chinese culture versus Japanese culture; famous examples are the Sannō Shrine mandala of the Hyakusaiji, or the Kumano Honjibutsu mandala of the Kōzanji. Another major type of painting used in ritual is called "shrine mandala." Depicting sacred landscapes of the shrine-temple complexes, they could serve as support for mental pilgrimages and as objects of meditation on syncretism. Famous examples are the Fuji mandala of the Fuji Hongū Sengen Shrine, the Kasuga Jōdo mandala of the Nōman'in, and the Kumano Nachi mandala of the Tōkei Shrine.

Since syncretism developed at the local level, and around a group of particular divinities, each major cult has its own art: the Kasuga cult, the Hachiman cult and so on. Shintō shrines did not support schools of painting as the government and later the schools of Buddhism did; this may be the reason why, outside of syncretism, one cannot find what could be called "Shintō painting." The exception to this rule is a minor one concerning the offering of votive tablets (EMA) by common people, or of representations emanating from popular cults during the Edo period, such as the catfish pictures of the Kashima cult. Many aspects of folk art (*mingei*) are also directly or indirectly connected to shrines, and may therefore warrant the inclusion of such pieces in the category of religious arts. A special place should be given to the genre of graphic emblems symbolizing shrines (shimmon); they are the object of a certain fascination in the contemporary Western world because of their simple appearance, yet intricate organization, which make them appear to be modern in the realm of graphic design. Their origin is most obscure; they show stylized animals (Tsuruoka Hachiman Shrine), stylized plants or flowers (Fushimi Inari Shrine, Suwa Shrines, Kitano Shrine), geometrical structures (Itsukushima Shrine, Takeda Shrine), or a mixture of these elements (Enoshima Shrine).

Finally, we should mention the varied styles of shrine architecture, which range from the stylized simplicity of Ise to the baroque complexity of Nikkō, and of the equally varied genres of music, ranging from single drum sentences or simple flute melodies to intricate orchestral pieces, which accompany the dances offered to the divinities at the festivals. Folk songs, music, and dances must be included, for they have helped to make the Shintō celebration (matsuri) a form of art in itself. See also SHINTŌ ARCHITECTURE.

——Engi Shiki, tr Felicia G. Bock as Engi-shiki: Procedures of the Engi Era, Books 1–5 (1970); Books 6–10 (1972). D. C. Holtom, Japanese Enthronement Ceremonies (1972). Haruki Kageyama, The Arts of Shinto, tr Christine Guth (1973). Kubota Osamu, Chūsei shintō no kenkyū (1959). Kuroda Toshio, Nihon chūsei no kokka to shūkyō (1975). William P. Malm, Japanese Music and Musical Instruments (1959). Murayama Shūichi, Shimbutsu shūgō shichō (1968). Murayama Shūichi, Honji suijaku (1974). Nishida Nagao, Nihon shintō shi kenkyū, 10 vols (1978–79).   Allan G. GRAPARD

Shintō and Buddhism, separation of

(shimbutsu bunri). The policy of the Meiji government (1868–1912) of separating Shintō and Buddhism in order to reinforce the Shintō-based divine status of the emperor. Some members of the new government who had been influenced by KOKUGAKU (National Learning), especially the school of HIRATA ATSUTANE, hoped to establish a Shintō-oriented government modeled on the rule of the legendary emperor JIMMU. They set out to separate Shintō and Buddhism, which since the early part of the Heian period (794–1185) had been partially syncretized. Buddhist priests, through the so-called Dual Shintō (RYŌBU SHINTŌ) system, had also gained administrative control of a large proportion of Shintō shrines. According to a March 1868 decree, these Buddhist priests were now ordered to relinquish their positions, and all Buddhist images were to be removed from Shintō shrines. Although the government did not intend to disestablish Buddhism as such, this decree set in motion a nationwide anti-Buddhist outburst (see HAIBUTSU KISHAKU).

Shintō architecture

Shintō architecture refers to the buildings located within the precincts of Shintō shrines. The precinct not only designates where a deity or deities, KAMI, are enshrined but serves as a place where people can worship and can stage ceremonies and festivals for the kami. Consequently, there are buildings for the kami and buildings for worshipers. Shintō architecture has its own distinctive style dating from prehistoric times, but from the Heian period (794–1185) shrines and other Shintō buildings have been influenced by Buddhist temple architecture. Because some Shintō shrines are dedicated to actual historic personages, Shintō architecture has influenced mausoleum design, especially after the Kamakura period (1185–1333).

Origin of Shintō Architecture —— Shintō is basically a pantheistic religion which believes in the kami's existence in practically every natural object or phenomenon. Often particularly beautiful mountains or deep forest areas were venerated as sacred sites (kannabi), e.g., the wooded area of Mt. Mikasa (Mikasayama) behind the KASUGA SHRINE in Nara. Active volcanoes such as Mt. Fuji (FUJISAN) and Mt. Aso (ASOSAN) were also considered sacred. The kami were thought to dwell in ponds, waterfalls, the confluence of rivers, giant trees, and large or strangely shaped rocks. Not only the kami but also the location where a kami might visit or reside were venerated. Thus a rocky crag or precipice might be considered a kami's seat and called iwakura. The temporary shelters for the kami during a festival (otabisho) were also sacred.

Thus, a natural object which was itself a kami or a place indicating a kami's existence was marked off as sacred, and a place for worship was created. This is the most basic level in the development of Shintō shrines, and the demarcation of the sacred area is accomplished simply by placing a straw rope (shimenawa) around the site. More elaborate fences can be used, such as a horizontally stacked wooden plank fence (mizugaki), which totally blocks the view into the enclosure, or the aragaki, which allows the worshiper to see between the vertically arranged planks in the fence. People worship in front of the TORII, a gatelike structure. The torii probably began as a gate in front of the sacred area and marked the furthest point within a sacred compound a worshiper could enter. The Ōmiwa Shrine in Nara Prefecture and the Kanasana Shrine in Saitama Prefecture illustrate Shintō shrine types without actual buildings.

Shrine Complexes and Their Buildings —— Because shrines are located in a variety of settings, from mountains to beaches, shrine buildings are sited to the environment and do not follow a uniform arrangement. The TŌSHŌGŪ at Nikkō in Tochigi Prefecture consists of a series of buildings forming courtyards staggered up a mountainside. The ITSUKUSHIMA SHRINE at Miyajima in Hiroshima Prefecture stands along the island's edge, and the buildings are completely surrounded by water at high tide. The worshiper knows he has entered a shrine complex because modest fences or a large torii usually mark the sacred precinct from the residential neighborhood buildings or from the surrounding forest or fields. Within this precinct a path or roadway will lead to the main shrine building, honden, and often stone lanterns will mark the route. To maintain the purity of the shrine precinct, water basins are provided for worshipers to wash their hands and mouth. Secondary buildings may be arranged around the honden to impart a formal symmetry or may be sited to suit the environment, thus appearing more asymmetric and informal. Often shrines are located in relationship with Buddhist temples, such as the Kasuga Shrine in Nara which adjoins the temple KŌFUKUJI.

There are two main sources for the architecture of the honden. One is the temporary building type constructed for special occasions to house the kami. This type probably dates to the early agrarian period in Japan, about 300 BC. Examples of this type of structure can be seen in the Suki and Yuki halls which are constructed as part of the ceremonies for the formal enthronement of an emperor. It is in these temporary buildings that the emperor partakes of the newly gathered rice crop with the kami in a ceremony called DAIJŌSAI. The buildings are rectangular, divided into two parts, and constructed of rough unbarked wood in a very simple style. The main shrine building of the SUMIYOSHI SHRINE in Ōsaka resembles the temporary building type, particularly in its roof and roof ornamentation, and is said to preserve the appearance of ancient religious buildings. The gabled roof, kirizuma, is supported by large round posts and the roofing is of Japanese cypress tree bark. At each gabled end, two ornamental members, chigi, cross above the roofing, and five short logs, katsuogi, lie horizontally across the ridges to weigh down the roofing material. The chigi and katsuogi are both symbolic and derived from functional construction techniques. Five posts support the roof on the long sides, and the interior is divided into two spaces. The entry is at one gabled end, and the rear gable has a centered post that runs to the ridge. This building form is called the Sumiyoshi style. A similar construction, but with three posts on the long side and an inner and outer sanctuary arrangement, was called the Ōtori style. The original Ōtori Shrine burned in 1905.

The second source for the architecture of the honden is domestic architectural forms, both storehouses (kura; see STOREHOUSES, TRADITIONAL) and dwellings. The so-called shimmei style is said to derive its simple two-bay by three-bay rectangular shape from the granaries and treasure storehouses of prehistoric Japan. The main shrine at Ise most clearly exemplifies this style and now enshrines the sacred mirror, yata no kagami, one of the three IMPERIAL REGALIA, symbols of the imperial succession. The inner shrine, Naikū, at ISE SHRINE is consecrated to AMATERASU ŌMIKAMI, the sun goddess and traditional ancestress of the imperial family. The Naikū is really two sacred sites, one which contains three buildings in the shimmei style, surrounded by four rows of fences, and one which will serve as the next shrine site. The Ise shrines are completely rebuilt every 20 years to purify the enclosure, and the buildings alternate between these adjacent sites. The Naikū buildings are raised above the ground and are entered via steps on the long side. The gabled ends have free-standing columns that support the ridge and are decorated with chigi. Ten katsuogi line the ridge, and a railed veranda encircles the building. The outer shrine, Gekū, at Ise is dedicated to the grain goddess, Toyouke no Ōkami, and is similar to the Naikū and also rebuilt every 20 years in the storehouse style. The buildings at Ise are distinguished by their simple design and natural woods, with few ornamental additions.

The shrine at Izumo in Shimane Prefecture, like that of Ise, dates from the "age of myths," and its buildings reflect the residential style of the Kofun period (ca 300–710). When ŌKUNINUSHI NO

Sumiyoshi style
Sumiyoshi Shrine, Ōsaka

Ōtori style
Ōtori Shrine, Ōsaka

shimmei style
Ise Inner Shrine, Mie Prefecture

Izumo Taisha style
Kamosu Shrine, Shimane Prefecture

nagare style
Kamo no Mioya Shrine, Kyōto

Kasuga style
Kasuga Shrine, Nara

Hachiman style
Usa Hachiman Shrine, Ōita Prefecture

gongen style
Tōshōgū, Nikkō, Tochigi Prefecture

Shintō architecture ——— Styles of main shrine building (honden)

MIKOTO, who ruled this area, built his own palace, he is said to have copied the Imperial Palace of the Yamato area, and the IZUMO SHRINE (Izumo Taisha) main building was modeled on this dwelling. The Izumo Taisha style of Shintō architecture reveals construction features suggestive of residential architecture with columns set directly into the ground and floors raised high above the earth. This raised flooring originated in damper southern regions of Asia and was introduced into Japan during the Yayoi period (ca 300 BC–ca AD 300). In the Kofun period it became a characteristic of the dwellings of powerful lords. The main shrine building at Izumo is two bays square with a central pillar, and a gabled *kirizuma* roof. The veranda that encircles the building is reached by stairs off-center on the gable end, and the doors to the shrine are on the right side. Another feature is the straight lines characteristic of wood residential construction, but the scale of the Izumo buildings has been greatly increased to show its special purpose to house the *kami*. These buildings too have been periodically rebuilt, and the present structure dates from 1744. Overall, though, the shrines at Ise and Izumo represent the most traditional of Japan's architectural styles that are still in use today, and these buildings are famed for their simple forms and use of natural materials.

After the introduction of Buddhism, the nature of Shintō worship changed, and shrine architecture evolved as well. Shrine buildings adopted elements from the Buddhist temple vocabulary, and many shrines were painted with Chinese red (cinnabar) on the columns and white over the walls. Metal and sculpted-wood ornaments were added, often using the same decoration motifs as Buddhist temples. The most important shrines increased the number of buildings within their precincts, and the *honden* itself was expanded to provide a roofed area for the worshipers. These changes occurred during the Nara (710–794) and Heian periods and four distinct building forms developed for the *honden*. These styles are the *nagare* style (*nagare-zukuri*), Kasuga style (*kasuga-zukuri*), Hachiman style (*hachiman-zukuri*), and the Hie style (*hie-zukuri*).

Among existing main shrine buildings, the *nagare* style is most common, with the Kasuga style a close second. The *nagare* is typified by the Kamo Shrines in Kyōto. They are distinguished by their small size in comparison to the more ancient shrines, and by their construction atop a raised earthen base. This may indicate their origin as small portable shrines (MIKOSHI), which were carried in festivities. A second characteristic is that a roof, or canopy, is extended to cover the stairs and area in front of the shrine. In the *nagare* style the whole roof on one side sweeps forward and down, and thus worship is conducted on the long side of these two-bay by three-bay structures. In the Kasuga style, named for the four small shrines that stand in a row at the KASUGA SHRINE in Nara, a pent roof has been added to the gable end of the one-bay square. This appended roof covers only the stairway leading to the shrine doors. In the Hachiman style, seen in the IWASHIMIZU HACHIMAN SHRINE and various other shrines dedicated to the war god HACHIMAN, a separate building for the worshipers has been added immediately in front of the main shrine building so that the roofs touch along the eaves. These three styles were established in the early Heian period and reflect the changes happening in BUDDHIST ARCHITECTURE as well, where halls were enlarged by extending the roof or adding a separate worship hall (*raidō*). Although Shintō and Buddhist buildings differed—main shrines originally had no pent roofs while Buddhist buildings often surrounded the hall with a pent-roofed corridor, *omoya*—the two developed in a similar manner during this period. The Hie style found primarily at the HIE SHRINE outside Kyōto has a pent roof added to the front and two sides of the main shrine and almost approximates the *omoya* of the Buddhist temple.

Among the group of shrine *honden* which join two buildings together, the problem of roof structures and water drainage led to two additional variations from the Hachiman style. In the Heian period the *ishinoma* style (later called the *gongen* style) separated the shrine from the worship hall by an intervening space. The area between these two parallel buildings, the *ishinoma,* is paved with stone, and covered with a gable roof set at 90° from the two parallel ridges. This style can be most clearly seen in the KITANO SHRINE, a shrine located in the northern part of Kyōto and dedicated to an actual historic figure, SUGAWARA NO MICHIZANE. Because of this association, the style was popular after the Kamakura period for mausoleums. The name *gongen* style was applied during the Edo period (1600–1868) after a title given the first Tokugawa shōgun, TOKUGAWA IEYASU, who is enshrined at the Tōshōgū in Nikkō, a building constructed in this style. Another solution to joining the main shrine and the worship hall was to construct a single large roof over both structures, as represented by the semigabled style of Yasaka Shrine in Kyōto. The main shrine at Yasaka closely resembles the Buddhist *hondō* style of architecture, which evolved in the late Heian period, in which the main hall (*hondō*) and worship hall (*raidō*) were joined. Again we see the parallel development of Shintō and Buddhist architecture.

Tradition of Periodic Reconstruction —— Even the oldest existing main shrine buildings date only as early as the 11th to 12th century. This results from loss by fire and natural disasters and also from the tradition of regular reconstruction. Shrine buildings were often rebuilt to purify the site and to renew the materials, a practice followed by most of the bigger shrines until the Edo period and still followed by the Ise Shrine. When these shrines were rebuilt, though, they invariably followed the traditional style and techniques, and so the shrines we see today are a fairly faithful preservation of the older styles. The development of Shintō architecture can be considered as practically completed in the Heian period, so that later buildings maintained the above-mentioned styles with only minor changes. In the area of ornamentation, however, Shintō architecture continued to change as more color and sculpture were applied to the basic forms. Rainbow-shaped beams, frog-legged struts, and elaborate bracketing were added to vary and beautify the shrines, and on the roof decorated gables contributed to the liveliness of the design. The ultimate example of decoration can be found in the *gongen* style, e.g., the Tōshōgū at Nikkō.

Other Shrine Complex Buildings —— A number of secondary building types besides the *honden* have developed in Shintō architecture. When the major shrines are rebuilt or repaired, temporary shrines (*karidono* or *gonden*) are constructed. During festivals or at times when shrine locations are changed, temporary structures are also built. The architecture for these temporary shrines does not significantly differ from the main shrine. At many shrines, buildings are used to house implements used by the *kami* or for offerings given to the *kami,* examples being the treasury (*hōko*) and the *sake* hall (*sakadono*). There are many such buildings at the Ise Shrine, the Kasuga Shrine, and the Kamo Shrines. These buildings follow the same basic style and do not have particularly distinguishing features.

The worship hall (*haiden*) can have a variety of plans—square, wide rectangular, and deep rectangular. The *haiden* is usually in front of or to one side of the *honden.* The square plan is often three bays wide and serves as an open-air dance platform (*maidono*). The wide rectangle plans are suitable for accommodating those who stay over and worship (*sanrō*), and often one area is made into the shrine office. The deep rectangular plans vary according to region and are suitable for a variety of services. A worship hall with a central bay of earthen floor is called a split worship hall (*wari haiden*). A prayer hall (*noritonoya*) and an offering hall (*heiden*) are other separate structures related to worship.

Within the shrine precinct, other structures aid in articulating the site or act as passageways. Among these are the gate, the fence, and the *torii.* One type of gate, the *rōmon,* developed as a two-story structure similar to the Buddhist temple gate in scale and detail. At some shrines, the fence has become a gallery (*kairō*) or a corridor to link various buildings. These corridors often have latticed windows or open-wash walls (*sukashibei*). But the most common element to nearly all Shintō shrines is the compatible relationship of the buildings to the site. Trees and rocks are protected, and within the increasingly dense urban centers of Japan, the shrines have become one of the few large plots of greenery and open space. As dwellings for the *kami,* who are often said to reside in nature, the architecture of Shintō shrines can be said to include both its buildings and the natural setting.

■ ——Haruki Kageyama, *The Arts of Shintō* (1973). Robert Treat Paine and Alexander Soper, *The Art and Architecture of Japan* (1975). Richard Ponsonby-Fane, *Studies in Shintō and Shrines* (1962). ITŌ Nobuo

Shintō art

Representation of the Shintō deity Hachiman in the guise of a Buddhist monk. Completed by the sculptor Kaikei in 1201, it is a noted example of *shūgō bijutsu,* the imagery produced through the merging of Buddhism and Shintō. Wood, painted. Height of statue 87.5 cm. Tōdaiji, Nara. National Treasure.

Shintō art

SHINTŌ, the native religion of Japan, is associated with a wide variety of art forms, including ritual objects, architecture, sculpture, and painting, in a tradition that dates from the 5th century. The range and style of Shintō-related arts are diverse. Whether in theme or usage, all forms of Shintō art radiate around the KAMI, the focal point of Shintō worship: loosely rendered in English as "deity," *kami* denotes any object or being possessed of a numinous quality.

Until the introduction of Buddhism to Japan in the 6th century, however, the forms of Shintō worship did not require elaborate edifices or accessories. Buddhism provided both the impetus and the artistic resources for the creation of Shintō statues and paintings, and made significant technical contributions in the field of architecture. Through contact with Buddhism there developed a heightened awareness of an image's potential as a devotional aid and of the shrine as the focal point for both individual and communal devotions.

Shintō art owes a great debt to Buddhism, but the influence of aristocratic values, practices, and symbols is also considerable. The incorporation of elements of court culture stems from the fact that the nobility traced its privileged status to descent from *kami* and that shrine priests were generally of the aristocratic class. The influence of aristocratic values is apparent in the forms of certain shrines, in the representation of *kami* in the guise of courtiers, and in the paraphernalia used in shrines.

Definition —— The term Shintō art (Shintō *bijutsu*) has come into usage by art historians only in recent decades and is still open to varying interpretations in terms of scope, significance, and even acceptability. Shintō art includes architecture, painting, sculpture, and the applied arts; the basis for their designation as such is subject matter, function, and in some instances style. A representation of a *kami,* a shrine, or a festival is readily recognizable as a form of Shintō art by merit of subject matter alone. Sometimes, as in wooden statuary, stylistic features, in combination with theme, may serve as guides in determining the nature of the work. Many forms of art are labeled Shintō on a contextual basis. Mirrors, swords, and the comma-shaped jewels called *magatama,* for instance, are included because of the symbolic role that they have long held in the Shintō tradition.

Because the term Shintō *bijutsu* can be used to denote any art form pertaining to *kami,* many scholars prefer *shūgō bijutsu* or *sui-*

Shintō art

Ninth-century representation of a female Shintō deity dressed in court robes. In this type of image, which diverges stylistically from contemporary Buddhist statuary, the influence of aristocratic tastes and values is strong. Wood, painted. Height 86.9 cm. Matsunoo Shrine, Kyōto.

jaku bijutsu. Shūgō bijutsu, which designates imagery produced through the merging of Buddhism and Shintō, is applied primarily to painting and statuary. The representation of the *kami* Hachiman in the guise of a Buddhist monk is a typical expression of *shūgō bijutsu. Suijaku bijutsu* refers to paintings and statues in which *kami* are presented as the traces or avatars *(suijaku)* of Buddhist deities who are their true forms *(honji).* Although Shintō art, *shūgō bijutsu,* and *suijaku bijutsu* are often used synonymously, they are progressively narrower in scope; whereas the two latter view art forms pertaining to *kami* from a Buddhist perspective, the former, while acknowledging Buddhist contributions, views them from a Shintō perspective. See also SYNCRETISM; HONJI SUIJAKU.

Imperial Regalia——Mirrors, swords, and comma-shaped *magatama* jewels constitute the most ancient known forms of Shintō art. Many examples both of Chinese and Japanese manufacture have been excavated from ritual sites such as the island of Okinoshima, between Korea and Japan, as well as from tombs of the Kofun period (ca 300–710). The place held within Shintō by these three items is attributive, for taken out of context, they do not immediately reveal themselves as forms of religious art. Indeed, initially they were rather attributes of power or personal ornaments. Their special esteem within the Shintō tradition stems in part from the combination of religious and political leadership embodied in the rulers of early Japan who possessed them. Today, possession of the mirror, sword, and jewels, which are regarded as IMPERIAL REGALIA, is solely the prerogative of the emperor.

As the special emblem of AMATERASU ŌMIKAMI, supreme goddess of the Shintō pantheon and ancestress of the imperial family, the mirror is the most highly revered of the three. The mirror given by this goddess to the founder of the imperial family is today the divine emblem housed in Ise Shrine. In other shrines also, ancient mirrors, swords, and jewels may function as *shintai,* or the material embodiment of the *kami.*

Numerous variations of the basic circular mirror with a reflecting surface on one side and a design on the other exist. One is the bell mirror, characterized by the knoblike bells attached to the mirror's circumference. Another, which developed in the late part of the Heian period (794–1185), is MISHŌTAI (or *kakebotoke),* embellished either with incised or raised representations of one or more Buddhist or Shintō deities and often used as the material embodiment of the divine spirit. One of the most ancient incised mirrors is dated 1001

and was unearthed from a sutra mound at the temple KIMBUSENJI in Nara Prefecture.

Architecture——The Shintō shrine, with its distinctive TORII gate, is the residence of the *kami* and the place where ceremonies and prayers are performed. The first shrines were either natural sites selected for their unusual configuration or strategic location, such as the island Okinoshima of the MUNAKATA SHRINE or the mountain MIWAYAMA of ŌMIWA SHRINE, or spots designated as sacred for the duration of a ceremony. The latter were comprised of groups of rocks or trees set off from their surroundings by a boundary of some sort. In both cases, the shrine was off limits to all but the priest or other properly purified individuals. The temporary nature of many primitive sanctuaries and the concept of the shrine as a place where ordinary men could not set foot have had a pervasive influence on the development of shrine architecture and its function. The former underlies *sengū,* or periodic reconstruction, once practiced at many shrines but today almost exclusive to Ise, which enabled ancient architectural forms to be preserved over extended periods of time; and the latter accounts in large part for the fact that individuals do not worship within the structure (*honden* or *shōden*) housing the deity. The special worship hall *(haiden)* is thought to have made a rather late appearance on the shrine compound.

The Ise, Izumo, and Sumiyoshi shrines all retain elements that may be traced to the initial stages of the development of shrine architecture. Each shrine is distinct in style, reflecting the particular local social, economic, and religious environment in which it emerged. While Ise Shrine on the Shima Peninsula in Mie Prefecture resembles a rice granary, IZUMO SHRINE at Taishamachi in Shimane Prefecture may have been modeled after a palace. The appearance of SUMIYOSHI SHRINE in present-day Ōsaka relates to that of temporary structures made for special religious observances such as enthronement ceremonies for the new emperor.

Ise's architectural style has an integrity and elegant simplicity of form that clearly reflect its original concept. The unpretentious buildings of Ise Shrine are rectangular, constructed of unpainted wood, and raised above the ground on pillars. They are further characterized by overhanging thatched roofs. Izumo stands out among shrines of all ages because of its tremendous scale and asymmetrical gable entryway, unusual in religious architecture. Both Ise and Izumo do, however, share certain important features, namely their raised floors, projecting finials at the end of the roof, and the nonfunctional sacred pillar located at the heart of each sanctuary. The two also have a series of four fences around the main compound. The elongated and low profile of Sumiyoshi Shrine has little in common with the two above shrines.

After the founding of the capital of Nara in 710, the influence of continental building techniques introduced to Japan through Buddhism became increasingly apparent in the preference for complex bracketing systems, curved, often multiple roofs, and vermilion-painted structures. The gabled KASUGA SHRINE in Nara is the forerunner of sanctuaries of this type. The style of the KAMO SHRINES in Kyōto, with the graceful sweep of the roofs devoid of projecting finials, also dates from the Nara period (710–794). Subsequently, this so-called flowing or *nagare-zukuri* style became one of the most widespread in shrine construction.

From the Heian period onward, the distinction between Buddhist and Shintō architecture became increasingly blurred. The architectural style known as *hachiman-zukuri,* which, as its name suggests, first appeared within the context of the Buddhist-influenced cult to the deity HACHIMAN, consists of a pair of adjoining gabled structures, one before the other. The rear building holds the divine emblem, and the front one is a worship hall. The tripartite structure resulting from the union of these two independent edifices by a corridor is yet another architectural form with Buddhist counterparts. TŌSHŌGŪ Shrine at Nikkō, although erected only in 1636, is the most illustrious example of its use. Other important types of shrine architecture may be distinguished from the above by the increasing complexity of their rooflines. The *irimoya* style has a hipped and gabled roof. This mode was also commonly employed for Buddhist temples and private residences. The Hie or Hiyoshi style has a roof that extends over the front steps and side eaves (see HIE SHRINE). Among the most elaborate structures are those in the so-called *yatsumune* or eight-roofed style, suggestive of the multiple levels and variety of the roofline, which is represented at KITANO SHRINE in Kyōto, and those in the Sengen style, which is two-storied, exemplified by the shrine of the same name (SENGEN SHRINE) at the foot of Mt. Fuji (Fujisan). See SHINTŌ ARCHITECTURE.

Sculpture——Shintō sculpture is comprised of portrayals of *kami* in various guises, of figures of human or animal guardians, and occasionally of images of personages who participate in ceremonies held on shrine precincts. Statuary may fulfill various roles in the Shintō system. The most important is that of *shintai,* either in an independent shrine or in a sanctuary on a Buddhist temple compound *(chinjusha).* In rare instances Shintō and Buddhist statuary might also be arranged so as to illustrate *honji suijaku* relationships, as at IWASHIMIZU HACHIMAN SHRINE in Kyōto Prefecture.

The earliest extant anthropomorphic portrayals of *kami* are in sculptural form. While this may be no more than a historical accident, wooden statuary has long held a special place among Shintō arts because of the deep reverence for certain kinds of trees, and indeed for all natural phenomena, within the Shintō tradition. Myths and legends describe many instances of trees being viewed as divinities and it is likely that initially statuary was frequently carved from such trees. This may be true of the earliest extant Shintō statues, a mid-9th century triad representing the HACHIMAN and two attendants in the sanctuary *(chinjusha)* in the temple TŌJI in Kyōto.

Shintō statuary falls into two categories. In one, both in style and in iconography, images are closely modeled after those current in Buddhist circles. In some cases, renowned Buddhist sculptors were commissioned to make these. The Hachiman of 1201 by KAIKEI at the temple TŌDAIJI in Nara is a case in point. In the other category, the influence of aristocratic tastes and values is strong. Deities, as those in the Matsunoo Shrine in Kyōto, are dressed in court garb, and stylistically, the development of this mode of statuary diverges considerably from contemporary Buddhist works. Generally, the identity of the artists of this type of sculpture is unknown. Some images, particularly those of the latter category, were carved by individuals without special artistic training but with a high degree of spiritual involvement in the act of creation. The origins of certain types of folk art may be sought in the compact, often ill-defined forms of Shintō sculpture of this type.

Painting——Among the varieties of Shintō arts, painting is unsurpassed in thematic range. It comprises portrayals of *kami,* individually or in groups, with or without their Buddhist *honji,* of maplike representations of shrines and their activities, of votive plaques, and of many variations thereof. It is likely that most types of painting emerged in the latter part of the Heian period as court culture reached a peak and the *honji suijaku* theory attained widespread acceptance. The Ujikami Shrine in Uji, on the outskirts of Kyōto, contains some of the earliest known pictorial representations of *kami.* They date from the 12th century. Documentary evidence indicates that depictions of the Kasuga Shrine compound were known about the same time.

Many forms of Shintō painting are designated as MANDALA, a term of Sanskrit origin that initially referred to a sacred circle, cosmic diagram, or arrangement of divinities showing their interrelationship and respective places in the universe. In Japan, however, the word mandala lost both its specificity and its purely Buddhist connotations and came to be applied to various forms of religious painting, including those with Shintō affiliations. Among Shintō mandalas are works of an iconographic nature illustrating the relationship between Buddhist and Shintō divinities *(honji suijaku* mandala), or those in which the *honji* or *suijaku* alone *(honji* or *suijaku* mandala) are depicted. In such works, the deities are generally arranged in rows within a structure resembling a shrine or in a landscape setting identifiable as that of the actual site in which the deities' shrine is located. The emphasis on re-creating the physical setting associated with a specific *kami* or group of *kami* is a characteristic of the Shintō mandala. Many such works were produced within the context of the Kumano (see KUMANO SANZAN SHRINES), Kasuga, Hachiman, and Sannō cults. In some cases, the shrine and its surroundings become the subject of a painting. The creation of these so-called shrine mandalas stem in part from the need for accurate records of the appearance of a shrine and of its boundaries for reconstruction purposes. Although the shrine mandala is a form of devotional painting, in some instances it comes close to pure landscape painting, as in a representation of the sacred Nachi waterfall in the Nezu Art Museum in Tōkyō. Closely related to the shrine mandala are the festival and pilgrimage mandalas in which the human activity at a shrine replaces the sanctuary as the composition's focus. This development in the late part of the Muromachi (1333–1568) and subsequent periods parallels the increasing role of genre-related themes in Japanese painting as a whole. One renowned example of this genre is the late Muromachi *Mt. Fuji Pilgrimage Mandala* (Fuji Hongū Sengen Shrine in Shizuoka Prefecture) illustrating an antlike

Shintō art

A section from the *Kitano Tenjin engi,* a set of handscrolls on the life of Sugawara no Michizane and the origins of the temple dedicated to his spirit. Shown is Michizane's attack, in his deified form as the God of Thunder, on a hall of the imperial palace. Colors on paper. Height of scroll 51.5 cm. Ca 1219. Kitano Shrine, Kyōto. National Treasure.

procession of devotees climbing the slopes of the mountain. The 16th-century *Chikubujima Festival Mandala* (Yamato Bunkakan in Nara), showing a procession of boats on Lake Biwa, is also characteristic of this type.

In contrast to the profusion of minute scenes and figures characteristic of the Shintō mandala, visions of *kami* are generally dominated by the single towering figure of a deity as he manifested himself to a devotee or as he was traditionally believed to appear. The portrayal of Kasuga Wakamiya in the John Powers Collection, New York, and the large body of paintings depicting the other deities of Kasuga Shrine astride deer or even the deer alone, are examples of this category.

Many paintings in the long EMAKIMONO or illustrated handscroll format may also be included among Shintō arts. Most numerous are those illustrating the origins of a shrine and miracles performed by its deities, such as the 13th-century *Kitano Tenjin engi.* Many such works, as well as the Shintō mandalas described above, were produced in painting workshops in shrine or temple compounds and show strong stylistic parallels with contemporary Buddhist painting.

Unlike the various forms of devotional painting enumerated above, whose basic function was didactic and devotional, the EMA is basically a form of votive art. *Ema* initially designated a representation of a horse. Painted on a wooden plaque, it was dedicated to a shrine for the fulfillment of a prayer, but in time, even the object of that prayer—a child, success in battle—also came to be depicted. In the Edo period (1600–1868) *ema* were often painted not only by the devotee but also by renowned painters of the day. *Ema* consequently serve both as important sources of information concerning the development of folk art and the interaction of popular art and established artists.

Applied Arts——As in most religious systems, ritual implements and other accessories were made for use within the Shintō tradition. Peculiar to Shintō is the *mikoshi,* or sacred palanquin, used to carry, hidden from public view, the emblem of the *kami* during festivals or other ceremonies. The appearance and use of the *mikoshi* reflects the influence of court practices. Elegant garments, fans, and other personal items prevalent among the aristocracy were also commonly presented to shrines for the use of the *kami.*

Many shrine accessories were modeled after those created for Buddhist establishments. These include the elongated embroidered banners and wreathlike ornaments hung both inside and outside the shrine.

Historical Development——The initial stages in the development of Shintō art coincided with the process of political centralization that led to the unification of Japan's cultural heartland under the leadership of an emperor and with the founding of its first permanent capital at Nara in 710. Sanctuaries designed as residences for *kami,* and the objects housed within them as the material emblems of those *kami,* may be viewed as the first manifestations of Shintō art. The few examples whose origins date from this period such as Ise and Izumo shrines, on Japan's east and west coasts respectively, or the mirrors, swords, and jewels found in various ritual sites, reveal themselves in different ways as products of an age when political and religious leadership were synonymous. This interdependence of political and religious symbolism is a characteristic of many of the early forms of Shintō art.

Many varieties of Shintō art, and the concept of Shintō as a religious institution, emerged only after the introduction of Buddhism and continental culture to Japan. Although its official introduction was said to have occurred in 538 (or 552), it was some time before Buddhism established itself firmly on Japanese soil. By the onset of the Nara period, however, Buddhism had become a state religion on a par with Shintō. Adjoining Buddhist temples and Shintō shrines were constructed under state and private sponsorship with *kami* functioning as the local guardians for the imported religion and its deities. Although the relationship between the two religions was not always conciliatory, Shintō absorbed many Buddhist elements. This period saw the emergence of Shintō sculpture and the formalization of more complex types of shrine architecture.

The Heian period (794–1185) saw the burgeoning and diversification of all art forms, including those of Shintō. While important examples of Shintō art of the Nara and earlier periods may be found in various regions, the new architectural types, statuary, and painting are concentrated in the vicinity of the capitals, first Nara and then later Kyōto, or along pilgrimage routes and sites popular at the time. Shrines of this period are characterized by a richness and complexity of form and scale previously limited to Buddhist edifices. Commissioned by Shintō priests, Buddhist monks, or members of the aristocracy, imagery of the time is often highly individualistic in style and subject matter.

While much of the art of the Heian period was created with the cooperation of individual Buddhist establishments, the codification and widespread acceptance of the Buddhist concept that Buddhist and Shintō deities were but two expressions of a single truth put the interaction of the two religions on a more formal footing. As a result, the imagery produced within this environment assumed a greater stylistic and iconographic uniformity. Art became one of the principal tools for the dissemination of the *honji suijaku* theory, and from the 12th through the 19th century, imagery graphically illustrating the relationship between specific Buddhist divinities and Shintō *kami* became a predominant mode of Shintō art.

Pictures of shrines, visions of *kami*, and legends and miracles associated with a particular deity were the focus of other forms of expression that emerged in the Kamakura period (1185–1333) and gained widespread currency in the Muromachi period (1333–1568). A strong popular undercurrent in which specifically Buddhist or Shintō elements are difficult to separate is evident in the character and function of such images, which were designed to encourage pilgrimages to the shrine and to extol the virtue of faith in its deities. Distribution throughout the country of much imagery of this type also contributed to the growth and spread of devotion to the deities depicted. Best represented are the Hachiman, Kasuga, Kumano, and Sannō cults, which assumed national stature, but others of a more limited regional nature also inspired an artistic output on a smaller scale.

The evolution of Shintō architecture over the 12th through the 19th centuries was also heavily influenced by Buddhism. The distinction, both formal and functional, between shrine and temple became blurred. Their appearance differed little; both had similar forms and rooflines, and were often painted vermilion, and even the pagoda, ubiquitous symbol of the Buddhist faith, was constructed on shrine compounds.

The structural elaboration and expanding role of the shrine that occurred over these years was accompanied by an increasing concern for shrine accessories. Guardian statues were installed in entryways; banners and other ornaments were suspended over open verandas. Offerings for the use of the *kami*, such as fans, lacquer boxes, and even elegant ceremonial garb, as well as votive plaques, further enhanced the appearance of the shrine and enriched its storehouses.

The establishment of the Meiji government of 1868, with its policy of strict separation of Buddhism and Shintō (see SHINTŌ AND BUDDHISM, SEPARATION OF) brought an abrupt halt to the production of most forms of Shintō imagery. Many Shintō images in Buddhist temples, as well as Buddhist objects in Shintō shrines, were destroyed by order of the government (see HAIBUTSU KISHAKU). Furthermore, the origins and history of many works of art were obscured when they were secretly transferred to more appropriate establishments. Many examples of Shintō art that were hidden from the Meiji authorities have only resurfaced in recent years.

———— Akiyama Aisaburō, *Shintō and Its Architecture* (1936). Kageyama Haruki, *Shintō no bijutsu* (1972). Kageyama Haruki, *The Arts of Shintō,* tr Christine Guth (1973). Kageyama Haruki and Christine G. Kanda, *Shintō Arts: Nature, Gods, and Man in Japan* (1976). Murayama Shūichi, *Shimbutsu shūgō shichō* (1957; 2nd ed, 1974). Murayama Shūichi, *Honji suijaku* (1974). Nara National Museum, *Suijaku bijutsu,* (1964). Oka Naomi, *Shinzō chōkoku no kenkyū* (1966). Tange Kenzō and Kawazoe Noboru, *Ise: Prototype of Japanese Architecture* (1965). Watanabe Yasutada, *Shintō Art: Ise and Izumo Shrines,* tr Robert Ricketts (1974).

Christine Guth KANDA

Shintō family altars

(*kamidana;* literally, "god shelf"). An altar placed in the home for the traditional worship of Shintō deities (KAMI). Typically, it is placed on a shelf built above a door lintel of the room in which visitors are received. It is customary to place talismans of gods such as those of the ISE SHRINE or the local tutelary deity (CHINJU NO KAMI) on the altar. The location of the altar may differ, however, according to the god or gods being worshiped: EBISU and DAIKOKUTEN, two of the SEVEN DEITIES OF GOOD FORTUNE, are usually lodged above a kitchen lintel; the fire and kitchen god KŌJIN has his own altar next to the oven. Not all *kamidana* are permanent structures: a temporary altar may be built to receive the TOSHIGAMI, gods who visit at NEW YEAR, or the returning ancestral spirits during the BON FESTIVAL. Often the *kamidana* is decorated with sprays of pine or the sacred SAKAKI tree, which serve to attract and lodge the gods. In some locations in the Ōsaka–Kyōto region, the *kamidana* is replaced by a so-called *kamidoko* on the floor of the *tokonoma* (alcove). Offerings placed on the *kamidana* include *sake* (rice wine), food, and candles. The number of households which have *kamidana* is fast declining.

Ōtō Tokihiko

Shin Tōhō Co, Ltd

Company engaged in film production, distribution, and exhibition. It was established in 1947 by several of the members and actors of the TŌHŌ CO, LTD, in the unrest leading up to the TŌHŌ STRIKE of 1948. Successful for a brief time, it produced several excellent pictures, including NARUSE MIKIO's *Okāsan* (Mother). It went bankrupt in 1961 after many of its staff returned to the reorganized Tōhō Co.

Shintō rites

SHINTŌ could well be termed a religion of ceremony. As a religion without official founders, Shintō has no tales of the conversion or revelations of early personalities, no official dogma, and no sacred texts (it does have several classics of myth, ritual, and history). Thus, Shintō is a popular religion based not on doctrine, but on elaborate ceremonial rites.

Various governments in Japanese history have attempted to codify Shintō rites. There were sections on Shintō rites in the Ritsuryō Code (see RITSURYŌ SYSTEM) and other statutes for warriors to observe in feudal times, including the Jōei Shikimoku (see GOSEIBAI SHIKIMOKU) in the Kamakura period (1185–1333) and the Statutes concerning Shintō Priests and Deacons issued in the Edo period (1600–1868). The Meiji government passed laws concerning Shintō and Shintō rites, as did the OCCUPATION forces following World War II.

More particularly, the *Ryō no gige* commentary of 833 has a section entitled "Rules on Shintō" which states that "all gods in the heavens and on the earth shall be revered according to the traditional rituals," and the ENGI SHIKI (927, Procedures of the Engi Era) includes a section on ceremonies at the Grand Shrine of Ise (ISE SHRINE) decreeing that ritual offerings follow precedent. Further, the section on chants and incantations states that traditional custom be followed for all matters not directly stipulated. In the case of ceremonies to be performed on short notice, a draft had to be presented to the appropriate bureau and the decision of the Office of Shintō Affairs received before performance of the ceremony in question was allowed.

These regulations show that Shintō has placed particular importance on ceremonial actions and on the transmission of ancient ceremonies, believing that in transmitting rites in their original form the power and dignity of the gods are made manifest.

Another important consideration is the history of Shintō in modern times. In the period before World War II, Shintō was divided into STATE SHINTŌ, SHRINE SHINTŌ, and SECT SHINTŌ, with rites classified as imperial house rites, rites conducted at the Grand Shrine of Ise, rites at other shrines, rites at sect shrines, and other ceremonies. The main rites in these categories were based upon laws dating from the Meiji period (1868–1912). However, at the end of World War II, many rites were either revised or completely revoked upon the abolition of the government offices concerning Shintō shrines and practices.

The Shintō Shrine —— Four elements are indispensable in a Shintō shrine: (1) deities, (2) a body of worshipers, (3) ritual as a means of communication between the deities and the worshipers, and (4) edifices for the above.

We can classify the enshrined deities *(saijin;* see also KAMI) into gods of heaven and earth *(tenjin chigi)* and tutelary deities (UJIGAMI) and further subdivide them into (a) ancestral gods, (b) nonancestral gods, (c) gods venerated as embodiments of virtues, (d) gods venerated for works, and (e) gods whose wrath is to be feared. Another possible classification is gods representing a certain idea, personal gods, and divine spirits.

Before Shintō deities began to be viewed as personal gods or ancestral spirits, they were worshiped at sites known as *saijō.* The *saijō,* whose ground was inviolable and holy, is the prototype of the *jinja.* At this stage, the *jinja* had not yet become a formal structure. Rather, the spirits of the gods were thought to be attracted to trees, forests, rocks, and other natural objects such as *himorogi* (a sacred place surrounded by evergreens), *kannabi* (a sacred mountain covered with forests), and *iwasaka* (a sacred place surrounded by rocks), all of which were revered as religious objects. The worship of groves, residing deities, the sky, and mountains (see MOUNTAINS, WORSHIP OF) were all forms of primitive Shintō.

The gods being given definite names and honored as such is a comparatively recent phenomenon. Before the gods were recorded in written records under definite names, shrines were known by place name, enshrined god's name, number of enshrined gods, the offerer's family name or original locality, a particular divine virtue, or a combination of place name, shrine guild name, and deity name or of place name and guild name. This shows that worshipers did not need to know the name of the god they were worshiping, and it was even thought to be disrespectful to utter the names of the gods aloud.

These gods were thought to approach the shrine from either a perpendicular or a horizontal direction or to occupy a certain fixed position. Thus gods ascended to heaven and descended to earth (the perpendicular category), approached and visited the shrine (the horizontal group), or had occupied certain areas since time immemorial, with other gods and the people being considered as their guests (the fixed category).

The *saijō* place of worship was the focus of a village as the place where the people felt nearest the sacredness of the gods. Places which might be considered as holy were those of particular importance for the residents, such as an area used as a fortress, springs or wells which did not dry up, a mine supplying iron for weapons, a central traffic point, a fork in a river, a hilltop, or a border. Factors such as the rise and fall of settlements, changes in the base of production, and the like sometimes caused a change in location of a shrine or the end of worship of one god and the welcoming of another god. In this sense, the god which was revered at a particular shrine was not necessarily a stationary entity.

Buildings and Facilities —— Shintō rites constitute a communion between the particular god to be revered and the body of worshipers. As Japanese culture developed, rites began to be performed in special buildings and facilities instead of in natural surroundings. These facilities include the *shinden* (sanctuary), *noritoya* (prayer hall), *heiden* (hall of offering), *haiden* (hall of worship), *shinsenjo* (culinary hall), *sanrōjo* (hostel for abstinence), *shamusho* (shrine affairs office), *chōzuya* (washing place), *haraijo* (place of exorcism), *rōmon* (entrance gate), *emaden* (votive picture repository), *kaguraden* (KAGURA dance platform), *hōmotsuden* (treasure repository), *torii* (ceremonial arch), and *mizugaki* (shrine fence). See also SHRINES; SHINTŌ ARCHITECTURE.

Body of Worshipers —— The worshipers were drawn from ancient settlements in Japan, often located near marshy areas at the base of hillsides. They formed an *ujiko chiiki* (a parish) surrounded by natural borders of mountains, hills, or rivers, with the shrine in the center. The number of the faithful belonging to a shrine was limited by the population the land could support, and the central area of the settlement was usually occupied by older families belonging to the ruling class. In the traditional village, branch families

and newcomers settled on the outer limits of the older family's territory.

The old families performed the village rites on a rotating basis and chose from among themselves officers *(tōnin)* to be in charge of the services held by shrine guilds (MIYAZA). Within certain limits imposed by family background, these ritual officers served as representatives for the services either in rotation, by drawing lots, or due to some religious perfection they had attained. Since the fate of the village and the success of the crops depended on these Shintō services, the ritual officers were obliged to observe strict abstinence.

This group of ritual officers in a sense belonged to "the territory of the gods." From this special group of people were chosen the *negi* and *hafuri,* the basis of the Shintō ministry (see KANNUSHI). The shrine ministry, particularly at larger shrines, grew more diversified as society became more complex, with varied names for different ministerial duties (see also PRIESTHOOD).

Although the shrine ministry during the Heian period (794–1185) was composed mainly of state-appointed positions, this did not apply throughout the entire country. Before the shrines were recorded under definite names in government records, they were indigenous to a particular province and called *mikansha* (nongovernmental shrine) or *densha* (local shrine). In this case, the shrine positions had their authority limited by local bodies of the particular province or settlement.

In the Heian period the Yoshida and Shirakawa families assumed assignment of state-appointed shrine positions, a system which continued up to the Meiji Restoration in 1868; these two families were also instrumental in passing down several ceremonial rites. The selection of the *negi* and *hafuri* for the local shrines depended on the character of that local area, and a particular ministerial position was traditionally held by one family for generations. Although the hereditary ministry was abolished at the time of the Meiji Restoration, no law alone could eradicate the family succession to ministerial positions, since this was based on the sacredness of the ministry, that is, the inviolability of those who inherited the Shintō offices and fulfilled the divine will.

Norito (Ritual Prayers) —— Shintō ritual prayers (NORITO) constitute the high point of the union between god and man in a Shintō ceremony. In this spoken ceremony, the officiant makes clear to the venerated god the meaning and purpose of the given ritual. The *norito* follows either the proclamation style of a deity addressing the faithful, or the reporting style of the faithful speaking to a deity. In the Engi Shiki, the most important source for *norito,* the proclamation style seems to be in use principally for official ceremonies, with the reporting style used for private ceremonies. The former style is older, but soon both styles came to be used in a mixed fashion.

Accessories and Offerings —— Shintō festivals center on the wait for the visitation of a god and entreaties and supplications preliminary to that arrival. Pillars, banners, and streamers are symbols employed to implore the gods to descend. Persons performing these actions belong to "the territory of the gods," and preparations for the festivals were traditionally performed by the devoted faithful (see also SACRIFICE). Since offerings had to be accepted by the gods, proper ritual objects such as sacred jewels, furniture, clothes, and food offerings were chosen according to various rites before the standardization of the Shintō rites.

These accessories and offerings tell much about the background of the modern ceremonies. Rituals have been classified by certain authors according to their purpose: (1) supplication, (2) thanksgiving, (3) memorials, (4) incantations, (5) divination, and (6) exorcism and purification. And the motive behind a particular ceremony is often a combination of two or more of the above.

Food offerings presently made at Shintō shrines include, in order, *nigishine* (husked rice), *arashine* (unhusked rice), rice wine, rice cakes, saltwater fish, wildfowl, waterfowl, sea plants, greens, sweets, salt, and water. In addition to these usual food offerings, special offerings are made at the ancient shrines; representative of these offerings are the *jōten mike* (ordinary foods) offered every morning and evening at the *mikeden* (culinary hall) in the Outer Shrine of the Grand Shrine at Ise.

The ancient order of offering foods differs in various respects from contemporary rites. Presenting water first, followed by cooked rice, salt, and *nie* (side dishes), demonstrates the order of importance these items had in ancient times. That is, obtaining pure, drinkable water was an absolute necessity for ancient population centers. A life without salt was also unthinkable and salt was thus held in great respect. These ritual accessories and food offerings occupy a central position in Shintō rites and ceremonies.

Festivals —— Shintō festivals *(matsuri)* attempt to renew the power of the gods, to renew the bond between god and worshiper. One early reference to Shintō festivals appears in the 8th-century *Yamashiro no Kuni fudoki* (Gazeteer of the Province of Yamashiro [now Kyōto Prefecture]), which makes mention of the festival days kept at the Inari shrines on HATSUUMA (the first horse day of the second month according to the sexagenary cycle; see JIKKAN JŪNI-SHI). A reenactment of the original rite held when the god was first enshrined, this festival is thus an annual event bringing back the god and his glory.

Shintō rites center on AGRICULTURAL RITES; these include the Toshigoi no Matsuri (a festival for good crops, observed in the second month of the year according to the lunar calendar), the Ōimi no Matsuri (a festival at the HIROSE SHRINE for good crops, observed in August), the Fūchinsai (a festival at the TATSUTA SHRINE for protection against wind disaster, observed in July), the Kanname no Matsuri or Kannamesai (a blessing of new rice at the Grand Shrine of Ise, observed in October), the Ainame no Matsuri (a rice offering to the 71 enshrined gods, held prior to the Niiname no Matsuri), and the Niiname no Matsuri or Niinamesai (an offering of new rice to the gods of heaven and earth by the emperor in November). Festivals praying for peace and happiness in daily life include the Hanashizume no Matsuri (a festival for protection against pestilence observed in the spring), the Ōmiwa no Matsuri (a festival of the god Ōmiwa), the Sai no Matsuri (a festival for the god Sai), the Saekusa no Matsuri (a spring festival at the Ikawa Shrine), the Kantoki no Kami no Matsuri (rites for the thunder god), the Hoshizume no Matsuri (rites for protection against fire, observed in June and December), and the Michiae no Matsuri (a festival to ward off evil spirits, observed in June and December).

In premodern times, some festivals were held according to the sexagenary cycle and others on a definite date each year. Most traditional festivals were divided according to the four seasons, with rural and agricultural ones taking place in spring and fall and urban ones in summer. Fixed festival days have sometimes changed following changes in society and in the lives of the worshipers. In modern times, for instance, festivals in the cities tend to be held on Sundays and holidays. See also FESTIVALS: matsuri.

Saikai (Purification Rites) —— Shintō rites also emphasize fasting and abstinence *(imi)*: it was believed that such practices prepared people for their approach to the gods. *Imi* includes both spiritual and physical mortification, involving the spirit, body, words, and actions, and necessitating an abandonment of everyday life during a period of abstinence. See also MISOGI; KEGARE.

The DAIJŌSAI (the first Niinamesai held after an imperial enthronement, and thus a major festival) in former times required a period of abstinence of one month. The period of abstinence for ordinary rites is three days and for lesser rites one day.

Abstinence is further divided into *sansai* (also called *araimi*) or preliminary purification rites and *chisai* (also called *maimi*) or main purification rites. The *chisai* rites are performed on the day of the festival itself and the *sansai* are performed on the days immediately preceding and following the festival. During the period of *sansai*, the daily routine at the shrine remains the same, but activities such as attending funerals, visiting the sick, banquets, trial and execution of criminals, profane music, and touching things considered unclean are all forbidden.

These acts of mortification are for avoiding uncleanness and spiritual disturbance. In the *sansai*, which was partly a preparation period for Shintō festivals, there were restrictions on the use of words; the Engi Shiki, for example, lists several *imikotoba* (see TABOO EXPRESSIONS), words forbidden at certain times and replaced by other expressions.

Since the Heian period, upon the assumption of the throne by a new emperor one of the emperor's female relatives was selected to serve at the Grand Shrine of Ise as a priestess called *saigū* or *saiō*. She underwent a period of three years of abstinence before entering the Grand Shrine of Ise to assume her duties. The first qualification for her serving at the shrine was the strict observance of this period of abstinence and purification. She was revered as having received the gods' will, which she then transmitted to the people.

For purification rites, Shintō officiants changed their clothes, performed *misogi* purification practices, cooked vegetarian meals on special purified fires, remained in the purification hall, and devoted themselves completely to the services. Similarly, in olden times the families performing shrine duties, including the head priest and his successor, his son, were not permitted to carry barrels of fertilizer, handle dead things, or the like. On festival days, they hung a rope *(shimenawa)* around their residence and set up a bamboo fence to prevent the entry of unclean persons and objects.

Religious Banquets —— These were the original form of Shintō rites, implying that ceremonies involving the entire population had more importance than ceremonies involving a single officiant. In this sense, banquets were the central focus of the ancient rites. In the practice known as NAORAI, the offerings are taken from the altar following a ceremony and eaten at the *ainame* ceremony, in which the participants receive the favor and blessing of the gods in the form of this food. *Naorai* refers to the dishes served at the *gesai,* or release from the period of abstinence, as well as to the ritual banquet held at the end of Shintō ceremonies. Regulations ordain that *sansai* take place both before and after the *chisai*. Thus the *gesai* may in a certain sense be considered a part of the purification rites *(saikai)*. *Gesai*, however, is also the final stage in a Shintō ceremony and demonstrates a return to everyday life from a unity with the gods. The stricter the *saikai*, the more festive the *gesai* ceremonies usually are. They consist primarily of ritual meals, singing, and dancing to assure a smooth return to everyday life.

At the climax of Shintō services, the *kagura* (ritual dances) or similar religious performances are staged as an act of praise to the divine virtues. At the ancient funerals for dead emperors, offerings of rice wine and food were served by the *asobibe* (clan for funeral services) on seven successive days and nights, which had incantatory implications. These were also accompanied by dances employing drums, flutes, and banners.

The Kanname no Matsuri and Niiname no Matsuri, held at the Grand Shrine of Ise and at the Imperial Palace, respectively, are held in autumn at harvest time to show respect for the power of the gods. By receiving the spirit of the rice *(uka no mitama)*, the celebrants reflect on the favor of the gods and dedicate themselves to a life where god and man are united. Thus ritual meals consisting of food offerings are a quite natural occurrence. See also SACRED, THE.

—— Iwamoto Tokuichi, *Shintō saishi no kenkyū* (1970). Kawade Kiyohiko, *Saishi gaisetsu* (1978). Nishitsunoi Masayoshi, *Saishi gairon* (1957). Saida Moriuji, "Saishi genron," in vol 1 of *Shintō kōza* (1929).   *Iwamoto Tokuichi*

Shintō Shrines, Association of

(Jinja Honchō). Umbrella organization of Shintō shrines established on 3 February 1946 with the ISE SHRINE as the principal shrine. When state administration over Shintō shrines was abolished with the end of World War II (see STATE SHINTŌ), Shintō organizations formed an association rather than a religious sect. Thus, although the Jinja Honchō does not regulate the doctrines of its member shrines, it promotes SHRINE SHINTŌ through public relations, setting up workshops for their priests, organizing devotees, and so forth. It supervises the prefectural associations of Shintō shrines. In 1979 it comprised the majority of Shintō shrines (79,523 shrines) and had registered 22,954 certified priests and 4,223 certified priestesses. It is a member of the Japan Religious League and the World Conference on Religion and Peace.   *Ueda Kenji*

Shinwa Kaiun Kaisha, Ltd

A steamship operator, Shinwa Kaiun Kaisha was founded in 1950 and is engaged primarily in the transporting of raw materials and finished products for the NIPPON STEEL CORPORATION. It is also engaged in the tanker business. An affiliate of NIPPON YŪSEN, it has had close relations with China, and currently imports Chinese iron ore and coal. It has subsidiaries in Hong Kong, London, and New York. Its fleet numbers 27 ships totaling 2 million deadweight tons. Annual revenue at the end of March 1982 was ¥127.5 billion (US $530 million), and the company was capitalized at ¥8.1 billion (US $33.6 million) in the same year. Corporate headquarters are located in Tōkyō.

Shin Yakushiji

A temple of the Kegon Buddhist sect; located in the city of Nara. It is said to have been founded in 747 by Empress KŌMYŌ for the recovery of her husband, Emperor SHŌMU, from an eye infection. Dedicated to the healing Buddha Yakushi Nyorai, the temple was called Shin, or "New," Yakushiji to distinguish it from the Yakushiji built earlier in another section of the capital. Only the main hall survives from the early 8th century. The main image of the temple is a 2-meter (6 ft) Yakushi Nyorai, dating from the early part of the

Heian period (794–1185); enshrined on a circular altar, it is surrounded by images of the Twelve Divine Generals.

Nancy SHATZMAN-STEINHARDT

Shinyei Kaisha

Commonly known as Shin'ei. Firm engaged in producing silk yarn and in trading. It was established in 1887 as a producer, wholesaler, and exporter of silk. After World War II it handled nylon and other synthetic textile products. It also commenced the production of secondary textile goods and electronic parts, and began to deal in housing. It has played a significant role in Japanese trade with China in recent years. The firm has a subsidiary in New York and a joint venture in South Korea. Sales for the fiscal year ending October 1982 totaled ¥61.1 billion (US $264.1 million) and the company was capitalized at ¥2 billion (US $8.6 million). Its head office is in Kōbe.

Shinzō inu tsukubashū

Two-volume collection of *haikai* verse and criticism by MATSUNAGA TEITOKU; published 1643. The volumes, entitled *Aburakasu* and *Yodogawa*, were written as a commentary on the *Inu tsukubashū* (ca 1540) to serve as a guidebook for novices of the verse form. In the process of demonstrating the weaknesses of earlier *haikai*, Teitoku's own theory emerges, particularly on the principles of *tsukeai* ("linking"). These and other rules of composition were codified in 10 verses of *waka* appended to the end of the first volume; these evolved to form the core of the first true guidebook of the Teimon school, *Haikai gosan* (1651).

Shiobara

Town in northern Tochigi Prefecture, central Honshū. It is known primarily for its complex of 11 hot springs. Rice cultivation and dairy farming are carried out at Nasunohara to the east. The area is noted for its scenic gorges; it is also a popular summer and winter resort, with good skiing on nearby mountains. Pop: 10,055.

Shioda Hiroshige (1873–1965)

Surgeon. Born in Kyōto Prefecture; graduate of Tōkyō University. Shioda is known for his achievements in the pathogenesis and treatment of actinomycosis (1911) and in other areas of visceral surgery. He was professor of surgery at Tōkyō University and president of Nihon Ika Daigaku (Nihon Medical School). He was a member of the Japan Academy from 1949.

Achiwa Gorō

Shiogama

City in central Miyagi Prefecture, northern Honshū. Situated on Matsushima Bay, in the Edo period (1600–1868) it developed as a fishing port and as a shrine town around the Shiogama Shrine. Its catch of salmon, bonito, and tuna is one of the largest in the prefecture. Principal industries are food processing and shipbuilding. A large number of people are drawn to the Shiogama port festival each August. Pop: 61,039.

Shiogama Shrine

(Shiogama Jinja). Shintō shrine in the city of Shiogama, Miyagi Prefecture, dedicated to Shiotsuchinooji no Kami (a deity associated with the sea) and two other deities. Although the precise origins of the shrine are not known, the ENGI SHIKI (927, Procedures of the Engi Era) records that the shrine received annual grants from the court to support its rituals. By the early 11th century it became the custom for each emperor to dispatch an emissary to the shrine once during his reign to make an offering there. During the Edo period (1600–1868) *daimyō* of the Date family provided ample patronage for the shrine. In 1874 another old shrine, the Shiwahiko (Shibahiko) Jinja was moved to the site from the nearby Iwakiri district; thus there are two shrines in the same precinct. The shrine was thought to offer particular protection to seafarers, saltmakers, and pregnant women. The annual festival, which is held on 10 July, includes a spectacular exhibition of YABUSAME (archery on horseback).

Stanley WEINSTEIN

shiohigari

(literally, "gathering at low tide"). Pleasure excursions for the purpose of gathering seashells, shellfish, and the like on tidewater beaches; they have been popular since the Edo period (1600–1868). The best time for such outings is in April, when the variation in tides is greatest. From very early times, excursions called *iso asobi* ("beach play") were among the events that marked the beginning of farm work in the spring. The modern shell-gathering picnics in April and the custom of serving clam soup at the DOLL FESTIVAL in March are thought to be derived from this ancient practice. In recent years this type of family recreation has declined because of seashore reclamation projects and pollution.

Shioiri Matsusaburō (1889–1962)

Agrochemist. Born in Nagano Prefecture. Graduate of Tōkyō University. Shioiri worked successively as a technician at the Agricultural Experiment Station of the Ministry of Agriculture and Forestry, professor at Tōkyō University, and president of the Prefectural College of Agriculture and Forestry, Shiga Prefecture. His many research achievements included the analysis of soil colloids, and his most outstanding study was on the chemical structure of rice paddy soil, completed during World War II. He clarified the functions of the oxidized and deoxidized layers of the wet rice field. He also developed techniques for fertilizing fields in every layer and for revitalization of deteriorated paddy fields, both of which helped contribute toward an increase in the yield of rice during a period of food shortages. He is the author of *Dojōgaku kenkyū* (1952).

Katō Shunjirō

Shiojiri

City in central Nagano Prefecture, central Honshū. In the Edo period (1600–1868) it prospered as one of the POST-STATION TOWNS on the highway Nakasendō. Grapes (used by the local wineries), lettuce, celery, and other vegetables are grown. There is also a well-developed electrical and precision instruments industry. The HIRAIDE SITE, an ancient settlement dating from the Middle Jōmon period (ca 3500 BC–ca 2000 BC), is located here. Pop: 52,711.

shioki

(criminal punishments). The general term for criminal punishments and their imposition during the Edo period (1600–1868). *Shioki* varied somewhat between shogunal and *daimyō* domains, but they generally followed the KUJIKATA OSADAMEGAKI (also called the Hyakkajō or Hundred Articles), a criminal code enacted by the Tokugawa shogunate in 1742. The punishments were in six categories. (1) *Seimeikei* (capital punishments) included *zanzai* (beheading) and *seppuku* (compulsory self-disembowelment; see HARAKIRI), imposed only on *samurai*. For commoners there were *nokogiri-biki* (sawing apart), *haritsuke* (crucifixion), *gokumon* (pillory and stocks), and *hizai* (burning at the stake). Such cruel punishments as *ushizaki* (drawing apart by oxen), *sakasa haritsuke* (head-down crucifixion), and *mizu haritsuke* (water crucifixion)—often imposed on Christians in the 17th century—were absent from the Hyakkajō. (2) *Shintaikei* (corporal punishments), imposed only on commoners, included *tataki* (beating) and *irezumi* (tattooing). Such earlier punishments as *teyubikiri*, *mimisogi*, and *hanasogi* (cutting off of fingers, ears, and nose, respectively) were no longer inflicted. (3) *Jiyūkei* (loss of liberty) included, for the samurai class, ENTŌ (exile to an island; earlier called RU), in severity considered second only to death; *tsuihō* (BANISHMENT from a particular region); and HEIMON, *hissoku*, *enryo*, *tojime*, and *oshikome* (various degrees and forms of house arrest). For commoners there were *jurō* (imprisonment) and *tejō* (placement in manacles under official seal). (4) *Zaisankei* (loss of property), applicable to all classes, included *kessho* (confiscation of property), often imposed in addition to exile; and *karyō* (fines). (5) *Mibunkei* (loss of status) included KAIEKI (demotion of a samurai and his family to commoner status), *hinin teshita* (demotion of a commoner to HININ, or pariah, status), and YAKKO (holding of a woman in servitude). (6) *Eiyokei* (loss of honor) included *inkyo* (dismissal of a samurai from office) and *shikari* (official reprimand to a commoner). The *shioki* punishments of the Hyakkajō code were abolished with the enactment of the Provisional Penal Code (Kari Keiritsu) in 1868. *Koyanagi Shun'ichirō*

Shipbuilding industry —— Table 1

Merchant Vessels Launched, by Country
(in percentage of world total gross tons)

	Japan	United Kingdom	West Germany	Sweden	Other countries
1913	2.0	58.0	14.0	0.6	25.4
1921	5.2	35.4	11.7	1.5	46.2
1924	3.2	64.1	7.8	1.4	23.5
1927	1.9	54.6	12.9	3.0	27.6
1930	5.3	51.9	8.7	4.6	29.5
1933	15.4	27.3	8.8	12.7	35.8
1936	14.1	40.9	18.3	7.4	19.3
1939	13.1	25.3	12.1	8.5	41.0
1950	7.8	29.5	3.5	7.8	51.4
1953	10.9	25.8	16.1	9.5	37.7
1956	26.2	20.7	15.0	7.3	30.8
1959	19.7	15.7	13.7	9.8	41.1
1962	26.1	12.8	12.1	10.0	39.0
1965	43.9	8.8	8.4	9.6	29.3
1968	50.8	5.3	8.0	6.6	29.3
1971	48.2	5.0	6.6	7.4	32.8
1974	50.9	3.7	6.2	6.4	32.8
1977	41.1	4.6	5.8	8.8	39.7
1978	31.9	5.3	3.9	8.5	50.4
1979	36.6	5.2	3.3	3.8	51.1
1980	52.3	1.8	3.3	2.4	40.2

NOTE: Prewar figures for West Germany are for all of Germany.
SOURCE: For 1913–30: League of Nations, *International Statistical Yearbook*. For 1933–80: United Nations, *Statistical Yearbook* (annual).

Shiomidake

Mountain on the border of Nagano and Shizuoka prefectures, central Honshū, in the central part of the Akaishi Mountains; composed of Paleozoic sandstone strata. The summit is divided into two peaks. Alpine flora abound. Height: 3,047 m (9,994 ft).

Shionogi & Co, Ltd

(Shionogi Seiyaku). Pharmaceuticals company engaged in the production, manufacture, distribution, export, and import of pharmaceuticals, industrial and agricultural chemicals, veterinary drugs, and cosmetics. Established in 1878 as a drug wholesaler by Shiono Gisaburō in Ōsaka, it assumed its present name in 1943. Its product line includes drugs licensed from international pharmaceutical companies such as Keflin and Keflodin (cephalosporin antibiotics) from Eli Lilly and Co, Rinderon (a synthetic corticosteroid) from Schering–Plough Corp, and Benzalin (a sleep-inducer) from F. Hoffmann–La Roche and Co, Ltd. Recently its research laboratories have succeeded in developing an injectable antibiotic, an antiinflammatory analgesic, and two antimammary tumor agents. The company has three overseas subsidiaries. Total sales for the fiscal year ending in March 1982 were ¥155.1 billion (US $644.3 million), and capitalization stood at ¥13.5 billion (US $56.1 million) in the same year. Corporate headquarters are located in Ōsaka.

Shionomisaki

Cape on southern Kii Peninsula, southern Wakayama Prefecture; projecting south into the Pacific Ocean, it is the southernmost point of Honshū (lat. 33°26′ N). Shionomisaki is noted for its fine scenery and a lighthouse. A fishing port, Kushimoto, and an island, Ōshima, 2 km (1.2 mi) off the coast, are popular resorts. It is part of Yoshino-Kumano National Park.

Shiozawa

Town in southern Niigata Prefecture, central Honshū. It developed as one of the POST-STATION TOWNS on the highway Mikuni Kaidō.

It is known for its fine silk fabrics such as *tsumugi* and *omeshi*. There are many skiing grounds in the area. Pop: 20,734.

Shiozawa Masasada (1870–1945)

Economist. Born in Ibaraki Prefecture. He first studied Chinese literature but later entered Tōkyō Semmon Gakkō (now Waseda University) and studied English. In 1896 he began his studies in the United States and Germany, later receiving his doctorate from the University of Wisconsin. Returning to Japan in 1902, he was appointed professor at Waseda University and later became its president. An influential member of the Nihon Shakai Seisaku Gakkai (Japanese Association for the Study of Social Policies), he was particularly active in the field of labor problems. Shiozawa's counsel was said to have been of great use to ŌKUMA SHIGENOBU, founder and first president of Waseda University. YAMADA Katsumi

shipbuilding industry

Japan has been the leading country in shipbuilding since 1956, producing from the mid-1960s to the mid-1970s about one-half of total world tonnage (see Table 1). Aimed at satisfying the domestic market in the pre–World War II period, shipbuilding became a major export industry after the war, with exports in 1975 amounting to more than 80 percent of total production and accounting for 11 percent of total exports. In 1975 the industry was composed of about 1,500 companies, of which 42 had the capacity to build or repair ships of more than 10,000 gross tons. The number of employees in shipbuilding reached 184,000, with an additional 74,000 in subcontracting firms.

The growth of the shipbuilding industry was generated by factors that account for Japan's economic development in general, among them dependence on imported raw materials, introduction and adaptation of foreign technology, and flexibility in conforming to changes in structure of domestic demand.

The Pre–1945 Period —— Under the self-imposed seclusion policy of the Edo period (1600–1868), construction of ocean-going ships was prohibited, and only toward the end of the period did the government realize the importance of shipbuilding for an island country. The ban on the construction of large vessels was lifted in 1853, dockyards were built in Uraga and Ishikawajima, foreign instructors and machinery were brought in from Holland and France, and a naval training school (KAIGUN DENSHŪJO) was opened in Nagasaki in 1855 under Dutch instructors. The first western-style ship, *Hedagō*, was built in 1853 under the supervision of a visiting Russian crew whose vessel, *Diana*, sank during an earthquake. In 1866 a steamship, with a 60-horsepower engine, *Chiyodagata*, was built by an all-Japanese team at Ishikawajima.

After the Meiji Restoration of 1868 shipbuilding became one of the first priority industries. The government took over the dockyards and began large-scale investment in them (see YOKOSUKA SHIPYARDS; NAGASAKI SHIPYARDS; HYŌGO SHIPYARDS). However, a few years later, the latter two were sold to private companies at very low prices. This did not signify the end of government involvement with the industry. In 1885 construction of the obsolete wooden *Yamato*-type boats was prohibited. In 1896 a subsidy plan was devised which promoted the construction of modern Western-style vessels under two laws: one, the Zōsen Shōrei Hō (Law to Promote Shipbuilding), gave a subsidy to vessels over 700 tons, the subsidy increasing with size of vessel; the other, the Kōkai Shōrei Hō (Law to Promote Shipping), applied to ships over 1,000 tons and a subsidy was given per mile of voyage. These two industries, shipbuilding and shipping, received about three-quarters of all government subsidies during the period between 1897 and 1913.

After the Russo-Japanese War of 1904–05 the navy became increasingly dependent on domestic ships and a main source of demand for the industry. A boom during World War I increased the total tonnage of ships launched from 65,000 gross tons in 1913 to 612,000 gross tons in 1919, and Japan became an exporter of ships to England, France, and the United States. Rising prices for ships in the international market enabled Japan to utilize mass-production methods and build ships before actual orders were received, ready to supply them on short notice. At the end of World War I, Japan became the third-ranking country in ship production with 8.3 percent of the world tonnage.

The boom, however, was short-lived, and, after the war, reduction in demand for ships brought about a large degree of excess capacity in the industry, with production in 1923 falling to as little as 10 percent of the previous peak. Government assistance in the form of tariff exemptions on steel imports and tariffs imposed on imports of vessels did little to alleviate the plight of the industry in the face of a reduction in both civilian and military demand. During the worst period of the world depression, in 1932, Japan launched ships with tonnage of a mere 50,000 gross tons.

Again the government came to the rescue of the industry with a "scrap-and-build" plan, according to which old vessels were scrapped and replaced by new, modern ones. After Japan declared in 1936 that all armament limitations imposed on it were void, military demand for warships was forthcoming, reactivating idle capacity and inducing further investment. In 1937 Japan became the second-ranking country after the United Kingdom, with 21.2 percent of total world production. This trend continued with even more vigor during World War II when the industry, under government control, supplied ships both to the Japanese navy and merchant fleet. (Note that Table 1 gives figures for merchant ships only.)

The Postwar Period —— Stripped of its colonies, its merchant fleet destroyed, and cut off from sources of raw material, Japan and its shipbuilding industry had to make a new start after the war. Although relying heavily on accumulated experience from the prewar period, the industry had to adapt to new conditions and change in several important respects. From an industry catering to the domestic market, civilian and military, it became an industry aiming mainly at export markets. Moreover, there was a complete change in shipbuilding technology, with the welding block-building method replacing riveting. The industry manifested a very high rate of growth, with total production amounting at its peak in 1974 to almost 17 million gross tons (see Table 2).

Several factors account for this rapid growth. Widespread technological borrowing coupled with highly skilled labor enabled Japan to catch up with the most advanced available technology. Paradoxically, the fact that Japan had to make a new start after the war enabled it to utilize the most advanced technologies without the need to scrap old ones. The organization of the Japanese labor force, where workers identify to a large extent with their companies, facilitated the influx of technology and reduced disruptions due to labor disputes, enabling Japanese dockyards to meet precise delivery dates. Government assistance again played a significant role through a system of *keikaku zōsen* (planned shipbuilding)—long-term, low-interest loans to shipping companies for the purchase of ships. After a hesitant start during the early Occupation period, when lack of raw materials coupled with administrative obstacles hampered the development of the industry, a considerable boost was provided by special procurements (TOKUJU) for the Korean War, so much so that in 1951 Japan launched more ships than in 1938. The "tanker boom" began in 1956 when Japan, taking advantage of growing demand for tankers, became the major supplier of tanker ships. The million-ton mark was surpassed the same year, and Japan became the undisputed first-ranking shipbuilding country.

The sky above the industry became cloudy after the "oil crisis" of 1973. A glut of tankers caused cancellation of orders and a substantial change in composition of production: cargo ships increased from 18 percent of total production in 1973 to 93 percent in 1975. There had been a reduction in the average size of ships from 47,000 tons in 1973 to 15,000 tons in 1975, and a larger share of exports was based on long-term loans provided by the EXPORT-IMPORT BANK OF JAPAN. Official predictions in the mid-1970s for trends in demand were not optimistic and measures were being taken to reduce capacity and employment and to assist small and medium companies, which were deemed to be the main victims of curtailed production.

Industrial Organization and Technology —— The shipbuilding industry is composed of a small number of large firms and a large number of medium and small firms, with the bulk of production concentrated in the former. In 1965, about 50 percent of total production was done by the 3 largest firms, 63 percent by the 5 largest, and 83 percent by the 10 largest firms. The five largest firms in 1978 were MITSUBISHI HEAVY INDUSTRIES, LTD; ISHIKAWAJIMA–HARIMA HEAVY INDUSTRIES CO, LTD; HITACHI ZŌSEN CORPORATION; MITSUI ENGINEERING & SHIPBUILDING CO, LTD; and KAWASAKI HEAVY INDUSTRIES, LTD. Many parts and gadgets are produced by subcontracting firms of small or medium size. The hard-core labor force consists of employees who enjoy the benefits of stable employment under the permanent employment system common to most Japanese firms, in which the worker joins the company after finishing his formal schooling and stays with it until retirement. The company provides the worker, in addition to his wages, with housing, educa-

Shipbuilding industry —— Table 2

Japanese Ship Production and Export
(in millions of gross tons)

	Total production	Export	Export as percentage of total production
1948	0.163	0.001	0.6
1950	0.227	0.076	33.5
1952	0.504	0.023	4.6
1954	0.412	0.111	26.9
1956	1.529	1.119	73.2
1958	2.285	1.351	59.1
1960	1.807	0.935	51.7
1962	2.154	0.857	39.8
1964	4.079	2.251	55.2
1966	6.396	3.777	59.1
1968	8.481	5.110	60.3
1970	10.172	6.225	61.2
1972	12.768	6.964	54.5
1974	16.782	13.997	83.4
1975	15.227	12.617	82.9
1976	15.263	11.866	77.7
1977	11.705	9.802	83.7
1978	6.295	4.871	77.4
1979	4.982	2.950	59.2
1980	6.189	3.411	55.1

SOURCE: Prime Minister's Office, Statistics Bureau, *Japan Statistical Yearbook* (annual): various years.

tion, and recreation and trains him in specific skills; the worker, on his part, identifies with the company (see EMPLOYMENT SYSTEM, MODERN). In addition to permanent workers, temporary workers are recruited to adjust for cyclical fluctuations in production. Although there is competition among shipbuilding companies for new orders, there is a considerable degree of cooperation, especially with respect to the sharing of technological know-how.

Shipbuilding companies not only produce ships but are involved in the production of other products, mainly various kinds of machinery. These "on-land activities" enable the companies to reduce risk through diversification and to withstand fluctuations in demand for any single product.

Shipbuilding is a good example of the role that imported technology played in Japan's economic growth and demonstrates the advantages of having both the opportunities and capability to assimilate foreign technology. In the early part of the Meiji period (1868–1912) foreign experts were brought to Japan, students were sent abroad, machinery was imported, and schools for shipbuilding engineering were founded (see FOREIGN EMPLOYEES OF THE MEIJI PERIOD; TECHNOLOGY TRANSFER). One outcome was that Japan could make a quick transition from wooden boats to steel ships, almost skipping the stage of iron vessels. As time went by, more formal ways of technological import were utilized, and contracts with foreign companies became the chief method through which new innovations were introduced. The most important types of technology introduced during the prewar period were the diesel engine and the steam turbine.

In the post–World War II period a complete revolution in shipbuilding technology took place, based on electric welding, automatic cutting of steel plates, and the block-building system. This technology called for an outlay of the dockyard and large capital investments. Growing world demand, absence of vested interests rejecting the introduction of new methods, and a highly motivated and skilled labor force enabled shipbuilding companies to adopt these new methods without delay. Dockyards unsuitable for implementing the new technology were used for repair while new ones were built to accommodate the new machinery. Widespread use of automation led to an increase in the output-labor ratio: the average tonnage associated with one worker went up from 3.7 gross tons in 1951 to 55.6 gross tons in 1968. Large capital investments caused a large increase in the capital-labor ratio from ¥0.1 million (US $278) per employee in 1951 to ¥2.6 million (US $7,222) in 1968. The large

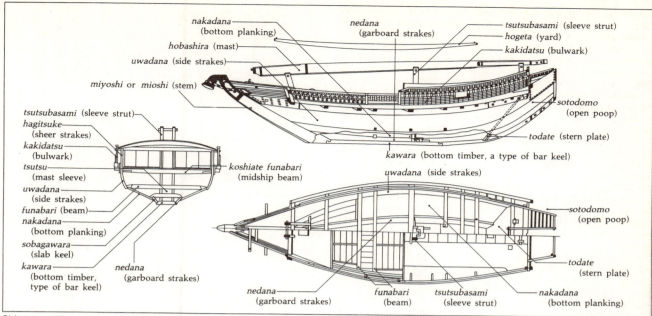

Ships ——— The structure of the benzaisen

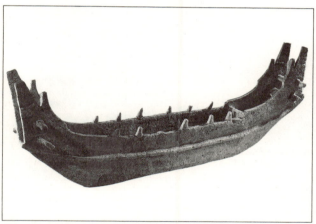

Ships ——— Clay model of early ship

An earthenware *haniwa* sculpture of a wooden dugout with bulwark planking to prevent flooding. No distinction is made between the bow and the stern. Tholepins are visible in the gunwales. Length 101 cm. 5th or 6th century. Excavated from the Saitobaru tomb cluster, Miyazaki Prefecture. Tōkyō National Museum.

increase in output can thus be explained by both the influx of capital and the high rate of productivity increase in the industry.

📖 ——— Tuvia Blumenthal, "The Japanese Shipbuilding Industry," in Hugh Patrick, ed, *Japanese Industrialization and Its Social Consequences* (1976). Kaneko Eiichi et al, *Zōsen*, vol 9 of *Gendai sangyō hattatsu shi* (1964). Katayama Shin, *Nihon no zōsen kōgyō* (1970).

Tuvia BLUMENTHAL

Shipbuilding Scandal of 1954

(Zōsen Gigoku). Also known as the Zōsen Oshoku (Shipbuilding Kickback) case. In January 1954 it was discovered that shipbuilding companies were paying bribes to high government officials in return for government contracts and subsidies. Between February and June 71 suspects were arrested, including the heads of Hitachi Shipbuilding & Engineering Co, Ltd, and Ishikawajima–Harima Heavy Industries Co, Ltd; several important politicians, including SATŌ EISAKU and IKEDA HAYATO, were indicted as well. Under pressure from Prime Minister YOSHIDA SHIGERU, however, Minister of Justice Inukai Takeru (1896–1960) refused to approve prosecution of Satō (who was secretary-general of the Liberal Party) citing the prerogative of administrative control of prosecutors as provided in article 14 of the

Public Prosecutors' Office Law. Although the investigation was thus impeded, a number of businessmen and government officials were eventually convicted of bribery and misuse of public funds, and Satō himself was eventually indicted for violation of the Political Fund Control Law. (He was released in a general amnesty before completion of his trial.) This incident, one of the largest postwar bribery cases, was one cause of the fall of the fifth Yoshida cabinet.

ships

Water transportation has been of great importance in Japanese history. That ships existed in Japan from ancient times is known from the discovery of primitive canoes at various archaeological sites and from numerous references to boats and ships found in ancient historical records. The occurrence of gaffs and fishhooks made of bone or horn in SHELL MOUNDS dating from the Jōmon period (ca 10,000 BC–ca 300 BC) shows that the inhabitants of the Japanese archipelago early on had ties to the sea and fishing. Jōmon-period sites have yielded specimens of dugout canoes, presumably made by burning and scraping with stone implements. Early Chinese accounts such as the *Han shu* (1st century AD) and the *Hou Han shu* (4th or 5th century) record that various communities among the inhabitants of Japan (Ch: Wo; J: Wa) sent tributes to China as early as the 1st century BC. From this it may be assumed that sea transportation between Japan and China existed even in the Yayoi period (ca 300 BC–ca AD 300). What sorts of ship were used, however, can only be conjectured from such scanty evidence as outlines found scratched on rock faces.

Japanese historical records such as the KOJIKI (712, Records of Ancient Matters) and NIHON SHOKI (720, Chronicle of Japan) and the 8th-century regional gazetteers called FUDOKI contain descriptions of many kinds of early boats: *ama no iwakusubune* (a dugout made from camphor wood, relics of which have been found at Yayoi-period diggings); *ashibune* (a type of raft made of papyrus reed); *morotabune* (a dugout rowed with oars by a large crew); *manashikatama obune* (a kind of coracle made of closely woven bamboo); and other types. The designs of these boats have not yet been made clear, though attempts are being made to reconstruct them through etymological study of their names and archaeological investigation. According to the *Nihon shoki* and the *Kojiki*, a boat named the *Karanu* was built during the reign of Emperor ŌJIN (late 4th to early 5th century). The same event is also mentioned in the *Kojiki*. No details are available concerning the boat except that it measured 30 meters (98 ft) in length. In the *Hitachi fudoki*, a gazetteer written in the 8th century, there is also a record of a large boat said to have measured 45 meters (148 ft) long and 3 meters (10 ft) wide.

The commonest boat of the time was the canoe or dugout made by hollowing out a single log. Compound-hulled craft were built by joining together two or more dugouts. Further technical development made it possible to build semicomposite boats, dugouts with vertically attached planking on each side for protection against waves, and finally composite craft.

The *Nihon shoki* reports that shipbuilding techniques were imported from the kingdom of SILLA on the Korean peninsula during the reign of the emperor Ōjin. A clay image of a ship (*fune haniwa*; see HANIWA) found at the SAITOBARU TOMB CLUSTER in Miyazaki Prefecture is said to date from the 5th or 6th century. It has six sets of oarlocks and is considered to be a copy of the largest of ships commonly in use at the time. Similar model ships dating from the same period have also been discovered in Korea.

In 600 the Japanese began sending missions to China on a systematic scale. Altogether some 20 missions were sent between the end and 894 to Sui (589–618) and Tang (T'ang, 618–907) China (see SUI AND TANG [T'ANG] CHINA, EMBASSIES TO). Japanese shipbuilding techniques improved considerably during this period, but precise data regarding the type of craft used by the envoys have not survived. We can only guess at the scale and structure of these ships from the number of crew members and passengers said to have been on board on each voyage and from paintings of scenes of early ocean voyages.

Ships used by the envoys sent to Sui China (*kenzuishi*) were apparently of the semicomposite type, but by the time of the second dispatch of envoys to Tang China (*kentōshi*) shipbuilding technology had developed to such a degree that in Aki Province (now part of Hiroshima Prefecture) it was possible to build seaworthy craft like the *kudarasen* (Korean-type ship), with room for about 120 people. From that time on the most common type of ship is believed to have been a continental-style single-masted ship of the junk type, estimated to have had a capacity of 1,500 *koku* (about 147 gross tons) and which could accommodate around 150 passengers. By comparison, a European sailing ship of this capacity was usually about 30 meters (98 ft) long, but the *kentōshi* ship must have been around 40 meters (131 ft) long, in view of its shallow-draft, flat-bottomed hull, and could have sailed only with a following wind. There are some reports of ships of this type splitting down the middle of the hull because of these characteristics.

The sending of embassies from Japan to China was halted after 838. The only development in shipbuilding between this time and the 12th century was in the size of ships constructed. There was little advancement in shipbuilding technology. During the Kamakura period (1185–1333) a number of merchant ships carried on limited trade with Song (Sung) China. The official exchange of envoys between Japan and China resumed under the government of the shōgun ASHIKAGA YOSHIMITSU, and continued from about 1401 to 1547, during which time 17 embassies were sent to Ming China (see TALLY TRADE). These envoys were called *kemminshi* and the ships they used were called *kemminsen*. Each *kemminsen* carried 150–200 people. Contemporary records describe their capacities as 500–2,500 *koku* (an estimated gross tonnage of 49–246 tons). They appear in picture scrolls as decked vessels with cabins and two masts fitted with simple square sails made of matting.

Foreign trade was conducted from 1592 under government license, and merchants in Nagasaki, Sakai, and Kyōto began to carry on a lively overseas trade. TOYOTOMI HIDEYOSHI, who wished to keep the NAMBAN TRADE under his control, took measures against pirates (see WAKŌ) and illegal traders by issuing to selected merchants official licenses with vermilion seals, which verified the protected status of their ships, referred to as *shuinsen* ("vermilion seal ship"; see VERMILION SEAL SHIP TRADE). Spanish and Portuguese influences are apparent in the shipbuilding techniques of the *shuinsen*, especially in their equipment and navigation system. Although based on the Chinese junk, which had fore-and-aft woven bambooleaf sails, the *shuinsen* skillfully adapted the European-style square-rigged cloth sail, in the manner of the Siamese junk. In the first decade of the 17th century, two English-style ships of about 80 and 120 gross tons were built under the direction of the Englishman William ADAMS. A galliot-type ship in the 500-gross-ton class, 35 meters (115 ft) long and 11 meters (36 ft) wide, was also built under the direction of the Spaniard Sebastian VISCAINO. These two instances show that Japanese shipbuilders were eager to learn new shipbuilding techniques from the West, but further development was suspended because of the policy of NATIONAL SECLUSION (Sakoku) imposed by the Tokugawa shogunate in 1639.

During the early period of the seclusion era, the shogunate strictly prohibited the construction of ships with capacities over 500 *koku* (about 49 gross tons). This restriction was soon lifted to encourage the development of coastal shipping. Various kinds of *wa-*

Ships——— Vermilion seal ship

A votive picture (*ema*) of a vermilion seal ship (*shuinsen*), illustrating one of the hybrid designs—a cross between a Chinese junk and a Western caravel—that evolved for overseas trade. Chinese lugsails are combined with sails rigged in the Western fashion. Colors on wood. 185 × 208 cm. 1634. Original owned by Kiyomizudera, Nagasaki.

Ships——— Coastal cargo ship

A Japanese-style ship (*wasen*) of the type used in coastal shipping from the early 17th century and known as the *higaki kaisen* ("lozenge-fenced cargo ship") after the pattern of the bamboo latticework of its outer bulwarks. From an Edo-period handscroll. Colors on paper. Height of scroll approximately 75 cm. Nippon Express Co, Ltd Collection, Tōkyō.

sen (Japanese-style ship) were built in accordance with local customs and requirements in different regions of the country. Typical examples are the two- or sometimes three-masted *hokkokubune* (northern province ship) found in areas along the Sea of Japan and the smaller *benzaisen*, a common type of coastal vessel in the Tōkai (Pacific coast) region. The latter may be considered the very model of the peculiar Japanese-type vessel (*yamatogata-bune*) in its perfected stage. In place of the keel and floor timber of European vessels, *yamatogata-bune* had a flat, rather wide and thick fore-and-aft bottom plank called *kawara*, to both sides of which planking (*nedana*) was installed horizontally. Next came a section of sloped planking (*nakadana*) and then an almost vertical third stage (*uwadana*), all held in place by numerous sturdy beams.

By 1670 the Tokugawa shogunate had established its own transportation system for military rice provisions. Internal shipping services grew more active, and gradually the *benzaisen* became the commonest type of vessel in use. One of the most traveled coastal sea routes was from ports located on the Sea of Japan counterclockwise (west to east) around Honshū via the Inland Sea to the ports of Ōsaka and Edo (now Tōkyō). The other prominent sea route was clockwise (east to west) from ports on the Sea of Japan northward through the Tsugaru Strait at the northern tip of Honshū and then down to Edo and Ōsaka.

Since the main purpose of the *benzaisen* was to transport as much cargo as possible, it was designed so that it had a width sometimes half the length of the main bottom plank. In the first half of the 17th century 300-*koku* (about 29 gross tons) vessels of the *ben-*

zaisen type were used in the Inland Sea. In the latter half of the century they became typical sailing ships of a larger size. The structure of the *benzaisen* had been firmly established by the middle of the 18th century, and its capacity reached around 1,000 *koku* (about 98 gross tons). It grew in scale to the point where ships capable of carrying 1,500–2,000 *koku* (about 147–196 gross tons) were common. The major reason for the popularity of sailing ships was that they did not have to increase the number of crew members in proportion to their size. Fifteen crew members were sufficient for a 1,000 *koku* ship (*sengokubune*), which would have required another 9–10 men if designed for rowing. Sailing ships yielded great economic benefits and were essential to the development of domestic trade in a country so mountainous as Japan (see KAISEN).

In 1854 Japan was opened to foreign intercourse. The authorities lost no time in introducing shipbuilding technology based on Western methods and Japanese shipbuilding advanced rapidly. See SHIPBUILDING INDUSTRY.

📖——Nihon Zōsen Gakkai, ed, *Shōwa zōsen shi* (1973). Nihon Zōsen Gakkai, ed, *Nihon kinsei zōsen shi*, 2 vols (1973–74). Sempaku Hyakunen Shi Kankō Kai, ed, *Sempaku hyakunen shi* (1958). Ueno Kiichirō, *Nihon no fune*, 3 vols (1952–58).　　　Mozai Torao

shirabyōshi

A type of song and dance performance, characterized by a strongly marked rhythm, that became popular in the 12th century; also, the female performers of this type of dance. The origin of the term is unclear; it may have come from the name for the beat accompanying Buddhist chants (*shōmyō*); this beat was called *shirabyōshi*, but the word was written with characters different from those denoting the song and dance performance type, which include the character meaning "white" (*shiroi*), presumably in reference to the fact that *shirabyōshi* performers invariably dressed in white, male attire. Their costume also included fans, court caps, and swords. Drums and small cymbals were the accompanying musical instruments. The performers sang songs and a kind of ballad called *imayō* as they danced. *Shirabyōshi* performances are recorded as part of court and temple festivities in the 12th and 13th centuries, but they declined in popularity thereafter, being largely replaced by a derivative dance form, *kuse-mai,* which in turn figured importantly in the development of the classical NŌ drama in the late 14th century. In the great medieval military romance HEIKE MONOGATARI (ca 1220; tr *The Tale of the Heike,* 1975), the origins of this performance type are attributed to the semilegendary figures Shima no Senzai and Waka no Omae (early 12th century); other famous semilegendary *shirabyōshi* performers are Giō, Hotoke Gozen (fl ca 1170), and SHIZUKA GOZEN, who formed liaisons with members of the nobility and the warrior class. See also DANCE, TRADITIONAL.　　　Barbara L. Arnn

Shiragi → Silla

Shirahama

Town in Chiba Prefecture, central Honshū. It is the center of the Minami Bōsō Quasi-National Park, with attractions like the AMA (women divers who dive for abalone, seaweed, and other sea products); flower greenhouses; and the Nojimazaki lighthouse, built by François VERNY in 1869. Pop: 7,503.

Shirahama

Town in southern Wakayama Prefecture, central Honshū, on the Pacific Ocean. It has been known for its hot springs since the Nara period (710–794). Visitors also come to see Senjōjiki and Sandanheki, rocky cliffs jutting out into the sea. Pop: 19,602.

Shirahone Hot Spring

(Shirahone Onsen). Located on the northern slope of Norikuradake at an altitude of 1,400 m (4,592 ft), western Nagano Prefecture, central Honshū. A hydrogen sulfide spring; water temperature 50°C (122°F). First opened in the middle of the Edo period (1600–1868), it features limestone caves and ball-shaped limestones that have been designated as natural monuments.

Shirai Kyōji (1889–1980)

Novelist. Real name Inoue Yoshimichi. Born in Kanagawa Prefecture, Shirai graduated from Nihon University. While working as a magazine editor he turned to professional writing around 1920. His major work is the lengthy period novel *Fuji ni tatsu kage* (1924–27) whose cheerful and virtuous hero, Kumaki Kōtarō, is often contrasted with Tsukue Ryūnosuke, the nihilistic hero in NAKAZATO KAIZAN's mammoth novel *Daibosatsu Tōge* (1913–41). These two novels, of which several film versions have been made, are representative works of modern POPULAR FICTION. As editor-in-chief of the magazine *Taishū bungaku,* Shirai was a leading critic in the field of popular literature. Other novels include *Shimpen goetsu-zōshi* (1922–24), *Shinsengumi* (1924–25), and *Bangaku no isshō* (1932).

Shirai Seiichi (1905–　　　)

Architect. Born in Kyōto. After graduating from Kyōto Technical School Shirai went to Germany to study philosophy and architecture at the universities of Berlin and Heidelberg and became interested in Gothic architecture. His early buildings, like the Kankisō House (1937), show obvious European influences, but his postwar designs are characterized by distinctive sculptural forms and closed, introspective spaces. His notable buildings include Akinomiya Town Hall (1949), Matsuida Town Hall (1955), the main temple building of Zenshōji in Asakusa (1958), the Shinwa Bank main office in Sasebo (1967–69) and its computer center the Kaishōkan (1975).

　　　Watanabe Hiroshi

Shiraito Falls

(Shiraito no Taki). Located on the upper reaches of the river Shibakawa, in the city of Fujinomiya, eastern Shizuoka Prefecture, central Honshū. It is said to resemble countless white threads dangling over a cliff; hence the name Shiraito no Taki, which means, literally, "White Thread Falls." Located at the foot of Mt. Fuji (FUJISAN) on its western side, and a part of Fuji–Hakone–Izu National Park, it attracts numerous tourists. It has been designated a natural monument. Height: 26 m (85 ft); width: 130 m (426 ft).

Shirakaba, Lake

(Shirakabako). Artificial lake in central Nagano Prefecture, central Honshū. Located on the western slope of the mountain Tateshinayama, the lake was completed for irrigational purposes in 1946. Popular for its summer camping grounds and winter skiing and skating. Area: 0.4 sq km (0.2 sq mi); circumference: 6 km (4 mi); depth: 10 m (33 ft); altitude: 1,400 m (4,592 ft).

Shirakaba school

(Shirakabaha, "White Birch school"). This so-called school of writers—most prominent among them MUSHANOKŌJI SANEATSU (1885–1976), SHIGA NAOYA (1883–1971) and the three brothers ARISHIMA TAKEO (1878–1923), Arishima Ikuma (1882–1974) and SATOMI TON (1888–1983)—takes its name from *Shirakaba,* a monthly journal of literature and art appreciation, published between 1910 and 1923, to which they were regular contributors.

From a cursory reading of the best-known works of Mushanokōji, Shiga, and the Arishima brothers, however, not to mention those of less famous contributors (e.g., the TANKA poems of KINOSHITA RIGEN [1886–1925] and the historical fiction of NAGAYO YOSHIRŌ [1888–1961]), it is apparent that these writers had no common literary program, much less the sort of consistency in style and theme that the designation "school" would imply. The critic Tsurumi Shunsuke (b 1922) contends that the real contribution of the Shirakabaha was simply the mutual moral support it afforded the individual "members" as they went their separate ways. Shiga himself would appear to support this view with his flat statement on the Shirakabaha: "Literary associations as such don't do much good."

For information on the careers and works of certain individual members, then, readers should consult the articles on them. Since much of what has been construed in the secondary literature as the "thought" of the Shirakaba group as a whole originated—and ended—with Mushanokōji, the reader should especially see the article on him.

The *Shirakaba* was a direct outgrowth of several little literary clubs and their magazines at the Peers' School (see GAKUSHŪIN UNIVERSITY), which all of its founding editors and contributors had attended. For the first few years after the inaugural issue of April 1910, it retained something of its original character as a forum for frankly amateurish writing: confessional stories about the authors themselves and each other, heady effusions on humanity, art, and so on (mostly by Mushanokōji) and introductory essays on an eccentric spectrum of Western literary and artistic figures including Tolstoy, Whitman, Ibsen, Strindberg, Romain Rolland, Courbet, Cézanne, Renoir, Van Gogh, Gauguin, and Rodin. The enthusiastic dilettantism of the journal's early years was perhaps both its principal strength and, in the long run, its chief weakness. The literary historian Honda Shūgo, an especially reliable writer on the Shirakaba group, comes close to concluding that the most durable impact of its cumulative output, much of it written by young men in the process of becoming authors of fiction, was not so much on literature as on art appreciation, an area where these writers (with a few exceptions to be noted below) could safely maintain their amateur standing.

Of new fiction, among the most notable works to be published in the pages of *Shirakaba* were several of Shiga's best early short stories ("Kamisori," "Han no hanzai," and "Kinosaki nite"), portions of what was to become *Aru onna* (tr *A Certain Woman*, 1978) by Arishima Takeo, and some promising juvenilia by Satomi Ton. The journal early established its role as introducer and interpreter of recent European art with the publication in November 1910 of a special commemorative number on Auguste Rodin, an artist with whom the group felt a special affinity (in response to their gift of a set of woodblock prints, Rodin sent the editors three small works—the first Rodin originals, though by no means the last, to reach Japan). Although the quality of both the essays on artistic subjects and the reproductions that accompanied them was uneven at best, *Shirakaba* was the widest conduit in this period for bringing the works of major impressionist and postimpressionist painters (also a few expressionists such as Edvard Munch) to the attention of a relatively large Japanese audience. Here the foundation was laid for the abiding and broad-based Japanese predilection for these styles of art, a fondness that has since produced several generations of dedicated collectors and a good deal of gifted amateur painting in the impressionistic manner.

Among the early contributors, who were already artists in their own right or went on to become so were Arishima Ikuma and Minami Kunzō (1883–1950) and, more notably, YANAGI MUNEYOSHI (1889–1961) and KISHIDA RYŪSEI (1891–1929). It was during the *Shirakaba* years that Yanagi and the British potter Bernard LEACH, who was closely associated with several of the group, began the collaboration that was later to develop into the widely influential "international" style in ceramics. In the last four or five years of the journal's publication, there was a significant increase in articles on various aspects of East Asian art and art history.

As arbiter of critical standards for reading more or less "modern" Western literature, *Shirakaba* was ultimately less influential, probably because of the availability of other forums for such knowledge and, through a growing body of translations on a scale seldom attempted by any of the journal's contributors, access to something closer to primary sources for a large readership. Indeed, a perusal of writings by Mushanokōji and Shiga, for example, on the subject of Tolstoy raises doubts about how much of the major work of this particular culture hero of theirs they had actually read. Rather, it would seem that they were most strongly attracted by the Tolstoy of the late Neo-Christian and quietist tracts, as they were by the gloomy, stoical humanism of extraliterary pronouncements by such as Romain Rolland and Anatole France (one of their few lasting contributions to the formation of Japanese literary taste may have been their advocacy of Rolland and France, whose works have surely enjoyed a higher reputation in Japan than in any Western country). Leaving to the individual entries their subsequent accomplishments in literary creativity, which varied widely, one may safely say that their collective role in educating their readers in literary matters was from the outset restricted by a youthful enthusiasm for, and an often very spotty reading of, the odd assortment of "major figures" with whom they had become infatuated in their student days.

There remains the nebulous question of the long-range effect of the image of the *Shirakaba* journal and its principal contributors—the so-called school. This shifting image has without doubt had a significant existence in standard literary and cultural histories and, to a degree of course unknowable, in the minds of various subsequent writers, some of whom may have drawn on the supposed ideology of the group, while others clearly reacted consciously against it. Of the founding members, Mushanokōji alone continued to assert the reality and the enduring strength of Shirakaba "tenets," most of

which were concocted by himself. Literary historians who have accepted him at his word have tended to view a conjectured opposition to the fancied "elitism" and overweening "egotism" of the Shirakaba-ha as a motive force in the careers of younger writers of a more egalitarian or "proletarian" persuasion during the 1920s and 1930s. And in the postwar period, the by and large hortatory, nonfictional utterances of such surviving members as Mushanokōji and Shiga, also the preoccupations of the journal *Kokoro* (generally regarded as a successor to the defunct *Shirakaba*) were widely interpreted as the last gasps of a quintessentially "Taishō" (i.e., Taishō period) blend of old-fashioned libertarianism, self-involved idealism, and a fundamental cultural conservatism.

📖 ——Honda Shūgo, *Shirakabaha no bungaku* (1954). Nihon Bungaku Kenkyū Shiryō Kankōkai, ed, *Shirakabaha bungaku* (1974). *William F. SIBLEY*

Shirakawa

City in southern Fukushima Prefecture, northern Honshū. In ancient times Shirakawa was a barrier station (SEKISHO) for travelers entering northeastern Japan (see SHIRAKAWA NO SEKI). During the Edo period (1600–1868) it developed as a castle town of the Matsudaira family, of which the most illustrious member was the reformer MATSUDAIRA SADANOBU. Principal industries are electrical appliances, furniture, construction materials, and clothing. Attractions include the remains of Komine Castle and the site of the barrier station. Pop: 43,184.

Shirakawa

Village in northwestern Gifu Prefecture, central Honshū, on the river Shōgawa. It is said to have been founded by surviving members of the TAIRA FAMILY, defeated by the Minamoto in the late 12th century. It is known for its farmhouses in the *gasshō-zukuri* style (see MINKA), which used to house as many as 40–50 family members. The Mihoro Dam, to the south of the village, is the largest rock-fill dam in East Asia. Pop: 2,132.

Shirakawa

River in central Kumamoto Prefecture, Kyūshū; originating from a caldera on the volcano Asosan and flowing west into Shimabara Bay. The city of Kumamoto as well as a large tract of reclaimed land are located on the lower reaches. The upper and middle reaches have a rapid current and are the site of numerous electric power plants. Length: 78 km (48 mi); area of drainage basin: 780 sq km (301 sq mi).

Shirakawa, Emperor (1053–1129)

The 72nd sovereign *(tennō)* in the traditional count (which includes several nonhistorical emperors); reigned 1073–87; son of Emperor GO-SANJŌ and Fujiwara no Moshi. Brought to the throne by his father's abdication, Shirakawa was not only active as an emperor but continued to dominate court politics for 43 years after his own retirement in 1087. Credited with establishing the system of "cloister government" (INSEI), Shirakawa united the imperial house, neutralized the Fujiwara REGENCY GOVERNMENT, and restored great political and economic power to the ruling dynasty during the reigns of his successors, emperors Horikawa (1079–1107; r 1087–1107), TOBA, and SUTOKU. Much of this he achieved by aligning himself with the newly emergent class of wealthy provincial tax managers (ZURYŌ) and with such warrior leagues as the TAIRA FAMILY and MINAMOTO FAMILY. He also established his own guard force, the HOKUMEN NO BUSHI, to protect his retirement palace. According to the military chronicle HEIKE MONOGATARI, Shirakawa, a strong-willed and unscrupulous man, asserted that he could control all but the waters of the river Kamogawa, the fall of the dice, and the warrior-monks of the mountain Hieizan. *G. Cameron HURST III*

Shirakawa no Seki

(Barrier of Shirakawa). One of the three ancient fortified barriers in northeastern Honshū (the others being NAKOSO NO SEKI and Nezu no Seki). Located on the border of the ancient provinces of Mutsu and Shimotsuke in what is now the city of Shirakawa, Fukushima Prefecture, it served from the 8th to 10th centuries to prevent southward incursions by the EZO people (regarded as barbarians by the Japanese) and to restrict travel to and from the north. Shirakawa no

Seki acquired many historical and literary associations. It appears in classical *waka* poetry as a conventionalized setting (UTA MAKURA), evoking the loneliness and desolation of remote and inhospitable frontiers. In 1800 MATSUDAIRA SADANOBU erected a stela to mark the site of the barrier. Excavations in 1959–63 show the barrier to have been an earthwork surrounded by a moat and surmounted by a palisade.

shiran

Bletilla striata. A perennial herb of the orchid family (Orchidaceae) which grows wild in bogs and on rocks from central Japan westward and is also widely cultivated as an ornamental. Five or six leaves grow alternately at the bottom of the stem. They are oblong, 29–30 centimeters (8–12 in) long, and have pointed ends and numerous lengthwise furrows. In late spring the plant produces a stalk about 50 centimeters (20 in) high from among the leaves and produces 6–7 attractive reddish purple flowers about 3 centimeters (1.2 in) across. Varieties developed through cultivation include the *shirobana shiran,* with very light red flowers, and the *fukurin shiran,* with white-margined leaves. The *shiran* is popular as a cut flower and its bulb is used both for medicinal purposes and as the source of a low-quality adhesive.   MATSUDA Osamu

Shiranesan

Also called Nikkō Shirane. Active volcano on the border between Gumma and Tochigi prefectures, central Honshū. Eruptions have been recorded from the Edo period (1600–1868) up to 1952. Erosion has created dammed lakes such as Marunuma and Suganuma. Oku Shirane Shrine is on the summit. Shiranesan is part of Nikkō National Park. Height: 2,578 m (8,456 ft).

Shiranesan

Also called Kusatsu Shirane. Active volcano in the Nasu Volcanic Zone, on the border between Gumma and Nagano prefectures, central Honshū. There are three craters: Karegama, Mizugama, and Yugama. Yugama is noted for the dense vapor clouds ascending from its center. Shiranesan is part of Jōshin'etsu Kōgen National Park. Height: 2,162 m (7,091 ft).

Shirane Sanzan

Also called Shiranesan and Kai Shirane. General name for the three-mountain group composed of KITADAKE (3,192 m; 10,470 ft), Ainotake (3,189 m; 10,460 ft), and Nōtoridake (3,026 m; 9,925 ft) extending from western Yamanashi Prefecture to the Yamanashi–Shizuoka prefectural border, central Honshū. The mountains are composed of Paleozoic strata and have ice-scoured regions. Wild animals and plants abound.

Shirase Nobu (1861–1946)

Explorer of the Antarctic. Inspired by Robert Falcon Scott's expedition to the South Pole, he embarked with 26 men aboard the 200-ton *Kainan maru* in 1910. In his second trial he succeeded in landing on the Antarctic continent from the Ross Sea in January 1912 and reached the point of 85°05′ south latitude and longitude 154°west, which he named Yamato Setsugen.

shirasu

(literally, "white sandbar"). Courtyards, spread with white gravel, in commissioners' offices of the Edo period (1600–1868). Usually attached to the offices of the commissioners of temples and shrines (JISHA BUGYŌ), city affairs (MACHI BUGYŌ), and finance (KANJŌ BUGYŌ), as well as the offices of regional intendants (DAIKAN), such courtyards were used for adjudicating both civil and criminal cases. Peasants, townsmen, and other members of the lower classes were made to sit on the white gravel during their trials, while priests, *samurai,* and other upper-class defendants sat on stairs leading from the gravel to the commissioner's desk. All entered the *shirasu* through a heavy door mounted on casters and had to pass a display of three weapons—*sasumata, sodegarami,* and *tsukubō* (see ARMS AND ARMOR)—used to capture criminals and symbolic of police and judicial powers.   INAGAKI Shisei

Shiratori Incident

(Shiratori Jiken). Controversial incident in which Shiratori Kazuo, an officer of the Sapporo Police Department, Hokkaidō, was shot and killed on 21 January 1952. The police apprehended and prosecuted two suspects, Murakami Kuniharu and Murate Hiromitsu, both members of the Japan Communist Party, on a charge of conspiracy to murder. Although nine other suspects, including one alleged to have been the killer, escaped arrest and fled to China, in May 1959 the Sapporo District Court found the two men guilty and sentenced Murakami to life imprisonment and Murate to three years in prison. As incriminating evidence the court cited the similarity of markings on the bullets recovered from Shiratori's body to those on two bullets found where the alleged conspirators engaged in target practice. On appeal the higher court reduced Murakami's sentence to 20 years, and in 1963 the Supreme Court upheld the higher court's decision. The inconclusive nature of the evidence and the disappearance of the remaining suspects aroused much public debate. By the end of 1980 seven of the nine escaped suspects had returned and not been indicted due to lack of evidence, and Satō Hiroshi and Tsuruta Tomoya, now thought by the police to be the true killers, had sent word from Beijing (Peking) that they wished to return. This incident, together with the SHIMOYAMA INCIDENT, MITAKA INCIDENT, and MATSUKAWA INCIDENT, is regarded by some as an example of government repression of communists during the Occupation years.

Shiratori Kurakichi (1865–1942)

Scholar of Asian history. Born in what is now Chiba Prefecture; graduate of Tōkyō University. After a period of study in Europe, he was appointed to the chair of the newly established department of Oriental history at Tōkyō University. Interested in the historical interaction of peoples on the Asian continent, particularly in terms of linguistics, he wrote on Korea, Manchuria, Mongolia, and Central Asia. Shiratori was also instrumental in founding in 1908 the Research Bureau of the SOUTH MANCHURIA RAILWAY to carry out studies of the area and in building up the collection of the TŌYŌ BUNKO library.

shirauo → whitebait

Shiretoko National Park

(Shiretoko Kokuritsu Kōen). Situated in northeastern Hokkaidō, on the SHIRETOKO PENINSULA. This virgin mountain region consists of forests, caldera lakes, waterfalls over sea cliffs, numerous species of wildlife, and volcanoes. The highest volcano is RAUSUDAKE (1,661 m; 5,448 ft) in the south; on its slopes is Rausu Hot Spring, a popular tourist resort. Sightseeing boats cruise along the peninsula's rocky coast up to Shiretokomisaki, the cape that forms its northernmost tip. The forests in the region consist mainly of Yeddo spruce (*ezomatsu*) and Sakhalin fir (*todomatsu*). Among the numerous species of wildlife that inhabit the region are the brown bear (*higuma*), a kind of fox called the *kita kitsune* (*Vulpes vulpes schrencki*), and the white-tailed sea eagle (*ojirowashi*). Area: 413.8 sq km (159.7 sq mi).

Shiretoko Peninsula

(Shiretoko Hantō). Located in eastern Hokkaidō and bounded on the northwest by the Sea of Okhotsk and on the southeast by the Nemuro Strait. One of the wildest and most remote regions of Japan, the peninsula is covered by dense coniferous forests and a massive volcanic range. It is famous for a long coastline, which includes overhanging precipices that are 100–200 m (328–656 ft) high, and rocks eroded by the sea. The cape of Shiretokomisaki is noted for its natural beauty. Fishing is the principal industry. Most of the peninsula has been designated as Shiretoko National Park.

Shiribetsugawa

River in southwestern Hokkaidō, originating near Lake Shikotsu and flowing west by Yōteizan, a volcanic mountain, to Kutchan where it changes to a southwesterly course before emptying into the Sea of Japan. Numerous electric power plants are located on the upper reaches. The river flows through several agricultural regions; asparagus and potatoes are cultivated in the basin. Length: 129 km (80 mi); area of drainage basin: 1,640 sq km (633 sq mi).

Shiroishi

City in southern Miyagi Prefecture, northern Honshū. In the Edo period (1600–1868) it developed as a castle town of the Katakura family and as one of the POST-STATION TOWNS on the highway Ōshū Kaidō. Traditional products are handmade Japanese paper (WASHI) and wooden dolls (KOKESHI); there are also flour mills and noodle factories. Pop: 41,274.

Shirone

City in central Niigata Prefecture, central Honshū. Situated between the rivers Shinanogawa and Nakanokuchigawa, it produces most of the grain in the region. Pears and grapes are also cultivated. Traditional products are sickles and Buddhist altars. A kite festival has been held every June for the past 300 years. Pop: 33,092.

Shiroumadake

Mountain at the junction of Niigata, Nagano, and Toyama prefectures, central Honshū, in the northern part of the Hida Mountains. Together with Shakushidake and Yarigatake, it is one of the three mountains of Shirouma and is made up mostly of Paleozoic strata. Near the summit are flower fields and the Shiroumayari Hot Spring. Shiroumadake has excellent ski slopes and is popular with climbers. It is part of Chūbu Sangaku National Park. Height: 2,933 m (9,620 ft).

Shiroyama

Small hill in the western part of the city of Kagoshima, Kagoshima Prefecture, Kyūshū. A battlefield during the Satsuma Rebellion (1877). The rebellion's leader, SAIGŌ TAKAMORI, committed suicide here, and it is now a historical site. The observation platform on the hill provides a view of SAKURAJIMA and Kagoshima Bay. Subtropical plants grow wild on the hill. Height: 108 m (354 ft).

Shiroyama Saburō (1927–)

Novelist. Real name Sugiura Eiichi. Born in Aichi Prefecture; graduate of Tōkyō Shōka Daigaku (now Hitotsubashi University). An economist by training, he is known for his many novels of the business and financial world. The 1958 Naoki Prize was awarded to his *Sōkaiya Kinjō* (1958), in which he revealed the behind-the-scenes workings of stockholders' meetings. He has continued to pursue in his novels the life and fate of the average person struggling to survive in a complex, capitalist society. He is also known as a biographer of modern business leaders and other historical figures. Principal works are *Shōsetsu Nihon ginkō* (1963), a novel, and *Rakujitsu moyu* (1974; tr *War Criminal: The Life and Death of Hirota Kōki*, 1977), a biography.

shiryō

(privately owned lands). (1) From the 10th century onward, lands held by private persons, as distinct from *kōryō* (public lands), which were held by the state or by communal bodies. *Shiryō* were not exempt from taxation by higher authorities, but their owners had the right to dispose of the land through trade, transfer, or donation. (2) In the Kamakura (1185–1333) and Muromachi (1333–1568) periods, lands obtained through reclamation or private acquisition, as distinct from *onryō*, lands granted by higher authorities such as the shogunate. (3) In the Edo period (1600–1868), lands owned by the *daimyō* or the shōgun's direct vassals (HATAMOTO and GOKENIN), as distinct from lands under the direct jurisdiction of the shogunate or those owned by temples and shrines. UEDA Nobuhiro

Shiryō Hensanjo → Historiographical Institute, Tōkyō University

Shisakajima

Group of islands in the central Inland Sea, approximately 18 km (11 mi) off the city of Niihama, Ehime Prefecture, Shikoku. The group consists of Minoshima, Ienoshima, Kajishima, Nezumishima, and Myōjinshima. These islands were uninhabited until 1897 when Sumitomo Metal Industries began building a smelting plant there. Area: 2 sq km (0.8 sq mi).

Shishi-mai

A group of *shishi-mai* dancers and musicians performing on the grounds of a Shintō shrine.

Shiseidō Co, Ltd

Company engaged in the manufacture and sale of cosmetics and soap. Its products are well known abroad under the brand names Moisture, Mist, Inoui, Murasaki, and Zen. Shiseidō is a leader in the Japanese cosmetics market and ranks high in the world cosmetics industry. Its forerunner was a small Western-style pharmacy which opened in Tōkyō's Ginza in 1872 and began selling cosmetic goods in 1897. Shiseidō is known for its high level of research and development; its corporate laboratories, located in Yokohama, conduct both basic and applied research, with results published in Japan and overseas. In 1976 the Ninth International Conference of the Association of Cosmetic Chemists presented Shiseidō with its highest award for research on the emulsification of amino acids. The company's domestic marketing system has a nationwide total of 25,000 chain stores under 98 sales companies. All sales personnel are specially trained in product use. In 1965 Shiseidō established a wholly owned subsidiary in the United States, and in 1968 it established another in Italy. It has a total of nine production and sales firms and two branches overseas. In the fiscal year ending in November 1981 sales totaled ¥302.3 billion (US $1.4 billion) and the company was capitalized at ¥10.4 billion (US $46.5 million). Its head office is in Tōkyō.

shisei system → uji-kabane system

Shishi Bunroku (1893–1969)

Novelist and theatrical director. Real name Iwata Toyoo. Born in Kanagawa Prefecture. Attended Keiō University. In 1937, with KISHIDA KUNIO and others, he organized the Bungakuza theatrical company and helped to introduce modern French drama to Japan. He wrote many works that attracted the public eye such as *Etchan* (1936–37), a popular novel rich in humor and irony; *Jiyū gakkō* (1950), a novel portraying the customs and manners of the immediate postwar period; *Musume to watashi* (1953–56), an autobiographical work; and *Kaigun* (1942), a work about the crews of the special submarines that attacked Pearl Harbor at the outset of World War II. ASAI Kiyoshi

Shishigatani Conspiracy → Shunkan

shishi-mai

A type of dance (often referred to in English as lion dance) performed in the guise of a *shishi*, an imaginary beast, supposedly a lion or, in some areas, a deer. Usually performers wear a headdress in the shape of a *shishi*. The type of *shishi-mai* in which two or more dancers form one lion belongs to the KAGURA (sacred dance) category. Originating from GIGAKU (masked dance) or *sangaku* (see SARUGAKU) introduced from the continent after the 7th century, this type spread throughout Japan during the medieval period (roughly 13th–16th centuries) as a form of exorcism. In the DENGAKU type of *shishi-mai*, the costume is worn by only one dancer. This form,

Shishi odori

The *shishi odori* being performed in Hanamaki, Iwate Prefecture.

found throughout eastern Japan, is derived from the deer dance (SHISHI ODORI) and influenced by a Pure Land Buddhist dance, NEMBUTSU ODORI. A large group of classical dance pieces with *shamisen* accompaniment derive from this tradition and form a category called *shishi-mono*, e.g., the NAGAUTA "Echigo-jishi." See also KADOZUKE; DANCE, TRADITIONAL. MISUMI Haruo

shishi odori

(deer dance). Also called *taiko odori*. A group dance of northeastern Japan (primarily Iwate and Miyagi prefectures) performed by 8 to 12, or, in some areas, 3 male dancers. They wear masks resembling a deer and beat two-headed drums attached to their waists. It was traditionally danced door-to-door during late summer or autumn so as to avert evil. The *shishi odori* should not be confused with the SHISHI-MAI. MISUMI Haruo

shishōsetsu → I-novel

Shisō

(Thought). Journal of philosophy put out by IWANAMI SHOTEN PUBLISHERS. The first issue appeared in 1921. Devoted to important philosophical problems, the journal's early contributors included KUKI SHŪZŌ, WATSUJI TETSURŌ, and NISHIDA KITARŌ. It has recently been publishing articles with wider audience appeal.

Shisōhan Hogo Kansatsu Hō → "Thought Criminal" Probation Law

Shisō no kagaku

(The Science of Thought). An intellectual movement and its journal of the same name founded in 1946 by seven young intellectuals who felt they had not opposed World War II vigorously enough. They were the physicists Taketani Mitsuo (b 1911) and Watanabe Satoshi (b 1910), the economist Tsuru Shigeto (b 1912), the political scientist MARUYAMA MASAO (b 1914), the sociologist Tsurumi Kazuko (b 1918), the philosopher Tsurumi Shunsuke (b 1922), and the intellectual historian Takeda Kiyoko (b 1917).

The pluralistic character of the movement was reflected in the different fields and intellectual backgrounds of the founders. Their aims were to carry out intellectual activity based on logic and experience and to introduce selectively Anglo-American philosophy and thought to a Japan hitherto enamored of German idealistic metaphysics. John Dewey's pragmatism, symbolic logic, psychoanalysis, and social anthropology thus found their way into Japan, as did new concepts of mass communication. Rejecting the idea that philosophy was exclusively the concern of scholars, the movement tried to develop a philosophy useful to the average person in everyday life.

In July 1949 the group formed the Shisō no Kagaku Kenkyūkai (Science of Thought Research Group), whose total membership reached over 200 in 1954. In addition to liberal scholars, researchers,

and journalists, the group also included educators, government workers, and laborers, embodying the movement's emphasis on "populist scholarship" as opposed to "government-university scholarship." Its journal welcomed manuscripts by nonprofessionals.

The group formed study circles in which specialists and nonspecialists from within and without the *Shisō no kagaku* group participated. These resulted in such publications as *Tetsugaku, ronri yōgo jiten* (1959, Dictionary of Terms in Philosophy and Logic), *Tenkō* (1959–62, Conversion), *Nihon no taishū geijutsu* (1962, Popular Arts of Japan), *Meiji ishin* (1967, The Meiji Restoration), *Shōdantai* (1976, The Small Group), *Nihon senryō* (1972, The Occupation of Japan), and *Nihon senryōgun* (1978, The Occupation Army in Japan). Most representative is the three-volume work on "conversion" (TENKŌ), the abandonment of antiwar positions by Marxists and liberals during the immediate prewar years. Reacting against the common practice of criticizing such people from an ethical viewpoint, *Shisō no kagaku,* with Tsurumi Shunsuke as a central figure, sought to place the phenomenon of *tenkō* in a historical context and to explore the psychological and intellectual makeup of those who succumbed. During the political turmoil over the renewal of the United States–Japan Security Treaty in 1960 (see UNITED STATES–JAPAN SECURITY TREATIES), the group attracted attention with its call for action from a nonpartisan, politicized citizenry. *Ōno Tsutomu*

shitaji chūbun

(literally, "halving of land"). Division of a private landed estate (SHŌEN) between its original proprietor (RYŌSHU) and its shogunate-appointed land steward (JITŌ), practiced mainly from the mid-13th to the mid-14th century. Disputes became inevitable, especially in the outlying areas, when the *jitō* took over many of the *ryōshu's* rights of tax collection and law enforcement. Various compromises, such as WAYO, were made, but when the concept of shared power proved unworkable, it was simplest to divide the estates. In most cases of *shitaji chūbun*, the land itself (*shitaji*) was divided into two parts, controlled separately by the *ryōshu* and the *jitō;* in other cases, the fruits of the land (*jōbun*) were divided between the two. The division was commonly on a 50-50 basis, but it was sometimes unequal, the stronger of the claimants obtaining as much as two-thirds or more of the estate. Divisions could be decided through "mutual understanding" (called *wayo-chūbun*), but more often one of the two parties involved—usually the *ryōshu*—would petition the shogunate to declare a territorial division in order to settle the dispute. However, as might be expected, actual territorial possession further strengthened the position of the *jitō* and speeded the disintegration of the *shōen* system.

Shitakiri suzume

(The Tongue-Cut Sparrow). Folktale. A sparrow owned by an honest old man eats some rice paste prepared by a greedy old woman (in some versions the man's wife). Enraged, the woman cuts out the tongue of the sparrow and drives it away. The grieving old man goes in search of his sparrow and is well treated by the sparrow's family. On leaving them, he is offered a choice of two boxes; he takes the lighter one, which turns out to be full of treasure. The greedy woman then pays a visit to the sparrows and demands the heavier box, from which emerge goblins and serpents; the woman dies of shock. The archetype of this story is found in the 13th century collection of tales, UJI SHŪI MONOGATARI. Variants tell of a sparrow in a melon (or a cage) floating downstream, suggesting a relationship to MOMOTARŌ, the tale of a small boy born from a peach found in a stream. *Suchi Tokuhei*

shitamachi

Traditional commercial districts of older Japanese cities, particularly Tōkyō (known as Edo until the Meiji Restoration of 1868). Although the term is often translated as "downtown," the *shitamachi* should not be confused with modern central business districts. Properly speaking, it refers to the merchant (*shōnin*) and craftsman (SHOKUNIN) quarters usually found in low-lying areas of feudal CASTLE TOWNS (*jōka machi*), and by extension to present-day neighborhoods with strong ties to the social and cultural traditions of preindustrial urban merchant life. Contemporary survival of those traditions is popularly associated with the so-called old middle classes—small-scale merchants and artisans—often clustered in older commercial neighborhoods. The *shitamachi* is often contrasted with the YAMANOTE (literally, "the foothills"), the districts and the traditions associated historically with *samurai* and now with the white-collar new middle class. Thus the *shitamachi* is a distinctive segment of urban society, distinguishable in terms of geography, historical background, social and cultural traditions, social identity, and economic subsistence.

The *shitamachi* was largely the product of the rigid geographic, economic, and social segregation imposed on the mercantile and manufacturing classes (the CHŌNIN or townspeople) by the feudal elite in the numerous castle towns established just prior to and early in the Edo period (1600–1868). Politically impotent, restricted in social and geographic mobility by hereditarily ascribed occupations, and forbidden emulation of the samurai by numerous sumptuary regulations, *chōnin* developed cultural pursuits, social patterns, and value systems markedly different from those of the samurai or the peasantry.

With the increasing economic prosperity of the *chōnin* in the middle and later Edo period, *shitamachi* blossomed, developing a sophisticated urbanity centering on the amusements of the great cities' pleasure quarters: Edo's Yoshiwara and Asakusa; Kyōto's Shimabara and Gion; Ōsaka's Shimmachi and Dōtombori. The *chōnin* subculture created the arts of the KABUKI theater, RAKUGO storytelling, the BUNRAKU puppet theater with its SHAMISEN music, the UKIYO-E print and the world of the GEISHA quarters it so often portrayed. Throughout *chōnin* residential, commercial, and manufacturing districts—such as Kanda, Shitaya, Nihombashi or Fukagawa in Edo, Shimogyō in Kyōto, Semba or Shimanouchi in Ōsaka, and the smaller merchant quarters of provincial *jōkamachi*—particular styles of dress, speech, spending and consumption were developed, as well as social norms of relative informality, spontaneity, emotionalism and candor, contrasting sharply with the severe standards of samurai society. There arose distinctive *chōnin* temperaments or personalities, such as the *edokko* ("children of Edo"), free-spending and studiously nonchalant in their adherence to the aesthetic canons of *iki* ("chic"; see IKI AND SUI) and *tsū* ("connoisseurship"). Their sentiment would find heightened expression on festive occasions such as the SANNŌ FESTIVAL, the SANJA FESTIVAL and the KANDA FESTIVAL in Edo and the GION FESTIVAL in Kyōto. There were, however, considerable local variations in *chōnin* life, and while *edokko* were famed as spendthrifts, citizens of Ōsaka were noted for their single-minded devotion to making money. In drama, Edo preferred swashbuckling kabuki, while Ōsaka followed *bunraku*'s domestic tragedies. In dialect, in the cut of their clothes, even in the preparation of SUSHI, *chōnin* life varied between these two great urban centers, and vestiges of these differing customs and temperaments remain even today.

Since the Meiji Restoration, however, the distinctiveness of the *shitamachi* and the *chōnin* tradition has lessened. Political changes and economic development have led to massive social and economic mobility and the rapid influx of migrants into major urban centers. Homogenization of social and cultural patterns has occurred because of mobility, mass education, mass media, and government policies intended to forge a unified national identity. In addition, *shitamachi* areas in many cities have suffered physical destruction and dispersion as a result of encroachments by growing central business districts, natural disasters (Tōkyō's *shitamachi* was largely destroyed in the TŌKYŌ EARTHQUAKE OF 1923), and the World War II firebombings that leveled many cities.

Though these have blurred direct continuities with *chōnin* life and the preindustrial merchant quarters, parallels exist and certain areas are still popularly considered *shitamachi*. Thus, while Tōkyō's Nihombashi is now largely a central business district, areas such as Asakusa and Ueno retain their *shitamachi* aura, and newer areas (e.g., Kōtō, Arakawa, and Sumida wards) have assumed many *shitamachi* characteristics. Here, and in similar districts in most Japanese cities, tightly packed shops and workshops with attached residences line narrow, winding streets and alleys, and neighborhood social life preserves much of the open informality that contrasts so noticeably with more reserved *yamanote* areas. Here, too, eschewing many Western-derived products and pursuits, some residents keep alive traditional cultural elements that evoke *chōnin* life: in Tōkyō's *shitamachi* one can still hear *edoben* (the Edo dialect), which does not distinguish the sounds "hi" and "shi" and ignores much of standard Japanese formality; kabuki and SUMŌ are still avidly followed; KIMONO are still selected with *iki* in mind. Writers such as NAGAI KAFŪ, KUBOTA MANTARŌ, and YAMAMOTO SHŪGORŌ drew upon the life of Tōkyō's *shitamachi* people for their literary works.

Typically, the present-day *shitamachi* is inhabited by members of the old middle class: independent or quasi-independent shopkeepers, artisans, wholesalers, and industrial subcontractors.

Though these tiny enterprises constitute a surprisingly large sector of the economy, their economic position is increasingly precarious. As in earlier periods, they often employ their own family members, perhaps supplemented by a few poorly paid workers in quasi-familial, paternalistic relationships with their employers. Compared with other sectors of society, the organization of the *shitamachi* family and the family enterprise resembles that of the traditional family, with corresponding emphasis on traditional norms and values: corporate solidarity, individual subordination, and hierarchical authority.

Beyond the household and the workplace, the *shitamachi*'s petty entrepreneurs are typically involved in other traditional social relationships. Extended kinship ties and particularistic patron-client, or fictive kinship, relationships (OYABUN-KOBUN) are important. Traditional values of GIRI AND NINJŌ (duty and human feeling) govern the conduct of social relations. Neighborly solidarity, based on reciprocity and mutual obligation, is encouraged through participation in neighborhood associations (CHŌNAIKAI) and other neighborhood activities, such as local festivals.

Many of these traditional aspects of *shitamachi* social organization and culture have been undermined by postwar legal reforms and pervasive changes in sociocultural values. As economic growth and urbanization proceed, promoting further changes in social, cultural, and economic patterns, and further eroding the economic position of the old middle class, the *shitamachi*'s distinctive way of life will further disappear. — *Theodore C. BESTOR*

Shitennōji

A Buddhist temple compound located in the Tennōji Ward of Ōsaka. The head temple of the Wa sect since the end of World War II, Shitennōji still retains close connections with the TENDAI SECT, with which it had been affiliated since 1010 (Kannin 4). Said to have been founded in 593, Shitennōji was strategically situated in the port city of Naniwa (present-day Ōsaka). The temple was repeatedly destroyed by fire and reconstructed. Gutted in an air raid in World War II, the site was excavated between the years 1950 and 1957 revealing the foundations to be intact. In the following years Shitennōji, originally made of wood, was reconstructed with every detail in reinforced concrete. It is the oldest temple compound in Japan which still preserves the original Asuka-period (latter part of the 6th century to 710) ground plan and building arrangement.

According to tradition, Shitennōji was founded by Prince SHŌTOKU in gratitude for a victory over his anti-Buddhist adversaries centered on MONONOBE NO MORIYA. In the heat of battle Shōtoku had vowed to establish a temple to honor the Shitennō (the Four Heavenly Kings; see TEMBU), who guard the cardinal points of the compass and who were popularly worshiped at that time.

The temple was laid out according to a traditional axial plan widely used in China and Korea, especially in the Kingdom of PAEKCHE (J: Kudara) whence it was introduced into Japan. The buildings are arranged along a north-south axis. The worshiper, entering through the south main gate (*nandaimon*), confronts the main compound of the temple which is surrounded by a cloister corridor (*kairō*). Upon entering through the central gate (*chūmon*), he stands before the most prominent building of the temple, the five-story pagoda, which contains a relic beneath its central mast. Immediately behind the pagoda is the rectangular image hall (*kondō*). Its dimly lit interior is dominated by a large altar-platform (*shumidan*) which symbolizes Mt. Sumeru (J: Shumisen), the cosmological center of the Buddhist universe. On it are placed the main image (*honzon*) and subordinate images of deities worshiped at the temple, originally by means of circumambulation around the altar. The lecture hall (*kōdō*) is built into the corridor to the north. Behind the main compound to the left and right are the belfry (*shōrō*) and the sutra repository (*kyōzō*). The building farthest to the north is the refectory (*jikidō*) which is flanked on either side by monks' quarters (*sōbō*). The Shitennōji plan, also known as the Kudara plan, was used for most temples built during the Asuka period. — *Lucie R. WEINSTEIN*

shitōkan

(the four ranks; also called *shibukan*). Collective term for the four highest ranks of bureaucrats under the RITSURYŌ SYSTEM of government during the Nara (710–794) and Heian (794–1185) periods. The *shitōkan* hierarchy was modeled, as was the *ritsuryō* system itself, after the practice of the Sui (589–618) and Tang (T'ang; 618–907) dynasties of China. The four ranks were: *kami* (bureau chief) and *suke* (assistant bureau chief), who were jointly responsible for administration; *jō*, who drafted documents; and *sakan*, who attended to clerical duties. In the most important bureaus there were several officials of each rank, while in smaller bureaus one or more of the ranks might be left unfilled.

Shizen shin'eidō

Principal work of ANDŌ SHŌEKI (1703?–62). The title means the laws (*dō*) whereby the truth (*shin*), which is active at the source of nature (*shizen*), creates (*ei*) all things. It is a book of social criticism purporting to demonstrate, through clarification of the laws of nature, that people suffer in existing society because their lives run counter to the laws of nature. It is also a medical book claiming to show the way to attain a sound mind and body. The book existed in a manuscript version in 93 volumes (101 chapters) and in a printed edition in 3 volumes (3 chapters). The latter was published in Edo (now Tōkyō) and Kyōto in 1753. Some of the manuscript volumes are thought to date from the years after 1755. In particular, the long introductory volume and volumes 24 and 25 present in the clearest and most concrete form Shōeki's social criticism and theories of social reformation. Volume 24, "The Tale of the Legal World," is known for its literary, allegorical criticism of human society. The manuscript volumes were discovered by KANŌ KŌKICHI in about 1899, but the bulk of them were lost in the Tōkyō Earthquake of 1923. Today there are only 15 volumes extant, including the three important ones whose contents are described above.

■ ——Modern editions of *Shizen shin'eidō*: *Nihon koten bungaku taikei*, vol 97 (Iwanami Shoten, 1966); *Nihon shisō taikei*, vol 45 (Iwanami Shoten, 1977); *Andō Shōeki zenshū*, vols 1–4 (Azekura Shobō, 1981). E. H. Norman, "Ando Shoeki and the Anatomy of Japanese Feudalism," in *Transactions of the Asiatic Society of Japan, Third Series*, vol 2 (1949).　　　　　　　BITŌ Masahide

shizen shugi → naturalism

shizoku

A term designating people of *samurai* descent. In 1869, the year after the MEIJI RESTORATION, it was decided to abolish the traditional class distinctions of *shi* (samurai), *nō* (farmer), *kō* (artisan), and *shō* (merchant) and to replace them with three broad categories, *kazoku* (former court nobles and *daimyō*; see PEERAGE), *shizoku* (those of samurai descent), and HEIMIN (commoners). The imperial family (*kōzoku*) formed a fourth class. Early the following year the government applied the name *sotsu* (or *sotsuzoku*) to those samurai with the rank of *ashigaru* (footsoldier) and below. In 1872 however, it reincorporated *sotsu* holding hereditary stipends into the *shizoku* class and made those with lifetime stipends or less *heimin*, or commoners.

To the modernizing Meiji-period (1868–1912) government, which had taken over from the domains the responsibility for paying hereditary stipends, the *shizoku* soon became a problem. They were a large class, making up 5 percent of the population. (According to the January 1873 census, there were 408,823 *shizoku* families, or 1,892,449 persons, in a population of 34.3 million.) Moreover, their stipends were an intolerable fiscal burden to the government, consuming one-fourth to one-third of the annual budget. The story of the *shizoku*, therefore, is largely the tale of the liquidation of their special samurai privileges. By 1882 their legal rights were gone, by 1914 the use of the term *shizoku* in the household registers (*koseki*) was ended, and in 1947, following the end of World War II, the very title was abolished along with all other distinctions.

Government Policy toward the Shizoku —— The government, which subordinated *shizoku* interests to its program for making Japan economically powerful, phased out their political, social, and economic privileges on a gradual but sustained basis in the 1870s. The most serious blow to the *shizoku* was the loss of their monopoly over military and civil office. The CONSCRIPTION ORDINANCE OF 1873 established the principle that military service, which had been an exclusive function of the samurai, would henceforth be a duty of all classes, including peasants. Some *shizoku* did hold rank as officers in the new Imperial Army, but this small force lacked billets for the majority of the hereditary warriors. Nor did *shizoku* long retain civil office as a matter of right. The Meiji leaders committed themselves to a merit bureaucracy, and in their search for "men of talent" they rejected ascriptive claims to office not only in the central gov-

ernment but, after the abolition of domains in 1871, in local offices as well.

The Meiji government also phased out special *shizoku* social privileges and symbols of rank or else made them available to all. A September 1871 edict gave *shizoku* freedom of choice in wearing the long and short swords and in putting up their hair in the traditional *chommage* style—the forepart of the head shaved, the remaining hair tied into a knot to be piled onto the bald pate. Informal pressure, however, encouraged *shizoku* to abandon both their swords and their distinctive hairstyle. At the same time commoners were allowed to wear the *haori* jacket and the *hakama* split-skirt, once exclusive to the samurai. The right of samurai to cut down commoners for "disrespect" was abolished (see KIRISUTE GOMEN). Class lines dissolved further with permission for marriages between *shizoku* and commoners, with the requirement that commoners take surnames like the *shizoku*, and with permission for *shizoku* to enter farming or business. The Sword Ban Order of 1876 (HAITŌREI) completed the process by denying *shizoku* their most cherished badge of rank. (More than one *shizoku* had used his long sword in attempted assassination of government officials.)

Finally, the *shizoku* lost their economic base. Voluntary, then compulsory, conversion of their hereditary stipends into cash settlements and government bonds brought ruin to many *shizoku*. Lacking experience, they failed at the businesses in which they invested their capital or else exhausted settlement money in meeting living expenses. In December 1873 lump-sum settlements became available to those *shizoku* whose stipends were below the 100-*koku* (see KOKUDAKA) level; and, before suspension of the offer in July 1875, about 130,000 *shizoku*, one-third of the total, had taken advantage of it. In August 1876 conversion of stipends became compulsory in conformity with Home Minister ŌKUBO TOSHIMICHI's policy of promoting industrial development. In his view the discontinuance of annual stipends would free government moneys for construction of model factories, subsidies to shipping interests, and agricultural experiment stations. His was a mercantilist policy to increase exports and diminish imports. Government bonds called KINROKU KŌSAI issued to *shizoku* to replace their stipends would also form capital investment in support of new private enterprise. The government paid ¥174,630,000 to the *shizoku* at the beginning of 1877, or an average of ¥563 per recipient. The bonds were issued on a sliding scale (see CHITSUROKU SHOBUN).

A fundamental policy Ōkubo adopted in the DAJŌKAN, which he controlled from 1873 to 1878, was SHIZOKU JUSAN, the economic rehabilitation of the former samurai class. Ōkubo's Home Ministry set up a bureau in 1876 specifically to deal with this policy. It was hoped that employment of the *shizoku* would soften their hostility to the government and that they would become a productive class, contributing to the industrialization of Japan. The implementation of the policy focused on land reclamation or settlement, the establishment of national banks capitalized with *shizoku* bonds, and government loans of industrial capital to *shizoku*. Government officials quickly recognized that agriculture was the most suitable occupation for the former samurai, and they moved early to "return" the samurai to the land. Title to existing paddy fields was assigned to others by the LAND TAX REFORM OF 1873–1881, and so *shizoku* entered farming by taking title to wilderness lands as part of their pension settlements, by migrating to Hokkaidō, where many of them became farmer-soldiers under the Colonization Bureau (see TONDENHEI) or by settling on land reclaimed by the government. The most ambitious reclamation project, promoted by Ōkubo as a model, opened about 50,000 acres of farmland by draining swamps in Fukushima Prefecture in 1879.

Shizoku entered banking through policies that led to their holding 75 percent of the stock in more than 100 banks set up under the National Banking Ordinance of 1872, but with indifferent results. The most successful program was that in which ¥53 million in industrial capital became available after 1878 from the central government, to be divided among the prefectures depending on the number of *shizoku*. The loans financed ventures in sericulture, silk reeling, mulberry cultivation, tea preparation, match manufacturing, and other small enterprises. Some *shizoku* became successful entrepreneurs; but on the whole "the way of the samurai in business" became synonymous with failure. Their land passed into the hands of others, their banks failed, and their industries went bankrupt. By 1889 the *shizoku jusan* program was suspended.

Shizoku Dissidence —— Rehabilitation programs often annoyed rather than mollified *shizoku* who were jealous of their more successful fellow samurai in government. Bitterness over loss of pensions and economic ruin expressed itself in assassinations, riots, and civil war and assumed more enduring form as part of the movement to establish representative government. "Righteous assassins," who had once cut down shogunate officials, now eliminated Meiji leaders. Vice-Minister of Military Affairs ŌMURA MASUJIRŌ was mortally wounded in October 1869 by discontented *shizoku* who resented his plans to conscript farmers as soldiers. Home Minister Ōkubo himself, the dominant figure in the modernizing government, fell under the swords of assassins on 14 May 1878 in Tōkyō. In their apologia the assassins charged that his industrialization policies had robbed *shizoku* of their livelihoods. Ōkubo's European-style dress and horse-drawn carriage only inflamed the six *shizoku* assassins who defiantly wore old-fashioned samurai clothing and carried forbidden swords.

The assassinations of Ōmura and Ōkubo bracketed a series of riots and rebellions that began in the northeastern domains defeated in the BOSHIN CIVIL WAR and finally centered in the southwest domains, whose troops had won the key battles. Chief among these were the HAGI REBELLION of October 1876, under the former government councillor MAEBARA ISSEI; the SAGA REBELLION of February 1874, which was personally suppressed by Ōkubo; and the JIMPŪREN REBELLION in Kumamoto in October 1876. That these armed revolts were localized and uncoordinated reflected their profeudal, backward-looking origins and accounted for their failure. The last and largest of these uprisings was the SATSUMA REBELLION of 1877 under SAIGŌ TAKAMORI; it was sustained through much of the year, but, after Saigō's death, quiescence generally prevailed among violence-prone *shizoku*. In the former domain of Tosa (now Kōchi Prefecture), *shizoku* expressed their dissidence through the FREEDOM AND PEOPLE'S RIGHTS MOVEMENT; in making a rather peaceful demand for representative government they developed a political consciousness that fed into the modern democratic tradition in Japan.

Shizoku dissidence in early Meiji Japan should not obscure the fact that the class also produced the elites who dominated the emerging society. The statesman IWAKURA TOMOMI called *shizoku* "the most useful group in society" in contributing so many "natural leaders." Most of the bureaucracy was made up of *shizoku*, and as noted, military officers were usually former samurai. Police were recruited almost exclusively from the class. Most teachers were former samurai, and even the business world had its contingent of *shizoku* entrepreneurs. One wing of the *shizoku* class resisted Japan's modernization, but another created modern Japan.

■ ——Sidney DeVere Brown, "Political Assassination in Early Meiji Japan: The Plot against Ōkubo Toshimichi," in D. Wurfel, ed, *Meiji Japan's Centennial* (1971). Fukuchi Shigetaka, *Shizoku to samurai ishiki* (1956). Gotō Yasushi, *Shizoku hanran no kenkyū* (1970). Harry D. Harootunian, "The Progress of Japan and the Samurai Class, 1868–1882," *Pacific Historical Review* 27 (May 1959). Harry D. Harootunian, "The Economic Rehabilitation of the Samurai in the Early Meiji Period," *Journal of Asian Studies* 19.4 (1960). E. Herbert Norman, "Feudal Background of Japanese Politics," in John Dower, ed, *Origins of the Modern Japanese State* (1975). Ōkubo Toshiaki, *Meiji ishin to Kyūshū* (1973). Kikkawa Hidezō, *Shizoku jusan no kenkyū* (1935; repr 1942).

Sidney DeVere BROWN

shizoku jusan

(employment for former *samurai*). An economic policy in effect during the early years of the Meiji period (1868–1912), it was designed to provide a livelihood for former samurai (SHIZOKU), who had been stripped of their hereditary stipends. As a result of the abolition of domains and the establishment of prefectures (1871; see PREFECTURAL SYSTEM, ESTABLISHMENT OF) and the adoption of a universal conscription system (see CONSCRIPTION ORDINANCE OF 1873), most members of the former samurai class were without means of sustenance. This was one of the most immediate problems facing the new government, for idle and dissatisfied warriors constituted a potentially serious threat to its stability. Economically, too, it was important to transform the samurai class into a productive segment of society. In 1873 the government gave money and bonds to those samurai who voluntarily surrendered their stipends. In 1876 all former samurai were ordered to relinquish their stipends in exchange for government bonds (see CHITSUROKU SHOBUN). In order to provide employment, the government established a colonist-militia system (TONDENHEI), sending former samurai to settle in Hokkaidō. It also sold them public land cheaply, lent them capital to form new businesses, and encouraged them to develop wasteland.

Although many former samurai obtained jobs through this policy, most of their endeavors ended in failure, since few of them were equipped with the skills required for modern commerce. Most of those with government bonds were forced to sell them, although the former *daimyō* tended to hold on to their government securities and invest them profitably in banks and other enterprises.

Shizugatake, Battle of

(Shizugatake no Tatakai). A major military encounter fought on 11 June 1583 (Tenshō 11.4.21) between the forces of the national unifier TOYOTOMI HIDEYOSHI and SHIBATA KATSUIE, the powerful *daimyō* of Echizen (now part of Fukui Prefecture) and Kaga (now part of Ishikawa Prefecture), at a site in northern Ōmi Province (now the town of Kinomoto, Shiga Prefecture) near the mountain Shizugatake. Shibata's defeat in effect ended the first stage of the succession struggle that had broken out among ODA NOBUNAGA's generals after his assassination the previous year. At a conference held at Kiyosu Castle on 16 July 1582 (Tenshō 10.6.27), Hideyoshi had stage-managed the designation of Nobunaga's infant grandson Sambōshi (Hidenobu; 1580–1605) as the dead hegemon's heir. Thoroughly discomfited by this political maneuver were Nobunaga's son Nobutaka (1558–83) of Gifu, the daimyō Takikawa Kazumasu (1525–86) of Ise Nagashima, and Hideyoshi's longtime rival Shibata. The three, however, were unable to act in concert against Hideyoshi, who outmaneuvered them militarily as well. In January 1583 (Tenshō 10.12), with Shibata tied down by the winter in his northern domain, Hideyoshi massed troops in Ōmi and obtained the surrender of Nagahama, Shibata's invaluable outpost in that province, and the submission of Oda Nobutaka. In April Hideyoshi invaded Takikawa's province of Ise (now part of Mie Prefecture); the next month, informed that Shibata was on the march, he moved to confront him in northern Ōmi, establishing his base at Nagahama. The news of Shibata's advance impelled Nobutaka once again to take up arms against Hideyoshi. On 7 June (Tenshō 11.4.17), Hideyoshi rushed from Nagahama to Ōgaki in Mino Province (now part of Gifu Prefecture) to put Nobutaka in check; but by the evening of 10 June he reappeared at Shizugatake to rally his troops, who had that day been mauled by Shibata's intrepid general Sakuma Morimasa (1554–83). The issue was decided the next day when, in the face of Hideyoshi's counterattack, the detachment of the daimyō MAEDA TOSHIIE of Noto (now part of Ishikawa Prefecture) left the field of battle, abandoning Shibata to his fate. Shibata committed suicide three days later, and Nobutaka a week after that; Takikawa Kazumasu capitulated and was pardoned. Hideyoshi's victory immensely strengthened his position, so that the next year he was fully able to confront Nobunaga's son Nobukatsu (or Nobuo; 1558–1630) and the future shōgun TOKUGAWA IEYASU in the KOMAKI NAGAKUTE CAMPAIGN, the second and final stage of the contest over the succession to Nobunaga's hegemonic heritage.

George ELISON

Shizuka Gozen (fl late 12th century)

SHIRABYŌSHI dancer and mistress of the tragic hero MINAMOTO NO YOSHITSUNE. When MINAMOTO NO YORITOMO turned against his younger brother Yoshitsune after the latter's brilliant victories in the TAIRA–MINAMOTO WAR (1180–85), Shizuka accompanied Yoshitsune in his attempt to flee to safety. Unable to keep up, Shizuka was left in the mountainous Yoshino region, south of Nara, where she was recognized and seized by monks loyal to Yoritomo. Taken to Kamakura for questioning, Shizuka—known as the best dancer in all Japan—was forced to perform for Yoritomo at the TSURUGAOKA HACHIMAN SHRINE, the tutelary shrine of the Minamoto. Her performance included thinly disguised references to Yoshitsune's success in eluding his brother, but it was so skillful that Yoritomo did not punish Shizuka. Instead, he allowed her to return to Kyōto, where she became a nun. Numerous works of medieval fiction give accounts of Shizuka's life, the most complete being that in the GIKEIKI, a 15th-century compilation of legends about Yoshitsune; that she was, however, a historical personage is attested by the mention of her performance at the Tsurugaoka Hachiman Shrine in the AZUMA KAGAMI, the history of the Kamakura shogunate.

Barbara L. ARNN

Shizuki Tadao (1760–1806)

Translator and scholar of the Dutch language. Born in Nagasaki, Shizuki was adopted into a family who had served as hereditary translators *(tsūji)* to Dutch traders. He contributed to the develop-

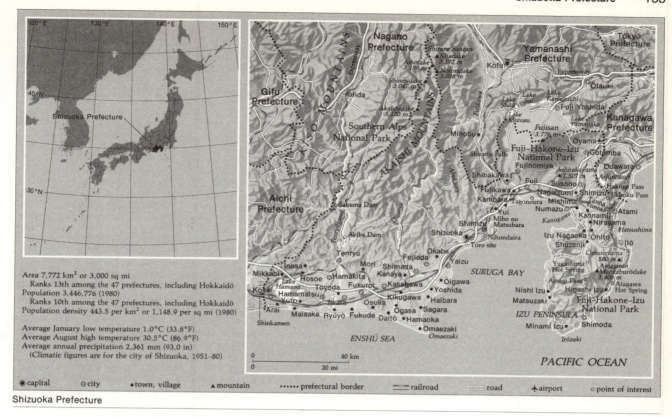

Area 7,772 km² or 3,000 sq mi
　Ranks 13th among the 47 prefectures, including Hokkaidō
Population 3,446,776 (1980)
　Ranks 10th among the 47 prefectures, including Hokkaidō
Population density 443.5 per km² or 1,148.9 per sq mi (1980)

Average January low temperature 1.0°C (33.8°F)
Average August high temperature 30.5°C (86.9°F)
Average annual precipitation 2,361 mm (93.0 in)
　(Climatic figures are for the city of Shizuoka, 1951–80)

◉ capital　　◎ city　　• town, village　　▲ mountain　　••••• prefectural border　　══ railroad　　══ road　　✈ airport　　○ point of interest

Shizuoka Prefecture

Shizuoka Prefecture

Workers harvesting tea near the town of Kikugawa in southern Shizuoka Prefecture.

ment of the study of astronomy in Japan by translating numerous works on astronomy from Dutch into Japanese. Particularly famous was *Rekishō shinsho* (1798–1802), a translation from the Dutch version of John Keill's commentaries on Newton's *Principia*. It was the first book in Japanese on modern physics and astronomy. In it Shizuki introduced much information acquired from his own studies of astronomy, including a theory concerning nebulas. See also NATURAL SCIENCES.

Shizuoka

Capital of Shizuoka Prefecture, central Honshū, on Suruga Bay. It was the site of Sumpu Castle, built by TOKUGAWA IEYASU in 1586, and his place of retirement after 1607. It also prospered in the Edo period (1600–1868) as one of the POST-STATION TOWNS on the highway Tōkaidō and as a distribution center of regional products. Traditional goods such as lacquer ware, sewing boxes, and *geta* (wooden clogs), as well as electrical appliances, textile goods, paper, and plastic models are made here. Principal agricultural products are tea,

mandarin oranges, strawberries, and horseradish. Of interest are the Late-Yayoi-period (ca 100–ca 300) TORO SITE, the Sengen Shrine, the ruins of Sumpu Castle (now a park), the Kunōzan–Tōshōgū Shrine commemorating Ieyasu, and the garden of the temple Togetsuhō-Saiokuji. Pop: 458,342.

Shizuoka Municipal Toro Site Museum

(Shizuoka Shiritsu Toro Hakubutsukan). Located in the city of Shizuoka, Shizuoka Prefecture, on the grounds of the Late Yayoi period (ca 100–ca 300) TORO SITE, now a historical park. Architecturally resembling a Yayoi-period raised storehouse, the museum, built in 1972, houses artifacts excavated from the site; the collection is noted for its wooden utensils and agricultural implements. Adjoining the museum are five Late Yayoi PIT HOUSES and two raised storehouse reconstructions. *Laurance ROBERTS*

Shizuoka Plain

(Shizuoka Heiya). Located in central Shizuoka Prefecture, central Honshū. Bordering Suruga Bay, it consists principally of the alluvial fans of the river Abekawa. A spectacular view of Mt. Fuji (Fujisan) can be obtained from the top of the hill called Udosan, on whose slopes strawberries are cultivated. The major city is Shizuoka, and the scenic area of MIHO NO MATSUBARA is an important tourist attraction. Area: approximately 110 sq km (42.5 sq mi).

Shizuoka Prefecture

(Shizuoka Ken). Located on the Pacific coast of central Honshū and bordered by Yamanashi and Nagano prefectures to the north, Kanagawa Prefecture to the east, the Pacific Ocean to the south, and Aichi Prefecture to the west. The terrain is principally mountainous, and the eastern half of the prefecture includes part of Mt. Fuji (Fujisan) and the rugged IZU PENINSULA. Rivers such as the FUJIKAWA, ABEKAWA, ŌIGAWA, and TENRYŪGAWA run between the mountains, creating deep gorges. The climate is humid and mild, especially in the southern part of the Izu Peninsula.

　Under the 7th-century system of provinces (KOKUGUN SYSTEM) the area was designated as the three provinces of Suruga, Tōtōmi, and Izu. The region gave rise to several important warrior families, such as the HŌJŌ FAMILY and TOKUGAWA FAMILY. The prefecture was created in its present form in 1876, with minor alterations in 1878.

Shizuoka is especially noted for its green tea and mandarin oranges. Fishery and forestry are also important, and eel cultivation is carried out in Lake HAMANA. The manufacture of textiles, musical instruments, looms, foodstuff, and paper dates from the late 19th century. Since World War II, the metal, machinery, motorcycle, automobile, shipbuilding, and oil refining industries have become important.

Proximity to the Tōkyō area and attractions such as FUJI–HAKONE–IZU NATIONAL PARK, SOUTHERN ALPS NATIONAL PARK, and numerous hot spring resorts make Shizuoka a popular tourist area. Area: 7,772 sq km (3,000 sq mi); pop: 3,446,776; capital: SHIZUOKA. Other major cities include HAMAMATSU, NUMAZU, SHIMIZU, and FUJI.

shō

The mouth organ of Japanese court music. The *shō* consists of a lacquered wooden cup-shaped body, into which 17 narrow bamboo pipes of varying length are inserted vertically to form a circular cluster. Two of the pipes are mute; the remainder are fitted with small metal tongues vibrating freely through a small slot, and made to speak by closing a fingerhole on the pipe. The instrument plays single notes and chords identified in the notation by the names of the pipes, and the player can maintain a continuous sound by sucking and blowing alternately. The *shō* is related to the Chinese *sheng* and to other East Asian mouth organs. In the 8th century there was also a deeper-voiced mouth organ, the *u*. See also GAGAKU.

David B. WATERHOUSE

Shōbara

City in northeastern Hiroshima Prefecture, western Honshū. It developed as an iron-mining center of the Chūgoku Mountains and later flourished as a market town. Principal activities are cattle raising, dairy farming, and *sake* production. It is the western gateway to the gorge known as TAISHAKUKYŌ. Pop: 22,874.

Shōbō genzō

(Treasury of the True Dharma Eye). The magnum opus of DŌGEN (1200–1253), founder of the SŌTŌ SECT of Japanese Zen Buddhism, is a collection of his sermons and commentaries on selected KŌAN, composed over a period of 22 years (1231–53). The corpus, which consists of 95 chapters, including "Genjō kōan" (Realization of *Kōan*), "Busshō" (Buddha nature), and "Bendōwa" (Discourse on the Practice of the Way), is written in Japanese, unlike other Japanese Buddhist works of the day which were customarily written in Chinese. Throughout the work Dōgen expounds matters of monastic life and examines Buddhist concepts and symbols at the limit of their semantic possibilities, revealing strikingly original and profound meanings. Dōgen conceived a 100-chapter work but died before its completion. Today the work is widely read as a Buddhist classic and is considered as one of the most important Japanese philosophical texts.

▰ ——Dōgen, *Shōbōgenzō* (1231–53; tr as *The Eye and Treasury of the True Law*, 1975 and 1977). Ōkubo Dōshū, *Dōgen zenji zenshū* vol 1 (1969). Terada Tōru, *Shōbōgenzō* in *Nihon shisōshi taikei*, vol 12 (1970), 13 (1972).

Hee-Jin KIM

shōbu

(sweet flag). *Acorus calamus* var. *asiaticus*. Often wrongly translated as "iris." An evergreen perennial herb of the arum family (Araceae) growing wild in colonies along the edges of ponds, marshes, and streams throughout Japan. The thick white rhizomes grow laterally and have numerous nodes with small fibrous roots. The sword-shaped leaves are narrow, pointed and about 80 centimeters (31 in) long, with a prominent midrib. In early summer the plant bears a finger-like light yellowish green inflorescence (spadix) in the middle of a leaflike stalk and crowded with minute light yellowish green flowers. In ancient times this herb was known as *ayame*, but that name is now used to refer to a species of iris (see IRISES).

The *shōbu* is known for the pleasant smell of its rhizome and leaves. The leaves were traditionally used to decorate the eaves of houses and added to bathwater during celebrations of Boys' Day (now CHILDREN'S DAY) in May; these customs were introduced from China and are based on an ancient Chinese folk belief that *shōbu* plants keep demons and plagues away.

A similar species called *sekishō* (*A. gramineus*) grows wild along mountain streams and is also cultivated in home gardens.

MATSUDA Osamu

shōbyōga → **screen and wall painting**

Shōchiku Co, Ltd

One of the largest entertainment companies in Japan. Aside from producing and distributing films, it also produces and promotes live shows and television programs. It was established in 1902 as a *kabuki* production company and expanded its business to movie production in 1920 when the Shōchiku Kinema Co was formed as a subsidiary. The company consolidated and assumed its present name in 1937. It is known for its many film dramas based on the lives of common people.

SHIRAI Yoshio

Shōchū Conspiracy

(Shōchū no Hen). An unsuccessful plot to overthrow the KAMAKURA SHOGUNATE; led by Emperor GO-DAIGO in 1324 (Shōchū 1). Since the time of Emperor FUSHIMI (r 1287–98) it had been the practice for members of the Jimyōin and Daikakuji lines of the imperial family to succeed to the throne in alternation. In 1321 the retired emperor Go-Fushimi (1288–1336; r 1298–1301) of the Jimyōin line sought to replace Go-Daigo's son (of the Daikakuji line) with his own son as heir apparent, and he succeeded in enlisting the support of the shogunate. Go-Daigo, who was strong-willed and moreover entertained hopes of renewed imperial glory, was incensed and conspired with the courtiers Hino Suketomo (1290–1332) and Hino Toshimoto (d 1332) to raise an army against the shogunate. The plot was discovered by the Rokuhara *tandai*, the shogunal deputy stationed in Kyōto, and arrests were made. Go-Daigo denied all knowledge of the plot and managed to survive the incident. This was the first of Go-Daigo's several attempts to wrest power from the shogunate; he failed again in the GENKŌ INCIDENT of 1331, but in 1333 he finally achieved his aims. See KEMMU RESTORATION.

Shōda Heigorō (1847–1922)

Businessman and leading figure of the Mitsubishi *zaibatsu* (financial and industrial combine). Born in Ōita Prefecture; graduate of Keiō Gijuku (now Keiō University). Shōda first taught at his alma mater but later joined Mitsubishi & Co through FUKUZAWA YUKICHI's introduction. He carried out a major organizational reform and modernization of the company's accounting practices and engineered its participation in capitalizing the Tokio Marine & Fire Insurance Co, Ltd. He became director of Nippon Yūsen upon the shipbuilding company's formation. He also became general manager of Mitsubishi & Co in 1886, taking a special interest in real estate and modern shipbuilding ventures. He masterminded the company's real estate acquisitions in Tōkyō's Marunouchi area, as well as the construction of office buildings, and the expansion and modernization of what is now MITSUBISHI HEAVY INDUSTRIES, LTD.

TATSUKI Mariko

Shōda Hidesaburō (1903–)

Businessman. Born in Gumma Prefecture, the third son of Shōda Teiichirō, founder of NISSHIN FLOUR MILLING CO, LTD. Graduated from Tōkyō Commercial University (now Hitotsubashi University). After first working for MITSUBISHI CORPORATION, Shōda joined Nisshin Flour Milling in 1929 and became its president in 1945. He devoted himself to the reconstruction of the company after World War II and added many new production lines, including formula feeds, foodstuffs, and chemicals. Shōda is the father of Crown Princess Michiko.

MAEDA Kazutoshi

Shōda Kenjirō (1902–1976)

Mathematician who led the development of abstract algebra in Japan. Uncle of Crown Princess Michiko. Born in Gumma Prefecture, he graduated from Tōkyō University in 1925. After studying in Germany, he became professor at Ōsaka University in 1933, later becoming its president. He also served as president of Musashi University. He received the Order of Culture in 1969.

Shōdoshima

Buddhist pilgrims, pictured here, come in large numbers to visit the 88 religious sanctuaries on the island.

Shōdan chiyō

(A Woodcutter's Chats on the Essentials of Government). An essay on government and the social conditions of the times, composed in 1480 by the high-ranking courtier and scholar ICHIJŌ KANEYOSHI, for the young shōgun Ashikaga Yoshihisa (1465–89; r 1474–89). The work contains interesting observations on the state of affairs in the aftermath of the ŌNIN WAR and is a valuable source on the political attitudes of the court aristocracy in that time of disorder and uncertainty.

Shōden Jiken → Shōwa Denkō Scandal

shodō → calligraphy

Shōdoshima

Island in the eastern Inland Sea, between southeastern Okayama Prefecture, southwestern Honshū, and northeastern Kagawa Prefecture, Shikoku. The second largest island in the Inland Sea after AWAJISHIMA, it is a level lava plateau averaging 700 m (2,296 ft) in elevation. Agricultural products include olives, green apples, and chrysanthemums. It is also known for its high-quality soy sauce, sōmen (noodles), and building stone. Part of the Inland Sea National Park, the island is also a tourist area. One of the attractions is the gorge called Kankakei. The 88 religious sanctuaries on the island also attract a large number of pilgrims. The highest point is the mountain Hoshigajō (817 m; 2,680 ft). Area: 155 sq km (59.8 sq mi).

shōen

(landed estate). One of the most important institutions for organizing the economic life of medieval Japan. The first landed estates appeared in the 8th century, and the last of them did not disappear until the 16th century during the turbulent Sengoku (Warring States) period (1467–1568). The mature estate, which had developed by the mid-11th century, proved to be an extremely successful way of securing a balance between the demands of the ruling class for income and the demands of the populace for a stable means of livelihood. Not only did the shōen serve as the primary means through which the ruling class tapped the wealth of the countryside, it also provided the residence, the workplace, and the source of sustenance for peasants and estate managers alike. Before the development of regional market economies in the 13th century, the workshops and craftsmen on the estate produced the hoes, plows, and other equipment needed by the farmers. Moreover, the estates frequently manufactured special products such as roof tiles, reed mats, and pottery to supply their proprietors in the capital. As one of the primary production units in medieval Japanese society, the shōen held a central place in the economic and social history of Japan, just as did the manors of medieval Europe, to which the shōen have often been compared.

At its mature stage, a shōen may be defined as a number of privately held parcels of land that had secured immunity from tax-

ation of the land and its cultivators as well as the right to refuse entry into the estate by government officials. These immunities placed the shōen and its residents outside the fiscal and administrative jurisdiction of the government and made it the private possession of a hierarchy of owners who shared, according to carefully negotiated schedules, the income it produced.

In discussing the long history of the shōen, most Japanese scholars divide their analysis into a consideration of the early shōen and the mature forms that either grew out of the early shōen or emerged independently from changed conditions of land tenure. This is a useful division because it makes very clear the structural differences between the early and the mature shōen and shows the developmental progression in types of land tenure.

The Early Shōen —— At the time when shōen first began to appear in the mid-8th century, the land allotment system promulgated under the RITSURYŌ SYSTEM had begun to fray at the seams (see HANDEN SHŪJU SYSTEM). Peasants and aristocrats alike were seeking a new and more compatible form of landholding. This search was aided unintentionally by the government's support of land reclamation to encourage the development of new paddy fields. Regulations issued by the government in 723 allowed newly developed fields to be held by the reclaimer for one to three generations as his personal property, though it was subject to rice tax (see SANZE ISSHIN NO HŌ). In 743 this condition was extended to tenure in perpetuity, thus removing the lands from the allotment system (see KONDEN EISEI SHIZAI HŌ). The creation of a new type of permanent tenure in which land was regarded as the reclaimer's personal property opened the way for the development of the landed estate. In fact, the term shō or shōen first referred to the storehouse for tools or the headquarters for a reclamation project, and it was not until the latter half of the 8th century that it was applied to the land itself. Not all early shōen had their origin in reclaimed land; purchase by court nobles or religious institutions of partly or fully productive rice land was another means of acquiring an estate. However, the development of new fields provided the richest source for estates.

Compared to later estates, the early estate was quite simple in both physical and administrative structure. For the most part, the lands granted for reclamation were located within a single district (gun), and, if several parcels were involved, they were in fair proximity to one another. This did not mean that fields brought into production were necessarily contiguous or in one enclosed area similar to a Western farm. Clusters of cultivated fields might be separated by unreclaimed tracts, since the order of reclamation was often dependent on the availability of irrigation and other geographical factors. Nevertheless, the early estate was a relatively compact unit that could be handled by a simple administrative structure.

Early shōen came under the direct control of the proprietor, court noble or religious institution that had supplied the capital for the reclamation project. Agents appointed by the proprietor resided on the estate and oversaw the day-to-day administration of the land and its cultivators. One of the agent's duties was the recruitment of peasants to till the fields, either from among cultivators of nearby public fields or from among peasants who had abandoned their allotment fields and become part of a drifting population. In the former case, the farmers worked estate land in addition to their own plots on an annual rental basis. In the latter case, the drifters often assumed a serf-like status, dependent on the proprietor for housing, tools, and seed. Another duty of the agent was the collection and transport of dues from the cultivators to the proprietor. Dues owed by the peasants included a fixed share of the grain production, a set amount of the special products of the estate, and a reasonable amount of labor at the demand of the proprietor, as well as the cost of transporting the dues to the proprietor's storehouses (see NENGU; KUJI). When the early estate was held by a local magnate, whose family often had ties to the area antedating the TAIKA REFORM of 645, he often resided on the estate and acted as his own manager. Regardless of whether the proprietor was in the capital or a local magnate, he managed the land for his own benefit and under his own administration. Thus, the early estate did not display the complex hierarchy of functions and rights to income that appeared in later estates.

A final feature of the early estate that differentiated it from later models was the ambiguity of its liability for taxation. Most dictionary definitions of shōen list immunity from government taxation as one of its distinguishing characteristics. This immunity was far from complete in the case of early shōen. Early estates gained their tax immunities in a variety of ways, often borrowing or extending exemptions from immune lands already acquired under different circumstances. This was especially true in the case of temples, which often gained tax immunity for their newly acquired estates by having them classified as temple land, a category not liable for grain tax under the provisions of the *ritsuryō* codes. A generally more secure method of gaining and insuring tax immunity was to submit a petition to the central government. When the petition was approved, the estate holder received a charter *(kanshōfu)* issued by the DAJŌ-KAN (Grand Council of State) and the Mimbushō (Ministry of Popular Affairs), which specified the location and area of the estate and the extent of its tax immunity.

An estate established through a government charter was known as a *kanshōfu shō;* the charter became irrefutable evidence in subsequent disputes that the estate had indeed received government sanction. Once a charter had been issued, officials of the estate and the local government surveyed the estate and established boundary markers. Records of the estate's fields and its boundaries were kept on the estate and in government offices. Both lay and religious institutions used this method to gain immunity. It is important to note that for early *shōen*, lands were granted for reclamation *before* they received tax immunity. Estate holders designated their lands and estates before any guarantee of immunity had been received. Tax immunity, then, was not necessarily a defining characteristic of the early estate, although most entities that were called *shōen* by their holders eventually received at least partial exemption from taxation. Those that did not simply failed to survive. It goes without saying that, from the viewpoint of the central government, an estate was liable for taxation regardless of its label or the holder's protestations until it received government documentation for its immunity.

During the 8th and 9th centuries the landed estate was not yet fully established as a distinct institution for the proprietary control of the land. The administration of some estates was similar to that of temple or shrine land *(jiden* or SHINDEN), and what fiscal immunity they had depended squarely upon their classification as religious land. Other early estates, because of their possession of charters, were officially recognized as *shōen* but nevertheless had to struggle constantly against encroachments by local government officials in order to maintain their existence.

The Mature Shōen——From the 10th century, as the central government's interest in the provinces declined, landed estates grew in both size and number. Established estates of court nobles and religious institutions enlarged their holdings by purchase of additional lands, by further reclamation, or by the outright aggrandizement of public fields (KŌDEN). Frequently, immunities were extended to these new holdings by the issuance of exemption certificates by provincial governors or district officials. Perhaps the most widespread means used to expand *shōen*, and the one that was to have the greatest impact on the development of tenurial relationships, was commendation *(kishin)*. This practice led to the formation of the conglomerate or commendation-type estates that flourished in the 12th and 13th centuries and formed the basis for the *shōen* system.

Though commendation was occasionally used by central proprietors, it was most often the local magnate who took this means of protecting his interests in the land. These small local proprietors usually held positions of influence in their areas, since most of them were provincial or district officials of some sort. They used the power and prestige of their offices to extend their landholdings. More important, however, their lands were held as "private lands" *(ryō)* over which they were recognized as proprietors or "lords" (RYŌSHU). This meant that the *ryōshu* possessed all fiscal and administrative power with regard to his land. The *ryōshu* faced recurrent disagreements with provincial authorities, not primarily over tax immunity, as was the case with central proprietors, but over his assertion of fiscal authority over cultivators. Because of the constant threat of provincial interference, the *ryōshu* sought protection for his interests. The most common way of securing protection became the practice of borrowing prestige from court nobles or powerful religious institutions. To do this the *ryōshu* commended his rights of ownership to a powerful figure or institution in the capital in return for political influence in securing protection. The practice of commendation added a new dimension to tenurial relationships and a new complexity to the estate hierarchy.

While in actuality the tenurial hierarchy of the conglomerate estate varied widely depending on the particular circumstances of its formation, location, and the prestige of its proprietors, it is possible to abstract a "typical" estate to serve as a general model. The organization of the conglomerate estate can be viewed as a pyramid with the cultivators *(shōmin)* at the base. Next came the resident managers, called variously SHŌKAN, *shōke*, *azukari-dokoro*, or *ryō-*

shu. Above the resident managers were the central proprietors or *ryōke* (see HONKE AND RYŌKE). At the peak of the hierarchy was the guarantor or *honke*. The key figure in the practice of commendation was the *ryōshu*, for he was the local magnate who generally took the initiative in commending his holdings to a central proprietor. In turning over title to his lands to the *ryōke*, he actually gave up very little in terms of income, though he relinquished the title of "lord" to the central proprietor. It became customary for the *ryōshu* to be appointed as manager under the terms of the commendation agreement, thus leaving much of the local administration in his hands. This document also specified his rights to income from the estate. The *ryōke*'s chief function was to act as legal protector for the estate, using his influence to maintain tax immunities and to intervene with government authorities when the necessity arose. In return, the *ryōke* received a specified share of income from the estate. If the *ryōke* felt additional weight or prestige was needed to further the interests of the estate, he could secure an even more influential court noble or religious institution to act as *honke* or guarantor. The *ryōke* commended a portion of his income share to the *honke*, who in return acted mainly to lend prestige to an estate's claim and generally took little interest in its administration.

Matters regarding the transmission, receipt, and distribution of income from the estate were handled by the *shōkan*'s administrative office, which communicated directly with the managerial office of the estate *(honjo)*. When the *honjo* was located on the estate, the original *ryōshu* or his descendants, as *shōkan*, were responsible for the day-to-day affairs of the estate. These included assignment of fields to cultivators, distribution of seed and implements, regulation of water supply, collection of revenues, and, if full immunity had been obtained, administration of justice. As one of the chief officials of the *honjo* of the estate, the *shōkan* was responsible for forwarding revenues to superior proprietors.

When the *honjo* of the estate was in the capital, the *shōkan* acted as agent of the absentee proprietor, working primarily as an overseer rather than as an administrator. In some cases, special agents were dispatched from the capital to serve as officials of the estate.

Although the basic hierarchy of estate land rights took the form of the *shōmin-shōkan-ryōke-honke* pyramid, there was room for a good deal of variation and flexibility within that form. Above all, it was possible for changes to take place at one level with little effect on the other levels. For example, a change in the *honke* or *ryōke* would scarcely be noticed in the day-to-day operations of the estate. The reason for this was that the estate system, as a means of economic profit from the land, was based not on direct proprietary control of land but rather on income from land. Total income, as defined by the goods and services provided by the cultivators, was conceived of as subject to allotment or sharing, according to the relationship of each level in the estate tenure hierarchy. These shares were defined for each estate in terms of *shiki*, which specified the share or amount of revenue due each rank in the estate hierarchy. There were, in other words, *shōmin shiki, shōkan shiki, ryōke shiki*, and so forth. Since *shiki* were alienable and divisible, it was possible for the income of the estate to be widely distributed. *Shiki* could change hands through sale, inheritance, or donation without disturbing the function of the estate as an economic unit. For the *shiki* holder, it was possible to receive income from a number of estates. As *shiki* gradually became divorced from the specific tenure function to which they were originally attached, one could hold variously a *shōkan shiki* in one estate, *ryōke shiki* in another, part of a *shōmin shiki* in a third, and so on in any imaginable combination.

In addition to accumulating numerous *shiki* in different *shōen*, from the mid-11th century central proprietors began to create conglomerates of estate holdings. Court nobles, the imperial family, and religious institutions grouped *shōen*, often from widely scattered provinces, together into portfolios and assigned the portfolios to family chapels, temples, or the like, as *ryōke* or *honke*. These portfolios then became one of the mainstays of the lineage's hereditary property. For example, the retired emperor GO-SHIRAKAWA (1127–92; r 1155–58) established a temple, the Chōkōdō, as *ryōke* for a portfolio consisting of almost 90 different proprietorships in 42 provinces. These estates supplied a wide variety of goods and services to the senior branch of the imperial family well into the 15th century (see CHŌKŌDŌ RYŌ).

While such changes were occurring at the top of the *shōen* hierarchy, important shifts were taking place in the cultivators' tenures as well. Some tenures had become sufficiently secure over the years so that the cultivators were viewed as having private tenurial rights in the land, and their names were attached to the plots. The cultivator became known as a MYŌSHU, or holder of "name land" (myō-den). By the late 11th century, myōden had become the basic unit of landholding in both shōen and public land. The myōshu was recognized as the person responsible for dues and labor services from his plots whether he farmed them himself or levied taxes on the cultivators working under him. He had, in effect, become a small-scale proprietor who exercised managerial rights over his own fields within the context of the shōen.

The estate's flexibility extended to the local level in other ways as well. It was able to absorb changes in the types of cultivators' tenures and changes in administration by the shōkan without altering the amount of income due the central proprietor. Thus, the tendency was for higher proprietors to take little interest in how their estates were administered at the lower levels, as long as they received the agreed-upon income. At the other end, the cultivators and the shōkan cared little who the higher proprietors were, as long as they provided legal protection and did not make excessive demands for income.

As the estate system matured in the 11th and 12th centuries, the critical feature that distinguished such holdings from publicly administered land (kokugaryō or kōryō) became the possession of complete immunity from taxation and from entry by government officials. The winning and protection of such immunities had been one of the main incentives for the small local ryōshu to commend their land to higher authority. The tax immunities gained at first applied only to those fields listed as cultivated in the charter and could not be extended to newly reclaimed fields within the estate's borders. To gain immunity for new fields inside or outside the boundaries of the estate required further petition by the ryōke to the central government. As time passed, new fields within the estate could have their immunity approved by provincial or even district officials. Immunities obtained in this way were only slightly less secure than those from the central government. The ryōke's role, therefore, did not end with the estate's initial receipt of immunities, for conflict between estate administrators and officials of the provincial government was pandemic. It was frequently necessary for the ryōke to intervene at court on behalf of the estate.

A shōen's immunity was not complete, therefore, until it was free from entry by government officials. Such freedom was acquired slowly and was not widespread until the middle of the 11th century. Security from entry applied at first only to government surveyors and tax collectors, but it was later extended to the police (see FUYU AND FUNYŪ). When this happened, the administrators of the estates had gained full power of jurisdiction over both land and cultivators (ICHIEN CHIGYŌ). They had become the true successors to provincial government in the territories that comprised their estates.

As shōen proprietors expanded their holdings in the 11th and 12th centuries, often at the expense of public lands, the imperial government made continuing efforts to put limits on this growth. Periodically, from as early as 902, emperors issued shōen limitation edicts. The most effective of these came from the era of the government of the retired emperors (INSEI, 1087–1192), a time of particularly rapid shōen expansion. The aim of these edicts was not so much to abolish all shōen as to weed out those holdings with improper charters and immunities. Edicts issued by the retired emperors were administered by the Shōen Records Office (KIROKU SHŌEN KENKEIJO), which confiscated the lands of some proprietors and reduced the immunities of others. But, although there was an imperial concern for keeping the estate holdings and the political influence of their proprietors to a certain desirable maximum, shōen nevertheless were seen as a legitimate and profitable kind of landholding. In fact, imperial shōen increased noticeably from the time of the retired emperors and provided a substantial portion of the imperial lineage's income.

Shōen and the Kamakura Shogunate—— With the establishment of the Kamakura shogunate (1192–1333) and the creation by MINAMOTO NO YORITOMO of the offices of SHUGO (military governor) and JITŌ (military estate steward), a new layer of tenurial rights was introduced into the shōen hierarchy. The insertion of jitō into the shōen would ultimately cause profound change in the allocation of income from the estates and in the locus of administrative functions. Appointment of jitō by the Kamakura shogunate marked the beginning of a long process that resulted in the diminution of the rights of the central proprietor and the growth of the warriors' authority over the land, its revenues, and inhabitants. And, by the 13th century, it is possible to identify some jitō who had acquired full proprietary rights to shōen lands. This process was most pronounced in the Kantō region and developed later in areas where the imperial court and central religious institutions had traditionally strong ties to land.

When Yoritomo first asserted his right to appoint jitō in 1185, the office was envisioned as one to aid the central proprietors, ensuring the collection of rents and allocation of services and their transmission to the central proprietors. The office of jitō was inserted into the shōen hierarchy at the shōkan level. In the early years of the shogunate, and especially for the Kantō area, the appointment of a Minamoto follower as jitō was often the reconfirmation of a position already held by the warrior within the shōen. As the office was extended to other areas of Japan, particularly after the JŌKYŪ DISTURBANCE of 1221, it was generally a new office imposed upon the shōen management. Although the jitō's main duties were to maintain the flow of income and services to the central proprietors and to keep the peace, as he established himself upon the land, he sought to extend his authority. This was usually at the expense of the managers appointed by the central proprietors.

In theory, the jitō was entitled to the income produced by one-eleventh of the land over which he had jurisdiction. In addition, he could levy a modest military surcharge (HYŌRŌMAI) based on cultivated area (5 shō of rice per tan of land; 1 shō=1.8 liters or 1.6 quarts, 1 tan=0.12 hectare or 0.25 acre), receive a share of income from legal cases, and take a portion of the produce from the mountains and streams. Altogether, this could amount to a sizable share of the total income of the shōen. In the early years of the shogunate, the military government was scrupulous in guarding the rights of the central proprietors, placing limits on the amounts and kinds of income the jitō could extract and upon his authority over the land and its inhabitants. As time went on, however, the jitō, using his military power, extended his fiscal and administrative authority over the shōen, often taking control out of the hands of the centrally appointed shōkan. This led to numerous disputes between the jitō and the central proprietors, particularly over revenues from the estate. At first the proprietors looked to Kamakura for judicial remedies, but since the settlements increasingly tended to favor jitō, or if they did not were often ignored by the jitō, the proprietors turned to out-of-court negotiations with the jitō. These settlements assumed various forms. The most important was known as SHITAJI CHŪBUN. This involved the physical division of the shōen lands into a part over which the jitō would have full authority and derive revenue, and a part under the control of the central proprietor. By the end of the Kamakura period the most common division was on a fifty-fifty basis, a major gain for the jitō from his original one-eleventh. Another method, and one that often represented an extension of the jitō's control after shitaji chūbun, is ukesho or jitō uke. In this instance, the jitō contracted with the central proprietor to send a fixed amount of revenue and services to the proprietor annually. In effect this put control of the estate into the hands of the jitō and moved him one step closer to being an autonomous local proprietor.

By the Kamakura period it is also possible to make a more accurate appraisal of how income from the estate was distributed among the many holders who had interests in the estate. Documents indicate that the tax or dues collection system had developed customary procedures complete with multicopy receipts, verification of transmission of taxes, and other paperwork. Income was derived from shōen in one of two ways. First, for officials of the shōen there was a small amount of demesne from which they received a direct yield. The major portion of the income derived from the rent and service payments from the myōden, assessed on a volume-per-area basis, the collection of which was the responsibility of the myōshu. Although local custom and the great variety of shiki agreements made for considerable diversity among shōen, it is possible to put forth a general estimate of how income from an estate was distributed among the various levels of the hierarchy. At the top of the hierarchy, the ryōke and the high-level managers took between 25 and 35 percent of the yield. Lesser officials of the estate claimed 7 to 10 percent. The remaining 55 to 68 percent stayed in the hands of the myōshu and the other cultivators. While these demands on the cultivators do not seem excessive, it must be remembered that tenant-cultivators also had to pay rent to the myōshu and were liable for payments for local products and for labor and military service duties. The demands of the ryōke and the myōshu combined often came close to 60 percent of the total yield. For the proprietors, the goods and services rendered in addition to the grain tax often proved to be the most valuable part of their holding.

Local control of the shōen had grown constantly throughout the Kamakura period. Complaints from central proprietors about not receiving income from their estates increased in both volume and rancor as the period progressed. They proliferated during the MON-GOL INVASIONS OF JAPAN (1274–1281), when the fighting made it possible for the military managers to justify keeping all of the revenue from the *shōen* for military expenses. This highlights the disagreement between the central proprietors and the *shugo* and *jitō* over whose services were the more valuable to the *shōen*.

Under the Muromachi shogunate (1338–1573), the balance between the civil and military authority that had prevailed during the Kamakura period shifted heavily toward the military. The civil government still existed in Kyōto, but actual governing authority extended from the shogunate directly to the *shugo* and *jitō* in the provinces. The old provincial governors were replaced almost entirely by the *shugo*, who functioned as both civil and military authorities. Thus, local administration was in the hands of the military governors and their followers. The basis for the administration of land law and management, however, remained the *shōen* system. Nevertheless, with local authority held by military administrators, the central proprietors were more or less at the mercy of the *jitō* and *shugo* for whatever income they wanted to send. At the shogunate level, the *shōgun*'s council was now the chief court in the land, and, as might be expected, decisions in disputes between court nobles and local military men consistently favored the latter.

This led the central proprietors to seek other ways to retain income from their estates. Some, especially those of lower rank, actually removed themselves to the countryside in an attempt to take over their proprietorships directly. Those who succeeded were soon virtually indistinguishable from the provincial military class (KOKU-JIN). Others, reluctant to leave the capital, acceded to the practice of HANZEI or half-rights. This had been made legal by the shogunate after the KEMMU RESTORATION (1333–36) to deal with rising military costs. Under this scheme, the *shugo* could hold back one-half of *shōen* proceeds due the central proprietor. This was not a division of proprietary rights as was *shitaji chūbun*, but it did eventually result in a physical division of the land base. In theory, estates of the imperial family, the main lineage of the FUJIWARA FAMILY, and the primary holdings of the great temples were exempted, but it was not long before many of these were made subject to *hanzei*. The *shugo*, not the *jitō*, had the responsiblilty for enforcing *hanzei*. This gave the military governors entrée into and fiscal rights in nonmilitary *shōen*. Moreover, they soon began to act as tax collectors for the proprietor's remaining half of the estate, just as the *jitō* had done earlier. To carry out tax collection under *shugo uke*, it was necessary to appoint agents to manage the estates. Thus, by the late 14th century, the central proprietors had lost most of their control and their income from the estates. If an estate had undergone *shitaji chūbun* with *jitō* in the Kamakura period, *hanzei* further reduced the income so that the proprietor received only one-fourth of his original share. With *shugo uke*, management was entirely in the hands of local military leaders. After the ŌNIN WAR (1467–77), both the shogunate and the *shugo* were greatly weakened, and control of the land and its inhabitants fell increasingly to local military leaders (SENGOKU DAIMYŌ). As political decentralization grew, many *shōen* disappeared, with new physical and political boundaries springing up to coincide more closely with the local military lord's scope of power. Those *shōen* that did survive into the 16th century were primarily those of great religious institutions, which could call not only on religious sanctions to protect their holdings, but also on sizable bands of WARRIOR-MONKS (*sōhei*), which made the temples local military powers.

🕮 —— Abe Takeshi, *Nihon shōen shi* (1972). Asakawa Kan'ichi, *Documents of Iriki* (1929). Asakawa Kan'ichi, *Land and Society in Medieval Japan* (1965). John Whitney Hall, *Government and Politics in Japan, 500 to 1700* (1966). John W. Hall and Jeffrey P. Mass, ed, *Medieval Japan: Essays in Institutional History* (1974). G. Cameron Hurst, *Insei: Abdicated Sovereigns in the Politics of Late Heian Japan* (1976). Inagaki Yasuhiko, ed, *Shōen no sekai* (1973). Kuroda Toshio, *Shōensei shakai* (1967). Jeffrey P. Mass, *Warrior Government in Early Medieval Japan* (1974). Nagahara Keiji et al, ed, *Chūsei shi handobukku* (1973). Elizabeth Sato, "Ōyama Estate and Insei Land Policies," *Monumenta Nipponica* 34.1 (1979). Yasuda Motohisa, *Shōen shi gaisetsu* (1957). Elizabeth S. SATŌ

Shōgakukan Publishing Co, Ltd

(Kabushiki-Gaisha Shōgakukan). One of Japan's major publishing houses, established in 1922 by Ōga Takeo. The company at first limited production to juvenile and educational publications and became known for its publication of magazines aimed at specific pri-

mary school grade levels. With the postwar rise in the birth rate and the subsequent changes in educational programs, the company expanded into a general publishing house and now publishes encyclopedias, collected works, dictionaries, and the *Nihon kokugo daijiten* (Dictionary of the Japanese Language). KOBAYASHI Kazuhiro

Shōgawa

River in Gifu and Toyama prefectures, central Honshū; originating in Eboshidake, a peak in the Hida Mountains, and flowing north into Toyama Bay. The villages of SHIRAKAWA and GOKAYAMA, located along the river, are noted for their houses with steeply pitched roofs in the style known as *gasshō-zukuri* (see MINKA). The water is utilized for electric power and for irrigating the Tonami Plain. Length: 133 km (82.6 mi); area of drainage basin; 1,180 sq km (455 sq mi).

shōgi

A board game involving two players and 40 pieces; commonly referred to in the West as "Japanese chess." The object of the game is to checkmate the opponent's king. There are many similarities to chess in the way the pieces move, but what is decidedly different is that a captured piece can be used again as one's own piece. There are said to be about 20 million *shōgi* players in Japan, or one person out of every six.

Origin and History —— The prototype of *shōgi* is believed to have originated in India, like that of Western chess. When it was transmitted to China, it became known as *xiang qi* (*hsiang-ch'i*; Japanese pronunciation *shōgi*). *Shōgi* may have been introduced to Japan in the Nara period (710–794) by Japanese envoys who were sent to Tang (T'ang; 618–907) China. It is unclear how the game was played in those days, but in the Heian period (794–1185) there were several forms popular among the noble classes. There were *shōshōgi*, *chūshōgi*, and *daishōgi* ("small," "medium," and "large" *shōgi*, respectively), which had boards of different sizes and varying numbers of pieces. There were also *daidai shōgi* ("larger" *shōgi*) and *makadaidai shōgi* ("great larger" *shōgi*). In the Muromachi period (1333–1568) the *hisha* (rook) and *kaku* (bishop) were adopted into *shōshōgi* from *chūshōgi*, and the rules were modified to allow utilization of captured enemy pieces, which up to that time were discarded. The result was a game very much like present-day *shōgi*.

In 1607 the Tokugawa shogunate established an office for *shōgi* and GO under the jurisdiction of the commissioner of shrines and temples; a monk named Hon'imbō Sansa (1558–1623) was made its head. Later the office was turned over to Ōhashi Sōkei (1555–1634), who was installed as its first lifetime *meijin* ("master"). The person chosen to head the *shōgi* office was given an annual stipend. This can be regarded as the beginning of professional *shōgi* in Japan. Every year a match called the *oshiro shōgi* took place in the shōgun's presence. During this time ranks up to the *meijin* were decided, and Sōkei's son Sōko (1613–60) standardized the game and committed to writing the prohibited moves and the rules that are in use today. The *meijin* rank was inherited within a *shōgi* "family"; a *meijin* remained one for life, with no alteration of status, despite any change in his actual ability. Following the Meiji Restoration (1868), there was a period of disarray, but in 1924 the Tōkyō Shōgi Remmei was founded. This was reorganized as the Shōgi Taiseikai in 1936. The present-day Nihon Shōgi Remmei (Japan Shōgi Federation) was founded in 1947. In 1935, at the suggestion of the 13th-generation *meijin* Sekine Kinjirō (1868–1946), the lifetime *meijin* system was abolished and annual contests for the title of *meijin* were begun. Kimura Yoshio (b 1905) was the first to win the title; he was followed by Ōyama Yasuharu (b 1923) and Nakahara Makoto (b 1948), the 16th and present *meijin*. Those who have won the rank of *meijin* more than five times are permitted to take the name of "permanent *meijin*" (*eisei meijin*).

The Japan Shōgi Federation —— The Japan Shōgi Federation is a corporation whose members are active professionals of the fourth rank and above (over 100 persons) and retired players. The federation pays professionals a monthly salary plus a fee for playing a game and decides on promotions. *Shōgi* players are ranked at nine levels (*dan*); below these are a number of classes (*kyū*). The federation sponsors title matches such as the *ōshō-sen*, *kisei-sen*, *jūdansen*, *ōi-sen*, and the *meijin-sen* (*sen* means tournament), in contract with individual newspapers. Some tournaments such as the NHK Cup and the "Quick Shōgi Tournament" are televised. The federation also issues licenses, trains new professionals, and publishes the monthly magazines *Shōgi sekai* (Shōgi World), which has a circula-

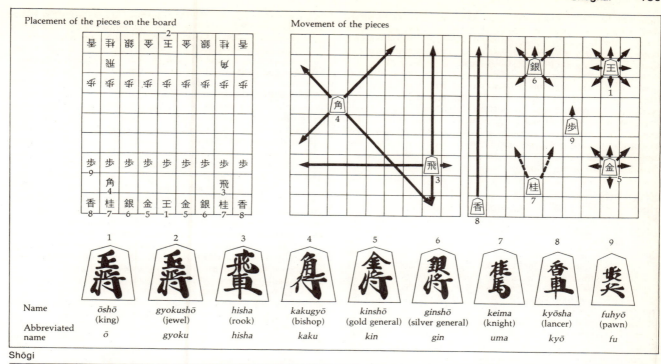

Placement of the pieces on the board

Movement of the pieces

	1	2	3	4	5	6	7	8	9
Name	ōshō (king)	gyokushō (jewel)	hisha (rook)	kakugyō (bishop)	kinshō (gold general)	ginshō (silver general)	keima (knight)	kyōsha (lancer)	fuhyō (pawn)
Abbreviated name	ō	gyoku	hisha	kaku	kin	gin	uma	kyō	fu

Shōgi

Although similar to chess in pieces, moves, and object of the game, *shōgi* differs in that captured pieces can be reentered into the game on the captor's side. The object, as in chess, is to checkmate the opponent's king, but the piece corresponding to the king is named *ōshō* (king) for one player and *gyokushō* (jewel) for the other. Abbreviated names (consisting of the first character of the two-character name) are used here to show placement and moves.

tion of 120,000, and *Shōgi Magajin* (Shōgi Magazine), with a circulation of 40,000.

Professional players sanction the promotion of amateurs, and the Japan Shōgi Federation approves and issues licenses to amateurs up to the sixth *dan;* there is no demotion in rank. Sometimes a handicap system during tournaments requires the higher-ranked player to remove some of his pieces from the board so the two can compete on roughly equal terms. Every year representatives from each prefecture compete in an amateur contest for the title of *meijin.* Competitions at places of employment are very popular; in 1978 there were 670 teams comprising 3,050 members. There are also matches on the primary school, middle school, high school, and college levels. The Japan Shōgi Federation has 568 chapters (including overseas branches) and a membership of about 20,000.

The Game —— The *shōgi* board is a square wooden block with a grid of 81 squares. Each player uses 20 flat wooden pieces of an elongated irregular pentagon shape: the pieces are placed on the grid with their apex pointing toward the opponent. The pieces are distinguished by characters written on each side. Captured pieces are placed to the player's right.

The *ōshō* (king; *ō* for short) and *gyokushō* (jewel; *gyoku* for short) are in essence the same piece, i.e., a king. Making one king a "jewel" (by adding one stroke to the character for "king") avoided having two kings on the same board, a custom that supposedly originated on the request of an emperor in ancient times. The better player has the king and the other player has the jewel. The *ōshō* or *gyokushō* can move one square in any direction, like a king in chess.

The *hisha* (abbreviated only in writing, as *hi*) resembles a rook and can move any distance horizontally or vertically. The *kakugyō* (*kaku* for short) moves any distance along the diagonals, like a bishop. The *kinshō* (*kin* for short) moves one square in any direction except diagonally backward. The *ginshō* (*gin* for short) moves one square in any direction except sideways or backward.

The *keima* (*kei* for short) can only move forward, and only to either of the two squares to the right or left of the square two spaces in front. Although the *kei* moves like a knight in Western chess, in contrast to a knight, which has eight squares available to it, the *kei* is limited to the two squares just mentioned. The *kei* is the only piece that can jump over other pieces.

The *kyōsha* (*kyō* for short) may advance to any square ahead of it; it cannot retreat. The *fuhyō* (*fu* for short) corresponds to the pawn in chess and advances straight ahead one square at a time.

The above pieces can take enemy pieces that are in range of their movements. The two aspects of *shōgi* that distinguish it from chess are *haru,* the use of captured pieces, and *naru,* the promotion of one's own pieces. A player may take a turn to place a captured piece on an open square. In order to promote a piece, one must move into the enemy territory: the first three ranks on one's own side are considered one's own territory. All the pieces except the *ō* or *gyoku* and *kin* can be promoted after penetrating enemy territory. The piece is turned over to show its new name. The *hisha* becomes a *ryūō* (*ryū* for short), which has the combined powers of a rook and king. The *kaku* becomes a *ryūma* (*uma* for short), which has the combined powers of a bishop and king. The *ginshō* becomes the *narigin,* which has the same powers as the *kin.* The *kei, kyō,* and *fu* can all be promoted to the powers of a *kin.* Their names after promotion are, respectively, *narikei, narikyō,* and *tokin.* To promote or not to promote is a matter of choice. There are positive aspects to using a *kei* or *gin* without promotion but in general it is better to promote. A promoted piece returns to its original status when captured.

To begin play, the board is placed between two players and the pieces are lined up as in the diagram. Players alternate, moving one piece at a time. There are three important restrictions: one cannot reenter a *fu* on a file in which there is already a friendly *fu,* one cannot reenter a piece where there is no room for its next move, and one cannot checkmate the enemy *gyoku* by reentry of a *fu.* It is permissible to checkmate using a *fu* on the board. One forfeits immediately upon violation of any of the above three rules. In the case of a stalemate, the game must be played over. When both players' kings enter enemy territory and neither player can check the other, victory is determined by the number of pieces left.

——Trevor Leggett, *Shōgi: Japan's Game of Strategy* (1966).

SAKAGUCHI Nobuhiko

Shōgitai

A military unit formed in Edo (now Tōkyō) by former retainers of the Tokugawa shogunate (1603–1867) to resist the Imperial Restoration (ŌSEI FUKKŌ) of January 1868. The unit was organized in March 1868 by Shibusawa Kisaku (1838–1912), who later left to form another group, the Shimbugun, and Amano Hachirō (1831–68); headquarters were established at Kan'eiji, a temple in the Ueno district. The group, some 2,000 strong, acted as police for the city, which was in confusion because of the impending attack by imperial forces, and as self-appointed protectors of the deposed shōgun, TOKUGAWA YOSHINOBU. Even after the city had been formally surrendered to imperial forces in April, the Shōgitai maintained resistance, but were finally defeated in the Battle of Ueno on 4 July 1868 (Keiō 4.5.15). Survivors escaped to northern Japan, and several participated in the Battle of GORYŌKAKU (1869), the last of the series of armed conflicts between imperial troops and Tokugawa diehards. See also BOSHIN CIVIL WAR.

Shōgoin

Head temple of the Honzan Shugenshū sect, located in Sakyō Ward, Kyōto. The Shōgoin, originally named Jōkōin, was built by the eminent Tendai monk ENCHIN (814–891) and reestablished in 1090 under its present name by Zōyo (1032–1116), a powerful monk from the temple Onjōji (MIIDERA). It has been the custom since the end of the 12th century to appoint only tonsured members of the imperial family to the abbacy (i.e., the temple was a *monzekidera*). The abbot also exercised jurisdiction simultaneously over the other temples belonging to the Jimon branch (i.e., the Miidera line) of the Tendai sect, as well as over the three Kumano shrines (KUMANO SANZAN SHRINES). In 1613 Shōgoin was designated the head temple for the Tendai line of SHUGENDŌ (Honzanha Shugendō), a Buddhist-Shintō syncretic mountain cult, and given control over the YAMABUSHI (mountain ascetics). Shōgoin was moved from the Karasuma Kamitachiuri section in Kyōto to its present site in 1676, one year after a disastrous fire had destroyed most of the temple complex. In 1946 Shōgoin became an independent religious organization; in 1979 it claimed about 73,000 followers. *Stanley* WEINSTEIN

shōgun

An abbreviation of *seii tai shōgun*, which is customarily translated as "barbarian-subduing generalissimo." Shōguns were in theory military dictators whose regimes dominated the Japanese polity for most of Japanese history between 1192 and 1867. Their regimes were known as *bakufu* or "tent governments," a term commonly translated as SHOGUNATE. There were three shogunates, the first (1192–1333) situated in Kamakura, the second (1338–1573) in the Muromachi district of Kyōto, and the third (1603–1867) in Edo (now Tōkyō).

During the Kamakura period the shogunal title was transmitted irregularly, but in the Muromachi period it was in the sole possession of the Ashikaga family, and during the Edo period, of the Tokugawa. Formally each shōgun was appointed by the emperor and was responsible for keeping the peace of the realm. In fact emperors were nearly powerless and approved shogunal appointments as instructed by the military figures who dominated affairs. Each shōgun headed an administrative organization that governed his direct vassals and his own domain while maintaining some degree of control over the domains controlled by other military families and by major Buddhist temples and Shintō shrines.

The title *seii tai shōgun* derived from an ancient set of titles bestowed on government officials who led expeditions against insurgents or indigenous tribal groups on the periphery of the realm. Most notably, the imperial government during the Nara period (710–794) ordered several officials in succession to lead forces against tribal groups known as EZO or Emishi, who occupied northeastern Honshū. These officials were given titles such as *chintō shōgun* ("east-pacifying general"), *chinteki shōgun* ("barbarian-pacifying general"), *seii shōgun* ("barbarian-subduing general"), and eventually *seii tai shōgun*. The most famous of these generals was SAKANOUE NO TAMURAMARO, who was commissioned to pacify the northeast in 791 and designated *seii tai shōgun* in 797.

The Kamakura Shōguns —— The borders subsequently became quiet, and the shogunal title fell into disuse. It was resurrected four centuries later during the TAIRA–MINAMOTO WAR, when the brilliant and ambitious warrior leader MINAMOTO NO YOSHINAKA drove the Taira leaders out of Kyōto and appropriated for himself the title *seii tai shōgun*. After Yoshinaka's death, his cousin MINAMOTO NO YORITOMO triumphed in the civil wars and established his military headquarters in Kamakura. In 1192 the emperor designated Yoritomo shōgun, giving him standing authority to undertake military action against anyone who might challenge his regime. The

title was only one of several that cumulatively gave Yoritomo effective and legitimate control over his own domains and vassals and the right to appoint supervisory officials (JITŌ and SHUGO) over much of the rest of the country.

Yoritomo's sons proved unable to dominate their powerful vassals the HŌJŌ FAMILY. The Hōjō seized power and, after the Minamoto line died out, settled on the practice of selecting malleable aristocrats from the Kyōto nobility who would go to Kamakura and receive the title of shōgun. By the time the Hōjō regents fell victim to rebellion in 1333 (see KEMMU RESTORATION), they had established the principle that the shogunal title would be held only by a man who nominally headed a shogunate (*bakufu*), a ruling military regime sanctioned by the imperial court. See also KAMAKURA SHOGUNATE.

The Ashikaga Shōguns —— The military leader ASHIKAGA TAKAUJI participated in the destruction of the Hōjō regime in 1333. Two years later he led his army east from Kyōto to suppress other insurgents, holding the title of *seitō shōgun* ("east-subduing general") for the occasion. In 1336 he overcame his rivals and upon establishing his own *bakufu* in Kyōto, claimed for himself the title of *seii tai shōgun* in 1338 on the grounds of his Minamoto ancestry. For the next 30 years Takauji and his son were continually at war fending off rivals. By the 1370s his grandson ASHIKAGA YOSHIMITSU was able to govern by maintaining a standing alliance with a few powerful regional warlords (SHUGO DAIMYŌ). During the next century he and his successors engaged in constant political maneuvering in attempts to consolidate their control over the country.

During the century after the ŌNIN WAR (1467–77), however, the shogunal position weakened as regional warriors (SENGOKU DAIMYŌ) came to control more and more of the country. In 1493 the shōgun Ashikaga Yoshitane (1466–1523) departed from Kyōto to suppress a rebellious warlord, and during his absence another warlord set up a new shōgun in his stead. In 1508 Yoshitane was able to return and oust his rival, only to flee the city again in 1521 and die in exile two years later. Finally in 1573 the 15th Ashikaga shōgun, ASHIKAGA YOSHIAKI, made the mistake of scheming against the hegemon ODA NOBUNAGA, who had installed him as shōgun five years earlier. He was driven out of Kyōto by Nobunaga, and the Ashikaga shogunate ceased to exist. See also MUROMACHI SHOGUNATE.

Neither Nobunaga nor his successor, the national unifier TOYOTOMI HIDEYOSHI, ever sought the title of shōgun or established a *bakufu*. Despite the enormous power they wielded, they seem to have accepted the tradition that the title was reserved for men of Minamoto descent, which neither of them could claim.

The Tokugawa Shōguns —— The period of civil war among regional warlords (DAIMYŌ) culminated in 1600 with a major battle at SEKIGAHARA. The leader of the triumphant army, TOKUGAWA IEYASU, was able to trace a tenuous link to Minamoto ancestors, and in 1603 he accepted the title of shōgun from the court. He also accepted other titles that had come to be associated with the title of shōgun from the time of Ashikaga Yoshimitsu, most notably that of *Genji no chōja* or chief of the Minamoto (see MINAMOTO FAMILY).

During the next century and a half his successors were able to retain governing power in their own hands by manipulating and balancing both their own vassals and the regional daimyō. However, the elaborate institutional structure, detailed regulations, and complex balancing mechanisms that held these groups in check also gradually deprived the shōguns of political flexibility. During the last century of Tokugawa rule the "barbarian-subduing generalissimo" was a nearly powerless figure in a political system whose survival rested in large part on the balance among the interest groups who participated in the governing process. See also TOKUGAWA SHOGUNATE.

In fine, then, most *seii tai shōgun* were rather less than military dictators. Of 9 Kamakura shōguns, apart from Yoritomo all were figureheads. Of 15 Ashikaga shōguns, none dominated the country, only 4 or 5 dominated all or part of central Japan, and the others were hard pressed merely to preserve their very limited patrimony. And of 15 Tokugawa shōguns, 5 or 6 were able to dominate the country while the others were more or less figureheads dominated by their own advisory officials and the governing system they maintained. See also WARRIOR GOVERNMENT. *Conrad* TOTMAN

shogunate

(*bakufu*; literally, "tent government"). Any of the three military governments that ruled Japan during most of the period from 1192 to 1867, as opposed to the civil government under the emperor at Kyōto. In ancient Chinese writings the word that is pronounced

Shogunate missions to the West

	Representatives	Countries visited	Purpose and accomplishment
13 February 1860– 9 November 1860	Shimmi Masaoki (head minister) Muragaki Norimasa (vice minister)	United States	Ratification of the Harris Treaty of 1858 (23 May 1860).
21 January 1862– 28 January 1863	Takenouchi Yasunori (head minister) Matsudaira Yasunao (vice minister)	Britain, France, Holland, Prussia, Russia, Portugal	Delay of the opening of the ports of Niigata and Hyōgo and the cities of Edo and Ōsaka. Agreement with Britain signed on 6 June 1862; agreement with Russia signed on 12 September 1862.
6 February 1864– 19 August 1864	Ikeda Nagaoki (head minister) Kawazu Sukekuni (vice minister)	France	Attempted to negotiate closing of Yokohama; rebuffed by the French. Conciliatory agreement signed in Paris on 20 June 1864, abrogated by the shogunate two months later.
27 June 1865– 12 March 1866	Shibata Takenaka	France	Purchase of machinery and arrangements for technical and military instructors to visit Japan.
18 November 1866– 10 June 1867	Koide Hidezane Ishikawa Toshimasa	Russia	Attempt to deal with friction between Japanese and Russians in Sakhalin.
15 February 1867– 16 December 1868	Tokugawa Akitake (bakufu representative) Mukōyama Ichiri (minister to France)	France	Attended Paris International Exposition.

bakufu in Japanese (Ch: *mufu*) referred to the field headquarters of a general on campaign. The Japanese in turn used it to refer to the Headquarters of the Inner Palace Guards (Konoefu), to the residence of the commander of the inner palace guards, or to the commander himself *(konoe no taishō)*. Thus, when MINAMOTO NO YORITOMO was appointed commander of the inner palace guards of the right *(ukonoe no taishō)* in 1190, his residence was called the *bakufu;* and after he was named SHŌGUN in 1192, the same term was applied both to Yoritomo and to the headquarters of the military government he established. In modern times the term *bakufu* and its English translation have been used by historians to designate the type of power structure presided over by a shōgun, specifically the KAMAKURA SHOGUNATE (1192–1333), the MUROMACHI SHOGUNATE (1338–1573), and the TOKUGAWA SHOGUNATE (1603–1867).

YASUDA Motohisa

shogunate missions to the West

(bakufu kengai shisetsu). Official missions sent to Western nations by the Tokugawa shogunate shortly before its collapse at the time of the MEIJI RESTORATION of 1868. There were altogether six missions, although the number would be higher if several minor missions were included, such as the one led by Ono Tomogorō (1867) to purchase warships and arms in the United States or the mission in the same year led by KURIMOTO JOUN to negotiate a loan from the French government and to settle problems over the Satsuma domain's (now Kagoshima Prefecture) decision to participate in the Paris International Exposition. One must also bear in mind that missions, both official and secret, were dispatched by the shogunate and several domainal governments.

One can distinguish two types of mission; the first includes the missions in 1860, 1862, 1864, and 1866, which were sent to negotiate problems connected with the ANSEI COMMERCIAL TREATIES of 1858. The second includes the missions of 1865 and 1867, which were sent primarily to obtain technological knowledge. The differences in these missions reflect both domestic changes and those taking place in Japan's relations with the outside world. In particular, the missions sent after 1864 reflect the disintegration of the traditional *shōgun–daimyō* BAKUHAN SYSTEM and the ensuing political flux. For example, the 1864 mission to negotiate the closing of the port of Yokohama, which had been opened in 1859 under the provisions of the Ansei treaties, was not only rebuffed by the French government but also resulted in Japan's agreement to pay reparations for damage to the French fleet during the SHIMONOSEKI BOMBARDMENT. The Japanese envoys furthermore, agreed to open the Shimonoseki Strait to navigation and to lower tariffs on imported goods. The decision of the chief ambassador IKEDA NAGAOKI to agree to such conditions no doubt reflected his own realistic assessment of the situation: that it was urgent to unify national policy and to build up economic and

military strength, and that this could be achieved only by opening Japan. The shogunate, however, was preoccupied with its own domestic problems, not the least of which was mollifying the imperial court and its supporters. It therefore punished Ikeda and notified the Western powers of its refusal to abide by these agreements.

In contrast, the missions of 1865 and 1867 demonstrate the shogunate's attempts to resolve the contradictions in its internal and foreign policies. They also reflect the influence of Léon ROCHES, the newly arrived French minister. The 1865 mission to France can be seen as an assertive and practical move, while the 1867 mission to the Paris Exposition can be interpreted as a gesture by the shogunate to show the world that it was still the sovereign representative of Japan. It was for this reason that the shogunate took such offense at Satsuma's decision to participate independently in the exposition.

But over and beyond their specific purposes, these missions were significant in that they opened up hitherto unexpected perspectives for the delegates and the students who accompanied them. Their xenophobic view of the world was shaken to its foundations; they began to question the wisdom of the traditional social and political order and to look to the West for a new model. It was not that they had been totally ignorant: Japan had gleaned since the end of the 1700s bits and pieces from the body of scholarship known as WESTERN LEARNING; but their knowledge was now confirmed by experience. Although they amounted only to a handful, these men were to stand at the forefront of the new Meiji government's policy of "civilization and enlightenment" *(bummei kaika;* see MEIJI ENLIGHTENMENT). And in spite of having been high shogunate retainers, many of them were to be chosen as members of the IWAKURA MISSION of 1871.

TANAKA Akira

Shōhaku (1443–1527)

Poet of WAKA (classical poetry) and *renga* (linked verse). Also known as Botange (Peony Blossom). He was a son of the court noble Nakanoin no Michiatsu. Of cultivated, patrician tastes, he enjoyed a combination of the life of the aristocratic aesthete and the hermit-poet. At about the age of 20, he embarked upon his first journey about the country to visit famous places celebrated in poetry, and at the same time was granted high court rank and privileges. When the imperial capital became a battleground during the Ōnin Wars of 1467–77, he took refuge at Ikeda in the province of Settsu (now part of Hyōgo Prefecture), where he built a hermitage, still making frequent visits back to Kyōto and continuing to journey about in search of famous poetic scenes. For reasons of health, he took partial Buddhist orders in 1511, and in 1518 he moved to the seaport town of Sakai. Having received a thorough grounding in classical poetry, he had already by 1475 or 1476 been initiated by the famous *waka* and *renga* poet SŌGI into the "secret mysteries" of the great classical anthology, the KOKINSHŪ (ca 905, Collection of Ancient and Modern

Times) and the TALE OF GENJI (ca 1000)—a tradition of artistic "laying-on of hands" which he perpetuated in the Sakai area.

In the early spring of 1488, Shōhaku participated with Sōgi and the younger poet SŌCHŌ in composing perhaps the most famous *renga* of 100 links, "Three Poets at Minase." In 1491 the same three poets met at the hot springs of Arima to compose another famous poem of 100 links, "Three Poets at Yuyama." Shōhaku's contribution to these poems show him to have been a master of the art of linked verse second only to Sōgi. In 1495 he collaborated with Sōgi, Kenzai, and other poets in compiling the *Shinsen tsukubashū* (Tsukuba Collection, Newly Selected), a very important and influential anthology of superior verses selected from various *renga*. He also wrote several commentaries, exegetical works, and treatises on both *renga* and *waka*. A collection of his own poetry entitled *Shummusō* (Book of a Spring Night's Dream) is in two parts, or versions. One contains some of his superior *renga* verses, and the other around 2,000 of his classical poems. His style, combining courtly elegance with homely, rustic touches, is particularly his own. See also RENGA AND HAIKAI.

📖 ——Earl Miner, *Japanese Linked Poetry* (1979).

Robert H. BROWER

Shōheikō

An official academy (KANGAKU) of the Tokugawa shogunate during the Edo period (1600–1868). Also called Yushima Seidō or Shōheizaka Gakumonjo. In 1630 HAYASHI RAZAN, under the patronage of the third shōgun, TOKUGAWA IEMITSU, built a school and library in the Ueno district of Edo (now Tōkyō). In 1632 a shrine honoring Confucius was donated to the school by Tokugawa Yoshinao (1600–1650), *daimyō* of the Owari domain (now part of Aichi Prefecture). In 1691 the school was moved to Yushima in the Kanda district of Edo where the fifth shōgun, TOKUGAWA TSUNAYOSHI, donated some property. The site was given the name Shōheizaka, a reference to the birthplace of Confucius, Changping (Ch'ang-p'ing; J: Shōhei) in Shandong (Shantung) Province. In 1691 the school was given official status by the shogunate. As a result of the KANSEI REFORMS (1787–93), the school was reorganized, and an official shogunal academy (*gakumonsho*) was established alongside it. This was named Shōheizaka Gakumonsho, though it was commonly referred to by the shorter alternative name Shōheikō. It served as a school for HATAMOTO and GOKENIN (shogunal retainers) as well as for the Confucian scholars from various domains. The Zhu Xi (Chu Hsi) school of Confucian teachings (SHUSHIGAKU) was taught as the official doctrine. After the Meiji Restoration of 1868, the school was taken over by the Meiji government but was discontinued in 1871.

Etō Kyōji

shōhekiga → screen and wall painting

shoin-zukuri

A style of Japanese residential architecture used in general in the mansions of the military, temple guest halls, and Zen abbot's quarters of the Azuchi-Momoyama (1568–1600) and Edo (1600–1868) periods. It forms the basis of today's traditional-style Japanese house. The *shoin* style developed out of the classic *shinden* style (see SHINDEN-ZUKURI) of domestic architecture in the Kamakura (1185–1333) and Muromachi (1333–1568) periods, the earliest extant structure incorporating a room that is clearly in the *shoin* style being the Tōgudō (at the temple GINKAKUJI in Kyōto) of the shōgun Ashikaga Yoshimasa, dating to about 1486. A typical example of the early mature *shoin* is the Kōjōin Guest Hall (1601) of the temple Onjōji (MIIDERA) in Shiga Prefecture. This structure retains a number of *shinden*-style elements such as a covered entrance arcade (*chūmonrō* or *chūmon*) projecting from one corner, a broad, southern veranda (*hiroen*), and, on the facade, latticed wall panels that swing open upward (*shitomido* or *shitomi*), hinged wooden doors (*tsumado*), and a slatted window (*renjimado*). The wooden doors are emphasized on the Kōjōin Guest Hall by a curved, "Chinese-style" gable (*karahafu*) above, and this combination serves as the formal entrance (*kurumayose*). The exterior of this structure also incorporates sliding, louvered doors (*mairado*) with one latticed, paper sliding screen (*shōji*) behind each pair. *Mairado* and *shōji* are not used in pure *shinden* structures. Other new developments include square posts and floors completely covered with woven rush mats (TATAMI). Moreover, unlike the *shinden*, the Kōjōin Guest Hall is subdivided into a number of fixed spaces by walls and sliding screens (*fusuma*).

Shoin-zukuri —— Kuroshoin, Ninomaru Palace, Nijō Castle

The first room (*ichi no ma*) of the Kuroshoin, Ninomaru Palace, an opulent example of the mature *shoin* style. The large room (24½ *tatami* mats) includes such characteristic features as *tokonoma* (back wall, left), *chigaidana* (corner), and *chōdaigamae* (right wall). The paintings are by artists of the Kanō school. Kyōto. National Treasure.

The main room of the Guest Hall, the Jōza no Ma, includes four characteristic *shoin* elements. These are the *tokonoma* (decorative alcove), located on the room's far wall, staggered shelves (*chigaidana*) next to it, a built-in desk (*shoin*), here located in a secondary space projecting off the main room at a right angle to the *tokonoma*, and decorative doors (*chōdaigamae*) on the wall opposite the veranda. In many cases, these four interior elements are located on a *jōdan*, a floor area raised one step above that of the surrounding spaces and fronted with decorative wooden molding (*kamachi*). All four built-in elements were originally functional but gradually became primarily decorative. In later *shoin* structures, the built-in desk is usually located directly on the veranda side of the *jōdan*, at right angles to the *tokonoma*, rather than in a secondary space. Furthermore, the *oshiita*-type *tokonoma*, with a thick plank for a floorboard, gives way in later structures to one with a thin floorboard and thick decorative molding (*tokogamachi*) in front. The Kōjōin Guest Hall also has ceilings, frieze rails (*nageshi*), and transoms (*ramma*). Primarily because of its incorporation of a *chūmonrō* entrance arcade, *hiroen* veranda, and *kurumayose* formal entrance, the Kōjōin Guest Hall is also traditionally considered to epitomize the *shuden* style of residential architecture, but most modern scholars prefer to include the *shuden* in the early *shoin* category.

The *shoin* style reaches full maturity in the early Edo period. The most opulent examples, such as the Ninomaru Palace (1624–26?) of NIJŌ CASTLE, have separate structures for public and private functions. In the case of the Ninomaru Palace, there are a Tōzamurai entry hall, Shikidai for formal greetings, Ōhiroma and Kuroshoin for formal audiences, and Shiroshoin for the private use of the master of the residence. In this period most *shoin* structures abandon the *chūmonrō* and *kurumayose* and incorporate a *genkan* (entry hall) instead. Exteriors are usually completely of *shōji* screens, an arrangement that allows twice the light of the earlier combination of two *mairado* and one *shōji*. The screens are protected from the elements by "rain doors" (*amado*), which are slid in front when necessary and stored in cabinets when not. The Ninomaru Palace is the most magnificent *shoin* extant, with elegant gold and polychrome paintings from floor to ceiling, gold nail-covers, carved openwork transoms, a double-coved-and-coffered ceiling over the *jōdan* of the Ōhiroma, and an expansive landscape garden.

At an early stage, some buildings in the *shoin* style came to include rustic teahouse elements perfected in the Azuchi–Momoyama period. This resultant *sukiya shoin* or simply SUKIYA-ZUKURI style is less formal in atmosphere, simpler in design, and richer in variation. It is this type of *shoin* that gradually diffused into the homes of the lower classes, despite Tokugawa sumptuary laws restricting the use of various *shoin* elements.

📖 ——Fujioka Michio and Tsunenari Kazunori, *Shoin*, 2 vols (1969). Fumio Hashimoto, *Architecture in the Shoin Style*, tr H. Mack Horton (1981). Kiyoshi Hirai, *Feudal Architecture of Japan*, tr Hiroaki Sato and Jeannine Ciliotta (1973). Hirai Kiyoshi, *Nihon jūtaku no rekishi* (1974). Teiji Itō, "The Development of *Shoin*-Style Architecture" in John W. Hall and Toyoda Takeshi, ed, *Japan in the*

Muromachi Age (1977). Harumichi Kitao, *Shoin Architecture in Detailed Illustrations* (1956). Ōta Hirotarō, *Shoin-zukuri* (1972).

H. Mack HORTON

Shōji Kaoru (1937-   )

Novelist. Real name Fukuda Shōji. Born in Tōkyō. Graduate of Tōkyō University. He first gained recognition, writing under his real name, with the short story "Sōshitsu" (1958, Loss), which received the Chūō Kōron New Writer's Prize. Following his initial success, however, he abandoned writing for ten years until May 1969, when *Akazukin-chan ki o tsukete* (Look Out, Little Red Riding Hood!), a novel published under his pen name, won the Akutagawa Prize and became a best seller. A first person narrative of the actions and emotions of an upper-middle-class youth born in the postwar baby boom, this book and its three sequels, known as the "Kaoru-chan series" from the name of their main character, established Shōji as the spokesman for young people in the 1970s. His informal, conversational style, replete with slang and teenage expressions, along with his positive view of life created a relaxed, warm atmosphere that attracted youthful readers.

Tsugumichi WATANABE

Shōkadō Shōjō (1584-1659)

Monk, painter, and one of the great calligraphers of his age. He was born in Yamato Province (now Nara Prefecture), and while a young man became a monk at the Hachiman Shrine at Otokoyama, southwest of Kyōto. Upon the death of his master Takimoto Jitsujō in 1627, Shōkadō became head of the shrine, which combined Shintō with Shingon Buddhism. He was good friends with the Zen abbots at Daitokuji and became known as an accomplished WAKA poet and painter and an expert on the tea ceremony. He was most famous, however, for his calligraphy, being counted as one of the Kan'ei no Sampitsu (Three Brushes of the Kan'ei Era), along with HON'AMI KŌETSU and KONOE NOBUTADA.

Shōkadō's calligraphic style shows a number of influences, including the writings of KŪKAI, FUJIWARA NO YUKINARI, and Konoe Nobutada. His brushwork is generally restrained in comparison with that of Kōetsu, but more elegant than that of Nobutada. His line ranges from thick to thin and his character shapes are rounded with occasional angularities. Shōkadō's paintings are considered ZENGA in that they are generally abbreviated and humorous inkplays in the manner of the Chinese painters Muqi (Mu-ch'i; J: MOKKEI) and Liang Kai (Liang K'ai).

◼ ——Haruna Yoshishige, *Kan'ei no sampitsu* (1971).

Stephen ADDISS

Shōkai shingo

(Kor: Ch'ŏphaesinŏ). Korean reference work on the Japanese language; first published in 10 volumes in 1676 but completed about 40 years earlier. Its author was Kang U-sŏng (J: Kō Gūsei; b 1581), who as a young boy was captured by the Japanese during the invasion of Korea in 1592 and taken back to Japan. After 10 years in Japan he was repatriated, but he visited Japan on three separate occasions thereafter as an interpreter. It is not known whether he was still alive when his work was finally published. The main part of Kang's work is based on conversations between Korean and Japanese officials, and it thus reflects the Japanese colloquial language of the late 16th and early 17th century. Japanese sentences and phrases are written in the *hiragana* phonetic syllabary with their pronunciation indicated in the Korean alphabet, *han'gul*. Each sentence or phrase is followed by a Korean translation.

Revised editions of this work were in use in Korea until the end of the 19th century. Extant today are the original edition, the 1871 revision, *Jūkan kaishū shōkai shingo* (Kor: *Chunggan kaesu ch'ŏphaesinŏ*), and a 1796 version, *Shōkai shingo bunshaku (Ch'ŏphaesinŏ munsŏk)*. The latter shows the Japanese words and phrases written in the normal combination of Chinese characters and the *kana* syllabary and is intended for the study of the Japanese writing system. These three existing versions of Kang's work are valuable materials for linguistic research, for, taken together, they reflect changes in the Japanese and Korean spoken languages during the 16th to 18th centuries.

YAMAZAKI Yukio

shōkan

(*shōen* managers). General term for a variety of functionaries who were responsible for management, assignment of duties, collection of taxes, and providing protection for landed estates (SHŌEN). Their specific titles were various and confusing, differing according to period, region, and individual estate; some of the most common were *azukari-dokoro* (proprietary deputy), *geshi* or *gesu* (steward), and *kumon* (clerk). There were originally two distinct types, those whom the estate proprietors dispatched from the capital and those chosen from among local notables. Since the latter normally had more agricultural experience, they tended to gain actual control of the *shōen* they were appointed to manage. Also, from the middle of the Heian period (794–1185), local proprietors began to commend their lands in name to powerful families or religious institutions in the capital, retaining or receiving some sort of *shōkan* title. With the appointment of military land stewards (JITŌ) by the Kamakura shogunate after 1185, conflict arose between these new officials and the previously appointed *shōkan*. By the 13th century most of the managerial and even the proprietary rights to many *shōen* had passed into the hands of the *jitō*.

G. Cameron HURST III

Shōkei (fl mid 15th–early 16th century)

Also known as Kenkō Shōkei. Zen monk and painter. Shōkei developed a distinctive style of landscape and figure painting that established a flourishing regional school of INK PAINTING in the Kantō area and influenced many followers. His official title at the Kenchōji, a Zen Buddhist temple in Kamakura, was that of record-keeper (*shoki*), hence his popular name, Kei Shoki. Later accounts relate that Shōkei initially studied painting with the Kenchōji monk-painter Chūan Shinkō (fl mid 15th century).

Significant contemporary biographical documentation of Shōkei's career comes from inscriptions on paintings. The inscription on *Viewing a Waterfall* (1480) by GEIAMI, aesthetic adviser to the Ashikaga shōgun and curator of the extensive shogunal collection of Chinese art, establishes that Shōkei studied with him in Kyōto for three years from 1478 to 1480. Another inscription, dated 1493, records Shōkei's second visit to Kyōto, of indefinite duration, and refers to him by the sobriquet Hinrakusai.

Shōkei's residence in Kyōto under Geiami's tutelage undoubtedly gave him access to the shogunal collection of Chinese paintings, a privilege shared by few other painters of the Muromachi period (1333–1568). His surviving works include excellent copies of Chinese paintings of the Southern Song (Sung; 1127–1279) and Yuan (Yüan; 1279–1368) dynasties, which in turn served as model paintings for Shōkei's many followers. Shōkei's landscapes from the period immediately following his first period of residence in Kyōto strongly reflect Geiami's distinctive style, itself evolved from Geiami's study of the work of the Southern Song academy painter Xia Gui (Hsia Kuei; fl ca 1195–1224). His late landscapes following his second visit to Kyōto reflect the influence of Japanese masterpainters of the mid-15th century, especially the circle of SHŪBUN, the leading monk-painter of Shōkokuji, the Kyōto Zen temple.

Shōkei's career, encompassing both periods of study in Kyōto and an influential role in establishing a provincial school of ink painting, is remarkably parallel to that of SESSHŪ TŌYŌ. Shōkei's followers embodied aspects of his style and diverse subject matter in their work, often overstressing repetition of typical forms and techniques derived from the style of Shōkei's midcareer, in which the angular forms and sharp, definitive brushwork of Xia Gui was most pronounced.

◼ ——Ann Yonemura, "Landscape . . . by Kenkō Shōkei," in Yoshiaki Shimizu and Carolyn Wheelwright, ed, *Japanese Ink Paintings from American Collections: The Muromachi Period* (1976).

Ann YONEMURA

Shō Ki

(Ch: Zhong Gui or Chung Kuei). A Chinese mythic being who dispels demons. The pictorial subject of "the demon queller" originated in the Chinese legend that the scholar-recluse Zhong Gui cured the ailing Tang (T'ang) emperor Xuan-zong (Hsüan-tsung; r 847–859) by driving away his devils in a dream. Zhong Gui is portrayed wearing a Chinese robe, high boots, and a black scholar's hat. He strikes a threatening pose with bulging eyes, abundant beard, and sword in hand. In Japan, he first appeared in the 12th-century JIGOKU-ZŌSHI (Scrolls of Hells) and has been painted by such artists as SESSHŪ TŌYŌ, Yamada Dōan (d ca 1573), and WATANABE KAZAN. He is associated with the Boys' Festival in May (see CHILDREN'S DAY), when his image is displayed to overpower evil and pestilence.

Carolyn WHEELWRIGHT

Shokkō Giyūkai

(Workers' Fraternal Society). The first modern Japanese labor organization, formed in April 1897 with the aim of initiating a labor union movement in Japan. The group's founders included TAKANO FUSATARŌ and Jō Tsunetarō (1856–1936), who had met while working in San Francisco, where they and other Japanese laborers had formed a labor union study group under the same name in 1890. The group was strongly influenced by the newly formed American Federation of Labor and adopted a moderate, reformist philosophy of trade unionism.

The Shokkō Giyūkai distributed pamphlets to factory workers, calling for the formation of labor unions. The social activist KATAYAMA SEN, the entrepreneur Sakuma Teiichi (1846–98), and the politician SHIMADA SABURŌ joined the organization. In July 1897 it changed its name to Rōdō Kumiai Kiseikai (Society for Formation of Labor Unions) to reflect its commitment to union organizing and soon became active nationwide. The Kiseikai published the first labor union magazine in Japan, Rōdō sekai (Labor World), and conducted nationwide speaking tours. Ironworkers were the most responsive to the group's message, and an ironworkers' union was formed in December 1897. The Kiseikai disbanded in 1901, after the ironworkers' union collapsed.

Shokkō jijō

(Conditions of Factory Workers). Five-volume report on labor conditions in the textile, iron, cement, glass, match, tobacco, and other industries published by the Ministry of Agriculture and Commerce in 1903. The investigative project was undertaken as preparation for legislation that eventually emerged as the FACTORY LAW OF 1911. The report contains data on work hours, rest days, wages, and labor relations in each industry, as well as records of interviews with factory managers, technicians, and laborers. It also contains information on housing, health care, welfare facilities, and general morale. Like YOKOYAMA GENNOSUKE's Nihon no kasō shakai (1899, Japan's Lower Classes), it is considered a classic study in the history of labor relations.

Shōkō Chūkin Bank

(Shōkō Kumiai Chūō Kinko; Central Bank for Commercial and Industrial Cooperatives). Semigovernmental institution established in 1936 to finance small businesses and small business-oriented organizations such as the Small and Medium Business Cooperative Association (Chūshō Kigyō Tō Kyōdō Kumiai). The largest bank of its kind in the world, it provides loans to small businesses of nearly every type, including the manufacturing, construction, wholesale, retail, transportation, and communications industries, as well as service businesses. Aside from its loan operations, the bank takes deposits, engages in exchange transactions, issues debentures, performs various trust functions, and provides business consultation and information services. To help smaller firms do business overseas, the bank maintains correspondent contracts with major foreign banks and also provides funds for investments abroad. Of the bank's ￥124.2 billion (US $516 million) capitalization at the end of March 1982, the share of the government's investment was ￥94.9 billion (US $394.2 million). The balance of loans in the same year was ￥5.9 trillion (US $24.5 billion). The head office is in Tōkyō.

Hirata Masami

Shōkōkan

The office where the DAI NIHON SHI (History of Great Japan) was compiled. Begun in 1657 by TOKUGAWA MITSUKUNI, daimyō of the Mito domain, at his mansion in the Komagome district of Edo (now Tōkyō), the massive history project continued until 1906 with as many as 59 people, including renowned historians, working on it at one time. The office was named Shōkōkan in 1672, when it was moved to Mitsukuni's mansion in the Koishikawa district of Edo. It was later moved permanently to the city of Mito (now in Ibaraki Prefecture). Converted into a library in 1907, the Shōkōkan houses many historically and culturally valuable works. Although the building was partially burned during World War II, the library continues to serve a large community of scholars.

Shokoku fūzoku toijō kotae → Yashiro Hirokata

Shōkokuji

Head temple of the Shōkokuji branch of the RINZAI SECT of Zen Buddhism, located in Kami-Gyō Ward, Kyōto. Shōkokuji was founded in 1383 under the sponsorship of the third Ashikaga shōgun, ASHIKAGA YOSHIMITSU. The construction of the temple was regarded as a national enterprise. Yoshimitsu is said to have participated personally in the construction as did the eminent Zen monk GIDŌ SHŪSHIN, and daimyō were obliged to contribute to the project in various ways. Shun'oku Myōha (1311–88), who as registrar of monks (sōroku) held a position of authority among the Zen clergy at the time, was appointed to serve as abbot but agreed only on condition that his master MUSŌ SOSEKI (1275–1351) be posthumously accorded the honorary position of first abbot. In 1386 Shōkokuji was designated second in rank among the GOZAN Zen temples in Kyōto. When the temple lost many of its new buildings in a fire in 1394, Yoshimitsu ordered its immediate restoration. Shōkokuji suffered extensive damage from fires in 1425, 1467, 1551, 1620, and 1788, but support for the temple was so constant that it was restored after each conflagration. Among the later influential patrons of the temple were the Toyotomi and Tokugawa families. Shōkokuji now consists of 15 subtemples. Its main hall (hondō), rebuilt by the warrior general TOYOTOMI HIDEYORI in 1605, is of great architectural significance, representing the karayō or Chinese style of building used in Japanese Zen temples from the 12th century on.

Stanley WEINSTEIN

shokudō

A general term for eating place or dining hall. Popular, inexpensive restaurants for serving the kinds of noodles called soba and udon (called sobaya in the Kantō region and udon'ya in the Kansai region) were first established in the latter half of the 17th century. Shops, chiefly teahouses (chamise) serving light meals, were built along the highways in the Edo period (1600–1868). From the Meiji period (1868–1912) these became luncheonettes (ichizen meshiya). In the Taishō (1912–26) and Shōwa (1926–) periods, inexpensive shokudō for the common people increased dramatically, including quick-lunch rooms and dining rooms in department stores. Unlike other more expensive restaurants, shokudō display realistic wax or plastic models of the food on their menus in their front windows. Some shokudō will deliver food and drinks, a service called demae. During the Edo period, soba and udon shops delivered food in a hand-carried wooden box called okamochi, but now the food is carried in a compartment attached to the back of a bicycle or motorbike. Recent years have also witnessed the rapid growth of fast-food places serving hot dogs, hamburgers, gyūdon (a beef and rice dish), and sushi.

Tsuchida Mitsufumi

Shokugenshō

(Origins of Office). A two-volume book on government offices compiled by KITABATAKE CHIKAFUSA during the period of dynastic schism between the Northern and Southern Courts (1336–92). Chikafusa is said to have written the book for the Southern Court's child emperor Go-Murakami (1328–68; r 1339–68) in 1340 while stationed at Oda Castle in Hitachi Province (now Ibaraki Prefecture). The book, the first of its kind, traces the development of government offices, both statutory and extrastatutory, since the establishment of the RITSURYŌ SYSTEM of government in the 7th century, and explains their functions. Of extant copies, the one in possession of the Imperial Household Agency is said to be the most faithful to the original.

Shokuhō seiken

(Shokuhō regime). The regime of national unification founded by ODA NOBUNAGA (1534–82) and developed by his successor TOYOTOMI HIDEYOSHI (1537–98). Shokuhō is an acronym formed from alternate pronunciations of the initial characters of their names: shoku is an alternate pronunciation of the character o in Oda, as is hō of the character toyo in Toyotomi. Hence the term "Shokuhō regime" is synonymous with "Oda-Toyotomi regime," that is, the central governmental system that evolved in Japan during the Azuchi-Momoyama period (1568–1600) and was succeeded by the

Tokugawa shogunate (1603–1867), which continued its major policies. In Japanese institutional history, the emergence of this regime marked the transition from the medieval period to the early modern age. The Shokuhō regime brought about the reconstruction of Japan's body politic after the collapse of its central organs in the Sengoku period (1467–1568). Under it, local barons were forced to submit to the national hegemon, the status of the *samurai* class and of the peasantry was redefined, and the country's economic base was reorganized through cadastral surveys (KENCHI). These effects are generally viewed as positive by Western historians, although Japanese scholars tend to emphasize the regime's brutal and authoritarian aspects. See also HISTORY OF JAPAN: Azuchi-Momoyama history.

George ELISON

shokunin

(artisans). A general term for makers of traditional handicrafts. Around the 8th century the construction, metalwork, and weaving needs of the state were handled by offices called *shiki*. From the 9th to the 12th century, throughout the country, groups of skilled workmen (also called *shiki*) were attached to estates (SHŌEN) under the control of court nobles and powerful temples. When the word *shokunin* came into general use, it referred not only to handcraftsmen but to entertainers and peddlers as well. Although the meaning of the word *shokunin* narrowed with the expansion of commercial activities, the types and number of *shokunin* increased; the Edo period (1600–1868) was the golden age of handcraft production. In the ranking of classes at this time *shokunin* fell below *samurai* and peasants, but above merchants (see SHI-NŌ-KŌ-SHŌ). Following the Meiji Restoration in 1868, mechanized factory production became widespread, with the result that many handcraftsmen became factory laborers.

In the past, master craftsmen were organized into a type of guild. The usual procedure was to become apprenticed to a master at age 12 or 13, learn the skill until about age 20, and spend a year working for, or sometimes with, one's master in gratitude and as repayment (called *orei bōkō*), before becoming an independent, full-fledged *shokunin* (see also APPRENTICE SYSTEM).

Today there are virtually no guilds, and competition is open. Although *shokunin* still work in fields such as carpentry, joinery, metalworking, woodworking, pottery, and lacquer art, their number is now very small. The Japanese government has begun to designate and protect both traditional handicrafts and those who possess traditional technical skills, but the lack of young people who might succeed these *shokunin* threatens the survival of traditional crafts. See also LIVING NATIONAL TREASURES.

MURAMATSU Teijirō

Shokuryō Mēdē

(Food May Day). Popular name for Shokuryō Kiki Toppa Jimmin Taikai (People's Meeting to Overcome the Food Crisis). Also known as Kome Yokose Mēdē ("Give Us Rice" May Day). A demonstration in front of the Imperial Palace in Tōkyō on 19 May 1946 that was organized by leaders of groups participating in May Day celebrations. Three hundred thousand people marched in what was the culmination of a series of nationwide demonstrations for food, the shortage of which had plagued Japan since the end of World War II. Resolutions were passed calling for the formation of a democratic popular front and the dissolution of the government. This demonstration, which occurred in the midst of a serious political crisis, was considered a threat to the democratic government and to law and order by the Occupation authorities (see SCAP) and on the following day General Douglas MacArthur issued a warning against future disorderly mob demonstrations.

Some of the demonstrators, members of the Communist Party, carried a placard saying "I, the Emperor, have eaten my fill, but you subjects can starve to death." As a result, one person was arrested and charged with LESE MAJESTY (*fukeizai*), but Occupation authorities declared that the emperor was not entitled to special protection, and the charge was changed to simple libel. The person arrested was sentenced to prison for eight months but was pardoned and released three days later, and lese majesty became in effect null and void as a criminal offense in Japan. Lese majesty was not included as a crime when the Penal Code was revised in October 1947.

Shokusan Jūtaku Sōgo Co, Ltd

A construction company specializing in building houses, stores, and apartment houses to order by standard construction methods, Sho-

kusan Jūtaku was established in 1950. It has grown rapidly, owing in large part to its method of taking payment for its construction work in monthly installments, and has come to boast the largest sales of individual homes in the country. In recent years the company has entered the real estate business through subsidiary firms. Sales for the fiscal year ending March 1982 totaled ¥146.6 billion (US $609 million), of which construction accounted for 71 percent, sales of goods 13 percent, and real estate 16 percent; capitalization stood at ¥7 billion (US $29.1 million) in the same year. Corporate headquarters are located in Tōkyō.

shokusan kōgyō

("Increase Production and Promote Industry"). Government policy of the early part of the Meiji period (1868–1912) to foster industries in order to realize the ideal of a "rich country and strong military" (FUKOKU KYŌHEI). The Ministry of Public Works (Kōbushō) was established in 1870, and the Home Ministry (Naimushō) in 1873, to organize industrialization. The two ministries were responsible for introducing modern technology from abroad, constructing railways, and supervising mining and other government enterprises. They also founded model factories for cotton-spinning and silk-reeling (see GOVERNMENT-OPERATED FACTORIES, MEIJI PERIOD), and emphasized the modernization of marine transport, agriculture, and other areas. Under the direction of ITŌ HIROBUMI, who became minister of public works in 1873, the policy produced positive results, but many of the government-operated enterprises encountered financial difficulties, and the government was forced to sell them to private entrepreneurs (see KAN'EI JIGYŌ HARAISAGE).

Shokushi, Princess → Shikishi, Princess

Shōmei Incident

(Shōmei Jiken; "Incident of the Bell Inscription"). The *casus belli* of the outbreak of hostilities between TOKUGAWA IEYASU and TOYOTOMI HIDEYORI in 1614. Hideyori had that year finished rebuilding the Hōkōji, a temple in Kyōto founded in 1588 by his father, the great national unifier TOYOTOMI HIDEYOSHI, and destroyed by an earthquake in 1596. The inscription on the bell commissioned for the rededication contained a phrase in which the two Chinese characters composing the name Ieyasu were split by a third; moreover, the characters of one couplet could, with some sophistry, be rearranged to read, "Make Toyotomi your lord and look forward to your progeny's prosperity." The authorities consulted by Ieyasu, notably the Neo-Confucian scholar HAYASHI RAZAN, interpreted these as imprecations to overthrow the Tokugawa, and Ieyasu seized this excuse to demand Hideyori's submission. When his ultimatum was rejected, Ieyasu mounted the massive campaign that resulted the next year in the destruction of Hideyori's Ōsaka Castle and the fall of the Toyotomi (see ŌSAKA CASTLE, SIEGES OF). That Ieyasu himself knew his justification for war to be specious is evident, for the bell was not destroyed and is still on view in Kyōto.

George ELISON

Shōmonki

(Record of Masakado). Also known as *Masakadoki*. Considered the prototype of GUNKI MONOGATARI, or war tales, it was written by an unknown author after TAIRA NO MASAKADO's death in the mid-10th century. Written in the heavily Japanized form of Chinese known as HENTAI KAMBUN, the tale follows the life of Masakado through the Jōhei and Tengyō rebellions. The only extant manuscripts are the version dated 1099, found in the temple Shimpukuji in Nagoya, and that in the Katakura Takeo collection in Tōkyō (formerly in the Yang Shoujing [Yang Shou-ching] library).

📖 —— *Shōmonki*, tr Giuliana Stramigioli as *Masakadoki* in *Rivista degli Studi Orientali* 53 1–2 (Università di Roma, 1979). Hayashi Rokurō, *Kōchū Masakadoki* (1975). Kajihara Masaaki, *Yakuchū Masakadoki*, 2 vols (1975–76). *Giuliana* STRAMIGIOLI

shōmono

A general term for Muromachi-period (1333–1568) commentaries on the classic texts of Buddhism, Confucianism, Chinese medicine, earlier Japanese literature, and so forth, by masters in these various fields. These commentaries typically consist of either notes made by the masters themselves preparatory to lecturing on the classic texts or notes taken down from the lectures by their disciples; they include not only interpretations of the wording of the classical Chinese (KAMBUN) or classical Japanese of the texts but also explanations of the thought they embody. Most *shōmono* are in an easy-to-understand form of the colloquial Japanese of the period, written in a combination of Chinese characters and the *katakana* (rarely *hiragana*) phonetic syllabary; some are in classical Chinese or a mixture of Chinese and Japanese. The term *shōmono* is also used to refer to similar materials of the early part of the Edo period (1600–1868); however, *shōmono* are usually distinguished from both the *hogo* or GOROKU (recorded oral teachings of Zen masters) of the Kamakura period (1185–1333) and the commentaries of Edo-period Confucian scholars. The *shōmono* that are written in Japanese contain abundant examples of contemporary colloquial expressions and are thus valuable materials for the study of the Japanese language of the Muromachi period. *YAMAZAKI Yukio*

Shōmu, Emperor (701–756)

The 45th sovereign *(tennō)* in the traditional count (which includes several nonhistorical emperors); reigned 724–749. He was eldest son of Emperor MOMMU, and his mother, Kyūshi, was a daughter of the influential minister FUJIWARA NO FUHITO; his consort, Empress KŌMYŌ, was also a daughter of Fuhito. During Shōmu's reign, the government was dominated first by the imperial prince Nagaya no Ō (684–729), later by the FUJIWARA FAMILY, and finally by a clique comprising TACHIBANA NO MOROE, KIBI NO MAKIBI, and the priest GEMBŌ. Political strife was a constant problem (see NAGAYA NO Ō, REBELLION OF; FUJIWARA NO HIROTSUGU, REBELLION OF), and during the period 741–745 the capital was moved from HEIJŌKYŌ (Nara), to three places in succession (KUNI NO MIYA, NANIWAKYŌ, and SHIGARAKI NO MIYA), only returning to Nara in 745.

Shōmu was an ardent Buddhist and in 741 ordered the establishment of state-maintained temples (KOKUBUNJI) in each province. His piety was further expressed in the building, with the aid of the priests RŌBEN and GYŌGI, of the temple TŌDAIJI and the casting of its great image of the Buddha (see DAIBUTSU), as well as generous donations of land to other temples, monasteries, and convents. Shōmu's reign was marked also by a flourishing of the arts under strong Chinese influence; the Tempyō era (729–749) is known as one of the most brilliant in the history of Japanese culture. This period probably witnessed a greater increase in government expenditure and consumption than any other of comparable length in early Japan.

In 749 Shōmu abdicated in favor of his daughter Empress KŌKEN, took holy orders, and spent the rest of his life in religious devotions. After his death, his personal possessions were donated to Tōdaiji, in whose treasure house, the SHŌSŌIN, they still remain today. See also HISTORY OF JAPAN: Nara history. *KITAMURA Bunji*

Shōnai Plain

(Shōnai Heiya). Located in northwestern Yamagata Prefecture, northern Honshū. Consisting of the flood plains of the lower part of the river Mogamigawa and other rivers, as well as deltas, and bordering the Sea of Japan, its straight coastline is characterized by a two- to four-kilometer-wide strip of high sand dunes. High-quality rice is produced. The major cities are Sakata and Tsuruoka. Length: 50 km (31 mi); width: 5–20 km (3–12 mi).

Shōnen

(Boy). A 1969 film directed by ŌSHIMA NAGISA. Written by Tamura Tsutomu. A mother (played by Koyama Akiko) and father (played by Watanabe Fumio) use their 10-year-old son to stage fake traffic accidents in order to collect accident insurance or extort money from drivers. This nuclear family, metaphor for the Japanese nation, survives only through deceit, violence, and repression. They make their living illicitly as they travel the length of the Japanese archipelago to the northern shores of Hokkaidō. There they realize that they cannot go beyond their homeland. The boy, who prefers his own fantasies to his parents' world, sees that his only way out will be rescue by creatures from outer space. Unlike most of Ōshima's work during this period, the narrative is largely conventional in structure. It originated in his attraction to current news stories as source material. The estranged visual style of *Boy* is dominated by unbalanced compositions that make full use of the edges of the wide screen and by a seemingly random mixture of monochrome and color photography. *J. L. ANDERSON*

Shōnai Plain

Newly harvested rice on the Shōnai Plain with the 2,230-meter Chōkaisan in the background.

Shōnen kurabu

(Boys' Club). One of the most popular boys' magazines in Japan in the first half of the 20th century. Published by KŌDANSHA, LTD, beginning in November 1914, the magazine completely changed the image of boys' magazines that had developed during the Meiji period (1868–1912) with its easy-to-read, interesting style and polished illustrations. Outstanding features of the magazine included the cartoon about a dog "Norakuro" (Blackie) in the early years of the Shōwa period (1926–) and novels such as YOSHIKAWA EIJI's *Shinshū temma kyō* (Seven Riders for Justice), SATŌ KŌROKU's *Aa gyokuhai ni hana ukete* (Ah! A Blossom in My Cup), and EDOGAWA RAMPO's *Kaijin nijūmensō* (The Man of 20 Faces). These made *Shōnen kurabu* the most widely read magazine among boys in Japan. Circulation of the magazine in 1936 reached 750,000. However, in the face of competition from numerous COMIC MAGAZINES, *Shōnen kurabu* was discontinued in December 1962.

Shōni family

Warrior family in northern Kyūshū from the 12th to the mid-16th centuries; they claimed descent from the 10th-century general FUJIWARA NO HIDESATO. The family founder, Mutō Sukeyori (fl 1189–after 1227), was appointed by MINAMOTO NO YORITOMO as junior-assistant governor *(shōni)* of Dazaifu, the government headquarters in Kyūshū; the position was hereditary, and his descendants adopted the title as their name. Sukeyori's son Sukeyoshi (1198–1281) became military governor *(shugo)* of Chikuzen, Hizen, and Buzen provinces (now parts of Fukuoka, Saga, Ōita, and Nagasaki prefectures) as well as of the nearby islands Iki and Tsushima. He and his sons Tsunesuke (1226–89) and Kagesuke (d 1285) were prominent commanders during the MONGOL INVASIONS OF JAPAN in 1274 and 1281. Tsunesuke's grandson Sadatsune (1272–1336) and great-grandson Yorihisa (1293–1371) allied themselves with ASHIKAGA TAKAUJI in the 1330s, and for the next 50 years the Shōni fought for the Ashikaga against supporters of the schismatic Southern Court (see NORTHERN AND SOUTHERN COURTS), notably the KIKUCHI FAMILY. The Shōni were deeply involved in the internecine military rivalries in Kyūshū during the late 14th and 15th centuries, and they gradually lost lands and power to neighboring *daimyō*, especially the ŌUCHI FAMILY. Finally, in 1559, the Shōni were destroyed by their vassals the RYŪZŌJI FAMILY, who were supplanted in turn, only 31 years later, by the NABESHIMA FAMILY, a surviving collateral branch of the Shōni.

shōnin

Translation of the Sanskrit term *ārya,* "noble person"; a title of respect given Buddhist monks distinguished for their wisdom, virtue, or good works. (The word can be written with either of two combinations of Chinese characters; the two are, for practical purposes, interchangeable.) Perhaps the first historical instance of its usage is in the appellation Ichi no Shōnin (Saint of the Marketplace) for the monk KŪYA (903–972). The term *shōnin* originally designated monks devoted to a life of seclusion or itinerant HIJIRI (ascetics endowed with charismatic powers) engaged in proselytization, but in later times it came to be applied in a more honorific sense, particularly in the Pure Land and Nichiren Buddhist traditions. It was even institutionalized as one of the honorary titles conferred upon Buddhist monks by the imperial court. *Robert RHODES*

Shōno Junzō (1921–)

Novelist. Born in Ōsaka; graduate of Kyūshū University. Shōno started to write after World War II while working for a broadcasting station. In 1954 he won the Akutagawa Prize for his short story "Pūrusaido shōkei," which describes the psychological crisis that befalls a typical middle-class housewife whose life is suddenly disrupted when her husband is unexpectedly fired from his job. Many of his subsequent novels in traditional autobiographical style deal with similar domestic situations. His novel *Yūbe no kumo* (1964–65) won the Yomiuri Literary Prize, and *E-awase* received the Noma Prize in 1971. Other works include *Seibutsu* (1960) and *Ukitōdai* (1961).

Shōriki Matsutarō (1885–1969)

Businessman and politician. Born in Toyama Prefecture and a graduate of Tōkyō University, Shōriki began a career in the Tōkyō Metropolitan Police Department, from which he resigned in 1924 after taking responsibility for the TORANOMON INCIDENT. He then became president of the YOMIURI SHIMBUN and developed it into Japan's most widely circulated newspaper. After World War II Shōriki promoted atomic power generation ventures by serving as director of the SCIENCE AND TECHNOLOGY AGENCY and chairman of the Atomic Energy Commission. He also inaugurated professional BASEBALL in Japan and was instrumental in the early development of commercial television. *TANAKA Yōnosuke*

Shōrui Awaremi no Rei

(Edicts on Compassion for Living Things). A series of edicts issued by the shōgun TOKUGAWA TSUNAYOSHI prohibiting cruelty to animals. The first of these edicts, issued in 1685, abolished the customary practice of leashing dogs and cats while the shōgun was traveling outside the castle. It prohibited hawking and ordered falconers and bird-catchers to take up other occupations. It strictly limited hunting to authorized persons and forbade the processing of certain horse-hide products. From 1687 onward the edicts became more and more extreme. The trapping and killing of all birds and animals was forbidden, and a government post, commissioner for living things (*shōrui bugyō*), was established to enforce the edicts. Dogs especially were to be cared for. In 1695 Tsunayoshi ordered large kennels erected at Yotsuya, Ōkubo, and Nakano in Edo (now Tōkyō) and appointed several vassals as kennel managers (*inugoya shihai*). The kennels, which were supported by levies imposed on the Edo populace, soon grew crowded. It is said that the Nakano kennel housed some 100,000 animals by the end of its first year of operation. In the countryside the hunting of hawks, eagles, doves, wild duck, and deer was forbidden, as was commerce in game fish and all living fish and fowl. To ensure obedience to these edicts, some of those found guilty of breaking the laws were punished by enforced suicide (*seppuku*), execution, imprisonment, or exile. It is said that some Edo residents grew so fearful that they began addressing dogs as "Sir Dog" (Oinu Sama).

The accepted explanation for these edicts is that Tsunayoshi, a learned and scholarly man, was distraught at the death of his young son and heir Tokumatsu in 1683 and by his subsequent inability to sire another. Steeped in the Confucian tradition, he saw his failure to beget an heir as evidence that in some way he was not governing properly. Ryūkō (1649–1724), a scholarly monk of the Shingon sect, who served as a religious adviser to Tsunayoshi and his devout mother, Keishō In (1624–1705), explained the problem in Buddhist terms as a consequence of Tsunayoshi's having taken the lives of many sentient beings in a prior incarnation. To nullify this malign karmic inheritance he advised the shōgun to show special compassion for living things, most particularly dogs, because he had been born in the year of the dog according to the Chinese sexagenary cycle (JIKKAN JŪNISHI). Further encouraged by his mother and his chief adviser, YANAGISAWA YOSHIYASU, Tsunayoshi issued the *shōrui awaremi* edicts. In the view of his contemporaries, Tsunayoshi's learning had undermined his sanity, and he was dubbed "the dog

shōgun" (*inu kubō*). His nephew and successor, TOKUGAWA IENOBU, rescinded the edicts soon after taking office in 1709. *Conrad TOTMAN*

Shōsenkyō

Gorge on the river Arakawa, a tributary of KAMANASHIGAWA, southwestern Yamanashi Prefecture, central Honshū. Originates in the Sengataki waterfalls and continues 5 km (3 mi) to Tenjimmori. Consists of towering granite cliffs and numerous strangely shaped rocks. Located within Chichibu–Tama National Park.

Shōshikai

Study group formed around 1832 by scholars and intellectuals interested in Western knowledge and its practical application to Japan. Also known as Bansha, an abbreviation of Bangaku Shachū, or "Companions of Barbarian Studies". Its members included noted scholars of Rangaku (Dutch studies; the study of Western science and culture through Dutch; see WESTERN LEARNING) such as WATANABE KAZAN, TAKANO CHŌEI, and OZEKI SAN'EI. The group, many of whose members were concerned about and critical of the backwardness of the shogunate's foreign policies, became the target of a governmental crackdown on progressive intellectuals that culminated in the BANSHA NO GOKU incident in 1839. (See also MORRISON INCIDENT.) The term *shōshikai* (literally, "honor-the-aged society") is otherwise a generic term used for informal groups that elderly people organized to share mutual interests such as poetry composition.

Shōshō Hakkei

(Eight Views of the Xiao and Xiang [Hsiao and Hsiang] Rivers). Painting subject. The term refers to paintings evocative of the humid lake and river scenery near Lake Dongting (Tung-t'ing), China. Originating with the painter Song Di (Sung Ti; ca 1015–80), by the 13th century the "Eight Views" became a standard theme in Chinese painting. The original eight titles were: *Geese Descending on Sandbanks, Returning Sails from a Distant Shore, Mountain Village in Clearing Rain, Evening Snow over the River, Autumn Moon over Lake Dongting, Night Rain over Xiao and Xiang, Evening Bell from a Misty Temple,* and *Sunset Glow over a Fishing Village.* The Ashikaga shōguns from ASHIKAGA YOSHIMITSU (1358–1408) onward acquired some remarkable examples that provided the core models for works in these modes by Japanese painters from the 15th to the 17th century. By 1437 ASHIKAGA YOSHINORI (1394–1441) owned Southern Song (Southern Sung; 1127–1279) handscroll versions attributed to painters Muqi (Mu-ch'i; J: MOKKEI), Zhang Fangru (Chang Fangju), and Yujian (Yü-chien), all in wash-oriented, "untrammeled" (*yipin* or *i-p'in*) styles, as well as a handscroll version attributed to Xia Gui (Hsia Kuei) and a folding-screen mounted version by Liu Yao, which were apparently in Southern Song academy-related styles. Fostered by the shōguns, literary monks of the GOZAN ("five mountains") temples, and court nobles as a favored mode for mural decoration, "Eight Views" paintings on folding screens and sliding doors, often bearing theme poems in Chinese by leading Gozan monks, flourished in the school of INK PAINTING started by SHŪBUN. Conditioned by the native penchant for seasonal structure, "Eight Views" works came to be arranged in a seasonal order; likewise, "Four Seasons" landscape compositions came to incorporate standard allusions to "Eight Views" themes. While mid-15th century works appear to have been modeled mainly on Song academic styles, the abbreviated style of Yujian gained favor in the SOGA SCHOOL and with the followers of SESSHŪ TŌYŌ. In the hands of SŌAMI, a landscape style in the manner of Muqi was perfected; it exerted a profound influence on the KANŌ SCHOOL. These three styles became prime representatives of the formal (*shin*), semicursive (*gyō*), and cursive (*sō*) modes of palatial and monastic decoration in the late 15th century. In the 16th century, native predilections increasingly favored wash-oriented modes, so that Yujian became the primary mode by the late 16th century. *Richard STANLEY-BAKER*

shōshū reijō

Draft notification slips first issued at the time of the IMO MUTINY in 1882; the last one was issued at the end of World War II. *Shōshū reijō* were issued by the commanders of the regimental districts into which Japan was divided. Printed on red paper, these notifications

Shōsōin

The 8th-century Shōsōin repository is built in a style of architecture known as *azekura* (log house); the structure utilizes no vertical supporting pillars, relying instead on the overlapping triangular wall logs for roof support. It houses several thousand precious objects from the 8th century. Nara.

Shōsōin

A corner of the Shōsōin repository, showing the interlocking construction of its log walls. 8th century. Nara.

Shōsōin

A rare five-string *biwa* (lute) of red sandalwood inlaid with mother-of-pearl, tortoiseshell, agate, and amber. Although the instrument's origin remains unclear, the inlaid design of a figure on camelback in Persian dress suggests a West Asian origin. Length 108.1 cm. 8th century. Shōsōin, Nara.

Shōsōin

Three-color ware bowl. The characteristic dappled effect results from application of green and yellowish brown glazes over a ground of white glaze. Thought to have been produced in Japan in imitation of Chinese Tang-dynasty (618–907) three-color ware. Glazed stoneware. Height 15.8 cm. 8th century. Shōsōin, Nara.

were commonly called *akagami* (red papers). Although *shōshū reijō* was a general term for conscription notices, it was usually used in connection with wartime draft.

Shōsōin

The wooden storehouse at the temple TŌDAIJI in Nara. It contains several thousand precious ornamental and fine art objects from the 8th century, many of which were donated by Empress KŌMYŌ in 756 or were used in the dedication ceremonies of the mammoth bronze statue of the Great Buddha (DAIBUTSU) of Tōdaiji in 752. In the 8th century the term *shōsō* described the imperial warehouses where rice and other items collected as tax were stored and the term *in* referred to a fenced enclosure. During the Nara (710–794) and Heian (794–1185) periods most large temples maintained such storage compounds, but today the word *shōsōin* applies only to the Tōdaiji treasure house. Managed by the temple under the supervision of the imperial court until early in the Meiji period (1868–1912), the Shōsōin is now under the jurisdiction of the Imperial Household Agency.

The Shōsōin is a huge, raised rectangular building made of Japanese cypress *(hinoki)*; it is divided into three sections and sits above the ground on 40 thick piles, each 2.4 meters (7.9 ft) in height. The north and south sections were built in the *azekura* style with triangular cross-section logs stacked horizontally, giving a smooth surface to the interior and a corrugated effect to the facade. The middle section joins the north and south sections with thick planks layered horizontally, and the whole building is covered by a *yosemune* hipped tile roof. The construction dates are not recorded but all three sections were in place by 761.

The Shōsōin, as an imperial repository, is not open to the general public. In October of each year, however, selected items are displayed at the NARA NATIONAL MUSEUM.

Bruce A. COATS

Shōsōin

Detail of an 8th-century painting of a bodhisattva. Like many objects in the Shōsōin, its provenance is unknown, although significant Chinese influence is evident in the brushwork. Ink on hemp cloth. Entire work 138.5 × 133.0 cm. Shōsōin, Nara.

Shōsōin

This folding-screen panel of plain silk dyed in the block-resist *(kyōkechi)* technique is an example of one of the three resist-dyeing *(sankechi)* processes of the Nara period. The symmetrical arrangement of deer and plants is reminiscent of Persian and other West Asian design motifs. 149 × 57 cm. 8th century. Shōsōin, Nara.

Treasures of the Shōsōin —— The treasures of the Shōsōin are from two main sources: the core collection of articles donated by the empress Kōmyō to Tōdaiji and the articles transferred to the Shōsōin from the storehouse of the Kensakuin, a subtemple of Tōdaiji, toward the middle of the Heian period (794–1185).

The donations by Empress Kōmyō were made beginning in June 756 to mark the end of the 49 days of official mourning for her husband, the emperor SHŌMU. In the next two years, she made several more donations, as attested by documents in the Shōsōin. Five such donations have been recorded, listing the types of object as well as the reasons for the donations. The scroll listing the first donation is the longest and contains a message from the empress praying for the repose of the soul of her husband as well as a detailed inventory of more than 600 objects. The principal objects in this first set were nine monk's robes *(kesa)* and articles used by the late emperor and at the imperial court, such as calligraphy samples, household implements, utensils, furniture, ornaments and accessories, musical instruments, and weapons. On the same day that these donations were made, the empress also donated 60 types of medicine to be given to the sick. These medicines are also described in detail in another scroll. Unfortunately, many of the articles donated by the empress have been lost through the centuries, and only a little more than a hundred treasures and thirty-nine types of medicine remain in the Shōsōin today.

The treasures from the Kensakuin seem to have been transferred to the Shōsōin because its storehouse had become greatly dilapidated by 950. Although there are no extant records of the treasures originally housed in the Kensakuin storehouse, we may assume they were considerable, judging from the great number of goods currently at the Shōsōin. Among them are objects used in the dedication ceremony of the Great Buddha in 752, at the funeral of the emperor Shōmu and the first anniversary ceremony commemorating his death, and at various annual observances. Most of these treasures bear inscriptions certifying their provenance, and even those without inscriptions can be identified by comparison.

Categories —— The treasures of the Shōsōin fall into the following categories: calligraphy samples, official documents, stationery, furniture and utensils, ornaments, Buddhist altar fittings, musical instruments, dance costumes, weapons and armor, objects used in annual observances, perfumes and medicines, and various art objects. Among the calligraphic works are transcriptions of Chinese classics and poems by Emperor Shōmu and Empress Kōmyō. The lists of donations themselves are written in the style of calligraphy then current in China and have merit as calligraphy. Official documents include the oldest extant Japanese household registers *(koseki),* written in 702, and documents concerning Tōdaiji in the Nara period. Among the furniture is a cabinet *(zushi)* and armrest used by Emperor Shōmu, as well as mirrors and screens used at the imperial court. There are 18 types of musical instrument, including wind, stringed, and percussion instruments. Tableware includes Persian-style vessels used for drinking and plates and bowls used for serving rice and other food during ceremonies at Tōdaiji.

Art objects include paintings, sculpture, metalwork, lacquer ware, handicrafts of wood, leather, horn, and shell, ceramics, glassware, and jade works as well as dyed and woven textiles. Paintings include *sai-e* (literally, "colored pictures") and ones decorated with bird feathers. Among the lacquer ware are examples of *heidatsu* and those that anticipate the technique of MAKI-E. In *heidatsu,* thin plates of gold or silver are cut up in patterns and pasted on the material which serves as the foundation. Several layers of lacquer are then applied over these patterns and polished so that the patterns come out in relief. Examples of wooden works are mosaics made by inlaying wood with various types of minute material. Among shell and horn works are *raden* (see MOTHER-OF-PEARL INLAY) and *bachiru,* in which designs are carved in dyed ivory with a picklike instrument. As for ceramics, there are pieces in three-color glaze—green, yellow, and white. Among the textiles are silken and brocaded fabrics, silk gauze, and fabrics dyed using the wax-resist, block-resist, and tie-dyeing processes (see SANKECHI). All these products display the high level of technique prevalent and the variety of materials imported into Japan during the Nara period.

In addition there are 56 mirrors, over 170 *gigaku* masks (see MASKS), more than 790 rolls of official documents, and nearly 300 strings of glass beads of different shapes and colors. These are but a fraction of the objects in the Shōsōin, and it is impossible to give a full list here, but suffice it to say that they provide a rich and detailed picture of the culture of the Nara period.

Although the majority of the Shōsōin treasures were made in Japan, many of them reflect foreign sources in their design motifs, materials, and production methods. These foreign sources are not limited to Tang (T'ang) China and neighboring areas but extend to more distant countries. The *hōsōge* (an imaginary flower based on the peony) motif is of Indian origin, the hunting scene motif and the *rempeki* round bead pattern are of Sassanid Persian origin, and the grapevine arabesque is from Greece. Foreign materials include ivory, rhinoceros horn, lapis lazuli, *shitan* (red sandalwood), and *byakudan* (white sandalwood) from Southeast Asia, India, and countries farther west. Practically all the medicines in the Shōsōin are products of China, Southeast Asia, India, Persia, and regions along the Mediterranean Sea.

Preservation of the Treasures ── In general, apart from some silk pieces, the treasures in the Shōsōin have been remarkably well preserved; indeed, some look almost new. One important reason for this is that the repository was built off the ground on pillars 2.4 meters (7.9 ft) high. The treasures were also placed in wooden chests which helped ward off damage from humidity. Further precautions were taken; for example, imperial permission had to be obtained to open the doors of the repository, and the treasures were not allowed to be handled without sufficient reason. Once in 1254, lightning struck the repository and a fire broke out near one of the doors, but this was soon extinguished by people living in the neighborhood. During the Edo period (1600–1868), when the treasures of the Shōsōin began showing signs of decay, repairs were initiated. Since 1883, the repository house has been opened for airing once a year in the fall. The greatest threats are fire and earthquake. To ensure their safety the treasures were recently transferred to two new ferroconcrete buildings, one completed in 1953 and one in 1962. A check of the items is conducted for some 40 days every fall, and an exhibition of selected treasures is held, principally at the Nara National Museum, for two weeks during this period.

📖 ── Ryōichi Hayashi, *The Silk Road and the Shōsō-in* (1975). Shōsōin Office, ed, *Treasures of the Shōsōin* (1965). Shōsōin Office, ed, *Glass Objects in the Shōsōin* (1965). Shōsōin Office, ed, *Musical Instruments in the Shōsōin* (1967). Shōsōin Office, ed, *Ceramic Objects in the Shōsōin* (1971). Shōsōin Office, ed, *Lacquer Works in the Shōsōin* (1975). Shōsōin Office, ed, *Metal Works in the Shōsōin* (1976). Shōsōin Office, ed, *Wood Work Objects in the Shōsōin* (1978).

ABE Hiromu

shotai

(script style; specifically, the style in which Chinese characters or KANJI are written). The three basic styles of Chinese calligraphy, in use in China and Japan since ancient times, are known in Japanese as *santai* (the three styles). They are, in the Japanese pronunciations of their Chinese names, *kaisho*, the standard angular, noncursive style, *gyōsho*, the semicursive style, and *sōsho*, the fluid cursive or "grass" style. *Kaisho* developed during the Later Han dynasty (AD 25–220) out of earlier styles, and *gyōsho* and *sōsho* had both developed on the basis of *kaisho* by the 5th and 6th centuries. A larger classification known as *gotai* (the five styles) consists of the above three plus two archaic styles: the *tensho* or seal script, dating from the Qin (Ch'in) dynasty (221 BC–206 BC) and the *reisho* or clerical script, dating from the Former Han dynasty (206 BC–AD 8).

Although the choice of script in personal writing is a matter of individual taste, certain general distinctions in usage are observed. *Kaisho* is the style taught in Japanese schools. It is used when clarity is called for, as in signs and official documents, and is in effect the style in widest use today. *Gyōsho* and *sōsho*, which abbreviate or stylize the strokes of the characters, are used for informal occasions such as personal correspondence or for calligraphy. The archaic *tensho* and *reisho* are not used in ordinary writing, and many of their forms are not readily recognizable to the general public. They are used decoratively, as in seals, trademarks, and sometimes the titles of learned books.

The most common styles of characters used in printing in Japan, all *kaisho*, are based on the printed styles of various Chinese dynasties. The *sōchōtai* 宋朝体 (Song or Sung dynasty style) and *seichōtai* 清朝体 (Qin dynasty style) are used for formal invitations and calling cards, while the *minchōtai* 明朝体 (Ming dynasty style) is the style used in most books, newspapers, and magazines. There is also a so-called *kyōkashotai* 教科書体 or textbook style.

YAMADA Toshio

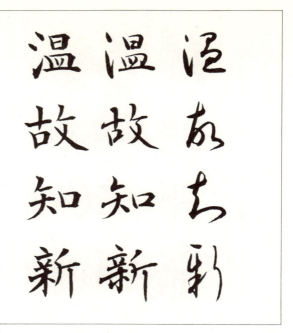

Shotai

Four Chinese characters written in the *kaisho* (left column), *gyōsho* (middle column), and *sōsho* (right column) styles. Read from top to bottom, they form the phrase *onko chishin* (to learn from the past; literally, "respect the old, know the new").

Shōtetsu (1381–1459)

Classical (WAKA) poet and critic, Buddhist priest. Shōtetsu stands out in his time with Imagawa Sadayo (also known as Ryōshun; b 1326) as one of the two foremost opponents of the dominant conservative Nijō poetic school. Shōtetsu's interest in poetry was encouraged by his father. During his family's residence in Kyōto in the 1390s he had an opportunity to meet Ryōshun and Reizei Tamemasa (1361–1417), head of the Reizei poetic school, hereditary adversaries of the Nijō group. Both Nijō and Reizei descended from Fujiwara no Teika (FUJIWARA NO SADAIE), the great arbiter of poetry in the golden age of the late 12th and early 13th centuries. At about the age of 16 Shōtetsu became an acolyte at Kōfukuji, a temple in Nara, and around 1417 became a secretary at Tōfukuji, a temple in Kyōto. From his forties to the end of his life, he was prominent in the area of the capital as a poet-priest, a scholar of classical literature, and an opponent of the Nijō school.

In his poetics Shōtetsu was somewhat at variance even with the Reizei school, calling for a return to the ideals and practice of Teika, whom he idolized, writing in his important poetic record known as *Shōtetsu monogatari* (Tales of Shōtetsu) that anyone who presumed to criticize Teika should be punished in the life to come. As this suggests, Shōtetsu was an outspoken critic and a man of strong ideas. The "return to Teika" he advocated was of course colored by his view of what aspect of the master's practice was most fundamental. He particularly admired Teika's love poetry, and his interpretation of the classical ideal of *yūgen*, or "mystery and depth" was actually closer to Teika's early poetic ideal of *yojō yōen*, the style of "overtones and ethereal beauty."

In addition to *Shōtetsu monogatari*, a valuable record of its time as well as of his poetic views, Shōtetsu left a collection of his own poems, *Sōkonshū* (Collection of the Roots of Plants), containing more than 20,000 poems. His distinctive style is both convoluted and elliptical and makes him one of the most difficult of the classical poets. It is indicative of the antipathy felt toward him by the conservative Nijō school that when one of its adherents compiled the *Shin zoku kokinshū* (New Collection of Ancient and Modern Times Continued), the last of the 21 imperial anthologies, in 1439, not one of Shōtetsu's poems was included.

📖 ── Earl Miner, *An Introduction to Japanese Court Poetry* (1968).

Robert H. BROWER

Shotai

The same four characters as on the facing page, written in the *tensho* (left column) and *reisho* (right column) styles. The phrase is from the *Lun yu* (*Lun yü; Analects*), a collection of sayings by Confucius and his disciples.

Shōtoku, Empress → Kōken, Empress

Shōtoku Nagasaki Shinrei

Also called Shōtoku Shinrei; officially known as the Kaihaku Goshi Shinrei (New Regulations on Ships and Trade). A set of regulations issued by the Tokugawa shogunate in 1715 (Shōtoku 5) to limit trade with China and the Netherlands, the only countries allowed to trade with Japan at that time under its NATIONAL SECLUSION policy (see also NAGASAKI TRADE). Drafted by the scholar and shogunate adviser ARAI HAKUSEKI, they were enacted to curtail the outflow of gold and silver resulting from excessive imports, to restrict the export of copper (Japan's largest export item at the time), and to reduce the growing practice of smuggling, particularly by Chinese vessels, by issuing certificates called *shimpai*. The regulations specified the number of ships (2 for the Dutch and 30 for the Chinese) and limited the volume of trade (not to exceed an estimated value of 3,000 *kan* or 11.3 metric tons [12.4 short tons] of silver for the Dutch and 6,000 *kan* or 22.5 metric tons [24.8 short tons] for the Chinese) to be allowed annually. These regulations remained in effect until the 1830s.

Shōtoku no Chi

A series of reforms undertaken during the reigns of the sixth and seventh Tokugawa shōguns TOKUGAWA IENOBU and Tokugawa Ietsugu (1709–16; r 1713–16); named for the era name *(nengō)* Shōtoku (1711–16). The main figures in the reforms were Ienobu's Confucian teacher and adviser, ARAI HAKUSEKI, who was responsible for drafting the reforms, and Ienobu's chamberlain *(sobayōnin)*, MANABE AKIFUSA, who supervised shogunate affairs as Ienobu's favorite. The reforms were intended to enhance the authority of the shōgun by transforming him into a Confucian monarch and were characterized by a conservative fiscal policy. They included discontinuation of currency debasement, stricter regulation of the NAGASAKI TRADE, change in the protocol for reception of embassies from Korea (CHŌSEN TSŪSHINSHI), adoption of monarchical ritual for shogunate ceremonies, and betrothal of the child shōgun Ietsugu to an imperial princess. The fiscal aspect of the Shōtoku reforms was continued under the eighth shōgun, TOKUGAWA YOSHIMUNE, but the ideological and ritual dimensions were abandoned.

Yoshiyuki NAKAI

Shōtoku, Prince (574–622)

Statesman of the Asuka period (latter part of the 6th century to 710); second son of Emperor Yōmei (r 585–587). As regent for the empress SUIKO (r 593–628), Prince Shōtoku exercised political leadership, instituting such measures as the KAN'I JŪNIKAI ("twelve cap ranks") and the SEVENTEEN-ARTICLE CONSTITUTION in order to centralize the government and strengthen the authority of the imperial institution. Devoted to Buddhism, he sought to extend its religious and civilizing influence. To enhance national prestige, he compiled histories with SOGA NO UMAKO and initiated diplomatic relations with the Sui dynasty (589–618) in China.

According to the account given in the NIHON SHOKI (720), Prince Shōtoku was born in the doorway of a horse shed *(umaya)*, when his mother, Anahobe no Hashihito no Himemiko, suddenly felt labor pains as she was making the rounds of the palace. For this reason, he was first named Umayado no Miko, or Prince of the Horse Shed. The legend of his birth, however, seems to be an embellishment added later by scholar-monks who had studied in Tang (T'ang; 618–907) China and heard about the birth of Christ from Nestorians. The prince was known by other names, such as Toyotomimi no Ōji (Prince Endowed with Intelligence and Judgment) and Jōgū Taishi, from the fact that he resided in the upper castle. But it is by his name Shōtoku Taishi (Prince of Sagely Virtue) that he is best known. It is only from the 8th century, however, that he is mentioned as such, an inscription at the temple Hokkiji (built in 706) being the earliest example.

Following the death of Emperor Yōmei in 587, a power struggle broke out between Soga no Umako and MONONOBE NO MORIYA over the question of imperial succession. Shōtoku and other princes sided with Umako. According to the *Nihon shoki* he prayed to the Shitennō (the Four Heavenly Kings) for victory and seems to have acted more prominently in a priestly function than in a military capacity. After Moriya was killed in the ensuing war, Shōtoku received some property owned by the Mononobe; he later donated it to the temple HŌRYŪJI.

The now all-powerful Soga no Umako succeeded in having Sushun installed as emperor. Sushun was murdered in 592 following a feud with Umako. It was at this critical juncture that Umako's niece and widow of the deceased emperor Bidatsu (r 572–585) was selected as the next ruler, Empress Suiko. After becoming empress in 593 Suiko appointed Shōtoku, then only 20 years old, as regent, delegating all powers to him. Her decision to abstain from politics was no doubt calculated to ensure her own safety and the stability of the imperial family, although some historians claim that Shōtoku's regency actually started a few years later.

The inauguration of the twelve cap ranks in 604 was Shōtoku's first administrative achievement. Tribal chieftains in service to the court were ranked on a completely new basis. Whereas the KABANE ranking had been determined within the larger framework of the UJI or lineage group to which one belonged by birth (see UJI–KABANE SYSTEM), status was now defined on a purely individual basis. (The order of ranking was marked by the color and pattern of the caps.) One could, furthermore, aspire to a higher rank. And by conferring each rank in the name of the emperor, Shōtoku hoped to convert tribal chieftains into faithful public servants of the emperor.

The same year Shōtoku promulgated the Seventeen-Article Constitution. Constitution, in this instance, meant a "splendid law," and stressing as it did the exalted personage of the emperor and the reverence and obedience due him, it resembled more a set of moral and political precepts. The text, with numerous quotations from Confucian, Buddhist, and Chinese Legalist works, is written in a highly literate style. Some scholars since the Edo period (1600–1868) have doubted whether it was in fact written by the prince, but opinion on the whole tends to attribute authorship to him. It is also questionable whether the document was ever presented to the public, but it does give a general idea of Shōtoku's political thought.

Shōtoku, who had been brought up by religiously zealous parents, was himself a devout follower of Buddhism. In 594, the year following his appointment, he issued an imperial edict calling for the promotion of Buddhism. He gave direct imperial support to the building of the temple ASUKADERA (Hōkōji), a project previously sponsored by the Soga, selecting it as the site of imperial ceremonies and appointing Umako's eldest son as a temple official. He also sponsored the building of the temples SHITENNŌJI and Hōryūji. It must be remembered, however, that in carrying out these good works he always sought to extend imperial influence over Buddhist institutions.

Shōtoku is also credited with having been the first Japanese to understand thoroughly the *Saddharmapuṇḍarīka* or Lotus (J: *Hokekyō*), *Vimalakīrti-nirdeśa* (J: *Yuimagyō*), and *Śrīmālādevī-siṃhanāda* (J: *Shōmangyō*) sutras, and to have written commentaries on these works (see SANGYŌ GISHO). The LOTUS SUTRA was of primary importance, and since the *Yuima* sutra recorded the teachings of a princely figure who, like Shōtoku, had elected to stay in the world, and the *Shōman* sutra centered on an imperial consort not unlike Suiko, it can be assumed that at the very least Shōtoku had a hand in selecting them. Be that as it may, the prince's role in spreading Buddhism remains undisputed.

In 620, together with Umako, Shōtoku compiled the historical chronologies, TENNŌKI AND KOKKI. Since the two manuscripts are recorded as having been burnt by Soga no Emishi when he committed suicide in 645, they must have been more or less completed. Yet the fact that they were kept at the Soga residence indicates that the histories were still unready for imperial presentation. What is of interest is the appearance of *tennō* (emperor) in the title. Whereas the title traditionally used, *daiō* (great king), emphasized the secular nature of the ruler, *tennō* (heavenly sovereign) stressed the ruler's religious aspect as well. One may assume that the *Kokki* (Record of the Nation) dealt with the founding of Japan and that it reflected Shōtoku's conception of the nation as an emperor-centered polity. In this sense, the compilation of history was for Prince Shōtoku an indispensable part of nation building.

Ever since the conquest of the Japanese enclave of KAYA by the adjacent Korean kingdom of SILLA in 562, successive emperors had made repeated efforts to regain a foothold on the Korean peninsula. Shōtoku too, in 602 appointed his brother Prince Kume (d 603) as head of an expeditionary force against Silla. When Kume died of illness in Tsukushi (Kyūshū), Shōtoku appointed his half-brother Tagima, but then Tagima's wife suddenly died. Although the plan to invade Silla thus ended in failure, it must be noted as yet another example of Shōtoku's leadership.

Shōtoku once more asserted his leadership in foreign affairs when he decided to dispatch an envoy to China in 600. His move was in response to the news that Yang Jian (Yang Chien; r 581–604) had overthrown the Chen (Ch'en) dynasty (557–589) and succeeded in unifying the country under his Sui dynasty (589–618). By sending the mission, the prince also hoped no doubt to thwart any untoward action on Silla's part. A second embassy was sent in 607, when ONO NO IMOKO was dispatched bearing a message from "the ruler of the Land of the Rising Sun to the emperor of the Land of the Setting Sun." The wording evidently incurred the displeasure of the Sui emperor Yangdi (Yang-ti; r 604–616). He nevertheless consented to send a return envoy, since he realized the advantages of allying with Japan in the event of a projected invasion against KOGURYŌ. When Imoko set off again the following year, he was accompanied by a large delegation of scholar-monks and students. They returned one by one over the years, many of them after Shōtoku's death. Some of these returned scholars contributed directly and indirectly to the TAIKA REFORM of 645. See SUI AND TANG (T'ANG) CHINA, EMBASSIES TO.

During the latter half of his regency, Shōtoku was curiously inactive. He may have been defeated in the power struggle against Umako, or he may have simply tired of politics. In any event the words attributed to Shōtoku in his declining years, "This world is empty and false; Buddha alone is real," testify not only to his disillusion in politics but to his whole-hearted embracing of religion. The prince died at IKARUGA NO MIYA. Some documents relating to him are preserved in the collection JŌGŪ SHŌTOKU HŌŌTEI SETSU. ◼ Ogura Toyofumi, *Shōtoku Taishi to Shōtoku Taishi shinkō* (1963). Ōno Tatsunosuke, *Shōtoku Taishi no kenkyū* (1970). Tamura Enchō, *Shōtoku Taishi* (1964).　　　　　　MAYUZUMI Hiromichi

Shōtoku Taishi → Shōtoku, Prince

Shoup mission

A group of seven American tax specialists, headed by Professor Carl S. Shoup of Columbia University, which arrived in Allied occupied Japan for its initial visit on 10 May 1949. The mission's purpose was to study and recommend revisions for Japan's system of taxes. These tax reforms were to complement the balanced budget and other stabilization measures implemented under the DODGE LINE and to aid in Japan's economic rehabilitation.

Shōtoku, Prince

Imaginary portrait of Prince Shōtoku holding a baton of rank and flanked by two young princes. Thought to date from the late 7th or early 8th century. Hanging scroll. Colors on paper. 125.0 × 50.6 cm. Imperial Household Agency.

By 1949 the Japanese tax system was in critical need of comprehensive revision. The United States government considered it inefficient and inequitable. Tax evasion was common, and enforcement generally arbitrary. Japanese taxpayers, moreover, were complaining that the postwar inflation had pushed them into higher and higher personal income tax brackets. The ratio of personal taxes to income had risen from 8 percent in the prewar period to 21 percent by 1947. The mission's recommendations centered on three major principles: (1) to generate most of the tax revenues through direct, rather than indirect, taxes; (2) to strengthen the fiscal autonomy of local governments; and (3) to encourage capital accumulation and sound business accounting. Specifically, the mission recommended that the central government rely on personal and corporate income taxes for the bulk of its revenue. Personal income tax rates were to be cut, but enforcement increased. The liquor tax was increased. Taxes on tobacco and commodities were retained, while those on such basic necessities as sugar, soft drinks, textiles, and travel were repealed. The net worth and inheritance taxes were added to replace revenue lost by the cuts in personal income tax.

In order to reduce the highly centralized power of the national government, the mission recommended that the revenue base of local governments be strengthened, the authority of local tax administrators be increased, and the tax jurisdictions for the respective levels of government be specified. Several local taxes were eliminated, but the prefectures were allowed a revised enterprise, amusement, and admissions tax. The municipalities were to rely mainly on a revised inhabitants' tax and property taxes. While national tax revenues were to decrease by 11 percent, that is, ¥59 billion (about US $164 million), prefectural revenues were to remain constant, and municipal tax revenues were to increase by 50 percent, that is ¥40 billion (about US $111 million). In order to facilitate capital accumulation, the mission recommended that corporations be allowed to revalue their assets with only a 6 percent tax on the revaluation profits, so that depreciation allowances would more accurately reflect the inflated replacement costs of capital. Excess profits taxes were also to be abolished. To encourage sound business accounting, the mission recommended that the tax and financial data of all corporations be certified by an independent public accountant.

After considerable debate, the Diet passed the Shoup mission's recommendations in 1950. Many of the measures, however, were subsequently modified or repealed. By 1953, the value-added, net worth, and corporate reserve taxes had been repealed. Other taxes had been altered to reflect economic conditions and to promote capital accumulation. Despite such changes, however, the Japanese system has remained essentially in the pattern established by the Shoup mission.

Carl Sumner Shoup (b 1902) was born in San Jose, California. He received his AB degree from Stanford in 1924 and his PhD from Columbia in 1930, where he taught economics from 1928 to 1971. He was awarded the Order of the Sacred Treasure by the Japanese government. See also ECONOMIC HISTORY: Occupation-period economy.

📖 ——Shiomi Saburō, tr Hasegawa Shōtarō, *Japan's Finance and Taxation, 1940–1956* (1957). Dick K. NANTO

Shōwa Aluminum Corporation

(Shōwa Aruminiumu). A company engaged in the manufacture of various types of aluminum products, Shōwa Aluminum is the largest aluminum roller and processor in Japan. It was established in 1935. It has concluded technical tie-ups with several companies in the United States, West Germany, and Australia, and serves as the manufacturer of processed aluminum products for SHŌWA DENKŌ. Sales for the fiscal year ending November 1981 totaled ¥115.9 billion (US $518 million); capitalization stood at ¥6.5 billion (US $29.1 million). Corporate headquarters are located in Sakai, Ōsaka Prefecture.

Shōwa Denkō

A general chemical company, Shōwa Denkō was founded in 1939 through the merger of Nippon Electric Industries and Shōwa Fertilizer Company. Its chief lines of business are manufacturing petrochemical products and smelting aluminum. The origin of the company dates back to 1908 when MORI NOBUTERU established an iodine-manufacturing company called Sōbō Suisan Co. This company was later absorbed by Tōshin Denki Co, but it became independent again in 1926 and took the name Nippon Iodine Co, Ltd. In 1928 Mori founded the Shōwa Fertilizer Co, Ltd, and succeeded in the domestic production of lime nitrogen and ammonium sulfate. At about the same time, Nippon Iodine started production of potassium chlorate, soda and carbide products, and other chemicals, and in 1934, it successfully developed an aluminum-refining technology using domestic resources. In that year it also changed its name to Nippon Electric Industries and began electrolytic refining of ferrous and nonferrous metals together with the mining of molybdenum ore in Korea, laying the basis for the creation of the so-called Mori Concern. After World War II the company was rebuilt centering on the manufacture of fertilizers, but in the latter half of the 1950s, it entered the petrochemical field. In 1966 Shōwa Denkō constructed a giant petrochemical plant in Ōita Prefecture, where it produces ethylene, polyethylene, polypropylene, acétaldehyde, and vinyl acetate. Its subsidiary firm, SHŌWA ALUMINUM CORPORATION, engages in the manufacture of aluminum products, and smelting companies have been established in New Zealand, Venezuela, and Indonesia to achieve vertical unification of aluminum production. Sales in 1981 were ¥384.5 billion (US $1.8 billion), of which petrochemical products accounted for 56 percent and other products 44 percent; exports composed 10 percent of the total sales. The firm was capitalized at ¥43.7 billion (US $199.6 million) in the same year. Corporate headquarters are located in Tōkyō.

Shōwa Denkō Scandal

(Shōden Jiken). A major political scandal of 1948 involving SHŌWA DENKŌ, Japan's largest fertilizer producer at the time, and many important political leaders and government officials. The scandal was first revealed before a special Diet committee in April 1948, when opposition party members accused several government officials of accepting bribes from Shōwa Denkō in return for special consideration in arranging a low-interest loan from the RECONSTRUCTION FINANCE BANK (established in 1946 and funded by the United States). Among those implicated were members of ASHIDA HITOSHI's coalition cabinet, and in October the cabinet was forced to step down. Hearings were drawn out, and it was not until 1962 that the final judgments were handed down by the Tōkyō Superior Court: 2 of the 64 indicted were found guilty, the rest having been acquitted earlier.

Shōwa Depression

(Shōwa Kyōkō). Great Japanese financial depression of the 1930s; so called from the Shōwa period (1926–). One of a series of world financial crises triggered by that in the United States in 1929; it began in early 1930 and lasted until 1935. The American crisis, which started with the Great Crash of the Wall Street stock market in October 1929, developed into a world financial crisis. Spreading to Europe, it provoked the German financial crisis of July 1931, and two months later caused England to go off the gold standard. As a consequence, the other chief capitalist countries, Japan, the United States, Italy, and France, also left the gold standard, putting an end to the worldwide gold standard system. The powerful capitalist countries strengthened political and economic bonds between themselves and lands under their hegemony—colonies, semicolonies, and self-governing territories—by forming bloc economies. Each bloc devised various strategies to increase its supply of raw materials and its share of the export market; adopted defensive measures in the form of import prohibitions and limitations, such as protective tariffs and systems of import licensing and allotment; and implemented aggressive policies such as currency devaluation and export dumping. As nations adopted such policies against one another, antagonism between blocs became unavoidable and escalated from economic opposition to military confrontation. The Japanese depression developed in close relationship with such world economic conditions.

In November 1929, believing that the American financial crisis would never lead to a world crisis, the Japanese government declared its intention to return to the gold standard, and in January 1930 it lifted the gold embargo. However, only two months later, as prices in the consumer and stock markets began to plummet and foreign trade took a turn for the worse, there was a huge gold outflow. Reeling from the double blow of the world economic crisis and the adverse effects of the return to the gold standard, the Japanese economy was thrust into an unprecedented depression. The steep drop in commodity prices throughout the world, the raising of import tariffs in every nation, and the shrinking of the Chinese and Indian markets caused by the sharp decline in the value of silver resulted in the cutting of exports by half from a valuation in 1929 of ¥2.1 billion to ¥1.5 billion in 1930 and ¥1.2 billion in 1931, and of imports from ¥2.2 billion in 1929 to ¥1.5 billion in 1930 and ¥1.2 billion in 1931.

The rate of decline in commodity prices was greater than that in England or the United States, and it was unique in that the prices of agricultural products meant for export, such as silk, cotton thread, unbleached muslin, and soy beans, fell rapidly. Among small- and medium-scale businesses the occurrence of bankruptcy, suspension of operations, absconding by factory owners, and failure to pay wages was common. Large businesses attempted to meet the situation by curtailing operations or forming cartels on the one hand, and by firing workers, reducing wages, and intensifying labor use on the other. The number of unemployed increased, reaching a total between 2 and 2.5 million. Labor disputes became violent, and their number grew rapidly, reaching a total of 2,456 incidents in 1931, the highest prewar figure.

The unique feature of the Japanese economic crisis was the severity and scale of the depression in the agricultural sector. The value of Japanese agricultural products fell from ¥3.5 billion in 1929 to ¥2.3 billion in 1930 and ¥2.0 billion in 1931. The severe reduction in the export of silk thread to the United States was immediately followed by a drop in the price of silkworm cocoons, the spring market price of cocoons in 1930 being half that of the previous year. At that time over 2 million families (36 percent of all farm families) were engaged in sericulture. Except for wage labor during temporary out-migration (DEKASEGI), sericulture was very nearly the farmers' only source of currency. Thus, the decline in silk prices was a calamitous blow to the farmer. Further, from October 1930, the price of rice began an unabated decline and, as a consequence, the agricultural depression entered its most serious and pervasive phase. It was during this period that there appeared newspaper stories, mostly from northern Honshū, of girls sold into prostitution, starving children, and unpaid schoolteachers and local bureaucrats. In rural communities there simultaneously arose a radical peasant movement and a reactionary agrarian nationalist movement (NŌHON SHUGI).

Late in 1930 the Japanese government took measures to combat the depression, such as relief loans financed by the Deposit Bureau of the Ministry of Finance and by the Bank of Japan, but it was not until the appointment of TAKAHASHI KOREKIYO as finance minister in the newly formed cabinet of INUKAI TSUYOSHI in December 1931 that an effective plan was instituted. Takahashi's task was twofold: to lead the country out of the economic crisis and to expand armaments production for the conquest of Manchuria. The course of action that he pursued was the opposite of that taken by the previous finance minister, INOUE JUNNOSUKE. Through retrenchment of government spending and maintenance of high interest rates, Inoue had tried to reduce commodity prices and improve the balance of international payments; by contrast, Takahashi sought to stimulate the economy, and thereby to promote economic recovery, by adopting an inflationary policy centering on the issue of government bonds and the granting of low-interest loans. Takahashi's program followed the Keynesian concept of a money-spending policy and marked a turning point in Japanese financial history as the pioneering example of a classic inflationary system of currency management. Takahashi's measures proved effective, and from the second half of 1933 the heavy and chemical industries led the way toward recovery. However, aggravated by a crop failure in 1934 due to unseasonal frost, the agricultural depression was not alleviated until the end of 1935. The belated recovery of the farming sector was one of the factors that led to the FEBRUARY 26TH INCIDENT, the 1936 coup attempt by radical young army officers, most of whom came from rural areas. NAKAMURA Masanori

Shōwa Electric Wire & Cable Co, Ltd

(Shōwa Densen Denran). Company engaged in the manufacture and sale of electric wires and cables, delay elements, components of electrical appliances and devices, and rubber and plastic products. Established in 1936, it is now one of the six major electric wire and cable companies in Japan. It has concluded technical assistance agreements with the General Electric Co and the Westinghouse Electric Corporation of the United States. Current plans call for expansion of its operations in sectors other than electric wire and cable. Sales for the fiscal year ending April 1982 totaled ¥104.4 billion (US $426.4 million), and capitalization stood at ¥6.7 billion (US $27.4 million) in the same year. Corporate headquarters are located in Tōkyō.

Shōwa Ishin → "Shōwa Restoration"

Shōwa Kenkyūkai

(Shōwa Research Association). Political study group founded in October 1933 and disbanded in November 1940. The association began as an informal organization founded by the politician GOTŌ RYŪNOSUKE. Gotō's original intention was to reassess Japan's constitutional politics in light of the demise of party cabinets following the assassination of Prime Minister INUKAI TSUYOSHI in May 1932 and the rise of authoritarian governments in Europe. Gotō was a close friend of KONOE FUMIMARO, who had political ambitions, and the latter hoped that the group would provide ideas for innovative national policies. Gotō asked Rōyama Masamichi (1895–1980), a political scientist from Tōkyō University, to head the association. To avoid a distinct ideological bias, membership was intentionally made diverse, encompassing scholars, journalists, socialist politicians, bankers, and representatives of the semiofficial Federation of Youth Groups of Japan (DAI NIPPON RENGŌ SEINENDAN), of which Gotō was an official. Retired General Shiga Naokata, a federation official, gave financial support. Konoe attended the first meetings of the association but soon ceased direct participation in its discussions.

Assuming the name Shōwa Kenkyūkai in 1935, the group soon formalized its structure while expanding its activity. A permanent executive board was established in 1936 to outline general policies, and an administrative bureau managed daily operations. Several large companies became major donors to the organization. Each year, a prospectus was drawn up indicating which topics the association should investigate through separate study groups; these were then staffed by invited specialists of varied backgrounds. In one year, for example, the association involved some 130 different participants in 10 major task forces covering issues of foreign affairs, politics, economics, culture, and education. The discussions of these groups were confidential, but their reports were passed on to Konoe and government officials and sometimes printed for limited distribution. Moreover, distinguished civil servants became leaders of the association and joined its study groups. These included GOTŌ FU-

MIO, home minister 1934–36, Kaya Okinori (1889–1977), finance minister 1937–38, ARITA HACHIRŌ, foreign minister in several cabinets, and Kazami Akira (1886–1961), cabinet secretary 1937–38. The popular press labeled the Kenkyūkai Konoe's "brain trust."

With the eruption of the SINO-JAPANESE WAR OF 1937–1945 shortly after Konoe's appointment as premier in June 1937, the problems of mobilizing national support for the war and ending the hostilities dominated the activity of the association. Convinced that Japan should become the leader of Asia, the group anticipated and probably influenced Konoe's declaration of a "New Order in East Asia" (TŌA SHINCHITSUJO) in November 1938, and some members became vocal exponents of an "East Asian Cooperative Body" (Tōa Kyōdōtai). The philosopher MIKI KIYOSHI headed a Culture Study Group that devised a theory of "cooperativism"—a deliberate blend of socialist, liberal, and fascist ideas—as the philosophical framework for a regional bloc of Asian nations. Academics, such as Rōyama and Yabe Teiji (1902–67; also called Yabe Sadaji), and journalists, such as OZAKI HOTSUMI and Sassa Hiroo (1897–1948), concentrated on political and foreign-policy issues. Believing liberal democracy to be outmoded, they argued that a new "national organization" based on occupational representation should replace the Diet; and they envisioned a political union of Japan with China. Other study groups prepared for the economic integration of Japan with Asia, while Ryū Shintarō (1900–1967), an editor of the newspaper *Asahi shimbun*, supervised research on implementing a state-planned economy.

These plans culminated in the NEW ORDER MOVEMENT, which Konoe initiated in June 1940. Konoe sought Gotō's help and asked Yabe to sketch its initial goals. Using ideas developed within the Kenkyūkai, Yabe proposed drastic reforms of Japan's economic and political systems. Although Konoe as prime minister endorsed Yabe's draft, it was clear by late autumn that such radical proposals would not succeed. In November, the association disbanded.

The influence of the Shōwa Kenkyūkai on the policies Konoe pursued as prime minister in 1937–38 and 1940–41 has been a controversial topic, as has the ideological orientation of the group. Its most prominent members have been labeled liberals, socialists, fascists, and reactionaries. The basic motivations of its leaders, and thus the aim of the initial New Order Movement itself, also remain debatable. Association members have argued in retrospect that they were attempting to curb the power of the military and to moderate Japan's military aggression. They did, however, stress Japan's mission to dominate Asia and sought to reduce the authority of the Diet and impose more state control over the economy.

━━━━Baba Shūichi, "Senkyūhyakusanjū nendai ni okeru Nihon chishikijin no dōkō," *Shakai kagaku kiyō* 41 (1969). Miles Fletcher, "Intellectuals and Fascism in Prewar Japan," *Journal of Asian Studies* 39.1 (1979). Sakai Saburō, *Shōwa kenkyūkai: aru chishikijin shūdan no kiseki* (1979). Shōwa Dōjinkai, ed, *Shōwa kenkyūkai* (1968).
Wm. Miles FLETCHER III

Shōwa Line, Ltd

(Shōwa Kaiun). A shipping firm chiefly operating tramp freighters, the Shōwa Line was established in 1944 and is one of the six largest companies of its kind in Japan. A member of the Fuyō group, it owns 31 ships totaling 2,713,000 deadweight tons. Sales for the fiscal year ending March 1982 totaled ¥195.7 billion (US $813 million); and capitalization was ¥7.7 billion (US $32 million) in the same year. Corporate headquarters are located in Tōkyō.

Shōwa literature

Shōwa is the reign name or period name adopted when the emperor Hirohito succeeded to the throne in 1926; it thus marks a change in the Japanese calendar (from the previous Taishō period, 1912–26) and bears no direct relation to the history of literature. Nevertheless, certain events took place around this time that the Japanese see as symbolic of the beginning of a new age in Japanese literature. Soon after the accession, in 1927 (Shōwa 2), the brilliant short-story writer AKUTAGAWA RYŪNOSUKE committed suicide, as though to seal the fate of the literature of the Taishō period with which his name is associated. In that same year there was a movement toward the political Left on the part of a number of literary figures; there was also a proliferation of the cheap editions called EMPON or "one-yen books," a development that was to have a great effect on the reading public. Thus Japanese literary historians have found the term Shōwa literature a useful one to mark the beginning of a new period. HIRANO KEN's study of contemporary literature, *Shōwa bungaku shi* (1959, History of Shōwa Literature), begins with the death of Akutagawa, but many scholars begin the literary period in 1924 (Taishō 13), since many distinguishing marks of the new literature were already evident by then. Although the Shōwa period continues after World War II, the literature since 1945 is commonly referred to as postwar literature. This article covers the literary history—centering on writers of fiction—of the period from 1924 to the eve of World War II in the late 1930s. For the succeeding decades, see WAR LITERATURE; POSTWAR LITERATURE.

What should be mentioned first in discussing this period is the fact that the writers of the Taishō years, who had sought to understand man as an individual (an idea foreign to the Japanese), had reached an impasse, as it were, and it was clear that there was a need to seek solutions elsewhere. The Taishō writers had tended to go in a number of different directions. Some authors of the SHIRAKABA SCHOOL, prominent among them MUSHANOKŌJI SANEATSU, thought that to develop one's individualism was naturally in conformity with human happiness; however, by the end of the Taishō period their idealism was considered naive. Some writers, like Akutagawa, sank into despair when, in their search for individualism, they encountered the ugliness of man's egotism. Certain writers of the Japanese naturalist school and their successors wrote of their daily lives, accepting the problems that surrounded them as presumably insoluble; these writers were apt to see only an infinite expanse of gray. NAGAI KAFŪ, TANIZAKI JUN'ICHIRŌ, and others who gave themselves to aestheticism, pursued a heterodox course but had not yet attracted major attention.

The early Shōwa years saw two responses to this situation. One was the PROLETARIAN LITERATURE MOVEMENT, which aimed at social revolution. Its adherents believed that man's consciousness was shaped by class relations and that when the proletarian revolution was realized not only would class exploitation be gone, but also the people would truly be able to develop their individuality; man would attain true freedom, unshackled by egotism. Proletarian literature emerged around 1921, the year that saw the first issue of the magazine TANE MAKU HITO (The Sowers). (The suicide in 1923 of ARISHIMA TAKEO, who had sympathized with Marxism but felt unable to participate, is also regarded as a turning point.) But it was with the first issue of BUNGEI SENSEN (Literary Battlefront) published in June 1924 that proletarian literature became a distinct force in the literary world.

The leading theoretician of *Bungei sensen* was AONO SUEKICHI; contributors included HAYAMA YOSHIKI, KUROSHIMA DENJI, and Satomura Kinzō (1902–45). In December 1925, members of the journal joined with other leftist groups to form the Japan Proletarian Literature League (Nihon Puroretaria Bungei Remmei). This organization was to dissolve and regroup many times, largely because of conflict between intellectuals and workers. One of its successors, the All Japan Proletarian Arts League (better known as NAPF from its Esperanto name: Nippona Artista Proleta Federacio), formed in March 1928, published the journal SENKI (Battle Flag). KURAHARA KOREHITO, KOBAYASHI TAKIJI, TOKUNAGA SUNAO, NAKANO SHIGEHARU, MIYAMOTO YURIKO, and SATA INEKO were some of its contributors. Another, the Worker-Farmer-Artist League (Rōnō Geijutsuka Dōmei, or Rōgei) continued the *Bungei sensen* beginning in June 1927. Besides Hayama and others mentioned above, Iwatō Yukio (b 1902) and HIRABAYASHI TAIKO were active members.

Another response was represented by members of the SHINKANKAKU SCHOOL (School of New Sensibilities), who founded the magazine BUNGEI JIDAI (Literary Age) in October 1924. They included YOKOMITSU RIICHI, KAWABATA YASUNARI, NAKAGAWA YOICHI, KATAOKA TEPPEI, and INAGAKI TARUHO. Writing a fast-paced prose with vivid images that sometimes bordered on the bizarre, they represented the reverse of Marxism as they explored futurism and Dadaism in an effort to enlarge the ego and break through the limitations of the individual. In this, the Shinkankaku writers were in no small measure influenced by avant-garde poets such as Hirado Renkichi (1893–1922), Kambara Tai (b 1898), TAKAHASHI SHINKICHI, and MIYAZAWA KENJI. With the exception of a few like Kawabata Yasunari and Inagaki Taruho, its members lacked intellectual conviction, however, and in the face of the ascendance of proletarian literature, dissension set in, and publication of *Bungei jidai* was suspended in May 1927.

Some Shinkankaku authors like Kataoka Teppei joined leftist writers in January 1928, but Yokomitsu Riichi and Nakagawa Yoichi remained with the Shinkankaku school and attacked, albeit ineffec-tively, proletarian literature from the viewpoint of literary theory.

Along with the rise of proletarian literature, the early Shōwa years were characterized by the rise of popular or mass literature (*taishū bungaku;* see POPULAR FICTION). The spread of universal education since the Meiji period (1868–1912) and the availability of cheap books were the main reasons for this. The majority of readers were more attracted to popular fiction than to serious literature, however, as evidenced in the success of such magazines as KINGU and *Kōdan kurabu*. A dispute arose among proletarian literature writers in 1928 over how one might enlighten the masses yet maintain literary quality. Several authors connected with the magazine BUNGEI SHUNJŪ, like KIKUCHI KAN, KUME MASAO, and Sasaki Mitsuzō (1896–1934), abandoned "pure literature" to write literature for popular consumption. Although a number of writers lost confidence during this period of turmoil, in its aftermath several fine works were produced both by writers for the masses and the art-for-art's-sake faction. Kobayashi Takiji's "Kani kōsen" (1929; tr "The Cannery Boat," 1973), Yokomitsu Riichi's *Shanhai* (1928–31; Shanghai), Tokunaga Sunao's *Taiyō no nai machi* (1929; City without Sun), and Kawabata Yasunari's *Asakusa kurenaidan* (1929–30; The Scarlet Gang of Asakusa) were produced in that productive period.

In April 1930 the younger generation of the writers who put primary emphasis on art formed the Shinkō Geijutsu Ha Kurabu (New Art School Club; see SHINKŌ GEIJUTSU HA). Typical writers of this group, which numbered over 30 members, were Ryūtanji Yū (b 1901), Kuno Toyohiko (1896–1971), Narasaki Tsutomu (1908–78), Nakamura Masatsune (1901–81), IBUSE MASUJI, and FUNAHASHI SEIICHI. Their works, which were referred to as "modernist" (in the Japanese sense), were characterized by urbanity and a fascination with "the erotic, the grotesque, and the nonsensical" (*ero guro nansensu*). Also members of the club, but producing works of a different sort than the above, were ABE TOMOJI, HORI TATSUO, and KAMURA ISOTA. Abe's works were more intellectual, Hori aimed at creating delicate psychological novels, and Kamura wrote typical examples of the Japanese genre known as the I-NOVEL (*watakushi shōsetsu*). The critic KOBAYASHI HIDEO was also a member of this club, but he rejected both the frivolousness of the so-called modernists and the adherence to the external ideology of Marxism on the part of some of the proletarian writers. He contended that writers should be faithful only to their own "inner truth."

It was about this time (the early 1930s) that ITŌ SEI, HAYASHI FUMIKO, and NIWA FUMIO, who were not members of the Shinkō Geijutsu Ha, began to be recognized. Itō, who had studied Freudian theory and found his literary models in the works of James Joyce, contrasted with Hori Tatsuo, who found his models in the works of Marcel Proust. Before Itō and Hori succeeded in developing their new psychological novels, however, Yokomitsu Riichi published his "Kikai" (tr "Machine," 1961) in September 1930. "Kikai" attracted much public notice and brought the new psychological novel into fashion. In opposition to the new emphasis on psychology in fiction ("psychologism," it was called), Kuno Toyohiko, Asahara Rokurō (1895–1977), and Yoshiyuki Eisuke (1906–40) advocated a new "social" fiction. (By this they did not mean social fiction, but only fiction that stressed the importance of the social and economic environment; Kuno quoted the economic theories of Paul Howard Douglas.) However, these writers did not succeed in producing a viable "social novel."

In the meantime various kinds of problems had arisen on the proletarian literature side. In March 1930 the leadership of NAPF decided on the communization of their artistic activities (i.e., that the present aims of the arts should be the same as those of the Communist Party). This policy was too overtly political for some members of NAPF, and the proletarian writers were not as successful in 1930 and 1931 as they had been in 1929. There was criticism of the leaders of the organization, and in November 1931 NAPF was dissolved and reorganized as KOPF or Federacio de Proletaj Kulturorganizoj Japanaj. (NALP or Nippona Alianco Proleta Literaturo was established as a subordinate organization of KOPF.) Problems had also arisen in the Artists Alliance of Farmers and Workers, and some members had left that organization in 1930 and 1931.

In September 1931 came the MANCHURIAN INCIDENT, and with it began what is known in Japan as the 15 Years' War (including the Sino-Japanese War that began in 1937 and World War II). Within Japan, ultranationalistic tendencies gradually intensified. The literature of the Japanese "modernists" was denounced because of its frivolousness and its superficial imitation of Western modes. In 1932 the magazines *Kindai seikatsu* (Modern Life) and *Bungaku jidai* (Literary Period), which had supported the Shinkō Geijutsu Ha, disappeared. That same year many proletarian writers were arrested by the police. In February 1933 Kobayashi Takiji, one of the best known proletarian writers, who had escaped arrest the year before, was seized and murdered in jail. In June of that year, jailed Communist Party leaders Sano Manabu (1892–1953) and Nabeyama Sadachika (b 1901) renounced communism; they were followed by other left-wing people, including writers. NALP was dissolved in February 1934, and KOPF in April of the same year.

At the beginning of the Shōwa period (i.e., from about 1926 to about 1931), many older writers who had begun writing in the Meiji or Taishō periods had either been silenced or eclipsed in public attention by the vogue of the proletarian writers and the modernists. Now, with both the leftists and the modernists removed from the literary stage, these older writers again began to write or to be noticed. Nagai Kafū came on stage again with his "Tsuyu no atosaki" (1931, During the Rains) and "Hikage no hana" (1934, Flowers in the Shade); TOKUDA SHŪSEI with his "Machi no odoriba" (1933, The Town Dance Hall); SHIGA NAOYA with his "Banreki aka-e" (1933); and UNO KŌJI with his "Kareki no aru fūkei" (1933, Landscape with Dead Tree). Tanizaki Jun'ichirō had continued to write steadily; however, he attracted new attention at this time with his "Shunkin-shō" (1933; tr "A Portrait of Shunkin," 1963) and other works. The I-novel was given new life by OZAKI KAZUO's "Nonki megane" (1933, Happy-go-lucky Viewpoint) and KAMBAYASHI AKATSUKI's "Bara tōnin" (1932, Rose Thief).

Writers who had begun their careers in the beginning of the Shōwa period now had to rearrange their attitude toward literature. In October 1933 Funahashi Seiichi, Abe Tomoji, and others founded Kōdō (Action), a magazine directed toward humanism and the social engagement of intellectuals. In the same month, the magazine BUNGAKUKAI (Literary World) was founded by TAKEDA RINTARŌ, HAYASHI FUSAO, Kobayashi Hideo, and Fukada Kyūya (1903–71). (Takeda and Hayashi were former proletarian writers; Kobayashi and Fukada were not.) Kawabata Yasunari and HIROTSU KAZUO also joined. Bungakukai attracted attention because writers of various persuasions had gotten together. These writers aimed to create a literature faithful only to their own "inner truth" without regard for external artifice or design. The Bungakukai group eventually came to include many strong writers such as Yokomitsu Riichi, KISHIDA KUNIO, and SHIMAKI KENSAKU, and it became the most influential force in the literary world of the late thirties.

Meanwhile, in 1934 and 1935, many writers who had been "converted" from (i.e., pressured into renouncing) communism wrote about the pain of their conversion. Such writings were referred to as tenkō bungaku (the literature of ideological conversion; see TENKŌ). Shimaki Kensaku's "Rai" (1934, Leprosy) and "Mōmoku" (1934, Blindness); Murayama Tomoyoshi's "Byakuya" (1934, White Night); and Nakano Shigeharu's "Dai isshō" (1934, The First Chapter) and "Mura no ie" (1935, The House in the Village) are examples of this kind of writing.

Among the writers who began their careers or first attracted general attention around 1935 were TAKAMI JUN, DAZAI OSAMU, ISHIKAWA JUN, and SAKAGUCHI ANGO. They were not proletarian writers, but they had experienced or been forced to think about communism in their youth; and so they shared some of the frustrations of the period. In their works they laughed at their own powerlessness, but the laughter was at the same time a kind of criticism of society. Among the other writers who made their debut in this period were ISHIKAWA TATSUZŌ, ISHIZAKA YŌJIRŌ, HŌJŌ TAMIO, and OKAMOTO KANOKO.

Some of the masterpieces of Shōwa literature appeared around the year 1935. Yokomitsu Riichi's Kazoku kaigi (1935, Family Conference), Kawabata Yasunari's Yukiguni (not completed until 1947 but the major parts written between 1935 and 1937; tr Snow Country, 1956), Takami Jun's Kokyū wasureubeki (1935–36, Should Auld Acquaintance Be Forgot), Hōjō Tamio's "Inochi no shoya" (1936, The First Day of a Life), and Hori Tatsuo's "Kaze tachinu" (1936–38, The Wind Has Risen) were among the fine works produced at this time.

With increasing ultranationalism, not only proletarian literature but even literature of a liberal character was suppressed. This tendency became especially pronounced after beginning of the Sino-Japanese War of 1937–45. Under these conditions the only literary groups that gained strength and influence were the Japanese Romantic school (NIHON RŌMANHA) and those groups associated with it. With such magazines as Kogito (1932–44, Cogito), Nihon rōmanha (1935–38), and Bungei seiki (1939–45, Literary Century) as their base, YASUDA YOJŪRŌ (1910–81) and Haga Mayumi (b 1903) provided theoretical leadership. Among other members were KAMEI KATSUICHIRŌ, NAKAGAWA YOICHI, HAGIWARA SAKUTARŌ, and Jimbo Kōtarō (b 1905). At first the group simply extolled the beauty of traditional Japanese culture and called for the revival of a spirit of dedication and self-sacrifice. As Japan became more involved in foreign aggression, however, it began to seek out and accuse those opposed to militarism.

As the war in China intensified, and as events led toward the outbreak of World War II, there was even more stringent government control of literature. Already in 1934, the Bungei Kondankai (Literary Conference) had been formed under the leadership of the head of the Police Bureau. In 1937 the Cabinet Information Bureau was set up and cultural control was greatly intensified. Shimaki Kensaku's Saiken (1937, Reconstruction) and Ishikawa Tatsuzō's Ikiteiru heitai (1938, Living Soldiers) were banned. Tokuda Shūsei's Shukuzu (1941, Epitome) and Tanizaki's Sasameyuki (1943–48; tr The Makioka Sisters, 1957) were censored. The periodical Jimmin bunko (1936–38, People's Library), put out by Takeda Rintarō and others who had left the Bungakukai, was forced to end publication in 1938. Between 1938 and 1939 many semiofficial literary groups were created. These included the Nōmin Bungaku Kondankai (Peasant Literature Conference) and the Kaiyō Bungaku Kyōkai (Marine Literature Association). Exponents of war literature were HINO ASHIHEI, who wrote Mugi to heitai (1938; tr Barley and Soldiers, 1939), Ueda Hiroshi (1905–66), and Hibino Shirō (b 1903). Many authors were drafted to write reports from the front. The poets TAKAMURA KŌTARŌ and MIYOSHI TATSUJI actively put their talents at the disposal of the war effort. In 1940 the cultural section of the IMPERIAL RULE ASSISTANCE ASSOCIATION was formed. In 1942 the NIHON BUNGAKU HŌKOKUKAI (Association of Patriotic Japanese Literature) with some 4,000 members was established. Literature had now become an instrument of the state.

HATORI Tetsuya

Shōwa Oil Co, Ltd

(Shōwa Sekiyu). Oil refining and sales company. Established in 1942, it concluded a tie-up with the Royal Dutch Shell group in 1949 for importation of crude oil, transfer of technology, and capital participation. Since then, Shōwa Oil has maintained close connections with Royal Dutch Shell. Its affiliated firms include the Shōseki Engineering Co, which is active abroad, and the Shōwa Yokkaichi Oil Co, which has one of the world's largest refineries in Yokkaichi, Mie Prefecture. Annual sales in 1981 were ¥1 trillion (US $4.6 billion); the firm was capitalized at ¥6.8 billion (US $31.1 million). Corporate headquarters are located in Tōkyō.

Shōwa period (1926–)

The reign of the present emperor, HIROHITO, who ascended the throne at the death of his father, Emperor TAISHŌ, on 25 December 1926. The longest reign in Japanese history, it covers World War II, the American OCCUPATION, and in its last two decades an extended period of peace and prosperity. For further information on this period, see the sections on Taishō and early Shōwa history, and on postwar history, in the article on the HISTORY OF JAPAN.

"Shōwa Restoration"

(Shōwa Ishin). Slogan used by right-wing extremists of the 1920s and 1930s (particularly the extremists of the early 1930s) who hoped for a sweeping national reform on the order of the MEIJI RESTORATION of 1868, Shōwa being the reign name of the current emperor, who succeeded the Taishō emperor in 1926. To radical young military officers and nationalists like TACHIBANA KŌZABURŌ, INOUE NISSHŌ, GONDŌ SEIKYŌ, and KITA IKKI, the term "Shōwa Restoration" meant social reform, reconstruction of the machinery of government, and a thorough reorganization of the national economic structure. These radicals regarded themselves as the 20th-century counterparts of the 19th-century shishi, the political activists who had sought to destroy the Tokugawa shogunate and reinstitute direct imperial rule, and they planned to achieve their objectives by "direct action," that is, by violence. When a group of young officers assassinated Premier INUKAI TSUYOSHI in May 1932 (see MAY 15TH INCIDENT), they issued a statement calling on citizens to "take up arms, eliminate the enemies of the people, and construct a brilliant restorationist Japan."

Besides national reform, restoration was understood to be synonymous with fukko, or "return to the ancient regime," and it connoted a revival of the traditional spirit of unity that was believed to have existed in an earlier, more virtuous age. According to the Shōwa-period restorationists, the original pure spirit of the Yamato race had been blemished by an unfortunate preoccupation with foreign ideas and techniques; they planned to purge foreign influences and to restore the original spirit of the Japanese people.

The ideology of "Shōwa Restoration" underlay a series of abortive coups d'etat by radical rightists in the 1930s that ended with the suppression of the revolutionary right-wing movement following the FEBRUARY 26TH INCIDENT of 1936.

——Ben-Ami Shillony, *Revolt in Japan* (1973).

Richard YASKO

Shōwa Sangyō Co, Ltd

A food processing company, Shōwa Sangyō was established in 1936 and produces flour, edible oils, dextrose, high fructose corn syrup, animal feeds, noodles, and tempura flour, besides engaging in grain storage and leasing of buildings. Its coastal plants are convenient for handling grain imports. The company is currently concentrating its efforts toward expanding the production of processed foods for home use. Sales for the fiscal year ending May 1982 totaled ¥168 billion (US $709 million), and capitalization stood at ¥7.7 billion (US $32.5 million). Corporate headquarters are located in Tōkyō.

Shōwa Shinzan

Volcanic hill, a parasitic volcano of USUZAN, south of Lake Tōya, southwestern Hokkaidō. When Usuzan erupted smoke and volcanic ash in 1943, the land adjacent to Lake Tōya rose and lava domes, including Shōwa Shinzan, were created. Shōwa Shinzan's volcanic activities ended in 1945, though it still emits steam and sulfuric fumes. Its rocks have a temperature of 600°C (1,112°F). It has been designated as a natural monument and is part of Shikotsu–Tōya National Park. Height: 408 m (1,338 ft).

shōya

(village headman). Village official in the Edo period (1600–1868). The term *shōya* was primarily in the Kansai region. In the Kantō region village headmen were called *nanushi,* and in the Hokuriku and Tōhoku regions of northern Japan they were called *kimoiri.* A village normally had only one headman; in towns, the leaders of individual wards *(chō)* were also sometimes called *shōya.*

The village headman stood at the second level of peasant officialdom, ranking below officials variously called *ōjōya, warimoto,* or *tomura,* who presided over groups of villages known as *gō, kumi,* or *tomuragumi.* In some areas, such as the Kaga domain (now Ishikawa and Toyama prefectures), there was a still higher stratum of peasant administrators who supervised the village group chiefs. The village headman acted as the principal intermediary between the villagers and higher authorities. He transmitted the decisions and orders of the village group chiefs and domainal officials to the villagers and presented requests and complaints from the villagers to the proper authorities.

As the chief administrator of the village, the headman was assisted by several *kumigashira* (household group leaders, also known as OSABYAKUSHŌ or *toshiyori*) and *hyakushōdai* (peasant representatives). The three offices were known collectively as *murakata san'yaku* or *jikata san'yaku.* The headman was responsible for the allotment and payment of the village's taxes. He supervised the maintenance and use of the village irrigation system and was generally responsible for preserving public order within the village. He was often instrumental in the introduction of new agricultural techniques. As compensation for his work the headman usually received a salary; sometimes his lands were exempted from taxation.

The broad official powers of the headman were reinforced by his relative wealth and high social standing, for he was chosen from among the richest and most prestigious villagers. The hereditary nature of the position in many villages allowed the headman's family to acquire broad social and economic privileges. For example, headmen frequently played an important role in local temple and shrine organizations (MIYAZA). As the "parent" of the village, he exercised considerable control over the personal lives of his villager "children."

In the 17th and 18th centuries headmen were leading advocates in disputes with neighboring villages over land and water rights, and they were frequently the leaders of peasant revolts (HYAKUSHŌ IKKI). But as they used their economic power to become large landholders, and as changing economic conditions increased social tensions within the villages, headmen often became the object of such revolts. Partly as a response to such pressures, headmen in some areas came to be elected by the villagers, and the position gradually lost its hereditary character. See also HYAKUSHŌ; MURA YAKUNIN.

Philip BROWN

shōyō jurin bunka

(laurilignosa culture). A term used to describe the culture specifically developed in the laurilignosa region of warm temperate Asia. The term laurilignosa is derived from the Latin *laures* for laurel and *lignosa* for woody; it refers to forests of evergreen oak-laurel trees with smooth, glossy, bright green leaves. Laurilignosa forests are sometimes termed lucidophyllus forests ("forests with shiny leaves"). Major tree species in these forests are the evergreen oak (beech family) and laurel (laurel family), as well as the tea plant, camellia, osmanthus, and chestnut. Laurilignosa forests flourish in areas with warm winters (in continental Asia, January mean temperature no less than 3.0–4.0°C; in the maritime Japanese archipelago, no less than 1.0°C). Centered mainly in southern China, the forests extend to the southern tip of Korea and southwestern Japan in the east, to the highlands of Vietnam, Laos, Thailand, and Burma (in contact with subtropical forests) in the south, and to the southern slopes of the Himalayas in the west.

Elements of Laurilignosa Culture——The term laurilignosa culture was first proposed in 1966 by the Japanese ethnobotanist, Nakao Sasuke (b 1916). In his comparative ethnobotanical studies of warm-temperate Asia, Nakao noted that the vegetational environment of Japan and other parts of East Asia characterizes certain material and nonmaterial cultural traits. Following are some traits commonly shared by traditional Japanese and laurilignosa cultures in general.

Material elements. These cultures all soak raw starchy foodstuffs in water to eliminate the harsh, poisonous bitter taste (*akunuki*). Deciduous and evergreen acorns, horse chestnuts, *kuzu* (*Pueraria thunbergiana*) roots and bracken fern rhizomes must first be soaked in water for a very long period before being eaten. Acorns, for example, are dried for a one- to two-month period; the edible part (embryo) is separated from the shells by crushing and winnowing and then stone-milled coarsely. The acorn flour is then put in a hemp bag and soaked in gently running water for about two months in winter. It is then dried for storage. Horse chestnuts must be heated, soaked in water, and reheated in ashes—a process taking two to three weeks. For the early Jōmon period (ca 10,000 BC–ca 300 BC) inhabitants of the entire archipelago who had no agricultural staple foods, these techniques of preparing naturally occurring wild foodstuffs were especially important for subsistence.

In primitive societies, people burned an uncultivated field or forest and then spread the ashes for fertilizing crops which were planted. When a particular plot of soil was exhausted by use, the people would move on to a new spot, eventually returning to the original plot after 10 to 20 years. This technique is known as shifting or slash-and-burn farming. With the exception of corn, sweet potato, turnip, and wheat, the principal crops (Italian millet, barn millet, buckwheat, soybean, *azuki* bean, and taro) of the slash-and-burn farming still practiced in the mountainous parts of Japan are identical with those produced in other areas in the laurilignosa zone. Although it is not clear when and how they arrived in Japan, these plants were introduced in waves over a long period of time.

In addition to these main subsistence techniques, peoples of the laurilignosa cultures use cakes (*mochi*) made of pounded sticky rice and millet for religious offerings and rituals, drink tea, produce rice wine (*sake*), soybean paste (*miso*), and soy sauce (*shōyu*) using *kōji* (a fermenting agent with a species of fungus, *Aspergillus oryzae*). They also produce fermented soybeans (*nattō*) and make lacquer wares and silk.

Nonmaterial elements. The prototype of the belief that ancestral spirits dwell in the mountains (see YAMA NO KAMI) is principally traced to the Yao tribe of Thailand and the agricultural rituals of slash-and-burn farmers in southern China. There is a myth in the KOJIKI and NIHON SHOKI that tells how the corpse of the goddess Ōgetsuhime produced several kinds of agricultural foods. Variations of this myth are found among slash-and-burn farmers along the Yangzi (Yangtze) River and in South China, through Laos to northeastern Assam. Furthermore, the customs of UTAGAKI (in which boys and girls gather at festivals to exchange sexually sugges-

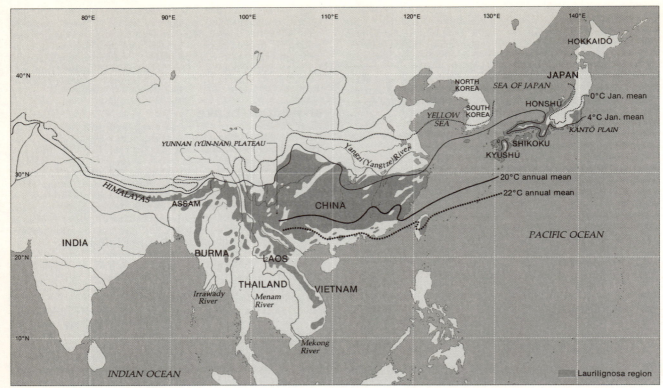

Shōyō jurin bunka——Laurilignosa region

tive songs and sexual favors afterwards) and *tsumadoi* (overnight visits by a male lover to his sweetheart's home before the official marriage), which were widespread in ancient Japan, are also found in modified form among the slash-and-burn farmers of the hilly zones of the laurilignosa region in continental Asia. The semiceremonial observance of a full moon in the fall (Jūgoya, see MOON VIEWING), is thought to have grown out of the yam and taro harvest festivals of these prehistoric farmers.

Laurilignosa and the Development of Agriculture——The mountainous region of Southeast Asia at the southern extreme of the laurilignosa zone, especially the Yunnan Plateau in China, is rich in floral variation. Many scholars believe that this region was one of the centers where agriculture began. Prehistoric inhabitants had been hunter-gatherers dependent primarily on chestnuts, walnuts, horse chestnuts, and acorns, along with other kinds of carbohydrate sources such as *kuzu*, bracken fern, arisaema (*Arisaema serratum*; J: *tennanshō*), konjak (*Amorphophalus konjac*; J: *konnyaku*), and other wild roots, tubers, and rhizomes. In developing techniques for extracting bitter poisons and tannins from these plants, their living pattern had become more settled, leading to experiments in cultivating plants. Since their hunting and gathering activities took them far afield, they no doubt discovered taros and yams and other plants that could be domesticated. This stage has been called the early laurilignosa cultural complex.

On the Asian continent the beginnings of shifting agriculture date back at least several thousand years. Among the most important crops cultivated in the Yunnan area were millet, kaoliang, buckwheat, and various strains of beans. None of these is indigenous to the Japanese archipelago. Italian millet, for example, is native to India, and kaoliang, to northern China. This suggests that prehistoric people traveled extensively.

The slash-and-burn farming which distinguished the laurilignosa culture proper later developed into wet-rice cultivation; in fact, the shifting and rice agricultures are together called the late laurilignosa cultural complex. It has been recently speculated that the rice plant originated and was first cultivated in the Yunnan highlands of China and the Assam district of India. It is also thought that the cultivation of rice, like taros, yams, and various grain plants, first relied on the slash-and-burn method. Rice farming then spread to India, southward along the Irrawaddy, Menam, and Mekong rivers, and eastward by way of the Yangzi River, reaching finally to the Korean peninsula and Japan across the Yellow Sea. In the first stages rice was grown either in burnt-over fields and paddies irrigated by rain water, with strains adaptable to both dryland and wetland conditions. It is believed that the practice of cultivating rice in carefully sectioned and irrigated wet paddies was influenced by the wheat agriculture of the loess plains of northern China, which was in full bloom by Longshan (Lung-shan) times of the late Chinese Neolithic culture (ca 2400 BC to ca 1500 BC). Systematic rice cultivation appeared as early as 4,000 years ago in the lower basin of the Yangzi River.

Laurilignosa and Jōmon Cultures——During the Incipient and Initial Jōmon periods (ca 10,000 BC–ca 5000 BC; see JŌMON CULTURE), evergreen oak and laurel forests were confined to the southern tip of Kyūshū, and the rest of Japan was covered by the more productive deciduous oak and beech forests (deciduilignosa). Acorns of deciduous oaks, chestnuts, walnuts, horse chestnuts, hazelnuts, and beechnuts are products of these forests. No laurilignosa impact on Incipient (ca 10,000 BC–ca 7500 BC) and Initial (ca 7500 BC–ca 5000 BC) Jōmon cultures has been seen, and hence it is not appropriate to assign these two periods to laurilignosa culture.

Some laurilignosa species had spread into the lowlands of Kyūshū by about 10,000 years ago and to almost all of southwestern Japan by about 7,000 years ago. It was about this time that the natural environment of present-day Japan was established, with the laurilignosa predominating in the southwest, including the Kantō Plain, and deciduilignosa in the northeast. The strong influence of the laurilignosa environment on prehistoric culture has been limited to southwestern Japan for approximately the past 7,000 years, and on Jōmon culture for about 4,500 years, from 5000 BC to 500 BC. The oldest Jōmon pottery dates back about 12,500 years. It is generally said that pottery-making cultures are agricultural. However, studies of the Jōmon period have so far only yielded evidence of hunting, fishing, and food-gathering, and some possible localized farming.

The initial slash-and-burn agricultural activity appears to have been adopted in areas south of the Kantō region at least from the Late Jōmon period (ca 2000 BC–ca 1000 BC) to the beginning of the Yayoi period (ca 300 BC–ca AD 300; see YAYOI CULTURE). However, fossil pollen and seed analyses show that buckwheat first appeared as early as 5,000 years ago in the Oshima Peninsula of Hokkaidō and 3,650 years ago in northernmost Honshū. Fossil buckwheat pollen dating back as early as 3,000 years ago has been identified in Kyūshū. The occurrence of insect-spread buckwheat pollen in these areas can be see as evidence of slash-and-burn farming. Palynologically, the cultivation of buckwheat can only be traced back to the Final (Latest) Jōmon period (ca 1000 BC–ca 300 BC), which would mean that slash-and-burn agriculture had also begun by this time. This was much later than the spread of shifting agriculture throughout the laurilignosa region on the Asian continent; it has been suggested that migrating groups from the continent brought the technique to the Japanese archipelago.

Wet rice cultivation reached northern Kyūshū and the southern tip of Korea by way of the Yellow Sea from the Yangzi lowlands as early as 3,000 years ago. Within a span of 500 years, it spread to almost all swampy locations scattered in the laurilignosa belt in southwestern Japan. Together with the introduction of the shifting farming method, rice agriculture radically affected the mode of food production and lifestyle and probably had a decisive effect upon subsequent cultures. Almost everyone was engaged in farming and other related activities, and a steady food supply through these agricultures was assured. Rice farming induced changes in the building of villages as well. The village was now established on flat low hills conveniently located near paddies of alluvial plains. A number of excavations show that in most cases a moat was constructed around the village. This was a continental system designed probably to protect villagers from enemies. The central plaza, which was an open space during the Jōmon period, was occupied by several rice storehouses, each with a raised floor. The new technological innovations were quickly assimilated also by Yayoi and KOFUN people in northeastern Japan.

Since the Japanese archipelago was characterized by deciduous hardwood forests in the south and boreal forests in the north until the Early Jōmon period, laurilignosa culture, from the gatherer and primitive agricultural complex to its full development of shifting and rice farming, should be placed after the full establishment of evergreen oak and laurel forests in southwestern Japan some 7,000 years ago. Thus one must not forget that it also has deep roots in the early Jōmon culture which developed in the deciduilignosa environment. See also HISTORY OF JAPAN: prehistory.

———Ho Ping-ti, *The Cradle of the East* (1975). Nakao Sasuke, *Saibai shokubutsu to nōkō no kigen* (1966). Sasaki Kōmei, *Inasaku izen* (1971). Tsukada Matsuo, *Koseitaigaku II: Ōyōron* (1974). Tsukada Matsuo, *Kafun wa kataru* (1974). Watabe Tadayo, *Ine no michi* (1977). Matsuo TSUKADA

shōyu → soy sauce

Shōyūki

Also known as *Yafuki*. Diary of the minister of the right Fujiwara no Sanesuke (957–1046), who was also known as Ononomiya Sanesuke because he had founded the Ononomiya school of rites and ceremony. The diary covers the years 978 to 1032 and is an important source of information on court ceremony and politics in the era when the regents FUJIWARA NO MICHINAGA and FUJIWARA NO YORIMICHI dominated Kyōto. It provides many details and critical comments about Michinaga, with whom the author was not on cordial terms. There are several alternative names for the diary, and the original number of chapters (*kan*) is unknown, extant manuscripts ranging from 5 to 32. G. Cameron HURST III

shōzei

Tax rice collected by the government and stored in provincial granaries (*shōsō*) under the Chinese-style RITSURYŌ SYSTEM of administration begun in the late 7th century. Of the three major forms of tax (SO, YŌ, AND CHŌ) levied by the government, the *shōzei* weighed the most; it was far more practical to store the rice in local warehouses and allocate it to the provincial government than to transport it to the capital. The locally stored tax rice was managed by the provincial governors (KOKUSHI), who used a large part of it for loans (SUIKO) to local farmers in the spring, to be repaid at high interest rates after the fall harvest. From the mid-8th century on, the term *shōzei* also began to be used more narrowly to mean the interest from such loans. The *kokushi* sent detailed annual reports (*shōzeichō*) to the Grand Council of State (DAJŌKAN) on their *shōzei* income and expenses; 25 of these reports, dated 729–739, are still preserved in the SHŌSŌIN repository at Nara.

shrikes

(*mozu*). In Japanese *mozu* is the common name for any member of the numerous species of predatory songbird of the family Laniidae, genus *Lanius;* it also refers specifically to the bull-headed shrike (*Lanius bucephalus*). Distinguished by its sharply hooked beak and longish tail, the typical shrike averages approximately 20 centimeters (8 in) in length. The male has an orange head, black eye lines, grayish streaked back, pale orange underbelly, and black wings and tail. The female has an overall brown plumage. As a resident or wandering bird, it breeds throughout Japan in plains or low mountains. Shrikes hunt insects, lizards, and other small animals and often impale their prey on sharp branches or thorns. From fall to winter each individual shrike stakes out the territory where it lives and hunts. Other members of the Laniidae family seen in Japan include the *akamozu* or Japanese red-tailed shrike (*L. cristatus*) and the *chigomozu* or thick-billed shrike (*L. tigrinus*), two species which summer in Japan; and the *ōmozu* or great grey shrike (*L. excubitor*) and *ōkaramozu* or Chinese great grey shrike (*L. sphenocercus*), which are occasional winter visitors. *Takano Shinji*

The *mozu* is first mentioned in Japanese literature in the MAN'-YŌSHŪ, the oldest extant anthology of Japanese poetry, dating from the latter part of the 8th century; following a Chinese literary convention, it is depicted as a spring bird. Centuries later, among *haiku* poets, the shrike became associated with autumn, perhaps because its habit of impaling its prey was regarded as the first offering (*hayanie*) of the fall harvest. More recent poets like KITAHARA HAKUSHŪ have been inspired by its shrill cry. *Saitō Shōji*

shrimps, prawns, and lobsters

(*ebi*). Crustaceans of the order Decapoda, suborders Natantia and Palinura are collectively called *ebi* in Japanese. They are found in freshwater, brackish, and saltwater environments, near the shore as well as deep in the sea. Major Japanese species include the *kurumaebi* (*Penaeus japonicus*), the *sakuraebi* (*Sergestes lucens*), the *tenagaebi* (*Macrobrachium nipponense*), the *iseebi* (Japanese rock lobster; *Palinurus japonicus*), and the *semiebi* (locust lobster; *Scyllarides squamosus*). *Nakane Takehiko*

In modern Japan, shrimp is best known as an ingredient in TEMPURA, SUSHI, and other forms of Japanese cuisine. In the premodern period deep red, boiled rock lobsters called *okazari ebi* ("decoration lobsters") were placed on round rice cakes, and these, along with bitter oranges, fern, and sea tangle, were put on a small wooden stand as a New Year's decoration. In some regions, rock lobsters were used to decorate the entrances or gates of homes; this custom is still practiced in some homes. The traditional conception of the *ebi* as an auspicious creature on occasions such as the New Year and wedding ceremonies may have resulted from the idea that its bent back symbolizes old age and thus a long life, but it may also be due to the *ebi*'s periodic shedding of its shell, which came to symbolize the renewal of life. These beliefs explain the traditional custom of eating shrimp during coming-of-age ceremonies. There is a reference to *ebi* in the *Honzō wamyō* (completed in 918), the oldest Japanese dictionary of natural history, and the ENGI SHIKI (completed in 927) records that *ebi* from various provinces were presented at the imperial court. *Ebi* appear in WAKA and HAIKU poetry, as well as woodblock prints. In cooking, the *kurumaebi* and *shibaebi* (*Metapenaeus joyneri*) are the most highly prized species. *Saitō Shōji*

shrines

(*jinja*). A Shintō shrine is an enclosed area containing a wooden sanctuary and several auxiliary buildings before which Shintō rituals are performed and prayers offered. The shrine constitutes the focal point for organized Shintō religious practice. In urban areas it provides a sense of community to those living within its parish. In rural areas it tends to create a feeling of kinship among villagers by stressing the common tie that all have to the shrine deity, who is often popularly, if not quite correctly, referred to as an UJIGAMI, that is, an ancestral deity worshiped by members of the same clan (*uji*). The parishioners of a given shrine are called *ujiko* (clan children), a term that suggests that they share a common ancestor who looks after them. The *matsuri* (see FESTIVALS) held annually at the shrine enhances the sense of community; KAGURA (sacred dance and music) performed on the day of the *matsuri* have been an important means of artistic expression for villagers.

Although there is considerable variation in the size, architectural style, and arrangement of buildings, a typical medium-size shrine might be laid out according to the following plan. Toward the rear of the shrine precinct, which is often rectangular in shape and surrounded by a fence marking it off as a sanctified area, stands the *honden* (main sanctuary) in which is housed the *goshintai* (august god body), a sacred object in which the spirit of the deity (KAMI) is believed to reside. Sometimes more than one deity is enshrined. Directly in front of the *honden,* and occasionally obscuring it from view, is the *haiden* (hall of worship or oratory), before which the priests conduct their rituals and individuals make their offerings.

Worshipers announce their presence to the diety or deities enshrined in the *honden* by loudly clapping their hands together and tugging on a heavy rope attached to a large bell hanging from the eves of the *haiden.* A huge, rectangular wooden box with a slatted top stands in front of the *haiden* to receive small monetary contributions from the worshipers. Laymen are never permitted to enter either the *honden* or the *haiden* lest they pollute the sacred area. The interiors of these buildings are usually also out of bounds for Shintō priests, who may enter only on very special occasions as, for example, when the *goshintai* must be moved because the sanctuary is undergoing repairs. Occasionally the *honden* and *haiden* are connected by a covered passageway.

Smaller shrines often have only a single sanctuary, the front half doing duty as the *haiden* and the rear half serving as the *honden.* In the case of some shrines the *haiden* and *honden* are located miles apart, typically with the *haiden* easily accessible in the village and the *honden* standing on an outlying peak where there is little chance of defilement from human contact. A shrine dedicated to a deity residing in a mountain, hot spring, or waterfall often may have only a *haiden,* since the natural phenomenon itself takes the place of a *honden* (see ŌMIWA SHRINE).

The entrance to a shrine is marked by a TORII, the characteristic shrine gateway that consists of two erect pillars pierced at the top by two crossbeams. A path, which may be arched by several additional *torii,* leads directly to the *haiden.* Somewhat removed from the path but close to the *haiden* stands a *temizuya* (pavilion for washing the hands), where worshipers are expected to purify themselves by a ritual washing of hands and mouth. Near the shrine entrance or flanking the stairs leading up to the *haiden* may be found a pair of highly stylized stone lions called *komainu* (Korean dogs) which guard the shrine. If a festival is in progress, a sacred rope made of twisted straw *(shimenawa)* with hanging white paper streamers will be stretched across the two pillars of the *torii* just below the second crossbeam. Other buildings in a medium-size shrine may include a storehouse for the shrine's ritual objects such as the portable shrine (MIKOSHI), a hall for preparing food offerings, a miniature shrine to protect the precincts, and a shrine office where amulets are sold. Sometimes a shrine may be a compound of equally important plural shrines, as is seen at the KAMO SHRINES or the ISE SHRINE, or comprised of main *(honsha),* associate *(sessha)* and subordinate *(massha)* shrines as is seen at HIE SHRINE. The spirit of a powerful divinity may be invited *(kanjō)* to establish an off-shoot shrine *(bunsha* or *bunshisha);* thus, for instance, the deity of INARI has more than 30,000 off-shoot shrines throughout the country (see also SUWA SHRINE, MUNAKATA SHRINES, HACHIMAN, TEMMANGŪ). Only the larger shrines have priests (see KANNUSHI) in residence. When a small shrine celebrates its annual festival, the services are arranged and often wholly conducted by members of the parish, although occasionally a priest is brought in from the outside to chant the liturgical texts (NORITO).

From around the time of the promulgation of the first legal codes (see TAIHŌ CODE) in the 8th century, the government had granted special status to divinities and shrines of particular importance. For instance, the ENGI SHIKI (927) singled out 3,132 divinities and shrines (called SHIKINAISHA), which it subdivided into imperial shrines *(kampeisha),* at which officials of the central government made annual offerings, and provincial shrines *(kokuheisha),* which, being distant from the capital, received offerings from provincial governors. Another category for shrines used by the Engi Shiki was that of *myōjin taisha* (eminent shrine), a designation it applied to 224 shrines whose deities were invoked in times of crisis. As the *ritsuryō* system disintegrated from the middle of the Heian period (794–1185), however, other ranking systems of shrines developed. For example, certain shrines in the Kansai area were given special recognition by the court from around the 10th century. These included Ise, Iwashimizu, Kamo, Matsunoo, Hirano, Inari, Kasuga, and other shrines, and this system was in practice into the 15th century.

Since the 12th century, it has been the unofficial practice to rank the leading shrines of each province in numerical order: *ichinomiya* (the foremost or first shrine), *ninomiya* (second shrine), and so on. A *sōja* (comprehensive shrine) was also selected for each province, close to the locus of provincial government, where all divinities within the province were worshiped together.

Following the decision in 1868 to use Shintō as the basis for a new official ideology, the Meiji government in 1871 divided shrines into six grades: *kampeisha, kokuheisha,* prefectural shrines, district shrines, village shrines, and unranked shrines. Of the 109,712 shrines that existed in 1945, the last two categories together accounted for 104,931 shrines (95.6 percent of the total). After 1871 the appointment of shrine priests required government approval; in 1875 the Board of State Ceremonials (Shikiburyō) took charge of shrine rituals, eventually prescribing the various rites to be performed at shrines and determining the appropriate liturgy to be used on each occasion. Government control of shrines was abruptly terminated in December 1945 on the order of the Occupation authorities. In 1979 there were 79,523 shrines registered with the government as independent religious organizations. The United Association for Shintō Shrines (Jinja Honchō; see SHINTŌ SHRINES, ASSOCIATION OF), a private body that coordinates Shintō affairs, reported for the same year that there were 22,954 certified priests and 4,223 certified priestesses in Japan. See also SHINTŌ ARCHITECTURE.

Stanley WEINSTEIN

Shrine Shintō

(Jinja Shintō). Before 1945 the term Shrine Shintō was occasionally used in contrast with SECT SHINTŌ and referred to that aspect of Shintō that was associated with all public shrines, of which there were 109,712 by the end of World War II. Sect Shintō was the designation applied to the 13 Shintō sects recognized by the government as independent religious organizations. Since the Home Ministry granted official status to shrines in 1870, appointed their priesthood, determined their liturgy, and generally used the shrines for the dissemination of the official ideology, Shrine Shintō was sometimes held to be synonymous with STATE SHINTŌ. In recent years, however, scholars have tended to employ the term Shrine Shintō to indicate one of several variations that make up the complex phenomenon known as Shintō. Although there is some disagreement among specialists, a typical classification might list the following: (1) Imperial Shintō, the rituals performed by or on behalf of the imperial family at the three palace shrines and the Grand Shrine of Ise; (2) Scholastic Shintō, the various schools of Shintō thought that emerged between the 13th and 19th centuries, usually under the influence of Buddhist or Confucian ideas (see WATARAI SHINTŌ, YOSHIDA SHINTŌ, SANNŌ ICHIJITSU SHINTŌ, SUIKA SHINTŌ); (3) Sect Shintō; (4) FOLK SHINTŌ, the religious activities that center on the small village shrines *(sonsha),* the SHINTŌ FAMILY ALTARS *(kamidana),* and private household shrines *(hokora),* and the voluntary religious associations (KŌ); and (5) Shrine Shintō, here defined as the religious observances performed at public shrines that were under government supervision before 1945. After a period of disarray in the wake of the OCCUPATION order in 1945 to separate religion and state and the consequent rescission of state support for shrines, most shrines were organized into an incorporated body, Jinja Honchō (see SHINTŌ SHRINES, ASSOCIATION OF), which is made up of about 90 percent (79,523 shrines in 1979) of all shrines in Japan, and gradually regained support among the people. There are now two chief seminaries for training priests, one at KOKUGAKUIN UNIVERSITY in Tōkyō, and the other at Kōgakukan University in Ise.

Stanley WEINSTEIN

Shūbun (?–ca 1460)

Also known as Tenshō Shūbun. Monk-painter of the Zen temple SHŌKOKUJI in Kyōto; the harbinger of the style of ink landscape painting *(suibokuga)* that arose in Kyōto during the second quarter of the 15th century. Followed by his pupil SESSHŪ TŌYŌ, Shūbun is considered the founder of the Japanese-Chinese style *(karayō)* of painting.

The earliest reference to Shūbun is as a Zen monk sent with a diplomatic mission to Korea by the Muromachi shogunate in 1423 to secure a printed edition of the Korean *Tripitaka.* Other sources record that he was the *tsukansu* (secretary-general) of Shōkokuji.

Shūbun learned painting from JOSETSU, a monk also affiliated with Shōkokuji. By 1438 Shūbun had attained a reputation as a

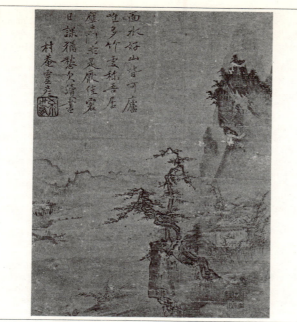

Shūbun——Reading in the Bamboo Study

Detail of a painting in the poetry-painting scroll format. On the mountain at the right can be seen a study or retreat nestling in a bamboo grove behind pine trees. One of the poetic inscriptions by various Zen monks is also visible. Ink and pale colors on paper. 134.8 × 33.3 cm. Ca 1445. Tōkyō National Museum. National Treasure.

painter of considerable importance and had painted the sliding-door panels for the residence of the imperial prince Fushimi Sadashige (1372–1456). It is recorded that he designed Buddhist sculptures as well, such as the image of Amida Buddha at the temple Ungoji and a portrait sculpture of Prince SHŌTOKU at the temple SHITENNŌJI.

Over several dozen ink paintings are traditionally attributed to Shūbun, although no authenticated seals or signatures are known. Based upon the datable inscriptions written directly on the paintings and through analysis of the style of the paintings, two works have been singled out as convincing examples of the Shūbun style: *Reading in the Bamboo Study* (*Chikusai dokusho zu*, ca 1445; Tōkyō National Museum) and *Color of Stream and Hue of Mountains* (*Suishoku rankō zu*, ca 1446; Fujiwara Collection, Tōkyō). The two paintings reveal common stylistic characteristics and themes that are typical of mid-15th-century ink landscape paintings. Both employ the *shigajiku* (poetry-painting scroll) format, with the combined impact of poetic inscriptions extolling the ideal retreat of scholar-monks and the lyrical, elusive landscapes that evoke precisely such idealized retreats.

The Shūbun style is distinctive in its handling of space. Although individual motifs—rocks, trees, hills, and huts—are inspired by Chinese landscapes of the 12th through the 14th centuries, the space that surrounds them permeates every corner of the composition in a manner surpassing that of their Chinese models and rendering the landscape images other-worldly. See also INK PAINTING.

■——Matsushita Takaaki and Tamamura Takeji, *Josetsu, Shūbun, San'ami*, vol 6 of *Suiboku bijutsu taikei* (Kōdansha, 1974). Shimada Shūjirō, ed, *Zaigai Nihon no Shihō*, vol 3 (1979). Tanaka Ichimatsu, *Shūbun kara Sesshū e* (1969), tr Bruce Darling as *Japanese Ink Painting: From Shūbun to Sesshū* (1972).   Yoshiaki SHIMIZU

shūdan shūshoku → group hiring

Shūeisha Publishing Co, Ltd

(Kabushiki-Gaisha Shūeisha). Established in 1926 as a subsidiary of SHŌGAKUKAN PUBLISHING CO, LTD, it initally published recreational magazines for school-age children. It became independent in 1949 and thereafter gained a reputation as one of Japan's leading magazine publishers. Since 1953 the company has also published books on literature and the fine arts.   KOBAYASHI Kazuhiro

Shufu no tomo

(The Housewife's Friend). The first magazine published in Japan for housewives; founded in 1917 by the publisher ISHIKAWA TAKEYOSHI. Since its inception, *Shufu no tomo* has taken the traditional ideal of "good wife and wise mother" as the theme of its articles on housekeeping and child rearing. In addition, it has offered serialized stories by such authors as KUME MASAO, YOSHIYA NOBUKO, YAMAMOTO YŪZŌ, and SHISHI BUNROKU. *Shufu no tomo*, with its combination of practical articles and fiction, became the prototype for subsequent women's magazines, and it continues as one of the major Japanese magazines in that category today.   INOUE Teruko

Shufuren

Abbreviation of Shufu Rengōkai (Japan Housewives Association). A consumer organization devoted to the improvement of family life through consumer education and public action. The association was founded in 1948 by OKU MUMEO, a member of the House of Councillors, in the midst of rampant inflation and scarcity of consumer goods. Oku believed that in order to improve the quality of life, housewives should organize and exert direct influence on government decisions. By the late 1970s Shufuren was a nationwide organization with over 460 locals, mainly composed of middle-class married women, with a membership of around one million.

In addition to political action, the organization engages in commodity safety research, presents lecture series, and, to a limited degree, operates consumer cooperatives. Its activity has focused on three major areas: consumer protection, inflation, and environmental issues. In the first of these areas it has argued for correct labeling and the elimination of harmful products, food additives, and pesticides. When the group can present scientific evidence to discredit a product, as it did in the case of chinaware containing lead, it has been highly effective in influencing the public and lawmakers. In dealing with economic and environmental problems, it stresses their impact on domestic life at the kitchen level, hence its insistence on extensive recycling and its warnings about the adverse effect of inflation on the household budget.

Shufuren leaders exert pressure by negotiating with politicians and industrialists and appearing at public meetings, while housewife members demonstrate on the streets, wearing aprons and carrying placards in the shape of *shamoji* (the wooden paddles used for serving rice). With its home-oriented image and its emphasis on the kitchen as the springboard of its argument, the organization has maintained a leading role in the CONSUMER MOVEMENT in postwar Japan, though its success with larger economic and environmental issues has been more limited.   Masako M. ŌSAKO

Shufu Rengōkai → Shufuren

Shūgaishō

(literally, "Collection of Dust"). Encyclopedic work in three volumes that classifies information into 99 categories, including Shintō affairs, Buddhist affairs, literature, customs, official ranks, historic and scenic sites, rites and ceremonies, arts, and so forth. *Shūgaishō* was compiled in the middle of the Kamakura period (1185–1333) and expanded somewhat later; several versions of the text exist. Although its authorship is unknown, it has variously been ascribed to such court officials as Tōin Sanehiro (b 1409) and Tōin Kinkata (1291–1360). It is a valuable source of information on court life in the period after the completion of the ENGI SHIKI (927) and has been so considered since the Muromachi period (1333–1568), as references in such works as SANETAKA KŌ KI attest.   G. Cameron HURST III

Shugakuin Detached Palace

(Shugakuin Rikyū). The detached Imperial Palace begun by the abdicated emperor Go-Mizunoo in the mid-17th century. Located in the foothills of Mt. Hiei (HIEIZAN) in the northeast part of Kyōto, the estate was originally planned as an imperial family retreat having three garden areas stepped down the hillside, separated and surrounded by ricefields, and connected by paths. Several small pavilions were completed by Go-Mizunoo in 1659, establishing the upper and lower gardens. After his death in 1680, his daughter Akenomiya built and occupied a nunnery, the Rinkyūji, which became the middle garden. The architecture of several pavilions exemplifies the *sukiya* style (see SUKIYA-ZUKURI) popular in the Edo period (1600–1868), and the gardens are famed for their ponds, paths, and so-called borrowed scenery (*shakkei*).

The buildings at Shugakuin are modest in size but highly refined in craftsmanship. The main structures in each of the three gardens are of wood post-and-beam construction, with plaster walls or movable panels (*fusuma*), mat flooring (*tatami*), and cypress bark on clay tile roofs. The details of joinery, the proportions and coloring of rooms, and the use of natural materials reflect certain Edo-period tastes in architecture. In particular, the Rin'untei and Kyūsuiken, two small belvederes in the upper garden, and the Sugetsukan, a residential structure in the lower garden, typify the *sukiya* style of design in which simple materials often associated with rustic dwellings are combined and finished in an elegant manner. The guest house of Rinkyūji was moved to the site from the Kyōto palace of Empress Tōfukumon'in, Go-Mizunoo's consort, and represents by contrast a more ornate palatial style. Several buildings at Shugakuin burned in the 18th century but were rebuilt in the 19th century.

Shugakuin is most noted for its gardens, particularly for the technique of *shakkei* in which views of distant hills are deliberately borrowed and included in the garden design. As the visitor walks along paths or climbs steps, trees and hedges are placed and cut to frame the scenery beyond and thus expand the small landscaped areas. Go-Mizunoo had a nearby stream diverted to create several waterfalls and to fill a large pond in the upper garden for boating. With bridges to three islands and paths connecting the several pleasure pavilions, this stroll garden is composed of carefully arranged and constantly changing views of the nearby mountains and looks out over the city of Kyōto. This garden type was popularized in the early 17th century by KOBORI ENSHŪ. The Shugakuin is administered by the Imperial Household Agency and permission to view the gardens and buildings must be arranged in advance.

Bruce A. COATS

Shugei Shuchiin

Private educational institute established for the sons of commoners in the early part of the Heian period (794–1185). Founded in 828 by the Shingon monk KŪKAI, the school offered education to people irrespective of their class background, in contrast to the DAIGAKURYŌ and the *kokugaku* (provincial academies), which trained candidates for the bureaucracy. The school gave instruction on Buddhist and Confucian teachings, emphasizing both moral discipline and intellectual development. After Kūkai's death in 835, the school, without anyone to carry on his ideal of private education, was closed.

Etō Kyōji

Shugendō

A religious order which prescribes ascetic practices in mountains in order to attain magic powers beneficial to the community. The order is syncretic, combining elements of ancient pre-Buddhist worship of certain mountains as holy ground (*sangaku shinkō;* see MOUNTAINS, WORSHIP OF) with the doctrine, ritual, and symbolism of esoteric Buddhism. Its members are known as YAMABUSHI.

The Shugendō emerged as a coherent religious group toward the end of the 12th century. Its predecessors were the HIJIRI, solitary Buddhist hermits who renounced monastic life to practice in the depths of certain mountains the ascetic disciplines of fasting, immersion in cold water, and the recitation of a holy text such as the LOTUS SUTRA (*Hokekyō*). By these means they sought to acquire the power to vanquish spiritual beings causing sickness, to render themselves impervious to heat and cold, and to enable the soul to leave the body and travel to heaven and hell. The *hijiri* was thus a healer and thaumaturge with much in common with the Siberian shaman.

In the course of the Heian period (794–1185) these solitary ascetics became organized into groups, with a prescribed body of ascetic exercises performed at stated seasons under the leadership of officers known as *sendatsu*. The order thus has no historical founder, though its members ascribe its origin to EN NO GYŌJA, the semilegendary magician described in the 8th-century chronicle *Nihon shoki* as acquiring his powers through ascetic disciplines.

The Shugendō was not until recently considered to be a separate religious sect, its members being affiliated with either the TENDAI SECT or the SHINGON SECT of Buddhism. The Shingon branch, or Tōzanha (see DAIGOJI), claims to have been organized by the monk Shōbō (834–909), and the Tendai branch or Honzanha (see SHŌ-

GOIN), by Zōyō (1032–1116) a century later (ca 1090). The difference between the two branches is confined to unimportant details of nomenclature and ritual practice.

Until the 16th century the teachings of the order were strictly secret, being communicated orally to those disciples who had undergone the required initiations. Recently, however, the esoteric tradition has collapsed, and descriptions of most of the rituals and symbolism have been published in full.

The principal ritual exercises of the Shugendō are known as *nyūbu* or *mineiri,* "entering the mountain." These comprise an ascent of a particular holy mountain at each of the four seasons. The mountain being invested with strong symbolism of a sacred "other world" and of the esoteric Buddhist mandala, the climb represents a passage from a profane to a sacred state. In the course of the ascent and subsequent sojourn in the mountain, austere exercises are enacted, which by symbolic action are intended to rouse the disciple's Buddha nature from its hidden state and bring about his transformation into a Buddha. Concurrently enacted is a second series of symbolic actions of an unmistakably initiatory kind, in which the mountain is seen as the mother's womb and the disciple as an embryo growing from conception to birth. These austerities are at the same time believed to endow the disciple with various magic powers, notably the power to subdue the spiritual entities, witch animals, and discontented ghosts responsible for sickness and possession. The *yamabushi* is and always has been chiefly sought as an exorcist and healer. The principal holy mountains where these exercises are performed are, ŌMINESAN (see also KIMBUSENJI), Katsuragisan (in Nara Prefecture, see KONGŌSAN), the mountains around Kumano (see KUMANO SANZAN SHRINES), DAISEN, Dewa Sanzan (see DEWA SANZAN SHRINES), and Ushiroyama (in Okayama Prefecture).

The order was proscribed in 1873 as part of the campaign by the Meiji government to purify Shintō from Buddhist elements. It nevertheless survived in many parts of the country, to be resuscitated in 1945 during the Occupation under the terms of Supreme Commander Douglas MacArthur's Religious Bodies Law. Since then it has continued to flourish in a number of officially registered groups, although the degree of ascesis practiced is much less severe than in former times. See also SHAMANISM.

■——Carmen Blacker, *The Catalpa Bow* (1975). Anne-Marie Bouchy, *Jitsukaga no shugendō* (1977). H. Byron Earhart, *A Religious Study of the Mount Haguro Sect of Shugendō* (1970). Gorai Shigeru, *Yama no shūkyō* (1970). Gorai Shigeru, *Shugendō nyūmon* (1980). Hori Ichirō, *Nihon no shāmanizumu* (1971). Miyake Hitoshi, *Shugendō girei no kenkyū* (1971). G. Renondeau, *Le Shugendō: Histoire, doctrines et rites des anachorètes dites Yamabushi* (1965). Wakamori Tarō, *Shugendō shi kenkyū* (1943). *Carmen BLACKER*

Shūgetsu Tōkan (ca 1427–ca 1510)

Priest-painter of the Muromachi period (1333–1568), direct pupil of the artist SESSHŪ TŌYŌ. Born to a *samurai* family serving the Shimazu *daimyō* of the Satsuma domain (now Kagoshima Prefecture), his original name was Taki Kantō (or Takagi Gonnokami). He entered the priesthood in 1462. In the mid-1460s he went to Yamaguchi to study painting with Sesshū at his Unkokuan studio, becoming one of the great master's closest disciples. In 1490, apparently in recognition of his pupil's artistic attainment after nearly 30 years, Sesshū presented his self-portrait to Shūgetsu. He inscribed the painting to "Tōkan Zōsu" (Tōkan, Head Sutra Keeper), indicating that Shūgetsu had achieved a high status in the Zen hierarchy. In 1492 Shūgetsu returned to Satsuma to serve the Shimazu daimyō. About 1494–95, he took a trip to China and probably followed the route Sesshū had taken on his 1467–69 trip. A painting of the scenic West Lake in Zhejiang (Chekiang), generally accepted as the work of Shūgetsu, bears an inscription written in Beijing (Peking) with a date corresponding to 1496. When he returned to Japan about 1497–98, Shūgetsu continued to paint at his home temple of Fukushōji in Satsuma for several more years; these later paintings are signed, "By Shūgetsu, who went to China."

Forming his style from the rigorous techniques of his master, Shūgetsu worked with a wide range of subject matter. He painted abbreviated landscapes in splashes of ink wash (see HABOKU), as well as detailed scenes constructed on the basis of strong outlines and linear texturing of forms. He created portraits in precise classical silhouettes filled in with heavy color (see YAMATO-E), as well as figure subjects painted with the viscous ink contours of the Muromachi INK PAINTING tradition. He designed bird-and-flower compositions within the elaborate matrix that Sesshū formed from his contact with Ming-dynasty (1368–1644) painting in China. In all these works, Shūgetsu created forms by repeating somewhat intricate brush patterns, which he balanced against equal areas of space within a dominant horizontal framework held in place by a few vertical elements in a clear, dry atmosphere. While he retained the angular contours and firm brush lines of his master, he applied them in consistent rhythms. Thus, although Shūgetsu remained outwardly faithful to Sesshū's style, his own characteristic tranquillity replaced his master's essential dynamism.

Carolyn WHEELWRIGHT

shūgi

A rite of celebration on happy occasions; a gift given at such an occasion; a tip or gratuity. These celebrations are usually public occasions for announcing the attainment of a new stage in life or a new state of affairs and usually require formal or traditional clothing and some kind of special food. The most important events requiring shūgi are births and marriages. Less important junctures in life, such as pregnancy, first eating of solid food, the "seven-five-three" celebration (see SHICHIGOSAN) or coming-of-age are also acknowledged. Later in life, the 60th, 70th, 77th, and 88th birthdays, respectively called kanreki, koki, kiju, and beiju, also require shūgi. The New Year, Doll's Festival (3 March), Children's Day (5 May), and the harvest in the fall are some of the calendrical occasions (nenchū gyōji) celebrated. In contrast, rites performed during inauspicious occasions, such as funerals and memorial services, are called bu-shūgi.

By extension, shūgi also refers to gifts given to the individuals in whose honor the rite is performed. Such gifts on formal occasions are wrapped in special white paper with an ornamental string (MIZU-HIKI) and a special symbolic element (NOSHI) signifying happiness, but on lesser occasions money may be placed in store-bought envelopes with these symbols printed in red (shūgibukuro).

Shūgi may also refer to tips given to a geisha, to the maid in a Japanese-style inn, and to other service personnel. In this sense, shūgi is synonymous with terms such as hana (tip given to geisha), KOKOROZUKE, and chippu (from "tip"). Harumi BEFU

shugo

(provincial constables; later, military governors). Shugo and JITŌ (estate stewards) represent the two major governing networks of the KAMAKURA SHOGUNATE (1192–1333). Shugo were assigned—one to a province—from among the regime's favored vassals and performed duties falling into two general categories: they exercised limited authority over Kamakura's vassals (GOKENIN) and limited criminal jurisdiction over certain types of offenders. Scholars have had difficulty, however, in discovering more about the post. There is no agreement, for example, regarding the origins of the office, the range of its jurisdiction in practice, its potential for growth, or even its overall importance. Much more is known about jitō than about shugo.

One puzzle concerns the initial appearance of these titleholders. There were no shugo during Heian times (794–1185), but the record is confusing and contradictory for the 1180s. The standard source for the history of the Kamakura shogunate, the AZUMA KAGAMI, refers to shugo as having been irregularly appointed during the years of the TAIRA–MINAMOTO WAR (1180–85) and authorized on a national basis only late in 1185. Accordingly, some Japanese scholars claim that the offices of shugo and jitō were simultaneously established and that the shōgun MINAMOTO NO YORITOMO became shugo- and jitō-in-chief for the whole of Japan. The main difficulty with this theory is the absence of any direct evidence with respect to the shugo. There appears to be no clear usage of the term as an office name until after 1190. Rather, there was another title—sō tsuibushi—whose holders exercised constabulary duties only vaguely suggestive of those of the later shugo. Whether these sō tsuibushi may properly be viewed as the forerunners of shugo remains uncertain. It is clear, at any rate, that shugo and jitō did not emerge from the same historical mold.

A pressing need of the shogunate after the helter-skelter expansion of the 1180s was to identify and register the warriors who deserved recognition as gokenin. This task came to be assigned to shugo, though it was not the shogunate's intention to interpose these shugo between itself and its men. After the initial registration of vassals, the shugo's only formal authority over them was in organizing and leading an occasional palace guard duty (ōban'yaku) in

Kyōto. This latter responsibility occurred but once or twice during a generation.

Besides the mustering of the imperial guard (ōban saisoku), the shugo was also given jurisdiction over punishment for two major crimes—murder and rebellion. This too dated from the 1190s, though these three resulting responsibilities (called DAIBON SAN-KAJŌ, "three regulations for great crimes") were not formalized until 1232 when they were included in the GOSEIBAI SHIKIMOKU. For the remainder of the Kamakura period (1185–1333), this definition served as the basis for the shugo's public authority. Scholars, however, have failed to agree on what any of this meant in practice. For example, were shugo free to initiate proceedings against criminals without receiving a formal complaint? Were they empowered to try offenders independently and confiscate their property? Did shugo exercise these privileges over Kamakura vassals? To what extent did shugo have access to estates with immunity rights (FUYU AND FU-NYŪ)?

Historians have a clearer idea of the shugo's auxiliary duties than of the more formalized Daibon Sankajō. Nowhere is this clearer than in the assistance rendered by shugo to the shogunate's judicial system. Kamakura regularly called on its provincial constables to conduct local investigations, forward results, and expedite summonses to trial. An overwhelming preponderance of source materials revealing shugo "at work" clearly belongs to this category. It is interesting that this actually worked to the disadvantage of the shugo themselves, for serving shogunate-issued injunctions and subpoenas cannot have won them much local favor.

To a considerable extent, in fact, the shugo of Kamakura times functioned as a buttress to the established order. On this point the contrasts with jitō are noteworthy and reflect the shogunate's greater leverage over its shugo appointees. Consequently, the limitations on shugo were: first, that there were far fewer shugo than jitō, and only families from the Kantō region could receive the appointment. This in turn meant that titleholders in areas beyond the Kantō were invariably outsiders. Second, shugo appointees only rarely took up residence in their assigned provinces. They were content to operate through regular deputies (shugodai). Third, shugo titles were not intended to be hereditary. The shogunate reserved to itself the right to dismiss or transfer an incumbent even without cause. One result was that only a handful of families held shugo posts continuously for the duration of the period. A fourth limitation centered on the Daibon Sankajō. The shogunate could, if it wished, compromise the regular authority of its shugo. Murder cases, for example, were sometimes handled directly by Kamakura. At the same time, the shogunate was ever watchful of shugo who sought to develop bonds with local gokenin. Shugo were prohibited from confirming the private land rights of these vassals, save for pro forma validations of Kamakura's own confirmations (ANDO). And of course no shugo was permitted to distribute new perquisites.

The office of shugo also did not include the right to income-producing lands. The post was viewed in this sense as a political lever to be used in Kamakura, which may have been a prime reason why so few appointees took up actual residence. Certainly it is clear that no shugo ever brought a lawsuit before the shogunate contesting infringement of his shugo lands (shugo ryō). On the other hand, families who were shugo did sometimes hold jitō rights in the same province, though it is noteworthy that the latter almost always predated or postdated the shugo tenure. In other words, they were not viewed explicitly as shugo perquisites.

A further limitation centers on the relationship between the shogunate, shugo, and shugodai. The Goseibai Shikimoku restricted the number of deputies to one per province, with whom Kamakura often communicated directly. There are many extant instructions from the shogunate in which the addressee is the shugodai. Moreover, since shugodai themselves often broke the law, Kamakura reserved the right to convey indictments directly. Though actual dismissals may have been made by the shugo, the relationship between constable and deputy was not considered inviolable by the shogunate. Not until the specter of the MONGOL INVASIONS OF JAPAN loomed in the 1270s did Kamakura order any of its shugo proper to take up local residence.

By that juncture another development was affecting the shugo institution. The shogunate's leading house, the HŌJŌ FAMILY, had come to possess a disproportionate share of shugo titles. Holding but 3 in 1200 and 15 in 1250, by the late 1280s it listed 28. Correspondingly, the number of non-Hōjō shugo posts dropped to 23 after 1285, distributed among 14 houses. How the Hōjō used these titles is a subject imperfectly understood. Moreover, since that family was totally destroyed in the 1330s, it is difficult to gauge the impact of their tenure on the rapid expansion of *shugo* powers during the next period. Indeed, the same question might be raised for non-Hōjō title holders, of whom only a handful were able to survive the demise of the Kamakura shogunate. The fact that only four or five Kamakura *shugo* retained the post under the MUROMACHI SHOGUNATE (1338–1573) suggests that its potential for local growth had failed to develop very far. By contrast, the new wave of *shugo* were drawn from two sources: kinsmen of the ASHIKAGA FAMILY and locally entrenched *jitō*. See also SHUGO DAIMYŌ.

📖 ——Jeffrey P. Mass, *Warrior Government in Early Medieval Japan* (1974). Jeffrey MASS

shugo daimyō

Term used by modern historians to refer to provincial military lords of the early and middle Muromachi period (1333–1568) as distinguished from the SHUGO (military governors) of the Kamakura period (1185–1333) and SENGOKU DAIMYŌ of the Sengoku period (1467–1568). Appointed as *shugo* by the MUROMACHI SHOGUNATE, they gradually increased their landholdings and power until they attained the status of semiautonomous lords (DAIMYŌ) ruling over one or more provinces. When MINAMOTO NO YORITOMO, first shogun of the Kamakura shogunate, created the office of *shugo*, their power was mainly limited to military and police oversight, but toward the close of the Kamakura shogunate and during the period of the rival NORTHERN AND SOUTHERN COURTS (1336–92) they gained increased political and economic authority. The shogunate permitted them to suppress roving bands of warriors who entered estates unlawfully to harvest rice *(karita rōzeki)*, to enforce the shogun's orders *(shisetsu jungyō)*, to exact corvées and special tributes for military expenses (HANZEI) from estates, and to distribute confiscated lands *(kessho)* among vassals. The acquisition of landholdings by *shugo* was accelerated when many court-based aristocratic estate (SHŌEN) proprietors, attempting to stem gradual encroachment upon their incomes, alienated their lands to the *shugo* in exchange for a fixed annual compensation *(shugo uke)*. In this way *shugo daimyō* eventually gained control over 30 to 40 percent of the country's rice land. Among these daimyō were the HOSOKAWA, HATAKEYAMA, SHIBA, IMAGAWA, ŌUCHI, TAKEDA, ŌTOMO, Sasaki, and YAMANA families. The Yamana alone were for a time masters of 11 of the 66 provinces of Japan, and as a consequence their family head was popularly called "lord of a sixth" *(rokubun no ichi dono)*. Under the Muromachi shogunate the *shugo daimyō* of central Japan were invested in important posts in Kyōto where they were obliged to reside. Increasingly, governance of the provinces was delegated to deputies *(shugodai)*. By the end of the 15th century most *shugo daimyō* had either been defeated in conflicts among themselves (see ŌNIN WAR) or overthrown by provincial proprietors (KOKUJIN) and *shugodai*. These victors over the *shugo daimyō* subsequently established themselves as Sengoku daimyō. John W. HALL

Shugō Incident

(Shugō Jiken; also called Title Incident). A controversy over the official title by which the Tokugawa shōgun should be addressed in diplomatic documents from Korea. Despite much opposition, in 1711 the shogunal adviser ARAI HAKUSEKI succeeded in replacing the customary term Nihonkoku *taikun* ("great ruler of Japan") with Nihon *kokuō denka* ("his highness the king of Japan"), a change that placed the shōgun on an equal level with the king of Korea diplomatically. Soon after Hakuseki's removal from influence, the title was changed back to Nihonkoku *taikun*. The English word tycoon is derived from *taikun*.

Shūhō Myōchō → Sōhō Myōchō

shuinjō

(vermilion-seal certificate). A diplomatic form originating in the Sengoku period (1467–1568); with the *kokuinjō* (black-seal certificate), it belongs to a category called *imbanjō*, i.e., documents authenticated by the impression of a seal *(imban; see* SEALS) rather than the subscription of a monogram or cypher (KAŌ), which had been the customary medieval practice. Seals were used in Japanese official documents during the Nara (710–794) and early part of the Heian (794–1185) periods; they do not appear, however, in the standard documentary forms (for example, KUDASHIBUMI, *migyōsho*, and *gonaisho*) adopted by the Kamakura (1192–1333) and Muromachi (1338–1573) shogunates, and their reemergence in public use is associated with the decline of shogunal authority and the rise of the *daimyō* institution. The earliest extant black-seal certificate is dated 1487, and the earliest *shuinjō* 1512; both were issued by Imagawa Ujichika (1473–1526), the daimyō of Suruga (now part of Shizuoka Prefecture). The Later Hōjō family (see HŌJŌ FAMILY) of Odawara, TAKEDA FAMILY of Kai Province (now Yamanashi Prefecture), and UESUGI FAMILY of Echigo Province (now part of Niigata Prefecture) were other 16th-century daimyō houses that pioneered the use of documents impressed with seals, which often incorporated a figure (such as a tiger, dragon, or lion) or a slogan symbolizing the daimyō's assertion of public authority over his domains. The most famous of such seals is that of the hegemon ODA NOBUNAGA, inscribed with the slogan *tenka fubu* ("the realm subjected to the military"). Nobunaga used *shuinjō* for various purposes, ranging from the confirmation of land rights (ANDO), the mobilization of vassals, and the grant of "off-limits" privileges *(kinzei)*, to correspondence with other daimyō. The very same seal was sometimes impressed in black ink on *kokuinjō* issued by Nobunaga; according to an early 17th-century work by the Jesuit missionary João RODRIGUES, the vermilion seal was applied to "more illustrious and public" purposes and the black seal to "lesser and private matters." *Shuinjō* were also issued by the other two national unifiers, TOYOTOMI HIDEYOSHI and TOKUGAWA IEYASU; their use as licenses for overseas voyages originated the term *shuinsen* (vermilion-seal ships; see VERMILION SEAL SHIP TRADE) for trading vessels of the early part of the Edo period (1600–1868). The diplomatic form of *shuinjō* and *kokuinjō* continued in use in shogunal state papers throughout the period of Tokugawa rule. See also DIPLOMATICS.

George ELISON

shuinsen bōeki → vermilion seal ship trade

Shūi wakashū

(Collection of Gleanings; the full title is usually abbreviated to *Shūishū* and sometimes simply to *Shūi*). The third imperial anthology *(chokusenshū)* of classical Japanese poetry (WAKA); 20 books, 1,351 poems.

With the first imperial anthology, the KOKINSHŪ (ca 905, Collection of Ancient and Modern Times), and the second, the GOSEN WAKASHŪ (after 951, Later Collection), the *Shūishū* is included in the collective term *sandaishū*, or "anthologies of three eras," the group revered over the centuries as the orthodox canon of classical poetry and the accepted source of elegant, decorous diction and expression. As the title suggests, the purpose of the anthology was to gather together good poems of earlier times which had for one reason or another missed inclusion in the first two imperial collections. It was ordered by former emperor KAZAN (968–1008; r 984–986), and was compiled perhaps by FUJIWARA NO KINTŌ (966–1041), the outstanding poetic arbiter of his generation, who is thought at least to have prepared a draft in 10 books containing 590 poems, which was circulated independently of the official anthology under the title *Shūishō* (Draft of the *Shūishū*), and came to be regarded by many as superior in quality to the final version. As for the latter, Kazan is said to have taken a direct hand in it, making substantial changes to materials submitted to him and adding many poems. There are also different traditions about the time of completion of the official version; the common dates given are between 996 and 1007.

The arrangement of the 20 books follows the general principles established by the *Kokinshū*, with differences in detail. Some 196 poets are represented. In terms of numbers of poems selected, the most important are: KI NO TSURAYUKI (872?–945), 106 poems; KAKINOMOTO NO HITOMARO (fl ca 685–705), 100 (of which many are dubious attributions); ŌNAKATOMI NO YOSHINOBU (921–991), 59; Kiyohara no Motosuke (908–990), 49; Taira no Kanemori (d 990), 38; ŌSHIKŌCHI NO MITSUNE (fl ca 900), 34; MINAMOTO NO SHITAGAU (911–983), 27; and Lady ISE (ca 877–940), 25.

As a collection intended merely to supplement the preceding two imperial anthologies, the *Shūishū* is marked by no radical new departures. Indeed, the tastes of the age and the preferences of the compilers emphasize conventionality and blandness at the expense of the robustness and high spirits of some 9th- and early-10th-century poetry, and the compositions by newer poets display an increasing refinement of technique within narrowing limits of sub-

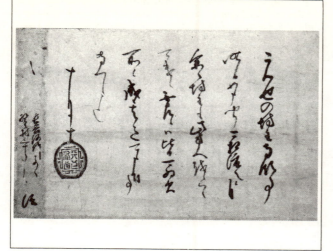

Shuinjō

Shuinjō impressed with Oda Nobunaga's *tenka fubu* seal. The document endows the Jōdo-sect temple Jōgon'in in Azuchi, Nobunaga's castle town, with landed income, promises similar grants to other temples who will move to Azuchi, and threatens those that will not with confiscation of their property. 28.7 × 43.6 cm. Ca 1576. Jōgon'in, Shiga Prefecture.

ject and treatment. In general, the collection reflects the times, during which the elegant, sophisticated, yet somewhat effete culture of the Heian court was at its height.

📖 ——Robert H. Brower and Earl Miner, *Japanese Court Poetry* (1961).

Robert H. BROWER

shūji → calligraphy

Shūkai Jōrei

(Public Assembly Ordinance). Ordinance restricting political assembly; issued in April 1880. Together with the PRESS ORDINANCE OF 1875, it was aimed at controlling the growing FREEDOM AND PEOPLE'S RIGHTS MOVEMENT. It required registration with, and prior approval from, local police authorities for all political organizations and meetings and provided for surveillance by uniformed police, who were empowered to break up meetings; it also prohibited outdoor meetings, contact between different political associations, and political activity by servicemen, police, teachers, and students. The ordinance was believed to have been specifically designed to suppress a nationwide meeting of the LEAGUE FOR ESTABLISHING A NATIONAL ASSEMBLY scheduled for that month in Ōsaka, and it provoked a general outcry. More restrictions were added in 1882. After further revision in 1890, the ordinance was replaced by the even more repressive PUBLIC ORDER AND POLICE LAW OF 1900.

shukkō

(temporary work transfer). A form of personnel reassignment in which an employee is temporarily sent or loaned to another organization (usually a related firm) while remaining on the home company roster. The term is also used to refer to similar transfers between government offices. In most cases it involves transferring an employee from the parent firm to a subsidiary or branch firm. Such transfers usually stem from a desire on the part of the parent firm to implement new systems of technology, conduct personnel development programs, or educate and train employees in a branch firm. Many corporations use this system to carry out promotions or demotions. During business slowdowns, employees are often sent to work in branch firms rather than dismissed. When the level of pay at the firm where one is transferred to is lower, the transferring firm makes up the difference in wages.   KURITA Ken

shukuba machi → post-station towns

Shukyūha → Sugup'a

shūmeigiku → anemone, Japanese

shūmon aratame

(religious inquisition). An institution of the Edo period (1600–1868) designed to eradicate Christianity throughout Japan. Under it, the population was screened for the presence of the religion's missionaries and believers; persons discovered to be Christian were forced to apostatize; the recalcitrant were subjected to psychological and physical tortures until they recanted, and those who refused to abandon their faith were executed. By the middle of the 17th century, the last priests had been captured, some 3,000 Japanese martyred, the majority of the religion's adherents driven into apostasy, and Christianity in Japan reduced to a few underground groups of believers, the KAKURE KIRISHITAN (crypto-Christians), among whom Catholicism was gradually transmuted into a syncretic folk creed. Far from being abolished, however, the inquisition developed into an elaborate mechanism of surveillance over the country's entire population: all persons were required to show that they were not Christian by affiliating themselves with approved Buddhist temples under the "temple guarantee" (TERAUKE) system. "Religious inquiry census registers" *(shūmon aratame nimbetsu chō)* compiled by the temples attested to their parishioners' religious purity for a government habituated to vigilance even after the "Christian peril" had in actuality passed.

Christianity had been defined as subversive by the national unifier TOYOTOMI HIDEYOSHI, who issued edicts restricting the religion's practice *(kinkyōrei)* in 1587 and martyred 6 European missionaries and 20 Japanese converts in Nagasaki on 5 February 1597 (Keichō 1.12.19). The Tokugawa shogunate likewise enacted prohibitions of Christianity from 1612 onward, in the lifetime of the first Tokugawa shōgun, TOKUGAWA IEYASU (r 1603–05), and under the shogunate of his son, TOKUGAWA HIDETADA (r 1605–23). In 1614 all Christian clergy were ordered to leave Japan. No fewer than 47 missionaries, including 27 Jesuits, defied the exile decree, however, and stayed in disguise with their flock; others were smuggled into the country on trading ships, the number of Jesuits actually increasing to 36 by 1621; between 1614 and 1624 the Jesuits alone registered 17,000 adult baptisms in Japan, and members of other religious orders also remained active under persecution. In 1616 Hidetada ordered the *daimyō* to "exert all effort to eliminate this religion among the populace," and there were sporadic martyrdoms throughout his regime, culminating in the "great martyrdom" of Nagasaki in 1622. Measures to stamp out the Christian faith were not systematized, however, until the shogunate of TOKUGAWA IEMITSU, who came to power in 1623. Under Iemitsu the methodical organization of the Tokugawa political order was completed, and the policies through which the shogunate asserted its supremacy prominently included the intensified persecution of Christianity within Japan and the country's isolation (Sakoku; see NATIONAL SECLUSION) from contact with Catholic lands.

The methods of the persecution were gradually worked out in Nagasaki, the terminus of foreign trade which in the first decades of the 17th century was an almost totally Christian city of 25,000, and in the neighboring, heavily Christianized areas of Kyūshū. From the beginning, the stress was on apostasy *(korobi)*. During the three-year term (1626–29) of Mizuno Kawachi no Kami Morinobu as shogunal commissioner in the city (Nagasaki *bugyō*), Japanese Christians were forced to apostatize or forfeit property invested in foreign trade; they were forbidden to have contact with foreign merchants for any purpose and particularly to provide them lodging (a measure aimed at shutting off one avenue of smuggling missionaries into Japan); artisans were told to abandon Christianity or quit their professions. This kind of intimidation was on occasion reinforced with torture. The pressures increased under Mizuno's successor Takenaka Uneme no Kami Shigeyoshi, Nagasaki *bugyō* until early 1633. Takenaka tested the Christians with macabre tortures (some of them pioneered by Mizuno), such as scalding them in the hot springs of nearby Unzen, but he also applied the subtler measures of psychological shock and intellectual persuasion to induce apostasy. Both Mizuno and Takenaka are credited with inventing the device of FUMIE (that is, forcing persons to tread upon a holy image to show that they disdained Christianity—an unconscionable sacrilege to genuine Christians and hence depended on to expose them).

The year 1633, when Soga Matazaemon and Imamura Denshirō were appointed to serve jointly as Nagasaki *bugyō*, proved fatal for the Jesuit missionaries of Japan. The new commissioners of Nagasaki came armed with the first of the shogunate's "national isolation directives" (*sakokurei*), issued on 6 March 1633 (Kan'ei 10.2.28), which included a paragraph offering financial rewards to anyone who informed against a *bateren* (Christian priest) or his aides; 10 Jesuit priests and a lay brother (*irmão*) were "in short order gathered in through this infernal design" in Nagasaki and vicinity, and another *irmão* was captured in Edo, leaving only six Jesuits at large. Moreover, in 1633 the inquisitors began using "a new type of most cruel torture," suspension head downwards in an ordure-filled pit (*anatsurushi*), and one of the captured Jesuits, Christovão Ferreira (1580–1650), the mission superior of Japan, apostatized under this torture. The Portuguese "apostate Padre" (*korobi bateren*) Ferreira, given the Japanese name Sawano Chūan, became a tool of the inquisitors, composing for them the manual of information on Christianity *Kengiroku* (1636; tr as *Deceit Disclosed*, 1973) and assisting them in the interrogation of other captured missionaries. None of the missionaries who sought to enter Japan after 1632 escaped immediate capture.

The search for Christians within Japan intensified in the middle 1630s, with the shogunate ordering its direct retainers to renewed vigilance and with daimyō domains from Sendai and Yonezawa in northern Honshū to Kagoshima in southernmost Kyūshū instituting stringent anti-Christian controls. The SHIMABARA UPRISING, a peasant rebellion which in 1637–38 swept what had once been a solidly Christian (and then a thoroughly purged) area of Kyūshū and which the shogunate adjudged to be inspired by a "regenerated" (*tachiagari*) Christianity, provided the impetus for yet another tightening of Tokugawa policy. The last few missionaries who had remained active in northern Japan were caught in the internal dragnet that resulted. In 1639 the final Sakoku directive (dated 4 August 1639; Kan'ei 16.7.5) ended the Portuguese trade and all traffic with Catholic lands. In 1640 the shogunate instituted the office of the *shūmon aratame yaku* (inquisitor) as the central organ for the supervision of its anti-Christian measures. On 10 January 1665 (Kambun 4.11.25), the daimyō were ordered to follow the shogunate's example and to appoint inquisitors charged with a yearly scrutiny of Christians; the analogous offices of *shūmon bugyō* and the like appeared in the tables of organization of domains from Yonezawa through Okayama to Kagoshima.

The shogunate's first *shūmon aratame yaku*, Inoue Chikugo no Kami Masashige (1585–1661), who concurrently served the shogunate as ŌMETSUKE (inspector general), had made his mark in 1639 by obtaining through torture the apostasy of two Jesuit priests examined by Shōgun Iemitsu himself. His headquarters in Edo (now Tōkyō), known as the Christian Mansion (KIRISHITAN YASHIKI), became the scene of grim sessions of torture interspersed with "arguments" which the inquisitor put to his victims "to awaken doubts in them, inextricably convince them, and cause them to apostatize." At some of these sessions, Inoue was assisted by Ferreira. Inoue's methods of torture and "thought control," summarized in the handbook *Kirisutoki* (Christian Records; German tr, *Kirishitoki*, 1940), were evidently successful: an entire group of five Jesuits and five of their acolytes, captured off Kyūshū in an attempt to enter Japan in 1643, apostatized under Inoue's ministrations; only one of the priests later revoked his apostasy. In 1657–58, however, more than 600 Christians were discovered in the Ōmura domain (now part of Nagasaki Prefecture) in Kyūshū; most of them died for their faith. Inoue resigned his posts, possibly as a result of this evidence that his success was less than total. Indeed, hidden remnants of Christianity were to come to light on several occasions over the next two centuries. In actuality, however, there was little left to do for the inquisitors after the 1660s, although *shūmon aratame yaku* continued to be appointed by the shogunate until 1792. But the routine set in motion for the purposes of the inquisition had developed an inertia and an identity of its own that made the *shūmon aratame* process continue in existence past the end of the Edo period.

That routine took the form of the compilation of "religious inquiry census registers" (*shūmon aratame nimbetsu chō*). These were prepared on the basis of periodic surveys which classified individuals according to their religious affiliation. The process utilized the "five-household neighborhood groups" (GONINGUMI), through which collective responsibility was enforced among the populace, and gave rise to the "temple guarantee system" (*terauke seido*), through which the Buddhist church was made into an instrument of the Tokugawa regime.

An early example of the association of *goningumi* and Buddhist temples with the inquisition is found in the orders for a roundup of Christians issued in 1634 by the shogunal deputy governing Kyōto (Kyōto *shoshidai*). Another comes from early 1636, when Sakai Tadakatsu (1587–1662), a senior councillor (*rōjū*) of the shogunate and daimyō of Obama in Wakasa Province (now part of Fukui Prefecture), ordered *goningumi* in his domain to certify the religious conformity of their members, setting down the principle: "Everyone must have a [Buddhist] temple he can go to for proof that he is not a Christian. Temple priests will therefore be required to issue attestations." The essential feature of a procedure subsequently adopted nationwide may be seen in the census register of a ward in Nagasaki which was prepared by heads of *goningumi* for submission to the Nagasaki *bugyō* in 1641: the document bears the seals of Buddhist temples attesting the religious orthodoxy of the persons enrolled, who are identified by name, age, sect, and temple of affiliation.

From 1645 an "apostate's oath" (*Kirishitan korobi kakimono*) appeared as a preamble to the census lists in Nagasaki. Its bizarre formula, which invoked eternal punishment from the Holy Trinity, the Virgin Mary, and the angels and saints upon any signatory who dared revert to Christianity, was certified to be effective by Ferreira and two other apostate priests, who also ascribed perfect efficacy to the ritual of treading the holy image (*fumie*) that accompanied entry onto the census rolls. The Nagasaki registers classified people as "originally" (*ganrai*) Buddhist or "fallen" (*korobi*) Christians. In 1687, as such former Christians were in fact dying out, the shogunate ordered the nationwide compilation of registers listing persons of *korobi* lineage (*ruizokuchō*) for submission to the *shūmon aratame yaku*; in 1695 that lineage was defined as male descent down to the sixth generation in the case of a lineage descending through a child of the original Christian born before his "fall" and to the fifth generation in the case of a lineage descending through a child born after the "fall." In this type of pedantry (as in other aspects of their work), the Japanese inquisitors proved the peers of their colleagues and contemporaries of the Spanish Inquisition, who were notoriously suspicious of "new Christians."

For all its thoroughness, the *shūmon aratame* did not succeed in totally extirpating Christianity in Japan. The hermetic religion of the Kakure Kirishitan survived its worst efforts. Four times between 1790 and 1865, groups of crypto-Christians were discovered near Nagasaki. (These incidents are known as the Urakami *kuzure*; see PERSECUTIONS AT URAKAMI). The persecution that followed the last and most spectacular of these discoveries carried over from the Tokugawa regime into the first years of the "modern" Meiji government, which punished 3,380 of these survivors of the Edo period's inquisition with exile to various provinces of Japan. Not until 1873 was the prohibition of Christianity ended. See also CHRISTIANITY; ANTI-CHRISTIAN EDICTS.

▣ ———*Kirishito-ki und Sayo-yoroku: Japanische Dokumente zur Missionsgeschichte des 17. Jahrhunderts,* tr Hubert Cieslik, S.J., and Gustav Voss, S.J. (1940). Fujii Manabu, "Edo bakufu no shūkyō tōsei," in *Iwanami kōza: Nihon rekishi,* vol 11: *Kinsei* 3 (Iwanami Shoten, 1963). Kataoka Yakichi, *Urakami yoban kuzure: Meiji seifu no kirishitan dan'atsu* (1963). Tamamuro Fumio, *Edo bakufu no shūkyō tōsei* (1971). George Elison, *Deus Destroyed: The Image of Christianity in Early Modern Japan* (1973). Ōkuwa Hitoshi, *Jidan no shisō* (1979). *Sakoku*, ed, Katō Eiichi and Yamada Tadao, *Kōza: Nihon kinsei shi,* vol 2 (Yūhikaku, 1981). Shimizu Hirokazu, *Kirishitan kinsei shi* (1981).

George ELISON

Shun'e (1113–ca 1190?)

One of the major poets and critics of the 12th century; the son of the famous poet MINAMOTO NO TOSHIYORI and the teacher of FUJIWARA NO TOSHINARI (Shunzei), one of Japan's greatest poets. In about 1130 he became a priest at the temple Tōdaiji in Nara, but continued to participate in the poetic activities of the nobility and made a considerable reputation for himself, although he did not appear in any of the truly prestigious poetry competitions until 1160. Thereafter he took part in several important competitions, but was never called upon to act as a judge. He named his dwelling the Karin'en (Garden of the Forest of Poetry) and held monthly poetry parties there, creating a type of literary circle. From these meetings he produced two anthologies, which have been lost. He was influential as a critic and poetic theorist, and although no treatise of his own is extant, his views have been preserved in the *Mumyōshō* (Nameless Notes) of his pupil KAMO NO CHŌMEI and in the *Eigyokushū* (Collection of Bright Jewels), a poetic treatise spuriously attributed to

Chōmei. He belonged to both of the rival poetic factions that had emerged by that time, the conservative Rokujō and the innovative Mikohidari, and to some extent helped to reconcile them. His ideal in poetry was profundity through simplicity and direct description, and he did much to foster the style of YŪGEN (mystery and depth), which was perfected by Toshinari and became one of the dominant styles of the middle and late 12th century. Toward the end of his life and after his death his style gave way to the more sophisticated and polished "new style" of the SHIN KOKINSHŪ. His own poetry is preserved in his collection, the *Rin'yōshū* (Collection of Forest Leaves) which he himself compiled in 1178, and he has 84 poems included in imperial anthologies from the SHIKA WAKASHŪ onward.

Phillip T. HARRIES

shunga

(literally, "spring pictures"). The Japanese term for erotic paintings, prints, and illustrations. As opposed to the native term *makura-e* ("pillow pictures"), *shunga* was originally an elegant, Chinese-derived expression but is today somewhat in disrepute in Japan, the term *higa* ("secret pictures") being considered more refined.

To the traditional Japanese, sex represented neither a romantic ideal of love nor a phallic rite of the gods; it was simply the joyful union of the sexes and a natural function. *Shunga* were thus considered a normal subject for the Japanese artist, no more improper or degrading than the painting of a nude or a classical love scene seemed to a contemporary Western artist.

Early Shunga —— Fragmentary evidence indicates that the earliest Japanese *shunga* were a diversion of Buddhist artists and artisans, graffiti sketched for relaxation in the midst of more serious endeavors. For example, an early, amateur *shunga* sketch has been found on the base of a statue in Japan's oldest extant temple, HŌRYŪJI in Nara (early 7th century), and fragments of early *shunga* (displaying, interestingly enough, use of both male and female sex implements) were discovered during the dismantling and repair of the Senju Kannon statue of the temple TŌSHŌDAIJI in Nara, a work of the latter part of the Tempyō era (729–749).

Sophisticated knowledge of sex was evidently widespread among the educated classes. We know, for example, that *shunga*-illustrated sex manuals were prevalent in the Nara period (710–794). The official TAIHŌ CODE of the year 701 even specified that physicians were required to study such illustrated texts, *osokuzu no e* ("posture-pictures"), as they were termed. And in 1288 the *Eisei hiyō shō* (Secret Essentials of Hygiene), a Japanese sex manual that summarized earlier Chinese texts, was even presented to the throne.

Pictorial erotica, naturally enough, was not suited to wide exploitation in the more public formats of Japanese art: hanging scrolls *(kakemono)*, screens, panels, and murals. It was only with the development of the EMAKIMONO, the lateral handscroll, that *shunga* became an established art form in Japan.

The first *shunga* scroll cited by name in literary sources is *Yōbutsu kurabe* (The Phallic Contest), ascribed to the abbot TOBA SŌJŌ (1053–1140). In subject this famous scroll depicts an imperial contest in which the most vigorous males of the empire gathered at the court, disrobed, and displayed their phallic splendors to be measured by the judges. Then the curtain was raised on the court ladies, who had been viewing the spectacle from concealment, and who now rushed out naked to engage the winners in a contest of sexual powers. As might have been expected, the ladies won and were conferred the imperial palm. A companion scroll, *Hegassen* (The Fart Battle), is not primarily erotic in nature but is, rather, the ribald account of a legendary wind-breaking contest between two groups of imperial courtiers.

Koshibagaki-zōshi (The Brushwood Fence Scroll), of the late 12th century, is the earliest scroll that can be termed truly erotic and aphrodisiac in nature. Here, for the first time, we are presented with a continuous study of sexual romance (based on a court scandal of the year 986), displayed in increasingly fervid states.

With the noted *Chigo no sōshi* (The Catamites' Scroll) preserved in the Sambōin temple of DAIGOJI, we come to the earliest *shunga* scroll extant in its original version in Japan. This scroll bears the colophon date 1321 and is probably the only extant *shunga* work which, except for its subject, would be officially classified a National Treasure. The text to the *Chigo no sōshi* consists of a series of short and sometimes ribald tales of pederasty among the Buddhist monks of medieval Japan. In *Fukuro hōshi ekotoba* (The Priest in the Bag) we find yet another early *shunga* scroll whose content, though erotic, makes humor its primary theme.

Shunga in Early Ukiyo-e —— It was with the Edo period (1600–1868) that erotic art came into its own as an object of appreciation by the urban populace in general, no longer merely a pleasure of the wealthier *samurai* and of the priesthood or aristocracy. A critical element in the popularization of the *shunga* art form was the expansion of woodblock printing—formerly limited to a few monastic presses—to the secular world. As with printing in general, the early 17th-century examples of *shunga* were yet very "limited" editions, produced in Kyōto by and for a restricted group of affluent connoisseurs. The first major development of printed *shunga* appeared not in the old imperial capital but in the new samurai administrative center of Edo (now Tōkyō). The year 1660 marks the first extant, dated *shunga* publication in Edo, and this may be taken as the general starting point of fully developed *shunga* in its printed form. The first Edo UKIYO-E artist of *shunga* was MORONOBU's anonymous mentor, the KAMBUN MASTER. It is of no little interest that *shunga* prints preceded the general appearance of nonerotic independent prints by fully two generations; clearly the audience for the relatively expensive prints was at the beginning limited to the more wealthy devotees of *shunga*.

The *ukiyo-e* pioneer Moronobu, in the two decades from 1672 until shortly before his death in 1694, produced some 150 separate sets of book illustrations, of which perhaps one-fifth are *shunga*—about average for the erotica output of an *ukiyo-e* artist. His noted follower SUGIMURA JIHEI (fl ca 1681–1703) was that rare *ukiyo-e* artist who devoted nearly half of his work to the erotic.

Of Moronobu's successors, TORII KIYONOBU I (1664?–1729), traditionally said to be the founder of the TORII SCHOOL of *ukiyo-e* which devoted its major production to the lively *kabuki* theater, was also a master of the erotic. Another Edo artist, OKUMURA MASANOBU (1686–1764), was a master of the album format in general, and his nine or more sets of erotic album prints are of consistently uniform quality.

The most devoted follower of the *ukiyo-e* master Moronobu was not an Edo artist at all, but an indirect pupil in Kyōto, NISHIKAWA SUKENOBU (1671–1750). He transformed Moronobu's austere vigor to a graceful, quiet charm most typical of the ancient capital of Kyōto. After Sukenobu, the major *shunga* artist in western Japan was his follower Tsukioka Settei (1710–86), an Ōsaka master who produced two or three sets of notable *shunga* prints and some two dozen *shunga* books.

Ukiyo-e in the "Golden Age" —— The Tokugawa shogunal government was more afraid of sedition than of erotica, and actual cases of censorship were infrequent, despite the sumptuary government edicts of 1722 and thereafter; yet the mere existence of such laws meant that *shunga* publication became more surreptitious and the number of prints and books fewer. At the same time, contrary to its intent, the official banning of artistic sex display seems to have created a popular demand for the semierotic that had hardly existed previously. This demand was soon met by the production of the so-called *abuna-e* (a punning compound implying "risqué pictures"): prints or paintings in which were featured the nude and seminude, hitherto hardly considered erotic at all.

The great revival of *ukiyo-e* in all categories came with the mid-1760s, one of the great epochs of the print. Suzuki HARUNOBU (ca 1725–70) thus appeared at a fortunate time, and his dozen albums of color prints in the smaller, *chūban*-style format mark one of the peaks of erotic *ukiyo-e*.

Harunobu's leading pupil and follower in the *shunga* genre was ISODA KORYŪSAI (18th century), an artist of *samurai* origin. The strange genius IPPITSUSAI BUNCHŌ (fl ca 1768–90) also produced important *shunga* prints, as did KITAO SHIGEMASA (1739–1820) and KATSUKAWA SHUNSHŌ (1726–92).

TORII KIYONAGA (1752–1815) is usually given credit for introducing the robust, "wholesome, magnificently normal" female figure to *ukiyo-e* design and to *shunga*. With Kiyonaga's close follower Katsukawa Shunchō (fl late 1770s–90s), this style found further expression in the *shunga* genre.

With the great Kitagawa UTAMARO (1753–1806) we come to a master who was known from his own time as the leading Japanese *shunga* artist—his prints are even said to have been exported as far as China. First studied by Edmond de Goncourt in the late 19th century, he is probably the best known abroad of any of the Asian masters of the erotic. Utamaro's most impressive *shunga* are found in his half-dozen sets of album prints. His most noteworthy single work of erotica was one of his first, the album *Uta makura* (Pillow of Song) of 1788. Utamaro literally dominated the *shunga* world during much of the last two decades of his life. Such noted contemporaries as KUBO SHUMMAN, UTAGAWA TOYOKUNI, HOSODA EISHI,

Chōkōsai Eishō, CHŌKYŌSAI EIRI, Rekisentei Eiri, and Ubunsai Gabimaru produced limited numbers of *shunga* prints or books—as did Utamaro's own pupils Kitagawa Kikumaro and Utamaro II—but these artists all worked in the shadow of the great master.

Later Shunga —— Japanese erotica during most of the first century and a half of *ukiyo-e*'s flourishing tended to retain much of the original, elemental force of the early *shunga*. From the "golden age" of Utamaro, however, decadent elements gradually came to predominate, and the innocent sexual curiosity of the earlier years was increasingly replaced by a manifestly lubricious, near-pornographic interest. This mutation is seen in one form or another throughout much of the art and taste of the later Edo period.

The great Katsushika HOKUSAI's (1760–1849) *shunga* activity seems mainly to fall in his middle years, ca 1814–20. His best-known works are undoubtedly *Tsuhi no hinagata* (Models of Loving Couples) and *Nami chidori* (Plovers above the Waves), each an album of 12 remarkable color prints.

After Hokusai, undoubtedly the most striking figure among the later *shunga* artists is KEISAI EISEN (1790–1848). Eisen's equally prolific contemporary UTAGAWA KUNISADA (1786–1865) worked extensively in the field of *shunga*-illustrated books. His confrere UTAGAWA KUNIYOSHI (1798–1861) is also famed for his erotic work.

The contemporaries and followers of Kunisada and Kuniyoshi are legion and it is their countless *shunga* works that are most commonly seen today. A checklist of these lesser 19th-century masters would include Utagawa HIROSHIGE, Utagawa Kuninao, Utagawa Kunimaru, Utagawa Kunimori, Koikawa Shōzan, Utagawa Kunisada II, Utagawa Sadatora, Utagawa Sadafusa, Utagawa Sadahide, Utagawa Yoshikazu, Utagawa Yoshiiku, Toyohara Kunichika, Toyohara Chikanobu, Kawanabe Kyōsai (see KAWANABE GYŌSAI), and such of Hokusai's pupils and followers as his daughter Oei, Teisai Hokuba, TOTOYA HOKKEI, Keisai Taigaku, and Harukawa Goshichi.

The *shunga* print followed the destiny of the figure print in general: it reached a peak with the last quarter of the 18th century, then declined gradually until, by the middle of the 19th century, it was a rare artist or publisher who could design or issue a print anywhere near the level of the earlier masters and publishers.

Over 90 percent of the *shunga* production of the Edo period consisted of the prints and printed books of the popular *ukiyo-e* school. But a survey of the remaining 10 percent—i.e., the hand-painted *shunga* of the Edo period—reveals that nearly all types and classes of artists at one time or another painted such works for their own amusement or on commission from their patrons. To judge from the literary sources of the time, a surprising number of the greatest 18th- and 19th-century painters of the MARUYAMA-SHIJŌ SCHOOL, BUNJINGA painters, and painters of other schools were known for their *shunga*. These include such artists as IKE NO TAIGA, MARUYAMA ŌKYO, Komai Genki, MATSUMURA GOSHUN, TANOMURA CHIKUDEN, TANI BUNCHŌ, WATANABE KAZAN, Takahisa Aigai, Kikuchi Yōsai, Kawanabe Kyōsai, and such female artists as Takenouchi Shōran and UEMURA SHŌEN. During the Meiji period (1868–1912), the final generation of *ukiyo-e* artists played their terminal role and sometimes produced *shunga* work of merit. However, in modern Japan—what with strong government censorship and prosecution—*shunga* have had only a minor role, in the hidden shadows of art.

——Works in Western languages: Marianne Densmore, *Les Estampes Érotiques Japonaises* (1961). T. and M. Evans, *Shunga, The Art of Love in Japan* (1975). Richard Lane, "The Shunga in Japanese Art," in P. Rawson, ed, *Erotic Art of the East* (1968). Richard Lane, *Shunga Books of the Ukiyo-e School, Series I–VI* (1973–82). Richard Lane, *Images from the Floating World: The Japanese Print—including an Illustrated Dictionary of Ukiyo-e* (1978). Richard Lane, *The Erotic Theme in Japanese Painting and Prints: I—The Early Shunga Scroll* (1979). Richard Lane, *Erotica Japonica: Masterworks of Shunga Painting* (1983). *Ukiyo-e: A Journal of Floating-World Art* (from 1962), a valuable source of current research on *shunga* prints, books, and paintings; texts in both English and Japanese. Works in Japanese (illustrations expurgated): Hayashi Yoshikazu, *Empon kenkyū*, 14 vols (Yūkō Shobō, 1960–76). Shibui Kiyoshi, *Genroku kohanga shūei: Estampes Érotiques Primitives du Japon*, 2 vols (1926–28). *Richard* LANE

Shunkan (1142?–1179)

Buddhist priest of the Shingon sect and administrative director *(bettō)* of Hosshōji, most prominent of the Six Great Temples (Rikushōji) founded by the imperial family in the 11th and 12th centuries in the Shirakawa area of Kyōto. In 1177 he met with several other intimates of the retired emperor GO-SHIRAKAWA in a villa at Shishigatani, in the eastern hills of Kyōto, to plan an uprising against TAIRA NO KIYOMORI, then the dominant power in the capital. Kiyomori discovered the plot (known as the Shishigatani Conspiracy) and arrested the conspirators, executing one of them and banishing three others, including Shunkan, to the island of Kikaigashima (believed to have been what is now Iōjima, Kagoshima Prefecture). The following year an amnesty was declared, but Shunkan's name was not included in the message of recall sent to Kikaigashima, and he remained there until his death. His grief and rage at the moment he realized he would not be recalled from exile provide the dramatic climax of several Nō, *bunraku,* and *kabuki* plays, the most famous of which is *Heike nyogo no shima* (1719) by CHIKAMATSU MONZAEMON. *Barbara L.* ARNN

shunran

Cymbidium virescens. An evergreen perennial herb of the orchid family (Orchidaceae) which grows wild on wooded mountains and hills from Honshū southward and is also cultivated. The leaves are 20–50 centimeters (8–20 in) long, broad linear in shape, and dark green; the upper half droops downward. In early spring a flower opens on the tip of a stalk that grows out laterally from the roots and is shorter than the leaves. The flower is 3–5 centimeters (1.2–2 in) across, pale yellow, and sometimes has reddish purple lines. The lip is white and spotted with reddish purple. The Japanese decorate bowls of soup with this flower and drink boiled water with the salted flower floating on it.

All the plants known as *ran* (orchid) and cultivated in Japan and China belong to the genus *Cymbidium,* which are referred to as *tōyōran* (oriental orchids) in distinction to *yōran* (Western orchids). Besides *shunran, tōyōran* species cultivated in Japan include Shina *shunran* or Chinese *shunran* (*C. forrestii*), and *surugaran* (*C. ensifolium*), both native to China. *MATSUDA Osamu*

Shunshoku umegoyomi → Tamenaga Shunsui

shuntō

(spring wage offensive). Sometimes referred to as "scheduled struggles." A strategy of organized labor designed to achieve a near-uniform pattern of annual wage increases throughout Japanese industry. It has been a yearly event, concentrated in the months of April and May, since the mid-1950s, during which labor unions conduct waves of industry-wide work stoppages of short duration as the means of bringing about basic wage settlements with employers for the ensuing 12 months. These "base-up" agreements have comprised a major part of wage bargaining in union-management negotiations in Japan and, compared to collective bargaining in other countries, appear to be a distinctive approach.

Origins of the Shuntō —— Japan's spring wage offensive had its formal beginnings in 1955. It developed under the leadership of ŌTA KAORU, then chairman of SŌHYŌ (General Council of Trade Unions of Japan) and IWAI AKIRA, Sōhyō's secretary-general. Sōhyō is Japan's major nationwide labor federation, embracing unions in both the private and public sectors of the economy. Essentially, the *shuntō* was a call for coordinating wage demands of the various enterprise-level unions in order to ensure the unity and solidarity of the labor movement at a time when it was threatened with division and possible decline. It took advantage of the fact that most hiring firms and the government formulated their annual budgets to coincide with the beginning of Japan's fiscal year in April, and that spring was the season when major enterprises usually hired the bulk of the new school graduates who would become career-long employees in their respective companies.

Wage Campaigns 1945–1955 —— Previously, the strategy of organized labor for achieving wage increases through collective bargaining and work stoppages under the leadership of national labor federations had resulted in sharp controversy among the unions themselves, and the effects had been dubious. Immediately after World War II, when unions spread rapidly, national federation wage demands were geared notably to left-wing or opposition political movements as well as to protecting the livelihoods of workers, and took the form of widespread drives which intermingled collective bargaining and political action. This approach culminated in the call for a nationwide general strike scheduled for 1 February 1947. The

Allied Occupation command, fearing that such a strike constituted a threat to its own authority, forced cancellation of this strike (see GENERAL STRIKE OF 1947). Nonetheless, for the next several years, the national labor centers attempted to continue to combine widespread wage and political campaigning without going so far as to resorting to a general strike. After the formation of Sōhyō in 1950, the secretary-general TAKANO MINORU stressed a strategy of community- or region-wide "struggles" involving not only union workers but all elements of the local population. Such drives were not yet concentrated at any particular time of the year, but occurred in each of the seasons in continual rounds of collective bargaining demands over different wage issues. In Japan, it should be noted, bargaining over wage increases is separated from negotiation of the general collective agreement between management and union. Theoretically, labor unions may make wage demands at any time.

Role of Enterprise-Level Unions ——— Such a diffuse approach, however, appeared to lose its effectiveness, since the actual wage settlements were made at the level of individual enterprises. While in the period immediately following Japan's surrender there were semblances of industry-wide collective bargaining in such industries as coal mining, private railways, and shipping, basically, from the beginning, workers formed unions at the plant and the enterprise level comprising both blue- and white-collar workers. It proved difficult for enterprise-level unions to focus demands upon management beyond the confines of a particular factory or company. This tendency became especially clear once the Supreme Commander for the Allied Powers (SCAP) began to retreat from its reformist policies in 1947, and industrial managements regained their authority in employer-employee relations soon thereafter. By the early 1950s, it was clear that a dominant characteristic of organized labor in Japan was its enterprise-level, rather than industry-wide or national, orientation. As a result, the basic problem facing the upper organizations of the labor movement was how to coordinate and unify the disparate approaches of the thousands of enterprise-level unions that had been formed.

By devising the *shuntō* strategy, Sōhyō's leadership succeeded in large measure in bridging the gap between the particularistic interests of the enterprise-level unions and the broader concerns of the national labor organizations. This was accomplished by concentrating almost exclusively on the wage increase issue at the one time of the year when there was generally a common concern among most enterprise-level unions.

Meaning of "Base-up" ——— There are several components which usually make up a Japanese employee's money wage, or salary, which is paid on a monthly rather than an hourly or weekly basis. The principal component is the basic wage, to which most other components are systematically related. Further, in the larger firms especially, the wage or salary is not closely related to the actual job performed, but rises with one's level of education, length of service in the firm, and age—a system called *nenkō joretsu* (SENIORITY SYSTEM). The *shuntō* demand for an increase in the base rate alone thus aims at raising the whole wage and salary structure by a fairly uniform amount or percentage within a company as well as across companies. Typically, the "base-up" is expressed as the increase in the basic wage for the average individual worker, say, a high school graduate of 30 years of age, with 10 years of service. When settled, the increase in a firm's total payroll is then distributed among the workers with little disturbance to the existing structure of the wage system. The union may or may not negotiate the actual distribution, depending on the negotiating relationship at the enterprise level. In general, the result is to treat all regular workers alike.

Intimately related to the "base-up" are other changes in the wage and benefit structure. Some are automatically adjusted upward, such as retirement and health insurance benefits, family allowances, and individual job pay. Others, especially the summer and year-end bonus, which in some cases may account for one-third of a worker's wages, are negotiated separately but geared closely to the increase obtained through *shuntō*. Thus, in a sense, while the *shuntō* "base-up" deals directly with only one element, it has a key influence on most other components of a worker's wages and benefits.

Spread of the Shuntō ——— At the outset in 1955, the *shuntō* was organized under Sōhyō leadership around a nucleus of a handful of industry-wide federations of unions which managed to mount waves of work stoppages involving about 800,000 workers in the aggregate. The spread of the *shuntō* as a general movement grew gradually year by year. Initially, Zenrō Kaigi (Japan Labor Council), Sōhyō's chief rival, later renamed DŌMEI (Japanese Confederation of Labor), condemned the *shuntō* strategy on the grounds that it ignored the particular economic conditions at the industry and enterprise level, and thus undermined efforts to develop full collective bargaining at the local level. With each year, more federations joined in, receiving a notable boost in support in the early 1960s after the founding of CHŪRITSU RŌREN (Federation of Independent Unions of Japan), which professed to take a neutral political stance between the left-socialist Sōhyō and right-socialist Dōmei. Moreover, while Dōmei has never joined the planning and coordinating bodies for the *shuntō* and has continued to condemn the advance scheduling of waves of strikes, its affiliated unions have in fact followed the *shuntō* wage demand strategy, especially those affiliated with the International Metal Workers' Federation–Japan Council (IMF–JC). By the 1970s, almost all of organized labor was participating in *shuntō*, with as many as 10 million workers engaging in stoppages and demonstrations. Throughout the era the trend has also seen a notable rise in the number of labor-management disputes, probably due in large measure to *shuntō*. Somewhat reminiscent of strike waves in France and Italy, the spread of *shuntō* as a nationwide movement has reached into the nonunion sectors, especially among medium and small firms. In a key sense *shuntō* settlements serve as a type of national wage policy. Throughout the boom years of the 1960s and early 1970s, *shuntō* settlements increased regularly, began to exceed productivity increases in the economy, and kept ahead of price inflation.

Shuntō Negotiations ——— While a central committee plans and directs the *shuntō* campaign, it does no actual bargaining. Planning begins months ahead of the spring drive, often accompanied by considerable publicity, with the major union federations and enterprise-level unions conferring on the appropriate demands to make and the strike tactics to undertake. On the employer side, too, there is considerable consultation; the government, especially through the MINISTRY OF LABOR and the labor relations commissions, keeps a close eye on developments. During this preparatory period there may also be direct discussion among unions, employers, and government concerning the eventual outcome.

By January, the union coordinating committee begins to announce the general aims for the *shuntō*, including the amount to be sought and the schedule of work stoppages likely to occur. Each participating industry-level union federation shortly thereafter makes similar pronouncements. Little formal collective bargaining occurs in this process, but rather begins only after the beginning of the strikes, usually lasting only a day or two at a time and confined to one or a few industries in any one instance. In scheduling the strikes, certain key industries, particularly steel and private railways, are considered leaders in the process.

Apparently, the use of the strike in this way is a means for demonstrating the resoluteness and solidarity of the union members. They do not usually result from impasses in the bargaining itself. In some instances, notably the steel industry, the scheduled strikes generally do not happen, as settlements are made before they do. While the waves of strikes run their course in April and May, settlements begin to appear at the enterprise level and then spread rapidly as a pattern throughout the industries and economy, although with some variation. Complete uniformity is by no means attained, although over the years there has been a notable decline in the disparity of settlements.

Throughout the process the CENTRAL LABOR RELATIONS COMMISSION tends to play a significant role in assisting the parties to reach agreements. Of special importance are mediation and arbitration awards made by the Public Corporations and Government Enterprises Labor Relations Commission for employees in government operations, who by law do not have the right to strike, although they do have the right to organize and engage in collective bargaining. The outcome of settlements in the private sector affects the award for the public workers, so that there is considerable political pressure upon and informal involvement of some of the highest figures in government in behind-the-scenes maneuvering in the *shuntō* process.

People's Shuntō ——— Especially as Japan moved from a high to a more moderate growth economy in the 1970s and faced the problem of economic readjustment with greater emphasis on welfare policy, there was serious questioning of the usefulness of *shuntō* with its near-exclusive emphasis upon the "base-up." Since the OIL CRISIS OF 1973 *shuntō* strategists have begun to broaden the concept with attempts to seek improvements in other areas, not only for workers but also the population at large. Dubbed the "people's *shuntō*," the new emphasis centers on such matters as income tax reductions, increases in retirement and health insurance benefits, and enlarged public housing construction, as well as general wage boosts. It remains to be seen how these new issues will affect the overall structure and effectiveness of the *shuntō* strategy. See also COLLECTIVE LABOR AGREEMENTS; COMPANY WELFARE SYSTEM; LABOR; KŌRŌKYŌ; LABOR DISPUTES; STRIKES AND OTHER FORMS OF LABOR DISPUTE.

📖 ——— Alice H. Cook, *Japanese Trade Unionism* (1966). Robert Evans, Jr., *The Labor Economies of Japan and the United States* (1971). Hanami Tadashi, *Rōdō sōgi* (1973). *Japan Labor Bulletin* (monthly). *Nihon Rōdō Kyōkai zasshi* (monthly). Kazuo Ōkōchi, Bernard Karsh, and Solomon B. Levine, ed, *Workers and Employers in Japan: The Japanese Employment System* (1973). Rōdōshō, *Rōdō hakusho* (annual). Shirai Taishirō, Hanami Tadashi, and Kōjiro Kazuyoshi, *Rōdō kumiai tokuhon* (1977). Sumiya Mikio, *Rōdō keizairon* (1965). Kōji Taira, *Economic Development and the Labor Market in Japan* (1970).   Solomon B. LEVINE

Shuppan Hō → Publication Law of 1893

Shuppan Jōrei → Publication Ordinance of 1869

Shuri castle remains

Early-15th-century castle site located at the highest point of the Shuri hills on the outskirts of the city of Naha, Okinawa Prefecture. The exact date of the castle's construction and its original size are not clear, but it is known to have been built by Shō Hashi (see CHŪZAN'Ō), founder of the first Shō dynasty, soon after his unification of the three Okinawan kingdoms in 1422. The castle was enlarged in the time of Shō Shin (r 1477–1526) and Shō Sei (r 1527–56) of the second Shō dynasty. Architecturally, the Shuri castle was a late representative of the Okinawan *gusuku* (castle) style that prevailed from the 9th through the 15th centuries. The castle was destroyed during World War II, but archaeological excavations have recently been undertaken.   KITAMURA Bunji

shuriken

Short, knife-like weapon for throwing; used in one of the traditional MARTIAL ARTS of the Edo period (1600–1868), although known since the 11th century. They averaged 21 centimeters (8 in) in length and were made of steel. The *shuriken* were thrown without a spin, except in the Yagyū school. The shape differed according to school; Yagyū school *shuriken* were shaped like small four-pointed stars; other schools used nail-shaped or needle-shaped objects. *Shuriken* throwing was widely practiced especially in such domains as Sendai (now Miyagi Prefecture), Aizu (now part of Fukushima Prefecture), and Mito (now part of Ibaraki Prefecture). Besides the Yagyū, the Tsugawa, Shirai, and Negishi were also well-known schools of *shuriken* throwing.   TOMIKI Kenji

Shushigaku

(Zhu Xi or Chu Hsi school). A general name in Japan for the so-called Neo-Confucianism that developed in Song (Sung) dynasty (960–1279) China. This, the most fully developed philosophical system of premodern China, was established by Zhu Xi (1130–1200), also known by the honorific appellation Zhuzi or Chu-tzu (J: Shushi; hence Shushigaku). Whereas the already established exegetical studies of the Han (202 BC–AD 220) and Tang (T'ang; 618–907) dynasties were concerned with practical ethics (i.e., proper forms of conduct, especially in terms of social and familial relationships) and based this concern on the ethically oriented "Five Classics" of Confucianism, the Zhu Xi School was, in addition, concerned with abstract metaphysical principles. It developed an interpretation of nature and society based on the more philosophically oriented "Four Books" of the Confucian tradition and, influenced by Buddhist and Taoist ideas, formed a philosophy integrating the metaphysical and the physical. It influenced not only China but also Japan, Korea, and Annam (now Vietnam) from the 12th to the 19th centuries.

Basic Teachings of the Zhu Xi School —— The basic concept in Zhu Xi Confucianism is the *li-qi* (*li-ch'i*) dualism. *Li* (J: *ri*) is the principle basic to the existence of all things as well as to natural law and social norms. Because *li* does not assume any shape, function, or motion, it cannot result in phenomena by itself; only in conjunc-

tion with *qi* (*ch'i*; J: *ki*) does it take on a concrete existence in the form of animate or inanimate beings. *Qi* is a kind of gaseous matter and by self-induced motion can become *yin* and *yang* and the five elements (wood, fire, earth, metal, and water) which determine the shape and quality of all things. Yet, the basis for the functioning of *qi* is found in *li*. When *li* and *qi* combine, *qi* is condensed, and beings are produced; when they separate, beings cease to exist.

Heaven (*tian* or *t'ien*; J: *ten*) presides over the changes in nature and the destiny of man. Heaven is sometimes described as *li* itself, but strictly speaking it is the combination of *li* and *qi*. The *li* in man is called *xing* (*hsing*; J: *sei*), that is, original or inherent nature. When it actually exists in combination with *qi*, *xing* is called *qi*-bound or physical nature. When a person's nature is unimpeded by *qi* and is the same as original nature, such a person is called a sage (*shengren* or *sheng-jen*; J: *seijin*). However, when original nature is clouded by the *qi* of physical nature, evil emerges. Such is the ordinary person. The actions of ordinary men are inclined toward selfish or personal interests. Moral effort aims to return to original nature that is not impeded by *qi*. This return is called the transformation of physical nature; it means an abandonment of selfish desires and a return to the *li* or heavenly principle. By denying that which is private or selfish in orientation and taking an impartial stand, that is, by actualizing *li*, even ordinary men can become sages. The actions of a sage have always coincided with *li*. His character and his actions have a wide influence. As a family member, he sets his family in order. If he is a ruler, he will govern the state perfectly and pacify the whole world, just as ancient sage kings did. Everybody is to cultivate himself, aiming at sagehood.

After Zhu Xi's death, a division occurred in the Zhu Xi school; one side inclined toward regarding *li* as substance, emphasizing *li* as the basis of existence of all things; the other side inclined toward regarding *li* as natural law and social norm. The first position, which pursued *li* as the eternally immutable substance underlying all changing phenomena, requires that man's physical nature be changed into man's original nature and emphasizes that the universal moral law and individual desires contradict each other. The latter position negates the substantiality of *li*, limits the validity of *li* to its working through *qi*, asserts that only man's physical nature is real, denies the existence or original nature as such, and attempts to confirm the existence of a universal moral law within individual desires. The school that became fixed as the national teaching in China was the former. In Japan, however, this division into two schools did not become particularly significant.

The Zhu Xi School in Japan: Shushigaku —— Zhu Xi's writings were introduced to Japan in the early years of the Kamakura period (1185–1333); but it was later, in the Muromachi period (1333–1568), that they were particularly studied by Zen monks of the GOZAN temples. In the last century of that period their influence appeared in the laws of *daimyō* domains (*kahō*). However, it was in the Edo period (1600–1868) that Zhu Xi's teachings, as Shushigaku, became rooted in the social fabric of Japan and became the official teaching of the shogunate.

Shushigaku is central to an understanding of the development of ideas in the Edo period. KOGAKU (Ancient Learning), a development within Japanese Confucianism and essentially a reaction against Shushigaku, advocated a return to the works of the ancient sages of China. Both KOKUGAKU (National Learning), which idealized Japan's earliest age and its ancient social mores and sentiments, and the so-called KOKUTAI ("national polity") theory, which found in the emperor system the special national characteristic of Japan, were also influenced in significant ways by the development of Shushigaku. With its emphasis on the investigation of the principle (*li*) of things, Shushigaku also played a part in the introduction and acceptance of modern European science, which entered Japan via the Dutch in the second half of the Edo period. See WESTERN LEARNING.

Confucianism and Buddhism had arrived in Japan by the 6th century as can be seen by the mention of them in Prince SHŌTOKU's SEVENTEEN-ARTICLE CONSTITUTION. These two teachings were regarded as more or less noncontradictory until the 16th century. Beginning with FUJIWARA SEIKA (1561–1619), however, Buddhism, with its other-worldly teachings, and Confucianism, with its socioethical teachings, became clearly distinguished. Seika found in Confucianism a system of practical ethics by which to live in society and consequently abandoned Buddhism. The recognition of this contradistinction was also the rediscovery of the attractiveness of the moral rigor of Shushigaku, and it was thus that the interest of the warrior class in Shushigaku was heightened. In 1607 the Edo shogunate employed HAYASHI RAZAN (the first important Japanese thinker to be exclusively identified with Shushigaku) as the shogunal Confucianist and then gave him funds and land to build a private school and a Confucian temple in Edo (now Tōkyō).

Razan, at the order of the shogunate, edited *Honchō tsugan* (a general history of Japan from the Confucian point of view) and KAN'EI SHOKA KEIZU DEN (a genealogy of the various *daimyō* families) and drafted the BUKE SHOHATTO, the basic legal codes for daimyō, as well as other laws and diplomatic tracts. At this time officials and townspeople of the merchant class such as MATSUNAGA SEKIGO (1592–1657) arose as scholars of Shushigaku. In 1690 the Confucian temple became a shogunal institution and the private school of the Hayashi family became its affiliate. The third-generation head of the family, HAYASHI HŌKŌ (1644–1732) was awarded the title *daigaku no kami* (head of the state university), the highest teaching title in Japan, which had been continuously bestowed since the Nara period (710–794). In 1790 MATSUDAIRA SADANOBU (1758–1829), senior councillor (*rōjū*) to the shōgun, brought about the so-called Kansei *igaku no kin* (Kansei era prohibition of unorthodox studies; see KANSEI REFORMS), which recognized Shushigaku as the orthodox teaching of the shogunate. The private school of the Hayashi family was made an official agency, Shōheizaka Gakumonsho (see SHŌHEIKŌ) in 1797, and from then on the teaching for Shushigaku as the only orthodoxy was conducted in the school for sons of the shōgun's vassals. After the Kansei Reforms, Shushigaku was advanced in the various domainal schools; by the end of the Edo period, 80 percent of all Confucianists teaching in domainal schools were Shushigaku scholars, the remainder being mostly KOGAKU and SETCHŪGAKUHA scholars. With the MEIJI RESTORATION of 1868 Shushigaku's status as the official teaching of the shogunate was abolished.

Until the mid-17th century, the Shushigaku of the Edo period was influenced by the Zen Buddhism of the Gozan or Five Monasteries, and was accommodating toward a *li-qi* monism, as seen in Fujiwara Seika and Hayashi Razan. Razan, however, came to take on the point of view of a *li-qi* dualism during his forties. YAMAZAKI ANSAI (1619–82) and his disciples ASAMI KEISAI (1652–1712), Miyake Shōsai (1662–1741), and Kinoshita Jun'an (1621–98) and Jun'an's disciple Muro Kyūsō (1658–1734) leaned toward regarding *li* as substance within a *li-qi* dualism. However, what is most characteristic of Shushigaku in Japan is its development of a position regarding *li* as law. The beginning of this development can already be seen in disciples of Ansai such as SATŌ NAOKATA (1650–1719). Yet others, such as YAMAGA SOKŌ (1622–85), ITŌ JINSAI (1627–1705), OGYŪ SORAI (1666–1728), and DAZAI SHUNDAI (1680–1747) developed a position regarding *li* as the law of *qi* and even arrived at a denial of the authority of Zhu Xi's interpretations of the classics; for they advocated a *qi* monism, which regards *qi* (or *yin-yang*) as the only actual existence and *li* as the law of *qi*. These last four are generally called Kogaku (Ancient Learning) scholars, among whom Itō Jinsai in particular was the theoretical propounder of *qi* monism. Shushigaku scholars were so influenced by *qi* monism that Matsudaira Sadanobu, who was responsible for the Kansei prohibition of unorthodox teachings, and the shogunal teacher BITŌ NISHŪ (1745–1813) also came to regard *li* as the law of *qi*.

The second most characteristic element of Edo-period Shushigaku is the greater importance it placed on loyalty (Ch: *zhong* or *chung*; J: *chū*) over filial piety (Ch: *xiao* or *hsiao*; J: *kō*). The lord-vassal relationship was considered to be the primary obligation, while the parent-child relationship was secondary. Further, loyalty became directed at the state or domain rather than at the lord as an individual. From Razan, Ansai, and ARAI HAKUSEKI (1657–1725) to Sokō and Sorai of the Ancient Learning school, this position can be found. Among the Confucianists of the MITO SCHOOL such as AIZAWA SEISHISAI (1782–1863) and FUJITA TŌKO (1806–55) loyalty to the emperor came to be emphasized, a tendency that developed into emperor-reverence toward the end of the shogunate.

The third characteristic of Edo-period Shushigaku is the union of Shintō and Confucianism. While an anti-Buddhist position was consistently held by the various Confucianist schools of the Edo period, especially Shushigaku, Satō Naokata and Miyake Shōsai were the only Shushigaku scholars who rejected Shintō. Ansai, claiming the intrinsic similarity of Shintō to Shushigaku, established SUIKA SHINTŌ and built a theory of Shintō according to his interpretations of Zhu Xi's teaching. This Shintō-Confucian syncretism developed hand in hand with the growing call for reverence for the emperor.

The final important characteristic of Edo-period Shushigaku is its advancement of philological research. The inclination to verify history, institutions, and phenomena resulted in the thorough studies

by Razan and Hakuseki of history and institutions, of astronomy by NISHIKAWA JOKEN (1648–1724), of natural history by KAIBARA EKIKEN (1630–1714), and research on the Confucian classics by NAKAI RIKEN (1732–1817), as well as the encyclopedic writings of YAMAGATA BANTŌ (1748–1821). The critical study of the Chinese classics by Jinsai, Sorai, and Shundai and the institutional history of the school of Ancient Learning by ITŌ TŌGAI (1670–1738) also belong in this context. See also CONFUCIANISM. —MIYAKE Masahiko

shūshin

("moral" training). Name of a course devoted to "moral" training in primary and middle schools before Japan's defeat in World War II. It was instituted by the Education Act of 1872 and attained special importance in the school curriculum as Japan embarked on an imperialist course.

The term *shūshin* is taken from the Analects of Confucius and means to "establish or conduct oneself." The value system of *shūshin* was basically Confucian, to which were added elements of modern civic morality as well as nationalistic tenets. The basic ideology underlying it was made clear in 1890 in the IMPERIAL RESCRIPT ON EDUCATION. The rescript spelled out filial piety and absolute loyalty to the emperor as the two great principles of moral conduct and exhorted the practice of friendship, fidelity, industry, philanthropy, and self-dedication. Discussion of the rescript was an important part of *shūshin* classes. Textbooks for moral training were made by the government, which used edifying stories and examples from everyday life. They gradually acquired a more nationalistic and militaristic tenor. *Shūshin* as a school subject was eliminated from the curriculum at the end of the war, but there has been a search since then for a new way to inculcate moral principles. See also MORAL EDUCATION. —NISHIMURA Makoto

Shu Shunsui (1600–1682)

(Ch: Zhu Shunshui or Chu Shun-shui). Expatriate Chinese scholar. Loyal to the Ming dynasty (1368–1644), he fled the rule of the succeeding Qing (Ch'ing) dynasty (1644–1912) and settled in Nagasaki in 1659. In 1665 he was invited by TOKUGAWA MITSUKUNI, *daimyō* of the Mito domain (now part of Ibaraki Prefecture), to live in Edo (now Tōkyō) under his patronage. There he cultivated the friendship of KINOSHITA JUN'AN, YAMAGA SOKŌ, and other Confucian scholars; lectured on various subjects, including Confucian etiquette, gardening, and agriculture; and greatly influenced the MITO SCHOOL of historical studies. He was noted also for his writing, the best-known example of which is the phrase he composed for inscription on the grave of KUSUNOKI MASASHIGE at the Minatogawa Shrine in Kōbe.

Shutoken → Tōkyō Metropolitan Area

Shuzenji

Town in eastern Shizuoka Prefecture, central Honshū. Situated on the river Kanōgawa, it developed as a hot spring resort in the Edo period (1600–1868). Of interest is the temple Shuzenji (after which the town is named), associated with MINAMOTO NO YORIIE, the ill-fated second shōgun of the Kamakura shogunate, and made famous by OKAMOTO KIDŌ's play *Shuzenji monogatari*. Pop: 17,720.

Sian Incident → Xi'an (Sian) Incident

Siberia, Japanese prisoners of war in

Soldiers and civilians captured by the Red Army and held for varying terms in prisons or labor camps throughout Soviet Asia between 1939 and 1959. Prisoners taken during the NOMONHAN INCIDENT along the Outer Mongolian-Manchurian frontier in 1939 spent several years at Karaganda in the Kazakh Soviet Socialist Republic (Kazakh SSR). Of the nearly 2 million Japanese captured by the Red Army offensive in Manchuria, North Korea, southern Sakhalin, and the Kuril islands during August 1945, several hundred thousand soldiers and a few civilian officials were transported to labor camps in Khabarovsk, Komsomolsk, and Chita in the Far East; Irkutsk, Tomsk, and Omsk in Siberia; Balkhash and Alma Ata in the Kazakh SSR; Tashkent (Uzbek SSR), Krasnovodsk (Turkmen SSR), and

Tbilisi (Georgian SSR). Most of these prisoners were repatriated between 1947 and 1950. On 22 April 1950, the Soviet news agency *Tass* announced that repatriation had been completed, but the Japanese Foreign Ministry replied that 370,000 of its nationals remained unaccounted for and were presumably in Soviet custody. There followed a "battle of figures" during which Tōkyō reduced its claim to 323,972 and Moscow conceded that an unspecified number of "war criminals" were serving sentences. In 1953 the Japanese and Soviet Red Cross organizations began talks on the repatriation problem, resulting in a boatload of 811 prisoners of war being returned to Maizuru in December. During the next six years, aided by the SOVIET-JAPANESE JOINT DECLARATION of 19 October 1956, some 4,500 were repatriated. The vast majority of those unaccounted for probably died at the end of the war and during the first few months of captivity. Many prisoners of war returned to Japan showing the effects of political indoctrination. Others evinced deep bitterness against fellow prisoners who had actively collaborated with the Soviet authorities. One prominent collaborator, nicknamed "Emperor of Siberia," prudently postponed his homecoming until 1976, reportedly for fear of his life.

📖 ——Edward Norbeck, "Edokko: A Narrative of Japanese Prisoners-of-War in Russia," *Rice University Studies*, 57.1 (1971).

John J. STEPHAN

Siberian Intervention

(Shiberia Shuppei). Expedition of Japanese troops to Siberia, 1918–22; part of a larger effort by Allied forces to intervene in the Bolshevik Revolution. The closing years of World War I witnessed the defeat of the Russian armies, the overthrow of the tsarist regime, and the conclusion of a separate peace treaty between the newly established Soviet government and Germany in March 1918. In due course, the railway towns of Siberia and the Russian Far East passed into Soviet hands. But some 750,000 tons of Allied munitions had accumulated at Vladivostok. Moreover, about 50,000 Czechoslovak troops, many of whom had deserted the Austrian armies to join the tsarist forces, were moving eastward through Siberia, hoping to reach the Allied front in Europe via Vladivostok and the Pacific. It was rumored that they had taken over sections of the Trans-Siberian Railway and formed an alliance with local anti-Bolshevik forces.

The issue was resolved by the decision of the Allies, with the concurrence and cooperation of the United States, to send troops to Vladivostok to protect the Allied supplies and to support the Czechoslovak troops. President Woodrow Wilson of the United States was also apprehensive lest Japan take advantage of the situation and act unilaterally to forward its long-standing territorial ambitions in Northeast Asia. In fact, in January of that year Japan had already dispatched two warships to Vladivostok "to protect its consular corps."

In July President Wilson suggested that Japan contribute 7,000 troops to a contingent of 25,000. After heated debate between the General Staff and several members of the TERAUCHI MASATAKE cabinet over whether Japan should act alone or join the Allies, the government replied that it would send 12,000 troops to Vladivostok, and beyond, if necessary.

Once the expedition was launched, the army took control, and troops poured into northern Manchuria and the Amur River valley; by November, more than 70,000 Japanese were entrenched in the Maritime Province and northern Manchuria. The Allies supported the counterrevolutionary forces of Admiral Aleksander Vasilievich Kolchak, but Kolchak was harassed by the Cossack leader Grigorii SEMENOV, a Japanese protégé. By February 1920 Kolchak had been captured and executed by the Bolsheviks, and in June of that year the Allied troops withdrew from Siberia.

The Japanese, however, remained for the avowed purpose of protecting their nationals and maintaining peace and order in the region. The military conflict now became localized in the Russian Far East and was carried on between the FAR EASTERN REPUBLIC, a buffer state set up by the Soviets, and the Japanese-supported Priamur government at Vladivostok. In the face of mounting criticism from all quarters within Japan—one billion yen had been expended, 3,000 soldiers had died, and many more were ill—and strong pressure from Britain and the United States at the WASHINGTON CONFERENCE, the Japanese finally withdrew in October 1922. See also RUSSIA AND JAPAN; NIKOLAEVSK INCIDENT.

📖 ——Hosoya Chihiro, *Shiberia shuppei no shiteki kenkyū* (1955). James W. Morley, *The Japanese Thrust into Siberia, 1918* (1957). Canfield F. Smith, *Vladivostok under Red and White Rule: Revolu-*tion and Counterrevolution in the Russian Far East, 1920–1922* (1975). John A. White, *The Siberian Intervention* (1950).

John A. WHITE

sickles → kama

Siddhaṃ

Also known as Siddhaṃatrka (J: Shittan). A script used to write the form of Sanskrit used in the Buddhist world. Deriving from a script which in turn developed out of Brāhmī, Siddhaṃ was introduced to Japan via China in the Nara period (710–794). The study of Siddhaṃ continued in conjunction with esoteric Buddhist studies until the Edo period (1600–1868). The traditional order of listing vowels and consonants in Siddhaṃ influenced the order of syllables in the traditional Japanese syllable chart (see GOJŪON ZU). Some premodern Japanese treatises on Siddhaṃ contain descriptions of the sounds of the Japanese language of their time and are thus valuable materials for the historical study of Japanese phonology.

YAMAZAKI Yukio

Sidotti, Giovanni Battista (1667–1714)

The last Roman Catholic missionary to penetrate Japan while the Tokugawa shogunate's policy of NATIONAL SECLUSION was in effect (1639–1854). Braving the ban on CHRISTIANITY, this Sicilian priest had himself dropped off by a ship from the Philippines on Yakushima, an island off Kyūshū, in 1708. He was captured immediately and transported first to Nagasaki and then to Edo (now Tōkyō) for interrogation. In late 1709 and early 1710 he was questioned four times by ARAI HAKUSEKI, the great Confucian scholar who was the principal policy adviser to the shōgun TOKUGAWA IENOBU. Hakuseki concluded that Christian missionary activity was not tantamount to external aggression but noted that the spread of Christianity inevitably led to internal subversion. Although he recommended that Sidotti be repatriated, the priest was imprisoned in the KIRISHITAN YASHIKI, the seat of the anti-Christian inquisition. When it was discovered that Sidotti had converted two of his caretakers to Christianity, he was confined in a hole in the ground and died there on 28 November 1714 (Shōtoku 4.10.21; his death date is often erroneously given as 1715). Sidotti's major contribution to Japanese history is that he gave Arai Hakuseki what the latter called "the wonderful chance of a lifetime" to inquire into Western conditions. The monument to their encounters is Hakuseki's treatise *Seiyō kibun* (Tidings of the West), drafted in 1715; because of laws prohibiting the spread of Christian information, however, the work could circulate only as a private manuscript during the Edo period (1600–1868).

George ELISON

Siebold, Philipp Franz von (1796–1866)

Pioneer of Japanese studies in Europe. Born in Würzburg, Bavaria, he studied medicine at the university there and took his degree in 1820. Two years later he entered Dutch government service as an army doctor and was dispatched to the Netherlands' East Indies. In 1823 he was appointed physician to the tiny Dutch settlement on DEJIMA, Nagasaki, where he had arrived in August. With fewer than 20 Dutchmen to look after, he had ample time for his own studies. His encyclopedic knowledge soon attracted many Japanese to study under him at this time of heightened interest in WESTERN LEARNING. In 1824 he established a boarding school, the Narutaki-juku, at Narutaki, then on the outskirts of the city of Nagasaki. He taught Western medicine and treated Japanese patients, accepting for payment the ethnographic and art objects that became the foundation of the Siebold collection. Upon his disciples he conferred "doctor's" degrees in exchange for "dissertations" that dealt with a wide variety of subjects and were later used by him in his compendium, *Nippon, Archiv zur Beschreibung von Japan* (1932–58, Nippon, An Archive for the Description of Japan). Among his outstanding students and collaborators were ITŌ GEMBOKU, TAKANO CHŌEI, Mima Junzō (1807–37), Ishii Sōken (1796–1861), Oka Kensuke (1799–1839), Kō Ryōsai (1799–1846), Totsuka Seikai (1799–1876), and Ninomiya Keisaku (1804–62). KAWAHARA KEIGA made zoological and botanical drawings as well as portraits and other pictures for him.

Early in 1826 Siebold, Ishii, Itō, Kawahara, Kō, and Ninomiya accompanied the *Opperhoofd* (chief merchant) of the Dutch settlement, J. W. de Sturler, and his suite on the "court journey" to Edo (now Tōkyō), where honors had to be paid to the shōgun. There he befriended the shogunate astronomer TAKAHASHI KAGEYASU, whose sobriquet was Globius, and who read Dutch, Manchu, and Russian. In exchange for Dutch books Takahashi gave him a map of Japan made by the famous cartographer and land-surveyor INŌ TADATAKA. He also met MOGAMI TOKUNAI, who furnished him with information concerning Sakhalin, the Kuril Islands, the Amur region, and the AINU LANGUAGE.

After his return to Dejima, Siebold kept up his correspondence with Takahashi, who sent him more maps in return for Dutch studies of geography, a barometer, and other objects. Eventually, enemies of Takahashi—Siebold assumed that MAMIYA RINZŌ was their leader—denounced him as a traitor and intercepted his correspondence with Siebold. Since Siebold was not a Dutchman by birth, he was suspected to be a spy in Russian service. Many of his Japanese friends were imprisoned, and after prolonged investigations he was expelled from Japan at the end of December 1829. He left behind his young mistress, Kusumoto Sonogi, and a two-year-old daughter, Ine (1827–1903), who were forbidden to accompany him.

Via Batavia he returned to the Netherlands, where he settled at Leyden in July 1830. The next two decades have been called his "period of harvest." In preparing his Japanese materials for publication he was assisted by Ko-Tsing-Dschang (pinyin spelling Guo Chengzhang; Wade-Giles spelling Kuo Ch'eng-chang), a Chinese he had brought with him from Batavia, and Johann Joseph HOFFMANN (1805–78), also from Würzburg, who became the first professor of Japanese at Leyden State University (1856). In 1831 King William I appointed Siebold adviser on Japanese affairs to the Ministry of the Colonies. In 1842 he was knighted as jonkheer (baronet). Two years later, when William II tried to persuade the Tokugawa shogunate to open the ports of Japan to all countries, his letter was drafted by Siebold. In 1847 Siebold, who had married Helene von Gagern two years earlier, moved to Germany.

In 1859 he returned to Japan, accompanied by his son Alexander, and worked for two years on behalf of the Netherlands Trading Company. Because he was anything but a diplomat, his mission ended in failure, and his policies were judged contrary to Dutch interests. His request to be appointed Dutch representative in Japan was refused in March 1863, and in October of that year he was pensioned.

His collection of Japanese ethnographic material was bought by the Dutch government in 1837 and became the foundation of the present National Museum of Ethnology (Leyden). He introduced to the Netherlands more than a thousand trees and plants, including ichō (Gingko biloba), sakura (Prunus serrulata), hydrangeas, varieties of chrysanthemums, lilies and irises, and several kinds of coniferous trees. His botanical and zoological collections are preserved at the Botanical Garden, the National Herbarium, and the National Museum of Natural History, all at Leyden.

📖 ——Works by Siebold: Fauna Japonica, 5 vols (1833–50). Flora Japonica, 2 vols (1835–70). Works about Siebold: Engelbert Kaempfer (1651–1716)—Philipp Franz von Siebold (1796–1866), suppl. 28 of Mitteilungen der Deutschen Gesellschaft für Natur und Völkerkunde Ostasiens (1966). Hans Körner, Die Würzburger Siebold: Eine Gelehrtenfamilie des 18. und 19. Jahrhunderts (1967). Hans Körner, Philipp Franz von Siebold: A Contribution to the Study of the Historical Relations between Japan and the Netherlands (1978). Kure Shūzō, Shīboruto sensei: Sono shōgai oyobi kōgyō, 3 vols (1967–68). Frits Vos

Siemens Incident

(Shīmensu Jiken). The Siemens Incident of January 1914 was one of several spectacular political scandals in the decade between 1905 and 1915, in this particular case one which involved collusion between the navy and the German firm of Siemens. It provoked mass demonstrations in Tōkyō that directly caused the resignation of the first YAMAMOTO GONNOHYŌE cabinet, which was backed by the majority party in the House of Representatives, the Rikken Seiyūkai. Yamamoto, an admiral from the former domain of Satsuma (now Kagoshima Prefecture), was the acknowledged head of the navy.

In the decade following 1905 both the army and the navy came under heavy criticism from the press and reformist party politicians in the lower house of the Diet. They were accused of overspending, concealing the details of their budgets on dubious grounds of security, and promoting the narrow interests of the military cliques led by men from the former domains of Satsuma and Chōshū (now Yamaguchi Prefecture). Rumors associating these cliques (HAMBATSU) with commissions from defense-related firms also spread from the budget committee of the lower house to the press. While these accusations were being made, the details of an actual bribery case were made public through the intrigues of a minor German employee of Siemens formerly stationed in Tōkyō.

The details revealed a story of deceit and trickery. The Siemens company had provided a 15-percent kickback to Japanese naval authorities in order to retain a monopoly over naval contracts, especially for ammunition and wireless materials. At the same time the navy had also contracted with the British firm of Vickers with a more favorable 25-percent commission. Hearing of this, the headquarters of Siemens demanded clarification through its Tōkyō office. At this point, an employee of Siemens in Tōkyō (a certain K. Richter) stole incriminating documents, sold them to a reporter for Reuters News Service, and returned to his home in Germany. The head of Siemens in Tōkyō informed the navy through Navy Minister SAITŌ MAKOTO, but the disclosures were withheld from the Diet and the press. In the meantime, the London Telegram reported on 21 January 1914 that Richter had been indicted in Berlin and sentenced to two years' imprisonment for his theft of valuable company documents. The article also noted that some of the documents exposed corrupt contractual agreements with the Japanese navy.

The response in Tōkyō was instantaneous and violent. The newspapers immediately reported the details of the scandal, including similar kinds of wrongdoing by Vickers through its agent, the Mitsui Bussan Company. In the lower house, members of the opposition Rikken Dōshikai party denounced the Yamamoto cabinet and the navy. Mass demonstrations followed in early February, culminating in violent confrontations with the police in Hibiya Park on the 10th and 14th. The crowds demanded the lowering of business taxes, the resignation of the Yamamoto cabinet, and the establishment of honest constitutional government. Naval officers in charge of bureaus of procurement and shipbuilding were made scapegoats and summarily discharged. On 24 March, challenged even by the House of Peers, Prime Minister Yamamoto resigned, bringing down the entire cabinet with him.

The Siemens Incident takes on significance in the broader historical context of the decade between 1905 and 1915. Beginning with the outbreak of popular protest against Prime Minister KATSURA TARŌ in 1905 for his alleged mishandling of the settlement of the Russo-Japanese War (1904–05), mass disturbances continued to erupt. Numerous demonstrations were held for the reduction of land, business, and consumption taxes and for the promotion of honest and reliable constitutional government to represent popular interests, as in the MOVEMENT TO PROTECT CONSTITUTIONAL GOVERNMENT during the TAISHŌ POLITICAL CRISIS of 1912–13. A common theme in these disturbances was the popular outcry against clique domination of the navy and army. Katsura, from Chōshū, was accused of arbitrarily promoting the army, and Yamamoto, from Satsuma, of favoring the navy. The Siemens Incident confirmed indisputably what the public had suspected about the leaders of the army and navy. The incident was also an embarrassment for the Rikken Seiyūkai, which, under HARA TAKASHI's leadership, had supported the Yamamoto cabinet to promote its policy of party expansion.

📖 ——Ōtsu Jun'ichirō, Dai Nihon kensei shi, vol 7 (1927).
Tetsuo NAJITA

signboards

(kamban). Traditional Japanese signboards came in an astonishing variety of shapes and lettering. Kamban became popular with the rapid development of commerce and industry in the 17th century. NOREN, cloth or rope curtains with the shop crest, apparently developed first. By the Edo period (1600–1868) signboards had become so gaudy that in 1682 the Tokugawa shogunate decreed that they must either be wooden boards inscribed with words or pictures in india ink or, in the case of metal boards, be made of copper. At night andon (paper-covered lamp stand) and chōchin (paper-covered lantern; see LIGHTING EQUIPMENT) bearing the store name were displayed. Among the more distinctive signboards were those of candle stores, umbrella shops, and fan stores, which hung out the ware itself or a representation of one. Grocery stores hung out huge wooden radishes, GETA shops an enormous sandal, while other more established shops were content merely to show their crest. Some shopowners invented puns for their shop names. A public bath or hot spring was easily identified by its sign depicting rising steam. Theatrical signboards were designed according to strict regulations regarding form and size, and KABUKI billboards today still use the picturesque KANTEI STYLE Chinese characters. In Kyōto, where streets were narrow, rooftop signs were favored; in Edo (now Tōkyō) hanging signs were more common. With the Westernization of buildings in the latter part of the 19th century, painted signboards, electric signboards, and neon signs became popular.

TANAKA Masaaki

silk

(kinu). Traditional Japanese textile and almost the only animal fiber widely used in Japan before the Meiji period (1868–1912). Silk cloth and SERICULTURE techniques were introduced to Japan around AD 200 from China. Until recently silk was used mainly by the upper class. To this day it is in great demand as material for formal clothing and especially for the KIMONO.

Fibers and Yarns——Silk fibers are extremely fine, elastic, and have a smooth surface, giving the silk cloth luster and strength. The fibers may be treated in different ways to produce either raw silk or glossed silk. In raw silk, the natural gummy substance called sericin, which adheres to the fibroin filaments of the silkworm cocoon, is left on the fibers. Several strands are twisted together to form the silk thread, which is then woven into cloth before being boiled in soap and water to remove the sericin. Types of raw silk fabrics produced in Japan include *habutae* (a fine, smooth silk), *chirimen* (crinkly silk crepe), *kurēpu de shin* (crepe de chine), and *kiginu* (raw silk). Of all silk fabrics, *chirimen* is produced in the largest quantities. The prefectures noted for their production of raw silk fabric include Kyōto, Niigata, Fukui, Ishikawa, and Fukushima.

Glossed silk is made from threads that have been dyed and have had the sericin removed. Traditional woven patterns of stripes, plaids, and KASURI (ikat) are particularly popular, as are the more modern, figured fabrics with complicated woven patterns made with a Jacquard loom. Japanese glossed silk fabrics include NISHIJIN-ORI (silk made in the Nishijin district of Kyōto), *omeshi* (a kind of *chirimen*), *hakata-ori* (silk made in Fukuoka Prefecture), and TSUMUGI (pongee). Most Japanese glossed silk fabrics are produced in Kyōto, Fukuoka, Gumma, Yamagata, and Tōkyō prefectures.

History——At the same time that silkworms and silk cloth were introduced into Japan from China, Chinese and Korean weavers and sericulture experts settled in Japan. They were assigned to official government workshops, where they began the production of fine silk *aya* (figured twill) and NISHIKI (brocade). These fine materials were for the use of the nobles and imperial family. Knowledge of sophisticated continental techniques spread, and domestic production increased in quantity and quality. Textiles produced by the common people, especially silk, became an important item of tribute (see SO, YŌ, AND CHŌ).

From the Kamakura period (1185–1333) textile production fell into decline; the internal wars of the 14th and 15th centuries dealt a blow to weaving nationwide. The silk industry revived in the 16th century, mainly in Hakata (now Fukuoka), Sakai (in Ōsaka Prefecture), and the Nishijin district of Kyōto, where imported silk from China (see ITOWAPPU) was readily available. Soon new Chinese weaves such as *shusu* (satin), KARA-ORI (an ornate brocade), KINRAN AND GINRAN (gold and silver brocade), and *donsu* (damask) were being produced.

The establishment of peace by the Tokugawa shogunate (1603–1867) and the encouragement of local domainal governments led to the development of new centers of production in many parts of Japan, particularly the northern and central regions. Restrictions on the importation of silk resulted in the improvement of domestic silk yarns and the overall development of the silk industry. Ashikaga and Kiryū, near Edo (now Tōkyō), emerged as silk-weaving centers rivaling Nishijin. The silk fabrics in greatest demand during this period were *chirimen*, *habutae*, and *tsumugi*, used for making *kosode* (an early form of kimono; see also CLOTHING).

The end of the NATIONAL SECLUSION policy in the mid-19th century brought another expansion in the Japanese silk industry. Exportation of silk products started in 1859, when Yokohama was first opened to foreign trade, and thereafter the new Meiji government regarded silk as the mainstay of its foreign trade.

The silk industry achieved its highest production in 1934: 45,243 metric tons (49,858 short tons). The major demand for Japanese silk, both in the United States and Europe, was for making silk stockings. With the invention of synthetic fibers such as nylon, Japanese silk

Silk

Production and Export of Raw Silk (in metric tons)			
	Production	Export	Import
1880	1,999	877	—
1890	3,458	1,266	—
1900	7,102	2,778	—
1910	11,904	8,908	—
1920	21,877	10,481	—
1930	42,618	28,646	—
1934	45,243	33,133	—
1940	42,768	17,621	—
1942	27,176	490	—
1944	9,242	61	—
1946	5,652	5,186	—
1948	8,659	4,802	—
1950	10,620	5,677	—
1960	18,057	5,299	327 (1965)
1970	20,515	75	2,958
1980	16,155	0	2,976

SOURCE: Nōrin Suisan Shō (Ministry of Agriculture, Forestry, and Fisheries), *Kiito jukyū chōsa* (annual): various years.

production decreased to less than half of what it had been at its peak. Today, Japan produces approximately 16,000 metric tons (17,600 short tons), or 33 percent of the world's silk. But since Japan consumes 50 percent of the total world production of silk, it must rely on imports to meet domestic demand. See also TEXTILES.

HOSODA Kazuo

Silk Road

The overland trade route by which Chinese silk was transported to Europe through Central and West Asia in premodern times. In a broader sense the term refers to all the ancient land and sea routes between East Asia and Europe. As the main artery for commercial, cultural, and religious exchanges between East and West for nearly two millennia, the Central- and West-Asian Silk Road in particular played a vital role in the evolution of Chinese and, ultimately, Japanese culture in the Nara (710–794) and Heian (794–1185) periods.

The Silk Road from China to the Mediterranean had many branches. All of them began in Chang'an (Ch'ang-an; now Xi'an or Sian), capital of the Former Han dynasty (206 BC–AD 8), or later in Luoyang (Loyang), capital of the Later Han dynasty (AD 25–220). From these great metropolises of Chinese civilization the Silk Road passed westward through Lanzhou (Lanchow) and Suzhou (Soochow) to Dunhuang (Tunhuang), the westernmost outpost of China proper.

From Dunhuang the most common route followed the southern foothills of the Tianshan (T'ien-shan) range (the northern rim of the Tarim Basin) through Turfan and Karashahr to Kashgar, in what is now western Xinjiang (Sinkiang) Province. It then crossed the Pamirs via the Terek-Davan Pass and passed through Fergana, Tashkent, Samarkand, and Bukhara to Merv (30 km east of what is now Mary in the Turkmen SSR). It next crossed the Iranian plateau via Ecbatana (now Hamadan), where it divided into a northern branch, through Maragheh and Edessa (now Urfa in Turkey) to Antioch, and a southern branch, through Baghdad and Palmyra to Damascus and Tyre on the eastern shore of the Mediterranean. From Kashgar an alternative, more southerly route crossed the Pamirs to the headwaters of the Oxus (now Amu Darya) River and on into Bactria, passing through Balkh to meet the northerly route at Merv.

Another branch of the Silk Road, after leaving Dunhuang, followed the northern foothills of the Kunlun range (the southern rim of the Tarim Basin) through Charklik to Khotan (in southwestern Xinjiang) and then crossed the Pamirs and descended through the Hindu Kush into Afghanistan, passing through Bagram (near what is now Kabul) and Kandahar and thence to the northwest through Balkh to Merv.

A third route went further south into Afghanistan and passed through Ghazna, Kandahar, and Zaranj before turning northward to connect with the above two routes at Merv. The region of southern Afghanistan that this third route traversed was irrigated by the Helmand River and was very rich in agriculture up to the time of Timur

(1336–1405), who destroyed the irrigation system in the course of conquering the region.

Yet a fourth route, independent of the others, went from Dunhuang to Turfan and then struck out northward, along the foothills of the Altai range, and passed north of the Tianshan over the Eurasian steppe in what is now the Kazakh SSR, crossing the upper reaches of the Irtysh, Ishim, and Tobol rivers, as well as the Ural Mountains and the Volga River, to arrive at Tana at the mouth of the river Don. Herodotus mentioned this route in the 5th century BC, and modern archaeological findings attest to the passage of Chinese silk along it in ancient times.

Through this continuum of high mountains, deserts, and grassy plains traveled large caravans of traders from Central and West Asia, India, Armenia, Greece, Italy, and other countries along the routes. Braving climatic extremes and brigands' attacks, they dealt in goods and currencies at the numerous markets along the way. They often gained admission to China by purchasing credentials from the states along the Silk Road to act as their emissaries to the Chinese emperor. The bulk of their China trade, however, was conducted with Chinese merchants, who were legally barred from leaving their country by land.

The Silk Road and Japan —— From the Nara period into the early years of the Heian period, Japan sent embassies to the Asian continent (see SUI AND TANG [T'ANG] CHINA, EMBASSIES TO). Along with the resulting import of much Chinese culture into Japan came the somewhat sinicized culture of Central and West Asia. Imported cultural artifacts from these areas, many of which still survive in the SHŌSŌIN repository in Nara, received lavish attention from Japanese emperors and their courts and helped to stimulate advances in Japanese arts and crafts.

Among the cultures of Central and West Asia, the civilization of Sassanian Persia was particularly influential in East Asia. During the Sui (589–618) and Tang (618–907) dynasties many Persians traveled to China, and some went on to Japan. For example, a Buddhist priest named Nyohō, who accompanied GANJIN from China to Japan in 754, is said to have been Persian. His participation in the construction of the temple TŌSHŌDAIJI perhaps explains the many traces of Central Asian influence in its architectural design and decorative motifs. Other things imported to Japan via the Silk Road include the following (description based on articles by Harada Yoshito listed in the bibliography of this entry).

Theater and acrobatics. The masked musical drama known as GIGAKU was derived from the Chinese Sui- and Tang-dynasty drama called *Xiliang ji* (*Hsi-liang chi;* J: *Seiryōgi*), itself an amalgam of folk music from the Dunhuang area in China and the music of Kucha in Central Asia. It was introduced to Japan in 612 by Mimashi, a musician from the Korean kingdom of Paekche, and has been regularly performed ever since. Among the characters in Japanese *gigaku* are the Gentleman and Lady of Wu, the Brahman, Kun Lun, Vajra, and the Drunken Persian King; their masks represent Chinese, Indian, and Central Asian facial types.

Acrobatics (*kyokugei*), which the Chinese practiced from ancient times, seem to have made their way into China from West Asia, probably from Parthia during the Han dynasty, and were still flourishing during the Tang. The Chinese referred to these performances as *za ji* (*tsa chi*) or *san yue* (*san yüeh;* J: *sangaku;* later corrupted to SARUGAKU).

Musical instruments and game objects. Among the musical instruments stored at the Shōsōin, the *kugo*, BIWA, and *genkan* especially display the brilliant colors characteristic of Central and West Asia. The *kugo* is a kind of harp, probably a Chinese variant of an instrument widely used in the ancient states of West Asia and in Egypt. The Shōsōin contains one restored *kugo* as well as two incomplete *kugo*, the only surviving originals.

Among the Shōsōin's lutelike *biwa*, there is a four-stringed instrument as well as the sole surviving five-stringed example, which is finished in rosewood and mother-of-pearl. The origin of these two *biwa* is unclear, but scholars have proposed a Persian, West Asian, or Indian origin for the five-stringed instrument. Its mother-of-pearl inlay depicts a Persian playing a *biwa* astride a camel, suggesting that the instrument is of West Asian origin. However, since *biwa* appear in the wall paintings at Kyzyl, a 7th-century site of Buddhist relics located near Kucha in Chinese Turkestan as well as the Ajanta wall paintings of India, the instrument could as easily have originated from either of those regions. The Shōsōin's *genkan*, a type of *biwa*, is again the sole surviving example in the world. Since this type of instrument appears in wall-painting fragments at Kyzyl, the Shōsōin example may have come from this region.

Among the game pieces of West Asian origin we find a board (*kyoku*), pieces (*koma*), two dice (*sai*), and a cylinder for shaking the dice, all employed in the dice game SUGOROKU. Of the Shōsōin's original 116 sets, only 6 now remain. Of Indian, or perhaps West or Central Asian, origin, *sugoroku* entered China from the West in the 5th century.

West Asian materials. Some Shōsōin objects are made of West Asian materials. For example, lapis lazuli, a semiprecious stone from the Badakhshan region in Afghanistan, is one of the materials in the Shōsōin's blue-stone belts, themselves probably of Chinese origin. A white bowl and ewer made of soda-lime glass have such exquisite workmanship that experts believe they originated in Persia.

West Asian objects and shapes. Of the many eating utensils and pieces of furniture manifesting Central and West Asian influence, we can cite chairs, pitchers, and 8- or 12-lobed drinking cups. The chair was used in ancient Egypt, and Japanese earthenware tomb objects (HANIWA) from about the 6th century AD include depictions of chairs, both backed and unbacked. We can surmise that chairs were possibly used earlier in China.

The slender Persian ewers (*kohei*) have long necks usually topped by a spout in the shape of a bird or animal and graced by well-crafted handles. These ewers, made in silver, glass, and gilt bronze, were widely used in Sassanian Persia. The Shōsōin also includes a ewer with strips of bamboo that form surface patterns (*rantai*) and with thin strips of silver, over which coats of lacquer were applied (*heidatsu* finish).

The treasures of the temple Hōryūji include a small silver vessel used to pour water into an inkstone. It has a dragon-shaped neck and a winged-horse design fashioned in gold on its main body. All of these motifs are believed to be Chinese versions of West Asian designs. The Shōsōin's 8-lobed drinking cups are made of gilt-bronze and its 12-lobed cups of glass. Both types are probably Chinese originals or Japanese copies. Recent archaeological work has excavated gilt-bronze and silver versions of these cups in China as well as in Iran, southern Russia, and Poland, thereby necessitating further research into the origins of these cups.

Motifs. Some fabrics and other artifacts of the Shōsōin have Chinese versions of flowing patterns that originated in Central and West Asia, Persia, India, and the Eastern Roman Empire. Two famous examples, the *Hunting Scene with Blue Background Brocade* (*Hekiji shuryō mon nishiki*) and the *Four Devas Brocade* (*Shitennō mon nishiki;* stored at Hōryūji), are either Chinese products of the early Tang or slightly later Japanese copies. The hunting-scene brocade, however, shows distinct Persian influence. Not only do the people depicted have Persian physical features but they are carefully arranged in the left-right symmetry characteristic of Persian art. There is also a dyed-fabric picture of a lion tamer that manifests the same Persian-style symmetry. This picture and a silver urn similarly decorated with a lion-taming scene attest to an origin in a region like West Asia, where the inhabitants actually raised and tamed lions. Furthermore, many surviving dyed fabrics from the Nara period contain bird and animal designs clearly based on Persian models.

In the Persian "nest pattern" (*kamon*) design one or two dragons, phoenixes, birds, or animals appear within a border composed of linked circles. In Sinicized versions of this design in the Shōsōin one finds animals with which the Chinese were familiar as well as Chinese mythical creatures. At times, animals not indigenous to East Asia, such as the elephant, rhinoceros, or camel, also form part of the designs. Since such animals were commonly used in designs and motifs in India, the East Roman Empire, and Sassanian Persia, the Chinese and Japanese quite possibly derived these patterns from these areas.

The Shōsōin treasures include shallow silver and gold vases as well as foot-rules of red-dyed ivory; on both types of object deer are drawn with one horn, which resembles a floral wreath. Although a similar design appears in wall paintings in the ancient Chinese colony of Gaochang (Kao-ch'ang) in the Turfan Basin of Central Asia, it is not certain that this is a representation of any real species of deer. What is certain is that many of the Shōsōin treasures contain motifs and designs that came to Japan via Tang China, often Chinese versions of patterns from West and Central Asia. The Japanese of the Nara period were thus unconsciously assimilating a considerable amount of Central and West Asian culture.

West Asian design composition. Pictorial representation of trees, birds, animals, and people was common in West Asia, particularly, as we have seen, in the lion-taming and hunting scenes of Persian silverware and fabrics. The beauty-under-a-tree motif (*juka bijin*) employed in the folding-screen painting *Woman Bedecked with Feathers (Torigedachi onna byōbu)* also originated in West Asia and came to Japan via the Silk Road and China.

📖 Yoshito Harada, "The Interchange of Eastern and Western Cultures as Evidenced in the Shōsōin Treasures," *Memoirs of the Research Department of the Toyo Bunko* 11 (1939). Harada Yoshito, "Saiiki bunka to Shōsōin hōmotsu," *Sekai no bunka* (1965). Ryoichi Hayashi, *The Silk Road and the Shoso-in* (1975).   ENOKI KAZUO

silkworms

(kaiko). The larvae of the silkworm moth *(Bombyx mori)* of the family Bombycidae, whose cocoon is collected and turned into silk. There are more than 3,000 varieties, divided into Japanese, Chinese, European, and tropical groups according to their origin. The native Japanese silkworm is sturdy, and it reproduces in great numbers; its principal food is mulberry leaves. The cocoon is peanut-shaped and colored white, yellow, or pale green. The breeding cycle of the silkworm moth is either six months or a year. Despite this long cycle, the insect is small in size. The silkworm was used in a series of experiments by TOYAMA KAMETARŌ in 1906 to establish the validity of Mendel's law of heredity in the insect world. See also SERICULTURE.   NIKI ISAO

Silla

(J: Shiragi). One of the Three Kingdoms of ancient Korea (see KOREAN THREE KINGDOMS PERIOD). Founded in 57 BC, Silla initially controlled the southeastern third of the Korean peninsula with its capital at Kyŏngju, 40 miles (64 km) north of modern Pusan. When Silla embarked on its unification of the peninsula with Tang (T'ang) Chinese military support in 660, the kingdom of PAEKCHE requested aid from Japan; the Japanese expeditionary force was defeated, however, at the naval battle of HAKUSUKINOE (663). Silla then conquered KOGURYŎ in 668 and ruled Korea until overthrown by the KORYŎ dynasty in 935. The art of Silla is admired throughout the world, especially its ceramics, royal crowns of gold decorated with curved, jade jewels (similar to the jewels of Japan's imperial regalia), roof tiles, and Buddhist sculpture. Much that is now considered indigenous Korean culture took form during the Silla period. See also KOREA AND JAPAN: premodern relations.

C. Kenneth QUINONES

Silver Seikō, Ltd

(Shirubā Seikō). One of Japan's major manufacturers of hand-operated knitting machines and typewriters, Silver Seikō was established in 1939. It is currently engaged in developing other high value-added products. Its knitting machines are sold overseas through the Singer Sewing Machine Co and Empisal (Europ) GmbH, while its typewriters are sold through two overseas sales subsidiaries, as well as through the Royal Co and Olivetti. Annual sales totaled ¥29.7 billion (US $123.4 million) in the fiscal year ending March 1982, of which 63 percent came from exports. The company was capitalized at ¥1.6 billion (US $6.6 million) in the same year. Corporate headquarters are located in Tōkyō.

sin → tsumi

Sin'ganhoe

(J: Shinkankai). A national coalition of Korean patriotic groups formed in 1927 with the goal of undermining Japanese rule from within Korea. Its founder was Yi Sang-jae (J: Ri Shōzai; 1850–1927), who devoted his life to Korea's independence and modernization, first as an official and diplomat of the Yi dynasty (1392–1910) and then as a Christian leader of the Korean YMCA and other youth organizations. Opposed to violence and political radicalism, his death shortly after the coalition's birth enabled radical elements, both left and right wing, to take control of the organization. The Sin'ganhoe turned violent, backing and coordinating the KWANGJU STUDENT RESISTANCE MOVEMENT of 1929–30. Korean communist involvement in the coalition and its violent tactics led to the arrest of many leaders, splintering the coalition and resulting in its membership voting for disbandment in 1931. See also KOREA AND JAPAN: Japanese colonial control of Korea.   C. Kenneth QUINONES

Singapore and Japan

As a trading center and port, Singapore has been of great importance to Japan throughout the modern era. Diplomatic relations were established in 1889, and by the end of the century, a number of large trading and shipping companies and banks had established offices in Singapore. These companies had been preceded by KARAYUKI SAN, women who were sold into prostitution and sent abroad, who first arrived in Singapore in the early part of the Meiji period (1868–1912). During World War I, Japan maintained the highest level of trade with the British crown colony, replacing European countries and establishing a dominant economic position. By 1941 there were about 3,600 Japanese in various professions in Singapore. Trade was by far their most important activity.

Japanese expansion into China in the 1920s and 1930s touched off anti-Japanese boycott movements by Chinese residents, who had been influenced by the rise of modern Chinese nationalism. The Chinese anti-Japanese movement, often agitated by Guomindang (Kuomintang; Nationalist Party) nationalists and Chinese communists, gained momentum after the Sino-Japanese War began in 1937. When Japanese forces attacked Malaya in December 1941, British colonial authorities released imprisoned Chinese communists and helped them organize an anti-Japanese voluntary force to fight against the Japanese. Their prewar and wartime anti-Japanese activities led to massacres of Chinese by Japanese following the 1942 fall of Singapore, which was renamed Shōnan. The Japanese military administration also coerced Singaporean Chinese to contribute 50 million Singapore dollars as reparations for their past activities against Japan.

Japan's postwar relations with Singapore were marred in 1962 when the so-called "BLOOD DEBT" INCIDENT renewed the Singaporeans' determination that Japan atone for past military atrocities. The controversy was settled amicably in 1966, aided by Prime Minister Lee Kuan Yew's conciliatory attitude and the Japanese government's willingness to pay reparations. Following the settlement, Japanese capital was used in Singapore to help finance government-sponsored industrial projects and to set up joint ventures with local Chinese partners. Official Japanese sources indicate that in 1978 Japanese investments reached US $174 million and that Japan's overall commercial involvement was estimated to amount to 10 percent of total foreign investment in Singapore. In trade, Japan-Singapore import-export volume reached US $5.4 billion in 1980.

Located at the entrance of the Malacca Strait connecting the Indian Ocean and the South China Sea, Singapore is extremely important to Japan's economy and security. In 1977 the Japanese government signed a treaty with Singapore, Malaysia, and Indonesia regulating navigation of the Malacca Strait, through which passes 80 percent of the oil Japan imports from Middle Eastern countries. The importance attached to Singapore is evident in Japan's active economic assistance program. The most important of Japan's aid projects is the construction of the Jurong Industrial Complex, which has employed tens of thousands of Singaporeans and contributes to the economic well-being of the country. Singapore is a recipient of Japanese assistance under the 1977 Fukuda Doctrine (Japan's economic aid commitment to help industrialize the countries of ASEAN or the Association of Southeast Asian Nations); Japan has promised Singapore to help build a diesel engine plant as part of a US $1 billion aid package to ASEAN under this doctrine.

Japan also contributes to Singapore's cultural programs. The JAPAN FOUNDATION sent professors and language teachers to Nanyang University (now integrated into the National University of Singapore) for some years, and the Japanese government assisted the National University of Singapore in establishing a department of Japanese studies, which opened in 1981. More than 200 Singaporeans have studied in Japanese universities under Ministry of Education scholarships, and several hundred others have come to Japan for further education under technical training programs with private funds. The Japan–Singapore Association is very active in cultural exchange programs. With 12,000 Japanese residents, Singapore, one of the most popular spots for Japanese tourists, receives thousands of Japanese visitors annually.

📖 —Yōji Akashi, *The Nanyang Chinese National Salvation Movement* (1970). Eric Robertson, *The Japanese File: Prewar Japanese Penetration in Southeast Asia* (1980). Shinozaki Mamoru, *My Wartime Experiences in Singapore* (1973). Shinozaki Mamoru, *Shingapōru senryō hiroku* (1976). Yano Tōru, *Nanshin no keifu* (1975).   AKASHI Yōji

Singh, Mohan (1909–   )

First commander of the anti-British INDIAN NATIONAL ARMY (INA) during World War II. Born in 1909 in Punjab, he graduated from the Indian Military Academy in 1934. He was stationed as captain in Malaya when the Japanese opened the Pacific War. Captured on 15 December 1941, Mohan Singh was immediately approached by Giani Pritam Singh, the founder of the Indian Independence League in Thailand, and Major Fujiwara Iwaichi of the Japanese Imperial Army, who hoped to win him over for collaboration. Mohan Singh finally gave in, and by January 1942 he had organized 200 men, who subsequently accompanied Japanese forward troops during the attack on Singapore.

In March 1942 Mohan Singh went to Tōkyō as a member of an Indian goodwill mission composed of Indians from the parts of Southeast Asia then under Japanese control. The mission's aim was to find out Japanese intentions regarding the setting up of the INA and the achievement of Indian independence. In June the same year the Bangkok Conference, a meeting of overseas Indians living in areas under Japanese control, took place. The conference elected its executive body, the Council of Action, presided over by Rash Behari BOSE. Mohan Singh was appointed commander of the envisaged INA. However, the resolutions approved in Bangkok by the Indian delegates were never confirmed by the Japanese authorities, which must have led to inevitable friction between Mohan Singh and Colonel Iwakuro Hideo (1897–1970), who replaced Fujiwara as the new chief of the liaison agency, the Iwakuro Kikan. Following the mass unrest in India after the Congress Party "Quit India" resolution in August 1942, Mohan Singh, back in Malaya, was allowed to raise the first INA division of about 16,000 men and appointed himself general. He pressed on for further expansion of the INA, aiming at a liberation army of 200,000 to 500,000 men strong. However, sanction for a second INA division was withheld by the Japanese military authorities. Mohan Singh began to lose confidence in the Japanese who still provided no answer to the Bangkok resolutions demanding that the Japanese government give full formal recognition to Indian independence and to the INA. In November 1942 the Council of Action demanded categorically the confirmation of the Bangkok resolutions as the price for the INA's cooperation in sending troops to Burma, but Iwakuro refused to forward the letter to Tōkyō. On 8 December, when Lieutenant Colonel Gill, the most senior Indian officer and together with Mohan Singh the chief architect of the INA, was arrested by the Japanese military police (kempeitai) on charges of being a secret British agent, all council members, with the exception of Rash Behari Bose, resigned.

On 21 December Singh issued secret instructions to disband the INA if he were arrested or assassinated. A week later he was arrested and the INA dissolved itself. Mohan Singh was first confined on a small island near Singapore and later in Sumatra. When in 1943 Subhas Chandra BOSE, the Indian nationalist leader, decided to raise the second INA, he hoped to use Mohan Singh's good offices, but the meeting between the two proved unsuccessful. After Japan's capitulation in August 1945, Mohan Singh was interrogated by the British, but never put before a court martial like some of his fellow officers. The main INA trial in the Red Fort of Delhi in early 1946 caused such an upheaval among hitherto loyal Indian units that the British authorities decided to call off the trials. Mohan Singh lives today in retirement in New Delhi and is a member of the upper house of parliament (Rajya Sabha).

——Mohan Singh, *Leaves from My Diary* (1946). Mohan Singh, *Soldiers' Contribution to Indian Independence* (1974). A. C. Chatterji, *India's Struggle for Freedom* (1947). Gerard H. Corr, *The War of the Springing Tigers* (1975). Fujiwara Iwaichi, *Efukikan* (1966), tr Yoji Akashi as *F Kikan* (1980). K. K. Ghosh, *The Indian National Army* (1969). Joyce Lebra, *Jungle Alliance, Japan and the Indian National Army* (1971). Shah Nawaz Khan, *My Memories of the I.N.A. and its Netaji* (1945). Hugh Toye, *The Springing Tiger* (1959).

Milan HAUNER

Sino-French War

War fought between China and France from 1884 to 1885 for domination of Vietnam, traditionally a tributary state of China. As a result of France's victory, Vietnam became a protectorate of France in June of 1885, in accordance with the TIANJIN (TIENTSIN) CONVENTION. During the war, pro-Japanese elements in Korea attempted, with Japanese help, to overthrow the pro-Chinese regime (see KAP-

SIN POLITICAL COUP). In Japan, the French victory was seen as the start of Western imperialism in East Asia, and leaders of the FREEDOM AND PEOPLE'S RIGHTS MOVEMENT, for example, turned with an emphasis on popular rights (*minkenron*) to that of national rights (*kokkenron*).

TANAKA Akira

Sino-Japanese Amity Treaty of 1871

(Nisshin Shūkō Jōki). First modern treaty between Japan and China; signed in Tianjin (Tientsin) on 13 September 1871 by special envoy Date Munenari (1818–92) and LI HONGZHANG (Li Hung-chang). The Tōkyō government initiated the treaty, which emphasized the regularization of commercial relations between the two countries. Provisions included the fixing of a minimum rate for maritime customs and establishment of mutual rights of extraterritoriality. A most-favored-nation clause was deliberately omitted. The treaty was abrogated with the outbreak of the SINO-JAPANESE WAR OF 1894–1895. See also CHINA AND JAPAN.

Sino-Japanese relations → China and Japan

Sino-Japanese War of 1894–1895

(Nisshin Sensō). A war between China and Japan that was formally declared on 1 August 1894 and concluded with the Treaty of SHIMONOSEKI on 17 April 1895. To the surprise of the Western world, Japan quickly and utterly defeated the superior forces of China and emerged as the dominant East Asian power. The war is a landmark in the modern history of Japan, China, Korea, and Asian international relations in general. In Japanese history it marked the point when the armed forces gained a controlling influence in official decision making, foreign policy came to emphasize territorial expansion and power politics, China became an object of Japanese exploitation, and industrialization began in earnest.

The immediate occasion for the war was political instability in Korea, where both China and Japan claimed special interests. Almost from the establishment of the Meiji government in 1868, Japanese in and outside the new regime had pressed for a bold interventionist policy in Korea. Former *samurai* were eager for military exploits, and many Japanese wished to do in Korea what the Western powers had done in Japan (see SEIKANRON). By the early 1880s, more definite interests had emerged. The nascent Japanese army, under the leadership of YAMAGATA ARITOMO, had come to the conclusion that Korea was the key to Japan's security and that Japan definitely needed some measure of control over the kingdom, even if it meant armed conflict with China. Also, opposition parties and opinion leaders believed that by supporting relatively progressive and pro-Japanese elements in Korea, they could press for more rights at home. In addition to these interests, Japanese merchants and fishermen had entered Korea and its environs under the provisions of the 1876 Treaty of KANGHWA and were anxious to have their rights protected from the sometimes hostile Koreans.

While the resolution of these and other issues depended on domestic developments in the two countries, China became directly involved in 1882, when it sent a fleet with 3,000 troops to Korea on the occasion of an anti-Japanese riot in Seoul. Two years later, when a Korean faction led by KIM OK-KYUN staged a coup d'etat with overt Japanese assistance, the reigning Queen MIN called in 1,500 Chinese troops (see KAPSIN POLITICAL COUP). From this time on, and especially after the signing of the TIANJIN (TIENTSIN) CONVENTION in 1885, it became impossible for Japan to interfere in Korean politics without incurring Chinese retaliation.

Historians agree that by 1884 the Japanese military had drawn up provisional plans for war with China in Korea. Ten years were to elapse, however, before hostilities broke out. It took time, as well as money (derived from taxes in the absence of foreign loans), to raise an adequate army and navy. Again, throughout most of the 1880s Japanese leaders were preoccupied with such issues as treaty revision (see UNEQUAL TREATIES, REVISION OF), legal and constitutional reforms, and the convening of the Diet. Furthermore, there was a strong current of opinion opposed to war overseas. By the 1880s many writers favored peaceful penetration of Korea and other lands, arguing that in the end national strength hinged on economic power, which in turn must be built on trade and industrialization. They felt that these activities must be promoted in a stable and peaceful domestic and international environment, and that militaristic adventures must be eschewed. This idea of "peaceful expansionism" had made a deep impression on the Japanese public.

By the early 1890s, however, domestic conditions were more favorable for undertaking a major foreign war. Competing political parties in the newly formed Diet frequently resorted to the strategy of embarrassing the government by attacking its irresolute foreign policy. Many political leaders came to feel that their survival depended on some dramatic achievement in foreign affairs. To be sure, the Western powers were now increasingly willing to discuss treaty revision with Japan; negotiations for tariff autonomy and abolition of extraterritoriality had begun in London in April 1894. But this was not enough. Peaceful expansionism too had lost some of its appeal, since during the 1880s France had established a protectorate over Indochina, Britain had annexed Burma, and in 1891 Russia had begun construction of the Trans-Siberian Railway. The Japanese military and public cited such moves as convincing evidence of the Western imperialists' penetration of East Asia. A case for bold initiatives in Korea now had greater plausibility and rising public support, and the possibility of war with China correspondingly increased. The cabinet of ITŌ HIROBUMI was put on the defensive. Foreign Minister MUTSU MUNEMITSU shrewdly advocated military action to prevent the military from imposing its will on the nation. By moving speedily and by confining military operations to certain designated objectives, Mutsu reasoned, the war could unite public opinion, end political divisiveness, confer prestige on the country, and enhance the position of men like himself who were committed to reducing, if not eliminating, the power and influence of the Meiji oligarchs (genrō).

That the outbreak of war came in 1894 rather than later was due, in part, to Korean developments and China's reaction. In the spring of 1893 a domestic uprising in Korea, which soon turned into the large-scale TONGHAK REBELLION, threatened the Korean dynasty. The ruler once again appealed to China for aid and received a force of 2,800 soldiers. The Japanese in turn dispatched troops almost immediately. Although the Tonghaks were easily suppressed, and the presence of Chinese and Japanese troops was no longer necessary, Tōkyō's leaders were determined to seize this opportunity for war. They believed that no Western power would intervene (Britain had signed the Aoki–Kimberley Treaty with Japan on 16 July), and they knew precisely what they wanted: control over Korea for strategic purposes. The Japanese decided to initiate military action against Chinese forces in Korea and off the Korean coast. After a series of encounters, all resulting in Japanese victories, Japan formally declared war on 1 August.

Virtually all Japanese enthusiastically supported the war and rejoiced at this demonstration of national power and enhancement of prestige; coupled with the new British treaty, victory persuaded Japan that it had at last established itself as a respectable, "civilized" nation in the eyes of the world. Greed was also involved; quick victories over Chinese land forces at P'yŏngyang (16 September) and Chinese warships in the Naval Battle of YALU RIVER (17 September), followed by the seizure of PORT ARTHUR (21 November) and the final destruction of the Chinese fleet at Weihaiwei (12 February 1895), whetted the appetite of a resource-poor nation for territorial acquisitions. Some called for the annexation of Taiwan and several Chinese provinces as trophies of war, while others insisted that Japan should demand concessions in southern Manchuria. Special-interest groups like merchants and fishermen, as well as those hoping to seek their fortune abroad, could now be assured of the protection of Japanese force and law. The war, however, also appealed to liberals like UCHIMURA KANZŌ and FUKUZAWA YUKICHI, who called it a war for "justice," bringing "freedom" and "human rights" to a neighbor hitherto oppressed by the Chinese.

The very unity of opinion, however, was destined to cause bitter disillusionment once the fighting was over. The Japanese had developed an inflated sense of their power, and their self-righteous pretensions had outstripped their capabilities as well as realistic objectives. For the Itō–Mutsu leadership, therefore, a peace treaty acceptable to a broad constituency became the principal goal. Mutsu, in particular, thought the peace treaty should deal primarily with the status of Korea, freeing it from Chinese suzerainty, and with indemnities, sorely needed by his war-exhausted nation. But the army was determined to establish itself on the Liaodong (Liaotung) Peninsula, and the navy had its eyes fixed on Taiwan. In the end, when the Chinese negotiator, LI HONGZHANG (Li Hung-chang), arrived in Shimonoseki in February 1895, the Japanese delegation, headed by Itō and Mutsu, presented what they considered the minimum terms acceptable to the wide spectrum of Japanese interests.

They demanded, first, the independence of Korea; second, the cession of the southern part of Fengtian (now Liaoning) Province (in Manchuria), Taiwan, and the Pescadores; third, the payment of 300 million taels (more than ¥500 million) as war indemnity; and, fourth, the conclusion of a new commercial treaty allowing Japan to navigate the Yangzi (Yangtze) River and to operate manufacturing establishments in the treaty ports, as well as the opening of four additional ports. Li strenuously resisted these demands, but he eventually yielded when the Japanese reduced the indemnity to 200 million taels (the indemnity was paid in Europe in British money) and confined territorial claims in Manchuria to the Liaodong Peninsula.

The Treaty of SHIMONOSEKI, signed on 17 April, marked a departure in Japanese diplomacy. Previously, Japanese expansionist impulses had stressed commerce and emigration rather than territorial control and colonization. With the conclusion of the treaty Japan became the first Asian imperialist power. In fact, the term "imperialism" (teikoku shugi) came into widespread use in Japan from about 1895, and it was usually employed to justify the nation's behavior. Territorial expansion, it was argued, was inevitable for a strong nation; to desist would be to watch passively while other powers expanded into the same territories. The acquisition of Taiwan and the Liaodong Peninsula was just the first step in what would be a sustained period of national expansion. National expenditures would increase enormously, but, most publicists agreed, they would be outweighed by the economic and political benefits of empire.

While most Japanese apologists viewed their country's new position in Asia in terms of shedding the negative aspects of traditional Asian culture, or datsu-a, to use Fukuzawa's famous phrase, some incipient pan-Asianists, such as KONOE ATSUMARO, saw it as a step toward a union of Japan and China against Western encroachment. Some Westerners feared that such a union would create a gigantic anti-Western bloc, combining China's people and resources with Japan's military and industrial strength.

Japan's "Manchurian empire," however, was soon aborted by the so-called TRIPARTITE INTERVENTION. Shortly after the signing of the peace treaty, Russia, France, and Germany "advised" Japan to give up the Liaodong Peninsula, since Japanese control over the area would threaten the independence of Korea, the security of China, and the stability of East Asia. Though not entirely unreasonable, such an argument imperfectly cloaked the three powers' desire to preserve the region for further Russian expansion. The Japanese government had no choice but to accept this "friendly advice" and to retrocede the peninsula to China in return for an additional indemnity of 30 million taels. This humiliating retreat only stiffened the Japanese resolve to persevere in the game of imperialist politics. Plans were made for eventual war against Russia; the ANGLO-JAPANESE ALLIANCE would be negotiated in order to isolate Russia and its ally, France; and Japan would intervene in the BOXER REBELLION in North China. In the meantime, as the Western powers took advantage of the proven weakness of the Manchu dynasty, Japan would establish a sphere of influence in Fujian (Fukien) Province in South China.

A significant by-product of the war should be mentioned: Japan's industrial revolution. The requirements of the enlarged armed forces and the newly opened markets of Korea and China provided an impetus for the growth of textiles, iron and steel, shipbuilding, and other industries. Although still backward by Western standards, within a few years Japan had significantly reduced imports of foreign manufactured items, replacing them with domestic products. Some Japanese products, notably cotton textiles, competed successfully in the China market. It may be argued, however, that industrialization would have proceeded even more rapidly and export trade expanded even more phenomenally if so much of the national wealth had not been diverted to military and colonialist adventures.

In sum, the Sino-Japanese War defined the framework in which Japan would deal with its external and internal problems for the next half-century. Not only did it mark modern Japan's active entry into international power politics, which would end in the disastrous war of 1941–45, but it also set the stage for internal economic, social, and cultural developments. A sense of national unity had been achieved, but this unity also called forth a rising tide of industrial disputes, labor movements, selfish pursuits, and extremist ideologies. The resulting tension would characterize the history of Japan over the next half-century.

■ ——Hilary Conroy, *The Japanese Seizure of Korea* (1960). Kajima Morinosuke, *Nisshin sensō to sangoku kanshō*, in *Nihon gaikō shi*, vol 4 (1970), tr *The Diplomacy of Japan*, vol 1 (1976).

Akira IRIYE

Sino-Japanese War of 1937–1945

(Nitchū Sensō). War between Japan and China, from 7 July 1937 to 15 August 1945. Fought on the Chinese mainland by forces of the Japanese Imperial Army against CHIANG KAI-SHEK's Nationalist army and MAO ZEDONG's (Mao Tse-tung) communist army centered in Yan'an (Yenan), the war claimed untold civilian lives and, by conservative estimate, 1,871,000 military lives (571,000 Japanese, 1,300,000 Chinese) and destroyed vast amounts of land and property. In addition to this legacy of destruction, the war greatly weakened the military strength and political credibility of the Chinese Nationalists, leaving the communist forces in a strong position in the struggle for control of China that loomed on the horizon in 1945. Ironically, the destruction of communist strength was one of the justifications used by Japan as it pursued its course of aggression.

Outbreak of Hostilities —— Lugouqiao (Lukouchiao) translates awkwardly from Chinese as "the bridge over the ditch where the reeds grow." Westerners called it the Marco Polo Bridge after the Venetian traveler who admired its graceful arches and stone carvings in the 13th century. In the 20th century the bridge, located about 19 kilometers (12 mi) southwest of Beijing (Peking; called Beiping or Peiping from 1928 to 1949), acquired a military significance because of its proximity to an important rail junction; and on the night of 7 July 1937, the Marco Polo Bridge acquired a historic status comparable to Sarajevo as the site where an incident began a war, the eight-year Nitchū Sensō or Sino-Japanese War (1937–45). The events of that night, however, have not been so incontestably defined as those at Sarajevo. This much is clear: Japanese troops, part of a brigade permitted in the area under terms of the Boxer Protocol of 1901 (see BOXER REBELLION), were conducting routine field exercises in the darkness when some blank shots were fired from a Japanese machine-gun position. These were answered by a round of live shots fired toward the Japanese position—perhaps from Chinese troops who were in the vicinity. When the Japanese detachment commander called roll, a soldier was found to be missing from the ranks. The Japanese officer demanded the right to search the nearby town of Wanping, the Chinese refused, and the Japanese responded by forcibly trying to breach the town's defenses. Historians have not recorded the name of the missing soldier who, if the Sarajevo analogy is pursued, compares with the assassinated Archduke Franz Ferdinand. It is a grotesque commentary on the role of chance in history that, according to an account by an informed Japanese diplomat, the "missing" soldier may simply have wandered off to urinate in the bushes.

The incident naturally prompted comparisons to the LIUTIAO-GOU (LIU-T'IAO-KOU) INCIDENT near Mukden (now Shenyang) in 1931, staged by Japanese officers searching for a pretext to expand Japanese control over Manchuria. Although the Marco Polo Bridge Incident has often been described as a repetition of that earlier event, which led to the MANCHURIAN INCIDENT, reliable postwar studies have concluded that the 1937 incident was not the result of prearranged planning by Japanese authorities—either those in Tōkyō or those on the scene. However, after a month of skirmishing in the Beiping–Tianjin (Peiping–Tientsin) area and a series of futile attempts to arrive at a local settlement in the north, the confrontation spread to Shanghai in August and then veered out of control. What had been called the North China Incident (J: Hokushi Jihen) now became the China Incident (J: Shina Jihen). By whatever name, it was full-scale war.

Background —— If historians have excused Japan from the charge of premeditating the Marco Polo Bridge affair, they have not exonerated it from the more serious charge that it created by its actions a climate of animosity in China in which a trifling incident could escalate into an eight-year war. To understand the intensity of anti-Japanese feelings among patriotic Chinese in 1937, it is necessary to mention only a few of the acts of Japanese aggression that had occurred in the immediate past: the invasion of resource-rich Manchuria in 1931, the creation there of the puppet regime of MANCHUKUO in 1932, the seizure of the province of Rehe (Jehol) in 1933, and the dictation of the humiliating HE-UMEZU (HO-UMEZU) AGREEMENT in 1935. In this agreement Japan called upon the Nationalist Party (Guomindang or Kuomintang) government of Generalissimo Chiang Kai-shek to withdraw all its party organs and armed forces from the province of Hebei (Hopeh), which included the cities of Beiping and Tianjin. This agreement was correctly interpreted by the Chinese as an early step in the Japanese sponsorship of a five-province autonomous North China state (Ch: Huabei *guo* or Hua-pei *kuo*), which would be linked, both economically and militarily, more closely to

Manchukuo and Japan than to the Chinese government at Nanjing (Nanking). The scheme had the enthusiastic support of Japanese expansionists, who had proven in Manchuria in 1931 that they were capable of defying and forcing the hand of their government, which they regarded as timid and irresolute. In Manchuria and in North China, Japan had thus embarked upon a policy that was frustrating the cherished dream of SUN YAT-SEN and his followers: the unification of all Chinese under the banner of the Nationalists.

Sun's disciple, Chiang Kai-shek, had been slow to respond to the challenge put to him by Japanese encroachment in North China, preferring to appease Japan in order to concentrate his energies on the annihilation of communism in China—in his mind a menace more deadly than Japanese imperialism. The hand of the generalissimo was forced, however, by the extraordinary episode at Xi'an (Sian) in December 1936 in which the Chinese leader was kidnapped and compelled to suspend the civil war against the communists and lead a resolutely anti-Japanese united-front movement (see XI'AN [SIAN] INCIDENT). When the incident at the Marco Polo Bridge occurred a half-year later, Chiang was in no mood to compromise with Japan—or more precisely, public opinion and pressure from his rivals made further appeasement of Japan politically impossible. Chiang now spoke of Japan as testing the limits of Chinese endurance and declared that the loss of even one more inch of Chinese territory was unacceptable; to tolerate it, he said, would be an "unpardonable crime against our race."

The initial response of the KONOE FUMIMARO government was to minimize the importance of the North China Incident, as the first stage of the war was designated in Japan. For many months, hopes remained high that a settlement favorable to Japan could be achieved through negotiations or, failing that, through application of military force.

Military Operations —— While Chinese armies withdrew after only token defense of Beiping and Tianjin in the north, Chiang Kai-shek ordered a determined defense of the lower Yangzi (Yangtze) River area, beginning with Shanghai. For three months, from August to November 1937, the city suffered first aerial and naval bombardment and then hand-to-hand combat as approximately 200,000 Japanese troops gradually forced a half-million-man Chinese army into retreat in savage street fighting. Foreign observers, scanning the battles from the relative safety of the international settlement, were divided, some giving high praise for gallantry to the Chinese defenders while others cited examples of cowardice and ineptitude. In one notorious example of the latter, poorly trained Chinese air force pilots, charged with sinking the Japanese battleship *Izumo*, tied up at the Bund, missed their target and sent half-ton bombs raining down on a hotel and department store, causing 3,500 casualties.

The Chinese resistance in Shanghai collapsed in November after a task force of about 30,000 Japanese troops landed unopposed at Hangzhou (Hangchow) Bay, about 48 kilometers (30 mi) south of Shanghai, outflanked Shanghai, and joined other units to begin a race westward to Nanjing. Chiang ordered a defense to the death in Nanjing, but while it had taken the Japanese three months to capture Shanghai, the capital fell after only a few days of fighting on 13 December 1937. Then commenced one of the most unambiguously sordid episodes of modern warfare, as Japanese soldiers in Nanjing were either turned loose or simply broke discipline—the question remains in dispute. What is certain, however, is that soldiers under the command of General Matsui Iwane (1878–1948; hanged as a war criminal after the WAR CRIMES TRIALS in Tōkyō) engaged in an orgy of looting, arson, torture, rape, and murder that lasted at peak intensity for three weeks. As an example of barbarism inflicted wholesale on a civilian population (and on surrendered soldiers as well), Nanjing fell into the same category as Guernica, Madrid, Coventry, Dresden, and Hiroshima. The casualty toll of the Rape of Nanjing will never be known with certainty, but credible estimates of wanton murder range upward from 42,000.

The capture of Nanjing, to the surprise and disillusionment of many Japanese, did not spell the collapse of Chinese resistance. The Nationalists simply withdrew from Nanjing and retreated farther inland to a new capital at Hankou (Hankow), about 967 kilometers (600 mi) upriver on the Yangzi. China's strategy sought to compensate for the weakness of its armies' training, equipment, and morale by yielding space, forcing Japan to extend its logistical lines into unfamiliar terrain, and in general by fighting a war of attrition. And in the north, Mao Zedong's partisans were developing techniques of guerrilla warfare that effectively tied down large numbers of Japanese and occasionally defeated the Japanese in pitched battles. The first significant Chinese victory in the war came in September 1937 when the communist general Lin Biao's (Lin Piao; 1908–71) 115th Division entrapped and decimated a Japanese division at Pingxingguan (P'ing-hsing-kuan) in northern Shanxi (Shansi). In addition, in order to retard the advance of Japan's mechanized units and render worthless the spoils of victory, the Chinese employed "scorched earth" tactics: the incineration of the city of Changsha and the intentional breaching of the dikes of the Yellow River near Zhengzhou (Chengchow), both in 1938, were examples of this tactic. It is doubtful whether the Chinese gained much military advantage from either. The rupture of the dikes released the silt-filled waters of "China's Sorrow" to inundate 4,000 villages in three provinces, causing a million casualties and leaving two million homeless. In the end, Japanese motorized columns were delayed for no more than six to eight weeks.

Japan's battlefield strategy was centered on the seizure of "points" (cities) and "lines" (railways) in the belief that the Nationalists could not long survive their loss. In the spring of 1938 attention was fixed on the crossroads city of Xuzhou (Hsuchow), which sits at the junction of the north-south Jinpu (Tsinpu) and east-west Longhai (Lunghai) railways. Surely, it was felt, the capture of Xuzhou would bring Chiang Kai-shek to his knees. The drive on the city began inauspiciously for Japan when Chinese forces under the personal command of Deputy Chief-of-Staff General Bai Chongxi (Pai Ch'ung-hsi; 1893–1966) badly mauled two Japanese divisions at Taier Zhuang (Taierh Chuang) in Jiangsu (Kiangsu), about 64 kilometers (40 mi) northeast of Xuzhou, in April 1938. To the consternation of many foreigners sympathetic to China's cause (including the US military attaché, Colonel Joseph W. Stilwell [1883–1946] and the German military adviser to the generalissimo, General Alexander von Falkenhausen [1878–1966]), Chiang failed to exploit his success at Taier Zhuang, pulled back, and allowed the Japanese to replenish their forces. Consequently, on 15 May 1938, Japanese armies encircled Xuzhou and four days later captured the city that for centuries had been regarded as a bellwether of dynastic strength. If Xuzhou fell, an ancient military prescription dictated, the dynasty was doomed. The surrender of Xuzhou, however, contradicted the maxim, and continued Chinese resistance forced the Japanese high command to turn its attention to Hankou.

Critics of the War —— There were a few critics of the war in Japan—but only a few—bold enough to challenge the prevailing myth that the war was nearly over, that Japanese victories had relegated Chiang Kai-shek to the status of a local warlord. It required an uncommon measure of courage to speak out against a war officially proclaimed as holy *(seisen)*, a war in which tens of thousands of Japanese had been killed, a war that must be won to save the honor of an exceptionally "face"-conscious army. This would be true of citizens in any country at war, but it was especially true in Japan, where citizens were predisposed to bend their will to policies established by superior authorities and where severe pressure—social, psychological, and legal—was brought to bear on dissidents who scorned consensus.

As the campaign for Hankou got under way, one such dissident was Major General ISHIWARA KANJI, a brilliant strategist who had masterminded the Manchurian Incident in 1931. Now, seven years later, Ishiwara felt that China had changed, largely because Japanese aggression had finally galvanized the Chinese into an awareness of the nation's peril. In 1937 Ishiwara used his influential position as chief of the First, or Operations, Division of the Army General Staff to caution his colleagues against the dangers of becoming mired in what he predicted would be a hopelessly protracted war with China. Ishiwara's condemnation of the Japanese leadership resulted in his assignment to garrison duty in Kyōto in 1939; two years later, on the eve of the Pacific War, he was reduced to the ranks of the inactive reserves. The voices of other critics were similarly muffled, and the drive to capture points and lines proceeded. The four-and-a-half-month pincer campaign to capture Hankou came to a climax when five Japanese columns poured into that city on 25 October. The Nationalist government had, however, already vacated the city. Government, industry, schools, hospitals—the working capacity of Free China—was relocated westward beyond the Yangzi gorges to Chongqing (Chungking) in one of the great mass migrations of human history. Meanwhile, the great southern city of Guangzhou (Canton), the last remaining seaport through which China could hope to import war matériel, fell to Japan on 21 October.

From that time on, the war fronts gradually stabilized. Chongqing was subjected to devastating air raids, but there were only a few large-scale land operations after October 1938. They included the largely unopposed seizure of the island of Hainan off the South China coast in February 1939; a year-long campaign to seal off the Guangxi (Kwangsi)–French Indochina border in 1939 to 1940 (made unnecessary because the rail link into Guangxi from the French colony was cut at the other end when Japan occupied northern Indochina in September 1940); and the drive upriver to capture the prosperous commercial port of Yichang (Ichang) on the Yangzi in western Hubei (Hupeh) in the spring of 1940.

Stalemate —— A peculiar aspect of the stalemate period beginning in late 1938, one that was a source of great irritation to China's American allies after 1941, was the casual approach to trade and commerce between occupied and unoccupied China. Mail was delivered across the lines, the Chinese postal service treating the war with Japan as no more an inconvenience than the warlord struggles of 20 years earlier. Travel across the lines posed no extraordinary difficulties. As Michael Lindsay observes in his book *The Unknown War* (1975), a Chinese citizen traveling from Beiping to Chongqing simply took the train to Zhengzhou, walked across some 20 miles (32 km) of no-man's land, and found himself in Nationalist China. At hundreds of locations along the 3,200-kilometer (2,000-mile) "front line," there was a lively trade in consumer products, bulk quantities of raw materials, narcotics, medicine, strategic goods, and military secrets. The flow of goods was sometimes merely tolerated but more often was actively encouraged because all parties managed to gain something from it. On balance, however, it would appear that Japan often gained strategically valuable products, while the Chinese participants gained consumer items that eased somewhat the bitterness of daily life in unoccupied China.

The expansion of the China Incident into WORLD WAR II (or the Greater East Asia War, as it was officially designated) on 8 December 1941, brought America into the Asian war. Although the China theater commanded only a low priority for material support—especially after the island-hopping strategy in the Pacific came to absorb more and more American energy after 1943—American airpower, provided through General Claire Chennault (1890–1958), helped to preserve Chongqing and other Chinese cities from Japanese attack. Joseph W. Stilwell, an able American general with years of experience in China, was designated as chief-of-staff to Chiang Kai-shek and assigned the task of defending Burma. The Chinese and British armies as well as the American advisers there, however, were overrun by Japan in the spring of 1942. The loss of Burma and its vital supply corridors to the west and the painfully slow recovery of that territory over the next three years heightened in American minds the needs for reform of the Nationalist army. Stilwell felt that Chiang was reluctant to commit his armies to battle with the Japanese in Burma and in China because he was using so many forces to blockade the communist guerrilla armies in the north. In addition, Stilwell felt that the generalissimo was hoarding many of his best troops for the inevitable clash with the communists that would ensue upon the defeat of Japan—a defeat that seemed only a matter of time after the tide of war turned against Japan in 1943. His criticism of the Nationalist armies' lethargic resistance to Japan was confirmed in May 1944 when Japan launched a highly successful half-year-long campaign on the China mainland. Known as OPERATION NUMBER ONE, this offensive overran the American base at Guilin (Kweilin) and was probing the approaches to Chongqing before Chinese lines finally held in late 1944. Almost a half-million Chinese soldiers were lost, and eight provinces with a population of more than 100 million fell under the control of the Japanese. While the weak Chinese response to this drive increased Sino-American tensions, fighting within China was no longer crucial to the outcome of the war. The decisive battles were being fought in the Pacific, and the devastating air raids on the Japanese home islands were already under way by the end of 1944.

Peace Initiatives and Collaborationist Governments —— From the time of the first shots at the Marco Polo Bridge until the end of the war eight years later, there was rarely a moment when, despite "fight-to-the-death" rhetoric from both sides, some efforts were not under way to end the war by negotiation. Some of these moves were private and informal, others enjoyed official support from one or both governments. Some were sincerely motivated, others were mere smokescreens designed to achieve some immediate tactical or propaganda goal. Some were conducted with agents of Chiang Kai-shek; others, notably the WANG JINGWEI (Wang Ching-wei) peace movement, sought to take advantage of long-standing enmities within the Guomindang, isolate Chiang, and bring about a separate peace with his rivals. Thus, "peace movements" *(heiwa undō)* and "collaboration movements" *(gassaku undō)* blurred indistinguishably. For the most part, however, they underscored the common conviction of many Japanese and Chinese that a protracted war served the interests of neither Nationalist China nor imperial Japan but weakened each and left them vulnerable to both imperialism and communism.

This recognition, however, did not impel Japan to soften the peace terms it offered China. The conditions Japan insisted upon always included variations on the following: an end to "anti-Japanese activities" in China; Chinese cooperation with Japan in a common struggle against communism; Chinese recognition of Inner Mongolian autonomy; and special economic and military privileges for Japan in North China and Shanghai, including Japanese control over the development of natural resources, transportation, and communications in those areas. In addition, especially in the early stages of the war, Japan frequently called upon China to give official recognition of the independence of Manchukuo and pay indemnities and reparations to Japan. Finally, making negotiations even more problematic was the frequent demand by Japan that Chiang Kai-shek retire from office and turn the peace settlement over to subordinates.

As Nationalist diplomats repeatedly turned a deaf ear to such harsh terms, mainland commands of the Japanese Imperial Army, not without a measure of intercommand rivalry, were busy recruiting pliable collaborators from outside the ranks of the Nationalist Party. It was hoped that they would aid the Japanese Imperial Army in controlling the areas that fell under Japanese occupation and at the same time lend legitimacy to Japanese aims in China. The first to act were agents of the GUANDONG (KWANTUNG) ARMY's *tokumubu* ("special services units"), charged with various clandestine operations of a political nature. After parts of Inner Mongolia as well as the northern portion of Shanxi and the southern part of Chahar provinces were overrun by the Guandong Army, these areas were amalgamated in November 1937 into a federation known as Mengjiang (Meng-chiang; J: Mōkyō; Mongolian Borderlands). Though the populations of the Shanxi and Chahar zones of the federation were distinctly Chinese rather than Mongolian, the Japanese recruited Mongolian tribal leaders, notably the prince De Wang (Te Wang; Mong: Demchukdonggrub; b 1902), to administer the federation, with ample guidance from the Guandong Army.

One month after the appearance of Mengjiang, agents of the North China Area Army sponsored the creation of the PROVISIONAL GOVERNMENT OF THE REPUBLIC OF CHINA in Beiping. This puppet regime, which survived until March 1940, when it was absorbed into the more ambitious scheme associated with Wang Jingwei, had jurisdiction over all or parts of the five provinces of North China. An understanding reached in April 1938 between the head of the Provisional Government, WANG KEMIN (Wang K'o-min), and the commander of the North China Area Army, General TERAUCHI HISAICHI, provided for a system of "cooperative assistance" from Japan. This was defined as prior unreserved consultation between appropriate Japanese advisers and officials of the Provisional Government in all matters of political administration. As an example of "cooperative assistance," Japanese advisers called upon the Provisional Government to charter so-called national policy companies *(kokusaku kaisha)* under rules that allowed Japan to increase its grip on virtually all industries related to resource development. Similar arrangements were made between the Central China Area Army and its REFORM GOVERNMENT OF THE REPUBLIC OF CHINA, launched in Nanjing in March 1938.

These regional collaborationist regimes meshed well with the ambitions of Japanese expansionists, who sought to fracture China politically so as to keep it weak. Predictably, however, the regimes attracted an especially opportunistic horde of Chinese job seekers, none of whom could be regarded as distinguished statesmen. Those who had national reputations were usually remembered as participants in the unsavory and ephemeral governments of the warlord era who had chosen the wrong side in the battles with the Nationalists that brought that tragic era to an end in the late 1920s. It is scarcely surprising that they constituted a poor advertisement for the merits of close partnership with Japan. In an effort to make such an alliance more palatable to China, Premier Konoe declared in November 1938 that Japan would strive for the creation of a "New Order in East Asia" (TŌA SHINCHITSUJO) based on an equal partnership between China and Japan. A month later, the deputy leader of the Nationalist Party, Wang Jingwei, defected from Chongqing and began to explore the possibilities of Chinese participation in Japan's New Order.

Wang had behind him an illustrious career as patriot and statesman that dated back to his revolutionary struggles against the Qing (Ch'ing) dynasty (1644–1912). He was an ardent champion of anti-communism who had pleaded the cause of reconciliation with Japan so that the two countries might pursue that goal jointly. After his defection from Chongqing, he faced the vexing task of negotiating the precise terms of collaboration with Japan, a process that lasted two years. In March 1940 Japan allowed Wang to inaugurate the REORGANIZED NATIONAL GOVERNMENT OF THE REPUBLIC OF CHINA and dissolve the earlier regional regimes. Japanese recognition of the new government was stalled until Japan had exhausted last-minute efforts to reach a peace settlement with Wang's longtime rival Chiang Kai-shek. Finally, on 30 November 1940, a "basic treaty" between Japan and the Reorganized Government was signed, and ambassadors were exchanged. The Wang regime proved to be almost as poor a showcase for the New Order as the earlier regional regimes had been. Japan's economic exploitation did not diminish; the adviser system through which Japan exercised political control persisted; Japan continued to regard North China as an area where it was entitled to extraordinary military and economic privileges; and perhaps most disappointing to Wang, Japan refused to give the Reorganized Government any meaningful guarantee of a timetable for troop withdrawal from occupied territories.

A "New Policy for China" —— By late 1942 battlefield reverses in the South Pacific and severe pressure from communist guerrilla forces in China caused the Japanese army to adopt a "New Policy for China," set forth at an imperial conference in December 1942. This policy, the work of SHIGEMITSU MAMORU, ambassador to the Reorganized Government, allowed Wang to acquire more of the trappings—though still far from the entire substance—of independent government. The new policy was translated by army commands into the so-called Program of Well-Meaning Assistance (Kōiteki Shien) in early 1943. There seems to have been a gradually developing awareness by the army that its "supervision" of the Wang regime amounted to intervention and that a new low-profile approach characterized by assistance and suggestion would better serve Japan's interests. The despised special services units were replaced by liaison units *(renrakubu),* whose officers were under explicit orders to refrain from using harsh or imperious language toward Chinese citizens or government officials. Wang's most signal success occurred in 1943, when he persuaded Japan to return the Shanghai International Settlement to Chinese administration. This gesture, made at the same time the Allies signed treaties ending their special privileges in China's foreign enclaves, came too late to have much influence on the credibility of Japan's promise of a New Order. Shigemitsu Mamoru, writing in his postwar memoirs, surmises that there might never have been a Sino-Japanese War if Japan had taken such a step in 1937 rather than in 1943.

Anticommunism —— Japan encouraged the Wang regime to maintain armed forces—known to the Nationalists as *weijun (weichün;* puppet armies). Defections from the Nationalist army swelled the size of these forces so that they numbered perhaps as many as 900,000 by the final year of the war. Japanese generals did not allow them to be very well armed and ordinarily did not assign them to major combat operations. They were, however, given garrison assignments in the cities and deployed to guard communication and transportation lines against communist attack in the countryside. As the war drew to an end—and indeed for several months thereafter—a preoccupation with the fear of communism became a common denominator that caused soldiers of the Nationalist army, the *weijun,* certain powerful warlords such as Yan Xishan (Yen Hsi-shan; 1883–1960), and the Japanese Imperial Army to put aside their differences in order to check growing communist strength.

The most critical issue was the transfer of power in the major cities controlled by Japan and the *weijun.* Near many of these cities communist forces were present in sufficient strength to contest the Nationalists in the race to accept the Japanese surrender. Shanghai, Nanjing, and other great Yangzi and coastal cities were eventually turned over by puppet and Japanese troops to Chiang's forces and denied to Mao's armies, but the process was far from routine or quick. It was not until the first week in September 1945 that the Nationalist troops began arriving in Shanghai, for example. On 10 September, the *New York Times* correspondent Tillman Durdin reported the "particularly important role" played by Zhou Fohai (Chou Fo-hai; 1897–1948) in the "puppets' shift to the Guomindang." (Zhou had succeeded Wang Jingwei as the most powerful figure in the Reorganized Government following Wang's death in November 1944.) In the North China countryside as well, communist attempts to take over the Shandong–Hebei region were hampered because Nationalist commanders received Japanese and *weijun* reinforcements in the immediate postsurrender period. On

23 November, well over three months after the Japanese surrender, the commanding general of United States forces in China, Albert C. Wedemeyer (b 1897), reported to his chief of staff that the disarming of Japanese by the Chinese was not proceeding rapidly because the Japanese were being employed to protect communication lines and installations against the communists. In Yan'an, Mao complained bitterly about this collusion of the Nationalist, puppet, and Japanese troops.

The outcome of Japan's war with China was not decided in China, which was all but bypassed by the grand strategy of the Allies. The fateful battles were fought on islands in the Pacific. With Japanese defeat there, the Allies were in a position to close the sea lanes connecting Japan to its empire and in the final years of the war to devastate its cities from the air. There were rumors that the relatively strong imperial forces stationed in China might fight on after the emperor's decision to terminate the war on 15 August 1945. With the exception of the local actions taken against the communists noted above, that did not happen. A Chinese representative was aboard the battleship *Missouri* in Tōkyō Bay on 2 September 1945 to witness the Japanese signing of the instrument of surrender. On 29 April 1952, Japan signed a peace treaty with the Republic of China. For many years political disagreements hampered efforts to reach an accord with the People's Republic of China. Finally, in October 1978, the formal end to the war came with the exchange of instruments of ratification of the CHINA–JAPAN PEACE AND FRIENDSHIP TREATY in ceremonies held in Tōkyō. See also GREATER EAST ASIA COPROSPERITY SPHERE.

—— John H. Boyle, *China and Japan at War, 1937–1941* (1972). James B. Crowley, *Japan's Quest for Autonomy* (1966). Frank Dorn, *The Sino-Japanese War, 1937–1941* (1976). Hattori Takushirō, *Dai Tōa sensō* (4th ed, 1966).   *John H. BOYLE*

sister cities

(shimai toshi). As of 1979, there were 306 Japanese cities linked with foreign sister cities. The first sister-city combination involving a Japanese city was arranged by the United Nations and linked Nagasaki with St. Paul, Minnesota, in 1955. These two cities actively exchanged messages, children's drawings, and mutual visists by mayors, citizens, and students. Thereafter, many Japanese cities became linked with other cities all over the world. The Kokusai Shinzen Toshi Remmei (International Federation for the Promotion of Sister Cities), founded in 1962, promotes activities between cities, collects information, and advertises programs.   *HOMMA Yasuhei*

Six National Histories → Rikkokushi

Sjahrir, Sutan → Syahrir, Sutan

slums

Slums in Japan date from the Edo period (1600–1868), when differentiations in social classes in CASTLE TOWNS were reflected by their proximity to the castle. Menial workers such as male servants, porters, peddlers, and low-class entertainers lived in the most remote areas.

With the development of the modern city and industrialization during the Meiji period (1868–1912), indigent peasants flocked to the cities, gathering in ghettos near urban factory districts. Called *himminkutsu*, these tenement quarters were home for ricksha men, ragpickers, peddlers, and day laborers, as well as prostitutes, criminals, and other social misfits. In the Meiji and Taishō (1912–26) periods some of the poorest districts were Yotsuya Samegabashi, Shiba Shin'amichō, and Shitaya Mannenchō in Tōkyō, and Ōsaka's Nagomachi (now the fashionable Nippombashi Suji) and Nishinari Gun, which developed into the Kamagasaki slum in the post–World War II era. Calamities such as the TOKYŌ EARTHQUAKE OF 1923, the great depression of the 1930s, and, particularly, the devastating air raids of World War II contributed to an increase in slum areas.

One particular type of slum which developed during the Meiji and Taishō eras is the ragpickers' community known as *bataya buraku*. In the years following World War II many such communities flourished in devastated areas of large cities, providing temporary homes for the uprooted and unemployed. These remained until the early seventies in several districts of Ōsaka and Tōkyō, with the largest concentration being in Motogichō, a part of Adachi Ward of Tōkyō. Typically, these communities were dominated by paternal-

istic OYABUN–KOBUN relationships. A boss *(shikiriya)* would rent to his ragpickers *(bataya)* a lodging place and a handcart for collecting recyclable refuse, pay them a small daily wage, and give them protection and assistance. Scrap material would then be sold by the boss to a dealer who worked for other agents linked through an intricate subcontracting network to the recycling industry. Under the impact of recent urban development projects and the increasing automation of the recycling industry the *bataya buraku* have gradually disappeared.

Another type of slum that became particularly prominent after the end of World War II is the flophouse district known as *doyagai* (from an inversion of *yado*, "inn," plus *gai*, "street"). With a largely migrant population swollen in the early postwar era by jobless or displaced rural men, this reservoir of unskilled urban laborers meets the large demand for temporary laborers in the construction and transport industries.

Daily jobs are provided by prefectural employment agencies but the low wages usually attract only the elderly and infirm. Most workers find jobs through a black market system involving labor contractors or *tehaishi*. Because much of the demand for labor comes from the construction industry, about half of the *doya* laborers move in winter to distant project sites under the direction of contractors (see HAMBA SEIDO) where work conditions are exploitative and sometimes illegal.

The *doyagai* population is predominantly male and single, and the districts are characterized by an absence of community organization and high rates of social alienation, alcoholism, crime, and disease. Riots, as in San'ya (Tōkyō) in the summer of 1960 and in Kamagasaki (Ōsaka) a year later, tend to occur in periods of severe unemployment or in cases of extreme exploitation. Presently leftist "struggle groups" are actively attacking the labor contracting system in *doyagai* areas.

The tenements of the *doyagai* may be wooden or reinforced concrete buildings. The size of a room varies from a minimum of one *tatami* (0.9 by 1.8 m or 3 by 6 ft) for a single person to 6 or 8 *tatami* for several people. Sometimes rooms are equipped with rows of bunk beds and can accommodate 6 to 12 people.

Since the mid-seventies the *doyagai* population has shown a general decreasing trend caused by a combination of factors, such as the continuing spread of automation, rising levels of education, decreasing demands for unskilled labor, and decreasing labor migration. Today the *doya* labor is roughly distributed as follows: 5,000 workers in the area of Kotobukichō (Yokohama), 11,000 in San'ya, 20,000 in Kamagasaki, and 10,000 in the so-called *rōdō geshuku gai* in Kita Kyūshū.

San'ya, a major *doyagai* located in Taitō Ward of Tōkyō, next to the former red-light district of Yoshiwara, covers an area of 0.845 sq km or 0.326 sq miles. It has had a flophouse district since the early Meiji period, but during World War II most of its buildings burned as a result of air raids. After the war temporary quarters were built in the area to house the homeless who had gathered in Ueno Park, and it gradually reverted to being a flophouse district. The demographic composition of San'ya is unusual in that there are few family units; it is estimated that only 10 percent of its population is female.

The area known as Kamagasaki in the Nishinari Ward of Ōsaka contains both ordinary slum dwellings and *doya* flophouses. Following a three-day riot in 1961, its name was formally changed to Airin, from the Airin welfare settlement built by Ōsaka Prefecture to sponsor various welfare programs on behalf of the residents. The area, which covers about 0.7 sq km or 0.27 sq mi, consists of three major districts: a *doyagai* section, a red-light district with hundreds of small retail stores and residences of prostitutes and underworld gang members, and a section characterized by a large concentration of tenements and substandard private houses. Kamagasaki, which dates from the Meiji period, is considered Japan's worst slum because of its large population and the complexity of its problems.

Low-income family slums are concentrated particularly in Adachi, Arakawa, and Taitō wards of Tōkyō, and in several districts of Ōsaka, Kōbe, and Kyōto. A large portion of the inhabitants, estimated as several tens of thousands, is Korean (see KOREANS IN JAPAN). They live in substandard houses and usually find employment on a daily or temporary basis and work in small enterprises.

The former outcaste BURAKUMIN communities form a special case of minority slums and are mostly concentrated in the urban and rural districts of the Kansai (Kyōto-Ōsaka-Kōbe) area and Fukuoka Prefecture. By conservative estimate, there are some 4,000 of these communities with about 1.5 million individuals. Many people with a history of personal and social failure also live in these slums.

Small and medium enterprises

Composition of Establishments by Number of Employees, 1978 (in percentages)				
Number of regular employees	Manufacturing	Wholesaling	Retailing	Services
0 [1]	35.6	21.4	59.2	50.7
1–4	30.8	40.4	31.7	33.1
5–9	13.8	19.5	5.6	8.5
10–19	9.3	10.8	2.2	4.4
(subtotal 0–19)	89.5	92.1	98.7	96.7
20 or more [2]	10.5	7.9	1.3	3.3
Total	100.0	100.0	100.0	100.0
Small and Medium Enterprises as percentage of total establishments	(99.5)	(99.6)		(98.6)

[1] Includes family-run establishments.
[2] 20–300 for manufacturing, 20–100 for wholesaling, 20–50 for retailing and 20–50 for services.
SOURCE: Chūshō Kigyō Chō (Small and Medium Enterprise Agency), *Chūshō kigyō hakusho* (annual): 1981.

The total population of urban slum areas in Japan, excluding the *burakumin,* is estimated at roughly 150,000 individuals. Current government policy, as in the past, is not particularly concerned with a direct approach to the solution of slum problems, except in the form of limited welfare assistance to those who are most in need. Slum problems are expected to resolve themselves naturally in the process of overall development aimed at raising the general socioeconomic standards of the population. Following the remarkable economic performance of Japan during the past few decades, the slum population has shown a decrease.

———Carlo Caldarola, "The *Doya-gai:* A Japanese Version of Skid Row," *Pacific Affairs* (Winter 1968–69). Fukuda Masumi, *Nihon toshi kasō shakai* (1972). Isomura Eiichi, *Suramu* (1959). Isomura Eiichi, *Nihon no suramu* (1962). Isomura Eiichi et al, *Kamagasaki: Suramu no seitai* (1960). Nasu Sōichi et al, ed, *Toshi chiiki no byōri* in *Toshi byōri kōza,* vol 3 (Seishin Shobō, 1973). Brett Nee, "San'ya: Japan's Internal Colony," *Bulletin of Concerned Asian Scholars* (September–October 1974). Ōhashi Kaoru, *Toshi no kasō shakai* (1962). Taira Kōji, "Urban Poverty, Ragpickers, and the 'Ants' Villa' in Tōkyō," *Economic Development and Cultural Change* (January 1969). Yokoyama Gennosuke, *Nihon no kasō shakai* (1898).
Carlo CALDAROLA

small and medium enterprises

(chūshō kigyō). Small-scale business establishments which predominate in production and employment throughout Japan's private sector. Small and medium enterprises in Japan were defined by law in 1972 as having no more than 300 employees (no more than 100 and 50 for wholesalers and retailers, respectively) or no more than ¥100 million (US $453,453) in paid-in capital (no more than ¥30 million [US $136,036] and ¥10 million [US $45,345] for wholesalers and retailers, respectively). In 1981 these enterprises totaled 6,229,572, or 99.4 percent, of all firms in Japan. This figure includes 837,098 manufacturers, 3,011,250 wholesalers and retailers, 1,334,709 companies in service industries, and 1,015,279 in other industries. It excludes agricultural, forestry, and fishery establishments, which were estimated at 4.8 million in 1977.

International Comparisons——Exact international comparison is difficult because of differences in definition by individual countries, as well as differences in, and unavailability of, statistics. But while small and medium firms generally constitute over 90 percent of the total number of enterprises in industrial countries, the share of such enterprises in Japan (99.4 percent, as stated above) is among the world's highest. The approximately 37.2 million workers employed by these firms in 1981 accounted for 81.4 percent of the total labor force, a figure which is also among the highest in the industrialized world.

Small and medium enterprises accounted for 52.1 percent of Japan's total shipments of manufactured goods in 1980, compared with 36.6 percent in the United States (1977, enterprises with fewer

than 250 employees) and 27.9 percent in Great Britain (1968, enterprises with fewer than 200 employees). Their value added in 1980 accounted for 56.9 percent of the national total, compared with 36.8 percent in the United States (1972) and 23.8 percent for British firms with no more than 500 employees (1968). Thus, although larger enterprises, accounting for only 0.6 percent of the total number of firms, are responsible for almost half of the total production, small and medium enterprises still play a significant role in Japan's economy.

Diversity of Industries——In most industrial sectors, smaller or family-owned enterprises are dominant in number. In manufacturing, for example, very small enterprises (*reisai kigyō,* generally defined as enterprises with fewer than 20 employees) constitute almost 90 percent of the total, and 35.6 percent of these enterprises have no regular employees and are operated by family members. This phenomenon is even more prevalent among retail and service enterprises, with as many as 59.2 percent of the former and 50.7 percent of the latter operated by family members (see table). Although the small and medium firms are widely distributed in all sectors, 84 percent of them are concentrated in four industries: manufacturing, wholesaling, retailing, and services (excluding finance and insurance).

Local industries consisting of a group of firms producing specific products by taking advantage of special management resources and materials in their local area are often included in discussions of small and medium enterprises. These local industries, generally referred to as *jiba sangyō,* formerly depended on families, especially women and the elderly, for their labor supply. Their wage levels were low, as was the quality of their labor. Low product prices resulting from low wages and mass production have in most cases been the small firm's sole competitive weapon; to take advantage of this, small local enterprises have frequently emphasized exports. Often a local economy has become heavily dependent on a single industry. When this industry declines for any reason, it becomes an acute social problem through a general decrease in the local income level and, sometimes, an increase in unemployment.

According to a survey by the Small and Medium Enterprises Agency of the MINISTRY OF INTERNATIONAL TRADE AND INDUSTRY, there were 326 such industries with 101,009 firms and 926,000 employees in 1976, whose shipments exceeded ¥6.3 trillion (US $21.2 billion). Textile companies were dominant in number, constituting 42 percent of these firms, followed by such industries as sundry goods, metal products, apparel, furniture and upholstery, and lacquer ware. In recent times there has been a tendency to place importance on local economic development, with local industries being viewed in a new light.

Relations with Large Companies——About 60 percent of all small and medium enterprises are *shitauke kigyō* (SUBCONTRACTORS), controlled to varying extents by large companies, generally through the supply of parts or semifinished goods and occasional financial or technical assistance. The large companies, through their overwhelming size and monopolistic position in the market, can control the prices of parts or semifinished goods they buy from their subcontractors. Through this control the larger firms often pass increased costs on to the smaller firms, sometimes even forcing them out of business. This is regarded as a salient example of social inequality and unfair competition in the Japanese economy.

On the average, subcontractors supply as much as 19 percent of all purchases by large corporations. This heavy reliance on subcontractors is characteristic of Japan's large corporations. The percentage is particularly high (25 to 30 percent) in four industries: machinery, electrical equipment, transportation equipment (automotive, shipbuilding, and rolling stock), and textiles. However, with increases in business volume in these industries, control by large companies has gradually abated. A 1974 survey showed that cases of absolute price control by "parent companies" (as the larger companies in such relationships are termed) had declined from 15 percent of total transactions in 1964 to 9 percent. Nonetheless, parent companies can still take advantage of their subcontractors by utilizing the subcontractors' low labor costs, economizing on capital investment, and passing on to subcontractors the financial burdens caused by increased inventories or by delayed customer payments. Recently, only the third of these advantages had been maintained, while the first two have lost their relative importance because of a smaller wage differential between large and small firms and greater increases in labor costs than in capital costs.

Continued Growth——One of the remarkable trends observed in the process of economic growth was the continued increase in the number of small and medium enterprises. From 1963 to 1978, small and medium enterprises increased by about 1.9 million from 3.9 million, while large enterprises increased by only 13,000 from 21,000. Since the OIL CRISIS OF 1973 especially, the number of large enterprises in the manufacturing sector has been decreasing, while only the rate of increase declined in most other sectors; industrial production and sales have grown equally in both categories of enterprises.

Between 1963 and 1978 the number of small and medium firms increased at an annual rate of 2.1 percent, while large firms grew more noticeably in size than in number. However, since the rate of "births" of small and medium enterprises is believed to be far higher than this annual growth rate, the rate of "deaths" for these enterprises must also have been high. The 1968 edition of the Ministry of International Trade and Industry's White Paper on Small and Medium Enterprises estimated their annual "birth rate" between 1964 and 1966 at 7.2 percent as against an annual "death rate" of 4.9 percent.

The trend of increase in the number of Japan's small and medium enterprises is significant when compared with their United States counterparts, which did not increase even during the period of rapid economic growth in the 1960s. It is also significant because it runs counter to the widely held assumption that small and medium firms are inferior to larger corporations in such areas as technology, management, labor, innovation, quality of products, productivity, and economy of scale, and that their number should shrink as they are taken over by larger enterprises. This type of reasoning led to the prediction of a "revolution" in the distribution system when supermarkets and mass merchandisers made their debut in Japan around 1962. It was thought that small retail shops with lower productivity and inferior services would give way to these superior larger firms and that retail stores, which numbered 1.3 million at that time, would decline rapidly, as would small secondary or tertiary wholesalers. However, this did not prove to be the case; instead, the numbers of small firms in both retail and wholesale businesses increased.

The increase in small and medium firms can be explained by such factors as expansion of market opportunities for goods and services based on high technology; marketing specialties which only small firms can provide (in the fashion or the leisure markets, for example); increased purchases of services by consumers; and the growth of industries requiring a large number of subcontractors, which in the process of expansion accumulated new technology, as seen in the automotive parts, electric appliance, and housing construction industries. The increase in small and medium enterprises accompanying the modernization of an industry is a good example of the capacity of the Japanese economy to adapt to changing situations.

Role in the National Economy —— There is no doubt that small and medium enterprises have contributed greatly to Japan's economic expansion since the end of World War II. In manufacturing industries, for example, small and medium enterprises contributed 51.5 percent to the growth of shipments in the 20 years from 1956 to 1976, and 70.1 percent to the increase in employment over the same period. For some time after the war, they absorbed many jobless people and supplied low-quality, emergency consumer and industrial products. During the period of economic reconstruction lasting until about 1955, they earned valuable foreign exchange credits by exporting such products as textiles, toys, watches, and Christmas decorations. They accounted for well over 50 percent of Japan's total exports, and their products secured a high foreign-currency earnings ratio.

Despite these contributions, scholars and policymakers considered the small and medium enterprises a hindrance to economic development during the period prior to rapid economic growth for several reasons. First, small and medium enterprises, content with extremely low productivity, were regarded as lacking the capacity for self-improvement. In 1956 their value added per employee stood at only 41 percent of that of large firms. In other industrial economies, the productivity gap between small and large firms was much smaller. Second, wage levels were too low compared with large firms to attract quality labor, and qualified management was also difficult to attract because of the firms' lower prestige and poorer future prospects. In 1956 average wages in small and medium firms were about half those of large firms. This wage difference has diminished considerably since then. In 1977 the difference stood at less than 30 percent, though the statistical bases are somewhat different. Third, a disproportionately large number of business failures

and layoffs occurred in small and medium enterprises, a fact that led banks to restrict credit, which in turn further limited small-business borrowing capability. Since bank borrowing by Japanese corporations is generally heavier than in foreign countries, this is a critical factor for the stability of any company. Fourth, products of small and medium enterprises were often characterized as low-quality goods on both domestic and overseas markets, hindering pricing policy and market development. These factors combined to create a vicious cycle, resulting in excessive competition among small firms and an even greater gap between small and large enterprises.

Recent Developments —— As the Japanese economy entered a high-growth stage in the late 1960s, and then a lower-growth stage after 1973, the situation of small and medium enterprises gradually improved. From the 1960s through the early 1970s, Japanese industry faced an acute labor shortage caused by an inadequate supply of middle and high school graduates and by general labor immobility. This problem was felt most keenly by small and medium enterprises, and led to wage increases, which helped reduce the wage gap between large and small companies. Furthermore, along with increased sales and profits, the productivity of small and medium enterprises improved so markedly during this period that the differential between small and large firms was reduced, owing to the composite effect of capital investment for labor saving and modernization of equipment and government assistance in strengthening small-business management.

Generally poor quality in all areas of management—planning, marketing, and technological development—has traditionally been another problem associated with small businesses, and improvement of managerial skill was too slow to catch up with growth in size. However, during the high-growth years, such industries as electronics, automobiles, machinery, and petrochemicals expanded rapidly. Small and medium enterprises, mostly subcontractors in these industries, grew in both number and size and could often overcome the problem of weak management capability, particularly in technological development, through their heavy dependence on large corporations. The expanded consumer market has also aided the growth of small and medium enterprises, as did government spending increases in the construction and civil engineering sectors. Thus, while wage, productivity, and skill differentials between small and large firms still exist, they are now much less conspicuous, and small firms sometimes show high levels of productivity and management skill.

The oil crisis of 1973 was followed by a sudden slowdown in economic growth, with two major problems hitting small and medium enterprises. One was an increase in business failures because of market shrinkage, abrupt price changes, poor management, and stricter lending policies. The other problem resulted from the appreciation of the yen, which not only decreased exports in both value and quantity, but also allowed products of developing countries to make inroads into domestic and overseas markets. However, many small and medium enterprises survived these economic vicissitudes, and some of them attained remarkable growth in spite of unfavorable circumstances.

Government Assistance —— The government's system for assisting small and medium enterprises is one of the most extensive of its kind in the world. It includes financial assistance for modernization, management consultation services, precautionary measures against possible bankruptcy, and guidance for organizing cartels. Financial assistance is offered by three government-affiliated institutions, Chūshō Kigyō Kin'yū Kōko (SMALL BUSINESS FINANCE CORPORATION), which supplies funds for equipment modernization and long-term operating funds; Kokumin Kin'yū Kōko (PEOPLE'S FINANCE CORPORATION), which focuses its activities on small-scale and family-owned firms; and SHŌKŌ CHŪKIN BANK (Central Bank for Commercial and Industrial Cooperatives), which makes loans to its members. All of these institutions provide loans with relatively favorable rates of interest and repayment terms. They also provide financing for special needs under the government's small and medium enterprise modernization program and facilitate emergency financing in the event of sudden appreciation of the yen or business failures. Other public financial institutions provide capital funds by underwriting new stocks or convertible bonds and offer credit insurance and guarantees.

The tax system helps alleviate the financial burdens of small and medium enterprises. The corporate tax for small firms (capitalized at less than ¥100 million, or US $329,913) is 28 percent for undistributed profits and 22 percent for dividend credits when annual income does not exceed ¥7 million (US $31,742), as compared with

40 percent and 30 percent, respectively, for large corporations. Unincorporated small firms with an annual income of less than ¥7 million are granted the option of an "assumed corporate tax," by which a proprietor receives a tax allowance for remuneration of family employees. Special depreciation allowances for bad debts are also granted to small corporations.

Other important government measures include management consulting assistance, technical assistance, and protection from the competition of larger firms. Emphasis in the government's policy for small and medium firms has gradually shifted from protection to cooperation with large firms, and then to assistance for modernization and improvement of technical and management skills. However, some of the original protective attitude still remains in the form of laws which restrict the construction of large-scale retail stores and call for a modification, in most cases curtailment, of business plans or activities when necessary to protect small retailers.

Advance of Medium Firms —— In the later stage of rapid economic growth, particularly after 1970, the emergence of a number of new high-growth companies with good business results drew much attention. These were medium-sized companies with between ¥50 million (US $226,727) and ¥1 billion (US $4.53 million) in capital, and over 300 but not more than 1,000 employees, known as *chūken kigyō* (leading medium firms). They number about 15,000, most of which are believed to have their own original markets and technologies, and all of which are quite independent of large corporations.

There are several features which distinguish these companies from large companies. Most of them are family-owned or family-controlled, and many have some degree of foreign ownership. Whereas large companies tend to have a long history of development, most of these *chūken kigyō* are relatively new entries. Only 20 percent were founded before 1945, and 35 percent were founded after 1966. Another distinction is their high concentration (26 percent) in wholesale and retail businesses. Other sectors where high concentrations of *chūken kigyō* are notable are printing and publishing, fashion, and pharmaceuticals.

The emergence of leading medium firms has been prompted by three major changes in economic conditions. The first is a rapid shift in production, employment, and consumption from manufacturing industries to service industries, where new business opportunities are available for smaller firms in such fields as restaurant chains, retailing and wholesaling, and fashion. The second change involves the development of high-technology assembly industries centering on large companies, which promoted the development of subcontracting firms. Automobiles and electric appliances are two major industries where a great number of subcontractors are part of the production system. With the assistance of parent companies, parts manufacturers have accumulated specialized high technologies which help increase both sales and profits. Many of the local assembly firms with good marketing capability have expanded their sales and joined the group of growing medium companies. Finally, diversifying and changing consumption patterns have helped create new market potentials which are not great enough for large companies, but which are adequate for *chūken kigyō* with aggressive, creative management, distinctive marketing practices, and a good market segmentation policy. Such fields include fast food, special toys, brand-name sportswear, do-it-yourself goods, sporting goods, housing and interior materials and related services, and educational materials.

Future Prospects —— Japan's small and medium industries are expected to expand the scope of their activities in the 1980s despite the prospect of a lower-growth economy. One of the key factors will be a further increase in the share of tertiary industries in Japan's economy, which will provide growth opportunities for sophisticated small enterprises. On the other hand, rapid changes in the industrial structure, larger fluctuations in foreign exchange rates and wholesale prices, and accelerated imports of comparatively lower technology products from newly industrialized nations are likely to press many small and medium enterprises into difficulties and necessitate major changes in management strategy. A probable result will be more business failures accompanied by a higher rate of new company formation. Three chronic problems which small and medium enterprises will continue to face are a shortage of managerial skills, an insufficient labor supply, and the lack of proper mechanisms for receiving information and guidance in a rapidly changing economic environment.

🔳 —— J. E. Bolton, *Small Firms—Report of the Committee of Inquiry on Small Firms* (1971). Katō Seiichi, ed, *Gendai chūshō kigyō kiso kōza* (Dōbunkan, 1976). Kiyonari Tadao, *Nippon chūshō kigyō no kōzō hendō* (1970). Kiyonari Tadao, *Gendai chūshō kigyō no shintenkai* (1972). MITI, Small and Medium Enterprises Agency, *Background Information White Paper on Small and Medium Enterprises* (1978). MITI, Small and Medium Enterprises Agency, *Chūshō kigyō hakusho* (annual). MITI, Small and Medium Enterprises Agency, *Chūshō kigyō shisaku no aramashi* (1978). Nakamura Shūichirō, *Chūken kigyō ron* (1976). Nomura Tatsuo, *Chūken kigyō no katsuryoku keiei* (1979). ABE Mikio

small and medium enterprises, laws concerning

A set of legislation centered on the Small and Medium Enterprises Basic Law (Chūshō Kigyō Kihon Hō, 1963) that forms the basis of Japanese government policy toward the large number of smaller enterprises that operate in the economy. Official policy, as stated in the basic law, is to rely chiefly on the independent efforts of the small and medium enterprises, with government assistance where appropriate, especially in the area of promoting cooperative efforts. Many laws have been passed to implement this policy. Measures designed to promote cooperative efforts include the Small and Medium Enterprise Group Organization Law (Chūshō Kigyō Dantai Soshiki Hō, 1957), the Smaller Enterprise Cooperative Association Law (Chūshō Kigyō Tō Kyōdō Kumiai Hō, 1949), the Environmental Sanitation Rationalization Law (Kankyō Eisei Tekisei Hō, 1957), and the Shopping District Promotional Associations Law (Shōtengai Shinkō Kumiai Hō, 1962).

Two basic policies, the modernization and improvement of the enterprises, are provided for by the following legislation: the Small and Medium Enterprise Modernization Law (Chūshō Kigyō Kindaika Sokushin Hō, 1963), which sets out concrete procedures for accomplishing this purpose, and the Small and Medium Enterprise Promotional Association Law (Chūshō Kigyō Shinkō Jigyōdan Hō, 1967), which facilitates the establishment of such associations. Measures designed to promote the restructuring of particular industries have also been enacted, including measures for the traditional crafts industry (1974) and for the textile industry (1967).

In the area of finance policy, special lending institutions have been established to provide public capital to small and medium enterprises. These include the pre–World War II SHŌKŌ CHŪKIN BANK, the postwar SMALL BUSINESS FINANCE CORPORATION (1953), and two other finance corporations. The following laws also serve this function: the Credit Guaranty Associations Law (Shin'yō Hoshō Kyōkai Hō, 1953), the Small and Medium Enterprise Credit Insurance Law (Chūshō Kigyō Shin'yō Hoken Hō, 1950), and the Small and Medium Enterprise Credit Insurance Finance Corporation Law (Chūshō Kigyō Shin'yō Hoken Kōko Hō, 1958). In the area of business guidance, there are the Small and Medium Enterprise Guidance Law (Chūshō Kigyō Shidō Hō, 1963), the Small and Medium Subcontractor Promotion Law (Shitauke Chūshō Kigyō Shinkō Hō, 1970), and measures to coordinate the business activities of small and medium enterprises with those of large corporations, department stores, and supermarket chains.

Measures to promote business stability include the Small and Medium Enterprise Bankruptcy Prevention Mutual Assistance Law (Chūshō Kigyō Tōsan Bōshi Kyōsai Hō, 1977), and the short-term Measures for Small and Medium Enterprises in Designated Economically Depressed Regions (Tokutei Fukyō Chiiki Chūshō Kigyō Taisaku, 1978) and Measures for Small and Medium Enterprises Affected by the Rapid Appreciation of the Yen (En Ichiba Kōtō Kanren Chūshō Kigyō Taisaku, 1978). Legislation concerning the welfare of employees of these enterprises includes the Small and Medium Enterprise Retirement Mutual Assistance Law (Chūshō Kigyō Taishoku Kyōsai Hō, 1959), the MINIMUM WAGE LAW (1959), the Home Labor Law (Kanai Rōdō Hō, 1970), and regulations regarding the LABOR RELATIONS COMMISSIONS (1949). ISOBE Kiichi

small business → small and medium enterprises

Small Business Finance Corporation

(Chūshō Kigyō Kin'yū Kōko). A government-funded financial institution established in 1953 to provide loans for small- and medium-sized businesses that have difficulty obtaining funds from commercial banks. It provides equipment funds for modernization and rationalization projects as well as long-term operating funds. During the high-growth period, which lasted through the early 1970s, these loans were principally used by small businesses for modernization and structural improvements, but since then most loans have been directed toward pollution control and the upgrading of safety and sanitary facilities. Of the total of ¥4.5 trillion (US $20.4 billion) loaned by the corporation as of 31 March 1981, equipment funds accounted for 51 percent. These loans constituted some 9.2 percent of all equipment loans made to smaller businesses by Japan's financial institutions. The corporation was capitalized at ¥29.2 billion (US $121.3 million) in 1982.

HIRATA Masami

smiths

(kajiya). In Japan this profession was passed down through family lines from early on. They belonged to the kajibe, one of many hereditary service groups that specialized in a craft (see BE); many of these smiths were naturalized immigrants (KIKAJIN) who introduced ironworking techniques from the Asian mainland. After the TAIKA REFORM (645) they came under the authority of the Bureau of Smiths (Kaji no Tsukasa) and lived in the capital area of Nara. They later scattered throughout the country to work on landed estates (SHŌEN). With the rise to power of the warrior class, professional sword-smiths appeared; there was further specialization when firearms were introduced by the Portuguese in 1543 (see FIREARMS, INTRODUCTION OF). During the Edo period (1600–1868) the increased demand for metal agricultural tools and household goods led to regional specialization: for example, cleavers were generally produced in Sakai, close to Ōsaka, and scythes and axes in Takefu (in what is now Fukui Prefecture). There were also traveling smiths who went from village to village at harvesttime to repair farm tools. In Echigo Province (now Niigata Prefecture), the smiths developed a plow rental system, and other such enterprises were not uncommon.

SAKURADA Katsunori

SMON disease

A disease of the nervous system associated with a disorder of the optical nerve known as subacute myelo-opticoneuropathy (SMON) and due primarily to the toxic effects of the drug chinoform (Iodo-chlorhydroxyquin), used for treatment and prevention of amoebic dysentery. The disease is characterized by progressive paralysis of the senses and movement, and usually is preceded by abdominal pain and diarrhea. Cases of SMON disease began appearing in Japan in 1955 and the number increased rapidly in the late 1960s, involving a total of about 11,700 patients, with 500 deaths. New outbreaks effectively stopped when the sale of chinoform was banned in 1970.

The etiology of SMON disease became a highly controversial issue. In October 1969 newspapers reported that public health experts believed it to be an infectious disease. Some sufferers subsequently committed suicide. The following August, a medical researcher announced a relationship between a worsening of SMON symptoms and chinoform. In September 1970 the Ministry of Health and Welfare prohibited the drug's sale and initiated measures to halt its use. A competing theory that the disease was caused by a virus nevertheless persisted. In March 1972 a special investigation commission appointed by the Ministry issued its final report, rejecting the virus theory and concluding that chinoform had caused the vast majority of SMON cases.

Although SMON disease is found in epidemic proportions in Japan, it does not commonly occur elsewhere. Some authors attribute the relatively high incidence in Japan to an interaction between chinoform and environmental factors, possibly chemical pollutants, nutritional characteristics, or infectious agents. Others cite the higher dosages of chinoform administered in Japan and aspects of the health insurance system that encourage the prescription of drugs. In 1972 the Ministry of Health and Welfare created a division in the Public Health Bureau to deal with "intractable diseases" (nambyō) like SMON by supporting research, advancing treatment facilities, and providing financial assistance.

By 1978 civil damage suits had been filed against the national government and three pharmaceutical companies in 23 areas of Japan by 4,100 plaintiffs. The largest trial, involving more than 2,000 plaintiffs in Tōkyō, reached a mediated agreement (wakai) in the fall of 1977. On 1 March 1978 the Kanazawa District Court handed down the first SMON decision. The court recognized nearly all of the plaintiffs' arguments, ruling that chinoform was a necessary cause of SMON disease, that the injury could have been foreseen,

and that the government and companies were negligent in failing to ensure the safety of the drug.

📖 ——Iijima Nobuko, Kōgai, rōsai, shokugyōbyō nempyō (1977). Takahashi Kōsei, "Nihon no yakugai no genten SMON," Iryō kakumei (1977).

Michael R. REICH

snakes

(hebi). In Japanese hebi is the general name for reptiles of the suborder Serpentes, order Squamata. Five families are found in Japan: Typhlopidae, Colubridae, Elapidae (Okinawa Prefecture), Hydrophiidae, and Viperidae. The most common species are the shima-hebi (Elaphe quadrivirgata); aodaishō (E. climacophora); and yamakagashi (Rhabdophis tigrinus) of the family Colubridae, which are distributed widely in paddy fields, dry fields, grasslands and woods; the shimahebi and aodaishō prey on rats and mice. The mamushi (Agkistrodon halys), the only poisonous snake widely distributed throughout Hokkaidō, Honshū, Shikoku, and Kyūshū, is commonly seen in paddy fields and other damp areas; it seldom harms humans or domestic animals because of its nocturnal habits and its general slowness of movement. The habu (Trimeresurus flavoviridis), which inhabits the Amami Islands and Okinawa, is aggressive and fatally poisonous. The Erabu umihebi (Laticauda semifasciata) sea snake is found southward from southern Kyūshū.

In ancient times snakes were venerated as beings possessed of an eternal life because their ability to shed an old skin and grow a new one was seen as a process of death and rebirth. The snake was also regarded as a deity of paddy fields, where it appears in the spring, and as a mountain deity, since it returns to the mountains in autumn for hibernation, as well as a guardian deity of houses, probably because it is an exterminator of vermin. Until recent years the habit of letting the aodaishō live in old houses to eat rats persisted in rural areas. Snakes gradually came to be detested later for a variety of reasons, one of which was the idea that they could violate women as described in the KONJAKU MONOGATARI, a collection of tales completed in the latter half of the Heian period (794–1185).

IMAIZUMI Yoshiharu and SANEYOSHI Tatsuo

Snow Brand Food Co, Ltd

(Yukijirushi Shokuhin). Producer of ham, meat, and canned food. A subsidiary of the SNOW BRAND MILK PRODUCTS CO, LTD, it was established in 1950 when the meat processing division of the Snow Brand Milk Products became independent of its parent firm. In 1970 it merged with the Andes Ham Co and became the fourth largest firm in its field. In the latter part of the 1970s, it moved into the fields of frozen and retort foods. It has a subsidiary firm in Brazil from which it secures raw material. Sales for the fiscal year ending March 1982 totaled ¥92.7 billion (US $385.1 million), and capitalization stood at ¥2.1 billion (US $8.7 million). Corporate headquarters are located in Sapporo, Hokkaidō.

Snow Brand Milk Products Co, Ltd

(Yukijirushi Nyūgyō). Manufacturer and seller of food products; Japan's largest dairy product company in annual sales. It was founded in 1925 as the Hokkaidō Dairy Cooperative by a group of dairy farmers who had suffered from the devastation caused by the Tōkyō Earthquake of 1923. In 1950 the company assumed its present name. It produces and sells a variety of products, including milk, butter, cheese, powdered baby formula, soft drinks, frozen foods, and wine. Some of its products are well known abroad and its powdered baby formula is widely used in Thailand, Malaysia, and the Middle and Near East. It has offices in Hamburg, New York, Melbourne, Bangkok, and Taipei. The company plans to increase product diversification in the years to come. Sales for the fiscal year ending March 1982 totaled ¥440 billion (US $1.8 billion), of which dairy products accounted for 73 percent and other products 27 percent; capitalization stood at ¥12.6 billion (US $52.3 million) in the same year. Corporate headquarters are located in Sapporo, Hokkaidō.

Snow Festival

(Yuki Matsuri). 1. A festival of prayer for a good harvest, held on 14–15 January at the Izu Shrine in the town of Anan, Nagano Prefecture. As part of the ceremony, snow, which is thought to bring about a bumper crop for the coming year, is offered before the gods.

2. A tourist-oriented festival held in Sapporo, Hokkaidō, in early February, featuring a contest of snow and ice sculptures. Similar festivals are held elsewhere in northern Japan.　　MISUMI HARUO

snow viewing

(yukimi). The custom of gathering to partake of food and sake (rice wine) while viewing a snow-covered landscape. Early records of such events appear in chronicles of the Nara period (710–794). In the Heian period (794–1185), aristocrats held gatherings or accompanied imperial excursions to view the snow. By the Edo period (1600–1868), the custom had been taken up by the common people, and continued to be a popular theme in literature.

INOKUCHI Shōji

Snyder, Gary (1930–)

American poet. Born in San Francisco. His family moved to the state of Washington when he was two, and he spent his childhood in the forests of the Pacific Northwest. From 1942 to 1951 he lived and attended schools in Portland, Oregon. Graduating in 1951 from Reed College, where he majored in anthropology and literature, he went to San Francisco and enrolled in 1953 as a graduate student in the Department of Oriental Languages of the University of California at Berkeley to study Chinese and Japanese. He wrote poetry from his days in Oregon and was gradually recognized by the poets of the San Francisco Bay area, including Kenneth Rexroth. In 1955 he met Jack Kerouac and Allen Ginsberg, and with them he participated in the "beatnik" movement on the West Coast, which is often referred to as the "San Francisco Poetry Renaissance." In his novel The Dharma Bums (1958), Kerouac portrayed the Snyder of this period as the "new hero of American Culture," Japhy Ryder. Having played a major role in this movement, in 1956 Snyder left for Japan, where he spent most of the following decade studying ZEN with Oda Sessō of the temple DAITOKUJI in Kyōto. His early interest in Oriental literature was further deepened during his years in Japan; notably he was much influenced by BASHŌ's haiku and MIYAZAWA KENJI's life and work as a Buddhist, poet, and agricultural worker in the mountains. Returning to the United States, Snyder published in 1968 The Back Country, a collection of poems in which he attempted to synthesize the work songs of the loggers of the Far West, his impressions of the American Pacific Northwest, and Bashō's Oku no hosomichi, the poetry of the wanderer-in-nature of the Far East. Appended to the collection were Snyder's translations of 19 poems by Miyazawa Kenji.

Snyder's belief in the incantatory power of language has led him to carry out a survey of various oral traditions surviving in today's world, such as Buddhist chants, NŌ drama recitation, and American Indian gambling songs. In Turtle Island (1974), a collection of poetry that won a Pulitzer Prize in 1975, he conjures up through incantations the past of the American continent, when bears, deer, coyotes, and the Indians were the masters of the land prior to conquest by the white man and machines. In search of primitive cultures around the Pacific, Snyder was in the late 1970s studying the moribund tradition of the AINU in Japan, which has much in common with the dying Indian culture of North America.

Snyder's poetry combines multiple elements deriving from both Western and non-Western origins. The European Romantics' praise of freedom in the forests, the American belief in the grass-roots democracy of independent workers, and the anarchists' hatred of modern institutions—these elements found in his poetic thought place him in the mainstream of Occidental poetry. However, he also has drawn much from the myths of the American Indians and from his extensive firsthand knowledge of Oriental literature: Buddhist texts, Chinese poetry, and the Japanese art of haiku. From Oriental poets he learned his laconic, intense style, the methodic pursuit of oneness with nature, and sensitivity to seasonal flowers, insects, and birds. In the late 1970s Snyder was involved in the movement for environmental preservation and was living in the mountains of the Sierra Nevada in northern California with his family.

Yoshiyuki NAKAI

sō

Also called sōchū, sōshō, or sōmura. Self-governing bodies, generally corresponding to a village unit, that existed in rural areas from the 14th through 16th centuries. As the estate (SHŌEN) system eroded and centralized control was disrupted by frequent warfare, many groups of cultivators (MYŌSHU and HYAKUSHŌ) began to manage village affairs independently, sometimes refusing to pay taxes to any higher authority. On occasion they even violently resisted attempts at outside control in uprisings called TSUCHI IKKI.

Each sō took care of its own irrigation, communal lands (IRIAI), law and order, and defense. Its decisions were reached at group meetings called YORIAI and were administered by the headmen (OTONA) and elders (TOSHIYORI), who were usually from among the leading landholders. The sō organization overlapped that of the local shrine association (MIYAZA) and was, for all practical purposes, identical in cases of arranging festivals and certain other joint activities.

Especially after the ŌNIN WAR (1467–77), sō often linked together into groups including whole districts (gunchūsō) and even cooperated in large-scale uprisings. As feudal control tightened from the mid-1500s on, many rural leaders became warrior retainers and placed their sō under the control of territorial daimyō (see GŌSON SYSTEM).

Sōami (ca 1455–1525)

Also known as Shinsō. Painter and connoisseur-curator of the Ashikaga shōgun's collection; the son of GEIAMI, whose duties he assumed after his father's death in 1485. Sōami's activities included mounting, restoration, and preparation of the text of labels of paintings in the collection. In 1485 one of his chief duties was to aid in the selection and transfer of paintings from the collection to be used by KANŌ MASANOBU as models for his religious paintings in Ashikaga Yoshimasa's Tōgudō, a famous building at the temple GINKAKUJI. He was highly regarded by contemporaries, including highranking monks and court nobles such as SANJŌNISHI SANETAKA, for his connoisseurship of Chinese art. He contributed to the historical Kundaikan sō chōki (1511) art records by adding notations taken from Xia Wenyan's (Hsia Wen-yen) paintings, together with his own opinions on works he had seen. He was very likely the author of Okazari ki (1524), a document outlining customs of ceremonial display for art objects during the Muromachi period (1333–1568). While very few authentic works from his hand remain, it is clear that by 1490 he was the master of a mature Chinese landscape style in the manner of the Ma-Xia (Ma-Hsia) school. He further appears likely to have mastered figure painting in the style of Muqi (Mu-ch'i; J: MOKKEI) and academic BIRD-AND-FLOWER PAINTING. The true measure of his genius may be found in his development of a landscape style based on very close study of works attributed to Muqi, notably the Eight Views of Xiao and Xiang (Hsiao and Hsiang; Shōshō hakkei zu, 1498) in the shōgun's collection. In this way he produced Japan's first truly "southern school" landscape style (see BUNJINGA). Sōami's paintings in the "Eight Views" style in the Daisen'in, a subtemple of Daitokuji in Kyōto (originally sliding door paintings; ca 1513) demonstrate that this mode had been perfected in such a way as to incorporate soft, rolling rhythms and a fluid interrelationship of parts, in a manner distinctly reminiscent of YAMATO-E traditions. See also AMI SCHOOL; INK PAINTING.

Richard STANLEY-BAKER

sobayōnin

(grand chamberlain). High-ranking aide of the Tokugawa shōgun whose function was to relay messages between the shōgun and the RŌJŪ, the shōgun's senior councillors (see TOKUGAWA SHOGUNATE). The influence of the sobayōnin's position, which was established in 1681, increased after 1684 when the assassination of rōjū HOTTA MASATOSHI in his office prompted the shōgun to move his own quarters farther away from the administrative offices. Sobayōnin like YANAGISAWA YOSHIYASU and TANUMA OKITSUGU took advantage of their direct access to the shōgun to enhance their power.

Sōbin → Sōmin

Sobosan

Mountain on the border of Ōita and Miyazaki prefectures, Kyūshū. The highest peak of the KYŪSHŪ MOUNTAINS. The mountain's upper part is covered with primeval forests of beech trees, and the lower part is covered with forests of fir and hemlock-spruce. The mountain is part of Sobo–Katamuki Quasi-National Park. Height: 1,757 m (5,763 ft).

Sōchō (1448–1532)

Master of linked verse *(renga)*, author, critic, Zen Buddhist priest. In his earlier years he was called Sōkan, first taking the name Sōchō in his late thirties. He was born the younger son of a blacksmith in the province of Suruga (now part of Shizuoka Prefecture), and at an early age entered the service of the local military overlord, Imagawa Yoshitada. He took Buddhist orders at 17, and on Yoshitada's death in battle in 1476, left the province and became a disciple of the Rinzai Zen master IKKYŪ at the Daitokuji monastery in Kyōto. He first met the eminent classical scholar and poet of linked verse SŌGI, at a *renga* gathering in 1466. Thenceforth he became Sōgi's disciple, studying classical poetry and linked verse with him and following him everywhere, accompanying him on his journey to Tsukushi (northern Kyūshū) in 1480–81. On returning to Kyōto, he found the capital laid waste by the destructive ŌNIN WAR of 1467–77, and went back to his native province, where he built a hermitage and performed various services of a political and diplomatic nature for Imagawa Ujichika, son of his old patron Yoshitada. In 1501 he went to Echigo Province (now part of Niigata Prefecture) to visit the ailing Sōgi, accompanying him the following year on his last journey and remaining at his side until his death. In 1504, Sōchō built a cottage at the foot of the mountain Utsunoyama and took a wife, who bore him a son and a daughter. For the most part he spent his remaining years in leisurely retirement, varied by frequent visits to Kyōto, often on missions for his Imagawa patrons, which made him a familiar figure in the mansions of powerful military barons.

Sōchō participated in a great many *renga* compositions of which the texts survive, the best known being "Three Poets at Minase" of 1488 and "Three Poets at Yuyama" of 1491. He also assisted Sōgi and others in compiling the *Shinsen tsukubashū* (Tsukuba Collection, Newly Selected), completed in 1495, an important anthology of superior *renga* verses. Collections of his own poetry, mostly *renga* verses, include *Kabekusa* (1512, Grasses on the Wall), *Nachigomori* (1517, Retreat at Nachi), and *Oi no mimi* (1526, An Old Man's Ear). He also wrote or compiled several *renga* handbooks and works of criticism, as well as travel accounts and diaries. Among the latter, his *Sōgi shūenki* (1502, Record of Sōgi's Last Days), an account of the master's last trip and death, is the most famous. A man of varied talents, Sōchō was also an enthusiastic and accomplished poet of *haikai* (informal or comic linked verse) and a capable musician. The *Kanginshū* (Collection of Tunes for Leisure Hours), an anthology of 15th-century popular songs, is also attributed to him. See also RENGA AND HAIKAI.

📖 ——Earl Miner, *Japanese Linked Poetry* (1979).

Robert H. BROWER

social insurance → social security programs

Socialist Democratic Party → Shakai Minshutō

Socialist Masses Party → Shakai Taishūtō

Socialist People's Party → Shakai Minshutō

social problems

Some of the major problems affecting contemporary Japanese society are high population density, environmental pollution, rapid population redistribution, care for the elderly, youth problems, discrimination, crime, suicide, and prostitution.

With a population of 115,280,000 living in 377,708 square kilometers (148,000 sq mi) in 1979, Japan had a population density of 305 persons per square kilometer (790 persons per sq mi). This high population density has led to extremely high prices for residential land, small residential spaces, and dense housing conditions (see LAND PROBLEM; HOUSING PROBLEMS). Dense housing, in turn, has created such problems as inadequate access to daylight (see RIGHT TO SUNSHINE) and increased risks of widespread injury and destruction in the case of NATURAL DISASTERS. In addition, because of the high cost of land, it is often impossible to implement large-scale road improvement, even where the narrow alleyways of premodern times are inadequate for auto traffic. With rapid development of automobile production and an increase in the number of cars per household, the conditions of roads have deteriorated and traffic jams are a matter of daily life. Finally, high population density in urban areas has had a detrimental effect on mental health as a result of friction in human relations and social alienation (see MENTAL ILLNESS).

Although recent industrial development in Japan has raised the general standard of living, the benefits have not always been equally distributed among all segments of society. Like most industrialized countries, Japan has problems with labor conditions, UNEMPLOYMENT, and POVERTY in some sectors of society. But the most serious problem resulting from rapid industrialization has been environmental pollution. Alarming instances of air, water, soil, noise, and chemical pollution have appeared in Japan. During the 1960s, CITIZENS' MOVEMENTS against pollution at the local level spread widely. While some pollution problems were improved by the enactment and enforcement of laws (see POLLUTION COUNTERMEASURES BASIC LAW), their growth in industry has not been entirely checked. New citizens' movements are expected to arise in the future. See ENVIRONMENTAL QUALITY.

Another problem caused by rapid economic growth was the movement, after 1955, of a large portion of the agricultural labor force to the industrial sector, so that population concentrated heavily in the cities. Problems of housing, traffic, pollution, waste disposal, and water supply resulted. These massive movements of people from rural to urban areas have also caused the "depopulation" of isolated islands and agricultural villages. In many of these areas only the elderly and women and children have remained, and a shortage of medical services and educational institutions and increased loneliness have become serious problems (see URBANIZATION). In the northeastern part of Japan, DEKASEGI, or seasonal relocation of labor to the cities during the agriculturally slack winter months, became common in the post–World War II period. This phenomenon placed serious strains on remaining family members. The practice of *dekasegi,* however, declined in the late 1970s, alleviating some of these problems.

In traditional Japan, the elderly were accorded great respect and occupied positions of authority and dignity within their families and society. Younger members of the family were obliged to take financial and spiritual care of the old. Since 1945, however, the young have increasingly tended to challenge the authority of their elders, while the elderly have become more reserved toward the young. The number of traditional FAMILY units which include several generations in one household has been decreasing, whereas the number of nuclear family households has increased.

The average life span has increased, but the elderly have had more and more difficulty in attaining long-term financial security. Particularly in urban areas, the number of elderly people who live alone has increased dramatically. They cannot depend for support on younger members of their families, and various welfare facilities and policies for them are not adequate, although improvements have been made since the early 1950s (see SOCIAL SECURITY PROGRAMS). Thus, the elderly are in an unstable position, caught between the gradual disintegration of the traditional family structure and incomplete social welfare policies. See also OLD AGE AND RETIREMENT.

For the younger generation, acute competition to enter certain higher education institutions has come to be recognized as a social problem. Since graduates of several famous universities have the best employment chances, the competition to enter these universities is intense and begins at a relatively young age (see ENTRANCE EXAMINATIONS). Though competition cannot be avoided in a free society, this phenomenon, the increasing number of so-called *rōnin* (high-school graduates who continue to study until they are able to pass the examinations for a specific university), and the increase of JUKU (private preparatory schools for primary and secondary school children) cannot necessarily be considered a good thing. The highly competitive examination system has distorted the formal education system, and time for play and other nonacademic activity for children has been sharply reduced. Carried to an extreme, such competition can block healthy physical and mental development. Since social position is largely determined by one's educational achievements, those who fail to excel sometimes abandon their dreams for the future at a young age and deviate from socially acceptable paths in life. For example, *bōsōzoku,* or groups of unlawful and sometimes violent young drivers of motorbikes and cars, have appeared in Japan, causing serious disturbances and occasionally committing crimes. See also DRUG ABUSE.

Social discrimination and prejudice against people living in areas customarily avoided by the general population (see BURAKAMIN) is also a serious problem. Most historians believe that the origin of this discrimination lays in the hierarchical system that came about during the Edo period (1600–1868). During this time, the Tokugawa shogunate designated certain groups of people as *eta* or *hinin;* they were responsible for certain lowly occupations, were forced to live in restricted areas, and were deprived of freedom of occupation, marriage, and religion. With the Meiji Restoration of 1868, the feudal ranking system was legally abolished, but discrimination against such people has continued and their rights have often been seriously violated. Movements have been organized to oppose discrimination toward people with this kind of background, and various local governments have also begun to take up this issue. Though the overall situation has improved, deep-rooted prejudices have not been eradicated. See also MINORITIES.

Another persistent problem is racial discrimination toward Koreans living in Japan and their descendants born in Japan. Most of this group are aliens under the law and face legal and social barriers that effectively keep them from enjoying full social benefits, hamper the attainment of citizenship, and handicap them in the job market. Many of them speak Japanese as their native language, yet they are prevented from entering the mainstream of Japanese society by virtue of their race. See KOREANS IN JAPAN.

Criminologists often argue that the CRIME rate increases proportionally with industrialization and urbanization, but this has not been borne out in Japanese society. In spite of rapid industrialization and urbanization since 1945, the crime rate, which reached a peak in 1948, has since gradually declined. However, organized crime rings, or gangsters called YAKUZA, require mention. The *yakuza* engage in various forms of blackmail and extortion. *Yakuza* groups are organized according to principles of fictive parent-child (see OYABUN-KOBUN) relationships, and loyalty and protection of the gang's interests are considered paramount. *Yakuza* groups numbered 2,525 in 1979, with a membership of 108,700. There are seven major *yakuza* groups, which collectively have 32,175 members. The largest group, Yamaguchi-Gumi, numbers 10,382.

In the past, the SUICIDE rate in Japan was quite high. Even after World War II, the suicide rate in Japan was the highest of the 10 major industrialized countries between 1955 and 1960. As in most industrialized countries, there is a high incidence of suicide among the elderly. In Japan, however, the suicide rate is also high among youth, and the number of suicides by young people accounts for almost 30 percent of the total. Since the 1960s, however, suicides among youth and the overall rate have been decreasing.

Suicides among women, particularly among the elderly, have been increasing. Suicides by women over 65 years of age account for almost one-third of all suicides. There is also a pattern of mothers committing suicide with their children. Love suicides (*shinjū*) were common in Japan during feudal times, but now occur rarely.

PROSTITUTION is prohibited in Japan by the PROSTITUTION PREVENTION LAW of 1956; however, it persists, particularly at Turkish bathhouses *(toruko)* and massage parlors. *Iwai Hiroaki*

social security legislation

Legislation establishing social insurance and public assistance programs to guarantee minimum standards of living for all citizens. Social security legislation in Japan authorizes the following types of program: public assistance for the impoverished and those with low incomes; social insurance programs, particularly for workers; social welfare programs for children, senior citizens, and the mentally and physically disabled; and programs of public hygiene or medical care.

The first national measure for the relief of the impoverished in Japan was enacted in 1874; this was followed by a famine relief fund law in 1880, a disaster relief fund law in 1899, a military relief law in 1917, and a general relief law in 1929. In response to the rapid development of factories, international pressures, and concern over the protection of workers, the FACTORY LAW OF 1911 was enacted, establishing the employer's absolute liability for injuries to workers. Under the influence of the International Labor Organization (ILO) Conventions, a workers' compensation law was enacted in 1931. A military policy of maintaining human resources led to the enactment of a national health insurance law in 1938, a seamen's insurance law in 1939, a pension law in 1941, and a welfare annuity insurance law in 1944. These various laws placed priority on mutual assistance

and were benevolent in character, while also reflecting the demands of the nation's industrial and military policies.

After World War II, the new constitution enacted in 1946 and effective in 1947 became the basis for social security legislation in Japan. The constitution guarantees the people's right to life and clearly establishes the responsibility of the state to promote and improve welfare, social security, and public health. Public assistance legislation—the LIVELIHOOD PROTECTION LAW—was also enacted in 1946. Social security legislation—the Workmen's Compensation Insurance Law and the Unemployment Insurance Law—were enacted in 1947 to supplement the prewar Health Insurance Law, Welfare Annuity Insurance Law, the National Health Insurance Law, and others. Social welfare legislation was also enacted—the CHILD WELFARE LAW in 1947, the PHYSICALLY HANDICAPPED WELFARE LAW in 1949, and the Social Welfare Activities Law in 1951. Subsequently, the National Health Insurance Law was completely revised in 1958, and additional legislation was enacted—the Mentally Disabled Welfare Law in 1960, the OLD-AGE WELFARE LAW in 1963, the Mother and Child Welfare Law in 1964, the Children's Maintenance Allowance Law in 1964, the Mother and Child Insurance Law in 1965, the Basic Policy Law for the Mentally and Physically Disabled in 1970, and the Children's Allowance Law in 1971. The social security system's quantitative expansion and qualitative improvement has been accomplished, but this has greatly increased the expenses borne by the nation, and ensuring the continued financing of these programs has become a major concern. See also MEDICAL AND HEALTH INSURANCE; NATIONAL HEALTH INSURANCE; PENSIONS; WORKERS' COMPENSATION. *Katō Shunpei*

social security programs

(*shakai hoshō seido*). The term "social security," defined as a government policy to ensure its citizens of a minimum standard of living, is supported by the twin pillars of social insurance and social aid. The main objective fulfilled by social security is to counter problems such as sickness, injury, disability, old age, death, unemployment, and large families. Consequently, social security programs can be defined as being made up of all systems and institutions providing social security to the citizens.

The term "social security" appears in article 25, section 2 of the 1947 CONSTITUTION, where it is referred to together with social welfare and public health. However, the Recommendations regarding the Social Security System, presented by the Cabinet Social Security System Deliberation Committee in 1950, employs the term in a wider sense and refers to it as a program consisting of social insurance, public aid, social welfare, and public health. This latter usage has since been widely adopted in Japan and will be used in this article.

In this connection, special attention must be paid to the use of the term "social welfare" in Japanese literature on social problems. Generally, as in this article, social welfare refers only to one of the four component parts of the social security program and should not be confused with a looser usage to mean social security.

Although the beginnings of a social security system can be traced to the first years of the Meiji Restoration (1868), when some form of public assistance was granted by the state, social security in the modern sense, as defined above, was not instituted until after World War II.

The first form of social assistance came in 1874 with the Poor Relief Regulation, which was followed by the Anti-Poverty Harvest Savings Act of 1880. Since government support was modest in both cases, various mutual aid associations, both on a governmental and private level, came into existence in 1888. It was not until 1922, with the passing of the Health Insurance Law (enforced in 1927), which was based on a German model, that most employees were provided with medical care and cash benefits (exceptions were agricultural and domestic workers and small-business employees). This move was largely seen as a conciliatory gesture on the government's part toward appeasing labor unrest during socially troubled times. With the outbreak of the second Sino-Japanese War in 1937 came further advances: in 1938 the NATIONAL HEALTH INSURANCE scheme was inaugurated (again benefits were inadequate and intended primarily to relieve conditions in farming and fishing villages). This was followed by the Seamen's Insurance Law and the Clerical Workers' Health Insurance Law in 1939. In 1941 the Employees' Pension Law was introduced, which was charged with raising funds to support the war effort in addition to providing security for workers in their old age. By 1944 this scheme was enlarged to cover women workers.

Social security programs

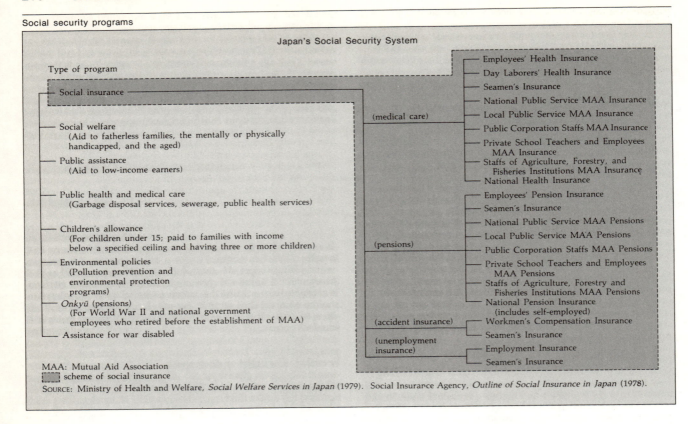

Japan's Social Security System

Type of program		
Social insurance	(medical care)	Employees' Health Insurance
		Day Laborers' Health Insurance
		Seamen's Insurance
		National Public Service MAA Insurance
		Local Public Service MAA Insurance
		Public Corporation Staffs MAA Insurance
		Private School Teachers and Employees MAA Insurance
		Staffs of Agriculture, Forestry, and Fisheries Institutions MAA Insurance
		National Health Insurance
Social welfare (Aid to fatherless families, the mentally or physically handicapped, and the aged)	(pensions)	Employees' Pension Insurance
Public assistance (Aid to low-income earners)		Seamen's Insurance
		National Public Service MAA Pensions
Public health and medical care (Garbage disposal services, sewerage, public health services)		Local Public Service MAA Pensions
		Public Corporation Staffs MAA Pensions
Children's allowance (For children under 15; paid to families with income below a specified ceiling and having three or more children)		Private School Teachers and Employees MAA Pensions
		Staffs of Agriculture, Forestry and Fisheries Institutions MAA Pensions
Environmental policies (Pollution prevention and environmental protection programs)		National Pension Insurance (includes self-employed)
Onkyū (pensions) (For World War II and national government employees who retired before the establishment of MAA)	(accident insurance)	Workmen's Compensation Insurance
		Seamen's Insurance
Assistance for war disabled	(unemployment insurance)	Employment Insurance
		Seamen's Insurance

MAA: Mutual Aid Association
⬚ scheme of social insurance
SOURCE: Ministry of Health and Welfare, *Social Welfare Services in Japan* (1979). Social Insurance Agency, *Outline of Social Insurance in Japan* (1978).

It was only after World War II that more serious consideration was given to social security programs. Faced with famine and escalating inflation and prompted by the presence of the OCCUPATION forces and insurgent labor movements, the LIVELIHOOD PROTECTION LAW to provide support for the needy was passed in 1946. Although relief was on a low scale, it nevertheless placed poor relief in the realm of the government's responsibility. With the passing of two new laws in 1947—the Unemployment Insurance Law and the Workmen's Compensation Insurance Law—the four areas of social insurance were covered, namely, medical care, pensions, accident insurance, and unemployment insurance. However, coverage was still not extended to the entire working populace, as workers in small enterprises were excluded.

In 1950 the Social Security System Deliberation Committee, established the previous year, submitted the recommendation that the government take measures to ensure that every Japanese be able to lead a life worthy of a civilized society. Because of confusion resulting from the existence of several systems of relief and financial complications within each area, especially in medical care, it failed to increase the amount of cash benefits substantially. Still, the extent of medical care coverage was enlarged, and the establishment of the New National Health Insurance Law of 1958 made medical care accessible to all people, at least in principle.

In subsequent years there was a call for complete adjustment of the various systems and drastic revision of medical insurance. The latter issue is becoming increasingly urgent as Japan faces the task of having to cope with a rapidly aging population. This factor has, in turn, diverted attention from medical care to the problem of pensions, a serious financial question especially in view of the fact that pension is pegged to the rate of inflation.

The present social security system is extremely complicated. It consists of several categories, namely, social insurance, children's allowance, public assistance, social welfare, public health and medical care, environmental policies, pensions, and assistance for war victims (see table). One characteristic of its diversified structure is that the organs controlling the system range from departments of the central government to sectors of local autonomous bodies. A case in point is medical care insurance and pension insurance, both governed by the type and locality of employment. In addition, gaps exist between the differing systems regarding supply and demand, types of benefits, standard rate of benefits, and the financing of the systems. A second characteristic is the broad extent of coverage

extended to the insured; in particular, medical care insurance is extended to almost all citizens. This application ratio has been further reinforced with the institution of children's allowance in 1972. A third characteristic is the low benefit rate, not only as compared to wages but also as a ratio of social security expenditure to national income. The most important task in the future is the problem of raising the rate of social security benefits when the Japanese economy is expected to enter a slow-growth period. See also SOCIAL WELFARE; PENSIONS.

——Kenkō Hoken Kumiai Rengōkai, ed, *Shakai hoshō nenkan* (annual, 1951–). Niwata Noriaki, *Shakai hoshō ron* (1973). Shakai Hoshō Kenkyūjo, ed, *Sengo no shakai hoshō* (1968).

NIWATA Noriaki

social welfare

(shakai fukushi). The development of social welfare in Japan may be seen as a response to the social problems resulting from industrialization and the breakdown of traditional supports. This process has been fundamentally similar to that in the West, although the Japanese industrial revolution came later and traditional social patterns have perhaps been more resilient.

Early Development —— The beginnings of modern social welfare came with the very start of modern government in the Meiji period (1868–1912). Development of a Western-style army was an early priority of the Meiji oligarchy, and a system of disability and retirement allowances was provided as early as 1871; similar benefits were extended to the navy in 1875, the police in 1882, and civilian officials in 1884. Aid for the general public did not come as quickly. The Poor Relief Regulation of 1874, a reaction to popular unrest, was little more than a codification of traditional (religious, family, neighborhood, or village) practices with modest national government support. A proposal by the Home Ministry to expand this system was rejected by the first Diet in 1890 on grounds that it would encourage indolence, and in fact the responsibility for public relief was turned back to local governments in 1912. A few institutions for needy children, the handicapped, and the aged developed during the Meiji period, but the initiative for these came first from Christian missionaries and then Buddhist organizations. Small government subsidies were granted only in 1909. One also notes an interest in urban poverty and slum clearance on the part of city governments from the late 1880s.

Industrialization——It was the acceleration of industrialization in the 20th century which brought real development. The plight of factory workers led to public concern and attempts at organization; one result was the establishment of mutual aid associations (kyōsai kumiai) in governmental and private corporations, based on German models, providing accident and illness compensation (and later, pensions) to members. In 1905 and 1911 came legislation requiring owners of mines and factories to compensate workers for injuries, illness, or death on the job. The first true social security legislation was the Health Insurance Law of 1922 (implemented in 1927), which came to provide medical care and cash benefits to employees except agricultural and domestic workers and those working in very small establishments. Then, in 1938 the National Health Insurance system was established to cover the rest of the population. An important motive for these measures was to ensure a healthy supply of manpower for industry and, later, for the rapidly expanding military. By the late 1930s, in fact, even most relief for the poor was going to families of soldiers, to support the war effort. Japan's first general pension program (Employees' Pension Insurance) was established in 1941, less for welfare purposes than to mobilize employers' and workers' contributions into a government-controlled capital fund for war industry.

Although modern social welfare was hardly well established before the war, the ideals of TAISHŌ DEMOCRACY combined with the need to cope with economic cycles and other new phenomena of industrial society had changed fundamental assumptions about the government's responsibility for its citizens' well-being. Social work achieved status as a legitimate activity, and the Social and Labor Affairs Bureau of the Home Ministry, created in 1920, became a source of social research and reform proposals (in 1938 it became part of the newly organized Ministry of Health and Welfare). It is notable that the semivolunteer welfare commissioners (minsei iin), organized by local governments around the time of the 1918 rice riots as a means of controlling as well as aiding the poor, had by 1929 come to spearhead the campaign to pass (and implement in 1932) the Poor Relief Law, which once again gave the national government a role in both home and institutional relief. Laws for the prevention of cruelty to children (1933) and for assistance to mothers (1937), and the Social Work Law (1938) covering management of various social welfare programs, did prepare the ground, in however piecemeal a fashion, for the major reforms of the postwar Occupation.

Postwar Period——The accomplishments of the Allied OCCUPATION in social welfare were threefold. First, the daily necessities of life were secured for the war-devastated population, which included millions of demobilized soldiers and repatriated civilians. Second, a new legal and philosophical basis for welfare was established, beginning with article 25 of the new constitution: "All people shall have the right to maintain the minimum standards of wholesome and cultured living. In all spheres of life, the State shall use its endeavors for the promotion and extension of social welfare and security, and of public health." Third, the administration of social welfare and many specific programs was extensively reformed. The most significant change was in public assistance, for which eligibility would depend on financial need rather than the character of the applicant or his reasons for being poor. New forms of social services for children and others were developed. American reformers also encouraged the growth of professionalism among social workers by instituting schools of social work, in-service training, and field supervision.

From the end of the Occupation to the 1960s, much of the structure of a modern social welfare system was being built, but benefit and service levels remained quite low by Western standards. As late as 1970–71, according to an International Labor Organization survey, only 5.7 percent of Japanese gross domestic product was devoted to social welfare (broadly defined), compared with 10.7 percent in the United States, 14 percent in Great Britain, and 20.6 percent in Sweden. During this period the implicit philosophy of the ruling Liberal Democratic Party was that living standards of all in society should be raised by encouraging rapid economic growth. It was beginning in the early 1970s that Japan moved toward the achievement of a welfare system comparable in many respects to those of other advanced nations. These developments may be examined in the categories of income maintenance, welfare for the aged, other welfare services, and social administration.

Income Maintenance——Cash payments to those temporarily or permanently dependent are of two types, insurance and welfare, depending on the extent benefits are related to individual contributions; most public insurance programs include some welfare compo-

nents. All Japanese are covered in principle by some form of pension insurance, providing old age, disability, and survivor benefits. The Employees' Pension Insurance program (Kōsei Nenkin, literally "welfare pension") was established in 1941 but substantially revised in 1954; it covers most employees in firms of five or more workers and is supported by equal employer and employee contributions proportionate to wages, plus some government subsidy. About 25 million were enrolled in 1980. National Pension Insurance (Kokumin Nenkin) was established in 1959; it is based on individual contributions at a flat rate plus a large public subsidy and covers over 27.8 million people not enrolled in other plans. About six million teachers and public employees are enrolled instead in several mutual aid associations (kyōsai kumiai), generally offering higher benefits, and about 5.7 million of those covered by the Employees' Pension receive additional benefits from Employees' Pension funds, established by firms with over 1,000 workers. Many needy Japanese have not participated in any of these contributory pension plans for long enough to be eligible for benefits and accordingly are granted means-tested Welfare Pensions (Fukushi Nenkin) under the National Pension. Finally, a declining number of Japanese (under three million) receive pensions (onkyū) based on their pre-1945 service or sacrifice.

Japanese pension benefits were extremely low by international standards until the early 1970s, when in many cases they were tripled or better. Mutual aid association and Employees' Pension average benefits came to approximate the international standard of 40–45 percent of average wage levels, but unfortunately fewer than one-fourth of recipients were covered by such generous plans. Payments under the National Pension, which will not provide full benefits for most until the system matures in 1984, are considerably lower. All contributory pensions are now indexed to consumer prices, and Employees' Pension benefits have also been linked to changes in wage levels.

Public assistance (seikatsu hogo, literally "livelihood protection") supplements income up to a minimum level. It goes to about 1.2 percent of the population, including disproportionate numbers of the aged, fatherless families and families with a handicapped member. Benefits are determined by a complicated formula which takes into account regional variation in living costs; age composition of the household; and necessary living, educational, housing, medical, maternity, vocational, and funeral expenses. Total benefits to a young family of four in Tōkyō in 1980 were over ¥150,000 (almost US $700) a month. Payment levels are revised upward each year in conformity with the principle (established in 1965) that the gap in consumer spending between recipient and ordinary households should be narrowed.

Public assistance is not particularly controversial in Japan, and poverty as such has not been perceived as a major social problem for many years. However, many have called for reform of social insurance, particularly for unification of the various programs to assure equal benefits and more rational administration. Since large firms, labor unions and many other interests benefit from the present system, radical change is unlikely. And even though all the pension programs currently produce large surpluses (which, as reserves, are invested by the government), there is concern in Japan as elsewhere for the future financial health of the system, because of the rapidly aging population.

Welfare for the Aged——Japan has had less need for public welfare programs for old people than other advanced nations, for two reasons: first, the proportion of the elderly in its population is low, and second, an astonishingly large number of the aged live with their children (some 70 percent of those over 65, against less than one-quarter in the West) and accordingly require less outside help. Nonetheless, in recent years the plight of the elderly has received much public attention. This concern is due in part to an impending demographic shift—the over-65 population is expected to go from under 9.1 percent in 1980 to over 13 percent in 1995—and in part to a belief that the traditional family system may be changing, so that more old people will be on their own, or at least that their children will not be willing to bear as many burdens as in the past.

The evolution of government policy for the aged has been shaped by these changing perceptions. In the early postwar period the emphasis was on homes (yōrōin) for the needy aged, particularly those without other recourse because their sons had been lost in the war. The Law for the Welfare of the Aged (Rōjin Fukushi Hō) of 1963, which guaranteed "a wholesome and peaceful life" to "those who have for many years contributed to the development of society" signaled a new direction. Old people's homes (now called yōgo rōjin hōmu) were removed from the public assistance framework and eligibility requirements were loosened. New categories of institutions were developed: nursing homes (tokubetsu yōgo rōjin hōmu, literally "special old people's homes") for the bedridden, and moderate fee homes (keihi rōjin hōmu) to provide sheltered housing for healthy old people with some means. New services were provided for noninstitutionalized old people, including a free annual health examination, a system of home helpers, and local welfare centers for the aged (rōjin fukushi sentā) to offer educational and recreation programs. The law also designated 15 September each year as Respect for the Aged Day (Keirō no Hi) and provided a small government subsidy for old people's clubs (rōjin kurabu)—in 1980, about half the elderly population was enrolled in over 120,000 such clubs, which meet at least once a month.

After a period of moderate growth in the 1960s, the early 1970s saw a spurt in new programs and in spending for the aged. In some cases, an innovation developed in a city run by progressive politicians would later be picked up by the conservative central government. The most notable example is payment of medical expenses (those not covered by health insurance) for the elderly, which was adopted by Tōkyō in 1969 and then nationally in 1973. Even today Tōkyō and other local governments may supplement the national program, as by extending coverage to those over 65 instead of 70 or eliminating the already rather liberal income ceiling. This free medical care program has continued to be controversial because of its heavy expense.

Japanese old people do face some distinctive problems. One is employment: the normal retirement age is well under age 60, which is when the Employees' Pension begins (the National Pension starts at 65 and the small welfare pension for the aged [rōrei fukushi nenkin] at 70), and even when receiving a pension many old people wish to work for economic and other reasons. The government has pushed successfully for higher retirement ages; developed services for job training, counseling, and referral; and even subsidizes companies which provide more jobs for the elderly; but the need well exceeds available employment. Given the declining proportion of working-age population in Japan, the government may be forced into a frontal attack on the traditional retirement system. Another problem is the relatively large number of bedridden or frail elderly living at home. Many localities have come up with imaginative and helpful programs, such as washing and drying of bedding, free diaper services, and even portable bathtubs and water heaters carried in vans to provide a once-a-month bath for those unable to bathe normally. However, very few areas provide the necessary visiting doctors and nurses, day-care centers or day hospitals, and short-stay facilities in homes. Financial allowances are also far from adequate to relieve the substantial difficulties faced by the bedridden and their families.

Other Welfare Services —— American Occupation officials were particularly concerned with the hardships of children whose lives had been disrupted by the war. The Children's Welfare Law (Jidō Fukushi Hō) of 1947 established the government's responsibility to protect children in need, through institutional or foster care, and to encourage a healthy and secure family life for children in general through counseling, public health, nutrition, recreation, and day-care programs. In recent years, one of the most popular programs in the social welfare field has been day-care centers (hoikujo), providing custodial care and education as well for preschool children. Strong demand has increased their number to 21,960, serving 2.1 million children (1980), and pressures continue for more facilities, lower fees, and longer hours. Recent years have also brought demands for playgrounds, which remain in short supply. In 1972 a children's allowance (jidō teate) was initiated for families with incomes under a liberal ceiling. In 1980 the allowance was ¥5,000 per month for each child after the second; it went to 2.8 million children.

The problems of the handicapped—particularly the mentally retarded—are perhaps the hardest to cope with in any society, and are especially difficult in Japan because of the persistence of traditional stigmas. Governmental programs include pensions, institutional care of various kinds, rehabilitation (although physical and occupational therapists are extremely scarce), special education, and cash allowances for families bringing up a handicapped child. Vocational training and sheltered workshops are provided for the older handicapped, as is assistance in getting started in such traditional occupations as masseur or proprietor of a tobacco stand. A law passed in 1960 made employment of a small percentage of handicapped workers mandatory for large firms. However, in terms of both popular attitudes and governmental programs, many experts consider aid for the handicapped the most undeveloped field in Japanese welfare.

Other categories of needy people have also been identified as eligible for aid. Widows with children receive financial and vocational help and counseling. "Borderline" families not quite eligible for public assistance are offered small business loans and piecework jobs at home or in workshops; lodging and some other facilities are provided for "day laborers" and inhabitants of metropolitan skid rows. BURAKUMIN villages, urban slums, and underpopulated rural areas are given preferential treatment in establishing public facilities. The government subsidizes consumer cooperatives for buying foodstuffs and insurance and provides loans and other aid to survivors of natural disasters. Specialists hope that as the social insurance system approaches maturity, the need for such fragmented social welfare measures will disappear.

Social Administration —— Most of the activities mentioned here are administered by the Ministry of Health and Welfare (Kōseishō), though the Ministries of Labor and of Education and many other agencies also have important social welfare functions. Within the Welfare Ministry, the Social Affairs, Children and Families, and Pension Bureaus are responsible for planning and high-level supervision, and the Social Insurance Agency handles administrative details of several pension plans. However, as is common in Japanese public administration, execution is mostly left to local governments rather than to branches of the central government: prefectural governments have bureaus covering health, welfare, and (often) labor matters; city, town, and village governments have sections with similar functions. In addition, there are welfare offices (fukushi jimusho) at the city and district level that are responsible for administration of public assistance and other welfare activities. Depending on size, their staffs may include caseworkers specializing in aiding the elderly, handicapped, and mentally retarded.

Volunteer agencies are not as well developed as in many Western countries—a matter of concern to Japanese specialists—but many private or quasi-public organizations play important roles. The Community Chest supports various local and national voluntary activities with annual fundraising campaigns. Social welfare councils (shakai fukushi kyōgikai), with mixed public and private membership, coordinate welfare activities at the local level and provide social services (home helpers, emergency loans, counseling) under contract with local governments. The prefectural and national level councils sponsor training sessions, disseminate information and are effective pressure groups for public welfare. A majority of welfare institutions—old people's homes, orphanages, and so forth—are owned and operated by social welfare corporations (shakai fukushi hōjin), which are nonprofit voluntary agencies regulated and financed by government.

A characteristic of Japanese social administration is a relative lack of influence by professional social work, in two senses: that social work education is dominated by the rather theoretical academic field of social welfare, and that many workers have not received even that degree of specialized training. Many important jobs are occupied by nonspecialist bureaucrats or retired bureaucrats. Much casework investigation, counseling, information and referral, and general social monitoring is carried out by the 160,000 semivolunteer welfare commissioners (minsei iin), who are designated by the welfare minister on local nomination. Commissioners are responsible for needy residents in their own neighborhoods, within which they are likely to be people of some social standing.

Prospects —— The Japanese social welfare system is nearing maturity and is drawing increased public attention. Debate in academic and official circles centers on classic welfare questions. Should services be universal or selective; should they go to all at high cost, or be concentrated on the most needy, requiring means testing? Should relatives of the needy be held responsible for their support? Should social services be free or should the "beneficiary principle" that recipients carry a portion of the costs (perhaps scaled to income) be applied? Should localities have the option of providing better services or should availability be equalized across the country? Today, the philosophy of welfare in Japan is quite eclectic, with programs at either extreme and in the middle of each of these dimensions. More generally, many worry about the fundamental problem of whether social welfare contradicts traditional Japanese values—particularly family values—and if so, is it the traditional or the modern road which should be chosen? This question became particularly acute when slower economic growth led to concerns about "big government." Echoing a theme heard in many variations since the Meiji period, many specialists today seek a Japanese-style welfare system to provide the benefits of the welfare state while still preserving the essence of the Japanese way.

🔲 ——Masayoshi Chūbachi and Kōji Taira, "Poverty in Modern Japan," in Hugh Patrick, ed, *Japanese Industrialization and its Social Consequences* (1976). Kagoyama Takashi, ed, *Shakai hoshō no kindaika* (1967). Kondō Bunji, *Nihon no shakai hoshō no rekishi* (1974). Shakai Hoshō Kenkyūjo, ed, *Gendai no fukushi seisaku* (1975). See also in English the Ministry of Health and Welfare's occasional publications, *Social Welfare Services in Japan* and *Outline of Social Insurance in Japan*. Useful annuals in Japanese are *Kōsei hakusho, Kokumin no fukushi no dōkō*, and *Hoken to nenkin no dōkō*.

John Creighton CAMPBELL

society

Japan today is one of the most industrially advanced societies of the world, highly urbanized, and reliant on advanced technology and communications. It is a society characterized by intricate forms of organized interdependency among highly specialized and differentiated social institutions. The web of interdependence extends throughout most of the world, as the postwar Japanese economy has been built on the assumption that free, stable, and growing international trade will provide the natural resources crucial to the nation's economy. Once the most culturally isolated of countries, Japan is now thoroughly integrated into the international sphere.

Japan has experienced a great deal of social change in the past century. Some of this change has come about in the course of industrialization and closely resembles the experience of other industrialized nations. Other elements of change have been unique, such as the dramatic transformation after the end of NATIONAL SECLUSION in 1853 and the rapid reform of the nation's basic institutions after defeat in World War II. Elements of tradition have mixed with modernization to produce a nation that shares a great deal with the rest of the modern world at the same time that it retains its own particular character.

Key Legacies of the Past——Traditional patterns of social relations and social ethics remain a significant part of the contemporary picture. These are best exemplified by the traditional household, village society, and Confucian morality.

Among farmers, warriors, and merchants, the household (IE) was the elemental form of social organization in the premodern period. Every individual understood his or her place in life first as a member of an immediate household. The extended family and primogeniture created an ancestral line, and ANCESTOR WORSHIP was in fact the worship of the household itself and its morality. All members shared resources, a common social identity, and responsibility for the enterprise upon which the existence of the household depended. To be a member was to be part of a highly interdependent group.

The internal organization of the household was based on a status hierarchy and a clear division of labor. Age seniority and male superiority were the two basic principles establishing rank. As the group was built upon the spirit of cooperative unity, however, adult members were often given a voice in decision making. The formal autocracy, in other words, was typically balanced by an informal democracy of joint discussion and consensus. See also KINSHIP.

The *ie* was also the basis for the organization of the traditional business enterprise. As enterprises grew, households expanded by adding outsiders to the business "family" through such practices as fictive kinship. Apprentices in the larger establishments worked their way slowly up the ranks to positions of responsibility, all the while being cared for in the style of a household servant-member. Several of the great commercial households of the premodern era, including the MITSUI and the SUMITOMO, survived and evolved into the most powerful ZAIBATSU of the modern era.

Agricultural villages, the economic backbone of premodern society, were characterized by considerable autonomy of internal affairs, but strict subordination to higher authority in such matters as taxation. Many common economic interests from irrigation to joint ownership of forests and communal labor activities fostered strong tendencies toward village solidarity, as did the common worship of local deities (UJIGAMI). Between villages, competition and hostility were strong, resulting in an "in-group" psychology for each village.

The internal structure of villages was characterized by a leadership hierarchy based on age, wealth, kinship, and length of household residence. Decision making, however, involved most or all households and followed a process aimed at consensus. Within this general framework, there was much variation and in some cases the ideals of cooperation and mutuality were far from realized. Conflicts occurred within the limits of a social framework that strongly discouraged schism, so interdependent were households. Compromise and accommodation to group norms were notable characteristics of village life.

The traditional household and village thus shared common characteristics of social solidarity based on common practical interests. Each had a particular religious focus, each was corporate in significant ways, and each combined the notion of participation in decision making with that of a status hierarchy and formal authority.

The morality of CONFUCIANISM was a further ingredient inherited from premodern days that shaped the natural evolution of modern institutions. It reinforced the heritage of practice in households and villages, but rather than being an outgrowth of everyday relationships, it was spread first as an official ideology. At the heart of the Confucian perspective was the notion of society as an ordering of different but interdependent roles and statuses. If each part followed its prescribed duties properly, the whole system would work well and all would prosper. The virtuous individual was one who was scrupulous in observing the duties and behavior proper to his or her social place. The family served as a model of this, with each generation and each sex having a distinct place. Morality centered on relationships, particularly the parent-child relationship, rather than on individual conscience or abstract principles. As in the family, Confucianism considered hierarchy the natural product of age and experience. Relationships were seen as reciprocal in nature, with nurturance and guidance from above being returned through obedience, loyalty, and eventually support from below. When both parties were sincere in their devotions to the other, relationships would be most fruitful and satisfying. Finally, Confucianism, as it was interpreted in Japan, permitted an extension by analogy of ideal family relationships to virtually any social situation. Familism, PATERNALISM, and LOYALTY became three dominant values of society in general. The EMPEROR was later to be seen as the father of the family comprising all Japanese (KAZOKU KOKKA), and contractual relationships such as that between employer and employee could be understood in the Confucian perspective as analogous to the parent-child bond. Note just how distant this conception is from the utilitarian philosophy popular at the time modern European and American society was being formed.

Social History, 1868–1945——The past century has been one of enormous change and modern development. No society in the world has experienced a higher rate of economic expansion than Japan. Within the span of less than one hundred years the country also experienced two great political upheavals, each dramatically altering the traditional social landscape.

The first moment of great change came in the years after the MEIJI RESTORATION of 1868, when the institutions of the Edo period (1600–1868) were replaced with a modern state dedicated to building an industrial nation. The sweeping changes were not created by a popular revolution, nor were they inspired by democratic or egalitarian ideals. Rather, the *samurai* who overthrew the Tokugawa government sought to restore the emperor to a central place in the life of the nation. The ideal was one of returning to the past. After consolidating power in a central government that they dominated, however, these ambitious men began to create a wholly new society based on modern institutions that they observed to be successful in Europe and America. By the turn of the century, a whole new social order had arisen as modern industries, public education, private stock companies, mass transportation, banks, national taxation, a conscripted military, and a host of other institutions replaced a less integrated, Confucian-inspired feudal order.

Much of the creative effort and the nurturance for the new institutions came directly from the government, the largest, most confident, and richest institution at the time. Private banks, for example, were largely founded with government bonds. Experiments in building heavy industry were initiated by the government and later sold to private entrepreneurs at low prices. Contracts for military procurement, for postal services and the like were often the most lucrative undertakings of private businesses. The process of generating a strong, modern society centered on cooperation between government and private businesses.

The bureaucrats' goal from the beginning was a powerful, independent Japan, one that could survive foreign imperialism and commercial pressure. No adversary relationship between government and large private interests developed. Rather, government policy favored large industries but put a heavy tax burden on farmers. This was an approach to economic development that left agriculture and consumers paying the price for industrial growth. An ideology of NATIONALISM that finally reached its apocalyptic peak in World War II served to legitimize this effort and the power of the BUREAU-CRACY that effected it.

The new social system matured as the nation entered the 20th century. Prominent among the new institutions were *zaibatsu*, or industrial and financial combines, comprised of many companies owned by a central holding company. Having purchased factories from the government and possessing considerable financial, managerial, and commercial strength, some older commercial houses and a few new dynamic enterprise groupings became innovative centers for much further industrial development. The gap between small and large enterprises widened progressively as intensive capitalization, foreign technology, skilled leadership, and government encouragement combined to create a few highly efficient enterprises that far outperformed the great multitude of small firms. The larger companies developed complex subcontracting networks utilizing the lower wage costs of smaller firms, while, to keep their own skilled labor, they gradually instituted SENIORITY SYSTEM and COMPANY WELFARE SYSTEM. The skilled elite of the laboring class thus came to be included in the benefits of a system of lifetime employment originally reserved for the managerial class. Productivity, working conditions, pay, and much else became differentiated according to the scale of the enterprise. A dual structure emerged in the economy, in which thousands of small, inefficient manufacturers paying low wages existed alongside internationally competitive industrial giants.

Occupation and Postwar Changes —— A second revolution came with defeat in World War II. Again change was the work of higher authority, this time the foreign OCCUPATION forces. The Americans who indirectly ruled Japan for nearly seven years intended to root out the social causes of prewar nationalism and to create a new, democratic Japan using an American blueprint. The centrality and power of the military was erased. Agricultural landholding was equalized. The public school system was strengthened and reorganized to offer equal opportunity to all students through the ninth grade. Trade unions were encouraged, and almost overnight millions of Japanese joined unions at their companies and offices. The prewar *zaibatsu* holding companies were abolished and ownership of *zaibatsu* companies was more widely distributed. Together with the great destruction and confiscation of property during the war, this resulted in a significant reduction in the gap between rich and poor. Women were made legally equal to men. Individuals, not households, became the legal units of society. The new CONSTITUTION made the emperor and what had been the imperial bureaucracy subordinate to the will of the people as expressed through their elected representatives. Leftist political parties were legalized, and universal suffrage instituted. Such basic structural and institutional changes were accompanied by a tremendous surge in popularity of all things Western.

Japanese social structure today is not simply a reflection of the Occupation blueprint, however. The democratic ideals of contemporary public culture have been in uneasy truce with more traditional values. Only by considering present Japanese society in greater detail can the historical legacy be appreciated in its complexity.

Urbanization and Rural Society —— POPULATION densities in urban areas are among the highest in the world, and urban sprawl extends to the very base of the mountains in many parts of the country. Three-quarters of the 112 million Japanese (1975) live in cities of 30,000 or more. The vast majority work in offices, factories, and shops. Millions commute from apartments, condominiums, and suburban homes in a daily mass scramble made possible by an intricate system of public transport. Fewer than one in ten households is now actively involved in agriculture. Even the small family farm, which dominates Japanese agriculture, is highly mechanized and oriented to commercial markets. A majority of farmers now work at second jobs in the modern sector. They too have become commuters.

Fishing and agriculture, once pillars of Japanese society, now play relatively minor roles in the overall economy. Both now center on complex national markets that are much affected by government policies, price supports, and import policies. Farmers must be businessmen, and like others they have learned to play interest-group politics to gain economic advantages. The central agency relating the village and the larger society today is the AGRICULTURAL COOP-ERATIVE ASSOCIATIONS. These associations serve as a sales and purchasing agent, savings and loan banker, agricultural extension agent, and community organizer throughout rural Japan. The cooperatives' national headquarters is also an active lobbyist and an important force for protectionist trade policies favoring farmers.

There is no significant difference between the standard of living of villagers and city dwellers today. Prosperity has brought consumerism to the villages. Farmers also save significant amounts of money, which the national cooperative invests largely in urban commercial schemes. Despite such progress the attraction of the city for young people is strong; young women in particular do not want to marry farmers as it has traditionally meant heavy work and burdensome family obligations. In response to these new social problems, many villages have come up with remarkable social innovations such as special apartment buildings for young newlyweds. The entry of small factories into the countryside has also changed patterns of living and social relations.

Rapid social change has now, however, reduced the significance of many older social ties. The importance of patrilineal kinship between main and branch households (establishing hierarchical groups known as *dōzoku*), as well as lateral relationships among in-laws and neighbors, has been weakened in economic terms, but patrilineal kinship continues to be important in other respects. Some hamlets remain more hierarchical and tightly structured than others. In general, local interests are being superseded by more distant ones, as the necessity for local cooperation diminishes and national and international forces make established patterns antiquated. The cooperative's significance lies in its position as a broker between localities and national forces. The postwar land reform and the increase in alternative sources of income for farmers combined to promote much greater equality of income in village society and thus has meant less hierarchical authority.

The most persistent ideal is that of hamlet solidarity. For centuries all households had to face crises together and this trait, learned under conditions no longer very significant, remains. Block voting in politics is one expression of this sentiment. In religious matters, too, there are powerful forces at work for conformity.

Marriage and Family —— In prewar days the typical MARRIAGE was arranged by parents. Prospective partners met perhaps once or twice and had, at most, some veto power over the arrangement. Today such marriages are not rare, but the dominant pattern is to marry by personal choice after courtship. Arrangements now are more flexible, and formal introductions can lead to romantic courtships. The rather elaborate traditional pattern is found primarily among the upper class or in cases where the two people have passed the proper age for marriage without finding a suitable partner. The average age at marriage remains high, 25 for women and 28 for men. Couples almost universally have small families for many reasons, including the housing shortage, the late age of marriage, the availability of abortion, and a general inclination to plan families carefully so as to preserve a middle-class lifestyle. See also FAMILY PLANNING.

Relationships between husbands and wives show a strong tendency to role separation, with the man away from home for long hours and the woman taking exclusive responsibility for home and children. The occasional efforts to adjust this pattern toward the American husband-wife centered family model have not led to basic changes. DIVORCE, though slightly on the rise in recent years, is quite low by Western standards, and the general stability of the family is a notable quality of Japanese society and an important ingredient in its overall stability. Japanese mothers are conscientious in child rearing, and the child is permitted considerable emotional license when of preschool age. Upon entering school, however, a much more disciplined regime begins. Parents look to schools to impose such discipline. See also FAMILY; YOUTH; LIFE CYCLE; CHILDHOOD AND CHILD REARING.

The notion of the household as an intergenerational corporate entity retains significance only in the case of family businesses and farms. Families with fame or fortune to preserve also are concerned with continuity, but in general, modern employment and urban living have severed all but personal ties with parents, once the children are grown.

Due to the shift from agriculture to wage employment, the inheritance of land is no longer significant to most Japanese and primogeniture is quite limited. Now the most significant contribution of parents to the children's future is to assist them in education. Most middle-class parents invest heavily in private tutoring, in lessons in the arts, and in other educational aids. Mothers spend much time helping with homework and worrying about grades. Over 70 percent of all elementary school children take music or other private art lessons. Saving to pay for college and to buy one's own house are the two major financial goals of parents. See also CONSUMPTION AND SAVING BEHAVIOR.

Education——— Japan has an elaborate and advanced educational system, one that presently produces the highest percentage of high school graduates in the world. Japan is second only to the United States in the percentage of its young going on to higher education, and a larger percentage of males obtain bachelors' degrees in Japan than anywhere else.

The government has always recognized the importance of having a highly educated populace, and the centrality of education to social status and income has produced a strong popular demand to match. Japan's system is meritocratic. Education is the central source of social mobility, and competition to get ahead, especially to do well on university ENTRANCE EXAMINATIONS, is intense. As a result, Japanese educational accomplishments are very high by international standards; in science and math, for example, Japanese eighth graders test highest in the world.

In 1977, 30 percent of all Japanese high school graduates went straight on to higher education, 48 percent took jobs, and nearly 20 percent (mostly males) continued studying on their own in hopes of doing better in the next year's entrance examinations. Only 8 percent of all ninth graders today do not go on to high school (which is not compulsory), and high schools have but a 2 percent dropout rate.

Since the capacity of UNIVERSITIES AND COLLEGES has not expanded any more rapidly than the increase in applicants, each year over 100,000 disappointed aspirants resign themselves to trying again, especially for the top universities. Competition ratios for particular universities run from an average of about 4 to 1 to extremes of 75 to 1. Entrance-exam pressure is naturally felt at the secondary school level, and education there is primarily geared to the task of preparing students for these examinations.

Children are throughly drilled to do careful work. Teachers also place great emphasis on training students to exhibit cooperative behavior, group discipline, and mutual empathy. The emphasis on socially ordered conduct rather than individualism or freedom lays a sound basis for good behavior at higher levels of the school system. Children clean their classrooms and their schools regularly and do many other socially significant tasks. Because students are kept together when learning to read, ability levels among elementary school children do not differ widely. Teachers in Japan have little difficulty handling larger numbers of students than are usual in the United States.

Teaching in high schools is highly formalized. Large classes (averaging around 45 in public schools and even more in private schools), nationally standardized textbooks, a lecture approach, little independent work or writing on the part of students, frequent tests, and a somewhat longer school year are features of the Japanese system (see EDUCATION).

Japanese student peer-group culture is limited. Except for after-school sports and school club activities, Japanese high school students do very little in groups. Study and a close friend or two dominate their private lives. Dating is still infrequent, and students typically spend much more time at home than do American teenagers. Part-time work and summer jobs are not common.

The intensity of exam competition has created numerous educational problems: rote learning of large quantities of detail, little opportunity for self-expression, too little time for nonacademic pursuits, and too much parental pressure are all widely appreciated faults of the system. Thousands of private-tutoring and CRAM SCHOOLS fuel competition by offering to provide their student clients with some advantage when exam time comes. Fully one-third of all middle-school students (more than half in Tōkyō) commute to these schools (JUKU) after their regular classes several days a week.

Upon finally entering a university, then, it is no wonder that students neglect serious study for the first two years. They tend to experiment with freedom and the temptations of the big city, with radical politics and French literature, with boy-girl relations and American-style leisure. College is a kind of hiatus between the heavy challenges of entrance exam preparations and the equally taxing early years of employment.

A highly educated population forms the basis for other general characteristics of Japanese society today. MASS COMMUNICATIONS are highly developed; the rate of newspaper readership per capita, for example, is among the highest in the world. The average Japanese is better informed and more internationally aware than the average American. Child mortality, the birthrate, divorce, and CRIME rates are all low by international standards, and, while education is but a factor in these matters, it remains that Japanese society, despite being crowded, busy, and rapidly changing, is remarkably orderly and stable. Lives are lived with a degree of care and circumspection that some observers find prejudicial to the growth of individualism and others consider worthy of international emulation.

Government and Business——— Japan has a capitalist economic system and a democratic form of government. These are appropriate labels, but there are subtle differences between Japan and other societies categorized in the same way. Business and industrial enterprises do operate quite independently from government control most of the time, and citizens exercise much economic free choice. On the other hand, Japanese capitalism has relatively few individual capitalists, and financial power is centered in the great banks and conglomerates. Businesses run largely on money borrowed from banks, and both debt levels and bank loan levels are high (see CORPORATE FINANCE). Behind this seemingly fragile arrangement stands the guarantee of a government anxious for economic stability and growth.

DEMOCRACY also works differently in Japan from the stereotypic ideal. The opposition parties (including the JAPAN SOCIALIST PARTY, JAPAN COMMUNIST PARTY, and the DEMOCRATIC SOCIALIST PARTY) have not succeeded in ousting the ruling LIBERAL DEMOCRATIC PARTY (LDP) from power in over 25 years. It is a "one-and-a-half party system." Nor are the leading parties built upon grass-roots bases. Rather, they are expressions in the political arena of large, well-organized interest groups. Government and business coordinate closely in a number of areas including technological development, financial policy, the management of foreign investment in Japan, and the promotion of Japanese international business interests. The national bureaucracy, small in numbers but led by a recognized elite that is largely immune to the debilitating practices of graft and patronage, plays a leading role in both generating official policies and mediating conflicting interests. Its traditional power, ironically, was reinforced during the Occupation as it exercised the power and prerogatives of Japan's American rulers, for it was Japanese bureaucrats who executed American directives. With the pre-war military taken out of the picture, the civil bureaucracy was boosted to a central role in government that it has retained.

By initially encouraging unions and leftist parties to develop and eliminating the imperial institution and the military as fulcrums of power, the Americans intended to create a two-party democracy or something resembling it. What resulted was a permanent opposition deeply rooted in the union movement and supported by urban intellectual culture. Its socialist ideology fit its stance as an opposition, but has limited its ability to achieve majority support. In order to challenge the ruling party and the remnants of the prewar establishment, the opposition has sometimes adopted tactics of confrontation, and its more radical elements prefer open conflict to compromise. The postwar establishment, centering on the LDP, for its part has tried to undermine this opposition through legislation and government power. Business interests, farmers, older voters, and others give the ruling party a regular majority of seats in the Diet and thus a legitimate monopoly of central power. Because ideology and basic economic interests are involved, the relationship between the LDP and the opposition parties is one that reflects some of the most fundamental divisions and contradictions within Japanese society. It also encourages schism and conflict by giving them a political coloration. Public school issues, union-management strife, and protest movements of most kinds tend to be drawn into the establishment-versus-opposition political struggle. Power is not shared, but the opposition often can frustrate LDP initiatives, and public issues are highly politicized in the media.

If left-right political conflict makes the headlines, silent struggles of a more significant nature occur within the established parties and institutions between factions and cliques and their competing leaders. Behind the establishment's face of cooperative unity lie tough decision-making processes that regularly set powerful but opposed internal interests on collision courses, especially in struggles over succession to leadership. See also BATSU; POLITICAL CULTURE; POLITICAL PARTIES; POLITICAL SYSTEM.

While group solidarity and the high degree of national integration have never failed to win the admiration (and jealous criticism) of foreigners, the fact remains that Japan is a highly competitive society. Just as individuals (indeed, whole families) compete intensely to get ahead in education, so do interest groups, businesses, localities, and religious groups.

Businesses exist in what tends to be a highly competitive environment, marked periodically by efforts to relieve insecurity through collusive practices or government intervention. The greatest firms have arch rivals in the same field and these rivalries naturally involve the distributors, suppliers, subcontractors, subsidiaries, company unions, and other corporate vassals and allies. The bureaucracy and ruling party are typically cast in the roles of referees and mediators. Their efforts to arbitrate, rearrange, and moderate the competitive pattern occur largely outside the democratic process. Besides the power of lobbyists of all sorts, there is the goal of national strength to be considered in analyzing how the process works. Oligopolistic competition among large units is the goal, as this is thought to produce the greatest efficiency and international competitiveness. An ideal of social harmony is accompanied by a national character in which competitive inclinations and loyalties to competing groups provide great dynamism. Japan is not divided by deep religious, ethnic, or racial schisms, but economic and political conflict it knows well. See also CONFLICT RESOLUTION.

Social Stratification——Differences of individual position and income based largely on education and employment are sources of a minutely graded status hierarchy of great concern to many Japanese. To begin, we can note a marked variance in the desirability of jobs. The favored career paths are within powerful, prestigious institutions—the bureaucracy, the largest companies, and the top universities. When the promotion and rank systems within these institutions are coupled to the order of institutional ranking and calibrated to age and sex, it becomes possible to judge just about any employed person's social status. Job security, salaries, levels of company welfare, marital prospects, access to loans, self-respect, and most every conceivable form of social differentiation, many very subtle, are graded according to this stratification. See also CLASS STRUCTURE; OCCUPATIONAL STRUCTURE.

The character of Japanese economic organization lies behind such hierarchical differentiation, while the educational system functions to allocate individuals to starting places in it. The differences between the smaller, less efficient organizations and the larger more efficient ones, the dual structure already mentioned, creates the basic conditions upon which employment is differentiated. The most talented individuals are naturally attracted to the larger companies and to government, while small firms have difficulty attracting employees of quality. Since those who enter desirable companies protect their advantage by staying until retirement, opportunities for upward social mobility are largely limited to the period of education. After graduation, employed persons rise in the world through promotion within a single organization.

Employment——Viewed in the widest sense, Japanese employment is composed of a "core" group consisting of workers enjoying permanent status in medium and large private companies or government organizations, and a "marginal" group including temporarily employed workers, those working part-time, and employees of enterprises too small to afford job guarantees. A rough approximation of the proportions of each would parallel the division between those employed in firms with 100 or more employees and those in smaller enterprises. In 1975, 44 percent of workers in manufacturing and 26 percent of all nonagricultural workers belonged to the first category. Some workers in firms of less than 100 enjoy what is essentially core-group status. On the other hand, between 10 and 25 percent of workers in large industrial organizations are temporary or part-time. In times of economic recession, when employment levels must be trimmed, it is the marginal group that begins to lose jobs. They do not, in other words, enjoy permanent employment. Japanese UNEMPLOYMENT levels remain low by international standards even in these circumstances, however, because of many factors including the reluctance of employers to move quickly to a policy of layoffs, the low percentage of the unemployed who apply for benefits, and the statistical basis of unemployment figures.

Differences between men and women employees are also important to note. Female employees in large companies actually occupy anomalous positions. While they formally have job security, the majority of women retire either at marriage or at the time of their first pregnancy. They rarely remain employed long enough to benefit from seniority status. Those that do stay rarely enjoy as rapid promotion or as many benefits as men. Finally, should women that have left to become HOUSEWIVES return to the labor force, as many do, they are employed and paid generally as marginal, temporary workers. We can further reduce the picture of the "core" employment group by subtracting most women from it. See also WOMEN IN THE LABOR FORCE.

Young male core employees, to make another basic distinction, are not so much the beneficiaries of a seniority-based WAGE SYSTEM as they are holders of options for a future share in it. In Japan, where the seniority pay scale in large firms has been quite steep, young workers accept low wages as part of a long-term contract in which raises occur regularly. Rapid growth from 1955 to 1974 permitted large firms to hire large numbers of young workers and thus gain from this arrangement. Slower growth and an aging work force are making this system a liability, and attempts are being made to reduce seniority pay scales.

University-educated males in the "core group" (the white-collar elite) receive faster pay raises and seniority promotions than high school and middle school graduates of the same companies. Blue-collar workers, along with workers in smaller firms, have always had seniority pay scales that were less steep.

Japanese "lifetime employment" reflects some aspects of this situation. In its most developed form it implies that the worker, after joining a large company or government agency directly from school, will not be fired, short of bankruptcy of the firm or criminal behavior; will receive steady seniority-based raises and some virtually automatic promotions; will enjoy a wide range of company welfare benefits and facilities; will become socially involved with his office or factory colleagues; and will have few employment alternatives, given the centrality of seniority. By his own choice, therefore, the core worker is inclined to stay with the same company until RETIREMENT (at age 55 or 60). The degree of identification between the worker and his organization implied in this arrangement would signify an alarming dependence to most Westerners, but to Japanese the security provided is highly valued and the fit can be a comfortable one. This close identification is reinforced by traditional values such as loyalty and familism, but it is undermined by other factors. Dissatisfied older core workers may not changes jobs often, but neither will they be strongly motivated. Many younger Japanese workers change jobs, especially in prosperous times. The high turnover rate among employees of smaller firms also attests to the fact that company loyalty is far from being the whole story.

Still, where employment is permanent, the company looms very large in the lives of its workers. While leisure and family are increasingly given the time and attention of workers who previously gave their jobs their full devotion, affiliation with a large company remains a most consuming matter by American standards. The hardworking "company man" is still a highly held ideal in Japan, one reminiscent of the loyal samurai, and this ideal is bolstered by the fact that such individuals tend to be rewarded with promotions. See also EMPLOYMENT SYSTEM, MODERN; CORPORATE CULTURE.

Income Distribution——An apparent contradiction arises when job stratification and company-centered differentials are examined from the point of view of simple income distribution. Research reveals that Japan is second only to Sweden among industrial nations in income equality. The reasons are not hard to discover, however, for Japan has fewer wealthy, fewer unemployed, and fewer poor farmers than other advanced countries. The war and the Occupation reforms destroyed most of the great private fortunes. Japan is a nation of company employees, small shopkeepers, and relatively prosperous farmers.

Despite an acute awareness of status, class consciousness is relatively weak. Horizontal social affiliations based on occupation or class lines appear here and there, but the great majority of people share middle-class incomes, ambitions, attitudes, and lifestyles. Class-based organizations, such as labor unions and leftist parties, prove on closer examination to be less rooted in class interests than their charters would imply. In the case of unions what might be termed "vertical" ties of affiliation to large companies have proven to be much more important than "horizontal" ties to class. Crucial here is the fact that rewards differ according to the size and success of the company. Self-interest enhances concern with company fortunes and undermines the conviction that the interests of employer and employee are antagonistic.

Unions——Unions are strongest precisely where employment advantages are greatest. One-third of all workers are union members. They work either in the largest companies or in government organizations. It is the core group (including women) that is organized. Their unions, furthermore, are constructed on an enterprise basis, not along occupational or industry-wide lines. Such "enterprise unions" have been instrumental in gaining for their members a sizable share in the economic prosperity of the country, and as a result they have helped raise the core group into a labor elite. Private sector unions seek to protect this achievement partly through cooperation with the management of their enterprise. In times of recession, they are ready to trade away wage increases to assure job security for their members in the company. The enterprise basis of unions has also meant the mixing of blue- and white-collar workers in the same labor organization and thus a blurring of class lines. The leadership of unions tends to be in the hands of white-collar employees on their way up in the company. Many are in line for management positions, in fact, and this too tempers negotiations. Those private sector unions wishing to express leftist ideological commitments do so primarily through support of national leftist parties. Public sector unions are not tied directly to the business fortunes of their employers, however, and are therefore much more inclined to engage in confrontation tactics. These unions also tend to be more ideologically committed. Since management in their case is a government controlled by the conservatives, public unions are inclined to oppose management on political and ideological grounds. See also LABOR.

Religion——Contrary to what is generally expected of industrialized societies, modern Japan is a field of lively religious development and change. The Meiji period (1868–1912) witnessed the growth of new sects of SHINTŌ, many of which are still active, particularly in rural areas. Following World War II another wave of fresh religious development passed over the land. Within a decade hundreds of NEW RELIGIONS (some Buddhist, some Shintō, and some highly syncretistic) captured the attention and loyalty of millions. They are centered in the cities and have their strongest appeal among shopkeepers, housewives, and "marginal" workers. As many as one-tenth of all households in Japan belong to one of these new religions. The largest of them, SŌKA GAKKAI, even spawned its own political party, the KŌMEITŌ.

Traditional religious institutions, on the other hand, have generally witnessed a slow decline in the modern period. The end of Tokugawa regulations requiring households to belong to a Buddhist parish set the stage for a decline in temple membership in most of the older sects of BUDDHISM. This trend has been exacerbated by urbanization, as migrants to the city have discarded their ancestral religious affiliations without renewing or finding alternative avenues for religious participation. The largest Buddhist organizations, all the same, remain viable and are making serious efforts to adapt to changing social conditions.

The modern vicissitudes of Shintō evidence a different pattern. The hamlet served as the foundation of popular Shintō practice. While older urban neighborhoods have shrines and festivals, most Japanese today are less oriented to their local neighborhoods than to their places of employment. Well-organized urban shrine institutions have survived not because of large membership, but because they have found ways of earning income based on special entertainments and services to the urban populations. Spectator-oriented festivals, the sale of sacred amulets for auto safety or success in entrance examinations, and nursery schools are three such activities.

Some two-thirds of all Japanese indicate they have no religion, but over 70 percent also say that a religious attitude is important. Japanese remain open to religious thinking and see religion as a counterweight to the secular and materialistic trends of the times. Noteworthy in this regard has been the fact that Japan's new religions typically have developed during times of great social change and cultural confusion. The older, established forms of Shintō and Buddhism could not capture the modern imagination when people sought some answer that was not of the Western secular mode, but new religions were able to flourish by dressing essentially traditional beliefs and practices in more contemporary clothes and adjusting their organizations to the modern social framework. In the formation of new religious organizations, membership has been recruited largely among those Japanese who do not already belong to other large organizations such as the large companies. The religious groups operate in much the same way as corporations and bureaucracies and provide a substitute institutional identification for their members. See also RELIGION; RELIGION AND SOCIETY; RELIGION AND MODERNIZATION.

Minorities——Japan has long been noted for its relatively homogenous population. There are MINORITIES, however, and they became a focus of political and public policy discussion in the 1970s. The largest minority group is the two to three million Japanese known as the BURAKUMIN, a euphemism for descendants of people who occupied outcaste villages in the Edo period. Today people belonging to this group are known primarily by their residence in traditional outcaste areas. Those who live outside in anonymity can be identified if their prior residence or even their parents' residence

was in one of these areas. It is illegal to discriminate against *burakumin* in employment, and the government has attempted to stop background investigations, yet cases of discrimination are discovered regularly, most involving marriage or jobs. The fact that large numbers of *burakumin* are still found in stigmatized occupations such as leather working and refuse collecting reflects the persistence of discrimination. Many are poor, and the group suffers high levels of unemployment. The government has spent large amounts of money lately to bring public facilities in *burakumin* areas up to national standards, to build housing and better schools, and to provide low interest loans. This policy, however, does not encourage assimilation and has caused resentment among other marginal Japanese as "reverse discrimination."

The next largest minority group is the Koreans. Totaling about 650,000, they do not enjoy Japanese citizenship or many of the civil rights that go with it despite the fact that more than 75 percent were born and raised in Japan. About three-fourths of all Korean youth attend Japanese schools and Japanese is spoken in most Korean households. The socioeconomic status of Koreans is quite low, and many work in small factories run by Koreans that suffer economic vulnerability and poor working conditions. The Korean population is divided politically into two groups, one loyal to North Korea, the other to South Korea. The trend among the young, however, is to concentrate on gaining greater civil rights in Japan. See KOREANS IN JAPAN.

Other minorities—AINU, Chinese, A-bomb victims, and children of mixed parentage (KONKETSUJI)—are very small in numbers. They too suffer discrimination, particularly in marriage and employment. All of the minorities combined comprise less than 4 percent of the population, however, and there is little reason to expect Japan to become a pluralistic society in its attitudes and laws. Rather, the insularity and ethnic solidarity of Japanese society, even with its widespread adoption of foreign cultural items, remains one of its distinguishing traits. See also FOREIGNERS, ATTITUDES TOWARD.

Social Problems——Ask Japanese about their society and typically they will list its problems. Housing is too expensive and insufficient, food costs too much; Japanese have little free time and they have not learned how to enjoy it; educational competition is too heavy a burden on the young; SOCIAL WELFARE is insufficient, especially for the aged; ENVIRONMENTAL QUALITY is deteriorating and urban congestion is almost intolerable; too many young people lack discipline and ambition; politics is open to corruption, and the national leadership offers little inspiration for the average citizen. All of these complaints underline the fact that economic success is accompanied by SOCIAL PROBLEMS that seem very great to Japanese. The problems reflect a set of governmental priorities that have placed economic growth first, and there is now much pressure and a growing consensus for a new set of priorities that places the quality of life ahead of growth for its own sake.

Among the most pressing problems in the last quarter of the century is the rapidly increasing proportion of older people in the population. This means higher average wages, greater welfare costs, and painful disorganization for the old (see OLD AGE AND RETIREMENT). There is also a need to find a set of meaningful national ideas to which the younger generation can orient itself. Japan and the Japanese, people complain, are economic animals, too materialistic, self-interested, and calculating. To emerge from this state, new ideas are needed. The multitude of inconveniences and costs that stem from the overconcentration of population in a few urban centers is another fundamental challenge to be met.

Slower economic growth may give Japan the latitude to focus on improvements in the quality of life, but it also will mean economic insecurity, new kinds of adjustments, and even perhaps a reduction in public resources available for social improvements. These are not the kinds of problems that demand a general overhaul of the social system, and the level of dissatisfaction among Japanese is not so high as to cause political instability. The system is delicate and finely tuned and the constraints on major change are great indeed.

Interpretations of Japanese Society——Scholars differ in their understanding and interpretation of contemporary Japanese society. Some emphasize the influence of tradition on interpersonal relations, psychology, and values, while others argue that traditional factors are of little significance. Some see a unique society formed out of recent Japanese history, while others see the same forces shaping modern Japan as have shaped other industrialized countries.

Psychological approaches to understanding Japanese society tend to focus on tradition and Japanese distinctiveness. For example, Doi Takeo and others have pointed to the relative strength of dependency relationships among the Japanese. According to their interpretation, dependency is cultivated by close and indulgent relationships between Japanese mothers and their children; later in life, it underlies the effectiveness of hierarchical relationships and the heavy reliance upon group membership. This interpretation points, in the final analysis, to an international comparison, that the Japanese are not raised to seek social independence as are Americans and Europeans, and that their social patterns are not based on an accommodation with individualism. See also AMAE; JAPANESE PEOPLE, PSYCHOLOGY OF.

The solidarity and hierarchical structure of small groups are emphasized by another approach that posits a Japanese distinctiveness. Popularized by anthropologist Nakane Chie, this interpretation is that the hierarchical ties between seniors and juniors are the building blocks for most groups in Japan. Such ties bind a set of people to a leader in an intimate fashion, with reciprocity of loyalty, obligation, and concern. The ubiquity of this pattern in face-to-face relations leads Nakane to conclude that Japan is a VERTICAL SOCIETY.

Critics of the above approaches point out that demographic, economic, and other factors have a similar influence on Japan and on other countries. They argue that, despite the existence of traditional values, psychological tendencies, and vertical personal ties, the Japanese tend to act and reason according to a universal logic of modern social life. A useful result of this critique is the separation of the interpersonal and institutional levels of analysis. Government bureaus and private companies are composed of many interpersonal relationships in which people may interact in a most Japanese manner, but this will not necessarily mean that the institutions will act in a uniquely Japanese way.

Marxists tend to see modern Japanese society suffering the same structural contradictions and conflicts between classes as other industrial societies. They note that rapid economic development left little time for the growth of a bourgeois class and popular democracy and that the state and large monopolistic enterprises have dominated. In this analysis, feudalism (as it survives in traditional social relations) and nationalism have inhibited the rise of class consciousness among average Japanese. The Marxists predict that the problems of unequal power and wealth are bound to push increasingly to the surface of political life.

A different, "liberal" interpretation of recent history emphasizes how the end of feudal institutions unlocked enormous amounts of popular energy for modern development. Japan had no revolution, but the transformation of society through social mobility, the rise of democracy, and widely distributed economic prosperity have brought about a relatively stable and healthy society. Tradition helped this process, as it served to legitimate and inspire much of the change. Japan could remain Japanese while it built a modern institutional superstructure, this interpretation concludes.

Finally, some scholars emphasize the peculiar geographic and economic situation of the country in explaining its social character. As residents of an overpopulated island with few natural resources, Japanese are acutely aware of the need to compete in a larger, essentially hostile world. Some scholars have argued that Japanese society is, out of necessity, closely integrated and prone to emphasize duties over rights. It is a place where choices are clearly bounded by physical circumstances. Many scholars part company with this analysis when the fact that Japan can only survive through social cooperation is generalized into a sweeping explanation of all behavior.

Each of these perspectives offers useful insight, but only taken in combination can they provide the necessary breadth of approach through which a reliable understanding of modern Japan is likely to be gained.

—— Richard K. Beardsley, John Hall, and Robert E. Ward, *Village Japan* (1959). Harumi Befu, *Japan: An Anthropological Introduction* (1971). Robert E. Cole, *Japanese Blue Collar* (1971). Ronald Dore, *British Factory-Japanese Factory* (1973). Ronald Dore, *City Life in Japan* (1958). Takeshi Ishida, *Japanese Society* (1971). Tetsuya Kobayashi, *Society, Schools and Progress in Japan* (1976). Takie S. Lebra, *Japanese Patterns of Behavior* (1976). Masao Maruyama, *Thought and Behavior in Modern Japanese Politics* (1963). Chie Nakane, *Japanese Society* (1970). K. Ōkōchi, B. Karsh, and S. B. Levine, ed, *Workers and Employers in Japan: The Japanese Employment System* (1973). Thomas P. Rohlen, *For Harmony and Strength: Japanese White-Collar Organization in Anthropological Perspective* (1974). Ōhashi Ryūken, *Nihon no kaikyū kōsei* (1971). Robert J. Smith, *Kurusu: The Price of Progress in a Japanese Village, 1951–1975* (1978). Ezra Vogel, *Japan's New Middle Class* (1963).

Ezra Vogel, *Modern Japanese Organization and Decision-Making* (1975).
Thomas P. ROHLEN

sociology in Japan

Sociology (J: *shakaigaku*), as a discipline of the social sciences, was introduced to Japan from the West at the time of the MEIJI RESTORATION (1868). The word SOCIETY *(shakai)* was also ' 'roduced at that time.

Meiji-Period Sociology —— Of the work of early Western sociologists, the theories of the British philosopher Herbert Spencer (1820–1903) were most widely and enthusiastically received in Japan. Beginning in 1877, some of his works, including *Social Statistics, Study of Sociology,* and *Principles of Sociology,* were translated. At the time, both proponents and opponents of the FREEDOM AND PEOPLE'S RIGHTS MOVEMENT (Jiyū Minken Undō), which played a decisive role in the formation of constitutional government in Japan, were profoundly influenced by Spencer's view of society. Activists in the movement advocated his theory of natural rights, while opponents justified their positions with his theory of social evolution.

In 1878 the American Ernest F. FENOLLOSA began lecturing on Spencer's theory of social evolution at Tōkyō University. His faculty position was later filled by TOYAMA MASAKAZU, the first professor of sociology in Japan, who lectured primarily on Spencer's view of society. The first systematized work of sociology was written by Ariga Nagao (1860–1921), whose writing was also strongly influenced by Spencer.

In the context of the Sino-Japanese (1894–95) and Russo-Japanese (1904–05) wars, radical nationalism began to prevail in Japan, and in the field of sociology the liberal aspects of Spencer were replaced with theories of extreme nationalism. Takebe Tongo (1871–1945) followed Toyama as lecturer in sociology at Tōkyō University and advocated an organic theory of society. He emphasized the establishment of a policy-oriented sociology in which he synthesized Auguste Comte's positivist theories of social reorganization with Confucian ideas of uniting knowledge and practice. Between 1905 and 1918 Takebe wrote a major work called *Riron futsū shakaigaku* (General Theory of Sociology), which was based on Comte's division of sociology into three areas of study: the physics, statics, and dynamics of society. Takebe contributed greatly to the establishment of sociology as a discipline in Japan.

Psychological and Formal Sociology —— Sociology in Japan entered a new phase in the 1910s. Psychological sociology was introduced at this time through the works of Albion W. Small and Franklin H. Giddings of the United States, Georg Simmel of Germany, and Jean Gabriel of France. Endō Ryūkichi (1874–1946), one of the early proponents of psychological sociology, objected to the organic theory of society in which society takes precedence over the individual and advocated an individual-oriented view. Yoneda Shōtarō (1873–1945) also emphasized the importance of psychological interaction between individuals.

The establishment of a scientific base for Japanese sociology was achieved by TAKATA YASUMA (1883–1972), who studied under Yoneda. His original theories raised the discipline to international standards and freed it from its total dependence upon the West for both theory and methodology. Even today, Takata's works represent the highest level of scholarship in the field of theoretical sociology in Japan. He made a penetrating and critical analysis of Marxism and greatly contributed to the development of the study of economics as well. Takata established a view of individuals as self-interested beings seeking power and used sociological theories to found the study of power economics. He thus raised the academic standards of both sociology and economics as theoretical disciplines in search of general principles. However, in the latter half of the 1920s his interests shifted to economics, and sociology in Japan once again came under the strong influence of Western sociology and Marxism.

Historical, Marxist, and Empirical Sociology —— In the 1930s both the historical and Marxist approaches to sociology became prominent. The historical approach was strongly influenced by historicism, which had become a major academic movement during the 1920s in Germany, where its advocates included Max Weber, Max Scheler, and Karl Mannheim. Historical sociologists in Japan criticized Takata's theoretical discipline, which they rejected as a formal approach. They attempted to formulate sociology as a science of realism and cultural study. Marxist sociologists were also critical of the established sociology, but their criticism was mainly directed toward its so-called bourgeois character. Both the historical and

Marxist schools rejected theoretical sociology, but the former attempted a reorganization of sociology, while the latter aimed to abandon it altogether.

During the 1930s empirical sociology also became popular. SU-ZUKI EITARŌ (1894–1966) and ARUGA KIZAEMON (1897–1979) conducted fieldwork using empirical observations. Suzuki, influenced by the American rural sociologist Charles J. Galpin, investigated social relationships in villages. Aruga focused on Japanese families and analyzed the dominance and dependence relationships among family members. Their methods depended on descriptive case study rather than analysis. Statistical methods were introduced by TODA TEIZŌ (1887–1955) during the 1930s, but were not widely used until after World War II.

Japanese Sociology Today——Sociology has experienced many changes in the period since World War II. The influence of European sociologists such as Marx, Weber, and Emile Durkheim increased markedly, but sociology was also affected by the Americanization that was taking place in society as a whole. The American influence was reflected in the growing use of statistical methods, particularly of public opinion polls, and in the motivational analyses of individual behavior. As a result, many sociologists who took a Marxist stance also adopted American statistical research methods, but their reports tended to be descriptive and emphasized simply the effects of social class and position on individual cases. These studies tended to omit the process of verifying research hypotheses. However, the studies on social stratification and mobility that were started in 1955 by the Japan Sociological Society (Nihon Shakai Gakkai) were exceptions to this pattern.

Meanwhile, there appeared a theory of sociology which could compete with Marxism: Talcott Parson's "general theory of action," based on his structural-functionalism. Most of the non-Marxist sociologists in Japan today are either structural-functionalists or heavily influenced by this approach. Tominaga Ken'ichi (b 1931) is a particularly distinguished scholar in the field. However, structural-functionalism has been losing popularity in the United States, and in Japan, as well, a number of other paradigms are appearing.

■——Fukutake Tadashi, *Gendai Nihon shakai ron* (1977). Fukutake Tadashi, ed, *Shakaigaku kōza 18: rekishi to kadai* (Tōkyō Daigaku Shuppankai, 1974). Kawamura Nozomu, *Nihon shakaigaku shi kenkyū* (1973).   NAOI Atsushi

Sōda Kiichirō (1881–1927)

Economic theorist. Born in Yokohama. After graduating from Tōkyō Higher Commercial School (now Hitotsubashi University) in 1904, he studied philosophy in Germany under Heinrich Rickert, well known for his Neo-Kantian writings. After returning to Japan, Sōda was appointed lecturer at his alma mater and established an original economic philosophy known as "Sōda philosophy", which was concerned with the methodological basis of economics. Also president of the Sōda Bank, he held numerous high positions in the business world. He was also a member of the House of Peers (1925). His works on economics include *Keizai tetsugaku no shomondai* (1917, Problems of Economic Philosophy) and *Geld und Wert* (1909, Currency and Value).   YAMADA Katsumi

Sōdōmei

(abbreviation of Nihon Rōdō Sōdōmei; Japan Federation of Labor). Organized originally as the YŪAIKAI (Friendship Association) in 1912, it was reorganized as the Dai Nippon Rōdō Sōdōmei Yūaikai in 1919. It took its present name in 1921. Although the federation was strongly influenced by radical theories of trade unionism at the time of its formation, it moved toward a more moderate reformist position after government suppression during the economic and social crisis following the TŌKYŌ EARTHQUAKE OF 1923. Ejecting the leftists in 1925 and the centrists in 1926, Sōdōmei eventually came to represent the right wing of the Japanese labor movement. Politically, it had a close relationship with the SHAKAI MINSHŪTŌ (Socialist People's Party). Emphasizing collective agreements and cooperation between labor and management, the federation took a stance supportive of World War II. Although Sōdōmei merged with centrist workers' unions in 1936, taking the new name of Zen Nihon Rōdō Sōdōmei (All Japan Federation of Labor), it split in 1939 and was dissolved in 1940 because of the government's policy of eliminating the labor movement in order to direct all energies toward the war effort. In 1946 the federation was reorganized as Nihon Rōdō Kumiai Sōdōmei (Japan Federation of Labor Unions) by its previous leaders, including MATSUOKA KOMAKICHI, and became a nationwide

organization in opposition to SAMBETSU KAIGI (Congress of Industrial Labor Unions of Japan). In 1950, at the time of Sōhyō's (General Council of Trade Unions of Japan) formation, it split again because of internal disagreements. After participating in activities with other anti-Sōhyō factions, the remaining members formally dissolved the organization in 1964 when DŌMEI (Japanese Confederation of Labor) was formed by the right-wing unions.

KURITA Ken

Soejima Taneomi (1828–1905)

Politician-statesman of the Meiji period (1868–1912). Born in the Saga domain (now Saga Prefecture). Influenced by his father and brother, both scholars of the nationalistic and proimperial KOKU-GAKU school of learning, he became a leader of the antishogunate movement in Saga. In 1867 he briefly studied law in Nagasaki with the American missionary Guido VERBECK. After the Meiji Restoration (1868), Soejima became a junior councillor *(san'yo)*, and together with FUKUOKA TAKACHIKA drew up the "Constitution of 1868" (SEITAISHO), the first official statement on the structure and functions of the new government. While the key government leaders toured in Europe (see IWAKURA MISSION), Soejima served as foreign minister, and in 1873 he led an ambassadorial mission to Beijing (Peking) where he secured the first audience granted to a foreign envoy by the Chinese emperor without performing the kowtow. His real purpose in Beijing was to lay the diplomatic groundwork for a program of Japanese expansion in both Korea and Taiwan.

In opposition to the government policy that rejected his own proposal to invade Korea (see SEIKANRON), a plan that he shared with SAIGŌ TAKAMORI, he resigned from the government in October 1873. He then joined ITAGAKI TAISUKE in forming the AIKOKU KŌTŌ, a political association, and in signing the memorial on the establishment of a representative assembly *(minsen giin setsuritsu kempaku)*. He did not, however, remain active in the FREEDOM AND PEOPLE'S RIGHTS MOVEMENT, nor did he participate in any insurrectionary movement. He was later appointed to the Privy Council, but he never returned to government service at the cabinet level except briefly in 1892 to serve as home minister in the MATSUKATA MASA-YOSHI cabinet.

■——Maruyama Kanji, *Soejima Taneomi haku* (1936). Wayne C. McWilliams, "East meets East: The Soejima Mission to China, 1873," *Monumenta Nipponica* (1975).   Wayne C. McWILLIAMS

Sōen (fl 1495–1499)

Priest-painter in the Muromachi-period (1333–1568) INK PAINTING tradition who studied with SESSHŪ TŌYŌ in Yamaguchi and returned with the new style to his home temple in Kamakura. Also known as Josui Sōen. Born in Sagami Province (now Kanagawa Prefecture), Sōen attained the high rank of *zōsu* (sutra keeper) in Kamakura's important Zen temple ENGAKUJI before going to Yamaguchi to become one of Sesshū's closest disciples. When Sōen completed his training and was about to return to eastern Japan, Sesshū presented him with his famous *Haboku Landscape* (1495; Tōkyō National Museum) with a long inscription to his pupil. After leaving Yamaguchi, Sōen stopped in Kyōto, where six high-ranking GOZAN monks added encomiums to the top of the painting. Four years later, when Sesshū was 80 years old, he wrote an affectionate letter to Sōen in Kyōto—an indication that Sōen was still in the capital in 1499. That he eventually returned to his Kamakura temple is witnessed by a painting of the deity Bhadrapāla in strong Sesshū style preserved at Engakuji and bearing Sōen's seal and signature. At this time, Kamakura painters were under the pervading influence of the Chinese Song (Sung; 960–1279) and Yuan (Yüan; 1280–1368) styles as they had been transformed by Japanese priest-painters of the 14th and 15th centuries. SHŌKEI, the Kamakura artist who had studied with GEIAMI in Kyōto, was predominant at the neighboring temple Kenchōji. To this environment, Sōen returned with the vision that Sesshū had created within the framework of the Ming (1368–1644) painting styles that he had seen on his 1467–69 trip to China. Strangely enough, however, there is no evidence that a school formed around Sōen at Engakuji. It has been suggested that he may have died soon after his return to Kamakura.

A relatively large number of Sōen's paintings survive, attesting to a breadth of subject matter characteristic of a Sesshū follower who was painting to meet the requirements of a Zen temple. His artistic foundation in Sesshū's style is undeniable in the brawny drapery

Soga family —— Genealogy

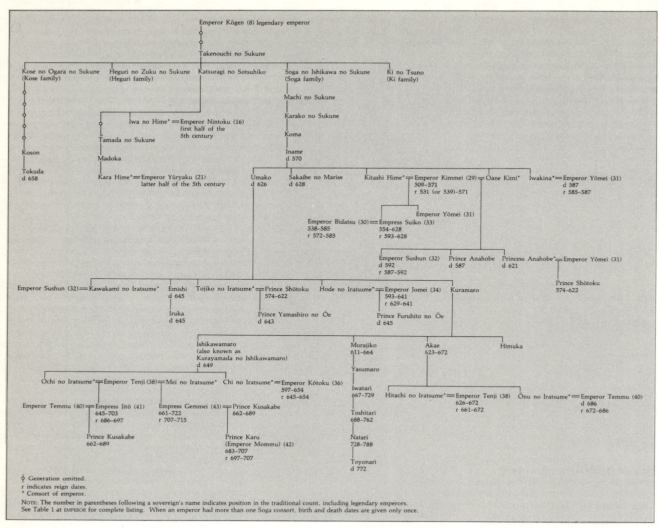

Emperor Kōgen (8) legendary emperor

Takenouchi no Sukune

Kose no Ogara no Sukune (Kose family) — Heguri no Zuku no Sukune (Heguri family) — Katsuragi no Sotsuhiko — Soga no Ishikawa no Sukune (Soga family) — Ki no Tsuno (Ki family)

Machi no Sukune

Karako no Sukune

Koma

Iwa no Hime* = Emperor Nintoku (16) first half of the 5th century

Tamada no Sukune

Koson

Madoka

Tokuda d 658

Iname d 570

Kara Hime* = Emperor Yūryaku (21) latter half of the 5th century

Umako d 626 — Sakaibe no Marise d 628

Kitashi Hime* — Emperor Kimmei (29) 509–571 r 531 (or 539)–571 — Oane Kimi* — Iwakina* = Emperor Yōmei (31) d 587 r 585–587

Emperor Bidatsu (30) 538–585 r 572–585 = Empress Suiko (33) 554–628 r 593–628

Emperor Yōmei (31)

Emperor Sushun (32) d 592 r 587–592 — Prince Anahobe d 587 — Princess Anahobe* = Emperor Yōmei (31) d 621

Prince Shōtoku 574–622

Emperor Sushun (32) = Kawakami no Iratsume* — Emishi d 645 — Tojiko no Iratsume* — Prince Shōtoku 574–622 — Hode no Iratsume* — Emperor Jomei (34) 593–641 r 629–641 — Kuramaro

Iruka d 645

Prince Yamashiro no Ōe d 643

Prince Furuhito no Ōe d 645

Prince Shōtoku 574–622

Ishikawamaro (also known as Kurayamada no Ishikawamaro) d 649

Murajiko 611–664 — Akae 623–672 — Himuka

Yasumaro

Ochi no Iratsume* = Emperor Tenji (38) = Mei no Iratsume* — Chi no Iratsume* = Emperor Kōtoku (36) 597–654 r 645–654

Iwatari 667–729

Hitachi no Iratsume* = Emperor Tenji (38) 626–672 r 661–672 — Ōnu no Iratsume* = Emperor Temmu (40) d 686 r 672–686

Emperor Temmu (40) = Empress Jitō (41) 645–703 r 686–697 — Empress Gemmei (43) 661–722 r 707–715 = Prince Kusakabe 662–689

Toshitari 688–762

Prince Kusakabe 662–689

Prince Karu (Emperor Mommu) (42) 683–707 r 697–707

Natari 728–788

Toyonari d 772

◊ Generation omitted.
r indicates reign dates.
* Consort of emperor.
NOTE: The number in parentheses following a sovereign's name indicates position in the traditional count, including legendary emperors. See Table 1 at EMPEROR for complete listing. When an emperor had more than one Soga consort, birth and death dates are given only once.

contours and substantial forms of his figure paintings; his landscapes bear ample evidence of the Sesshū techniques. But Sōen's personal style is softer than that of his master and is distinguished by his smooth handling of moist ink to create atmospheric effects.

Carolyn WHEELWRIGHT

Sō family

Daimyō family of the island of Tsushima (now part of Nagasaki Prefecture). Because the island was situated between northern Kyūshū and Korea, the family was constantly involved with the interactions between Korea and Japan. The Sō became military governors (*shugo*) of Tsushima under the Kamakura shogunate (1192–1333) and were nearly destroyed when the island was overrun in the first of the MONGOL INVASIONS OF JAPAN (1274). In 1419 they repulsed a Korean force sent in retaliation against Japanese pirates (see ŌEI INVASION) and in 1443 concluded a treaty with Korea to regularize the foreign trade on which Tsushima throve. In 1592 and 1597 they contributed troops to Toyotomi Hideyoshi's Korean expeditions (see INVASIONS OF KOREA IN 1592 AND 1597). After Hideyoshi's death in 1598, Sō Yoshitomo (1568–1615)—still trusted by the Koreans—led the peace negotiations and in 1605 established diplomatic relations with Korea on behalf of the Tokugawa shogunate (1603–1867), in reward for which the Sō domain was enlarged to 100,000 *koku* (see KOKUDAKA). The Sō continued to serve as intermediaries between Korea and Japan throughout the Edo period (1600–1868).

soft drinks

With the opening of Japan to foreign influences after the Meiji Restoration (1868), carbonated drinks with names derived from English such as *saidā* (from cider) and *ramune* (from lemonade) became popular, as did lactic-acid beverages. At present beverages flavored with cola and various fruits are also sold. The long-favored Calpis (a trade name), made with milk, sweetener, artificial color, and lactic-acid bacteria, has been replaced in popularity by cola drinks.

ŌTSUKA Shigeru

Soga brothers → Soga monogatari

Soga family

A family (UJI) of the Yamato region (now Nara Prefecture) whose leading members in the 6th and 7th centuries came to exercise political influence rivaling that of the imperial house. Accounts in the chronicles NIHON SHOKI (720) and *Kogo shūi* (807) link the Soga to financial administration, foreign relations, and the promotion of Buddhism and other aspects of continental culture. They were closely associated with the AYA FAMILY of Korean immigrant (KIKAJIN) descent.

The name Soga is thought to have come from a place name in the Yamato basin. The SHINSEN SHŌJIROKU, 9th-century genealogical compendium, traces the Soga origins to TAKENOUCHI NO SUKUNE, but some scholars believe that the 5th-century official Soga no Manchi, the first member of the family mentioned in historical sources, is identical with an official and foreign affairs activist of the Korean state of PAEKCHE whom the Korean chronicle SAMGUK SAGI calls "Mongna Manchi" and the *Nihon shoki* "Moku Manch'i."

Soga no Iname (d 570), the first of four generations of Soga who consecutively held the post of *ōomi* (chief minister) at the YAMATO COURT, showed much interest in Korean affairs and was one of the first converts to Buddhism, recently introduced from Paekche. He is said to have made his home into a small temple called the Mukuharadera. Two of his daughters were married to Emperor KIMMEI (r 531 or 539 to 571) and three of his grandchildren reigned in succession as Emperor Yōmei (r 585–587), Emperor Sushun (r 587–592) and Empress SUIKO (r 593–628).

SOGA NO UMAKO (d 626), who was Iname's son, is said to have been a zealous Buddhist (he built the temple ASUKADERA as the Soga family temple) as well as a man of scholarly interests who helped Prince SHŌTOKU compile two histories, TENNŌKI AND KOKKI, both now lost. He is credited with promoting a consultative system of balancing the interests and opinions of various factional leaders. No stranger, however, to violence and intrigue, he and his supporters in 587 waged a victorious battle against the anti-Buddhist MONONOBE FAMILY and Nakatomi family. In the same year he is said to have arranged the murder of his nephew Prince Anahobe; five years later he accomplished the assassination of another nephew (and son-in-law), Emperor Sushun. Umako's almost obsessive hatred of the Korean state of SILLA caused international friction and unnecessary bloodshed. One military expedition, sent to southeastern Korea in 600, was commanded by Umako's brother Sakaibe no omi Marise.

Umako's son Emishi (d 645) and grandson SOGA NO IRUKA (d 645) increasingly abused their authority. They met enmity and distrust when in 641 they requisitioned other people's private groups of laborers *(kakibe)* to build for themselves grandiose twin mausoleums; and Iruka's armed attack on the residence of Shōtoku's surviving son, Prince YAMASHIRO NO ŌE, brought even greater condemnation. Emishi and Iruka seem to have foreseen trouble when in 644 they built two fortress-like residences atop a hill west of the Asukadera and overlooking the imperial palace.

But their fortifications, armed guards, and buckets of fire-extinguishing water, a precaution against arson, did not save them from the coup d'état of the summer of 645, a major aim of which was to eliminate the Soga abuses of power. During a reception for Korean envoys, Iruka was killed in the audience hall of the palace by Prince Naka no Ōe, the future emperor TENJI. Emishi committed suicide the next day after his militia deserted him. A fire, which presumably was set to his residence, is said to have consumed the manuscript of the *Tennōki,* although a fragment of the *Kokki* was rescued from the blaze.

It seems possible that the compilers of the *Nihon shoki* deliberately exaggerated the negative aspects of the Soga, and much about the family's activities is unclear. Iruka was perhaps not entirely the villain that the chronicle depicts. According to the *Taishoku kanden,* a biography of FUJIWARA NO KAMATARI, one of the main planners of the 645 coup, Iruka and Kamatari had once studied together under the priest Min (see SŌMIN) after his return from China, and Min is said to have highly praised Iruka's deportment and eagerness to learn. Some members of the Soga family had opposed the excesses of Emishi and Iruka, and the family was by no means exterminated in 645. Soga no Akae, a grandson of Umako, served as ōomi during the TAIKA REFORM.

📖——Kadowaki Teiji, *Asuka* (1977). Naoki Kōjirō, *Kodai kokka no seiritsu* (1973). William R. CARTER

Soga monogatari

(Tale of the Soga Brothers). A medieval prose tale of revenge. Kudō Suketsune, angry at being deprived of his inheritance by his uncle Itō Sukechika, has Sukechika's son murdered. Eighteen years later, the dead man's two young sons exact revenge by killing Suketsune, now a henchman of Minamoto no Yoritomo, at a hunt near Mt. Fuji (Fujisan) in 1193. The elder Soga brother (the surname is that of their stepfather), Jūrō Sukenari, is killed in the melee, but the younger, Gorō Tokimune, is captured and brought before Yoritomo who, impressed by his filial piety, would have pardoned him had not Suketsune's son demanded his execution.

This historical incident has stirred and excited the Japanese ever since. It is treated in several NŌ plays and ballad dramas (KŌWAKA). The form of the Soga prose tale most widely current in the 15th and 16th centuries contained many dramatic and romantic elements ideally suited for later adaptation to the popular theater (see KABUKI). However, many of these elements are absent from the earliest known form of the story, that written in Chinese *(kambun)* perhaps between 1300 and 1350. The earliest Soga tales are thought to have grown out of religious rituals to appease the angry spirits of the boys. As literature, *Soga monogatari* is rather tedious, being overloaded with religious propaganda, but its evolution in various literary genres well repays study.

📖——D. E. Mills, "*Soga monogatari, Shintōshū* and the Taketori Legend," *Monumenta Nipponica* 30.1 (1975). Douglas E. MILLS

Soga no Iruka (?–645)

Court official of the 7th century; son of Soga no Emishi (d 645) and grandson of SOGA NO UMAKO. He was a shrewd and daring political manipulator who with his father worked to preserve the SOGA FAMILY's control of the imperial throne. The death in 628 of the Soga-created Empress SUIKO led to a succession dispute between Prince Tamura, supported by the Soga, and Prince YAMASHIRO NO ŌE, son of Prince SHŌTOKU. Prince Tamura prevailed and ascended the throne as Emperor Jomei (593–641; r 629–641). On Jomei's death the Soga intervened again to install his widow, Empress Kōgyoku (later Empress SAIMEI), on the throne. Yamashiro no Ōe, still a threat to Soga ambitions, was forced by Iruka to commit suicide in 643. Emboldened by their success, Emishi and Iruka flaunted their power by assuming high ranks, arbitrarily managing state affairs, and building pretentious mansions for their personal use. Finally, in 645, Prince Naka no Ōe (later Emperor TENJI) conspired with Nakatomi no Kamatari (later FUJIWARA NO KAMATARI), whose family had been eclipsed by the Soga in the 580s, and succeeded in assassinating Iruka. Thereupon the supporters of the Soga dispersed, Emishi committed suicide, and Empress Kōgyoku was deposed. These events marked the end of Soga tyranny and paved the way for the TAIKA REFORM, of which Naka no Ōe (then crown prince) was a leading proponent.

Soga no Umako (?–626)

Political figure of the YAMATO COURT (ca 4th–mid-7th centuries). Son of the chieftain Soga no Iname (d 570), Umako sought to establish the SOGA FAMILY's dominance over the court through kinship ties with the imperial house and patronage of Buddhism. He achieved his aims in an imperial succession dispute of 587, when he destroyed his arch rivals, the anti-Buddhist MONONOBE FAMILY and installed his nephew on the throne as Emperor Sushun. When Sushun resisted his high-handed conduct of government, Umako had him assassinated in 592 and set up a niece as the reigning empress SUIKO. As chief minister *(ōomi)* under Suiko, Umako collaborated with the regent and heir-apparent Prince SHŌTOKU in strengthening the central government. Some scholars believe that he is buried in the ISHIBUTAI TOMB in ASUKA (Nara Prefecture).

📖——Michiko Y. Aoki, *Ancient Myths and Early History of Japan* (1974). Michiko Y. AOKI

Soganoya Gorō (1877–1948)

Comic actor, playwright, and director known as the father of modern Japanese comedy. Born Wada Hisakazu in Sakai, the port city near Ōsaka, he spent 10 years touring the provinces in second-rate KABUKI troupes until he met Ōmatsu Fukumatsu (1869–1925). Both actors were attracted to each other because each wanted to develop his own comic talents beyond what was possible in traditional theater. They borrowed the names of the Soga brothers (see SOGA MONOGATARI) of revenge-story fame to become Soganoya Gorō and Soganoya Jūrō.

Gorō was especially inspired by translations of Molière and by *niwaka* (improvised comic skits customarily performed in brothels and at shrine festivals). Along with Jūrō, he sought to create a contemporary form that would be the comedy counterpart to the flourishing melodramatic SHIMPA theater.

Both men were forerunners of the modern Japanese phenomenon of multitalented individuals who write, direct, produce, and star in their own plays. Although the stories of their comedies were contemporary, the initial Soganoya staging techniques remained close to kabuki. Invariably their plays were tempered with traces of the didactic, conflicts between obligation and feeling (see GIRI AND NINJŌ), and obligatory sentimentality. The highest goal of the unbroken Soganoya tradition is to make audiences laugh through their tears.

Gorō played low-life, carefree churls in a bombastic manner to contrast with Jūrō's restrained interpretations of pessimistic semi-intelligentsia. Gorō also originated the definitive caricature of the nasty, crafty old woman that remains the standard for such portrayals in comedy and comic strips.

Primarily due to the incompatibility between Jūrō's older age and Gorō's leadership, the two separated in 1913. After Gorō returned from a European trip where he studied comedy, he organized the

Heimin Gekidan (Plebian Troupe). Jūrō set up his own company which he ran independently until his death.

The entertainment conglomerate Shōchiku eventually took over Soganoya interests and integrated them into their Shōchiku Kateigeki (Family Drama) troupe. Under the subsequent leadership of comedians Shibuya Tengai II and Fujiyama Kambi, this troupe evolved into the present Shōchiku Shinkigeki (New Comedy) company, which remains active on stage and in television.

Using the pen name Ikkai Gyojin, Gorō wrote more than a thousand short comedies. His major works include *Sanjūroku kaishō* (Thirty-Six Big Laughs), *Yu no machi* (Resort Town), *Ushi* (Cow), *Warai o wasureta hitobito* (They Forgot How to Laugh), *Namida no suteba* (The Dumping Ground for Tears), *Hariko no tora* (Paper Tiger), *Ryōshin* (Conscience), and *Kokoro no uzumaki* (Whirlpool of Feelings). Soganoya Jūrō, whose pen name was Warōtei Tōrō, also wrote many comedies.

■ ———Soganoya Gorō, *Soganoya Gorō jiden: Kigeki ichidai otoko* (1948).   J. L. ANDERSON

Soga school

A school of painters active from the 15th century into the 18th century who specialized in INK PAINTING. Patronized by the Asakura family of Echizen Province (now Fukui Prefecture) and connected with the Zen master Ikkyū Sōjun (1394–1481; see IKKYŪ), the early Soga artists centered their activity around the Kyōto temple of DAITOKUJI. Traditional art histories cite Soga Dasoku as the primary figure in the development of the school but give contradictory accounts of his identity. Lack of firsthand information about artists surrounding and following Dasoku extends this confusion to the entire group. Existing Soga-school paintings reflect a manner evolved from the style of the great Shōkokuji priest-painter SHŪBUN, but they also contain Korean elements, giving some credence to the claim that the founder of the line was Yi Chuman (J: Ri Shūbun), a Korean artist who came to Japan in 1424. Soga-school paintings include the important panels in the Daitokuji subtemple Shinjuan, as well as numerous scrolls treating a wide range of subject matter: portraits of Ikkyū, Zen figure themes, bird-and-flower paintings, ink landscapes in both a neatly crystalline manner and an impromptu HABOKU ("break ink") style. Some of these works bear seals with the names Bokkei, Saiyo, and Sekiyō, and Soga-school lineage charts include the names Sōjō, Nara Hōgen Kantei, Shōsen, Sōyo, and Shōshō.

Although Soga Nichokuan wrote a Soga-school lineage in 1656 claiming that his father, Chokuan, was heir to Soga Shōshō, there was probably no strong connection between the early group of Soga painters and the later school founded by Chokuan. When ODA NOBUNAGA destroyed the Asakura house in 1573, the artists dispersed and Chokuan probably went to the city of Sakai (in what is now Ōsaka Prefecture) to establish a patronage basis among wealthy merchants. Chokuan's biography is unknown, but a votive panel at KITANO SHRINE in Kyōto inscribed in 1610 and painted for TOYOTOMI HIDEYORI provides a date for his activity and an indication of his patronage. Records indicate that he did wall paintings for Kyōto subtemples, but today only his folding screens and hanging scrolls remain. Most of these are bird-and-flower subjects in a rather conservative style: clearly detailed, brightly colored flowers and birds quietly arranged across an ink monochrome landscape setting. Noted especially for his treatment of hawks, Chokuan was a favored artist of the warrior class. Nichokuan, active during the first half of the 17th century, preserved his father's style and used his father's seal, which has resulted in frequent confusion of their works. A series of painters continued to work in the Soga style, culminating in the innovative eccentricities of the great 18th-century master SOGA SHŌHAKU.   Carolyn WHEELWRIGHT

Soga Shōhaku (1730–1781)

Painter whose works exemplify the spirit of experimentation and diverse, innovative modes of expression that are characteristic of 18th-century painting in Japan. Shōhaku's birthplace and family background are unclear, but there is evidence suggesting that he may have been a member of a merchant family from Kyōto and that his family name was Miura. As a young man he studied painting under Takada Keiho (1674–1755), an independent artist whose works are often highly personal in conception and utilize a lively and assertive inventory of brush-strokes, characteristics that are apparent in more mature and dynamic forms in the works of his student Shōhaku.

Shōhaku felt a strong artistic affinity with the ancient SOGA SCHOOL painters, founded by Soga Dasoku in the 15th century, but he stands apart, both in temperament and creative predilection, from any of the institutionalized schools of painting of his time. Chinese legend and folklore provided the subjects for most of his figurative works, and a broad variety of personalities appear in them: exemplary sages and paragons of moral rectitude, poets, priests, and literati, as well as more unconventional types such as rustic hermits, eccentric anchorites, and SENNIN ("immortals"), mysterious figures possessed of supernatural powers. A similar inventory of traditional pictorial components is evident in his landscapes, features drawn in a broad manner from the *suibokuga* (INK PAINTING) of the Muromachi period (1333–1568), with its dependence on Chinese traditions, but inspired more directly by the concepts and methods of the 17th-century KANŌ SCHOOL and UNKOKU SCHOOL and their preoccupation with crisp, explicit brushwork and strong linear contours. At Shōhaku's hands this pastiche of varied subjects and stylistic components from the past are combined into a new and unique form of pictorial expression.

A good deal of Shōhaku's time seems to have been spent on the road, working independently as an itinerant painter. He apparently moved at a leisurely pace, accepting commissions wherever he found them; and it is clear that he pursued his peripatetic activities for protracted periods in both the Harima and Ise regions (roughly equivalent to modern Hyōgo and Mie prefectures), for significant numbers of his paintings have been preserved in these areas. Moreover, he seems to have made a strong impression on the natives in both places, for lively anecdotes about his eccentric behavior and unconventional painting methods were still alive in oral traditions there as late as the Meiji period (1868–1912).

Information about Shōhaku and his painting appears in certain of the writings on artists compiled during the later years of the Edo period (1600–1868), such as the *Gadō kongōsho* and *Chikutō garon* by NAKABAYASHI CHIKUTŌ; the *Hampaku zawa* by Morishima Nagashi; the *Gajō yōryaku* by Shirai Kayō; the *Kinsei meika shogadan* by Anzai Un'en; and the *Kinsei itsujin gashi* by Okada Heiji, which notes in part: "He traveled about widely in the Kyōto and Settsu (Ōsaka) regions, and people thought he was mad. His paintings were multiform and free. Among his 'grass'-style paintings, there were some where he applied ink to a straw brush and literally swabbed about. On the other hand, when it came to painting meticulous works, others could not equal him."

Although Shōhaku experimented with colors occasionally, his most representative works are in monochrome ink. These are characterized by a broad range of incisive brushwork as well as the distinctive manner in which subjects are depicted, a trenchant, unambiguous style marked by great spontaneity. These features are apparent in one of the finest of Shōhaku's mature works, a pair of folding screens in the Museum of Fine Arts, Boston, depicting the Four Sages of Mt. Shang, a theme drawn from Chinese legend.

■ ———Money L. Hickman, "Bosuton bijutsukan shozō no shōhakuga ni tsuite," in *Jakuchū, Shōhaku, Rosetsu*, vol 14 of *Suiboku bijutsu taikei* (Kōdansha, 1973). Money L. Hickman, "Soga Shōhaku and the Museum of Fine Arts, Boston," in *Bukkyō geijutsu* 90 (February 1973). Matsuo Katsuhiko, "Paintings by Shōhaku Soga in Harima Province," in *Kobijutsu* 39 and 40 (December 1972; March 1973). Tsuji Nobuo, Kōno Motoaki, Money Hickman, *Jakuchū/ Shōhaku*, vol 23 of *Nihon bijutsu kaiga zenshū* (Shūeisha, 1978).
                                                                         Money HICKMAN

Sōgi (1421–1502)

The leading *renga* (linked verse; see RENGA AND HAIKAI) poet of the late 15th century, and a renowned scholar of classical court literature. He was revered by later generations as the epitome of the traveler-poet and served as the chief compiler of the second honorary imperial *renga* anthology, the SHINSEN TSUKUBASHŪ (1495). He presided as senior poet at the composition of *Minase sangin hyakuin* (1488), the single most celebrated sequence in the *renga* canon.

The details of Sōgi's early life are obscure. Born in either Kii Province (now Wakayama Prefecture) or Ōmi Province (now Shiga Prefecture), he was of humble origin, perhaps the son of a GIGAKU (an ancient masked dance drama) performer; his surname was Iio. In early adulthood he moved to Kyōto and entered the Buddhist priesthood at Shōkokuji, a Zen temple of the RINZAI SECT. Taking advantage of the cultural contacts this provided, Sōgi began the study of *renga* at about the age of 30 under the instruction of Sōzei (d 1455). During his first decade in the capital he also studied with Senjun (ca 1418–81) and SHINKEI, the greatest *renga* master of the day. In this early period his most important patron was ICHIJŌ KA-NEYOSHI, the famous scholar and high court official. He tutored Sōgi in the Chinese classics, Japanese classical poetry (WAKA), traditional tales (monogatari), and court customs, and provided access to the highest social circles.

Motivated at least in part by a desire to visit places celebrated in Japanese poetry, Sōgi embarked upon his first major journey in 1466, traveling along the TŌKAIDŌ to the eastern provinces. He remained outside the capital for most of the next eight years, enjoying the lavish hospitality of provincial barons eager to acquire the culture of the nobility. In this fashion he avoided the disturbances in Kyōto caused by the Ōnin War (1467–77), and was able to visit other poets who had taken up residence in the east, including Shinkei. During this period he wrote two critical works, Chōrokubumi (1466) and Azuma mondō (1470), both chiefly concerned with technical matters of renga composition, and a travel diary, Shirakawa kikō (1468).

While in Izu Province (now Shizuoka Prefecture) in 1471, Sōgi received the KOKIN DENJU—the transmission of a secret body of knowledge concerning the KOKINSHŪ (ca 905), the first imperial waka anthology—from TŌ NO TSUNEYORI (1401–84), a waka poet of the orthodox Nijō school. This scholarly pedigree qualified Sōgi as an official authority on court literature, despite his low birth. For the rest of his life he lectured frequently on the Kokinshū and such classics as ISE MONOGATARI (The Tales of Ise) and the TALE OF GENJI.

Returning to the capital in 1473, Sōgi built a hermitage in the northeast part of the city, the Shugyokuan. In this proverbial "grass hut"—within the tradition, an important symbol of serious devotion to poetry—he conducted renga sessions and gave lectures attended by the highest nobility. Wasuregusa, the first of three personal renga anthologies, was completed in 1474; two years later he compiled the Chikurinshō, an anthology of verses by the seven most famous renga poets of the mid-15th century; in 1479 he analyzed verses by these same poets in Oi no susabi.

Sōgi continued to travel, and in 1480 he made an extended visit to the estate of Ōuchi Masahiro (1400–1494), the powerful lord and art patron of Yamaguchi in Suō Province (now part of Yamaguchi Prefecture), and then continued on to Kyūshū, where he recorded Tsukushi no michi no ki, a travel diary later admired by the great HAIKU poet BASHŌ (1644–94). After Kaneyoshi's death in 1481, Sōgi became the leading literary figure in the capital.

In the spring of 1488—the same year he was appointed by the shogunate to administer the Kitano Shrine renga sessions, the highest official honor accorded a renga poet—Sōgi and his disciples SHŌHAKU and SŌCHŌ gathered at Minase (between Kyōto and Ōsaka), at the site of retired emperor Go-Toba's (1180–1239) detached palace. To commemorate Go-Toba's achievements as poet and chief compiler of the famous imperial waka anthology the SHIN KOKINSHŪ (1205), they composed the celebrated Minase sangin hyakuin, a majestic and dignified 100-verse sequence. Three years later the same three poets produced the more informal but highly praised Yuyama sangin hyakuin at the Arima Hot Spring, near modern Kōbe. In 1495 Sōgi was commissioned for the Shinsen tsukubashū; succeeding the great renga masters NIJŌ YOSHIMOTO and GUSAI—compilers of the original TSUKUBASHŪ (1356)—he considered this his greatest honor. Sōgi died while on a journey with Sōchō to Suruga Province (now part of Shizuoka Prefecture) in 1502.

As a poet, Sōgi was a conservative. His verses are based upon the classic waka ideals of loftiness (taketakaki), emotional conviction (USHIN), and mystery and depth (YŪGEN). Stylistically, he preferred the elegant yet simple, unadorned expression of the orthodox Nijō school of waka, in contrast to the elliptical style Shinkei adopted from the more experimental Kyōgoku–Reizei poets. Neoclassical in attitude, his best poetry contains allusions to the court literature he knew so well, adding a resonance and depth rarely achieved before. Bashō and others admired verses of Sōgi which exhibit a melancholy tone (SABI) and subdued autumnal imagery, consonant with his reputation as a solitary traveler-poet. However, many of his best verses reveal a predilection for a more resplendent beauty (miyabi), reminiscent of Yoshimoto.

Sōgi's greatest achievement was to realize the full potential of the extended (usually 100-verse) renga form; in Minase sangin and Yuyama sangin, his aim was to orchestrate the tempo, mood, and variety of the sequence, rather than merely to produce outstanding individual verses. For Sōgi, an ideal sequence contained mostly subdued "background" (ji) verses, balanced by a few well-placed "pattern" (mon) verses exhibiting strong emotion or striking imagery. Thus he generally preferred close linking between verses (shinku)

over the more obscure and often ostentatious distant linking (soku) valued by Shinkei.

◼ ——Steven D. Carter, "Three Poets at Yuyama: Sōgi and Yuyama sangin hyakuin," Monumenta Nipponica 33.2–3 (1978). Etō Yasusada, Sōgi no kenkyū (1967). Ijichi Tetsuo, Sōgi (1943). Konishi Jin'ichi, Sōgi (1971). Earl Miner, Japanese Linked Poetry (1979), contains translations of Minase sangin and a solo 100-verse sequence by Sōgi.

Arthur H. THORNHILL III

Sogō Co, Ltd

One of Japan's largest department store chains, with branches in Ōsaka, Kōbe, and Tōkyō. Its history can be traced back to an Ōsaka clothing store that opened in 1830. It has subsidiary stores throughout the country in such cities as Matsuyama (Ehime Prefecture), Chiba and Kashiwa (Chiba Prefecture), Hiroshima, and Sapporo. Sales for the fiscal year ending February 1982 totaled ¥195.6 billion (US $831.7 million); leading components were clothing (40 percent), accessories (9 percent), sundry goods (16 percent), household goods (12 percent), foodstuffs (20 percent), restaurants (2 percent), and others (1 percent). In the same year Sogō, ranked 10th among the major department stores in Japan, was capitalized at ¥4.2 billion (US $17.9 million). The company's head office is located in Ōsaka.

sōgō shōsha → general trading companies

sōhei → warrior-monks

Sōhō Myōchō (1282–1337)

Also known as Shūhō Myōchō. Monk of the RINZAI SECT of Zen Buddhism. Born in Harima Province (now part of Hyōgo Prefecture), he first studied TENDAI SECT teachings but later traveled to Kyōto where he practiced Zen under the noted master Kōhō Kennichi (1241–1316) and subsequently under RANKEI DŌRYŪ's disciple Nampo Shōmyō (or NAMPO JŌMYŌ; 1235–1308). Following the death of Nampo Shōmyō, he returned to Kyōto and there led the life of a recluse until 1315 when he established a temple in Murasakino, then north of the city. With his great virtue, he attracted many followers, who also built temples on the same site. It eventually developed into the complex known as DAITOKUJI. His adherents included the emperors Hanazono and Go-Daigo. The former bestowed on him the title Daitō Kokushi ("National Teacher of the Great Lamp") by which he has been remembered.

MATSUNAMI Yoshihiro

Sōhyō

(abbreviation of Nihon Rōdō Kumiai Sō Hyōgikai; General Council of Trade Unions of Japan). Japan's largest nationwide federation of labor unions. Sōhyō was formed in 1950 through a merger of Sambetsu Minshuka Dōmei, which had seceded from SAMBETSU KAIGI (Congress of Industrial Labor Unions of Japan), and the left and neutral factions of Nihon Rōdō Sōdōmei (General Federation of Japan Trade Unions). Since its formation, it has been the leading labor organization in Japan. Although Sōhyō originally took an anticommunist position and planned to join Kokusai Jiyū Rōren (International Confederation of Free Trade Unions or ICFTU), it soon took a leftist stand in opposing the Korean War and formed a close relationship with the left wing of the JAPAN SOCIALIST PARTY. Sōhyō maintained its leading position even after the secession of its rightwing faction in 1953 and has organized a nationwide spring wage offensive (SHUNTŌ) every year since 1955. In 1960 it led a political strike in opposition to the revision of the United States-Japan Security Treaty, but then shifted to a policy emphasizing economic struggle. Since the yen revaluation of 1971 it has led spring labor offensives centered on the development of social welfare programs and the interests of those with low-income levels.

While Sōhyō includes almost all unionized government employees in Japan, it has not extended its power comparably in the private sector. Especially in large enterprises, Sōhyō is surpassed by DŌMEI (Japanese Confederation of Labor), another major labor organization. The appearance of groups within Sōhyō such as Tekkō Rōren (Japanese Federation of Iron and Steel Workers' Unions) with close relationships with the International Metalworkers Federation–Japan Council (IMF–JC) and Dōmei has recently jeopardized the stability of the organization. Although Sōhyō has traditionally maintained a cooperative relationship with the Japan Socialist Party, it has shown a tendency toward abandoning the policy of supporting a particular political party in recent years. In 1978, Sōhyō consisted of 50 trade unions with a membership of 4,550,000. See also LABOR.

Kurita KEN

Sōja

City in southern Okayama Prefecture, western Honshū. It developed as a shrine town around the Sōja Shrine and as the seat of the provincial capital (kokufu) of Bitchū Province. Formerly a farming area known for its rice, vegetables, and rush (igusa) for making the covering of tatami mats, Sōja now has spinning, foodstuff, machinery, and metal plants. Numerous mounded tombs (KOFUN), the Kibi Historical Prefectural Park, and the remains of the ancient state-established provincial temple (kokubunji) are of interest. Pop: 49,107.

Sōjiji

One of the two major centers, along with EIHEIJI, of the SŌTŌ SECT of ZEN Buddhism in Japan. Originally founded in 1321 by Keizan Jōkin (1268–1325) in Noto Province (now part of Ishikawa Prefecture), the center was moved in 1911, after a fire had destroyed it some years earlier, to its present location in Tsurumi Ward in the city of Yokohama. A branch temple was subsequently rebuilt on the original site and has remained a center of worship for faithful followers.

In 1267 Tettsū Gikai (1219–1309) was appointed the third abbot of Eiheiji, founded in Echizen Province (now part of Fukui Prefecture) by DŌGEN as the first Sōtō Zen monastery. He actively sought to propagate the sect throughout Japan, but he was opposed by those monks who preferred to remain in seclusion, away from secular concerns. After twice serving as abbot of Eiheiji, Tettsū eventually moved to Kaga Province (now part of Ishikawa Prefecture) to become the first Zen abbot of Daijōji, formerly a TENDAI SECT temple. Tettsū's successor, Keizan Jōkin, furthered the expansion of the sect and in 1321 converted Morookaji, a RITSU SECT temple, into the original Sōjiji, a Sōtō Zen monastery, and established it as a training center for monks from all regions of Japan. Since Noto and Kaga provinces had traditionally been under the heavy influence of Tendai esoteric Buddhism, Keizan and his followers were conciliatory toward esoteric Buddhist teachings. In 1322 Emperor GO-DAIGO officially recognized Sōjiji as a Sōtō monastery. The second abbot of Sōjiji, Gazan Jōseki (1275–1365), devoted his entire career to the propagation of Sōtō sect teachings, from Kyūshū in the south to the Kantō (eastern Honshū) region and even farther north. In 1615 the Tokugawa shogunate designated Eiheiji and Sōjiji as the two major centers of Sōtō sect Zen. As one of the largest and most active Buddhist institutions in the eastern part of Japan, Sōjiji serves Zen followers in the Tōkyō and Yokohama areas.　T. James KODERA

sōjutsu

The ancient martial art of attack and defense with a spear. Japanese spears are divided into two types according to the method used to attach the spearhead to the long wooden shaft: the fukuroho style and nakago style. The former type is called hoko, a long-shafted spear with a double-edged head primarily employed as a thrusting weapon. The hoko was used in combat and ceremony through the first half of the Kamakura period (1185–1333) but was replaced by the latter type, which is also called yari. Becoming especially popular after the Mongol Invasions of Japan (1274; 1281), the yari played an important role on the battlefield as one of the major weapons of war at the end of the Muromachi period (1333–1568), a time of contending warlords. The yari commonly has a double-edged blade or head ranging in size from 30 to 75 centimeters (12 to 29 in); an especially long-bladed type is called ōmiyari. The shaft length varies depending on the size of the spearhead; some are as long as 5.45 meters (17.9 ft). The suyari is a single-head spear. Two kinds of yari with fork-shaped spearheads are called kamayari and jūmonji-yari. Spears with two or more prongs can be used not only to lance but also to pull down an object by hooking it.

Various methods of spear handling were developed by experts using different kinds of yari. The Tenshin Shōden Shindō school, established by Iishino Chōisai, and the Hōzōin school, founded by Kakuzen Hōin'ei, are two famous schools. During the Sengoku period (1467–1568) infantry divisions armed with long spears, called

yaribusuma ("screen of spears"), often played a decisive role in battle. After the harquebus (see HINAWAJŪ) was introduced in 1543, however, the yari suddenly lost importance. In the peace of the Edo period (1600–1868), the yari became a symbol of samurai status, and whenever high-ranking warriors made formal trips, they were accompanied by retainers bearing these spears.

Sōjutsu is counted as one of the seven primary military arts together with KYŪDŌ (the art of shooting with bow and arrow), bajutsu (the art of horsemanship), KENDŌ (the art of swordsmanship), JŪDŌ, hōjutsu (gunnery), and heihō (military strategy). Sons of daimyō were encouraged to learn the art of spear handling as part of their necessary military accomplishments. There are 148 different schools of sōjutsu currently on record. See also MARTIAL ARTS.

TOMIKI Kenji

Sōka

City in southeastern Saitama Prefecture, central Honshū; contiguous with Adachi Ward in Tōkyō. In the Edo period (1600–1868) it developed as one of the POST-STATION TOWNS on the highway Ōshū Kaidō. Leather, textiles, and machine industries are active. A well-known local product is sembei (rice crackers). Today the city is a dormitory suburb of Tōkyō. Pop: 186,618.

Sōka Gakkai

(Value-Creating Society). One of Japan's new religious movements (see NEW RELIGIONS). Founded on 18 November 1930 in Tōkyō by MAKIGUCHI TSUNESABURŌ, a school teacher who became its first president. Sōka Gakkai is a juridically independent lay organization of the Nichiren Shō sect (Nichiren Shōshū) of Buddhism. The head temple is TAISEKIJI in the city of Fujinomiya, Shizuoka Prefecture. It is the largest of the new religious organizations in Japan; in early 1980 it claimed an active membership of 6,000,000 people; sister organizations overseas comprise some 430,000 people in about 50 countries. In addition to its religious activities, it has been active in numerous cultural and social projects.

At the time of its establishment, the organization was called the Sōka Kyōiku Gakkai (Value-Creating Educational Society) and was composed mainly of school teachers interested in Makiguchi's educational theories. Makiguchi had originally intended to introduce various reforms to Japanese society through a fundamental reform of its educational system, but his educational theories received little attention from the academic world of his day. Makiguchi was converted to Nichiren Shōshū in 1928. He became convinced that his educational ideals could best be realized through its founder NICHIREN's teachings, and it was to advocate an educational reform integrated with religious values that he founded the organization in 1930.

The Sōka Kyōiku Gakkai grew slowly during the 1930s. The first general meeting was held in 1939. There were about 300 members in 1940 and about 3,000 in 1942. On 6 July 1943 Makiguchi and his chief disciple, TODA JŌSEI, the general director of the organization, were jailed by the government along with 19 other associates, having been charged with violating the 1941 revision of the PEACE PRESERVATION LAW OF 1925 for advising their followers not to venerate Shintō, then the state religion, and for opposing the government's war policy. Makiguchi died in prison on 18 November 1944.

Toda began to reconstruct the organization following his release from prison in July 1945; the name was changed to Sōka Gakkai (Value-Creating Society) to reflect its greater emphasis on religious rather than educational aims. Toda assumed the presidency of the Sōka Gakkai in May 1951 and embarked on a vigorous campaign to consolidate and expand the organization. At the time of his death in 1958, the Sōka Gakkai claimed a membership of 750,000 family units.

Toda was succeeded by IKEDA DAISAKU (b 1928), who became president in May 1960. Ikeda, who had been converted to Nichiren Shōshū in 1947, had served as Toda's closest associate in organizing and expanding Sōka Gakkai activities throughout the 1950s. Under his leadership the Sōka Gakkai grew rapidly during the 1960s and 1970s and also expanded abroad, primarily in North and South America. He also traveled frequently throughout Japan and to Europe, North America, China, India, and the Soviet Union. He resigned in 1979 and was succeeded by Hōjō Hiroshi (1923–81). The latter was succeeded by Einosuke Akiya (b 1930) in 1981.

The Sōka Gakkai upholds the Nichiren Shōshū teachings as its basic doctrine. It assumes as a central idea that the Buddha nature is inherent in each human being who can manifest this nature through religious practices. The Buddha nature is regarded as the dynamic force that can change an individual's bad "karma," or destiny, into a good one. The Buddha nature, regarded as a motivating force, is identical with the *myōhō*, or "ultimate law," that permeates all phenomena and natural laws. With this idea as a basis, the Sōka Gakkai advocates reformation from within ("human revolution") and holds that changes in individuals affect society and help bring about happiness and peace in the world.

The essence of its teachings can be summarized as faith, practice, and study. By faith is meant unwavering belief in the doctrines of Nichiren Shōshū. A person practices this faith by chanting the *daimoku* (a repetition of the phrase NAMU MYŌHŌ RENGE KYŌ, literally, "Devotion to the Lotus Sutra," here meaning the ultimate truth of life) before the object of worship installed in the family altar, known as the Gohonzon, and by reciting parts of the Lotus Sutra. The Gohonzon is a copy of a scroll originally inscribed by Nichiren in Chinese characters with later inscriptions by high priests of Nichiren Shōshū; it is regarded as the manifestation of the essence of the universal law indicated in the Lotus Sutra. Practice signifies the incorporation of Buddhist activities into the pattern of one's daily life. The most important of these activities is the communication of the doctrines of Nichiren Shōshū to other people. Study means the study of Nichiren's teachings to deepen one's faith.

The Sōka Gakkai holds frequent seminars, guidance meetings, and community discussion meetings to enhance the members' understanding of orthodox Nichiren Buddhism and to give followers an opportunity to share their faith and experiences. It also carries out a broad range of educational, cultural, and social programs to transform its religious ideals into social realities. It has launched a campaign for world peace and, in accordance with the founder's ideas, it has also developed its own educational system, including Sōka University, founded in Tōkyō in 1971. The organization publishes numerous books and periodicals; its daily newspaper, *Seikyō shimbun*, claimed a circulation of about 4,540,000 in 1983. It also founded a political party, KŌMEITŌ, in 1964 but separated the party from itself in 1970.

📖 ——Kiyoaki Murata, *Japan's New Buddhism* (1969). James W. White, *The Sōkagakkai and Mass Society* (1970).

sōkaiya

("professional stockholder"). Certain individuals or groups of individuals who sell their services as "protection" for companies. They are so called because they generally own a small amount of the company's stock and attend the shareholders' meeting, ostensibly to keep order.

The high degree of dependence on financial institutions for provision of capital for equipment and operating funds in postwar Japan has led to the relative neglect of the rights of the individual shareholder and to an emphasis instead on joint stockholding among corporations. Although high priority is placed on the payment of dividends by corporations and on protecting other basic rights of shareholders, there has been a tendency to treat the annual shareholders' meeting, required under Japanese commercial regulations for approval of the annual statement of accounts, as a necessary evil. As a result of the presence of the *sōkaiya* strong-arm types, it is not unusual for the shareholders' meeting of a large corporation to last just long enough for the company president to make a few remarks and answer a number of "planted" questions. This procedure may last from 15 to 30 minutes. For their services, the *sōkaiya* generally receive "assistance money"; they also charge for advertisements in publications that they sponsor. These publications have the purpose of providing a forum to influence important corporate decisions which require stockholders' approval.

The system of using *sōkaiya* is generally recognized as antiquated, and leading corporations have banded together, with the cooperation of law enforcement authorities, to protect themselves against the *sōkaiya's* excessive exactions and other abuses. Nevertheless, it has proved extremely difficult to remove the influence of these elements because of their skill at intimidation, including the threat of acting in just the opposite way from their basic purpose—that is, they can disrupt the meeting just as easily as they can "pacify" it.

C. Tait RATCLIFFE

sokushin jōbutsu

("Buddhahood in this very body"). A central tenet of the SHINGON SECT of Buddhism which holds that perfect enlightenment can be attained in one's present lifetime and is as much a bodily as a spiritual process. The doctrine was explicated by KŪKAI (774–835), who, in his *Sokushin jōbutsu gi* (817–818), traced its origins to the treatise known in Japanese as *Bodaishin ron* (Treatise on the Bodhicitta "Mind of Enlightenment") attributed to the Indian sage Nāgārjuna.

The concept of *sokushin jōbutsu* derives from the radically immanentalist view that the potentiality to become a Buddha exists fully developed, though latent, in all creatures and needs not so much to be developed as simply evoked. This understanding is related to the immanentalist emphasis upon HONGAKU (primordial enlightenment) as contrasted with the developmental *shigaku* (incipient enlightenment) viewpoint. Broadly construed, *sokushin jōbutsu* suggests an organic, pantheistic view of the universe, and the doctrine was easily accommodated to the pantheistic inclinations of Shintō. Thus it became important for Japanese Buddhism not only as an explicit doctrine but also as an interpretive tendency. As a philosophical and religious tenet, the doctrine shows some similarities both to the "sudden enlightenment" (J: *tongo*) ideal of the so-called Southern school of Chinese ZEN (see RINZAI SECT) and to the "liberation in this life" (Skt: *jīvan mukta*) concept of Indian tantrism. Like the latter, *sokushin jōbutsu* in its extreme interpretations served at times as a justification for strongly antinomian doctrines and practices such as those of the notorious Tachikawa sect.

📖 ——Kūkai, *Sokushin jōbutsu gi* (817 or 818), tr Yoshito S. Hakeda as "Attaining Enlightenment in This Very Existence," in *Kūkai: Major Works* (1972). James H. SANFORD

sōkyoku

Music for KOTO. The *koto* was used in the 11th century to accompany court songs from the SAIBARA and *imayō* repertoires; as a solo instrument from at least the Kamakura period (1185–1333); and to accompany Buddhist chant from at least the late 15th century. *Ninchi yōroku* (1192), by Fujiwara no Moronaga (1138–92), and other sources preserve early notation and other information about medieval practice. However, the term *sōkyoku* (sometimes *zokusō*) is generally applied to the solo repertoire developed from the late 15th century onwards, when Kenjun, a former Buddhist monk from Kyūshū, composed a group of song suites (*koto kumiuta*) inspired partly by Japanese court music and partly by the technique and music of the Chinese *qin* (*ch'in*; a 7-string zither). This new music was known as Tsukushi *sō* or Tsukushi *gaku*; the melodies of certain pieces were based closely on court music, especially on the famous piece *Etenraku*; and various other pieces in Tsukushi *sō* included some more purely instrumental music. These last pieces inspired a series of instrumental solos, the so-called *dammono*, which are usually credited to the blind SHAMISEN master Yatsuhashi Kengyō (1614–85), one of Kenjun's pupils. The *dammono* are sets of variations, all using the same thematic material and having similar structures; the most famous are *Rokudan no shirabe*, *Hachidan no shirabe*, and *Midare rinzetsu*. *Midare*, which has an irregular structure, is based on the Tsukushi *sō* piece *Rinzetsu*. Yatsuhashi also rearranged the old *kumiuta* of Tsukushi *sō*, composed new *kumiuta*, and established *hira-jōshi* and *kumoi-jōshi* (with prominent minor seconds) as the two basic tunings for the *koto*. At present there are very few players in the two schools Tsukushiryū and Yatsuhashiryū, but many of their pieces were adopted and modified by later schools, and their influence on later *koto* music has been of fundamental importance.

It is not entirely clear what happened after Yatsuhashi's death. Thirteen *kumiuta* composed by him were printed in *Kinkyokushō* (1695), and some 21 others were gradually added to the repertoire by later composers. Among Yatsuhashi's followers, Kitajima Kengyō (d 1690) and his pupil Ikuta Kengyō (1655–1715), together with others, were active in Kyōto; and other Yatsuhashi offshoots developed in the Ryūkyū Islands, Ōsaka, Kaga Province (now part of Ishikawa Prefecture), Edo (now Tōkyō), and northern Japan. Many of these were influenced by Ikutaryū, which in modified form gradually came to be the leading school in western Japan.

Meanwhile the repertoire was being extended under the influence of *shamisen* music, especially JIUTA, a genre which comprised both *kumiuta* and concert arrangements of theater pieces, particularly *nagauta* and *hauta*, and which was associated above all with western Japan. *Shamisen* pieces were rearranged for *koto* or as *sankyoku* trios; and the later 18th century saw the flowering of a new form, the *tegoto-mono*, composed by such men as Fujinaga Kengyō (1719–57), Minezaki Kōtō (fl 1790s), Matsuura Kengyō (d 1822), Kikuoka Kengyō (1791–1847), and many others. *Tegoto-mono* have two or more 31-syllable songs which are separated by instrumental interludes *(tegoto)* that give the performer an opportunity to display his technique. Yaezaki Kengyō (d 1766) had popularized the use of a second *koto* part *(kaede)* in *sōkyoku,* and this became customary in *tegoto-mono.*

At the same time a new movement was led in Edo by Yamada Kengyō (1757–1817), the blind son of a NŌ actor, whose 36 *koto* compositions include some elaborate pieces of program music. These works, with specially written texts, often on themes from classical literature, have long, flowing vocal lines and dramatic contrasts in mood. The *koto* parts are relatively simple, but may use unusual tunings and special effects. Yamada Kengyō also made innovations in *koto* technique. Since his day there have been two main schools of *sōkyoku,* Ikutaryū (centered in Kyōto) and Yamadaryū (in Tōkyō).

The leading composers of the mid-19th century were Mitsuzaki Kengyō and Yoshizawa Kengyō II (d 1872), who led a revival of *kumiuta.* Yoshizawa introduced a new tuning, *kokin-jōshi,* for a group of compositions based on texts from the KOKINSHŪ. During the Meiji period (1868–1912) the *koto* world was in some disarray, but a few neoclassical works composed then are still performed. In the 20th century the two leading composers and performers have been MIYAGI MICHIO (1894–1956) and NAKANOSHIMA KIN'ICHI (b 1904). At present *koto* music flourishes as never before, and its future seems assured.

—— W. Adriaansz, *The Kumiuta and Danmono Traditions of Japanese Koto Music* (1973). Kishibe Shigeo, ed, *Sōkyoku, shakuhachi,* vols 3 and 4 of *Hōgaku taikei* (1970–71). Kishibe Shigeo and Sasamori Takefusa, *Tsugaru sōkyoku Ikutaryū no kenkyū: Rekishi hen* (1976). Tafuji Seifū, *Yamadaryū sōka kōwa zempen* (1965). Tōyō Ongaku Gakkai, ed, *Sōkyoku to jiuta no kenkyū* (1967). Bonnie C. Wade, *Tegotomono: Music for the Japanese Koto* (1976). Yamazaki Shinko, *Yatsuhashiryū koto kumiuta no kenkyū* (1977).

David B. WATERHOUSE

solatium

(isharyō). In Japanese law, compensation for pain and suffering. Compensation for damages arising out of torts (Civil Code, art. 709) can be divided into compensation for economic loss and compensation for pain and suffering.

Solatium is usually paid in cases of injury to person or reputation, but even in the case of invasion of property rights, it is provided that compensation must be paid for nonfinancial damages (Civil Code, art. 710). However, in the case of invasion of property rights, solatium is limited to intentional damage and to damage to property of great sentimental value. Solatium may be included not only in compensation for damages arising from torts but also in compensation for damages arising out of the nonperformance of obligatory duties (Civil Code, arts. 415–6). However, in practice, such consolation payments are usually limited to special cases such as personal injury, defamation, or injury to property of great sentimental value. In the past, solatium was paid to the wife in divorce cases, but this has now been almost completely absorbed into the distribution of property system (Civil Code, art. 768) that was established after World War II.

Personal injuries caused by traffic accidents, pollution, and pharmaceutical products are prime examples of cases in which payment of solatium is required. In cases where the victim has died, special provisions allow the victim's mother or father, spouse, or child to claim consolation payments as compensation for his or her own suffering (Civil Code, art. 711). Moreover, case law recognizes the right of the decedent's successor to inherit the deceased's claim for solatium and to bring such a claim in his capacity as successor. The person making the claim may choose either method, but there is no great difference in amounts awarded. However, no one can claim for solatium through both methods.

At trial, it is the judge who decides whether solatium is to be paid and, if so, the amount to be awarded (in Japan there is no jury system). The judge makes this determination at his discretion after considering all relevant factors. There is a trend for the amount of the solatium to be determined not by such subjective factors as the relative amount of actual pain and suffering, but rather in a more standardized fashion, on the basis of objective factors. For example, in the case of death resulting from an automobile accident, the typical consolation payment is currently somewhere between ¥7 million ($31,742) and ¥13 million ($58,949) with ¥10 million ($45,345) per victim the norm, regardless of the number of survivors of the decedent (1981 figures). The amount of solatium has risen rapidly in response to the high growth rate of Japan's economy and the increased consciousness of individual rights. The trend has been reinforced by the increased number of automobile accidents and the guarantee of compensation by liability insurance. KATŌ Ichirō

Sōma

City in northeastern Fukushima Prefecture, northern Honshū, on the Pacific Ocean. Sōma developed as a castle town of the Sōma family. It is now a distribution center for rice. Stockbreeding and sericulture are carried on in the outlying areas. A tourist attraction is the Sōma Nomaoi Festival, a horseback tournament held every year from 23–25 July. Pop: 38,335.

Sōma family

Provincial leaders and later *daimyō* of the northern part of what is now the northeastern corner of Fukushima Prefecture (originally the southern part of Mutsu Province) from the 12th century through the Edo period (1600–1868). The family claimed descent from the 10th-century military hero TAIRA NO MASAKADO. In 1189 Sōma Morotsune (1139–1205) was awarded the Namekata district of Mutsu Province for helping MINAMOTO NO YORITOMO, the founder of the Kamakura shogunate, to subjugate the northern region. During the civil wars of the Sengoku period (1467–1568), the Sōma family was alternately in conflict and in alliance with other nearby daimyō, especially the DATE FAMILY in Sendai. Then Sōma Yoshitane (1548–1635) allied himself with TOYOTOMI HIDEYOSHI, and the family confirmed its landholdings. When TOKUGAWA IEYASU confronted the Toyotomi family in the Battle of SEKIGAHARA (1600), the Sōma family refused to side with the Tokugawa and its domain was confiscated. In 1604, however, the family was again granted its traditional lands in a general amnesty and settled in Nakamura (now the city of Sōma, Fukushima Prefecture) with an assessed income of 60,000 *koku* (see KOKUDAKA).

Sōmagahara Incident → Girard case

Sōma Kokkō (1876–1955)

Businesswoman and patron of the arts. Original name, Hoshi Ryō. Born in Sendai, niece of the feminist SASAKI TOYOJU. She entered the Meiji Girls' School (Meiji Jogakkō) in 1895 and also attended the Ferris Girls' School in Yokohama. In 1897 she married Sōma Aizō (1870–1954), and in 1901 they opened the Nakamuraya, a bakery and restaurant still flourishing in the Shinjuku district of Tōkyō. The store became famous for its Western pastries and curried rice. The Sōmas encouraged the artists and writers who gathered there, such as the sculptor OGIWARA MORIE and the drama group centered on SHIMAMURA HŌGETSU. The couple also befriended the exiled Indian independence movement leader Rash Behari BOSE and hid him from the police; Bose married their daughter Toshiko in 1918. At about the same time, they also helped the blind Russian poet Vasilii EROSHENKO find refuge. Among Sōma Kokkō's works are her memoirs, *Mokui* (1934, Silent Transition).

Sōma ware

(sōma-yaki). Ceramics produced in two centers, one in Nakamura in the city of Sōma, the other at Ōbori in Namie, both in Fukushima Prefecture. The products of the former, which some consider true Sōma ware, are also called Nakamura *sōma-yaki* or *koma-yaki* (because of their *koma* or horse motif), while those of the latter are known as Ōbori *sōma-yaki.*

The Nakamura kiln was set up by Tashiro Gengoemon, a retainer of the lord of the domain, Sōma Yoshitane, around 1630. Encouraged by Yoshitane, Gengoemon spent seven years in Kyōto, where he learned the techniques of Omuro pottery under NONOMURA NINSEI, from whom he later received the name Seijiemon. On returning to the Sōma domain he set up a kiln for the production of stoneware for the exclusive use of the SŌMA FAMILY. Initially the kiln produced wares in the Ninsei style. Not until the mid-19th century was it possible to purchase the ware on the open market. The wares are made from clay obtained from Tsubota near Sōma. The traditional pale, honey-colored transparent glaze is made from a mixture of feldspar and zelkova wood ash. *Koma-yaki* is easily identified by the underglaze painted design of a leaping horse that appears on almost all vessels and that is said to have been based upon a painting by Kanō Naonobu (1607–50). It gives the ware its name and was first used by Seijiemon II in the 1690s.

The kiln, designated an Important Cultural Property in 1968, was constructed in the late 1640s. It is a six-chambered climbing kiln (noborigama) having an unstepped sloping floor of 15°. It is fired four or five times a year and is one of the oldest kilns still in continuous use in Japan. The atmosphere in the kiln is predominantly an oxidizing one, and hence the wares tend to be buff to off-white. The present potters, now in the 14th generation, still produce the traditional range of shapes, including teabowls, jars, and dishes.

Ōbori sōma-yaki is thought to have been established by a servant of Hangaya Kyūkan, himself a retainer of Sōma Masatane, in the 1680s. The kiln produces a wide range of wares and the varieties of glaze and decoration used are numerous. Today around 22 kilns are engaged in making the ware. *Brian* HICKMAN

Sōmin (?–653)

Buddhist priest and scholar in the service of the YAMATO COURT; also known as Bin, Sōbin, or Min. In 608 he accompanied a mission to the Sui dynasty of China headed by ONO NO IMOKO. He remained in China until 632, studying Buddhism, Confucianism, divination, and other subjects. Because of his extensive knowledge of Chinese institutions, together with TAKAMUKO NO KUROMARO he was appointed state scholar (kunihakase) in 645 and assisted Prince Naka no Ōe (later Emperor TENJI) in drawing up the provisions of the TAIKA REFORM. The reform, inaugurated in the following year, was intended to establish in Japan the systems of land tenure, government, and taxation then current in China.

Sompi bummyaku

(August and Humble Genealogical Lines). A comprehensive collection of genealogical tables begun sometime in the late 14th century by the court noble Tōin Kinsada (1340–99) and continued by his adopted son Mitsusue (dates unknown) and Mitsusue's son Sanehiro (1409–57). The work as originally planned comprised three parts: (1) a genealogy of the imperial family, the "august" line referred to in the title; (2) genealogies of leading families such as the FUJIWARA, TAIRA, and MINAMOTO; and (3) lines of transmission of the largely hereditary learned traditions officially recognized by the court, such as law and mathematics. Passing out of the hands of the Tōin line, the work was further elaborated and also somewhat distorted by the later editors, notably Kanroji Chikanaga (1424–1500), SANJŌNISHI SANETAKA, and Nakamikado Noritane (1442–1525). The imperial genealogy appeared as an independent work, called the Honchō kōin jōun roku (A Record of Imperial Descent and Succession in This Realm). This later work was compiled in 1416 by Tōin Mitsusue. Despite its flaws, *Sompi bummyaku* is an invaluable source of genealogical and biographical information. *Cornelius J.* KILEY

Sone no Yoshitada (fl ca 985)

Classical (WAKA) poet, bold and eccentric innovator, and rebel against the "Fujiwara style" that was inherited from the 9th and early 10th centuries and became increasingly monotonous and decadent in the late 10th and 11th centuries.

Yoshitada came from obscure origins and never achieved important office, his highest appointment being secretary of the province of Tango (now part of Kyōto Prefecture). From the combination of the first character of his surname with his official title, he is said to have been nicknamed So-Tango; when this was, much to his annoyance, further abbreviated to So-Tan, he is said to have angrily sputtered, "Why not go all the way and call me just So-Ta?" Tales and anecdotes about Yoshitada's eccentricities abound: he is depicted as an odd, somewhat irascible character, ill-clothed and badly groomed, and completely unperturbed by the impression he made. On one occasion, it is told, he appeared without invitation at a poetry gathering sponsored by ex-Emperor En'yū (959–991; r 969–984), at which the most prominent poets of the day were present in formal court dress. Yoshitada appeared dressed in an informal robe and cap and sat himself down in the lowest place. When it was demanded that he explain himself, he replied, "I came because I heard that 'the poets' were invited, and I am a poet no less than any of you." And as he made no sign of going away, the courtiers found themselves obliged to suffer his presence.

Yoshitada's poetic eccentricities were mostly confined to the use of startling colloquialisms, crude images, and "low," "vulgar" metaphors. On reading one of Yoshitada's poems in which the expression "stacks of mugwort" (yomogi ga soma) was used, the arch-conservative Fujiwara no Nagatō (940?–1015?) is said to have exploded, "The man is mad! Whoever heard of 'stacks of mugwort'?" Despite his idiosyncracies, however, Yoshitada seems to have been on the whole content with his low rank and office and free of selfish ambition or guile. His experiments with unusual diction, in which he persisted despite the indignation of his contemporaries, are so unique in the age that the phenomenon demands some explanation: It is said that Yoshitada was inspired in part by the coarse, homely imagery of early Japanese poetry as preserved in the first great anthology, the MAN'YŌSHŪ (ca 759), and in part by the example of Chinese poetry, particularly the colloquial verse of the very popular Bo Juyi (Po Chü-i; 772–846). Whatever the source of inspiration, Yoshitada stands out alone in a rather homogeneous and not very interesting poetic age. Unfortunately, he often erred in his use of colloquial and archaic diction, making himself ridiculous by his frequent misidentification and misuse of words. On the other hand, Yoshitada sometimes composed in a more quiet, reflective mode of natural description quite new in the age and foreshadowing the descriptive poetry of retirement in nature practiced in the 11th century by MINAMOTO NO TSUNENOBU and his son MINAMOTO NO TOSHIYORI, and preeminently by FUJIWARA NO TOSHINARI (Shunzei) and FUJIWARA NO SADAIE (Teika) and their adherents in the 12th and 13th centuries. Thus Yoshitada was not merely an eccentric personality, but a poet of importance who left his mark on tradition. Nor was he wholly unappreciated as a poet by his contemporaries, who esteemed his more graceful compositions. Nine of his poems were chosen for the third imperial anthology, the SHŪI WAKASHŪ (ca 1005, Collection of Gleanings), while 89 more were included in various imperial anthologies from the Goshūishū (Later Collection of Gleanings) on. His personal collection, Sotanshū (Collection of the Secretary of Tango Province) contains some 625 poems.

➤——Robert H. Brower and Earl Miner, *Japanese Court Poetry* (1961). *Robert H.* BROWER

Song Hŭi-gyŏng (1376–1446)

(J: Sō Kikei). Korean government official of the Yi dynasty (1392–1910); also known by his pen name, Nosongdang (J: Rōshōdō). Song came to Japan in 1420 as an envoy from King Sejong to reciprocate a visit by a Japanese delegation sent by the shōgun Ashikaga Yoshimochi (r 1395–1423) to request Buddhist scriptures. His record of the trip, *Nosongdang Ilbon haengnok* (J: *Rōshōdō Nihon kōroku*), provides valuable information on Japanese society, religion, and customs of the time.

Song Jiaoren (Sung Chiao-jen) (1882–1913)

(J: Sō Kyōjin). An anti-Manchu revolutionary, follower of HUANG XING (Huang Hsing), and founder of the Guomindang (Kuomintang; Nationalist Party), Song Jiaoren studied Western political thought while a student in Japan. His assassination in 1913 marked the end of the initial period of optimism concerning democratic government in the new Republic of China. Song fled to Japan in 1904 after the failure of plans by Huang Xing's Huaxing Hui (Hua-hsing Hui; Society for the Revival of China) for an uprising in Hunan. In Tōkyō Song studied at the Kōbun Institute, Hōsei University and, under the assumed name of Song Lian (Sung Lien), at Waseda University. As a participant in the anti-Manchu movement among Chinese students in Tōkyō, he founded the journal *Ershi shiji zhi Zhina* (Erh-shih shih-chi chih Chih-na; Twentieth Century China), which was later named *Min bao* (Min pao; People's Journal) when it became the organ of the revolutionary United League (Tongmeng Hui or T'ung-meng Hui) led by SUN YAT-SEN. During this period, Song became a close friend of KITA IKKI, the Japanese socialist and nationalist. In 1910 Song returned to China, where he worked closely with Huang. Song was convinced of the necessity of creating a strong party which would counter the growing authoritarianism of President YUAN SHI-KAI (Yüan Shih-k'ai) and in August 1912 he formed the Guomindang, a predecessor of Sun's Guomindang and China's first modern democratic party. On 20 March 1913 Song was fatally shot by followers of Yuan.

➤——Song Jiaoren, *Wo zhi lishi* (Wo chih li-shih; 1920). Chün-tu Hsüeh, *Huang Hsing and the Chinese Revolution* (1961). K. S. Liew, *Struggle for Democracy: Sung Chiao-jen and the 1911 Revolution* (1971).

Song Zheyuan (Sung Che-yüan) (1885–1940)

(J: Sō Tetsugen). A military figure in modern China, directly involved in Sino-Japanese confrontations in North China in the 1930s. From early in his career, until 1930, Song was a subordinate of Feng Yuxiang (Feng Yü-hsiang; 1882–1948), a warlord in northwest China, and not directly loyal to CHIANG KAI-SHEK, the Guomindang (Kuomintang; Nationalist Party) leader and unifier of China. With the outbreak of the MANCHURIAN INCIDENT of 18 September 1931, Song, then commander of the 29th Army in Chahar and Rehe (Jehol) provinces, issued a telegram to the Guomindang, calling for war against Japan. He resisted the Japanese GUANDONG (KWANTUNG) ARMY when it invaded Rehe in the spring of 1933 and fought on until the TANGGU (TANGKU) TRUCE of 31 May. In December 1935 Song assumed the chairmanship of the JI-CHA (CHI-CH'A) AUTONOMOUS POLITICAL COUNCIL created by the Japanese military. In the face of anti-Japanese student demonstrations (see DECEMBER NINTH MOVEMENT), he informed the Japanese that he would not be responsible for order in Beiping (Peiping, as Beijing [Peking] was called, 1928–49) if they continued to agitate for the separation of North China. In this, Song showed that, although he was not dependent on Chiang's Nationalist government in Nanjing (Nanking), neither was he necessarily pro-Japanese. Immediately after the MARCO POLO BRIDGE INCIDENT (7 July 1937) in which Japanese troops fired on Chinese soldiers, Song went to Tianjin (Tientsin) to negotiate a settlement with Japan. Japanese troops moved toward Beiping, and Song evacuated the city on 28 July. Forced to retreat southward, the remains of Song's troops were defeated in the autumn at Xinxiang (Hsin-hsiang), a strategic point in Henan (Honan) near the borders of Hebei (Hopeh) and Shandong (Shantung), marking the end of what had been a major military force in North China.

Sonkeikaku Library

(Sonkeikaku Bunko; more correctly, Maeda Ikutoku Kai Sonkeikaku Bunko). The MAEDA FAMILY library; located in Komaba, Meguro Ward, Tōkyō. It is regarded as one of the finest private collections of the Edo period (1600–1868), when daimyō did much to influence the development of culture by collecting important manuscripts, books, and works of art. Five generations, beginning with MAEDA TOSHIIE (1538?–99), the founder of the family, collected the riches of Ming-dynasty (1368–1644) Chinese classics and printed scriptures, old manuscripts and household records, rare Heian (794–1185) and Kamakura (1185–1333) books and art works, as well as valued Edo-period handicrafts, including publications. By the time of the fifth family head, MAEDA TSUNANORI (1643–1724), there were counted among the holdings of the library some 80 priceless works that are today recognized as National Treasures and Important Cultural Properties by the Japanese government. A handwritten copy by FUJIWARA NO SADAIE of KI NO TSURAYUKI's Tosa nikki (Tosa Diary) is just one of the many treasures in the library. Part of the collection is now housed in the Kanazawa City Public Library.

Theodore F. WELCH

sonnō jōi

(literally, "Revere the Emperor, Expel the Barbarians"). The idea that Japan should be unified under imperial rule and that incursions by foreigners should be resolutely repelled. Sonnō jōi as a political doctrine developed during the latter part of the Edo period (1600–1868), and as the guiding principle of the movement to overthrow the Tokugawa shogunate, it played a significant role in bringing about the MEIJI RESTORATION. Even after the Restoration, it served as the prototype of the state-oriented nationalism of modern Japan.

The tendency to hold foreigners in contempt as "barbarians" can be traced back to ancient China. The necessity of defending the Middle Kingdom against foreign invaders was a recurrent theme throughout Chinese history. Particularly during the Song (Sung) dynasty (960–1279), when China's northern frontiers were constantly threatened by nomadic invaders, the idea of "foreigner-as-barbarian" was stressed by many thinkers including Zhu Xi (Chu Hsi; 1130–1200). In the Chinese instance, however, the basis for differentiating native and foreigner was always cultural or moral, and sonnō jōi did not develop into a racial or statist ideology. Indeed, the expression sonnō jōi was never used by the Chinese.

In Japan the sacrosanct character of the imperial institution and the superiority of Japan over other nations were upheld by such 17th-century Confucian scholars as YAMAZAKI ANSAI and YAMAGA

SOKŌ. In the 18th century the view was vigorously expounded by MOTOORI NORINAGA and other scholars of the Japanese classics (see KOKUGAKU). As Russian and British ships intruded into Japanese waters in the closing years of the 18th century and as social unrest erupted in the form of peasant rebellion, anxiety arose about the viability of the 150-year-old policy of NATIONAL SECLUSION. Confronted with this crisis, scholars and intellectuals put forth all manner of theories and proposals to ensure Japan's independence and future development.

One of the more prominent ideas to emerge was the amalgamation of the concepts sonnō and jōi, and the first thinker to do so systematically was AIZAWA SEISHISAI, a scholar of the Mito domain (now part of Ibaraki Prefecture). In his treatise SHINRON (1825), Aizawa stressed the importance of uniting the people's will toward a national purpose. To achieve this, he proposed the establishment of a political order based on the quasi-religious authority of the emperor, and the heightening of national consciousness through a sense of confrontation with foreign enemies. In formulating his sonnō jōi ideas into a political theory and strategy, Aizawa was no doubt influenced by the Confucian scholar OGYŪ SORAI and by Kokugaku.

This sonnō jōi doctrine was subsequently to become a distinguishing mark of the MITO SCHOOL of historical studies. In fact, the expression first appeared in Kōdōkan ki (1838), a manifesto drafted by FUJITA TŌKO and read in public under the name of the Mito daimyō, TOKUGAWA NARIAKI, explaining the purpose of the domainal school, Kōdōkan, and expressing the spirit of Mito studies. In that work, the phrase sonnō was used to describe admiringly the respect and reverence paid to the imperial court by TOKUGAWA IEYASU, the founder of the shogunate, while jōi was used to mean the proscription of Christianity. It did not carry any antishogunal overtones, nor did it call for a blind and senseless xenophobia.

With the partial opening of Japan under pressure from the Western powers, however, the weakness of the shogunate both within and without was exposed. Fervent advocates of sonnō jōi like YOSHIDA SHŌIN and MAKI IZUMI put forth incisive criticisms of the shogunal institution and called for its abolition. The expression came to represent a militant antishogunate stance and was soon taken up as the rallying cry for the gathering movement to overthrow the shogunate and restore imperial rule. Since the sonnō jōi movement originally envisioned a unified nation centering on the shogunate, some historians have regarded it as no more than a conservative ideology aimed at maintenance of the shogunal ruling structure. However, the fact that sonnō jōi had as its main object the preservation of national unity meant that, in the face of shogunal impotence, it would lead inevitably to an antishogunate position. In this light, one must stress the positive role of sonnō jōi as an impetus in the formation of modern Japan.

📖 ——Bitō Masahide, "Sonnō jōi shisō," in Iwanami kōza: Nihon rekishi, vol 13 (Iwanami Shoten, 1977). David M. Earl, Emperor and Nation in Japan (1964). Matsumoto Sannosuke, Tennōsei kokka to seiji shisō (1969). BITŌ Masahide

Sono Ayako (1931–)

Pen name of the novelist Miura Chizuko. Maiden name Machida. Born in Tōkyō. In 1953 she married the novelist MIURA SHUMON, even before her graduation from Seishin Joshi Daigaku (Sacred Heart Women's College). Part of the first wave of talented women writers to emerge after World War II, she gained prominence with her story "Enrai no kyakutachi" (1954, Guests from Afar), about the US Occupation forces. An eloquent and graceful narrator, she has written many short stories and novels analyzing society from the standpoint of an intellectual Catholic woman. Her principal works include Tamayura (1959, A Moment); Rio Gurande (1961, Rio Grande); and Ikenie no shima (1970, Island of Sacrifice), about the fate of schoolgirls on war-torn Okinawa.

Sony Corporation

Japan's leading electronics manufacturer, which produces mainly audio and visual electronic equipment. It was established in 1946 by IBUKA MASARU and MORITA AKIO. In 1958 it changed its name from Tōkyō Tsūshin Kōgyō (Tōkyō Telecommunications Engineering Corporation) to its present one. Sony has introduced many new products both in Japan and abroad, including the first tape recorder and all-transistor radio in Japan and the world's first all-transistor, direct-view, eight-inch television. It also developed the one-gun, single-lens Trinitron color television and the Betamax video cassette system for home use. The Sony trademark is now registered in 177 countries and territories around the world. Its exports are distributed overseas through locally managed subsidiaries. It has established production facilities in various countries, including a color television plant in San Diego, California, a magnetic recording tape plant in Dothan, Alabama, and a color television plant in Wales. Its stocks are listed on 18 major stock exchanges in 10 countries, including those in Great Britain, the Netherlands, and Hong Kong. Its AMERICAN DEPOSITARY RECEIPTS, issued in 1961, were the first shares offered by a Japan-based enterprise on the US stock market. At the end of October 1981 its consolidated net sales were ¥777.9 billion (US $3.4 billion), of which overseas sales accounted for 71 percent. Sales were distributed as follows: televisions 23 percent, video cassette recorders 27 percent, tape recorders and radios 17 percent, audio equipment 7 percent, and other products 26 percent. In that same year the company was capitalized at ¥11.5 billion ($49.7 million). Its head office is in Tōkyō. See also ELECTRONICS.

Sophia University

(Jōchi Daigaku). Located in Chiyoda Ward, Tōkyō. A private, Catholic, coeducational university based on the Jōchi Gakuen, which was founded by the German Hermann Hoffman in 1913; it was granted university status in 1928. It maintains an international division for foreign students, and faculties of letters, economics, law, theology, foreign languages, and science and engineering. It is known principally for its foreign language studies and for the following institutes: Counseling Institute, Iberoamerica Institute, Institute of Christian Culture, Institute of Medieval Thought, and Life Science Institute. Enrollment was 9,723 in 1980.

Sorge Incident

On 18 October 1941 the Tōkyō police took into custody the following: Dr Richard Sorge, a leading German newspaper correspondent; Branco Vukelic, a Yugoslav national who worked for a French news agency; and Max Klausen, a German businessman. Some days earlier the police had arrested a Japanese artist named MIYAGI YOTOKU and OZAKI HOTSUMI, a political commentator and journalist.

It transpired that these five men were the principal figures in a spy ring organized and directed by Soviet military intelligence in Moscow. However, the brief press release by the Ministry of Justice in May 1942—the first inkling the Japanese public had of the case—stated that the five men, together with certain other persons, were charged with espionage "on behalf of the Communist International." By its reference to the Comintern rather than to Soviet military intelligence, thereby creating the fiction that Sorge and his associates were essentially members of an international communist organization (the Comintern), the Ministry of Justice could take the view that the Soviet Union itself, then linked to Japan by a nonaggression pact, was not involved in the affair. Moreover, the accused, as members of a communist party, could be tried for violation of the 1941 revision of the PEACE PRESERVATION LAW OF 1925 (which came within the ministry's jurisdiction) instead of for a breach of the National Defense Security Law, which, it could be argued, would have to be dealt with by the military authorities—specifically, the kempei.

At their trials in September 1943 Sorge and Ozaki were sentenced to death and Vukelic and Klausen to life imprisonment. Miyagi died in custody before being brought to trial. Sorge and Ozaki were hanged at Sugamo on 7 November 1944. Vukelic died in Abashiri Prison, northern Hokkaidō, in January 1945. Klausen survived to be released in October of that year, following the advent of the Allied Occupation forces. He and his wife (who had also been imprisoned) proceeded to the Soviet Union and subsequently to East Germany.

Although it did not become a matter of full public knowledge until after 1945, the Sorge Affair profoundly disturbed justice officials and others at the time, for Dr Sorge was known to be on terms of close friendship with Major General Eugen OTT, the German ambassador. Furthermore, he had won the confidence of Colonel Josef Meissinger, the police attaché at the embassy charged with the political surveillance of the German community. Meissinger had evidently come to regard Sorge as a thoroughly reliable and congenial fellow Nazi. Indeed, from the outbreak of war in Europe in September 1939 Sorge had been formally associated with the embassy, though without diplomatic status, as editor of the daily German news bulletin compiled from the official news service cabled from Berlin.

Even more shocking to the authorities, however, was the case of Ozaki Hotsumi. Ozaki had been a member of the Shōwa Research Society (SHŌWA KENKYŪKAI), founded late in 1936 by friends and admirers of KONOE FUMIMARO, then prime minister. Through this society, which embraced some of the best brains in Japan, Ozaki came close to Kazami Akira (1886–1961), chief secretary to the Konoe cabinet; and in 1938 Kazami invited Ozaki to become a temporary cabinet consultant (naikaku shokutaku). If we are to believe Ozaki's statement to the preliminary judge, this appointment enabled him to pass "accurate and valuable information" to Sorge. In fact Ozaki's direct access to cabinet papers was confined to a period of a few months, for in January 1939 Konoe resigned, and when he formed his second cabinet the following year, Ozaki did not rejoin him as a consultant. Ozaki nevertheless remained in close contact with more than one member of Konoe's inner circle. Thus Konoe himself and certain of his friends faced some questioning by prosecutors of the Ministry of Justice. The arrest, trial, and execution of Ozaki set up shock waves of which the ripples did not die down for many years.

Possibly the third most important member of the Sorge ring was the artist Miyagi Yotoku, who had lived as a boy in Okinawa and as a young man in California. It was in Los Angeles, as a member of the Communist Party of the United States, that he was recruited in 1933 as a Comintern agent. In accordance with his secret instructions he went to Japan in October of that year. After some weeks he made contact with Sorge through a prearranged advertisement placed in the Japan Advertiser. Over the next seven years and more, Sorge was to rely heavily on Miyagi for the translation of material provided by Ozaki and by himself. Miyagi himself organized a small group of his own trusted informants.

Branco Vukelic, who had been recruited by a Russian Comintern agent in Paris, was of much less importance as a provider of Japanese intelligence than either Ozaki (whom he never met) or Miyagi. His main value to Sorge may have been that of a photo technician, for its was his function to make photocopies of long background reports passed to him by Sorge. The results, which were usually in the form of microfilm, reached Moscow through courier contacts in Shanghai.

Klausen, who had previously worked with Sorge in China behind his cover as a businessman, operated a clandestine radio transmitter and sent Sorge's messages to the Soviet Union. This was a risky undertaking, for the Japanese authorities became aware that illegal transmissions were taking place.

A great deal of intelligence material, some of it from German sources, was sent to the Soviet Union by the Sorge ring. The range of material covered economic as well as military and political information of a top-secret and confidential nature. For something like eight years no real danger of detection appeared to threaten Sorge and his associates. He himself wrote in his statement to the police: "I was surprised that I was able to do secret work in Japan for years without being caught by the authorities."

Possibly the two most dramatic items of intelligence sent to Moscow by Sorge were an almost perfect order-of-battle chart of the Japanese army in June 1941 and an assurance that Japan would not attack the Soviet Union in 1941, following Germany's assault in the summer, but would move south, probably against the British and Dutch possessions in Southeast Asia.

The discovery of the Sorge ring arose through the arrest of a Japanese Communist who revealed, in the course of being questioned, the name of an elderly women living in Wakayama Prefecture. She had lived at one time in Los Angeles, and Miyagi had lodged at her home there. After she returned to Japan, Miyagi kept in touch with her. When interrogated by the police in September 1941 she mentioned Miyagi's name. His arrest soon followed. Under interrogation Miyagi attempted suicide, without success. From him the inquisitors learned of Ozaki, Sorge, and the others.

It was in the fall of 1945 that fuller coverage of the Sorge Affair was given by the Japanese press. Ozaki emerged as a resistance leader, as a symbol of the opposition in high circles to Japan's entry into the war, and as a victim of Japanese "fascism." In 1946 his letters from prison to his wife and daughter were published and became a best-seller. Three years later, SCAP (the headquarters of the Allied Occupation of Japan) released to the press an account of the Sorge Affair. This created an upheaval in the leadership of the Japan Communist Party, since the SCAP account suggested that the discovery of the Sorge ring in 1941 could be traced to the indiscretions of a communist who had become a member of the Politburo of the JCP central committee after the war.

In 1956 a society was founded in Tōkyō to keep alive the memory of Ozaki and his associates, Japanese and European. This society raised the money for Sorge's tombstone in Tama Cemetery, Tōkyō, which bears the inscription: "Here sleeps a brave warrior who devoted his life to opposing war, and to the struggle for the peace of the world."

For many years Moscow denied every allegation that Sorge had been a Soviet-controlled agent. But in November 1964 Sorge was suddenly "accepted" by the Soviet authorities as a heroic intelligence officer, and he was given the posthumous decoration of Hero of the Soviet Union. A series of tributes to him appeared in the Russian press; a street in Moscow and a new ocean-going tanker were named after him; and in 1965 a Russian postage stamp, showing his face, was issued in his honor.

——F. W. Deakin and G. R. Storry, *The Case of Richard Sorge* (1966). Ishidō Kiyotomo, ed, *Zoruge jiken*, in *Gendaishi shiryō*, vol 24 (Misuzu Shobō, 1971). Chalmers Johnson, *An Instance of Treason: Ozaki Hotsumi and the Sorge Spy Ring* (1964). Kawai Teikichi, *Aru kakumeika no kaisō* (1953). Kazama Michitarō, *Aru hangyaku* (1959). Obi Toshito, ed, *Zoruge jiken*, in *Gendaishi shiryō*, vols 1–3 (Misuzu Shobō, 1962). Charles A. Willoughby, *Shanghai Conspiracy: The Sorge Spy Ring* (1952).　　　Richard STORRY

Sorge, Richard → Sorge Incident

Sōrifu → Prime Minister's Office

soroban → abacus

sōrōbun

(epistolary style). A style of literary or classical Japanese, used mainly for letters; a development of certain types of documentary style called HENTAI KAMBUN (modified, i.e., Japanized, classical Chinese) in the latter part of the Heian period (794–1185) and the Kamakura period (1185–1333). The distinctive feature of *sōrōbun* is the frequent use of the polite auxiliary verb *sōrō* (a verb that originally meant "to serve," later simply "to be"), having entirely lost its capacity to convey an independent meaning and roughly corresponding in function to the polite verbal suffix *-masu* of modern Japanese.

History——Unlike official documents, which were customarily written in Chinese (KAMBUN), personal documents, including letters, were written in Japanese. This was to some extent a colloquial form of Japanese containing abundant honorific and humble expressions (see HONORIFIC LANGUAGE). In the Nara period (710–794) the verb *haberi* was used as a humble or polite auxiliary in place of the verb *ari*, "to be," whereas, in the Heian period the same type of verb *saburafu* (later pronounced *sōrō* or *soro*) came to be used as a polite auxiliary verb interchangeably with *haberi*. In MEIGŌ ŌRAI (ca 1058, [Fujiwara no] Akihira's Letter Writer), the oldest collection of models for letter writing, for example, both *haberi* and *saburafu* appear. In the Kamakura period the word *saburafu* changed phonologically to *sōrō* and was also employed for certain types of official document. In the Edo period (1600–1868), not only personal letters but also official letters were written in *sōrōbun*. This custom was continued in the Meiji period (1868–1912), and until a few years after the end of World War II *sōrōbun* was required for all formal correspondence and was sometimes used even in commercial notices and advertisements.

Writing System——*Hentai kambun,* the Japanized form of classical Chinese from which *sōrōbun* was derived, follows Chinese word order without KANA letters to indicate Japanese inflections, but the words are always read as Japanese words and in Japanese word order.

Since *sōrōbun* follows the style described above, particles and conjugational suffixes are, as a rule, omitted wherever possible; thus, the verb *sōrō* is written simply as 候 , and never as 候ふ. Even when *kana* letters are necessary for transcribing certain particles and conjugational suffixes, the *kana* letters are replaced, if possible, by Chinese characters used to express either the sound or meaning of the Japanese particle in question, for example:

降而	*kudatte*	for my part
謹而	*tsutsushinde*	respectfully
就而者	*tsuite wa*	in this connection

Sōrōbun —— Table 1

Nonpast, Past, and Tentative Forms of Itasu

Affirmative	Negative
Nonpast	
"I/we do" *itashi sōrō* 致候	"I/we do not do" *itasazu sōrō* 不致候 (*itashi sōrawazu* 致候はず)
Past	
"I/we did" *itashi sōrō* 致候 (*itashi sōraiki* 致候ひき)	"I/we did not do" *itasazu sōrō* 不致候 (*itasazu sōraiki* 不致候ひき)
Tentative	
"I will do/ let's do" *itasubeku sōrō* 可致候 (*itashi sōrawan* 致候半)	"I will not do/let's not do" *itasumajiku sōrō* 致間敷候

宜敷	*yoroshiku*	well
候得共	*sōraedomo*	although

Chinese word order, which requires reading in reverse order in Japanese, appears idiomatically in adverbial phrases and predicates:

不悪	*ashikarazu*	without offense
不得已	*yamu o ezu*	unavoidably
乍憚	*habakari nagara*	hesitatingly
為念	*nen no tame*	for making sure
有之候	*kore ari sōrō*	there is
難有存候	*arigataku zonji sōrō*	I appreciate it

Grammar——The grammatical structure of *sōrōbun* is essentially based on that of CLASSICAL JAPANESE, but the verb *sōrō* has become an irregular verb lacking a continuative form *(renyōkei).*

Verbal predicates. The auxiliary verb *sōrō* is appended to the continuative form of verbs and corresponds semantically to the polite verbal suffix *-masu* in modern Japanese. The form *sōrō,* which is the nonpast (i.e., present or future tense) form, ordinarily serves also as the past tense form (although the past tense form of *sōrō* is *sōraiki,* this form is usually replaced by *sōrō* and the tense is implied by context). This means in effect that the form *sōrō* denotes all tenses, since the nonpast form of Japanese verbs denotes both present and future tenses.

The negative nonpast form is *sōrawazu,* but normally the negation of any verb is expressed by appending *sōrō* to the negative form of the verb (i.e., the main verb followed by the negative verbal suffix *-zu*).

The tentative form of *sōrō* is *sōrawan,* but this form is rarely seen. It is usually replaced by a form made up of *sōrō* added to a verbal suffix: *-beku sōrō.* The corresponding form *-majiku sōrō* expresses the negative tentative. (The meanings expressed by the tentative form are: volitive, with a first person subject: "I will . . . "; hortative, with a first person plural that includes the addressee: "let's . . . "; and presumptive, with the third person: "he/she/it/they may . . .") In Table 1 these forms are summarized with the verb *itasu* "to do" as an example.

The verb *itasu,* or its humble equivalent *tsukamatsuru,* is used only with a first person subject, i.e., the writer or his associates. For second person or honorific third person subjects, *nasare, nashikudasare,* or *asobasare* (from the verb *nasu* "to do," the formalized compound verb *nashikudasu,* or the honorific verb *asobasu,* respectively, with the honorific verbal suffix *-re* attached) is followed by *sōrō.* Thus:

仕候	*tsukamatsuri sōrō*	I/we humbly do
被成候	*nasare sōrō*	
被成下候	*nashikudasare sōrō*	(esteemed) you/he/ she/they do
被遊候	*asobasare sōrō*	

The desiderative verbal suffix *-taku* is used in expressing wishes. The writer's request is expressed by the desiderative suffix preceded by the honorific suffix *-re/-rare,* that is, *-retaku/-raretaku,* plus *sōrō.* This form is often used in place of the honorific-obligatory compound suffix *-rubeku/-rarubeku* plus *sōrō* in order to soften its meaning. Thus:

Sōrōbun——Table 2

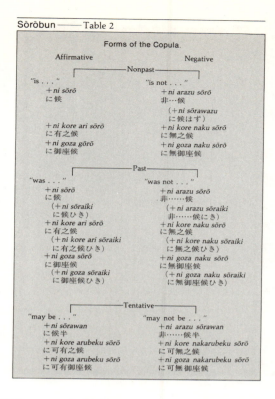

Forms of the Copula.

Affirmative	Negative
Nonpast	
"is . . ."	"is not . . ."
+*ni sōrō* に候	+*ni arazu sōrō* 非…候
	(+*ni sōrawazu* に候はず)
+*ni kore ari sōrō* に有之候	+*ni kore naku sōrō* に無之候
+*ni goza gōrō* に御座候	+*ni goza naku sōrō* に無御座候
Past	
"was . . ."	"was not . . ."
+*ni sōrō* に候	+*ni arazu sōrō* 非……候
(+*ni sōraiki* に候ひき)	(+*ni arazu sōraiki* 非……候にき)
+*ni kore ari sōrō* に有之候	+*ni kore naku sōrō* に無之候
(+*ni kore ari sōraiki* に有之候ひき)	(+*ni kore naku sōraiki* に無之候ひき)
+*ni goza sōrō* に御座候	+*ni goza naku sōrō* に無御座候
(+*ni goza sōraiki* に御座候ひき)	(+*ni goza naku sōraiki* に無御座候ひき)
Tentative	
"may be . . ."	"may not be . . ."
+*ni sōrawan* に候半	+*ni arazu sōrawan* 非……候半
+*ni kore arubeku sōrō* に可有之候	+*ni kore nakarubeku sōrō* に可無之候
+*ni goza arubeku sōrō* に可有御座候	+*ni goza nakarubeku sōrō* に可無御座候

致度候	*itashitaku sōrō*	I/we should like to do
被成度候	*nasaretaku sōrō*	I/we should like you to do
可被成候	*nasarubeku sōrō*	you have to do

To decline the addressee's request, a writer would use compound verbs with *-kane* (from *-kanu* "to be unable"): e.g.,

致兼候	*itashikane sōrō*	I am not in the position to do

To express modesty, a writer would use the humble auxiliary verb *tatematsuru*, which originally meant "to offer":

存候	*zonji sōrō*	I believe
奉存候	*zonji tatematsuri sōrō*	I humbly believe

The verb *mōsu* "to state" (or the formalized compound verb *mōshiagu*) is used as a humble verb "to do" when preceded by a noun indicating action: e.g.,

御願申候	*onnegai mōshi sōrō*	I beg of you
御願申上候	*onnegai mōshiage sōrō*	I beg of you

The auxiliary verb *sōrō*, unlike the modern Japanese polite verbal suffix *-masu*, is appended also to adjectives (*keiyōshi*), *sōrō* being added to the continuative form *-ku* in affirmative statements and to the negative form *-karazu* in negative statements:

嬉敷候	*ureshiku sōrō*	I am glad
不苦候	*kurushikarazu sōrō*	I do not mind

Nominal predicates. The copula in *sōrōbun* is *ni sōrō* or a derivation thereof. It corresponds to *nari* "is," the copula of classical Japanese, in that the latter is a contraction of the particle *ni* plus the auxiliary verb *ari* (*sōrō* thus corresponding to *ari*).

Sentences ending with a nominal predicate, i.e., a noun plus copula, are classified into three styles, corresponding to the three polite styles in the copula of modern Japanese; that is, *ni sōrō* corresponds to *desu* in modern Japanese, *ni kore ari sōrō* to *de arimasu*, and *ni goza sōrō* to *de gozaimasu*.

Here too the indicative form *sōrō* denotes both the nonpast and past tenses depending on the context, and the past tense form *sōraiki* rarely appears. The negative form *sōrawazu* is seldom used either. The forms of the copula are summarized in Table 2. It should also be noted that *ni te* is sometimes used instead of *ni* in the copula and its derived forms, thus giving *ni te sōrō*, *ni te kore ari sōrō*, and so on.

Clause final expressions. Interrogative sentences are formed by appending the sentence-final particle *ya* 哉 to any declarative sentence. In sentences ending with the seldom used past tense form

sōraiki, the latter changes to *sōraishi* 候ひし when followed by the interrogative particle *ya*. The imperative form of the verb *sōrō* is *sōrae* 候へ but it is also rarely used.

In general, attributive clauses that modify a noun also include the auxiliary verb *sōrō*. The sentence-ending form *sōrō* also functions as the attributive form. The past tense attributive form, *sōraishi*, is commonly replaced by *sōrō*. The attributive form *sōrō* (or *sōraishi*) immediately precedes the noun that it modifies as do the verbs that end attributive clauses in modern Japanese.

In complex sentences, adverbial clauses always precede the main clause, just as attributive clauses precede the modified noun. With few exceptions, a subordinate adverbial clause ends either in a verbal suffix affixed to the stem of the verb *sōrō* or in a bound noun modified by an attributive clause.

The following are examples of some peculiar clause final expressions for coordinate and subordinate clauses in *sōrōbun* (Table 3).

Sōrōbun——Table 3

Coordinate and Subordinate Clause Final Expressions

sōrōte	候而	(copulative)	". . . , and"
sōrō tokoro	候處	(adversative)	". . . , but"
sōraedomo	候得共	(concessive)	"although . . ."
sōrō tomo	候共	(concessive)	"even if . . ."
sōrawan ka	候はんか	(conditional)	"provided that . . ."
sōrawaba	候はゞ	(conditional)	"if . . ."
sōrō aida	候間	(causal)	"because . . ."
sōrō ni tsuki	候に付	(causal)	"inasmuch as . . ."
sōraeba	候得者	(causal)	"since . . ."
sōrō mama	候儘	(causal)	"as . . ."
sōrō jō	候條	(causal)	"in view of the fact that . . ."
sōrō omomuki	候趣	(hearsay)	"as I heard that . . ."
sōrō yoshi	候由	(hearsay)	"as they say that . . ."

When verbs consisting of a noun stem of Chinese origin and the verbalizer *-itashi sōrō* occur at the end of coordinate clauses, the verbalizer may be omitted; e.g., *Goshomen sakujitsu haidoku* . . . "I perused your letter yesterday, and . . ." instead of *haidoku-itashi* (or *haidoku-tsukamatsuri*) *sōrōte* . . .

Epistolary Form——A Japanese letter consists of three parts; the opening, the body, and the closing. It is customary to begin a letter with a salutation such as *haikei* 拝啓 "humble greetings," or, if the letter is a reply, with *haifuku* 拝復 "I humbly reply" or a similar expression. This is followed by polite phrases that almost always mention the season, the state of weather, concern about the addressee's health, and so forth. The body, i.e., the message that the writer wishes to convey, is introduced in a new paragraph by a word like:

偖	*sate*	now then
陳者	*nobureba*	if one were to say

After the body, a short paragraph of closing remarks is included, which usually contains a note on the weather, greetings to others, and so on. The closing ends with such a complimentary close as:

敬具	*keigu*	with respect

Some business letters and less formal personal letters are written occasionally without these opening and closing remarks. Even in these cases, however, in the beginning of the letter a salutation like *zenryaku* 前略 "opening abbreviated" must still generally be given to apologize for omission of the usual opening; in the end, a less formal complimentary close such as *sōsō* 草々 "hurriedly" is given. No punctuation marks are used in any letters written in the *sōrōbun* style.

Sōrōbun and *mairase sōrōbun*, a variant written only by women, may soon be obsolete. Nevertheless, many epistolary forms, rules, and diction (including wording and phrasing) which developed in *sōrōbun* are now common in Japanese correspondence in the modern spoken language.

━━━━Ishikawa Ken and Ishikawa Matsutarō, *Nihon kyōkasho taikei*: vols 1–4: *Ko ōrai* I-IV (Kōdansha, 1967–70); vol 8: *Shōsoku* (1972); vol 15: *Joshiyō* (1973). Yamada Yoshio, *Keigohō no kenkyū* (1924).

Gisaburō N. Kiyose

Sōtatsu

A pair of two-panel folding screens entitled *Wind and Thunder Gods*. Based on a mythological theme, this work typifies Sōtatsu's mature style. Colors and gold leaf on paper. Each screen 157 × 173 cm. First half of the 17th century. Kenninji, Kyōto. National Treasure.

sōryō system

Internal organization of regional landholding families on the basis of divided inheritance under the absolute leadership of a main heir *(sōryō)*, who was usually the eldest son. The practice, which continued through the Kamakura period (1185–1333), first emerged as a system of property management in the latter half of the Heian period (794–1185). All sons and even daughters were originally entitled to a share of each family's property, but the *sōryō* came to be responsible for the distribution and overall administration of the fields *(myōden)* and cultivators controlled by his family (see MYŌSHU and RYŌSHU). The system is generally viewed as a transitional stage leading to a feudal lord-vassal relationship as regional landholders became militarized and members whose kinship was fictive were accepted into families (see BUSHIDAN; IENOKO AND RŌTŌ).

Stimulated by increased population, warfare, and the encroachments of local officials of the imperial government, most landholding families came to rely on the guidance and military leadership of one member, i.e., the *sōryō*. The most powerful *sōryō* served as vassals (GOKENIN) under the Kamakura shogunate (1192–1333). The system initially provided the frame for shogunal administration and family heads were held responsible for the behavior of all members. However, toward the close of the Kamakura period the shogunate circumvented the authority of *sōryō* by directly confirming collateral family members' rights of proprietorship (ANDO), thus making the system ineffective.

Sosei (fl ca 859–923)

Classical (WAKA) poet, Buddhist priest. His lay name was Yoshimine no Harutoshi and he was also called Yoshiyori no Ason. One of the "Thirty-Six Poetic Geniuses" (SANJŪROKKASEN). His father, the poet HENJŌ (Yoshimine no Munesada), insisted that he enter the priesthood, claiming it to be unseemly for his son to remain a layman after he himself had taken orders in 850. He was active in poetic events at court, and 36 of his poems are included in the first imperial anthology of classical poetry *(chokusenshū)*, the KOKINSHŪ (Collection from Ancient and Modern Times), while some 25 more are found in later imperial anthologies. His personal collection, *Soseishū*, exists in several versions, of which the most reliable contains 65 poems. His poetry displays the mannered elegance and technical and rhetorical skill typical of the *Kokinshū* age.

Robert H. BROWER

sōsen

(literally, "Song [Sung] coins"). Copper coins minted in China during the Song dynasty (960–1279). After the last minting of Japanese coins (KŌCHŌ JŪNISEN) in 958, coins imported from China and Korea were used in increasing numbers. *Sōsen*, in particular, circulated widely in Japan as a result of flourishing trade in East Asia in the 13th century. In fact *sōsen*, together with KŌBUSEN and EIRAKUSEN

minted by the Ming dynasty (1368–1644), were the major currency until coins were once again minted in Japan, by the national unifiers ODA NOBUNAGA and TOYOTOMI HIDEYOSHI. The general use of these coins stimulated the money economy to the extent that they were sometimes used in place of rice for paying taxes.

Sosogi Coast

(Sosogi Kaigan). Coastal area on the northern Noto Peninsula, Ishikawa Prefecture, central Honshū. Noted for its oddly shaped rocks, rugged cliffs, and the Tarumi Falls, with some of the rocks designated as natural monuments. Part of Noto Peninsula Quasi-National Park. Length: about 2.5 km (1.6 mi).

Sōtan → Oguri Sōtan

Sōtatsu (?–1643?)

Also known as Tawaraya Sōtatsu. Artist and founder of the RIMPA style of painting. Sōtatsu headed the workshop Tawaraya in Kyōto, which flourished between 1600 and 1640, and is said to have attempted a revival of the tradition of medieval painting. The repertoire of his workshop comprises paintings done in color and gold and silver on screens and sliding-wall panels, fans, writing paper, and album leaves, as well as paintings done in ink.

Sōtatsu's family name may have been Kitagawa or Nonomura. He may have been related by marriage to the great calligrapher HON'AMI KŌETSU and to Ogata Dōhaku (d 1604), owner of a brocade manufactory and the great-grandfather of Sōtatsu's later follower KŌRIN. While the general characteristics of Sōtatsu's style are easy to define, there are only a few works that can with surety be attributed to his hand, since his seals (Taiseiken, Taisei, and Inen) and his signatures (Hokkyō Sōtatsu and Sōtatsu Hokkyō) were in some cases later additions.

Sōtatsu's artistic connection with Kōetsu is confined to the years between 1605 and 1615. Kōetsu's early handscrolls and poem leaves show under-paintings *(shita-e)* in gold and silver *(kingindei-e)*, and some have the seal Inen. The same floral patterns, animals, birds, and scenic details recur in the *shita-e* of Kōetsu's later scrolls, which were printed with mica from wooden stamps. This may be an indication that Sōtatsu first specialized in ornamental design and only later developed his workshop into a painting atelier.

The earliest documents of Sōtatsu's style are restorations done in 1602 of frontispieces of three medieval sutra-scrolls contained in the *Heike nōkyō* (1164) owned by the Itsukushima Shrine. Sōtatsu's only dated work is a 1630 copy of the now-lost picture scrolls *Saigyō monogatari emaki* (ca 1500). The text of this copy (formerly Mōri Collection) was written by the courtier KARASUMARU MITSUHIRO. Paintings on sliding doors in the Kyōto temple Yōgen'in traditionally attributed to Sōtatsu, may date from the time of the temple's restoration in 1621. It is believed that the Buddhist honorary title *hokkyō* was bestowed on Sōtatsu shortly thereafter.

Some of the literary sources for Sōtatsu's illustrative works are the classical tales HEIJI MONOGATARI, HŌGEN MONOGATARI, ISE MONOGATARI, and the TALE OF GENJI. The themes of major works like the *Genji* screens (Seikadō Foundation, Tōkyō), the *Waves at Matsushima* screens (Freer Gallery, Washington, DC), the *Wind and Thunder Gods* screens (Kenninji, Kyōto), and the *Bugaku Dancers* screens (Daigoji, Kyōto) come from literature, lyrics, mythology, and classical music and dance, respectively. Although one can see traces of an influence by the TOSA SCHOOL and other contemporary painting schools, the greater part of Sōtatsu's figurative repertoire is taken from medieval picture scrolls (EMAKIMONO), which he used as his source book. Surprisingly, there are no genre paintings in Sōtatsu's oeuvre.

In his ink paintings Sōtatsu chose mostly bird-and-flower and Zen Buddhist subjects. He created a new, "boneless" technique by applying several wet layers of ink or paint on specially prepared paper, producing an accidental fusion of the pigments, a technique known as *tarashikomi*.

Sōtatsu's art reveals the difference between painting in the Chinese mode as represented by the KANŌ SCHOOL and the indigenous Japanese tradition of YAMATO-E painting. From the 15th century onward the *yamato-e* tradition had been monopolized by the Tosa school, but it had become obsolete by the time the Tosa family moved from Kyōto to Sakai about 1570. Sōtatsu stepped into this vacuum and combined *yamato-e* subject matter with the new preference for grandiose compositions and lavish materials, such as gold and silver, that had developed in the Azuchi–Momoyama period (1568–1600).

Sōtatsu had an enormous impact on later Japanese painting, especially in his use of color and ink, which allowed tonal modulation similar to that of watercolor technique. In the genre of flowers and grasses, Sōtatsu's school started a new tradition of realistic representation based on detailed observation. Most important, however, Sōtatsu monumentalized the compositional principles of *yamato-e* by organizing his large picture planes through geometrical means. His paintings reveal a charming informality that reflects the aestheticism of the tea circles of Kyōto in the early part of the Edo period (1600–1868). In the late 19th and early 20th centuries, his tradition became one of the major roots of modern Japanese-style painting (NIHONGA).

——Doris Croissant, *Sōtatsu und der Sōtatsu-Stil.* (Münchener Ostasiatishe Studien, Sounderreihe, Band 3, 1978). Elise Grilli, *Sōtatsu* (1956). Mizuo Hiroshi, *Edo Painting: Sōtatsu and Kōrin*, tr John M. Shields (1972). Yamane Yūzō, *Sōtatsu* (1962). Yamane Yūzō, *Sōtatsu to Kōrin*, vol 14 of *Genshoku Nihon no bijutsu* (1969).

Doris CROISSANT

sotetsu

(Japanese sago palm). *Cycas revoluta.* An evergreen tree of the family Cycadaceae, commonly cultivated as an ornamental and found growing wild in warm regions, such as southern Kyūshū and the Ryūkyū Islands. Its rough, dark, columnar stem grows erect from 1–4 meters (3–13 ft) high. Atop the stem is a crown of stiff, glossy, dark green frond-like leaves, 0.5–2 meters (2–7 ft) long, which uncoil like fern leaves. Around August the *sotetsu* produces male and female flowers on separate trees; its reproductive system is among the simplest of all seed-bearing plants. In 1896 IKENO SEIICHIRŌ (1866–1943) discovered the sperm of the *sotetsu* and clarified its reproduction process and thereby its genealogical relation to other gymnosperms. In the past, starch taken from the stem was used as food in times of emergency, and the seeds were used for medicinal purposes.

MATSUDA Osamu

Sotomo

Coastal area on the Uchitomi Peninsula, city of Obama, Fukui Prefecture, central Honshū. Noted for its granite joints, oddly shaped rocks, caves, and cliffs created by the erosion of the sea. Pleasure boats are available from the port of Obama. Part of Wakasa Bay Quasi-National Park. Length: 2 km (1.2 mi).

Sōtō sect

One of the two major schools of Zen Buddhism introduced to Japan from Song (Sung) China (960–1279) early in the Kamakura period (1185–1333). Sōtō Zen was established in Japan by DŌGEN, who returned from study in China in 1227. Previously, in 1191 the RIN-ZAI SECT of Zen had been introduced by EISAI, who was followed by a succession of Japanese and Chinese Rinzai Zen masters. The Sōtō sect initially grew under the shadow of Rinzai but eventually moved from Kyōto into the provinces where it became one of the largest of Japanese Buddhist sects.

Basic Teachings——Zen, together with other schools of Mahāyāna Buddhism, teaches that all men are inherently possessed of the Buddha nature and that, by awakening to this Buddha nature, man may achieve enlightenment. Many Buddhist schools practice meditation as a means to the acquisition of this enlightenment; Zen, however, places extensive emphasis on the practice. Zen was the principal school of Buddhism in Song China; two branches, the Rinzai (Linji; Lin-chi) and Sōtō (Caodong; Ts'ao-tung), flourished, although the Rinzai sect was dominant. During the 13th and 14th centuries Zen monks visited China and Chinese masters came to Japan. Dōgen was one of the few to study under a Sōtō sect master; his teacher, Tiantong Rujing (T'ien-t'ung Ju-ching; J: Tendō Nyojō; also known as Zhangweng Rujing or Chang-weng Rujing; J: Chōō Nyojō; 1163–1228) was a disciplinarian who advocated an intense devotion to Zen meditation. The teaching of these two schools of Zen was substantially the same. Intensive meditation on a KŌAN, or brief Zen story, under the direction of a Zen master was characteristic of the Zen of the time. Sōtō and Rinzai differed in that the Sōtō sect placed a greater emphasis on a tranquil form of meditation sitting, characterized as *mokushō* Zen, or "silent illumination Zen," whereas Rinzai advocated the more active *kanna* Zen, or "*kōan*-introspection Zen."

Early History——When Dōgen returned from China in 1227, he went first to the Rinzai temple, KENNINJI in Kyōto, but was dissatisfied with the mixture of Zen and esoteric teachings practiced there. In 1230 he moved to Fukakusa, south of Kyōto (now in the city of Kyōto), where he set up (in 1233) a Song-style meditation temple, Kōshōji, in which Zen practice and a strict observation of the precepts were observed. Dōgen attracted only a small number of students, and those who came to study under him were largely former members of a school known as Nihon Daruma Shū (Japan Bodhidharma sect). This school had been founded by Dainichi Nōnin (d 1189), a self-enlightened Zen master of whom very little is known. Its members left Kyōto in 1194 when the propagation of Zen by Eisai and Nōnin was forbidden, and several of them, including Ejō (1198–1280), Gikai (1219–1309), and Gien (d 1314) came together to study under Dōgen.

In 1243 Dōgen, pressured by the presence of the huge Rinzai temple complex at TŌFUKUJI nearby, set out for the remote province of Echizen (now Fukui Prefecture), where he eventually settled at EIHEIJI. By then Dōgen was in poor health and he turned over all ceremonial duties and official functions to Ejō in order to concentrate on his writings. In 1253 he died. Ejō took over Eiheiji and devoted himself to teaching his master's students and editing his writings. Because of ill health, he in turn handed the duties of running the temple to Gikai. Gikai was one of the few Sōtō priests who had studied in China, and he had brought back architectural designs that were used in the temple buildings at Eiheiji. An opposing faction, centering on Gien and Jiyuan (Chi-yüan; J: Jakuen, 1207–99), both of whom had been followers of Dōgen, objected to Gikai's attempts to enlarge the temple, to add elements from esoteric Buddhism, and thus to gain a local following, protesting that the simple and austere style Dōgen had established was being violated. This quarrel is known as the *sandai sōron* or "third-generation dispute." For several years the struggle continued until Gikai with his followers finally left Eiheiji for Kaga Province (now Ishikawa Prefecture), where he changed a former Tendai temple, Daijōji, into one of the Sōtō sect. Meanwhile, Gien and Jiyuan maintained a precarious hold on Eiheiji. From this time until the end of the Muromachi period (1333–1568) there was absolutely no connection between the successors of Gikai and those of Gien and Jiyuan. Eiheiji lost its local support and fell into disrepair. The school stemming from Gikai and his descendants spread throughout Japan, dominating the Sōtō school of Zen, which grew enormously in prosperity throughout the centuries.

Popularization——With the emergence of the fourth patriarch, KEIZAN JŌKIN, Gikai's heir, Sōtō began to gain a more popular appeal. Keizan is spoken of, along with Dōgen, as one of the two founders of the Sōtō sect. Until recent times he was revered as a patriarch of the sect at a level equal to or perhaps even higher than Dōgen. Under Keizan and his disciples Sōtō spread west to Kyūshū and Chūgoku, east to the Tōkai and Kantō regions, and north to Ōu. Keizan made no attempt to preserve Dōgen's austere style but sought rather to enlarge his religious group. He incorporated elements from mountain religious activities, Hakusan Tendai beliefs in KANNON, various local Shintō guardian deities, and absorbed ascetic practices of the SHUGENDŌ mountain monks. By emphasizing prayers and incantations, esoteric tendencies were strengthened. When new temples were established, esoteric elements were given prominence; when old temples were taken over, existing elements of popular beliefs were adopted and incorporated into temple practices. There was a conscious effort to cater to the local populace, to provide them with some sort of solace and help in the unsettled feudal society in which they lived. Great emphasis was placed on public works and services: the building of bridges, digging of hot springs, irrigation projects, curing of diseases, and driving away of evil spirits. A similar pattern of development was followed by later leaders of Keizan's new religious group, until the Sōtō sect spread throughout a large part of Japan, attracting men from all schools of Buddhism and revitalizing temples as attractive new places of worship.

Until the middle of the Muromachi period the monks had maintained a strenuous life style in Sōtō temples, with intensified meditation practice, periods of work, and regular *sanzen*, or interviews with the Zen master. But from this time the practice of *sanzen* gradually deteriorated in both the Rinzai and Sōtō sects. *Missan roku, kōan* answer books, circulated widely. Practicing monks knew the answers their predecessors had made and they memorized these answers; *kōan* practice developed into a fixed form and lost all vitality.

While *sanzen* practice deteriorated, assemblies such as the *gōkoe*, gatherings of monks from throughout the country, and *jukaie*, gatherings for conferring the precepts, flourished. These assemblies were originally designed to assist in the practice of meditation and *sanzen*, and at times as many as a thousand monks attended. As the temples came under the protection of the Sengoku-period (1467–1568) *daimyō*, large-scale affairs were held throughout the country and, since the general public was allowed to attend, these meetings gained great popularity and furnished the public with a general knowledge of Zen. The *jukaie* was also a great factor in spreading the teaching. A temple would invite a famous priest as preceptor-master and he would confer the precepts on the people, from daimyō to commoner. Since these ceremonies conferred precepts on several hundred people at a time, they were extremely effective both as an educational and as a promotional activity.

Edo Period and Revitalization——By the Edo period (1600–1868) the Sōtō sect had spread throughout the country, but it, along with Rinzai Zen, had virtually abandoned any serious Zen study and practice. With the advent of the Tokugawa shogunate, a rigid control was put on all forms of Buddhism. In 1612 *hatto*, or regulations, for the Sōtō sect were handed down, establishing fixed relations between the main temple and its branches and setting up rules for the internal affairs of the sect. In 1615 an order establishing both Eiheiji and Sōjiji as *honzan*, or main temples, where people might enter the priesthood, was issued. A census for 1745 listed a total of 17,549 Sōtō temples, 16,179 associated with Sōjiji and 1,370 with Eiheiji.

The Edo period, partly because of the rigid governmental control and partly because of the emergence of Neo-Confucian and other teachings, has been described as a time of Buddhist decline. Yet the strict regulations imposed on Buddhism served to turn the priests toward an academic study of their own schools and a revitalization of the teaching as a whole. Gesshū Sōko (1618–96) was one of the leaders of a movement known as *Shūtō fukko*, or restoration of the lineage. By the end of the Sengoku period the system of a direct transmission of the teaching from master to disciple had deteriorated. Monks paid no attention to their own original lineage and, in order to enter a temple of higher rank than their own, simply changed the name of the person from whom the teaching had been inherited or acquired an additional line. Teaching lineage and temple lineage had become completely confused. Gesshū and his disciples were eventually successful in bringing order to the Sōtō lineage. Gesshū was also one of the leaders in the renewed interest in Dōgen's major work, the SHŌBŌ GENZŌ (literally, "storehouse of the eye of the true dharma"), making a copy of the 60-volume manuscript. The Edo period saw a succession of Sōtō sect scholars who made extensive study of Dōgen's work, bringing about a reassessment of his position as the founder of Sōtō Zen and a reevaluation of his teaching, which led to the first publication of the *Shōbō genzō* between 1796 and 1811.

During the Genroku era (1688–1704) a school, the Sendanrin, was established in Edo (now Tōkyō). While its primary function was to instruct Sōtō monks in the teachings of their own sect, Chi-

nese studies and poetry were also taught. The school is said to have had a thousand monks; it was the forerunner of present-day Komazawa University. Sōtō has continued today to have a large popular following as well as organized and effective training facilities for its monks. Recent statistics show the Sōtō sect to have 14,699 temples and 6,748,616 adherents (1980).

📖——Imaeda Aishin, *Zenshū no rekishi* (1969). Imaeda Aishin, *Dōgen to sono deshi* (1972). Suzuki Taizan, *Zenshū no chihō hatten* (1942). Suzuki Tairan, "Sōtō Zen no gufu to sono gegosha," *Kokumin seikatsu shi kenkyū* 4 (1960). Yokozeki Ryōin, *Edo jidai tōmon seiyō* (1938).   Philip YAMPOLSKY

Sōunji Dono Nijūikkajō

(The Twenty-One Articles of Lord Sōunji). A set of household precepts (KAKUN) attributed without direct evidence to HŌJŌ SŌUN (1432–1519), a Sengoku-period (1467–1568) adventurer who rose from obscure origins to lordship over Izu and Sagami provinces (now comprised in Shizuoka and Kanagawa prefectures) and founded the Later Hōjō Family (see HŌJŌ FAMILY). Unlike other documents of the same category, these articles are addressed principally not to the author's family and descendants but to the vassals of his house, who are provided here with basic rules of conduct. The *samurai* are told to believe in the Buddhas and the gods, to practice reading and writing no less than riding, and to be prudent, straightforward, and under all circumstances truthful; repeated homilies on the topic of "early to bed and early to rise" give the precepts a certain homespun quality, perhaps justifying in part the attribution of authorship to a rough-hewn and "practical-minded" soldier.

George ELISON

Sōunkyō

Gorge near the upper reaches of the river Ishikarigawa, central Hokkaidō. Located in the town of Kamikawa on the northern fringe of Daisetsuzan National Park. Its sheer cliffs reach a height of more than 200 m (656 ft) on both sides of the gorge, presenting a grand spectacle of columnar joints and waterfalls. Sōunkyō Hot Spring is located here. Length: approximately 24 km (15 mi).

South China Sea, Battle of

(Marē Oki Kaisen; literally, Battle off the Malay Coast). Naval engagement between Japan and Great Britain at the beginning of World War II. On 10 December 1941 the British Far Eastern Fleet, consisting of the battleship *Prince of Wales*, the battlecruiser *Repulse*, and four destroyers, and commanded by Admiral Sir Thomas Phillips, went into action to prevent the Japanese forces from landing on the Malay Peninsula. Both the *Prince of Wales* and *Repulse* were sunk by Japanese naval airplanes; the Japanese lost only three aircraft. The battle, together with the attack on Pearl Harbor several days earlier, proved conclusively the importance of air power and altered the course of naval strategy.   ICHIKI Toshio

Southeast Asia, the Pacific Islands, and Japan

Prior to World War II, the Japanese used the terms Nan'yō (the South Seas) and Nampō (the South) to refer to Southeast Asia and the Pacific Islands, occasionally including Australia and New Zealand. Although the term "Southeast Asia" (Tōnan Ajia) is sometimes used more narrowly to refer to the Malay Archipelago and the Indochinese Peninsula, it will be used in this article in its larger sense.

Relations between Japan and Southeast Asia first flourished after the middle of the 16th century. It was an age of adventure and navigation; the Tokugawa shogunate (1603–1867) promoted trade with the countries of Southeast Asia (see VERMILION SEAL SHIP TRADE), and an increasing number of Japanese formed settlements (NIHOMMACHI) in several places, including Manila in the Philippines and Ayuthaya in Siam (Thailand). However, Japan's relations with Southeast Asia came to an abrupt end with the enforcement of the NATIONAL SECLUSION policy in the early 17th century, and it was not until the middle of the 19th century that relations were resumed.

Meiji Period——It is unfortunate that most of the Japanese who went to Southeast Asia in the early part of the Meiji period (1868–1912) were prostitutes known as KARAYUKI SAN. Groups of these women, who were sold into prostitution, left Japan as early as 1868; they spread throughout the entire area of Southeast Asia, especially on the Malay Peninsula. Of the Japanese living in Southeast Asia at this time, it is estimated that 80 to 90 percent were women engaged in prostitution and related jobs. Japanese men were primarily engaged in roadside entertainment; others worked as masseurs, ricksha men, and itinerant vendors of medicine.

Toward the turn of the century, private Japanese shipping companies opened sea routes between Japan and various Pacific Islands. The Foreign Ministry established diplomatic and consular offices. Communities of Japanese merchants scattered throughout Southeast Asia. In the Dutch East Indies, a chain of Japanese stores called *toko jepang* became popular among local inhabitants. In Davao in the Philippines the Japanese developed a manila hemp industry, while on the Malay Peninsula, the Japanese began operating rubber plantations. At the same time, large trading firms and banks opened a network of branches throughout Southeast Asia.

Japanese Expansion—— At least three important changes in relations occurred after the outbreak of World War I. The first was the Japanese occupation of a number of Pacific Islands that had been German protectorates (including the Marshall, Palau, Caroline, and Mariana islands); these were put under a military administration in October 1914. The Versailles Peace Treaty of 1919 stipulated that the islands would become Japan's mandated territories. Civilian administration was established on the islands in July 1921, and the Pacific Islands Agency (Nan'yōchō) was officially opened on 1 April 1922. It was stipulated that its director-general would be under the supervision and guidance of the prime minister. The Japanese considered the Pacific islands an important part of Southeast Asia, and possession of the islands represented a strong tie to the region.

A second change was related to the expansion of Japan's national economy. During the so-called war boom between 1914 and 1920, the industrial structure of the country underwent substantial change and trade volume increased greatly. The export item that registered the most dramatic increase was cotton fabric. Exports of this item to the Dutch East Indies increased by an average 424 percent annually from 1913 to 1915. Exports to Siam increased 167 percent. The area, as a new trade market, became a key outlet for a burgeoning Japanese capitalism. Overseas Japanese capital investment also increased. Investments by large corporations in rubber and coconut plantations were especially noteworthy. The financial crisis of 1920 reduced the flow of Japanese goods and capital to Southeast Asia. However, while the crisis served to weed out financially weak enterprises, it also made it possible for financially strong companies to lay deeper roots in Southeast Asia.

The third change was closely related to the second one: there was a sudden increase in the number of Japanese settling in Southeast Asia. This migration coincided with Japan's increasing economic penetration, but another important reason was the increase in shipping routes between Japan and the areas. In general Japanese expansion into Southeast Asia during this period was characterized by conscious planning and policy making on the part of business and government authorities, in contrast to the previous period of rather haphazard migration by individuals.

Southern Expansion and World War II—— The SOUTHERN EXPANSION DOCTRINE, which had been advocated by some Japanese since the late 19th century, was adopted as national policy in 1936. The doctrine held that the whole of Southeast Asia was destined to come within Japan's sphere of influence and that the Pacific Ocean should be turned into a "Japanese lake." By July 1940 Japan had decided to implement the doctrine, which was incorporated into the larger plan to establish a GREATER EAST ASIA COPROSPERITY SPHERE.

In September of the same year, Japan occupied northern French Indochina. A Pacific Islands Bureau (Nan'yōkyoku) was created within the Ministry of Foreign Affairs in November, and in the following year Japan seized New Guinea and the Solomon Islands. After the outbreak of the Pacific War, Japan took in quick succession the Philippines, Singapore, the Dutch East Indies, and Burma, before being turned back by American forces at the Battle of Midway in June 1942. On 1 November 1942, a Greater East Asia Ministry was formed; a year later the Greater East Asia Conference was held in Tōkyō.

During this period, as if to compensate for the failure of its China policy, virtually 90 percent of Japanese foreign affairs concerned Southeast Asia. With defeat in August 1945, all Japanese nationals, military and civilian, were repatriated. See also WORLD WAR II; COLONIALISM.

Post-World War II Relations—— The first issue in postwar relations was the payment of war reparations to the Southeast Asian countries. Article 14 of the SAN FRANCISCO PEACE TREATY between Japan and most of the Allied powers required Japan to pay reparations to countries it had occupied during the war. On the basis of this peace treaty, the Philippines and Vietnam demanded reparations and started negotiations with Japan. Although Burma did not attend the peace conference and Indonesia signed the treaty but did not ratify it, both countries demanded reparations from Japan individually. Cambodia and Laos renounced their claims for indemnity. Japan began to pay reparations to Burma, the Philippines, Indonesia, and Vietnam in 1954. The reparations negotiations played a major role in the establishment of formal relations between Japan and these countries. See REPARATIONS FOR SOUTHEAST ASIA.

The Japanese economy benefited much from the payment of these reparations, which was conducted on a long-term basis, with payments in services and products, principally capital goods. The automobile and electric machinery industries were boosted by contracts for capital goods, while stockpiles of ceramic wares, rayon, canned fish, and galvanized iron sheets were utilized for reparations payments, which aided the revitalization of depressed industries.

Even more important was the fact that reparations payments proved to be "priming the pump" for the advance of trading firms and other enterprises into Southeast Asia. Particularly noteworthy was the fact that the Japanese construction industry, which had little overseas involvement before the war, established itself abroad by providing services. Payment in the form of such capital goods as trucks, buses, bicycles, sewing machines, household electrical appliances, and pumps paved the way for later sales of Japanese products. After the reparations payments were completed, these goods became firmly established as some of Japan's most important commodities in Southeast Asia.

Reparations also boosted capital formation in the recipient countries. For example, reparations constituted between 20 and 34 percent of Burma's total capital expenditures, while the payments accounted for 30 to 75 percent of the overall financial assistance received by Burma from foreign countries during the years reparations were paid.

Japanese Influence in Southeast Asia—— The postwar Japanese advance into Southeast Asia has been remarkable, especially since Japan had conducted some of the most destructive battles of the war in that area. Its relative ease may be explained primarily by the emergence of the cold war. The overcommitment of the United States in Asia both during and after the Korean War enabled Japan, with American encouragement, to reestablish itself as an economic and political power in Asia. And it could do this while passively depending on the military security provided by the UNITED STATES–JAPAN SECURITY TREATIES.

There is little doubt that the United States put pressure on the countries of East and Southeast Asia to open their markets to Japan. The substitution of Southeast Asia for the China market was expressed by Prime Minister YOSHIDA SHIGERU in a Diet speech in June 1953: "At a time when we cannot anticipate much from trade with China, it is not necessary for us to repeat here the importance of Japan's relations with Southeast Asia. The government is willing to extend full cooperation in capital, technology, and services for the prosperity of the countries of Southeast Asia."

One other historical development favored Japan's expanding role in Southeast Asia. This was the emergence of the so-called "North-South problem," a two-system framework in which the destinies of the advanced (north) and developing (south) countries were seen as inexorably linked. Developing countries began to put increasing demands on the advanced countries for assistance in economic development. As the only industrialized country in Asia, the expectation grew that Japan would become involved in the development of the region. In October 1954 Japan became a signatory of the Colombo Plan and in April of the same year joined the United Nations' Economic Commission for Asia and the Far East (ECAFE). Both these affiliations helped open the way for expanded Japanese activities.

From the mid-1960s economic ties between Japan and Southeast Asia became stronger. The governments of Thailand and Indonesia legislated laws to facilitate the introduction of foreign capital and began to implement policies aimed at industrialization. Japan entered aggressively into the markets of Southeast Asia and succeeded in turning the entire area into a key market for Japanese goods. In 1964 Japanese exports to Southeast Asia totaled $1.8 billion, while imports amounted to $1.3 billion. By 1978 the figures had increased to $23.1 billion for exports and $17.3 billion for imports. The figures for 1978 represented 23.7 percent of Japan's exports and 21.8 percent of its imports.

Anti-Japanese Sentiment———However, because some businesses violated norms of proper behavior in the attempt to monopolize the markets, anti-Japanese voices rose in various parts of Southeast Asia, culminating in violent anti-Japanese demonstrations and riots, particularly in Bangkok and Djakarta in January 1974 when Prime Minister TANAKA KAKUEI visited the ASEAN nations. The antagonism had deeper roots: memories of the atrocities committed by Japanese forces during the Pacific War; cultural differences, including criticism from the elite class (who had been educated in Europe and the United States) of the unrefined manners of some Japanese; charges that the economic advance of Japan was obstructing the development of the region's economies and the welfare of their people and having adverse effects on the political systems of Southeast Asian countries.

After the United States withdrew from Southeast Asia at the end of the Vietnam War in 1975, the role of Japan in Southeast Asia grew quickly. Southeast Asian countries also came to expect expanded Japanese contributions to their development. In response, Prime Minister FUKUDA TAKEO issued the so-called Manila Declaration (also called the Fukuda Doctrine) in Manila in August 1977, in which he stated that Japan not only desired close economic and cultural relations with the five countries of ASEAN, but would also make constructive contributions to the three socialist countries on the Indochinese peninsula (see ASEAN AND JAPAN).

See also INTERNATIONAL RELATIONS. For relations between Japan and the individual countries of Southeast Asia, see BURMA AND JAPAN; CAMBODIA AND JAPAN; INDONESIA AND JAPAN; MALAYSIA AND JAPAN; PHILIPPINES AND JAPAN; SINGAPORE AND JAPAN; THAILAND AND JAPAN; and VIETNAM AND JAPAN.

━━━━Gaimushō Baishōbu, ed, *Nihon no baishō* (1963). Nagasu Kazuji, *Nanshinsuru Nihon shihon shugi* (1971). Nihon Bunka Fōramu, ed, *Hannichi kanjō no kōzō* (1975). Yano Tōru, *Tōnan Ajia seisaku* (1978).
                                                                  YANO *Tōru*

Southern Alps → Akaishi Mountains

Southern Alps National Park

(Minami Arupusu Kokuritsu Kōen). Situated in central Honshū, in Shizuoka, Nagano, and Yamanashi prefectures. The park extends 55 km (34 mi) north to south and has a maximum width of 18 km (11 mi). It is set in an entirely mountainous region, and its chief features are towering peaks, gorges, waterfalls, and granite cliffs. Unlike the more rugged Northern Alps (see HIDA MOUNTAINS), the Southern Alps, also called the AKAISHI MOUNTAINS, are not volcanic in origin but are composed mainly of granite, sandstone, and clay slate. KOMAGATAKE (2,966 m; 9,728 ft) lies at the northernmost edge of the park. To its south is SENJŌGATAKE (3,033 m; 9,948 ft), followed by HŌŌZAN (2,841 m; 9,318 ft) and KITADAKE (3,192 m; 10,470 ft), the highest of the three peaks called SHIRANE SANZAN, and the second highest mountain in Japan after Mt. Fuji (FUJISAN). At the southern end of the park is AKAISHIDAKE (3,120 m; 10,234 ft). Three large rivers, the TENRYŪGAWA, ŌIGAWA, and FUJIKAWA, flow southward into the Pacific.

The park is noted for forests of Japanese beech (*buna*), Japanese stone pine (*haimatsu*), and hemlock spruce (Amerika *tsuga*). Such wild birds as the ptarmigan or snow grouse (*raichō*) inhabit it, as well as the Japanese antelope (KAMOSHIKA). Area: 357.5 sq km (138 sq mi).

southern expansion doctrine

(*nanshinron*). The doctrine that regarded Southeast Asia and the Pacific Islands as Japan's sphere of interest; it was used until World War II to justify Japan's territorial and political expansion into the area. The term was used in contrast to the "northern expansion doctrine" (*hokushinron*), which advocated Japanese expansion into Korea and Manchuria. A related phrase was "guard the north and advance to the south" (*hokushu nanshin*). The southern expansion doctrine concerned the area referred to as Nan'yō ("the southern seas," or the southwest Pacific), an area including the Caroline, Marshall, Palau, and Mariana islands (those Pacific Islands lying north of the Equator). Southeast Asia was also considered part of Nan'yō, but, in its original sense, the primary focus of the doctrine was on the Pacific Islands.

Some consider the doctrine's origin to be in the Edo period (1600–1868), but it took shape as a modern political doctrine only after Japan had opened its doors to the West in the mid-19th century. The doctrine underwent periodic changes between the Meiji (1868–1912) and the Shōwa (1926–) periods, but it occupied an increasingly important place in modern Japanese diplomacy through these years. However, from the Meiji to the beginning of the Shōwa period, the theory was expounded principally by private citizens, and it was not until the 1930s that the Japanese government adopted the southern expansion doctrine as official policy.

Elements of the Doctrine———A common set of assumptions ran through the various formulations of the doctrine. Among these was the belief that overseas expansion into Southeast Asia held greater potential value for Japan than any other area. The doctrine stood in opposition to the northern expansion doctrine, which held that expansion into Russia, the Korean peninsula, and China was more vital to national defense. Southeast Asia was seen as an economically undeveloped, politically backward area that could benefit from Japanese guidance. The doctrine refused to concede that Southeast Asia was historically within the sphere of influence of Western powers. For example, SUGANUMA TEIFŪ, one of its formulators, called the area "the new Japan's choice territory that Heaven had placed temporarily in the custody of other countries." The doctrine also challenged the ability of advanced Western countries to bring about development and questioned the validity of the relations between the West and Southeast Asia.

The doctrine placed more emphasis on control of the sea rather than the Asian continent. In the words of the scholar TAKEGOSHI YOSABURŌ: "Our future lies not in the north but in the south, not in the continent but in the sea. The Japanese people should be aware that their biggest task is to transform the Pacific Ocean into a Japanese lake." The doctrine thus advocated the strengthening of the Imperial Navy, the expansion of Japan's shipbuilding capability, the extension of sea routes, the promotion of trade, and free immigration. The Japanese people were criticized for lacking an interest in the Pacific Islands and the sea in general, and it was argued that expansion to the south would contribute to the resolution of domestic social and economic problems.

History of the Doctrine———The first formulations of the doctrine can be dated to about 1887. Around this time, the "domestic colonization doctrine" (*naikoku shokumin ron*), which emphasized the settlement of Hokkaidō, was replaced by the "overseas colonization theory" (*kaigai shokumin ron*), and interest in overseas emigration grew considerably. Also, in the background of such thought was the fact that Germany had established a protectorate over the Marshall Islands in 1886. Representative advocates of the southern expansion doctrine during this period were TAGUCHI UKICHI, Suzuki Keikun, SHIGA SHIGETAKA, Inagaki Manjirō (1861–1908), and Suganuma Teifū. At the end of the Meiji period, the primary advocates of the doctrine were Takegoshi Yosaburō, Yamada Kiichi (1848–1923), and Soejima Yasoroku (1875–1950).

The outbreak of WORLD WAR I in 1914 presented an opportunity to apply the doctrine: Japan occupied the Pacific Islands that had been held by Germany (the Caroline, Palau, Marshall, and Mariana islands), and in 1919 these islands came under the mandate of Japan. Supporters of the doctrine next turned their attention toward the Dutch East Indies and British Malaya. At the same time several Japanese magazines, notably the *Jitsugyō no Nihon*, tried to promote public support for the doctrine.

By the 1930s many Japanese came to regard southern expansion as Japan's manifest destiny. In the summer of 1936 Murobuse Kōshin (1892–1970), a leading advocate, published his *Nanshinron* (Southern Expansion Doctrine). On 7 August 1936 the doctrine was incorporated for the first time in national policy in a statement issued by a conference of five ministers. The national policy of southern expansion was to be implemented forcefully in the coming years.

A number of factors contributed to the growing emphasis on the doctrine. The first was Japan's colonization of TAIWAN after the Sino-Japanese War (1894–95); it bolstered the belief that Japan's future was tied to the south. Secondly, there was the Japanese navy's strong insistence on southern expansion from the end of the Meiji period. After it was decided in September 1933 that the navy would be utilized in Japan's strategy in South China, the navy's advocacy of southern expansion came out into the open. A third factor was the role played by General KOISO KUNIAKI. A series of articles that he wrote in the summer of 1940 concerning the concept of a "Tōa *keizai ken*" (East Asia economic sphere) was exceptionally well articulated.

It was from this background that the concept of the GREATER EAST ASIA COPROSPERITY SPHERE emerged. Shortly after the formation of the second KONOE FUMIMARO cabinet on 22 July 1940, Japan launched its southern expansion on a broad front. In September 1940 Japan occupied northern French Indochina; it took New Guinea and the Solomons in 1941, and the Philippines, Singapore, the Dutch East Indies, and Burma in early 1942. It was only with Japan's defeat in the Pacific War that an end was put to the southern expansion doctrine. See also PAN-ASIANISM; COLONIALISM; SOUTHEAST ASIA, THE PACIFIC ISLANDS, AND JAPAN.

📖——Yano Tōru, *Nanshin no keifu* (1975). Yano Tōru, *Nihon no Nan'yō shikan* (1979). YANO TŌRU

South Korea, Japanese relations with → Korea and Japan

South Manchuria Railway

(Minami Manshū Tetsudō; abbreviated as Mantetsu; often referred to as South Manchurian Railway). A semiofficial Japanese company engaged from 1906 to 1945 in the management of railways, initially between Kuanchengzi (K'uan-ch'eng-tzu; now part of Changchun [Ch'ang-ch'un]) and Dalian (Ta-lien; J: Dairen); in the administration of the railway zones; and in the economic construction and development of Manchuria. It served to perpetuate Japan's domination of Manchuria, a potential base for further penetration in East Asia.

Founding of the Company——The Treaty of PORTSMOUTH, ending the Russo-Japanese War of 1904–05, provided for the transfer of Russia's rights and leases on the Liaodong (Liaotung) Peninsula and the South Manchuria Railway (SMR) to Japan. In 1896 Russia had obtained from China the right to build the CHINESE EASTERN RAILWAY across Manchuria to its port of Vladivostok. When two years later Russia obtained a 25-year leasehold to the southern portion of the Liaodong Peninsula, it also acquired the right to build a southward extension (the SMR) of this line to Port Arthur (Ch: Lüshun, now part of Lüda [Lü-ta]) and Dalian. The construction of the SMR portion was completed in 1902 (see map at MANCHURIAN INCIDENT).

Initially, government leaders were divided on how the railway should be operated: Prime Minister KATSURA TARŌ favored a proposal by E. H. Harriman of the United States endorsing joint international operation of the SMR, while chief of the general staff KODAMA GENTARŌ and the governor of Taiwan GOTŌ SHIMPEI advocated the "Japan alone" policy. The issue was resolved in favor of the latter when Gotō became the first president of the SMR.

The operation and control of the railways were crucial for establishing Japanese control over Manchuria. From the beginning, the company was dominated by the Japanese government and especially by its military policies. The Japanese government was the major supplier of capital and major authority on personal and financial matters. The administration of the GUANDONG (KWANTUNG) TERRITORY (as the leased area was now called) controlled the company's railway guards and police. Furthermore, the company relied on government banks for the supply of money. Seventy-eight percent of the funds invested abroad by the Japan Industrial Bank (Nihon Kōgyō Ginkō) between 1905 and 1914 was in SMR bonds.

Administration of the Railway Zone, 1906–1937——The SMR exercised special jurisdictional and administrative power in its railway zone. The zone included not only the land along the railway but also many cities and settlements. The Chinese government was excluded from exercising its sovereign power within the zone. The SMR had the power to levy taxes, maintain police forces, handle real estate, operate schools, undertake public works, and provide medical services. These privileges were supplemented by Japan's extraterritorial rights and consular jurisdictions. The population of the zone was 30,000 in 1908 and had reached about 545,000 by the mid-1930s. The zone was like an independent state. In 1937, however, Japan formally relinquished these special powers to MANCHUKUO, the puppet state established by the Guandong Army in 1932.

The SMR's Economic Empire, 1906–1931——Between 1906 and 1931 the SMR dominated and monopolized the economic life of Manchuria through the management of harbors, water transportation, railways, warehousing, coal mines, electric power, real estate, iron works, industrial plants, natural resources, the labor market, and monetary facilities. The giant Anshan steel works, the Fushun coal mine, and other mines operated by the railway contributed tremendously to the economic development of Manchuria. Moreover,

the SMR invested in and gained control over a growing number of business and industrial companies. However, the Chinese were not the beneficiaries. Wages of Chinese laborers were kept at a minimum; worker casualties were high. More than 114,000 Chinese were either killed or seriously injured on the job during 1909–31.

Conflict with China——The SMR's ever-increasing control of Manchuria raised the foreign powers' suspicions regarding Japan's intentions on the Asian continent, and the encroachment into Chinese territory led to a conflict with China that threatened the Japanese hegemony. The assassination of ZHANG ZUOLIN (Chang Tso-lin), the Chinese warlord based in Manchuria, by radical elements in the Guandong Army, and the subsequent decision by his son, ZHANG XUELIANG (Chang Hsüeh-liang), to join the Nationalist Chinese unification movement in 1928 intensified the Chinese-Japanese conflict. Chinese efforts to build competing railways and the fall of the silver price undercut SMR profits. In 1931 the SMR was in deficit for the first time in its history.

In 1931 the Guandong Army used a bombing incident engineered by some of its officers as a pretext to occupy almost all of Manchuria (see MANCHURIAN INCIDENT). This use of force indicated the military's shift from its previous policy of indirect colonial rule through the SMR to one of direct control. The SMR collaborated fully with the Guandong Army.

After the creation of Manchukuo in 1932, SMR profits rose tremendously. The management of the entire nationalized railway system in Manchuria was placed under the control of the SMR in 1932. In 1935 the Chinese Eastern Railway was purchased from the Soviet Union and also placed under its control. The company's major function thus gradually narrowed from a broad program of economic development for the entire area to the management of railways and the construction of militarily important railways.

SMR after 1937——In 1937, with a view to strengthening Japan's defense and developing resources in Manchuria, the Guandong Army asked the Nissan (Nihon Sangyō Kabushiki Kaisha) interests under AIKAWA YOSHISUKE to organize the Manchuria Heavy Industry Company to manage the region's coal, iron, steel, light metals, airplane, and automobile industries. Although SMR capital had increased to ¥1.4 billion, all its heavy industries, technicians, and facilities, including the Shōwa Steel Works, were transferred to the new corporation. While the SMR attempted to expand its operations into North China, its primary function remained the transportation of goods and people, especially military personnel in Manchuria; these efforts reached a peak in 1942, two years after the outbreak of World War II, when SMR transported over 80 million tons of freight and millions of passengers. In addition, the Research Department, with its budget of ¥20 million and a staff of over 2,000 researchers in 1939, greatly intensified its activities and achieved excellent results, especially in its survey of agricultural and mineral resources. However, military pressure in the form of the requisitioning of the railway for military maneuvers, the transportation of settlers to north Manchurian regions, and the construction of strategic railways caused a decline in profits. For instance, a special military operation during the summer of 1941 that involved transporting troops to the north caused a 40-percent reduction in passengers and a 26-percent reduction in freight income. With the reduced rate for the military and the disruption of regular passenger and freight operation, the SMR lost income. The economic deterioration was hastened by greater difficulty in floating bond issues (the total assets of the SMR had almost doubled between 1937 and 1943) and in obtaining raw materials and facilities. A rapid rise in inflation also contributed to the economic decline.

Japan's position in the war deteriorated in 1944; Anshan and Mukden (now Shenyang) were bombed. The SMR was forced to transport more and more troops and war materials. SMR employees were drafted en masse. With the Japanese surrender in 1945, the SMR, now under the control of Soviet troops who invaded Manchuria in August, was perilously caught between the competing Chinese Communist and Nationalist forces. The SMR continued to operate under the control of the Chinese Changchun Railway, a joint Chinese-Soviet operation, until July 1947, when SMR's president, Yamazaki Motomiki, who had been appointed adviser, left Manchuria.

The military conflicts of the 20th century directly affected the SMR's fortunes. Created as a result of a military victory, the SMR had evolved together with the military as an instrument to penetrate Manchuria. When the military employed direct force to conquer Manchuria, it became an adjunct to the military. When the Manchurian Industrial Development Company was created under the military's direction, the SMR withdrew from other economic involvements and confined itself to transportation, construction, and operations for military purposes. When the Japanese military collapsed in 1945, the SMR collapsed too.

It is true that the SMR's achievements in railway, industrial, agricultural, and research developments were spectacular. But these achievements were neither intended, nor resulted in benefits, for the Chinese people. Not even the Japanese people in the end were the beneficiaries.

📖 ——Manshikai, *Manshū kaihatsu yonjūnen shi* (1964). Minami Manshū Tetsudō Kabushiki Kaisha, *Minami Manshū tetsudō kabushiki kaisha jūnen shi* (1919). Minami Manshū Tetsudō Kabushiki Kaisha, *Minami Manshū tetsudō kabushiki kaisha dainiji jūnen shi* (1928). Minami Manshū Tetsudō Kabushiki Kaisha, *Minami Manshū tetsudō kabushiki kaisha daisanji jūnen shi* (1938). Sadako Nakamura Ogata, *Defiance in Manchuria: The Making of Japanese Foreign Policy, 1931–32* (1964). Elizabeth B. Schumpeter, George C. Allen, E. F. Penrose, and M. S. Gordon, *The Industrialization of Japan and Manchukuo, 1930–1940* (1940). Carl Walter Young, *Japan's Special Position in Manchuria: Its Assertion, Legal Interpretation, and Present Meaning* (1931). John Young, *The Research Activities of the South Manchurian Railway Company, 1907–1945: A History and Bibliography* (1966).　　　　　　　John YOUNG

Soviet-Japanese Basic Convention

(Nisso Kihon Jōyaku). Signed at Beijing (Peking) between Lev Mikhailovich KARAKHAN and YOSHIZAWA KENKICHI on 20 January 1925, the convention embodied the basic rules of the relations between Japan and the Union of Soviet Socialist Republics (USSR). The secret alliance that Japan had concluded with tsarist Russia during World War I had been shattered by the Bolshevik Revolution and the subsequent SIBERIAN INTERVENTION by Allied troops. The convention constituted Japanese recognition of the new regime. It terminated the intervention by providing for the withdrawal of Japanese troops who had remained in northern Sakhalin (J: Karafuto) to secure compensation for the NIKOLAEVSK INCIDENT in which Japanese nationals had been murdered, and it restored diplomatic relations between the two countries. In exchange, the Soviet government, which had unilaterally abrogated the treaties concluded by the tsarist regime, agreed that the Treaty of PORTSMOUTH (1905) ending the RUSSO-JAPANESE WAR remain in full force and that the other treaties, conventions, and agreements signed between Japan and tsarist Russia be reexamined at a conference between the two governments.

The Basic Convention furthermore provided for the revision of the Fishery Convention of 1907, the conclusion of a treaty of commerce and navigation, and the granting of concessions to Japanese individuals and companies for the exploitation of natural resources in the USSR. It also guaranteed reciprocal freedom of movement and protection for its nationals in each other's territories. In attached protocols Japan promised to hand over the old Russian embassy and consulates, until then occupied by anticommunist Russians. The Soviet government assented to further negotiations concerning the debts owed by the tsarist regime to Japan and agreed on a formula for working out contracts for Japanese oil and coal concessions in northern Sakhalin. See also RUSSIA AND JAPAN.

📖 ——Gaimushō, ed, *Nisso kōshō shi* (1942, 1969). George Alexander Lensen, *Japanese Recognition of the U.S.S.R.: Soviet-Japanese Relations, 1921–1930* (1970).　　　　George Alexander LENSEN

Soviet-Japanese development of Siberia

An ongoing series of joint projects undertaken since 1968 to develop a region extending from the Ural Mountains to the Pacific, with Japan providing capital, technology, and equipment in exchange for raw materials, principally timber, coal, copper, iron ore, oil, and natural gas.

Japanese interest in Siberian resources dates from the late-18th-century writings of HONDA TOSHIAKI. Japanese investment started in 1875 with commercial privileges in Sakhalin accorded by the Treaty of ST. PETERSBURG. After 1907 Japanese merchants and bankers became active in the Russian Far East, but their enterprises contracted and eventually terminated between 1920 and 1922 as a result of the advent of Bolshevik power. When Japan and the USSR established diplomatic relations in 1925 (see SOVIET-JAPANESE BASIC CONVENTION), the former secured oil and coal concessions in northern (Soviet) Sakhalin, which were retained until 1944.

Although Soviet-Japanese economic ties did not cease entirely in 1945, their restoration to pre-World War II levels was handicapped

by the absence of full diplomatic relations until 1956. In 1962, within a context of burgeoning bilateral trade, Soviet officials proposed the joint development of a number of Siberian projects. Subsequent negotiations resulted in an agreement signed in Moscow on 1 July 1965 between representatives of the Japanese Federation of Economic Organizations (KEIDANREN) and the Japan Chamber of Commerce on one hand, and the president of the All-Union Chamber of Commerce on the other, to establish the Soviet-Japanese Joint Economic Committee (JEC), a mechanism to oversee and coordinate future joint projects in Siberia. The JEC in turn produced subcommittees concerned with specific projects as they materialized.

In 1968 the first project to be agreed upon provided for the joint exploitation of timber resources along the Amur River. This agreement was renewed in 1974. The second project, inaugurated in 1970, entailed the joint construction of a US $300 million (¥108 billion) port at Wrangel Bay, near Nakhodka, to handle the transshipment of containers. Contracted in 1971, the third project called for the exchange of US $50 million (¥18 billion) worth of Siberian pulp and wood chips for Japanese machinery, textiles, and consumer goods. Two agreements, involving American participation, dealt with geological exploration: for natural gas in the Yakut Autonomous Soviet Socialist Republic (signed in 1974), and for oil and natural gas off the coast of Sakhalin (signed in 1975). As of 1976 Japanese investment in Siberia totaled more than US $1.5 billion (¥450 billion).

Oil and gas offer much potential for Soviet-Japanese cooperation. Siberia contains extensive deposits of both. The USSR places high priority on their development. Japan wants to stabilize and diversify its sources of energy supplies, particularly since the 1973 Arab oil embargo (see OIL CRISIS OF 1973). For over a decade, Moscow and Tōkyō have negotiated the terms of Japanese participation in the construction of an oil pipeline from the Tyumen fields in western Siberia to the Far East and in the transportation of gas from the Yakut fields to the Pacific littoral and beyond. A variety of economic and political problems have inhibited progress in these negotiations.

Siberia's inadequate transportation facilities render much of the raw materials inaccessible or, in Japanese eyes, economically less attractive than alternative sources in Alaska, Australia, Indonesia, and the Middle East. Secondly, capital-short Japanese businesses are reluctant to make long-term, low-interest investments whose return is usually deferred. Thirdly, fundamental differences in the Soviet and Japanese economic systems have been only partially bridged by such mechanisms as the JEC. Finally, there are several political obstacles which from Japan's point of view hinder greater participation in Siberian development: the still unsolved Northern Territory Issue (Japan's claims to the Soviet-occupied southern Kuril Islands); sensitivity to Chinese displeasure at Soviet-Japanese collaboration (especially evident in connection with the Baikal–Amur Railroad project in which the Japanese finally declined to become involved); and reluctance to become dependent upon Soviet resources given the unpredictability of Soviet-Japanese relations.

Despite the slow progress of their cooperation in Siberia's development, Soviet-Japanese trade continues to grow at 10 to 15 percent annually and exceeded US $3 billion (¥900 billion) in 1976.

📖 ——Violet Conolly, *Siberia Today and Tomorrow* (1976). Paul Dibb, *Siberia and the Pacific* (1972). Suzuki Keisuke, *Nisso keizai kyōryoku* (1974).　　　　　　　John J. STEPHAN

Soviet-Japanese Joint Declaration

(Nisso Kyōdō Sengen). A joint declaration issued on 19 October 1956 by the governments of Japan and the Soviet Union, ending the state of war that had existed between them since 9 August 1945 and reestablishing diplomatic relations. The Soviet Union did not sign the SAN FRANCISCO PEACE TREATY of 1951, but on 25 January 1955 Moscow approached Prime Minister HATOYAMA ICHIRŌ with a proposal to move toward normalizing relations. Negotiations began that June in London and continued intermittently until March of the following year, hampered by an impasse over the disposition of territories (southern Sakhalin, the Kuril Islands, Shikotan, and the Habomai Islands) seized by the USSR immediately before and after the end of World War II. After complex bargaining among factions in the ruling Liberal Democratic Party, Hatoyama flew to Moscow on 10 October and nine days later issued a declaration with Nikolai Bulganin, the Soviet premier. In the declaration, both sides agreed to terminate the state of war between them, to restore diplomatic and consular relations, to adhere to principles set forth in the United Nations Charter with respect to the right of self-defense and noninterference in one another's internal affairs, to mutually waive claims arising out of World War II, to activate a fisheries and marine safety treaty concluded the previous May, and to continue negotiations for commercial agreements and a peace treaty. In addition, the Soviet Union pledged to support Japan's entry into the United Nations, to repatriate all remaining Japanese prisoners of war, and to hand over Shikotan and the Habomai Islands after the signing of a peace treaty. The peace declaration marked an important step toward Japan's re-entry into the international community after World War II, but it also highlighted the importance of the territorial issue. The Soviet-Japanese impasse over Japan's claims to KUNASHIRI and ETOROFU in the southern Kurils still prevents the two countries from concluding a peace treaty (see TERRITORY OF JAPAN).

■——Donald C. Hellmann, *Japanese Domestic Politics and Foreign Policy: The Peace Agreement with the Soviet Union* (1969).
John J. STEPHAN

Soviet-Japanese Neutrality Pact → Russia and Japan

Sōyamisaki

Cape in the city of Wakkanai, northern Hokkaidō. Forms the north-ernmost tip of Japan at latitude 45°31′ north. An extension of the Sōya plateau, its cliffs jut out into the Sōya Strait. Until World War II, Sōyamisaki held a vital position as a base for transportation to Sakhalin (J: Karafuto).

Sōya Strait

(Sōya Kaikyō). Between the cape Sōyamisaki, the northernmost tip of Hokkaidō, and Sakhalin (J: Karafuto) in the Soviet Union, con-necting the Sea of Japan and the Sea of Okhotsk. Narrowest width: 43 km (27 mi); average depth: 50 m (164 ft); deepest point: 74 m (243 ft).

soybeans

(*daizu*). *Glycine max*, annual herb of the family Leguminosae, now cultivated throughout the world. Said to have first been cultivated in the area ranging from North China to Siberia in ancient times, soy-beans were introduced to Japan in the early years of the Yayoi pe-riod (ca 300 BC–ca AD 300) and have continued to be one of Japan's main food crops.

Soybeans are rich in protein and fat and traditionally have been an important source of these nutrients for the Japanese, who rarely ate meat in premodern times. MISO, a paste made from cooked soybeans mashed and fermented with malted rice, is used for a soup which is an indispensable part of the daily Japanese diet. Soybeans are also a material for SOY SAUCE (*shōyu*). TŌFU (bean curd), which is made with the protein extracted from soybeans, is another food highly favored by the Japanese. Besides these, soybeans are used to make fermented beans (NATTŌ) and to grow bean sprouts. Parched beans and bean flour are used in confections. Of the annual Japa-nese consumption of about 3,500,000 metric tons (3,850,000 short tons), about 2,600,000 metric tons (2,860,000 short tons) are made into soybean oil. Besides being used for cooking, it has many indus-trial uses.

Domestic production of soybeans has long been insufficient to meet Japanese demand. Before World War II large quantities were imported from Manchuria, and after the war, from the United States. At present, domestic production is about 190,000 metric tons (209,000 short tons) a year (1978), with Hokkaidō producing the most. Besides these, about 100,000 metric tons (110,000 short tons) of soybeans are produced in Japan for green soybeans (*edamame*), which are boiled in the pods and shelled while eaten as a snack, often with beer. Small quantities are also grown for green livestock feed.
HOSHIKAWA Kiyochika

so, yō, and chō

Basic taxes under the RITSURYŌ SYSTEM of law and administration established in the 7th century. In earlier times there had been a rice tax (*tachikara*), a handicraft or local-products tax (*mitsugi*), and a corvée labor requirement (*edachi*). With the adoption of Chinese institutions following the TAIKA REFORM (645), however, taxation was modified to conform with the new land-allotment system

whereby all rice land became public domain and was parceled out to the peasantry (see HANDEN SHŪJU SYSTEM). A census registration made clear those who were eligible for land and liable to taxation, and the various categories for taxes were increased.

So, the rice tax, was imposed on the KUBUNDEN, the plots of land distributed to every male and female over six years of age. The tax generally amounted to 3 percent of the harvest. Most of the rice tax was paid to the district (*gun*) or provincial (*kuni*) granaries and used for local expenses. A part of it was lent out with interest as seed rice (see SUIKO). *Yō*, also known as *chikarashiro*, was a handicraft or local product tax paid in lieu of the 10 days of corvée labor required each year (see YŌEKI). It was exacted from all able-bodied males (*seitei*) between 21 and 60 years of age (later changed to between 22 and 59 [each figure is one year less in Western reckoning]) and was usually paid in the form of a certain length (7.9 m or 26 ft) of cloth, although salt, silk floss, and other local products could be substi-tuted. *Chō*, also called *mitsugi*, referred to handicrafts or local prod-ucts paid to the imperial court. Initially levied on each household or plot of riceland, it was later imposed on individuals. Every adult male was required to pay silk, rough-silk, thread, silk floss, cloth, iron, salt, and the like in specified amounts. Those rendering mili-tary service were exempted from *chō*, *yō*, and *zōyō* (corvée labor). The proceeds of the *yō* and *chō* taxes went to the national treasury to pay the stipends (FUKO) of nobles and officials. Responsibility for transporting these goods to the capital lay with the adult males of each household, who were also expected to pay for their own food during the trip. The *so*, *yō*, and *chō* were an enormous burden on the peasants, and they resorted to every subterfuge to evade these taxes. From the 10th century onward, with the breakdown of central authority and the gradual abandonment of population census, these taxes were gradually diverted by the proprietors of private estates (SHŌEN).
KITAMURA Bunji

soy sauce

(*shōyu*). The basic flavoring agent used in Japanese cuisine; made by fermenting water, salt, and a yeast made from soybean and wheat, a process that may take over a year. Its prototype, a pasty substance called *hishio*, made by adding fish to salt, is known to have been made in the Yayoi period (ca 300 BC–ca AD 300). *Shōyu* as we know it today was first made in Japan in the Muromachi period (1333–1568).

Shōyu is distinguished according to the ingredients and the length of fermentation. *Koikuchi shōyu*, widely used, is fermented for a longer time and is thick; *usukuchi shōyu* is fermented for a shorter period. The addition of *amazake* (a sweet rice wine) gives the latter a delicate color, flavor, and aroma, making it suitable for seasoning vegetables, white-fleshed fish, and clear soups. There are also local variations: the sweeter *tamari*, made in central Honshū; the pale yellow *shottsuru* of Akita Prefecture, made with fish; and the white *shiroshōyu* of the Nagoya area. Since aroma is most impor-tant, it is advisable to add *shōyu* just before a dish is ready to be served. Also, once the container is opened the flavor and color of *shōyu* begin to deteriorate, so it should be used quickly.
ŌTSUKA Shigeru

sozō

Modeled statues of naturally dried, unbaked clay. *Sozō* sculpture flourished in the Nara period (710–794) when it was used in produc-tion of large-scale, realistically conceived Buddhist images. A high degree of control was attained through the technique of wrapping straw around a wooden armature over which clay, fortified with fiber and glue, was applied in layers of increasingly fine detail. Some-times thin layers of clay were applied to a wooden image carved to an almost finished state. After drying, appropriate colors were added; mica powder previously mixed into the surface layers of clay facilitated the adherence of pigments. Ancient examples of *sozō* have been found in northern India and Afghanistan, and in China. *Sozō* reached Japan in the 7th century; the earliest extant example is considered to be the image of the bodhisattva MIROKU in the Nara temple Taimadera. The best-known *sozō* are the figures of Nikkō and Gakkō Bosatsu in the *hokkedō* of the temple TŌDAIJI at Nara. Post-Nara-period *sozō* are rare.

space technology

(*uchū kaihatsu*). Space technology is relatively new to Japan, al-though there were attempts at developing military rockets near the end of World War II. Some years after the war, research was resumed with the development of sounding rockets, followed by a series of successful launchings of scientific satellites and applications satellites. In launching heavy stationary satellites, however, Japan currently depends on the United States. Studies are in progress to increase the economic efficiency of Japanese launch vehicles as well as to increase the weight of the satellites that can be put into orbit.

Sounding Rockets ——— Work on rockets for military use was in progress in Japan during the last years of World War II. The army was working on an antitank rocket shell and a guided rocket for use over short distances, and the navy was developing the manned rocket Ōka for suicide attack. Both forces worked jointly on the manned liquid fuel rocket Shūsui. However the foundations laid by this work were lost with Japan's defeat in the war.

As interest in the peaceful use of rockets grew throughout the world, plans to use rockets for an extensive survey of the upper atmosphere were developed for the International Geophysical Year (IGY) of 1957–58. Japan decided to take part in the IGY activities and to launch a sounding rocket. The altitude aimed at was 80–100 kilometers (50–62 mi), too difficult a feat for the Japanese technology of that time.

Rocket research had been resumed only in 1954. The tiny, so-called pencil rocket of that year, 23 centimeters (9 in) long and 1.8 centimeters (0.7 in) in diameter with a speed of only 200 meters (656 ft) per second on horizontal launch, was followed by the "baby" rocket of 1955 which was 124 centimeters (48.8 in) long and 8 centimeters (3.2 in) in diameter and weighed 8 kilograms (17.6 lb). The Kappa series began in 1956 with model 1 which was 2.2 meters (7.2 ft) long and 13 centimeters (5.1 in) in diameter, weighed 33 kilograms (72.6 lb), and climbed to a height of 5.4 kilometers (3.4 mi). The two-stage model 6 rocket of 1958 (with which Japan participated in the IGY) was 5.6 meters (18.4 ft) long and 25 centimeters (9.8 in) in diameter, weighed 260 kilograms (572 lb), and climbed to 60 kilometers (37.3 mi). Later, in 1964, the three-stage Lambda rocket which was 19.2 meters (63 ft) long and 73.5 centimeters (29 in) in maximum diameter raised the altitude range of Japanese rockets to 1,000 kilometers (621 mi). With the development of the Lambda rocket, the launch site was moved from Michikawa in Akita Prefecture to Uchinoura in Kagoshima Prefecture.

These sounding rockets advanced work in X-ray astronomy, including the study of cosmic X rays and solar X-ray flares, and knowledge about the nature of the ionospheric plasma.

Scientific Satellites ——— The sounding rockets were followed by scientific satellites, and the Mu rocket series was developed to launch them. The diameter of the first stage was enlarged to 1.4 meters (4.6 ft), the total length was 23.7 meters (77.7 ft), and the weight exceeded 40 metric tons (44 short tons). The first of the Mu series was the four-stage Mu-4S, followed by the three-stage Mu-3C and Mu-3H. All of these used composite solid propellant.

After four consecutive failures, the launching of an experimental satellite was achieved in February 1970. The satellite, Ōsumi, weighed 23.8 kilograms (52.4 lb), had a perigee of 337 kilometers (209 mi) and an apogee of 5,151 kilometers (3,198 mi). The launch vehicle was the four-stage Lambda L-4S. Ōsumi was the first Japanese artificial satellite to orbit, making Japan the fourth country to achieve satellite launch capability, following the Soviet Union, the United States, and France. Ōsumi was nonguided, with only attitude control, and deviated from its intended orbit. A year later, in February 1971, the experimental satellite Tansei weighing 63 kilograms (138.6 lb) was launched into orbit using the Mu-4S; its perigee was 990 kilometers (614.8 mi) and its apogee 1,100 kilometers (683.1 mi). Tansei was followed by the launch of the first full-scale Japanese scientific satellite, Shinsei, in September 1971. Put into orbit with a perigee of 870 kilometers (540 mi) and an apogee of 1,870 kilometers (1,161 mi), it made observations of the ionosphere, measuring cosmic rays and solar waves.

In August 1972 the second Japanese scientific satellite, Dempa, was put in orbit; its weight was 75 kilograms (165 lb), the perigee 250 kilometers (155.3 mi), and the apogee 6,560 kilometers (4,073.8 mi). Dempa was intended mainly for study of the area from the ionosphere to the magnetosphere; it produced data concerning the measurement of plasmic waves, plasmic concentration, electronic flux, and electromagnetic undulation.

The third experimental satellite, and first to be launched using the Mu-3C, Tansei 2, went up in February 1974. The launch rocket was improved and the satellite's attitude control system changed to one utilizing the earth's magnetic field. Tansei 2 weighed 56 kilograms (123.2 lb), the perigee was 290 kilometers (180 mi), and the apogee 3,240 kilometers (2,012 mi).

A year later, in February 1975, Japan's third scientific satellite, Taiyō, was placed in orbit by the Mu-3C. It weighed 86 kilograms (189.2 lb), the perigee was 260 kilometers (161.5 mi), and the apogee 3,140 kilometers (1,950 mi); it measured solar X rays, ultraviolet radiation, and coronal bright lines.

Next the experimental satellite Tansei 3 weighing 134 kilograms (294.8 lb) was launched in February 1977 using the Mu-3H with a perigee of 790 kilometers (490.6 mi) and an apogee of 3,810 kilometers (2,366 mi).

The fourth Japanese scientific satellite was launched using the Mu-3C in February 1976. It failed, but the fifth one, Kyokkō, weighing 126 kilograms (277.2 lb), was placed in orbit in February 1978 using the Mu-3H with a perigee of 636 kilometers (395 mi) and an apogee of 3,977 kilometers (2,470 mi). It measured plasmic concentration, temperature, and composition and carried out television observation of the aurora. In February 1979 the sixth Japanese scientific satellite, Hakuchō, was placed in orbit using the same Mu-3H rocket. Having a perigee of 541 kilometers (335 mi) and an apogee of 649 kilometers (402 mi), it conducted observations of cosmic X rays.

The sounding rockets, scientific satellites, and rocket-powered launch vehicles described above were largely developed by Tōkyō University.

Applications Satellites ——— The development of applications satellites and their launch vehicles in Japan has been conducted mainly by the NATIONAL SPACE DEVELOPMENT AGENCY OF JAPAN which was established in 1969. These satellites have been used in the areas of communications, meteorology, and observation of the earth. The launch vehicle used for the Japanese applications satellites was the N rocket; it consisted of an American Y Delta rocket for its first and third stages, and the Japanese-developed LE-3 rocket for its second stage. Using liquid propellants for the first and second stages and solid propellants for the third stage, it was 32.6 meters (106.9 ft) long, 2.44 meters (8 ft) in maximum diameter, weighed 90 metric tons (99 short tons), and was equipped with three solid-propellant auxiliary boosters. The launch site was the Tanegashima Space Center on the island of Tanegashima in Kagoshima Prefecture.

The first Japanese applications satellite, Kiku, was launched in September 1975. An experimental technology satellite, it weighed 83 kilograms (182.6 lb) and had a perigee of 980 kilometers (608.6 mi) and an apogee of 1,100 kilometers (683.1 mi). It was followed by Ume, launched in February 1976 to make observations of the ionosphere preparatory to the development of communications using the ionosphere. It weighed 139 kilograms (305.8 lb) and had a perigee of 980 kilometers (608.6 mi) and an apogee of 1,010 kilometers (627.2 mi).

Plans were then made to put an experimental technology satellite into a stationary orbit. This was successfully realized in February 1977 when Kiku 2, weighing 130 kilograms (286 lb), was placed in a stationary position at 130° E. Later Japan decided to put much heavier satellites into stationary orbit and, in the absence of a suitable launch vehicle in Japan, to commission the United States to make future launches until domestic vehicles became available.

The first such satellite was a stationary weather satellite, Himawari, which weighed some 350 kilograms (770 lb) and was launched using a Y Delta rocket in July 1977. Stationary at 140° E, Himawari continues to send back photographs of the distribution of clouds covering Japan to aid in weather forecasting. It was followed by the stationary experimental communications satellite Sakura, weighing 340 kilograms (748 lb), which was launched in the same way and became stationary at 135° E. It uses the submillimeter wave band (20–30 GHz) for communication. In April 1978 an experimental broadcasting satellite of medium size, Yuri, was launched using a Y Delta from Cape Kennedy and put into a stationary orbit at 140° E. It is equipped with a three-axis attitude control system and has a weight of 350 kilograms (770 lb).

In February 1979 another experimental broadcasting satellite, Ayame, was launched using an N I rocket at the Tanegashima Space Center. Cylindrical with a diameter of 1.4 meters (4.6 ft) and a height of 1 meter (3.3 ft) and weighing 130 kilograms (286 lb), it failed to separate from the third stage of the rocket. This was followed by the launching in February 1980 of Ayame 2, which also failed to attain a stationary orbit.

Future Plans ——— Work is being carried out in Japan to prepare equipment that can be used in space shuttles. One type of such equipment is designed for the study of electromagnetic undulation and of the movement of charged particles in ionospheric plasma through the use of particle acceleration. New types of rockets are also being developed. Work is continuing on the N II rocket, a modified N rocket with improvements in the second stage, and on the H I rocket, which will be fueled by liquid oxygen and liquid hydrogen. This H I rocket will be able to place a satellite weighing 500 kilograms (1,100 lb) into a stationary orbit.

─── Keizai Dantai Rengōkai Uchū Kaihatsu Suishin Kaigi, ed, *Uchū kaihatsu handobukku* (biennial, from 1969). Shinra Ichirō, *Nihon no uchū kaihatsu* (1969).   SHINRA Ichirō

Spain and Japan

Spain was among the first European nations to open relations with Japan; although its cultural influence was slight because of the short duration of contact, its political influence was great.

The dispatch of a mission to the governor of the Philippines by TOYOTOMI HIDEYOSHI in 1592 led to the opening of diplomatic relations, conducted through Spain's colonies in the Philippines and Mexico. Spanish Franciscan monks came to Japan the following year as Philippine envoys and also began missionary activities. The Franciscans had no specific policies of proselytization, as did the Jesuits, and mainly practiced acts of charity for the sick and the poor. Spanish Dominicans and Augustinians came to Japan after 1602; the former in particular worked hard to organize groups of believers known as *cofradía* (J: *kumi*). These groups proved to be essential in providing mutual aid and maintenance of faith among believers, especially after missionary activities were restricted and eventually banned altogether in 1614 (see ANTI-CHRISTIAN EDICTS). The Dominicans published in Manila two books of faith, *Rosario kiroku* (1622) and *Rosario no kyō* (1623), in romanized Japanese for the benefit of Japanese believers under persecution.

From the Spanish the Japanese also acquired knowledge concerning Europe and the New World. However, these contacts intensified the suspicions that the Japanese authorities entertained about the Christian missionaries—that their missions were a precursor of eventual territorial aggression. The pilot of the galleon *San Felipe*, for example, made statements to the effect that the activities of the Spanish missions were the first step in the conquest of Japan (see SAN FELIPE INCIDENT). The 1611 Pacific expedition of Sebastian VISCAINO, in which he visited Japan as the envoy of the viceroy of Nueva España (Mexico), seemed to provide more grounds for mistrust of the Spanish. The anti-Spanish campaign of the Dutch and the English further damaged Spain's reputation, and diplomatic relations were severed by the Japanese in 1624. It is conceivable that the aggressive nationalism of the Spanish gave the Japanese leaders a stronger sense of nationalistic pride and contributed to the proscription of Christianity and the later policy of NATIONAL SECLUSION.

Following the Meiji Restoration of 1868, formal relations between the two countries were resumed. After World War II diplomatic relations were broken for a while and then reestablished. Today, commercial relations between Spain and Japan are growing stronger, and exchange of technology in such industries as iron manufacturing is being pursued. See also MEXICO AND JAPAN; PHILIPPINES AND JAPAN; CHRISTIANITY; NAMBAN TRADE.

KISHINO Hisashi

sparrows

(*suzume*). In Japanese, *suzume* is the common name for small brownish, streaked, songbirds of the genus *Passer*, family Ploceidae. They average approximately 14.5 centimeters (5.7 in) in length and live in close proximity to human habitation. The most typical species found in Japan is the Japanese tree sparrow (*Passer montanus saturatus*), a variation of the Eurasian tree sparrow (*P. montanus*). Another typical member of this genus indigenous to Japan is the *nyūnai suzume* or russet sparrow (*P. rutilans rutilans*). The common house sparrow (*P. domesticus*) is not found in Japan. Japanese farmers have long regarded the sparrow as an injurious bird, since it feeds on grain seeds and rice. However, in urban areas it is credited with combating certain insect pests.   TAKANO Shinji

The *suzume* is first mentioned in Japanese literature in the ancient chronicle KOJIKI (712). No doubt reflecting Chinese influence, the *Kojiki* account attributes to the sparrow certain supernatural powers. The noted Heian court lady SEI SHŌNAGON categorized the *suzume* among things that are lovable in her early 11th century work *Makura no sōshi* (The Pillow Book), and the sparrow occupies an especially high place in the fauna of court literature. The familiar folktale SHITAKIRI SUZUME (The Tongue-Cut Sparrow), about a sparrow which repays kindness with fortune, is found in the UJI SHŪI MONOGATARI, a 13th-century collection of tales. The *suzume*

has also been a favorite bird of Japanese poets like the *haiku* poet Kobayashi ISSA (1763–1827).   SAITŌ Shōji

special education

(*tokushu kyōiku*). Special education, in the wording of the SCHOOL EDUCATION LAW OF 1947, is directed at the blind and nearly blind, the deaf and nearly deaf, and the mentally retarded, as well as those with speech impairment, emotional disorders, and multiple disorders. Special education facilities are of three types: for the blind, for the deaf, and for the mildly handicapped (*yōgo gakkō*). In addition, there are also special education classes for the mildly handicapped within the regular primary and middle school systems.

The need for education of the handicapped was first officially recognized in the EDUCATION ORDER OF 1872, and the founding of the Kyōto Institute for the Blind and Deaf in 1878 marked the beginning of comparatively systematized special education. In 1880 the Rakuzenkai Institute for the Blind opened in Tōkyō, and subsequently came under the direct control of the Ministry of Education in 1885. This school was the forerunner of the Tōkyō University of Education (now Tsukuba University), which has continued to play a central role in the preparation of teachers in special education.

Regulations concerning the opening and closing of schools for the blind and deaf were made in 1890 and followed in 1891 by the establishment of regulations concerning teacher qualifications and use of staff. With these steps came a gradual establishment of a legal basis for this work. However, particularly in areas other than education for the blind and deaf, the establishment of public systems has been slow, despite the invaluable contributions made by private institutions such as Takinogawa Gakuen, Shirakawa Gakuen, Tōka Juku, and Fujikura Gakuen.

Compulsory education was extended to include schools for the blind and deaf from 1948, and to *yōgo gakkō* in 1979. As of 1979, the number of special schools was: schools for the blind 73, schools for the deaf 110, and schools for the mildly handicapped (*yōgo gakkō*) 654. The number of children within the compulsory education age bracket (ages 6–15) who were enrolled at these schools was 69,038. In addition there were 115,711 children enrolled in special education classes within the regular school system.

Special education in Japan is moving from quantitative expansion to qualitative improvement, with a positive attitude toward such problems as integration and communication with ordinary schools and classes, education of children with multiple disorders, and early education of handicapped children.

─── Mombushō, *Tokushu kyōiku hyakunen shi* (1978). Tsujimura Yasuo, *Nihon no shinshin shōgaiji kyōiku* (1977).

TAKUMA Shinpei

Special Higher Police

(Tokubetsu Kōtō Keisatsu; often abbreviated as Tokkō). A police organization created in 1911 primarily to prevent the spread of dangerous foreign ideologies and to investigate and control the activities of politically motivated groups. These police, who were also known as "peace police" (*chian keisatsu*) or "thought police" (*shisō keisatsu*), achieved great notoriety as the eyes and ears of the powerful HOME MINISTRY until the end of World War II.

While the direct origins of the Special Higher Police, at least in its most recognizable form, date from 1911, its roots extend back into the early part of the Meiji period (1868–1912) and more indirectly even to the Edo period (1600–1868). The rigid social regulations and "spy system" established by the Tokugawa shogunate and the creation of a political police by the Meiji government prepared the way for the creation of the Special Higher Police.

The appearance of leftist groups and labor organizations early in the 20th century made government officials acutely aware of the need to strengthen political controls. The government's response took the form of highly restrictive laws and tighter surveillance of suspected radicals. Under the provisions of the PUBLIC ORDER AND POLICE LAW OF 1900 (Chian Keisatsu Hō), political groups were required to register with the police and obtain special permission to meet, police were empowered to dissolve such meetings and disband political organizations, and people were forbidden to join secret organizations. (Unions were destroyed, since they were classified as secret societies.)

The sensational HIGH TREASON INCIDENT OF 1910, in which Japan's leading anarchist, KŌTOKU SHŪSUI, and others were hanged for plotting to assassinate the emperor, appears to have been the direct stimulus for the creation of the Special Higher Police. By 1912 these so-called thought police had independent sections within the Tōkyō Metropolitan Police Headquarters and the Ōsaka Prefectural Police Headquarters. They were charged with investigating and suppressing the activities of radical and other suspect groups who spread dangerous foreign ideologies or organized intellectuals, laborers, and farmers against the government.

After 1912 leftist activities declined, and the Special Higher Police force grew only slowly; but the Russian Revolution, the RICE RIOTS OF 1918, the upsurge of strikes and agrarian disputes, the huge SAMIL INDEPENDENCE MOVEMENT in Korea in 1919, and the generally unsettled conditions in the closing days of World War I prompted the thought police to increase its numbers and devise more sophisticated methods. Bureaucrats under the HARA TAKASHI cabinet (1918–21), which was anxious to control leftists and contain the rapidly developing suffrage movement, expanded police investigations; there were more numerous and more frequent reports, more factual data on individuals, and more research concentrating on specific organizations. Three new sections were added in the 1920s to oversee labor, arbitration, and Koreans in Japan.

The real period of growth and power, however, did not begin until after the passage of the PEACE PRESERVATION LAW OF 1925 (Chian Iji Hō). Using this broad law, the thought police, in cooperation with justice officials, launched a sustained campaign to destroy the JAPAN COMMUNIST PARTY. Students were the first target during the winter of 1925–26. Then the authorities struck directly at the Communist Party on 15 March 1928, catching about 1,600 suspected members in their legal net (see MARCH 15TH INCIDENT). Other nationwide arrests followed, until the Communist Party ceased to exist as an effective nationwide organization. These incidents had implications for socialists, liberals, Christians, radical rightists, and followers of "radical" indigenous religions as well: they, too, soon became targets for the police, who were spurred on by the internal and external pressures that plunged Japan into an era of semiwar after 1931 and war after 1937; the thought police made it their duty to stamp out "unhealthy" thoughts in every corner of society. The scope of the Peace Preservation Law was extended to allow prosecution for many formerly legitimate activities. By 1941 arrests of those involved in leftist-related violations of the peace law totaled nearly 66,000.

The increasing importance of the Special Higher Police was reflected in their numbers and organizational structure. Prior to the 15 March 1928 mass arrest, thought police units were in Tōkyō, Ōsaka, Kyōto, Kanagawa, Aichi, Hyōgo, Fukui, Nagano, Yamaguchi, Fukuoka, Nagasaki, and Hokkaidō. Agents were also stationed in Beijing (Peking), Shanghai, and Harbin. After the March arrest the number of thought police in Tōkyō was increased, and they were also assigned to all prefectures; a budget was requested to install special telephone lines between the capital and other key cities and to send agents to places like Chicago, New York, London, and Berlin. In 1932 the Special Higher Police was enlarged to include a section for external affairs and given the status of a full department. The phenomenal growth can be seen in the number of personnel in the Tōkyō headquarters: 70 persons in 1928 and 380 just four years later. The expansion in Ōsaka was similar.

Much has been said by scholars and the popular press about the brutality of the Special Higher Police, suggesting that police torture to force confessions and to punish "reds" was savage. Often, those who indict the police for brutality point to the cruel fate of KOBAYASHI TAKIJI and to his 1928 novel, Senkyūhyakunijūhachinen sangatsu jūgonichi (The Fifteenth of March, 1928), which exposed police tactics in Otaru, Hokkaidō. A more balanced view is that although there were instances of torture and beatings and although conditions in some jails were harsh and the indeterminate length of detention while awaiting trial became a kind of "psychological torture," terror was never a general policy; furthermore, police actions in Japan were mild compared to those of Nazi Germany, Stalinist Russia, and Maoist China.　　　　　　　　　Richard H. MITCHELL

special tax measures

(sozei tokubetsu sochi). Measures adopted mainly under the Special Tax Measures Law (Sozei Tokubetsu Sochi Hō) of 1957, in which certain tax bases are assessed at reduced rates or exempted from taxation in order to achieve specific economic policy objectives. The first such measures were instituted shortly after World War II to spur the rebuilding of lost capital stock. Postwar Japanese economic policy aimed at achieving economic recovery as quickly as possible without causing inflation, and special tax measures were initiated to

achieve this objective through the favorable treatment of savings and the promotion of investment. Interest and dividend incomes were exempted from taxation, or given lower tax rates, until the economy entered into the period of rapid growth after 1955.

In the meantime, the increasing concentration of population in larger cities exacerbated the housing shortage, which had existed since the end of World War II. In 1969 special tax measures were instituted to induce the conversion of privately held land to residential property. The tax on individual long-term capital gains was reduced sharply in order to encourage land sales. As a result, land transactions increased, and speculation drove up the price of real estate. Controversy continues to surround the special taxation of land.

Another controversial tax measure levies a low tax rate upon payments to physicians for medical services under social insurance programs. Corporation tax measures include special depreciation allowances and exemptions for special reserves which have been authorized to promote rationalization. See also TAXES; TAX LAW.
　　　　　　　　　　　　　　　　　　　　　UDAGAWA Akihito

spiders

(kumo). In Japanese, kumo is the common name for arthropods of the order Araneae. Japanese spiders belong to three suborders, and about 1,000 species have been identified; some of the most common of these are the kimuragumo (Heptathela kimurai), the jigumo (Atypus karschi), the onigumo (Araneus ventricosus), the koganegumo (Argiope amoena), and the ashidakagumo (Heteropoda venatoria).
　　　　　　　　　　　　　　　　　　　　　NAKANE Takehiko

Japanese folklore frequently casts the spider in the role of the villain or the pursued, probably because of the association of spiders with a legendary race of cave dwellers known as tsuchigumo (literally, "earth spiders"), who are said to have lived in parts of Japan until the 7th or 8th century. Such spider legends have been used as material for various macabre tales and are a theme in Nō and kabuki plays.
　　　　　　　　　　　　　　　　　　　　　SAITŌ Shōji

Spirit of Jesus Church

(Iesu no Mitama Kyōkai Kyōdan). A Christian sect founded in 1937 by Murai Izuru, who claimed to have had a divine vision in 1941. It purports to restore the original church of Jesus and emphasizes the coming of the Holy Spirit to individual believers. The church has no foreign affiliation; there are no paid clergy. It claimed 89,604 adherents in 1977.
　　　　　　　　　　　　　　　　　　　　　Kenneth J. DALE

sports

Sports and sports-related activities are extremely popular in Japan. Over the years, the Japanese government has made efforts to encourage people to participate in various sports for leisure, health, and physical fitness. As a result, most secondary schools and universities provide facilities for team sports, and many large companies encourage and support sports activities for their employees. As in other modern, industrialized countries, professional spectator sports draw large crowds into stadiums and arenas.

Modern Western-style sports were first introduced during the Meiji period (1868–1912) by foreign teachers (see FOREIGN EMPLOYEES OF THE MEIJI PERIOD) and by Japanese students returning from abroad. BASEBALL was introduced in the 1870s by Horace Wilson, an American teacher. At about the same time, Archibald Douglas, a British naval instructor, introduced track and field, billiards, and rugby to Japan. Other contributions were made by such notables as Theodor von LERCH, who introduced skiing (see WINTER SPORTS) to the Japanese army in 1911, and Dr. George A. Lealand, who popularized GYMNASTICS and TENNIS. Another Englishman, Fredric W. Strange, introduced rowing and crew, and founded the Imperial Universities Athletic Association. The emphasis placed on team sports in the military and in the schools contributed to the popularization of athletic competition in general.

In the first two decades of the 20th century, secondary schools nationwide engaged in a mixture of traditional Japanese and Western sports, including KENDŌ (swordsmanship), JŪDŌ, archery, track and field, rowing, and baseball. Since the traditional Japanese samurai education had stressed martial training and competition as well as scholarship, sports were readily accepted as part of the new general education program.

The JAPAN AMATEUR SPORTS ASSOCIATION (JASA) was first organized in 1911 to direct the training of athletes for the Olympic games. During the 1920s more than 14 other amateur sports organizations, each dealing with an individual sport, also came into being to train athletes for such events as the Meiji Shrine Games held between 1924 and 1943. In the days preceding World War II, however, Western sports were discouraged in the schools, and traditional martial arts received official support.

After World War II, following the first NATIONAL SPORTS FESTIVAL in 1946, JASA was reorganized to form the governing body for all amateur sports. Currently, JASA is made up of 39 individual sports groups, the Japan Sports Art Association, and 47 prefectural sports associations. Outside JASA's jurisdiction are the Japan High School Sports Association and the All Japan Middle School Sports Association.

In a public opinion poll conducted by the Prime Minister's Office in 1976, 67 percent of those polled said they enjoyed sports. Of these, 45 percent participated in one or more individual sports. According to the poll, the most popular leisure sports are baseball, TABLE TENNIS, CYCLING, skiing, and fishing. The most popular spectator sports are baseball, SUMŌ wrestling, and VOLLEYBALL. Fully 20 percent of those polled listed various forms of gymnastics and calisthenics, such as those led by radio programs that have been broadcast regularly since 1928, as their principal form of fitness exercise. Running, too, has gained popularity in the past two or three years, and the number of participants in local marathons has increased markedly. The Ōme-Hōchi Marathon, which has been held annually since 1967, drew more than 15,000 participants in 1980.

Professional sports in Japan include baseball, sumō, boxing, tennis, bowling, skiing, and GOLF. Of these, baseball and sumō are the most popular. First organized in 1936, professional baseball drew more than 14 million spectators in 1978. Today, there are around 700 professional sumō wrestlers in Japan competing in the six scheduled tournaments held annually. More than a million spectators attend the tournaments each year. Golf, too, has become extremely popular in recent years; more than 50 professional tournaments were held in 1978. Although its status as a sport can be questioned, professional wrestling also deserves mention as the largest box-office sports attraction in recent years.

The first Japanese athletes to go abroad were the members of the Waseda University baseball team who visited the United States in 1905. Since 1912 Japan has participated in such international events as the Olympic Games, the Far Eastern Championships (1913–34), and the ASIAN GAMES. In 1940 the 12th Olympic Games were to be held in Tōkyō, but because of the wars in Europe and China, the games were cancelled; Japan was not invited to participate in the London Olympics in 1948. However, Japan hosted the 1964 TŌKYŌ OLYMPIC GAMES and the 1972 SAPPORO WINTER OLYMPIC GAMES. Japanese teams also participate in the World University Games and the Stokes Mandeville Games for the handicapped. In recent years the number of international sports meets held in Japan and the number of Japanese participating in foreign sports meets have increased steadily.

WATANABE Tōru

spring wage offensive → shuntō

squid and cuttlefish

(ika). In Japanese, ika is the general name for cephalopods of the order Decapoda. About 120 species live in waters off Japan and many are important in fishery. The thick-shelled kōika (Sepia esculenta), a species of edible cuttlefish, spawns on seaweed beds in shallow water from spring through summer, when it is caught and eaten raw or cooked. The thin-shelled surumeika (Todarodes pacificus), yariika (Loligo bleekeri), and kensaki ika (L. edulis), which migrate in groups, are eaten raw, or dried (surume). The luminous hotaruika (fire squid; Watasenia scintillans) is caught when the female migrates to the shallow water of Toyama Bay to spawn in early summer. It has been designated as a natural monument for its beautiful luminescence. The himeika (Idiosepius pygmaeus paradoxus), the world's smallest squid with a body length of about 5 cm (about 2 in), lives in sea grass (eel grass; Zostera marina) in bays; the daiōika (Architeuthis japonica) is a large species growing to about 6 m (20 ft).

HABE Tadashige

Raw squid has become a popular food in modern Japan since the development of refrigeration technology, but squid was eaten in dried form (surume) in ancient times. Descriptions in the ENGI SHIKI (completed in 927) reveal that surume was presented to the imperial court from various provinces. As surume was traditionally used as an offering to Shintō deities, the Japanese still use it for presents on auspicious occasions.

SAITŌ Shōji

standard-form contract

(yakkan). A prepared contract containing standard terms and conditions pertaining to specified transactions. Such contracts are used to execute a large number of transactions promptly and with uniform conditions. They are often used in banking, carriage, warehousing, insurance, and maritime transactions.

Because standard terms and conditions are used in daily commercial practice, they assume a self-governing legal and regulatory character, controlling the trade practices of certain transactions. A CUSTOMARY LAW (kanshūhō) has developed to the effect that transactions of a certain type are generally undertaken pursuant to standard terms and conditions. All contractual provisions of a transaction can be stipulated in standard terms and conditions. Usually, however, the enterprises that prepare standard-form contracts are in a stronger position relative to those with whom they are doing business; thus, it becomes important to determine independently the validity of the various clauses in the contract. Particularly problematic is the validity of provisions that reduce or eliminate the statutory liabilities of debtor enterprises. Accordingly, legislative and administrative regulations and judicial remedies come into play. Standard-form contracts are not interpreted through examination of the circumstances and intent of the concerned parties, as is the case in interpreting an individualized contract. Rather, the method of interpretation more closely resembles that of interpretation of statutory provisions, in that the meaning of the contractual terms, as they are reasonably, uniformly, and objectively understood within the business circles concerned, must be established. See also CONTRACTS.

NAGAHAMA Yōichi

standard of living

(seikatsu suijun). A measure of the economic well-being of average citizens of a society at a given point. The term describes a norm and may provide a greatly distorted picture of the society if there is a highly unequal distribution of income. Although this is not the case in Japan, it should be stressed that the following discussion is confined to the average level.

The standard of living is related mainly and most importantly to the current flow of goods and services available for immediate consumption during a specified time span (e.g., a year). At the same time, however, it is affected significantly by the natural environment as well as by the stock of national wealth accumulated previously.

Measurement poses a series of serious problems involving which types of goods and services should be chosen in assessing the standard of living, and the importance given to each of the goods and services chosen. Thus, any indicator of the standard is necessarily an approximation and should be interpreted with caution.

Living Conditions of an Average Family —— An ordinary family in Japan in the mid-1970s consisted of three to four members (husband and wife with one or two children) who lived in a residential unit with a floor space of about 77 square meters (829 sq ft), or, if in a metropolitan area such as Tōkyō or Ōsaka, about 60 square meters (646 sq ft). The family would earn a monthly income of about ¥236,000 (equivalent to US $770), about 9 percent of which would be deducted for taxes and social security payments. For various reasons, the family would set aside about 22 percent of its disposable income as savings.

The household would typically be equipped with a washing machine, an electric rice cooker, a vacuum cleaner, a refrigerator, a telephone, a color television set, and one or two radio receivers. There was a 50 percent chance that the family would own a motor vehicle. The number of registered passenger vehicles in 1975 was 0.15 units per person, compared with 0.49 units per person in the United States.

In the mid-1970s, working hours were relatively long: 38.6 hours per week for a production worker in a manufacturing industry, compared with 36.5 hours in the United States and 35.1 hours in West Germany. This meant, of course, that the head of a household had less time for family outings and other entertainment than his Western counterpart. However, a visitor would probably find a fair quantity of reading material on the family book shelf, as the number of new books published per 1,000 persons in Japan in 1975 (0.30 titles) was only slightly smaller than in the United States (0.40) and approximately half the number published in the United Kingdom (0.64) and West Germany (0.66).

The average family was reasonably healthy, as evidenced by the relatively low infant-mortality ratio (0.93 percent in 1976), which was roughly equivalent to the Swedish ratio (0.87 percent in 1971–75) and superior to those of England and Wales (1.4 percent in 1973) and the United States (1.5 percent in 1975). By the same token, the life expectancy of a male at birth, 72.0 in 1976, was not inferior to that in the Western countries; the corresponding figures were 72 in Sweden (1971–75) and 69 in both the United States (1975) and England and Wales (1973).

Japan has managed to keep its CRIME at a fairly low level by international standards: the annual number of crimes committed per 100,000 inhabitants in 1975 was 1,495, as opposed to 5,285 in the United States. On the other hand, Japan scored poorly in the area of social overhead capital (monies expended for improvement of social conditions). The per capita park area in Tōkyō, for instance, was only 1.5 square meters (16.1 sq ft) in 1976, whereas it was 13.1 (141.0 sq ft) in Frankfurt, 30.4 (327.1 sq ft) in London, 45.7 (491.7 sq ft) in Washington, DC, and 80.3 (864.0 sq ft) in Stockholm. In 1975, only 23 percent of Japan's citizens had access to a public sewage system, compared with 71 percent in the United States, 79 percent in West Germany, 80 percent in Sweden, and 94 percent in the United Kingdom.

Levels and Contents of Personal Consumption —— Standard of living may be measured by investigating the level and content of personal consumption. This can be accomplished by studying per capita personal consumption as expressed in standardized monetary units such as base year (constant) prices. Another measuring technique examines the physical quantities involved in basic consumption of goods and services, like calorie intake or physical spaciousness of dwellings. In the following, several such attempts will be briefly reviewed, using one or the other method.

The United Nations study on international comparison of real purchasing power of national currencies provides the most comprehensive monetary measure currently available. By employing an internationally standardized scale of measurement and using multicountry comparison techniques, the study concluded that the Japanese level of personal consumption in 1973 was, on the average, approximately half that in the United States (see Table 1). It should be noted here that the gap was much wider in 1967 (43.4 for Japan as against 100 for the United States) and that the differential narrowed toward the end of the 1960s.

If the data is looked at more closely, it becomes apparent that an ordinary Japanese citizen in 1973 expended approximately 30 percent more on beverages, 30 percent less on food, and 70 percent less on housing than an average American. Furthermore, an examination of food intake reveals that the Japanese ate 3.5 times more fish and about twice the quantity of cereals (inclusive of rice), while consuming only 25 percent of the meat and 40 percent of the dairy goods that an American would consume (Table 2).

Changes in Japanese Consumption Patterns —— According to estimates by the economist Shinohara Miyohei and the government of Japan, the per capita consumption in constant prices increased at an annual rate of about 1.4 percent between 1874 and 1940 and at about 7.9 percent between 1952 and 1971. The upward trend stopped during World War II, but the prewar peak level (attained in 1938) was recovered by 1956 and followed by a rapid rate of improvement (about 8 percent per annum between 1960 and 1973). The advance was again disturbed by the OIL CRISIS OF 1973, after which a slower rate of improvement ensued (about 3 percent per annum between 1974 and 1978).

The rapid rise in the living standard was accompanied by changes in the pattern of consumption. A notable example of this was the declining trend in the proportion of total consumption expenditures devoted to food items (the Engel coefficient). In the mid-19th century, the national average was over 65 percent, and the corresponding figure for the working-class family easily exceeded 70 percent. The coefficient decreased to some 60 percent by the beginning of the 20th century, to some 50 percent in the 1930s, and further to less than 50 percent in the post–World War II years (see Table 3).

The above records are corroborated by statistics of the calorie intake of an average Japanese. In the second decade of this century, the economist Morimoto Kōkichi observed that the Japanese adult diet was inferior to that of an adult American by as much as 43 percent. By contrast, the World Bank's 1976 figures show that the

Standard of living —— Table 1

Comparison of Per Capita Consumption in Japan and the United States, 1973
(US = 100)

Beverages	128.7
Medical care	122.7
Personal care and miscellaneous services	86.8
Clothing and footwear	68.1
Food	66.5
House furnishings and appliances	58.3
Tobacco	51.7
Recreation and education	39.5
Gross rent and fuel	32.0
Transport and communication	12.1
Average	53.5

SOURCE: I. B. Kravis, A. Heston, and R. Summers, *International Comparison of Real Product and Purchasing Power* (1978).

Standard of living —— Table 2

Comparison of Per Capita Food Consumption in Japan and the United States, 1973
(US = 100)

Fish	356.8
Bread and cereals	196.3
Fruits and vegetables	68.6
Spices, sweets, and sugar	51.6
Milk, cheese, and eggs	42.2
Coffee, tea, and cocoa	27.5
Meat	25.8
Oils and fats	24.0
Average	66.5

SOURCE: I. B. Kravis, A. Heston, and R. Summers, *International Comparison of Real Product and Purchasing Power* (1978).

Standard of living —— Table 3

Changes in the Engel Coefficient in Selected Countries
(in percentages)

Period roughly covered	Italy	Japan	United Kingdom	US	Sweden
1880–1900	67.3	62.8	48.0	37.7	36.5
1900–1920	67.0	60.3	45.9	35.5	35.6
1920–1940	60.7	53.1	43.1	31.8	—
1950–1960	57.3	47.9	44.4	29.4	38.6

NOTE: Computed on the basis of current-price data.
SOURCE: Japan: Miyohei Shinohara, "Consumption," in Kazushi Ohkawa and Miyohei Shinohara, ed, *Patterns of Japanese Economic Development, A Quantitative Appraisal* (1979). Other countries: S. Kuznets, *Modern Economic Growth: Rate, Structure and Spread* (1966).

per capita calorie supply of the nation fully satisfied its physical requirements in 1960, at which time Sweden exceeded the requirements by 11 percent, West Germany by 17 percent, the United States by 18 percent, and the United Kingdom by 16 percent. Meanwhile, the diet pattern of the average Japanese went through a process of drastic transformation, as Western cuisines slowly but steadily gained acceptance. Rice was in part substituted by bread, fish by meat, and so forth.

Compensating for the relative decline in food expenditure has been an increase in the proportion of expenditure on clothing and

Standard of living —— Table 4

Changes in the Composition of Consumption Expenditures, 1874–1971
(in percentages)

	Nominal values	Real values	Changes in relative prices
Food, beverages, and tobacco	−55	−53	Little change
Clothing	+42	+290	−37
Gross rent and household furnishings [1]	+175	+16	+135
Fuel and lighting	−53	+85	−31
Other [2]	+118	+104	Little change

[1] Inclusive of consumer durables.
[2] Medical and personal care, transport and communication, social expenses, education, recreation, etc.
SOURCE: Miyohei Shinohara, "Consumption," in Kazushi Ohkawa and Miyohei Shinohara, ed, *Patterns of Japanese Economic Development, A Quantitative Appraisal* (1979).

consumer durables (Table 4). For instance, by the end of the 1960s virtually every household was equipped with a washing machine, a refrigerator, a vacuum cleaner, and a television set. During the succeeding decade, there was another surge in demand for automobiles, air conditioners, and color televisions.

The Task Ahead —— Housing is one of the few areas where Japan still lags far behind by Western standards, particularly in urban areas. In terms of the number of dwelling units per person, Japan (0.29 in 1973) was surpassed by the United States (0.36 in 1975) by only a small margin. The total floor space of a Japanese residential unit in 1970, however, was about 50 percent of that in the United States.

Additional negative factors in the quality of housing services include the substandard provision of flush toilets, running water, private baths, and garden space. One could estimate the extent to which Japanese housing is inferior to that in the United States by using the market values of different types of dwelling units as well as the density of occupancy. According to such a computation, the quantity of Japanese housing was equivalent to roughly 40 percent that of the United States in 1970. This was partly a result of natural forces (geography, population density, and so forth) but also ascribable to the government's failure to develop a rational policy on land allocation and use. See also HOUSING PROBLEMS.

📖 ——Masayoshi Chūbachi and Kōji Taira, "Poverty in Modern Japan: Perception and Realities," in Hugh Patrick, ed, *Japanese Industrialization and Its Social Consequences* (1976). R. P. Dore, *City Life in Japan* (1969). Alan H. Gleason, *Postwar Housing in Japan and the United States,* University of Michigan, Center for Japanese Studies Occasional Paper No. 8 (1964). Alan H. Gleason, "Economic Growth and Consumption in Japan," in W. W. Lockwood, ed, *The State and Economic Enterprise in Japan* (1965). Hiroshi Hazama, "Historical Changes in the Life Style of Industrial Workers," in Hugh Patrick, ed, *Japanese Industrialization and Its Social Consequences* (1976). I. B. Kravis, A. Heston, and R. Summers, *International Comparison of Real Product and Purchasing Power* (1978). I. B. Kravis, Z. Kenessey, A. Heston, and R. Summers, *A System of International Comparison of Gross Product and Purchasing Power* (1975). Kōkichi Morimoto, *The Standard of Living in Japan* (1918). Kōnosuke Odaka, "Housing Conditions in Japan and the U.S.: A Comparison," in Japan Society for the Promotion of Science, ed, *Comparison of Levels of Living in Real Terms in Japan and the United States* (1971). Miyohei Shinohara, *Personal Consumption Expenditures,* vol 6 of *Long-Term Economic Statistics* (1967). Miyohei Shinohara, "Consumption," in Kazushi Ohkawa and Miyohei Shinohara, ed, *Patterns of Japanese Economic Development: A Quantitative Appraisal* (1979).   ODAKA Kōnosuke

State Shintō

(Kokka Shintō). A term used by Japanese chiefly after 1945 to designate those Shintō ideas, rituals, and institutions that were fostered by the government with the aim of creating an official national ideology. At the core of State Shintō was the belief in the divinity of the emperor and the uniqueness of Japan's "national polity" (KOKUTAI). Strongly influenced by the RESTORATION SHINTŌ movement of the early 19th century, State Shintō is often thought to represent a fusion of Shrine Shintō with Imperial Shintō, i.e., the rituals and traditions transmitted within the imperial family.

The beginnings of State Shintō go back to 1868, when the new Meiji government proclaimed as its goal the realization of the ancient ideal of *saisei itchi,* "the unity of religious ritual and government administration." One of the first acts of the newly established Shintō Worship Bureau (Jingi Jimukyoku), staffed by students of the ultranationalist thinker HIRATA ATSUTANE (1776–1843), was to order the complete separation of Buddhism and Shintō, which resulted in the immediate removal of all Buddhist images and symbols from Shintō shrines and in the ban on the participation in shrine rituals by Buddhist monks. In 1869 the Imperial Palace was purged of Buddhist influences: the Buddhist altars with their ancestral tablets were transferred to Buddhist temples, the annual Buddhist palace rituals were terminated, and members of the imperial family who had become Buddhist monks were laicized.

To give concrete expression to the ideal of *saisei itchi,* an Office of Shintō Worship (Jingikan) was created in 1869 and ranked above the Grand Council of State (Dajōkan). Attached to the former was an Office of Propaganda (Senkyōshi) responsible for disseminating the "Great Teaching" (Taikyō), that is, reverence for the Shintō deities and obedience to the imperial will. In 1872 the Office of Propaganda was reorganized as the Agency for Spiritual Guidance (Kyōdōshoku), to which all Shintō priests were appointed, in effect transforming them into government functionaries. The goal of using Shintō as a unifying ideology remained unchanged even though the modernization of governmental institutions inevitably necessitated, in 1871, the replacement of the Office of Shintō Worship with a Ministry of Shintō Religion (Jingishō), which, in turn, was absorbed in 1872 by the Ministry of Religion (Kyōbushō).

The formal structure of State Shintō was created in 1871 with the issuance of a series of decrees declaring that (a) shrines were places for the observance of "national rites" *(kokka no sōshi),* that is, they were government institutions; (b) priests were to be appointed by the government and could not occupy their office solely by hereditary right; (c) all citizens must register with their local shrines as parishioners *(ujiko);* and (d) shrines would be assigned an official rank that would determine the degree of support they would receive from the state. The highest rank was accorded to the Grand Shrine of Ise, which was sacred to the divine imperial ancestress, the sun goddess Amaterasu Ōmikami. The government subsequently stipulated in detail the various rituals that were to be performed at the shrines, the dress of the priests, and even the wording of the liturgy *(norito).*

The constitution of 1889 reaffirmed the central concept of State Shintō by declaring the emperor to be "sacred and inviolable." The special position of State Shintō was recognized in 1900 by placing Shintō under the jurisdiction of the newly created Bureau of Shrines (Jinjakyoku) in the Home Ministry, whereas Buddhism, the independent Shintō sects, and Christianity were put under the supervision of the Bureau of Religion. In 1911 the Ministry of Education ordered that schools should take their pupils to local shrines on festival days to pay homage to the shrine deities. Particularly important to State Shintō were the group visits to YASUKUNI SHRINE, which housed the spirits of all soldiers who fell in the imperial cause since 1853. After a group of Catholic university students declined to participate in the Yasukuni service in 1932 on the grounds that the constitution expressly guaranteed freedom of religion, the Ministry of Education declared definitively that shrines were nonreligious institutions whose primary purpose was to foster patriotism and loyalty. In this way the government established the principle that all Japanese, regardless of religious affiliation, could be required to take part in shrine rituals. State Shintō was represented in virtually all homes by the presence on the Shintō altar of an amulet *(ofuda)* from the Ise Shrine (these were called Jingū *taima*).

State Shintō came to an abrupt end on 15 December 1945 when General Douglas MACARTHUR issued his "Shintō Directive" ordering the Japanese government to dissociate itself from all shrine affairs and cease financial support. This principle of separation of church and state was subsequently incorporated into the constitution

Stock exchanges

Major Stock Exchanges, 1980					
	Tōkyō	New York	United Kingdom	Frankfurt	Paris
Number of listed companies	1,402	1,533	2,659	197	586
Value of listed shares (in billions of dollars)	379.7	1,242.8	204.5	63.5	53.1
Value of transactions (in billions of dollars)	179.8	382.4	36.7	5.6	12.6
Rate of turnover (in percentages)	49.9	36.1	6.4	8.9	30.7

SOURCE: Tōkyō Shōken Torihikijo (Tōkyō Stock Exchange), *Shōken* (December 1981).

of 1947. Today the 81,000 shrines in Japan, including such one-time pillars of State Shintō as the Ise and Yasukuni shrines, are private religious organizations supported by voluntary donations. See also SHRINE SHINTŌ.

■ ——D. C. Holtom, *The National Faith of Japan* (1938). D. C. Holtom, *Modern Japan and Shinto Nationalism* (1943, rev ed 1947).

Stanley WEINSTEIN

Statistical Mathematics, Institute of

(Tōkei Sūri Kenkyūjo). Institute belonging to the Ministry of Education. Located in Tōkyō. It was established in 1944 for the purpose of studying statistical concepts as the basis of scientific technology and developing statistical methods and techniques. Its publications include the *Annals of the Institute of Statistical Mathematics,* which appears thrice yearly.

steel industry → iron and steel industry

Stein, Lorenz von (1815–1890)

German scholar whose conservative views on government influenced the framers of the Meiji CONSTITUTION. In 1882 ITŌ HIRO-BUMI, a leader of the Meiji government, headed a mission to Europe to study constitutional systems. The members of the delegation, which included ITŌ MIYOJI and AOKI SHŪZŌ, went first to Berlin, where they were instructed privately by the jurist Rudolf von GNEIST. They went on to Vienna to listen to Stein, who was lecturing on administration, legislation, and diplomacy at the university there. Like Gneist, Stein was opposed to universal suffrage and party government and held that the state should be above society, that its aim was to bring about social reform, and that the latter be implemented by a "social monarchy." Although Stein refused Itō's invitation to become an adviser to the Japanese government, his ideas, as well as Gneist's, had a strong influence on the final drafting of the 1889 constitution.

stick dance

(*bō odori*). Any of several folk dances (mainly ceremonial in nature) involving the clashing of sword-length sticks or poles. These are usually vigorous dances performed by groups of young men who form various configurations while dancing. In Kyūshū and Shikoku, stick dances are often conducted at festivals honoring the UJIGAMI (local tutelary deity), or at the BON FESTIVAL and harvest festival; in the Kantō (eastern Honshū) region the stick dance serves as a preliminary for the lion dance (SHISHI-MAI). In some areas the sticks are replaced by scythes or long swords. The Okinawan stick dance is clearly martial. In most regions, however, the clashing of sticks seems not to symbolize fighting but is thought simply to have the power to exorcise evil spirits.

MISUMI Haruo

stilts

(*takeuma*; literally, "bamboo horse"). Japanese stilts are made of bamboo poles with wooden footstands attached. The word *takeuma* is also used to refer to hobbyhorses made of one bamboo pole. The present form of stilts, in use since the 17th century, is a variation of a kind of footgear used in the performance of DENGAKU.

SAITŌ Ryōsuke

Stimson Doctrine → nonrecognition policy

Stimson, Henry Lewis (1867–1950)

American lawyer, statesman; twice US secretary of war (1911–13, 1940–45), secretary of state (1929–33), and governor-general of the Philippines (1928–29); a Republican whose name is identified with the so-called NONRECOGNITION POLICY applied to Japan as a result of its military takeover of Manchuria in 1931. His presence in Franklin D. Roosevelt's cabinet, along with that of Secretary of Navy Frank Knox, reflected the bipartisan nature of United States policy in the years leading to World War II.

Stimson became Herbert Hoover's secretary of state, following a successful year as governor-general of the Philippines. He was chief delegate at the London Naval Conference of 1930 (see LONDON NAVAL CONFERENCES). His nonrecognition policy was formulated in response to the Japanese army's occupation of Manchuria and the setting up of a puppet regime (see MANCHURIAN INCIDENT). Together with the LYTTON COMMISSION report of the League of Nations, it effected a moral condemnation of Japan in the eyes of the world, but failed to deter further action and eventuated in Japan's withdrawal from the league.

During World War II it was Stimson who as head of the War Department made the decision to evacuate Japanese, alien and citizen alike, from the West Coast of the United States into relocation camps (see JAPANESE AMERICANS, WARTIME RELOCATION OF). He recognized that the move ran counter to constitutional guarantees, but he also believed it was necessary for the safety of the nation and those of Japanese descent. The War Department was given the task of developing the atomic bomb, for which Stimson was directly responsible to the president. He took an active part in determining policy on the dropping of the bomb, and he eliminated Kyōto from the list of possible target cities. Stimson worked closely with Under-Secretary of State Joseph C. GREW in making it possible for Japan to accept the surrender terms of the POTSDAM DECLARATION without renouncing its imperial institution.

■ ——Otis Cary, "Mr. Stimson's 'Pet City'—The Sparing of Kyōto, 1945," *Moonlight Series* 3 (Kyōto, Dōshisha University, 1975). Elting E. Morison, *Turmoil and Tradition* (1960). Henry Lewis Stimson and McGeorge Bundy, *On Active Service in Peace and War* (1948).

Otis CARY

stock exchanges

(*shōken torihikijo*). Japan's stock market, organized into eight exchanges, is one of the largest in the world in terms of the value of listed issues and total transactions. As the table illustrates, the number of companies listed with Japan's major exchange is comparable to its counterpart in the United States. The market value of listed shares in 1980 was nearly twice that of any European stock exchange, and the value of total transactions was about half that of the United States but far above the value for major European exchanges.

The Tōkyō Stock Exchange is far and away the dominant one in Japan, accounting for 78.4 percent of all transactions in 1974. The Ōsaka Stock Exchange, the next largest, tallied 17.4 percent the same year. Additional exchanges are located in Nagoya, Kyōto, Hiroshima, Fukuoka, Niigata, and Sapporo. In 1961 a second section was added at the Tōkyō, Ōsaka, and Nagoya exchanges to trade stocks that had been handled over the counter; each section maintains its own listing requirements.

The development of Japan's stock exchanges, which handle not only stock but also bonds, bank debentures, and other types of securities instruments in separate sections, began in the late 1870s when legal provisions were enacted to provide for the trading of government bonds issued to members of the former *samurai* class (see KINROKU KŌSAI). The market experienced particularly rapid growth and development during and after World War I, as manufacturing entered a period of growing importance in the Japanese economy. The securities exchanges were placed under strict control during World War II, and trading was suspended just prior to the end of that conflict. The markets were reopened in 1949, after the formulation of a SECURITIES EXCHANGE LAW patterned on similar legislation in the United States.

Although the financing of Japan's development during the postwar period has been dominated by banks and other financial intermediaries, Japan's stock market continued to grow apace with the economy, both in terms of the market value of listed issues and the volume of transactions. There are several distinguishing features of the stock market in Japan. One is that the predominant form of issuance of new shares prior to the early 1970s was through granting stock subscription rights to shareholders. The rights permitted shareholders to purchase new shares at a subscription price below market, generally set at the par value of the stock or ¥50 for most companies. A major implication of this method of issue was that equity issued became an expensive form of capital for corporations, which had to pay dividends from aftertax income and were generally under pressure to maintain dividends because of the high percentage of financial institutions holding shares. Another result was that shareholders were able to increase the effective yield on their holdings despite dividends fixed on par value, but continued reinvestment was required to accomplish this end. A second distinctive feature of the Japanese stock market is that a common means of rewarding shareholders with higher effective dividends has been through the free distribution of shares, which is very similar in principle to the stock split in other markets. Also, beginning in the early 1970s, Japanese companies were permitted to commence new stock issues at market rather than par value. However, the law requires that the difference between par and market gained from the issue must be returned to shareholders over a period of five years. This is generally accomplished through a free distribution. As a result of this system, the apparent yield per share is understated. This and other factors result in significantly higher price-earnings ratios than stock markets in other nations. C. Tait RATCLIFFE

stockholders' general meeting

(kabunushi sōkai). An essential organ of JOINT-STOCK COMPANIES *(kabushiki kaisha)* that determines fundamental corporate matters by resolution of the stockholders. Stockholders' general meetings can be in the form of either annual meetings *(teiji sōkai)*, which must be convened at least once in each fiscal year, or extraordinary meetings *(rinji sōkai)*, which may be convened as necessary. Matters to be decided by stockholders' general meetings are specified in the COMMERCIAL CODE or a company's articles of incorporation.

Under the Commercial Code, stockholders' general meetings are to decide on such matters as election and replacement of corporate directors (see BOARD OF DIRECTORS), OVERSEERS, and liquidators; approval of financial records; stock dividends; ex post facto incorporation (German: *Nachgründung*); remuneration of directors and overseers; amendment of the articles of incorporation; reduction of stated capital; dissolution of the corporation; continuation of the corporation; mergers and consolidations; and transfers of all or substantially all assets of the corporation.

As a general rule, stockholders' general meetings must be convened at the seat of the registered principal office of the corporation or in its immediate vicinity. All shareholders who possess voting rights must be given prior written notice of a meeting. Attached to the notice of an annual meeting must be a copy of the corporation's balance sheet, its profit and loss statement, its dividend plan, and the overseer's report on each of the above-mentioned items. Unless otherwise specified in the Commercial Code or the company's articles of incorporation, a quorum is constituted if the shareholders present at a general meeting hold a majority of the issued shares, and passage of a resolution requires a majority of the votes to which those in attendance are entitled. The Commercial Code generally specifies the conditions for passage of resolutions on matters the law stipu-

lates must be determined at stockholders' general meetings. With regard to other matters, however, the articles of incorporation generally eliminate the quorum requirement. Determination of the identity of shareholders is based either on the shareholders' register or, in the case of share certificates in bearer form, on actual deposit with the corporation. Shareholders generally may vote by written proxy, but in the case of listed corporations, this practice is regulated under the SECURITIES EXCHANGE LAW. Furthermore, a corporation is required to keep minutes of each meeting, including a summary of the proceedings and results and bearing the signatures of the chairman and attending directors. These minutes must be kept at the corporation's registered principal and branch offices and made available to shareholders and creditors of the corporation for inspection and copying. NAGAHAMA Yōichi

stone tools

(sekki). The origin of stone tools in Japan probably dates back 100,000 years to the early paleolithic period (see HISTORY OF JAPAN: prehistory). This age was characterized by the use of rough or chipped stone implements, in contrast to the polished stone tools common in the subsequent neolithic period.

Sites remaining from the early paleolithic period are extremely rare. Stone tools that have been excavated include chopping implements, prototype hand axes, and elliptical stone tools. These are comparable in shape and function to the implements used in the chopping tool culture on the Asian continent. In the late paleolithic period, various types of backed-blade stone tools were developed. In the Kinki and Setouchi regions of Japan there appeared a type of backed blade called the Kō type; in the Chūbu and Kantō regions, the Moro type; and in the Tōhoku region, the Sugikubo type. Other stone implements which appeared are cutting tools, elliptical stone tools, burins, side scrapers, end scrapers, and small stone spearheads. Some semipolished stone axes also can be found in this period. During the transition between Japan's paleolithic and neolithic periods, small stone tools called microliths came into wide use. These, measuring from 2 to 3 centimeters (0.8–1.2 in) long, were inserted into handles made of wood or bone and sharpened to serve as blades or points for an arrow or sickle. Another stone tool or point had a sharpened tip and was used to cut open or to pierce things. See also PALEOLITHIC CULTURE.

Japan's neolithic period included the Jōmon (ca 10,000 BC–ca 300 BC) and part of the Yayoi (ca 300 BC–ca AD 300) periods. The Jōmon period can be divided into six stages: Incipient (ca 10,000 BC–ca 7500 BC), Initial (ca 7500 BC–ca 5000 BC), Early (ca 5000 BC–ca 3500 BC), Middle (ca 3500 BC–ca 2000 BC), Late (ca 2000 BC–ca 1000 BC), and Final (ca 1000 BC–ca 300 BC). Throughout the period stone tools were used not only for labor but also in daily life for religious ceremonies and festivals and for personal adornment.

Work tools were mostly arrowheads, axes, and adzes, including polished stone tools and chipped stone implements. Chipped stone axes and adzes were mainly formed from slate and shale. Principal types are *tanzaku-gata* (oblong), *fundō-gata* (balance weight), and *bachi-gata* (plectrum). During the Middle Jōmon period, the oblong type increased in use. In the Late Jōmon period, the balance-weight type appeared. These are considered to have been tools for digging, and evidence of them supports theories that primitive farming methods such as slash-and-burn agriculture existed in the Kantō and Chūbu regions during the Middle Jōmon period. Polished stone axes and adzes were made of serpentine, sandstone, diorite, and other stones. There were also varieties of implements with cross sections that were *hen daenkei* (elliptical lacking a top position), *nyūbōjō* (pestle shaped), or *teikakushiki* (rectangular), used mainly for cutting down trees.

Arrowheads were practically all chipped products, but a few semipolished ones have been discovered. Although of numerous shapes, the common arrowhead is triangular with a concave or straight base. They were made mostly from obsidian, quartzite, andesite, hard shale, and slate. Stone spearheads from the Initial, Early, and Middle Jōmon periods in the shape of tree leaves have been found in eastern Japan. *Ishisaji* (scrapers) were stone tools used to strip hides from animals. There was a handle on the upper part of the tool and two varieties, vertical and lateral, were made. Stone sinkers were also used for fishing nets, made by chipping off both sides of a natural pebble or by scraping out a groove around a pebble and tying it with a string.

Ishizara (stone querns) developed from the Middle Jōmon period. These were oval or rectangular. Because the center was concave, it is referred to as a stone plate; it was used with a stone grinder or hammer to crush hard shelled nuts for food. *Sekibō* were phallus-shaped stone rods used at religious ceremonies or festivals during and after the Middle Jōmon period. Some stone rods measured more than 1 meter (3.3 ft) long during the Middle period, but thereafter size diminished, although ornamentation became more elaborate. In the Late and Final Jōmon periods there were certain tools whose uses are unknown. These are called *gyomotsu sekki, sekkan, dokkoishi,* and *seiryūtō-gata sekki* (scimitar-shaped stone tools).

The Yayoi period in Japan was a transition from the neolithic period to the metal age. It can be divided into the Early (ca 300 BC–ca 100 BC), Middle (ca 100 BC–ca AD 100), and Later (ca 100–ca 300) periods. All stone tools disappeared in the Later period. Since rice cultivation began during the Yayoi period, there are numerous stone tools related to rice cultivation. Also, many stone implements of this era were modeled after counterparts on the Asian continent. Among the polished axes and adzes used as work tools were the *futogata hamaguriba sekifu,* used for chopping down trees and carving, and the *chūjō kataha sekifu,* used for cutting and shaping wood. Together with *ishibōchō* (stone harvesting knives) and *ishigama* (stone sickles), these were distributed among the early agricultural societies of East Asia. There were also chipped and polished harvesting knives that differed according to region. Polished harvesting knives had backs shaped like a half-moon, with two holes, usually in the back, and a piece of string passed through to serve as a finger grip. The stone harvesting knife and the stone sickle, both used for harvesting, were distributed mainly in northern Kyūshū.

Arrowheads were used chiefly for hunting during the Jōmon period, then as battle weapons in the Yayoi period along with stone spearheads. There exist both chipped and polished arrowheads. The latter are said to have been patterned after bronze arrowheads. The spread of bronze tools from the end of the Early Yayoi period led to their use as models for stone tools (see BRONZE WEAPONS). Like the polished stone arrowhead, polished stone swords and stone halberds indicate the close contact between Japan and the Korean peninsula. The point of a polished stone sword imbedded in human bone has also been discovered, suggesting the importance of this type of sword as a weapon. Together with these stone implements from the Asian continent and the Korean peninsula, traditional Japanese stone tools from the Jōmon period and after have been excavated. These include awls, chipped stone axes and adzes, as well as *kanjō sekifu* (stone rings).   GŌDA Yoshimasa

storehouses, traditional

(*kura*). Farmers in Japan have long used storehouses, known for their unique architectural design, for storing rice and other grains. The court nobility and major Buddhist temples constructed repositories to house their treasures, archives, and sutras beginning in the Nara period (710–794), and as commerce, industry, and transport developed in the latter part of the Edo period (1600–1868), storehouses for raw materials and merchandise were constructed.

Farming requires that one not consume the next year's seed rice. This axiom became ritualized in the form of worship of the grain deity, to whom the first rice of the harvest was offered. The offering was then stored in the granary under communal supervision, and the remainder of the harvest was used as food. The granary reconstructed from the ruins of a Yayoi-period (ca 300 BC–ca AD 300) farm village in the Toro district of Shizuoka Prefecture, built in a log-cabin style (see TORO SITE), was probably used as a storehouse for seed rice.

The architectural style of the ISE SHRINE, preserved through successive rebuildings every 20 years, is clearly a form of storehouse architecture (see SHINTŌ ARCHITECTURE). The main sanctuaries and the treasure repositories have raised floors and ridge purlins supporting gable roofs held up by free-standing ridge supports. The hall of offerings behind the outer shrine best preserves the ancient architectural style of the shrine buildings. Pillars support the base of the structure, and the planks of the walls are joined at the corners in log-cabin fashion. In ancient times the east and west treasure repositories also conformed to this log-cabin style of architecture. The YAMATO COURT of the 4th to the 7th centuries, in order to extend its control over the country, set up outpost granaries in many areas for storing the harvest, and the architecture of the buildings that compose Ise Shrine may well be that of the outpost granaries built in the three shrine districts of Watarai, Iino, and Take. Just as the buildings of the Ise Shrine were constructed in the style of the grain

Traditional storehouses

A storehouse in Matsumoto, Nagano Prefecture. Designed to provide protection against fire, it is characterized by thick plaster walls and small, easily closed windows. A ball of *sugi* (cryptomeria) leaves hanging to the right of the storehouse marks it as that of a *sake* brewer. 1878.

storehouse, the ancient palace of the Yamato court, which combined religious with residential functions, is believed to have been built in the storehouse fashion, with gable roof and raised floor.

Relationship to Residential Architecture —— The Japanese term *kura* does not refer to storehouses alone. Originally the word meant "seat," as can be seen from the terms *uma no kura* (horse saddle), *kurai* (meaning where one sits, and hence social position), and *agura* (sitting cross-legged). Such words as *iwakura* (sacred spot) lead one to believe that *kura* often referred to places where the gods deigned to sit. Granaries were regarded as the seat of the grain spirit and so were viewed as sacred. Thus they came to be called *kura*. Consequently the emperor, who was considered to be an incarnation of the grain spirit, also had to live in a palace patterned after the raised granaries; a palace with a raised floor naturally symbolized high social position (*kurai*).

Dwellings with gable roofs and raised floors clearly had their origin in the south, for they are cool in summer but cannot withstand cold winter weather. Despite this shortcoming, the emperor's palace assumed the granary style of gable roof and raised floor at an early period. For nobles other than the emperor, raised-floor palaces were used only for religious rites and other formal functions. Archaeological evidence indicates that for daily living there must have been separate dirt-floor dwellings and privies. But in time the nobles, too, came to have raised-floor dwellings furnished with braziers and toilets.

The Heian raised-floor mansion was built so that the outside air could enter just as easily at night, when the latticed shutters were lowered, as during the day, when they were raised. Breezes readily permeated the large, unpartitioned, wooden-floor interior. Various furnishings were set out where and when they were needed. Furnishings and accessories for ceremonies and formal functions were numerous, and separate storehouses were built to store all such articles.

In the open, Heian-style dwelling, the area used as the master's sleeping quarters was surrounded by plastered clay walls. In farmhouses these quarters also served as storerooms for household articles, and were called *nema* (bedrooms) or *nando* (storerooms), depending on the region. They were the predecessors of the *dozō,* unique clay-walled structures used solely for the purpose of storage, which later became widespread throughout Japan.

Storehouses in Premodern Times —— It is said that early in the Edo period (1600–1868), farmers on the Noto Peninsula on the coast of the Sea of Japan stored their seed rice at the nearby estate of the Tokikuni clan so that they would not use it up when they had a bad crop or a famine. Farmers in villages that had such wealthy households were thus able to recuperate more quickly after a crop failure or a natural disaster.

Storehouses also played an important role in urban areas. Although Edo (now Tōkyō) was the scene of frequent conflagrations, businesses always recovered quickly. Fire insurance was unknown, so funds for reconstruction must have come from some form of stock. Such stocks also helped the newcomers from the countryside who moved to the capital to work for large commercial establishments. Instead of working for wages, these people indentured themselves so that someday they could be set up in business with their own stores or become artisans in their own right. The masters of storehouses provided a base for these people, furnishing support for their shop clerks and apprentices even after they had established their own businesses.

Contributions to Modernization——In Japan no single concentration of commercial wealth existed at the close of the Edo period. Yet there was sufficient stock in Japan's storehouses to enable the nation to follow in the footsteps of the West and achieve rapid industrialization and modernization after the 1868 Meiji Restoration. In many villages the stocks contained in the community granaries were used to finance primary schools, while Edo's rice storehouses provided the public funds to modernize Tōkyō with bridges and gas lamps. The privately owned clay-walled storehouses of the nation's towns and villages, however, played the most important role. Although these storehouses were not very significant on an individual basis, the combined volume of their stock was tremendous. This is probably one of the reasons for the uninterrupted growth and development of small businesses in the cities and of traditional industries in the rural areas during the process of industrialization. However, Japan's transformation from an agricultural to an industrial nation has meant the end of the historical role of the storehouse.

📖——Futagawa Yukio, Itō Teiji, *Nihon no minka* (1957–59). Kawashima Chūji, *Horobiyuku minka* (1976). Kawazoe Noboru and Itō Teiji, *Kura: The Japanese Storehouse* (1979). Naitō Akira, "Edo no machiya," in *Edo jidai zushi* (Chikuma Shobō, 1976). Ueda Atsushi and Tsuchiya Atsuo, *Machiya: kyōdo kenkyū* (1975).

Kawazoe Noboru

Straight, Willard Dickerman (1880–1918)

American diplomat, financier, and journalist. Born in New York. Graduating from Cornell University, Straight went to China to work for the Imperial Maritime Customs Service. He then went to Korea as correspondent for the Reuters News Agency. After a stay in Mukden (Ch: Shenyang) as the US consul general, he worked at the State Department in Washington. In 1909 he returned to Asia to consider the possibility of developing railways in Manchuria and North China, but meeting opposition from Russia and Japan, he decided against it. He also tried to secure an international loan for the Chinese government. In 1912, shortly after the Chinese Revolution, Straight returned to the United States and worked for J. P. Morgan and Company as its Far Eastern expert. Interested in public affairs, he and his wife financed the magazine the *New Republic*. He also founded a monthly magazine, *Journal of the American Asiatic Association* (later called *Asia*).

Strategic Bombing Survey, United States

A study of the effectiveness of Allied bombing of Japan and Germany during World War II; made at the request of President Harry S. Truman and carried out under the auspices of the US Department of the Army. The survey pertaining to Japan was initiated in August 1945; between September and December of that year a group of 1,150 military and civilian personnel headed by Franklin D'Olier gathered a vast body of documents, including transcripts of conversations with Japanese government administrators, high ranking military officers, and industrialists. From this they drew up 108 reports in 1946–47. These dealt with the effect of bombing on the Japanese government, the military, the livelihood of the people, and the economy. The reports also analyzed the events leading to the war, the stages of its development, effects of the atomic bombs dropped on Hiroshima and Nagasaki, and miscalculations on the part of the United States in evaluating the Japanese war effort.

straw boots → waragutsu

straw raincoats

(*mino*). A type of rainwear woven from the stalks or leaves of straw, sedge, or miscanthus; used in Japan since ancient times and still occasionally worn by farmers and others. Today there are six varieties of straw raincoats: the *koshimino* hangs from the mid-section of the upper torso and covers the waist and hips; the *katamino* is worn over the shoulders and covers the entire back; the *dōmino*

extends from the shoulders down to the mid-calf; the *marumino* protects the entire body from the shoulders down; the *seimino* is a small protective piece covering only the shoulders and top of the back; and the *minobōshi* covers the head as well as the upper torso.

Miyamoto Mizuo

straw sandals → waraji

straw ware

Rice straw and, less frequently, barley straw, have traditionally been employed in Japan in the production of utilitarian as well as sacred objects.

The religious significance of straw is best demonstrated by the *shimenawa,* sacred straw ropes used in Shintō shrines to set apart a holy space or to suspend offerings to the deities. Such ropes, adorned with purificatory paper strips (GOHEI), are also used to decorate gateways during the observance of the New Year's festivities. Straw is also connected with the BON FESTIVAL for the souls of the dead in midsummer, when *shōryōbune* ("boats of the blessed ghosts"), miniature straw boats whose sails are inscribed with the posthumous names of the dead (*kaimyō*), are launched in a traditional rite. It is also customary during the Bon Festival to spread a new rice straw mat, specially made for the occasion, in front of the household Buddhist altar (*butsudan*).

An ancient festival involving the construction of a straw snake is still celebrated in certain districts of the Ōsaka–Kyōto area and Shimane Prefecture. A rope is constructed from straw in the symbolic form of a snake, or sometimes a dragon, and employed in a rainmaking fertility ritual, which usually takes place at the beginning of the year. Elaborate ceremonies are connected with the construction of these giant snake ropes, some of which are over 60 meters (200 ft) long and about 1 meter (3 ft) wide. The rite itself varies from place to place, consisting in the suspension of the straw snake from a tree, across a road, or in front of a shrine, or casting the snake into a river or the sea.

Straw has also played a significant role in traditional Japanese architecture. Straw or pampas grass is employed in the large thatched roofs or *kayabuki* of Japanese peasant houses (see MINKA), the most splendid examples of which may be found in the village of Shirakawa in Gifu Prefecture. The straw mats or TATAMI in Japanese houses are made in large part of thickly wadded straw matting (*toko*) covered with rushes. In ancient times, prior to the development of *tatami*, wooden floors were typical, and straw cushions (*enza*), wadded sitting mats (*okidatami*), and sleeping mats (*shikidatami*) were used. Simple straw mats called *mushiro* are still in use today.

Straw and grass are also used widely, especially in rural areas, for all kinds of utensils such as baskets, boxes, and bags. Of particular interest are the boxes made with straw mosaic decorations. Straw is also used for traditional STRAW RAINCOATS (*mino*) and rain hats (*amigasa*; see HEADGEAR) as well as for sandals, both light ZŌRI and sturdier WARAJI. In northern Japan straw boots (WARAGUTSU) and gloves may also be seen. Straw folk toys, especially straw horses, are popular in all parts of Japan. See also FOLK CRAFTS; MINGU.

📖——Hugo Münsterberg, *The Folk Arts of Japan* (1958). Tsujimoto Yoshitaka, *Washū saireiki* (1938). *Hugo Münsterberg*

street entertainment

Public entertainment performed in the open air. The varieties of such entertainment increased rapidly during the Edo period (1600–1868), and they assumed importance among the masses along with the staged dramatic arts of KABUKI and JŌRURI. Street entertainment had its beginnings in ancient times when sacred entertainment was performed for the imperial family in order, it was thought, to convey the blessings of the gods. Low-ranking religious functionaries maintained similar practices at shrines and temples until medieval times, when street entertainment gained in popularity along with the growth of cities.

Street entertainers existed outside normal society, since they owned no property and drifted throughout the country. The people they met and entertained as they traveled were becoming increasingly settled under a system of landholding and tenancy in the largely agricultural economy. Early in the Edo period, the shogunate created an official hierarchy of classes (*samurai,* peasant, artisan, and merchant; see SHI-NŌ-KŌ-SHŌ), and street entertainers found themselves treated as outcasts.

There were perhaps 300 different types of street entertainers, of which only a few remain. Among them were such illusionists as the rubber-necked man, who could stretch and shrink his neck at will, the bear woman, and the snake woman. People with physical deformities were also on display. There were performances of simple dramas, exhibitions in makeshift shelters, and peep shows with stories narrated; many of these could be found in the grounds of temples and shrines during religious festivals. There were also candy and medicine peddlers who could gather a crowd of hundreds with their quick monologues and dexterous gestures.

Few of these entertainments are performed today as other diversions have taken their place. Nonetheless, a few traditions from the earlier period have been preserved. For example, on the island of Sado in Niigata Prefecture, performers enact the *haru koma* (spring horse) ceremony. In early spring (corresponding to the first month of the lunar calendar), performers make the rounds of the town, wearing or carrying a horse-head costume. Stopping at the gate of a house, they recite a phrase of celebration and perform a dance. This custom was observed throughout the country in the past, but now survives primarily on Sado.

The SHISHI-MAI (lion dance) was performed throughout Japan, but that of the *daikagura* tradition was considered especially felicitous. The *daikagura* were troupes of performers organized to distribute talismans from the ISE SHRINE wherever they traveled throughout the country. They performed the lion dance and acrobatic feats using plates, balls, and tops. The dance is still performed in Kuwana, Mie Prefecture, and at centers for folk performing arts in Tōkyō (see YOSE).

Many of the street performances involved trained animals; monkeys, which were the object of devotion in folk religion, were the most important performing animals in medieval times. The *saru mawashi* (monkey show) was performed from house to house at the beginning of the new year; the monkeys were made to dance and bestow blessings. This was the most popular form of street performance in the Edo period, and the monkeys were able to perform tricks of considerable complexity and sometimes acted out dramas in small "monkey theaters." This form of entertainment can be seen today in Hikari, Yamaguchi Prefecture, where it is maintained by a small society for that purpose.

MANZAI (witty dialogues), GOZE (troupes of blind women singers), *daikoku-mai* (dances performed by people wearing the costume of Daikoku, one of the SEVEN DEITIES OF GOOD FORTUNE), and *ningyō mawashi* (street puppeteers) can also be seen today, although the future of some of these forms of entertainment is somewhat uncertain.

📖 ——Misumi Haruo, *Sasurainin no geinō shi* (1974). Miyao Shigeo, *Edo shomin no fūzoku shi* (1970). Ozawa Shōichi, *Nihon no hōrōgei* (1974). ORITA Kōji

street stalls

(*rotenshō*). Stalls set up to sell miscellaneous articles for daily use, food, and so forth, usually on a busy street corner. The word *rotenshō* also applies to the keepers of such stalls, who are distinguished from STREET VENDORS, who travel throughout the country, and from shopkeepers, who have a fixed, permanent shop. Stalls that appear only at night are called *yomise;* these first appeared in the latter part of the Edo period (1600–1868) in Ōsaka. The lighting for these night stalls, originally candles and oil lamps (*andon*), changed to Western-style oil lamps, acetylene gas lights, and finally modern electric lights. Some stalls open only on special days such as festival or temple-fair days (ENNICHI), but many stalls, including night stalls, appear every day in a regular location. *Rotenshō* who attract their customers by some performance such as top-spinning, sword-drawing exhibitions, or hypnotism are called *yashi* or *tekiya*. At festivals, the head *yashi* used to have the authority to assign places for each stall. Presently, the officials of the Cooperative Association of Street-Stall Keepers have that power.

In the early years of the Shōwa period (1926–), the word *gimbura* referred to strolling along the Ginza in Tōkyō and looking at the night stalls that appeared there each night. In 1951 Occupation authorities ordered the closing of night stalls in the streets of Ueno, Shibuya, Shinjuku, Ikebukuro, Ginza, and other sections of Tōkyō. At that time many street-stall keepers joined together to form jointly run shops. TSUCHIDA Mitsufumi

street vendors

(*gyōshōnin*). Itinerant merchants and peddlers have a long-established tradition in Japan beginning in the 6th century. In the Heian period (794–1185), peddlers went out from Heiankyō (now the city of Kyōto) into the countryside, and vice versa, at regular intervals. In the Edo period (1600–1868), the Ōmi (now Shiga Prefecture) peddlers were so successful that they soon established large shops in Edo (now Tōkyō), Ōsaka, Kyōto, and other cities. In the latter part of the Edo period, medicine dealers from Toyama created a nationwide sales route and sales distribution system: peddlers would leave medicines in the customer's home and calculate the amount actually used the following year when they returned to receive payment and to replace the used products. Many peddlers could be distinguished by their cries. In recent years, however, most peddlers hawking wares such as roasted sweet potatoes, bamboo poles, and so on, use microphones or recordings. See also STREET STALLS.

TSUCHIDA Mitsufumi

Strike, Clifford Stewart (1902–)

American engineer and industrial expert. As a consultant to the US Department of the Army he led two missions to Japan after World War II to study the reparations issue in the light of Japan's industrial needs and economic potential. The report of Overseas Consultants, Inc, also known as the Strike report, was issued in February 1948. It concluded that in order to achieve a self-sustaining economy, Japan would require much greater productive capacity than that prescribed by the existing US policy, which was based on the report of the mission (headed by Edwin Wendell PAULEY) and on later modifications by the FAR EASTERN COMMISSION. Born in Marion, Illinois, Strike graduated with a degree in engineering from the University of Illinois in 1924. He spent much of his career as a senior executive of engineering firms. Richard B. FINN

strikes and other forms of labor dispute

(*sōgi kōi*). The withholding of labor by labor unions, workers' associations, or unorganized groups of workers in order to achieve demands from an employer. The Japanese use the English word "strike" (*sutoraiki*) to describe full-scale strike activity; a broad range of tactics is encompassed by the term "dispute activities" (*sōgi kōi*). The latter is defined by the Labor Relations Adjustment Law (Rōdō Kankei Chōsei Hō) as "a walkout, slowdown, lockout, or other action, taken by labor or management in pursuit of its own demands or in opposition to the demands of the other party, which obstructs the normal operation of an enterprise."

Japanese labor disputes have the following characteristic features. First, it is rare to encounter all-out strikes which continue until the workers' demands are either met or abandoned. Most Japanese strikes are short ones of scheduled duration (*jigen suto*); an example is the "spring offensive" (SHUNTŌ), which lasts one or two days, according to a schedule agreed upon by the major labor organizations, before collective bargaining begins. Strikes do not usually involve the entire enterprise work force; often only one group of workers engages in a so-called partial strike (*bubun suto*) or a designated workers' strike (*shimei suto*).

Second, the dispute activity takes place at the enterprise facilities, and an attempt is often made to interfere with the employer's control over the facilities and the means of production. The extreme form of this tactic, production control (*seisan kanri*), was prevalent for a number of years after World War II but was eventually suppressed by the Occupation authorities. Similar tactics currently in use include the occupation of job sites, the seizure of vehicles at taxi and bus companies, the posting of leaflets throughout an enterprise, demonstrations on the grounds of a factory or business, and organized picketing.

Third, a partial rather than a complete work stoppage is often employed. While continuing to work, employees will engage in slowdowns, refuse to answer the telephone, or refuse to go on business trips. Ribbons, armbands, and headbands are also worn as a sign of protest. A similar disruptive tactic is the JUMPŌ TŌSŌ (work-to-rule struggle); in these cases, workers will exercise their contractual rights in an intentionally disruptive manner. For instance, all workers will take a holiday on the same day, refuse to work overtime, or enforce safety rules in an extremely strict manner. These measures are often employed by public employees, to whom the RIGHT TO STRIKE is denied.

The special characteristics of Japanese labor disputes can be explained in part by the following factors. Japanese unions organize within individual enterprises, rather than throughout an industry. As there is a different union at each enterprise, they are often not strong enough to carry out a full-scale strike. The right to strike is given broad protection by the constitution and the courts, which makes a wide range of tactics legally permissible. Since strikes by public employees are strictly prohibited, public employee unions often resort to alternative dispute tactics in order to press their demands. Finally, the peculiar wage increase mechanism of the spring offensive preserves the employer paternalism that characterizes much of Japanese labor relations, since the bitterness of open-ended confrontation is avoided. See also GRIEVANCE PROCEDURE; LABOR; LABOR DISPUTES; LABOR DISPUTE RESOLUTION PROCEDURES; LABOR LAWS; SUTO KEN SUTO.   *Sugeno Kazuo*

student movement

(gakusei undō). A vocal and well-organized Marxist student movement has been a conspicuous feature of the Japanese political scene ever since the 1920s—with the obvious and important exception of the years leading up to and during World War II. At certain times, most dramatically in 1968–69, student radicalism has become the center of national attention. On the whole, the immediate political gains of the student movement have been far less than its generalized impact on national and especially intellectual opinion. Within the left-wing movement as a whole, students have served as a constant source of new talent and revitalizing energy, while at the same time exacerbating theoretical disputes and inviting attack on students as unreliable and bourgeois. Within the universities, which provide their institutional base, student radicals have come to play an even more dominant role, determining much of the tone and even organization of student life. More broadly, the student movement has served as a critical mechanism in the institutionalization of Marxism as the dominant ideology of the post–World War II intellectual class.

Of course not all student political activists in Japan are Marxists. Liberal and anarchist student organizations have long existed in Japan, and a wide range of traditionalist and patriotic student groups has flourished in constant and self-conscious opposition to the Marxist Left. But in the end, it is the Marxist mainstream that has been by far the most conspicuous and influential and has come to monopolize the conventional understanding of the term "student movement" in Japan.

Origins of the Student Movement—— The roots of student political activity in Japan may be found in late Edo-period (1600–1868) patterns of *samurai* education, which while emphasizing the "feudal" virtues of loyalty and obedience also tended to encourage a Confucian spirit of political activism and criticism. The young samurai leaders of the Meiji Restoration (1868) may be seen as having set a pattern by which well-educated young men, imbued with idealistic concern about the state of the nation and society, engage in heated debate and concerted political action to realize their ideals. But it remained for the creation of the modern Japanese university system in the late 19th century to provide the framework of the modern student movement. The close linkage of university education with positions of power in both private and public life has conferred on Japanese students an elitist sense of mission that has done much to encourage political activism.

Large-scale student political activity dates from the late 19th century. On the university campuses, strikes and boycotts over issues of education and student living conditions were common, setting a pattern of protest that has continued to the present. At the same time, students came to participate in national protest movements, first in the FREEDOM AND PEOPLE'S RIGHTS MOVEMENT of the 1880s and then on a far more conspicuous scale in the socialist movement of the early 1900s. Such off-campus student political activity was viewed with concern by the government, which issued numerous—and generally ineffective—directives aimed at restricting the students.

But it was not until 1918 that the Japanese student movement took durable organizational form, under the combined influences of international Wilsonian idealism, the victory of the Bolsheviks in Russia, and the widespread popular discontent which was epitomized by the RICE RIOTS of that year. Under the influence of such progressive intellectuals as YOSHINO SAKUZŌ and KAWAKAMI HAJIME, various new student groups were founded in late 1918 in support of political and social reform. The most important were the

Rōgakkai (Study of Labor Society) at Kyōto University, the SHINJINKAI (New Man Society) at Tōkyō University, and the Minjin Dōmeikai (People's League) at Waseda University.

The Prewar Gakuren—— The liberal-democratic spirit which dominated the early months of this vigorous new student movement gave way steadily to the growing influence of Marxism–Leninism as propagated by the Comintern. This process was closely involved with the emergence of a Communist Party movement in Japan, culminating in the founding of the first JAPAN COMMUNIST PARTY (JCP) in 1922. Several students and young alumni were active in the early JCP, setting a pattern of symbiotic linkage between the student movement and the communist movement that would become even more pronounced with time.

The JCP was thus to some degree involved in the organization in November 1922 of Japan's first national left-wing student federation, the Gakusei Rengōkai (Student Federation), generally known as the Gakuren. After a slow start, the Gakuren by September 1924 claimed a membership of 1,600 students, in 53 groups on 49 campuses. Throughout the seven years of its existence, the Gakuren membership remained at around this level and served as the central leadership of the student Left. In the fall of 1924 the official name was expanded to Gakusei Shakai Kagaku Rengōkai (Student Federation of Social Science), to which the prefix Zen Nihon (All-Japan) was added a year later. The member groups in most cases came to be known as *shaken*, an abbreviation of Shakai Kagaku Kenkyūkai, or Social Science Study Group. The term "social science" had by this time become a euphemism for Marxism–Leninism.

The tasks of Gakuren members in the mid–1920s were many. Foreign languages had to be learned and Marxist texts laboriously studied and translated. The rapid growth of the university population combined with the periodic economic depression of the 1920s to make students a distinct interest group, and the student Left took the lead in organizing student governments and cooperatives to deal with campus issues. Another major target of Gakuren protest was the institution of required military training in secondary schools and colleges in 1925. And throughout the 1920s, Gakuren activists continued to join, and often lead, the broader movements outside the campus: the labor movement, the proletarian cultural movement, the rural tenant movement, and the socialist and communist party movements.

Suppression and Decline—— The first case of large-scale suppression of the student Left was the dramatic KYŌTO UNIVERSITY INCIDENT in the winter of 1925–26, in which 38 Gakuren activists from several universities (mostly Kyōto and Dōshisha) were arrested and convicted under the PEACE PRESERVATION LAW OF 1925, becoming the first victims of this new piece of anticommunist legislation. Suppression of the campus Left escalated greatly in the wake of the 15 March 1928 mass arrests of communists, in which students were conspicuously involved (see MARCH 15TH INCIDENT). In response to these pressures and to directives from Moscow favoring a closer integration of students with the communist movement, the Gakuren was formally dissolved on 7 November 1929, and its functions were assumed by the underground Japanese Communist Youth League.

Ironically, the police suppression of the student Left after 1928 coincided with, and itself stimulated, a tremendous wave of on-campus student rebellion that swept Japan, reaching a peak in the winter of 1930–31 and affecting virtually every major institution of higher education and many minor ones as well. Partly a reflection of increasing economic pressures on students in the wake of the world depression and partly the result of agitation and organization by the student Left, the dozens of student strikes and boycotts were limited almost exclusively to on-campus issues relating to student life.

Following the MANCHURIAN INCIDENT of 1931, however, the wave of campus protest rapidly subsided under increased suppression and the mounting mood of nationalism. Off campus as well, underground student communists were arrested and jailed in increasing numbers, precluding any continuity of the student movement. In 1933 the student movement enjoyed a brief revival in a spirited defense of Professor TAKIKAWA YUKITOKI of Kyōto University, whose resignation had been forced on grounds of allegedly left-wing scholarship. This proved to be the effective end of the prewar student Left, despite sporadic attempts at reorganization for the remainder of the 1930s. Meanwhile, nationalistic student groups rapidly multiplied after 1931 and came to dominate the political tone of Japanese universities until the end of World War II.

Postwar Reconstruction—— The early postwar years were a period of reconstruction and reorganization by the student Left. Strong antiwar feelings among many students combined with a generally favorable attitude by the American OCCUPATION (1945–52) to create an environment hospitable to the student movement. The first tasks were the purging of right-wing professors, the replacement of wartime patriotic student unions with new democratic forms of student government (known generically as *jichikai*, "self-governing associations"), and the defense of student economic interests in a time of acute scarcity.

The creation of a new national student federation came slowly, complicated and delayed by the restructuring of higher education under the Occupation authorities. A league of student governments at national universities was founded in November 1946, but it was not until 1948 that it was expanded to include, first, all public universities, and then, finally, private universities with the founding in September 1948 of the ZENGAKUREN (an abbreviation for Zen Nihon Gakusei Jichikai Sōrengō, or All-Japan Federation of Student Self-Governing Associations). The system of compulsory membership for all students in a *jichikai* enabled the Zengakuren from the start to claim a massive membership of 300,000 students on 145 campuses, although in fact only a tiny fraction of these were committed radicals. Nevertheless, the hospitable environment and the continued explosive growth of the entire university population guaranteed that the Zengakuren-led student movement would be on a far larger scale than that of the prewar Gakuren.

The Early Zengakuren —— The Zengakuren was founded by student members of the Japan Communist Party, and the activities of its early years were closely coordinated with official party policy. For the first year after the founding of the Zengakuren, the student Left focused on militant protests against various educational reforms of the Occupation and began to win considerable public attention. From 1950, however, with the emergence of a strongly anticommunist policy by the Occupation, the Zengakuren, along with the JCP, was put on the defensive. The factional split within the JCP from this point between the mainstream and international factions also greatly weakened the Zengakuren. Zengakuren students played a leading role in the protests against the RED PURGE of 1950 and were again in the vanguard in the extremist "Molotov cocktail struggle" of the JCP in the winter of 1951–52. The violent May Day demonstrations (see MAY DAY INCIDENT) of 1952 in particular worked to discredit the student movement in the eyes of the general public.

The end of the Korean War in 1953 and the reunification of the JCP in the mid-1950s led to a new phase of aggressive activity by the student Left, notably in support of the movement to ban the hydrogen bomb and in opposition to the American military presence in Japan under the terms of the United States–Japan Security Treaty of 1952 (see UNITED STATES–JAPAN SECURITY TREATIES). Zengakuren students played the central role, for example, in the protracted protest against the expansion of an American base at Sunagawa in suburban Tōkyō in 1955–57 (see SUNAGAWA CASE). It was through such activities that the Japanese student movement began to win international attention.

The Break with the JCP —— A development of great significance in the late 1950s was the emergence from within the Zengakuren of factions in clear and articulate opposition to the Japan Communist Party. Denounced by the JCP rather imprecisely as Trotskyites (although they did include self-professed Trotskyite elements) and known from the mid-60s as the New Left, these anti-JCP forces of the extreme Left introduced a wholly new phase in the history of the student movement in Japan, which ever since the early 1920s had been tightly integrated with the JCP. It was in 1958, following the 11th Congress of the Zengakuren in June, that a majority of the representatives (the "mainstream") broke completely with the JCP. The anti-JCP forces were themselves already divided, however, between the Revolutionary Communist League (Nihon Kakumeiteki Kyōsan Shugisha Dōmei, or Kakkyōdō, founded November 1957) and the Communist League (Kyōsan Shugisha Dōmei, founded December 1958 and popularly known as the "Bunto"). On the eve of the Security Treaty Crisis of 1960, the Zengakuren mainstream was controlled by the "Bunto," although some 40 percent of all the representatives remained loyal to the JCP.

Zengakuren activists won new levels of national and international attention for their leading role in the protests against the revision of the United States–Japan Mutual Security Treaty in 1960, culminating in the violent demonstration of June 15 and the death of a Tōkyō University student. Throughout the Security Treaty protests, however, the Zengakuren forces were badly divided, with pro-JCP students often holding demonstrations separately from their ri-

vals in the anti-JCP mainstream. The anticlimactic outcome of the struggle led to much mutual recrimination, which left the Zengakuren in a factional shambles. See also PEACE MOVEMENT.

Armed Confrontation —— The early 1960s were years of organizational regrouping, and the Zengakuren split into several wholly separate federations, each claiming the title of Zengakuren. The JCP-led group came to be known from 1964 as the MINSEI (an abbreviation of Minshu Seinen Dōmei, or Democratic Youth League) Zengakuren and throughout the tumultuous late 1960s claimed control of some two-thirds of all left-wing *jichikai*. The anti-JCP New Left forces were fragmented into several different factions, although an alliance known as the Sampa (Three-Faction) Zengakuren was in force from December 1966 to July 1968 among the Chūkakuha, Shagakudō, and Shaseidō. Student movement factionalism in these years was extremely complex, turning on issues of personality, tactics, and interpretations of revolutionary strategy.

Mounting problems within the system of higher education itself did much to create the setting for the protracted campus disturbances of the middle and late 1960s. The first major dispute occurred at Waseda University in the winter of 1965–66, resulting in a total student strike of over five months and a massive paralysis of the school. The major issue at Waseda was a proposed tuition raise, but as in other campus confrontations of the late 1960s, a variety of other issues were involved, centering broadly on the trend to rising costs and decreasing educational quality, particularly at the large private universities.

The growth of student revolt against the universities was paralleled by an intensification of the broader political movement in opposition to the security treaty with the United States, particularly as a result of the war in Vietnam. The specific goal of this movement, which closely paralleled similar antiwar protests in the United States, was the revocation of the Security Treaty ("Ampo") in mid-1970. It was this emerging "Ampo 70" campaign that gave birth in late 1967 to a dramatic new mode of left-wing student protest that came to be known as *geba*. The *geba* (short for *gebaruto*, from the German *Gewalt* meaning force) was an armed confrontation with the riot police, in which students wore helmets and masks for protection and used rocks, wooden staves (metal pipes later), and firebombs as offensive weapons. The first full-dress *geba* occurred near Haneda airport in Tōkyō on 8 October and 17 November 1967, when extremist Zengakuren forces attempted to prevent Prime Minister SATŌ EISAKU's departure on trips to South Vietnam and the United States.

The *geba* techniques became the standard mode of operation of the student Left and were used in further protests in 1968 in opposition to the American military presence in Japan. In January, Zengakuren students gathered at the port of Sasebo in Kyūshū in an effort to prevent a visit by the nuclear carrier *Enterprise*. In April students led a series of violent confrontations in protest against a military hospital at an American base at Ōji that was used to treat soldiers wounded in Vietnam. New Left student radicals also came to play a major role in the protracted movement in opposition to the construction of a new international airport at Narita. Beginning in early 1968 and continuing for almost a decade, this protest resulted in many armed confrontations with the police, and the death of three policemen in September 1971 and one student in May 1977.

The Crisis of 1968–1969 —— From mid-1968 into early 1969, these off-campus campaigns against the "Ampo" system were joined by a new wave of on-campus revolts, beginning at Tōkyō University and Nihon University and then spreading to dozens of other campuses. The turning point came in January 1969 with the mobilization of riot police to evict radical students who had blockaded much of the Tōkyō University campus. From this point, the student movement began to lose momentum both on and off campus, the victim of severe interfaction rivalry, mounting public opposition, and increasingly severe control measures by police and educational authorities. The passage of a law to control university disturbances in August 1969 led to a sharp drop in on-campus unrest, while the decision on the reversion of Okinawa to Japan, made in late 1969, worked to undercut the anti-Ampo drive. The great struggle envisioned for June 1970 proved an anticlimactic failure.

In the early 1970s, the student Left turned increasingly against itself in the form of the *uchigeba* ("internal *geba*") in which rival factions fought with one another. Strongly criticized by the pro-JCP Minsei forces, these incidents among the anti-JCP factions reached a peak in 1973 and 1974, in the course of which 332 incidents left 20 students dead and 641 wounded. It was also in the aftermath of the 1968–69 crisis that the Sekigunha (RED ARMY FACTION) emerged with a program of guerilla terrorism. In Japan the Sekigunha activists carried out a series of bombings and robberies, finally collapsing under police pressure and internal violence in February 1971. An international wing of the same group, known as the Japanese Red Army (Nihon Sekigun), was responsible for a spectacular series of international terrorist attacks and hijackings throughout the 1970s. See also UNIVERSITY UPHEAVALS OF 1968–1969.

📖 ——Stuart Dowsey, ed, *Zengakuren: Japan's Revolutionary Students* (1970). Kikukawa Tadao, *Gakusei shakai undō shi* (1931). Nihon Gakusei Undō Kenkyūkai, ed, *Nihon gakusei undō no kenkyū* (1966). George R. Packard III, *Protest in Tokyo: The Security Treaty Crisis of 1960* (1966). San'ichi Shobō, ed, *Shiryō sengo gakusei undō*, 8 vols (1968–70). Henry D. Smith II, *Japan's First Student Radicals* (1972). Suzuki Hiroo, *Gakusei undō—Daigaku no kaikaku ka, shakai no henkaku ka* (1968). Takakuwa Suehide, *Nihon gakusei shakai undō shi* (1955). Kazuko Tsurumi, *Social Change and the Individual: Japan Before and After Defeat in World War II* (1970).

Henry D. SMITH II

student protests of 1968–1969 → university upheavals of 1968–1969

study abroad

Japan, an island country, has always regarded sending students abroad as an effective means of absorbing foreign culture and technology. Prior to the Meiji period (1868–1912), the Japanese primarily studied the culture of China. The eight students, headed by ONO NO IMOKO, who went with the embassy to the Sui dynasty in 607 constituted Japan's first overseas students (see SUI AND TANG [T'ANG] CHINA, EMBASSIES TO). Students continued to be sent to study in China until the Japanese embassies to the Tang (T'ang) dynasty were abolished in 894. From that time to the end of the Edo period (1600–1868), no government students were sent abroad, although some Buddhist priests studied in China during the Muromachi period (1333–1568). After the Meiji Restoration in 1868 the government actively encouraged students to go overseas in order to study European and American culture and technology. In 1872, a government-financed Ministry of Education scholarship was established, and by 1945 over 3,200 students had studied overseas in this program.

Post–World War II foreign study programs for Japanese students can be roughly divided into three categories: those sponsored by foreign governments, those sponsored by the Japanese government, and those sponsored by private organizations. The first major program sponsored by a foreign government was the United States GARIOA scholarship system of 1949 (see GARIOA–EROA). This was replaced by the Fulbright exchange program in 1952 (see JAPAN–UNITED STATES EDUCATIONAL COMMISSION); by 1978, this program had sent 5,800 students to the United States. Since 1979 the Fulbright program has been financed on an equal basis by the Japanese and the United States governments. Other foreign scholarship programs were started by France in 1950 and by West Germany and England (the British Council) in 1952. In 1979, 28 countries (other than the United States) provided scholarships to 320 Japanese students. Foreign-government-sponsored Japanese students in 1979 included 60 in France, 35 in West Germany, 15 in England, 104 in Mexico, and 20 in China.

There are three types of programs for foreign study sponsored by the Japanese government: an international student exchange program which promotes educational exchange among colleges and furthers the internationalization of Japanese higher education, a program sending education students abroad in order to give them an international outlook and knowledge, and a program sending students to Asian countries for training as Asian area specialists. In addition, the Ministry of Education operates a program sending faculty members of universities or research institutes abroad to study; 622 persons went abroad through this program in 1979. There is also an overseas study program for artists. In addition to these foreign and Japanese government programs there are those sponsored by private organizations such as the Sankei Scholarship Foundation, the AFS (American Field Service), and the Alexander von Humboldt Foundation. Privately funded students abroad far exceed those funded by the government, and most of them go to the United States.

KATŌ Kōji

Subarjo, Raden Akhmad (1897–1978)

Indonesian nationalist and minister of foreign affairs after World War II. He studied for nine years in the Netherlands, where he led an anticolonial organization of Indonesian students. From 1942 to 1945 he worked for the Japanese navy in Djakarta; upon Japan's defeat in 1945 he supported the decision of SUKARNO and Mohammad HATTA to declare Indonesia's independence. In the 1950s he played an instrumental role in Indonesia's negotiations with Japan on war reparations. See also INDONESIA AND JAPAN.

NAGAZUMI Akira

Subaru

(The Pleiades). Literary magazine published from January 1909 to December 1913. Launched as a successor to MYŌJŌ, an earlier influential literary journal, with financial backing provided by Hiraide Shū (1878–1914), this monthly opposed the so-called Japanese naturalism, publishing poetry and prose works in a style often labeled as decadent or neoromantic. MORI ŌGAI intervened to reunite the defunct *Myōjō's* feuding poets in this new attempt to stem the naturalist tide. Members and contributors included ISHIKAWA TAKUBOKU, TAKAMURA KŌTARŌ, KINOSHITA MOKUTARŌ, YOSANO AKIKO, KITAHARA HAKUSHŪ, SATŌ HARUO, and YOSHII ISAMU. NAGAI KAFŪ and UEDA BIN introduced translations of European poetry, and Ōgai and TANIZAKI JUN'ICHIRŌ published prose works. The magazine was weighted in favor of poetry, putting out several special numbers of TANKA, but also devoted space to original critical essays, stories, and plays. A chief characteristic of much of the writing in *Subaru* was its curious blending of urbanity, exoticism, aestheticism, and fin de siècle decadence. Taking a generally antinaturalist position at a time when the literary world was under the sway of naturalism, *Subaru* is viewed from the perspective of literary history as one of the most influential magazines of the period. It eventually stagnated and ceased publication with the rise of idealism.

Theodore W. GOOSSEN

subcontractors

(*shitauke kigyō*). Firms occupying lower tiers in multilevel production structures. Subcontractors exist in many forms in Japan. Some barely survive by performing simple processing operations on consignment, while others are deeply embedded in the production structures of their parent or chief purchaser companies. Some of the latter boast advanced, specialized technologies and outstanding management.

A survey by the Small and Medium Enterprises Agency (Chūshō Kigyō Chō) of the MINISTRY OF INTERNATIONAL TRADE AND INDUSTRY divides subcontractors into two categories by subcontracting ratio (the proportion of subcontracting in the total value of manufacturing). Specialist subcontractors have subcontracting ratios of more than 80 percent, and nonspecialists less. Specialist subcontracting has both advantages and disadvantages. On the plus side, a given level of orders is assured, so production rather than sales can be emphasized. On the minus side, they are at the mercy of parent company decisions and are more seriously hurt by aggregate business fluctuations. Nonspecialist contractors, on the other hand, resemble ordinary manufacturers. They market products and develop technology on their own. Since the OIL CRISIS OF 1973, subcontractors have been forced to rationalize, especially through cost cutting. Moreover, many parent organizations now rely more on internal production. A growing number of subcontractors are responding to these challenges by improving technology and consolidating sales networks.

Subcontractors comprise a significant portion of Japan's SMALL AND MEDIUM ENTERPRISES, which constitute the second tier of the dual structure of the Japanese economy. Some large enterprises, such as those in the automotive industry, rely on subcontractors for as much as 50 percent of their production. Wages and working conditions are considerably lower than in large corporations, and job security is nonexistent. In times of recession, orders to subcontractors are cut first. Unemployment in this sector functions as a "safety valve" to relieve the pressures of permanent employment in the large companies. See also EMPLOYMENT SYSTEM; INDUSTRIAL ORGANIZATION.

MASUDA Yūji

subsidiary companies

(*kogaisha*). A joint-stock or limited liability company whose majority stocks or shares are owned by another company (*oyagaisha*, or

Subways

	Tōkyō						
Facts about Subways in Japan, May 1982							
	Teito Rapid Transit Authority	Transportation Bureau of Tōkyō Metropolitan Government	Tōkyū Corporation	Total	Ōsaka Municipal Transportation Bureau	Nagoya Municipal Transportation Bureau	Sapporo Municipal Transportation Bureau
Operating distance (km)	131.8	54.9	9.4	196.1	89.1	54.4	31.6
Lines in operation	7	3	1	11	6	4	2
Cars owned	1,738	440	216	2,394	792	445	320
Passengers carried daily (1,000)	4,698	1,116	410	6,224	2,346	939	558
Minimum headway (minutes)	1:50	2:00	4:00	—	2:00	2:00	3:30
Maximum train composition (cars)	10	6	8	—	8	6	8
Minimum fare (yen)	100	120	120	—	120	120	120

	Kōbe					
	Kōbe Rapid Transit Railway Corporation	Kōbe Municipal Transportation Bureau	Total	Yokohama Municipal Transportation Bureau	Fukuoka Municipal Transportation Bureau	Kyōto Municipal Transportation Bureau
Operating distance (km)	7.6	5.7	13.3	11.5	7.2	6.6
Lines in operation	2	1	3	1	1	1
Cars owned	0	32	32	70	48	36
Passengers carried daily (1,000)	312	58	370	132	71	136
Minimum headway (minutes)	3:20	6:00	—	5:00	7:00	5:00
Maximum train composition (cars)	8	4	—	5	6	4
Minimum fare (yen)	60	120	—	120	120	100

Source: Teito Kōsokudo Kōtsū Eidan (Teito Rapid Transit Authority), *Chōsa tōkei geppō*, no. 418 (September 1982).

parent company) as defined by the COMMERCIAL CODE, article 274 (3).

The OVERSEER of the parent company is authorized, when necessary, to request a business report from the subsidiary company and to inspect the condition of the subsidiary company's business and property. The overseer of the parent company may not concurrently be a director, manager, or other employee of the subsidiary company (art. 276). Under the SECURITIES EXCHANGE LAW (Shōken Torihiki Hō), a parent company is required to attach consolidated financial statements covering all subsidiary companies to the Report of Securities (Yūka Shōken Hōkoku Sho) and the Notice of Securities (Yūka Shōken Todokede Sho). KITAZAWA Masahiro

Subversive Activities Prevention Law

(Hakai Katsudō Bōshi Hō; abbreviated Habō Hō, SAPL). An internal security law, enacted in 1952, which permits the government to restrict the activities of or dissolve organizations engaged in terroristic subversive activities. The rationale for this law was the need, from the government's point of view, to respond to and control violent tactics used at that time by the Japanese Communist Party and its supporters, inside and outside of Japan. The SAPL was the first major law enacted by the Diet after Japan regained its independence in April 1952. Fears that this would be the beginning of a reinstitution of the prewar thought control system that had been made possible by the PEACE PRESERVATION LAW OF 1925 aroused against the passage of the SAPL what was at the time the largest and most vehement demonstration since the end of World War II. Probably because of this strenuous opposition, but also because of restrictions written into the law and the government's apparent policy of using it only in unusual circumstances, the SAPL was invoked by the government only about 10 times between 1952 and the late 1970s.

"Terroristic subversive activities" are described in two broad categories: (1) insurrection and aiding and assisting foreign military action on Japanese soil (arts. 77–79, 81–82, 87 of the Criminal Code)

and instigation (kyōsa) of these acts, the incitement (sendō) of most of these acts, use of wired broadcasting and wireless communication, public posting, distribution, and printing of documents or drawings which would lead to the execution of these acts; (2) riot, arson, setting off and use of explosives, endangering the passage of or wrecking of public conveyances, murder, robbery, and interference in the exercise of duties of, and coercion of, public officials (principally arts. 95, 106, 108–109, 117, 125, 126, 236 of the Criminal Code) carried out for political purposes, and incitement and instigation of these acts.

The potential danger of this law to civil liberties lies in the interpretation and enforcement of the ambiguous terms incitement (sendō) and instigation (kyōsa) as stipulated in the SAPL—especially in light of Japan's pre–World War II experience with the expanded interpretation and enforcement of the notorious Peace Preservation Law. The Public Security Investigation Agency (Kōan Chōsa Chō) was created to investigate possible violations of the SAPL. If it finds violations, it can recommend to the Public Security Examination Commission (Kōan Shinsa Iinkai) restriction of the activities of, or dissolution of, organizations engaged in such activities. The commission's decisions, in turn, may be appealed to the courts.

Cecil H. UYEHARA

subways

(chikatetsu). Since the Tōkyō Underground Railway Co opened up a 2.2 kilometer (1.4 mi) track in Tōkyō between Asakusa and Ueno on 30 December 1927, the subway has become an increasingly common feature of Japanese urban life. Other cities gradually followed Tōkyō's lead: Ōsaka in 1933, Nagoya in 1957, Kōbe in 1968, Sapporo in 1971, Yokohama in 1977, and Kyōto and Fukuoka in 1981. In 1982 a subway system was being built in Sendai and 409.8 kilometers (254 mi) of subway track were already in operation in Japan. New lines are continually being constructed in cities that already have subway systems to meet increasing demand. (Subway systems in service in 1982 are listed in the table.) In 1982, construction costs in

Tōkyō were estimated to have ranged between approximately ¥18 billion (US $72 million) and ¥23 billion (US $92 million) per track kilometer, 60 percent of which was subsidized by the central government and local public bodies.

Subway lines have assumed an increasingly prominent role in the urban transportation system, with surface transportation being unable to expand in congested areas. In Tōkyō the subway system has seen an 8-fold increase in track and a 13-fold increase in passengers during the past 25 years. Since 58 percent of the subway passengers in Japan are commuters and students, rush-hour congestion is extreme, with passengers numbering two to three times the prescribed capacity of the system. In every city the fare is determined by the distance traveled. Commuters and students, however, benefit from fare reductions of 30 and 76 percent, respectively, through purchase of special passes.

Three characteristics of the Japanese subway system deserve mention. First, most of the recently constructed subway lines are designed to connect with (and the same trains to run on) surface railway lines in the suburbs, allowing passengers to travel between downtown and the suburbs without changing trains. Second, subway cars specially designed to consume less electric power and generate less heat are increasingly used in large cities. Third, rubber tires have been placed on Sapporo subway trains to reduce noise and vibration. *WATANABE Takeshi*

Sūden (1569–1633)

Also known as Ishin Sūden, Konchiin Sūden, and Honkō Kokushi. Zen cleric of the RINZAI SECT; diplomatic and political adviser to the first three Tokugawa shōguns and a major figure in the early institutional development of the Tokugawa shogunate (1603–1867).

Born into the Isshiki family, important vassals of the Muromachi shogunate (1338–1573), in early childhood Sūden entered the temple NANZENJI in Kyōto, a major Rinzai center, and studied Zen under several masters, including Saishō Shōtai (1548–1607), who was diplomatic adviser to both TOYOTOMI HIDEYOSHI and TOKUGAWA IEYASU. Sūden became abbot of Nanzenji in 1605 but was called to Ieyasu's retirement capital at Sumpu (now the city of Shizuoka) in 1608 to succeed Shōtai as his diplomatic adviser. His duties quickly expanded to include domestic political affairs and legislation. He was responsible for drafting Ieyasu's diplomatic correspondence and for overseeing the *shuinsen* system of trade licenses (see VERMILION SEAL SHIP TRADE). In 1612 Ieyasu charged him with overseeing all Buddhist institutions and with drafting the first shogunal act suppressing Christianity. In the same year he began to draft legislation for Ieyasu, particularly laws dealing with the control of the imperial court, the warrior houses, and various Buddhist sects (see BUKE SHOHATTO; KINCHŪ NARABI NI KUGE SHOHATTO).

Sūden was elevated to the rank of *kokushi* (national teacher) by the imperial court in 1626 and granted the right to wear purple robes. He nonetheless argued successfully for severe punishment of the principals in the Purple Robe Incident (SHIE INCIDENT) of 1627, in which Emperor GO-MIZUNOO made similar awards to other Zen monks without shogunal permission, in defiance of legislation Sūden himself had drafted. In this manner throughout his career as shogunal adviser he worked to secure the supremacy of shogunal authority over all segments of Japanese society. His diplomatic papers, included in IKOKU NIKKI (Register of Foreign Affairs), and his office log, *Honkō Kokushi nikki* (Diary of Honkō Kokushi), are important sources for early Edo-period (1600–1868) history.

Ronald P. TOBY

Sue

Village in southern Kumamoto Prefecture, Kyūshū. Sue is known primarily in the West as the subject of a book, *Suye Mura: A Japanese Village* (1939), by John F. EMBREE. About 60 percent of the village is public forest land. Some rice cultivation is also carried out. Pop: 1,562.

Suehiro Izutarō (1888–1951)

Legal scholar; born in Yamaguchi Prefecture. A 1912 graduate of Tōkyō University, Suehiro joined its faculty in 1914. His exposure during studies abroad (1918–20) to the case-study method at the University of Chicago and, in Switzerland, to the ideas of Eugen Ehrlich (1862–1922), founder of the discipline of the sociology of law, led him to take a positivist approach to civil law. He stressed

the importance of judicial precedent and organized a study group, the Mimpō Hanrei Kenkyūkai, at the university. He also became interested in the problems of farming villages and of labor and was the first scholar before World War II to lecture on labor law. Suehiro retired from the university in 1946 to become the first chairman of the CENTRAL LABOR RELATIONS COMMISSION and arbitrated numerous labor disputes. Among his publications are *Nōson hōritsu mondai* (1924, Legal Problems of Farming Villages), *Rōdōhō kenkyū* (1925, Studies on Labor Law), *Hōgaku nyūmon* (1934, Introduction to Law), and *Mimpō zakkichō* (2 vols, 1940, 1949; Notes on Civil Law). *KATŌ Ichirō*

Suehiro Tetchō (1849–1896)

Politician, journalist, and novelist. Real name Suehiro Shigeyasu. Born in what is now Ehime Prefecture. Suehiro joined the staff of the liberal newspaper *Chōya shimbun,* and was jailed twice during the 1870s for his resistance to government oppression of freedom of speech. In 1881 he participated in founding the JIYŪTŌ (Liberal Party), Japan's first political party. During the next few years, he wrote such political novels (SEIJI SHŌSETSU) as *Nijūsannen miraiki* (1886) and *Setchūbai* (1886); the former, about his plan for Japan's future political system, was a best-seller. In 1890, he was elected to the lower house of the newly founded Diet as a member of the RIKKEN KAISHINTŌ.

Suekawa Hiroshi (1892–1977)

Legal scholar; born in Yamaguchi Prefecture. He graduated from Kyōto University in 1917, joined its faculty in 1919, and taught there until 1933, when he resigned in the wake of the KYŌTO UNIVERSITY INCIDENT. In 1940 he became a professor at Ōsaka Municipal University, and in 1945 president of Ritsumeikan University in Kyōto, where he remained until 1969. While at Ritsumeikan he raised the quality of its staff and developed a faculty council system aimed at democratizing the university administration. Suekawa made many significant contributions to the study of the CIVIL CODE. His book *Kenri shingai ron* (1930, Theory of Infringement of Rights) led to a basic change in the law of torts in Japan. Other works include *Mimpō ni okeru tokushu mondai no kenkyū* (1925, Study of Special Problems in the Civil Code), *Kenri ran'yō no kenkyū* (1949, The Abuse of Rights), *Bukkenron* (1956, Real Rights), *Keiyakuhō* (1958, Contract Law), and *Sen'yū to shoyū* (1962, Possession and Ownership).

——Suekawa Hiroshi, *Suekawa Hiroshi hōritsu rombunshū,* 4 vols (1970). *AWAJI Takehisa*

Suematsu Kenchō (1855–1920)

Politician and scholar. Born in what is now Fukuoka Prefecture. He worked for the newspaper *Tōkyō nichinichi shimbun* and attracted the attention of the government leader ITŌ HIROBUMI, whose daughter he later married. In 1878 Suematsu went to England to work in the Japanese embassy and to study at Cambridge University, remaining there until 1886. He won a seat in the first Diet elections of 1890 and went on to serve in various government posts, including communications minister and home minister in the Itō cabinets of 1898 and 1900, respectively. He was later appointed to the Privy Council and the Imperial Academy (Gakushiin). Suematsu is also remembered for his studies in literature, having produced the first English translation of the TALE OF GENJI, and for his compilation of BŌCHŌ KAITEN SHI, a 12-volume history of the Chōshū domain (now Yamaguchi Prefecture), a domain which had played a leading part in the MEIJI RESTORATION.

Suetsugu Heizō (?–1630)

Overseas trader. Born into a family of wealthy merchants of Hakata (now Fukuoka). His father moved to Nagasaki in 1571, when that port was opened to foreign trade, and amassed a great fortune. Heizō succeeded to his father's business and in 1619 was appointed local intendant *(daikan)* of Nagasaki. After obtaining from the shogunate an official license to engage in the VERMILION SEAL SHIP TRADE, he dispatched ships to Luzon (the main island of the Philippines) and Siam (now Thailand). One of his captains, HAMADA YAHYŌE, fought with the Dutch factor in Taiwan and brought Taiwanese hostages back to Nagasaki. Because of this skirmish, on Heizō's advice the shogunate discontinued trade with the Dutch for a time. The Suetsugu family business continued to flourish, but in 1676 Heizō's grandson was discovered by the authorities to have been secretly trading with Cambodia, a violation of the strict NATIONAL SECLUSION policy of the Tokugawa government. He and his entire family were severely punished and the Suetsugu family name and business were discontinued.

sue ware

(*sueki*). A gray stoneware manufactured in Japan from the 5th through 10th centuries. This pottery was known as *iwaibe doki* or Chōsen *doki* (Korean pottery) until the 1950s, when the word *sue*, derived from a reference to the vessels in the 8th-century anthology MAN'YŌSHŪ, was generally adopted. Originally a ceramic tradition of the southern part of the Korean peninsula, *sue* ware was one of several crafts to be transmitted to Japan by immigrant (KIKAJIN) craftsmen during the 5th and 6th centuries.

Differing greatly from the native HAJI WARE—a porous, reddish earthenware—*sue* ware was fired stone-hard at temperatures exceeding 1,000°C (1,832°F); the atmospheric oxygen was then reduced to produce a gray color. Simple combed or punctate designs make up the decorative repertoire, although rarer ceremonial pieces were elaborately adorned with sculptures of human and animal figures and miniature vessels. *Sue* ware was generally unglazed in its early stages, except for natural ash deposits that formed during the firing process.

Contrary to popular belief, *sue* vessels were mainly coil-made and beaten, smoothed, or carved into shape rather than wheel thrown. Wheel throwing was first used in the 9th century, but even then only small pieces—especially bowls, as evidenced by string-cut bases—seem to have been made this way. Many other vessels were formed in several parts, then joined together, and finally finished on a turntable.

Sue kilns have been described as tunnellike (*anagama*), being dug into and utilizing the natural slope of a hillside. Lacking a separate firebox or partitioned firing rooms, these simple kilns with sloping flat or stepped floors were the forerunners of the true *noborigama* ("climbing kilns") used from the 1600s onward.

Sue production was initially established in the rolling hills of southern Ōsaka Prefecture, at a place that still bears its name, Suemura; but the new pottery technology spread quickly throughout Japan. By the 6th century, kilns existed in several localities along the Inland Sea, the Sea of Japan coast, and the eastern seaboard. This early *sue* was produced for the political elite, most probably by the production corporations (BE) that supplied the YAMATO COURT with basic necessities. Many of the finely decorated vessels, such as pedestaled bowls, jars, and spouted beverage containers, were filled with ceremonial food offerings and deposited in the mounded tombs (KOFUN) of the protohistoric era.

In the early 7th century, *sue* began to be mass produced; replaced as an elite product by new imports such as three-color ware from China, *sue* became available to a larger sector of society and was used for utilitarian purposes. Kilns were built in many Nara-period (710–794) provincial capitals to supply local needs, in addition to consignments to government offices and temples, as evidenced by inked characters on the vessels showing their delivery destinations. Specific kilns, especially in modern Okayama and Aichi prefectures, were taxed to supply the Nara court; and many other kilns in and around the Kinai (Ōsaka–Kyōto–Nara) area specialized in certain *sue* shapes, testifying to an increased demand and the development of a more elaborate distribution system.

Continuing throughout the Heian period (794–1185) as a utilitarian ware, *sue* gave birth to a number of regional wares (e.g., YAMACHAWAN) and gave way to new glazed versions using the native ash glaze or imported green and three-color glazing techniques. The successors of *sue* were the medieval pottery traditions of unglazed, heavy farmhouse crockery—IGA WARE, BIZEN WARE, and SHIGARAKI WARE. See also CERAMICS.

——Haraguchi Shōzō, *Sueki*, in *Nihon no genshi bijutsu*, vol 4 (Kōdansha, 1979).

Gina Lee BARNES

Sueyoshi Magozaemon (1570–1617)

Wealthy merchant and overseas trader of the early Edo period; also known as Sueyoshi Yoshiyasu. At the behest of TOKUGAWA IEYASU, Sueyoshi and his father helped establish an office for minting silver coins (the Ginza) in 1601. During the Ōsaka campaigns of 1614–15 (see ŌSAKA CASTLE, SIEGES OF), he constructed the military headquarters for the Tokugawa and in recognition of his contributions was appointed *daikan* (intendant) of two districts in Kawachi Province (now part of Ōsaka Prefecture). He also received a SHUINJŌ (vermilion-seal certificate) granting him official permission to engage in foreign trade and dispatched ships (known as *sueyoshibune*) annually to Luzon in the Philippines and Tonkin in Vietnam. His family remained involved in the VERMILION SEAL SHIP TRADE until the prohibition of voyages abroad in 1635 under the NATIONAL SECLUSION policy. Three famous *ema* (votive pictures) donated by the Sueyoshi family in gratitude for a safe voyage are preserved in the temple KIYOMIZUDERA in Kyōto. Dated 1632, 1633, and 1634, they depict three-masted ships manned by crews—one man a Western pilot—playing cards and smoking pipes.

suffrage → Universal Manhood Suffrage Movement; women's suffrage

Sugadaira

Highland in northeastern Nagano Prefecture, central Honshū. On the southwestern slopes of Azumayasan and Nekodake. The central part is a swamp created by lava flows. Principal agricultural products are highland vegetables and potato seedlings. Stock farming is also carried out. In winter skiing is available; in summer it is a resort area. Part of Jōshin'etsu Kōgen National Park. Elevation: 1,200–1,500 m (3,936–4,920 ft).

Sugae Masumi (1754–1829)

KOKUGAKU (National Learning) scholar and writer; known for his descriptions of local folk customs. Born near Toyohashi (now in Aichi Prefecture). Real name Shirai Hideo. He began to write about his travels in 1783 and eventually completed over 70 accounts, consisting of dated journal entries, poems, and drawings and generally concerning rural life. He traveled mainly in the central and northeastern regions of Japan's main island, Honshū, but he also visited briefly the northern island Hokkaidō. In 1811, Sugae was commissioned by Satake Yoshikazu, *daimyō* of the Akita domain, to write a geographical description of the six districts (*gun*) of Dewa Province (now Yamagata and Akita prefectures), reflecting the wide esteem in which he was held as a writer and as a chronicler of regional lifestyles. His works, long circulated in manuscript form, were published under the title *Sugae Masumi yūranki* in 13 volumes in 1966–71. A study of Sugae has been written by Japan's most eminent folklorist, YANAGITA KUNIO.

Ōtō Tokihiko

Suganuma Teifū (1865–1889)

Scholar of economic history. Born in Nagasaki Prefecture. Educated at a domainal school, he later completed a survey of the history of trade in HIRADO, Japan's foreign trade center until the early 17th century. He entered the classics department of Tōkyō University in 1884 and at the same time studied economics at the Senshū Gakkō (now Senshū University). In 1888 he became a professor at the Tōkyō Higher Commercial School (now Hitotsubashi University) and began a study of Japanese commercial history. Six months later he resigned his post. While investigating industrial and economic conditions in Southeast Asia, he died of cholera in Manila. His principal work, on Hirado trade, is *Dai Nippon shōgyō shi: Fu Hirado bōeki shi* (1888).

Yamada Katsumi

Sugawara no Michizane (845–903)

Leading court scholar, poet, and political figure of the Heian period (794–1185) who challenged the powerful FUJIWARA FAMILY and was sent into exile where he died in disgrace.

The Sugawara were descended from the ancient Haji family, hereditary makers of ceramic funerary objects (HANIWA). During the 8th century the family abandoned this tradition, and in 781 Michizane's great-grandfather changed his name to Sugawara. Thereafter, members of the family established a new tradition as scholars, poets, and diplomats. In particular, Michizane's father and grandfather were actively involved in Japan's enthusiastic adoption of Chinese culture during the 9th century. They helped edit Japan's imperially sponsored anthologies of poetry in Chinese, served as presidents and professors of literature at the Confucian-oriented court university (DAIGAKURYŌ), and participated in early Japan's last two official missions to China (see SUI AND TANG [T'ANG] CHINA, EMBASSIES

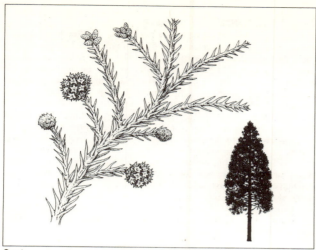

Sugi

TO). Following in their footsteps, Michizane had a career which resembled that of a typical Chinese scholar-official.

Michizane began his studies of Chinese classics and literature under his father's supervision and at the age of 11 wrote his first poem in Chinese. He entered the university in 862 as a student of literature and eight years later completed his studies, passing the difficult civil-service examination to gain admission to the court bureaucracy. After holding a variety of minor posts that called upon his ability to draft documents in elegant Chinese, in 877 he was appointed professor of literature, an office he held for 10 years. During those years he greeted two embassies from the Manchurian kingdom of BOHAI (Po-hai), offered scholarly opinions on current political issues, and regularly composed poetry in Chinese both at court functions and for his own edification. In 886 he was named to a four-year term as governor of Sanuki Province (now Kagawa Prefecture) in Shikoku. This was his first extended period away from the capital and, although he lamented his separation from friends and family, he wrote some of his best poetry in Sanuki, much of it reflecting a concern for the common man rare in the literature of his day.

After his return to the capital, he was rapidly promoted to high court office by Emperor UDA, who sought to rule without interference by the powerful Fujiwara family. Uda selected Michizane as a counterbalance to the Fujiwara in accord with the Confucian theory that men of ability, particularly scholarly ability, ought to run the government. Michizane reached the peak of his power in 899 when he was appointed minister of the right (udaijin), the second highest regular office at court. By this time, however, his patron Uda had abdicated in favor of his young son Emperor DAIGO, who had closer ties with the Fujiwara. In 901 Fujiwara leaders falsely accused Michizane of plotting against the throne and he was transferred to DAZAIFU, the government headquarters in Kyūshū, an appointment tantamount to exile. He died there in 903 after writing a series of famous poems bemoaning his fate and protesting his innocence.

During his years in high office, Michizane's most important contribution was his proposal that Japan abandon its official missions to China because of the unstable political conditions there. The proposal was accepted in 894 and thus Michizane helped bring to an end the period when early Japan was most strongly influenced by Chinese culture. Michizane's poetry in Chinese survives in two anthologies that he himself compiled. He is considered early Japan's greatest master of poetry in Chinese and his poetry in Japanese is also highly regarded. In addition, he helped write the *Nihon sandai jitsuroku*, last of Japan's six official histories (RIKKOKUSHI), and compiled a version of all of them arranged topically rather than chronologically (the RUIJŪ KOKUSHI). Michizane's poetry continues to be read, and his histories are of great value to modern scholars.

After Michizane's death, a number of misfortunes at court were ascribed to his angry spirit. To placate the ghost, Michizane was posthumously pardoned and promoted to the highest of court ranks. His descendents were reinstated and became hereditary court scholars. Shrines dedicated to him were established in Kyōto (KITANO SHRINE) and Dazaifu (DAZAIFU SHRINE). Deified as Karai Tenjin, Michizane came to be venerated as the patron saint of scholarship,

and even today countless Japanese students buy amulets at the many shrines dedicated to him before taking their school entrance examinations (see TEMMANGŪ).

———Sugawara no Michizane, *Kanke bunsō* and *Kanke kōshū*, ed Kawaguchi Hisao, in *Nihon koten bungaku taikei*, vol 72 (Iwanami Shoten, 1966). Robert Borgen, "Sugawara no Michizane: Ninth-Century Japanese Court Scholar, Poet, and Statesman," PhD dissertation, University of Michigan (1978). Ivan Morris, *The Nobility of Failure: Tragic Heroes in the History of Japan* (1975). Sakamoto Tarō, *Sugawara no Michizane*, in *Jimbutsu sōsho*, vol 100 (Yoshikawa Kōbunkan, 1962). Burton Watson, tr, *Japanese Literature in Chinese*, vol 1 (1975). Robert BORGEN

Sugawara no Takasue no Musume (1008–?)

(Sugawara no Takasue's Daughter). Writer of the middle Heian period. Real name unknown; usually identified by her father's name. Born into a family of scholars, she was a sixth-generation descendant of SUGAWARA NO MICHIZANE and niece of the author of KAGERŌ NIKKI (974; tr *The Gossamer Years*, 1964). She spent her childhood in the province of Kazusa (now Chiba Prefecture), where her father was stationed. She was very fond of reading tales *(monogatari)* about life at the Kyōto court, the TALE OF GENJI being her favorite. She returned at the age of 12 to Kyōto and eventually entered service at the court. At about age 33 she married Tachibana no Toshimichi. Two years after her husband's death, when she was 51, she wrote the SARASHINA NIKKI (ca 1060, The Sarashina Diary; tr *As I Crossed a Bridge of Dreams*, 1971), in which she recorded her experiences from childhood. She is also said to be the author of YORU NO NEZAME (ca mid-11th century, Nights of Fitful Waking) and HAMAMATSU CHŪNAGON MONOGATARI (11th century, Tale of the Hamamatsu Middle Counselor).

sugi

(Japanese cedar). *Cryptomeria japonica*. An evergreen tree of the family Pinaceae, common throughout Japan. The largest Japanese conifer, it grows to a height of 40 meters (131 ft) with a straight columnar trunk 2 meters (7 ft) in diameter. Its bark is reddish brown and fissured vertically. The crown has a distinctive conical shape; the short needles are aligned in spiral fashion on twigs. In early spring, the yellowish male flowers and the green, ball-shaped, female flowers are borne on the tips of twigs of the same tree (monoecious), and the fruit turns brown in October.

All *sugi* belong to a single species, but shape or color of needles and bark may vary according to region, giving rise to such names as Akita *sugi*, the cedar of Akita Prefecture, and Yaku *sugi*, the cedar of Yakushima, an island off the coast of Kagoshima Prefecture. The *yawarasugi* (*C. japonica* var. *elegans*) has soft needles which turn reddish brown in winter. The *enkō sugi* (*C. japonica* var. *araucarioides*) has whorled branches which grow long and pendulant to a height of 1 to 4 meters (3–13 ft). The *yoresugi* (*C. japonica* var. *araucarioides* f. *spiralis*) has needles which spiral tightly about twigs and grows to about 2 meters (7 ft).

Some *sugi* grow very large. For example, the larger of a famous pair of *sugi* in Kōchi Prefecture, Shikoku, both more than a thousand years old, is 13 meters (43 ft) in girth. The principal use of *sugi* today is as construction material for buildings, bridges, ships, and furniture. It has been traditionally prized as *sake* cask material for its crisp scent, and its needles were formerly tied together into a large ball which was hung from the eaves of a *sake* shop to serve as a sign. *Sugi* bark was once used for house roofing and is still used for incense powder and incense sticks. MATSUDA Osamu

Sugi Michisuke (1884–1964)

Corporate executive and business leader. Born in Yamaguchi Prefecture. Graduated from Keiō Gijuku (now Keiō University). After working for a time at Kuhara Kōgyōsho, a mining firm, Sugi shifted to the textile business in Ōsaka, serving as an executive in a number of textile firms there. He became president of Yagi Shōten in 1938. He had close connections with the Ōsaka Chamber of Commerce and Industry from 1929, and acted as its chairman from 1946 through 1960. Sugi made great contributions to the resurgence of the Kansai (Ōsaka–Kōbe area) business and industrial community and at the same time promoted foreign trade by helping to establish the Japan External Trade Organization (JETRO) and serving as its chairman. KATSURA Yoshio

Sugimoto Eiichi (1901–1952)

Economist. Born in Tōkyō. After graduating from the Tōkyō University of Commerce (now Hitotsubashi University), Sugimoto studied at the universities of Berlin, Kiel, and Frankfurt, and became a professor at his alma mater upon his return to Japan. He was primarily interested in econometrics, still in its infancy at the time, and his brilliant contributions to the field included a classic analysis of the principles of supply and demand in regard to rice. Sugimoto touched off a series of debates in postwar academic circles by maintaining that the analytical tools of modern economics could be utilized to perfect Marxist economic theory. Sugimoto also contributed to the development of the theory of dynamics. Sugimoto's published works on economics include *Riron keizaigaku no kihon mondai* (1939, Basic Problems of Theoretical Economics) and *Kindai keizaigaku shi* (1953, History of Modern Economics).

YAMADA Katsumi

Sugimura Jihei (fl ca 1681–1703)

Prominent early UKIYO-E print artist and illustrator. The most striking of Hishikawa MORONOBU's followers, Sugimura (who, unlike other traditional Japanese artists, preferred to use his surname on his works) illustrated at least 70 novels and picture books, as well as several series of SHUNGA (erotica) prints. He seems to have specialized in *shunga*, and in this field his flamboyant, decorative style often surpasses Moronobu in erotic effectiveness. His peak years also coincided with the rising popularity of large-sized prints, and his extant works include several of the early masterpieces in this format.

■ ——Richard Lane, *Images from the Floating World* (1978). Richard Lane, *Shunga Books of the Ukiyo-e School: VI—Sugimura Jihei*, eight volumes of reproductions plus text volume (1982).

Richard LANE

Sugimura Kōzō (1895–1948)

Economic theorist. Born in Hokkaidō. After graduating from Tōkyō Higher Commercial School (now Hitotsubashi University), he studied under SŌDA KIICHIRŌ in the school's graduate department. He later lectured on philosophy and economic history as an assistant professor at the Tōkyō University of Commerce (presently also part of Hitotsubashi University). He resigned from his post in 1935 when he failed to obtain committee approval for his doctoral thesis "Keizai shakai no kachironteki kenkyū," which concerned the theory of value. He began to work in business and became a director of the Shanghai Chamber of Commerce and Industry and an auditor of Mitsubishi Shōji (MITSUBISHI CORPORATION). Continuing the work of his mentor Sōda Kiichirō, he was the first to give definition to economic philosophy in Japan. His works on economics include *Keizai tetsugaku no kihon mondai* (1935, Basic Problems of Economic Philosophy) and *Keizai rinri no kōzō* (1938, Structure of Economic Ethics).

YAMADA Katsumi

Sugimura Sojinkan (1872–1945)

Real name Sugimura Kōtarō. Newspaper reporter and essayist. Born in Wakayama Prefecture, Sugimura joined the newspaper ASAHI SHIMBUN in 1903. While in England as a foreign correspondent for the newspaper (1904–05), Sugimura established a reputation for his informative coverage. After returning to Japan, he convinced the *Asahi shimbun* to adopt several features of leading foreign newspapers, such as setting up a research department and a data-checking system. He also persuaded the company to publish reduced-size editions of the newspaper as well as a photogravure magazine. *Sojinkan zenshū*, a 16-volume collection of his articles and essays, was published in 1937–39.

ARASE Yutaka

Suginami Ward

(Suginami Ku). One of the 23 wards of Tōkyō. On the Musashino plateau. During the Edo period (1600–1868), it was a farming area along the Ōme Kaidō (Ōme Highway). Beginning in the 1920s, it became a residential and commercial area, with shopping centers developing around stations of the Chūō Line of the Japanese National Railways. Pop: 542,450.

Sugita Gempaku (1733–1817)

Physician and scholar of WESTERN LEARNING. In 1769 he succeeded his father as personal physician to the *daimyō* of the Obama domain (now part of Fukui Prefecture). As he relates in his book RANGAKU KOTOHAJIME, in 1771 he was invited to witness the dissection of the body of a female criminal executed in Edo (now Tōkyō) and compared his observations with the *Ontleedkundige Tafelen* (1734, Anatomical Tables), a Dutch translation of the German work *Anatomische Tabellen* (1722) by Johann Adam Kulmus (1689–1745). Impressed by the accuracy of the book, he began the following day to translate it into Japanese, aided by MAENO RYŌTAKU, NAKAGAWA JUN'AN, KATSURAGAWA HOSHŪ, and others. Published in 1774, this translation, entitled *Kaitai shinsho* (New Book of Anatomy), aroused great interest in Western scientific knowledge and methods. As the first Japanese translation of a European medical work, it marked the beginning of a new era in the diffusion of Western learning, especially medicine. Many of Sugita's disciples, including ŌTSUKI GENTAKU, played leading roles in this movement.

■ ——Katagiri Kazuo, *Sugita Gempaku* (1971).   Frits Vos

Sugiura Shigetake (1855–1924)

Also known as Sugiura Jūgō. Educator and thinker of the Meiji (1868–1912) and Taishō (1912–26) periods. Born into the family of a Confucian scholar of the Zeze domain in Ōmi Province (now Shiga Prefecture), Sugiura traveled to Tōkyō in 1870 to study at the Daigaku Nankō (the forerunner of Tōkyō University). In 1876 he went to England where he studied for several years under the sponsorship of the Ministry of Education. There he undertook research in chemistry and physics. Upon his return to Japan, Sugiura served as director of the Tōkyō Daigaku Yobimon (the forerunner of the First Higher School), and later for a period as assistant director of the Education Ministry's higher studies division. He also served as an administrator for Kokugakuin University, ran a private school called Shōkōjuku, and established the Tōkyō English Institute (later the Nippon Middle School). Sugiura joined journalist MIYAKE SETSUREI and others in publishing the periodical NIHONJIN (The Japanese) in 1888; this was followed by the tabloid *Nippon shimbun* (Japan News) in 1889. While using these publications to promote nationalist ideology, Sugiura applied the principles of physics in his work to "explain human affairs and to interpret life." Here we can find his peculiar viewpoint: an emphasis on human development rooted in a fusion of Western natural science and nationalist ideology. In his later years, the conservative educator Sugiura lectured the then crown prince and princess (Emperor Hirohito and Empress Nagako) as an imperial household official, a position he held from 1914 to 1921.

TANIKAWA Atsushi

Sugiyama Gen → Sugiyama Hajime

Sugiyama Hajime (1880–1945)

Also known as Sugiyama Gen. General of the Imperial Japanese Army. Born in Fukuoka Prefecture, the son of a former *samurai*. Graduated from the Army Academy in 1900. Holding several important positions, including that of army minister in the first KONOE FUMIMARO cabinet, Sugiyama rose to become chief of the ARMY GENERAL STAFF OFFICE in 1940 and remained in that post until February 1944. He then held the positions of the inspector general of military education and army minister of the KOISO KUNIAKI cabinet. In July 1945 he became commander of the First Theater Army to direct the defense of the Japanese mainland against the anticipated Allied invasion. On 12 September 1945, after finishing preparations for the final dissolution of Japan's military forces, he shot himself in his office; the same day, his wife, the daughter of an army general, killed herself.

KONDŌ Shinji

Sugiyama Naojirō (1878–1966)

Professor of law and founder of comparative legal studies in Japan. Graduate of Tōkyō University. After studying in France, Switzerland, and Germany, he taught at Nagasaki University (then Nagasaki Kōtō Shōgyō Gakkō) from 1908 to 1913. In 1916 he was named the first Japanese professor to teach French law at Tōkyō University. After World War II he was director of the Institute of Comparative Law at Chūō University in Tōkyō. In his theories on comparative jurisprudence, he was strongly influenced by such French scholars as

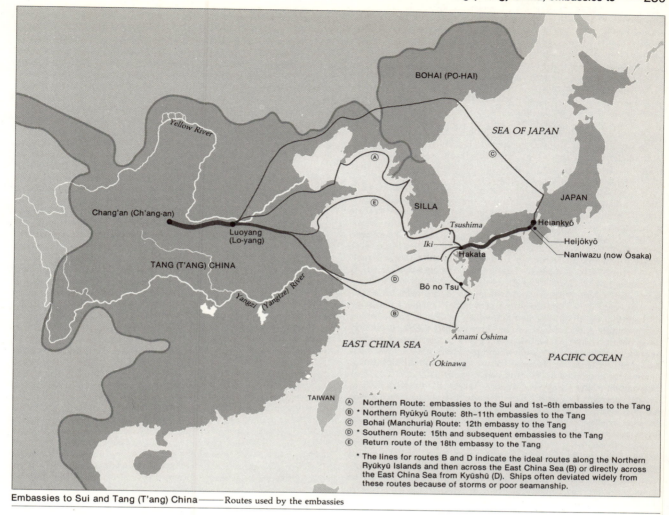

Embassies to Sui and Tang (T'ang) China —— Routes used by the embassies

Ⓐ Northern Route: embassies to the Sui and 1st–6th embassies to the Tang
Ⓑ * Northern Ryūkyū Route: 8th–11th embassies to the Tang
Ⓒ Bohai (Manchuria) Route: 12th embassy to the Tang
Ⓓ * Southern Route: 15th and subsequent embassies to the Tang
Ⓔ Return route of the 18th embassy to the Tang

* The lines for routes B and D indicate the ideal routes along the Northern Ryūkyū Islands and then across the East China Sea (B) or directly across the East China Sea from Kyūshū (D). Ships often deviated widely from these routes because of storms or poor seamanship.

Raymond Saleilles (1855–1912) and François Gény (1861–1959), who stressed free scientific inquiry. Sugiyama insisted that students of foreign law be disinterested and that in adopting foreign systems Japan should first consider the historical sources of each law. His principal publication is *Hōgen to kaishaku* (1957, Source and Interpretation of Law).

TANIGUCHI Yasuhei

Sugiyama Sampū (1647–1732)

HAIKU poet of the early Edo period. A prosperous fish wholesaler in Edo (now Tōkyō), he was a faithful disciple of BASHŌ, giving him both moral and financial support. Bashō's cottage in Fukagawa (now part of Tōkyō) had originally been a warehouse of Sampū's, and was named "Bashōan" after a plantain tree *(bashō)* in its yard; from this Bashō took his pen name. Sampū's main collection of haiku is *Sampū kushū* (1785).

sugoroku

A board game like backgammon played by two or more persons using dice. There are two main varieties of *sugoroku*. In *bansugoroku* ("board *sugoroku*"), introduced from China in the 8th century, two people advance their pieces (15 each) across a wooden board according to the numbers on the dice. The player who succeeds in advancing all his pieces into enemy territory wins. Popular at the court and in the houses of the nobility, it went out of fashion in the Edo period (1600–1868). *Esugoroku* ("picture *sugoroku*"), developed during the 17th century, is played on a large sheet of paper divided into sections with various colored illustrations. The first *esugoroku* games had religious themes and were didactic in nature: called *Jōdo sugoroku* ("Pure Land *sugoroku*") and illustrated with religious scenes, the goal was to reach heaven and avoid being dropped into hell. Today these picture *sugoroku* have illustrations

of popular tourist spots or pictures of famous theater personalities. The game is mainly played at New Year's by children.

SAITŌ Ryōsuke

Sugup'a

(J: Shukyūha; Conservative Faction). A Korean political clique active in the late 19th century that advocated the maintenance of traditional ties with China. It is sometimes referred to as the Sadae party, because it backed the policy of *sadae* (J: *jidai*; literally, "serve the great") that symbolized Korea's ritual submission to imperial China and adherence to Confucian ideology. The TAEWŎN'GUN, father of Korean King KOJONG, was a strong supporter of this group. The clique was involved in numerous clashes with advocates of Westernization between 1880 and 1900. See KOREA AND JAPAN: early modern relations.

C. Kenneth QUINONES

Sui and Tang (T'ang) China, embassies to

(*kenzuishi* and *kentōshi*). Japanese diplomatic embassies sent to China during the Sui dynasty (589–618) and the Tang (T'ang) dynasty (618–907). Between 600 and 614, 4, or possibly 5, missions were sent to the Sui, and in the period 630–894 at least 19 missions to the Tang were appointed; of the latter, however, some did not actually make the trip, and others were not designated *kentōshi*. In addition to their diplomatic functions, these embassies fostered trade and cultural exchange with China.

Envoys from WA, an early name for Japan, are recorded sporadically in Chinese histories from as early as the end of the 2nd century BC. Such embassies appear to have been particularly frequent during the 5th century when the Japanese were very much involved in affairs on the Korean peninsula (see KAYA).

Embassies to the Sui —— Although short-lived, the Sui dynasty unified China after nearly 400 years of political division and provided a model for the Japanese, who had already begun to adapt China's more advanced culture to their own needs. Japan's first mission to the Sui in 600 was a carryover from an earlier age, as it seems to have been intended to gain Chinese support for Japanese activities in Korea. In 607 the regent Prince SHŌTOKU appointed the court official ONO NO IMOKO to lead a second embassy, which returned to Japan the following year accompanied by the Sui envoy Pei Shiqing (P'ei Shih-ch'ing). The embassies did result in diplomatic relations, but their real significance was largely in the cultural sphere.

In two important respects missions to the Sui set the pattern for later relations with the Tang. First, the Japanese did not readily submit to the Chinese form of international relations, which treated all foreign nations as tributary vassals of China. The embassy of 607 bore a message in which the Japanese sovereign addressed his Chinese counterpart as an equal, and the latter was greatly affronted. When the Japanese envoy returned home, he claimed that Korean brigands had stolen the Chinese emperor's message of reply. More likely, he had diplomatically "lost" a document that the Japanese sovereign in turn would have found insulting. Problems of this sort recurred when Japan attempted to deal with the Tang as an equal.

A second feature of Japan's later missions to the Sui, repeated in embassies to the Tang, is that they included students sent to learn more about Chinese culture and institutions. Some were lay scholars, but many were Buddhist priests sent to perfect their knowledge of that religion, which was then flourishing in China. For example, eight scholars and Buddhist priests accompanied the third mission (608), among them such well-known figures as TAKAMUKO NO KUROMARO, MINABUCHI NO SHŌAN, and the priest SŌMIN; these men had great influence on Japanese culture and on the administrative innovations embodied in the TAIKA REFORM of 645.

Embassies to the Tang —— Japanese relations with the new Tang dynasty began smoothly with the first embassy of 630, which was honored with a Chinese escort on its return. In the mid-7th century, however, friendly relations were briefly interrupted when China and Japan allied themselves with opposing sides in a Korean internal conflict. In 663 a Japanese fleet was defeated by a joint Chinese-Korean force in the Battle of HAKUSUKINOE, and for the next 10 years the Japanese built up their defenses in fear of a Chinese invasion. But China's interests lay elsewhere, and after a flurry of diplomatic exchange—six Chinese missions to Japan and three Japanese missions to China—the tension was eased.

In the 8th century the Japanese resumed sending envoys to the Tang in a peaceful and increasingly grand manner. A typical embassy came to be led by an ambassador (kentō taishi) and vice-ambassador (kentō fukushi), plus one administrative officer (kentō hangan) for each of four ships. To make a good impression, particularly accomplished courtiers were selected for these posts, and indeed Chinese records make special note of the learning and deportment of the Japanese envoys. In addition to such officers and the customary scholars and priests, a variety of specialists were also sent to China. Some were men whose skills were needed to complete the mission successfully, including navigators, carpenters, physicians, diviners, archers, and interpreters. Others, such as painters, musicians, and jewelers, were sent to perfect their arts. Of the students and priests, a few remained in China for long periods (see ABE NO NAKAMARO) and many, upon their return, made important contributions to Japan's increasingly sinified culture (see KIBI NO MAKIBI; GEMBŌ; ENNIN). The number of men sent on a mission sometimes exceeded 600, almost half of them sailors needed to row the vessels when winds were unfavorable.

The voyages to China were very dangerous, in part because of poor seamanship. The Japanese tended to set sail when the monsoon winds were blowing in the wrong direction, hence the many oarsmen. In addition, after Japan's 7th-century troubles in Korea, Japanese ships were no longer welcome there and so had to sail directly to China. This was an exceedingly difficult voyage for Japan's primitive ships, many of which were lost at sea.

Abandonment of the Embassies —— In 894 the eminent scholar SUGAWARA NO MICHIZANE was named ambassador to the Tang. He responded by proposing that the mission be canceled because of political instability in China—the Tang dynasty collapsed not long afterward—and because the journey was too dangerous. His proposal was accepted, and regular diplomatic relations were not resumed until the 15th century.

Japan had many reasons for abandoning its missions to China. In addition to those stated by Michizane, there were economic consid-

Embassies to Sui and Tang (T'ang) China

Embassies to Sui China

Year of departure from Japan	Year of return to Japan	Comments
?	?	In 600, Chinese sources note a Japanese envoy at the Sui Court; not mentioned in Japanese sources
607	608	Accompanied by Chinese envoy on return
608	609	Escorted Chinese envoy back to China
614	615	Mentioned only in Chinese sources; not accepted by some scholars

Embassies to Tang China

Year of departure from Japan	Year of return to Japan	Comments
630	632	Accompanied by Chinese envoy on return
653	654	Two ships sent with separate ambassadors; one ship lost
654	655	Departed before previous mission returned
659	661	One of two ships lost
665	667	Escorted Chinese envoy back to China
667	668	Escorted Chinese envoy, possibly only as far as Korea
669	?	
702	704	One official did not return until 707, another not until 718 with the next mission
717	718	First time four ships sent; Kibi no Makibi and Abe no Nakamaro sent as students
733	734–736	Two of four ships lost; one returned late; Kibi no Makibi brought back
752	753–754	One ship drifted to Annam; Japanese ambassador eventually entered service of Chinese court; Chinese priest Ganjin brought to Japan
759	761	Unsuccessful attempt to bring previous Japanese ambassador back to Japan; accompanied by Chinese envoy on return
761 762	— — }	Two missions appointed to escort Chinese envoy back to China with military supplies requested by Chinese court then facing civil war; both missions abandoned because of bad weather
777	778–779	One ship lost; accompanied by Chinese envoy on return
779	781	Escorted Chinese envoy back to China
804	805–806	Brought priests Saichō and Kūkai to China; two ships departed late after having been blown back to Japan; one ship lost; another brought Kūkai back to Japan
838	839–840	One ship lost; brought priest Ennin to China; returned on Korean ships
—	—	In 894, Sugawara no Michizane named ambassador to the Tang, but at his suggestion mission was abandoned

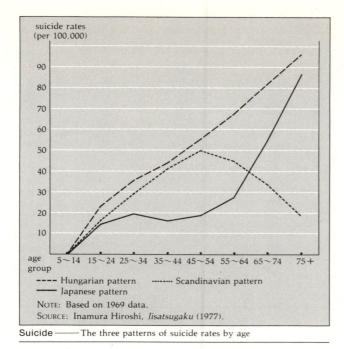

suicide rates
(per 100,000)

age
group 5~14 15~24 25~34 35~44 45~54 55~64 65~74 75+

---- Hungarian pattern   .... Scandinavian pattern
—— Japanese pattern

NOTE: Based on 1969 data.
SOURCE: Inamura Hiroshi, *Jisatsugaku* (1977).

Suicide —— The three patterns of suicide rates by age

erations. The opportunity for trade had been an important aspect of the missions, but in the 9th century Chinese merchants began to appear in Japan, providing safer and cheaper means to acquire goods from China. Also, throughout that century, the Japanese received regular missions from the Manchurian kingdom of BOHAI (Po-hai), and so, even without sending missions, they were able to maintain regular diplomatic contact with the Asian mainland.

From the mid-9th century, Japan's enthusiasm for Chinese culture gradually began to wane, and the Chinese cultural elements imported by the missions and adopted by the Japanese came to be either assimilated or replaced by indigenous counterparts. Although the Japanese did not completely lose interest in China, they felt less need to maintain active diplomatic relations.

📖 ——Mori Katsumi, *Kentōshi* (1955). Edwin O. Reischauer, *Ennin's Travels in T'ang China* (1955). Ryusaku Tsunoda, tr, L. Carrington Goodrich, ed, *Japan in the Chinese Dynastic Histories* (1951).

Robert BORGEN

suibokuga → ink painting

suicide

Japan has a relatively high suicide rate, a characteristic shared with other industrialized nations. In addition, however, it has traditions of ritual suicide (HARAKIRI; more properly called *seppuku*) and plural suicide *(shinjū)*, that have attracted world attention to the moral and aesthetic attitudes Japanese people have held, and to some extent still hold, regarding suicide.

Generally speaking, highly industrialized countries in central and northern Europe (Hungary, Austria, Czechoslovakia, Germany, Sweden, Denmark, Finland) as well as Japan have historically shown higher rates of suicide, whereas most Latin American and some southern European countries (Italy, Spain, Portugal) manifest consistently lower rates. France, the United States, and Canada rank somewhere in the middle.

Historical Trends —— Japan has long been known for a highly stylized and ritualized form of self-disembowelment known as *seppuku* or *harakiri*. For centuries it had been a badge of courage and honor reserved for the *samurai* class. Even today it is a source of popular attention and inspiration for numerous plays, novels, television dramas, and movies. During World War II, countless numbers of Japanese officers committed *seppuku* in the South Pacific. Immediately after Japan's surrender to the Allies, some patriotic men and women committed *seppuku* on the grounds of the Imperial Palace as an "apology" to the emperor for having lost the war. In 1970 the world was shocked by the *seppuku* of MISHIMA YUKIO, one of the most celebrated novelists in postwar Japan, following his failure to

trigger a coup d'etat. Nevertheless, *seppuku,* long practiced among the samurai in feudal Japan and among military officers after the Meiji Restoration (1868), has virtually disappeared in postwar Japan.

The first official statistics on suicide in Japan were compiled in 1882. The suicide rate during the Meiji and Taishō periods (1868–1926) remained constant, ranging from 16 to 19 per 100,000 in 1902–12, and 17 to 20 per 100,000 in 1912–26, accounting for 1 percent of total deaths. The rate slowly began to inch up to 20–22 per 100,000 in 1925–35. The year 1936 was marked by a coup d'etat, the Niniroku Jiken (see FEBRUARY 26TH INCIDENT), which pushed Japan onto the road to militarism. The suicide rate began to decline steadily thereafter, finally plummeting to an all-time low of 12 per 100,000 in 1943. Such a decline is consistent with worldwide trends, which show suicide rates usually decreasing sharply in times of war and revolution. After the end of World War II, the rate began to climb up again, from 15.7 per 100,000 in 1947 to an all-time high of 25.7 in 1958, accounting for 3.5 percent of total deaths and occupying the top rank in suicide rates in the world. After 1958, however, the rate began to decline again, to 13–17 per 100,000 in 1962–67, with the lowest postwar rate (13) in 1967. Since 1967 it has been on a steady rise again, registering 15.6 in 1970 and 17.3 in 1973. Though Japan no longer has the highest suicide rate, it still ranks as one of the more suicide-prone countries of the world.

Despite fluctuations in overall rates over the years, one still finds, when age, sex, and regional rates are compared, surprising degrees of constancy and similarity between suicide rates today and the first reliable statistics taken in 1882.

Some Characteristics of Suicide in Japan ——(1) *Age.* There seems to be a definite correlation between age and suicide in most countries. At present there are three discernible patterns of suicide rates by age: the Hungarian, Scandinavian, and Japanese models (see graph). In the Hungarian pattern, the suicide rate increases steadily and sharply with age. Such patterns are equally observable in other Eastern and Western European countries: France, Austria, Belgium, the Netherlands, West Germany, Italy, Portugal, Bulgaria, Czechoslovakia, and Yugoslavia. In the Scandinavian pattern, the rate increases steadily with age but begins to decrease after age 60; such trends are observed in Finland, Norway, Denmark, Sweden, the United Kingdom, Australia, New Zealand, the United States, and Canada. The Japanese pattern shows a bimodal trend (i.e., with two peaks) in which the rate increases steadily with age and reaches one peak in the age group 25–34, tapers off slightly in middle age, and then rises again very sharply after age 55. Such bimodality is also observed in other countries, mostly Asian and Latin American (Taiwan, Hong Kong, Singapore, the Philippines, Thailand, Iceland, Chile, Colombia, Dominican Republic, Mexico, Panama, and Venezuela).

In recent years there has been a general increase in the suicide rate among youths in Japan in the age group 10–19. For example, in one three-day period in January 1979, 13 children between 11 and 17 years of age committed suicide. The figure for youthful suicide in 1979 surpassed that of 1978, when 900 people under 19 killed themselves, an average of nearly 3 a day. This is a big increase from the 784 young people who killed themselves in 1977. It is still too early to tell whether the recent increase in youthful suicide in Japan indicates a long-term trend or a temporary aberration.

(2) *Sex differential.* It has generally been observed that in most countries the male suicide rate outranks that of the female by at least two to one. Suicide in Japan, however, has always been characterized by high female rates. Especially in the postwar years, suicide was the primary cause of death for females 20–29 years of age and the second major cause for females aged 15–19 and 30–34. The rate for women over 65 is very high: 85 per 100,000 in 1936, 84 in 1940, 105 in 1950, 92 in 1955, 72 in 1960, 80 in 1965, 73 in 1970, and 77 in 1971. High female suicide rates are also observed in Taiwan, Singapore, Czechoslovakia, Thailand, and Hong Kong.

(3) *Region.* In Japan higher suicide rates are generally seen in rural areas rather than in urban areas and cities, showing a reverse trend in comparison to industrialized countries in the West. In terms of prefectures, higher rates have usually been observed in Wakayama, Kōchi, Shimane, Shiga, Kagawa, and Iwate, whereas Miyagi, Tōkyō, Ibaraki, Saga, Fukushima, and Saitama have lower rates. Likewise, the Kyōto-Ōsaka-Kōbe metropolitan region has had higher rates than the more populous Tōkyō-Yokohama metropolitan area.

(4) *Marital status.* For both males and females, suicide rates are generally lower for the married than for those without spouses. Japan's suicide rates can be ranked from the highest to the lowest as

follows: (i) widows and widowers, (ii) the divorced, (iii) the separated, (iv) the nonmarried, and (v) the married. Evidently, the loss of a spouse through death or the breakup of a marriage as well as the single status all seem to be correlated to suicide rates. Family size has also been found, in both Japan and other countries, to correlate negatively with suicide—that is, the more children there are in the family, the lower the suicide rate.

(5) *Occupation.* In many countries it has often been observed that suicide rates are higher for those employed in business and industry than for those engaged in agriculture and fishing. The rates are also higher for those who are in upper managerial positions, proprietors of business, and highly trained professionals. In Japan, however, the rates are generally higher for the unemployed, unskilled, or semiskilled workers, employees in small enterprises, fishermen, and farmers.

(6) *Plural suicide.* Collective orientation and group cohesion are two of the hallmarks of Japanese society and are reflected in the prevalence of plural suicides. Plural suicides may be divided into two major types: (i) group suicide, involving a group of people unrelated to one another, and (ii) *shinjū*, involving a small number of closely related persons.

Group suicide was common in times of war in feudal Japan and during World War II. It has occurred among the members of tightly knit cohesive socio-religious groups and communities; examples in Japan include the many incidents during World War II of collective suicide by Japanese fighting men as well as civilians on Saipan, Okinawa, and other Pacific islands and the KAMIKAZE SPECIAL ATTACK FORCE. Since the end of the war, however, there have been no incidences of collective suicide in Japan.

Shinjū may be subdivided into *jōshi* (love suicide) and *ikka shinjū* (family suicide). *Jōshi* typically involves two lovers who may be either heterosexual or homosexual. It was fairly common in feudal times. Stifling customs and rigid social codes in the Edo period (1600–1868), for instance, resulted in numerous love suicides, providing a rich source of material for plays and novels. The gifted playwright CHIKAMATSU MONZAEMON (1653–1724) popularized some of these love suicides in his plays. Though Japan's social codes have become far less rigid and social relations more casual and relaxed than in prewar times, *jōshi* remains a frequent form of plural suicide in contemporary Japan.

Ikka shinjū involves at least two persons in a family. It can take such forms as husband-wife, father-child, mother-child, and parents-child. Inadequate social welfare measures, relative indifference to, and a lack of concern for, those outside one's own family and kin, and the long-standing Japanese tradition of considering one's children as one's property—all these circumstances seem to lead some parents to think that it is more "humane" to take their children along in suicide than to leave them behind.

Love suicide and family suicide can further be classified according to whether the suicide is committed by mutual consent or not. When it is committed by mutual consent, it is called *gōi shinjū*, and when it is done without the consent of the partners, it is classified as *muri shinjū* (forced *shinjū*). Hence, *muri shinjū* is a combined form of homicide and suicide. In a love suicide, therefore, lovers may kill their partners and then commit suicide immediately afterward; in a family suicide, the parents kill the children first and then commit suicide afterward.

Theories of Suicide —— At present there is no definitive and uniform theory of suicide that is cross-culturally valid and applicable to all cases of suicide. To date, theories of suicide are generally divided into two major types in terms of etiology: psychoanalytic and sociological. Psychoanalytic theory and its derivative postulates, based mainly on observations and analysis of individual case histories, are primarily credited to Sigmund Freud. It assumes that the human psyche has dual impulses, *eros* (life instinct) and *thanatos* (death instinct), both of which coexist in the individual. The death instinct is primarily destructive and is expressed as aggression and hostility. When it is turned against others, it may take the form of homicide; when it is internally directed against the self, it is often expressed in the form of suicide.

A major sociological approach to suicide comes from a theory originally proposed by the French sociologist Emile Durkheim at the turn of the century. It assumes that the phenomenon of suicide is an index of an individual's integration into social groups and hence into society at large. It presents a classification of suicide into three major types: egoistic, altruistic, and anomic suicide. Egoistic suicide occurs among people who are characterized by excessive individualism and are least integrated into social groups in terms of social

Suicide

Plural Suicide Incidents by Type, 1956–1963

Type	Combination	A. Total incidents of plural suicides[1]	B. Total incidents of homicide-suicides[2]	B as % of A
Family suicide (*ikka shinjū*)	husband-wife	810	108	13.3
	father-child	241	197	81.7
	mother-child	1,542	1,280	83.0
	parents-child	217	142	65.4
Love suicide (*jōshi*)	male-female	4,937	337	6.8
	male-male	129	9	6.9
	female-female	232	13	5.6

[1] *Shinjū*; includes both plural suicides by mutual consent (*gōi shinjū*) and homicide-suicides (*muri shinjū*).
[2] *Muri shinjū*; cases in which one or more of the partners kill the others (e.g., their lover or their children), then kill themselves.
SOURCE: Okazaki Ayanori, "Jisatsu no seitaigaku" in Ōhara Kenshirō, ed, *Jisatsugaku 3: Jisatsu no shakaigaku, seitaigaku* (1978).

bonds and relations. Altruistic suicide is seen among people who have an excessive sense of duty to the community and whose social and personal existence is inexorably tied to the existence of their community; in short, it is a case of an individual's overintegration into society. The anomic suicide occurs when society and social norms lose their control over some members of society. It takes place among people who are suddenly thrown off balance, their accustomed lifestyles and values disrupted by swift and massive social change such as might accompany sudden prosperity or economic depression.

Another sociological theory is a combination of both psychoanalytical and sociological orientations. Proposed by the American sociologists Andrew H. Henry and James F. Short, this theory assumes an inverse correlation between homicide and suicide. In other words, in a highly formalized and cohesive society, where externalization of aggression and hostility in the form of homicide would be discouraged and curbed, aggression would be internalized and expressed in the form of suicide. In such a society one would expect low homicide rates and high suicide rates. Conversely, in a loosely organized and highly heterogeneous society one would expect high homicide rates and low suicide rates.

Durkheim's theory suffers from vagueness, making it almost impossible to study suicide in terms of inner motives, but his typology of suicide is useful. Many incidents of *seppuku*, and in the last war the suicide flights of *kamikaze* pilots and group suicides, are the altruistic type of suicide. This altruistic suicide represents a supreme act of responsibility and of belonging in which individual behavior is subordinate to the needs of a cohesive society. In this form of suicide, the individual's purpose or meaning is defined so strongly in terms larger than himself that he readily sacrifices his life in the name of his social role. If altruistic suicide explains many incidents of suicide before and during the last war, egoistic and anomic suicides seem to explain many suicides in postwar years, including those of many Japanese writers.

The theory proposed by Henry and Short, which assumes an inverse relationship between homicide and suicide, has been a source of lively controversy among suicidologists for decades. Some data seem to support the theory, whereas other data refute it. In the case of Japan, the relationship between homicide and suicide was found to be parallel rather than inverse. Although the suicide rate is much higher than the homicide rate (19.6 versus 3.5 in 1960, and 15.6 versus 1.5 in 1970), homicide and suicide rates in Japan either increase or decrease together, as has also been the case in France.

In addition to the classical theories, some other theoretical approaches to suicide in Japan have been proposed by behavioral and social scientists. One theory emphasizes the importance of AMAE (the wish for dependency) in the personality formation of the Japanese as a clue to suicide (Doi, 1974). Another approach considers the weak ego-formation in the Japanese personality as a major contributing factor to a propensity for suicide (Iga, 1967). According to these two theories, the fundamental psychological orientation of the

Japanese is a desire for dependency nurtured by the warm, indulgent, and consuming love of the mother and constantly reinforced by stories of the brutal and cruel outside world. The need for dependency is further enhanced by an authoritarian and group-oriented social structure that demands strict conformity and selflessness. Selflessness is upheld as one of the supreme virtues and ideals among the Japanese and runs deep in Japan's religious and moral values. But dependency contributes to weak ego-structure in the personality, which in turn predisposes a person to society's demand for conformity and selflessness and finally to the elimination of the self by suicide.

Another theory holds that suicide in Japan stems from excessive "role narcissism." According to this idea, suicide is a response to the sudden frustration of a constant need for social recognition and response deriving from a narcissistic preoccupation with the self in respect to status and social role. Many Japanese tend to become excessively involved with their social roles, which become the ultimate meaning of life for them. Such individuals are often unable to cope with social disturbances or personal mistakes that may bring about a change in role definition (DeVos, 1973).

Suicide in Japan may also be understood in terms of the philosophy and aesthetics of death long held by the Japanese (Lebra, 1976; Fusé, 1978). In Japan a heroic, romantic, aesthetic, and moral aura surrounds death in general and voluntary death in particular. Circumstances and accounts of suicides in Japan suggest that the Japanese resort to suicide often to break through a blocked communication channel so that a person's ideas, beliefs, or sufferings can become known through his death. This may explain some of the underlying motives behind love suicide, family suicide, and other suicides related to interpersonal difficulties.

▬▬——George DeVos, "Role Narcissism and the Etiology of Japanese Suicide," in George DeVos, *Socialization for Achievement* (1973). Doi Takeo, *Amae no kōzō* (1971), tr as *Anatomy of Dependence* (1973). Emile Durkheim, *Le Suicide* (1897). Sigmund Freud, *Civilization and Its Discontents* (1930). Toyomasa Fusé, "To Be or Not to Be: Analysis of Suicide in Japan in Comparative Perspective," *Stress* 1.3 (1980). Andrew F. Henry and James F. Short, *Homicide and Suicide* (1954). Iga Mamoru, "Japanese Adolescent Suicide and Social Structure," in Edwin S. Scheidman, ed, *Essays in Self-Destruction* (1967). Inamura Hiroshi, *Jisatsugaku* (1977). Inamura Hiroshi, *Jisatsu no shinri to jisatsu bōshi* (1978). Takie S. Lebra, *Japanese Patterns of Behavior* (1976). Ōhara Kenshirō, *Nihon no jisatsu* (1965). Ōhara Kenshirō, *Shinjūkō* (1973). Ōhara Kenshirō, *Jisatsugaku*, vols 1–5 (1974–75). Toyomasa FUSÉ

suigun

General term for naval forces in Japan from ancient times to the 1850s before the advent of a modern navy. According to the chronicle NIHON SHOKI, the military commander ABE NO HIRAFU led a number of naval expeditions between 658 and 660 in a successful campaign to subdue the EZO tribes of northern Japan. Abe's navy was, however, defeated in 663 at the Battle of HAKUSUKINOE in Korea. In the Heian period (794–1185) sea forces were maintained by strong local families along the coastal areas of the Inland Sea and northern Kyūshū. They participated in the Taira–Minamoto War (1180–85) and played an important role in the Battle of DANNOURA. Naval forces were also mobilized at the time of the MONGOL INVASIONS OF JAPAN in the late 13th century. During the Edo period (1600–1868), because of the policy of NATIONAL SECLUSION, daimyō were prohibited from building large ships. Some domains did have small programs of naval instruction, but they were of no value in actual warfare. After the mid-1850s, when the Tokugawa shogunate began to modernize its military forces in the face of foreign military pressure, the term *kaigun* (navy) was used.

suijakuga

A genre of Shintō paintings derived from Buddhist iconography, often showing Shintō deities (KAMI) portrayed with, or in the form of, their Buddhist avatars. This eclectic genre developed in the Heian period (794–1185) in response to the increasing popularity of Buddhism. Shintō had no independent tradition of pictorial representation, and these paintings were based on the belief that Shintō *kami* were incarnations of Buddhist deities (see HONJI SUIJAKU). The oldest surviving *suijakuga* date from the Kamakura period (1185–1333), when the genre flourished; later examples are generally of less aesthetic interest. *Suijakuga* were anonymous and were often in the "shrine mandala" format, depicting a shrine and its natural setting along with related deities. Some *suijakuga* portrayed Shintō or Buddhist deities alone, without a shrine. The most notable examples of this genre are the Kasuga Shrine Mandala (Nōman'in, city of Sakurai, Nara Prefecture) and the Kumano Mandala (Nezu Art Museum, Tōkyō), both dating from the Kamakura period. See also SHINTŌ ART.

suijin

A type of god whose domain is water; known variously as god of the river, god of the waterfall, god of the well, and so forth. Dragons and serpents are commonly regarded as incarnations of the water god, while the mischievous KAPPA, an imaginary creature combining the features of a human, frog, and turtle, may also be a degenerate form of the water deity. Since water is absolutely essential for the cultivation of rice, many rice-planting songs refer to the gods of the fields (TA NO KAMI) or of rice harvests as having been born of the sun and a female water deity. In farming communities in Japan, special fraternities *(suijinkō)* are established to see that the deity is properly honored. In some households a stone statue of a *suijin* is placed near the well. Festivals honoring water gods are held in June and December throughout the country; vegetables such as cucumbers are offered, and in some areas rice cakes are tossed into the river to ward off floods and other disasters. ŌTŌ Tokihiko

Suijinroku

Collection of the financial records of the Tokugawa shogunate (1603–1867); published in 1890. It was compiled at the behest of Finance Minister MATSUKATA MASAYOSHI by KATSU KAISHŪ and a team of men who had been involved with shogunal finances. Besides containing data on the land system, irrigation, rice yields, population, foreign trade, currency, and commerce, it is an important source of information on the financial policies of the Tokugawa regime. A supplement, the *Suijin yoroku,* was published later in the same year.

Suika Shintō

An eclectic school of Shintō founded by YAMAZAKI ANSAI (1619–82). Ordained as a Buddhist monk at Myōshinji, a leading Zen monastery, Yamazaki returned to lay life in 1646 to devote himself to the study of the Zhu Xi (Chu Hsi) school of Confucianism (see SHUSHIGAKU), eventually becoming a resident scholar in the household of the influential *daimyō* of Aizu, Hoshina Masayuki. Having developed a serious interest in Shintō in his twenties, Yamazaki in his fifties traveled about Japan studying the doctrines of the major schools. Among his teachers were such eminent Shintō thinkers as Yoshikawa Koretari (the founder of the Kikkawa Shintō school), Deguchi Nobuyoshi (a prominent exponent of WATARAI SHINTŌ), and Kawabe Kiyonaga (the chief priest of the Grand Shrine of Ise). The school that ultimately emerged from Yamazaki's studies represented a grand synthesis of Neo-Confucian metaphysical, cosmological, and ethical concepts with the doctrinal traditions of various Shintō schools, notably the Yoshida, Kikkawa, Watarai, and Tsuchimikado.

The school is called Suika ("grace and protection") in honor of Yamazaki, who was given this appellation by his teacher Yoshikawa Koretari in 1671. The term *suika,* which in Yamazaki's view signified the essence of Shintō, is taken from a passage in the *Yamatohime no Mikoto seiki* (one of the five scriptures of Watarai Shintō), which states, "To receive divine grace *(sui),* prayer must be foremost in your mind; to enjoy the protection *(ka)* of the deities, uprightness must be the root of your conduct." From Neo-Confucianism Yamazaki borrowed the Chinese concept of *jing (ching;* J: *kei;* reverence), which he held to be the basis of all human behavior. He also appropriated the Neo-Confucian Chinese notion of *li* (J: *ri),* "the all-pervading and unifying principle," to establish the fundamental unity between the Shintō deities and man, as well as between the emperor and his subjects. Despite the heavy reliance on Chinese concepts in his interpretation of the Japanese creation myths, Yamazaki stressed the uniqueness and divinity of the imperial line, which he said must be preserved and protected above all else. His followers, who numbered in the thousands, spread his ideas throughout Japan after his death. Although Suika Shintō was criticized by the great scholar of National Learning MOTOORI NORINAGA (1730–1801) because of its philologically unsound and often irrational reading of the early classics, its ideas nevertheless exerted a great influence on the Mito school of historical scholarship as well as on HIRATA ATSU-TANE (1776–1843), a leading exponent of Restoration Shintō, and contributed to the movement that led to the divinization of the emperor and overthrow of the shogunate. *Stanley WEINSTEIN*

suiko

(loans). Loans of public and private goods, often seed rice, made to peasants in Japan from the 7th through 12th centuries. The loans originated with the practice of wealthy individuals lending food and seed to peasants as relief in the spring and summer before the harvest. Religious institutions, provincial governors, and eventually the government itself came to extend such loans to peasants at interest rates that varied from 30 to 100 percent annually. Private lenders generally charged higher interest rates. *Suiko* were widely used by the mid-7th century; an edict issued in 675 specifies that public loans (*kusuiko*) be limited to poorer peasants.

Since many borrowers were unable to repay their loans, they were forced to sell their lands to pay off their debts. The heavy burden of interest caused many peasants to abandon their land and flee to other districts. Repeated government measures to deal with this problem by prohibiting private loans (*shisuiko*) or by offering compensatory tax reductions generally failed. Indeed, the government realized that interest from such loans could be an important source of revenue, and eventually the peasants were forced to take loans from the government. By the 12th century the government was collecting "interest" on permanent "loans" that were never repaid. In effect, such government loans had become a part of the tax burden. *Philip BROWN*

Suiko, Empress (554–628)

Reigning empress (*tennō*), the 33rd sovereign in the traditional count (which includes several nonhistorical emperors); reigned 593–628. The third daughter of Emperor KIMMEI (509–571; r 531 or 539 to 571), her mother came from the powerful SOGA FAMILY. She became empress (*kōgō*) to Emperor Bidatsu (r 572–585), her half-brother. When Emperor Sushun (r 587–592; another half-brother) was killed in a plot masterminded by her uncle SOGA NO UMAKO, Suiko ascended the throne with the support of her maternal kinsmen. She ruled with the help of her nephew Prince SHŌTOKU.

Suiko's reign saw the establishment of the so-called twelve cap ranks (KAN'I JŪNIKAI), the promulgation of the SEVENTEEN-ARTICLE CONSTITUTION, the beginning of diplomatic contact with the Sui dynasty of China (see SUI AND TANG [T'ANG] CHINA, EMBASSIES TO), the compilation of the national histories TENNŌKI AND KOKKI, the building of the HŌRYŪJI and other temples, and a general efflorescence of Buddhist arts. The early part of her reign was marked by political tension and growing antagonism between the Soga, who were eager to accept Buddhist culture, and religious conservatives like the MONONOBE and Nakatomi families. It may be that Suiko's elevation to the throne was meant to maintain a balance of power among contending factions. According to the chronicle *Nihon shoki* (720), even in a period so steeped in Buddhist influence, Suiko did not neglect the proper veneration of Shintō deities, and she strictly regulated the activities of monks and nuns. She also drew a sharp line between sovereign and subject, on one occasion refusing Soga no Umako's request for a large tract of land near his birthplace. *KITAMURA Bunji*

suiren → water lilies

Sui shu

(J: *Zuisho*). History of the Sui dynasty (589–618) of China, compiled in the mid-7th century. Its chapter "Records of the Eastern Barbarians" ("Dongyi zhuan" or "Tung-i chuan"; J: "Tōiden") contains a section on "the country of Wo" (J: Wakoku; see WA), or Japan, which is called in Japanese "Tōiden Wakoku no jō" or "Zuisho wakokuden." Much of the general information on Japan in this section is taken from such earlier Chinese histories as *Hou Han shu* (History of the Later Han Dynasty), *Wei lüe* (Wei lüeh; Summary of the Wei Dynasty), the WEI ZHI (Wei chih; Records of the Wei Dynasty) section of *Sanguo zhi* (San-kuo chih; History of the Three Kingdoms), and *Song shu* (Sung shu; History of the [Liu-] Song Dynasty [420–479]). Nonetheless, *Sui shu* contains valuable records

of Sino-Japanese diplomatic relations in the late 6th and early 7th centuries, as well as objective descriptions of Japan absent from early Japanese chronicles, and is thus an important historical source. —— Ryusaku Tsunoda, tr, and L. C. Goodrich, ed, *Japan in the Chinese Dynastic Histories* (1951). *KITAMURA Bunji*

Suita

City in central Ōsaka Prefecture, central Honshū. A residential suburb of Ōsaka, Suita has many metal, paper, chemical, and other industrial plants, including a brewery of the Asahi Breweries, Ltd. Located in its northern section are Kansai University and Senri New Town, with a population of about 150,000 and an area of 1,160 hectares (2,865 acres). East of Senri New Town is the former site of the Ōsaka EXPO '70. Pop: 332,413.

Suita Incident

A disturbance of 24–25 June 1952 created by leftist groups in Suita, near the American military base in Itami, Ōsaka Prefecture. On 24 June, the eve of the second anniversary of the outbreak of the Korean War, about 1,300 demonstrators gathered at Toyonaka to protest the presence of American military bases and the continuation of the war. After the rally, several hundred went on to Suita station. On the way they damaged police stations and patrol cars, throwing stones and Molotov cocktails. In the ensuing confrontation, 42 policemen and 12 demonstrators were injured. Of 102 tried, 46 were found guilty in 1968 under the Riot Law. The incident was ultimately regarded as a result of the decision by the mainstream faction of the JAPAN COMMUNIST PARTY to resort to violence in pursuit of their goals.

Suiyuan Incident

(Suien Jiken). Military excursion into Inner Mongolia by the Japanese GUANDONG (KWANTUNG) ARMY in November 1936. Seeking to create a buffer zone between MANCHUKUO (the Japanese-controlled puppet state in Manchuria) and China, the Japanese government had earlier called for the neutralization of five provinces of North China—Shandong (Shantung), Hebei (Hopeh), Shanxi (Shansi), Chahar, and Suiyuan. The Guandong Army had also fostered an anti-Chinese Inner-Mongolian separatist movement led by a certain De Wang (Te Wang; Mongolian: Demchigdonrob; J: Toku Ō). A combined force of Guandong Army and Inner-Mongolian troops attacked Chinese troops in eastern Suiyuan, but was routed within a week. The Tōkyō government, embarrassed by the independent action taken by the field army, issued an official statement denying that Japanese troops had been involved in the fighting. The incident further stimulated the growth of Chinese nationalism and resistance.

Sujin, Emperor

The legendary 10th sovereign (*tennō*) in the traditional count (which includes several other nonhistorical emperors). In the account given in the chronicle NIHON SHOKI (720) he is said to have reigned 97 BC–30 BC, an implausibly early date. The KOJIKI (712) and *Nihon shoki* accounts of his reign have a decidedly legendary cast. Sujin is said to have sent the so-called generals of the four quarters (*shidō shōgun*, referring to four regions of Japan still known as San'yōdō, San'indō, Hokurikudō, and Tōkaidō) throughout the country to extend the authority of the imperial court. He is credited with having developed agriculture through the construction of ponds and irrigation canals and is said to have greatly improved court finances by levying taxes called *yuhazu no mitsugi* (edible birds and animals, provided by men) and *tanasue no mitsugi* (woven goods, provided by women). His rule having brought peace and tranquillity to the land, Sujin was known by the laudatory name Hatsukunishirasu Sumeramikoto, which in part suggests "being first" in ruling the country and would seem to be appropriate for a sovereign engaged in nation-building. Interestingly, the same name, though written with different characters, is traditionally ascribed to the putative first emperor, JIMMU. In light of this and various other legends attributed in common to the two sovereigns, some scholars have concluded that the chronicles' accounts of an Emperor Jimmu of doubtful historicity are projections of an Emperor Sujin who did exist. *KITAMURA Bunji*

Sukiya-zukuri

The first room *(ichi no ma)* of the Chūshoin at the Katsura Detached Palace in Kyōto. A celebrated example of the *sukiya-zukuri* style, it was built in the 17th century. The upper walls are earthen and the columns not fully squared, typical features of the style.

Sukagawa

City in central Fukushima Prefecture, northern Honshū. Situated on the river Abukumagawa, Sukagawa developed as one of the market towns and POST-STATION TOWNS on the highway Ōshū Kaidō during the Edo period (1600–1868). It has small- and medium-sized textile, watch component, and printing plants. There is a large peony garden with more than 280 species. Pop: 57,109.

Sukarno (1901–1970)

Indonesian nationalist leader and statesman. Born in Surabaya, he became a prominent opponent of colonial rule in the Dutch East Indies even before his graduation from Bandung Technological Institute in 1925. From February 1934 to March 1942 he was exiled to the islands of Flores and Bengkulu. Forced to collaborate with Japanese occupation authorities during World War II, he held a series of leading positions in Japanese-sponsored bodies but remained committed to the goal of Indonesian independence. Two days after the Japanese surrender in 1945, he proclaimed Indonesia's independence, which was followed by years of struggle with the Dutch. At the Hague Conference of 1949 he finally succeeded in achieving a formal transfer of sovereignty to the Republic of Indonesia. He served as president of Indonesia until 1967, becoming a major spokesman for the nonaligned nations; toward the end of his presidency he married Nemoto Naoko, a Japanese woman whom he had met during a visit to Tōkyō. See also INDONESIA AND JAPAN.

NAGAZUMI Akira

Sukayu Hot Spring

(Sukayu Onsen). Located in the Hakkōdasan Mountains, in the southern part of the city of Aomori, central Aomori Prefecture, northern Honshū. A sulfur spring; water temperature 48–60°C (118–140°F). Located within Towada-Hachimantai National Park, it is a base for skiing and mountain climbing. Designated as a National Health Resort Hot Spring.

sukegō

Labor service requisitioned by the Tokugawa shogunate (1603–1867) from peasants living near post stations. Villages supplying this corvée labor were also called *sukegō*. The shogunate had established SHUKUEKI or post stations along the main highways (GOKAIDŌ), holding the post station officials responsible for providing labor, horses, and other supplies. With the increase in travel in the 17th century, especially with the institution of the SANKIN KŌTAI system, under which *daimyō* were required to spend alternate years in the shogunal capital of Edo (now Tōkyō), it became necessary to requisition supplementary labor. At first temporary, in time the levying of *sukegō* became permanent. In some cases substitution of money payment for labor was accepted, particularly from those living far from the post stations; the money was then used to hire homeless drifters (KUMOSUKE) as porters. The burden on peasants, especially during the harvest season, was enormous, and they frequently rose up in rebellion. *Sukegō* was abolished soon after the Meiji Restoration (1868).

suki

Traditional Japanese spade. An agricultural implement used for shoveling and tilling the soil, consisting of a hollowed-out blade or scoop attached to a handle. Historically, its use precedes that of the hoe (KUWA) in ancient Japan. Its functions parallel those of the shovel or scoop found in the West. Examples of spade-shaped *suki* dating back to the Yayoi period (ca 300 BC–ca AD 300) have been unearthed at the KARAKO SITE in Nara Prefecture. These consist of a blade extending more or less straight out from a wooden handle. Japanese spades fall into two types: the "common spade" *(futsū suki)* and the "shovel spade" *(fumi suki)*. The former consists of a blade attached to the handle at an angle of nearly 180 degrees and is used by holding it in front of the body and digging into the soil while walking backwards. The latter has a blade fixed to a long handle at more or less 150 degrees and is pushed into the ground with the foot. Both types are common in Japanese farming communities.

NOGUCHI Takenori

sukiyaki

A dish consisting of thinly sliced beef, vegetables, bean curd, and other ingredients flavored with soy sauce and sugar and cooked at the table in a large skillet or pot. *Sukiyaki* is a relatively new dish in Japan, having been created to suit the taste of the Japanese after eating meat became common in the Meiji period (1868–1912).

The word *sukiyaki* first appeared in documents from the beginning of the 19th century as a name given to a dish prepared from the meat of wild geese, ducks, or deer that was broiled *(yaku)* on top of a spade *(suki)* and basted with *tamari* (a thick soy sauce). Traditionally, there was a religious (Buddhist) injunction against eating the meat of four-legged animals, especially cattle and horses, although in actuality some meat was undoubtedly consumed. With the rapid adoption of Western culture in the Meiji period, however, the eating of meat became widespread. Restaurants began serving a dish with thinly sliced beef and coarsely cut scallions flavored in the Japanese style with MISO (fermented bean paste). Flavoring meat with soy sauce and sugar soon became popular, and in Tōkyō a dish called *gyūnabe* (beef pot), beef cooked in broth, was regarded as "Western." In Ōsaka, however, the traditional Edo-period (1600–1868) method of preparing *sukiyaki* was preserved, with flavorings added after first roasting the beef in an iron pot. *Sukiyaki* can refer to either of these two methods of preparation, with variations, regional or personal. In addition, there are such variations as *uosuki*, in which fish rather than beef is used, and *udonsuki*, in which *udon* noodles are combined with the other ingredients.

Usually a high-quality, tender beef, especially well-marbled roast, is selected and sliced as thinly as possible. Other ingredients might include spring onions, *shirataki* noodles, *fu* (a kind of gluten bread), bean curd, *shungiku (Chrysanthemum coronarium)*, and mushrooms.

TSUJI Shizuo

sukiya-zukuri

A style of residential architecture. *Suki* refers to the enjoyment of the elegantly performed tea ceremony; *sukiya* denotes a building in which the tea ceremony was performed. *Sukiya-zukuri* is a style of residential architecture incorporating features characteristic of the *sukiya*.

The Azuchi-Momoyama period (1568–1600) saw the perfection of not only the *sukiya* as a distinctive style but also the SHOIN-ZUKURI as a contrasting style of residence of the warrior class. The *sukiya* comprised a small space, simple and austere. The *shoin-zukuri* was meant for a large, magnificent reception area, the setting for the pomp and ceremony of the feudal system. In the fusion of the two styles, the delicate features of the *sukiya* were introduced into *shoin-zukuri*, and the result was *sukiya-zukuri*. In the Edo period (1600–1868) *sukiya-zukuri* became popular among the townspeople, and the majority of houses came to be built in this style.

A comparison with *shoin-zukuri* makes the stylistic features of *sukiya-zukuri* clear. In *shoin-zukuri*, "frieze rails," called *nageshi* (horizontal timbers), connect grooved square columns, the wall surfaces are finished and covered with paintings, sculpture decorates the transom, and the ceiling is coffered or railed with a hexagonal rail. The *toko* (alcove), *tana* (shelves), and *shoin* (built-in desk) are arranged according to a fixed formula. By contrast, in the *sukiya-zukuri*, columns *(hashira)*, which are simply tree trunks with the bark removed, may be used. There are also instances in which the corner columns are square and the *nakabashira* (central post) is a barked column. The wall is earthen, and though there may be sculpture in the transom it is kept simple. The boarded ceiling is railed with a flat, rectangular rail. Although there are *toko, tana,* and *shoin* in the main room, their disposition and treatment are free. The beauty of *sukiya-zukuri* comes from the delicate sensibility, the slender wood elements, the use of natural materials, and the elimination of ornament.

Sukiya-zukuri was first used in the private areas of residences and in villas. An example of the former is the Kuroshoin, a building at the temple Honganji in Kyōto. As *sukiya-zukuri* this is still relatively formal. An example of the latter is KATSURA DETACHED PALACE. In particular, the Koshoin, the Chūshoin, and the Shinshoin there can be considered representative works of *sukiya-zukuri*.

Itō Nobuo

Sukumo

City in western Kōchi Prefecture, Shikoku, on Sukumo Bay. It developed in the Edo period (1600–1868) as a castle town. Agricultural products are rice, *igusa* (material for making *tatami* mats), and citrus fruits. There is also fishing for sardines and yellowtail. Sukumo is known for its cultured pearls and coral. Pop: 26,079.

Sukumo Bay

(Sukumo Wan). Inlet of the Pacific Ocean on the coast of southern Ehime and southwestern Kōchi prefectures, Shikoku. Between the Nishiumi and the Ōtsuki peninsulas. Site of the city of Sukumo. Principal activities are pearl culture and the cultivation of oysters and yellowtail. A scenic bay, with a heavily indented coastline, it forms part of the Ashizuri-Uwakai National Park.

Suku site

One of several archaeological sites of the Yayoi period (ca 300 BC–ca AD 300) located on some low hills projecting out into the Fukuoka Plain in the Suku section of the city of Kasuga, Fukuoka Prefecture. The site consists mainly of a cemetery where a burial jar containing more than 30 Former Han dynasty (206 BC–AD 8) Chinese BRONZE MIRRORS, bronze daggers and spearheads, and glass *magatama* (see BEADS, ANCIENT) was discovered in 1899. Excavations in 1929 and 1962 unearthed more than 50 additional jar burials with similar objects. Bronze daggers and halberds, as well as stone molds for casting BRONZE WEAPONS, have been found in the vicinity. Although similar burial grounds with magnificent funerary objects are found throughout northern Kyūshū, the Suku site is by far the richest. This site is thought to be the burial place of the rulers of the ancient country of NAKOKU. See also PREHISTORIC BURIALS.

Abe Gihei

Suma

District in the western part of the city of Kōbe, Hyōgo Prefecture, western Honshū. This scenic coastline facing Ōsaka Bay has been famous since ancient times for its pine trees and white sandy beaches. Suma is mentioned in the 8th-century poetry anthology *Man'yōshū* and is the setting for a chapter in the *Genji monogatari (Tale of Genji)*. It was a battlefield during the Taira-Minamoto War (1180–85), and was a resort area in the early modern period. Land reclamation and the construction of housing complexes have greatly altered its aspect today.

Sumidagawa

River in Tōkyō, central Honshū; the lower reaches of the ARAKAWA. It originates in the Kantō Mountains and flows through the eastern part of Tōkyō Prefecture into Tōkyō Bay. It flows north to south through Tōkyō's SHITAMACHI (the eastern half of Tōkyō) and is connected with a network of canals. Numerous wholesale stores, warehouses, and industrial plants are located along the river. The lower reaches are called Ōkawa or Asakusagawa. The riverside of Ōkawa (Ōkawabata) has long been described in poems and songs. Industrial waste has been causing pollution since the 1960s, but the quality of the water has been improved greatly by strong measures to control effluents. Length: 23.5 km (14.6 mi).

Sumida Ward

(Sumida Ku). One of the 23 wards of Tōkyō. On the east bank of the river Sumidagawa. A farming area until the end of the Taishō period (1912–26), after the Tōkyō Earthquake of 1923 the area developed into an industrial district with numerous plants manufacturing beer, timepieces, and cosmetics. It is part of the Kōtō Delta area. Also the site of many amusement centers. Pop: 232,755.

sumi-e → ink painting

suminagashi

("ink-flow"). A design technique used to produce marbled patterns in handmade paper and pottery and hand-dyed textiles. In paper and textiles, swirling designs are created by adding drops of ink to a pan of oily water. The surface of the water is gently disturbed by blowing or touching it lightly with the tip of a brush; the ink, prevented by the oil from diffusing, forms delicate patterns following the natural surface movements of the water. The paper or cloth is then applied to the surface and the pattern is absorbed. In ceramics, an unfired leather-hard piece is coated with slip (liquid clay), followed by a few drops of slip in a contrasting color. The two are swirled together by moving the piece through several angles until the desired marbled effect is achieved. The piece is then fired. In the Heian period (794–1185), *suminagashi* paper was used primarily for poetry and calligraphy. The Sanjūrokunin Kashū (Anthology of the 36 Poets) in the temple Nishi Honganji in Kyōto, and the *Semmen koshakyō* sutras in the temple Shitennōji in Ōsaka, both dating from the 12th century, are the earliest extant examples. In the Edo period (1600–1868), when indigo and crimson inks were added to the previous gray-black repertoire, *suminagashi* paper became a famous local product of Echizen (now a part of Fukui Prefecture). *Suminagashi* paper is still being made in Imadate, Fukui Prefecture, today by certain families who have preserved the technical process over many generations.

Aya Louisa McDonald

Suminokura Ryōi (1554–1614)

Wealthy merchant and overseas trader of the Azuchi-Momoyama and early Edo periods. Born in Kyōto as Yoshida Mitsuyoshi, scion of a family of physicians who had made a fortune as moneylenders (DOSŌ). Ryōi was his pen name and Suminokura the name his family had adopted for business purposes. Having begun his career in moneylending, sometime in the 1590s he obtained from the hegemon TOYOTOMI HIDEYOSHI an official license (SHUINJŌ; see also VERMILION SEAL SHIP TRADE) to engage in overseas commerce and began to send trading ships to Annam and Tonkin (both now part of Vietnam). The ships, known as *suminokurasen*, brought in huge profits for Ryōi and his son Soan (1571–1632) until all foreign trade was ended under the shogunate's NATIONAL SECLUSION policy. Ryōi also devoted himself to riparian engineering projects such as the opening of the rivers Ōigawa, Fujikawa, and Kamogawa to navigation.

sumire → violets

Sumitomo

Merchant house founded in the early 17th century, major business combine (ZAIBATSU) of the pre–World War II era, and enterprise grouping (KEIRETSU) of the postwar period. Sumitomo started in copper mining and refining, but beginning in the Meiji period (1868–1912) it branched out into other fields, developing by the 1920s into a leading *zaibatsu*, the third largest after MITSUI and MITSUBISHI. Unlike these other combines, however, Sumitomo was industrial from the outset, and its activities, despite diversification, continued to center on mining and metallurgy.

The House of Sumitomo was founded by Sumitomo Masatomo (1585–1652), who learned from his adopted son, Sumitomo Tomomochi (born Soga Rihei) a technique for refining copper that allowed one to extract its silver content. (Tomomochi's real father, Soga

Riemon [b 1572], had learned the technique from Europeans in Kyūshū.) Of great importance to the Sumitomo House was the discovery and acquisition of the Besshi Copper Mine in Shikoku in 1690. Many of Sumitomo's later industrial undertakings were to be directly related to this mine. Further, after acquiring Besshi, Sumitomo became the official purveyor of copper to the Tokugawa shogunate and a major exporter of copper, presumably through the NAGASAKI TRADE with China and the Netherlands, for the remainder of the Edo period (1600–1868). Sumitomo also became chartered agent (GOYŌ SHŌNIN) for the three senior branches of the Tokugawa family, managing their annual tax receipts.

Sumitomo faced a crisis at the time of the Meiji Restoration of 1868, for it had been closely allied with the losing Tokugawa side. The daimyō of Tosa (now Kōchi Prefecture) confiscated the Besshi mine on behalf of the new government. However, the manager of Sumitomo, HIROSE SAIHEI, persuaded the government to allow the company to continue operating the mine and eventually recovered its ownership. Hirose also greatly increased production, which had been declining since the early 18th century, by modernizing the operation with the help of a French engineer.

During the Meiji period Sumitomo branched out from copper production into copper rolling, steel manufacture, and other fields. During the 1910s and early 1920s, under the general manager SUZUKI MASAYA, many of the Sumitomo enterprises were separately incorporated as joint-stock companies. In 1921 the firm was reorganized as Sumitomo, Ltd (Sumitomo Gōshi Kaisha), a limited partnership capitalized at ¥150 million, and the family budget was strictly separated from the business operation. Although it managed some enterprises directly, Sumitomo, Ltd, served mainly as a holding company for the joint-stock subsidiaries. During the 1920s and 1930s Sumitomo expanded into other fields, notably machinery and electricity, becoming the third most important zaibatsu with diverse business interests centered in a top holding company controlled by the House of Sumitomo. In 1937 the top holding company itself was reorganized as a joint-stock company with paid-up capital of ¥150 million.

Sumitomo was much more centralized than other prewar business combines. Not only was the House far more dominant in the top holding company, but the holding company itself was in much firmer control of the subsidiaries. The house rules of the Sumitomo prescribed primogeniture at its most extreme. Unlike the families controlling other combines, the Sumitomo remained a single house with its wealth concentrated accordingly. In 1937 the head of the House of Sumitomo, the 16th in line from the founder, held over 98 percent of the shares. At the end of World War II he held 78.3 percent of the shares, other family members held 5 percent, and the remainder was held by the three financial institutions of the group, SUMITOMO BANK, LTD, SUMITOMO TRUST & BANKING CO, LTD, and SUMITOMO MUTUAL LIFE INSURANCE CO.

Owing to wartime expansion, the number of companies controlled by the Sumitomo holding company increased from 40 firms with a total paid-up capital of ¥574 million in 1941 to 135 firms with a total paid-up capital of ¥1.92 billion in 1946. The paid-up capital of the holding company was ¥225 million in 1946. In February 1948, as a result of the ZAIBATSU DISSOLUTION measures of the Allied Occupation, the holding company was dissolved.

In the 1950s the Sumitomo group was reconstituted in keiretsu form, and the role of the family was greatly diminished. In place of the top holding company, a presidents' club, composed for the most part of the presidents of the former key subsidiaries, serves as a consultative forum for the grouping but has no power to direct overall business activities or to appoint officers as the holding company did. The Sumitomo group, as it is known, today comprises some 80 firms, 21 of which are represented in the presidents' club. See also CORPORATE HISTORY.

—— Eleanor M. Hadley, Antitrust in Japan (1970). Johannes Hirschmeier and Tsunehiko Yui, The Development of Japanese Business, 1600–1973 (1975). W. W. Lockwood, The Economic Development of Japan (1954). Mission on Japanese Combines, Report to the Department of State and the War Department, pt 1 (1946). Mitsubishi Economic Research Institute, ed, Mitsui, Mitsubishi, Sumitomo (1955). Charles David Sheldon, The Rise of the Merchant Class in Tokugawa Japan (1958). Eleanor M. HADLEY

Sumitomo Bakelite Co, Ltd

(Sumitomo Bēkuraito). A company engaged in the production and sale of various types of plastic, including raw materials and semifin-

ished and finished products. Established in 1932, it is currently Japan's largest manufacturer of phenolic resins. Its products are known abroad under the brand names Sumilite, Sumikon, and others. It has a joint venture operation in Japan with the Hooker Chemical Co of the United States, overseas affiliated companies in the United States and Singapore, and a joint venture in Indonesia. Future plans call for the company to develop and produce high-value-added goods, such as medical instruments and products for the electronics industry. Annual sales totaled ¥93.3 billion (US $426.1 million) in 1982, and capitalization stood at ¥6.8 billion (US $31.1 million). Corporate headquarters are located in Tōkyō.

Sumitomo Bank, Ltd

(Sumitomo Ginkō). One of the three largest city banks in Japan and a central member of the SUMITOMO group. Its history can be traced back to a money-changing business founded by Izumiya Rihei in 1743. It was Sumitomo Kichizaemon VII (real name Sumitomo Tomoito, the 15th head of the Sumitomo family; see SUMITOMO KICHIZAEMON) who established the Sumitomo Bank in 1895. Until the end of World War II it was the principal financial organ of the Sumitomo ZAIBATSU and expanded together with the various enterprises under the Sumitomo wing. It also absorbed a great number of smaller local banks to become one of Japan's major banks with a huge network of branches throughout the country. After the war, it concentrated its efforts on capturing the deposits of the general public and at the same time worked at diminishing bad debt losses and decreasing management costs by modernizing its operations. It also entered the consumer credit field at an early date. Sumitomo Bank was the first private bank in Japan to expand its business abroad, establishing branches in San Francisco and Hawaii in 1916. In 1925 it established the Sumitomo Bank of California, and in 1958 it set up a subsidiary in Brazil. It currently has a total of over 200 branches, including 9 overseas. In parallel with the expansion of overseas activities by the members of the Sumitomo group, the bank has established joint multinational financial institutions in Djakarta, London, and the Cayman Islands. In March 1982 total assets were ¥20.7 trillion (US $86 billion), with operating profits of ¥105.2 billion (US $437 million), and capitalization at ¥111.4 billion (US $462.8 million). Deposits were broken down as follows: time deposits 50 percent, ordinary deposits 10 percent, current deposits 8 percent, and others 32 percent. Assets were loans 52 percent, negotiable securities 12 percent, cash and deposits 16 percent, and others 20 percent. Headquarters are located in Ōsaka.

Sumitomo Cement Co, Ltd

(Sumitomo Semento). Cement company. An affiliate of the SUMITOMO group. Established in 1907 under the name of Iwaki Cement Co, Ltd, in Fukushima Prefecture, it developed rapidly into one of the major cement companies in Japan with the absorption and merger of numerous smaller cement companies. The Iwaki company joined the Sumitomo group in 1963. It completed construction of its ultramodern Akō plant in 1975 and is currently modernizing the equipment and facilities of six older plants throughout the country. Sales for the fiscal year ending March 1982 totaled ¥159.5 billion (US $662.6 million), and capitalization stood at ¥11.9 billion (US $49.4 million) in the same year. Corporate headquarters are located in Tōkyō.

Sumitomo Chemical Co, Ltd

(Sumitomo Kagaku Kōgyō). A general chemical company producing a wide range of petrochemical and fine chemical products; one of the mainstays of the SUMITOMO group. Its forerunner was the Sumitomo Fertilizer Manufacturing Co, established in 1925 to produce chemical fertilizer and sulfur by utilizing byproducts of copper ores refined at the Sumitomo ZAIBATSU's Besshi Copper Mine. Since then, the company has expanded its operations to include the production of ammonia, methanol, formalin, synthetic resins, and tar products. It took its current name in 1934. In the same year, it established the Sumitomo Aluminum Reduction Co (now Sumitomo Aluminum Smelting Co) as a result of its success in developing aluminum-refining technology. After World War II the company imported new technology and equipment from the United States and Europe for the modernization of its plants. It entered the petrochemical field in the 1950s, constructing petrochemical plants in Ehime and Chiba prefectures to produce such substances as vinyl chloride, ethylene, polyethylene, polypropylene, acrylics, and caprolactam. The company produces many other chemicals ranging from intermediate to finished products; industrial raw materials; and consumer goods, including agricultural chemicals, pigments, synthetic rubber, dyes, and pharmaceuticals. It has joint venture production affiliates in Taiwan, Thailand, Singapore, and Brazil; another joint venture company in the United States produces an agricultural chemical known as Sumithion. Together with other members of the Sumitomo group, the company is currently constructing a giant petrochemical plant in Singapore. Sales for the fiscal year ending December 1981 totaled ¥641 billion (US $2.9 billion), of which industrial chemicals and fertilizers accounted for about 54 percent, synthetic resins and rubber 21 percent, dyestuffs and chemicals 12 percent, agricultural chemicals 6.5 percent, and pharmaceuticals 6.5 percent; the export ratio was 10 percent. The company was capitalized at ¥74.9 billion (US $342.1 million) in the same year. Corporate headquarters are located in Ōsaka and Tōkyō.

Sumitomo Construction Co, Ltd

(Sumitomo Kensetsu). Comprehensive construction company affiliated with the SUMITOMO group and engaged in public engineering projects as well as construction. It was established in 1950. The ratio of orders from Sumitomo-affiliated companies is relatively low, and that from government offices high. It has undertaken construction projects in Iraq, Kenya, Indonesia, Malaysia, Singapore, and Thailand, and is also engaged in the real estate business. Sales for the fiscal year ending March 1982 totaled ¥204.7 billion (US $850.4 million), with public engineering works and construction making up equal parts. The company was capitalized at ¥5.6 billion (US $23.3 million) in the same year. Corporate headquarters are located in Tōkyō.

Sumitomo Corporation

(Sumitomo Shōji). One of Japan's largest GENERAL TRADING COMPANIES (sōgō shōsha) and a leading member of the Sumitomo group. The company was first established in 1919 as Ōsaka Hokkō Kaisha, but was reorganized after World War II as part of the ZAIBATSU DISSOLUTION program, its name being changed to Nihon Kensetsu Sangyō, and the sales department of the holding company, Sumitomo, Ltd, relegated to it. Although the new company was a late starter, with the cooperation of the companies of the Sumitomo group it increased its sales rapidly, centering on heavy industrial products such as iron and steel, nonferrous metals, machinery, electrical equipment, and chemical products, all of which are specialties of the Sumitomo group. The company changed its name to Sumitomo Shōji in 1952, with Sumitomo Shōji Kaisha, Ltd, as its English name. (The English name was changed to Sumitomo Corporation in 1978.) During the years between 1956 and 1965, the company increased its sales more than fivefold, and in 1971 it ranked fifth among the trading firms in Japan. During the 1960s, the company established numerous overseas offices and incorporated firms in Europe, the United States, Southeast Asia, and Australia, as well as engaging in the development and import of iron ores and copper ores from Canada and Australia. It also traded with communist bloc nations. During the period between 1966 and 1975, in parallel with the expansion of its established lines of business, it entered the fields of plant exports, resource development, regional development, and ocean development. By thus diversifying its operations, Sumitomo not only strengthened its function as a general trading company but also increased its sales 10 times. The company is known for its sound management despite the fact that its scale of operations has grown so swiftly, and its earnings are quite stable. It has a total of 128 overseas offices, branches, and companies incorporated abroad. Sales for the fiscal year ending March 1982 totaled ¥11 trillion (US $45.7 billion), of which metals constituted 30 percent, machinery 27 percent, chemical products and fuel 26 percent, foodstuffs 6 percent, and textiles and others 11 percent. It was capitalized at ¥28 billion (US $116.3 million) in the same year. Corporate headquarters are located in Tōkyō and Ōsaka.

Sumitomo Electric Industries, Ltd

(Sumitomo Denki Kōgyō). Japan's largest manufacturer of electric wire and cable. Established in 1897, it is one of the major enter-

prises in the SUMITOMO group today. The company also produces special steel wires, sintered alloy products, disk brakes, rubber and plastic products for industrial use, traffic and vehicle control systems, and electronics materials. It has been active abroad since before World War II, maintaining a capital tie-up with the International Standard Electric Co of the United States until recently. It has offices in New York, Los Angeles, Chicago, London, Singapore, Sydney, São Paulo, and Hong Kong, and operates nine joint enterprises in Thailand, South Korea, Singapore, Nigeria, Australia, Venezuela, and the United States. The company's main products, electric wire and cable, are used in many projects around the world. The company also provides over half of all the material used for III–V compound semiconductors worldwide. Sales for the fiscal year ending March 1982 totaled ¥455.6 billion (US $1.9 billion); capitalization was ¥26.8 billion (US $111.3 million) in the same year. Corporate headquarters are located in Ōsaka.

Sumitomo Forestry Co, Ltd

(Sumitomo Ringyō). Forestry company established in 1948; a member of the SUMITOMO group. Its lines of business include forestry management, lumber processing, imports of forest products, and the manufacture and sale of building materials for housing. It has overseas offices in Seattle, Manila, Hong Kong, Djakarta, and Malaysia. Sales for the fiscal year ending September 1981 totaled ¥191.8 billion (US $833.8 million), of which building materials accounted for 35 percent, imported lumber 20 percent, domestic timber 26 percent, housing 18 percent and others 1 percent. It was capitalized at ¥3.3 billion (US $14.3 million) in the same year. Corporate headquarters are located in Ōsaka.

Sumitomo Heavy Industries, Ltd

(Sumitomo Jūkikai Kōgyō). A company engaged in the manufacture of industrial machinery and ships, Sumitomo Heavy Industries was established in 1969 through the merger of the Sumitomo Machinery Industries Co (established in 1934) and the Uraga Heavy Industries Co (established in 1897). A member of the SUMITOMO group, it is the largest manufacturer of reduction gears in Japan and one of the three top producers of steelmaking machinery, presses, and haulage machinery. Some 90 percent of its technology used in large-scale cranes has been developed by the company itself. It also exports a large amount of its technology. Overseas it has eight affiliates, eight offices, and two companies to which it provides technical know-how. At present the company is curtailing its shipbuilding activities and expanding its mass-production machinery department. Sales for the fiscal year ending March 1982 totaled ¥281.6 billion (US $1.2 billion), with exports occupying 40 percent, and capitalization standing at ¥21.9 billion (US $91 million) in the same year. Corporate headquarters are located in Tōkyō.

Sumitomo Kichizaemon

Name adopted by successive heads of the SUMITOMO merchant family, beginning in the late 17th century and continuing, with some exceptions, to the 20th. The first Kichizaemon (real name Sumitomo Tomonobu; 1647–1706) was the third head of the family and fifth son of Sumitomo Tomomochi, the second head. He tried his hand at developing several copper mines but was largely unsuccessful. In 1690 his son Tomoyoshi or Kichizaemon II (1670–1719) discovered extraordinarily rich copper deposits at Besshi (in what is now Ehime Prefecture) and obtained from the Tokugawa shogunate exclusive rights to establish a mining and refining operation at the site. He later diversified into the money changing, minting, and lumbering businesses, but copper remained the mainstay of his enterprises. The successful commercial ventures of this second Kichizaemon laid the foundation for SUMITOMO CORPORATION, one of the largest financial and industrial combines (ZAIBATSU) in Japan before World War II.

Sumitomo Light Metal Industries, Ltd

(Sumitomo Keikinzoku Kōgyō). Nonferrous metal company principally producing rolled aluminum products; it also manufactures rolled copper products. A member of the SUMITOMO group, the company traces its roots to the pre–World War II aluminum operations of the Sumitomo ZAIBATSU, centered on the SUMITOMO METAL INDUSTRIES, LTD, which manufactured duralumin for aircraft bodies. In 1959, with the expansion and reinforcement of Sumitomo

Metal's steel-manufacturing division, the nonferrous division became independent of the parent firm to create the present Sumitomo Light Metal Industries. It started out producing rolled aluminum products, and in 1973 it established a subsidiary, the Sumikei Aluminum Industries Co, which handles the smelting of aluminum. At the same time it continued to expand the scale of its rolling operations, developing into Japan's largest manufacturer of rolled aluminum goods. It has also moved into the field of aluminum foil and invested in bauxite mines in Australia to complete a so-called perpendicular unification system for producing aluminum products. Sales for the fiscal year ending March 1982 totaled ¥178.7 billion (US $742 million), and capitalization stood at ¥12.6 billion (US $52.3 million). Corporate headquarters are located in Tōkyō.

Sumitomo Metal Industries, Ltd

(Sumitomo Kinzoku Kōgyō). An iron and steel maker and leading member of the SUMITOMO group, Sumitomo Metal Industries has the longest history of any major enterprise in Japan, with its origin dating back to 1590, when the Sumitomo family started the refining of copper in Kyōto. In 1897 the Sumitomo Copper Works was opened in Ōsaka, and in 1901 the Sumitomo Steel Works was established; after several reorganizations, the two plants were merged to form Sumitomo Metal Industries in 1935. During the ZAIBATSU DISSOLUTION program following World War II, the company changed its name to Fusō Metal Industries, but it reverted to its original name in 1952. In the following year, after absorbing the Kokura Steel Manufacturing Co, Ltd, it launched a long-term equipment modernization program and started installation of large blast furnaces and construction of new steel mills in coastal areas. By 1976 its production capacity of blister steel had reached 22.7 million metric tons (25 million short tons). At the same time, it constructed new processing plants and established a technical research institute. The company's steel tubes and pipes are among the best in the world, both qualitatively and quantitatively. It also can supply 30 percent of the total world demand for wheels for rolling stock. It is active in overseas projects and technological cooperation with foreign companies, and has three affiliated companies in the United States and one in Thailand and Saudi Arabia, as well as offices in the United States, Brazil, Venezuela, West Germany, Australia, the United Kingdom, Iran, and Singapore. Future plans call for the improvement of its products and an advance into the engineering and steel structure fields utilizing its accumulated technologies. Sales for the fiscal year ending March 1982 totaled ¥1.5 trillion (US $6.2 billion), third in the country after NIPPON STEEL CORPORATION and NIPPON KŌKAN, and consisted of steel plates 31 percent; steel pipes 46 percent; steel wire 7 percent; and rolling stock, castings, forgings, and other products 16 percent. In the same year the export ratio was 48 percent and the company was capitalized at ¥124.3 billion (US $516.4 million). Corporate headquarters are located in Ōsaka.

Sumitomo Metal Mining Co, Ltd

(Sumitomo Kinzoku Kōzan). Manufacturer of nonferrous metals and member of the SUMITOMO group. The history of the company dates from 1590, when Soga Riemon (b 1572), brother-in-law of Sumitomo Masatomo (1585–1652), founder of the Sumitomo family, started a copper smelting operation in Kyōto; this was followed by the discovery in 1690 of the Besshi Copper Mine in Shikoku, which the family started to manage on a commercial basis in the following year. In the process of developing this mine, heavy and chemical industries, a banking business, and other operations were organized and developed, leading to the formation of the present Sumitomo group. The activities of the company have diversified from mining, smelting, and metal processing into a wide area including electronics materials, construction materials, catalysts, lubricants, nuclear fuels, industrial pollution control technology, and development of deep seabed mineral resources. Overseas activities include prospecting, mining, purchasing of mineral resources, technological assistance, and sale of the company's products. Sales for the fiscal year ending March 1982 totaled ¥290.8 billion (US $1.2 billion) and consisted of copper (22 percent), nickel (16 percent), gold (27 percent), cobalt (3 percent), construction materials (5 percent), zinc (5 percent), and other products (22 percent). The company was capitalized at ¥17.4 billion (US $72.3 million) in the same year. Corporate headquarters are located in Tōkyō.

Sumitomo Mutual Life Insurance Co

(Sumitomo Seimei Hoken Sōgo Kaisha). One of the three largest life insurance companies in Japan and a member of the SUMITOMO group. Founded in 1907, it became a mutual company in 1947. It achieved rapid growth through an aggressive expansion of its sales force and a sophisticated policyholder service system. The components of the company's assets are financial loans, securities, real estate, and policy loans; it also owns and rents space in 100 office buildings. Recently it has substantially increased its purchases of foreign bonds and its loan activities overseas. Sumitomo Mutual has business tie-ups with Metropolitan Life and Equitable Life in the international group life insurance business and maintains an office in New York and representatives in London. In the fiscal year that ended in March 1982, new life insurance sales totaled ¥13.5 trillion (US $56.1 billion), life insurance in force amounted to ¥84 trillion (US $349 billion), and total assets were ¥3.7 trillion (US $15.4 billion). Corporate headquarters are located in Ōsaka.

Sumitomo Rubber Industries, Ltd

(Sumitomo Gomu Kōgyō). Company engaged in the manufacture and sale of automobile, bicycle, and other types of tires, as well as such sporting goods as golf and tennis balls. It is known abroad for its products under the brand names Dunlop and Sumitomo. Sumitomo Rubber Industries, Ltd, was established in 1909. It has capital and technical tie-ups with the Dunlop Co of the United Kingdom and a total of eight overseas offices. The company is a member of the SUMITOMO group. Its annual sales totaled ¥171 billion (US $781 million) in 1981; it was capitalized at ¥6.3 billion (US $28.8 million) in the same year. Corporate headquarters are located in Kōbe.

Sumitomo Trust & Banking Co, Ltd

(Sumitomo Shintaku Ginkō). One of Japan's leading financial institutions, providing not only trust and banking services but also a full line of real estate, corporate agency, securities, and investment advisory services. Established in 1925 as a trust company for the SUMITOMO group, it added commercial banking to its business activities in 1948. It contributed to Japan's postwar economic recovery and expansion by supplying mainly long-term loans to such key industries as electric power, steel, chemicals, and shipbuilding. Sumitomo Trust maintains four overseas branches (in London, New York, Los Angeles, and Singapore), four representative offices (in Frankfurt, Bahrain, Sydney, and São Paulo), and two wholly-owned subsidiaries (in Hong Kong and London). Efforts are being made to expand further its international business. As of March 1982 total employable funds amounted to ¥8.83 trillion (US $36.7 billion) broken down roughly as follows: loan trusts 50 percent, deposits 29 percent, money trusts 10 percent, and pension trusts and others 11 percent. The bank's total loans were ¥5.2 trillion (US $21.6 billion). The bank was capitalized at ¥37.5 billion (US $156 million) in the same year. Headquarters are located in Ōsaka.

Sumitomo Warehouse Co, Ltd

(Sumitomo Sōko). Company engaged in warehousing, harbor and land transportation, and the operation of container terminals. Established in 1923, it now ranks as the third largest company in Japan's warehousing business. Its efficiently controlled computer service ensures smooth operation and control of import and export cargoes. It has played a pioneering role in international freight forwarding and is actively engaged in intermodal transportation services. Sales for the fiscal year ending March 1982 totaled ¥37.2 billion (US $154.5 million), and the company was capitalized at ¥5.6 billion (US $23.3 million) in the same year. Corporate headquarters are located in Ōsaka.

Sūmitsuin → Privy Council

Sumiyaki chōja

(The Charcoal-Maker Millionaire). Folktale. Variations are known as Asahi chōja (The Rising-Sun Millionaire) or Imohori chōja (The Potato-Digger Millionaire). A poor and honest charcoal maker makes a fortune when his wife finds a gold mine. Stories about discovery of gold exist in China and Korea and throughout Japan. This version is believed to have been spread by itinerant ironcasters, who made their own charcoal as well as the pots and kettles that they sold.   Suchi Tokuhei

Sumiyoshi monogatari

Anonymous tale of the early part of the Kamakura period (1185–1333). Believed to be a revision of an earlier Heian-period (794–1185) work, now lost, of the same title. The plot is a Japanese version of the Cinderella story. The councillor Saemon no Kami begets two daughters by one wife and another daughter, Himegimi, by a second wife, who dies when Himegimi is yet a child. Shii no Shōshō, the son of a high minister, hears of Himegimi's beauty and asks for her hand in marriage. Himegimi's stepmother, who is concerned only for the fortunes of her own daughters, tricks him into marrying one of them instead. Learning that her stepmother is plotting to have her kidnapped by a lecherous old man, Himegimi runs away to Sumiyoshi (now part of Ōsaka) in the company of her wetnurse's daughter, Jijū. Shii no Shōshō realizes he has been deceived, finds Himegimi, and takes her back to Kyōto. Informed of the duplicity of his wife, Saemon no Kami banishes her from his house. The stepmother dies impoverished, while Himegimi and her husband thrive, he becoming regent to the emperor.

Sumiyoshi school

A school of painting founded by Sumiyoshi Jokei (original name Tosa Hiromichi; 1599–1670) in 1662; an offshoot of the TOSA SCHOOL. The Sumiyoshi painters worked primarily for the shogunate in Edo (now Tōkyō), while the Tosa family served the imperial court in Kyōto. The Sumiyoshi artists worked in the Tosa style, revitalizing to some extent its depleted traditions, but they are remembered mainly for their services as art historians and connoisseurs to the Tokugawa shōguns.

Like their colleagues of the Tosa school, the Sumiyoshi artists claimed an elaborate and largely fictional genealogy. They traced their artistic lineage to a 13th-century painter known as Sumiyoshi Keion, whose identity is not clear.

Hiromichi, probably the younger brother of painter Tosa Mitsunori (1583–1638), changed his family name to Sumiyoshi at the order of the emperor Gosai (1637–85, r 1655–63), who appointed him the official painter of the Sumiyoshi Shrine in Ōsaka. He received from the court the title hokkyō and then hōgen, and took the priestly name Jokei. More important to his career, however, was his success in attracting the attention of the shogunate. This brought his move to Edo, where he set up the Sumiyoshi school and worked as goyō eshi (official painter). Jokei's son Gukei (original name Hirozumi; 1631–1705) followed a career very similar to that of his father. He too received the titles of hokkyō (in 1674) and hōgen (in 1691), taking the name Gukei when he became hokkyō. In 1682 he was appointed oku eshi (private painting master) to the shōgun TOKUGAWA TSUNAYOSHI.

Father and son worked together on such projects as the Tōshōgū engi of 1665, a pictorial history of the shrine of TOKUGAWA IEYASU at Nikkō. Both were noted for their studies of older YAMATO-E paintings. Jokei's copy of the 12th-century handscroll Nenchū gyōji emaki (Annual Rites and Ceremonies), commissioned by the emperor GO-MIZUNOO in 1626, is now the only surviving trace of what must have been a major EMAKIMONO, or illustrated handscroll. Also of art historical importance is Gukei's study of early illustrations of HEIKE MONOGATARI (Tale of the Heike).

Both Jokei and the young Gukei followed the traditional yamato-e style closely in their works, producing finely detailed, colored paintings that were truer to the old Tosa style than were the works of many of their Tosa-school contemporaries. Gukei's artistic range was somewhat broader than his father's. He became known as a painter of genre scenes, the most famous of which is the scroll Rakuchū rakugai (Scenes in and around Kyōto), now in the Tōkyō National Museum. Because of his humorous depictions of scenes from contemporary life, he is sometimes regarded as an early UKIYO-E artist. In his later works the influence of the KANŌ SCHOOL is frequently apparent.

The tradition of connoisseurship of ancient Japanese writings begun by Jokei and Gukei was carried on by later Sumiyoshi painters. Particularly famous in this regard was Gukei's grandson Hiromori (1705–77), together with his adopted son Hiroyuki (1755–1811) and Hiroyuki's son Hironao (1781–1828). Their certificates of authentication and attribution are found on many ancient examples of yamato-e. The excellence of Hiroyuki's own painting in the eyes of the shogunate was indicated by a commission he received in 1809 to paint screens to be sent as official gifts to Korea. At court the Sumiyoshi school ranked officially below the Kanō school until the time of Hiroyuki's younger son Hirotsura (1793–1863), the last major Sumiyoshi painter, whose prowess caused the Sumiyoshi family to be made equal in status to the Kanō.

In the 18th century two minor painting schools were founded by pupils of Sumiyoshi Hiromori. One such pupil was Sumiyoshi Hiromasa (1729–97), the real father of Hiromori's adopted son Hiroyuki. His religious name, by which he is generally known, was Keishū; when he established himself as an independent painter in 1782 he took the surname Itaya, founding an Itaya school. His main pupil was his son Itaya Hironaga (1760–1814), later called Keii; Hironaga's son Hirotaka (1786–1831) took his grandfather's name, Keishū. All of the Itaya painters served as goyō eshi to the shogunate, and the younger Keishū was awarded the title of hōgen. Another pupil of Hiromori who founded his own school was Awataguchi Naoyoshi (1723–91; religious name Keiu). Naoyoshi's original name was Kondō Gorōbei; the name Awataguchi was probably chosen to suggest descent from the 15th-century Tosa-school painter Awataguchi Takamitsu. His son Naotaka (1753–1807) and grandson Naoki (also Keiu; 1779–1821) continued to work as painters for the shogunate.   Sarah THOMPSON

Sumiyoshi Shrine

(Sumiyoshi Taisha). Shintō shrine in Sumiyoshi Ward, Ōsaka, dedicated to four deities. Three of the deities, born of the god Susanoo no Mikoto, are called collectively Suminoe no Ōkami (i.e., Uwatsutsunoo no Mikoto, Nakatsutsunoo no Mikoto, and Sokotsutsunoo no Mikoto). The fourth is Okinagatarashihime no Mikoto (i.e., the legendary empress Jingū deified). According to legend, this shrine was founded by Empress Jingū upon her return to Japan, after her successful campaign in Korea (an episode related in the chronicle NIHON SHOKI of 720 but discounted by modern historians), to express gratitude to the three deities who guarded her during the expedition. Sumiyoshi Shrines (Sumiyoshi Jinja) with the same deities are found in the cities of Fukuoka and Shimonoseki, the island of Iki, and more than 2,000 other places in the country. In time the shrine in Ōsaka, because of its proximity to Kyōto, became the largest and best known of its kind. The shrine was believed to offer protection and prosperity for mariners, fishermen, waka poets, and merchants. The four buildings, each housing one deity, are in the so-called sumiyoshi-zukuri style of architecture, and are designated a National Treasure. The annual festival is held on 31 July.
                                                                Stanley WEINSTEIN

Summers, James (1828–1891)

British scholar and teacher of English literature. Born in Ritchfield, England. Summers was interested in a diplomatic career but, unable to afford a university education, he traveled to China and studied dialects in Hong Kong, Shanghai, Guangzhou (Canton), and Beijing (Peking). In 1848 he accepted a position as tutor at St. Paul's School in Hong Kong. He returned to England in 1851 and became professor of Chinese at King's College, London University, the following year. One of his students was Ernest Mason SATOW. Summers studied Japanese while in London and, when the IWAKURA MISSION visited England in 1872, he was invited to teach English in Japan. In 1873, along with his family, he traveled to Japan to teach English literature at Kaisei Gakkō (a predecessor of Tōkyō University). He was probably the first to introduce Shakespeare and Milton to Japan. His students included INOUE TETSUJIRŌ, Wadagaki Kenzō (1860–1919), OKAKURA KAKUZŌ, KATŌ TAKAAKI, and KANŌ JIGORŌ. Summers also taught English at other schools, moving to Niigata in 1876 and to Sapporo in 1878. He resettled in Tōkyō in 1882 and opened his own English school.

sumō

A unique form of wrestling with a 2,000-year-old history that easily qualifies as the national sport of Japan. Sumō became a professional sport almost 300 years ago in the early part of the Edo period (1600–1868), and although it is practiced today by clubs in high schools, colleges, and amateur associations, it has its greatest appeal as a professional spectator sport, rivaling even baseball in popularity.

Sumō

The decisive moment in a *sumō* match. The ancient origins of this sport are evident in the traditional hairstyle of the wrestlers and the costume of the referee at the lower left.

At first glance, to Western eyes, nothing about *sumō* seems to make sense. Up onto a cement-hard ring climb two blubbery behemoths, 90 percent naked and apparently without an ounce of lean muscle between them for all their astonishing size and weight. The next four minutes are spent in a bewildering ritual of stamping, squatting, puffing, glowering, tossing salt in the air, and seemingly going nowhere. Suddenly they charge each other in unison like two football tackles. An audible thud, a frantic tussle, and both inexplicably fly out of the ring and into the laps of the cheering audience. Elapsed time, 7.5 seconds. A winner is declared by a referee dressed in the court costume of a 14th-century nobleman brandishing a warrior's war fan *(gumbai)*. Without a pause two more giants stomp into the ring and the procedure is repeated.

This is not the sort of sport to which most Westerners are accustomed, to be sure, and yet it is Westerners who often become the most avid fans of what must be one of the world's great spectator sports—a sport rich with tradition, pageantry, and elegance and filled with action, excitement, and heroes—dedicated to an almost impossible standard of excellence down to the last detail.

The world of modern professional *sumō* is so complex and filled with fascinating details that it is challenging indeed to give an explanation that is both concise and comprehensive. The following are some of the institutions whose influence plays an important part in shaping its unique character. The adjective "modern" is used because although *sumō* may appear to be totally medieval in every respect, it has changed constantly throughout its long history and continues to do so.

The Dohyō or Ring —— Hardly a ring in the Western sense, the *dohyō* is a 54-centimeter (1.7-foot) high, 5.45-meter (17.9-foot) square mound of special clay packed hard and sprinkled with sand. The borders of this mound are defined by the tops of 28 bales made of straw bags filled with earth and sunk in the clay during construction. Another 20 bales are similarly sunk in the center to form a circle 4.55 meters (14.9 ft) in diameter. In the middle of the circle are two white lines about 90 centimeters (3 ft) long, which face each other about 120 centimeters (4 ft) apart. These are the *shikirisen* (literally, "dividing lines"), where the two wrestlers meet to glower at each other during their psychological buildup for the match. And it is from the *shikirisen* that they finally leap at each other in the *tachiai* (initial charge). Over the *dohyō* hangs a roof *(yakata)* designed in a Shintō style of architecture called *shimmei-zukuri*. In Edo times when *sumō* was performed outdoors, the *yakata* served a functional purpose of weather protection and was supported at its four corners by colored pillars representing the four seasons, against which the four judges sat. Now the two-ton *yakata* is slung from the ceiling by steel cables for better viewing, and the pillars have been replaced by four huge silk tassels *(fusa)*—green for spring, red for summer, white for autumn, black for winter.

The Object of a Sumō Match —— A wrestler wins by forcing his opponent out of the center circle or by causing him to touch the surface of the *dohyō* with any part of his body other than the soles of his feet. To decide who has stepped out or touched down first is

often extremely difficult and requires the closest attention of a referee *(gyōji)* on the *dohyō* and judges *(shimpan)* sitting around the *dohyō* at floor level. Judges are all ex-wrestlers and members of the Japan Sumō Association (Nihon Sumō Kyōkai).

Techniques —— The Japan Sumō Association, the governing body of professional *sumō*, officially lists 70 winning techniques consisting of assorted throws, trips, lifts, thrusts, shoves, and pulls. Of these, 48 are considered the "classic" techniques but the number in actual daily use is probably half of that. Kicking or punching with a closed fist are not allowed, but a thrusting slap *(tsuppari)* delivered toward the chest-throat region is. Most wrestlers settle on 6 to 8 techniques for their fighting repertoire, with emphasis on 2 or 3 that become their ring specialities. There are always a few, known as "technicians," who keep a much wider arsenal of attacks and counterattacks at their command. Unlike Western professional wrestling, in *sumō*, ring decorum and sportsmanship are of the highest order, making even cricket seem somewhat rowdy by comparison.

The Belt —— There are many elements that set *sumō* apart from other forms of wrestling, and perhaps the most significant is the use of a belt or belly band called a *mawashi*. Ten to 13 meters (33–43 ft) long, depending on its owner's girth, and 80 centimeters (32 in) wide, the *mawashi* is first folded over six times to a width of about 13 centimeters (5 in), looped over the groin as a breechclout, then wrapped tightly around the waist (about five times) and knotted in the rear. Practice *mawashi* are made of cotton, blue for beginners, white for high-ranked seniors. During tournaments wrestlers in the two top divisions wear *mawashi* made of silk or satin costing several hundred thousand yen (several thousand dollars) or more. Once limited to navy blue, purple, or black, the colors of these tournament *mawashi* are now brightly varied. The lower four divisions are limited to dark blue cotton.

Most *sumō* matches center on the wrestlers' attempts to get a firm, two-handed grip on their opponent's *mawashi* while blocking him from getting a similar grip on theirs. With the right grip they then have the leverage to execute a throw, trip, or lift. Wrestlers who are "good at the belt" usually enjoy the longest and most successful careers in *sumō*.

During tournaments, but not in practice, a curious string apron *(sagari)* is also worn tucked into the front folds of the *mawashi*, from whence it falls frequently in the heat of the fray. The "strings" of the *sagari* are actually 40-centimeter (1.3-foot) lengths of silk, twisted and starched. There are usually 19 such strands—or 17 or 21 depending on a wrestler's whim—but never an even number, for the *sagari* is patterned after the sacred rope *(shimenawa)* that hangs before a Shintō shrine to ward off evil. There is nothing in *sumō* that does not have some very special significance.

The Wrestlers —— Traditionally, *sumō* has drawn the majority of its recruits from the rural communities of the poorer prefectures with representation from the Tōhoku (northeast) region and Hokkaidō running ahead of other areas. The logic is simple. A big boy from a poor farm or fishing village is thought to arrive preconditioned to the hard knocks and spartan discipline typical of *sumō* life and to be filled with incentive to strive for a wealth and fame he could never achieve at home. In the past such recruits might be as young as 13, with no particular limits on height or weight. Now they are usually 15 or have finished middle school and should be 173 centimeters (5 ft 8 in) tall and weigh 75 kilograms (165 lb) to pass the Japan Sumō Association's acceptance examination.

Wrestlers grow to an average height of 183 centimeters (6 ft) and an average weight of 137 kilograms (300 lb), with successful exceptions running from as light as 110 kilograms (240 lb) to as heavy as 200 kilograms (440 lb). Most wrestlers retire from this rigorous sport in their early thirties, which is not surprising, considering that they start in their mid-teens.

In the early 1980s, the total number of wrestlers officially listed by the Japan Sumō Association hovers around 700—up about 150 from the early 1970s. This growth surprises even members of the association, who assume that the alternatives offered by Japan's increasingly affluent society would dim the luster of the distant rewards that might be made possible by a difficult and demanding career in *sumō*. And though it is true that some of the harsher aspects of *sumō* life have been deliberately softened in recent years, perhaps the unexpected increase is better explained by the allure of the idea that "only the toughest need apply."

Divisions and Ranks —— The 700-odd wrestlers in professional *sumō* are organized into a large and somewhat lumpy pyramid. Progress from the ranks of beginners at the bottom to the grand champion's pinnacle at the top depends entirely on ability. Winners go

oshidashi—pushing the opponent out of the ring with hands applied to the front of his body

yorikiri—forcing the opponent out of the ring with one or both hands going below his arms or behind him

uwatenage—grabbing the belt of the opponent and throwing him down while pinning his arm under one's outer arm

tsuridashi—grabbing the belt of the opponent and carrying him out of the ring

Sumō——Basic winning techniques

up. Losers go down. The speed with which a wrestler rises or falls depends entirely on his win-loss record at the end of each tournament. Based on this, his ranking is calculated for the next tournament and then written with his name and those of other wrestlers in Chinese characters on a graded list called the *banzuke*. The names of the highest rankers are written large and those of the lowest so small that they are called "magnifying-glass letters." The pretournament posting of the *banzuke* is one of the great and often bitter moments of truth in *sumō*.

Not included on the *banzuke* are the names of the young apprentices of pre-*sumō* (*maezumō*). Here are the six official divisions of the *banzuke* listed in order from bottom to top with literal translations of their names and typical numbers of wrestlers in each to give a sense of their relative size. *Jonokuchi*, "the beginning," 75. *Jonidan*, "the second step," 262. *Sandamme*, "the third step," 180. *Makushita*, "below the curtain," 120. *Jūryō*, literally "ten ryō" (an old unit of coinage), but more accurately, "junior wrestler," 26. *Makuuchi*, "within the curtain," 36.

Unlike the other divisions, the number of wrestlers in *jūryō* is presently fixed at 26. The limitation on *makuuchi* is that it cannot exceed 38. The *makuuchi* division is broken down internally in another set of rankings starting at the bottom with *maegashira*, "senior wrestler," which includes about 24 to 28 wrestlers in all. Next up are *komusubi*, "champion third-class," *sekiwake*, "champion second-class," *ōzeki*, "champion," and *yokozuna*, "grand champion." There are usually about 10 wrestlers in the champion ranks, distribution varying from tournament to tournament, depending on promotions, demotions, injuries, and withdrawals. The three ranks of *komusubi*, *sekiwake*, and *ōzeki* are called *san'yaku* collectively.

For purposes of competition, all divisions are divided arbitrarily into East-West camps on the *banzuke*. For example, a wrestler's position for one tournament might be listed as "West, maegashira 12." If he did well, he might be promoted to "East, maegashira 5" in the next tournament. But if he did badly, he would probably be dropped back down into the *jūryō* division. Anyone with a losing record is liable to demotion except the *yokozuna*, whose rank is permanent. But a *yokozuna* who cannot maintain a certain level of championship performance is expected to retire.

Only wrestlers in the top two divisions, *jūryō* and *makuuchi*, receive regular salaries. They also enjoy many other distinctions such as the title *sekitori*, "top-ranking wrestler" and the right to have their long, oiled hair combed into the elegant *ōichōmage* (ginkgo-leaf knot) during tournaments. Rank very clearly has its privileges in the world of professional *sumō*.

Sumō Ceremonies——The world of *sumō* is filled with ceremonies large and small, all of which must be performed precisely down to the last detail; to describe each one of them would become an essay in itself. The following two have been chosen in the hope that they will speak eloquently for all.

The ceremony known as the *yokozuna dohyōiri*, "the ring entrance of the grand champions," presents the very essence of splendiferous success achieved through superhuman skill, strength, and effort.

Before the *jūryō* and *makuuchi* division matches, a much simpler ring-entrance ceremony is performed. First the wrestlers representing the East file down their *hanamichi* ("flower way") aisle wearing their richly embroidered and very expensive *keshōmawashi* (ornamental aprons). A referee calls out the name of each wrestler as he mounts the ring and parades around the center rope circle to stop, facing the audience. When all are on the *dohyō*, they turn at a

signal, face in, clap their hands, raise their aprons slightly with both hands, throw up their hands, and file out, followed immediately by wrestlers from the West, filing down their *hanamichi* and onto the *dohyō* to perform the same ceremony.

Following this, the *jūryō* matches begin at once. But after the *makuuchi dohyōiri* the best is yet to come.

Down the East *hanamichi* comes the *yokozuna* procession led by the top-ranked referee, who only officiates at *yokozuna* bouts. Next comes a herald, the *tsuyuharai* ("dew-sweeper"), then the *yokozuna*, then his *tachimochi* ("swordbearer"), who is indeed bearing a richly mounted ceremonial sword. The *tsuyuharai* and *tachimochi* must be *makuuchi* wrestlers and, if possible, from the same *heya* (stable; see below) as the *yokozuna*. All three wear matching *keshōmawashi* woven in heavy silk, rich with colorful designs accented with the sparkle of gold and silver thread. A sum of ¥5 million ($22,000) is not too much to pay for a splendid *keshōmawashi*, but they are given gladly by members of the *kōenkai* (supporters group or fan club) of the wrestler or his *heya*.

Knotted around the *yokozuna*'s waist is a huge white rope, the *tsuna*, which only he can wear and which gives his rank (*yoko*, "sideways' + *tsuna*, "rope") its name. Hanging from the *tsuna*—which may weigh 13 kilograms (29 lb) or more—are five strips of paper folded in zigzags (these are called GOHEI). Similar ropes with *gohei* can be found over the main entrances to Shintō shrines.

All three enter the ring and squat at the West side facing East. The *yokozuna* spreads his arms wide and brings them together in a mighty clap, rubs the palms together, sweeps his arms out again, turning the palms up, and repeats the gesture, which is supposed to symbolize purifying the hands and body with grass before battle and also indicates "no hidden weapons."

The *yokozuna* then stands, strides grandly into the middle of the ring and turns to face north, which is the *dohyō*'s *shōmen* ("front") and the side on which the emperor sits. Placing his feet wide apart he then proceeds to do a very elegant form of *shiko*, the basic *sumō* exercise, complete with graceful and strangely evocative arm and hand movements. When he slams his foot down in the sand, the crowd roars its approval. Performed three times, this stamping ritual is supposed to frighten evil spirits from the ring and at the same time demonstrate the champion's determination to trample his opponents in the dust. The *yokozuna* then returns to his original position, squatting between his two attendants, repeats the hand-body purifying ritual, and leaves the ring. The *yokozuna* for the West enters the ring immediately from the opposite side to repeat the ceremony. Following this, the final *makuuchi* matches of the day begin.

At the other end of this moment of glory is the *dampatsushiki*, the "hair cutting ceremony" performed at a senior wrestler's public retirement (*intai-zumō*). *Intai-zumō* is a great spectator event where one can enjoy such *sumō* specialities as *shokkiri* ("comic *sumō*" that is genuinely comic) and *jinku* (*sumō* songs, often extemporaneous), both performed by *makushita* wrestlers. But the *dampatsushiki* is the main event and a very moving one indeed, especially if the retiring wrestler is a *yokozuna*.

The wrestler, dressed in his best formal *kimono*, his oiled hair combed into the handsome *ōichōmage* knot, sits in the middle of the *dohyō*. Beside him stands a high referee in ceremonial tournament dress holding a pair of scissors (usually gold-plated). One by one friends, relatives, fellow wrestlers, celebrities, *kōenkai* members climb into the ring to take a ritual snip at the back of the knot. When the *yokozuna* Wajima (now the *oyakata* Hanakago) retired in November 1981, it took 320 men an hour and a half to cut his hair, the longest *dampatsushiki* in *sumō* history.

The last and final cut, which completely removes the topknot, is usually made by the wrestler's *oyakata* (see the section on the stable system, below). At this point it is not unusual to see tears streaming down the now ex-wrestler's face.

Annual Tournaments —— Traditionally, with a brief exception in the late 1920s and early 1930s, only two tournaments were held in a year until 1949. By 1959 this number had grown to six, where it stood in the early 1980s. The big six are held every other month in four different cities as follows: January, Tōkyō; March, Ōsaka; May, Tōkyō; July, Nagoya; September, Tōkyō; November, Fukuoka.

In 1949 the length of a tournament increased from the traditional 10 days to 15 days. A tournament opens on whatever Sunday is close to the 10th of the month and closes on a Sunday. A tournament day starts around 10:00 AM with the apprentices of *maezumō* fighting qualifying rounds. Interest increases around 11:00 AM, when the long march of the four lower divisions across the *dohyō* begins. The boy-men in these divisions—*jonokuchi, jonidan, sandamme,* and *makushita*—wrestle on alternate days for seven days. For them, a winning record (*kachikoshi*) begins with four wins against three losses, which ensures promotion. Anything less is a losing record (*makekoshi*) and demotion. A *zenshō* record (all wins, no losses) of course boosts a wrestler way up the ladder, usually into a higher division.

Sekitori in the two top divisions—*jūryō* and *makuuchi*—wrestle once a day for 15 days. Each of their bouts takes around 5 minutes, most of which is consumed by ritual preliminaries. Actual fighting time averages 30 seconds per bout. *Sekitori* must win 8 of their 15 bouts for a *kachikoshi* record. *Makekoshi* starts with 8 losses. The entire tournament is won by the *makuuchi* wrestler with the most wins—usually a *yokozuna* with a 13–2 or 14–1 record. Should two *sekitori* end the tournament with identical records, they must fight again soon after the last bout even though one of them may have been in it.

The *jūryō* division begins to wrestle around 3:00 PM, *makuuchi* at 4:00, and the tournament is over for the day at 6:00 except on the last Sunday, when prizegiving takes longer.

The Stable System —— The *sumō* stable system is another of the sport's unique and influential institutions. Its purpose is to train young wrestlers into senior champions while inculcating them with the strict etiquette, discipline, and special values which are the foundations of *sumō*'s world-apart society. In this it is most successful.

Physically, a stable (*heya;* literally, "room") is a self-contained unit complete with all living-training facilities. Upstairs are dormitories for the juniors and semiprivate and private rooms for the seniors. Downstairs, the unheated training room has a hard-packed earthen floor with a 4.55-meter (14.9-ft) rope circle just like a *dohyō* except that the floor is not raised. Adjacent is an open room, usually with *tatami* mats, where coaches and visitors sit to observe practice. Other areas include a large washroom with Japanese-style tubs, a kitchen, a dining-living room, and a reception room.

There are 30 or so *heya* currently active, and every professional *sumō* wrestler belongs to one, making it his home throughout his ring career and often even into retirement. The only exceptions to the live-in rule are the married *sekitori,* who may live outside with their wives and commute to daily practice at the *heya.* In fact, few wrestlers are married until they are well established in the upper ranks. Depending on the state of its fame and fortunes, a *heya* may boast several dozen wrestlers or carry on with barely a handful. Each *heya* has a name taken from the champion or retired elder (*toshiyori*) who founded it, and its wrestlers fight under this aegis. Some *heya,* like Sadogatake, have a 200-year-old history. Some, like Taihō-Beya, named for the brilliant *yokozuna* who retired in 1971, have been founded within the past 20 years.

A stable is managed under the absolute control of a single boss (*oyakata*). All *oyakata* are ex-senior wrestlers and members of the Japan Sumō Association. The stable they run is usually the stable where they wrestled. For example, the present boss of Dewanoumi-Beya, traditionally one of the biggest and most powerful stables, is ex-grand champion Sadanoyama, who succeeded his boss (after marrying his daughter) to become the ninth-generation Dewanoumi Oyakata.

Oyakata are generally married and live in special quarters with their wives, who are known by the title of *okamisan,* the only women to live in *heya.* *Okamisan* play an important behind-the-scenes role in the smooth operation of a stable, but their duties never include cooking or cleaning for the wrestlers. These and all other housekeeping chores outside the *oyakata*'s quarters are performed by apprentices and low-ranked wrestlers who receive no pay at all for all their pains and must in addition serve as *tsukebito* (servant-valet) for *jūryō* and *makuuchi* wrestlers. *Heya* expenses are paid for by regular allowances from the Japan Sumō Association and gifts from the *heya* fan club (*kōenkai*).

Occasionally in the past and still today, a retiring champion will leave his old stable to found his own. If this break is amicable, he will be allowed to enter the main stable's *ichimon* ("clan"), thus establishing a beneficial and typical parent-child relationship. Powerful and established stables may have three or four related *heya* in their *ichimon.* In the past this practice dulled competition, since *ichimon* wrestlers were not required to fight against each other. Today this rule applies only to wrestlers in the same stable.

Traditionally, the greatest geographical concentration of *heya* has been and still is in the Ryōgoku area of Tōkyō, by the river Sumidagawa, an area perhaps more widely known through Hiroshige's print "Fireworks at the Ryōgoku Bridge." Other high population areas for *heya* are nearby Edogawa and Kōtō wards.

Sumō Practice —— *Keiko,* "practice," is a sacred word in *sumō,* and a brief description of the morning practice that takes place every day in every *heya* will give an idea of the *sumō* way of life.

The day begins at 4:00 or 5:00 AM for the youngest, lowest-ranked wrestlers, who ready the ring and begin their exercises. The higher a wrestlers's rank, the longer he may lie abed. *Makushita* are up at 6:30 and in the ring at 7:00. *Jūryō* wrestlers enter the ring around 8:00 and *makuuchi* shortly after.

The physical essentials for success in *sumō* are balance, agility, and flexibility, combined with a pair of powerful thighs and the lowest possible center of gravity. To achieve all this, wrestlers practice endlessly three traditional exercises, *shiko, teppō,* and *matawari,* which every coach and *oyakata* will agree are the absolute basics of *sumō.*

For *shiko,* one stands with feet wide apart, draws in the breath, tips the body to the left, raises the right leg sideways as high as possible, and then stamps it down with a hissing exhale. The action is repeated with the left foot, and so on. Beginners should practice *shiko* at least 500 times a day.

Matawari involves sitting in the dirt with legs spread as wide as possible, the closer to 180° the better. Next, one leans forward until the entire upper body from the navel to the cheekbone is pressed against the ring. If one can't quite make it, a senior wrestler will help by standing on his back, an incredibly painful procedure. "Are you crying?" he asks. "No, just sweat in my eyes," the junior wrestler groans.

Teppō is the *sumō* punching bag, but the object one hits is a pillar of wood sunk in the earth. Stepping forward and back with rhythmical, sliding footwork one slams ones open hands against the pole—right, left, right, left—to develop timing and coordination while strengthening arms and hands, legs and back.

Wrestling techniques are learned by watching and in practice bouts (*mōshiai*), there being no formal, Western-style teaching of the various throws and lifts. Instead the wrestler learns from wrestling with a senior and then practicing with one of his peers.

When the session is almost over, wrestling ends and *butsukari-geiko* (literally, "collision training") begins. This requires the younger wrestlers to charge a senior and drive him across the ring in one long slide, turn and drive him back and repeat until the junior is tottering with exhaustion. Along the way he is occasionally thrown down so that he will learn how to hit the cement-hard *dohyō* and roll without hurting himself. After *butsukari-geiko* comes *matawari,* and then all join in a final round of *shiko.*

Now it is 11:00 AM and the senior wrestlers head for the baths, where their backs are scrubbed by their *tsukebito* attendants. When they are out, the lower ranks can get in. Next it is time for brunch, the first and largest *sumō* meal of the day. This consists of *chanko-nabe,* the famous, high-calorie stew which is another one of the *sumō* basics. To make *chankonabe* one begins with a big pot of seaweed-base stock and then dumps in chicken, pork, fish, *tōfu,* bean sprouts, cabbage, carrots, onions, etc, etc. The senior wrestlers eat bowl upon bowl of this stew together with bowl upon bowl of rice washed down with quarts of beer. Around 1:00 PM the skinny youngsters who got up at 4:00 AM sit down to eat what is left. Ample incentive to go for the top.

Except for the housekeeping chores of junior wrestlers and *tsukebito*-type errands, the official business of the day is over at the *heya* after lunch and does not begin again until next morning's *keiko.* Supper is usually a poor affair, and most wrestlers prefer to eat out if they can afford it. Most young wrestlers cannot. Whenever a wrestler leaves the *heya* he must be dressed neatly in a *kimono;* and his hair, if it is long enough, must be carefully oiled, combed, and tied in the *chommage* topknot of the 18th-century townsman. This is done by the *heya's* resident barber or *tokoyama*.

The Japan Sumō Association—— Every aspect of professional *sumō* is controlled down to the last detail by the Japan Sumō Association (Nihon Sumō Kyōkai). This association is composed of 105 retired wrestlers known as elders *(toshiyori)* and includes representation from *sumō's* "working ranks," i.e., active wrestlers, referees *(gyōji)*, and ring stewards *(yobidashi)*. Thus one could say that *sumō* is one of the few professional sports, if not the only one, to be run entirely by insiders.

To become a member of the Japan Sumō Association one must first qualify as an ex-wrestler who has competed in 24 tournaments in the *jūryō* division or in a tournament in *makuuchi*. Next, a vacancy among the 105 memberships must exist. Finally, one must purchase a share in the association—*toshiyorikabu*—which sold for ¥5 million ($22,000) in 1982. As always in *sumō* there are exceptions, and as of February 1982 there were actually 106 association memberships, 96 of which were actually filled. This is because, although there were no vacancies at the time of his retirement in 1971, ex-yokozuna Taihō was permitted to buy a share and join the association in recognition of his outstanding career. This practice is called *ichidai toshiyori*—"one-generation elder"—and it was expected that when Taihō Oyakata reached the retirement age of 65, the position would retire with him and the number of *toshiyori* revert to 105.

The Japan Sumō Association is organized in six divisions: Business, Judging, Off-Season Tours (Jungyō), Out-of-Tōkyō Tournaments (Chihō Basho), Training, and Guidance. All this is supervised by an elected, 10-man board of directors under the leadership of a president or managing director *(rijichō)*. The *rijichō* in 1982 was a fine example of the *sumō* success dream come true. Entering Kasugano-Beya at age 13, he fought his way from apprentice at the bottom to grand champion at the top, competing under the wrestling name *(shikona)* of Tochinishiki. On retirement from competition he joined the association and became boss of his old stable with the *toshiyori* name Kasugano Oyakata. In 1974 he was elected president of the Japan Sumō Association, the top of the line.

The Kokugikan—— Located in the Kuramae section of Taitō Ward in Tōkyō, the Kokugikan (National Sport Arena) is in every respect the home of professional *sumō*. Its complex includes an amphitheater with a seating capacity of over 10,000, where the three Tōkyō tournaments and other *sumō*-related events are held, with changing rooms and baths for the wrestlers, a medical clinic, and all the various offices of the Japan Sumō Association.

The main entrance leads through an arcade lined with small, numbered booths staffed by men in Edo-period costume. These are the *chaya* (literally, "tea house") and each "controls" a block of *sajiki* (small boxes on the main floor of the garden with *tatami* mats and no chairs) into which four average people can cram with only moderate discomfort. On presenting one's ticket to the *chaya* booth in charge of one's box, an attendant will escort one there and take one's order for such refreshments as beer, *sake,* and *sushi.*

Also within the Kokugikan are a Sumō Museum and a Sumō School (the Sumō Kyōshūjo). All new wrestlers must attend a six-month course at this school, which presents a core curriculum evenly balanced between physical and classroom education.

The first Kokugikan was built across the river right in the Ryōgoku section in 1909. Destroyed by fire in 1917, it was quickly rebuilt. This second building, though damaged in World War II, was repaired and used until the early 1950s and is now an auditorium for Nihon University. The Kuramae Kokugikan, as the new one is called, was completed in 1954. In a courtyard area between the *chaya*, museum, and main garden sections is a memorial stone inscribed with a poem written by the then head of the Imperial Household Agency to express the feelings of the emperor—a lifelong *sumō* enthusiast—after his visit to the Kokugikan in 1955 during the May tournament. It had been 18 years since His Majesty was able to attend a match, and the poem reads, "How enjoyable! The wrestlers straining . . . the people applauding. It had been so long since I saw *sumō*." His Majesty still visits the Kokugikan every May, thus maintaining a tradition of *tenran-zumō*, "*sumō* performed before the emperor," a tradition which supposedly began when, according to a legend in the chronicle NIHON SHOKI (720), Nomi no Sukune fought and beat Taima no Kehaya in a command performance before the legendary emperor Suinin—the first written reference to a *sumō* bout.

◼◼ —— Andy Adams and Ryo Hatano, *Sumo History and Yokozuna Profiles* (1979). Patricia L. Cuyler, *Sumo: From Rite to Sport* (1979). Japan Sumō Association, *Sumo* (1978). J. A. Sargeant, *Sumo:*

the Sport and the Tradition (1959). John Wheeler, *Takamiyama: The World of Sumō* (1973).　　　　　　　　John E. THAYER III

Sumoto

City on the island of Awajishima in the Inland Sea; administratively a part of Hyōgo Prefecture. A castle town during the Edo period (1600–1868), it is the political and economic center of the island. There is convenient transportation between Sumoto and Honshū. Principal industries are spinning and electrical appliances manufacture. It is part of the Inland Sea National Park. Pop: 44,131.

Sumpu

The *kokufu* (seat of provincial goverment) of "Sunshū" (that is, Suruga Province) under the RITSURYŌ SYSTEM formed in the 7th and 8th centuries. The town's name euphonically combines the syllables *"sun"* and *"fu"* from these two terms. Sumpu was renamed Shizuoka in 1869 and has been the capital of Shizuoka Prefecture since 1871. From the 14th century, it was the seat of the IMAGAWA FAMILY, the military governors *(shugo)* of Suruga; with the collapse of the Imagawa at the end of 1568, Sumpu was occupied by the powerful *daimyō* TAKEDA SHINGEN; after the destruction of the Takeda in 1582, Suruga came into the possession of TOKUGAWA IEYASU, who moved his headquarters to Sumpu in early 1587. In the massive redistribution of fiefs *(kunigae)* undertaken by the national unifier TOYOTOMI HIDEYOSHI in 1590, Ieyasu was transferred to Edo (now Tōkyō), and Sumpu was allotted to Hideyoshi's old vassal Nakamura Kazuuji (d 1600). After his great victory at the Battle of SEKIGAHARA, however, Ieyasu displaced the Nakamura from Sumpu; and in 1607, two years after he retired from the shogunate, Ieyasu returned to Sumpu, where he established a governmental apparatus (the so-called Sumpu *seiken*) that had national responsibilities and overshadowed the shogunate itself, in effect creating a dyarchy which Ieyasu dominated as retired shōgun *(ōgosho)*. Ieyasu died in Sumpu on 1 June 1616 (Genna 2.4.17) and was buried on KUNŌZAN, a mountain southeast of the town. Although his remains were moved to the shrine TŌSHŌGŪ in Nikkō the next year, Kunōzan with its own well-endowed Tōshōgū continued to be the sacred ground of the Tokugawa shogunate. Sumpu Castle, built by Ieyasu in 1607–08, ranked with ŌSAKA CASTLE as one of the shogunate's most important fortifications outside Edo.　　　　　　　　　*George* ELISON

Sumpuki

(Chronicle of Sumpu). Work in diary form covering the period from 1611 to 1615, when TOKUGAWA IEYASU was living in retirement at his castle in Sumpu (now the city of Shizuoka); variously attributed to GOTŌ MITSUTSUGU, an official of the shogunal mint, and to HAYASHI RAZAN, the Confucian scholar. It contains valuable information on Ieyasu's relations with TOYOTOMI HIDEYORI and his family, whom Ieyasu eventually crushed in 1615 (see ŌSAKA CASTLE, SIEGES OF), and on his views concerning foreign trade, literature, religion, and the arts.

Sunagawa

City in western central Hokkaidō, on the river Ishikarigawa. Sunagawa has been a vital transportation center since the opening of a railway line in 1891. Principal industries are chemical fertilizer, plywood, and concrete. Thermoelectric plants of the Hokkaidō Electric Power Co, Inc, are located here. Pop: 25,355.

Sunagawa case

(Sunagawa Jiken). A criminal trial in which seven Japanese, indicted for trespassing on an American army base, challenged the stationing of the US Security Forces in Japan on the grounds that it violated article 9, the controversial RENUNCIATION OF WAR clause, of the constitution.

The facts of the case are undisputed. The United States desired to extend a runway at its Tachikawa Air Base in the village of Sunagawa, Tōkyō Prefecture, and had won permission from the Japanese authorities to procure adjoining private farmland. When it was surveyed in July 1957, more than 1,000 opponents of the American military gathered to protest. Seven rioters broke down part of the fence and entered the base. They were accused of having violated a special law that, in accord with the Administrative Agreement between the two nations, set more severe penalties for such trespassing than the general law did with regard to other property.

The Tōkyō District Court, composed of three judges under the presidency of Judge Date Akio, on 30 March 1959 reached a verdict of not guilty and acquitted all defendants.

The court ruled that the stationing of US forces in Japan did violate article 9 of the constitution. It held that article 9 prohibits "war potential" even for self-defense. Japan retains a right of self-defense but may exercise it only by resorting to the United Nations. It argued further that article 9 derives from the will of the Japanese people, who, in the spirit of the preamble and in "self-reflection on the past," aim at being pioneers of eternal world peace.

As to the stationing of the US forces, the court ruled that the United States–Japan Security Treaty permits the United States to deploy its forces in areas outside Japan as well. The treaty therefore may involve Japan in a war that does not concern Japan and so runs counter to the pacifism of the constitution. Moreover, even the use of the US forces for the defense of Japan would make Japan a belligerent, since the treaty's Administrative Agreement provides that in the event of hostilities in the area of Japan the two governments shall confer and take joint measures necessary for the area's defense. Although Japan has no command or control over the US forces, their stationing was the result of a mutual agreement and therefore also an act of the Japanese government.

On the basis of these considerations, the court concluded that, since the stationing of the US forces in Japan is unconstitutional, their privileged treatment by the special law for violation of which the defendants were prosecuted was null and void under the due-process-of-law principle of article 31 of the constitution.

The decision was rendered in the explosive atmosphere of national debate over the revision of the security treaty, which the Japanese government was then renegotiating with the United States. The leftist parties, with the support of some other groups, were bitterly opposed to any renewal of the treaty and advocated neutrality and nonalignment. Soviet Russia and China supported this stand. The acquittal of the defendants was therefore hailed as a great victory by all antagonists of the renewal. It also made the troubled government even more vulnerable to its political critics. Hence, the public prosecutor, omitting the middle instance of the High Court, appealed directly to the Supreme Court for JUDICIAL REVIEW (Japanese law permits appeals by the state, even in the case of acquittals). The prosecution was confronted with a defense council consisting of a huge battalion of lawyers and other jurists.

In its verdict of 16 December 1959 the Grand Bench of the Supreme Court quashed the first-instance decision and remanded the case to the Tōkyō District Court for retrial. The judgment was unanimous, but 10 justices submitted supplemental opinions, either elaborating the majority ruling or objecting to its reasoning.

The majority opinion held that article 9 embodies the spirit of pacifism in the constitution. Although it renounces war and prohibits the maintenance of war potential, it in no way denies Japan the right of self-defense that a sovereign nation inherently possesses. It does not require defenselessness or nonresistance. The preamble recognizes that "all peoples of the world have the right to live in peace." That includes Japan, which therefore has the right to maintain her own peace and security and take the measures necessary for her self-defense. Since under paragraph 2 of article 9 the Japanese people are not allowed to maintain war potential and are thereby practically disarmed, they are free to select any means deemed suitable for self-defense and not at all limited to the United Nations, as the District Court believed. The selection depends upon the prevailing international conditions.

What article 9 bans, the court ruled, is the devising of aggressive war through the maintenance of war potential, as well as the exercise of command and control over it, *by Japan*. This ban does not extend to foreign military forces retained in Japan, since Japan's agreement in a treaty to their retention does not make them *Japanese* war potential.

Nonetheless, the court felt that to decide whether such retention violated the constitution would require an examination of the constitutionality of the security treaty on which it was based. That treaty is closely connected with the SAN FRANCISCO PEACE TREATY (1952) signed by 40 of the then 60 members of the United Nations. The peace treaty explicitly permits the stationing or retention of foreign military forces on Japanese soil. Hence, Japan was justified in entering into collective security arrangements with the United States. The security treaty was duly executed by the Japanese cabinet, and after careful consideration, including discussion of the question of constitutionality, it was approved by both houses of the Diet. In view of the highly political nature of the treaty, the court, as a judicial body, is not authorized to render a legal decision on its constitutionality "unless there is clearly obvious unconstitutionality or invalidity."

That decision must be left primarily to the two other branches of government. The court's examination, however, led it to the conclusion that the retention of US forces, the main purpose of the security treaty, "must certainly be in accord with the intent of article 9 and of article 98, paragraph 2 (which requires faithful observation of treaties and established laws of nations), and it absolutely cannot be admitted that it is in violation of the said provisions or that it is clearly obvious that it is unconstitutional and invalid." The same conclusion was reached with regard to the treaty's Administrative Agreement. The principal reasoning behind this judgment appears to be that the US forces are not war potential of Japan, since command and control over them are left completely to the United States, and that the purpose of their retention is the maintenance of peace and security in East Asia in view of the inadequacy of Japan's defensive strength.

Some of the supplemental opinions took issue with the majority ruling's profession of self-restraint in view of the political nature of the security treaty. Others made the criticism that, while judicial review of the treaty is limited to clearly obvious unconstitutionality, the majority opinion nevertheless thoroughly reviewed and judged it as if this self-imposed limitation did not exist. Justice Otani Katsushige characterized this departure from the self-restraint principle as "a self-consoling excuse." Chief Justice TANAKA KŌTARŌ, a prominent teacher and advocate of natural law, elaborated on the international spirit of the constitution and on the interdependence of nations as reflected in the preamble. He believed that self-defense in its strict meaning was no longer possible, since self-defense is the defense of others, and the defense of others is self-defense.

The Tōkyō District Court, to which the case was remanded, was bound by the Supreme Court's ruling of constitutionality. It had to accept the legal validity of the special law under which the defendants had been indicted, and its role was restricted to merely determining the appropriate punishment. The trespassers were punished with a fine.

The legal and political significance of the Supreme Court's decision at home and abroad can hardly be overstated. For the first time Japan's highest tribunal had interpreted the problematic war-renunciation clause and made a ruling on judicial review of international treaties. Although a finding on the constitutionality of the Japanese Self Defense Forces was explicitly omitted from the Supreme Court's ruling, it is not difficult to deduce from the court's reasoning how this hotly disputed question will be finally decided. While dealing with this issue in the early 1970s, the Sapporo High Court evidently used the Sunagawa ruling as a precedent in the NAGANUMA CASE.

With its reversal of the first-instance court decision, the Supreme Court had deprived Japanese and foreign opponents of Japan's alliance with the United States of their major legal weapon. Still, the political crisis brought on by the revision of the security treaty continued and culminated in mass demonstrations, an assassination attempt against Prime Minister KISHI NOBUSUKE, who had been accused of pushing the treaty through the Diet, and his resignation and replacement by IKEDA HAYATO. In this climate of unrest the visit of President Eisenhower planned for the Tōkyō signing of the revised treaty had to be cancelled. This embarrassment to the conservative government was insignificant compared to the incalculable domestic and international damage it would have suffered had the Supreme Court upheld the original decision.

📖 ——John Maki, *Court and Constitution in Japan* (1964). Alfred C. Oppler, "The Sunakawa Case: Its Legal and Political Implications," *Political Science Quarterly* 76 (1961).　　Alfred C. OPPLER

sunao

An important concept in Japanese interpersonal relationships. Used in the adjectival form *sunao na*, meaning "upright and compliant." (The prefix *su* adds emphasis to *nao*, meaning "straight"; *naosu*, a verb derived from *nao*, means "to straighten, correct, or cure.") *Sunao* is considered one of the most desirable personality traits in young Japanese, male and female. *Sunao na* is the opposite of *hinekureta* (warped, twisted). According to the psychologist Doi Takeo, when a Japanese person's AMAE (dependency need) is not satisfied, he feels acute frustration and resorts to the kind of sulking described by the verb *suneru* (to pretend indifference to one's *amae* or dependency needs) or the verb *higamu* (to pretend not to need to depend, while envying others who are apparently favored). When this becomes a chronic attitude and is seen as an integral part of the personality, the person is described as a *hinekureta* person (distrustful, embittered, begrudging, and resentful). In contrast, a *sunao na* person, whose *amae* has been sufficiently gratified since childhood, continues to have a basic trust in authority, finds it easy and natural to follow the directives of others, and acts on the assumption that he will be taken care of should special needs arise. See also JAPANESE PEOPLE, PSYCHOLOGY OF.

■ ——Doi Takeo, *Amae no kōzō* (1971), tr John Bester as *The Anatomy of Dependence* (1973).   *Hiroshi* WAGATSUMA

sundry goods industry

A general term used to refer to a large group of various kinds of relatively minor industries. It includes manufacturers of musical instruments, sporting goods, stationery, kitchen utensils, tableware, accessories, shoes and other footwear, suitcases, handbags, lacquer ware, bamboo ware, pottery and porcelain ware, glass products, toys, and other miscellaneous goods. Although each of these is an independent industry, they are often collectively referred to as the sundry goods industry because of their similar methods and scale of production. Most of the companies are labor intensive and small or medium sized. Production in many cases is concentrated in specific areas. The city of TSUBAME, Niigata Prefecture, for example, is known for its production of eating utensils, while the city of TAJIMI, Gifu Prefecture, is a center for chinaware manufacture. Until around 1970, because the average wage in Japan was lower than in Western countries, many companies in the sundry goods industry had expanded their business through exports. However, with the growth of similar industry in developing countries and the revaluation of the yen in 1971, the competitive power of Japan's sundry goods industry in the international market declined rapidly. As a result of this decrease in export markets and of increased imports from developing countries, numerous Japanese firms have been forced to shut down or switch to another industry. In order to counter this trend, Japanese enterprises are striving to reduce costs or to specialize in high-quality products. Some enterprises are contemplating the establishment of plants in developing countries.
                                                                              TOMISAWA Konomi

Sung Che-yüan → Song Zheyuan (Sung Che-yüan)

Sung Chiao-jen → Song Jiaoren (Sung Chiao-jen)

sun goddess → Amaterasu Ōmikami

Suntory, Ltd

(Santorī). The oldest and largest distiller of whiskey in Japan and a major producer of spirits, beer, wine, and soft drinks. Suntory, Ltd, is one of the world's top three whiskey producers, and its Old Suntory (sold in Japan as Suntory Old) is the world's best-selling whiskey (over 10 million cases in 1981). Founded in 1899 by TORII SHINJIRŌ, the firm produced a sweet wine called Akadama and subsequently began distilling the first Japanese whiskey. Under Torii's son, SAJI KEIZŌ, the company played a major role in making the Japanese whiskey market the second largest in the world. The company exports its products to more than 60 countries and has several overseas subsidiaries. It also owns a restaurant chain with a total of eight branches overseas. Future plans include ventures into the pharmaceutical, fast-food, mail-order, and housing businesses. Suntory is involved in cultural activities as well, operating the Suntory Foundation, whose goal is to promote cultural exchange between Japan and foreign countries, as well as the Suntory Museum of Art and the Suntory Music Foundation. Sales for the fiscal year ending March 1982 totaled ¥722 billion (US $3 billion), distributed as follows: whiskey, wine, and spirits 80 percent; beer 15 percent; and soft drinks 5 percent. In the same year the company was capitalized at ¥2.2 billion (US $9.1 million). Its head office is in Ōsaka.

Sun Wen → Sun Yat-sen

sun worship

Sun worship has been practiced in Japan since ancient times. According to Japanese mythology the sun goddess, AMATERASU ŌMI-KAMI, is the highest deity and a direct ancestor of the imperial family. One story associated with this goddess describes her as hid-

ing in a cave and having to be coaxed out. The story is believed to have its origin in the agricultural rite seeking the return of the sun at the winter solstice. In the Kansai and Kyūshū regions there are several Shintō shrines where a sun deity, *amateru kami*, is still worshipped. Traces of sun worship are also seen in festivals held on the days of the solstice or equinox (HIGAN), and in the custom of welcoming the rising sun on the peak of a mountain, especially on New Year's Day.   FUJITA Tomio

Sun Yat-sen (1866–1925)

(Mandarin: Sun Yixian or Sun I-hsien; original name Sun Wen). Leading revolutionary against the Qing (Ch'ing) dynasty (1644–1912), first provisional president of the Chinese republic, and to all Chinese the father of their country. During a total of six years' residence in Japan he secured considerable Japanese political and financial aid for the Chinese republican cause, particularly between 1897 and 1907.

Born in Guangdong (Kwangtung) Province, he went in 1879 to join his elder brother in Honolulu, where he attended an Anglican missionary school. Four years later he returned home, but his disrespect for village customs soon forced his family to send him to Hong Kong. He next studied Western medicine in Guangzhou (Canton) and Hong Kong and graduated as a doctor in 1892.

While in medical school, Sun made acquaintances who later joined his Xingzhong Hui (Hsing Chung Hui; Revive China Society), organized in 1894 with funds raised in Honolulu. After his first, unsuccessful, uprising against the Qing in 1895, he traveled to Japan, Southeast Asia, Europe, and North America to raise money for the revolutionary cause. During a visit to Japan in 1897 he adopted the Japanese alias by which he is commonly known to Chinese today—Nakayama (Mandarin: Zhongshan or Chung-shan); more important, he began his close, lifelong friendship with the pan-Asianist MIYAZAKI TŌTEN. Through Miyazaki, Sun became a friend of TŌYAMA MITSURU and Kayano Chōchi (1873–ca 1940) and made the acquaintance of the eminent politicians ŌKUMA SHIGENOBU and INUKAI TSUYOSHI. Inukai in particular provided Sun with living quarters and funds. Several of Sun's Japanese friends participated in the unsuccessful Huizhou (Waichow) uprising in 1900; one of them, Yamada Yoshimasa (1868–1900), became the first foreigner to sacrifice his life for the Chinese revolution.

In 1905 Sun organized the revolutionary United League (Tongmeng Hui or T'ung-meng Hui) in Tōkyō and urged its members to intensify their efforts in Central China. Under Qing pressure Sun was expelled from Japan in 1907. He proceeded to seek support elsewhere in Asia, Europe, and the United States. Abroad at the time of the successful Chinese Revolution of October 1911, Sun arrived in Nanjing (Nanking) on 1 January 1912 to accept his fellow revolutionaries' offer of the post of provisional president of the Republic of China.

One month later Sun resigned in favor of YUAN SHIKAI (Yüan Shih-k'ai), the general who had engineered the abdication of the last Qing emperor. When Yuan began to remove Sun's associates from office in preparation for his own enthronement as emperor, Sun launched the abortive Second Revolution of 1913. Fleeing to Japan, he again sought financial and political support from Japanese bureaucrats, militarists, and industrialists. MORI KAKU of the Mitsui Company and KUHARA FUSANOSUKE reportedly gave him considerable financial aid in return for promises of territorial concessions for Japan. In 1914 Sun set up the Guomindang (Kuomintang; Nationalist Party) to wrest power from Yuan Shikai.

For brief periods between 1916 and 1924 Sun was leader of a separatist government. Unable to gain support from Western nations, he turned to Soviet Russia. In 1923 the Comintern sent Mikhail Borodin (1884–1951) to China to help Sun reorganize the Guomindang along Bolshevik lines. The following year Sun elaborated in public lectures his three famous principles of nationalism, democracy, and people's livelihood. During a visit to Beijing (Peking) to confer with political leaders, he fell ill and died on 12 March 1925. In 1929 his remains were moved from Beijing to an impressive mausoleum outside Nanjing, where they lie today.

■ ——Marius B. Jansen, *The Japanese and Sun Yat-sen* (1954). C. Martin Wilbur, *Sun Yat-sen: Frustrated Patriot* (1976).
                                                                          Susan H. MARSH

Suō Province

(Suō no Kuni; also called Bōshū). One of the eight provinces of the San'yōdō ("South of the Mountains Circuit") in southern Honshū;

Supreme Court

Chief Justices of the Supreme Court, 1947–1982		
Chief justice	Term	Age at time of appointment
1st Mibuchi Tadahiko	4 August 1947–2 March 1950	67
2nd Tanaka Kōtarō	3 March 1950–24 October 1960	59
3rd Yokota Kisaburō	25 October 1960–5 August 1966	64
4th Yokota Masatoshi	6 August 1966–10 January 1969	67
5th Ishida Kazuto	11 January 1969–19 May 1973	65
6th Murakami Tomokazu	21 May 1973–24 May 1976	66
7th Fujibashi Ekizō	25 May 1976–25 August 1977	68
8th Okahara Masao	26 August 1977–31 March 1979	68
9th Hattori Takaaki	2 April 1979–30 September 1982	66
10th Terada Jirō	1 October 1982–	66

established under the KOKUGUN SYSTEM in 646, it comprised what is now the southeastern part of YAMAGUCHI PREFECTURE. In the 8th through 10th centuries the copper produced in the region was used to mint Japan's earliest coins, the KŌCHŌ JŪNISEN. During the Heian period (794–1185) large landed estates (SHŌEN) were established in Suō by temples and shrines of the Kyōto-Nara area. In the Kamakura period (1185–1333) the entire province was designated revenue land for the temple TŌDAIJI in Nara; it was administered by the FUJIWARA FAMILY, the HŌJŌ FAMILY, and, later, the ŌUCHI FAMILY. Under the Ōuchi, the castle town of Yamaguchi became a major cultural center of western Japan. In 1551 ŌUCHI YOSHITAKA was destroyed by a retainer, who in turn was overthrown by MŌRI MOTONARI. The Mōri family ruled both Suō and the neighboring province of Nagato (or Chōshū) throughout the Edo period (1600–1868). Traditional products included rice, salt, paper, and wax. With the establishment of the PREFECTURAL SYSTEM in 1871, Suō was combined with Nagato to form Yamaguchi Prefecture.

support

(fuyō). Furnishing funds or sustenance to persons who cannot provide their own financial resources. Under the Civil Code of 1898, which was influenced by the traditional Japanese family system, the head of the household was responsible for the support of the family. Today, however, support is construed primarily as economic assistance determined by the relationships of rights and obligations between individuals. Book IV, chapter 6 of the present Civil Code makes support obligatory only in relationships between parent and child and among siblings. Under extenuating circumstances, the FAMILY COURT may impose the obligation of support upon blood relatives outside the immediate family. The obligation to provide support arises when two conditions exist: first, a person with a right to receive support requires it; and second, the party obliged to provide support is capable of providing it while still maintaining his own livelihood. The second, limiting condition does not apply, however, to a parent's responsibility to support a minor child or to one spouse's responsibility to support the other, since a distinction is made between these and other familial relationships.

The method, extent, and precedence of support were explicitly delineated in the Civil Code of 1898, but in the present Civil Code these matters are decided by deliberation between the parties involved, with the Family Court arbitrating only if no agreement can be reached. Along with the establishment of a welfare state, increasing emphasis has been placed on the state's obligation to ensure a minimum guarantee of support for the public. Nevertheless, the support provisions of the Civil Code take precedence and the state's assistance is only supplementary. See also CIVIL PROCEDURE, CODE OF.   Bai Kōichi

Supreme Commander for the Allied Powers → SCAP

Supreme Court

(Saikō Saibansho). Highest tribunal in Japan. The Supreme Court is roughly equivalent to the prewar GREAT COURT OF CASSATION (Dai-

shin'in), but the Daishin'in was the highest tribunal only in civil and criminal cases and had no jurisdiction in administrative law cases, which were exclusively handled by a special tribunal, the ADMINISTRATIVE COURT. Under the Meiji Constitution of 1889 there were other special tribunals, beyond the control of the Daishin'in, such as courts-martial, a court of the imperial household, and so on. Moreover, the Daishin'in, as well as lower courts of civil and criminal law, was not empowered to examine the constitutionality of statutes enacted by the Diet; prewar courts including the Daishin'in were not involved in the construction of constitutional law. In addition, the Daishin'in was only a legal court, without powers of justice administration, rule-making powers, and the like. Powers of justice administration (control of personnel, financial, and organizational matters) belonged to the Justice Department. In short, the prewar Great Court was not significant in a political sense and its prestige was not as great as that of the present Supreme Court.

The 1947 constitution states: "(1) The whole judicial power is vested in a Supreme Court and in such inferior courts as are established by law. (2) No extraordinary tribunal shall be established, nor shall any organ or agency of the Executive be given final judicial power" (art. 76). The Supreme Court is literally the highest organ of judicial power in civil and criminal cases, as well as in administrative law cases or any other forms of legal litigation. Furthermore, article 81 of the constitution makes the Supreme Court "the court of last resort with power to determine the constitutionality of any law, order, regulation or official act." This reflects the obvious influence of the American system of judicial review and extends judicial powers to include judgments about constitutional issues. However, the Supreme Court, not a "constitutional court" in a Western European sense, decides issues of constitutionality only in the context of controversies involving parties with proper standing.

The Supreme Court consists of a chief justice and 14 associate justices. The chief justice is formally appointed by the emperor in accordance with the designation by the cabinet. Other justices are appointed by the cabinet, and their appointments are reviewed by voters in the first general election of members of the House of Representatives after each appointment. The justices' retirement age is 70. The Supreme Court is divided into three petty benches and each bench is able to decide most cases. The grand bench, consisting of full members of the court, examines cases referred by one of the petty benches because of the importance of issues involved in terms of constitutional questions, context of precedents, and so on. The Supreme Court is now regarded as the highest organ of justice administration: judges of the inferior courts are appointed by the cabinet from a list of persons nominated by the Supreme Court. The court has powers in matters of personnel and finance which once belonged to the prewar Justice Department. Furthermore, the constitution invests the court with a rule-making power, which also reflects an American influence. According to the constitution, therefore, the Supreme Court should enjoy great prestige in constitutional matters, as well as in other aspects of the governmental process. In practice, however, constitutional guarantees of the Supreme Court's status have not been rigorously fulfilled, and the court is perhaps not held in as much esteem as was intended.   Okudaira Yasuhiro

Su, Prince (1863–1922)

Known in Japan as Shuku Shinnō. Prince Su was the hereditary title of Su Shanqi (Su Shan-ch'i), a member of the Manchu imperial family in China whom the Japanese supported in a movement to foster independence in Manchuria and Inner Mongolia. After the overthrow of the Manchu dynasty in the 1911 revolution, the Japanese military concluded that China's new president, YUAN SHIKAI (Yüan Shih-k'ai), was not favorable to their interests in China and began to work toward the formation of a separate Manchu state in Manchuria. In 1912, with the help of Kawashima Naniwa, a China adventurer, Su was brought to Japanese-controlled PORT ARTHUR in the Liaodong (Liaotung) Peninsula as future head of the proposed puppet state. The plot was discovered and halted by the Japanese Ministry of Foreign Affairs, for the Tōkyō government had already decided to support Yuan's government by participating in the REORGANIZATION LOAN. During 1914, however, Japanese policy toward Yuan Shikai began to shift and, when Yuan proclaimed himself emperor of China at the end of 1915, Japan gave aid both to SUN YATSEN's movement against Yuan in South China and to Prince Su's separatist movement in Manchuria and Inner Mongolia. The latter collapsed in 1916, and Prince Su retired to Port Arthur.

suretyship

(hoshō). Legal duty (hoshō saimu or the suretyship obligatory duty) of a third party (hoshōnin or the surety) to perform the principal obligatory duty to the obligee when the principal obligor fails to perform the principal obligatory duty, or a contract (hoshō keiyaku or suretyship contract) giving rise to such a duty. Suretyships are most commonly given by relatives or friends, but suretyship by public or cooperative surety organizations is becoming frequent. The suretyship obligatory duty is secondary to the principal obligatory duty: for example, when the principal obligatory duty ceases to have force because of invalidation or cancelation or when it is discharged, the suretyship obligatory duty also ceases to have force or is dissolved. The suretyship obligatory duty also accompanies the principal obligation: when the principal obligatory duty is transferred, the suretyship obligatory duty is transferred along with it. In addition, the suretyship obligatory duty is supplementary to the principal obligatory duty. That is, when the obligee demands performance of the obligatory duty from the surety, the surety can demur by demanding that the principal obligor be called upon to perform the obligatory duty first (right to demur by call upon principal obligor). The obligee, on the other hand, must seek performance from the principal obligor first, if the surety proves that the principal obligor has the means to discharge easily the obligatory duty (right to demur by referring the obligee to the principal obligor). However, the right to these two pleas is lost if the surety has undertaken joint and several obligation with the principal obligor. *Awaji Takehisa*

surimono

(literally, "printed thing"). Specifically, surimono refers to a luxurious kind of print on unsized paper, made to special order and used for greetings, announcements, etc, notably as New Year's gifts. Surimono are approximately shikishiban or poem card size: 21.2 by 15.8 centimeters (8.3 by 6.2 in). There are some as small as 6 by 8 centimeters (2.4 by 3.1 in) and as large as a double nagaban (67 by 15.8 cm or 26.4 by 6.2 in). Some of the surimono from the late 19th century exceed the nagaban size by as much as one-third in depth. Most surimono include one or more poems, usually KYŌKA. Many were commissioned by kyōka clubs in order to feature poems by their members.

Surimono are distinguished from other woodblock prints in several ways: they are invariably made in short editions, as few as one of a kind; in addition to the usual woodblock printing, much embossing (blind printing) is used to give texture and depth to the impressions; frequently, the prints are enhanced with gold, silver, and copper onlays. Surimono subjects cover the entire gamut of Japanese wood block print art: history, landscape, kachō (bird-and-flower prints), animals, marine life, folklore, mores, traditional arts, still life and religious subjects.

Surimono emerged from the calendar prints which came into vogue in the 1770s. They reached a peak of excellence between 1795 and 1835, with many designed by HOKUSAI (1760–1849) and his pupils. Although many exceptional surimono were made by KUBO SHUMMAN (1757–1820) and other UKIYO-E artists before and after the early 19th-century surge of surimono art, the two outstanding surimono artists were Gakutei (1786?–1868) and Hokkei (1780–1850).

As the production of surimono tapered off, elegant stationery was made, incorporating fine surimono art with space for adding a poem or special message. Late in the 19th century many large surimono were made to announce commercial ventures such as restaurants. Some had calendars on the reverse side of the surimono: Japanese giveaways which predated American advertising calendars. *Edythe Polster*

Surrender, Instrument of

(Nihon Kōfuku Bunsho). The formal document whereby Japan surrendered to the Allied Powers. Signed on 2 September 1945 aboard the USS *Missouri* by Foreign Minister SHIGEMITSU MAMORU and Chief-of-Staff General UMEZU YOSHIJIRŌ, it was accepted by General Douglas MACARTHUR, supreme commander for the Allied powers, and formally concluded World War II. In the instrument, Japan agreed to the immediate cessation of all hostilities, formal acceptance of the terms of the POTSDAM DECLARATION (which it had accepted earlier, on 14 August), and the placement of all administrative powers of the Japanese government under the supreme commander for the Allied powers. The document thus established the basic conditions for the OCCUPATION of Japan. On the same day the emperor issued a proclamation stating that he had ordered the government to sign the Instrument of Surrender and commanding his subjects to adhere to its provisions.

Suruga Bay

(Suruga Wan). Inlet of the Pacific Ocean, on the southern coast of Shizuoka Prefecture, central Honshū. Extends from OMAEZAKI, a cape in the west, to IRŌZAKI, a cape on the southern tip of the Izu Peninsula in the east. The warm Kuroshio Current makes this area a fertile fishing ground, now threatened by pollution resulting from industrialization. Much of the eastern coast of the bay along the Izu Peninsula is included in the Fuji–Hakone–Izu National Park. Width: 55 km (34 mi); length: 58 km (36 mi).

Susaki

City in western central Kōchi Prefecture, Shikoku. Located on Tosa Bay, it has a good natural harbor. Principal occupations are fish (yellowtail) farming and the cultivation of rice, vegetables, and citrus fruits. Cement plants make use of abundant limestone deposits. Pop: 31,852.

Susanoo no Mikoto

A complex and composite deity in Japanese mythology, Susanoo no Mikoto figures variously as god of the storm, the underworld, agriculture, the waters, and disease. In the Yamato myth cycle, centering on the lineage group that eventually ruled Japan, he is the son of Izanagi (see IZANAGI AND IZANAMI), one of the creators of the Japanese islands, and the capricious younger brother of the sun goddess AMATERASU ŌMIKAMI, from whom the Yamato line claimed descent. When Susanoo's offensive behavior drives Amaterasu into a cave, bringing darkness and calamity on the world, he is banished from the High Celestial Plain (TAKAMAGAHARA) and descends to Izumo in western Japan. The Izumo cycle, however, which centers on a local lineage group that submitted to the Yamato line, portrays Susanoo as its hero and ancestral deity. In his most famous exploit, he intoxicates and slays the YAMATA NO OROCHI, a great, eight-headed, eight-tailed serpent, thereby rescuing a maiden and acquiring the sword later known as Kusanagi, one of the IMPERIAL REGALIA. Susanoo later came to be associated with the tutelary deity Gozu Tennō and as such is worshiped at the YASAKA SHRINE in Kyōto. See also MYTHOLOGY. *Gine Johnson*

sushi

Japanese dish in which various ingredients, such as raw fish, are added to vinegar-flavored MESHI or boiled rice. Consisting of many colorful varieties, it is widely enjoyed at seasonal events, at home, in box lunches, as an accompaniment for *sake*, and so forth. *Sushi* may be roughly divided into four categories:

1. *Nigirizushi* (*sushi* shaped by hand) is made by adding a dab of *wasabi* (Japanese horseradish) to a bite-sized amount of *sushimeshi* (freshly cooked and cooled rice flavored with vinegar, sugar, and salt) on which is firmly pressed fresh raw seafood, such as fileted sea bream, sole, tuna, shrimp, squid, arkshell, or abalone. Also used as ingredients are broiled conger, egg, and salmon roe. The freshly made *sushi* is picked up with the fingers, dipped in soy sauce on the fish side, and eaten.

2. *Hakozushi* (boxed *sushi*) is made by pressing the flavored rice into a wooden box about 13 centimeters (5 in) square; fish marinated in vinegar, shrimp, broiled conger, mushrooms cooked in sweetened soy sauce, and the like are arranged on top of the rice. A lid is placed on top and pressed down, after which the rice is taken out and cut into bite-sized pieces.

3. *Makizushi* (rolled *sushi*) is made by placing NORI (dried seaweed), which has been lightly toasted over a flame, on a bamboo mat, evenly spreading vinegared rice on it, placing cooked dried gourd, mushrooms, dried bean curd, egg, *mitsuba* (*Crytotaenia japonica*; trefoil), or other ingredients in the center, rolling it into a cylinder about 5 centimeters (1–1.5 in) in diameter, and slicing it crosswise. It can also be made into narrow rolls, with cucumber or raw tuna in the center, or into very thick rolls with numerous ingredients in the middle.

4. *Chirashizushi* ("scattered" *sushi*) is made by mixing minced vegetables with vinegared rice and arranging colorful strips of seafood and egg on top. *Bōzushi* (stick *sushi*) and *sugatazushi* (figure

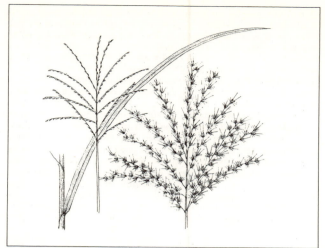

Susuki

sushi) are made by placing marinated fish such as mackerel, sea bream, sweetfish, and horse mackerel on the vinegared rice and then pressing it. There is also *inarizushi,* made by mixing vinegared rice with roasted poppy seeds or sesame seeds and scooping it into a piece of fried bean curd *(aburage)* that has been cooked in sweetened soy sauce.

Sushi cuisine originated in South China, where fish was preserved by salting and fermentation. The word *sushi* is thought to have originally been an adjective, meaning sour or vinegary, the modern form of which is *sui.* Later, in order to hasten the fermentation of the fish, boiled rice was added to the salt. After lactic fermentation had taken place, the rice was discarded and the fish eaten. This method is still used today in making certain regional specialties. An even later method, departing from the original purpose of preserving fish, omitted the fermentation process; boiled rice was flavored with vinegar and then left overnight to blend with the fish.

Tsuji Shizuo

Susono

City in eastern Shizuoka Prefecture, central Honshū. Automobile, aluminum, and electrical cable plants have been established here recently. Cattle are raised on the slopes of Mt. Fuji (Fujisan). Pop: 41,025.

susuki

(eulalia). *Miscanthus sinensis.* Sometimes referred to as Japanese pampas grass. One of the traditional "seven autumn plants" *(aki no nanakusa),* this reedlike perennial herb of the family Gramineae grows wild on hills and in fields, often in large masses, throughout Japan and the rest of East Asia. Its narrow stem grows straight up to a height of 100–150 centimeters (39–59 in). The leaves are narrow and grow alternately. From late summer through autumn several flower spikes develop at the top of the stem; from their resemblance to animal tails, these spikes have given *susuki* the nickname *obana* ("tail flower"). From each spike node grow two spikelets at the base of which are fluffy white hairs.

Dried *susuki* stalks have been used to make roofs, sacks, sandals, ropes, and curtains, and young leaves have been used as fodder.

Several varieties of *susuki* grow wild in Japan. The *itosusuki* has very slim leaves and a larger spike and is often planted in gardens or used for BONSAI (miniature trees) because of its graceful form. The *shimasusuki* has leaves covered with white spots and is also planted in gardens and commonly used for IKEBANA (flower arrangement). Besides these, there are *murasaki susuki,* which has purple spikes, and *hachijō susuki,* a large semievergreen plant which grows along the seashore in warm areas. A separate species, *tokiwasusuki (Miscanthus japonicus),* is an impressive plant with evergreen leaves which grows in warm spots in fields, or along the seacoast from central Honshū westward. Since its leaves do not die in winter, it is also called *kan* (cold weather) *susuki.* *Matsuda Osamu*

Susukida Kyūkin (1877–1945)

Poet, essayist. Real name Susukida Junsuke. Born in Okayama Prefecture. He left middle school to study on his own, and at about 20 years of age, he went to Tōkyō to write poetry. In 1899 his first poetry collection, *Botekishū,* was published, and the following year he became editor of a literary magazine in Ōsaka. His second collection of poems, *Yuku haru* (1901) established him as a poet. Known as one of Japan's early symbolist poets, he first wrote in a romantic style and later turned to symbolist expression. After 1910, as chief literary editor of the newspaper *Ōsaka mainichi shimbun,* he became known as an essayist. Other works include *Hakuyōkyū* (1906), a collection of poems, and *Sōmoku chūgyo* (1929), a collection of essays.

sutego

Abandoned children; also, the abandoning of children. The term *sutego* refers both to actual abandonment of unwanted children and to ritual abandonment for purposes of exorcism, a custom that was once fairly widely practiced in Japan. Ritual abandonment was practiced when an infant was weak and sickly or if it was born in an unlucky year according to Chinese and Japanese zodiacal traditions (see JIKKAN JŪNISHI) and thus considered destined to lead a life of misfortune. The parents left the infant at a crossroad or on the bank of a river, and a previously chosen "finder parent" *(hiroioya)* then took the child and returned it to its real parents. Those selected for the task were usually parents who had raised strong and healthy children, powerful and respected members of the community, Shintō priests, or Buddhist monks. In many cases, ritual abandonment led to a lasting relationship between the *sutego* and the *hiroioya.* *Inokuchi Shōji*

Suto Ken Suto

(Strike for the Right to Strike). An illegal eight-day strike carried out by Japanese public employees in 1975 to demand the legal right to strike. Regular government employees and employees in public corporations are prohibited from striking according to the PUBLIC CORPORATIONS AND GOVERNMENT ENTERPRISES LABOR RELATIONS LAW (Kōkyō Kigyōtai Tō Rōdō Kankei Hō) enacted in 1948, but government employee labor unions have consistently sought to secure revision of this law and win a guarantee of the right to strike. A number of unions involved in the reform effort complained to the International Labor Organization (ILO) about the government's infringement of fundamental labor rights. In 1965 an ILO survey team, the Dreyer Commission, visited Japan and in August of that same year issued a report stating that the commission did not feel strike prohibition to be necessary. At this point the government created the Public Service System Council (Kōmuin Seido Shingikai) to study the problem, but no opinion was ever issued by the council. In the meantime, a decision was handed down in a district court that made lawful those strike actions carried out on the local level. This led to strikes being carried out on a larger scale. On each such occasion the government as well as the public corporations took punitive action against strike participants. In order to settle this dispute, the involved labor unions (members of KŌRŌKYŌ, the Council of the Public Corporation and National Enterprise Workers' Unions) went on an eight-day strike beginning on 26 November 1975 to demand government recognition of the right to strike by public employees. The strike was suspended on the condition that the government quickly make an investigation and issue an opinion, but as of the early 1980s no resolution had been reached. *Kurita Ken*

Sutoku, Emperor (1119–1164)

The 75th sovereign *(tennō)* in the traditional count (which includes several nonhistorical emperors); reigned 1123–42. Son of Emperor TOBA and Taiken Mon'in, Sutoku was enthroned as a small child and remained powerless while first his great-grandfather, the former emperor SHIRAKAWA, and later his father ruled in his stead from retirement (see INSEI). Relations with his father were further strained when in 1142 Toba forced Sutoku to relinquish the throne to a young half-brother (Toba's son by another consort), who became Emperor Konoe (1139–55; r 1142–55). Sutoku tried to secure the succession for his own son after Konoe's death but was thwarted when another half-brother was enthroned as Emperor GO-SHIRAKAWA. After Toba's death in 1156, Sutoku conspired with

Minister of the Left Fujiwara no Yorinaga (1120–56) and others to depose Go-Shirakawa (see HŌGEN DISTURBANCE). Failing in his attempt, he was exiled to Sanuki Province (now Kagawa Prefecture), where he died.

sutra mounds

(kyōzuka). Small earthen mounds beneath which Buddhist sutras were buried. The practice of burying sutras is said to have been introduced from China by the monk ENNIN in the 9th century. It was especially popular late in the Heian period (794–1185), when people believed that theirs was the last, degenerate period of history (mappō; see ESCHATOLOGY) and that it was necessary to preserve sutra texts. Later, texts were buried for other purposes, such as ensuring one's rebirth into paradise, worldly gain, or the repose of the souls of the dead. The practice continued through the Edo period (1600–1868). Copies of the sutras were placed in stone or metal containers that were inscribed with the depositor's intentions or wishes. These containers, together with other articles such as BRONZE MIRRORS and knife talismans, were then placed in stone-lined pits 1 to 4 meters (3.3–13 ft) in diameter and about 1 meter (3.3 ft) deep. Earth was mounded over the pit, and a stone stupa or GORINTŌ was usually erected on the spot. In the late Heian period tiles inscribed with passages from the sutras were also buried, and in the Edo period it was common to bury small stones on which one or several characters from a sutra were written in black ink.

KITAMURA Bunji

Suwa

City in central Nagano Prefecture, central Honshū, on Lake Suwa. In the Edo period (1600–1868) it developed as a castle town of the Takashima family. The traditional paper-making industry was replaced after World War II by precision instrument (watches and cameras), miso (bean paste), and woodwork industries. Local attractions are Lake Suwa, the Kami Suwa Hot Spring, the Kirigamine highland, and Suwa Shrine. Pop: 50,558.

Suwa Basin

(Suwa Bonchi). A graben basin in central Nagano Prefecture, central Honshū. It spreads around Lake Suwa, forming a delta and fans and is basically a rice-producing area. In some areas natural gas seeps out of the ground. The basin is also noted for the production of raw silk, agar-agar, and precision instruments. The major cities are Suwa and Okaya. Area: 714 sq km (275.6 sq mi).

Suwa, Lake

(Suwako). In Suwa Basin, central Nagano Prefecture, central Honshū. The lake boasts some of the most abundant fishing in Japan with catches including carp, crucian carp, and pond smelt. It is popular for ice skating in winter. Numerous hot springs are located on the eastern bank and also within the lake. Area: 14.1 sq km (5.4 sq mi); circumference: 17 km (11 mi); depth: 7.6 m (24.9 ft); altitude: 759 m (2,490 ft).

Suwa Shrine

(Suwa Jinja). A shrine in Nagano Prefecture combining two shrines, the Kami Sha (Upper Shrine) and the Shimo Sha (Lower Shrine). The former is located in the city of Suwa, and the latter is some 10 kilometers (6.3 mi) away, in the town of Shimo Suwa. The gods enshrined in Suwa Shrine are Takeminakata no Kami, Yasakatome no Kami, and Kotoshironushi no Kami. The shrine has approximately 10,000 branch shrines throughout the country, the most numerous in Japan. The date of its founding is not certain. According to mythology, Takeminakata no Kami was the second son of ŌKUNINUSHI NO MIKOTO, who came to this part of the country from Izumo (now part of Shimane Prefecture) before the descendants of the sun goddess AMATERASU ŌMIKAMI, the mythical ancestor of the imperial family, descended to earth. He is said to have developed and ruled the province, refusing to submit to the descendants of the sun goddess. For this reason it is believed that he was originally a local deity. The Suwa family, who claimed direct descent, subsequently enshrined him.

The Kami Sha consists of a Mae Miya and a Moto Miya; the Moto Miya has no main hall (honden) and the surrounding forest itself is called the Miya Yama and is venerated as the sacred abode of the god. The Shimo Sha consists of a Haru Miya and an Aki Miya; the god enshrined stays in the Haru Miya from February to July and in the Aki Miya from August to January. Consequently, on the first of February and August, a switch of shrines ceremony is held every year. In ancient times, the gods enshrined were revered as hunting deities; they were later revered as farming deities, and during the age of warrior rule, they were honored as the preeminent gods of war.

Of the numerous religious ceremonies performed at the shrine, the most famous and perhaps the most unusual one is the Ombashira Matsuri, held every sixth year, i.e., during the year of the monkey and the year of the tiger (according to the sexagenary cycle). Tall fir trees are cut down, brought to the shrine by some 1,000 men, and used to replace four posts at each of the two miya of the Kami Sha and Shimo Sha. Called the ombashira, these are regarded both as the habitats of gods as well as serving to mark the borders of the sacred precinct. The annual festival of the Kami Sha is on April 15 and that of the Shimo Sha on August 1.

Suzaka

City in northeastern Nagano Prefecture, central Honshū. It prospered as a silk-reeling town from the Meiji period (1868–1912), but since World War II, it has become the center of an electronics industry. Apples and grapes are grown. A prefectural agricultural experimental station is located here. It is the gateway to the Jōshin'etsu Kōgen National Park and to Manza Hot Spring and Minami Shiga Hot Spring. Pop: 52,543.

Suzu

City in northeastern Ishikawa Prefecture, central Honshū, on Noto Peninsula. It is known for its portable cooking stoves (konro) and refractory bricks. There is also farming and fishing. A part of Noto Peninsula Quasi-National Park, it has a beautiful coastline. Pop: 27,352.

suzu

(bell). A small enclosed bell with a tiny pellet for a clapper, much like a jingle bell or sleigh bell; also, a small bell with a dangling clapper. The word kane is used for larger bells. Objects thought to be clay bells have been found among artifacts of the Jōmon period (ca 10,000 BC–ca 300 BC). Suzu came to be made of metal after the introduction of Chinese culture in about the 5th century. Funerary goods excavated from tombs of the Kofun period (ca AD 300–710) indicate that suzu were used to decorate hats, BRONZE MIRRORS, and horse trappings (see HORSE TRAPPINGS, ANCIENT). A string of suzu are traditionally used in KAGURA dances for the repose of departed souls.

Suzuka

City in northern Mie Prefecture, central Honshū. Known as Suzuka no Seki, an important barrier station (SEKISHO), from the 8th to the 12th centuries, it developed as one of the castle towns and POST-STATION TOWNS on the highway Tōkaidō during the Edo period (1600–1868). Synthetic fiber and transport machinery industries are active. The technique for patterned paper made in the Shiroko district has been designated an Important Intangible Cultural Property (see LIVING NATIONAL TREASURES). The Suzuka Circuit is known for its car races. Pop: 156,249.

Suzuka Mountains

(Suzuka Sammyaku). Mountain range forming the border between Mie and Shiga prefectures, central Honshū. It consists of numerous mountains in the 1,000 m (3,280 ft) range including Gozaishoyama (1,210 m; 3,969 ft). During the Nara period (710–794) the check stations of Fuwa no Seki to the north and Suzuka no Seki to the south were established in the mountains, forming a boundary between the Kantō and Kansai regions.

Suzuka Pass

(Suzuka Tōge). Located in the Suzuka Mountains, on the border of Mie and Shiga prefectures, central Honshū. Important pass connecting the Kinai (Kyōto–Nara–Ōsaka) region with eastern Japan in ancient days, with the Suzuka Barrier Station (Suzuka no Seki) located on the southeastern slope. The POST-STATION TOWNS of Sakashita and Tsuchiyama on the Mie and Shiga sides of the pass, respectively, flourished in the Edo period (1600–1868). The Mie side of the pass is steep, and National Route No. 1, which runs over the pass, sometimes becomes impassable due to heavy winter snowfall. The pass is mentioned in the famous song "Suzuka magouta" ("Song of the Suzuka Pack-Horse Man"). Altitude: 378 m (1,240 ft).

Suzuki Akira (1764–1837)

Confucian scholar and Japanese grammarian of the Edo period (1600–1868). Born in Nagoya to a medical family in the service of the Owari domain (now Aichi Prefecture). In his late twenties, Suzuki developed an interest in Japanese grammar, became a student of MOTOORI NORINAGA (1730–1801), and was instrumental in the synthesis of the grammatical work on the Chinese language of Confucians like OGYŪ SORAI (1666–1728) and Minagawa Kien (1734–1807) with the work on Japanese of Norinaga and FUJITANI NARIAKIRA (1738–79). His ideas in turn influenced MOTOORI HARUNIWA (1763–1828) and TŌJŌ GIMON (1786–1843).

Suzuki's most noted contribution to Japanese grammar was his theory of word classes, reminiscent of the parts of speech in traditional European grammar. His major classes were *tai no kotoba* (substance words), corresponding to nouns; *arikata no kotoba* (state words), corresponding to adjectives; *shiwaza no kotoba* (action words), corresponding to verbs; and *tenioha* (particles), corresponding to nonderived adverbs, prepositions, conjunctions, and interjections. He made a distinction between the first three classes, which express concepts used by the mind to organize experience, and the fourth class, which expresses the mind's activity directly. This distinction was later developed further by the modern grammarian TOKIEDA MOTOKI (1900–1967).

Suzuki's best-known works on Japanese grammar are two short treatises. *Gengyo shishu ron* contains the theory of word classes described above; it was probably written near the turn of the 19th century and first printed in 1824. *Katsugo danzoku fu* deals with the inflectional paradigms of Japanese verbs and adjectives; it too was probably written by 1803 but was not published during Suzuki's lifetime. He also wrote a treatise on the origin of language, *Gago onjō kō*, first printed in 1816. See JAPANESE LANGUAGE STUDIES, HISTORY OF.

George BEDELL

Suzuki Bokushi → Hokuetsu seppu

Suzuki Bunji (1885–1946)

Labor leader. Born in Miyagi Prefecture. While a student at Tōkyō University, he became a Christian, and, under the influence of YOSHINO SAKUZŌ and ABE ISOO, became interested in social problems. After the arrest of socialists and anarchists in the HIGH TREASON INCIDENT OF 1910, he gave up his job as a newspaper reporter to join the administrative staff of the Unitarian Church, devoting himself to social work. In 1912 he founded the YŪAIKAI, a society to promote the welfare of workers, which gradually acquired the characteristics of a labor union. His development as a labor leader was influenced by his contact with the American labor movement during a trip to the United States in 1915 and by his attendance in 1916 at a conference of the American Federation of Labor. By 1919 the Yūaikai had over 30,000 members and was reorganized as the Dai Nippon Rōdō Sōdōmei Yūaikai. Suzuki was elected to the Diet for three terms, beginning in 1928 as a candidate of the Shakai Minshūtō (Socialist People's Party) and later of the Shakai Taishūtō (Socialist Masses Party). He advocated moderation, attempted to reconcile labor and management, and opposed communism. He was four times elected as a Japanese representative to the International Labor Organization (ILO), and served as vice-chairman of the general assembly at the 14th ILO conference in 1932. In the first Diet election after World War II he was selected to run as a candidate of the Japan Socialist Party, but died before the campaign started. His works include *Nihon no rōdō mondai* (1919, Labor Problems of Japan), *Rōdō wa shinsei nari* (1922, Labor Is Holy), *Rōdō undō nijūnen* (1931, Twenty Years of the Labor Movement).

KURITA Ken

Suzuki, Daisetz Teitarō (1870–1966)

Known in Japan as Suzuki Daisetsu. Philosopher who, through his numerous books in both Japanese and English (the latter signed D. T. Suzuki), was instrumental in engendering the current worldwide popularity of ZEN Buddhism. He was born in Kanazawa, Ishikawa Prefecture, the youngest of five children. He entered Tōkyō University and concurrently undertook Zen training at the temple Engakuji in Kamakura under its abbot, SHAKU SŌEN. In 1897, at the age of 27, he went, through Shaku Sōen's introduction, to La Salle, Illinois, to assist Paul Carus of the Open Court Publishing Company with the translation of Oriental philosophical and religious works into English. Suzuki stayed there for 11 years, editing Carus's magazines, *Open Court* and *The Monist*, and translating various works, including *Daijō kishin ron* (Ch: *Dasheng qixin lun* or *Ta-sheng ch'i-hsin lun*; tr *Açvaghosha's Discourse on the Awakening of Faith in the Mahāyāna*, 1900), the first translation of this pivotal Chinese Buddhist text. In 1907 he published *Outlines of Mahāyāna Buddhism*, the first book of its kind in English.

Upon his return to Japan in 1909, Suzuki was appointed lecturer and later professor of English at the Peers' School (now Gakushūin University). In 1911 he married Beatrice Lane, who was his close collaborator until her death in 1939. In 1921 he became professor of Buddhist philosophy at Ōtani University, Kyōto, where he began the publication of the magazine *Eastern Buddhist*. Articles which he published in this journal became the nucleus of his three-volume *Essays in Zen Buddhism* (1st ser, 1927; 2nd ser, 1933; 3rd ser, 1934). These works, virtually the first exposition in any Western language on Zen, served to catalyze European and American interest in Zen Buddhism. Meanwhile, he also published two works on the *Lankāvatāra-sūtra*, a text central to early Chinese Zen: his *Studies in the Lankavatara Sutra* (1930) and his English translation of the sutra, *The Lankavatara Sutra* (1932). In 1938 appeared another major work, *Zen Buddhism and its Influence on Japanese Culture*. In 1949, he was elected to the Japan Academy and received the Order of Culture the same year. From this year, he began to spend much time lecturing on Zen outside Japan, most notably as visiting professor at Columbia University for several years, contributing firsthand to the growth of Western interest in Zen Buddhism.

Besides Zen, Suzuki's interest ranged to the philosophy of the *Kegonkyō* (Skt: *Avataṃsaka-sūtra*), which plays an important role in Zen thought, and Pure Land philosophy. In the latter, he was particularly drawn to the lay practitioners known as MYŌKŌNIN, such as Asahara Saichi (whose verses he edited as *Myōkōnin Asahara Saichi shū*, published posthumously, 1967). In these unlettered and simple Pure Land believers, Suzuki discovered profound expressions of enlightenment.

Suzuki's collected works in Japanese number 32 volumes. His English works also number about 30.

Robert RHODES

Suzuki decision

(Suzuki *hanketsu*). A landmark legal decision of 8 October 1952, comparable to *Marbury* v. *Madison* in the United States, in which the Japanese SUPREME COURT asserted its power of JUDICIAL REVIEW for the first time. It was important also as the first Supreme Court decision to touch on article 9, the RENUNCIATION OF WAR clause, of the 1947 constitution of Japan.

The case arose from a suit filed on 15 March 1952 by SUZUKI MOSABURŌ, chairman of the Left Faction (Saha) of the JAPAN SOCIALIST PARTY. Suzuki claimed that the establishment by the Japanese government in July 1950 of the NATIONAL POLICE RESERVE violated the constitutional ban on "war potential" in Japan. His claim assumed that the Supreme Court held a sweeping power of judicial review under article 81 of the constitution, which states: "The Supreme Court is the court of last resort with power to determine the constitutionality of any law, order, regulation or official act." The court, however, did not agree that it possessed such broad authority. In its decision it stated that it did possess the power of judicial review, but that, as the judicial branch of the government, its charge was to resolve concrete legal disputes. Consequently it regarded abstract consideration of the constitutionality of the National Police Reserve to be beyond its jurisdiction, absent a specific legal dispute.

The decision has had mixed consequences for the Supreme Court. The court set a historical precedent by asserting its power of judicial review. In declining to rule on the constitutionality of the Police Reserve, however, it left open the question of the conflict between article 9 and the presence of instruments of war potential such as the SELF DEFENSE FORCES (which replaced the Police Reserve in 1954), a question that has reappeared in a series of subsequent constitutional cases including the SUNAGAWA CASE and the NAGANUMA CASE and has yet to be resolved. See also CONSTITUTION, DISPUTE OVER REVISION OF.　　　　Kenneth M. TAGAWA

Suzuki Eitarō (1894–1966)

Sociologist. Born in Nagasaki Prefecture. A graduate of Tōkyō University, he later held professorships at Hokkaidō University and Tōyō University. Suzuki is held in high regard for having devised a system of rural and urban sociology, as well as an original theory of local sociology. While engaged in the study of American rural and urban sociology, he developed a sociological theory based on conditions in Japan. Conducting studies on the family, he demonstrated how life cycles developed within the context of the Japanese family, also basing these studies on American models. He said that in the case of the Japanese farming community, the basic local social unit known as the *buraku* (settlement) was most important and labeled it the "natural village" (*shizenson*). After World War II, Suzuki did research on urban sociology and criticized urban studies for tending to focus on slums and crime. He then turned to the structural pattern produced by the lives of the average population of a city. Maintaining that the city serves as a medium for social intercourse, he theorized that the size of a city is determined by the size of the integrative organization and class composition. His publications include *Nihon nōson shakaigaku genri* (1940), *Toshi shakaigaku genri* (1957), and his collected works, *Suzuki Eitarō chosakushū* (Miraisha, 1967–77).　　　　HASUMI Otohiko

Suzuki Harunobu → Harunobu

Suzuki Kantarō (1867–1948)

Admiral and prime minister of Japan's last wartime cabinet. Born in Ōsaka; graduate of the Naval Academy and the Naval War College. Suzuki saw action in the Sino-Japanese (1894–95) and Russo-Japanese (1904–05) wars and was successively appointed principal of the Naval Academy and commander of the Kure Naval Station. Promoted to admiral in 1923, he was named chief of the Naval General Staff two years later. The same year that he was put on the reserve list (1929) he was appointed grand chamberlain (*jijūchō*). Suzuki resigned from this post when he was seriously wounded in the FEBRUARY 26TH INCIDENT, an attempted coup by army officers in 1936. Late in World War II, following the resignation of General KOISO KUNIAKI on 5 April 1945, Suzuki became prime minister. With the landing of American forces in Okinawa six days earlier and Russian notification that it would not extend the Soviet-Japanese Neutrality Pact (see RUSSIA AND JAPAN), Japan's military situation had become desperate; although Suzuki publicly maintained an unyielding posture, he secretly asked the Soviet Union to mediate for peace; his overtures were rebuffed. In early August Hiroshima and Nagasaki were destroyed by atomic bombs; on the 8th the Soviet Union declared war. A series of imperial conferences (GOZEN KAIGI) were held, and on the 14th the Suzuki cabinet decided to accept the terms of the POTSDAM DECLARATION. The following day the cabinet resigned.

Suzuki Kiitsu (1796–1858)

Artist of the RIMPA style and a favorite disciple of SAKAI HŌITSU. Real name Suzuki Motonaga. The son of a dyer, Kiitsu was born in Ōmi Province (now Shiga Prefecture) and moved to Edo (now Tōkyō). He married the elder sister of a fellow student of Hōitsu, Suzuki Reitan (1782–1817). When Reitan died Kiitsu became head of the Suzuki family, who were vassals to the Sakai *daimyō* family, and was appointed *tsukebito* (attendant), or close retainer, to Hōitsu. Kiitsu specialized in paintings of figures and birds and flowers. He was also known as an accomplished HAIKU poet and a master of the various polite classical arts (*geinō*) practiced by members of the nobility.

Suzuki Kisaburō (1867–1940)

Conservative bureaucrat and a leader of the political party RIKKEN SEIYŪKAI. Born in Kawasaki, Musashi Province (now part of Kana-

gawa Prefecture), and graduated from the law faculty of Tōkyō University in 1891, Suzuki entered the Ministry of Justice that same year and became a protégé of HIRANUMA KIICHIRŌ, who was then a rising young official in the Office of the Prosecutor. In 1907, now a judge, Suzuki accompanied Hiranuma to Europe to observe how Western nations dealt with strikes and radicalism.

As prosecutor for the Great Court of Cassation (1912), prosecutor-general (1921), and minister of justice in the KIYOURA KEIGO cabinet (1924), Suzuki worked to suppress heterodox social movements and was influential in securing passage of the PEACE PRESERVATION LAW OF 1925. Joining the Rikken Seiyūkai in 1927, Suzuki was awarded the post of home minister in the TANAKA GIICHI cabinet. Under Suzuki the Home Ministry arranged the mass arrests of Communist Party members in 1928 (see MARCH 15TH INCIDENT). However, his high-handed interference in the national elections of 1928 (see SENKYO KANSHŌ) incurred severe criticism, and he was forced to resign in May 1928.

With the assassination of Prime Minister INUKAI TSUYOSHI in May 1932, Suzuki, who had been Inukai's home minister, became president of the Seiyūkai and a strong candidate to succeed Inukai as prime minister. The elder statesman (*genrō*) SAIONJI KIMMOCHI, however, could not tolerate Suzuki's antiliberalism, and when important army cliques (GUMBATSU) told Saionji that they would not support another party cabinet, Suzuki was passed over in favor of Admiral SAITŌ MAKOTO. Leading his party in a period of decline, Suzuki, seriously ill, resigned as president of the Seiyūkai in 1937. 📖——Yamaoka Mannosuke, ed, *Suzuki Kisaburō* (1955).

Richard YASKO

Suzuki Masatsugu (1889–)

Civil engineer. Authority on harbor construction and systems concepts applied to the design of large-scale industrial areas. Born in Nagano Prefecture, he graduated from Kyūshū University in 1914 and entered the Department of Public Works (Dobokukyoku) of the Home Ministry (Naimushō), serving until 1945. He later became professor at Nihon University. He received the Order of Culture in 1968. His publications include *Kōwan kōgaku* (1933, Harbor Engineering) and *Dobokuya san* (1956, Mr. Civil Engineer).

Suzuki Masaya (1861–1922)

Businessman. Leader of the SUMITOMO *zaibatsu* (financial and industrial combine) in the early 20th century. Born in Miyazaki Prefecture, Suzuki graduated from Tōkyō University in 1887. He joined Sumitomo in 1896 after serving in the Home Ministry and the Agriculture and Commerce Ministry. As manager of Sumitomo's Besshi Copper Mine, he promoted construction of the Shisakajima smelting works. He became executive director of Sumitomo's main office in 1904 and promoted the diversification, consolidation, and modernization of Sumitomo-affiliated businesses by inviting able personnel from outside and turning Sumitomo Sōhonten, the combine's private holding company, into Sumitomo Gōshi Kaisha, a limited partnership.　　　　ASAJIMA Shōichi

Suzuki Miekichi (1882–1936)

Novelist, writer of children's stories. Born in Hiroshima Prefecture. Graduate of Tōkyō University. While still a student, he associated with the noted author NATSUME SŌSEKI and his disciples, writing his first lyrical short stories, "Chidori" (1906) and "Yamabiko" (1907). After graduation he continued to write while teaching school, and from around 1917, when he became a father, his interest turned to children's stories. In July 1918 he founded *Akai tori* (Red Bird), a magazine for children's literature, stories, and songs. This was a landmark in the history of CHILDREN'S LITERATURE in Japan, enlisting such prominent authors as AKUTAGAWA RYŪNOSUKE and KITAHARA HAKUSHŪ as contributors. Other works include *Kosui no onna* (1916), a collection of children's stories, and *Kotori no su* (1910), an autobiographical novel.

Suzuki Mosaburō (1893–1970)

Politician and leader in the socialist movement. A native of Aichi Prefecture, Suzuki worked his way through Waseda University, graduating in 1915. He then worked for the newspaper *Hōchi shimbun* and, while covering the SIBERIAN INTERVENTION and the RICE RIOTS OF 1918, became interested in socialism. He joined the *Tōkyō* nichinichi shimbun (now the *Mainichi shimbun*) in 1922 and became increasingly involved in socialist politics. During the late 1920s and the 1930s Suzuki helped to found several proletarian parties, among them the Proletarian Masses Party (Musan Taishūtō, 1928), the Japan Masses Party (Nihon Taishūtō, 1928–30), and the Japan Proletarian Party (NIHON MUSANTŌ, 1937). In December 1937 he was arrested along with other socialists and communists in the POPULAR FRONT INCIDENT. After World War II he helped to form the JAPAN SOCIALIST PARTY, serving as secretary-general from 1948 and as chairman in 1951. He was elected to the first of nine terms in the Diet in 1946. When his party split in 1951, Suzuki became chairman of the Left Faction (Saha); when it was reunited in 1955 he was reelected chairman. In 1960 he withdrew from all formal posts but continued to act as an adviser to the party. The author of several books, including an autobiography, he collected a library, the Shakai Bunko (now open to the public), of materials related to the socialist movement in Japan.

Suzuki Motor Co, Ltd

(Suzuki Jidōsha Kōgyō). Company manufacturing minicars, motorcycles, and outboard motors; it is the largest producer of minicars in Japan and the third largest manufacturer of motorcycles after HONDA MOTOR CO, LTD, and YAMAHA MOTOR CO, LTD. It is affiliated with General Motors Corporation and Isuzu Motors, Ltd. The company's predecessor was the Suzukishiki Loom Co, established by Suzuki Michio in the city of Hamamatsu in 1920. With the decline of the textile industry during the Korean War, it switched to the manufacture of motor vehicles. In 1952 it succeeded in the development and mass production of a two-cycle, 36-cc light motorbike; it took on its current name in 1954 and started selling its two-cycle, 360-cc minicar in the following year. For three years, starting in 1962, its 50-cc motorcycles won first prizes at the famous annual races on the Isle of Man (in the United Kingdom), leading to a sharp rise in exports. Sales of its minicars have expanded substantially in recent years because of the rising price of gasoline. Suzuki has motorcycle assembly plants in Thailand, the Philippines, Indonesia, and Pakistan. Sales for the fiscal year ending March 1982 totaled ¥551.5 billion (US $2.3 billion), with an export ratio of 44 percent. The company was capitalized at ¥13.2 billion (US $54.8 million) in the same year. Corporate headquarters are located in Hamamatsu, Shizuoka Prefecture.

Suzuki Shigetane (1812–1863)

Classical scholar of the latter part of the Edo period (1600–1868); born on the island of Awaji (now part of Hyōgo Prefecture). In 1832 Suzuki took up the study of National Learning (KOKUGAKU), the school of learning that sought to return to the true Japanese spirit through study of the Japanese classics. He journeyed north to visit the eminent Kokugaku scholar HIRATA ATSUTANE; Hirata had died, but Suzuki considered himself his disciple and attached himself to the school. He settled in Edo (now Tōkyō) to write; in 1848 he completed *Engi shiki norito kōgi* (Discourse on Shintō Rituals in the Engi Legal Code), and in 1853 he began his *Nihon shoki den*, a voluminous commentary on the mythical sections of the 8th-century chronicle NIHON SHOKI. His ideas clashed with those of his fellow disciples, however, and he was cut off from the Hirata school. Suzuki was murdered in his home in 1863 for motives that have never been clear.

Suzuki Shin'ichi (1898–   )

Creator of the world-famous SUZUKI VIOLIN METHOD. Son of a noted violin maker, he studied violin in Japan with Andō Kō (1878–1963). Later, he studied violin in Germany. In 1946, while living in Nagano Prefecture, he started the Talent Education Movement with the motto "Anyone's talent can be developed through education." When he achieved striking results, his method spread worldwide. There are about 12,000 studying his method in Japan, and about 300,000 students abroad. Among his published works are *Sainō kyōiku* (1948, Talent Education). KOJIMA Tomiko

Suzuki Shōsan (1579–1655)

Zen teacher and moralist. Born in Mikawa (now part of Aichi Prefecture). He fought as a minor Tokugawa vassal at the Battle of SEKIGAHARA (1600) and at the sieges of Ōsaka Castle, then in 1621

became a monk. Shōsan acknowledged no master and therefore was outside both Sōtō and Rinzai Zen, although he supported Sōtō. He also had no successor. Intensely combative and loyal, he aspired personally to conquer all fear of death and publicly to have the shōgun proclaim true Buddhism—his own simple and strenuous teaching—as the moral guide for Japan. He succeeded in the first aim but failed in the second. His message probably never reached the government at all. Shōsan taught that each man's work as a warrior, farmer, artisan, or merchant was deeply worthwhile and itself a path to enlightenment. Indeed he would not ordain monks. He taught individuals to contemplate the foulness of the body and to meditate with clenched fists, gritted teeth, and a glare so fierce as to terrorize the demon host of the desires. Hence his teaching has been called Niō Zen after the menacing deities who guard temple gates. He also urged recitation of the NEMBUTSU, a formula unorthodox but sometimes present in Zen: it had the virtue of being universally known and easy for anyone to do anywhere. Shōsan's writings include *Ninin bikuni* (1664, Two Nuns), a KANA-ZŌSHI tale; *Bammin tokuyō* (1661, Right Action for All), a moral essay; and other stories and tracts. Of interest too is *Roankyō* (1648), a collection of Shōsan's sayings. *Royall* TYLER

Suzuki Shōten

A trading firm active during the Meiji (1868–1912) and Taishō (1912–26) periods; founded by Suzuki Iwajirō around 1877. Initially dealing in sugar and camphor, the firm grew rapidly under the aggressive leadership of Kaneko Naokichi (1866–1944), manager of the firm after Suzuki's death. When the island of Taiwan, a major producer of camphor, was acquired by Japan after the SINO-JAPANESE WAR OF 1894–1895, Kaneko skillfully used his political connection with GOTŌ SHIMPEI to obtain the right to sell 65 percent of the camphor produced there. The company grew substantially larger when Kaneko's speculative investment in a sugar refinery paid off, realizing in a few years a profit three times the original investment. He continued to manage the firm in a speculative manner, acquiring smaller companies and establishing subsidiaries. When World War I broke out, he expanded his firm's holdings in ships, agricultural products, and iron ore. World demand for such products intensified as the war continued, bringing enormous profits to the firm. It soon rivaled MITSUI and MITSUBISHI, establishing offices all over the world. In the economic slump after World War I, however, its position began to deteriorate. The firm was further weakened by disclosures of improprieties in its relationship with its major source of credit, the Bank of Taiwan (TAIWAN GINKŌ), and it finally collapsed in the FINANCIAL CRISIS OF 1927. Several new corporations emerged as a result of the firm's liquidation and reorganization. They presently include KŌBE STEEL, LTD; TEIJIN, LTD, a textile firm; and Harima Shipbuilding, now a part of ISHIKAWAJIMA–HARIMA HEAVY INDUSTRIES CO, LTD.

Suzuki Umetarō (1874–1943)

Agricultural chemist and one of the pioneers of biochemistry in Japan. He was born in Shizuoka Prefecture and graduated from Tōkyō University in 1896. In 1901 he went to Germany to do research on proteins under Emil Fischer. He returned to Japan in 1906 and became a professor at Tōkyō University. In 1910 Suzuki succeeded in extracting the substance later known as vitamin B_1, an important contribution to the foundations of vitamin theory. Later he became a member of the INSTITUTE OF PHYSICAL AND CHEMICAL RESEARCH (Rikagaku Kenkyūjo), taking an active part in various research fields, such as the chemistry of nutrition; he successfully compounded synthetic *sake*. Suzuki received the Japan Academy Prize in 1924 for research on secondary nutrients and the Order of Culture in 1943. *TANAKA Akira*

Suzuki violin method

Method of early musical talent development. The Suzuki violin method was established and developed by the violin teacher, SUZUKI SHIN'ICHI. The principle of the method is simple: all talent is "equal," and any child can develop his or her talent provided that adequate training is given. Children are started on the violin when they are still very young, using small-size instruments; the parents are encouraged to participate at all levels. Suzuki started a music school in the city of Matsumoto in Nagano Prefecture, and taught many famous violinists, such as Etō Toshiya, Toyoda Kōji, and Kobayashi Kenji. Today there are about 100 affiliated schools in Japan, and the method is well known all over the world.   *ABE Yasushi*

Suzuki Zenkō (1911–   )

Politician. Prime minister (1980–82). Born in Iwate Prefecture. Suzuki graduated from the Agriculture and Forestry Ministry's Fisheries Institute (now Tōkyō University of Fisheries). He worked for various fishery organizations and engaged in fishery cooperative movements. In 1947 he was elected to the House of Representatives as a candidate of the Japan Socialist Party. He switched to the Shakai Kakushintō (Socialist Reform Party) the next year, and in 1949, claiming that he would be more effective as a member of a larger party, he changed to the Minshu Jiyūtō (now LIBERAL DEMOCRATIC PARTY) and was elected to the Lower House. Elected thereafter 14 times, he was minister of posts and telecommunications in the first IKEDA HAYATO cabinet (1960), chief cabinet secretary in the third Ikeda cabinet (1964), and welfare minister in the first Satō Eisaku cabinet (1965–66). Suzuki also served as chairman of the Executive Board of the Liberal Democratic Party. In 1980, upon the sudden death of Prime Minister ŌHIRA MASAYOSHI, Suzuki was appointed successor. Two years later, in the fall of 1982, he abruptly resigned and was succeeded by Nakasone Yasuhiro (b 1918). Suzuki was known more for his skill in mediating differences than for strong leadership.

swallows

(*tsubame*). Birds of the family Hirundinidae; the name *tsubame* may be used to refer to all species in this family or specifically to the barn swallow (*Hirundo rustica*). The barn swallow measures approximately 17 centimeters (7 in) in length and has a black back, reddish brown throat, and white belly. The wings and tail are long and the tail is deeply forked. It migrates to Japan from Southeast Asia in the spring, appearing in settled areas throughout the country, and builds nests of grass and mud under the eaves of houses and other buildings. In autumn it moves to reedy marshes along seacoasts and at river mouths. Some barn swallows spend the winter in Japan near rivers and lakes, particularly along the shores of Lake Hamana in Shizuoka Prefecture. The species is also very common in Eurasia and North America. Other swallow species found in Japan include the *koshiaka tsubame* (Japanese striated swallow; *H. daurica*); the *iwatsubame* (house martin; *Delichon urbica*); the *ryūkyū tsubame* (Pacific swallow; *H. tahitica*); and the *shōdo tsubame* (sand martin; *Riparia riparia*).   *TAKANO Shinji*

Because barn swallows have the unusual habit of building their nests in peoples' houses and because pairs of swallows may return to the same house spring after spring, they came to be revered by the Japanese people as "sacred birds." Their arrival was welcomed as a joyful sign of the rebirth of life and warmth in the spring and constituted an important stage in the annual agricultural cycle. The swallow has appeared relatively infrequently as a theme in Japanese art and literature, but it has long been a familiar bird in daily life, and its taking up residence in a house was considered a sign of good fortune. It has also been seen as a symbol of motherhood, an idea probably borrowed from classical Chinese literature.

📖 ——Nakahara Magokichi, *Nihon no dōbutsu kisetsu* (1940). Saitō Shōji, *Nihonjin to shokubutsu dōbutsu* (1975).   *SAITŌ Shōji*

swearwords

There are no Japanese swearwords with as strong religious or sexual connotations as those commonly employed in other languages. Perhaps the major exception is *chikushō* ("beast"), an insult with religious overtones because of the Buddhist belief that one could be consigned to the realm of beasts in a future existence as a result of actions in this life. Another Japanese swearword is *kuso* (excrement, filth), but this lacks the taboo connotations of the English "shit" and is much milder in effect. There are many even milder expressions of disdain, roughly equivalent to "fool" or "idiot," like *baka, baka yarō, ahō,* and *manuke*.   *YAMAZAKI Yukio*

swimming

(*suiei*). The earliest recorded reference to swimming in Japan is found in the KOJIKI, an 8th-century book of history. From the medieval period (1185–1600) it was one of the *bujutsu* (see MARTIAL ARTS), or combat skills, developed by the *samurai* warrior class.

Techniques were developed for swimming while carrying weapons, for moving underwater, and for swimming silently. During the Edo period (1600–1868) various domains developed schools of swimming, guarding their secret techniques carefully. When the domain system was abolished in 1871, these methods became public and contributed to the popularity of swimming as a sport. Some of these traditional swimming methods are still taught today, along with the international styles developed in the West.

The first competitive swimming meet in Japan, between a group of Japanese and some American sailors, was held in 1884. An international meet between foreign residents of the Yokohama settlement and members of the Ōta school of swimming in 1898 increased the popularity of swimming races throughout the country. Japan sent swimmers to the Antwerp Olympics in 1920, and in the Amsterdam Olympics of 1928 TSURUTA YOSHIYUKI became the first Japanese swimmer to win an event. In the Los Angeles Olympics of 1932 five of the six events for men were won by Japanese.

HAYASHI Yūzō

sword-guards → tsuba

sword hunt

(*katanagari*). Programs of weapons confiscation carried out by military authorities especially during the 16th century. The best-known of these was ordered in 1588 by TOYOTOMI HIDEYOSHI. There had been sword hunts in Japan from early times, and Hideyoshi and other 16th-century *daimyō* had already carried out confiscations directed toward certain specific areas or against specific groups, such as the armed monks of certain temples. The 1588 order was distinguished by the fact that it applied to the entire nation. Hideyoshi's order to this effect read in part:

"1. The farmers [*hyakushō*] of all provinces are strictly forbidden to possess swords, short swords, bows, spears, and guns or other types of weapons. Those who possess unnecessary weapons make the collection of annual dues difficult; they are encouraged to engage in collective resistance and to give trouble to the holders of fiefs. For this they are, of course, punished. But as a consequence, their fields are left uncultivated, causing unnecessary reduction [in proceeds from the land]. Therefore provincial lords [*daimyō*], their fief holders, and their stewards must collect all the above types of weapons and deliver them up [to Hideyoshi].

"2. The swords and short swords collected will not be wasted but will be used as nails and cramps for the great statue of Buddha now being built [in Kyōto]. This will benefit farmers both in this life and the next.

"3. Farmers, when they possess only agricultural tools and devote themselves exclusively to cultivation, will benefit their children and grandchildren [to all generations]."

Despite these pious protestations, the sword hunt was clearly a means of reducing the level of violence in the countryside to the benefit of higher military authority. In the edict, the word *hyakushō* (farmers) is ambiguous. At the time, the separation of pure cultivator from rural *samurai* had not fully taken place. It is thought by some that the real object of the confiscation was to eliminate the farmer-samurai who remained a threat to the pacification of the countryside.

How thorough and effective the confiscation was is not well documented. In many cases, such as that of the monastery KONGŌBUJI on the mountain of Kōyasan, the order had to be repeated several times before Hideyoshi was satisfied that the confiscation was complete. Moreover, in large areas of Japan, Hideyoshi could not intrude his own officials to oversee the collection process. In such instances he had to rely on vassal daimyō of uneven reliability to conduct the confiscations. However, it was probably as much to the daimyō's advantage as to Hideyoshi's to have the farming class disarmed. Records of actual enforcement of the confiscation and the resulting number of weapons impounded are quite rare. A list of the take from one district (*gun*) in Kaga Province (now part of Ishikawa Prefecture) has survived. It lists 1,073 swords, 1,540 short swords, 160 spears, 500 guns, and 700 knives.

Whether the 1588 sword hunt was completely successful or not, the effort to disarm the nonsamurai classes continued for several decades. Nor was it the only means used to make the status of samurai and the authority of the daimyō secure. The one that had the most profound effect was undoubtedly the series of national cadastral surveys (KENCHI) also ordered by Hideyoshi. As a result of

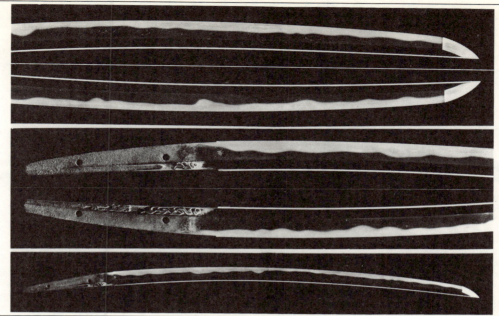

Swords——Five views of the Kanze Masamune, a 14th-century sword

Named after the Kanze family, its original owner, and Sōshū Masamune, the swordsmith. The *hamon* is a combination of the *notare* and *gunome* patterns. Sanskrit characters adorn the tang. No signature. Length of blade (excluding tang) 64.2 cm. Tōkyō National Museum. National Treasure.

these surveys, those samurai who still lived in their village fiefs were obliged to move to the castle towns of the daimyō lords or give up their samurai status. The result was the phenomenon known as *heinō bunri* (separation of samurai from *hyakushō*). Increasingly, also, daimyō and national military hegemons like Hideyoshi began to define class differences by law. Hideyoshi's edict of 1591 envisaged a society composed of three main classes: samurai, farmers, and townsmen and forbade movement from one to another. By the start of the Edo period (1600–1868) the pacification of the countryside was complete. The wearing of two swords had become the samurai's badge of status, denoting the monopoly of arms bearing by the warrior aristocracy.

📖 ——Kuwata Tadachika, *Toyotomi Hideyoshi kenkyū* (1975).

John W. Hall

swords

The origins of the Japanese sword *(nihontō)* and related weapons go back to the 8th century and the earliest development of steel in Japan. But Japanese swords are different from the swords of all other cultures not only because of the early technical mastery achieved in Japanese steelmaking, but also because of the elegant shape, lines, and texture and the shades of color of the steel fabric. Furthermore, for more than 12 centuries the sword has had a spiritual content and religious identification for the Japanese; along with the mirror and jewels, it is one of the three IMPERIAL REGALIA. The Japanese sword is considered by most scholars who have studied it as a supreme form of artistic expression.

From as early as the 8th century, the Japanese sword was fabricated from steel of controlled carbon content rather than iron. From the first the sword was made with varying degrees of hardness appropriate to the different parts of the blade. Generally the cutting edge exhibited sharply defined martensitic crystal structure while the body of the sword was of a softer and tougher steel, crystallized in pearlitic structure. Even the earliest examples are characterized by a very densely forged, many times folded, cross-welded, laminar structure with as many as 10,000 layers of steel, of alternating higher and lower carbon content hammered to exceptional toughness. In later years swords were made from forged blocks of steel, selected and combined according to their degree of hardness. The carefully assembled composite mass was hammered to its final shape, a process of hardening that provided nearly the hardness of file steel at the edge with resultant unsurpassed sharpness. With the crystalline structure forming the cutting edge locked into and supported by the tough but somewhat softer body of the blade, the sword was better

able to resist cracks or chips at the edge and capable even of being bent and later straightened without destruction of the sharp edge.

Swordsmiths——The Japanese swordsmith, traditionally held in high regard, possessed what must have seemed an almost magical skill, one that was essential to the life of the communities dependent upon him. The earliest swordsmiths were often *yamabushi*, members of the SHUGENDŌ sect, who with their student apprentices lived an austere and religiously dedicated life beginning each day with bathing, dressing in ceremonial costume, and prayers to the gods that the day's work might succeed.

There was a total of approximately 200 schools of Japanese swordsmith-artists, 120 during the Kotō (Old Sword) period from about 900 to 1590, and 80 in the Shintō (New Sword) period from 1590 to the Meiji Restoration in 1868. These schools contained about 1,000 outstanding master smiths, whose schools, teachers, dates of production, and blade characteristics are recorded in some detail, and with some personal history that covers both their predecessors and descendants. An additional 10,000 to 12,000 smiths of somewhat lesser skill are listed in standard references. These 200 schools were scattered throughout Japan, each with its own history and its own identifiable and surprisingly consistent blade characteristics which can be traced down through the centuries.

The file marks *(yasurime)* on the tang *(nakago)* of the blade, the shape and style of finishing, the texture, tempering, and color of the steel, and the refinements of contours are all taken into consideration in establishing the provenance of a sword. From as early as the 10th century the signature of the smith was often chiseled on the tang; the earliest existing dated sword was made by a smith named Yukimasa in 1159. In the case of individual schools, notably in Bizen Province (now Okayama Prefecture), the inscription often included not only the name of the smith, but the province, the name of the town, and the date when the blade was tempered.

A large proportion of the older long swords was later shortened for use in hand-to-hand combat, and consequently the tang with all its inscribed information was often cut off. These swords usually were converted from 1 to 1.2 meters (3.3 to 3.9 ft) to .75 meters (about 2.5 ft) in length from sword guard to point. Fortunately, in many instances the smith who did this shortening preserved the signature, sometimes welding the original inscription onto the opposite side of the new tang, or simply cutting out the signature portion and welding it into a slot made for this purpose on the new tang. Many such inscriptions, however, are difficult to authenticate.

Forging——In Japan there was a progression of use of stone, bronze, and iron weapons from about the 3rd century BC to the 3rd century AD. Iron-working technology was probably introduced to

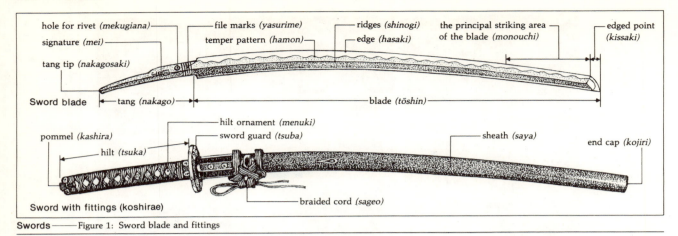

Swords —— Figure 1: Sword blade and fittings

Japan through Korea from about the 4th to the 5th century AD; the smiths who made the swords that are found in the SAITOBARU TOMB CLUSTER in Kyūshū were probably Korean. Thus, for all practical purposes as far as weapons are concerned, the BRONZE AGE in Japan was quickly succeeded by the IRON AGE, which was still more quickly followed by the steel age. As early as the 8th to 10th centuries, sword blades of excellent quality steel were being made in Japan.

In order to produce reliable tough and hard but nonbrittle steel, the carbon content had to be carefully controlled. The Japanese use of carefully prepared charcoal made from selected types of wood rather than coal helped to eliminate such trace impurities as sulphur and phosphorus. Early Japanese furnaces for the production of iron were very small with pits no more than 1.5 to 2 meters (4.9 to 6.6 ft) deep. They could not produce heat of sufficient degree to melt the iron that had been reduced from the iron oxide but only enough heat to produce a spongy mass of iron at the bottom of the furnace when a batch had been completed. It was not until the middle of the 18th century that the *tatara* furnace, which could process a much larger mass of iron ore, came into wide use; having very large bellows it supplied a sufficient amount of heat to produce molten iron as was beginning to be done in Europe (see TATARA-BUKI). This process had the advantage that impurities present in the original ore could be separated as slag from the pure metal.

After the steel was forged, an intensive process of hammering and repeated folding and welding tended to cause some of the slag to be extruded from the billet of steel. Importantly, however, the hammering thinned out traces of the slag into microscopic layers and then interwove it by the cross-welding of the billet of steel so that it became an intrinsic part of the finished work. This gives the Japanese blade, in addition to its other characteristics, one of its unique qualities—a texture (*jihada*) like that of the grain of wood, often of great beauty and variety, depending upon the smith and the practice of his school.

The smith traditionally selected the steel to be used in the various parts of the blade by hammering a red hot rough block to a thin plate, which was quenched in water, then hardened and broken into coin-sized pieces. This not only permits rejection of major slag inclusions but also allows the smith to learn, by examining the degree of granular structure and color of the fractured edge of each of the pieces, how to sort them so as to provide a mass of steel of predictable carbon content when they are rewelded together. When the forging process has been completed, the smith roughs out the blade with hammer and scraper to its final form which is then tempered and ground to its final polished state. These latter processes are both unique to the Japanese sword.

Tempering and Polishing —— The *hamon,* or temper pattern of the blade, is one of the most noticeable and beautiful features of the sword; for the connoisseur, it is also an important means of identifying the sword's origin. The tempering on the earliest swords was usually a straight, narrow zone of martensitic crystallization parallel to and forming the edge of the blade and running around the curve of the point. With the beginning of the Kamakura period (1185–1333), however, and even earlier in some instances, this *hamon* was made to exhibit many shapes and forms of great beauty. There was a gradual transition from a straight, narrow tempering pattern, or *suguha,* to a wavy pattern likened to a long succession of sectioned clove flowers, termed *midare* or *chōjimidare.* Many other *hamon* variations, some with long waves, others with short waves like a turbulent sea, many with a succession of points like a row of fir trees, are found; generally a specific type of temper or group of types was employed by an individual school or an individual smith.

The tempering is done in the last stage of making the blade. The blade is first covered with a mud formed of a mixture of water and clay, polishing-stone powder, fusible salts, and various other materials handed down in secret recipes from teacher to apprentice over the centuries. This mixture, coated thickly on the body of the blade and shaped with a bamboo knife or scraped to a thin layer along the edge, is baked to ceramic-like hardness. When the blade is heated by the smith to the exact proper temperature, judged in the darkened forge by the glowing red color of the metal, it is thrust into a trough of water, edge down and point foremost. Because the edge is thinner than the back portion of the blade, and because the baked-on clay coating is thin on the edge but thick on the back of the blade, the edge cools much more rapidly than the body. This results in the formation of martensite steel along the edge, a eutectic mixture of iron carbide compound (cementite, Fe_3C) combined with the pure or nearly pure metallic iron. This martensite area combines great beauty of shapes and colors along with the capability of being ground to extreme sharpness.

The edge of the blade is nearly white, contrasting with the body of the blade which is much darker and close to a blue-gray. Between the martensite of the edge and the pearlitic structure of the body of the blade is a transition area, a boundary zone consisting of tiny round mirror-like areas of hard steel or martensite embedded in the pearlitic structure. When these are large enough to be visible to the naked eye, they are called *nie,* but when they are more minute, such that they can only be seen discretely with a low-powered lens but still as individual bright, shiny dots, they are called *nioi,* the two differing only in size. If the sword is held point foremost toward a small light source in a darkened room, this line of *nie* or *nioi,* being brilliant and highly reflective, appears fiery, almost glowing, like the edge of a cloud illuminated at sunset. Another type of structure, called *utsuri,* generally a sign of a good blade, consists of a shadowy area bordering the edge pattern of the blade, and is seen as a faint, brightened, misty area.

The final polishing of the sword is done by the sword polisher rather than the swordsmith. With nothing but his eye and practiced hand to guide him, the polisher carefully grinds the sword by delicate, controlled motions, using a series of stones of increasing degrees of fineness, with liberal amounts of water as a lubricant. This cuts off, without distorting the structure, the roughened surface left by the smith and permits the crystallized, intricate pattern of the tempered edge and the grain structure of the body of the blade to become fully visible.

When completed, the final curving outlines of the sword exhibit extraordinary symmetry, its surfaces not planes but sections of parabolic curves. The curved lines outlining the body of the sword are also all sections of parabolas rather than arcs of circles, tapering toward each other toward the point but with such perfection that when sighting along the blade no irregularity or deviation of surface or line can be seen. A cross section of the blade itself shows that the two sides meeting at the edge form a slim Gothic arch, a stable structure that lends greatly to the strength of the edge. Any ten-

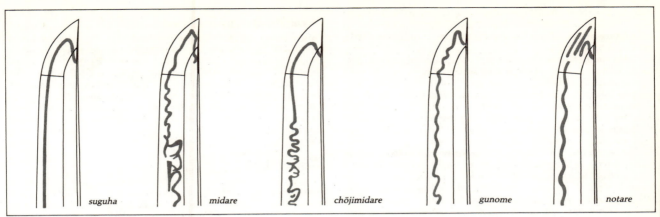

suguha   *midare*   *chōjimidare*   *gunome*   *notare*

Swords——Figure 2: Temper patterns (hamon)

dency of any crystal plane in the edge to slip out of position, producing a rolled-over edge, chip or crack, is blocked by the supporting curvature beneath it. A blade made with flat sides would lose enormously not only in strength but in cutting ability as well.

Jōkotō (Ancient Sword) Period——*Jōkotō*, or ancient swords, have come down to us almost exclusively from the ancient burial mounds of the Kofun period (ca AD 300–710), and in a badly rusted state. Swords preserved in the 8th-century SHŌSŌIN imperial art repository in Nara have been kept in near perfect condition for centuries; these reveal the beautiful texture of well-forged steel and a straight *suguha* temper pattern along the edge, or very rarely, a small convoluted *midare* pattern. These ancient blades were straight in almost every instance, with a very small and sharply angled slanted point *(bōshi)*. They were produced by essentially the same techniques as were the swords of succeeding periods. Swords of the Nara period (710–794) and the early part of the Heian period (794–1185) were similar to those found in the mounds. It is probable that the early, straight blades with beveled, angled points were derived from swords in use on the mainland, in China and Korea, and being rather short and lightweight, were probably used for thrusting rather than slashing. From approximately the 9th and 10th centuries, blades were made longer with a slightly curved shape and with ridge lines on both sides of the blade, a far more efficient weapon for mounted warriors.

Kotō (Old Sword) Period——There was a great improvement in the quality of the sword in the middle Heian and early Kamakura periods, or from approximately the 10th to the early 13th century when the use of the sword, especially by mounted warriors, increased so much that it was employed equally with the bow and arrow.

The early *tachi* (long sword) was worn at the left side, slung edge down where it could be efficiently brought into play by the mounted warrior. The *tachi* was graceful in shape with an elegant curvature and very marked taper in width from the sword guard (TSUBA) to the point, the handle *(tsuka)* set at a slightly oblique angle. Other types of steel weapons were also being used. The halberd (NAGINATA) with a blade as wide and as long as the sword, but generally with greater curvature, mounted on a staff approximately 1 or 2 meters (3.3 or 6.6 ft) long, was commonly and increasingly employed. A shorter blade, or dagger *(tantō)* was worn with the *tachi* and employed in hand-to-hand combat. More rarely, a shortened saber *(ko-dachi)* was used as a companion sword to the *tachi*. Very few of the *tantō* or *ko-dachi* of this early period still exist.

The swords of the Kamakura period (1185–1333) are of the highest quality, both artistically and technically, and most of the National Treasure (Kokuhō) blades derive from this period. In the early and middle Kamakura period, the *tachi* remained about the same length it had been in the middle to late Heian period, but with improvements in armor, the sword became longer and heavier of necessity. In the late Kamakura period the sword became very long—in many instances as long as 1 to 1.5 meters (3.3 to 4.9 ft)—and was used exclusively by mounted warriors.

This golden age of the Japanese sword, from approximately 1050 to 1400, was also the period when schools of swordsmiths arose in most of the principal provinces of Japan. But in the Muromachi period (1333–1568), as a result of prolonged strife and feudal combat, the production of swords increased greatly in numbers but qual-

ity declined. The earlier method of transmitting secret techniques from master swordsmith to disciple-apprentice gradually broke down, and old skills were lost, never to be wholly regained. Smiths were appreciated primarily for the numbers of weapons they could produce. Nevertheless, many beautiful blades were made, particularly in Bizen Province, between 1400 and 1450.

Another change also began during the Muromachi period. With warriors dismounting and doing nearly all of their fighting on foot, the speed required to draw a sword and complete a stroke was decisive. In earlier periods *tachi* had been slung at the side, edge down, but now the shorter *katana* began to be worn straight down at the side with the edge to the rear, or sometimes slightly angled back to the rear with the edge up, permitting the sword to be drawn and a blow struck in a single continuous motion. Swords also became somewhat heavier and less curved, wider and considerably shorter, so that they could cut through the heavier armor beginning to be used. This new blade shape, with the smith's signature on the opposite side from that which had been customary with the *tachi*, is called *katana*. It was soon accompanied by a shorter blade, *wakizashi*, somewhat less than 60 centimeters (2 ft) in length, and having duplicate mountings. The *wakizashi* was worn thrust through the sash edge up, parallel to or crossing the *katana* in the sash. This pair of swords was called *daishō*, "long and short," and was to provide an opportunity for the development of highly decorative metal fittings and scabbards in the long period of peace that was to come.

Shintō (New Sword) Period——During the Azuchi–Momoyama (1568–1600) and Edo (1600–1868) periods there arose a great interest in Japanese history and arts, including the largely lost skills of the swordsmith. Patronized by the powerful *daimyō* families, individual swordsmiths, especially in the major castle towns, founded new schools of swordmaking and began to produce swords of ever-increasing quality. They attempted to copy the swords of the past, but influenced by the requirements of hand-to-hand combat, their copies tended to be of shortened *tachi* rather than full-length *tachi*, but reduced in size; as a result, they somewhat lacked the graceful contours, tapered shapes, and elegant curves of the earlier periods. However, many had extraordinarily brilliant tempering patterns, substantial structure of well-hammered and well-tempered steel, and beautiful chiseled engravings *(horimono)* and grooves. The color of the steel varied with the use of different forms of iron ore, reworked iron, and *namban* (Southern Barbarian) iron imported by the Dutch. The blades of this period tend to be light in color with brilliant crystal structures in the edge patterns.

The increasingly tight control of the Tokugawa shōguns curtailed opportunity for the use of swords, and as a result there was a brief period, principally during the 18th century, when the practice arose of testing blades on the corpses of executed criminals (tameshigiri). Occasionally found on swords from this period are the recorded results of these tests, inlaid in gold on the tang of the sword and dated and signed by the official executioner.

Sword guards *(tsuba)* and metal fittings for the *samurai*'s long and short sword and for daggers became more gorgeous and highly ornate, often with a profusion of gold and silver and colored lacquer that would have been considered out of place in earlier periods. Some nonsamurai, especially the wealthy Ōsaka merchants, also began to wear swords, although the practice was controlled by the government. In any case, nonsamurai were forbidden to wear more than one sword, which had to be less than 60 centimeters (2 ft) long. Hence many elegant *wakizashi* blades just under 60 centimeters in length were made for wealthy merchants especially by the Ōsaka and Edo schools.

There were, additionally, many types of spears and halberds produced during this time. *Yari*, or long spears, sometimes with staffs as long as 2 meters (6.6 ft) and with various shapes of blades, most often had short, straight blades with triangular cross sections. Occasionally these were as long as 1 meter (3.3 ft) made like a sword but sharp on both edges. An especially distinctive type of Edo-period blade was known as *jūmonjiyari*, a spear in cross form with two sharp projections on either side of the spear point.

The period from 1800 to the close of the Edo period is known in sword history as Shinshintō (New, New Sword Period). It was a brief renaissance and a final effort to revive the beauty and quality of the ancient sword. An exceptionally skilled and literate swordsmith, Masahide, working in Edo (now Tōkyō) around 1800, left written records of his observations and efforts to produce swords of high quality copied after the schools and patterns of the ancients. The swords of Masahide and others, though highly regarded today, never attained the perfection of the ancient sword.

Modern Period —— It is probably impossible to estimate the number of genuine Japanese swords still extant. Enormous numbers of swords were destroyed in battlefields in ancient times, rusted away in storerooms, temples, and castles, or were destroyed by fire and earthquake. In the Meiji period (1868–1912), as a result of the effort to modernize the country as rapidly as possible, the old culture of Japan, together with the Japanese sword, was literally cast aside, and many Japanese swords found their way to Europe and America. But probably the great majority of extant Japanese swords are owned by connoisseurs or are family heirlooms in Japan, with a remaining 25,000 in private collections and museums all over the world.

In 1868 the Emperor Meiji promulgated regulations forbidding the making or wearing of swords. He was himself, however, very much interested in swords and permitted a small number of smiths to continue work in an effort to keep the art alive. A further quickening of interest occurred during the Russo-Japanese War of 1904–05, and also with the renewed ascendance of the military before and during World War II. For the most part these later military swords are not genuine art swords (*nihontō*), being made from machine-made steel of homogeneous structure, neither hand-forged nor hand-tempered.

After World War II, the Allied Occupation forces ordered all swords destroyed, but with the help in particular of the provost marshal of the Eighth Army, Colonel Victor Cadwell, the order was modified. Arrangements were made with a small but determined group of Japanese connoisseurs for this directive for destruction to be applied principally to modern battlefield swords in war mounts; art-swords of artistic, religious, or spiritual significance belonging to museums, shrines, or in private collections were allowed to be preserved. Even so, an enormous quantity of good swords were destroyed, and a very large number were taken out of the country as souvenirs during the immediate postwar period, when it became mandatory that all swords be registered with the police, as is still the case in Japan today.

Since the end of World War II there has been a gradual renewal of interest in the art of the ancient sword and currently a number of smiths doing work of high quality are attempting to restore the ancient skills. The Agency for Cultural Affairs has in recent years designated two swordsmiths and two sword polishers as LIVING NATIONAL TREASURES; this has provided a great impetus to cultivate the ancient skills. The swords of some modern swordsmith artists currently bring very high prices. Nevertheless, their work does not in most instances match the extraordinary beauty, grace, and balance of the swords of the 10th to the 14th centuries. See also ARMS AND ARMOR; IRON AND STEEL.

—— Fujishiro Yoshio, *Nihon tōkō jiten* (rev ed, 1974). W. M. Hawley, ed, *Japanese Swordsmiths*, 2 vols (1967). Homma Junji and Satō Kan'ichi, ed, *Nihontō zenshū*, 9 vols (Tokuma Shoten, 1966–68). Japan Society, Inc, The Walter A. Compton Collection, *Nippon-To; Art Swords of Japan* (1976). H. Joly and H. Inada, *The Sword Book and Book of Samé* (1912). Ōtsuka Kōgeisha, ed, *Nihontō taikan*, 7 vols (1966–72). B. W. Robinson, *A Primer of Japanese Sword Blades* (1955). B. W. Robinson, *Art of the Japanese Sword* (1961). J. Yumoto, *The Samurai Sword* (1958).

Walter Ames COMPTON

Syahrir, Sutan (1909–1966)

Also spelled Sjahrir. Indonesian nationalist and prime minister (1945–47). After studying in the Netherlands for two years, he helped to establish a national education movement in the Netherlands East Indies in 1931, but he was exiled by the Dutch in 1934. He returned to the East Indies in 1942, after the Japanese occupation began, but he refused to cooperate with the Japanese. He served as prime minister during the struggle for independence, but his conciliatory diplomatic policies met with disfavor in Indonesia, and he was forced to resign.

NAGAZUMI Akira

syncretism

A conscious or unconscious admixture of two or more different, or sometimes even contradictory, traditions or ideas—cultural, philosophical, or religious. In modern usage, "syncretism" signifies "mixing" or "blending" and is sometimes regarded as interchangeable with "eclecticism." In the broadest sense some regard it as synonymous with "synthesis."

Terms —— The traditional Japanese equivalents of "syncretism" are *setchū* and *konkō*, two terms borrowed directly from literary Chinese. *Setchū* (Ch: *zhezhong* or *che chung*) originally meant "the just sentencing (of a crime)" or "proper and balanced judgment"; the meaning of "mixing" or "blending" seems to have evolved in Japan with a somewhat derogatory connotation in certain contexts, as in phrases such as *wayō setchū* (mixing of Japanese and Western styles). *Konkō* (Ch: *hun'yao* or *huen yao*), meaning "random admixture and resulting confusion," has a more pejorative connotation than *setchū*. Probably because of the ambiguity of these two terms, the neologism *shūgō* was used by Shintō scholars of the late 17th century in terms such as Ryōbu Shūgō Shintō (Dual Shintō), a syncretism of Shingon Buddhist doctrines and Shintō beliefs. In modern times, *shūgō* has come to be commonly used by itself to mean "syncretism" by Japanese scholars, especially in such fields as religion and philosophy. *Shūgō* is often translated into English as "unification." It must be noted, however, that *shūgō* signifies more than "unification" does. *Shū* (Ch: *xi* or *hsi*) initially meant "the act of laying one over another," and hence "repetition," and *gō* (Ch: *he* or *ho*) "to collect and place things into an enclosure." Syncretism, especially in Japanese culture, has produced essentially multilayered constructs, and thus the creation and usage of the word *shūgō* implies more than a simple unification of diverse elements.

Evolution of Syncretism in Japan —— Various interesting cases of syncretism are found in Japanese history and culture. Some of them are similar to those found in other cultural traditions, but syncretism can be said to be an especially dominant trait of the Japanese mind, and an underlying disposition toward syncretism may be found in the ethnic origin of the Japanese people.

Although the homogeneity of the Japanese is often referred to by social scientists, they also acknowledge that ethnically the Japanese are of mixed ancestry. Since prehistoric times, waves of migrants, presumably from the northern and southern regions of the Asian continent and the islands in the southeastern region of the Pacific Ocean, settled in the Japanese archipelago. After much warfare, coercion, and also natural domination by newly arrived carriers of superior material culture over earlier inhabitants with inferior material culture, Japan proceeded toward gradual unification. By the time of the federation of powerful tribes led by the YAMATO COURT, perhaps around the 5th century AD, a considerable degree of ethnic and cultural uniformity seems to have been attained. Japanese racial homogeneity is thus the result of a fusion process that had continued for centuries, and the so-called indigenous Japanese culture is thus the product of a long process of syncretism. This process consisted of both conscious and unconscious efforts by the inhabitants of the Japanese archipelago to meet political, social, and cultural needs arising from the movement toward a unified state. This gradual process of syncretization and the foundation of an early syncretistic Japanese culture, the indigenous culture, are evidenced by archaeological findings, historical and comparative linguistic studies, accounts of Japan in the first few centuries AD found in Chinese and Korean chronicles, and recorded Japanese mythology and historical traditions.

As an integral part of this indigenous culture, another national trait that gave further impetus to syncretism was formed. This is the characteristic Japanese way of thinking in which intuitive cognition and attainment of unity with the essence of reality are emphasized over objectivization and rationalization of reality, and in which subjective and emotive values are more appreciated than objective and abstract concepts. Thus when the Japanese met new ideas from alien traditions, instead of confronting them with rational analysis and finding contradictions with their indigenous tradition, they would move toward compromise and attempt to find proper places for these new ideas within the indigenous culture. New ideas from outside might be substituted for their counterparts in the indigenous tradition, but without a total replacement of any segment of the traditional culture. The dynamics of particular cases of Japanese syncretism, therefore, may have to be characterized differently depending upon the circumstances of their occurrence. Typologically, then, the modern Japanese lifestyle can be called an example of an "inclusive" type of syncretism; early Buddhists' efforts to incorporate native beliefs can be called "accommodating"; Shintō scholars' continued attempts, especially since the 13th century, to regain initiative by systematizing Shintō theories while borrowing heavily from Confucian and Buddhist doctrines can be called "defensive"; and the nativism of 18th- and 19th-century KOKUGAKU thinkers, who covertly syncretized "foreign" ideas while overtly rejecting them, can be called "exclusive."

Some Examples of Japanese Syncretism —— With the introduction of Buddhism and Confucianism between the 4th and 6th centuries and again with the influx of Western culture after the Meiji Restoration of 1868, syncretism in Japan has been constantly increasing in scope and depth, and it continues to be in evidence in all aspects of Japanese culture to this day. *Wayō setchū* has already been mentioned. This phrase reflects the syncretistic new lifestyle of the modern Japanese. Much earlier we find the phrase WAKON KANSAI, in which *wakon* means "Japanese spirit" and *kansai* (or *karazae*), "Chinese learning." In early usage, for example by SUGAWARA NO MICHIZANE (845–903), it signified the practical application of Chinese learning to Japanese situations. As *wakon* (or YAMATO-DAMASHII) changed into the ambiguous concept of a unique "Japanese spirit," it began to connote the syncretistic ideal of the selection and practice of Chinese learning based upon indigenous Japanese principles. It was in the same fashion that the phrase WAKON YŌSAI (Japanese spirit, Western learning) was later created.

There are a few examples of syncretism in Japanese expressions of political thought and ideals. For instance, the traditional separation of the symbols of state power and its actual exercise is a syncretistic political philosophy which made the continuation of the Japanese imperial institution possible and is now embodied in the constitution of 1947. The SEMMYŌ (imperial edicts) of the ancient past are distinct examples of the syncretism of Buddhist, Confucian, and indigenous Shintō beliefs. In his various edicts, Emperor SHŌMU (701–756) referred to himself by the Shintō term "living deity" *(akitsumikami),* the Confucian term "sage king" *(hijiri no kimi),* and the Buddhist term "servant of the Three Treasures" *(sambō no miyatsuko).* He also professed that he was "inept and inferior" *(tsutanaku ojinashi:* Buddhism), while the gods of heaven and earth revealed "their will" *(ametsuchi no kokoro:* Confucianism) by "omen" *(shirushi:* Confucianism). Another case is the Jūshichijō Kempō (SEVENTEEN-ARTICLE CONSTITUTION) of Prince SHŌTOKU (574–622). Shōtoku adopted Confucian ethics and political doctrines but, at the same time, strongly advocated Buddhism. However, the *semmyō* and the Jūshichijō Kempō do not show a clear grasp of Confucian and Buddhist doctrines by their authors. Instead, these syncretistic documents were constructed of diverse ideas in isolation from the systems of thought to which they originally belonged. Two main systems among them, Buddhism and Confucianism, were not always compatible in many of their main tenets. The authors of these documents might not have been aware of their own syncretistic orientation, but they were selective of ideas and motivated by the need to accommodate the social and political realities of the time.

Religious Syncretism —— In religious syncretism we see the assimilation of the native cult, Shintō, with Buddhism, Confucianism, and religious Taoism. Shintō-Buddhist syncretism, known as *shimbutsu shūgō* or *shimbutsu konkō,* spread among the masses and had a lasting and important impact on Japanese culture. One of the first policy decisions of the new Meiji government in 1868 was to order the complete separation of Shintō and Buddhism (see SHINTŌ AND BUDDHISM, SEPARATION OF), but by this time Shintō-Buddhist syncretism had been so throughly integrated into Japanese religious beliefs and practices that it has never been totally eradicated. It is very much alive in modern Japan.

There are a number of possible causes for the development of this Shintō-Buddhist syncretism. First, the indigenous Shintō cult was not a well-defined religious system. When it encountered Buddhism, there was no possibility for their dialectic confrontation. Second, the Buddhism that reached Japan through China and Korea had already assimilated many local deities from these countries into its pantheon. This rich variety of deities had the potential to be easily identified with the innumerable deities of native beliefs. Third, the indigenous Shintō cult was primarily community-oriented. The welfare of a community, especially agrarian, and the cohesiveness of kinship groups were the primary goals of its religious activities. Shintō could not meet individual spiritual needs nor answer existential questions as Buddhism could. Thus, Buddhism filled the spiritual gap left by the native beliefs. Many Japanese sought direct answers to these problems through religious experiences in Buddhism rather than through speculation about abstract ideas. Fourth, the religious "hospitality" of the native cult and the Buddhist doctrine of accommodation *(hōben)* provided grounds for syncretism. Fifth, Buddhism was transmitted on a large scale to the upper echelon of Japanese society. When the political leaders of the time accepted Buddhism after serious political strife, they found in it an ideological base for a unified state. In turn, Buddhists, for the purpose of establishing a firm footing on the new soil, took positive steps to syncretize their religion with the native beliefs, as long as syncretization did not violate their own doctrines. Advocates of Shintō were aware of their incapability to confront Buddhism ideologically. They found no sociopolitical and economic advantage in fomenting any conflict with the Buddhists, who had strong backing from powerful elements in the state. It would not be cynical to point out that syncretism was exploited by institutionalized Shintō for the practical purpose of its own survival.

Japanese Buddhists devised a particular form of religious syncretism that also resulted in the enrichment of the doctrinal content of Shintō. Commonly known as HONJI SUIJAKU theory, this syncretism reflected different structural relationships between Shintō and Buddhism at various stages of its development. *Honji suijaku* refers to a manifestation of a Buddha or bodhisattva *(honji)* in the temporary form of a Shintō deity *(suijaku).* The common use of the term *bosatsu* (BODHISATTVA) or *gongen* (temporary manifestation, incarnation) as part of the name of a Shintō deity, as in Usa Hachiman Daibosatsu or Kumano Gongen, is an explicit application of this theory.

The Shingon sect of Buddhism constructed a system of Dual Shintō (RYŌBU SHINTŌ), in which the deities of the Inner Shrine (Naikū) and Outer Shrine (Gekū) of the ISE SHRINE (Amaterasu Ōmikami and Toyoukehime no Kami) are respectively identified with Mahāvairocana (the Great Sun Buddha; J: Dainichi Nyorai) in the Matrix World (J: Taizōkai) and the Diamond World (J: Kongō-kai) of the mandalas. In the Sole Reality Shintō (Ichijitsu Shintō or SANNŌ ICHIJITSU SHINTŌ) of the TENDAI SECT, the native deities of Mt. Hiei (HIEIZAN) were first made protectors of Buddhism and of the temple erected on that mountain (ENRYAKUJI), and later identified with various Buddhas and bodhisattvas.

With the rise of strong national sentiments and advances in theoretical sophistication from around the 13th century, Shintō theorists were motivated to develop a system in which Shintō deities were regarded as *honji* and the Buddhas and bodhisattvas as *suijaku.* The basic logical structure of this counter-*honji suijaku* theory is the same as that of the original theory, but it lacks real philosophical depth.

Another unique form of religious syncretism is SHUGENDŌ (mountain asceticism), which emphasizes the attainment of magico-religious powers. The founding of Shugendō is attributed to the legendary figure EN NO GYŌJA (also called En no Ozunu or En no Ubasoku). Legends tell of his possession of magical powers and his practice of asceticism and Tantrism in the mountains. They reveal that Shugendō is a syncretistic mixture of elements of the native belief in the sacredness of certain mountains, esoteric Buddhism, and religious Taoism. This indicates that the roots of Shugendō belong to prehistoric Japan, in that many native religious rites are associated with sacred mountains where tutelary deities and the spirits of the dead are believed to reside. The later addition of Buddhist and Taoist elements endowed the acts of climbing and living on these mountains with new ascetic and mystical implications. Shugendō was widely practiced in all parts of Japan, and traveling Shugendō ascetics (YAMABUSHI) contributed greatly to the spread of religious syncretism among the masses. Because of its syncretistic nature, Shugendō was prohibited by the Meiji government in 1873, but again the tradition survived, and a Shugendō revival is currently under way.

Confucianism also found its way into religious syncretism. As Shintō gradually began to develop its own systematized metaphysical, cosmological, and ethical doctrines around the 13th century, it borrowed heavily from Confucianism and Neo-Confucianism as well as from Buddhism. During the Edo period (1600–1868), when Neo-Confucianism (SHUSHIGAKU) was made the orthodox state philosophy, many scholars attempted to create a syncretism of Shintō and Neo-Confucianism which purportedly eliminated Buddhistic elements. For example, Ritō Shinchi Shintō was advocated by HA-YASHI RAZAN (1583–1657), SUIKA SHINTŌ by YAMAZAKI ANSAI (1619–82), and Rigaku Shintō by YOSHIKAWA KORETARI (1616–94). Although their attempts to rationalize Shintō were not truly successful, it is ironic that Neo-Confucianism served to stimulate the development of more sophisticated esoteric concepts.

Thus, the Japanese mind has endeavored through syncretism to maintain and enrich the "indigenous" Japanese culture, which itself is syncretistic and defies efforts at precise characterization. It has been this ambiguity that has led the Japanese mind to produce a complex and essentially multilayered syncretistic culture, with the indigenous culture as its substratum. Syncretism can be found in practically all phases of Japanese culture, but it has never formed a coherent system. Its most conspicuous form (and the form that has been the object of most research) is religious syncretism, which has affected all segments of the Japanese society. The ramifications of popularized syncretism in Japanese literature, fine arts, and folklore have yet to be extensively studied and analyzed. See also SETCHŪ-GAKUHA; THOUGHT AND CULTURE.

——Carmen Blacker, *The Catalpa Bow* (1973). Sven S. Hartman, ed, *Syncretism* (1969). J. H. Kamstra, *Encounter or Syncretism: The Initial Growth of Japanese Buddhism* (1967). Alicia Matsunaga, *The Buddhist Philosophy of Assimilation* (1969). Robert E. Morrell, "Mujū Ichien's Shintō-Buddhist Syncretism: Shasekishū, Book 1," in *Monumenta Nipponica* (1973). Birger A. Pearson, ed, *Religious Syncretism in Antiquity* (1975). Herbert E. Plutschow, "Is Poetry Sin? *Honjisuijaku* and Buddhism vs. Poetry," in *Oriens Extremus* (1978).

Hiroshi MIYAJI

T

Tabaruzaka

Hill in the town of Ueki, northeastern Kumamoto Prefecture, Kyūshū; formerly an important transportation center of the area and the site of an engagement between rebel and imperial troops during the SATSUMA REBELLION in 1877. A monument and museum commemorating the battle are located in the town. Height: 50–100 m (164–328 ft).

Tabei Junko (1939–)

Alpinist; first woman to climb Mt. Everest. Born in Fukushima Prefecture. In 1970 she reached the summit of Annapurna III in the Himalayas. In 1975 she challenged Mt. Everest, along with 13 other Japanese women. Despite injuries received in an avalanche, she and Ang Tzering, the Sherpa leader, reached the summit at 12:30 PM on 16 May. ___TAKEDA Fumio___

tabi

A kind of sock worn with traditional Japanese clothing. Originally *tabi* were made of deer or monkey skin (*kawa tabi*) and had no separation between the toes, but as thonged ZŌRI sandals became popular in the Kamakura period (1185–1333), *tabi* were divided between the big toe and the other four toes to accommodate the thong. They were fastened at the ankles first with a string, later with buttons, and finally with two to five metal clasps called *kohaze*. Because of the scarcity of skins, after the 17th century silk and cotton were used. White *tabi* were worn with formal or festive *kimono,* while solid colors such as dark blue, black, or purple were for ordinary occasions. Today *tabi* come in white or colored cotton or satin, as well as stretch nylon. ___ENDŌ Takeshi___

Tablada, José Juan (1871–1945)

A noted Mexican poet, essayist, and journalist. Many of his poems, though written in Spanish, were modeled on the form of the Japanese HAIKU. These innovative poems are said to have had a significant influence on Latin American literature. Tablada's work as a whole helped to form Latin America's view of Japan in the early 20th century.

Tablada started his literary activities while working as a proofreader for *El Universal,* a noted Mexican newspaper. He became interested in Japanese culture early on, through his reading of the works of Pierre Loti, Judith Gautier, and the Goncourt brothers. In May 1900 Tablada went to Japan as a correspondent for the literary journal *Revista Moderna* and stayed in the Chinatown section of Yokohama for several months. This was his only visit to Japan. After he returned to Mexico, he became a wine merchant, temporarily leaving the literary scene. In 1911, right after the outbreak of the Mexican revolution, he went to Paris for several months. Interest in Asian culture and particularly in Japanese haiku was very high there, and Tablada's literary career revived: when he returned home, he published a number of essays on Japanese art and artists, as well as a book on the *ukiyo-e* artist HIROSHIGE. In 1914 he moved to New York City, a political exile; however, four years later he was appointed second secretary of the Mexican embassy in Colombia and Venezuela. In 1919 he published a collection of short poems in haiku form entitled *Un Día.* That same year he also published *En el País del Sol,* a collection of essays that he had written during his stay in Japan in 1900. Impressed with the visual potential of Chinese characters to convey poetic meaning, Tablada experimented with similar possibilities in his own language in *Li-po y otros Poemas* (1920). He spent his later years in New York City, devoting himself to the diffusion of Mexican and Japanese culture to the rest of the world. ___Atsuko TANABE DE BABA___

table tennis

Table tennis was introduced into Japan around 1900. In 1921 the Japan Imperial Table Tennis Association was founded, and in 1922, All-Japan Table Tennis Championships began. At first, a softer nonstandard ball, unique to Japan, was used exclusively. According to an agreement in 1934, however, the standard ball also began to be used, and about the same time international matches began to be played. For a long time, the penhold grip, in which a player grips the racket with thumb and forefinger and hits the ball with only one side of the racket, was dominant in Japan. Currently, however, the handshake grip, predominant in Europe, is also common. Since both the softer ball and the standard ball are still in use, national table tennis matches are separated into two classes. Since 1952 Japan has participated in the World Table Tennis Championships and has gained excellent records in both men's and women's competitions. As of the late 1970s, the number of players registered with the Japan Table Tennis Association was approximately 520,000, but it is estimated that roughly 10 million Japanese enjoy this sport. ___WATANABE Tōru___

taboo

Ritual avoidance (*imi*) of things, persons, places, times, actions, or words believed to be inauspicious or, on the contrary, sacred. The concept of taboo is closely allied to the notion of ritual impurity (KEGARE): anything impure must be avoided so as not to offend or defile the sacred; at the same time, the sacred itself must occasionally be avoided to insure that no offense to its sanctity occurs. Examples of the former category are the traditional taboos surrounding birth, menstruation, and death. Inauspicious words (*imikotoba*) or numbers (*imikazu*) which are homonyms of tabooed phenomena may also be taboo: hence the avoidance of the number four (*shi*) which is a homonym of the word for death (*shi*). In the Heian period (794–1185), directional taboos (KATATAGAE) were observed so as to avoid transgressing the direction believed to be occupied by certain deities. See also TABOO EXPRESSIONS. ___FUJITA Tomio___

taboo expressions

(*imikotoba*). Words or expressions considered among certain groups of people to bring or be associated with bad luck; also, the euphemisms and alternative expressions used in their place. For example, in Shintō ceremonies Buddhist terms such as *hotoke* (Buddha) and *sō* (Buddhist monk) are generally avoided (Buddhism being associated with funerals), as are words like *shi* (death) and *chi* (blood). Certain expressions are avoided at New Year's, when the God of the New Year (Toshi no Kami) is supposed to visit the home; going to bed (*neru*) is called *ine tsumu* (to store the rice plants) and a mouse (*nezumi*) is more auspiciously termed *yomegakimi* or *yomesama* (bride). There are expressions to be avoided after nightfall; instead of saying *shio* for salt (near-homophone of *shi,* death), one says *nami no hana* (flowers of the waves). In speeches at wedding parties, words like *kaeru* and *modoru* (to go back home) are carefully avoided. Among *imikotoba* used by fishermen are *nagamono* (long object) for snake (*hebi*), *etekō* ("honorable monkey") for monkey (*saru,* homophone of the verb "to depart"), while hunters and charcoal makers refer to the bear (*kuma*) as *yamaoyaji* (old man of the mountains), and so forth. Some *imikotoba* have become part of the secular argot used exclusively by particular communities or groups, such as craftspeople, entertainers, and gangsters, to reinforce in-group solidarity and exclusivity. ___INOKUCHI Shōji___

Tachibana Akemi (1812–1868)

WAKA poet of the late Edo period. Born in Echizen (now part of Fukui Prefecture). Pen name Shinobunoya. An admirer of the classical style based on the MAN'YŌSHŪ and advocated by KAMO NO MABUCHI, he strove for simplicity of expression. With Tanaka Ōhide (1776–1847), a student of the KOKUGAKU (National Learning) scholar MOTOORI NORINAGA, he read widely and at the age of 35, entrusting his family responsibilities to his half-brother, he turned to a life of austere and impoverished seclusion. Nevertheless, he was a fervent champion of the emperor and supported the SONNŌ JŌI (Revere the Emperor, Expel the Barbarians) movement. His chief works include a collection of poetry, *Shinobunoya kashū* (1878), and a volume of essays, *Irori tan* (date unknown).

Tachibana family

A noble family (UJI) of ancient Japan who distinguished themselves particularly during the Nara period (710–794). In 708 Agata no Inukai no Michiyo, the wife of Prince Minu, a descendant of Emperor Bidatsu (538–585), was granted the name Tachibana no Sukune in recognition of her services to the court (see AGATA NO INUKAI NO TACHIBANA NO MICHIYO). After her death in 733, her son Prince Katsuragi was allowed to change his name to TACHIBANA NO MOROE and later received the honorific cognomen of *ason* (see YAKUSA NO KABANE), indicating his status as a kinsman of the imperial house. Moroe's son Naramaro (721–757) in 757 dared to challenge the power of FUJIWARA NO NAKAMARO. His rebellion was suppressed, and the influence of the Tachibana greatly declined. A few generations later, however, Tachibana no Kachiko (786–850) became principal consort *(kōgō)* to Emperor SAGA and the mother of Emperor Nimmyō (r 833–850). Popularly known as Empress DANRIN after Danrinji, a temple she built, she took responsibility for educating members of the extended family. The Tachibana thus enjoyed a period of renewed good fortune, but they were soon eclipsed by the northern branch of the FUJIWARA FAMILY; and after TACHIBANA NO HAYANARI's involvement in the JŌWA CONSPIRACY (842) and the downfall of the imperial favorite Tachibana no Hiromi (837–890) in the AKŌ INCIDENT OF 887, the family's influence declined even further. By the latter part of the Heian period (794–1185) people bearing names of the central nobility had become common in the provinces. The Tachibana were no exception, becoming one of the "Four Great Surnames" together with the Fujiwara, Taira, and Minamoto families.

KITAMURA Bunji

Tachibana Kōzaburō (1893–1974)

A farm educator, rural utopian, and agrarian nationalist who helped to plan an unsuccessful coup d'etat to rescue Japan from excesses that he attributed to capitalism, bureaucracy, and the urban way of life. On 15 May 1932 two dozen of Tachibana's students and an equal number of young military officers attacked power stations, civilian leaders, and the Tōkyō police headquarters. Prime Minister INUKAI TSUYOSHI was assassinated in the incident (see MAY 15TH INCIDENT). Convicted at a sensational trial, Tachibana spent six years in prison and turned to a quiet life of scholarship after World War II.

Born the third and youngest son of a prosperous merchant in Mito, Ibaraki Prefecture, Tachibana studied European literature at the First Higher School in Tōkyō. Forsaking his studies, he founded a "fraternal village," Kyōdai Mura, near his native place in November 1915. This utopian community became the basis for a producers' cooperative he founded in November 1929 and a school known as the AIKYŌJUKU (Academy for the Love of One's Community) in April 1931. INOUE NISSHŌ, the ultranationalist ideologue who founded the Ketsumeidan (League of Blood) and inspired political terrorism in early 1932, is known to have visited Tachibana occasionally in Mito starting in December 1929. But Tachibana did not take part in the LEAGUE OF BLOOD INCIDENT of February and March 1932. He first met GONDŌ SEIKYŌ, Japan's leading prewar agrarian nationalist, shortly before the first League of Blood Incident, but he claimed never to have read any of Gondō's works until after the May 15th Incident.

Tachibana believed that the essence of Japanese life was "mutual love and cooperation," qualities he thought were found mainly in rural society. In a 1932 lecture to young military officers, he denounced the "materialistic civilization of modern capitalism," which oppressed farmers, and called for a "patriotic reform" to cleanse Japan of selfishness and privilege. Like all agrarian nationalists, he vilified absentee landlords for leaving the soil to join the urban monied classes. However, he thought that the chasm between city and village was the most crucial social division in Japan, not the gap between tenants and landlords.

To remedy these evils, Tachibana proposed economic reforms based on cooperation and progressive taxation to minimize the monopoly on private wealth enjoyed by the urban elite. He also sought local controls on corporate enterprise and advocated rural political autonomy by restoring village self-rule. He opposed social revolution, affirmed the rural hierarchy, and hoped to restore, not erode, both private property in general and land ownership in particular.

Tachibana's romantic agrarian doctrines had less to do with inspiring political violence than did his forceful personality and his insistence on uniting theory and action. Tachibana feared centralized military rule fully as much as he hated business and bureaucratism. His impact on the young officers of the 1930s was confined to showing them the flaws of modern capitalist society. See also NŌHON SHUGI.

———— Thomas R. H. Havens, *Farm and Nation in Modern Japan: Agrarian Nationalism, 1870–1940* (1974). T. R. H. HAVENS

Tachibana Moribe (1781–1849)

KOKUGAKU (National Learning) scholar and WAKA poet of the late Edo period. Tachibana was born in Ise (now part of Mie Prefecture), but lived mainly in Edo (now Tōkyō). Largely self-taught, he evinced a boldly imaginative approach to scholarship and in *Itsu no kotowaki* (1847–50), an annotated study of the songs contained in the 8th-century chronicles KOJIKI and NIHON SHOKI, took a stand in opposition to the eminent but xenophobic Kokugaku scholar MOTOORI NORINAGA. His works number over 60 volumes, including inductive analyses of the rhetoric of *waka* and prose and etymological studies of the Japanese language based on phonemic principles. Among his disciples were wealthy farmers and weavers of the provinces north of Edo, who supported him and the publication of his work.

Tachibana no Hayanari (?–842)

Court official of the early years of the Heian period (794–1185). He was a member of an official mission to China in 804 that included the Buddhist monks KŪKAI and SAICHŌ. In 842 he was charged with being a ringleader in the JŌWA CONSPIRACY, a probably fictitious plot to enthrone Prince Tsunesada (825–884), the heir apparent. Hayanari was arrested, stripped of his rank and surname, and banished from Kyōto; he died on his way into exile. He was a distinguished calligrapher and was ranked, together with Kūkai and Emperor SAGA, as one of the so-called Sampitsu ("Three Brushes") of his time. See also CALLIGRAPHY. Dennis M. SPACKMAN

Tachibana no Moroe (684–757)

Court official of the Nara period (710–794); sixth-generation descendant of Emperor Bidatsu (538–585); son of the imperial prince Minu and the court lady AGATA NO INUKAI NO TACHIBANA NO MICHIYO, who later became the wife of the statesman FUJIWARA NO FUHITO and the mother of Empress KŌMYŌ, consort of Emperor SHŌMU. Originally called Prince Katsuragi, he received his first court post in 710 and in 731 was made a councillor *(sangi)*. In 736 he renounced his royal status and assumed his mother's family name, Tachibana. In the following year, the influence of the FUJIWARA FAMILY was greatly reduced when four of Fuhito's sons died in an epidemic, and Moroe, now appointed great counselor *(dainagon)*, became by default the principal figure in the court, which he dominated with the help of the priest GEMBŌ and the scholar-official KIBI NO MAKIBI. In 738 Moroe became minister of the right *(udaijin)* and in 743 rose to minister of the left *(sadaijin)*. During this period he suppressed the Rebellion of FUJIWARA NO HIROTSUGU (740), an attempt to return the Fujiwara to power. In 749 Moroe was elevated to the senior first rank *(shōichii;* see COURT RANKS) with full administrative control of the state; but his power was almost immediately eclipsed by that of FUJIWARA NO NAKAMARO, a favorite of Empress KŌKEN, who succeeded to the throne in that year. In 755 Moroe was accused of plotting a coup d'etat and, although spared punishment through the intercession of his half-sister, the dowager empress Kōmyō, was forced to withdraw from public life. Immediately after Moroe's death two years later, his son Naramaro (721–757) attempted to overthrow Nakamaro but was captured and killed. Moroe was responsible for the construction of two imperial palaces between 740 and 745—the KUNI NO MIYA and the SHIGARAKI NO MIYA palaces—and is also remembered as a poet. Several of his verses are preserved in the 8th-century anthology *Man'yōshū*.

YAGI Atsuru

Tachibana Shiraki (1881–1945)

Sinologist. Born in Ōita Prefecture, Tachibana studied at the Fifth Higher School in the city of Kumamoto. He took a job with a Hokkaidō newspaper in 1905. In 1906 he went to Manchuria to work as a reporter for a local Japanese language newspaper. He became interested in Chinese agriculture, economics, and folk beliefs and traveled widely, collecting material. He later worked for the SOUTH MANCHURIA RAILWAY and became editor in chief of the magazine *Manshū hyōron* (Manchurian Review) in 1931. In the course of his studies he came to view Confucianism as the guiding principle of the Chinese social revolution and to criticize Japan's imperialistic policies on the Asian mainland. Because of his first-hand knowledge of China, his opinion carried considerable weight at the South Manchuria Railway Research Institute. He also influenced many Japanese intellectuals through his published works on Chinese culture, history, and philosophical thought such as *Shina shisō kenkyū* (1936, Studies on Chinese Philosophy). His collected works in three volumes were published posthumously as *Tachibana Shiraki chosaku-shū* (Keisō Shobō, 1966).

Tachibana Shūta (1865–1905)

Army officer. Born in Hizen Province (now Nagasaki and Saga prefectures). He graduated from the Army Academy in 1887 and served successively as military attaché to the crown prince and as an instructor at the army's Toyama School and at the Cadet School in Nagoya. He was killed during the RUSSO-JAPANESE WAR of 1904–05 while serving as commander of the First Battalion of the Thirty-Fourth Infantry Regiment. Together with the naval officer HIROSE TAKEO, he was honored as a *gunshin* ("war god") until the end of World War II.

IWASHIMA Hisao

Tachihara Masaaki (1926–1980)

Novelist. Real name Yonemoto Masaaki. Born in Korea. Studied at Waseda University. His works are noted for their intricate construction, sensitive depiction of human psychology, and evocation of human loneliness. He was awarded the Naoki Prize for his novel *Shiroi keshi* (1965). Other novels include *Tsurugigasaki* (1965) and *Kinuta* (1972).

ASAI Kiyoshi

Tachihara Michizō (1914–1939)

Poet. Born in Tōkyō. Graduate of Tōkyō University, where he studied architecture. Attracted more to poetry, however, Tachihara became a frequent contributor to the poetry magazine *Shiki*, founded in 1933 by poet HORI TATSUO. His health was poor, and he died at the age of 25. Known as a lyrical poet, he left two collections of poems, mostly in a sonnetlike form, *Wasuregusa ni yosu* (1937) and *Akatsuki to yūbe no shi* (1937).

Tachikawa

City in central Tōkyō Prefecture. An army airfield was constructed here during the Taishō period (1912–26). During World War II it was a center for aircraft production. After the war it was the site of a United States Air Force base; this was returned to Japan in 1977. Part of this air base is now used by the Japanese Self Defense Force. Formerly a regional railroad center, the city has now developed into a residential and commercial area as well. Industrial products include automobiles and machinery. Pop: 142,600.

Tachikawa Bunko

(Tachikawa Library). A series of books—mostly period pieces read by boys and girls—published by an Ōsaka firm named Tachikawa (more properly pronounced Tatsukawa) Bummeidō between 1911 and the mid-1920s. In Japan, there is a tradition of oral storytelling called KŌDAN whose stories were often highly dramatized retellings of historical events. The Tachikawa Bunko consisted of *kōdan* stories that were adapted by the *kōdan* storyteller Tamada Gyokushūsai for juvenile readers and published as paperback books. Almost 200 such books were published in a period of 15 years. The movie director MAKINO SHŌZŌ completed a series of *samurai* adventure movies based on the Tachikawa books. These movies became one of the most popular forms of entertainment in the Taishō period (1912–26). The Tachikawa Bunko books occupy an important posi-

tion in the history of mass culture as a transitional style in the development of the modern genre called *taishū bungaku* (see POPULAR FICTION).

ARASE Yutaka

tachimono

(literally, "that which is cut off"). Certain types of food that an individual voluntarily abstains from eating for a set period of time as an ascetic practice in preparation for the observance of an important festival or to fulfill a personal or religious vow (see GANKAKE). In many cases it involves abstinence from a favorite food or a basic food such as tea, salt, rice, or *sake*. Usually this is an individual practice, but there are examples of whole villages avoiding *tachimono* on special occasions.

INOKUCHI Shōji

Tada Fumio (1900–1978)

Geographer. Born in Tōkyō; graduated from Tōkyō University in 1924. Professor at Tōkyō University, Komazawa University, and Hōsei University. President of the ASSOCIATION OF JAPANESE GEOGRAPHERS and vice-president of the International Geographical Union. Tada was an expert on physical geography and applied geography, particularly in regard to the topographical formation of plains in Japan. His works include *Shizen kankyō no hembō* (1964, Changes in the Natural Environment).

NISHIKAWA Osamu

Tadamigawa

River in western Fukushima Prefecture, northern Honshū; originating in the lake called Ozenuma, which straddles the border of Fukushima and Gumma prefectures, it flows into the Agagawa in the Aizu Basin. (The latter flows into Niigata Prefecture, where it is known as the Aganogawa, and eventually empties into the Sea of Japan.) The upper reaches of the Tadamigawa are noted for scenic gorges. Large electric power plants, including the Oku Tadami and Tagokura, are located on the river. Its great volume of water is due to melting snow. Length: 137 km (85 mi); area of drainage basin: 2,260 sq km (872 sq mi).

tadokoro

Private rice lands and granaries owned by local chieftain families (*gōzoku*) before the TAIKA REFORM (645), when all land was proclaimed public domain; the term is used in distinction to *miyake*, rice lands owned by the ruling family in Yamato. *Tadokoro*, like the imperial estates, are thought to have been worked by serfs or service groups (BE) belonging to the landowners. As the Yamato ruling family extended its authority, it acquired many *tadokoro* either as gifts or by confiscation. Although *tadokoro* were formally abolished by the Taika Reform, many of their administrative features survived in the private landed estates (SHŌEN) that developed in the Heian period (794–1185).

Taehan Empire

(Kor: Taehan Cheguk; J: Daikan Teikoku). Replaced Chosŏn (J: Chōsen) as the official name of Korea in August 1897. *Tae* means great, while *han,* not to be confused with the Han dynasty of China, was the name of ancient Korean tribes living in southern Korea prior to the KOREAN THREE KINGDOMS PERIOD. The name was intended to symbolize Korea's independence not only from Qing (Ch'ing) China but from all foreign powers, and continued to be used until Japan's annexation of Korea in 1910. See KOREA AND JAPAN: early modern relations.

C. Kenneth QUINONES

Taewŏn'gun (1820–1898)

The father of the Korean king KOJONG (r 1864–1907); personal name, Yi Ha-ŭng; enfeoffment title, Hŭngsŏn'gun. *Taewŏn'gun* (J: *taiinkun;* grand prince) is a royal title reserved for a monarch's father who has not occupied the throne; the term is widely used to refer to the specific individual, Yi Ha-ŭng.

After his son's succession to the throne in 1864, the Taewŏn'gun became the dominant figure at court. He was a strong-willed Confucian reformer whose efforts were intended to strengthen the authority of the throne, create a counterweight to the entrenched officialdom, revitalize the traditional military system, and secure the dynasty's fiscal base. He implemented an exclusionist foreign policy, its essence being the rejection of all efforts by Western nations and Japan to replace Korea's traditional tributary relations with European-style treaty relations. This policy resulted in a number of confrontations with foreign powers, including the 1866 French assault following the persecution of French Catholic missionaries and their converts, the 1871 American raid in retaliation for the destruction of an American merchant ship in 1866 and, most significantly, the Japanese SEIKANRON affair of 1873.

The Taewŏn'gun retired from the palace in late 1873, opening the way for the Treaty of KANGHWA with Japan in 1876 and the ascent of Queen MIN's clique at court. He did remain, however, a rallying point for Confucian conservatives and anti-Japanese sentiment until his death in 1898, and he was involved in many of the factional disputes prevalent during this period. The Taewŏn'gun was returned to power briefly after the IMO MUTINY of 1882, only to be abducted by Chinese forces and taken to Tianjin (Tientsin), where he was held until 1885. The Japanese reinstalled him in the summer of 1894, just prior to the outbreak of the Sino-Japanese War of 1894–95, but he sided with the rebels of the TONGHAK REBELLION, which had been breaking out intermittently since 1893, and was again removed from power. The Taewŏn'gun also played a role in the Japanese assassination of his long-time rival, Queen Min, in 1895. See also KOREA AND JAPAN: early modern relations.

▬ ——Choe Ching Young, *The Rule of the Taewŏn'gun, 1864–1874* (1972). Kikuchi Kenjō, *Chōsen saikin gaikōshi Taiinkun den* (1910). James Palais, *Politics and Policy in Traditional Korea* (1975). Yi Sŏn-gŭn, *Han'guksa ch'oegŭnse p'yŏn* (1961).

C. Kenneth QUINONES

Tagajō

City in central Miyagi Prefecture, northern Honshū; 11 km (7 mi) northeast of Sendai. In the 8th century Tagajō was the site of a military outpost for subduing the Ezo tribesmen. It is now a residential and industrial suburb of Sendai and Kamaishi. Industries include the manufacture of electric and electronic machinery and appliances, cans, and industrial edged tools. Pop: 50,784.

Tagajō

(Taga Castle). The civil and military headquarters established in northern Honshū in the 8th century primarily to prosecute the war against the aboriginal EZO people. Called Taga no Ki (Taga Stockade) when it first appears in the documents in 737, following destruction in a local rebellion and rebuilding after 780 it was known as Tagajō (Taga Castle) and served as the provincial headquarters of Mutsu (now Fukushima, Miyagi, Iwate, and Aomori prefectures).

Situated south of the modern city of Shiogama in Miyagi Prefecture, Tagajō crowned a 30 meter (98.4 ft) high hill and was girdled by an earth mound running 1,000 meters (0.6 mi) north-south by 800 meters (0.5 mi) east-west. Several formally grouped buildings stood in the walled central area on the crest of the hill, the main office looking rather like the lecture hall of a temple. The plan of these buildings underwent a number of modifications over a 200-year span of time. Recovered tiles are chiefly of the 7th through 9th centuries. By the end of the 8th century there was an elaborate entrance gate with flanking colonnades and a simple central main hall. This hall kept its initial dimensions throughout Tagajō's history, but the gates were changed as were several side and back office buildings. After the Ezo were crushed by SAKANOUE NO TAMURAMARO in 802, the military headquarters moved farther north to IZAWAJŌ. Tagajō was left understaffed and was eventually evacuated completely.

The well-preserved site of the guardian temple of the castle is located in the southeast sector of the precinct, the base stones for a pagoda, main hall, lecture hall, and other buildings all *in situ*. The plan was modeled after the temple Kawaradera in Asuka (see KAWARADERA REMAINS).

▬ ——Miyagi Ken Kyōiku Iinkai, ed, *Tagajō shi* (1977).

J. Edward KIDDER, Jr.

Tagawa

City in central Fukuoka Prefecture, Kyūshū. Close to the Chikuhō Coalfield, it was once the center of a thriving coal-mining industry. The closing down of all the mines has led to a drastic drop in the population. Efforts are being made to introduce cement and garment industries. Pop: 60,077.

tageta

A type of footwear formerly worn when working in paddy fields. Also called *ōashi*. Based on the same principle as the snowshoe and consisting of a sandal for the foot resting on a large wooden frame that distributed the weight and enabled the wearer to walk in muddy fields. Also used for trampling the bed of the seedling nursery or the paddy before transplanting. *Tageta* have been excavated from the Yayoi-period (ca 300 BC–ca AD 300) Toro site in Shizuoka Prefecture. See also KANJIKI. NOGUCHI Takenori

Tagokura Dam

Located on the upper reaches of the river TADAMIGAWA, southwestern Fukushima Prefecture, northern Honshū. Completed in 1959, the dam created Lake Tagokura, now a popular tourist attraction. The dam is utilized for electric power generation with a maximum output of 380,000 kilowatts. Height: 145 m (476 ft); length of embankment: 462 m (1,515 ft); storage capacity: 370 million cu m (13,061 million cu ft).

Tagonoura

Coastal area near the mouth of the river Fujikawa, Shizuoka Prefecture, central Honshū. Celebrated in ancient poems, the coast offers a beautiful view of Mt. Fuji (FUJISAN). Tagonoura Port, in the city of Fuji, is an important port. There are large chemical and starch manufacturing plants on the coast. Sludge pollution, a serious problem in 1965, is now under control.

Tagore, Rabindranath (1861–1941)

Indian poet and philosopher; recipient of the Nobel Prize (1913) in literature. Born in Calcutta; son of Debendranath Tagore, the Bengali philosopher and religious reformer. Tagore wrote plays, novels, and literary criticism, composed music, and painted, but it is for his Bengalese poems that he is best remembered. He was also interested in political and social problems and worked for the independence movement in India. When OKAKURA KAKUZŌ traveled to India in 1902, he met with Tagore; Okakura's works, *The Ideals of the East* (1903), *The Awakening of Japan* (1904), and *The Book of Tea* (1906), all bear witness to Tagore's influence. Tagore visited Japan on three occasions as part of a worldwide lecture tour.

Taguchi Ukichi (1855–1905)

Economist and cultural historian. Born in Edo (now Tōkyō), the son of a foot soldier (*ashigaru*) in the Tokugawa shogunate's army. He completed a course of study in economics and English in the Translation Bureau of the Ministry of Finance in 1874 and later did translation work in the ministry's Currency Bureau until 1878. In 1879 Taguchi founded his own journal, the *Tōkyō keizai zasshi* (Tōkyō Journal of Economics), modeled after the British journal *The Economist*, through which he helped to introduce the theories of the British classical "liberal" economists. In his articles he criticized protectionist theories and government economic policies from the standpoint of laissez-faire economics, earning for himself the sobriquet "the Japanese Adam Smith." He was the author of *Nihon kaika shōshi* (1877–82, A Short History of the Enlightenment of Japan), a systematic study of Japan's political, economic, religious, and literary history. He is also noted for having edited the KOKUSHI TAIKEI and the modern edition of the GUNSHO RUIJŪ, two major compilations on Japanese history and culture. He was also active in politics and business, serving first in the Tōkyō prefectural and municipal assemblies and, from 1894 on, in the lower house of the Diet, as an overseer of the Tōkyō Stock Exchange, and as president of the Ryōmō Railway Company.

▬ ——*Teiken Taguchi Ukichi zenshū*, 8 vols (Teiken Taguchi Ukichi Zenshū Kankōkai, 1927–29).

Tahata Eitai Baibai Kinshi Rei

Also known as Dempata Eitai Baibai Kinshi Rei. Ordinance issued by the Tokugawa shogunate (1603–1867) in 1643 forbidding the sale and purchase of farming land. Issued to check the accumulation of land by rich peasants, who were taking advantage of a severe famine the previous year, it was also intended to prevent the pauperization of the peasants, their flight from rural areas, and the deterioration of farmland. Punishment for offenders was severe: sellers were thrown into jail and later banished, and buyers had their land confiscated and were imprisoned. Similar ordinances were issued in individual domains. Decrees reinforcing the ordinance were issued periodically thereafter, but since peasants were allowed to put up their land as security against loans *(shichiire)* in order to pay their taxes (NENGU), land did in effect change hands, and by the 18th century the law had become almost meaningless. Criticisms were leveled against the ordinance throughout the period: the Confucian scholar OGYŪ SORAI contended that since the land belonged to the peasant, it was therefore at his disposal. The magistrate ŌOKA TADASUKE argued that the law might as well be abolished, since no one gave up his land voluntarily but only as a last resort, and it was at his suggestion that punishments were mitigated. The ordinance was finally revoked in 1872, five years after the Meiji Restoration.

tai → sea bream

Tai Chi-t'ao → Dai Jitao (Tai Chi-t'ao)

Taiga → Ike no Taiga

Taigyaku Jiken → High Treason Incident of 1910

Taiheiki

A GUNKI MONOGATARI (war tale) of unknown authorship recounting the inception and course of the conflict between the NORTHERN AND SOUTHERN COURTS over the period 1318–67. In 40 volumes, the work, which translates as "Chronicle of the Great Peace"—no doubt reflecting the author's hopes for more stable and peaceful times—was probably completed about 1370–71. In contrast to the lyricism of the HEIKE MONOGATARI, and its Buddhist-oriented emphasis on the transience of life, this account of internal disorder and shifting loyalties emphasizes the natural order of cause and effect and seems Confucian in outlook. The *Taiheiki* depicts a period of turmoil, a world in which the low displace the high (GEKOKUJŌ), but it also portrays the spirit of the common people. It was initially recited as entertainment by storyteller-priests known as *taiheiki-yomi* without musical accompaniment in a style that was popular well into the Edo period (1600–1868). The narrative, written in *wakan konkōbun*, mixed Chinese-Japanese style, is embellished with tales from the Chinese classics and Buddhist mythology.

The *Taiheiki* falls into three sections. The first section covers Emperor GO-DAIGO's plot to overthrow the HŌJŌ FAMILY, who controlled the Kamakura shogunate, and the establishment of the KEMMU RESTORATION (Kemmu no Chūkō). The second section covers the rebellion of ASHIKAGA TAKAUJI, the dissolution of the restoration government, the split between the Southern and Northern Courts, and the death of Go-Daigo. The third section covers the gradual emergence of the Northern Court, the establishment of the Ashikaga shogunate (see MUROMACHI SHOGUNATE), and the appointment of Hosokawa Yoriyuki (1329–92) as shogunal deputy.

The question of authorship is complicated not only by the tale's oral origin but also by the existence of a number of variant texts. Various people are considered to be possible authors, including several monks and *samurai*. Kojima Hōshi, perhaps a YAMABUSHI of the SHUGENDŌ sect, is thought to be at least partly responsible for the tale reaching its final form. The number of variants, as well as variation in the quality of the writing, reflects the number of participants in composition, as well as interaction between reciters and their audiences.

📖 ——Okami Masao and Kadokawa Gen'yoshi, ed, *Taiheiki, Soga monogatari, Gikeiki*, vol 21 of *Kanshō Nihon koten bungaku* (Kadokawa Shoten, 1976). Helen Craig McCullough, tr, *Taiheiki: A Chronicle of Medieval Japan* (1959), a translation of vols 1–12.
                                                    William R. WILSON

Taiheiyō Kouhatsu, Inc

(Taiheiyō Kōhatsu). A company dealing in real estate and the sale of coal, Taiheiyō Kouhatsu was established in 1920 as the Taiheiyō Coal Mining Co. With the deterioration of the coal-mining industry, the company stopped its mining operations and switched to real estate and coal sales. In recent years coal has sold well as a substitute for oil, and the company has established a joint enterprise in Australia to develop coal mines and import coal. Sales for the fiscal year ending March 1982 totaled ¥81.1 billion (US $336.9 million), with coal accounting for 60 percent and real estate 21 percent, and the company was capitalized at ¥3.1 billion (US $12.9 million) in the same year. Corporate headquarters are located in Tōkyō.

Taihō Code

(Taihō Ritsuryō). Legal code of the early 8th century consisting of 6 volumes of penal law *(ritsu)* and 11 volumes of administrative law *(ryō)*. It is believed to have been a revision of the ASUKA KIYOMIHARA CODE (689), which in turn had been modeled on the legal code of the Tang (T'ang) dynasty (618–907) of China. It was compiled by an imperially appointed commission that included Prince Osakabe (d 705), FUJIWARA NO FUHITO, and Awata no Mahito (d 719). Completed in 701, it became effective in 702 (Taihō 2). The Taihō Code was the first code in which penal and administrative laws were drawn up together; it was also the first code to be formally promulgated. Although the original text of the code has not survived, a 9th-century commentary, the RYŌ NO SHŪGE, indicates that it was quite similar to the YŌRŌ CODE, which superseded it in 757. See also RITSURYŌ SYSTEM.

Taihō Ritsuryō → Taihō Code

Taika no Kaishin → Taika Reform

Taika Reform

(Taika no Kaishin). Designates in its strictest sense the political and economic reforms carried out in the name of Emperor KŌTOKU from 645 to 649. After eliminating the SOGA FAMILY in a coup d'etat in the sixth month of 645 (Taika 1), a faction at court led by Nakatomi no Kamatari (later FUJIWARA NO KAMATARI) and Prince Naka no Ōe (later Emperor TENJI) took measures to break the independent power of the various UJI (chieftain families) and to place the imperial house in direct control of the people and land throughout Japan. To this end, in the first month of 646 they issued an edict in which Prince Naka no Ōe and Emperor Kōtoku announced plans to establish a new system of regional administration, to compile household registers regularly and allocate land to peasants, and to collect three kinds of head tax from all male adults. Thus the reformers aimed for the gradual formation of a Chinese-style centralized state (see RITSURYŌ SYSTEM), but since the development of this state had to await the enactment of the ASUKA KIYOMIHARA CODE in 689 and the compilation of the Kōinnen-Jaku population register in 690, in its broadest sense the term Taika Reform refers to political changes throughout the second half of the 7th century.

Emergence of the Yamato Court —— The major theme during the century prior to the Taika coup is the gradual formation of a centralized, despotic imperial system. Formed in the Kyōto–Ōsaka region around 400, the YAMATO COURT had been steadily expanding in two dimensions since its inception. The first dimension was the growth of a vertical service nobility surrounding the Yamato hegemon. Important milestones in this development include the establishment of the UJI-KABANE rank system during the reign of Emperor Yūryaku (mid-5th century), the victory of the Soga over nativist conservatives like the MONONOBE FAMILY in 587, and the articulation of a bureaucratic ethic by Prince SHŌTOKU in his SEVENTEEN-ARTICLE CONSTITUTION (604). The second dimension was the outward expansion of Yamato control into eastern Japan and Kyūshū by means of regional administrative units called *miyake* (imperial domains) and *agata* (local districts; see AGATANUSHI).

In studying the Taika Reform it is important to consider the international setting as well. During most of the 6th century both China and the Korean peninsula were divided into numerous contending states. By 589, however, Emperor Wen of the Sui dynasty (589–618) had united China into a vast empire. The Chinese empire applied military pressure on the states of the Korean peninsula (SILLA, PAEKCHE, and KOGURYŌ) to submit to its imperium. This pressure extended to Yamato and its foothold on the Korean peninsula called KAYA. The overbearing diplomatic and military force of the Sui and Tang (T'ang; 618–907) empires resulted in coups in Paekche in 641, Koguryō in 642, and Silla in 647. All of them led to imitation of the Chinese model of a centralized, despotic state. With the Taika coup of 645, Japan's centralizing regime emerged.

The 645 Coup —— Ever since their victory over MONONOBE NO MORIYA in 587, the Soga family had occupied the preeminent position at court. In fact, the Soga had become the "mating line" for the imperial family; Soga women produced male children who eventually ascended the throne and remained under the influence of Soga relatives. Soga preeminence was also based on avid assimilation of continental culture (notably Buddhism) and technology, and intervention in Korean affairs.

Prince Shōtoku and SOGA NO UMAKO died in 622 and 626, respectively. When it became necessary to choose a new emperor in 628, Soga no Emishi (Umako's son) supported Prince Tamura (593–641), a grandson of Emperor Bidatsu (538–585, r 572–585), over other, more logical candidates. Tamura became Emperor Jomei (r 629–641); his sons included Prince Naka no Ōe, Prince Ōama (later Emperor TEMMU), and Prince Furuhito no Ōe.

Jomei died in 641, and his consort ascended the throne as Empress Kōgyoku (later Empress SAIMEI) in 642. With the throne in their control, Soga no Emishi and his son SOGA NO IRUKA began to arrogate certain privileges that belonged to the imperial line, and Iruka eliminated Prince YAMASHIRO NO ŌE, Shōtoku's son and a leading contender for the throne. An anti-Soga clique developed at court, headed by Prince Naka no Ōe and Nakatomi no Kamatari (later FUJIWARA NO KAMATARI). On the 12th day of the sixth month in 645, Naka no Ōe had Soga no Iruka assassinated in Kōgyoku's presence at the Itabuki Palace. On the 13th Emishi committed suicide at his private residence. Naka no Ōe replaced Kōgyoku with her younger brother (Emperor Kōtoku) and assumed the position of heir apparent, which gave him control over government affairs. The chronicle NIHON SHOKI (720) notes that a new era called Taika ("Great Reform") began with Kōtoku's accession.

Immediate Reform Efforts —— One of the first major steps of the new leaders was to dispatch officials called *kokushi* or *kuni no mikotomochi* to all Yamato-controlled areas in eastern Japan and also to the six districts *(mutsu no agata)* under direct court control in Yamato Province (now Nara Prefecture). Those sent east consisted of eight groups with jurisdiction over local chieftains (KUNI NO MIYATSUKO). The officials were given four principal duties. First, they were to survey the land, count the population, and guarantee communal rights to forests. Second, they were to prevent the exaction of excess taxes by local rulers or the exercise of vigilante justice. Third, they were to report all false claims to KABANE titles such as *kuni no miyatsuko*. Finally, they were to collect all weapons and keep them in storehouses, although in areas threatened by attack from the EZO tribesmen to the north, owners were allowed to keep their arms.

In sending these officials, the court hoped to strengthen its hold on the militarily important Kantō area. Often in the past, local chieftains, particularly those in eastern Japan, had been hostile to Yamato interests. While other local chieftains usually found it in their interest to comply with the court from the 500s on, the confiscation of weapons and registration of population would now ensure their cooperation.

The *Nihon shoki* reports other reform efforts in 645. Complaint boxes were installed throughout the country to register popular opinion. Rules for interclass marriage and divorce were established. Laws for state support of certain Buddhist temples and the nomination of monks to posts of authority in their monasteries were promulgated. On the 19th day of the ninth month of 645, court emissaries were sent to count the national populace. This practice was undoubtedly limited to lands under direct court control. Finally, Kōtoku's court moved to Naniwa (see NANIWAKYŌ) on the Inland Sea to facilitate communication with the continent.

The Reform Edict —— In the first month of 646 Emperor Kōtoku and Prince Naka no Ōe welcomed the new year by proclaiming the Taika Reform edict. The edict had four articles. The first article abolished both imperial and local-magnate service communities (*koshiro, kakibe;* see BE) and lands (*miyake,* TADOKORO), setting up a system of government stipends in their stead. Second, the edict made arrangements for the establishment of a permanent imperial capital and a new system of local government. In the third section the proclamation ordered the drawing up of population and tax registers and the state allocation of land (HANDEN SHŪJU SYSTEM). It described land measurements (see JŌRI SYSTEM) and village government. The fourth section substituted a produce tax for the prior labor tax. The produce tax was levied both on paddy land and households (see SO, YŌ, AND CHŌ). Thus the goal of the reform was government control of land and populace (*kōchi kōmin*).

Other Reforms —— Besides the edict, the *Nihon shoki* lists one other major verifiable reform in the Taika era. This is the so-called Hakusōrei of 646, a sumptuary law that limited the size of burial mounds (KOFUN) and the number of workers employed in their building. This reform was probably meant to strike at the *kabane* system in operation before 645, for its restrictions correlated with the rank system of Emperor Kōtoku. Some proof of the implementation of the burial reform may be derived from the virtual disappearance of the mounds after this period.

Opposition to the Reforms —— There was opposition to the new government from the outset. The first disturbance involved Prince Furuhito no Ōe, a son of Emperor Jomei and one of the prime candidates for the throne at the time of Kōgyoku's abdication. In the 11th month of 645 it was discovered that he was plotting against Kōtoku and Prince Naka no Ōe, and he was quickly eliminated.

In 649 Soga no Ishikawamaro and Abe no Uchimaro grew discontented as their position in the new government weakened. After the death of Abe in that same year, Ishikawamaro was accused of plotting to assassinate Prince Naka no Ōe. The prince's soldiers captured and killed Soga along with a number of his clansmen.

The most serious domestic revolt occurred after Emperor Kōtoku's death in 654, when Naka no Ōe set aside the designated heir, Prince ARIMA, in favor of the former empress Kōgyoku, who reascended the throne as Empress Saimei. Arima retired to Kii Province (now Wakayama Prefecture), where he and several other leaders planned to sweep into the capital and burn the palace. At the last moment the plot was uncovered, and Prince Arima was beheaded.

The Emergence of the Ritsuryō State —— An event of major import during the early stages of state centralization was the Battle of HAKUSUKINOE in Korea. The defeat of Japanese forces by the combined forces of Tang China and Silla in 663 seriously damaged the authority of Naka no Ōe (now Emperor Tenji) and drained the nation's resources. It also necessitated further government centralization through reforms. Thus in 664 (a year designated *kasshi* in the sexagenary cycle) Tenji had his brother Prince Ōama proclaim the Kasshi Reform, which established a 26-step rank system for government offices and ordered the selection of *uji* representatives *(uji no kami)*, recognizable by the swords they were allowed to carry.

Other notable actions were taken during Tenji's reign. In 667 he moved his capital to ŌTSU NO MIYA. The following year, as one source indicates, Japan's first statutes, the ŌMI CODE, were proclaimed. In 670 Tenji carried out the first nationwide census of population, the KŌGONEN-JAKU. In this register people were granted surnames and their statuses were fixed.

A period of instability followed Tenji's death in 672 (see JINSHIN DISTURBANCE), but in 672 Prince Ōama ascended the throne as Emperor Temmu (he was formally enthroned in 673). During his reign and that of his empress JITŌ, who succeeded him, two important milestones in the creation of a Chinese-style centralized state were achieved: The first was the compilation and implementation of the first verifiable statutes, the Asuka Kiyomihara Code of 689, the direct ancestor of the TAIHŌ CODE and YŌRŌ CODE of the 8th century. Second, in 690 the Kōinnen-Jaku was compiled as a preliminary to the first nationwide allocation of state land (*handen shūju* system). This land system was the basis of the *ritsuryō* state.

In the last 25 years much doubt has been cast on the authenticity of the 646 reform edict, which appears in the *Nihon shoki*. That the reforms described in the edict actually took place is not questioned; the new systems of regional administration, citizen registry, and male taxation were the basic institutions of the full-fledged archaic state of the 8th century. All scholars agree, though, that these institutions were not implemented until the 690s, specifically with the enactment of the Asuka Kiyomihara Code in 689 and the compilation of the Kōin register in 690. What is at issue is whether the impetus for these reforms can be attributed to the farsightedness of the emperor Kōtoku after the coup of 645, or whether these reforms were adopted in reaction to other events of the late 600s, especially to the defeat of Japanese armies in Korea in 663 and the Jinshin Disturbance of 672.

Most Japanese scholars agree that the 646 edict was altered to some extent by the compilers of the *Nihon shoki* when they inserted it into the chronicles in 720. According to the historian Inoue Mitsusada (1916–83), large parts of the edict are later additions, sometimes containing words that did not come into use until the early 8th century. However, Inoue believes that each article of the edict contains a kernel of historical truth, usually to be found in the introduction to the article before the longer explanatory section. Although this kernel does not prove that the reforms were carried out on the stated schedule, Inoue believes that at least it represents the plans for reform as conceived by Emperor Kōtoku and Prince Naka no Ōe.

The historian Kadowaki Teiji, on the other hand, sees no reason to accept any part of the edict as dating from 646. Rather, he believes that the defeat of Japanese armies at Hakusukinoe by the Tang Chinese forces and the succession struggle of 672 were more important stimuli for change than the Taika coup of 645. His explanation for the *Nihon shoki* presentation of the edicts is that the chroniclers, working within the ideology of the time, preferred to attribute the development of the new state to the active participation of the emperor rather than to less visible forces of social change. In this way, Kadowaki imagines, the edicts were made up after the fact and projected back to the reign of Emperor Kōtoku. Moreover, he notes that the term Taika no Kaishin itself dates from the 1880s when certain Meiji scholars seized on the reforms described in the *Nihon shoki* as a historical parallel to the MEIJI RESTORATION. Just as the Meiji emperor had granted the new constitution by his own imperial will, so the imperial line was seen as the source of the reforms and the archaic state in the 8th century.

Unfortunately, many scholarly works in English on the early Japanese state still unquestioningly accept the *Nihon shoki*'s version of the 7th-century reforms without taking into account the motives from which it was written. According to the historian Yagi Atsuru, the first of these was the need to portray the development of the centralized state as inevitable for 645 and to magnify the role of the emperor in its establishment. Thus the evils of the Soga and the extent of the reforms can be said to have been exaggerated by the ideology of the 8th-century court. Second was the wish of the compiler FUJIWARA NO FUHITO to enhance his power at the court by embellishing the role of his father, Fujiwara no Kamatari, in the formation of the state. Finally, the national need to backdate the origin of reformed institutions, gaining credit in the Chinese-oriented world and discrediting unified Silla, should not be discounted.

📖 ——— John W. Hall, *Government and Local Power in Japan, 500 to 1700* (1966). Hara Hidesaburō, "Taika no kaishin ron hihan josetsu," *Nihonshi kenkyū* 86 (1966), 88 (1967). Inoue Mitsusada, *Taika no kaishin* (rev ed, 1970). Kadowaki Teiji, *Taika no kaishin ron* (1967). Cornelius J. Kiley, "State and Dynasty in Archaic Yamato," *Journal of Asian Studies* 23.1 (1973). *Nihon shoki* (720), in *Nihon koten bungaku taikei*, vols 67–68 (Iwanami Shoten, 1965). Nomura Tadao, *Kenkyūshi: Taika no kaishin* (1973). Robert K. Reischauer, *Early Japanese History*, 2 vols (1937). *Ritsuryō*, in *Nihon shisō taikei*, vol 3 (Iwanami Shoten, 1976). Sakamoto Tarō, *Taika no kaishin no kenkyū* (1938). George Sansom, *A History of Japan to 1334* (1958). Suzuki Osamu, *Hakusukinoe* (1972). Yagi Atsuru, "Taika no kaishin," in *Kodai no Nihon*, vol 1, *Yōsetsu* (Kadokawa Shoten, 1971). Kozo Yamamura, "The Decline of the Ritsuryō System," *Journal of Japanese Studies* 1.1 (1974). Wayne FARRIS

Taika Shakkandan

(International Banking Consortium for China). A group of European, American, and Japanese banks that sought to coordinate their loan policies toward China in the first decades of the 20th century. As originally organized in 1909, it consisted exclusively of European banks, but the US and Japanese governments soon succeeded in gaining participation by their banks as well. The idea was to pool the banks' resources in cooperative efforts to develop the Chinese economy and stabilize the country's monetary affairs.

When the Republican revolution broke out in China in 1911 (caused in part by opposition to railway development programs financed by the consortium), the banks found it difficult to do their work. It was only in 1920, after World War I, that the consortium was reactivated. However, unstable conditions in the country discouraged bankers, and when the consortium was dissolved after World War II (1946), it had failed to extend a single joint loan to China.

The importance of this organization in modern Japanese history lies in the fact that it provided one framework for Japan's economic activities in China. It was intended to internationalize loan and investment activities and thus from the beginning tended to conflict with Japan's unilateral initiatives and policies. On the other hand, the consortium was also a symbol of great-power status; failure to join it would have isolated Japan. Thus when the consortium was revived in 1919–20, political and financial leaders such as HARA TAKASHI and INOUE JUNNOSUKE endorsed Japanese participation, even though it meant that thenceforth loan and investment activities in

China would first have to go through the international organization. (Japan's existing rights in Manchuria and Inner Mongolia were excepted, however.) Despite the consortium's dismal record, it is significant as a precursor of more recent multinational endeavors by capitalist, industrial nations to undertake joint projects in developing areas of the world.   Akira IRIYE

Taiki

Diary of the Heian-period (794–1185) court official Fujiwara no Yorinaga (1120–56); also known by other names, *Ukaiki* being the most common. The diary, in 12 sections, covers the years from 1136, when the young Yorinaga was appointed inner minister (*naidaijin*), to 1155, but the entries are sporadic, and many years are missing entirely. Yorinaga was a leading scholar of his day, and his career was greatly advanced by the patronage of the retired emperor TOBA. As the result of political rivalry with his elder brother, the powerful regent Tadamichi (1097–1164), however, he lost his influence and the favor of his patron; thereupon he joined forces with Minamoto no Tameyoshi (1096–1156) and Taira no Tadamasa (d 1156) in an unsuccessful coup d'etat, the HŌGEN DISTURBANCE of 1156, and died of his wounds. His diary is an important source for the cultural life and political developments of the late Heian period, when retired emperors controlled the government (see INSEI).
                          G. Cameron HURST III

taiko

Any of various kinds of large drum. (1) Three types of *taiko*, known collectively as *gakudaiko*, are used in court music: *dadaiko*, an enormous laced drum; *tsuridaiko*, a nailed drum, the most commonly used type; and *ninaidaiko*, a laced drum on a carrying pole, played in processions. (2) The large *shimedaiko* of the NŌ drama, an hourglass-shaped laced drum, is also used in KABUKI and popular KAGURA music. (3) The *ōdaiko*, a large barrel-shaped, nailed drum, which may sometimes be mounted on wheels, is used in festival music and also to announce kabuki performances. (4) The *hirazuridaiko*, a thin barrel-shaped drum suspended on a stand, is used in kabuki and in popular Sino-Japanese music.
                          David B. WATERHOUSE

taikō

Honorific title applied in the Heian period (794–1185) to the grand minister of state (*dajō daijin*) or the regent of the realm (SESSHŌ) and later used in referring to an imperial regent (KAMPAKU; see REGENCY GOVERNMENT) who had passed on his office to his son. The most famous bearer of this title was the great national unifier TOYOTOMI HIDEYOSHI, who was called *taikō* after the office of *kampaku* was transferred to his nephew and adopted son TOYOTOMI HIDETSUGU on 11 February 1592 (Tenshō 19.12.28); hence the term *taikō* is in some contexts synonymous with the name Hideyoshi.
                          George ELISON

Taikō kenchi → kenchi

Taikyō Sempu

(Proclamation of the Great Doctrine). The policy of the government immediately after the Meiji Restoration (1868) to promote SHINTŌ as the national religion as part of an effort to foster national unity. Because a renewed interest in Shintō had been part of the movement to restore direct rule to the emperor in the early 19th century, some of the leaders in the new government sought to revive the ancient Japanese ideal of "unity of religion and government" (*saisei itchi*). In 1869 the Office of Shintō Worship (Jingikan) was established, with a section for missionary activities, and in 1869 the office was ranked above the Grand Council of State (DAJŌKAN) in the administrative hierarchy. In 1870 the government issued the Proclamation of the Great Doctrine, which declared the "way of the gods" to be the guiding principle of the state. The government also ordered (in 1871) compulsory registration at local Shintō shrines. These efforts to promote Shintō as a national religion encountered severe criticism, particularly from Buddhists; in 1871 the Office of Shintō Worship was renamed the Ministry of Shintō Religion (Jingishō). This, in turn, was replaced in 1872 by the Ministry of Religion (KYŌBUSHŌ), and more restrained religious policies were adopted. The Kyōbushō was absorbed by the Home Ministry in 1877. See also STATE SHINTŌ.

Taira family ——— Genealogy

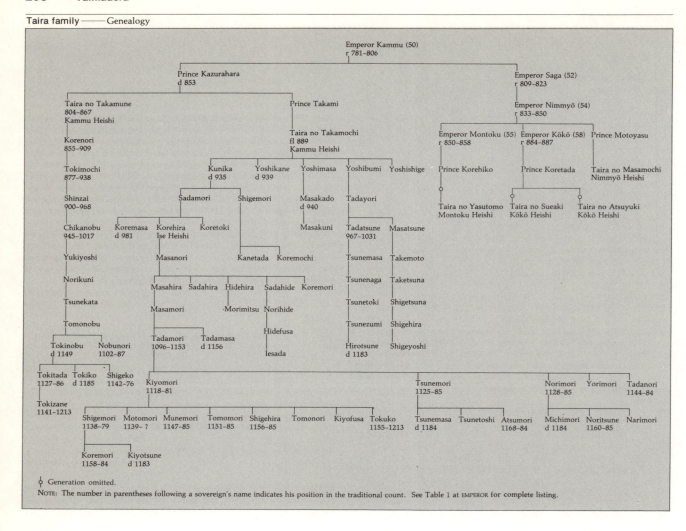

Generation omitted.

NOTE: The number in parentheses following a sovereign's name indicates his position in the traditional count. See Table 1 at EMPEROR for complete listing.

Taimadera

A temple of the Shingon and Tendai sects of Buddhism; located in the village of Taima in Nara Prefecture. According to temple tradition, in 612 Prince Maroko, the son of Emperor Yōmei (d 587), built the monastery Mampōzōin in Kawachi Province (now part of Ōsaka Prefecture); in 682 the monastery was moved to its present site and called Zenrinji. Its name was later changed to Taimadera. The back half of the Mandala Hall dates from the Nara period (710–794), but its front half was rebuilt around 1242. It houses the *Taima mandara* of 763, one of the oldest surviving mandalas in the world. It is said to have been donated by the lady Chūjō (753–781), daughter of Fujiwara no Toyonari (706–765).

The central image in the main hall *(kondō),* rebuilt in 1184, is of Maitreya Buddha. The structure also houses a set of the Four Heavenly Kings (see TEMBU) from the Nara period. In front of the *kondō* are the three-storied East and West pagodas, both from the 8th century. The Taimadera lecture hall *(kōdō),* burned in 1180 and rebuilt in 1303, houses a 4.9-meter (16-foot) wooden image of the Buddha Amida from the 10th or 11th century.

Nancy SHATZMAN-STEINHARDT

Tainoura

Coastal area in the town of Amatsu Kominato, southern Chiba Prefecture, central Honshū; part of Uchiura Bay. It is famous for sea bream viewing. A boat takes the tourist some 800 m (0.5 mi) off the coast, where bait is thrown into the sea, and sea bream *(tai)* leap out

of the water by the dozen at the sound made by slapping the side of the boat. Birthplace of the monk NICHIREN, founder of the Nichiren sect of Buddhism, and site of the temple Tanjōji.

Taira family

One of the four great families, including also the MINAMOTO FAMILY, FUJIWARA FAMILY, and TACHIBANA FAMILY, that dominated court politics during the Heian period (794–1185). The Taira family, like the Minamoto and Tachibana, was an offshoot of the imperial family. In pre-Heian times, indeterminate succession practices led to numerous succession disputes and depleted imperial finances. To help solve these problems, imperial offspring five or six generations removed from the ruler were cut off from the dynasty and given surnames like other nobles, a practice known to anthropologists as dynastic "shedding." Since the royal house had no surname, these persons are known in Japanese as "surname-receiving royalty" *(shisei kōzoku).*

In the Heian period, dynastic shedding continued for much the same reasons as well as to create houses which might bolster imperial house power against the growing power of the Fujiwara. Now, however, sons and daughters of sovereigns were also periodically shed from the dynasty. In 814 Emperor SAGA created the surname Minamoto for several of his children, and in 825 Emperor KAMMU awarded the surname Taira to his grandson Takamune. Thereafter all members cut off from the imperial line were surnamed either Minamoto or Taira. The Taira family is better known through alternate pronunciations of its Chinese characters (Taira *[hei]* and family *[shi]* or *[ke]* = Heishi or Heike). Besides the Kammu Heishi, there were the Nimmyō Heishi, Montoku Heishi, and Kōkō Heishi, each descended from an emperor.

Several other descendants of Kammu were also made Taira, establishing several branches of the Kammu Heishi. The branch destined to flourish, however, traced its origin not to Takamune, whose descendants remained as middle-level officials in the capital, but to Prince Takamochi, Kammu's great grandson, who became a provincial official in Kazusa (now part of Chiba Prefecture) sometime toward the end of the 9th century. After his tour of duty, Takamochi settled in the area, and his descendants traditionally held provincial posts in eastern Japan, many of them achieving a notable reputation as warriors. For example, a number of families which would play major roles in the TAIRA–MINAMOTO WAR of the late 12th century trace their beginnings to Takamochi's son Yoshibumi: the Ōba, MIURA, and Kajiwara among them. Together, these provincial warriors came to be known as the "Eight Bands of Taira from the East" (Bandō Hachi Heishi).

The Taira thus played a prominent role in eastern Japan during the mid-Heian period, but two major rebellions involving Taira leaders diminished their influence: the defeats of TAIRA NO MASAKADO in 940 and TAIRA NO TADATSUNE almost 100 years later in 1030. When Minamoto warrior chieftains, notably Yoriyoshi and Yoshiie, moved into the area, Taira-related families became their vassals. Later they were crucial in helping MINAMOTO NO YORITOMO, the chieftain of the Seiwa branch of the Minamoto, establish his shogunate in Kamakura. In fact, upon the death of Yoritomo, it was the HŌJŌ FAMILY, claiming descent from the Taira, who controlled the reins of power in the shogunate.

Another branch of this Kammu Heishi moved to Ise Province (now part of Mie Prefecture) in central Japan, when Taira no Korehira became governor there. His great grandson Masamori began to establish a military reputation for this branch, known as the Ise Heishi, having first become a client of the retired sovereign SHIRAKAWA by commending some landholdings (see SHŌEN) in his home province to a chapel built in honor of Shirakawa's daughter.

Masamori's son TAIRA NO TADAMORI also served Shirakawa and the next retired emperor, TOBA, as well. Both father and son were amply rewarded for participation in the subjugation of piracy and provincial rebellions. Even at the time, however, there were numerous rumors to the effect that these Taira chieftains had in actuality not won significant military victories but had been rewarded with promotions in rank and office because of their close relationship with the retired emperors.

Nevertheless, the Taira did rise in power and Masamori became the object of some open hostility at court when he was raised to a position allowing attendance upon the emperor. Despite such hostility, however, by the mid-12th century the Ise branch of the Taira and the Seiwa branch of the Minamoto were known as the two leading warrior houses in Japan. It was in fact, Taira no Masamori who was deputized by Shirakawa to chastise MINAMOTO NO YOSHIIE's rebellious son Yoshichika in 1106.

The high point of Taira influence came in the late Heian period under Tadamori's son TAIRA NO KIYOMORI, victor in the HŌGEN DISTURBANCE of 1156 and HEIJI DISTURBANCE of 1160. As Taira power increased, however, considerable envy and open hostility was focused upon Kiyomori and his house. Plotting against Kiyomori, who ultimately rose to the position of prime minister, became an open secret in the late 1170s.

In 1180 Minamoto no Yoritomo rose in rebellion against the Taira. In a five-year struggle known as the Taira–Minamoto war, Yoritomo's forces crushed the Taira and established warrior government in Japan (see KAMAKURA SHOGUNATE). Kiyomori and all the major Taira leaders, including his infant grandson, Emperor ANTOKU, died or were killed during the period, and the house never again achieved prominence. Only provincial families descended from the Taira played important roles at a local level.

The story of the rise and fall of the Taira in three short generations is recounted in Japan's major military chronicle, *The Tale of the Heike* (HEIKE MONOGATARI).

■——John W. Hall, *Government and Local Power in Japan, 500 to 1700* (1966). "Heishi" entry in *Nihon rekishi daijiten,* vol 8 (1969). G. Cameron Hurst, *Insei: Abdicated Sovereigns in the Politics of Late Heian Japan, 1085–1186* (1976). Ishimoda Shō, *Kodai makki seiji shi josetsu,* (1964). Jeffrey P. Mass, *Warrior Government in Early Medieval Japan* (1974). Yasuda Motohisa, *Insei to Heishi* (1975). G. Cameron HURST III

Taira Incident

(Taira Jiken). The seizure of a police station in Taira, Fukushima Prefecture, on 30 June 1949 by several hundred people, mostly local members of the JAPAN COMMUNIST PARTY (JCP) and labor unions. The incident was incited by police removal of a billboard that had been put up by the local JCP in front of the city's railway station; angered by this action, demonstrators occupied the police station for about eight hours. Several people were injured in the disturbance. More than 150 demonstrators were indicted on the charge of participating in a riot (sōjōzai, article 106 of the Criminal Code). The incident attracted national attention because this was the first time under the postwar constitution that article 106—often used by the prewar government to suppress the freedoms of press and assembly—had been invoked. In 1955 most of the demonstrators were acquitted by the local court, which ruled that the disturbance had been an accidental occurrence. The prosecution appealed the decision to a higher court, however, and it reversed the lower court's ruling and found the defendants guilty of rioting charges. In 1960 the Supreme Court dismissed the defendants' appeal.

Taira–Minamoto War

(Gempei no Sōran). A nationwide conflict that engulfed Japan between 1180 and 1185, the Taira–Minamoto War was on the surface a battle between two major warrior leagues, one under the TAIRA FAMILY (Heishi or Heike), who were in power, and another under the MINAMOTO FAMILY (Genji), who were out of power. Yet beneath the surface it was an opportunity for warriors in eastern Japan to vent long-held frustrations and assert themselves against control of their homelands by the court nobility. It was a socioeconomic upheaval of major proportions, and for most warriors the conflict between the Minamoto and the Taira simply provided a vehicle for seeking a solution to local political and economic problems.

The Minamoto——By the late 12th century the Seiwa Genji branch of the Minamoto family had established a formidable warrior reputation and hegemony in eastern Japan after the victories of Minamoto no Yoriyoshi (988 or 994–1075) and his son MINAMOTO NO YOSHIIE in the northeast. From that time, however, the Seiwa Genji went into a decline. In the HŌGEN DISTURBANCE (1156), much of the main line was killed or executed by the Taira. In 1160, after the HEIJI DISTURBANCE, the Seiwa Genji leader MINAMOTO NO YOSHITOMO was killed. His three surviving sons—MINAMOTO NO YORITOMO, Minamoto no Noriyori (d 1193), and MINAMOTO NO YOSHITSUNE—were exiled and placed under the watchful eyes of Taira guardians. Minamoto power was effectively extinguished.

The Taira——The other major military lineage of the latter part of the Heian period (794–1185), the Ise branch of the Taira family, had risen to power somewhat later than the Minamoto. Their base was in central Japan, and under Taira no Masamori and his son TAIRA NO TADAMORI they achieved a military reputation. More important, they entered the service of the retired emperors SHIRAKAWA and TOBA and succeeded in infiltrating the ranks of the court nobility.

As the power of the Minamoto disappeared with the death of Yoshitomo, that of the Taira under TAIRA NO KIYOMORI's leadership increased. Between his victory in the Heiji Disturbance and his death in 1181, Kiyomori rose from a middle-level courtier to the post of grand minister of state (dajō daijin). When his infant grandson was enthroned as Emperor ANTOKU in 1180, Kiyomori was the most powerful member of the small noble oligarchy that controlled court politics, and other Taira family members had likewise penetrated the councils of state.

Outbreak of War——By 1180 the Taira had become so powerful that most other elements at court, including their long-time patron the retired emperor GO-SHIRAKAWA, turned against them. In March 1180 (Jishō 4.2) Go-Shirakawa's second son, Prince Mochihito (1151–80), frustrated at having twice been passed over for the succession, and MINAMOTO NO YORIMASA, the sole remaining Minamoto in a Taira-dominated court, plotted an uprising. The prince issued an edict, calling for all Minamoto bands, loyal warriors, and others to rise up against the Taira. Unable to recruit a sufficient force of armed monks in Kyōto and Nara, Mochihito and Yorimasa lost their lives in a battle near the river Ujigawa. Kiyomori also took revenge on the temples that had tried to support the two; such great institutions as the TŌDAIJI and KŌFUKUJI were burned to the ground. The anti-Taira revolt seemed crushed.

Yoritomo's Revolt——But Mochihito's edict reached Yoritomo in Izu (now part of Shizuoka Prefecture), where he had been in exile since age 13. He had developed a close relationship with his captor HŌJŌ TOKIMASA, now his father-in-law. For three months Yoritomo carefully evaluated the potential for a successful uprising. In September (Jishō 4.8), Yoritomo was able to gather 300 men, whom he sent to destroy the headquarters of the local deputy (Izu *mokudai*). He then seized control of the province, and on the basis of the prince's edict claimed authority over the provinces of eastern Japan. This was the first of many lawless acts by Yoritomo, who was soon branded a rebel by the court.

Marching eastward into Sagami (now Kanagawa Prefecture), Yoritomo confronted a major Taira force at the Battle of Ishibashiyama. Outnumbered, he was soundly defeated and barely escaped with his life to the Hakone Mountains. Later that month he fled to Awa Province (now part of Chiba Prefecture), and over the course of the next two months he managed to gather from surrounding provinces a force of warriors said to have numbered 200,000. Having established a headquarters in the town of Kamakura, Yoritomo rode off to Suruga (now part of Shizuoka Prefecture) to meet a large Taira army sent out from the capital in November (Jishō 4.10).

In the Battle of FUJIGAWA Yoritomo won his first major victory with little trouble. Traditional accounts say that a flock of geese rose screeching into the night sky and sent the frightened Taira forces fleeing to the capital. Presented with the opportunity to pursue the Taira to Kyōto and perhaps avenge his father's death, Yoritomo instead heeded the advice of his major commanders, who urged him to stay in the east and consolidate his power. Their worry was less the Taira than the security and preservation of their own territory.

From late 1180 to 1183 warfare virtually ceased, except for certain provincial skirmishes between partisans of one side or another seeking to settle long-standing grievances of local origin. Yoritomo's role during these years was more that of a ruler than a general, and he devoted himself to the consolidation of recently seized powers in the east. After an offer to share national authority with the Taira on an east-west basis was rejected, Yoritomo turned to improving social and economic conditions in his new territory, brought recalcitrant Minamoto and former enemies into his band, and solidified his authority as a feudal lord.

Yoritomo issued edicts of confirmation (ANDO) of his major vassals' rights to their home lands and rewarded others by distributing lands seized from defeated enemies. He established the SAMURAI-DOKORO (Board of Retainers) in December 1180 to regularize the various rights and responsibilities tying him to his growing body of vassals (GOKENIN), which now included nobles from the capital who had joined Yoritomo's ranks.

Yoshinaka and the Resumption of Fighting —— The uneasy peace was disrupted late in 1183 by the actions of Yoritomo's cousin MINAMOTO NO YOSHINAKA, a rough provincial *samurai* from the province of Shinano (now Nagano Prefecture) in north central Japan. While both sides watched with apprehension his military growth during the period 1181–83, the Taira had more to fear and sent a large force against him in the seventh month. Yoshinaka routed the Taira troops and chased them back to the capital. Taira supporters fled westward with Emperor Antoku when Yoshinaka entered the city late in the same month.

Yoshinaka and Yoritomo's uncle Yukiie (d 1186) now replaced the Taira in control of the capital, but they were even less acceptable to the court, since their men created havoc throughout the city. The two were also reluctant to pursue the Taira, Yoshinaka in particular fearing that Yoritomo might march on the capital during his absence. Estrangement between the cousins reached the point that Yoshinaka had the court designate him to chastise Yoritomo, a rebel once again.

Yoritomo reacted by sending his brothers Noriyori and Yoshitsune to Kyōto, where Yoshitsune's military prowess was well displayed in his quick defeat of Yoshinaka late in February 1184 (Juei 3.1). Almost immediately the Minamoto commanders pursued the Taira to the west, winning a major victory at Ichinotani early in the following month.

Again the fighting was interrupted. The Taira fled to Yashima on the island of Shikoku, and the Minamoto, lacking boats, had no immediate opportunity to attack. The next months were devoted to procuring boats, sending provisions and horses from the east, and trying to win support among the warriors of the Taira-dominated west. Yoritomo once again entered into negotiations with Go-Shirakawa and the court, offering to chastise the Taira on their behalf.

Yoritomo was forced to create new institutions to handle the administrative burden created by the extension of his government in the field. In particular, there was a great increase in complaints from landholders claiming that warriors had illegally seized their holdings. Yoritomo established the KUMONJO (Public Documents Office) to deal with the additional paperwork, and the MONCHŪJO (Board of Inquiry) to review and decide cases of land seizure by Kamakura vassals. Thus the bodies that later formed the core of Yoritomo's governmental administration were all established during the fighting to meet the exigencies of war.

Defeat of the Taira —— During this period Yoritomo and Yoshitsune became alienated over the matter of Yoshitsune's acceptance of certain court titles without his brother's permission. Nevertheless, by early 1185 Yoritomo had appointed Yoshitsune commander of the Minamoto to replace his brother Noriyori, who had been ineffective. Yoshitsune quickly launched a successful attack against the fortress of Yashima in March (Juei 4.2) and sent the Taira fleeing farther west with their young emperor.

The Minamoto and Taira fleets met for what was to be the final battle of the war at DANNOURA, off the southern tip of Honshū, on 25 April 1185 (Juei 4.3.24). The Minamoto victory was complete: the major Taira figures were killed or took their own lives, Emperor Antoku was drowned, and it is believed that even the sacred jewels and sword of the IMPERIAL REGALIA sank beneath the waves.

The Aftermath —— Although Yoritomo emerged as the victor over the Taira and the most powerful figure in Japan, he still faced a number of problems. One was contending with his estranged brother Yoshitsune, another was obtaining *de jure* recognition from the court of his de facto powers, and a third was the subjugation of regions still independent of his control.

Yoritomo was successful in having Yoshitsune branded a rebel by the court and received from Go-Shirakawa the right to post his men as stewards (JITŌ) on landed estates (SHŌEN) and as constables (SHUGO) at the provincial level and to levy commissariat rice (HYŌ-RŌMAI) nationwide to prosecute his war against Yoshitsune; he also effected the removal of anti-Minamoto nobles at court. When Yoshitsune ultimately sought refuge with the ŌSHŪ FUJIWARA FAMILY in northeastern Japan, Yoritomo focused his attention in that direction. Although Yoshitsune was eventually forced to commit suicide by his hosts, Yoritomo nevertheless reduced the Ōshū Fujiwara capital at HIRAIZUMI and brought the north under his control.

By the end of the decade Yoritomo was master of most of Japan, which was a far different place from what it had been when the war broke out in 1180. The Taira–Minamoto confrontation had been settled in favor of the latter, but a wholesale social, economic, and political upheaval had also taken place. Yoritomo had initially emerged as a symbol of the challenge by eastern warriors against a political order that had been controlled by the court nobility. At the end of the Taira–Minamoto War a new WARRIOR GOVERNMENT had come into being, one that, in one form or another, was to continue until the MEIJI RESTORATION of 1868. See also KAMAKURA SHOGUNATE; HISTORY OF JAPAN: Kamakura history.

◾️—— Kan'ichi Asakawa, "The Founding of the Shogunate by Minamoto-no-Yoritomo," in Kan'ichi Asakawa, *Land and Society in Medieval Japan* (1965). Endō Motoo, *Gempei shiryō sōran* (1966). John W. Hall, *Government and Local Power in Japan, 500 to 1700* (1966). John W. Hall and Jeffrey P. Mass, ed, *Medieval Japan: Essays in Institutional History* (1974). Ishii Susumu, "Kamakura bakufu ron," in *Iwanami kōza: Nihon rekishi*, vol 5 (Iwanami Shoten, 1962). Jeffrey P. Mass, *Warrior Government in Early Medieval Japan* (1974). Nagahara Keiji, *Minamoto no Yoritomo* (1958). Minoru Shinoda, *The Founding of the Kamakura Shogunate* (1960). Watanabe Tamotsu, *Genji to Heishi* (1955).   G. Cameron HURST III

Taira no Atsumori (1168–1184)

Son of the warrior Taira no Tsunemori (1125–85) and nephew of the powerful leader of the Taira family, TAIRA NO KIYOMORI. Atsumori is famous only for the poignant literary accounts of his death at the age of 16 in the Battle of Ichinotani during the TAIRA–MINA-MOTO WAR. Following the main encounter, which took place near the shore of the Inland Sea, the Minamoto warrior KUMAGAI NAO-ZANE saw Atsumori attempting to reach the safety of the Taira ships waiting offshore. Kumagai pursued Atsumori and caught him but was so moved by the youth's beauty and resemblance to his own son that he wished to spare him. At that movement several other Minamoto warriors appeared, and Kumagai, seeing that they would kill Atsumori if he did not, killed the boy himself. It is said that remorse over this deed so haunted Kumagai that he became a priest after the war. This probably apocryphal story became a favorite subject of literature and drama including the NŌ play *Atsumori* and the play entitled *Kumagai* in the BUNRAKU and KABUKI repertoires.

Barbara L. ARNN

Taira no Kiyomori (1118–1181)

Prominent political figure at the end of the Heian period (794–1185). Of warrior origin, he rose to dominate the court and saw his grandson become emperor. He is the central figure in Japan's greatest war chronicle, HEIKE MONOGATARI.

Kiyomori was born into the Ise Heike branch of the TAIRA FAMILY. His grandfather, Masamori, and his father, TAIRA NO TADAMORI, were military commanders who gained prominence at the court in the service of the retired emperors SHIRAKAWA and TOBA. Although official genealogies record Kiyomori as Tadamori's son, the *Heike monogatari* asserts that he was in fact the son of Shirakawa. The retired emperor is said to have presented a pregnant concubine to Tadamori with instructions that, if the child were a boy, he should be raised as a warrior. A growing number of scholars accept this story.

Nonetheless, it was as the son of a middle-ranking warrior that Kiyomori began his career at court. Little is known of his early life, but his rapid advancement in office can only have been due to the patronage of the imperial house. As Tadamori's nominal son, he must have received military training, but the sources indicate that he spent most of his boyhood in the capital. In any case, Kiyomori's later rise to power was due less to military prowess than to his skillful navigation of the traditional channels to political influence— marriage and patronage. From 1137 to 1156 Kiyomori held important governorships in the southwestern provinces, where he established alliances and landholdings that later enabled him to dominate the trade with Song (Sung) China.

Kiyomori's position at court was strengthened greatly by his participation in two major factional struggles. In the HŌGEN DISTURBANCE of 1156 Kiyomori and MINAMOTO NO YOSHITOMO defended Emperor GO-SHIRAKAWA against an attempted coup. Although Kiyomori contributed less to the victory, he was rewarded more generously than Yoshitomo. The disgruntled Yoshitomo then attempted to eliminate both Kiyomori and Go-Shirakawa (now retired) in the HEIJI DISTURBANCE of 1160, but Kiyomori swiftly crushed the uprising and eliminated Minamoto influence from the court.

Kiyomori now held military control of the capital, and he dominated the court for the next 20 years, placing dozens of his Taira kinsmen and partisans in high official posts. In 1160 he became an imperial adviser *(sangi)* and the first member of a warrior house to sit in the Grand Council of State (Dajōkan). In 1167 he was made grand minister of state *(dajō daijin)*, a post seldom filled, and then only by men of the highest lineage and exemplary character. Kiyomori's rise to eminence and power was bitterly resented by the old nobility, but his daughters were so successfully married into the imperial house and the Fujiwara regents' family that he could not be challenged. When Kiyomori tried to arrange the enthronement of a Taira prince, however, opposition to him grew, and finally even his patron Go-Shirakawa turned against him.

By the late 1170s, opposition to Taira rule was widespread. In 1177 a plot by several of Go-Shirakawa's associates was discovered and harshly suppressed. In 1180 Prince Mochihito (1151–80), a son of Go-Shirakawa passed over for the succession, in league with the elderly MINAMOTO NO YORIMASA (1104–80) enlisted the aid of warrior monks of the temple Onjōji at what is now the city of Ōtsu and called for the Minamoto and other loyal warriors to rise against the Taira. This revolt, too, was quickly put down. To guard against further conspiracies, Kiyomori transferred the court, together with the reigning and retired emperors, to FUKUHARAKYŌ (now part of Kōbe) in his own domain; but public protests forced him to return the government to Kyōto after six months. Late in 1180, Kiyomori placed his grandson Emperor ANTOKU on the throne.

After Kiyomori's death in 1181 the Taira clung to power, but their downfall was assured. Prince Mochihito's earlier call to arms had reached the eastern provinces, where MINAMOTO NO YORITOMO, a son of Yoshitomo spared by Kiyomori after the Heiji Disturbance, had raised the standard of revolt in 1180 (see TAIRA–MINAMOTO WAR). In 1183 Minamoto forces drove the Taira from Kyōto, in 1184 dislodged them from their base of power in the west, and in the spring of 1185 finally destroyed them in the Battle of DANNOURA.

Although he is the central figure in the *Heike monogatari*, Taira no Kiyomori is not treated sympathetically. He is presented as a man arrogant beyond his talents, whose success was due to calculation, ruthlessness, and a great measure of good luck.

——*Heike monogatari* (ca 1220?), tr Hiroshi Kitagawa and Bruce T. Tsuchida as *The Tale of the Heike* (1975). G. Cameron Hurst, *Insei: Abdicated Sovereigns in the Politics of Late Heian Japan* (1977). Jeffrey P. Mass, *Warrior Government in Early Medieval Japan* (1974). Ivan Morris, *The Nobility of Failure* (1977). Ryō Susumu, "Rokujō In ryō to Taira no Masamori," in Ryō Susumu, *Heian jidai* (1962). Takada Minoru, "Taira no Kiyomori," in *Jimbutsu Nihon no rekishi*, vol 3 (Yomiuri Shimbun Sha, 1966). Takeuchi Rizō, "Go-Shirakawa In to Taira no Kiyomori," in Takeuchi Rizō, ed, *Heian ōchō: Sono jitsuryokusha tachi* (1965).

G. Cameron HURST III

Taira no Masakado (?–940)

Warrior of the Heian period (794–1185) who led the first major rebellion by the rising warrior class against the central government. A grandson of Taira no Takamochi (fl 889), the princely founder of the TAIRA FAMILY, Masakado was based in Shimōsa (now part of Chiba and Ibaraki prefectures) in the Kantō region, where the Taira held considerable influence and controlled extensive landed estates. According to the military chronicle SHŌMONKI (ca 940; also known as *Masakadoki*), an intrafamily quarrel over a woman erupted in 931. It soon developed into a military struggle (935–936) for predominance and control over land between Masakado on the one side and his kinsmen and their allies on the other, with Masakado emerging the winner. His fame as a warrior and commander spread throughout the eastern provinces, gaining him the support of many local forces. Thus, from 938 the intrafamily conflict widened into a struggle for preeminence in the whole of the Kantō. It turned into a rebellion against the state when, early in 940 (Tengyō 2.11–12), in defiance of Kyōto, Masakado attacked and occupied first the Hitachi (now Ibaraki Prefecture) government quarters and then those of the other Kantō provinces, installing governors of his choosing. He then took an even graver step: he assumed the title "New Emperor," making the Kantō into an autonomous state. The central government issued on 21 February 940 (Tengyō 3.1.11) an ordinance commanding the suppression of the rebels, but before the imperial envoy who was to lead the campaign reached the scene, Masakado was killed by forces under FUJIWARA NO HIDESATO on 25 March 940 (Tengyō 3.2.14). His army dispersed, and his allies were captured and executed. Thus ended the rebellion which had caused great alarm to the central government not only for its gravity but also because its leader had arrogated to himself a title and prerogatives belonging to the sovereign. This rebellion and a contemporaneous revolt in Shikoku led by FUJIWARA NO SUMITOMO are collectively known as the rebellions of the Jōhei (931–938) and Tengyō (938–947) eras.

——Hayashi Rokurō, ed, *Ronshū Taira no Masakado kenkyū* (1975). Kajiwara Masaaki and Yashiro Kazuo, *Masakado densetsu* (1966). Saeki Arikiyo et al, *Kenkyūshi Masakado no ran* (1976). Giuliana Stramigioli, "Preliminary Notes on *Masakadoki* and the Taira no Masakado Story," *Monumenta Nipponica* 28.3 (1973).

Giuliana STRAMIGIOLI

Taira no Munemori (1147–1185)

Warrior in the latter part of the Heian period (794–1185). Third son of TAIRA NO KIYOMORI, he succeeded to the family headship at his father's death (1181) and assumed leadership of Taira forces in the TAIRA–MINAMOTO WAR (1180–85). Despite initial military successes, in 1183 Munemori and his brothers were forced to abandon the capital city of Kyōto under pressure from the general MINAMOTO NO YOSHINAKA, and the Taira fled to the western provinces with their kinsman, the child emperor ANTOKU. Munemori was a commander in the Battle of Ichinotani (1184), in which MINAMOTO NO YOSHITSUNE inflicted a severe defeat on the Taira. When Yoshitsune finally crushed the Taira in the naval battle at DANNOURA (1185), Munemori cast himself into the sea but was captured and sent to the rival leader MINAMOTO NO YORITOMO in Kamakura. Refused an audience by Yoritomo, Munemori was ordered sent back to Kyōto under escort but was killed by Yoshitsune en route.

Barbara L. ARNN

Taira no Shigehira (1156–1185)

Warrior; fifth son of TAIRA NO KIYOMORI. In 1180 Shigehira defeated at Uji (near Kyōto) the forces led by MINAMOTO NO YORI-

MASA in support of the imperial prince Mochihito (1151–80), whose rising against Taira authority marked the outbreak of the TAIRA–MINAMOTO WAR. Late in the same year Shigehira led a punitive expedition against the warrior-monks of the temple Onjōji or MIIDERA (in what is now the city of Ōtsu) for their support of Mochihito. Two weeks later Shigehira's forces, in a similar raid against the monks of Nara, burned the Great Buddha Hall (Daibutsuden) of the TŌDAIJI, the chief temple of the imperial government, and razed the nearby KŌFUKUJI, a temple of the aristocratic Fujiwara family. In 1182 Shigehira was given command of Taira forces on campaign in the eastern provinces, and in 1184 he led a wing of the Taira army in the Battle of Ichinotani, where he was captured. After the decisive Minamoto victory in the Battle of DANNOURA in 1185, Shigehira was delivered into the hands of the monks of Nara and was beheaded for his sacrileges.

Barbara L. ARNN

Taira no Shigemori (1138–1179)

Eldest son of TAIRA NO KIYOMORI and reputedly a moderating influence on his father in the series of civil disturbances leading up to the TAIRA–MINAMOTO WAR (1180–85). Shigemori's posthumous reputation was that of a cultivated, devout, and filial gentleman who combined the best qualities of the warrior and the aristocrat, although his contemporary, the courtier and diarist KUJŌ KANEZANE, blamed him for initiating at least one serious confrontation between the Taira family and the court in 1170. Shigemori fought alongside his father in the HŌGEN DISTURBANCE of 1156 and the HEIJI DISTURBANCE of 1160, both incidents arising from intrigues by factions of the imperial house, the court nobility, and their warrior supporters. Because of his father's power, Shigemori was rapidly promoted at court and in 1177 became inner minister (naidaijin), an unusual honor for a scion of a warrior family. In the same year Kiyomori discovered the so-called Shishigatani Conspiracy against him, led by the priest SHUNKAN; only Shigemori's intercession prevented his father from incarcerating the retired emperor GO-SHIRAKAWA, who was closely involved with the conspirators. Shigemori resigned as inner minister in 1179.

Barbara L. ARNN

Taira no Tadamori (1096–1153)

Warrior and leader of the TAIRA FAMILY; father of TAIRA NO KIYOMORI; later married to IKE NO ZENNI. Following in the footsteps of his father, Masamori, he consolidated the economic and military strength of his family and established it as an important force in the politics of the imperial court through his faithful service to the retired emperors SHIRAKAWA and TOBA. Tadamori led at least two major expeditions to suppress piracy on the Inland Sea, in 1129 and again in 1135, both times parading captured pirates through the streets of Kyōto. The court also used Tadamori and his warriors as a police force to control the unruly WARRIOR-MONKS of the ENRYAKUJI, the great monastic complex northeast of Kyōto, and of temples in the old capital city Nara. Tadamori's successful supervision of building projects for Toba gained him permission to attend the emperor at court, a privilege unprecedented for a warrior and resented by courtiers. Only three years after Tadamori's death from illness, the political and military alignments he had participated in turned to armed conflict in the HŌGEN DISTURBANCE of 1156.

Barbara L. ARNN

Taira no Tadanori (1144–1184)

Warrior and poet at the end of the Heian period (794–1185); youngest brother of TAIRA NO KIYOMORI. Tadanori studied poetry under the renowned court poet FUJIWARA NO TOSHINARI. With the outbreak of the TAIRA–MINAMOTO WAR in 1180, he was made a commander of the Taira armies. He was killed while leading a wing of the Taira forces in the Battle of Ichinotani in 1184. Poems widely attributed to Tadanori are included in the imperial anthologies SENZAI WAKASHŪ and GYOKUYŌ WAKASHŪ, but they are listed as anonymous, supposedly because the compilers did not wish to offend the court by naming a member of the defeated Taira family as author.

Barbara L. ARNN

Taira no Tadatsune, Rebellion of

Rebellion of 1028 in which Taira no Tadatsune (967–1031), a magnate and former vice-governor of Kazusa Province (now part of Chiba Prefecture), killed the governor of neighboring Awa Province (now also Chiba Prefecture), seized control of the entire region, and defied the central government. Because the military strength of the court had greatly declined since its suppression of the rebellion of TAIRA NO MASAKADO (940), Tadatsune was able to maintain his independence in the area for nearly three years. Taira no Naokata led court forces against Tadatsune in 1028 but was defeated. Finally, in 1031, Minamoto no Yorinobu (968–1048) succeeded in forcing Tadatsune to surrender without a fight. Tadatsune died of illness while being transported to the capital. From this time the MINAMOTO FAMILY began to consolidate their power in the Kantō region of eastern Japan; the descendants of Tadatsune's sons, who became retainers (kenin) of Yorinobu, flourished there as the Chiba family.

G. Cameron HURST III

Taira no Tomomori (1151–1185)

Fourth son of TAIRA NO KIYOMORI; warrior active throughout the TAIRA–MINAMOTO WAR (1180–85). In 1180 Tomomori and his younger brother TAIRA NO SHIGEHIRA defeated the forces of the imperial prince Mochihito (1151–80) and MINAMOTO NO YORIMASA in an early battle of the war, and in the next year, with his elder brother TAIRA NO MUNEMORI, he defeated Minamoto no Yukiie (d 1186). In 1183 Tomomori was in command of the Taira forces when they abandoned the capital city of Kyōto and fled with the child emperor ANTOKU to the western provinces. He also led Taira armies in the Battle of Ichinotani in 1184 and at the final destruction of the Taira in the naval battle at DANNOURA in 1185. There Tomomori, seeing that the day was lost, leaped into the sea and drowned. In the Nō and kabuki plays entitled Funa Benkei (Benkei and the Boat), Tomomori's ghost, leading the spirits of the Taira warriors killed at Dannoura, rises from the waves to obstruct the passage of MINAMOTO NO YOSHITSUNE across the Inland Sea; only the prayers of Yoshitsune's retainer BENKEI can subdue the vengeful Taira spirits.

Barbara L. ARNN

Taira no Yoritsuna (?–1293)

A vassal and house official of the HŌJŌ FAMILY late in the Kamakura period (1185–1333). When Hōjō Sadatoki (1271–1311) succeeded as shogunal regent (shikken) in 1284, Yoritsuna became an important house steward (naikanrei or uchikanrei). He soon came into conflict with Sadatoki's powerful father-in-law, Adachi Yasumori (1231–85), and falsely accused Yasumori's son of plotting against the Hōjō, thus bringing about the destruction of the Adachi in the so-called Shimotsuki Incident of 1285. Thereafter Yoritsuna's power overshadowed that of the regent himself; but when he schemed to have his second son named regent, his eldest son betrayed him to Sadatoki, who destroyed Yoritsuna's family.

G. Cameron HURST III

tairiku rōnin

(rōnin or wanderers on the continent; an allusion to the RŌNIN or masterless samurai of the Edo period). An expression referring to Japanese civilians who were active on the Asian mainland in the late 19th century and early decades of the 20th century, supporting Asian revolutionaries and promoting Japan's imperialist aims in China, Korea, and Manchuria. These activists often served as agents of Japanese military officers, politicians, and businessmen, by whom they were secretly funded and for whom they gathered intelligence and engaged in covert political activities. Many of them were affiliated with such ultranationalist organizations as the GEN'YŌSHA and the AMUR RIVER SOCIETY. Some, like MIYAZAKI TŌTEN, were idealistic pan-Asianists who worked selflessly for the Chinese revolution and the Philippine independence movement in the early 1900s. Others were mere adventurers, taking advantage of their status as privileged foreigners and their connections with the Japanese military to engage in illegal profiteering.

TANAKA Akira

tairō

(great elder). Nominally the highest-ranking position below that of shōgun in the TOKUGAWA SHOGUNATE (1603–1867), the post of tairō was in fact rarely occupied and then only occasionally by a person of noteworthy political influence. During the 17th century several shōguns promoted distinguished advisers such as SAKAI TADAKIYO to the office. From the 18th century until the demise of the shogunate in 1867 only FUDAI daimyō of the Ii family of Hikone held the title, and then only as an infrequent political sinecure, until 1858, when

the willful II NAOSUKE took decisive control of the shogunate as *tairō* and pursued repressive policies that eventuated in his assassination.
Conrad TOTMAN

Tairo Dōshikai

(Anti-Russia Society). Political organization formed in August 1903, on the eve of the RUSSO-JAPANESE WAR, by KONOE ATSUMARO and others to advocate a strong foreign policy toward Russia. The Russians had used the Chinese BOXER REBELLION of 1899–1900 as an excuse to send a large contingent of troops to southern Manchuria. After the rebellion the troops had stayed on; Russia, moreover, was pressing the Chinese government to declare Manchuria a Russian protectorate. To protest this, in 1901 Konoe, a prominent politician who had long been interested in Asian problems, founded an association, the Kokumin Dōmeikai (Nationalist Alliance). In 1902 Russia agreed to withdraw its troops, and the Dōmeikai disbanded. But in the following year it became evident that Russia had no intention of withdrawing all its troops, and former members of the Kokumin Dōmeikai established the Tairo Dōshikai. Working together with Professor Tomizu Hirondo (1861–1935) and other prowar academics (see SHICHIHAKASE JIKEN), the organization sought to rally public opinion and bring pressure on the government to declare war on Russia. In July 1905, protesting what it considered the humiliating terms of the Treaty of PORTSMOUTH concluding the war, it merged with other groups to form the Kōwa Mondai Dōshi Rengōkai (Joint Council of Fellow Activists on the Peace Question). See also HIBIYA INCENDIARY INCIDENT.

Taisei Corporation

(Taisei Kensetsu). General construction company engaged in public works, designing and erecting of buildings, plant engineering, housing, and real estate. The company traces its origins to the Ōkura-Gumi Shōkai, founded in 1873 by ŌKURA KIHACHIRŌ. It became independent and took on its current name in 1946 as a result of the post–World War II ZAIBATSU DISSOLUTION program. It expanded tremendously during the postwar reconstruction of Japan and the ensuing years of high economic growth. In 1956 it became the first major construction company to offer its shares for public subscription, and in an industry where family partnership is the rule rather than the exception, Taisei is making great progress in modernizing its management. It is now the second largest construction company in Japan, after KAJIMA CORPORATION, and has numerous subsidiary firms, including Taisei Road Construction Co, Taisei Prefab Construction Co, and Yūraku Real Estate Co. The Taisei group leads all other construction groups in annual sales. Current plans call for the further reinforcement of the company's two main areas of operations: public works on bridge, tunnel, water, and sewerage projects and the construction of office buildings, factories, housing, hotels, and other units. At the same time, Taisei is concentrating its efforts on urban redevelopment projects and the exploitation of the sea through new technologies. Some 70 percent of the company's employees are technicians, of whom 60 percent are engaged in executing the projects and the remainder in the designing, computer, and development departments. Taisei has been involved in construction projects in over a dozen countries in Southeast Asia, the Near and Middle East, and Africa. Orders received by the company in the fiscal year ending March 1982 totaled ¥811.7 billion (US $3.4 billion), of which construction occupied 67 percent, public engineering 30 percent, and real estate 3 percent. It was capitalized at ¥38.6 billion (US $160.3 million) in the same year. Corporate headquarters are located in Tōkyō. See also ŌKURA & CO, LTD.

Taisei Hōkan

(Return of Political Rule to the Emperor). A formal statement issued by the last shōgun, TOKUGAWA YOSHINOBU, on 9 November 1867 (Keiō 3.10.14)—two months before the actual MEIJI RESTORATION—surrendering to the emperor the shōgun's de facto right to rule the country. By midsummer of 1867, anti-Tokugawa forces led by the Satsuma (now Kagoshima Prefecture) and Chōshū (now Yamaguchi Prefecture) domains had decided to take up arms in order to restore imperial rule. However, a group of more moderate restorationist *samurai,* including SAKAMOTO RYŌMA and GOTŌ SHŌJIRŌ of the Tosa domain (now Kōchi Prefecture), tried to avoid war by advancing a compromise plan (the KŌGI SEITAI RON), according to which the shōgun would voluntarily relinquish his political authority, act as

head of a council of *daimyō,* and retain his domainal holdings. At Gotō's behest, YAMANOUCHI TOYOSHIGE, the daimyō of Tosa, persuaded Yoshinobu to relinquish political authority. After consulting with his retainers, Yoshinobu issued a formal statement, the Taisei Hōkan, thus bringing to an end the Tokugawa shogunate, which had ruled Japan since 1603. This act, however, did not satisfy the leaders of Satsuma and Chōshū, who continued to press for military defeat of the supporters of the shōgun, and in December their troops moved into Kyōto. On 3 January 1868 Satsuma and Chōshū forces surrounded the palace and proclaimed an "imperial restoration" (ŌSEI FUKKO). Their move precipitated a civil war in which the Tokugawa forces were defeated (see BOSHIN CIVIL WAR).

Taisei Yokusankai → Imperial Rule Assistance Association

Taisekiji

Head temple of the Buddhist sect Nichiren Shōshū, located in the city of Fujinomiya, Shizuoka Prefecture. Taisekiji was built in 1290 by Nikkō (1246–1333), a prominent disciple of NICHIREN (1222–82), with support from Nanjō Tokimitsu (1259–1332), a local official and lay follower. Taisekiji subsequently became a center for the Fuji Tradition (Fuji Monryū), a subschool based on Nikkō's interpretations of Nichiren's teachings. In 1900 Taisekiji seceded from the Hommon sect, which had been formed a year earlier from subschools of the Fuji Tradition, and announced the formation of its own independent religious organization under the name of Nichirenshū Fujiha (The Fuji Branch of the Nichiren Sect). In 1912 the latter name was changed to Nichiren Shōshū (True Nichiren sect), around which later arose the SŌKA GAKKAI, the largest lay Nichiren Buddhist organization in Japan. Today Taisekiji is a massive temple complex, daily receiving a large number of Sōka Gakkai pilgrims. See also NICHIREN SECT.
Stanley WEINSTEIN

Taisha

Sometimes called Taishamachi. Town in northern Shimane Prefecture, western Honshū. On the Shimane Peninsula. Taisha developed around the IZUMO SHRINE (Izumo Taisha) and is still economically dependent on it. Grapes are cultivated in the surrounding areas. Pop: 18,203.

Taishakukyō

Gorge on the river Taishakugawa (a tributary of the TAKAHASHIGAWA), eastern Hiroshima Prefecture, western Honshū. Created by the river cutting through a limestone area of the plateau called Kibi Kōgen, it is dotted by numerous fantastically shaped rocks, deep pools, and caves. It is the location of the artificial Lake Shinryū and a National Vacation Village. Length: 20 km (12 mi).

Taishakusan

Also called Taishakuzan. Mountain in northern Tochigi Prefecture on the border with Fukushima Prefecture, northern Honshū; the highest peak in the Taishaku Mountains. There are relatively level areas near the summit and numerous swampy areas. Natural forests of hemlock-spruce, Japanese black pine (*Pinus thumbergii),* and oak cover the slopes. Height: 2,060 m (6,757 ft).

Taishin'in → Great Court of Cassation

Taishō and early Shōwa history → history of Japan

Taishō Democracy

A term coined by Japanese historians after World War II to refer to the democratic ideals, practices, and movements of early 20th-century Japan; generally used to refer to political currents in the period between the end of the Russo-Japanese War in 1905 and the end of party government in 1932, a period spanning the Taishō period (1912–1926). The term implies a contrast with the less democratic Meiji period (1868–1912) and the militaristic 1930s, and also with post–World War II democracy.

The term is used rather loosely to refer to government institutions and political parties as well as to ideas and movements in society at large. The period was one of great social ferment, and major changes also took place in cultural and intellectual circles, in education, and in popular media; here we will be concerned primarily with social and political aspects of the time.

One major feature of Taishō Democracy was increased power for the popularly elected House of Representatives (Shūgiin) of the IMPERIAL DIET. As a political ideal, this was expressed in terms of party government, whose cabinets would be based on the strength of political parties in the House of Representatives. Such cabinets would have predominant influence over the other, nonelected organs and forces of government—the GENRŌ (elder statesmen), the HOUSE OF PEERS (Kizokuin), the PRIVY COUNCIL (Sūmitsuin), the military, and the career bureaucracy. Another important aspect of Taishō Democracy was the expansion of popular involvement in politics. This meant primarily expansion of male suffrage and more widespread freedom of political expression.

Thus the main emphasis was on political democracy in a fairly strict sense of the term. There was also some emphasis on broader ideals of social democracy including the recognition of labor and tenant-farmer unions and of greater equality for women. Even here, the democracy sought was essentially within the framework of the existing capitalist system. "Political democracy" may be too narrow to describe Taishō Democracy, but it may be characterized, even in ideal terms, as "liberal" or "bourgeois" democracy. In fact, the socialist movement largely disassociated itself from Taishō Democracy.

While the strictly political aspect does stand out, Taishō Democracy was nevertheless a part of a broad social trend toward asserting the value of the individual, or at least of nonstate entities, against the interests of the state. Besides providing some of the rationale for popular participation in government, this trend gave some sanction to the representation of competing special interests in politics.

Strengthening Elected Bodies —— Institutionally, the age of Taishō Democracy was marked by the growing prominence of the political parties, whose strength lay in their control of seats in the House of Representatives. The electorate for that body, while never more than one quarter of even the adult male population before 1925, was still over 1.5 million persons as early as 1908, making the parties the only political force responsible in any direct sense to a substantial popular base.

Japan's government leaders found that in their experience with the Diet since its inception in 1890, support in the House of Representatives was essential to govern effectively. The RIKKEN SEIYŪKAI, which emerged as the strongest party in the decade after 1905, capitalized on this need for support to aggrandize its position in the political system as a whole. After 1910 there was growing acceptance of party government, either as an ideal or as a practical necessity. Some politicians who had devoted their careers to elective office understandably supported this view. Moreover, many who had gained prominence as career bureaucrats came to see leadership of a political party as the path to their further advancement.

Party government meant different degrees of democracy to different persons. In its fullest form, it meant free competition between parties and formation of the government by the majority party. HARA TAKASHI, de facto leader of the Seiyūkai since 1905 and its president after 1914, had long had as his ultimate aim cabinets organized by a party. Although he was less concerned to have alternation between competing political parties, he accepted more than did many the legitimacy of special-interest representation in politics. Moreover, unlike KATŌ TAKAAKI and some other party leaders, Hara contested regularly and successfully for a seat in the House of Representatives. KATSURA TARŌ, prime minister for 8 of the first 12 years of the century, exemplified a more restricted commitment. He aspired after 1910 to lead a government based on his control of, but not membership in, a strong party in the House of Representatives, preferably one that harmonized all conflicting interests. But Katsura reached this from an earlier position adamantly opposed to any form of party government, and he shortly afterward bowed to the realities requiring a more partisan base.

Hara's formation of a cabinet in 1918 composed of Seiyūkai members except for the army, navy, and foreign ministers was hailed as the advent of true party government. From then until 1922, and from 1924 to 1932, although prime ministers continued to be selected by the genrō and resigned for other reasons than loss of Diet support, the premiership was held by the leader of a major party.

Party government also meant, for many, reducing the independent power of nonelected bodies and their ability to interfere in the work of cabinets. The genrō continued to claim an informal but potent voice as the emperor's chief advisers. After 1910 resentment of genrō interference was virtually in direct proportion to cries for party government. In cabinet positions as early as 1906, Katō Takaaki registered resistance to genrō interference in his ministry; although Hara approached them with greater tact and patience, he was equally determined to end their influence, which he regarded as an anachronism.

Curbing the independence of the career bureaucracy had long been a rallying cry of the party politicians. Some steps were taken in the Taishō period, notably by Hara, both to make top bureaucrats responsive to party leadership, and to end the virtual monopoly by the career service of positions below the ministerial level.

While Taishō Democracy generally supported imperial rather than popular sovereignty, its theorists were forthright about the desirability of limiting the emperor's powers. They acknowledged this as part of the concept of democracy and argued that in any case the emperor did not make policy decisions in Japan and that the selection of prime ministers by the genrō limited the emperor's sovereignty just as much as selection by the popularly elected house. Professor MINOBE TATSUKICHI of Tōkyō University asserted that under the constitution the emperor was an organ of the state, and Minobe sought to preclude mystical and irrational invocation of the emperor in politics. Hara as prime minister arrived at a position similar to these theorists from another standpoint. His concern for bringing the military under cabinet control was motivated in part by fear that the emperor might have to take responsibility—and criticism—for political decisions if the military continued to act independently in his name.

Expansion of Popular Involvement —— As the parties with their explicit base in the populace at large sought to expand their influence, so too did the public increase the scale and intensity of its involvement in politics. The most direct form of this involvement, the mass demonstration, became markedly more prominent under Taishō Democracy. In fact, the choice of 1905 as the beginning of Taishō Democracy may be based primarily on the outbreak in that year—particularly in the so-called Hibiya riots (see HIBIYA INCENDIARY INCIDENT)—of popular indignation over the peace settlement following the Russo-Japanese War. Mass demonstrations that sometimes turned into riots became frequent, and perhaps reached a peak, in the first decade of the Taishō period. The riots in early 1913 sparked by genrō interference with the Saionji Kimmochi government led to the resignation of the successor cabinet two months after its formation (see TAISHŌ POLITICAL CRISIS). The RICE RIOTS OF 1918, wider in scope though less political and specific in their objectives, are further evidence of a growing tendency to mass expression and involvement in public issues. Again in 1919 and 1920 mass rallies of the UNIVERSAL MANHOOD SUFFRAGE MOVEMENT were a notable feature of politics.

The demonstrations that were characteristic of Taishō Democracy reflected the emerging urbanization of Japan. Within the period, the early prominence of service trades workers, sometimes identified as lumpen proletariat, gave way to that of industrial and white-collar workers. Evolution can be seen also in the causes espoused, from the support of others' interests to issues touching more directly on the demonstrators' own interests.

Universal manhood suffrage represented a less direct but more focused and clearly political form of involvement in public issues. While the suffrage campaign dates from the late 1890s, its development into a mass movement roughly coincided with the early years of the Taishō period and became a major political issue in 1919 and 1920. Public enthusiasm for universal suffrage waned somewhat after 1920. In this sense its enactment into law in 1925 was anticlimactic, but the movement and its achievement have been seen by some as the central feature of Taishō Democracy.

Private Interests vs. State Interests —— In these same years there was growing participation by businessmen in antitax movements, suggesting a decline in the earlier unquestioning acceptance of the sacrifices required for the state's military preparedness. Even some of the populist-chauvinist groups (kokumin shugi teki taigai kōha) dissociated themselves from the government on foreign as well as domestic policy, opposing increased military expenditures and condemning ultranationalist groups that did collaborate with the government.

The refusal to identify individual—perhaps more accurately private—interests with state interests is a major trend in Taishō Democracy. It appeared in areas other than business, such as the emphasis in the scholarly world on academic freedom and intellectual cultivation for its own sake. It took still another form politically, as in the Seiyūkai's call for a railroad policy that would serve particular local interests rather than national strategic needs.

The populist-chauvinist leaders found their mass appeal declining markedly at this time. They continued to play a significant if not dominant role in the universal suffrage movement, an issue that permitted an appeal to all segments of the public. But people were tending more and more to think of themselves rather as members of particular classes or interest groups.

Limits of Taishō Democracy ——— The limitations of Taishō Democracy deserve some attention. The trend away from personal identification with the state took in notable cases the form of withdrawal from (rather than autonomous participation in) public affairs. Even as a movement of participation, Taishō Democracy had limits in its predominantly political, or at least liberal-democratic, emphasis. The socialist movement at the time was as a whole severely critical, or at best unsympathetic, to this emphasis. Whether this was a weakness of Taishō Democracy or of the socialist movement is still a subject of disagreement among Japanese scholars.

Taishō Democracy scarcely rejected the sovereignty of the emperor in favor of popular sovereignty, and this imposed some limit on its theoretical, if not its practical, horizon. The achievement of universal manhood suffrage in 1925 may well be the central accomplishment of Taishō Democracy. Still, political competition was materially inhibited by restrictions on freedom of expression including the PEACE PRESERVATION LAW OF 1925 (Chian Iji Hō). While the aim of party cabinets was attained in some real sense at least before 1932, party cabinet control over the other organs of government was only partially attained. Indeed, by the time party cabinets were realized, there was also considerable general popular disillusionment with the parties as bearers of democracy.

The question of how large these limitations should loom in evaluating Taishō Democracy remains open. Apart from disputing its intrinsic value, one can focus on Taishō Democracy's "failure" to survive into the 1930s and early 1940s; or see it as providing the indigenous roots essential for the "success" of democracy after 1945.

■———Tatsuo Arima, *The Failure of Freedom: A Portrait of Modern Japanese Intellectuals* (1969). Peter Duus, *Party Rivalry and Political Change in Taishō Japan* (1968). Matsuo Takayoshi, "The Development of Democracy in Japan: Taishō Democracy: Its Flowering and Breakdown," *The Developing Economies*, 4.4 (1966). Matsuo Takayoshi, *Taishō demokurashī* (1974). Mitani Taichirō, *Taishō demokurashī ron: Yoshino Sakuzō no jidai to sono ato* (1974). Miyachi Masato, *Nichiro sengo seiji shi no kenkyū: Teikoku shugi keisei ki no toshi to nōson* (1973). Tetsuo Najita, *Hara Kei in the Politics of Compromise 1905–1915* (1967). Nezu Masashi, *Hihan: Nihon gendai shi* (1958). Shinobu Seizaburō, *Taishō demokurashī shi* (1954–1959). Bernard S. Silberman and H. D. Harootunian, ed, *Japan in Crisis: Essays on Taishō Democracy* (1974). Yoshino Sakuzō, "On the Meaning of Constitutional Government and the Methods by Which It Can Be Perfected," in Ryusaku Tsunoda et al, comp, *Sources of Japanese Tradition* (1958).   Edward G. GRIFFIN

Taishō, Emperor (1879–1926)

The 123rd sovereign (*tennō*) in the traditional count (which includes several nonhistorical emperors); so called posthumously from the name of the era, Taishō (1912–26), during which he reigned. The third son of Emperor MEIJI, his mother was Yanagihara Naruko (1855–1943), an imperial concubine. His personal name was Yoshihito.

In contrast to his father, Taishō did not play an active role in the political process, largely because of his ill health. Soon after his birth on 31 August 1879 he contracted what appeared to be meningitis. Consequently his upbringing, at first in the care of Emperor Meiji's maternal grandfather, Count Nakayama Tadayasu (1809–88), stressed physical fitness more than formal study; but his health remained poor and of constant concern to court and government leaders. Although Yoshihito was deemed competent to ascend the throne on the death of his father in 1912, his health deteriorated rapidly thereafter. By 1919 he had become unable to perform such basic state ceremonies as convocations of the Imperial Diet, and he spent longer and more frequent periods at imperial villas away from the palace in Tōkyō. Finally, in 1921, Crown Prince HIROHITO was made regent (*sesshō*) for his father. Emperor Taishō died on 25 December 1926 and was succeeded by Hirohito.

The traditional upbringing of imperial princes changed greatly after Yoshihito was designated crown prince in 1887. He was the first imperial heir to be educated publicly. He attended the Peers' School (now Gakushūin University). He studied Western subjects as well as the Japanese and Chinese classics. After eight years of formal schooling he was assigned tutors and lecturers, among them Frenchmen, Englishmen, and Americans. Practices within the imperial family were reformed as well. After 1905 the emperor's children were allowed to reside with him, a departure from past custom. In 1924 monogamy was established, and the ancient system of imperial concubinage was abolished.   David A. TITUS

Taishō Marine & Fire Insurance Co, Ltd

(Taishō Kaijō Kasai Hoken). One of the largest insurance companies in Japan and a member of the Mitsui group. Established in 1918, it engages in insurance business other than life insurance both in Japan and overseas. After establishing a liaison office in London in 1924, it expanded its network throughout the world and in 1982 it had 26 overseas branches and offices, 22 underwriting agencies, 50 associated companies, and 13 subsidiaries and affiliates, as well as a total of approximately 430 claims survey and settling offices. Current plans call for increasing the number of insurance contracts concluded with enterprises in Japan and expanding its base in regional mass markets. Overseas, the company's goals include the further expansion of its business network and the strengthening of its foundation in various markets through direct insurance and reinsurance operations. Net premiums totaled ¥264 billion (US $1.1 billion) in the fiscal year ending March 1982, and the company was capitalized at ¥33 billion (US $137 million) in the same year. Corporate headquarters are located in Tōkyō.

Taishō period (1912–1926)

The reign of Emperor TAISHŌ, father of Emperor Hirohito. Although less dramatic than the achievements of the Meiji (1868–1912) and Shōwa (1926–) periods, the events of the Taishō period represent to many Japanese their nation's introduction to participatory democracy (see TAISHŌ DEMOCRACY) and to the problems of a modern industrial state. See HISTORY OF JAPAN: Taishō and early Shōwa history.

Taishō Political Crisis

(Taishō Seihen). Political crisis of the Taishō period (1912–26) in which the third cabinet of KATSURA TARŌ was overthrown in 1913 by the first MOVEMENT TO PROTECT CONSTITUTIONAL GOVERNMENT, a popular protest movement organized by opposition political parties, journalists, and businessmen. In December 1912 the second cabinet of SAIONJI KIMMOCHI fell with the army's refusal to replace former Army Minister UEHARA YŪSAKU, who had resigned when the government rejected the army's demand for two new divisions. General Katsura, who had ostensibly retired from politics and was then serving as lord keeper of the privy seal (*naidaijin*), was named to form the next cabinet. He was unpopular, however, with the public, which identified him with the authoritarian oligarchs who had ruled Japan since the Meiji Restoration of 1868 (see HAMBATSU). Many believed that he had arranged the army's overthrow of the Saionji cabinet and then used his influence with the emperor to secure the premiership for himself. When the navy threatened to withhold its minister if its demand for new battleships was not met, Katsura had an imperial edict issued ordering the navy to furnish a minister. Critics saw this action as further proof of Katsura's undemocratic nature. The first Movement to Protect Constitutional Government, begun after the overthrow of the Saionji cabinet to protest GENRŌ (elder statesmen) interference in politics and to press for the establishment of cabinets responsible to the Diet, now took the form of a popular front against Katsura and quickly won support throughout the country. Katsura countered by forming his own party, the RIKKEN DŌSHIKAI, and by proroguing the Diet three times, on one occasion to avoid a vote of no confidence. His highhanded tactics infuriated the public, and on 10 February 1913 thousands of angry demonstrators surrounded the Diet building, set fire to police stations, and raided several progovernment newspaper companies. Katsura resigned the following day, barely 53 days after taking office. The Taishō Political Crisis was the first instance in modern Japanese history in which a popular movement brought down a cabinet.

Taishō Seihen → Taishō Political Crisis

Taiso Yoshitoshi (1839–1892)

The major UKIYO-E artist of the early part of the Meiji period (1868–1912). Born in Edo (now Tōkyō). Although his real name was Yoshioka Kinzaburō, he was adopted by the ukiyo-e artist Tsukioka Sessai (d 1839) and so became known as Tsukioka Yoshitoshi (alternate pronunciation, Tsukioka Hōnen). As a youth he studied with UTAGAWA KUNIYOSHI, and by the age of 15, he was producing his first ukiyo-e prints. His formative years spanned the socially and politically troubled time of the Meiji Restoration (1868). He soon became famous for vivid, often shockingly realistic prints based on sketches made from life. In the treatment of historical subjects he is said to have been influenced by the eclectic style of Kikuchi Yōsai (1788–1878). After 1868 he worked in Tōkyō as a newspaper illustrator for the Yūbin hōchi shimbun and the E-iri jiyū shimbun, pioneering in the adaptation of print designs for journalism. Although Yoshitoshi drew from a broad range of subject matter, including portraits of beautiful women (bijinga), landscapes, popular heroes, and cartoons (MANGA), he is particularly remembered for his realistic depictions of sadistic, bloody scenes. After recovering from a nervous breakdown around 1873, he began to call himself Taiso Hōnen ("Hōnen the Resurrected"). At the height of his activity, between 1882 and 1890, he had more than 80 disciples. He died insane at the age of 53. Aya Louisa MCDONALD

Taitō Co, Ltd

Major sugar manufacturer, affiliated with MITSUI & CO, LTD. Its forerunner, the Taiwan Seitō Co, was founded in 1900 to develop sugar plantations in Taiwan. It expanded by amalgamating a large number of small and medium-sized sugar firms, but lost the greater part of its operations with Japan's loss of Taiwan after World War II. Reorganized as the Taitō Co in 1946, it started operations in Kōbe at its only remaining factory in Japan. It refined and sold crude sugar imported on an allotment basis, and also began producing penicillin, of which it became Japan's leading maker. In 1955 the pharmaceuticals division was transferred to Taitō Pfizer Co, Ltd, a joint venture with Pfizer Co of the United States. Following the liberalization of crude sugar imports in 1963, the company was faced with overproduction of refined sugar relative to the decline in consumption. With the support of Mitsui & Co, it is currently developing new products, including medications for treating cancer. Sales in the fiscal year ending March 1982 totaled ¥46.6 billion (US $193.6 million), of which refined sugar accounted for 99 percent. In the same year the company was capitalized at ¥2 billion (US $8.3 million). Its head office is in Tōkyō.

Taitō Ward

(Taitō Ku). One of the 23 wards of Tōkyō. On the west bank of the river Sumidagawa. With an area of 10 sq km (3.8 sq mi), Taitō Ward is the smallest of the wards. It has numerous small and medium-sized factories and wholesalers and various recreational, commercial, and cultural facilities. Site of UENO PARK. Pop: 185,980.

Taiwan

The island of Taiwan (Formosa), because of its strategic location and resources, has figured intermittently in Japanese trade and politics. Situated some 1,060 kilometers (660 mi) southwest of Japan and only about 130 kilometers (80 mi) east of China's Fujian (Fukien) Province at the nearest point, Taiwan may have been visited by Japanese pirates operating along the Fujian coast as early as the 14th century. By the latter part of the 16th century, Japanese merchant adventurers began to make use of the yet-unclaimed island as an intermediate station for commercial contacts between Japan and China. This early Japanese presence in Taiwan ceased during the 1630s in accordance with Tokugawa seclusionist policies. Nevertheless, the Dutch, who gained control of the island in 1624, continued to trade with Japan from southern Taiwan until 1661, as did the Zheng (Cheng) family members who ruled there for the next 22 years.

After Taiwan came under the rule of China during the Qing (Ch'ing) dynasty (1644–1912) in 1683, the island had few contacts with Japan over the remainder of the Edo period (1600–1868). Japa-

nese trade and political ventures involving Taiwan resumed upon the "opening" of Japan in the 1850s. Although a Japanese military expedition sent to Taiwan in 1874 proved abortive, China was forced to cede Taiwan to Japan in 1895 at the end of the SINO-JAPANESE WAR OF 1894–1895. Over the next 51 years this mountainous island, slightly larger in area than Japan's southern island of Kyūshū, prospered as a Japanese colony. The colony included Penghu (P'eng-hu, the Pescadores), a small, low-lying island group, situated in the Taiwan Strait 48 kilometers (30 mi) to the west, that had been a dependency of Taiwan since the late 17th century.

Taiwan and Penghu were restored to China in 1945 at the end of World War II. Relations between Japan and Taiwan resumed in 1952, when Japan signed a separate peace treaty with the Republic of China, represented by the nationalist regime based in Taiwan. Twenty years later, in Beijing (Peking), Japan recognized the People's Republic of China as the sole legal government of China, including Taiwan and Penghu. Yet Japan continued to carry on economic relations with Taiwan and became its most important trading partner.

Early Period of Japanese Contact——Whereas bands of Japanese pirate-traders, termed WAKŌ, may previously have sojourned in Taiwan, historical records indicate that such seafarers definitely rendezvoused there in the late 1560s. By then the Ming dynasty (1368–1644) of China had severed all relations with Japan. Hence these enterprising Japanese began to use Taiwan as a convenient station for illicit trade between southeastern China and Japan, as did seafaring Chinese. Initially, the Japanese kept to the harbors of Jilong (Keelung) and Danshui (Tanshui) in northern Taiwan, while the Chinese clustered along the western coastline, where Anping (Anp'ing) served as the major seaport. Some decades later, Japanese merchants also established small settlements near Anping and to the south at Gaoxiong (Kaohsiung; J: Takao). In this southern coastal strip, which they named Takasago, Japanese residents maintained commercial contacts with Chinese traders and, later, the Dutch as well. There they fitted out vessels and entered into trade with Annam, Siam, Java, Portugese-held Macao, and nearby Luzon in the northern Philippines.

Such mercantile activities in Taiwan were encouraged by powerful rulers in Japan in their efforts to foster overseas trade. TOYOTOMI HIDEYOSHI in 1593 issued licenses to merchants of Nagasaki, Kyōto, and Sakai, authorizing them to open offices on the island. Early in the 17th century TOKUGAWA IEYASU issued voyaging permits bearing his vermilion seal, as Hideyoshi had done, and endeavored to safeguard the increasing VERMILION SEAL SHIP TRADE with Taiwan and Southeast Asia.

These two ambitious rulers were also attracted by Taiwan's strategic location. Hideyoshi, as part of his plan to create an Asiatic empire, desired to gain control of Taiwan, along with the Philippines to the south and the Ryūkyū Islands extending northeastward toward Japan. Late in 1593 he dispatched an envoy to Taiwan with a formal demand of submission. Subsequently, Ieyasu arranged for expeditions to be sent to Taiwan in 1609 and again in 1616 in further unsuccessful attempts to extend Japanese hegemony over the island.

The Dutch and Zheng (Cheng) Family Periods——Japanese merchant activities in Taiwan reflect the expansion of East Asian maritime trade that began in the latter half of the 16th century. The main thrust of this commerce involved importing Chinese silk to Japan and exporting Japanese silver in exchange. The Dutch in their efforts to compete in the lucrative silk and silver trade, occupied Taiwan in 1624, and constructed Castle Zeelandia (Fort Orange) at Anping as a trading center. There they sought to collect raw silk and other Chinese commodities for reshipment to Japan. At Zeelandia they also exported Taiwan sugar and deerskins to Hirado, or Nagasaki after 1641, together with merchandise sent from their East India Company headquarters at Batavia or acquired at company factories and Asian ports along the way.

Situated in this favorable island location, the Dutch encountered fierce competition from maritime rivals. At the outset they contended with resident Japanese merchants who brought in valuable cargoes that enabled them to buy up the costly goods shipped to the island by the Chinese. The Dutch, lacking sufficient capital to compete in this exchange, tried unsuccessfully to prevent it. Relations with the Japanese worsened in 1628, when Dutch authorities at Zeelandia clashed with the crew of a vermilion seal ship. Angered by this incident, the Tokugawa shogunate (1603–1867) suspended all Dutch trade at Hirado until 1632. After trade resumed the following year, the shōgun stopped issuing vermilion seal permits to vessels sailing to Taiwan and sought to prohibit overseas voyages by Japanese subjects. Japanese trade with the island soon ceased, and Dutch-Japanese rivalry there came to an end.

The Spanish also became Taiwan-based trading rivals after an expeditionary force from Manila established a settlement at Jilong in 1626. With an eye to resuming trade with Japan, the Spanish envisioned making Jilong an entrepôt for Chinese silk exports in competition with Zeelandia and Macao. However, the Spanish lacked sufficient capital to engage in sizable transactions with the Chinese, and trade with Japan by way of northern Taiwan failed to materialize prior to the time they were ousted from the island by the Dutch in 1642.

Moreover, Dutch authorities at Zeelandia constantly had to cope with powerful Chinese merchant adventurers engaged in the silk and silver trade. These included Li Dan (Li Tan; alias Captain Andrea Dittis), a shipping magnate with headquarters at Hirado, whose agents controlled much of the Chinese junk trade with Taiwan, and Zheng Zhilong (Cheng Chih-lung; alias Iquan), who subsequently seized power in Xiamen (Amoy) and extended his operations to Taiwan and Japan. When Zheng capitulated to the new Manchu rulers of Qing China, his son ZHENG CHENGGONG (Cheng Ch'eng-kung; J: Kokusenya; known in the West as Coxinga), a staunch Ming loyalist, took over the family's maritime operations. Born at Hirado of a Japanese mother, Zheng Chenggong annually sent large numbers of his junks to Nagasaki, the Ryūkyūs, and various ports in Southeast Asia. He also monopolized the supply of Chinese goods shipped to Zeelandia prior to the time he attacked Taiwan in 1661 and drove the Dutch from the island the following year.

Under Zheng-family rule Taiwan served as a major center of the Chinese junk trade in Asian waters. Zheng Chenggong's eldest son, Zheng Jing (Cheng Ching), who succeeded his father as ruler of the island, continued to depend primarily on this extensive maritime trade to support his pro-Ming regime and warfare against the Qing. Trade with Japan remained most important in this respect. Zheng Jing dispatched junks to Nagasaki and appealed for aid from the Tokugawa rulers as his father had done. However, following the Qing ban imposed on Chinese overseas trade in 1661, the number of Chinese junks that traded with Japan, including those operated by the Zheng family, decreased sharply.

The Qing Period——After the Qing takeover in 1683, Taiwan no longer served as an important entrepôt for trade with Japan and other Asian countries. Yet an overseas market prevailed for Taiwan sugar and deerskins. When the Qing ban on overseas trade was lifted in 1684 Fujian officials administering Taiwan tried to profit from the demand in Japan for these two major exports, as the Dutch and Zheng family rulers had previously done. However, their government junks were turned back at Nagasaki by seclusion-minded Tokugawa authorities. Over the remainder of the 17th century, the island's sugar and deerskin trade was handled mainly by southern Fujian merchants who reexported the bulk of these commodities to Japan. By the early 18th century, lower Yangzi (Yangtze) merchants came to dominate the Chinese junk trade with Japan. In their hands Taiwan sugar became an important supplement to local silk exports, despite the decline of trade at Nagasaki due to the stringent quotas imposed on foreign shipping.

Trade between Taiwan and Japan experienced a gradual upswing in the 1860s when Western steamships began to call at the island's treaty ports. After the SINO-JAPANESE AMITY TREATY OF 1871 was ratified, Japanese vessels entered this trade. Japan's demand for sugar increased appreciably by the late 1870s and absorbed the greater part of Taiwan's rising sugar exports over the next two decades.

With the "opening" of Japan in the 1850s, a few *samurai* advocating national expansion included Taiwan in their proposals for overseas conquest. Meiji Japan's course of action toward Taiwan fit in with expansionist policies. Early in 1874, a Japanese expeditionary force was dispatched to the island in response to an incident involving 54 shipwrecked Ryukyuan seamen who had been slain by Taiwan aborigines over two years previously. This force landed in a remote coastal area of southwestern Taiwan and engaged in skirmishes with hostile aborigines before withdrawing in December after China and Japan finally came to terms (see also TAIWAN EXPEDITION OF 1874).

The cession of Taiwan and Penghu was added to Japan's list of demands upon China in 1895 at the close of the first Sino-Japanese War. Prior to the signing of the peace treaty, a Japanese naval force seized the Penghu Islands during a four-day engagement in March. The subsequent takeover of Taiwan proved more difficult. A makeshift island government, labeled the Taiwan Republic, was created in

an attempt to attract Western support and foster a local resistance movement. Although foreign assistance failed to materialize and the Qing court cut off aid from the Chinese mainland, Japan encountered almost five months of organized resistance and had to use some 50,000 troops to complete the takeover.

Colonial Rule——Having acquired Taiwan, Meiji leaders were anxious to emulate the achievements of Western colonial powers. Hence, the colonial system devised for Taiwan was modeled closely after European rule prevalent in overseas colonies elsewhere. Under this system Taiwan was governed separately by a governor-general appointed by the throne, and the island's economy was subordinated to the needs of Japan. Moreover, care was taken to isolate the colony from China and much of the outside world. Tight control was also exerted over internal affairs, and preferential treatment was accorded the Japanese resident population. Although burdens were imposed on the Taiwanese, colonialism not only yielded many benefits to Japan but brought about modernization and economic growth in Taiwan as well.

Japanese colonial rule was formally inaugurated in Taibei (Taipei; J: Taihoku) on 17 June 1895 by the first governor-general, Admiral KABAYAMA SUKENORI. Extraordinary powers were vested in his office. These included military command within the colony, control over the judiciary and police, and jurisdiction over levels of government subordinate to the government-general (*sōtokufu*), the central organ that he headed. The power of the governor-general was significantly lessened in 1919, when Japanese civilians were allowed to hold office and the Taiwan garrison was placed under separate command, and again in 1921, after the Imperial Diet limited the authority of the governor-general to issue ordinances (*ritsurei*) in lieu of duly legislated laws of Japan. Later on, however, extensive wartime controls were assigned to that office, and military command was eventually restored in 1944, when the commander of the Taiwan garrison was appointed the 19th and last governor-general.

Meanwhile, over the first half of the colonial period the lower units of government were frequently reorganized and their territorial boundaries shifted. Not until 1920 was the colony permanently divided into five provinces (*shū*) and two lesser districts (*chō*), with the Penghu Island District (Hōkotō Chō) added in 1926.

Early Reforms——Initially, the governors-general of Taiwan were preoccupied with the banditry, guerrilla warfare, and disease that prevailed as an aftermath of the takeover. Widespread disorder did not subside until early in the 1900s, after the fourth governor-general, KODAMA GENTARŌ, and his chief of civil administration, GOTŌ SHIMPEI, had revamped the police system, adopted appeasement policies, and reinstated the Chinese *baojia* (*pao-chia*; J: *hokō*) system of mutual surveillance among registered Taiwanese households. Gotō launched a successful long-range public health program as well.

Kodama and Gotō, who assumed office in 1898, laid the foundation for extensive economic development in Taiwan. To stimulate the agricultural sector, as well as to develop commerce and industry, they introduced a modern-type infrastructure and technology. Under their auspices shipping between Taiwan and Japan was subsidized, the harbors at Jilong and Gaoxiong improved, and work on the trunk railway connecting these two chief seaports continued. Moreover, the Bank of Taiwan (TAIWAN GINKŌ) was established in 1899 and assigned the task of introducing standard Japanese currency throughout the colony. Postal and telegraph facilities were expanded as well, and telephone service was introduced at the turn of the century. Also, scientific improvements in agriculture were initiated by the government and the heavily capitalized sugar industry, then implemented through the village police network and the first farmers' associations.

In addition, the Kodama administration devised fiscal policies to finance such costly undertakings. Larger revenues were secured principally through increased income derived from monopoly bureaus and, later on, the land tax after a comprehensive land reform program had been carried out. Public loan bonds were also issued. Despite considerable deficit spending, sufficient revenue was generated to make Taiwan self-supporting and no longer dependent on subsidies from the home government by 1905, a year before Kodama and Gotō were reassigned to posts elsewhere.

Economic Policy and Development——Thereafter, until the late years of World War II, Taiwan proved to be an economic asset to Japan. Agricultural growth continued to be stressed as a means of keeping the colony self-sufficient in food production and enabling a large volume of Taiwan's major crops, sugar and rice, to be exported. Since the bulk of the colony's trade was confined to the home country, such policies helped satisfy Japan's growing demands for agricultural products and raw materials. Moreover, because of the low rate of consumption maintained in Taiwan, the colony managed to export more than it imported. This favorable trade balance allowed additional profits to be extracted from Taiwan and transferred to Japan. Profits from Japanese holdings were also partly retained in the colony, where favorable investment opportunities prevailed.

In the mid-1920s the colonial authorities began to concentrate more on Taiwan's industrial development. They were encouraged to do so by the rapid increase in agricultural productivity as well as by a greater availability of investment capital. This capital came from savings and reinvested profits, Taiwan's credit and banking institutions, and business interests in Japan, including the ZAIBATSU. Undertakings requiring expenditures and fixed investments on the part of the government-general also helped to pave the way for industrialization. These included extended transportation facilities, new commercial and technical schools, and the first large-scale hydroelectric installations.

At this stage, however, modern industrial production involved mainly light industry and processing plants for food and fertilizer. Not until Japan began to prepare for war in the mid-1930s were there concerted efforts on the part of the home government and colonial authorities to create a broader industrial base in Taiwan. During the late 1930s and early 1940s factories were rapidly built, chiefly for the processing of raw materials and the production of chemicals and metals to complement Japan's heavy industry. This late surge of industrialization in Taiwan was highlighted by the opening of large aluminum plants in Gaoxiong and on the east coast at Hualian (Hualien; J: Karenkō).

Modernization and Change——Modernization under colonial rule also brought about demographic and social change in Taiwan. This was reflected by the rising rate of population growth recorded for the colony after 1905, as the number of Taiwanese increased from approximately 3 to 6 million by 1943. Change was most apparent in the island's nine main cities where, collectively, the urban population more than doubled during the 1920s and 1930s. These municipalities attracted excess Taiwanese labor from the countryside. Japanese with managerial and technical skills also migrated to Taibei and the major provincial and port cities where most such civilian residents tended to congregate. This essentially urban Japanese population increased from around 50,000 in 1905 to almost 350,000 by 1943.

Taibei best symbolized the colony's progress with its well laid-out Jōnai section, which had once been enclosed by a Chinese city wall. This area contained imposing Western-style buildings belonging to the government-general, as well as parks, boulevards, Japanese-style residences, and a modern business district. Other cities with sizable Japanese populations also acquired parks and broad avenues, along with modern institutions conspicuous by their Western design: banks, hospitals, schools, and police and railway stations. Again, most Taiwan cities developed water supply and sewage systems as well as gas and electric utilities.

Technological advances also affected life in the towns and countryside with the advent of modern transportation and communication systems. Government-run railway lines served many towns, and narrow-gauge private lines—designed for trains of a smaller model or manually operated pushcarts (daisha)—linked rural districts and extended to remote mountainous areas. By the mid-1920s, a network of roads spanned the island as well. Motor-bus services increased rapidly thereafter, as did the number of bicycles in use. By then, the towns and most large villages had already acquired telephone and telegraph services. During the 1930s electrical service became more widespread in areas of the countryside. Newly opened radio broadcasting stations, transmitting from major cities, then began to serve the outlying areas.

Colonial Society——Although the impact of modernization was widespread in Taiwan, traditional ways still prevailed. Long-standing Chinese customs remained dominant in the towns and villages, while in the cities contrasts between the congested Taiwanese sections and the more spacious Japanese districts were often striking in terms of the architecture, living standards, and general environment. Furthermore, handicraft industries and customary forms of enterprise were maintained by the Taiwanese, who continued to invest more heavily in the traditional than the modern industrial sector. In agriculture, too, modern processes and techniques tended to supplement rather than supplant the enduring modes of local marketing and labor-intensive farming still engaged in by the native population.

Adherence to traditional ways tended to set the Taiwanese off from the Japanese residents in the colonial setting. By and large, the Taiwanese were products of a conservative rural society. Moreover, the large majority continued to live in the tradition-bound countryside. The Japanese, on the other hand, were the chief beneficiaries of modernization and change, as evidenced by their more affluent urban lifestyle. Discriminatory practices, fostered under colonialism, did much to perpetuate the marked social distinctions and differences in well-being that prevailed between these two components of the colonial population. Japanese nationals were assured the best openings in professional and official positions and were recruited as technicians and skilled workers. Again, regulations stipulated that Japanese were to control and help manage all registered corporate enterprises in the colony.

Discrimination also prevailed in the colonial system of education which was initially segregated. Schools above the primary level were integrated early in the 1920s. However, a disproportionate number of Japanese still were admitted to the secondary schools and the several institutions of higher learning, including the prestigious Taihoku University established in 1928. Relatively high literacy rates were eventually achieved among a large majority of Taiwanese males and females by way of the numerous primary schools. Nevertheless, this educational system afforded better opportunities for economic and social advancement to the Japanese residents, a privileged minority in the colony.

Colonial rule also affected Taiwan's aborigines, whose numbers doubled to well over 200,000 by the end of the period. After the colonial police were assigned to deal with aboriginal affairs around the turn of the century, policemen manned the guard lines (aiyūsen) that served to fence in restive mountain tribes. They also supervised the activities of tractable groups and taught the young. By the 1940s, a sizable proportion of the aborigine youth were attending police-directed education centers where training in the Japanese language was stressed, as was the case in primary schools maintained for the Taiwanese population at large. At times the colonial authorities launched military campaigns against hostile tribes inhabiting the central and northern ranges. These proved most severe during a five-year period beginning in 1911, when the government-general strove to gain access to the forest reserves and other resources in the mountainous interior.

Colonial Politics——Political dissent within the colony changed in character as the Taiwanese accommodated to modernization and foreign rule. Although sporadic uprisings occurred until 1915, new leaders, educated in Japanese ways, had already begun to take action. These Taiwanese activists suffered a setback in an initial endeavor to gain equality under Japanese rule when their short-lived assimilation movement was suppressed by the colonial authorities in 1914.

Subsequently, a few prominent leaders launched a home rule movement. Soon their movement was challenged by radical Taiwanese intellectuals who in general manifested more of a national consciousness and espoused liberal and left-wing sentiments current among the growing number of Taiwanese students in Japan. These intellectuals formed various organizations and movements advocating socioeconomic change as well as political autonomy for Taiwan.

Taiwan's colonial administration was more directly affected by the party government and liberal trends in politics that developed in Japan following World War I. After HARA TAKASHI became premier, he chose an experienced bureaucrat, Den Kenjirō (1855–1930), to serve as Taiwan's first civilian governor-general. Den introduced somewhat more liberal policies during his four years in office, beginning in 1919, and created advisory councils with partial Taiwanese representation. It was also during his incumbency that the Diet limited the legislative authority of the Taiwan governor-general so that constitutional laws of Japan might be applied in the colony as much as possible.

Despite these reforms, educated Taiwanese continued to call for autonomy for their island homeland. Between 1920 and 1934 leaders of the home rule movement submitted 15 annual petitions to the Diet in Tōkyō. Slightly more self-government was conceded to the colony, but soon their movement was dissolved prior to the outbreak of war with China in 1937. As liberal tendencies gave way to militarism in both Japan and Taiwan during the 1930s, all left-wing Taiwanese organizations were disbanded as well.

The Wartime Period——The colony served Japan well during the war with China and the ensuing Pacific War. Taiwan and Penghu were used as staging areas for the coastal occupation of Fujian and Guangdong (Kwangtung), beginning in 1938, and again for the invasion of Luzon in December 1941 and subsequent Japanese thrusts in

Southeast Asia. During the early wartime period the colony was assessed heavy contributions. Later on, young Taiwanese males were mobilized for labor and military purposes to help supply Japan's growing manpower needs. Other segments of the colonial population were required to volunteer for local wartime duties, and an "imperialization" *(kōminka)* movement was launched in an attempt to assimilate the Taiwanese as loyal imperial subjects.

Not until 1944 did the colony begin to suffer from the direct effects of war after Allied submarines had interrupted shipping between Taiwan and Japan and heavy American air strikes commenced late in that year. By then, severe shortages and inflation had already disrupted the economy. Finally, on 25 October 1945, the last governor-general, General Andō Rikichi (1884–1946), relinquished control over Taiwan and Penghu to representatives of the Republic of China following Japan's surrender to the Allied powers in August. The next year Taiwan's entire Japanese civilian and military population, totaling approximately half a million by the war's end, was repatriated.

The Postwar Era —— Taiwan and Penghu were turned over to China in accordance with the decisions reached by the Allied leaders at the CAIRO CONFERENCE of 1943 and in the POTSDAM DECLARATION of July 1945. Later on, in the bilateral peace treaty concluded with the Republic of China on 28 April 1952, Japan formally renounced "all right, title and claim" to its former colony. However, when extending diplomatic recognition to the People's Republic of China in a joint communiqué signed at Beijing on 29 September 1972, Japan acknowledged Taiwan and Penghu to be an inalienable territory of the mainland communist government.

Within two months after this formal diplomatic rupture with the Taiwan-based Nationalist government, Japan and the Republic of China established mutual exchange associations in Tōkyō and Taibei, respectively. These ad hoc agencies enabled the commercial links formed between Japan and Taiwan since 1952 to remain essentially intact. Hence the import and export trade that had ensued during the 1950s and burgeoned thereafter was not disrupted. Japanese industrial investments in Taiwan and tourist travel to the island, both of which underwent rapid growth during the 1960s, also continued to increase.

📖 ——General histories: James W. Davidson, *The Island of Formosa, Past and Present* (1903; repr 1961). Inō Yoshinori, *Taiwan bunkashi*, 3 vols (1928; repr 1965). Specialized studies: C. R. Boxer, "The Rise and Fall of Nicholas Iquan," *T'ien Hsia Monthly* 11 (1941). Iwao Seiichi, "Li Tan, Chief of the Chinese Residents at Hirado: Japan in the Last Days of the Ming Dynasty," *Memoirs of the Research Department of the Toyo Bunko* 17 (1958). Ts'ao Yung-ho, "The Acceptance of Western Civilization in China: A Brief Observation in the Case of Taiwan," *East Asian Cultural Studies* 6 (1967). Yamawaki Teijirō, "The Great Trading Merchants, Cocksinja and His Son," *Acta Asiatica* 30 (1976). Sophia Su-fei Yen, *Taiwan in China's Foreign Relations, 1836–1874* (1965). Works on the Japanese colonial period: George H. Kerr, *Formosa: Licensed Revolution and the Home Rule Movement, 1895–1945* (1974). Kō Sekai (Xu Shijie or Hsü Shih-chieh), *Nihon tōchika no Taiwan* (1972). Kō Shōdō (Ng Yuzin Chiautong), *Taiwan minshukoku no kenkyū* (1970). Tō Shōgen (Tu Zhaoyan or T'u Chao-yen), *Nihon teikoku shugi ka no Taiwan* (1975). E. Patricia Tsurumi, *Japanese Colonial Education in Taiwan, 1895–1945* (1977). The postwar period: Ralph N. Clough, *Island China* (1978).   *Harry J.* LAMLEY

Taiwan Expedition of 1874

(Taiwan Shuppei or Seitai no Eki). A punitive expedition by Japanese military forces. Using as a pretext the murder of 54 shipwrecked Ryūkyū islanders by Taiwanese aborigines in December 1871, the Japanese government—which had protested to the Chinese without result—in May 1874 sent a force of more than 3,000 men led by SAIGŌ TSUGUMICHI to southwestern Taiwan. The ulterior aims of the expedition were to force Chinese acknowledgment of Japanese claims of sovereignty over the RYŪKYŪ ISLANDS, gain a foothold in Taiwan, and indirectly exert pressure on the Korean government to accede to Japanese demands to open the country. After suffering disease and meeting fierce resistance from the Taiwanese, Japanese forces withdrew without significant military gains. A settlement was reached through the mediation of Thomas F. Wade (1818–95), the British minister in Beijing (Peking). China agreed to pay an indemnity of 500,000 taels for the murdered Ryukyuans and for "improvements" left by the Japanese expeditionary force, thus tacitly acknowledging Japanese suzerainty over the Ryūkyūs. The first foreign military adventure by the new Meiji government, the expedition served to mollify those in the government pressing for a more assertive foreign policy.

Taiwan Ginkō

(Bank of Taiwan). A semiofficial colonial bank established by the Japanese government in 1899 to serve as the central bank for Taiwan, a Japanese colony from 1895 to 1945; to promote the resource exploitation and economic development of that island; and to facilitate the expansion of trade between it and South China and the South Sea Islands. The bank's initial task, the unification of Taiwan's currency, was completed by 1909. From around that time it began lending extensively to primary industries in Taiwan engaged in the production of sugar, tea, camphor, and the like. During World War I it moved aggressively into Japan proper and by the 1920s was lending more to businesses in Japan than to those in Taiwan. Disclosure of its reckless lending to the Suzuki conglomerate, in particular, helped to bring on the FINANCIAL CRISIS OF 1927, during which the bank was forced to close temporarily most of its branches outside of Taiwan. With government assistance it later carried out a major reorganization, once again focusing its lending operations on Taiwan. During World War II it helped to finance the administration of the Japanese-occupied areas of South China and Southeast Asia. Following the war the bank was ordered dissolved by the OCCUPATION authorities, its liquidation being completed by 1957. See also COLONIALISM.

Taiwan Shuppei → Taiwan Expedition of 1874

Taiyō

(The Sun). One of Japan's first general-interest magazines; published by HAKUBUNKAN, a leading Tōkyō publishing house, from 1895 to 1928. Launched in January 1895, along with *Shōnen sekai* and BUNGEI KURABU, in a move by Hakubunkan to consolidate its magazine division, *Taiyō* came out monthly (bimonthly from 1896 to 1899). It published articles on an extraordinarily wide variety of practical and intellectual topics and was among the leading periodicals of the late Meiji to early Taishō periods (roughly 1900–1920). Its literary columns attracted especial attention because of the critical articles of literature editor TAKAYAMA CHOGYŪ, who engaged such writers as MORI ŌGAI and TSUBOUCHI SHŌYŌ in literary debate. Chogyū's series of essays on romanticism and, later, HASEGAWA TENKEI's on the so-called Japanese naturalism were extremely influential. Chogyū died in 1902, but in 1906 Tenkei took over as literary editor and quickly established *Taiyō* as one of the pivotal journals, along with WASEDA BUNGAKU and *Bunshō sekai*, in the naturalist movement. Other writers who helped to make it a leading voice during this important period of modern Japanese literature include UEDA BIN, TOKUDA SHŪSEI, KUNIKIDA DOPPO, SHIMAZAKI TŌSON, and TAYAMA KATAI, to name but a few. *Taiyō* also carried a broad selection of translations, including works by Poe, Balzac, Turgenev, Chekov, Shakespeare, Flaubert, Twain, Maeterlinck, Hauptmann, Maupassant, and Tolstoy. When naturalism declined, *Taiyō* lost its literary influence but continued to publish original works by major writers and poets. With the rise of TAISHŌ DEMOCRACY and changing social trends after World War I, it was overshadowed by CHŪŌ KŌRON and KAIZŌ and ceased publication in February 1928. Generally speaking, the wide assortment of essays, stories, poems, and translations published in *Taiyō* during its 33-year history reflects the changing literary trends of its time.

Two other magazines with the same name were later published by CHIKUMA SHOBŌ PUBLISHING CO, LTD (October 1957–February 1958) and HEIBONSHA, LTD, PUBLISHERS (July 1963 to the present).
                                                          Theodore W. GOOSSEN

Taiyō Fishery Co, Ltd

(Taiyō Gyogyō). One of the leading fishery companies in the world. It was founded in 1880 by Nakabe Ikujirō. Originally called Hayashikane Shōten, it was engaged in the purchase and distribution of fish. It is now a widely diversified food-producing conglomerate. It centers its activities on the fishing industry, including whaling, and has expanded its line of business to include shipping, shipbuilding, and cold storage. It also owns a professional baseball team, the Taiyō Whales. The company has a total of 84 domestic subsidiaries, with 28 joint enterprises and 20 representative offices overseas. Sales for the fiscal year ending January 1982 totaled ¥612.9 billion

(US $2.7 billion) and the company was capitalized at ￥15 billion (US $66.8 million). Its head office is in Tōkyō.

Taiyō Kōbe Bank, Ltd

City bank based in the Kinki (Kōbe–Ōsaka–Kyōto) district and in Tōkyō. It was established in 1936 but took its current name in 1973 after the merger of the Kōbe and Taiyō banks. It ranks midway among the 13 city banks in Japan but has the largest number of branches, with a total of 342 at home and abroad. The bank holds no specific corporate group membership, and it handles individual clients as well as small-, medium-, and large-scale businesses. It has seven branches, twelve representative offices, and two firms incorporated overseas. It finances enterprises operating domestically and abroad, and concentrates on internationalization through short- and medium-term loans to foreign banks, public agencies, and foreign enterprises. As of March 1982 the bank's total assets were ￥11.9 trillion (US $49.4 billion), deposits ￥9.4 trillion (US $39.0 billion), and capitalization stood at ￥70 billion (US $290.8 million). Its head office is in Kōbe.

Taizōkai

(Skt: Garbhadhātu; Matrix or Womb Realm). A realm symbolizing one of two aspects of the Dharmakāya Buddha Mahāvairocana (J: DAINICHI Nyorai), the central Buddha in ESOTERIC BUDDHISM. The Taizōkai refers to Mahāvairocana's dynamic enlightenment aspect, which is immanent in the universe. This eternal enlightenment is the all-embracing principle underlying and nurturing all phenomena; hence the use of the word womb. The Taizō mandara (Skt: Garbha-maṇḍala), also called Taizōkai mandara (mandala of the Garbhadhātu), is the pictorial representation of this realm, and the Dainichikyō (Mahāvairocana-sūtra) is the sacred text that expounds the mandala. The mandala, in the shape of a long rectangle, consists of 12 great sections or "halls," with the eight-lobed central pedestal, on which Mahāvairocana is seated, as the central section. The Taizōkai and the KONGŌKAI (Diamond or Thunderbolt Realm), which is the other aspect of Mahāvairocana, are often paired and known as Kontai Ryōbu. Together these realms formulate the two central tenets of SHINGON SECT esoteric Buddhism. See also RYŌBU MANDARA; MANDALA. MATSUNAMI Yoshihiro

Tajima Naoto (1912–)

Athlete; specialist in the triple and broad jump. Born in Yamaguchi Prefecture; graduate of Kyōto University. Professor of physical education at Chūkyō University from 1966. Tajima won a gold medal in the triple jump in the 1936 Berlin Olympic Games, setting a world record of 16 meters (52.5 ft), and also won a bronze medal in the long jump. Japan won the triple jump event in the Olympics three consecutive times: ODA MIKIO won in 1928, NAMBU CHŪHEI in 1932, and Tajima in 1936. Tajima became a member of the Japanese Olympic committee in 1969. TAKEDA Fumio

Tajimi

City in southeastern Gifu Prefecture, central Honshū. Tajimi has been known since ancient times for its MINO WARE. With the opening of the Chūō Main Line of the Japanese National Railways in 1900, Tajimi's ceramic industry developed further. Today, it manufactures tile and tableware. Pop: 74,311.

taka → hawks and eagles

Takabatake Motoyuki (1886–1928)

Social theorist. Born in Gumma Prefecture; attended Dōshisha University. He was imprisoned for two months in 1908 for publishing a socialist magazine in his home prefecture. It was during his confinement that he began translating Marx's Das Kapital (1919–24, Shihonron). In 1911 he joined SAKAI TOSHIHIKO's socialist organization, the BAIBUNSHA, and wrote articles for the leftist magazine Shin shakai (New Society), introducing the ideas of Karl Kautsky, the German Marxist. In 1919 he joined the Rōsōkai, a discussion group formed by KITA IKKI and ŌKAWA SHŪMEI, and under their influence moved toward national socialism. In his last years, he became even more conservative, joining forces with ASŌ HISASHI and other ultranationalists.

Takachiho

Town in northwestern Miyazaki Prefecture, Kyūshū. The locale is mentioned in several legends concerning the mythic beginnings of Japan. The principal activity is stock raising; agricultural products include rice, vegetables, and tobacco. The yokagura, a sacred Shintō dance performed at night at the Amanoiwato Shrine, claimed to be the site of the cave where the sun goddess AMATERASU ŌMIKAMI supposedly hid in displeasure (see MYTHOLOGY), has been designated as an Important Cultural Property. Takachiho is part of the Sobo–Katamuki Quasi–National Park. Pop: 19,957.

Takachihokyō

Gorge on the upper reaches of the river GOKASEGAWA, northern Miyazaki Prefecture, Kyūshū. Famous for its rocky formations and for its spring and autumn foliage. The area is associated with the mythic beginnings of Japan as recounted in the Kojiki (702) and the Nihon shoki (720).

Takachihonomine

Craterless stratovolcano, on the southeastern edge of the Kirishima Volcanic Group, on the border between Miyazaki and Kagoshima prefectures, Kyūshū. Legend has it that the grandson of AMATERASU ŌMIKAMI, the sun goddess, descended from heaven to the summit of this mountain. Takachihonomine is known for the alpine plant miyamakirishima (a kind of azalea); it is part of Kirishima–Yaku National Park. Height: 1,574 m (5,163 ft).

Takada Hiroatsu (1900–)

Western-style sculptor and art critic. Born in Ishikawa Prefecture. He learned Italian at the Tōkyō University of Foreign Languages and later studied sculpture with TAKAMURA KŌTARŌ. Strongly influenced by the SHIRAKABA SCHOOL, a movement of young writers and artists, in 1927 he helped found a short-lived artists' commune on the outskirts of Tōkyō. In 1931 he left for Paris, where he associated with Romain Rolland, Georges Rouault, Jean Cocteau, and other leading French artists. In Paris he published a newspaper, Nichifutsu tsūshin (Japan French News) to keep Japanese abreast of events in Europe. Toward the end of World War II he stayed in Berlin, where he was later detained by Allied troops for over a year. He then returned to Paris as a correspondent for the newspaper Yomiuri shimbun and went back to Japan in 1957. In addition to his original writings and numerous translations, he is noted for his portrait sculptures, especially the busts of his Paris friends.

Takada Kenzō (1939–)

Fashion designer. Born in Hyōgo Prefecture. Graduate of Bunka College of Fashion. Kenzō's "big silhouette" designs attracted worldwide attention, and his work has come to be regarded as an indicator of trends in fashions for the young throughout the world. He has shown his originality in combining the spirit of Paris with Japanese sensibilities. He is esteemed highly in Japan as a pioneer who opened the way for world appreciation of the work of Japanese designers. HAYASHI Kunio

Takada Sanae (1860–1938)

Educator and politician. Born in Edo (now Tōkyō). Upon graduation from Tōkyō University in 1882, he helped ŌKUMA SHIGENOBU to found Tōkyō Semmon Gakkō (now WASEDA UNIVERSITY). In 1887 he became editor-in-chief of the newspaper Yomiuri shimbun and engaged the services of such famous writers as OZAKI KŌYŌ and KŌDA ROHAN. In 1891 and on five later occasions he was elected to the House of Representatives from Saitama Prefecture. In 1915 he was appointed to the House of Peers. In addition, he held such eminent posts as director-general of the Ministry of Foreign Affairs and of the Ministry of Education and later served as education minister in the second Ōkuma cabinet (1914–16). His greatest achievement, however, lay in the sphere of private university management, particularly at Waseda. He was appointed its provost (gakuchō) in 1907 and became its third chancellor (sōchō) in 1921. TERASAKI Masao takagari → falconry

Takagi Kenkan (1849–1920)

Also known as Takagi Kanehiro. Naval surgeon and medical educator. Born in Hyūga Province (now Miyazaki Prefecture), Takagi studied under Ishigami Ryōsaku and William WILLIS and graduated from St. Thomas's Hospital Medical School in London. Upon returning to Japan in 1880, he became director of the Tōkyō Naval Hospital. The following year he founded the Seiikai School (now the Jikei University School of Medicine) and Japan's first nursing school at the Yūshi Kyōritsu Tōkyō Hospital (now the hospital attached to the Jikei University School of Medicine). Takagi became medical inspector general of the navy in 1885 and as a member of the Beriberi Investigation Committee proved that beriberi was mainly related to a dietary imbalance resulting from a diet of polished rice. NAGATOYA Yōji

Takagi Teiji (1875–1960)

Mathematician. The leading figure in modern Japanese mathematics, Takagi is known for his far-reaching contributions in algebraic number theory. Born in Gifu Prefecture, he graduated from Tōkyō University in 1897. From 1898 to 1901 he studied at the universities of Berlin and Göttingen under such prominent mathematicians of the day as Immanuel Fuchs, Georg Frobenius, and David Hilbert. Shortly after returning to Japan, he attracted international attention by proving for the Gauss imaginary-number fields the German mathematician Leopold Kronecker's "dearest dream of youth," a theorem concerning Abelian extensions of imaginary quadratic fields. In 1904 Takagi became professor at Tōkyō University, where he taught until his retirement in 1936. He made his most significant contribution to the advance of modern mathematics in 1920 with the introduction of the Takagi class-field theory. The theory generalized and gave structure to Hilbert's concept of a class field, and became the framework for the study of algebraic number theory. In 1929 he received an honorary doctorate from Oslo University and in 1932 was elected to the selection committee for the prestigious Fields Prize. He received the Order of Culture in 1940. His publications include Kaiseki gairon (1938, Introduction to Analysis) and Daisūteki seisūron (1948, Algebraic Number Theory).

Takahagi

City in northeastern Ibaraki Prefecture, central Honshū, on the Pacific Ocean. The Abukuma Mountains occupy about 70 percent of the city's area. Formerly a coal mining center, it now has pulp and lumber mills. The Ibaraki Satellite Communication Station of Kokusai Denshin Denwa Co, Ltd (KDD), Japan's overseas telephone and telegraph company, is located here. Pop: 32,436.

Takahama

City in central Aichi Prefecture, central Honshū; on Chita Bay. Long known for its tiles, with the completion of a coastal reclamation project it has diversified into machinery, and other industries. Poultry farming is also active. Pop: 31,548.

Takahama Kyoshi (1874–1959)

HAIKU poet and novelist. Real name Takahama Kiyoshi. He is noted for his leading role in the haiku world during the first half of this century; for his achievements, principally as editor of the magazine HOTOTOGISU, in introducing the work of other writers; and for his experiments with new types of poetic prose.

He was born in Matsuyama in Ehime Prefecture. His father, a former domain official, dabbled in WAKA, the 31-syllable traditional poetic form, and the amateur recitation and performance of NŌ plays; his mother also showed literary taste. In 1876 his father moved the family back to the country amidst scenery which, as Kyoshi later wrote, made a lasting impression on him. In 1881 the family returned to Matsuyama, where he attended primary and middle school. It was at middle school that he first revealed a literary bent, editing several student-produced school magazines together with his schoolmates. He also made the acquaintance of KAWAHIGASHI HEKIGOTŌ, who for many years was to be his closest literary confidant and collaborator. Impressed by his reading of the novels of KŌDA ROHAN, TSUBOUCHI SHŌYŌ, and MORI ŌGAI, he was inspired by a desire to write fiction himself. His friend Hekigotō confessed a similar ambition. The two were also interested in haiku poetry; they got to know the poet MASAOKA SHIKI, who also came from Matsuyama, and Kyoshi began to show Shiki his own work for comment. In 1892 the two young aspiring writers entered the Third Higher School in Kyōto and formed a haiku circle with other friends.

In 1894 Kyoshi left school and went to live in Tōkyō, where he studied Edo-period (1600–1868) literature and boarded at Shiki's home. Yet despite Shiki's devotion to poetry, Kyoshi still cherished the desire to become a novelist. He returned briefly to school in Kyōto, then moved to the Second Higher School in Sendai, but took a dislike to it and left. Around this time, he and Hekigotō sent some stories to Shiki, who severely criticized their immaturity. Shiki was already looking hopefully to Kyoshi as his natural successor in the field of haiku studies, but in some ways Kyoshi seems to have felt this to be a burden.

Returning to Tōkyō in 1895, Kyoshi entered Tōkyō Semmon Gakkō (now Waseda University) but soon abandoned his studies and instead took a job with the magazine Nihonjin (The Japanese) as haiku editor and critic. Shiki also arrived in Tōkyō late that year and asked Kyoshi to carry on his studies, but Kyoshi refused, saying that he preferred to concentrate on the actual writing of poetry. The decision seems to have had a liberating effect. The poems that Kyoshi produced during the following years are notable for their experimentation with lines containing irregular numbers of syllables and for carrying on the general tradition of the haiku poet BUSON but with an increased emphasis on human affairs and a greater complexity in the idea underlying each verse.

Kyoshi married in 1897. In the same year, the magazine Hototogisu was founded in Matsuyama. Kyoshi contributed verse and, when the magazine fell into difficulty, took it over, bringing it to Tōkyō in 1898 and using it henceforth as the principal outlet for his own literary activities. These included the regular contribution of shaseibun ("sketch pieces"), short, poetic pieces inspired by the methods of Western painters. Following the death of Shiki in 1902, Kyoshi's prose-writing activities gradually inclined more toward the short story. Hototogisu published more and more prose, including such works as NATSUME SŌSEKI's Wagahai wa neko de aru (1905–06; tr I Am a Cat, 1961). Criticized for this trend, Kyoshi insisted that he was merely extending the spirit of the haiku to other forms of literature. Stimulated by Sōseki's example, he published a number of his own stories in the magazine; a collection of them, Keitō (Cockscomb), published in 1908, had a preface by Sōseki in which he described them as "leisurely tales," thus giving rise to the appellation "Leisure School" (Yoyū Ha).

In 1908, Kyoshi began serialization of his first full-length novel, Haikaishi (The Haiku Master), and joined the newspaper Kokumin shimbun as literary editor, a post he left two years later. In 1909 a second volume of short stories, Bonjin (An Ordinary Person), appeared. This increasing preoccupation with fiction gradually estranged him from Hekigotō. Trips to Korea in 1911 inspired another novel, Chōsen (Korea), but from 1912 on the pages of Hototogisu showed a renewed interest in haiku, stimulated in part by opposition to a movement launched by Hekigotō to get away from traditional form and themes. In Susumubeki haiku no michi (1915–17, The Path Haiku Ought to Take), Kyoshi stressed objective observation as the basis of the haiku, and in the ensuing years up to the outbreak of World War II emerged as champion of the conservative outlook.

He continued to write his own poetic types of prose, including short stories and the novel Kaki futatsu (1915, Two Persimmons), while his activities as editor of Hototogisu helped to launch the careers of many other poets and novelists. He took an interest in Nō theater, writing some new plays himself. Visits abroad inspired him to write several travel pieces as well as helping to widen the scope of his verse. His major postwar work was the novel Niji (1947, Rainbow). He was awarded the Order of Culture in 1954.

■——Takahama Kyoshi, Teihon Kyoshi zenshū, 12 vols (Sōgensha, 1948). R. H. Blyth, A History of Haiku, vol 2 (1964). Mizuhara Shūōshi, Takahama Kyoshi (1952). Narusawa Kaken, Kyoshi kanshō (1971). Makoto Ueda, Modern Japanese Haiku: An Anthology (1976). John BESTER

Takahashi

City in western Okayama Prefecture, western Honshū. A regional commercial and agricultural center. Local products include tobacco, lumber, Christmas decorations, and straw hats. Bitchū Matsuyama Castle on the summit of Gagyūzan (altitude: 420 m or 1,378 ft) has the highest elevation of all mountain castles remaining in Japan. Pop: 27,259.

Takahashigawa

River in western Okayama Prefecture, western Honshū; originating in the mountains on the border of Tottori Prefecture and flowing south into the Inland Sea at the city of Kurashiki. The middle reaches flow through the plateau Kibi Kōgen and form beautiful V-shaped valleys. The stalactite grottos where the river has carved through limestone are well known. The lower reaches form the agricultural belt of the Okayama Plain, and the Mizushima Industrial Area is located at its mouth. The water is utilized for drinking, irrigation, industry, and electric power. Length: 111 km (69 mi); area of drainage basin: 2,670 sq km (1,031 sq mi).

Takahashi Kageyasu (1785–1829)

Geographer and scholar of WESTERN LEARNING who produced some of the earliest scientifically surveyed maps of the Japanese archipelago and who paid with his life for sharing his work with a foreigner. Born in Ōsaka. Succeeding his father, TAKAHASHI YOSHITOKI, as shogunal astronomer in 1804, he published a series of maps of Japan based upon the surveys of INŌ TADATAKA and two northern explorers, MAMIYA RINZŌ and MOGAMI TOKUNAI. In 1811, he established a translation office for foreign books and personally translated part of Engelbert KAEMPFER's history of Japan. Eagerness to acquire new Western materials led him to ignore a strict prohibition against giving maps to foreigners when the Bavarian naturalist Philipp Franz von SIEBOLD visited Edo (now Tōkyō) in 1826. When Japanese maps were discovered among Siebold's effects in 1828, shogunal authorities arrested Takahashi and a number of his disciples, reportedly after Mamiya Rinzō had informed upon them. Takahashi died in prison, and his corpse was formally "executed."

John J. STEPHAN

Takahashi Kazumi (1931–1971)

Novelist; scholar of Chinese literature. Born in Ōsaka. Graduate of Kyōto University, where he specialized in Chinese literature. He established his name as a novelist with *Hi no utsuwa* (1962), which depicts the fall of a university dean from prominence and power as a result of his self-centered love affairs. During the nationwide student uprising of the late 1960s, he conscientiously supported the radical students, with whom he was very popular. His widow, Takahashi Takako (b 1932), is also a writer. His principal works include the novels *Yūutsu naru tōha* (1965) and *Jashūmon* (1965–66), and an essay "Waga kaitai" (1971).

Takahashi Kenji (1871–1929)

Archaeologist. Born in Miyagi Prefecture, he graduated from Tōkyō Higher Normal School (later Tōkyō University of Education), where he studied under MIYAKE YONEKICHI. He then began archaeological research in Nara Prefecture while employed as a middle school teacher. In 1904 Takahashi joined the staff of the Tōkyō Imperial Household Museum (now Tōkyō National Museum). With Miyake he also helped to direct the Archaeological Society of Nippon. Among his publications are *Dōhoko dōken no kenkyū* (1925) on bronze weapons; *Kagami to ken to tama* (1911) on bronze mirrors, swords, and beads; *Nihon fukushoku shi ron* (1927), a study of ancient Japanese clothing; and *Kofun to jōdai bunka* (1922) on mounded tombs (KOFUN) and ancient culture.

ABE Gihei

Takahashi Korekiyo (1854–1936)

Politician and financial expert. Prime minister, November 1921–June 1922; president of the RIKKEN SEIYŪKAI political party, 1921–25; and intermittently finance minister in six cabinets between 1913 and 1936. Long an advocate of economic rather than military competition with the Western powers, he was assassinated by the "young officers" in the FEBRUARY 26TH INCIDENT.

Born in Edo (now Tōkyō), the son of an artist in the service of the Tokugawa shogunate, he was adopted by a *samurai* of the Sendai domain (now Miyagi Prefecture). He began to learn English at age 11 while a servant in Yokohama. In 1867 his domain sent him to the United States for further study. After his return the next year, he became a *shosei* (student-houseboy) to the statesman MORI ARINORI. Having served as a low-ranking bureaucrat in various government ministries, he became the first chief of the Patent Office in

1887. He was swindled out of his inheritance in an 1889 silver-mine venture in Peru, but his abilities were still sufficiently recognized to gain him employment in the BANK OF JAPAN in 1892. Appointed a director of the YOKOHAMA SPECIE BANK in 1895, he encouraged Finance Minister MATSUKATA MASAYOSHI to put Japan on the gold standard in 1897. The following year Takahashi became vice-president of the Bank of Japan. For his services in obtaining foreign loans amounting to about ¥1.3 billion during and immediately after the Russo-Japanese War of 1904–05, he was appointed to the House of Peers in 1905. He continued his rise in the banking world, attaining the presidency of the Yokohama Specie Bank in 1906 and of the Bank of Japan in 1911.

In 1913 Takahashi was appointed finance minister in the first cabinet of YAMAMOTO GONNOHYŌE and joined the Rikken Seiyūkai party. From 1918 to 1921 he again served as finance minister in the cabinet of HARA TAKASHI. He worked to increase Japan's naval power but earned the reputation of being more friendly to industrial-commercial interests than to the military. After Hara's assassination in 1921, he took over leadership of the government and of the Seiyūkai, despite the opposition of younger party members. His term as prime minister lasted less than seven months, mainly because of his inability to control factions within his own party. When one faction bolted the Seiyūkai to support the nonparty cabinet (see "TRANSCENDENTAL" CABINETS) of KIYOURA KEIGO in 1924, Takahashi, with the rest of his party in tow, joined with the leaders of the other major parties, KATŌ TAKAAKI and INUKAI TSUYOSHI, in the second MOVEMENT TO PROTECT CONSTITUTIONAL GOVERNMENT. He renounced his peerage and won election to the lower house. Thus, when Katō formed a coalition cabinet (see GOKEN SAMPA NAIKAKU) later that year, Takahashi was appointed minister of agriculture and commerce.

Resigning from the Seiyūkai presidency in 1925, he served as finance minister in the cabinets of TANAKA GIICHI (1927–29), Inukai Tsuyoshi (1931–32), SAITŌ MAKOTO (1932–34), and OKADA KEISUKE (1934–36). His major accomplishments then were to bring under control the FINANCIAL CRISIS OF 1927 and to help the economy to recover rapidly from the SHŌWA DEPRESSION. His program for combatting the depression entailed the December 1931 suspension of the the gold standard and increased government expenditures, especially on armaments, through deficit financing. Seeking to accommodate the demands of financial interests as well as the military, he resisted military demands for all-out armaments expansion as fiscally irresponsible. After he was assassinated by some of his severest army critics, the government's fiscal policy grew even more attuned to the military's plans for a "national defense state."

Takahashi Mutsuo (1937–)

Poet. Born in Fukuoka Prefecture, Kyūshū, he had a difficult childhood marked by the death of his father, separation from his mother, poverty, and, finally, Japan's defeat in World War II. He began writing very early, the poetry of his teens being collected in his first published work *Mino, atashi no oushi* (1959, Mino, My Bull). In 1962 he graduated from Fukuoka University of Education and moved to Tōkyō, where his second collection of poems, *Bara no ki: Nise no koibitotachi* (1964, The Rose-Tree: Imitation Lovers) was published. Since that time he has published prolifically: not only numerous collections of powerful and original poetry, but also the autobiographical work *Jūni no enkei* (1970, Twelve Perspectives); short stories ("Sei sankakukei," 1972, The Holy Triangle); aphoristic reflections on single words (*Dōshi*, 1974, Verb); a full-length novel (*Zen no henreki*, 1974, Zen's Pilgrimage) in which a young provincial journeys through Tōkyō's erotic underground, seen as a transmutation of the various realms of the Buddhist cosmos; and travel essays (e.g., an account of a trip to Mt. Athos, center of Greek monasticism).

Running through his works is an intense dual preoccupation with eroticism and religion. His eroticism is homosexual and ranges from the soft, rather sentimental, lyricism of his adolescent poems to the massive, Whitmanesque catalog-poem "Homeuta" (1971, Ode). In the area of religion, Takahashi's interests extend from Roman Catholicism (especially in his earlier work) to Eastern Orthodoxy and Mahayana Buddhism. He presently lives in Tōkyō, where he continues his unique and prolific literary activities.

——Takahashi Mutsuo, *Takahashi Mutsuo shishū* (Shichōsha, 1969). Takahashi Mutsuo, *Poems of a Penisist*, tr Hiroaki Satō (Chicago Review Press, 1975).

Paul McCARTHY

Takahashi no Mushimaro (fl ca 730)

Poet; court official. Practically nothing is known of his life apart from references in the MAN'YŌSHŪ (ca 759, Collection for Ten Thousand Generations or Collection of Ten Thousand Leaves), the first great anthology of Japanese vernacular poetry. These indicate that he was a petty bureaucrat serving at the Nara capital and also as a local official, especially in the northeastern province of Mutsu (now Aomori, Iwate, Miyagi and Fukushima prefectures). He is believed to have had a hand in collecting local dialect songs and poems included in the *Man'yōshū* under the rubric Azuma *uta* (Poems of the East). Only two poems in the anthology are indisputably his—a *chōka* (long poem) and *hanka* (envoy) addressed to his superior, Fujiwara no Umakai (d 737) on the latter's departure for provincial military duty in 732. However, an additional 31 poems—12 *chōka*, 18 *tanka*, and 1 *sedōka* (see WAKA for an explanation of these terms)—in the *Man'yōshū* are indicated as being from the "Takahashi no Mushimaro Collection," and all or most are believed to be by him. He is unique among *Man'yō* poets for his verse treatments of local myths and legends, several of which are among the best-known poems of the period. Many of his other poems are on travel. He is thought by some authorities to have compiled Books 9 and 14 of the *Man'yōshū* while on duty in Mutsu.   Robert H. BROWER

Takahashi Oden (1851–1879)

Murderess; the most notorious *dokufu* (wicked woman) of the modern era. Accused of several sex-related murders, Oden was the first woman to be executed by beheading after the Edo period (1600–1868). Born in what is now Gumma Prefecture, she was known from girlhood for her beauty and promiscuity. Her life of crime began after her husband contracted leprosy and sought the aid of Dr. James C. HEPBURN in Yokohama. When the disease proved incurable, Oden allegedly poisoned her husband and embarked on a career of prostitution, larceny, and homicide. Arrested in 1877 for slitting the throat of a used-clothing merchant at an inn in Asakusa, she was convicted and ultimately executed. It was the most sensational crime story of the day, and lurid accounts of Oden's escapades filled the newspapers. The popular author KANAGAKI ROBUN wrote a spicy novel based on her life, *Takahashi Oden yasha monogatari* (1879, Tale of Takahashi Oden, the She-Devil), which Kawatake MOKUAMI adapted as a *kabuki* play in the same year. Because she was thought to have been possessed of an extraordinary sexual drive, certain parts of her body were removed in an autopsy and preserved as specimens in the crime laboratory of the Tōkyō Metropolitan Police.

▅——Nanjō Norio, *Akujo no keifu* (1970). Togawa Masako, *Nihon dokufu den* (1971).   James T. KENNEY

Takahashi Satomi (1886–1964)

Philosopher. Born in Yamagata Prefecture. After graduating from Tōkyō University in 1910, he spent three years (1924–27) studying in Germany and France. Upon his return to Japan, he became a professor at Tōhoku University. Early in his life, he was influenced by the Marburg school of Neo-Kantianism and NISHIDA KITARŌ's philosophy of "Absolute Nothingness," but later became critical of Nishida and Tanabe Hajime (whose position is related to Nishida's) and came to expound his own philosophy of the "comprehensive dialectical whole" *(hō benshōhōteki zentaisei).* This philosophical system aims to embrace and transcend the dialects of Hegel, Marx, Nishida, Tanabe, and Buddhism from the standpoint of Absolute Nothingness, which is considered to be identical with love. His writings, which include *Hō benshōhō* (1942) and *Tetsugaku no honshitsu* (1947), are collected in the *Takahashi Satomi zenshū* (Iwanami Shoten, 1973).   TAKAHASHI Ken'ichi

Takahashi Shinkichi (1901–   )

Poet. Born in Ehime Prefecture. As a young man Takahashi was deeply moved by the manifestos of dadaism by the Rumanian poet Tristan Tzara, which were carried in a Tōkyō newspaper, and started to write dadaist poems. These were collected in *Dadaisuto Shinkichi no shi* (1923), which created an immediate sensation. Takahashi combined the dadaist opposition to all convention and tradition with a Buddhist sense of nihilism, often achieving an effect in his poems reminiscent of the Zen KOAN. Other collections include *Gion matsuri* (1926) and *Nisshoku* (1934).

Takahashi Yoshitoki (1764–1804)

Astronomer of the middle part of the Edo period (1600–1868). Along with his son TAKAHASHI KAGEYASU, he did much to advance the study of astronomy and the calendar in Japan. Born in Ōsaka, he studied under ASADA GŌRYŪ, the leading Japanese astronomer of the day. In 1795, he was made official astronomer to the Tokugawa shogunate and, along with Hazama Shigetomi (1756–1816), who had also studied with Asada, was directed to devise a new calendar. The product of this work, the Kansei Calendar, was officially adopted in 1798. Takahashi also translated a Dutch version of a work by the French astronomer Joseph Lalande and published it as *Rarande reki-sho kanken.*

Takahashi Yuichi (1828–1894)

Western-style painter. Born in Edo (now Tōkyō), he studied the orthodox KANŌ SCHOOL style of painting until his interest in Western art was aroused by Western lithographs. In 1862 he entered the shogunal Institute for the Investigation of Western Books (SEE BANSHO SHIRABESHO), where he studied under KAWAKAMI TŌGAI. In 1866 he furthered his study of Western art under the direction of the English illustrator Charles WIRGMAN in Yokohama. That same year Takahashi traveled to Shanghai to meet Western artists resident there. In 1870 he became professor at Daigaku Nankō, the predecessor of Tōkyō University. In 1873 he left to found his own art school, Tenkai Gakusha, and held monthly Western-style art exhibits. In the late 1870s he became acquainted with the Italian art teacher Antonio FONTANESI, who helped him to improve his technique. In 1880 he began publication of Japan's first art magazine, *Gayū sekichin.* He often painted portraits and landscapes of Tōkyō in the academic manner popular in 19th-century Europe. He is best known, however, for his realistic still lifes.

Takahata Seiichi (1887–1978)

Businessman. Born in Ehime Prefecture. After graduating from Kōbe Kōtō Shōgyō Gakkō (now Kōbe University), Takahata joined the firm SUZUKI SHŌTEN in 1909. Handpicked by its head manager KANEKO NAOKICHI to act as London branch manager in 1913, he involved Suzuki Shōten in third-country trade (trade not involving Japan) and helped build the firm into a leading trading company in the course of World War I. After the company's failure in 1927, Takahata established the general trading firm Nisshō & Co (now NISSHŌ IWAI CO, LTD) in 1928. He served as the company's chairman from 1945 through 1963.   KATSURA Yoshio

Takahira Kogorō (1854–1926)

Diplomat. Born in what is now Iwate Prefecture, he attended the Kaisei Gakkō, a precursor of Tōkyō University. Initially employed by the Kōbushō, the early Meiji Ministry of Public Works, in 1876 Takahira joined the Ministry of Foreign Affairs. He served as minister to Italy and Austria before becoming vice-foreign minister in 1899. As minister to the United States from 1900, he helped negotiate the Treaty of PORTSMOUTH (1905) concluding the Russo-Japanese War; and in 1908, as ambassador, he signed the TAKAHIRA–ROOT AGREEMENT, which sanctioned the status quo in the Pacific and provided equality of commercial opportunity to Japan and the United States in China.

Takahira–Root Agreement

An agreement between Japan and the United States regarding their respective roles in China and the Pacific Ocean area following the RUSSO-JAPANESE WAR of 1904–05; negotiated by Secretary of State Elihu Root and Ambassador TAKAHIRA KOGORŌ, it was signed on 30 November 1908. The agreement consisted of an official recognition of the status quo; provisions included affirmation of the independence and territorial integrity of China, mutual respect for national interests in the Pacific area, and maintenance of free and equal commercial opportunities. In effect, the agreement ensured Japanese recognition of American priority in Hawaii and the Philippines and American recognition of Japan's special position in Manchuria. See also KATSURA–TAFT AGREEMENT; OPEN DOOR POLICY.

Takai Kitō (1741–1789)

HAIKU poet. Born in Kyōto. A faithful disciple of BUSON, he compiled and edited the texts of his master's school and devoted himself to the haiku revival movement of the late 18th century. His verses, noted for their delicacy and subtlety, are mainly collected in *Seikashū* (1789).

Takaishi

City in southwestern Ōsaka Prefecture, central Honshū, on Ōsaka Bay; some 20 km (12 mi) southwest of Ōsaka. It was once an exclusive suburb of Ōsaka, but since the 1960s, it has undergone rapid industrialization with the construction of a large petrochemical complex. An older textile industry produces woolen yarn, blankets, and cotton fabrics. Pop: 66,810.

Takakura Ken (1931–   )

Screen actor known for his tough-guy roles in numerous YAKUZA (gangster) films. Real name Oda Gōichi. He was born in Fukuoka Prefecture. After graduating from Meiji University, he joined the acting stable of Tōei Motion Picture Company (see TŌEI CO, LTD) in 1955 as a so-called new face. His first role was in *Denkō karate uchi* in 1956. After playing the lead in *Jinsei gekijō: Hishakaku* in 1963, Takakura became the undisputed archetypical hero of yakuza movies for his performance in an 18-segment *yakuza* movie series collectively titled *Abashiri bangaichi* (1965–72). This and another series, *Shōwa zankyō den* (1965–72), made him one of Japan's most popular box-office stars. He is known to American moviegoers for his appearance in 1975 in *The Yakuza* with Robert Mitchum. He left Tōei in 1976 to become a free-lance actor. His memorable films since then include *Hakkōdasan* (1977) and *Shiawase no kiiroi hankachi* (1977).   SHIRAI Yoshio

Takamagahara

(literally, "High Celestial Plain"). Also called Takamanohara. A term for the abode of the heavenly divinities (*tenjin* or *amatsukami*) in Japanese MYTHOLOGY. It was subject to multiple interpretations in the course of Japanese history. It is generally considered that the High Celestial Plain is opposed to the "Land of Roots" (Nenokuni), to which some dead persons go; between these two realms, the human world, the "Central Land of Reeds" (Ashihara no Nakatsukuni), is located. This term therefore symbolizes the vertical view of the universe and suggests its association with shamanistic tradition. It is of some importance in the mythology, for it represents not only the abode of AMATERASU ŌMIKAMI, the solar divinity, but also the abode of the formless and anthropomorphic heavenly divinities, the last one of which, NINIGI NO MIKOTO, "descended" to the islands in order to pacify them.

The High Celestial Plain was interpreted by Shintō scholars according to their various philosophico-religious inclinations. Those who were influenced by Taoism qualified it as the "void," those who emphasized ritual purity termed it the "ultimate space of purity," whereas those who were influenced by Buddhism identified it with the realms of form and of formlessness, or with Mt. Sumeru. Yoshida Kanetomo (1435–1511), founder of the Yuiitsu School of Shintō (see YOSHIDA SHINTŌ), associated the practice of meditation on the *a* sound in esoteric Buddhism with meditation on the same sound as found in Takamagahara, which he saw as the beginning and end of all things. The SHUSHIGAKU scholar HAYASHI RAZAN (1583–1657) viewed it as the void and as the ultimate principle (Ch: *li*) of all things, which was to be found in the midst of the heart-mind. Another interpretation holds that the term applies to the imperial residence, in association with the classical term *unjō* ("above the clouds") which refers to the aristocracy. Another interpretation held a different version of the triple organization of the cosmos: "at the level of heaven, Takamagahara represents what is above the sky; at the level of earth, it represents the imperial residence; at the level of human beings, it represents the heart-mind." The Shintō popularizer Masuho Nokoguchi (1655–1742) wrote: "*taka* is heaven, *ma* is human beings, *hara* is earth," thereby suggesting the pervasive aspect of the divine. But MOTOORI NORINAGA (1730–1801) stated that "Takamagahara is in heaven and is the residence of the heavenly divinities," and this has become the standard definition.
                                                    Allan G. GRAPARD

Takamatsu

Capital of Kagawa Prefecture, Shikoku, on the Inland Sea. Takamatsu developed as a castle town after Ikoma Chikamasa con-

Takamatsuzuka tomb

A portion of the wall paintings on the east wall of the tomb. Shown is a group of four women, thought to represent mourners, dressed in jackets and pleated skirts of Korean type. One of the two groups of figures on the east wall. Ca 700. Asuka, Nara Prefecture. National Treasure.

structed a castle in 1588. Later, in the Edo period (1600–1868), it came under the rule of the Matsudaira family. The opening in 1910 of a ferryboat service between Uno in Okayama Prefecture and Takamatsu led to its emergence as a transportation center. Its main industries are machinery and foodstuffs. Traditional products are LACQUER WARE, tissue paper, and *udon* (noodles). The first successful artificial breeding of prawns was carried out in the Ikushima district. Attractions include the remains of Takamatsu Castle, RITSURIN PARK, and YASHIMA, the site of a battle in the TAIRA–MINAMOTO WAR. Pop: 316,662.

Takamatsu, Prince (1905–   )

(Takamatsu no Miya Nobuhito). Third son of Emperor TAISHŌ and younger brother of Emperor Hirohito. Named Teru no Miya Nobuhito, in 1913 he succeeded to the headship of the Takamatsu family, a princely house established in 1625 by a son of Emperor Go-Yōzei (1571–1617; r 1586–1611) that had died out. He graduated from the Naval Academy and the Naval Staff College and married a daughter of Tokugawa Yoshihisa (1884–1922), a son of the last Tokugawa shōgun. Attached to the military command during World War II, the prince was involved in a conspiracy to overthrow the cabinet of TŌJŌ HIDEKI. He serves as president of several organizations interested in promoting international goodwill.

Takamatsuzuka tomb

(Takamatsuzuka *kofun*). A small tomb mound with plastered and painted walls located in the southern hills of ASUKA, Nara Prefecture. It is the sole Japanese example of the artistic technique in the so-called international style then current in East Asia. The tomb was excavated in March 1972 by the Nara Kashiwara Archaeology Research Institute. The mound is 5 meters (16.4 ft) high and 18 meters (59 ft) in diameter, and the internal dimensions of its stone chamber are 2.6 by 1.0 by 1.1 meters (8.7 × 3.4 × 3.7 ft) in length, width and height, respectively. Although illustrated and identified in documents of the Edo period (1600–1868), as the mausoleum of the 7th-century Emperor Mommu, the Takamatsuzuka was dropped from the list of imperial tombs when a large mound to the south was later identified with Mommu. The excavation yielded skeletal remains of a male in his forties (Mommu had been cremated), fragments of a lacquered coffin, and grave artifacts that included a Chinese grape and lion bronze mirror, silver and gilt bronze ornaments used possibly for weapons, and glass beads. The east and west walls bear four groups of four human figures each, the groups being segregated by sex: men at the south end and women at the north end, divided by representations of the Azure Dragon of the east and the White Tiger of the west, the sun and moon respectively above them. The tomb had been previously looted, badly damaging the paintings at the south ends of the walls. The "Black Warrior" (the snake and tortoise) appears on the north wall. Overhead are 72 red dots, some still showing a little gold; a few are grouped in recognizable constellations. The women wear jackets and pleated skirts as seen in Sui dynasty (589–618) China but more familiar in Korea, and the men wear long robes and trousers best known in China. The deceased stands by a man holding a portable canopy over him, the chief of many status symbols. All the objects in the paintings—satchels, spear-like wrapped rods, round fans, and priests' staffs—with the exception of the folding stool, have their counterparts in China. The Azure Dragon of the Takamatsuzuka and the one on the bronze base under the Yakushi Buddha (NYORAI) in the temple YAKUSHIJI in Nara bear crosses on their necks, both similar to the cross on the Azure Dragon in the vault of the Four Deities Tomb in Tonggou (Tung-kou), China, then part of the Korean kingdom of Koguryŏ. From the fact that the Yakushiji is described in the chronicle NIHON SHOKI (720) as having celebrated the completion of its statues in 697, some art historians date the tomb to around AD 700; however, the 697 date itself is disputed by other art historians, who date the statues to the period 719–729. Some scholars consider it to be the tomb of Prince Takechi (654–696), a son of the 40th emperor, TEMMU. See also KOFUN.

■——*Bukkyō geijutsu (Ars Buddhica)*, 87, 89 (1972), special issues on the Takamatsuzuka and Korean wall paintings. Suenaga Masao, ed, *Hekiga kofun Takamatsuzuka* (1972). Suenaga Masao, ed, *Asuka Takamatsuzuka kofun* (1972).   J. Edward KIDDER, Jr.

Takami Jun (1907–1965)

Novelist, poet. Real name Takama Yoshio. Born in Fukui Prefecture. Graduate of Tōkyō University. The avant-garde literary movement of the mid-1920s inspired him to write. He participated actively in left-wing politics, but after being arrested he gave up Marxism. He wrote about the mental anguish of this ideological "conversion" (see TENKŌ) in *Kokyū wasureubeki* (1935–36, Should Auld Acquaintance Be Forgot). Gaining recognition for this novel, he went on to write similar autobiographical novels. His works, including those written after World War II, are characterized by ironic self-pity over his decadence and intellectual confusion following his "conversion" in the 1930s. In 1962, he joined several others to found the Nihon Kindai Bungakukan (MUSEUM OF MODERN JAPANESE LITERATURE). In 1964, his poetry collection *Shi no fuchi yori* (By the Abyss of Death) received the Noma Prize. Other works include the novels *Ikanaru hoshi no moto ni* (1939–40, Beneath What Star) and *Iya na kanji* (1960–63, A Disagreeable Feeling).

Takamine Hideko (1924–   )

Film actress. Real name Matsuyama Hideko. Born in the city of Hakodate, Hokkaidō. She joined Shōchiku (see SHŌCHIKU CO, LTD) studios at the age of six, earned a name for herself as a child actress and then, maintaining her reputation into her adult years, became a star through her appearance in numerous dramatic roles. Two of her best pictures were YAMAMOTO KAJIRŌ's *Tsuzurikata kyōshitsu* (1938, Composition Class), about a young girl, excelling at composition, who is sold as a *geisha* so her family can pay off debts, and the award-winning NIJŪSHI NO HITOMI (1954, Twenty-Four Eyes) directed by KINOSHITA KEISUKE, with whom she made several pictures. In Japan's first color picture, *Karumen kokyō ni kaeru* (1951, Carmen Comes Home), the first of Kinoshita's popular light comedy series, she played a good-hearted stripper and in this role won great acclaim. She also scored a critical triumph as the wife in the film *Na mo naku mazushiku utsukushiku* (1961, Nameless, Poor, Beautiful) of her husband MATSUYAMA ZENZŌ, the well-known scriptwriter and director. The picture portrays a deaf-mute couple who communicate eloquently in sign language. In 1976 she published her autobiography entitled *Watashi no tosei nikki*.   ITASAKA Tsuyoshi

Takamine Hideo (1854–1910)

Meiji-period educator; born in the Aizu domain (now part of Fukushima Prefecture); graduate of Keiō University. In 1875 Takamine went to the United States, where he studied teacher training in Oswego, New York. After returning to Japan in 1878, he took a teaching post at Tōkyō Normal School (later Tōkyō University of Education). He became president of this school and, subsequently, of Tōkyō Women's Higher Normal School (now Ochanomizu Women's University) and Tōkyō Bijutsu Gakkō (now Tōkyō University of Fine Arts and Music).

The state college at Oswego, where Takamine studied, was then the center of Pestalozzianism, a pedagogical school based on the theories of the Swiss educator Johann Heinrich Pestalozzi (1746–1827). This pedagogy stressed the need for education utilizing student participation and paced to follow the child's natural development. Takamine played a key role in introducing and spreading these ideas in Japan. He translated J. Johonnot's *Principles and Practices of Teaching* into Japanese as *Kyōiku shinron* (1885).

TAKAKUWA Yasuo

Takamine Jōkichi (1854–1922)

Applied chemist. Born in Takaoka, Etchū Province (now Toyama Prefecture). After graduating (1879) from the applied chemistry course of the Kōbu Daigakkō (now Tōkyō University), Takamine went to England and studied there until 1883. Returning to Japan, he worked for the Agriculture and Commerce Ministry. In 1890 he went to the United States, where he produced a powerful digestive, Taka-Diastase (patented in 1894 in the United States). He also succeeded in isolating adrenaline in crystalline form from bovine adrenal glands (patent right obtained in 1901 in the United States). In 1917 he founded a chemical laboratory in Clifton, New Jersey. In 1912 Takamine was awarded an Imperial Academy Prize for his work on adrenaline. He contributed much to the development of Japan–United States cultural exchange during his long stay in the United States. He died in New York in 1922.

Takami Senseki (1785–1858)

Official of the Koga domain (now part of Ibaraki Prefecture) and scholar of WESTERN LEARNING. Appointed chief retainer (*karō*) to the *daimyō* Doi Toshitsura in 1831, he went to Ōsaka with Doi, who had been named keeper (*jōdai*) of Ōsaka Castle, and was instrumental in capturing ŌSHIO HEIHACHIRŌ, the leader of a rebellion in 1837. He also accompanied Doi to Edo (now Tōkyō) when the latter was appointed a senior councillor (*rōjū*) of the Tokugawa shogunate. Takami took the opportunity to study about the West, associating with official interpreters and scholars of Western Learning such as ŌTSUKI GENTAKU, MITSUKURI GEMPO, and WATANABE KAZAN. He was particularly interested in maps and built up a considerable collection of atlases. Having thus become knowledgeable about the outside world, after Commodore PERRY's visits in 1853 and 1854 Takami urged the shogunate to open the country to trade, invite foreign advisers, and send study missions abroad. There is a famous portrait of Takami by Watanabe Kazan that can be seen at the Tōkyō National Museum.

Takamuko no Kuromaro (?–654)

Scholar and adviser on government at the YAMATO COURT. Descended from an immigrant (KIKAJIN) family that had come to Japan from Korea in about AD 400, in 608 Takamuko was sent with a group led by ONO NO IMOKO to study in China, where he remained for 32 years. With the advent of the TAIKA REFORM in 645, he and the priest Min (see SŌMIN), who had been a fellow student in China and shared his deep knowledge of Chinese political institutions, were named state scholars (*kuni hakase*); in that capacity they were charged with establishing the central administrative organs (*yatsu no suburu tsukasa*, or eight ministries) of the new Japanese government. In 654 Takamuko was sent as an envoy to the Tang (T'ang) dynasty of China; he died at the Tang capital in the same year.

William R. CARTER

Takamura Kōtarō (1883–1956)

Sculptor and poet. Eldest son of the noted sculptor TAKAMURA KŌUN. Kōtarō's work in both fields covers a wide range: as sculptor, he fashioned small wood carvings of insects and fish and chiseled the monumental nude figures that grace the shore of Lake Towada; as a poet, he utilized both the classical literary language and the modern spoken language to write on such themes as nature and marital love. Almost all of his poems of note are in free verse.

Born in Tōkyō, Takamura Kōtarō was raised with the idea that he would eventually succeed his father as head of a studio that turned out traditional Japanese wooden sculpture to order. While still a boy, Kōtarō was introduced to the tools and techniques of his father's trade; eventually he was sent to the Tōkyō Bijutsu Gakkō (now Tōkyō School of Fine Arts and Music). As the culminating stage of his training, he went abroad in 1906 for study in America, England, and France. Whatever technical benefits he might have gained from this experience, Kōtarō returned to Japan three years later irrevocably opposed to the idea that genuine sculpture could be produced upon order for a patron or customer. Above all, the example of Rodin had instilled in him a notion of artistic freedom incompatible with the purpose of his father's studio. Like many other intellectuals of the Meiji period (1868–1912), Kōtarō had come to associate the West with freedom and his native Japan with duty. Increasingly estranged from his family, he began spending his days in the company of the decadent writers and artists who styled themselves the Pan Society (PAN NO KAI).

It was not merely the example of such poets as KINOSHITA MOKUTARŌ and KITAHARA HAKUSHŪ of the Pan Society which turned Kōtarō's primary creative energies toward poetry at this point. Like other writers of modern colloquial verse, Kōtarō composed both HAIKU and TANKA during his youth and, before his trip abroad, was associated with the circle of poets behind the influential poetry magazine Myōjō (Bright Star). Nonetheless, in poems like ''Mona Lisa'' and ''Loneliness,'' composed soon after his return to Japan, the weary tone and satirical edge suggest the manner of the decadent poets of the Pan Society. At the same time the commitment to simplicity which emerges so prominently in the later poetry can already be noticed in the defiant ''Journey,'' the title poem which Kōtarō composed for Dōtei, his first collection of verse published in 1914.

In certain reminiscences written later in life, Takamura Kōtarō claimed that he was rescued from a decadent existence by Naganuma Chieko, a student of Western painting who eventually became his wife. According to Kōtarō's own account, marriage to Chieko provided a haven from the distractions of society. The image Kōtarō creates in certain poems and prose memoirs of their life together—an image of husband and wife surviving within the confines of their own home on little other than mutual affection—is subject to qualification; but there can be no doubt about the quality of the love poems Chieko inspired in Kōtarō. Composed over the years from 1912 to 1952, the 40-odd poems of Chieko shō (tr Chieko's Sky, 1978) are especially remarkable during a period when marital love was seldom evoked in Japanese poetry. For approximately the last seven years of her life, Chieko was schizophrenic, a condition which allowed Kōtarō considerable scope to delineate her as an individual alienated from both reality and himself.

World War II followed shortly after Chieko's death and Kōtarō emerged as a writer firmly committed to the policy of the militarists. As head of the Poet's Division of the Japanese Literature Patriotic Association (Nihon Bungaku Hōkokukai), Kōtarō took a very public stance on the war and, when defeat came, he determined to go into a kind of exile. For seven years he led a hermit-like existence in a rural cabin in Iwate Prefecture. Some of the poems from this period picture him as a fool; but there is also a striking work entitled ''Reverence'' which, in its depiction of a child compelled to bow before the emperor Meiji on parade, serves indirectly as an apologia for the poet's wartime conduct.

Altogether, Kōtarō seems more prominent in modern Japanese culture as poet than sculptor. Japanese critics customarily treat his sculpture in relation to his poetry; but while Kōtarō himself in his own writings often did this, for him, unlike the majority of the critics, the sculpture took precedence over the poetry. Though he abandoned the kind of sculpture for which he was trained, he continued to think of himself primarily as a sculptor. In certain essays he envisions poetry as an outlet for the sentiment and emotion which he tried to eliminate from his sculptures. Even with close observation of such famous works as the bronze hand in the Tōkyō Museum of Modern Art and the wooden carvings of fish, it is difficult to declare that Kōtarō was wholly successful in eliminating from his sculptures the emotional gestures that found expression in his poems.

📖———Works by Takamura: Takamura Kōtarō zenshū, 19 vols (Chikuma Shobō, 1957–58). Takamura Kōtarō zenshishū (1966). Takamura Kōtarō zenshikō (1967). Takamura Kōtarō shishū (Kadokawa Shoten, 1968). Chieko shō, tr Soichi Furuta as Chieko's Sky (1978). Chieko and Other Poems of Takamura Kōtarō, tr Hiroaki

Satō (1980). Works about Takamura: Itō Shinkichi, Takamura Kōtarō kenkyū (1966). Kakuta Toshio, Takamura Kōtarō kenkyū (1972). Takamura Toyochika, Kōtarō kaisō (1962). Yoshimoto Takaaki, Takamura Kōtarō (1967).

James A. O'Brien

Takamura Kōun (1852–1934)

Sculptor. Born Nakajima Mitsuzō in Edo (now Tōkyō), apprenticed in 1863 to the traditional-style Buddhist sculptor Takamura Tōun, and later adopted into the Takamura family. On the recommendation of OKAKURA KAKUZŌ, he was appointed professor of Tōkyō Bijutsu Gakkō (now Tōkyō University of Fine Arts and Music) in 1889. His most distinguished pupil was HIRAGUSHI DENCHŪ. Kōun worked in wood, ivory, and bronze in an exceptionally realistic style that reflected Western influence. His statue of KUSUNOKI MASASHIGE, the 14th-century warrior known for his devotion to the imperial house, stands in front of the Imperial Palace in Tōkyō, and his statue of SAIGŌ TAKAMORI, one of the heroes of the Meiji Restoration (1868), stands in Ueno Park, Tōkyō. The Aged Monkey, an early sculpture in wood exhibited at the Chicago World's Fair in 1893, won international acclaim. His eldest son, TAKAMURA KŌTARŌ, was a well-known poet and sculptor.

Aya Louisa McDONALD

Takamure Itsue (1894–1964)

Historian and feminist, known for her pioneering research in women's history. Born in Kumamoto Prefecture. Her formal schooling was interrupted by illness and financial problems; she worked briefly in a textile factory and then as a primary school teacher. In 1919 she married Hashimoto Kenzō (1897–1976), who later helped with her studies of social issues and women's history. In 1930 she joined with several other feminists, including HIRATSUKA RAICHŌ, in forming the Musan Fujin Geijutsu Remmei (Proletarian Women's Art League), a group sympathetic to anarchism; she wrote spirited articles for its monthly magazine, Fujin sensen (Women's Battlefront; 16 issues). Her direct involvement with activism was brief, however, and today she is best known for her many historical studies, especially those tracing the development of Japanese marriage patterns. Her major works include Bokeisei no kenkyū (1938), a study of matrilineal practices in ancient Japan; Shōseikon no kenkyū (1953), a study of the matrilocal pattern of marriage; and her monumental history of Japanese women, Josei no rekishi (4 vols, 1954–58). She also published an autobiography, Hi no kuni no onna no nikki (1965, Diary of a Woman from the Land of Fire [i.e., Kumamoto]). To commemorate her work, her husband published the magazine Takamure Itsue zasshi (1968–76; 31 issues).

Takano Chōei (1804–1850)

Scholar of Rangaku, or Dutch studies, as WESTERN LEARNING was known in the Edo period (1600–1868). Born in Mizusawa, Mutsu Province (now the city of Mizusawa in Iwate Prefecture) the son of a physician, he was adopted by an uncle who had studied with the Rangaku scholar SUGITA GEMPAKU. In 1820 he went to Edo (now Tōkyō) to study with Sugita Hakugen (1763–1833), Gempaku's adopted son. Five years later Takano went to Nagasaki to study medicine at the Narutakijuku, the school operated by Philipp Franz von SIEBOLD, and in 1826 he was awarded the degree of ''Doktor.''

In 1830 Takano, who had relinquished the headship of his family, began medical practice in Edo, at the same time lecturing and working on his book Seisetsu igen sūyō (1832, Outline of Principles of Western Medicine), one of the first Japanese treatises on modern physiology. It was at about this time that he formed, together with WATANABE KAZAN, OZEKI SAN'EI, and other Rangaku scholars, an informal study group called the SHŌSHIKAI. On learning that the Tokugawa shogunate had decided to enforce its NATIONAL SECLUSION policy and turn away the American ship Morrison, which had offered to return Japanese castaways (see MORRISON INCIDENT), Takano wrote Bojutsu yume monogatari (1838, Tale of a Dream), in which he criticized the government's short-sighted policies. As a result, in 1839 he was arrested in the shogunate's roundup of Rangaku scholars known as the BANSHA NO GOKU. Takano was sentenced to life imprisonment but in 1844 he escaped during a prison fire. Traveling incognito, he managed to elude the authorities, even lecturing for a while in the Uwajima domain (now part of Ehime Prefecture). Takano returned to Edo under an alias in 1850, having first altered his features with chemicals, but in December of that year he was captured by shogunal officials and committed suicide.

In addition to his translations and writings on medicine, Takano wrote on physics, chemistry, and military science. His autobiography, *Tori no naku ne* (The Song of a Bird), is included in his collected works.

——Takano Chōei, *Takano Chōei zenshū*, vols 1–4 (Takano Chōei Zenshū Kankō Kai, 1930–31; repr Daiichi Shobō, 1978), vols 5–6 (Daiichi Shobō, 1980–82). Takano Chōun, *Takano Chōei den* (1943). KATAGIRI Kazuo

Takano Fusatarō (1868–1904)

Pioneer in the labor movement in Japan. Born in what is now Nagasaki Prefecture. He went to the United States in 1886 and worked as a laborer in the San Francisco area. In 1890, with fellow Japanese immigrants, he organized the Shokkō Giyūkai (Fraternal Society of Workers) for mutual aid and for study of American labor problems with a view to future reference in Japan. He returned to Japan in 1896, and in 1897, while working for the *Japan Advertiser*, an English-language paper, he formed, together with KATAYAMA SEN and other labor leaders, the SHOKKŌ GIYŪKAI (Workers' Fraternal Society), Japan's first significant labor organization. He also founded Japan's first consumers' union in 1899. With the government's enactment of a new oppressive PUBLIC ORDER AND POLICE LAW (Chian Keisatsu Hō) the following year, the embryonic labor movement suffered an immediate setback. Takano, discouraged, left Japan for China, where he died. KURITA Ken

Takano Iwasaburō (1871–1949)

Statistician. Born in Nagasaki Prefecture. He was the first in Japan to apply social statistics to labor problems. After graduating from the Law School of Tōkyō University in 1895, he studied statistics in Germany under George von Mayer. After returning to Japan he was appointed professor at the law and economics schools of his alma mater, and gave the first lectures in Japan on statistics. He later became director of the ŌHARA INSTITUTE FOR SOCIAL RESEARCH and conducted the first family budget survey of working people, concentrating on the study of labor problems. TAKANO FUSATARŌ, an early labor leader, was his elder brother. His statistical studies include *Tōkyō ni okeru nijū shokugyō kakei chōsa* (1916, Family Budget Survey of Twenty Occupations in Tōkyō), and *Tōkeigaku kenkyū* (1915, Study of Statistics). YAMADA Katsumi

Takano Minoru (1901–1974)

Labor union leader. First secretary-general of SŌHYŌ (General Council of Trade Unions of Japan). Born in Tōkyō. Takano began to participate in the labor movement while he was a student at Waseda University, becoming a member of the JAPAN COMMUNIST PARTY in 1922. After he was expelled from Waseda, he devoted himself completely to the labor union movement, playing an active part in various labor groups until 1940. After World War II he was engaged in the reorganization of SŌDŌMEI (Japanese Federation of Labor) and was appointed its secretary-general in 1948. When Sōhyō was established in 1950, he became its first secretary-general and held the post until 1955. During his tenure, Takano was known for his support of the so-called three principles of peace (*heiwa sangensoku*): a comprehensive peace treaty, neutrality in the cold war, and opposition to military bases in Japan. He also believed in injecting his left-wing politics into the activities of the union as comprehensively as possible; he did this through practice of *gurumi undō* (inclusive movement), in which the family and local neighbors of union members were encouraged to participate in the activities of the union. KURITA Ken

Takano Sujū (1893–1976)

HAIKU poet; physician. Real name Takano Yoshimi. Born in Ibaraki Prefecture; graduate of Tōkyō University, where he specialized in medicine. Although a long-time professor of medical jurisprudence, he is best remembered for his haiku poems. He studied with the well-known poet TAKAHAMA KYOSHI and contributed regularly to the popular literary magazine HOTOTOGISU (published since 1897), which Kyoshi edited from 1898. From 1915 to 1925 Sujū was one of the "Four S's," the Hototogisu haiku school that also included MIZUHARA SHŪŌSHI, YAMAGUCHI SEISHI, and AWANO SEIHO. His po-

ems are noted for pure descriptions that are simple, yet buoyant. His collections of haiku include *Hatsugarasu* (1947) and *Seppen* (1952).

Takaoka

City in northwestern Toyama Prefecture, central Honshū. In the Nara period (710–794) Takaoka developed as a private estate (SHŌEN) of the temple TŌDAIJI and as the seat of a provincial capital (*kokufu*) and provincial temple (*kokubunji*). It was briefly a castle town after a castle was built in 1609 by Maeda Toshinaga. It is now a major commercial and industrial center, with traditional products such as copper ware and lacquer ware, and emerging pharmaceutical, pulp, and metal goods industries. Pop: 175,055.

Takaosan

Mountain in the city of Hachiōji, southwest of Tōkyō Prefecture, central Honshū, on the eastern edge of the Kantō Mountains. It has been an object of worship since ancient times. Because of its proximity to Tōkyō, it is a crowded recreational spot throughout the year. A cable car runs up to the summit, where there is an observation platform and the temple Yakuōin, of the Shingon sect of Buddhism. It is part of Meiji no Mori Takao Quasi-National Park. Height: 600 m (1,968 ft).

Takarabe Takeshi (1867–1949)

Navy minister, 1923–27 and 1929–30, and delegate to the London naval arms limitation conference of 1930; a central figure in the ensuing controversy over ratification of the London naval treaty. Born in Hyūga Province (now Miyazaki Prefecture). After graduating from the Naval Academy and the Naval Staff College, he served in the Sino-Japanese War (1894–95). Takarabe studied for two years in England and, returning to Japan, held a series of posts that prepared him for distinguished service in the naval section of Imperial Headquarters during the Russo-Japanese War of 1904–05. He married the eldest daughter of Admiral YAMAMOTO GONNOHYŌE, the "father" of the modern Japanese navy.

In 1909 Takarabe was promoted to rear admiral and became vice-minister of the navy. He held this post until 1914 when, together with Prime Minister Yamamoto Gonnohyōe, he resigned, taking "political responsibility" for the SIEMENS INCIDENT, a scandal involving naval construction contracts. Although in no way personally implicated, Takarabe suffered a temporary professional setback. He was brought back to prominence by Navy Minister KATŌ TOMOSABURŌ, who made him commander of the Sasebo Naval Station in 1918, promoted him to full admiral in 1919, and named him commander of the Yokosuka Naval Station in 1922. The following year Takarabe became navy minister in the Katō Tomosaburō cabinet.

As navy minister Takarabe presided over a navy beset with problems. Senior officers were caught between their commitment to the principle of arms limitation embodied in the WASHINGTON NAVAL TREATY OF 1922 and their desire to possess more and newer auxiliary surface ships, aircraft, and submarines. As the size of the officer corps declined and the struggle for Diet approval of naval budgets became more bitter, navy men felt increasingly isolated and humiliated. The navy was also frustrated in efforts to define strategic priorities. While Admiral Takarabe and the chief of the Naval General Staff worked out a new strategic posture and a force level definition with their army counterparts in 1923, the two services could not agree on specific war plans. In 1927 the navy agreed to seek further arms limitation at the Geneva conference. The collapse of the talks in Anglo-American discord led to the continuance of Japanese demands for a strength ratio of 7 in auxiliary craft against 10 each for the United States and Great Britain.

In 1929 Takarabe was appointed a delegate to the first of the LONDON NAVAL CONFERENCES. He hoped to attain a 10:10:7 ratio in cruiser strength. The conference ended with a compromise that imposed a 10:10:6 ratio on eight-inch gun cruisers but allowed the Imperial Japanese Navy its desired 70-percent strength ratio in other cruisers and destroyers and parity in submarines. This settlement angered the chief of the Naval General Staff, Admiral KATŌ HIROHARU, who protested that the cabinet had not taken his views into proper consideration (see TŌSUIKEN). Right-wing groups and opposition party leaders took up Katō's arguments to attack the HAMAGUCHI OSACHI cabinet, and when Admiral Takarabe returned to Japan in May 1930, he was presented with a suicide dagger by an ultranationalist.

Determined to overcome opposition, Takarabe replaced his vice-minister and the vice chief of the Naval General Staff and acquiesced in Katō Hiroharu's resignation as chief of the Naval General Staff. Prime Minister Hamaguchi and former Navy Minister Admiral OKADA KEISUKE were able to neutralize dissent among navy members of the Supreme War Council and within the Privy Council, and the treaty was approved by both bodies. Exhausted by the struggle over the treaty and fiscal 1931 budget, Takarabe resigned as navy minister on 3 October 1930, the day after the ratification of the treaty.
📖——Bōeichō Bōei Kenshūjo Senshishitsu, ed, *Daihon'ei kaigunbu rengō kantai,* vol 1 (1975). Itō Takashi, *Shōwa shoki seiji shi kenkyū* (1969). *Japan Biographical Encyclopedia and Who's Who* (1964). Thomas F. Mayer-Oakes, ed and tr, *Fragile Victory* (1968).
Roger DINGMAN

Takarai Kikaku (1661–1707)

Also known as Enomoto Kikaku. HAIKU poet of the early part of the Edo period (1600–1868); born in Edo (now Tōkyō), son of a physician. Considered a leading disciple of BASHŌ. After his master's death in 1694, Kikaku founded the Edoza school of haiku, which diverged from Bashō's style in its urbane spirit and its emphasis on novelty, wit, and rhetorical flourish. With HATTORI RANSETSU, Kikaku edited *Minashiguri* (1683), the first collection of haiku by Bashō and his disciples. The most complete collection of his own haiku is *Gogenshū* (1747).

takara kuji → lotteries, public

Takara Shuzō Co, Ltd

A distiller of such alcoholic beverages as SAKE, it is the largest domestic producer of the sweetened cooking wine called *mirin,* and of *shōchū,* a distilled drink made from rice or sweet potatoes. Established in 1842, after World War II it expanded to become a comprehensive liquor maker. It also engaged in beer brewing from 1957 to 1967. Since the 1970s it has been developing new fermented products, including pharmaceuticals and feedstuffs. Sales for the fiscal year ending March 1982 totaled ¥71 billion (US $295 million) and the company was capitalized at ¥10.6 billion (US $44 million). Its head office is in Kyōto.

Takarazuka

City in southeastern Hyōgo Prefecture, western Honshū. Known for its hot springs since the 8th century, it is now a residential satellite city of both Ōsaka and Kōbe. Tree and plant nurseries, as well as several zoological and botanical gardens, are located here. The city's name is most often associated with its all-female revue troupe (the TAKARAZUKA KAGEKIDAN), founded in 1914. Pop: 183,628.

Takarazuka Kagekidan

(literally, "the Takarazuka Opera Company"; prior to 1940 the Takarazuka Girls Opera Company). All-female troupes which specialize in musical spectacles. Entertainment tycoon and politician KOBAYASHI ICHIZŌ (1873–1957) organized the troupe in 1913 as the principal attraction for his Takarazuka resort area near Ōsaka. He proclaimed that his young girl singers and dancers would provide "strictly wholesome entertainment suitable for women and children from good families." Within a few years, several Takarazuka troupes were touring the major cities as they capitalized on the growing popularity of European-influenced popular music. Kobayashi subsequently opened a school in Takarazuka to develop talent for the company and constructed large Takarazuka theaters in Takarazuka (1922) and Tōkyō (1934).

Since 1930, Takarazuka has been divided into four separate troupes: Tsuki (Moon), Hana (Flower), Yuki (Snow), and Hoshi (Star). Each has its own distinct characteristics and loyal supporters.

Along with the all-male KABUKI and NŌ theaters, Takarazuka is yet another manifestation of the pervasive Japanese obsession with the androgyne performer. The major stars are "beauties in men's clothing" who perform the male roles. With its official motto of "clean, proper, and beautiful," Takarazuka has generally appealed to teenage girls. Although alumnae of the company have often gone on to become distinguished film and stage actresses, the writers and other principal talents behind Takarazuka are all men.

Like many other Japanese theatrical forms, a Takarazuka program is usually a potpourri arranged to show off the versatility of its performers. Takarazuka features spectacular production numbers (often on the scale of Hollywood musicals of the 1930s), tabloid operettas, and star turns. Materials range from Japanese traditional dances to romantic musical tales in overseas settings. The distinctive achievement of Takarazuka is the scope and amazing depth of its singers. Their pasticcio ranges from European operatic aria, chanson, and the latest international pop tunes through Japanese classic NAGAUTA and folk songs.

The rival Shōchiku (see SHŌCHIKU CO, LTD) entertainment organization created its own Girls Opera Company in 1922 and eventually replicated the success of Takarazuka. The Shōchiku version emphasizes dancing instead of singing (despite the name of the troupe), scale (larger theaters and wider stages with up to 300 performers in one show), and a shift in basic appeal away from daughters of the middle class who follow Takarazuka toward those of small shop owners.

During the past half century, landmark Takarazuka shows have included *Mon Pari* (Mon Paris), *Shinderera* (Cinderella), *Hofuman monogatari* (Tales of Hoffman), *Pari no kishi* (Parisian Chevaliers), *Ningen banzai* (Hurrah for Humanity), *Burigadōn* (Brigadoon), and *Kareinaru sembyōshi* (The Splendor of a Thousand Rhythms).
📖——Takarazuka Kagekidan, ed, *Takarazuka Kagekidan no rokujūnen* (1974). Hata Toyokichi, *Takarazuka to Nichigeki* (1948).
J. L. ANDERSON

Takasago

City in southern Hyōgo Prefecture, western Honshū, on the Inland Sea. The city developed as a port and rice-shipping center during the Edo period (1600–1868). It has textile, machinery, concrete, firebrick, pharmaceutical, and paper factories. Its once lovely coastline provided the setting for the Nō play *Takasago.* Pop: 85,463.

Takasago Thermal Engineering Co, Ltd

(Takasago Netsugaku Kōgyō). The largest Japanese company specializing in the design and installation of air conditioning equipment. Established in 1923. Its branch in Singapore handles installation of air conditioning equipment throughout Southeast Asia and provides technical guidance to nine countries. In the early 1980s it expanded its operations in the field of industrial air conditioning. Sales for the fiscal year ending March 1982 totaled ¥81 billion (US $336.5 million) and the company was capitalized at ¥1.8 billion (US $7.5 million). Its head office is in Tōkyō.

Takasaki

City in southern Gumma Prefecture, central Honshū. During the Edo period (1600–1868) it was a flourishing POST-STATION TOWN on the highways Nakasendō and Mikuni Kaidō. Traditional products include silk, dyes, and flour. Machinery, chemicals, and metal goods are also manufactured. A huge statue of the bodhisattva KANNON (42 m or 138 ft) and an annual DARUMA FAIR in January, at which *daruma* dolls are sold, attract visitors. Pop: 221,432.

Takasakiyama

Volcano near Beppu Bay, Ōita Prefecture, Kyūshū. Covered with warm-climate broadleaved trees, it is a habitat of wild monkeys. It is currently a natural zoo and part of the Inland Sea National Park. Height: 628 m (2,060 ft).

Takasegawa

Canal in the southern part of the city of Kyōto, central Honshū. It flows north to south from Nijō parallel to the river KAMOGAWA before joining the BIWAKO CANAL at Fushimi. Built in the Edo period (1600–1868) by SUMINOKURA RYŌI, it was a vital link in a system of waterways for transporting passengers and produce such as rice, lumber, and firewood between Kyōto and Ōsaka. Length: 10 km (6 mi).

Takashima Coal Mine

(Takashima Tankō). One of the largest and most important mines in Japan; located on the small island of Takashima, south of Nagasaki.

It was discovered in the early 18th century and came under the control of the Saga domain in the Bunka era (1804–17). In 1868 the domain established joint management of the mine with the British firm Glover & Company (see GLOVER, THOMAS BLAKE) and installed a ventilating system and steam-driven machinery for hoisting coal. In 1870 Glover went bankrupt and was replaced by the Dutch company Bauduin. With the abolition of domains (see PREFECTURAL SYSTEM, ESTABLISHMENT OF) in the following year, the mine came under government ownership for a time but later was sold to GOTŌ SHŌJIRŌ (see KAN'EI JIGYŌ HARAISAGE), who in turn sold it to MITSUBISHI in 1881. The mine was an important source of income for Mitsubishi in its formative years. During the period of government control, convicts were used for labor, and as a result of harsh working conditions, the Takashima mine was the scene of outbreaks of violence. There were incidents even after it came under Mitsubishi management, and an exposé, published by the magazine *Nihonjin* (The Japanese) in 1888, brought the problem to national attention.

TANAKA Akira

Takashima Shūhan (1798–1866)

Pioneering authority in Western military science. Popularly regarded as the introducer of modern Western artillery to Japan. Born in Nagasaki, Takashima became interested in Western arms through contact with Dutch traders. In 1814 he was placed in charge of the fortification at DEJIMA, and thereafter he imported Western firearms and tried to reproduce them. The Tokugawa shogunate (1603–1867) ordered him to give a demonstration of Western artillery in 1841, but it disapproved of the wide dissemination of Takashima's specialized knowledge, and in 1842 he was jailed. He was banished in 1846 and placed in the custody of the Annaka domain (in what is now Gumma Prefecture) until 1853. Two years later he was appointed head instructor of the newly established shogunal military training center and thereafter was invited by many *daimyō* to instruct their men in his teachings, known as Takashimaryū. Takashima exerted a major influence on military tactics in the last two years of the Edo period.

Takashimaya Co, Ltd

Major department store company, ranking first in Japan in annual domestic sales. Established in 1919, its forerunner was a cotton goods store established in Kyōto in 1831. The company has department stores in Ōsaka, Tōkyō, Kyōto, Sakai, Rakusai, and Wakayama. It has created separate companies to operate stores in other cities, and now leads a department store group of 11 companies with 18 stores. It has also formed a group that distributes commodities to provincial department stores. In 1982 it had one store in the United States and one in France, as well as six overseas offices. Sales in the fiscal year ending February 1982 totaled ¥441 billion (US $1.9 billion); sales for the entire Takashimaya group amounted to ¥762 billion (US $3.2 billion). In the same year the company was capitalized at ¥10.6 billion (US $45.1 million). Its head office is in Ōsaka.

Takasugi Shinsaku (1839–1867)

A retainer of the Chōshū domain (now Yamaguchi Prefecture) and a central figure in the movement to overthrow the Tokugawa shogunate (1603–1867). He was born in the castle town of Hagi, the eldest son of Takasugi Kochūta, a low-ranking *samurai*. He attended the domain school, Meirinkan, but from 1857 he studied at the Shōka Sonjuku, the school run by the noted proimperial ideologue YOSHIDA SHŌIN. During this period he became acquainted with SAKUMA SHŌZAN through Yoshida's introduction. In 1860 Takasugi studied navigation at the shogunate training school Gunkan Kyōjusho and put his knowledge to use by sailing to Edo (now Tōkyō). In 1862 he was sent by his domain in a shogunate ship to Shanghai, where he heard the guns of the Taiping (T'ai-p'ing) Rebellion and saw at first hand the realities of a country reduced to semicolonial status. From that experience he became convinced that Japan must strengthen itself to avoid a similar fate and came to the opinion that the shogunate must be overthrown by force.

On 25 June 1863 (Bunkyū 3.5.10) Chōshū artillery fired on foreign ships passing through the Shimonoseki Strait, and Takasugi was ordered to organize a militia, the KIHEITAI, to defend the domain from retaliation. The Kiheitai, which enlisted samurai and commoners alike, became the core of Chōshū's fighting forces and provided a base for Takasugi's political activities. In 1864 he was

imprisoned for leaving Chōshū without official permission. In the meantime Chōshū had continued its attacks on foreign ships, and in September a fleet of 17 Western vessels demolished its coastal fortifications (see SHIMONOSEKI BOMBARDMENT). The Western powers also demanded indemnity, and the domain called on Takasugi to deal with them. Later in 1864 Chōshū was defeated by a punitive expedition mounted by the shogunate (see CHŌSHŪ EXPEDITIONS). This led to the replacement of the reformist faction by a conservative one, and Takasugi fled to Kyūshū. He soon returned, and from late 1864 to the beginning of 1865 he led Kiheitai units in a coup against the conservative clique in Chōshū and together with KIDO TAKAYOSHI took over the leadership of the domain. In 1866 another shogunate expedition was sent against Chōshū for failure to observe the terms of its surrender two years earlier. This time, domainal forces under Takasugi repelled the shogunate army. Chōshū's victory thoroughly discredited the shogunate and opened the way for other antishogunate domains to take united action. Takasugi had long suffered from tuberculosis, and he died in 1867, the year before the MEIJI RESTORATION.

TANAKA Akira

Takataya Kahei (1769–1827)

A wealthy trader of the early 19th century who opened new trade routes to EZO (now Hokkaidō and the Kuril Islands) and helped the Tokugawa shogunate to develop the area for defense against possible encroachment by Russia. Born into a poor family in Awaji Province (now part of Hyōgo Prefecture), Kahei went to the port of Hyōgo (now Kōbe) and worked as a pilot before founding his own shipping business in 1795. He specialized in transporting commodities such as clothing, tobacco, and salt to northeasten Japan, with lines extending as far as Hakodate in Ezo. In 1799 the shogunate, wary of the Russian presence in that area, decided to carry out a survey of Etorofu, the largest of the Kuril Islands. Hoping to win sole trading rights for Ezo products, Kahei volunteered his services as an aide to KONDŌ JŪZŌ, a shogunate official who explored in Ezo. He was suitably rewarded in 1806 and, establishing his headquarters in Hakodate, built up a thriving business between Ezo and the home islands. In 1812 Kahei and four members of his crew were seized by a Russian ship off the Kuril Islands in retaliation for Japan's detention of the Russian naval officer Vasilii Mikhailovich GOLOVNIN a year earlier. Kahei was taken to Kamchatka but persuaded his captors to free him and returned to Japan in 1813. He then worked successfully to have Golovnin released. Kahei was once again awarded exclusive trade rights in Ezo, but he soon retired and left the business to his brother and an adopted son.

Takata Yasuma (1883–1972)

Sociologist and economist who contributed significantly to the development of sociological theory in Japan before World War II. Born in Saga Prefecture. After graduating from Kyōto University, he taught at Tōkyō Shōka Daigaku (now Hitotsubashi University), Kyūshū University, and Ōsaka University. He strove to establish sociology as a separate and independent scientific discipline in Japan, criticizing the then dominant school of sociology, which heavily influenced by Herbert Spencer and Auguste Comte, sought to incorporate the principles of political science and other social sciences. Influenced by the theories of Georg Simmel, Ferdinand Tönnies, Franklin H. Giddings, and Robert MacIver, he adopted a psychological approach. Takata was also critical of Marxist theory; he felt that the cause of all social change lay in population growth and called his approach the third or sociological view of history in contrast to materialistic and idealistic interpretations. Representative writings are *Shakaigaku gairon* (1922), *Kaikyū oyobi daisan shikan* (1925), and *Shakai to kokka* (1922).

HASUMI Otohiko

Takatō

Town in south central Nagano Prefecture, central Honshū. During the Edo period (1600–1868) Takatō developed as a castle town of the Naitō family. The cherry blossoms at the site of Takatō Castle attract visitors in April. Pop: 8,761.

Takatori ware

(takatori-yaki). Ceramics made at kiln sites in or near present-day Nōgata and Fukuoka, Fukuoka Prefecture, Kyūshū. Produced from 1601 to almost the end of the Edo period (1600–1868), this ware was made for both everyday and TEA CEREMONY use, but is best known for the latter. The kilns were operated under the auspices of the Kuroda *daimyō* family and started by Korean potters. The early kilns were Takuma (1601–14) at the foot of the mountain Takatori-san, Uchigaiso (1614–24), Yamada (1624–30), and Sengoku (1624–?). After 1610 the kilns came under the direction of the Korean potter Pal San (J: Hachizan, later known as Takatori Hachizō). They produced thickly and freely potted everyday and tea-ceremony wares with emphasis on the former, employing sea slug glazes or thick, opaque white-straw or wood-ash glazes resembling those found on old KARATSU WARE. During the "Enshū period" (1630–65) the Kuroda *daimyō* sent Hachizan and his son to the famous tea master KOBORI ENSHŪ for guidance in making tea wares, and they began producing sophisticated, elegant, thin-walled pieces with what was to become a characteristic lustrous, dark toffee-brown glaze. During the "Koishiwara period" (1665–late Edo), the Tsuzumi kiln in Koishiwara made only tea wares, most notably tea caddies, and the Nakano kiln produced everyday pieces. The "Fukuoka Sarayama period" (1716–late Edo) runs consecutively with the "Koishiwara period." Two kilns were operated near Fukuoka Castle, one making tea wares for *daimyō* use and the other, everyday wares for general consumption. Porcelains were also made at a number of kilns, but these have not been closely studied. In 1860 the 11th-generation Kuroda *daimyō* reopened the Sarayama kilns for the mass production of high-quality porcelains. Production has not been continuous. Among the modern ceramists who specialize in Takatori ware, the best known is the 11th-generation woman potter, Takatori Seizan (b 1907). *Frederick* BAEKELAND

Takatsuki

City in northeastern Ōsaka Prefecture, central Honshū. During the Sengoku period (1467–1568) Takatsuki developed as a POST-STATION TOWN on the highway Saigoku Kaidō. It then became a castle town of the 16th century Christian *daimyō* TAKAYAMA UKON, who was later expelled from Japan for his beliefs. It is a residential and industrial suburb of Ōsaka; principal products are electric appliances, machinery, chemicals, metals, and foodstuffs. Tumuli (KOFUN) and other prehistoric remains are located here. Pop: 340,722.

Takayama

City in northern Gifu Prefecture, central Honshū. Takayama developed from 1586 as a castle town of the Kanamori family. It came under the direct jurisdiction of the Tokugawa shogunate in 1692. Its chief industry is lumbering. *Shunkei-nuri*, a type of LACQUER WARE, has long been famous. With its beautiful setting and old houses, several of which have been converted into folk art museums, the city draws visitors throughout the year. The Takayama Festival in April and skiing in the northern Japanese Alps and on the mountain Norikuradake are added attractions. Pop: 63,813.

Takayama Basin

(Takayama Bonchi). In northern Gifu Prefecture, central Honshū. Situated along the river Miyagawa and the upper reaches of the Jinzūgawa. This basin is located at a high altitude, which accounts for its severe winters. Rice is cultivated along the Miyagawa. The area draws numerous tourists. The major city is Takayama. Area: approximately 30 sq km (12 sq mi).

Takayama Chogyū (1871–1902)

Literary critic, novelist. Real name Saitō Rinjirō. Born in Yamagata Prefecture. Graduate of Tōkyō University. After gaining recognition for his historical romance *Takiguchi Nyūdō* (1894), he wrote critical essays for the magazines *Teikoku bungaku* and *Taiyō*. Regarding the TRIPARTITE INTERVENTION of Western powers after Japan's victory in the Sino-Japanese War of 1894–95 as a national humiliation, he vigorously advocated a Japanese nationalism (Nihon shugi) that went so far as to reject not only Christianity but also Buddhism as alien to the Japanese character. He is best remembered for his later enthusiasm for the philosophy of Nietzsche and for the 13th-century Buddhist leader NICHIREN, who, in his eyes, embodied the Nietzschean heroic ideal. In his essay "Biteki seikatsu o ronzu" (1901), he called for reliance on instinct and the veneration of genius. His brand of romantic individualism, extremely popular during the 1890s and early 1900s, profoundly influenced the thought and literature of the period.

Takayama

Two of a number of elaborate high-wheeled floats pulled through the streets during the Takayama Festival held in April.

Takayama Hikokurō (1747–1793)

Emperor worshiper famed for the extremity of his infatuation with the nobility and the imperial line. Born in Kōzuke Province (now Gumma Prefecture), the son of a rural *samurai* (GŌSHI). Takayama made several trips to the imperial capital of Kyōto to visit the graves and residences of court nobles and royal personages and to persuade all he could of the legitimacy of the emperor's authority. The Tokugawa shogunate exerted pressure on Takayama and his hosts in an attempt to stop his activities, even destroying the home of a noble who had housed him. Takayama then left Kyōto for Kyūshū, hoping to inspire more imperial loyalists, but, unable to escape hounding by shogunate authorities, he finally committed suicide. Takayama's bizarre acts of homage (well-known examples are his practice of prostrating himself at the Sanjō Bridge in Kyōto in the direction of the Imperial Palace and his whipping the grave of ASHIKAGA TAKAUJI, a villain to all imperial loyalists) earned him inclusion among the Three Eccentrics (Sankijin) of the Kansei era (1789–1801), together with GAMŌ KUMPEI and HAYASHI SHIHEI.

Takayama Sōzei (?–1455)

Poet of *renga* (linked verse), critic, and Buddhist priest. He was born into a military family, but took holy orders at least before 1427. He studied classical poetry with the great SHŌTETSU, and linked verse with the master ASAYAMA BONTŌ. In 1448 he was appointed grand master (*sōshō*) of the official Renga Center at the Kitano Shrine in Kyōto, a prestigious office which he occupied until his death. One of the most eminent linked-verse poets of the 15th century, he was ranked by the master SŌGI as one of the "Seven Sages of Renga" (Renga Shichiken), on a par with SHINKEI. He was instrumental in reviving linked verse in the early 1400s, collaborating with the great scholar and court noble ICHIJŌ KANEYOSHI on important enterprises, including preparing a revised and enlarged edition of the official rules of linked verse known as *Renga shinshiki kon'an* (Current Revision of the New Rules of Renga), completed in 1452. He was also the author of several handbooks and critical works, especially: *Shoshin kyūei shū* (Principles of Composition for Aspiring Poets), a collection of his teacher Bontō's pronouncements written shortly after the latter's death; *Hana no magaki* (Blossoms by the Sacred Fence), an exposition of various kinds of *renga* linkings and styles written for a pupil in 1452; and *Kokon rendan shū* (Discussions of Renga, Ancient and Modern), a treatise written in the late 1440s on important poetic masters and schools, together with exemplary verses with critical and exegetical notes. See also RENGA AND HAIKAI.

📖 ——Earl Miner, *Japanese Linked Poetry* (1979).

Robert H. BROWER

Takayama Ukon (1552?–1615)

The best known of the CHRISTIAN DAIMYŌ. The son of Takayama Zusho (d 1594), one of the first protectors of the Jesuit mission in the Kyōto area, Ukon was baptized Justo in 1564. He first made a name for himself in the fashion of the Sengoku period by killing his lord Wata Korenaga in 1573, and thereby obtained the domain of Takatsuki (southwest of Kyōto) for the Takayama. In 1578 Ukon betrayed his new lord, Araki Murashige (d 1586), in favor of the hegemon ODA NOBUNAGA to prevent a threatened persecution of Christianity; thereafter he ordered the Christianization of the people of Takatsuki. Ukon played a key role in the Battle of YAMAZAKI (1582), in which TOYOTOMI HIDEYOSHI won for himself the succession to the murdered Nobunaga's hegemony, and also served Hideyoshi in other campaigns. In 1585 Ukon was transferred from Takatsuki to the richer domain of Akashi in Harima Province (now part of Hyōgo Prefecture); here he again endeavored to convert the entire populace. When Hideyoshi issued his ANTI-CHRISTIAN EDICTS in 1587, he dispossessed Ukon, castigating him for his religious zeal. In 1588 Ukon was placed under the supervision of the *daimyō* MAEDA TOSHIIE of Kaga Province (now part of Ishikawa Prefecture); eventually he attained high status in the Maeda house but was dispossessed again when the Tokugawa shogunate undertook a general persecution of Christianity in 1614. Banished from Japan in November 1614, Ukon died in Manila on 5 February 1615. A highly cultivated man, Ukon was particularly accomplished in the arts of tea, ranking among the "Seven Great Disciples" (Rikyū Shittetsu) of the tea master SEN NO RIKYŪ.

George ELISON

Takayanagi Kenjirō (1899–   )

Electrical engineer. The father of Japanese television. He successfully engineered the first television transmission in Japan in 1926, and in 1933 developed an iconoscope (the main component in a television camera) only months behind the work of Vladimir K. Zworykin (b 1889) of the United States. Born in Shizuoka Prefecture, Takayanagi studied at a technical school in Tōkyō. He became professor at Hamamatsu Kōtō Kōgyō Gakkō (Hamamatsu Higher Technical College) in 1930. Then in 1937 he joined the Japan Broadcasting Corporation (NHK). He was director of NHK's Technical Laboratory when he joined VICTOR CO OF JAPAN, LTD, in 1946. His publications include *Terebijon kōgaku* (1959, Television Engineering) and *Terebijon* (1950, Television).

Takayanagi Kenzō (1887–1967)

Scholar of Anglo-American law. Born in Saitama Prefecture, he graduated from Tōkyō University in 1912 and, apart from a period of study in the United States and Europe (1915–20), taught in its law faculty until his retirement in 1948. Takayanagi was particularly interested in legal history and comparative law. In 1946, as a member of what was then the House of Peers, he was appointed to a committee to discuss the draft of the new CONSTITUTION. When the question of revising the 1947 constitution arose in the 1950s, Takayanagi was named chairman of the COMMISSION ON THE CONSTITUTION (1957–65) and, because of his impartiality, became one of the most respected defenders of the new constitution. *John M. MAKI*

Takebe Ayatari (1719–1774)

HAIKU and WAKA poet, author of YOMIHON, and artist of the middle part of the Edo period (1600–1868). Real name Kitamura Kingo Hisamura. Born in Edo (now Tōkyō), the son of a house elder (*karō*) in the Hirosaki domain (now part of Aomori Prefecture). His mother was the daughter of DAIDŌJI YŪZAN, the famous theoretician of BUSHIDŌ (the *samurai* code). At the age of 20, he ran away when his love affair with his elder brother's wife was discovered, embarking on a variegated career. He went first to Kyōto and then to Edo (now Tōkyō), where he studied haiku and became established as a poet and master, writing under the name Ryōtai. He advocated that haiku should be returned to older forms and attempted to revive a verse form known as *katauta*. In his 30s, he went to Nagasaki, where he studied the literati style of painting known as NANGA and

painted under the name Kan'yōsai. In his later years, Takebe wrote novels that are chiefly noteworthy as early examples of the *yomihon* genre. Said to be eccentric and to have pursued art for art's sake, he did not find complete success in any one area. His best known novels are *Nishiyama monogatari* (1768) and *Honchō suikoden* (1773).

Takebe Katahiro (1664–1739)

Mathematician. Coauthor of *Taisei sankyō* (1712), a 20-volume compilation of the achievements of Japanese mathematics. Born in Edo (now Tōkyō), he entered the school of SEKI TAKAKAZU at the age of thirteen. His published works on algebra, actually commentaries and notes on algebraic techniques developed by Seki, helped to spread knowledge of higher mathematics in Japan.

Takechi no Kurohito (fl ca 690–710)

Court official; poet. The correct pronunciation of his name is uncertain: it may be Takaichi instead of Takechi and Kuroto rather than Kurohito. Very little is known about him apart from notes accompanying his poems—comprising a total of only 19 *tanka*—in the MAN'YŌSHŪ (ca 759), the first great anthology of Japanese vernacular poetry. It is believed that like KAKINOMOTO NO HITOMARO, YAMABE NO AKAHITO, and other court poets of the *Man'yō* age, he was an official of low rank who served as one of the small but important group of "poets laureate" who accompanied sovereigns on excursions, composing auspicious and laudatory poetry on demand. That all of Kurohito's surviving poems are on travel is not surprising, but that he is so celebrated for such a relatively meager number of surviving poems is due to his skill at "objective description" of nature—a mode of which he is considered one of the pioneers of his age and which is highly prized by modern critics and enthusiasts.

📖 ——Ian H. Levy, *The Ten Thousand Leaves* (1981–). Nippon Gakujutsu Shinkōkai, *The Man'yōshū: One Thousand Poems* (1940, repr 1965).

Robert H. BROWER

Takechi Zuizan (1829–1865)

Master swordsman and proimperial activist from the Tosa domain (now Kōchi Prefecture). The son of a rural *samurai* (GŌSHI), Zuizan early established himself as a master of swordsmanship. In 1856 and 1857 he studied at fencing academies in Edo (now Tōkyō) and associated with other fencing students, many of whom would later become SONNŌ JŌI (Revere the Emperor, Expel the Barbarians) activists. He opened his own school after returning to Tosa, but early in 1861 he went again to Edo, where he met *sonnō jōi* activists from the Satsuma (now Kagoshima Prefecture) and Chōshū (now Yamaguchi Prefecture) domains. Influenced by their ideas, he returned to Tosa and organized 192 men, largely lower-ranking and rural samurai, into a loyalist group called the Tosa Kinnōtō (Tosa Loyalist Party). Members included SAKAMOTO RYŌMA and NAKAOKA SHINTARŌ. In 1862 his group murdered YOSHIDA TŌYŌ, an influential domainal adviser who supported the MOVEMENT FOR UNION OF COURT AND SHOGUNATE. The group was temporarily able to control domainal politics, but after the expulsion of *sonnō jōi* extremists from Kyōto in the summer of 1863, Tosa once again reverted to a position favoring reconciliation between the court and the shogunate. Zuizan and other loyalist leaders were arrested and in the summer of 1865 ordered to commit suicide.

Takeda Chemical Industries, Ltd

(Takeda Yakuhin Kōgyō). Manufacturer of pharmaceuticals and other chemical products. Founded in 1781, the company ranks first in the sale of pharmaceutical products in Japan. Its products include, besides fine chemicals, various chemical products such as food additives, industrial and agricultural chemicals, and animal health products. Active in overseas markets, the company exports many varieties of fine chemicals, such as vitamins and raw materials for local processing. Fine chemicals are shipped mainly to the United States and Europe, while some 70 kinds of raw materials are shipped to developing countries. In recent years, however, raw materials together with technology have increasingly been shipped to the West as well. There has also been an increase in the export of Ribotide, a new flavor enhancer; TDI, a material used in the manufacture of polyurethanes; and Padan, an agricultural insecticide.

Processing plants have been established in Southeast Asia and Mexico, and subsidiary distribution centers have been established in the United States, West Germany, and several locations in Southeast Asia. Recently sales promotion centers as well have been established in West Germany, and France. Sales for the fiscal year ending March 1982 totaled ¥460.4 billion (US $1.9 billion), of which pharmaceutical products accounted for 61 percent and nonpharmaceuticals 39 percent. In the same year the company was capitalized at ¥31.6 billion (US $131.3 million). The head office is located in Ōsaka.

Takeda family

Prominent military house of the Kamakura (1185–1333), Muromachi (1333–1568), and Azuchi-Momoyama (1568–1600) periods. The family traced its provenance back to Shinra Saburō Yoshimitsu (d 1127), a famous scion of the Seiwa Genji branch of the MINAMOTO FAMILY; its name derives from the residence of Yoshimitsu's great-grandson Nobuyoshi (d 1186) in Takeda, Mukawa no Shō, Kai Province (now the city of Nirasaki, Yamanashi Prefecture). Takeda Nobuyoshi fought for the future shōgun MINAMOTO NO YORITOMO in the TAIRA–MINAMOTO WAR (1180–1185); his son Nobumitsu (d 1248) distinguished himself in the service of the Kamakura shogunate during the JŌKYŪ DISTURBANCE of 1221, eventually being appointed SHUGO (military governor) of Aki Province (now part of Hiroshima Prefecture). It is assumed that the family played a major role in its home province of Kai during the Kamakura period, but the scanty historical records on shugo in Kai during that period show only that a Takeda served in that post between 1331 and 1333; the Takeda did, however, hold it throughout the Muromachi period. This shugo family came close to being destroyed when it took the losing side in the Rebellion of Uesugi Zenshū in 1416–17: Takeda Nobumitsu lost his life, and his heir, Nobushige (d 1450), fled Kai to seek refuge in the Shingon monastery on Mt. Kōya (Kōyasan). Nobushige was appointed military governor of Kai in 1423 but could not enter the province until 1438 because of the opposition of powerful local barons (KOKUJIN), such as the Hemmi and Anayama families, collaterals of the Takeda. In the Eikyō Disturbance, which broke out that year, the Takeda helped the shogunate to destroy its rebellious governor-general of the Kantō (Kamakura KUBŌ), Ashikaga Mochiuji (1398–1439), and reestablished themselves in Kai. Their hold on the province was, however, by no means secure: from 1492 to 1517, for instance, they were constantly threatened by family conflicts, vassals' revolts, and the incursions of their neighbors, Imagawa Ujichika (1473?–1526) of Sumpu and HŌJŌ SŌUN of Odawara. The family's position was finally consolidated by Takeda Nobutora (1498–1574), who succeeded to its headship in 1507 and over the next two decades managed to fend off external enemies while subduing the kokujin; Nobutora established the Takeda as a SENGOKU DAIMYŌ house. The house's fortunes reached their apogee under TAKEDA SHINGEN, who displaced his father Nobutora in 1541; but the Takeda house of Kai fell in 1582, when the hegemon ODA NOBUNAGA destroyed Shingen's son TAKEDA KATSUYORI.

The Takeda of Kai are the best known, but other branches of the family are as noteworthy. At least 10 Takeda were shugo of Aki Province under the Muromachi shogunate from 1336 to 1520, when they were supplanted by the ŌUCHI FAMILY. An offshoot of this lineage were military governors of Wakasa Province (now part of Fukui Prefecture) from 1440; there the Takeda supplanted the Isshiki family. The Takeda of Wakasa were known for their cultural pursuits: Kuninobu (1442–90) and his son Motonobu (1472?–1521), in particular, were noted amateurs of poetry. Successive heads of this house were devoted to compiling the rules of chivalrous bearing, especially of mounted archery (YABUSAME), developing a "Takeda school" of military etiquette (kyūba kojitsu). By the middle of the 16th century, this branch of the Takeda was in decline, unable to control Wakasa's local barons; by 1570 Wakasa was nothing more than an arena of contention for the outsiders Oda Nobunaga and ASAKURA YOSHIKAGE. The province fell under Nobunaga's sway; in 1582, when Nobunaga was killed in the HONNŌJI INCIDENT, Takeda Motoaki adhered to the assassin, AKECHI MITSUHIDE, but was captured and committed suicide, as had his relative Takeda Katsuyori of Kai. Thus the two major branches of the Takeda family were destroyed within four months and one week of each other.

George ELISON

Takeda Izumo

The name of a succession of managers of the Takemotoza, a puppet theater located in Ōsaka and first established in 1685. According to

tradition, Takeda Izumo I (d 1747) assumed control of the Takemotoza in 1705 and founded the well-known line. Besides attending to business affairs, he also demonstrated his skill as a writer and director of JŌRURI puppet plays. Kokusen'ya kassen (1715; tr The Battles of Coxinga, 1951), a renowned masterpiece by CHIKAMATSU MONZAEMON, is said to owe much of its original success to the spectacular staging conceived by Izumo I.

Like his father, Takeda Izumo II (also known as Geki, Koizumo I, and Senzenken; 1691–1756) was a gifted dramatist and director who began writing plays with encouragement from Chikamatsu. While Izumo II wrote several plays independently, he is best recognized for his collaborative efforts with NAMIKI SŌSUKE (1695–1751?), Miyoshi Shōraku (1706?–1772?), and others. His puppet plays are equally esteemed in KABUKI adaptations. His collaborations include Natsumatsuri Naniwa kagami (1745, The Summer Festival in Naniwa), Sugawara denju tenarai kagami (1746; tr Sugawara's Secrets of Penmanship, 1959), Yoshitsune sembonzakura (1747, The Thousand Cherry Blossoms of Yoshitsune), and Kanadehon chūshingura (1748, The Treasury of Loyal Retainers; tr Chūshingura, 1971).

After the death of Takeda Izumo II, his son Izumo III inherited Takemotoza. However, he could not stem the steadily declining fortunes of the puppet theater when, after the mid-18th century, kabuki swiftly regained the dominant position. By 1767, Takemotoza was forced to close temporarily. Eventually, Izumo III relinquished title to the theater, thus ending the Takeda Izumo succession.

■ ——Kitani Hōgin, Jōruri kenkyū sho (1941). Kuroki Kanzō, Jōruri shi (1943).

Ted T. TAKAYA

Takeda Katsuyori (1546–1582)

Daimyō of the Azuchi-Momoyama period (1568–1600); also known as Takeda Shirō. At the death of his father, TAKEDA SHINGEN, in 1573, Takeda rule extended over the provinces of Kai (now Yamanashi Prefecture), Shinano (now Nagano Prefecture), and Suruga (now part of Shizuoka Prefecture), as well as parts of Kōzuke (now Gumma Prefecture) and Hida (now part of Gifu Prefecture). This was a vast but unconsolidated domain, and Katsuyori, neither an effective nor a popular administrator, was not the man to preserve it in the face of the enmity of ODA NOBUNAGA and TOKUGAWA IEYASU, which he had also inherited from his father. He attempted to contest Tōtōmi (now part of Shizuoka Prefecture) with Ieyasu and maintained a foothold there from 1574 to 1581; when he invaded Ieyasu's home province of Mikawa (now part of Aichi Prefecture), however, he was routed by the combined forces of Nobunaga and Ieyasu in the Battle of NAGASHINO. Although Katsuyori recovered from this blow, his position became precarious when his ally Hōjō Ujimasa (1538–1590), the powerful daimyō of Odawara, transferred his support to Nobunaga and Ieyasu. Early in 1582 some of Katsuyori's most important vassals, such as Anayama Nobukimi (d 1582), went over to Nobunaga, who thereupon launched a massive invasion of the Takeda territories. Katsuyori was unable to resist this assault. Abandoned by all but a handful of his closest retainers, he fled into the mountains of Kai but was hunted down and committed suicide on 3 April 1582 (Tenshō 10.3.11). His domains were parceled out to Nobunaga's generals, but the destruction of the house of Takeda was Nobunaga's last great victory.

George ELISON

Takeda Kōunsai (1803–1865)

Samurai activist of the Mito domain (now part of Ibaraki Prefecture) and leader of the 1864 antiforeign MITO CIVIL WAR. As a high-ranking official, Takeda supported TOKUGAWA NARIAKI's domainal reforms and shared his SONNŌ JŌI (Revere the Emperor, Expel the Barbarians) ideology. In response to the growing sentiment against the Tokugawa shogunate for having opened the country, in 1864 hundreds of antiforeign activists gathered at Mt. Tsukuba under Fujita Koshirō, son of the sonnō jōi ideologue FUJITA TŌKO, to press for expulsion of foreigners from Japan. Takeda attempted to pacify the activists but in the end decided to lead them in a march to Kyōto to present their demands to the shōgun, who was then in attendance at the imperial court. The shogunate ordered the domains en route to suppress the revolt; after three months of hard fighting the insurgents were defeated. Takeda escaped but was captured and executed soon after.

Takeda Rintarō (1904–1946)

Novelist. Born in Ōsaka Prefecture. Studied at Tōkyō University. Influenced by the SHINKANKAKU SCHOOL of writers, he also participated in the labor movement while still a university student. He gained recognition as a writer of the so-called PROLETARIAN LITERATURE MOVEMENT with his antiwar short story "Bōryoku" (1929). Partly because of the government crackdown on leftist literature, he developed a more conventional style, borrowing from 17th-century novelist Ihara SAIKAKU's techniques to depict the life and character of peripheral members of urban society in such novels as *Nihon sammon opera* (1932) and *Ginza hatchō* (1934). His works are commonly referred to as *shiseimono* (urban life stories), although behind the trivial details describing urban life, there is sharp criticism of social injustice. Other works include the short story "Ichi no tori" (1935) and the unfinished novel *Ihara Saikaku* (1936).

Takeda Shingen (1521–1573)

Prominent *daimyō* of the Sengoku period (1467–1568) and the Azuchi-Momoyama period (1568–1600). He was named Harunobu at his coming of age in 1536; Shingen is a Buddhist name which he began using in about 1559.

The house of Takeda had been well established in Kai Province (now Yamanashi Prefecture) since the Kamakura period (1185–1333), and members of the family held the post of military governor *(shugo)* there throughout the Muromachi period (1333–1568). Shingen succeeded to this position in 1541 in true Sengoku fashion by expelling his father, Nobutora (1498–1574), and usurping the family headship. Having consolidated his hold on Kai, Shingen in 1542 invaded Shinano Province (now Nagano Prefecture). This vast and mountainous territory was divided among a multitude of petty arms-bearing landholders *(dogō)* whose mutual contentiousness facilitated Shingen's task. Nevertheless, it was not until 1559 that he succeeded in occupying most of the province's northern reaches. In that year the shōgun Ashikaga Yoshiteru (1536–65) appointed him *shugo* of Shinano, in effect legalizing the conquest.

The advance into northern Shinano inevitably brought Shingen into conflict with UESUGI KENSHIN, the great daimyō of Echigo Province (now part of Niigata Prefecture); after 1553 the two were involved in almost incessant warfare against each other. Their rivalry is the most famous in all of Sengoku history. Particularly celebrated is the series of battles they fought at KAWANAKAJIMA, a spot in northern Shinano dominating the approaches to Echigo, between 1553 and 1564.

In order to secure his southern and eastern flanks, Shingen in 1554 formed a tripartite alliance with the daimyō IMAGAWA YOSHIMOTO of SUMPU (now the city of Shizuoka) and Hōjō Ujiyasu (1515–71) of Odawara. That coalition began to crumble in 1565, when Shingen established ties with ODA NOBUNAGA, who had destroyed Yoshimoto at the Battle of OKEHAZAMA; it had collapsed by 1568, when Shingen and Nobunaga's ally TOKUGAWA IEYASU entered a compact to divide up the Imagawa provinces of Suruga and Tōtōmi (parts of what is now Shizuoka Prefecture). Shingen could not invade Suruga without clashing with the Later Hōjō family (see HŌJŌ FAMILY) of Odawara. He tried to safeguard himself in 1568 by proposing an alliance to none other than Uesugi Kenshin, but the project was foiled by a Hōjō demarche to Kenshin. Shingen's energetic advance into Suruga caused Ieyasu in 1570 also to ally himself with Kenshin; the next year, the erstwhile partners in the partition of the Imagawa domains were fighting over the spoils in Tōtōmi, and Shingen pressed the attack into Ieyasu's home territory of Mikawa Province (now part of Aichi Prefecture). Shingen's attentions were being drawn westward; hence, at the end of 1571, Shingen and the Hōjō were reconciled and again signed a treaty directed against Kenshin. The futility of 16th-century daimyō politics is perfectly illustrated by these tergiversations: the pattern of alliances formed and dissolved for the sake of a temporary advantage, without a governing long-range plan, is a Sengoku paradigm.

In 1572 Shingen mounted an offensive toward the west. Its purpose is unclear: commonly described as a march on Kyōto to eliminate Nobunaga and seize the hegemony over Japan's heartland, it was most likely just another regional foray. Its only lasting effect was indirect: Shingen's early successes, particularly his victory over the combined forces of Ieyasu and Nobunaga at Mikatagahara in Tōtōmi on 6 January 1573 (Genki 3.12.3), enticed the shōgun ASHIKAGA YOSHIAKI into an open break with Nobunaga, a move that led to the downfall of the Muromachi shogunate. A mortal disease forced Shingen to break off the campaign, and he died on his way home in Shinano on 13 May 1573 (Genki 4.4.12). Nine years later, Nobunaga eliminated his heirs and partitioned his domains.

——— Inoue Toshio, *Kenshin to Shingen* (1964). Isogai Masayoshi, *Takeda Shingen* (1971). Kōsaka Nobumasa, *Kōyō gunkan* (ca 1625), ed Isogai Masayoshi and Hattori Harunori, in *Sengoku shiryō sōsho*, vols 3–5 (Jimbutsu Ōraisha, 1965). Okuno Takahiro, *Takeda Shingen*, vol 19 of *Jimbutsu sōsho* (Yoshikawa Kōbunkan, 1959). Watanabe Yosuke, *Takeda Shingen no keirin to shūyō* (1971).

George ELISON

Takeda Taijun (1912–1976)

Novelist. Born in Tōkyō, son of a JŌDO SECT Buddhist priest. He entered Tōkyō University in 1931 to study Chinese literature but became involved in various left-wing activities; after several arrests and a month in jail he withdrew from school. In 1932, following in the family tradition, he was ordained a Buddhist priest. With a number of other young sinologists he founded the magazine *Chūgoku bungaku geppō* (later renamed *Chūgoku bungaku*) in 1934 for the publication of translations and research concerning Chinese literature and culture. In October 1937 Takeda was drafted into the army and served two years in China, stationed chiefly in the Shanghai area. Discharged in 1939, he returned to Japan. In 1943 he published *Shiba Sen*, a critical biography of the famous Chinese historiographer Sima Qian (Ssu-ma Ch'ien). Takeda returned to Shanghai in 1944 to work for the Japan–China Cultural Association and was repatriated after the war's end in 1946. In October 1947 he was appointed assistant professor of Chinese literature at Hokkaidō University, but resigned the following May. Thereafter he published a number of essays and novels and gained recognition as an important postwar writer.

A major influence on the intellectual formation of Takeda's work was his Buddhist upbringing, from which he gained an appreciation of the concept of the impermanence of life. Coupled with this were the disillusionment he experienced as a member of a leftist group, feelings of inadequacy in his role as a priest, and a sense of guilt stemming from his participation in a war of aggression against the Chinese people. Takeda was a prolific writer whose narrative style was much influenced by Chinese literature. He wrote 9 full-length novels, 9 novellas, 126 short stories, and 3 plays, as well as 33 books of essays. *Shiba Sen*, his most noted work, was reissued as *Shiba Sen: Shiki no sekai* in 1952. In this work, Takeda maintains that the world described by Sima Qian in his voluminous history the *Shiji (Shih chi)* is a complete negation of the society of Sima Qian's day. An admirer of Chinese culture and yet a participant in the invasion of China, Takeda felt that his life, like Sima Qian's, was a disgrace; a self-appraisal reflected in his treatment of the Chinese historian. *Fūbaika* (1952, A Flower Pollinated by the Wind) is a confessional piece laying bare the author's feelings of guilt toward China and its people. In it Takeda describes his relationships with the former members of his Chinese culture study group. "Hikarigoke" (1954; tr "Luminous Moss," 1967) is a dramatic work dealing with the themes of cannibalism and human survival. Some of his other works are *Mamushi no sue* (1947; tr "This Outcast Generation," 1967), set in Shanghai at the time of Japan's defeat, *Igyō no mono* (1950; tr "The Misshapen Ones," 1957), *Mori to mizuumi no matsuri* (1955–58, The Festival of Woods and Lakes), and *Fuji* (1969–71, Mt. Fuji Sanitarium).

——— *Takeda Taijun zenshū*, 21 vols (Chikuma Shobō, 1979). Hyōdō Masanosuke, *Takeda Taijun ron* (1978). Matsubara Shin'ichi, *Takeda Taijun ron* (1970). Takeishi Haku, *Takeda Taijun ron* (1977).

TAMAI Kensuke

Takefu

Also known as Takebu. City in central Fukui Prefecture, central Honshū. Takefu developed as a castle town in the Edo period (1600–1868). It has been known for its cutlery since the Kamakura period (1185–1333). Silk and linen textiles, handmade Japanese paper *(washi)*, furniture, chemical products, and electrical machinery are also produced. Pop: 67,104.

Takegoshi Yosaburō (1865–1950)

Historian and politician; also known as Takekoshi Yosaburō. Born in what is now Saitama Prefecture, Takegoshi attended Keiō Gijuku (now Keiō University). As a writer for the liberal *Jiji shimpō* and several other newspapers, he came to the attention of the oligarch SAIONJI KIMMOCHI, who chose Takegoshi as editor-in-chief of his magazine, *Sekai no Nihon* (Japan in the World). On Saionji's recommendation Takegoshi then worked for the Education Ministry.

He was elected to the Diet in 1902 as a member of the political party RIKKEN SEIYŪKAI and was subsequently reelected four times. Takegoshi was appointed to the House of Peers in 1923 and to the Privy Council in 1940. He early established his reputation as a historian with his *Shin nihonshi* (A New History of Japan), published in 1891–92, but his principal work is *Nihon keizai shi* (1920, Economic History of Japan), which is still highly regarded. Other works include *Nisengohyakunen shi* (1896, 2,500 Years of History), *Tōankō* (1930), a biography of Saionji, and an English publication, *The Economic Aspects of Japan* (3 vols, 1930).

Takehara

City in southern Hiroshima Prefecture, western Honshū, on the Inland Sea. A private estate (SHŌEN) of the Shimo-Gamo Shrine in Kyōto during the Heian period (794–1185), Takehara flourished as a salt-making town during the Edo period (1600–1868). It is also known as the boyhood home of the Edo-period man of letters RAI SAN'YŌ (1781–1832). Its principal industries are metallurgy, food processing, *sake,* and ceramics. Pop: 36,895.

Takehashi Insurrection

(Takehashi Sōdō). Uprising in 1878 by soldiers of the elite Konoe Artillery, First Battalion, stationed near Takehashi bridge in Tōkyō. Angered by a reduction of wages and an insufficiency of rewards following the SATSUMA REBELLION (1877), over 260 soldiers led by Mizoe Unosuke and Nagashima Takeshirō rose up on the night of 23 August 1878 and killed the battalion commander and the officer on weekly duty. They occupied the barracks and fired shots into the residence of the finance minister. They planned to proceed to the Imperial Palace nearby, capturing high government officials on the way, but were thwarted by soldiers sent out from the Tōkyō garrison. At the military trial held on October 15, Mizoe and 52 others were sentenced to death and 118 were banished from Tōkyō. The incident prompted the government to reinforce army discipline and to issue in the name of Army Minister YAMAGATA ARITOMO the Admonition to Soldiers (Gunjin Kunkai), which stressed fidelity, courage, and obedience as the supreme military virtues. The admonition was further elaborated in the IMPERIAL RESCRIPT TO SOLDIERS AND SAILORS (1882).

Takehisa Yumeji (1884–1934)

Painter, illustrator, and poet. Real name Takehisa Shigejirō. Born in Okayama Prefecture. After he left a vocational school in Tōkyō, he became associated with socialist periodicals such as the HEIMIN SHIMBUN, to which he contributed sketches and caricatures. He later joined the newspaper YOMIURI SHIMBUN, where he became established as an illustrator and prose writer. In 1909 he published his first collection of prints, *Haru no maki,* which created a sensation. Said to be a composite image of the women in his life, this type of feminine beauty, slightly consumptive, with large eyes and sad expression, became the basic theme of his work. In addition to his oil paintings, watercolors, Japanese-style paintings, and prints, Yumeji was a talented designer of book and magazine covers. He also wrote some fiction and poetry. One of his poems, "Yoimachigusa," was set to music and is still a popular song. Yumeji traveled in America and Europe from 1931 to 1933 and died in a sanatorium the year following his return to Japan. His work is said to epitomize the lyricism of the Taishō period (1912–26), capturing the spirit of the UKIYO-E print while at the same time being distinctively modern. See also NIHONGA.

Takeiri Yoshikatsu (1926–)

Politician. Born in Nagano Prefecture, he attended the Military Academy during World War II and worked for the Japanese National Railways in Tōkyō after the war. Falling ill, in 1953 he joined the religious organization SŌKA GAKKAI. Upon his recovery, which he attributed to his new faith, he became a dedicated and effective missionary. In 1959 Takeiri resigned from the National Railways to enter municipal politics, and in 1961 he became a central committee member of the Kōmei Political Federation (Kōmei Seiji Remmei), the political arm of the Sōka Gakkai. Following the formal establishment of the KŌMEITŌ party in 1964, Takeiri served in several central posts. He was elected to the House of Representatives in 1967, and under his leadership the Kōmeitō made significant advances on the political front. Since the decision by IKEDA DAISAKU in 1970 to separate the religious and political activities of the Sōka Gakkai, Takeiri has devoted himself exclusively to politics.

Takemitsu Tōru (1930–)

Composer. Born in Tōkyō, but spent his first eight years in Manchuria, where his father was stationed. His father died in 1938, but he inherited from him a taste for jazz. During and after World War II he was exposed to mainly military and light music, but in 1946 he got to know Suzuki Hiroyoshi (b 1930), FUKUSHIMA KAZUO (b 1930), and others, and first heard the music of modern French and other composers. He began composing the following year, mainly teaching himself, but also studied privately with Kiyose Yasuji (b 1900) and with Hayasaka Fumio (1914–55), who wrote music for Kurosawa Akira's films. From about 1950 his work began to attract attention; he was active in the Experimental Workshop (Jikken Kōbō) and gradually established an international reputation with his many sensitive works for film, ballet, orchestra, small ensembles, and electronic media. Takemitsu has also written for Japanese instruments, especially the SHAKUHACHI and BIWA. His compositions include *Coral Island* (1962), *Arc* (1963–66), *Woman in the Dunes* (film, 1964), *Kwaidan* (film, 1964), and *Face of Another* (film, 1966). 📖 ——Recording: *Takemitsu Tōru no ongaku,* Victor Records, SJV 1503/6 (4-record set). David B. WATERHOUSE

Takemoto Gidayū I (1651–1714)

Chanter *(tayū)* in the JŌRURI form of dramatic narrative chanting that is associated with the BUNRAKU professional puppet theater. Originator of the GIDAYŪ-BUSHI style of chanting. Born in Ōsaka.

In 1685 the chanter now known as Gidayū I (i.e., Gidayū the First), who had previously performed under a number of other names such as Kiyomizu Gorobei, took the name Takemoto Gidayū, established the Takemotoza puppet theater in Ōsaka, and, through stylistic and repertorial innovation, soon brought to *jōruri* an unprecedented popularity. Although Gidayū's voice alone ranked him as the preeminent figure in contemporary *jōruri,* it was his collaboration with the playwright CHIKAMATSU MONZAEMON (1653–1724) that was to have the most profound effect on *jōruri* as an art. In plays such as *Shusse Kagekiyo* (1686, Kagekiyo Victorious) and *Sonezaki shinjū* (1703; tr *The Love Suicides at Sonezaki,* 1961), whose subject matter touched upon popular themes familiar to the audience, the collaborators gave to *jōruri* a new dramatic appeal. The *gidayū-bushi* style of chanting continues to predominate in the modern puppet theater. MOTEGI Kiyoko

Takenaka Kōmuten Co, Ltd

A construction company which traces its history back to the year 1610. Takenaka Kōmuten places greater emphasis on special construction orders than on contracts obtained by bidding; one of the company's main characteristics is that it adopts an integrated process system, from the designing to the completion of construction projects. The company's technology is highly regarded; particularly well known is the TACSS (Takenaka Aqua-reactive Chemical Soil Stabilization) method for strengthening foundations, which the company and DAINIPPON INK & CHEMICALS, INC, developed jointly. It has been active overseas, with two subsidiaries in the United States, and seven more in other countries, including West Germany. It also has an office in Singapore. Future plans call for further strengthening of the integrated process system and the active development of new technologies, as well as the expansion of engineering operations. Sales totaled ¥622.8 billion (US $2.8 billion) in 1981, and the company was capitalized at ¥50 billion (US $228.4 million). Corporate headquarters is located in Ōsaka.

Takenouchi no Sukune

A legendary figure who supposedly served several early Japanese emperors, most of whom were themselves legendary. According to the chronicle KOJIKI (712) and the NIHON SHOKI (720), Takenouchi was the great grandson of the legendary emperor Kōgen and served under the legendary emperors Keikō, Seimu, and Chūai, as well as the emperors ŌJIN (late 4th to early 5th century) and NINTOKU (early 5th century). He is said to have made inspection tours to northeastern Honshū and recommended to the emperor that he send troops to these areas to subjugate the inhabitants. He is supposed to have played an active role in Empress JINGŪ's expedition to Korea and was said to be successful in expanding the territories of the Yamato court. It is difficult however, to distinguish these legends from historical fact. The five families of Kose, Soga, Heguri, Ki, and Katsuragi all claimed to be descendants of Takenouchi no Sukune, but this too is doubtful.

Takenouchi Shikibu (1712–1767)

Japanese classical scholar and early proponent of imperial loyalty. The son of a physician in Echigo Province (now Niigata Prefecture), Takenouchi lived with the noble Tokudaiji family while studying Shintō, military arts, Confucianism, and Buddhism in Kyōto. He later opened a school in Kyōto; in his lectures he placed great emphasis on loyalty and spoke of the need to curb the arrogance of the Tokugawa shogunate toward the emperor. Some of his students, young nobles in service at the court of Emperor Momozono (1741–62; r 1747–62), relayed Takenouchi's ideas to the emperor; they also began to hope for a weakening of the shogunate and a revival of court power. When their activities came to the attention of the Kyōto shoshidai (shogunal deputy), several nobles were sentenced to domiciliary confinement. In 1759 Takenouchi was banished from Kyōto (see HŌREKI INCIDENT). He sought refuge with a Shintō priest at Ise but, in the wake of the MEIWA INCIDENT, was sentenced to exile on Hachijōjima. He died before reaching the island.

Takenouchi Tsuna (1840–1922)

Politician and entrepreneur. Born in Tosa Province (now Kōchi Prefecture). Takenouchi fought with the imperial forces in the BOSHIN CIVIL WAR, and after the establishment of the Meiji government, he was appointed to the Ministry of Finance. For a time he operated the TAKASHIMA COAL MINE on an island of Kyūshū with GOTŌ SHŌJIRŌ, but was imprisoned briefly for attempting to incite an antigovernment insurrection in Tosa in response to Saigō Takamori's SATSUMA REBELLION (1877). He joined the JIYŪTŌ, Japan's first political party, upon its formation in 1881 and was elected to the Diet for three terms from 1890. Active also in business, Takenouchi was involved in several enterprises in Korea, including the Seoul–Pusan Railway. The postwar prime minister YOSHIDA SHIGERU was his fifth son.

Takenouchi Yasunori (1806–?)

Official of the Tokugawa shogunate and leader of a shogunal mission to Europe in 1862–63. Takenouchi, who was born in Edo (now Tōkyō) into a hatamoto (direct shogunal vassal) family, began his career in the shogunate's Finance Office (Kanjōkata). In 1854 he was appointed commissioner (bugyō) of Hakodate in EZO (now Hokkaidō), where he dealt with the problem of developing Japan's northernmost island and handled territorial disputes with Russia. In 1861 he was appointed commissioner of finance (kanjō bugyō) and then commissioner of foreign affairs (gaikoku bugyō). The following year he was sent abroad as the head of a 35-member mission to Britain, the Netherlands, France, Prussia, Russia, and Portugal; with the aid of the British envoy Sir Rutherford ALCOCK, the mission succeeded in obtaining agreements to delay until 1868 the opening of Japan's major ports to foreign trade as provided by the ANSEI COMMERCIAL TREATIES. After his return in 1863, Takenouchi fell into disfavor when national sentiment temporarily turned against dealing with the Western powers. He held one last post, as city commissioner (machi bugyō) of Ōsaka, before retiring from government service in 1864. See also SHOGUNATE MISSIONS TO THE WEST.

Takeo

City in western Saga Prefecture, Kyūshū. Takeo has long been known for its hot springs, being mentioned in an 8th-century gazetteer (fudoki). Traditional products include the pottery wares known as kuromuta-yaki and tatarō-yaki. Rice is cultivated in the lowlands and mandarin oranges, tea, and persimmons are grown in the hills. Several prehistoric sites are situated in the area. Pop: 34,237.

Takeshima

An uninhabited island in the Sea of Japan that has become the focus of a territorial dispute between Japan and the Republic of Korea.

Located just south of the 38th parallel and approximately equidistant from Honshū and the Korean peninsula, the island is called Takeshima by the Japanese and Tokto by the Koreans. It is also known as the Liancourt Rocks, after the French ship Liancourt which discovered it in 1849. Small (0.23 sq km; 0.09 sq mi) and barren, the island is little more than a cluster of reefs that was used as a stopover by fishermen. During the Edo period (1600–1868), conflict occasionally erupted over the issue of territorial rights. Japan occupied the island for strategic reasons during the Russo-Japanese War (1904–05), and it was incorporated into Shimane Prefecture in 1905. Since the end of World War II, the Republic of Korea has claimed rights to the island and has control over it. Attempts to resolve the dispute have been unsuccessful, and the issue, more symbolic than real, reflects lingering tensions between the two countries. See also TERRITORY OF JAPAN; KOREA–JAPAN TREATY OF 1965, SUPPLEMENTARY AGREEMENTS.　　　　　　　　　　　　　C. Kenneth QUINONES

Taketa

City in southwestern Ōita Prefecture, Kyūshū. Taketa developed as a castle town after a castle was built in the 12th century by Ogata Koreyoshi. Principal products are rice, tobacco, and shiitake (a species of mushroom). It was the childhood home of TAKI RENTARŌ, whose well-known song, "Kōjō no tsuki" (Moon over Castle Ruins), was supposedly composed at the site of the castle. TANOMURA CHIKUDEN, the Edo period (1600–1868) painter, was born here; his residence is open to viewers. Of interest also are the remains of secret Christian chapels (see KAKURE KIRISHITAN) that have been found in caves and a cluster of mounded tombs (KOFUN). Pop: 22,770.

taketombo

("bamboo dragonfly"). A children's toy made of bamboo carved into the shape of a propeller with a shaft attached at the center. It is set in motion by rubbing the shaft between the palms of the hands and then releasing it upward in the air to fly. It supposedly originated in the 18th century, and is said by some to have been invented by HIRAGA GENNAI (1728–80), a scholar of Western learning. Today they are often made of plastic. Taketombo are popular because they can easily be made by hand and are often made in primary school arts and crafts classes.　　　　　　　　　　　　Saitō Ryōsuke

Taketomijima

Island 4 km (2.5 mi) southwest of the island of Ishigakijima, southwestern Okinawa Prefecture. One of the YAEYAMA ISLANDS. It is a level island surrounded by beautiful coral reefs, with beaches covered with hoshisuna ("star sand"), the remains of tiny sea animals. The principal activity is sugarcane cultivation. Area: 6.3 sq km (2.4 sq mi).

Taketori monogatari

(Taketori no okina no monogatari; tr The Tale of the Bamboo Cutter, 1956). An early Heian-period (794–1185) prose work, probably written between 850 and 950, about a supernatural being found in a bamboo stem by a bamboo cutter and brought up as his daughter under the name Kaguyahime, "The Shining Princess," on account of her radiant beauty. Miraculously, he becomes rich and urges her to marry one of five noble suitors, to each of whom she sets a fantastic quest; all either fail or resort in vain to trickery. She also refuses the suit of the emperor. Eventually she explains to her parents that she is from the Palace of the Moon, whence messengers are coming to take her back. All human efforts to keep them away are fruitless, and sad though she is to go, she dons a robe of feathers that obliterates her memories of the world and departs. She has left a letter and an elixir of life for the emperor, but loath to prolong life without her, he has both burned on the mountain top nearest heaven (i.e., Mt. Fuji).

This is obviously a composite of several distinct folklore elements, none exclusively Japanese. For the finding of the supernatural child, foreign sources, both Buddhist and secular, have been suggested; however parallels of a more general kind do exist in Japan (cf the finding of MOMOTARŌ in a peach). The last section of the story reflects Taoist beliefs about immortality, but the most noteworthy feature is the robe of feathers, apparently linking the story with the worldwide Swan Maiden theme, which was certainly known in 8th-century Japan.

The part about the quests set to suitors, again a worldwide folklore theme, is here used with some literary effect of humor and realism, but whether the author himself brought together disparate elements, or retold, possibly from a text written in Chinese, an already composite tale, we do not know. (A version differing in detail appears in KONJAKU MONOGATARI 31.30, while post-Heian versions not only differ markedly, in many cases describing the girl as born from a bush warbler's egg and in some cases having her marry a provincial governor, but also localize the tale in the area of Mt. Fuji, mentioned only at the end of *Taketori monogatari*.) Stylistically simple and lacking elegance, *Taketori monogatari* represents an early stage of Japanese prose literature; *Genji monogatari* refers to it as "the archetype and parent of all romance." See FOLKTALES.

🔲——Donald Keene, tr, "Taketori Monogatari: The Tale of the Bamboo Cutter," *Monumenta Nipponica* 11.4 (1956). Douglas E. Mills, "Soga Monogatari, Shintōshū and the Taketori Legend," in *Monumenta Nipponica* 30.1 (1975).   *Douglas E. MILLS*

Takeuchi Kyūichi (1857–1916)

Japanese-style sculptor. Born in the Asakusa district of Edo (now Tōkyō). In 1880, after studying ivory carving for several years, Takeuchi visited the temples of Nara and Kyōto and decided to devote himself to the study and revival of traditional techniques of Japanese painted wood sculpture. When the Tōkyō Bijutsu Gakkō (now Tōkyō University of Fine Arts and Music) opened in 1889, he became an instructor in the sculpture department, and on the advice of OKAKURA KAKUZŌ, de facto director of the school, he made several reproductions of Nara-period (710–794) sculptural masterpieces. His image of Gigeiten, the Buddhist feminine deity of the arts, was exhibited at the Chicago World's Fair in 1893. Takeuchi is considered one of the three leading sculptors of the early Meiji period, along with TAKAMURA KŌUN and Ishikawa Kōmei (1852–1913).

Takeuchi Seihō (1864–1942)

Japanese-style painter who for close to half a century was the dominant force in the Kyōto art world. The only son of a Kyōto restauranteur, his real name was Takeuchi Tsunekichi. Seihō studied painting first with a minor Shijō artist, Tsuchida Eirin, and then from 1881 to 1887 with Kyōto's predominant painter-educator, the MARU-YAMA–SHIJŌ SCHOOL painter KŌNO BAIREI. Bairei also secured his entry to major exhibitions and introduced him to important officials.

His early paintings were traditional enough to gain prizes from the conservative establishment, yet innovative enough to win him publicity. He soon established a private school that attracted promising pupils and, from 1895 to 1924, also taught at the Kyōto Prefectural Painting School (Kyōto Fu Gagakkō). Many of the leading Kyōto painters of the succeeding generation were his students, including Nishiyama Suishō (1879–1958) and TSUCHIDA BAKUSEN.

Takeuchi became the first exponent of Japanese-style painting (*nihonga*) to be sent abroad by the government when he was included in an official delegation to attend the Paris exposition of 1900. He spent six months touring England and the major European countries and brought back casts, photographs, books, and paints that greatly influenced his work. His attempt to adapt Western subjects, principles, and pigments to the traditions of Japanese painting drew both censure and praise.

An able administrator and adroit politician, Takeuchi played an influential role in the government exhibitions, or BUNTEN, to which he submitted a remarkable series of paintings, beginning in 1907 with a pair of screens of willows and herons, *After the Rain*, that acknowledged his indebtedness to BUSON and MATSUMURA GO-SHUN. This was followed by *Tame Rabbits and Monkeys* in 1908, which displayed his skill at depicting animals, and in 1909, by a bold and refreshingly original interpretation of the hackneyed theme of the *maiko* (see GEISHA), entitled *In the Summer Shower*. His gleanings from Western art were completely transmuted in the landscape *The Estuary*, which he exhibited in 1918. His highly sophisticated and elegant works of the Shōwa period (1926–) are now the most sought after.   *Ellen P. CONANT*

takeuma → stilts

Takezaki Suenaga (1246–?)

A warrior of Higo Province (now Kumamoto Prefecture) who distinguished himself in the defense of the northern Kyūshū coast during the MONGOL INVASIONS OF JAPAN of 1274 and 1281. In the repulse of the second invasion, he boarded enemy ships and engaged in hand-to-hand combat. Takezaki is immortalized in a pair of polychrome painted scrolls, entitled *Mōko shūrai ekotoba* (Scrolls of the Mongol Invasion) or *Takezaki Suenaga ekotoba*, preserved in the Tōkyō National Museum. The scrolls bear the date 1293 and are tentatively attributed to Tosa Nagataka; they vividly depict Suenaga's exploits and illustrate the arms and armor of the period in great detail.   *G. Cameron HURST III*

takiguchi no bushi

(literally, "warriors of the mouth of the waterfall"). A unit of armed guards in the Imperial Palace. First established during the reign (887–897) of Emperor UDA, they were attached to the KURŌDO-DOKORO (Chamberlain's Office or Bureau of Archivists). They were named for their station at the waterfall in the garden of the Seiryō-den, the emperor's living quarters. The unit originally comprised 10 warriors, was later expanded to 20, and at one time numbered as many as 30. Selected for their skill in archery, these guards also served as imperial messengers, accompanied the emperor on outings, and performed other miscellaneous services. Although they lived in rotation within the palace, they were not admitted to imperial audience. During the reign of Emperor Horikawa (1079–1107; r 1087–1107), some of the *takiguchi no bushi* were seconded to the service of the retired emperor SHIRAKAWA and became known as HOKUMEN NO BUSHI.   *G. Cameron HURST III*

Takii Kōsaku (1894–)

Novelist, HAIKU poet. Haiku pen name Sessai. Born in Gifu Prefecture. He started to write haiku in his early teens, and became a disciple of the haiku poet KAWAHIGASHI HEKIGOTŌ, who is known for his nontraditional "new trend" haiku. Later, while working as an editor for a Tōkyō newspaper and magazine, he became acquainted with two prominent writers, AKUTAGAWA RYŪNOSUKE and SHIGA NAOYA, both of whom encouraged him in his literary attempts. He established his reputation as a novelist with *Mugen hōyō* (1921–24), an autobiographical account of his love for and marriage to a prostitute who died soon after their marriage. Like those of Shiga Naoya, his lifelong mentor, his works depict interpersonal family relationships. However, most of his later works are plotless essays that reflect the haiku tradition. Other works include the haiku collection *Sessai kushū* (1931) and the short stories "Kekkon made" (1927) and "Yokuboke" (1933). In 1959 he became a member of the Japan Art Academy.

Takikawa

City in central Hokkaidō, at the confluence of the rivers Ishikarigawa and Sorachigawa. Takikawa was developed from 1889 by colonist militia (TONDENHEI) from Honshū. It is a mining and agricultural distribution center; principal products are rice, fruit, and onions. Pop: 51,192.

Takikawa Incident → Kyōto University Incident

Takikawa Yukitoki (1891–1962)

Also known as Takigawa Kōshin. Law professor and central figure in the Takikawa Incident of 1933 (see KYŌTO UNIVERSITY INCIDENT), in which university autonomy and academic freedom were seriously undermined by the government. Born in Okayama Prefecture, Takikawa graduated from Kyōto University and served as a judge before joining his alma mater's faculty. He became a full professor in 1924. He was attacked in 1932 by right-wing groups for his liberal views. The Ministry of Justice banned his textbooks, *Keihō kōgi* (1926, Lectures on Criminal Law) and *Keihō tokuhon*

(1932, Reader on Criminal Law), and he was eventually forced out of his job in 1933 by Education Minister HATOYAMA ICHIRŌ, despite resistance from the university president, faculty, and students and widespread support from other academics. His dismissal prompted several other members of the law faculty to offer to resign. After World War II Takikawa was reinstated at Kyōto University (1946) and became its president in 1953. Thereafter Takikawa's postwar conservatism ironically led to several clashes with radical students. His most representative work is *Hanzai ron josetsu* (1937, Introduction to Criminology).

━━━━Takikawa Haruo, ed, *Aru shōgai, Takikawa Yukitoki* (1965).   *George Oakley* TOTTEN III

Taki Mototaka (1695–1766)

Edo-period (1600–1868) physician and founder of a long line of physicians to the TOKUGAWA FAMILY. Born in Edo (now Tōkyō). A descendant of TAMBA YASUYORI, a court physician of the 10th century, Taki taught medicine at his own school and later served as the administrator of the shogunate medical bureau; he was regarded as the highest medical authority of the time. His direct descendants include Taki Motonori, Taki Motoyasu, and Taki Motokata.

YAMADA Terutane

Taki Rentarō (1879–1903)

Composer; pianist. Born in Tōkyō, he attended school in Ōita, Kyūshū (where his father was an official), before entering in 1894 the music school founded in Tōkyō by IZAWA SHŪJI (1851–1917). There he studied Western music, one of his teachers being Kōda Nobu, whose sister Andō Kō had studied violin for six years in Germany with Joseph Joachim. Taki was also influenced by Raphael von Koeber (1848–1923), who came to Japan in 1893 and taught him piano and composition. In 1900 he went to Germany and the following year entered the music academy in Leipzig; but, falling ill, he returned to Japan in 1902 and died in Ōita at the age of 24. He left a small body of songs and piano pieces that are the first serious Western-style songs by a Japanese composer, yet are pervaded with Japanese sentiment, notably "Kōjō no tsuki" (1901) and "Hana" (1900).

━━━━Endō Hiroshi, *Taki Rentarō no sakuhin to shōgai* (1950).
David B. WATERHOUSE

Takita Choin (1882–1925)

Real name Takita Tetsutarō. Editor of the monthly magazine CHŪŌ KŌRON. Born in Akita Prefecture. While still a student at Tōkyō University, Takita joined the staff of CHŪŌ KŌRON SHA, INC, the publisher of a then relatively obscure monthly. Soon after his promotion to editor in chief in 1912, the magazine became one of Japan's leading general interest magazines. Much of his success was owing to his efforts to introduce writers like TOKUTOMI SOHŌ, NATSUME SŌSEKI, TAYAMA KATAI, TOKUDA SHŪSEI, and SHIMAZAKI TŌSON. He also encouraged the spread of liberal ideas during the 1920s by inviting YOSHINO SAKUZŌ to write social criticism.

ETŌ Fumio

Takita Minoru (1912–)

Labor leader. Born in Toyama Prefecture. President of DŌMEI (Japanese Confederation of Labor) from 1948 through 1972. Takita joined the Nisshin Spinning Co in 1931 and became active in the labor movement after World War II. After serving as president of the Nisshin Spinning Co labor union and ZENSEN (Japan Federation of Textile Industry Workers' Unions), Takita became president of Zenrō (Congress of Trade Unions of Japan) when it was formed in 1954 as a splinter group of SŌHYŌ (General Council of Trade Unions of Japan). When Zenrō was expanded to become Dōmei in 1964, Takita became its first president. As a leader of the anticommunist trade union movement, Takita was instrumental in building Dōmei into a larger labor presence than Sōhyō in Japanese private industry. He successfully led Dōmei in the Ōmikenshi Co strike and other major labor conflicts, but usually advocated cooperative relations between labor and management. Since his retirement from the labor movement, Takita has headed a research organization.

KURITA Ken

Takizawa Bakin → Bakin

tako → kites

Taku

City in central Saga Prefecture, Kyūshū. Under the rule of the Taku family (vassals of the Kamakura shogunate) from the 12th century, it later came under the Ryūzōji, and subsequently the Nabeshima family. It became a center of Confucian studies in the Edo period (1600–1868); a shrine dedicated to the Confucian sages, built in 1708, may still be seen. It later flourished as a coal-mining town, but all the mines have now been closed and new industries are being encouraged. The southern section has long been noted for its loquats and, more recently, for its mandarin oranges. Pop: 25,635.

Takuan Sōhō (1573–1645)

Zen monk, calligrapher, and painter. Born in Izushi (in what is now Hyōgo Prefecture), he was given the name Sōhō in 1594 at Daitokuji, the leading Rinzai Zen temple in Kyōto. After serving in other temples, he returned to Daitokuji to become abbot at the remarkably young age of 35. Takuan served with distinction, but in 1629 he had a disagreement with the shogunate about temple succession and was banished for three years to Kaminoyama (in what is now Yamagata Prefecture). In 1632 Takuan returned to Kyōto and won the friendship of the former emperor GO-MIZUNOO. He journeyed to Edo (now Tōkyō) and so impressed the shōgun TOKUGAWA IEMITSU that at the latter's behest he founded the temple Tōkaiji in 1638. Takuan's calligraphy in poems and letters shows his personal strength of character. Like other Daitokuji abbots of the early part of the Edo period (1600–1868), he produced writing that was bold, rough, and free, emphasizing angular rather than fluid movements of the brush. His paintings exhibit a similar brushwork, achieving a maximum of expression with a minimum of lines. His painting *The Fifth Patriarch Planting Pines* with his poetic inscription shows the use of dry, sharp, and occasionally stubby lines. The painting also indicates the importance of manual work to Zen monks, as the patriarch is shown walking through the mountains to plant pine seedlings. Takuan is also known as a poet and tea master. See also ZENGA.

━━━━Tachibana Daiki, *Daitokuji rekidai bokuseki seisui* (1977).
Stephen ADDISS

Takuma Eiga (fl late 14th century)

Buddhist painter (*ebusshi*). Eiga's precise relationship to other painters of the TAKUMA SCHOOL is not clear, and there is no documentary evidence to place him in the direct lineage of such painters as TAKUMA TAMETŌ or TAKUMA SHŌGA. A number of paintings survive, however, bearing his seal or signature. The inscription on his painting of the poet KAKINOMOTO NO HITOMARO in the Tokiwayama Collection, Kamakura, may be dated 1395, thus providing one point of reference for his activity as a painter toward the end of the 14th century. His other surviving paintings include a set of 16 hanging scrolls in the Fujita Art Museum, Ōsaka, depicting the 16 arhats, or RAKAN; a painting of the Buddhist deity Fudō in the Seikadō Collection, Tōkyō; and three hanging scrolls of Shaka (Śākyamuni Buddha) and the bodhisattvas Monju (Mañjuśrī) and Fugen (Samantabhadra) in the Chōmyōji, a Kyōto temple as well as a painting of Fugen in the Freer Gallery of Art, Washington, DC.

Eiga's paintings show a remarkable diversity of style, which is attributable in part to the historical milieu in which he worked. His paintings of Buddhist subjects range from fully colored icons based on traditional Japanese and Chinese iconographic and stylistic models to paintings executed entirely in ink. The latter type, represented by the Freer painting, reflects the trend among 14th-century Buddhist painters toward assimilation of newly introduced stylistic and thematic ideas from Chinese paintings of the day. The newly fluent and vigorous use of the brush learned from Chinese ink paintings is most evident in Eiga's ink paintings, but the period's tendency toward a more expressive use of the brush is apparent in his more conservative Buddhist paintings as well. Eiga's versatility as a painter in both traditional and recently introduced modes and his mastery of both Buddhist and secular subjects parallel the career of Ryōzen, a mid-14th-century painter of the Tōfukuji, a Kyōto Zensect temple.

Ann YONEMURA

Takuma school

A school of EBUSSHI (artists specializing in Buddhist painting) that flourished from the mid-12th to the late 14th centuries. Its founder was claimed to be the artist TAKUMA TAMETŌ (fl mid-12th century). However, its association with the temples KŌZANJI and JINGOJI, in the northwest section of Kyōto, did not occur until sometime between the late 12th and early 13th centuries, during the lifetime of the founder's oldest son, TAKUMA SHŌGA. After Shōga, there followed a succession of noted artists such as Takuma Tamehisa (fl ca 1184–85), Takuma Shunga (fl 1201–32), Takuma Ryōga (fl 1202–17), and others. Within a generation after the death of the last great Takuma painter, TAKUMA EIGA (fl late 14th century), the school ceased to exist.

If the lives of these painters are obscure, so also is their artistic development. There is a large body of art thought to be by Takuma painters, but except for three by Takuma Chōga (fl ca 1253–70) and a few by Eiga, none are signed or stamped with seals. Consequently, it is nearly impossible to date or attribute individual pieces.

The Takuma school has traditionally been considered a pioneer of a new realism in painting, characterized by vigorous brushwork inspired by Chinese works of the Song (Sung) dynasty (960–1279). The school rivaled the KOSE SCHOOL of ebusshi in Nara, which specialized in Buddhist paintings in the refined, decorative Heian-period (794–1185) style.

Joseph SEUBERT

Takuma Shōga (fl late 12th century)

Buddhist painter. Son of TAKUMA TAMETŌ. Shōga attained the priestly rank of *hōgen*. Surviving paintings attributed to Shōga indicate his important role in incorporating stylistic and iconographic elements from Song (Sung) dynasty (960–1279) Chinese painting. He is one of the earliest professional Buddhist painters to manifest a knowledge of Song painting, which helped to bring about a pronounced shift in stylistic trends in Japanese painting of the Kamakura period (1185–1333). Paintings attributed to Takuma Shōga include the *Jūniten byōbu* (Screen Paintings of 12 Devas), dated 1191, in the collection of the Kyōto temple TŌJI, the *Ryōkai mandara* in the same temple collection, and the *Jūniten* in the JINGOJI, a temple northwest of Kyōto. All these works show the delicate color harmonies associated with Song Chinese paintings. Nevertheless, attribution continues to be debated among scholars.

Ann YONEMURA

Takuma Tamenari (fl mid–11th century)

Buddhist painter known only through a later account recorded in the Kamakura-period (1185–1333) collection of anecdotes, *Kokon chomonjū*. According to this account, Tamenari painted the door panels of the BYŌDŌIN. The extant paintings of the Hōōdō (Phoenix Hall) of the Byōdōin were executed in 1053. There is no reliable contemporary documentation of Tamenari's participation in the Byōdōin project, however, nor is there any other biographical documentation. His relationship to later TAKUMA SCHOOL artists such as TAKUMA TAMETŌ and TAKUMA SHŌGA, both active in the second half of the 12th century, is also unverified.

Ann YONEMURA

Takuma Tametō (fl mid–12th century)

Buddhist painter. Tametō is the earliest painter whose name has been associated with the TAKUMA SCHOOL, which was especially active in Buddhist painting of the 12th to the 14th centuries, and he has been claimed as its founder. As a Buddhist priest he took the ecclesiastical name Shōchi and attained the rank of *hōin*. He is recorded to have executed paintings for the interior of the Kakuōin, a subtemple of the temple KONGŌBUJI at Kōyasan in Wakayama Prefecture at the request of Emperor Konoe (r 1142–55). The extant work attributed to Tametō, and likely to be authentic, comes from the *Kontai butsuga chō*, an album of iconographic drawings in ink and light colors that once belonged to the temple Ganjōji in Kyūshū. Twelve pages are in the Yamato Bunkakan in Nara, and other pages have been dispersed to collections in Japan and abroad. The drawings, executed fluently in ink and light colors, represent the *Kongōkai mandara* (Diamond Realm Mandala; see RYŌBU MANDARA) and its deities. Tametō's son, TAKUMA SHŌGA, also specialized in painting Buddhist subjects.

🔲——Tanaka Ichimatsu, "Kontai butsuga chō to Takuma Tametō," in *Yamato bunka* 12 (December 1953). *Ann* YONEMURA

Tale of Genji

(Genji monogatari). By general repute the supreme masterpiece of Japanese prose literature. Written in the early 11th century, when prose literature scarcely existed in the West, it has been called the first great novel in the literature of the world. A very long work, upwards of a thousand pages in translation, or some three-quarters of a million words, it has an essentially simple plot, describing the life and loves of an erstwhile prince known, from his family name, as "the shining Genji," and, after his death, the less successful loves of a youth who passes before the world as his son, but is in fact the grandson of his best friend.

The earliest surviving texts are fragmentary, from late in the Heian period (794–1185), and it is only from the medieval period (13th–16th centuries) that complete texts can be put together. The absence of a holograph manuscript and the absence as well of detailed information about the author, a court lady known as MURASAKI SHIKIBU, means that no final answers can be given to questions concerning the circumstances of composition. From evidence in the work known as *Murasaki Shikibu nikki* (Murasaki Shikibu Diary), it does not seem possible to deny that at least a part of the work is from the hand of Murasaki Shikibu, or that at least a part of it was written before she entered court service, in the first decade of the 11th century. From the SARASHINA NIKKI, the diary or memoirs of another court lady, it seems equally certain that a long prose work, approximately the length of the present *Genji,* had been completed and widely circulated by the end of the first quarter of the 11th century.

The major questions that ask for answers include these: may Murasaki Shikibu be given credit for the whole of the work, or were there other authors? Over how long a period was it written? Is it finished or unfinished?

The available evidence does not permit of a final answer to any of these questions. Possible answers will emerge from the description below of the contents and the stages of composition. Scrutiny of medieval texts, of which there are many, brings a plausible answer to another major question: how closely do texts from several hundred years later resemble the text that originally came from the hand of the author? Medieval texts differ from one another in a great many points of detail, most of which may be described as minor; and so it seems likely that the general shape and configuration of the tale went fundamentally unchanged through the centuries for which no texts survive. It seems unlikely that anything of major proportions was added to or lost from the tale read by the *Sarashina* diarist in about the year 1020.

The action covers almost three-quarters of a century. Genji is born in the first chapter and is 52 by the Oriental count in the 41st chapter, "The Wizard," the last in which he is still living. (Chapter titles are from the most recent English translation. See the bibliography at the end of this article.) Kaoru, the youth who passes as his son, is 5 by the Oriental count in "The Wizard," and 28 in the last of the 54 chapters which make up the present *Genji.*

There is a very clear break at the end of "The Wizard." In the first sentence of the next chapter, "His Perfumed Highness," we are informed that Genji is no longer living. His death is not described, nor are his last years, though in later chapters there is a suggestion that he lived in seclusion. Presently it becomes clear that several years have elapsed between the two chapters. With the 45th chapter, "The Lady at the Bridge," the major action moves to the village of Uji, some distance to the south and east of the capital, Kyōto, where almost all of the events have thus far taken place. So much of the remaining action is set outside the capital that the last chapters are commonly known as "the 10 Uji chapters."

The Early Stages——The tale can thus be divided very clearly into two parts, the 41 chapters, more than two-thirds of the whole narrative, of which Genji is the hero, and the 10 chapters of which Kaoru and his good friend and rival, Prince Niou, a son of Genji's only daughter, are the principal characters. The 3 chapters between, 2 of them much under the average length of the chapters, may be described as transitional. They seem in many respects tentative and hesitant.

The first great division, the 41 chapters centered upon Genji's career, may be further subdivided. The long "New Herbs" chapters, the 34th and 35th, are a watershed. Taken together, and it may be that they were not originally divided, they form about a tenth of the whole tale. Though there have been setbacks along the way, Genji's career has thus far been a happy and successful one. His public career continues to be successful, but great sadness comes into his

Tale of Genji

A fragment from the *Genji* scrolls (*Genji monogatari emaki*) illustrating the 36th chapter, "The Oak Tree" ("Kashiwagi"). Genji (upper left) holds the baby Kaoru, son of Genji's wife and Tō no Chūjō's son, Kashiwagi. Colors on paper. 12th century. Tokugawa Reimeikai, Tōkyō. National Treasure.

private life, and the tone of the narrative is altogether more somber. The halfway point in the long narrative comes at about the beginning of the first "New Herbs" chapter.

Genji is born the son of the reigning emperor by his best-loved wife, a lady of not very distinguished lineage. She dies before Genji is old enough to remember her. He is his father's favorite son, but, for complex reasons, the possibility of his succeeding to the throne is early dismissed, and he is given commoner status and the family name Genji or Minamoto, commonly bestowed by emperors upon sons not granted royal status.

After the death of Genji's mother, the emperor transfers his affections to a princess, Fujitsubo, who is brought to court because she so resembles the dead lady. (It should be pointed out that none of the characters, except for a few in subordinate positions, are mentioned by name. Thus we never learn Genji's given name. Such designations as "Fujitsubo," from her apartments in the palace, have become traditional.) Knowing of the averred resemblance, Genji is strongly attracted to her as a substitute for the mother he never knew. He has a brief affair with her, and the son who is the result presently succeeds to the throne, and is known after his abdication as the Reizei emperor.

The search for affinities with his dead mother also prompts Genji to take in the girl who is to be the great love of his life. Known as Murasaki—and it is quite possible that the "name" by which the author has traditionally been known derives from this designation—she is a niece of Fujitsubo, whom she closely resembles. Her marriage to Genji and his love for her form the principal strand of the plot. She dies in the 40th chapter, "The Law," and the next chapter is the last in which Genji himself appears.

Genji has already made a political marriage, to Aoi, a lady somewhat older than he, the daughter of the Minister of the Left. Aoi dies after the birth of a son, Yūgiri, who is to rise to great eminence and figure prominently in the later plot. Genji is persuaded that the jealous spirit of the Rokujō lady, with whom he has had an affair, is responsible for the death. The Rokujō lady is the extremely sensitive and artistically gifted widow of a former crown prince. A belief that disturbed spirits wander forth and do great mischief was prevalent in the Heian period.

The youthful Genji has a variety of love affairs, with, among others, the lady of the evening faces, a former mistress of his best friend, Tō no Chūjō; the comic safflower lady, an impoverished princess to whom Genji remains steadfast (and we are repeatedly told that steadfastness is among his more conspicuous traits), despite her uncomeliness; and Oborozukiyo, a daughter of the Minister of the Right, the most powerful political rival of Genji's father-in-law and Tō no Chūjō's father, the Minister of the Left.

The abdication of Genji's father is announced at the beginning of the ninth chapter, "Heartvine," the eventful chapter in which Aoi dies. Three chapters later Genji is driven into exile, largely as a result of the abdication and the affair with Oborozukiyo. The Minister of the Right and another daughter, the Kokiden lady, who is the

mother of the new emperor and greatly dislikes Genji, come into political ascendancy with the abdication, and the Oborozukiyo affair gives them the occasion they need for driving Genji into exile.

It is the one major setback of his career, which after a few years recovers brilliantly. Ill and determined to abdicate, the Suzaku emperor, his brother and Kokiden's son, summons him back from exile, and with the accession of Genji's son, the Reizei emperor, thought by the world to be his brother, his future prospects are secure. He and the new emperor are very close despite the fact that the paternal relationship cannot be recognized. His prospects are further brightened by the fact that a liaison with a lady of Akashi, one of his places of exile, gives him a much-needed daughter. He does as the FUJIWARA FAMILY did through much of the Heian era; he marries the girl to the crown prince, and so gains control of future emperors.

There are deaths in the early chapters, to bring sorrow into Genji's life: of Aoi; of the Rokujō lady, after some years in Ise, where her daughter has served as high priestess; of Fujitsubo; of Genji's father. His career is triumphantly successful, however. By his 40th year, which comes in the climactic "New Herbs" chapters, he is the most powerful statesman in the land, and he has been accorded the honors and emoluments of a retired emperor.

In the 21st chapter, "The Maiden," Genji moves into a magnificent new mansion at Rokujō, and in the following chapter, "The Jeweled Chaplet," he discovers and brings into his house Tamakazura, Tō no Chūjō's lost daughter by the lady of the evening faces. In the chapters between the "The Jeweled Chaplet" and "New Herbs," there is a lyrical review of the seasons at Rokujō, so delicate and detailed that it almost seems that the description of nature has become Murasaki Shikibu's chief concern; and the affairs of the second generation come to the fore. Yūgiri courts his cousin Kumoinokari. The courtship is initially thwarted by the girl's father, Tō no Chūjō, but presently brought to a happy conclusion. Genji makes Tamakazura unhappy by his too-open designs upon her, but in the end she makes a prudent if loveless marriage to a man with a bright political future.

In recent years several theories have been proposed to the effect that the early chapters were not composed in the order in which we have them today. The most persuasive of the theories have as their starting point the remarkable fact that some of Genji's lesser ladies are mentioned nowhere in the first score or so of chapters, except in the chapters of which they are the heroines. This suggests that episodes concerning such ladies were not in existence when the main narrative was written, but were written later and inserted into their present positions. It suggests, for instance, that the fourth chapter, "Evening Faces," was written later, and perhaps considerably later, than the fifth, "Lavender." If accepted, these theories would explain why, in matters both of style and of sensitivity, the fourth chapter should seem so much more mature than the fifth.

The first great division of the tale can thus be broken into three subdivisions: those of the first 21 chapters in which the main story of

Genji, his love for Fujitsubo and Murasaki, his marriage to Aoi, and his public career is carried forward; self-contained episodes having to do with lesser ladies, which may well have been added later to the main narrative; and the 12 chapters following upon the move to Rokujō. Through the three subdivisions, a steady refinement of narrative technique and a bolder originality are to be seen. Although even at the outset the narrative is recognizably superior to 10th-century romances, it still bears very clearly the marks of its antecedents. By the time of the move to Rokujō, romance has been left behind, and realism prevails, for the first time perhaps in the literature of the world. The idealization of Genji is altogether less pronounced than in earlier chapters, the incident has very strongly the feel of actuality, and the characters are believable and likable. Though no larger than life, they emerge with a vividness that is wanting in the earlier, idealized Genji. If it is realism, it is a genial sort of realism.

The Later Stages

A harsher, darker realism emerges in the next division, the eight chapters from "New Herbs" through "The Wizard." Genji's career reaches a brilliant climax in "New Herbs," and he prepares to go into retirement; tragedy enters his private life. Murasaki falls seriously ill and indeed is briefly taken for dead. Although she makes a partial recovery, she never fully regains her strength, and in the seventh of the eight chapters she dies. At the behest of his brother, the Suzaku emperor, now abdicated, Genji takes as his wife the emperor's favorite daughter. She is seduced by Kashiwagi, the oldest son of Tō no Chūjō, and the result of the liaison is Kaoru, the principal character of the last 10 chapters. Though in no way responsible for what has happened except through a certain carelessness, the princess is so consumed with guilt that she becomes a nun.

In the six chapters following "New Herbs," the bright alternates with the dark, to very beautiful effect. Kashiwagi languishes and dies, and the Third Princess, Genji's young wife, is seen in her nunnery; and in alternation with these somber episodes Yūgiri is followed in his earnest, somewhat ludicrous, and finally successful pursuit of Kashiwagi's widow, a sister of the Third Princess. The 41st chapter, "The Wizard," sees Genji through the first full year of his bereavement, and at the beginning of the next chapter his death is suddenly announced. Formally, the 41st chapter is a return to the *uta monogatari* (lyrical episodes; see MONOGATARI BUNGAKU), which are among the literary antecedents of the *Genji,* and its content is like a sad echo of the chapters following upon the removal to Rokujō, with their delicate, essentially happy review of the seasons. From the medieval period there has been the tradition of a lost chapter telling of Genji's death. If indeed there was such a chapter, only the title survives, and both the content and the form of "The Wizard" suggests that the grand story of Genji's private and public life is being brought to a conclusion on a muted lyrical note.

The three chapters that follow are the most difficult to justify and fit into general schemes and summaries. The first two are short, and do serve the purpose of introducing the characters who are to dominate the last 10 chapters, and to inform us of events having to do with the houses of Genji and Tō no Chūjō. The third, "Bamboo River," describes the activities of lesser characters who are not heard from again. Both because of the style and because of the content, persuasive argument can be made that it is spurious.

At the commencement of the 45th chapter, "The Lady at the Bridge," we are introduced to an "Eighth Prince," a brother of Genji and the Suzaku emperor who, at the end of a life of disappointment, is living in the village of Uji and pursuing religious devotions. Kaoru visits him and becomes interested in his two daughters, especially the older. She turns him away with something like terror, and in effect starves herself to death after her father dies. Kaoru has meanwhile acted as intermediary for his good friend Prince Niou, Genji's grandson and the son of the reigning emperor, in his courtship of the younger princess. Niou makes her his wife and takes her off to the city, and Kaoru is left with bitter regrets that he should have brought the two together. He has learned, from an old lady in attendance upon the two Uji princesses, the secret of his birth, which intensifies his unhappiness and sense of ineffectuality.

Another daughter of the Eighth Prince is introduced after the removal of the second princess to the city. Traditionally known as Ukifune, she is an unrecognized daughter, the result of a brief liaison after the death of the prince's wife. Kaoru is interested in her and thinks of making her a concubine, but she has the misfortune of also attracting the interest of Niou, and of returning it. Paralyzed at the prospect of choosing between two gentlemen so much higher in rank than herself, she attempts to drown herself. She is rescued and

taken off to a nunnery in the hills east of Kyōto, where she becomes a nun. The story ends on an uncertain note as she refuses to see her own brother, Kaoru's emissary, and Kaoru permits himself a suspicion that Niou has spirited her away and hidden her.

If in the earlier sections the narrative has moved from romance to comic realism to sad realism, in this last section the reality of the phenomenal world seems to recede from the author's interest. The court and the city are left behind for the secluded world of the Eighth Prince and his daughters, and presently this too is left behind and one last, sad lady is left alone with her fate. This withdrawal from society and the material world, however, is accompanied by no evidences of weariness or uncertainty on the author's part. Rather it is as if, at each of the successive stages in the narrative, she found herself aware of new possibilities and willing to have a try at more difficult things.

In the narrative itself, and the process of growing and maturing so apparent therein, is to be found the most persuasive argument for single authorship. The narrative literature of the 10th century provides very little by way of anticipating the *Genji*. It is known, through references in the *Genji* itself and in other works, that numbers of 10th-century romances have been lost, but the likelihood is that the important ones survive. Even in its early, romantic stages the *Genji* is much superior to any of them. The appearance of a talent so far in advance of its times is remarkable; but to suggest that, at some point in the process of composition, a second talent took over, maintained the narrative at its high level, and pushed it to yet higher levels, is to suggest the unbelievable. Although there may be spurious chapters or passages, the internal evidence argues that the *Genji* is for the most part from the hand of a single author. The fact that later Heian romances are so greatly its inferior would seem to point to the same conclusion. If two or more geniuses produced the *Genji,* then other masterpieces might have been expected from other geniuses.

The internal evidence argues further that the composition of the *Genji* required many years. The process of maturing, and especially the withdrawal from society in the last chapters, suggests an aging author. If Murasaki Shikibu went on writing to the end of her life, then it may be that another of the unanswerable questions becomes meaningless. The last chapter has both the look of a new beginning and the look of an ending, and it may be that for Murasaki Shikibu, at the end of her life, it had the look of being sufficient for the time, and that she herself would not have been able to say that there would be more at another time. The *Genji* does not seem to be one of those stories that are carefully planned out in advance. There are hesitations and false leads, and the narrative does not come full circle in the Proustian fashion; and whether or not it is finished might therefore not have meant very much to Murasaki Shikibu.

Themes, Textual History, and Influence

There are persuasive reasons, having to do largely with music and festive events, for thinking that the *Genji* is set at a time perhaps three-quarters of a century before the writing. It is not, strictly speaking, a historical novel, with the setting carefully established and maintained and the action moving across an identifiable expanse of history. Yet Murasaki Shikibu does seem to have thought of her great hero as living in another day, and in her idealization of that day she passes judgment on her own. One of the chief points implicit in her story is that the latter is a day of smaller people and possibilities. A deep pessimism pervades the work. The great day was that of Genji, and it is over. Kaoru and Niou are lesser men, she seems to be saying, and Genji's kind will not come again. Kaoru in particular is such a figure of frustration and indecision that he has been called, with much justice, the first antihero in the literature of the world.

There is an element of social criticism in the pessimism. Genji comes from the royal family and not from the Fujiwara clan, which quite dominated affairs of state in Murasaki's day. His successes would have been unthinkable in that day, with which Murasaki is implicitly expressing her dissatisfaction. She has also been called a prophet, foreseeing the breakdown of the Fujiwara hegemony, and foreseeing as well the subjugation to which women were reduced by the development in the medieval period of husband-centered marriage. Genji's marriage to the Murasaki of the story is such a marriage, unconventional for the times, and, it may be, looking ahead to the medieval period.

The pessimism has a religious as well as a social grounding. The Buddhist notion of the ephemeral was among those which the Japanese found most congenial. It is everywhere in the *Genji*. Certain forms of Buddhism went to the extreme of applying the principle of evanescence to Buddhism itself. The day would come when the

Good Law would wither away. The final decline (*mappō*; see ES-CHATOLOGY) was to begin in the mid-Heian era, it was thought, and Murasaki's grand story of decline can be read as a parable, a symbolic recounting of this ultimate decline. The falling away of society as Ukifune is left alone with her fate becomes the withering away of the Buddhist law itself.

The *Genji* can be read as another sort of Buddhist parable. The principle of karma, or retribution, is another to which the Japanese were strongly attracted. Early in the story Genji has an affair with one of his father's wives. Towards the end of his career he is similarly cuckolded. He is aware of this last happening, and wonders whether his father was also aware and remained silent. He is convinced that his youthful misdeeds have come back to make him unhappy. There can be little doubt that Murasaki Shikibu meant her story to be read as an instance of the inexorable workings of karma.

Other readings are possible, for the *Genji* is a rich and complex story. It can be seen as a kind of archetypal myth, telling of the quest for a lost parent. Genji is too young when his mother dies to remember her. He is drawn to Fujitsubo because he has been told of her resemblance to his mother. When first he sees Murasaki he is aware of a close resemblance to Fujitsubo, though he does not yet know that they are aunt and niece. Murasaki becomes the great love of his life, and with her death his life too is at an end, at least for purposes of the narrative, and the quest has worked itself out.

It is resumed, though less explicitly, in the Uji chapters. A vague uneasiness about the circumstances of his birth leads Kaoru to Uji, where he finds in the Eighth Prince a father figure, and his relations with the prince's daughters make it abundantly clear that none of the unhappiness would have occurred had this surrogate father not also left him. The quest for a parent is a favorite theme of modern literature, and may be taken as one of the elements giving the *Genji* its remarkable immediacy, as if it were modern.

It is above all the characterization that supports the claims of the *Genji* to be the oldest of novels. The total number of characters runs into the hundreds, and of major characters the count is perhaps 50 or 60. Although there is not a great deal by way of explicit inquiry into emotions and states of mind, the characters are skillfully delineated and kept distinct one from another with remarkable consistency. It has been averred that the *Genji* takes the form of theme and variations, with the theme announced in the second chapter in a famous discussion of the states and varieties of femininity, and the several varieties of courtly love introduced in subsequent episodes. Although this view suggests a neater and better-ordered structure than in fact the *Genji* has, it is valuable in drawing attention to the vigor and inventiveness of the characterization. Incident may repeat itself in a kind of cyclical pattern, but characterization does not. For so long a work, the plot is essentially simple, and the hold upon the reader's attention depends chiefly on characterization. There are no extremes of good and evil, except perhaps in the earlier, more romantic chapters. The illusion of life is achieved for the most part without exaggeration or caricature. A number of themes may be abstracted from the narrative, but they depend on the vigor and subtlety of the characterization and do not alter the fact that in it is the final and irreducible significance of the work.

Initially read to and by a small circle of court ladies, the *Genji* seems to have gained immediate popularity. Its popularity has not flagged in the years since. It is not among the works that went into eclipse and later emerged again. The history of criticism and commentary begins late in the Heian period, and it too has been continuous. In the medieval period criticism tended strongly towards the didactic, being in the hands of men who considered prose narrative an inferior, womanish form of literary endeavor, and who therefore felt compelled to give it a higher purpose than the mere entertainment they deemed of the genre. Modern *Genji* criticism is usually held to begin in the 18th century with the work of MOTOORI NORI-NAGA. Norinaga insisted that the good and evil of the *Genji* are not those of the traditional religions. He held that for Murasaki Shikibu good and evil were to be defined in terms of a quality which he called *mono no aware*, a delicate awareness of the pathos of the human condition. Norinaga's definitions are by no means precise and his argument is sometimes confused, but in emphasizing the humanity of the *Genji* he did indeed break with earlier centuries and concentrate on what is most important. It takes little modification to make of his *mono no aware* a recognition of the psychological realism that is at the heart of the *Genji*.

A confusing proliferation of medieval texts—and it is from the medieval period that the earliest complete texts survive—makes the establishment of a definitive text impossible. In the early medieval period the preferred text was the "Kawachi Book," deriving from the work of two scholars who were active in the city of Kamakura. Since the late middle ages the "Blue Book" (Aobyōshi) has been preferred. It derives ultimately from the work of FUJIWARA NO SADAIE (Teika), the great poet and scholar of the late Heian and early Kamakura periods. There are numerous medieval texts that seem to fit into neither line.

The *Genji monogatari* has been an enormous influence on later literature and other art forms and on popular lore as well. It is one of the principal sources for the NŌ drama. There have been fictional recountings and adaptations in more recent centuries, as well as adaptations for the KABUKI stage, the cinema, and television. Of several renditions into modern Japanese, more than one has become a best seller. The remoteness of the language from modern Japanese means that few save specialists read the whole of the *Genji* in the original, but every high-school student gets a smattering. The *Genji* has been a continuing source of inspiration for artists. The 12th-century *Genji* scrolls, traditionally known as the Takayoshi scrolls, are the earliest and most famous of many graphic representations. See also GENJI MONOGATARI EMAKI.

—— Edward Seidensticker, tr, *The Tale of Genji* (1976). Arthur Waley, tr, *The Tale of Genji* (1925–33). Ivan Morris, *The World of the Shining Prince* (1964). Ryusaku Tsunoda et al, *Sources of Japanese Tradition* (1958). Abe Akio et al, *Genji monogatari*, in *Nihon koten bungaku zenshū* (Shōgakukan, 1970–76). Abe Akio et al, *Genji monogatari*, in *Kokugo kokubungaku kenkyū taisei* (1960–61). Abe Akio, *Genji monogatari no kenkyū* (1974). Akiyama Ken, *Genji monogatari no sekai* (1964). Akiyama Ken, *Genji monogatari* (1968). Enchi Fumiko, tr, *Genji monogatari* (1972–73), a translation into modern Japanese. Enchi Fumiko, *Genji monogatari shiken* (1974). Ikeda Kikan, *Genji monogatari taisei* (1953–56). Ikeda Kikan, *Genji monogatari jiten* (Tōkyōdō, 1960). Imai Gen'e, *Genji monogatari no kenkyū* (1962). Ishida Jōji and Shimizu Yoshiko, *Genji monogatari*, in *Shinchō Nihon koten shūsei* (1976–). Kazamaki Keijirō, *Genji monogatari no seiritsu*, in *Kazamaki Keijirō zenshū*, vol 4 (1969). Kitayama Keita, *Genji monogatari jiten* (Heibonsha, 1957). Matsuo Satoshi, et al, *Zenshaku Genji monogatari* (1958–63). Matsuo Satoshi, *Genji monogatari nyūmon* (1958). Motoori Norinaga, *Genji monogatari tama no ogushi*, in Ōno Susumu, ed, *Motoori Norinaga zenshū*, vol 4 (Chikuma Shobō, 1969). Nomura Seiichi et al, *Genji monogatari nyūmon* (1979). Oka Kazuo, *Genji monogatari jiten* (Shunjūsha, 1964). Oka Kazuo, *Genji monogatari no kisoteki kenkyū* (1954). Orikuchi Shinobu and Ikeda Kikan, *Genji monogatari kōza*, III (1953). Shimazu Hisamoto, *Murasaki Shikibu no geijutsu o omou* (1959). Takeda Sōshun, *Genji monogatari no kenkyū* (1954). Tamagami Takuya, *Genji monogatari hyōshaku* (1964–69). Tanizaki Jun'ichirō, tr, *Shinshin'yaku Genji monogatari* (1964–65); a translation into modern Japanese. Yamada Yoshio, *Genji monogatari no ongaku* (1934). Yamagishi Tokuhei, *Genji monogatari*, in *Nihon koten bungaku taikei*, vols 14–18 (Iwanami Shoten, 1958–63).
Edward G. SEIDENSTICKER

Tale of the Heike → Heike monogatari

tally trade

(*kangō bōeki*). Trade carried on between Japan and the Ming dynasty (1368–1644) of China from the beginning of the 15th to the middle of the 16th century. Although the Ming government prohibited Chinese merchant ships from trading in foreign countries, they permitted ships of "tributary" countries to trade by issuing *kangō* (Ch: *kanhe* or *k'an-ho*) or tallies. The tally trade was the only avenue of trade between Japan and China aside from smuggling. Other countries allowed to trade with China under the tally system were the Ryūkyū Islands, Annam, Siam, Java, and Korea.

In 1401 the retired shōgun ASHIKAGA YOSHIMITSU sent an envoy to China and complied with its request to prohibit the activities of the WAKŌ (Japanese pirates). The following year formal diplomatic relations were opened, the Ashikaga shōgun thereafter signing all diplomatic correspondence with China as the "king of Japan." In 1404 an envoy arrived in Japan from China, bearing tallies and a register for the shōgun. Thenceforth all official ships going to China carried sequentially numbered tallies, which were verified at the port of Ningbo (Ningpo) and once again at Beijing (Peking). Between 1404 and 1547 a total of 87 tally ships made 17 voyages.

In principle, the tally trade represented tribute on the part of the "king of Japan" to the Ming emperor, and the ships flew banners that read "tribute-bearing ship of Japan." The goods that the Japanese received in return were "gifts" from the emperor to his loyal subject the "king." The actual operation, however, was carried out by powerful regional *daimyō* and Buddhist temples, who were sometimes joined by Hakata (see FUKUOKA) and SAKAI merchants. Because the Zen priests of the leading monasteries (see GOZAN) were the most highly educated group of the period, they were enlisted to write memorials to the Chinese emperor and to serve as heads of the missions.

Three kinds of transaction took place:

Tribute trade: horses, swords, sulfur, gold screens, and fans were presented in return for silver coins, silk textiles, and copper coins. The greatest number of copper coins were received during the rule of Yoshimitsu. At a time when Japan did not have a unified currency, these copper coins played an important role in its monetary economy (see EIRAKUSEN and KŌBUSEN).

Official trade: exchange carried out in Beijing by the Ming government and representatives of the shogunate, regional daimyō, temples, and merchants. Swords, sulfur, copper, Indian redwood (sappanwood), and gold lacquerware were exchanged for Chinese copper coins, silk, and textiles.

Private trade: trade with licensed Chinese merchants in Beijing and Ningbo. This was by far the most profitable trade; it was said that when Chinese raw silk was brought back to Japan, its value increased 20 times, while copper from Japan was sold in China at five times its domestic value. The huge cost of the overseas expeditions required a broad mobilization of capital, and the profits encouraged many individuals to make comparatively small investments.

As the power of the Ashikaga declined, the HOSOKAWA FAMILY and ŌUCHI FAMILY, influential daimyō families, competed with each other for the right to send tally ships. Following a clash in 1523 between the delegations of these two families in Ningbo, the Ōuchi gained a monopoly. With the collapse of the Ōuchi in 1551, the tally trade ceased to exist.

■——Tanaka Takeo, *Chūsei taigai kankei shi* (1975). Tanaka Takeo with Robert Sakai, "Japan's Relations with Overseas Countries," in John W. Hall and Toyoda Takeshi, ed, *Japan in the Muromachi Age* (1977). TANAKA Takeo

Tama

City in southern Tōkyō Prefecture; on the river Tamagawa. Formerly a farming village, Tama is now a residential area with large housing complexes. One development, Tama New Town, covers an area of 30 sq km (11 sq mi) and has a projected population of 400,000. Pop: 95,248.

tama

Name applied in the Shintō tradition to a metaphysical substance of being. Different from *mono* and *mi,* which are spiritual entities inseparable from material being, *tama* (also called *mitama*) functions through the medium of material substance but is independent from that substance. Disease or misfortune occurs when the function of *tama* declines, and death when this *tama*-spirit escapes from the corporeal body. Religious services have been devoted to *tama;* from ancient times rituals to prevent the spirit from leaving the body *(tamashizume)* and to reactivate the spirit *(tamafuri)* were practiced at the imperial court and among the people.

Historically, four aspects or functions of *tama* have been recognized: the harmonious and harmonizing *nigimitama,* the active and valiant *aramitama,* the gracious and beneficent *sakimitama,* and the wondrous and wonder-working *kushimitama.* The fact that deities are distinguished and worshiped according to their functions is well illustrated by the separate enshrinement and worship of the *aramitama* of the sun goddess and imperial ancestress AMATERASU ŌMIKAMI at the Aramatsuri no Miya, a subshrine of the ISE SHRINE, and the *sakimitama* and *kushimitama* of the god ŌKUNINUSHI NO MIKOTO at the ŌMIWA SHRINE. Thus Shintō deities have proliferated and been ranked in accordance with the recognition of difference in degree and function of *tama. Tama* whose function is maleficent are regarded as vengeful spirits (*onryō* or GORYŌ) that must be placated through rites of pacification. UEDA Kenji

Tamagawa

River in Tōkyō Prefecture, central Honshū, originating in Yamanashi Prefecture in the Chichibu Mountains and flowing east through the western part of Tōkyō Prefecture into Tōkyō Bay. The lower reaches separate Tōkyō from Kanagawa Prefecture. The upper reaches beyond the city of Ōme, an especially scenic area known as OKU TAMA, are part of Chichibu–Tama National Park. Tōkyō International Airport (Haneda) is located on the northern bank of the river's mouth. The water has been utilized for drinking since the Edo period (1600–1868), and Lake Oku Tama, a lake created by a dam in the upper reaches of the river, is now a major source of drinking water for Tōkyō. Length: 126 km (78 mi); area of drainage basin: 1,240 sq km (479 sq mi).

Tamagawa Aqueduct

(Tamagawa Jōsui). In Tōkyō Prefecture, central Honshū, extending from the Musashino Plateau to the Yotsuya district of Tōkyō. One of the three main aqueducts of Edo (now Tōkyō) during the Edo period (1600–1868) together with the KANDA AQUEDUCT and the Senkawa Aqueduct, it accelerated the creation of new rice fields in the Musashino area. Construction was completed in 1654 on orders of Matsudaira Nobutsuna. It provided Tōkyō with water until 1965. Length: approximately 50 km (31 mi).

Tamagawa University

(Tamagawa Daigaku). Private, coeducational university located in the city of Machida, Tōkyō Prefecture. Founded in 1929 by the progressive educator Obara Kuniyoshi as Tamagawa Gakuen, it adopted its present name in 1949. It has departments of letters, agriculture, and engineering. It is known for its Institute of Pedagogy. Enrollment was 5,492 in 1980.

Tama Hills

(Tama Kyūryō). Group of hills in southern Tōkyō and Kanagawa prefectures, central Honshū. Portions of the hills have been incorporated into a series of parks serving as major recreation areas for Tōkyō residents. In the 1960s numerous large housing projects were built in and around many of the hills.

Tama, Lake

(Tamako). Also called Murayama Reservoir. Artificial reservoir in north central Tōkyō, central Honshū. It was constructed in 1927 and is one of the main sources of water for Tōkyō. Located in the densely wooded region of the Sayama Hills, the lake is noted for its clear water and is a popular recreation area and the site of a major amusement park. Area: 1.4 sq km (0.5 sq mi); storage capacity: 14.8 million cu m (522.4 million cu ft).

Tamana

City in northwestern Kumamoto Prefecture, Kyūshū. Situated on the Ariake Sea, Tamana has been an active port since the 14th century. Principal industries are printing, foodstuffs, and rubber. Laver (a seaweed) and shellfish are cultivated in the coastal areas; grapes and mandarin oranges are grown in the hilly regions. Tamana Hot Spring attracts visitors. The ETA FUNAYAMA TOMB is known for its rich yield of Kofun period (ca 300–710) artifacts. Pop: 44,714.

Tamano

City in southern Okayama Prefecture, western Honshū, on the Inland Sea. Following the completion of the port of Uno in 1909, regular boat service to Shikoku was initiated. The construction of the shipyard of Mitsui Engineering & Shipbuilding Co, Ltd, in 1919 resulted in rapid industrialization. Copper smelting and the manufacturing of school uniforms and golf balls are also important. It is part of the Inland Sea National Park. Pop: 77,807.

Tamatsukuri Hot Spring

(Tamatsukuri Onsen). Located southwest of the city of Matsue, northeastern Shimane Prefecture, western Honshū. A sulfate spring; water temperature 60–70°C (140–158°F). Famous since ancient days, it is one of the representative hot-spring spas in the San'in region. Agate is a specialty product of this area.

Tamba Mountains

(Tamba Sanchi). Mountain range running from north-central Kyōto Prefecture to eastern Hyōgo Prefecture, central Honshū. Aside from the monadnocks of Mikunidake (959 m; 3,146 ft), ATAGOYAMA (924 m; 3,031 ft), and HIEIZAN (848 m; 2,781 ft), most of the range is 600–700 m (1,968–2,296 ft) in height. The Yuragawa and Ōigawa rivers have carved the mountains to create basin lands such as Kameoka, Fukuchiyama, and Sasayama. Special products are *matsutake* (a kind of mushroom) and chestnuts.

Tamba ware

(tamba-yaki). Ceramics produced in the southwestern part of ancient Tamba Province (present-day town of Konda, Hyōgo Prefecture). Archaeological data are limited, but production appears to have begun early in the Kamakura period (1185–1333) as a farming sideline.

Many art historians and collectors equate Tamba pottery's florescence with the initial phase of production, lasting until the early 1600s, when potters fired in single-chamber *anagama* (through-draft kilns), hollowed out high in mountain slopes. These wares addressed the daily needs of the local farming population. Among the most abundantly produced objects were thick, asymmetrical storage jars, hand built by the coil method and unfolding from small bases into broad-shouldered, narrow-mouthed vessels. Except for some incised designs and inscriptions, surface decoration grew out of the firing process: falling wood ash formed an accidental greenish glaze on the shoulders of pots, and flame flashing resulted in variegated reddish hues elsewhere.

The diffusion of advanced Korean ceramic technology to Tamba by the early 17th century helped potters adapt to the burgeoning Edo-period (1600–1868) economy. Wooden kick-wheels facilitated production speed as well as variety and refinement in shape. In addition, long, low, brick and mud-plaster kilns built on lower mountain slopes, *noborigama* (climbing kiln) prototypes often called *tamba-gama,* held more pottery and required less firing time than *anagama.*

Pottery produced in *tamba-gama* tended to retain the sturdy, utilitarian character of earlier times. Besides storage jars, expanding inventories emphasized such items as rice bowls, small *hibachi* (braziers), mortars, and *sake* bottles. Although reddish brown, black, or amber glazes were used, simple designs predominated; typically, potters used a bamboo tube or ladle to superimpose contrasting glaze or slip on an overall glazed pot before firing. The small number of ceramics produced for the elite during the Edo period from the first included tea-ceremony ware and, later, delicate *sake* bottles and vases, often decorated with bird or flower motifs. *Tamba-gama* output reached distant and urban locales, much being destined for *sake* or condiment manufacturers. Marketing increasingly revolved around middleman-wholesalers. By the 19th century, the regional government (the Sasayama domain) was exercising at least partial control over production and distribution.

Demand for Tamba pottery declined rapidly after the Meiji Restoration (1868). For almost half a century after 1915, production centered on a variety of industrial and commercial ware, all produced in quantity by electric jigger wheels (a mold technique). However, after the early 1960s, the growing momentum of the FOLK CRAFTS *(mingei)* movement encouraged potters to revitalize the Tamba tradition.

Today, approximately 55 ceramic workshops—many small, household-based enterprises hiring few, if any, employees—operate in the villages of Shimo- and Kami-Tachikui. The majority produce folkcraft ceramics. Vases reminiscent of old-fashioned jars and *sake* bottles provide clearest continuity with old Tamba pottery and, along with tea-ceremony ware, constitute the villages' most artistic and expensive pottery. In addition, workshops produce both Japanese- and Western-style tableware and teapots. Electric potters' wheels as well as gas, oil, or electric kilns are widely used; wood-burning kilns, smaller than *tamba-gama,* are usually reserved for artistic production lines.

■ ——Daniel Rhodes, *Tamba Pottery: The Timeless Art of a Japanese Village* (1970). Sugimoto Katsuo, *Tamba no kogama* (1969). Yabuuchi Kiyoshi, *Tachikui kama no kenkyū* (1955).

Jill KLEINBERG

Tamba Yasuyori (912–995)

Heian-period (794–1185) physician and author of the *Ishimpō* (982), the oldest extant medical treatise in Japan. Born in Tamba Province (now part of Kyōto and Hyōgo prefectures) of a naturalized Chinese family, he served as a high-ranking court physician. The *Ishimpō* is a compilation, in 30 fascicles, of Chinese medical books of the Sui (589–618) and Tang (T'ang; 618–907) periods, many of which have otherwise been lost.

YAMADA Terutane

Tamenaga Shunsui (1789–?)

Late-Edo-period GESAKU fiction writer. There are various theories as to the year of his death, some placing it in 1842 and some in 1844, but it is in any case unknown. He is generally regarded as having originated, or at least brought to maturity, the genre of fiction known as the NINJŌBON. Shunsui's real name was Echizen'ya Chōjirō, and he was originally the proprietor of a commercial lending library *(kashihon'ya)* in Edo (now Tōkyō). He acquired a taste for fiction in his boyhood, and tradition pictures him as a young man making his rounds as an itinerant booklender walking the streets of Edo with his nose always in a book, heedless of the bustle around him. Sometime in his twenties, he became a student of the KŌDAN storyteller Itō Enshin (1761–1840), and for many years thereafter appeared irregularly on the YOSE stage as a raconteur under the name Tamenaga Shōsuke, though never to great popular acclaim. Whether out of a serious desire to learn the writer's craft or to procure manuscripts for publication, Shunsui became a student of SHIKITEI SAMBA late in Samba's career, and also formed an association with RYŪTEI TANEHIKO.

In 1821, using the pen name Nansenshō Somabito with the permission of that earlier writer's heirs, Shunsui published the first three volumes of a work entitled *Akegarasu nochi no masayume,* on which he had collaborated with Ryūtei Rijō (d 1841). (Two more volumes appeared in 1824.) Rijō, an associate of Shikitei Samba's and a writer of contemporary repute, is described in some sources as Shunsui's elder brother. This work, Shunsui's first popular success, deals with a disaster-filled love affair between a young married merchant and a courtesan. Its plot, intricately convoluted and filled with intrigues and murderous villains, marks the work as close kin to GŌKAN ("bound volumes"), a form of popular illustrated fiction, and YOMIHON ("reading books"), a genre of *gesaku* fiction usually serious in tone, but it is regarded as Shunsui's first important essay in the *ninjōbon* field.

The decade of the 1820s saw Shunsui's gradual emergence as a popular writer, although by his own admission, a great number of his works, all published under the name Somabito, were either plagiarisms or written to his outlines by assistants while he continued to operate his lending library. Few of the works dating from this period of his career have attracted much critical attention. Several of them, however, are clearly in the line of development from *Akegarasu nochi no masayume* to his later *ninjōbon* masterpieces, although it is debatable how much of a role Shunsui played in their composition.

Shunsui announced in 1829 that he was abandoning the name Somabito and would hereafter call himself Tamenaga Shunsui. His reputation for using collaborators and for downright plagiarism survived this change of names, however, and in later years he felt compelled to insist repeatedly that he had indeed turned over a new leaf and was working independently. There is litte doubt that Shunsui's best works, chief among them his masterly *Shunshoku umegoyomi* (1832–33, Spring Love: A Plum-blossom Almanac), were entirely his own, although he admitted that at least two of his later books were written in part by assistants.

Shunshoku umegoyomi, published in four volumes in 1832 and 1833, met with such success that some of Shunsui's contemporaries doubted that he and the unprincipled hack writer Somabito II of previous years could be one and the same. *Umegoyomi,* like all *ninjōbon,* shows much influence from the SHAREBON, as well as elements derived from *gōkan* and *yomihon* sources, the earlier UKIYO-ZŌSHI tradition, and the KABUKI stage, but it is distinguished from these forms and from earlier *ninjōbon* by its unique blend of social and psychological realism and sentimental romance. It is a rambling and somewhat shapeless tale, describing a complex of human relationships centering upon Tanjirō, the adopted heir to a YOSHIWARA brothel who is falsely accused of theft and done out of his inheritance by a treacherous brothel clerk. Tanjirō is a striking contrast to the wealthy, witty, and suave hero of the classic *sharebon;* he is living in penury, driven to his bed by a vague illness brought on by his disappointments, weak-willed, and unable to disguise his emotions. He is, however, extremely handsome, and his very weakness makes him appealing to the female characters in *Umegoyomi* and, presumably, to the women who seem to have made up a majority of Shunsui's readers. Tanjirō's principal lover is the passionately devoted *geisha* Yonehachi, portrayed as alternately self-sacrificing and viciously jealous of the attraction Tanjirō feels toward Ochō, the orphaned daughter of the brothelkeeper who originally adopted Tanjirō. Subplots and tangents enrich and sometimes mar the narrative, but Shunsui's focus is always on Tanjirō's shifting emotional entanglements.

Umegoyomi caused a sensation because Shunsui's honest, sympathetic portrayal of romantic love was a novelty in the fiction of his day. The *sharebon* treated love as a lapse in taste on the part of the sophisticated brothel patron and an emotion that was wholly alien to the geisha or prostitute, whose very job was to be deceitful and coldly dedicated to the appearance, not the reality, of love. Love was either absent from *gōkan* and *yomihon* stories or treated as a snare to be avoided. *Umegoyomi* and its sequels and imitators, on the other hand, portrayed characters absorbed in reading each other's emotions and motivated not by the orthodox virtues of honor, family, or thrift, but by pursuit of a new ideal of life governed by honest feeling. Shunsui's gift for dialogue, honed by his training as a storyteller and probably by his study with Shikitei Samba, allowed him to present his characters almost wholly in their own words, a device that, combined with his efforts to deal with real, unstereotyped emotions, produced characterizations of unprecedented vividness. In a larger sense, *Shunshoku umegoyomi* gave legitimacy to feelings and motivations that had long been repressed both in fiction and in its readers.

Shunsui attempted to capitalize on the success of *Umegoyomi* with several sequels (chief among them *Shunshoku tatsumi no sono*, 1833–35), but none of the two dozen or more books he subsequently produced was as popular or as influential as his first great achievement. While his *ninjōbon* are often subtly erotic, they are in no way pornographic; nonetheless Shunsui ran afoul of the moral conservatism that undergirt the TEMPŌ REFORMS initiated by shogunate leader MIZUNO TADAKUNI. He was arrested and charged with harming public morals. The details of the proceedings against him and the consequences are somewhat unclear, but Shunsui spent several months in manacles, his publisher and illustrator were fined heavily, and the blocks from which his books were printed were confiscated and destroyed. Broken in health and spirit, reduced once again to writing adventure stories for which he had no particular gift, Shunsui died soon after. The *ninjōbon* never regained the eminence to which Shunsui raised it, but *Umegoyomi* and the best of Shunsui's other works maintained their popularity and would have a considerable influence on modern Japanese fiction.

Robert W. LEUTNER

Tamiya Hiroshi (1903–)

Plant physiologist. Born in Tōkyō. Graduate and professor of Tōkyō University. With his former teacher, SHIBATA KEITA, he carried out research on the activities of enzymes, especially respiratory enzymes, in living creatures and joined in the worldwide debate concerning these matters. In connection with his research in photosynthesis, he devised a method for the synchronized culture of CHLORELLA, making its mass cultivation possible. He was awarded the Order of Culture in 1977.

Suzuki Zenji

Tamiya Torahiko (1911–)

Novelist. Born in Tōkyō. Graduate of Tōkyō University. As a young man, Tamiya participated in various literary groups. After World War II, he gained recognition for his historical novel *Kiri no naka* (1947). He continued writing other historical novels such as *Rakujō* (1949), and he developed an autobiographical form of fiction exemplified by *Ashizurimisaki* (1949). Tragic historical figures or contemporary people in adverse situations are the main characters in his often sentimental works. He later wrote novels of unhappy marriages and other family situations. *Ehon* (1951) is a collection of his short stories.

Tamon'in nikki

(Tamon'in Diary). A journal of 46 volumes *(kan)* kept by successive heads of the Tamon'in chapel of the temple KŌFUKUJI in Nara between 1478 and 1618. The original manuscript does not survive, and the oldest extant copy dates from the early 18th century. Although the *Tamon'in nikki* spans nearly a century and a half, its reliability as a historical source is greatest in its later portions, especially the period 1534–96, when entries were kept by the priest Eishun (1518–96). The scope of the work is broad, and it is a rich source of information for political, social, economic, and cultural history during a dynamic period when Japan was transformed from a fragmented country at war into a unified national entity.

H. Paul VARLEY

Tamura Ransui (1718–1776)

Also known as Tamura Gen'yū. Specialist in *honzōgaku* (traditional pharmacognosy) known for his cultivation of ginseng (Chōsen *ninjin*). He was a student of ABE SHŌO. During and after the rule of shōgun TOKUGAWA YOSHIMUNE, he is said to have worked as an adviser to help carry out the government's plan of encouraging an increase in domestic production of certain products including ginseng. The first national trade fair was held in Edo (now Tōkyō) in 1757 mainly through his efforts. One of his students was HIRAGA GENNAI. He wrote *Ninjin kōsakuki* in 1747.

Suzuki Zenji

Tamura Taijirō (1911–)

Novelist. Born in Mie Prefecture. Graduate of Waseda University. He started writing before World War II and participated in many literary coteries. Shortly after the war, he created a sensation with his novel *Nikutai no mon* (1947, Gateway of the Flesh), which describes the world of prostitutes. Its motif, that the liberation of man is realized through the liberation of the flesh, particularly appealed to the postwar public. Other works include the novels *Shumpuden* (1947) and *Jiraigen* (1964).

Tamura Toshiko (1884–1945)

Novelist. Original name Satō Toshi. Born into a merchant family in Tōkyō, she studied briefly at Nihon Joshi Daigaku (Japan Women's University) but left because of illness. She began writing as a disciple of KŌDA ROHAN. Also interested in dance and theater, she became an actress for about two years in the dramatic troupe of OKAMOTO KIDŌ. In 1909 she married the novelist Tamura Shōgyo (1874–1948). When her novel *Akirame* (1911, Resignation) won first place in the *Ōsaka asahi shimbun* newspaper fiction contest, she was launched immediately as a best-selling writer of naturalistic and passionate works, reflecting the new women's consciousness. She became involved with a journalist, Suzuki Etsu (1886–1933), and left her husband to follow him in 1918 to Vancouver, British Columbia, where he was employed by the Japanese-language newspaper *Tairiku nippō*. There they married, and there she lived for a total of almost 18 years, remaining after Suzuki's death in 1933. She returned to Japan in 1936 and resumed her writing career with only limited success. She had a difficult affair with the leftist KUBOKAWA TSURUJIRŌ, and in 1938 she went to Shanghai, where she edited a women's literary magazine before her death there. Her works include *Miira no kuchibeni* (1913, Lip-Rouge on a Mummy), *Onna sakusha* (1913, Woman Writer), and *Yamamichi* (1938, Mountain Road). The posthumous royalties from her works were used to establish a literary prize for women in her name; its first winner in 1960 was SETOUCHI HARUMI for the biography *Tamura Toshiko*.

Tanabata Festival

One of Japan's traditional five festivals, or *gosekku* (see SEKKU), currently observed on 7 July, or in some locales, 7 August. Its celebration originated in a Chinese folk legend concerning two stars—the Weaver Star, i.e., Vega, and the Cowherd Star, i.e., Altair—who were said to be lovers who could meet only once a year on the seventh night of the seventh lunar month. The Ji Qiao Tian (Chi Ch'iao T'ien), the commemoration of this occasion in ancient China, was observed mainly by women, who burned incense and prayed to the Weaver Star for success in love and proficiency in such skills as sewing and calligraphy. The festival was introduced to Japan, where it merged with native legends concerning a celestial weaving maiden (Tanabatatsume) believed to fashion clothing for the gods. Termed Tanabata (a shortened form of Tanabatatsume), this festival became one of the annual events (*nenjū gyōji*; see FESTIVALS) observed by the imperial court. Since Tanabata fell close to the time of the BON FESTIVAL for the souls of the dead, its celebration also became associated with certain taboos, rites of purification, and other practices

Tanabata Festival

Brightly colored paper decorations hang from bamboo poles in downtown Hiratsuka during the Tanabata Festival.

involved in welcoming and seeing off the spirits of one's departed ancestors.

Although the modern celebration of Tanabata varies widely according to locale, a common feature of this festival is the display of bamboo branches decorated with long narrow strips of colored paper and other small ornaments and talismans. The paper strips are inscribed with poems expressing the wish for fulfillment of romantic aspirations, and legend has it that if the ink for these poems is made of dew gathered from the leaves of the taro plant on the morning of Tanabata one's calligraphy will also be improved. The decorated bamboo branch is tied to a pole and placed in front of the house. At the end of the Tanabata festivities, the bamboo branches are thrown into a river to be carried away, thereby dispelling misfortune, or are placed in rice paddies as a means of repelling insects or as a thanksgiving offering for what is hoped will be a bounteous harvest. The display of bamboo branches may be connected with their function as *yorishiro,* places for visiting ancestral spirits to reside; and their disposal in a river is exemplary of rites of purification by water (MISOGI) basic to Shintō ritual. Other rites of ablution connected with the observance of Tanabata are the ceremonies of the Tanabata *bune* (boat) and Tanabata *ningyō* (doll), in which straw figures of men and animals are set afloat in small boats. It was believed that, by means of this practice, one's sins and the stain of evil could be transferred to these straw figures and floated away. This kind of rite is called *nemurinagashi* (literally, "floating away sleep"), based on the notion that evil or misfortune could be cast off like shaking off harmful sleep (see also NEBUTA FESTIVAL).

The cities of Sendai and Hiratsuka are particularly known for their elaborate celebrations of the Tanabata Festival as a tourist attraction. Both cities observe Tanabata on 7 August, which is closer to the traditional festival date.   *INOKUCHI Shōji*

Tanabe

City in southern Wakayama Prefecture, central Honshū; on Tanabe Bay. An ancient port town, military base, and transportation center, Tanabe later became a castle town of the Andō family. Principal industries are lumber and fishing. Plums and mandarin oranges are also grown. Scenic attractions include the gorge Kizetsukyō and the Kikyōiwa, a strange rock formation. Pop: 69,550.

Tanabe Hajime (1885–1962)

Philosopher. Born in Tōkyō, he graduated from the philosophy department of Tōkyō University, and from 1922 studied phenomenology in Europe, chiefly under the direction of Edmund Husserl (1859–1938). He became professor at Kyōto University in 1927. Tanabe first worked on a philosophical theory of science under the influence of the Neo-Kantian school. Following this, he took a critical stance on German idealism, Marxism, and the philosophical views of NISHIDA KITARŌ and went on to develop his own philosophical system based on the theory known as the "logic of species" (*shu no ronri).* After World War II, Tanabe came out with *Zangedō to shite no tetsugaku* (1946, Philosophy as the Way of Atonement) in which he criticized his own philosophical methods up to then for their tendency to make absolutes of what he called "species." He moved from this stance to a position stressing the TARIKI (salvation through the power of the "other") tenets found in the Jōdo Shin sect of Buddhism. His works are collected in the 15-volume *Tanabe Hajime zenshū* (1963–64).   *FURUTA Hikaru*

Tanabe Seiko (1928–   )

Novelist. Born in Ōsaka, she graduated from Ōsaka Shōin Women's College. Most of Tanabe's stories are set in the Ōsaka area, and her use of Ōsaka dialect is a prominent feature of her writing. Her novel *Senchimentaru jānī* (1964, Sentimental Journey), which won the Akutagawa Prize, humorously describes an incongruous love affair between a frivolous middle-aged woman screenwriter and a young communist. She has also written many scripts for TV and radio dramas, as well as a novel based on the life of the poet YOSANO AKIKO, titled *Chisuji no kurokami* (1972, A Thousand Strands of Black Hair). In the 1970s she also became a widely read newspaper columnist.

Tanabe Seiyaku Co, Ltd

Company engaged in the manufacture and sale of pharmaceuticals. A member of the SANWA BANK, LTD, group, it traces its roots back to 1678. It was organized in its present form in 1933 and currently ranks fifth in the industry. It has wholly owned subsidiaries in the United States, Belgium, and Brazil and joint venture companies in Taiwan and Indonesia. Future plans call for the development of new medications and imports from pharmaceutical companies. It has had to pay considerable compensation to SMON DISEASE patients. Sales for the fiscal year ending April 1982 totaled ¥124.6 billion (US $508.9 million) and the company was capitalized at ¥8 billion (US $32.7 million). Its head office is in Ōsaka.

Tanabe Taichi (1831–1915)

Diplomat who served both the Tokugawa shogunate (1603–1867) and the Meiji government (1868–1912). The son of a Confucian scholar, Tanabe attended the Shōheikō, the shogunate's Confucian academy. He developed an interest in foreign affairs and became friends with FUKUZAWA YUKICHI and other scholars interested in the West. In 1864 he accompanied an unsuccessful Tokugawa mission to Europe to seek the closing of the port of Yokohama—a revision of the ANSEI COMMERCIAL TREATIES. He traveled again to Europe in 1867 as a member of the shogunate delegation to the Paris International Exposition (see SHOGUNATE MISSIONS TO THE WEST). After the MEIJI RESTORATION (1868) he entered the Ministry of Foreign Affairs and accompanied the IWAKURA MISSION abroad (1871–73) as chief secretary. Late in 1874 he traveled to Beijing (Peking) with ŌKUBO TOSHIMICHI to settle a dispute over Taiwan (see TAIWAN EXPEDITION OF 1874). He was later appointed to the GENRŌIN (Chamber of Elders, a protosenatorial body); as an official of the Committee for the Compilation of Documents on the Meiji Restoration (Ishin Shiryō Hensankai) he helped to edit *Bakumatsu gaikōdan* (1898, History of Foreign Relations in the Late Edo Period).

Tanaka Chikao (1905–   )

Playwright and director. Born in Nagasaki Prefecture. Graduate of Keiō University. A one-time student of acting, he became established as a playwright when his one-act play *Ofukuro* was well received at the Tsukiji Little Theater in Tōkyō in 1933. Influenced by French existentialism and interested in Catholicism after World War II, he explored such themes as female sexuality and the concept of original sin. In 1935 he married the playwright and novelist TANAKA SUMIE. In 1953 his play *Kyōiku* won the Yomiuri Literary Prize. Other major plays include *Kumo no hatate* (1947) and *Maria no kubi* (1959). Since 1981 he has been a member of the Japan Art Academy.

Tanakadate Aikitsu (1856–1952)

Geophysicist. Father of Japanese seismology and geophysics. Born in Iwate Prefecture, he graduated in 1882 from Tōkyō University, where he studied with Thomas C. MENDENHALL. He studied in England and Germany from 1881 to 1891 and became a professor at Tōkyō University upon his return to Japan. He took measurements of gravity and terrestrial magnetism at many locations throughout Japan and was a prime mover behind the establishment of the Latitude Observatory of MIZUSAWA. He received the Order of Culture in 1944, the first time it was awarded. He also had a lifelong interest in the movement to replace the traditional Japanese writing system with Roman letters, having devised a system of his own.

Tanaka Fujimaro (1845–1909)

Meiji-period politician; active in the promotion of progressive educational administrative policies during the 1870s. Born in Owari Province (now part of Aichi Prefecture) of *samurai* stock, Tanaka joined the new government after the Meiji Restoration (1868) and was placed in charge of administering educational policy. As a member of the IWAKURA MISSION, which toured the United States and Europe from 1871 to 1873, he carefully observed Western educational systems. After his return home he was appointed vice minister of education in 1874. Since the post of minister was vacant at the time, he was the top-ranking official of the Ministry of Education. From 1876 to 1877, Tanaka again visited the United States to make a more detailed inspection of the American school system. Upon his return to Japan he set out to reform the Japanese school administration system on the American model. He revised the EDUCATION ORDER OF 1872, which he criticized for making the educational system too highly centralized and uniform, and thus paved the way for the enactment of the EDUCATION ORDER OF 1879, which was based on the more decentralized American system. The new order aimed at giving more freedom to local school bodies and curtailing intervention by the central government. However, it was severely criticized as inviting confusion and decadence in education and resulted in Tanaka's leaving the Ministry of Education and becoming minister of justice in 1880. He served as minister to Italy (1884) and France (1887) and was a member of the Privy Council from 1890 to 1891 and again from 1892 to 1909 after having served as minister of justice from 1891 to 1892.　　　*Satō Hideo*

Tanaka Fuyuji (1894–1980)

Poet. Real name Tanaka Kichinosuke. Graduate of Rikkyō Middle School in Tōkyō. Born in Fukushima Prefecture. As an employee of the Yasuda Bank, he lived in different cities throughout Japan. He began writing poems around 1920 and contributed to *Shiki,* the magazine started in 1933 by the lyrical poet HORI TATSUO. Tanaka's poems are reminiscent of HAIKU, being short, concise, and unadorned in style, and reflect the life and landscape of the places where he lived. His poems have been translated into English, French, and other languages. Principal collections are *Umi no mieru ishidan* (1930) and *Banshun no hi ni* (1961).

Tanaka Giichi (1864–1929)

General, prime minister (1927–29), foreign minister, and president of the party RIKKEN SEIYŪKAI. Born in the Chōshū domain (now Yamaguchi Prefecture), he attended the Army Academy (1883–86) and the Army War College (1889–92). During the SINO-JAPANESE WAR OF 1894–95, Tanaka served under YAMAGATA ARITOMO in Manchuria. Sent to Russia by the chief of staff in 1898 to study military and social conditions, he returned in 1902 to become head of the Russian section of the General Staff.

During the RUSSO-JAPANESE WAR (1904–05) he served as an aide to KODAMA GENTARŌ, chief of staff of the Manchurian army, and accompanied Kodama to Tōkyō in March 1905 to support arguments for ending the war before Japan became exhausted. The next year he drafted a comprehensive defense plan, which, after revisions by Yamagata, became basic policy. In 1911, now a major general, he became director of the Military Affairs Bureau of the Army Ministry and advocated expansion of the army by two divisions. The army's insistence on expansion precipitated the downfall of the SAIONJI KIMMOCHI cabinet. Tanaka was also pivotal in the founding of the IMPERIAL MILITARY RESERVISTS' ASSOCIATION. Following the outbreak of World War I, Tanaka wrote extensively about Sino-Japanese economic cooperation and he helped to negotiate the 1918 Sino-Japanese Joint Defensive Military Agreement, which gave Japan the option of challenging either Soviet or Austro-Hungarian troops from the Amur Basin to Lake Baikal. Ironically, as HARA TAKASHI's army minister (1918–21), Tanaka was pitted against the General Staff over withdrawal of Japanese troops sent on the SIBERIAN INTERVENTION.

In September 1923 Tanaka, now a full general, became army minister in a cabinet formed by YAMAMOTO GONNOHYŌE. He also became known as a military man with close ties to civilian politics, and when leaders of the Seiyūkai in April 1925 invited him to be party president, he accepted and transferred to the inactive reserve. Tanaka became prime minister when a major banking crisis (the FINANCIAL CRISIS OF 1927) and criticism of the moderate China policy of SHIDEHARA KIJŪRŌ brought down the WAKATSUKI REIJIRŌ cabinet in April 1927. He served concurrently as foreign minister and minister of colonization. Loans guaranteed through an imperial ordinance restored order to the economy, but many small and medium-sized banks and businesses failed. In the so-called MARCH 15TH INCIDENT of 1928 and of the APRIL 16TH INCIDENT of 1929 the Tanaka cabinet ordered large-scale arrests of members of the Communist and other leftist parties and the dissolution of all suspect organizations. Moveover, through an imperial ordinance the cabinet had the PEACE PRESERVATION LAW OF 1925 amended to include the death penalty and lifetime sentences for those suspected of subversive activities.

In foreign policy Tanaka took a "positive" stance toward China (see TŌHŌ KAIGI; TANAKA MEMORANDUM). He promised CHIANG KAI-SHEK limited support for the Chinese Nationalist Revolution but sought some form of autonomy for Manchuria under a client warlord such as ZHANG ZUOLIN (Chang Tso-lin). Moreover, in 1927 and 1928, ostensibly to protect Japanese residents, the Tanaka cabinet on three occasions sent troops to Shandong (Shantung). Clashes in 1928 at Jinan (Tsinan) resulted in the death of more than 3,000 Chinese. In June of the same year Zhang Zuolin was assassinated by Guandong (Kwantung) Army officers near Mukden (now Shenyang). Tanaka called the murder an "unthinkable disaster" and promised the emperor, who was much displeased, to punish those responsible, presumably through a court-martial. The army, however, proposed some sort of administrative punishment. Meanwhile, the Privy Council and other conservatives objected that a phrase in the KELLOGG–BRIAND PACT, to which Japan was a signatory ("in the names of their respective peoples"), violated the concept of national polity *(kokutai).* In the face of mounting criticism, especially from the emperor over Tanaka's handling of the Zhang Zuolin affair, the Tanaka cabinet resigned in July 1929.

📖 ——Nobuya Bamba, *Japanese Diplomacy in a Dilemma: New Light on Japan's China Policy* (1972). Hosokawa Ryūgen, *Tanaka Giichi* (1958). Kawatani Tsuguo, *Tanaka Giichi den* (1929). William Fitch Morton, *Tanaka Giichi and Japan's China Policy* (1980). Takakura Tetsuichi, ed, *Tanaka Giichi denki,* 2 vols (1960).

　　　William F. MORTON

Tanaka Hidemitsu (1913–1949)

Novelist. Born in Tōkyō. Graduate of Waseda University. During his student years at Waseda, he participated in the rowing events of the 1932 Olympic games held in Los Angeles. Influenced by his brother, who was a newspaper reporter, he subsequently became a communist sympathizer, but was disenchanted by the corrupt leadership of the Communist Party. He participated in the founding of a literary coterie and started writing for its magazine. After graduation from Waseda, he continued to write, while working for a rubber company, and became acquainted with his lifelong mentor, the novelist DAZAI OSAMU. During the early 1940s he wrote two novels based on his experience at the Los Angeles Olympics: *Orimposu no kajitsu* (1940) and *Tantei sōshu* (1944). After World War II he joined the Communist Party, but again became disenchanted and was eventually expelled. His later years were colored by drugs, alcoholism, and decadence. He committed suicide in 1949 at the grave of Dazai Osamu.

Tanaka Hisashige (1799–1881)

Also known as Tanaka Giemon. Inventor. Born in Kurume (now in Fukuoka Prefecture). Even as a child he was known for his cleverness with mechanical devices. Among his numerous and varied inventions were a pump for extinguishing fires and a "perpetual" clock. In 1854 he entered the service of the Saga domain and made contributions to the manufacture of cannons and rifles as well as boiler power plants for ships. He was the founder of Tanaka Manufacturing Works, the forerunner of the Tōshiba group.

Tanaka Kakuei (1918–   )

Politician; prime minister from 1972 to 1974. Born in Niigata Prefecture. As a young man he formed his own construction firm, having worked his way through middle school as an apprentice to a contractor. His company prospered during World War II, enabling him after the war to make substantial contributions to the Nihon Shimpotō (Japan Progressive Party) and easing his entry into politics. Elected to the House of Representatives in 1947 as a candidate of the MINSHUTŌ (Democratic Party), the following year he joined the newly formed Minshu Jiyūtō (Democratic Liberal Party), a forerunner of the Liberal Democratic Party (LDP; formed in 1955). He served as minister of postal services and communications in the first KISHI NOBUSUKE cabinet and as minister of finance in the second and third IKEDA HAYATO and first SATŌ EISAKU cabinets. As minister of international trade and industry in the third Satō cabinet he pushed for high economic growth. With his private wealth he built up a following in the LDP and was twice secretary-general of the party before becoming party president and prime minister in 1972. He was the first Japanese prime minister since World War I without a university background. As prime minister he opened diplomatic relations with the People's Republic of China, visiting Beijing (Peking) in September 1972, and advocated the "remodeling" of the Japanese islands, that is, a geographical redistribution of Japanese industry (see NIHON RETTŌ KAIZŌ RON); the latter program served only to spur an inflationary rise in land prices. He resigned from the government in December 1974 amid allegations of involvement in financial scandals and was arrested in 1976 in connection with the LOCKHEED SCANDAL, but he continued to be an influential politician and factional leader into the 1980s.

Tanaka Kinuyo (1910–1977)

Film actress and director, one of only a handful of women in Japanese film history to work in both capacities. She is better known for her work as an actress in a career that spanned over 50 years. She worked with most of Japan's leading directors, but her best-known films and greatest critical acclaim came from her long association with director MIZOGUCHI KENJI, for whom she worked in such memorable film roles as Oharu in Saikaku ichidai onna (1952, The Life of Oharu), the potter's wife in Ugetsu monogatari (1953, Ugetsu), and the mother in Sanshō-Dayū (1954, Sansho the Bailiff).

After a brief apprenticeship in musical theater, Tanaka joined the Shōchiku (see SHŌCHIKU CO, LTD) production company in 1924 and made her film debut that year in Genroku onna (Woman of Genroku). From there she went on to appear in a number of popular silent films. She appeared in Japan's first successful talkie, GOSHO HEINOSUKE's Madamu to nyōbō (1931, The Neighbor's Wife and Mine), and went on to become the most popular female star of the 1930s, playing a wide variety of parts ranging from sweet innocents to seductive vamps.

She remained popular through the war years, but her star faded slightly after she traveled abroad with Mizoguchi in the early 1950s to promote Ugetsu. She did not remain out of favor long, however. Some of her best and most popular performances were made after she had turned 40, in sympathetic roles as a downtrodden wife, a working woman, or a prostitute.

Tanaka began her directorial career in 1953 with Koibumi (Love Letter). The films she directed, though generally undistinguished, show evidence of Mizoguchi's influence with their long, sweeping panoramic shots and their stately grace. In all, she directed six films.

She continued to act in films and on television through the 1960s and 1970s. Her last film appearance once again earned her plaudits. For her part as an old prostitute in KUMAI KEI's Sandakan hachiban shōkan: Bōkyō (1974; shown abroad as Sandakan No. 8; Brothel No. 8), she won the Kinema Jumpō Prize for best actress, the Japanese film industry's highest award. She was appearing in a television serial at the time of her death.

Upon her death, one commentator wrote that Tanaka had been sister, girl friend, and mother to the generations that had grown up with her films. Her career of over 50 years in films is unmatched in Japan and is a rarity in international film history. *David* OWENS

Tanaka Kōtarō (1890–1974)

Legal scholar and second chief justice of the postwar Supreme Court. Born in Kagoshima Prefecture, he graduated from Tōkyō University in 1915. After serving in the Home Ministry, in 1917 he joined the faculty of Tōkyō University, where he taught jurisprudence and commercial law. He was minister of education (1946) in the first YOSHIDA SHIGERU cabinet and a member of the House of Councillors (1947–50). As chief justice of the Supreme Court, 1950–60, Tanaka took part in many historic rulings, including those on the TEIGIN INCIDENT and the SUNAGAWA CASE. Politically a conservative, he was a devout Roman Catholic who believed that the antiwar, democratic 1947 constitution embodied what medieval scholastics termed natural law. He had little tolerance for journalistic criticism of trials, dismissing it as "static." He served on the International Court of Justice from 1960 to 1970. His writings include Hō to shūkyō to shakai seikatsu (1927, Law, Religion, and Life in Society), Sekaihō no riron (3 vols, 1932–34, Theory of World Law), Hō no shihai to saiban (1960, Courts and the Rule of Law), and Kyōiku kihonhō no riron (1961, The Theory of the Basic Education Law). *TANAKA Shigeaki*

Tanaka Kyūgu (1663?–1729)

Civil administrator of the Edo period (1600–1868). Born in Hachiōji, Musashi Province (now Tōkyō Prefecture), he was adopted into the family of a village official in the POST-STATION TOWN of Kawasaki (now in Kanagawa Prefecture). After establishing himself as an able local administrator, he went to Edo (now Tōkyō), where he studied under such Confucian scholars as Narushima Kinkō (1689–1760) and OGYŪ SORAI. In 1721 he published Minkan seiyō, a 15-volume treatise on taxation, flood control, and other aspects of civil administration. In 1723 he was commissioned by the shōgun TOKUGAWA YOSHIMUNE to supervise river control and irrigation projects on the rivers Arakawa and Tamagawa. Later he completed the dikes of the river Sakawagawa. For his services he was made an intendant (daikan), or administrator, over Tokugawa land valued at 30,000 koku (see KOKUDAKA), a singular honor for a commoner.

Tanaka Memorandum

A memorandum, dated 25 July 1927, supposedly presented to the emperor by Prime Minister TANAKA GIICHI following the Far Eastern Conference (TŌHŌ KAIGI); it contained a detailed plan for the conquest of Manchuria and Mongolia. Its text was published in 1929 in the Nanjing (Nanking) Chinese-language monthly review Shishi yuebao (Shih-shih yüeh-pao) and in 1931 in the Shanghai English-language China Critic. The latter version became the basis for anti-Japanese pamphlets circulated in China (by the Comintern) and in the United States, while the former was translated into Japanese, reportedly by the Japan Communist Party. The Japanese government officially denied the authenticity of the memorandum, but opposition-party politicians could use it to embarrass Tanaka and the Rikken Seiyūkai party by exposing the aims of their "positive" policy toward China; and as Japanese armies occupied Manchuria in 1931 and later advanced into China, the memorandum gained credibility among the Western powers. Close examination of the texts, however, reveals important discrepancies of fact and of formal style. Moreover, no corroborative archival material has been found, and at the WAR CRIMES TRIALS, where it was discussed, OKADA KEISUKE, and on subsequent occasions other diplomats and military leaders contemporary with Tanaka, such as ARITA HACHIRŌ, Hayashi Kyūjirō (1882–1964), MATSUOKA YŌSUKE, Morishima Morito (1896–1975), SHIGEMITSU MAMORU, Suzuki Teiichi (b 1888), and UGAKI KAZUSHIGE, all denied that such a memorandum had ever been written.

—— Etō Shinkichi, "Nankin kokumin seifu to Tanaka gaikō," in Fashizumu to dainiji taisen (1962). Hashikawa Bunzō, "Tanaka jōsōbun no shūhen," vol 39 of Seikei ronsō (March 1972). Inō Tentarō, "Tanaka jōsōji o meguru ni san no mondai-I," nos 3 and 4 of Kokusai seiji: Nihon gaikōshi kenkyū—Nihon gaikō shi no shomondai (July 1964). William Fitch Morton, Tanaka Giichi and Japan's China Policy (1980). John J. Stephan, "The Tanaka Memorial (1927): Authentic or Spurious?," Modern Asian Studies 7.4 (1973). *William F.* MORTON

Tanaka Mitsuaki (1843–1939)

Government official of the Meiji period (1868–1912). Born in the Tosa domain (now Kōchi Prefecture). Tanaka early joined the proimperial, antishogunate faction formed in Tosa by TAKECHI ZUIZAN. After the Meiji Restoration of 1868, he served the new government in various military and civil posts, including positions as head of the Audit Bureau, chief of the Tōkyō Metropolitan Police, and principal of the Peers' School. In 1898 Tanaka became imperial household minister. As a confidant of Emperor Meiji he exercised great authority in the palace during his 11-year tenure.

Tanaka Ōdō (1867–1932)

Pen name of Tanaka Kiichi; popular essayist for CHŪŌ KŌRON and other journals during the latter part of the Meiji period (1868–1912) and the Taishō period (1912–26). An unusual Japanese thinker known for his support of individualism, liberalism, and democracy. He began his development of these positions during a nine-year term of study in the United States, especially with the philosopher John Dewey.

Tanaka's decision to study in the United States was influenced and supported by Christian missionaries. Born the third child and second son of a well-to-do landlord family in the village of Naka-tome (now the city of Tokorozawa) in Saitama Prefecture, Tanaka left home in his early teens to attend several missionary schools in Tōkyō and Kyōto. Before graduating he joined the American missionary Eugene Snodgrass (Disciples of Christ) as a translator and English teacher in the city of Tsuruoka in Yamagata Prefecture. He was baptized by Snodgrass in March 1889 and five months later boarded a steamship for the United States, where he attended Snodgrass's alma mater, the College of the Bible (now Lexington Theological Seminary), in Kentucky for four years.

Tanaka's education took a secular turn, which greatly influenced his later writings, when he transferred to the philosophy department of the University of Chicago in September 1894. He studied with the four men who formed the nucleus of the Chicago school of pragmatism: James H. Tufts (history of philosophy), George Herbert Mead (logic and the methodology of psychology), James R. Angell (experimental psychology), and John Dewey (the history of logic and the logic of ethics). John Dewey particularly supported Tanaka as "a most deserving man" for the doctoral program, but Tanaka was unable to find financial support and returned to Japan in 1897 without having earned a graduate degree.

Before beginning his studies with Dewey and the Chicago pragmatists, Tanaka was searching for solutions to the problems he perceived in Meiji Japan. His letters to his family criticized American racism and ignorance about Japan and deplored the jingoism which accompanied Japan's victories in the SINO-JAPANESE WAR OF 1894–1895. In his view Japan's progress to greater "civilization" required more than the mastery of Western technology. Though eager for social reform, Tanaka rejected the socialist notion of class conflict and expressed a profound faith in education. These concerns were very compatible with the Chicago school of pragmatism, an experimental approach to gradual reform. All Tanaka's later writings showed Dewey's imprint in the ideas of scientific method in philosophy and society, the evolutionary and indeterminate nature of humanity, the interrelationship of society and the individual, and the necessity of individual liberty and self-expression within a context of social cooperation.

As a Japanese writer, Tanaka addressed a different spectrum of issues than those which preoccupied his American teachers. Rising to prominence in the journalistic boom which followed the RUSSO-JAPANESE WAR (1904–05), he attacked government censorship and paternalism, repressive education, and the patriarchal family system. He also articulated the social function and responsibilities of the essayist (hyōronka) in the formation of public opinion and public policy. During the 1910s, in harmony with the rising TAISHŌ DEMOCRACY movement, he attempted to reinterpret the MEIJI RESTORATION, the beginning of Japan's modern experience, as a commitment to cosmopolitanism and representative government; to develop a conception of national and cultural autonomy which would advance democracy and respect for the autonomy of other nations; and to promote democratic reforms—such as universal suffrage—which would ensure a more representative relationship between government and people.

During the 1920s Tanaka fell out of step with new trends in Japanese intellectual life, Marxism and Neo-Kantian culturalism, and in doing so, lost his prestige as an essayist and his reading audience. Nevertheless, his influence remained strong among a small group of his former students at Waseda University, where he taught philosophy. His most prominent and devoted follower was

ISHIBASHI TANZAN, who became the editor of the financial journal TŌYŌ KEIZAI SHIMPŌ in 1924 and served a brief term as prime minister after World War II.

Tanaka's leading publications were his critical biographical studies, *Ninomiya Sontoku* (1911) and *Fukuzawa Yukichi* (1915), about an Edo period (1600–1868) agriculturalist and a leading Meiji thinker respectively, and anthologies of his journal articles such as *Shosai yori gaitō ni* (1911, From the Study to the Streets) and *Tettei kojin shugi* (1918, Radical Individualism).

■——Tanaka Ōdō, *Tanaka Ōdō senshū*, 4 vols (1948–49).

Sharon H. NOLTE

Tanaka Shōsuke (fl early 17th century)

(Western name, Don Francisco de Velasco). Kyōto merchant thought to have been the first Japanese to cross the Pacific. In 1610, at the head of a party of some 20 Japanese, he accompanied to New Spain (Mexico) Don Rodrigo VIVERO DE VELASCO, the former viceroy of the Philippines, who had been shipwrecked on the coast of Kazusa (now Chiba Prefecture) in the previous year. Bearing a personal message and gifts from the shōgun TOKUGAWA IEYASU, Tanaka hoped to establish Japanese trade relations with Mexico. Unsuccessful, he returned to Japan the following year with Sebastian VISCAINO, the Spanish envoy sent to thank the shogunate formally for its hospitality to Don Rodrigo.

Tanaka Shōzō (1841–1913)

Pioneer environmentalist and reformer. His lifelong campaign on behalf of the peasants against political oppression and industrial pollution is a striking demonstration of an active, defiant humanism that owed nothing to Western influences. His career contrasts interestingly with those of other radicals of the modern period, such as KITA IKKI and KŌTOKU SHŪSUI.

Resistance to Provincial Misgovernment——As a son of the headman (shōya) of a small village in what is now Tochigi Prefecture, Tanaka received a traditional education at the village school (terakoya) based mainly on the Chinese classics. In his twenties, when he had succeeded his father as headman, a four-year struggle against the exactions of a corrupt domain official resulted in his imprisonment, torture, and, on his release a year later in 1869, exile from the domain; but the real victory was his, for simultaneously with his release, the official was dismissed in disgrace. This was the first of the three "tests" that together constituted what Tanaka called "my university." The second came shortly afterward. Friends had procured for him a government post in a remote district of the far north, where he proved himself an efficient and just administrator. Late in 1870 his superior was found brutally murdered. Wrongly convicted of the murder, Tanaka spent three more years of extreme hardship in a primitive jail before new evidence brought about the reversal of the verdict and his release.

Undaunted by these experiences, he now decided with characteristic single-mindedness to eschew any private career and to devote the rest of his life to the public good. Soon he became a leader of the FREEDOM AND PEOPLE'S RIGHTS MOVEMENT in his native Tochigi and a moving spirit in the launching of its first liberal newspaper, the *Tochigi shimbun*. The third "test" followed in 1883. This time his opponent was the new prefectural governor MISHIMA MICHITSUNE, an autocratic modernizer and developer whose methods were as cruel as his aims were, arguably, admirable. Tanaka encouraged the peasants to resist. Once again he was arrested and imprisoned; but once again the defeat was only temporary, the governor being dismissed after less than a year in office. Shortly afterward, Tanaka was elected chairman of the prefectural assembly.

Pollution: Industry vs Agriculture——Thus far, Tanaka's career had been similar to those of earlier leaders of popular protest. The last 20 years of his life, however, made it unique and led in the 1970s to a general recognition of his lasting significance after 60 years of near oblivion.

When the Meiji Constitution, with its promise of a national Diet, was promulgated in 1889, Tanaka was deeply moved by what he saw as "this manifestation of the imperial benevolence." He was never a revolutionary in the usual sense of the word. Elected by a large majority to the first Diet in 1890, he at once showed himself a vigorous and capable member. Almost immediately the issue that was to preoccupy him throughout his 10 years in the Diet crystallized. This was the pollution of a wide area of the Kantō Plain by effluent from the huge copper mine at Ashio, in the mountains to the northeast of Tōkyō (see ASHIO COPPER MINE INCIDENT). The exploitation of the Ashio Mine was undoubtedly one of the economic miracles of the early Meiji period. It was carried out at breakneck speed, and Ashio copper played a large part in the electrification of Japan. But large quantities of waste copper-bearing rock were dumped into the nearby headwaters of the river Watarasegawa, contaminating the stream as it flowed across the rich farmlands below, and ultimately, through its frequent flooding, poisoning crops and severely affecting the livelihood of many thousands of households. The first signs of pollution had appeared in 1878, when the peasants and fishermen saw it only as a mysterious natural calamity. By 1891 it was serious and widespread, and copper effluent had been authoritatively recognized as the cause.

Tanaka, as the Diet member for some of the worst-affected areas, called on the government to order the closure of the mine, as it had the power to do. The government took little notice. For a nation whose first priority was the establishment of a powerful industrial base on the Western model, the hardships incurred in the process by some thousands of peasants were of very minor importance. But Tanaka refused to withdraw or to moderate his demand. With an intransigence that alienated many who might otherwise have supported him, he insisted on two principles that to him were fundamental: first, that agriculture is the true basis of a nation's life and must therefore always take priority over industry, and second, that in no circumstances must a people, even a minority, be sacrificed to the demands of what is called "industrial progress." Eventually his untiring campaign appeared to bear some fruit when in 1897 the government imposed stringent pollution-control regulations on the mine. But these measures proved ineffective, at least in the short term; and twice, in 1898 and in 1899, peasant anger erupted in mass marches on Tōkyō, while in the Diet Tanaka continued to demand tougher government action on the basis of his two principles. Nothing further was done. In 1901 he resigned from the Diet in disgust at its indifference to his appeals. Two months later, in a final attempt to rouse the nation's conscience, he tried to thrust a petition into the emperor's state carriage when the latter was on his way back from opening the Diet. Police arrested him, but he was soon released; the opinion was widely expressed that to protest in such a bizarre, unseemly way only showed that he was mad.

Fight for a Village —— This was the end of Tanaka's career on the national stage, but not of his fight on behalf of the peasants against an indifferent, authoritarian bureaucracy, nor of his own inner development. At first he busied himself with organizing private relief for the pollution victims. Then, in 1903, a huge scheme for the containment of the floodwaters of the Watarasegawa was drawn up by the government. (When it was finally carried out, over many years and at enormous expense, this scheme did reduce the pollution effectively; but it was never eradicated, and sporadic outbreaks continued to occur for over 50 years.) One of its main features was the creation of a vast overflow reservoir, which necessitated the destruction of the old and prosperous village community of Yanaka. Tanaka at once joined the villagers in their rejection of this scheme. He went to live with them and for three years inspired and led their resistance against both the prefectural and central governments. Such an unequal struggle could never have been more than symbolic, but the little group of peasants persevered until July 1907, when Tanaka and the small minority of villagers who had resisted all official efforts to get them to leave had to watch the demolition of the last remaining houses.

During the years in Yanaka his outlook underwent a remarkable change. His earlier life had been an acting out on a larger stage of his inherited role as a representative and leader of the rural community. Now he came to see himself as a humble fellow-worker with the peasants from whom he had as much to learn of their qualities of simplicity and quiet endurance as he had to give by way of encouragement and wider vision. His diaries and voluminous correspondence record with an almost childlike directness this new humility and openness to fresh experience of an elderly man of action. They reveal also the secret of the serenity that, despite unceasing physical hardship and constant surveillance by the police as a potential "danger to public order," impressed all who met him in these last years: a deeply religious understanding of life, in which Buddhism, Confucianism, and Christianity (a chance reading of the Gospels during another spell in prison in 1902 had given him a new understanding of the meaning of his own long fight for justice) all played their part.

A Pioneer Ecologist —— With a few of the survivors, Tanaka stayed on in Yanaka in makeshift huts. Apart from attempts to persuade friends in Tōkyō to campaign for the rebuilding of the village, the last great effort of his life was to expound to any who would listen—and few did, for he was far in advance of his time—the need for man to respect the natural environment if he were to survive. Convinced that the government's plan for controlling floods and pollution by expensive projects such as reservoirs and river diversion was wasteful and inefficient, he argued that only a "loving understanding" of rivers, hills, and forests would point the way to lasting solutions. In support of this belief he tramped hundreds of miles, studying the behavior of rivers and recording his observations in meticulous detail. It was on one of these journeys that he collapsed in the summer of 1913, to die a month later in a peasant's house nearby. Though in Tōkyō he had been largely forgotten by the political establishment, some 50,000 people, including several hundred priests, gathered for his funeral.

Tanaka's long career of protest was rooted in traditional values whose relevance was scarcely perceived during his lifetime. Today, however, he is seen with some justice as the prophet of an age when the ideal harmony between man and nature, as well as between man and man, will win permanent acceptance, and when all industrial and other economic activities will be conducted, in E. F. Schumacher's phrase, "as if people mattered."

——Tanaka Shōzo, *Gijin zenshū*, 5 vols (Chūgai Shinronsha, 1927). Amamiya Yoshito, *Tanaka Shōzo no hito to shōgai* (1971). Arahata Kanson, *Yanaka Mura metsubō shi* (1907). Hayashi Takeji, *Tanaka Shōzo no shōgai* (1976). Kinoshita Naoe, *Tanaka Shōzo Ō* (1921). Kinoshita Naoe, *Tanaka Shōzo no shōgai* (1928). Mitsue Iwao, *Tanaka Shōzo: Sono shōgai to shisō* (1961). Nakagome Michio, *Tanaka Shōzo to kindai shisō* (1972). F. G. Noteh elfer, "Japan's First Pollution Incident," *Journal of Japanese Studies* 1.2 (1975). Kenneth Strong, *Ox against the Storm: A Biography of Tanaka Shozo* (1977). *Kenneth* STRONG

Tanaka Sumie (1908–)

Playwright and novelist. Maiden name: Tsujimura Sumie. Born in Tōkyō; graduate of Tōkyō Women's Higher Normal School (now Ochanomizu University). In 1935 she married playwright TANAKA CHIKAO. From the early 1930s she began publishing plays which examine women's psychology and often show the influence of her own Catholic faith. She has also written many radio dramas and screenplays. Her plays include *Tsuzumi no onna* (1958, The Woman with the Drum), retelling an Edo-period tragedy; *Garashiya Hosokawa fujin* (1959), based on the life of the 16th-century Christian woman HOSOKAWA GRACIA; and *Genshi, josei wa taiyō de atta* (1971, In the Beginning, Woman Was the Sun), recounting the struggles of the feminist HIRATSUKA RAICHŌ. Some of her short stories are collected in *Kakitsubata gunraku* (1973, A Clump of Irises).

Tanaka Yoshio (1838–1916)

Natural history scholar, known for creating the variety of loquat called the Tanaka *biwa*. Born in Iida in present day Nagano Prefecture, he was a student of ITŌ KEISUKE. Active in many fields, he worked for the government after the Meiji Restoration (1868), establishing museums, writing textbooks for children, and so forth. The Tanaka *biwa* is an improved version of a superior type of Japanese loquat he obtained in Nagasaki. He wrote *Nihon yūyō shokubutsu zusetsu* (1891), a work in seven volumes containing illustrations and descriptions of Japanese flora. *Suzuki Zenji*

Tanaka Yutaka (1888–1964)

Civil engineer and authority on bridge engineering and design in Japan. He was born in Nagano Prefecture and served as professor at Tōkyō University. After the TŌKYŌ EARTHQUAKE OF 1923, he directed the design and construction of numerous bridges in the Tōkyō area.

Tanashi

City in central Tōkyō Prefecture. In the Edo period (1600–1868), Tanashi developed as a POST-STATION TOWN on the highway Ōme Kaidō. It is principally a residential area, although many industrial plants have been constructed in recent years. There are several public housing complexes. Pop: 66,972.

tandai

(shogunal deputies). Officials appointed in strategic areas by the Kamakura (1192–1333) and Muromachi (1338–1573) shogunates to oversee political, military, and judicial affairs. Among those appointed by the Kamakura shogunate were the ROKUHARA TANDAI (an office established after the JŌKYŪ DISTURBANCE of 1221 for the protection of Kyōto and surveillance over the imperial court), and the Chinzei tandai, established in Kyūshū in 1293 after the MONGOL INVASIONS OF JAPAN. The Muromachi shogunate set up the Ōshū tandai and the Ushū tandai in northwestern Honshū and the Chūgoku tandai in southwestern Honshū.

The term tandai originally referred to high-ranking priests who examined novices on the Buddhist scriptures. It later came to mean the extemporaneous composition of a poem on a theme drawn by lot at literary gatherings.

Taneda Santōka (1882–1940)

HAIKU poet; remembered for his anthology containing 701 free-verse haiku, Sōmokutō (1940, Monument of Grass and Trees), which he edited from over 9,000 poems composed between 1925 and 1940, and Gochū nikki, a five-volume diary, published posthumously, which he kept in his hut called the Gochūan. His best haiku are written in simple and lucid language filled with a lyricism reflecting his love of drink and travel and his appreciation of nature.

Santōka was the son of a landlord in Yamaguchi Prefecture. His mother committed suicide when he was 10 years old. He studied at Waseda University in Tōkyō but did not graduate. In 1904 he started a sake brewery with his father near his hometown. When the business failed, Santōka moved to Kumamoto with his wife and son and ran a picture-frame store. Later he returned to Tōkyō and was employed at several different jobs. In 1925, having divorced his wife, he became a Buddhist monk of the Sōtō sect, serving as a sexton at a small temple in Kumamoto Prefecture. In 1926 he left the temple and became a mendicant priest.

For the remainder of his life, except for intermittent stays in his hut in Ogōri, Yamaguchi Prefecture, during the 1930s, he was on the road, begging, visiting his friends, composing haiku, and writing travel diaries. His trips frequently covered the Kyūshū, Shikoku, and Chūgoku (western Honshū) regions, but in 1936 he went as far as Sendai in northeastern Japan on a trip reminiscent of the haiku poet BASHŌ's famous journey north in 1689. He died in Matsuyama, Ehime Prefecture.

■——Taneda Santōka, Teihon Santōka zenshū, 7 vols (Shun'-yōdō, 1972–73). Ōyama Sumita, Haijin Santōka no shōgai (1971). Ueda Toshi, Santōka no shūku (1977).   Kyōko Iriye SELDEN

Tanegashima

Island approximately 40 km (25 mi) south of the Ōsumi Peninsula, Kagoshima Prefecture, southern Kyūshū. Nishinoomote is the only city on the island; there are also two towns. The climate is warm, and subtropical plants flourish on the coasts; the island is frequently struck by typhoons. The chief agricultural activities are the cultivation of sweet potatoes and sugarcane, and stock raising. The first musket was introduced to Japan by a Portuguese whose ship was stranded on Tanegashima in 1543. A space center for launching rockets and satellites is located on the cape Takezaki. Area: 446 sq km (172 sq mi).

Tanegashima Tokitaka (1528–1579)

The lord of Tanegashima, an island south of Kyūshū where the first Portuguese to come to Japan arrived in 1543. Tokitaka obtained from the traders samples of the harquebus, a portable shoulder gun; he had them reproduced, and firearms constructed after the Western model soon became known as tanegashima. By 1549 Tokitaka was receiving inquiries about these guns from the Muromachi shogunate; by the 1570s, various daimyō and warlike monastic institutions had organized units of musketeers (teppō ashigaru), and the massed use of troops so armed revolutionized Japanese military tactics. See also FIREARMS, INTRODUCTION OF.

Tane maku hito

(The Sowers). Small but influential leftist literary monthly that was published from February 1921 to August 1923 and marked the beginning of the so-called PROLETARIAN LITERATURE MOVEMENT. The first three issues were in leaflet form and printed in Tsuchizaki in northern Akita Prefecture, of which five of its six original members, including founder Komaki Ōmi (b 1894) and Kaneko Yōbun (b 1894), were natives. After six months of reorganization, it shifted to Tōkyō and adopted a magazine format. New members were added, including leftist critics HIRABAYASHI HATSUNOSUKE and AONO SUE-KICHI and journalist HASEGAWA NYOZEKAN. Tane maku hito's varied supporters also included noted writers MAEDAKŌ HIROICHIRŌ, MUSHANOKŌJI SANEATSU, and ARISHIMA TAKEO (the latter also lent financial support). The journal was antiwar, supported the Russian revolution, and called for the liberation of all oppressed peoples. It billed itself as the "magazine of internationalism" and listed such foreign writers as Vasilii Eroshenko and Anatole France as contributing members, thus attracting the attention not only of the literary world but of the intelligentsia at large. Influenced by Hirabayashi and Aono's criticism, Tane maku hito moved steadily leftward until the TŌKYŌ EARTHQUAKE OF 1923 and the increasing clampdown on all leftist activities forced its closure. As a parting shot, it published a special issue in January 1924 detailing police atrocities committed against leftists in the aftermath of the earthquake. It was eventually succeeded by BUNGEI SENSEN.   Theodore W. GOOSSEN

Tange Kenzō (1913–)

An architect and city planner of international recognition, Tange is known for his boldly shaped, distinctive buildings and urban complexes that show that functionalism does not demand a rigidly geometric style. He introduced a number of modern technological developments to architecture, notably the shell structure, and he is acclaimed for his conscious blending of modern expression with traditional Japanese aesthetics.

Born in the city of Imabari in Shikoku, Tange graduated from Tōkyō University in 1938 and went to work for the firm of MAE-KAWA KUNIO. He returned to the university for postgraduate study (1942–45), became an assistant professor (1946–49), and then in 1949 was appointed professor. Early in his career he won recognition for his Hiroshima Peace Center (1949); within the next decade he established himself as a major architect by designing an impressive series of public buildings including: the Tōkyō prefectural offices (1957); the Shizuoka assembly hall (1953), which employed a hyberbolic paraboloidal system to span a distance of 114 meters (375 ft); and the Kurayoshi (1957) and Kurashiki (1960) city halls. Another outstanding structure was the Kagawa prefectural office building in Takamatsu (1958), which was widely hailed for its restrained style and synthesis of modern form with aesthetic tradition.

In the 1960s, Tange's work assumed a more dramatic form, partly under the influence of modern American architecture. For the 1964 Tōkyō Olympic Games he designed two dynamically paired structures that comprise the YOYOGI NATIONAL GYMNASIA (1964), a noted example of steel suspension roofing. Two other striking examples of his work from this period are the Yamanashi Press and Broadcasting Center (1966), which experimented with a columnar grid spatial plan that attracted much attention, and the theme pavilion for Expo '70 in Ōsaka. Tange's work has been expressive of the continual physical transformations that cities undergo.

From 1960 on, Tange devoted himself increasingly to urban planning, such as his ambitious Tōkyō Plan of 1960, which incorporated the use of megastructures, and the reconstruction of the city of Skopje, Yugoslavia (1965), after its destruction by a disastrous earthquake.

Tange has also written widely on various aspects of architecture and its history in Japan. He has been a prime mover in international architectural circles; his approach to architecture, his spatial solutions, and his attention to materials and detail have influenced many younger architects.   WATANABE Hiroshi

Tanggu (Tangku) Truce

(Tankū Teisen Kyōtei). An armistice between the Japanese GUAN-DONG (KWANTUNG) ARMY and Chinese officials concluded on 31 May 1933 at Tanggu, a coastal city near Tianjin (Tientsin). The truce designated the Great Wall as the boundary between Chinese and Japanese forces in Hebei (Hopeh) Province and established a demilitarized zone north and east of the Tianjin–Beiping (Peiping; now Beijing or Peking) area up to the Great Wall. In December 1932 the SAITŌ MAKOTO cabinet had given permission to the Guandong Army, which was already in possession of Manchuria, to expand its territory. In January 1933 the army annexed Rehe (Jehol) Province and moved south into Hebei, toward Beiping, but withdrew as far as the Great Wall after the truce was negotiated. Within two years the Guandong Army again exerted pressure southward, and the movement of Chinese troops into the demilitarized zone in response to the MARCO POLO BRIDGE INCIDENT of 7 July 1937 provided one of the pretexts for the expansion of the incident into the SINO-JAPANESE WAR OF 1937–1945.

Tango

Town in northern Kyōto Prefecture, central Honshū. Main industries are agriculture and fishing, although with a decline in the catch, there has been a major effort to introduce fish farming. Textiles, most notably Tango *chirimen,* are also an important local product. The beautiful peninsular coastline attracts many sightseers. Pop: 8,955.

Tango Mountains

(Tango Sanchi). Mountain range forming the border between Kyōto and Hyōgo prefectures, west central Honshū. ŌEYAMA (833 m; 2,732 ft) is the highest peak. Composed primarily of granite, it is located between the rivers Maruyamagawa and Yuragawa, and much of it is level ground. It is known for its Tango beef cattle.

Tani Bunchō (1763–1840)

Painter who introduced BUNJINGA (literati painting) to Edo (now Tōkyō); author of and contributor to many illustrated books. Born Tani Masayasu of a *samurai* family in Edo, Bunchō was the son of the poet Tani Rokkoku (1729–1809). He first studied the KANŌ SCHOOL style under Katō Bunrei (1706–82), then worked with the Chinese academic-style painter Kitayama Kangan (1767–1801), whose repertoire included Western-influenced subjects. Bunchō also received instruction in the *bunjinga* tradition and BIRD-AND-FLOWER PAINTING. On his own initiative, he studied other styles of Japanese painting, including those of the TOSA SCHOOL, UKIYO-E, and the MARUYAMA-SHIJŌ SCHOOL. His career was sponsored by MATSUDAIRA SADANOBU, regent to the shōgun Tokugawa Ienari. Bunchō's command of a broad range of subjects and styles, together with his influential patrons, contributed to the success that he enjoyed. His reputation as a leading artist of the Edo period (1600–1868) brought him a great number of pupils, including WATANABE KAZAN, TANOMURA CHIKUDEN, and TSUBAKI CHINZAN.

Many of Bunchō's landscapes of the 1790s utilize a compositional formula derived from Chinese academic painting. Like their Southern Song (Southern Sung; 1127–1279) prototypes, these works are characterized by a lyric quality achieved through stylistic features and the media employed. Bunchō favored the use of ink and light colors on silk and developed a repertoire of motifs that he employed repeatedly throughout this period.

Bunchō realized the importance of direct observation of nature, a recognition most graphically demonstrated by the sketches he made while accompanying the regent on an inspection tour of the coastal defenses in the provinces. These sketches reveal the influence of Western artistic principles that preoccupied the artist at the turn of the century.

In later works, Bunchō achieved a synthesis of the Northern and Southern schools of Chinese landscape painting (see NANGA). These works display neither the lyricism of earlier landscapes nor the spontaneity of his later style. The latter category is characterized by the use of heavy, wet inks in less tightly constructed compositions. An example of Bunchō's mature style is his painting *Mt. Hiko* (1815) in the Tōkyō National Museum.

Bunchō also devoted time to book publication and theoretical writings. He executed illustrations for some 30 to 40 books, often in collaboration with other artists. His most noteworthy publications include *Honchō gasan* and a collection of reproductions of famous Japanese paintings called *Nihon meizan zue* (1807, Famous Mountains of Japan); his treatise on painting, *Bunchō gadan,* is also well known.　　　　　　　　　　　　　　　　　　　*Wendy* HOLDEN

Tanigawadake

Mountain on the border between northern Gumma Prefecture and Niigata Prefecture, central Honshū. The Niigata side has gentle slopes but the Gumma side forms a precipitous wall of rocks, pro-

viding a variety of routes for rock climbing. Because of the easy access by public transportation from the Tōkyō area it attracts many climbers, but its precipices and changeable weather have claimed many lives. It is part of Jōshin'etsu Kōgen National Park. Height: 1,963 m (6,439 ft).

Tanigawa Kotosuga (1709–1776)

Classical scholar of the middle years of the Edo period (1600–1868). Born in Ise (now Mie Prefecture) to a family of physicians, he went to Kyōto to study medicine and Shintō. On his own he studied KOKUGAKU (National Learning), the Shintō-oriented school of classical learning, and corresponded with MOTOORI NORINAGA. In contrast to Norinaga, however, who devoted his life to the study of the KOJIKI (712), Kotosuga valued the history NIHON SHOKI (720) and wrote *Nihon shoki tsūshō* (1748, Commentary on the *Nihon shoki*). He also compiled a dictionary of the Japanese language, WAKUN NO SHIORI (A Guide to Japanese).

Taniguchi Masaharu (1893–)

Religious leader and founder of SEICHŌ NO IE, a contemporary religious organization. Born in Hyōgo Prefecture. In his early life he was troubled by financial, physical, and spiritual problems. From 1917 to 1922 he was an adherent of the religious group ŌMOTO. In 1929, claiming to have received revelations, he began writing profusely on ways to solve life's problems. His magazine *Seichō no ie,* the first publication of which in 1930 marked the beginning of his organization, gained wide circulation among the common people. In 1934 he moved to Tōkyō and began popularizing his doctrines through writings and lectures. During World War II he supported the emperor-centered ideology of the militarist regime and his church grew rapidly, but he was purged after the war. Later he became more inclined to Shintō teachings and advocated a return to traditional morality.　　　　　　　　　　　　　　*Kenneth J.* DALE

Taniguchi Yoshirō (1904–1979)

Architect. Born in the city of Kanazawa, Ishikawa Prefecture. Taniguchi graduated from Tōkyō University and went on to a long-term teaching career at the Tōkyō Institute of Technology. Neo-classicist in spirit, his designs were in contrast to the work of the more conventional modern architects. His Hotel Ōkura (1962) was one of the first modern buildings to incorporate extensively traditional motifs. His representative works include Keiō University Hiyoshi Dormitory (1938), Tōson Memorial Hall (1948), Shiga House (1955), and the Tōkyō National Museum of Modern Art (1969). As head of the MEIJI MURA, an open-air museum in Inuyama near the city of Nagoya, he played a key role in the preservation of Meiji-period (1868–1912) architecture; he was also an eminent architectural historian.　　　　　　　　　　　　　　　　　　*WATANABE Hiroshi*

Tani Jichū (1598–1649)

Confucian scholar of the early part of the Edo period (1600–1868); associated with NANGAKUHA, the branch of Zhu Xi (Chu Hsi) Confucianism (see SHUSHIGAKU) in the Tosa domain (now Kōchi Prefecture). As a youth Jichū entered a local Buddhist temple and studied with the abbot Tenshitsu. He later studied Confucianism with Minamimura Baiken, the founder of the Nangakuha, and abandoned Buddhist orders to devote himself to teaching. Among his disciples were NONAKA KENZAN and YAMAZAKI ANSAI.

Tani Kanjō (1837–1911)

General and politician; also known as Tani Tateki. Born in the Tosa domain (now Kōchi Prefecture). He went to Edo (now Tōkyō) to study with the Confucian scholar YASUI SOKKEN. On his return to Tosa he became associated with the antishogunate, proimperial movement that culminated in the MEIJI RESTORATION of 1868. He joined the new Meiji government and occupied various important army posts, distinguishing himself as the commander of the defense of Kumamoto Castle during the SATSUMA REBELLION in 1877. Tani also served as head of the Army Academy. After he retired from active duty in 1881, he and another military man, Torio Koyata (1847–1905), founded the Chūseitō, a conservative political group. In 1885 he joined the first ITŌ HIROBUMI cabinet as minister of agriculture and commerce but resigned in objection to what he considered the insufficiently forceful demands of Foreign Minister INOUE KAORU for revision of the so-called Unequal Treaties with Western nations. See UNEQUAL TREATIES, REVISION OF.

Tanikawa Shuntarō (1931–)

Poet. Born in Tōkyō as the son of the philosopher Tanikawa Tetsuzō (b 1895). He made his debut with *Nijūoku kōnen no kodoku* (1952), a collection of poems on the theme of man's universal insignificance and isolation. Tanikawa joined the group of poets behind the poetry journal *Rekitei* and in 1953 became a member of Kai no Kai, a Tōkyō circle of poets who did much to foster a new spirit in postwar lyric poetry; it included ŌOKA MAKOTO, Ibaragi Noriko (b 1926), Yoshino Hiroshi (b 1926), and others. Since then he has been exploring with various poetic forms attempting to bring new life to the sonority and rhythms of the Japanese language. Among his volumes of poetry are *Rokujūni no sonetto* (1953), *Rakushu kyūjūkyū* (1964), and *Kotoba-asobi uta* (1972). *ASAI Kiyoshi*

Tanimoto Tomeri (1867–1946)

Educator. Born in the Takamatsu domain (now part of Kagawa Prefecture). Studied philosophy and education (the latter under Emile HAUSKNECHT) at Tōkyō University. Taught at Kyōto University and Bukkyō Daigaku (now Ryūkoku University). At first an advocate of the educational theories of the German philosopher and educator Johann F. Herbart (1776–1841), Tanimoto later turned against Herbart's ideas and advocated education for the benefit of the state. But then, during the liberal Taishō period (1912–26), he again shifted his stance to one favoring education for the sake of the individual and became one of the leaders of the progressive education movement (SHIN KYŌIKU UNDŌ) in Japan. *SUGIYAMA Akio*

Tanino Setsu (1904–)

Public official especially concerned with labor and women's problems. Graduating from Nihon Joshi Daigaku (Japan Women's University) in 1926, she entered the Home Ministry. She thereafter held responsible posts in the Welfare Ministry and Labor Ministry. As head of the Women's and Minors' Bureau of the Labor Ministry from 1955 to 1965, Tanino worked especially for the adoption of protective measures for working women.

Tani Tateki → Tani Kanjō

Tanizaki Jun'ichirō (1886–1965)

Novelist. Tanizaki made his literary debut in 1910 as an adherent of the romantic movement in Japanese literature, which had emerged in opposition to Japanese naturalism, then at the height of its influence. In his later writings he went on to explore his own sexual conflicts and sought to discover how man could wrest spiritual salvation from the baser struggles of the flesh. The Great Tōkyō Earthquake of 1923 marked an important turning point in Tanizaki's career. At that time, he moved from the cosmopolitan atmosphere of Tōkyō to the more traditional Kansai area. Inspired by this intimate and intense contact with a pure form of Japanese culture, Tanizaki forced his imagination to new heights of richness and vigor.

During the years of World War II, Tanizaki did not reflect the exigencies of the time in his writings. Instead, he delved into his own creative powers, turning toward wholly fabricated tales, seeking to discover the essential truths of literature through imaginary works, not in current events. In his masterly storytelling and loving appreciation of traditional Japanese concepts of beauty, Tanizaki, more than any of his contemporaries, carried on the classical literary tradition of the Heian period.

Any reader of Tanizaki will be struck by his preoccupation with women. Whether it is women in their protective, nurturing role as mothers, or women as purely sensual creatures whose bodies are the source of unending and confusing temptations for men, Tanizaki, with a tenacity that occasionally verges upon the pathological, traces the dreadful yearning for women. In work after work, Tanizaki describes the humiliations, the pitifully small victories, and always the persistent desires that drive his male characters to ignominy. But the force of his prose and a sheer confidence in his own imagination bring illuminative insights to his writings about this very fundamental human struggle.

Most writers of the Japanese naturalist school, concerned with actual situations in contemporary life, took as their subject conflict with traditional paternal authority and the subsequent process of reconciliation. In their studies of individuals striving against father figures and entrenched mores, these writers of the naturalist school could often do little more than make sociological observations. Tanizaki had the daring to dwell upon the subject of women in endlessly varied writings and through this obsession created works that went beyond social detail to quite startling psychological perceptions.

Tanizaki Jun'ichirō was born in the Nihombashi district of Tōkyō which, in the first half of the Meiji period (1868–1912), represented a unique mix of the old traditions of the Edo period (1600–1868) and the new influences of the West. Raised in this setting, Tanizaki possessed an urbanite's sophistication in his frankly sensual approach to life. His complex sensibility required more than the bare, inelegant "true to life" aesthetic of the naturalists, many of whom came from the provinces. When Tanizaki published the short story "Shisei" (1910; tr "The Tattooer," 1963), it was quite predictably received with enthusiastic praise by NAGAI KAFŪ, another urbane Tōkyō author whose own early work *Amerika monogatari* (1908, American Stories) had deeply impressed the young Tanizaki.

The success of "Shisei" launched Tanizaki's literary career. In this first short story, a tattoo artist inscribes a gigantic spider, symbolic of evil, upon the flesh of a beautiful young woman. Suddenly her beauty seems to take on a compelling, demonic power. The tattoo artist cannot resist and he prostrates himself before her. In this chilling tale, masochism is seen to be an inescapable component of erotic yearnings. This theme is repeated in most of Tanizaki's other early short stories, including "Kirin" (1910), "Shōnen" (1910), "Hōkan" (1911) and "Akuma" (1912).

The masochistic tentacles within Tanizaki's sensibility could not resist reaching out to touch, to praise, to abhor the complexities of the female nature in which he saw beauty and evil commingled. Tanizaki hoped to make sense of these contradictory elements and also free himself from his own pain, achieving a salvation tinged with his own diabolism. His Taishō-period (1912–26) works "Shindō" (1916) and "Oni no men" (1916) reflect these autobiographical tendencies.

Both Tanizaki's first marriage in 1915 and the so-called Odawara episode—a triangular relationship between Tanizaki, his wife Chiyoko, and the writer SATŌ HARUO—had great psychological effects upon him. Once again the masochistic edge to Tanizaki's vision of the world surfaced. In several works, including the play *Aisureba koso* (1921, If Indeed One Loves) and the novel *Kami to hito no aida* (1924, Between Men and the Gods), Tanizaki seems to believe that complete happiness can only be achieved out of the anguish and guilt that result from the struggle of two men for the love of one woman. In *Chijin no ai* (1924–25, A Fool's Love), Tanizaki succeeded in setting this theme against the background of the rapid modernization of Taishō society. The writing of this book was interrupted by the Great Tōkyō Earthquake. Afterwards, Tanizaki moved from Tōkyō to the Kansai (Kyōto-Ōsaka-Kōbe) area.

Two transitional works followed. The novel *Manji* (1928–30) shows the new influence of the Kansai area as Tanizaki, inspired by the feminine charms of the Kansai dialect, wrote about lesbianism. *Tade kuu mushi* (1928–29; tr *Some Prefer Nettles*, 1955) shows how the superficial effects of Tōkyō culture were effaced by stronger, more traditional strains.

Tanizaki's return to classical literature and the traditional storytelling techniques that had developed over the centuries since the advent of the Heian period began with *Yoshinokuzu* (1931, The Arrowroot of Yoshino), a fine study of maternal love.

While still married to Furukawa Tomiko, his second wife, Tanizaki became involved with Morita Matsuko, who was then also married to someone else. The effects of his relationship with Matsuko, who eventually became his third (and last) wife, figured in many of his later works. Matsuko had been brought up in an old Ōsaka household which was on the verge of financial ruin. From an extremely cultured background, Matsuko caused in Tanizaki the kind of suffering seemingly so necessary to his masochistic side. Inspired by Matsuko, Tanizaki began to produce a number of his best works in rapid succession.

"Mōmoku monogatari" (1931; tr "A Blind Man's Tale," 1963), "Ashikari" (1932; tr "Ashikari," 1936), and "Bunshoshō" (1935) were Tanizaki's chief works during this period. These are the stories of men who find their ultimate happiness in absolute devotion to a woman who is either haughty, or pure and unapproachable. The male protagonists all cower in fear before these women and although they experience countless humiliations, the men do not seem to be crushed spiritually; instead their subjugation seems to help them transcend their own sorry state, elevating them to an undefiled, almost religious realm of existence.

In 1939 Tanizaki took up the formidable task of rendering the entire *Genji monogatari* (TALE OF GENJI) into modern Japanese. The novel *Sasameyuki* (tr *The Makioka Sisters*, 1957), which Tanizaki started writing in 1942, was probably prompted by the affinity he felt with the splendid but sorrowing court ladies in the *Genji monogatari*. For the background material of *Sasameyuki*, Tanizaki turned to his own family and that of his third wife, Matsuko. His novel is an elegy to a bygone era, an exaltation of "beauty in ruin," as depicted in the decline of the once proud and prosperous family. The protagonist, Teinosuke, is portrayed as an average and placid family man, with the usual masochistic impulses so often found in Tanizaki male characters held tightly in check. *Sasameyuki* is not merely the story of Teinosuke, but also a leisurely, detailed study of the daily lives of the four sisters who surround him (to one of whom he is married). The novel also describes contemporary social trends and succeeds in capturing the spirit of a particular culture at a certain moment in time. The graceful heroine Yukiko, whose marriage is delayed by a strange combination of circumstances, is particularly notable for her pathos and beauty. The serialization of *Sasameyuki* began in 1943 but was immediately halted under the pressure of the military authorities. Tanizaki nevertheless continued working on the manuscript amid the devastation of World War II, completing it in 1948.

In the years after the war, Tanizaki was afflicted by high blood pressure, but continued to write tirelessly and with staggering productivity. *Shōshō Shigemoto no haha* (1949–50; partially tr as "The Mother of Captain Shigemoto," 1956) represents another aspect of Tanizaki's treatment of the femme fatale. It is, so to speak, a brilliant culmination of other works that deal with the theme of love between mother and son, and the concluding scene, in which mother and son are reunited, is one of the most beautiful in modern Japanese literature. At the same time, one cannot overlook the introduction of another theme—the problem of sexuality in old age, a theme further developed in *Kagi* (1956; tr *The Key*, 1961). *Kagi* is a lurid psychological study that chronicles, in diary form, the sexual struggle between an aging professor and his wife. To stimulate his flagging sexual desire and restore his similarly dulled taste for life, the protagonist cunningly sets the stage for his wife to commit adultery, while she, though pretending to submissively meet his demands, actually deceives him. Once again, the masochistic paradox of being unable to find true happiness except by living through a sheer hell is studied to its utmost.

In his next work, "Yume no ukihashi" (1960; tr "The Bridge of Dreams," 1963), Tanizaki again explored the search for redemption from sexuality. Nevertheless, it was only with one of his last novels, *Fūten rōjin nikki* (1961–62; tr *Diary of a Mad Old Man*, 1965), that Tanizaki combined his former themes of the femme fatale and the mother-figure, with that of incest between mother and son to bring his protagonist toward a resolution that allows him a final, troubled salvation. In this work, the "evil woman," resembling the heroine in *Chijin no ai*, is the aged protagonist's daughter-in-law. The old man carries on a flirtation with this woman and becomes fascinated by her feet, for him the alluring essence of woman. These feet, so much on the protagonist's mind throughout, bring back memories of his beloved mother. He requests that after his death he be buried beneath a Buddhist gravestone inscribed with a faithful tracing of his daughter-in-law's feet. Of course the bizarre and ludicrous nature of the old man's desires keep the narrative of this novel extremely lively. But aside from his memorable descriptions of the old man's absorption in his daughter-in-law and her feet, Tanizaki, through the old man, seems to have made peace at last with his own tortured yearnings. An imprint of the daughter-in-law's perfect feet on the gravestone will remain above the old man for all eternity. In death, the old man does not find salvation in absolute otherworldly purification, but in a wise acceptance of his own ineffaceable human perversities.

📖 Works by Tanizaki: Collected works in Japanese: *Tanizaki Jun'ichirō zenshū*, 28 vols (Chūō Kōron Sha, 1966–70). Translations: *Seven Japanese Tales*, tr Howard Hibbett (1963), includes several of the short works mentioned in this article. *Tade kuu mushi* (1928–29), tr Edward G. Seidensticker as *Some Prefer Nettles* (1955). *Sasameyuki* (1943–48), tr Edward G. Seidensticker as *The Makioka Sisters* (1957). *Shōshō Shigemoto no haha* (1949–50), Chaps 9 and 10 tr by Edward G. Seidensticker as "The Mother of Captain Shigemoto," in Donald Keene, ed, *Modern Japanese Literature* (1956). *Kagi* (1956), tr Howard Hibbett as *The Key* (1961). *Fūten rōjin nikki* (1961–62), tr Howard Hibbett as *Diary of a Mad Old Man* (1965). Works about Tanizaki: Edward G. Seidensticker, "Tanizaki Jun'ichirō 1886–1965," *Monumenta Nipponica* 21.3–4.

NOGUCHI Takehiko

tanka

(literally, "short poem"). A 31–syllable poem consisting of five lines in the pattern 5–7–5–7–7; the dominant form in classical Japanese poetry (WAKA) from the 7th to the early 20th century. *Tanka* are still composed by many people, especially amateurs and students of all ages. In the oldest anthology of native poetry, the 8th-century MAN'YŌSHŪ (Collection for Ten Thousand Generations or Collection of Ten Thousand Leaves), the term *tanka* is used to distinguish the short 31–syllable poem from the "long poem" (CHŌKA or *nagauta*), a form consisting of an indefinite number of pairs of 5– and 7–syllable lines, with an extra line of 7 syllables at the end. *Tanka* is also used for the 31–syllable "envoys" (also *hanka* or *kaeshiuta*) that were attached to *chōka* with growing frequency and in increasing numbers from the mid-7th century. Such *tanka* tended more and more to become the lyrical focus of the "long poems," which began to lose vitality and significance. At length, following the decline and virtual disappearance of the *chōka* as well as of other less important genres by the end of the 8th century, the *tanka* became essentially the only form of sophisticated Japanese vernacular poetry. Amazingly, it retained its dominance, if not always its vitality, for 1,200 years. For this reason, *tanka* came to be synonymous with *waka* ("Japanese poetry" as distinguished from *kanshi*, "Chinese verse"). Indeed, during the classical and postclassical periods *waka* was the common term for the 31–syllable vernacular poetry of the aristocratic court tradition, whereas the term *tanka* was only found in treatises and handbooks, where it was employed in its original sense to distinguish the 31–syllable form from other genres, such as the earlier *chōka* and the linked verse (RENGA AND HAIKAI), that came into prominence from the late 13th century.

Since about 1900, *tanka* has in turn replaced *waka* as the preferred generic term for poetry in the 31–syllable form. Revived by the nationalistic scholar-poets of the 17th, 18th, and early 19th centuries, from around the turn of the 20th century the word began to be deliberately used by innovating poets for their own compositions in order to distinguish them clearly from the ultraconservative verse of the traditional schools. Thus, the word *tanka* took on new connotations of freshness of diction, spontaneity, personalism, "realism" in subject matter and expression, "sincerity" of feeling, modernity, and freedom from conventional restraints. At the same time, the term *waka* has come to be increasingly used for the older, more traditional classical and postclassical poetry in the 31–syllable form.

Owing to these historical developments, poets of the 31–syllable form active prior to 1900 are, in this encyclopedia, called "waka poets," whereas those active from 1900 to the present are called "tanka poets." Thus, Ki no Tsurayuki (872?–945) and Fujiwara no Sadaie (1162–1241) are *waka* poets; Yosano Akiko (1878–1942) and Saitō Mokichi (1882–1953) are *tanka* poets. Robert H. BROWER

Tankai (1629–1716)

Also called Hōzan Tankai. Buddhist monk and sculptor of the early part of the Edo period (1600–1868). At age 17 he became a priest of the SHINGON SECT and left his home in Ise Province (now part of Mie Prefecture) to practice austerities at various mountain temples. He lived for several years in a cave on the mountain IKOMAYAMA near Nara before founding the temple Hōzanji in Nara in 1678. He is best known for his statues of Fudō Myōō (Skt: Acalanātha), which are preserved in the temples Hōzanji, HŌRYŪJI, and TŌSHŌDAIJI. See also MYŌŌ.

Tankei (1173–1256)

Sculptor of Buddhist images in the Kamakura period (1185–1333). A member of the KEI SCHOOL of sculpture, he was the eldest son and principal pupil of UNKEI; his grandfather was the sculptor KŌKEI. One of the most distinguished sculptors of the period, Tankei assisted in the restoration of the temples Tōdaiji and Kōfukuji and received the honorary Buddhist titles of *hokkyō* (1194), *hōgen* (1208), and *hōin* (1213). Among his best-known works are the Senju Kannon (Skt: Sahasrabhujā; 1254) in the temple Rengeōin in Kyōto, and the figures of Bishamonten (Skt: Vaiśravaṇa) and two attendants in the temple Sekkeiji in Kōchi Prefecture. They are noted for their understated and refined realism.

Tankū Teisen Kyōtei → Tanggu (Tangku) Truce

Tannishō

Religious treatise of the 13th century compiled as a summary of the basic ideas of SHINRAN, founder of the JŌDO SHIN SECT of Buddhism, by his disciple Yuien. The text contains the words of Shinran as remembered and recorded by Yuien soon after his master's death and purports to make explicit the true teaching of PURE LAND BUDDHISM in order to settle doctrinal disputes which had arisen among Shinran's followers; hence the title, which means "Lamenting the Deviations." It is a collection of sayings and insights concerning the Primal Vow of AMIDA, the entrusting of self to the Primal Vow, good and evil, self-power and other power, filial piety and universal ethics, limited and unlimited compassion, good works and the authentic religious life. Such issues as the legalistic interpretations of faith, antinomian tendencies among followers, and other related problems are discussed as well. Before its popularization by the late-19th-century thinker and reformer KIYOZAWA MANSHI, the Tannishō was largely unknown even to followers of the Jōdo Shin sect. Today it is one of the most widely read of Japanese Buddhist classics.

——Imadate Tōsui, tr, "Tannishō," in D. T. Suzuki, ed, Collected Writings on Shin Buddhism (1973). Ryūkoku Translation Series II, The Tannishō: Notes Lamenting the Differences (1962).

Taitetsu UNNO

Tanno Setsu (1902–)

Labor activist and social reformer. Born in Fukushima Prefecture. In 1913 her father went to work in the Hitachi mines, and at age 15 Setsu too began working for the Hitachi company, later becoming a nurse in the company hospital. Spurred to action by Hitachi's brutal suppression of the activities of the YŪAIKAI, Japan's first labor organization, she went in 1921 to Tōkyō, where she joined the socialist women's group SEKIRANKAI and was involved in the 1923 KAMEIDO INCIDENT. In 1924 she married a fellow labor activist, WATANABE MASANOSUKE; the next year they helped to form the leftist labor group Hyōgikai (Japan Labor Union Council), a radical offshoot of the SŌDŌMEI. Later they helped to organize major strikes at the Kyōdō Insatsu printing plant and the Hamamatsu Musical Instruments factory. Setsu joined the outlawed JAPAN COMMUNIST PARTY in 1926, four years after her husband, and became the first head of its women's section. With many other leftists, she was arrested in the MARCH 15TH INCIDENT of 1928, and later that year her husband committed suicide while fleeing from the police in Taiwan. She was released from jail because of illness but continued her underground activities and was imprisoned again from 1932 to 1938. After World War II she turned her attention mainly to health-care reforms and hospital administration.

ta no kami

(god of the paddies). The Shintō god who protects rice plants and brings about abundant rice crops. Also known as sakugami and sukurigami. Festivals to this god are often observed in conjunction with the various stages of rice cultivation. These include the major festivals "welcoming of the god of the fields" (kamimukae), which takes place just prior to spring planting; "the festival of the water gates" (minakuchi matsuri), held on the day when seed rice is sown in the rice plant nurseries; the festival of the first rice planting (saori); the festival held on the final day of planting of the rice seedlings in the irrigated paddies (sanaburi); and many harvest festivals. In the annual Aenokoto Festival of Noto in Ishikawa Prefecture, held just after the harvesting of the year's rice, the god of the paddies is "welcomed," escorted into the home, and then honored with a large banquet. The god is then escorted back out to the fields on the following New Year's Day. It is believed that the god of the paddies does not dwell in the human world but descends at times of festivals (kyoraishin). Old legends tell that the god of the mountain (YAMA NO KAMI) comes down to the villages in the spring in the form of the god of the paddies to protect the growth of the rice and returns to his permanent abode after the fall harvest, once again becoming the god of the mountain.

NOGUCHI Takenori

Tanomura Chikuden (1777–1835)

A painter in the Chinese manner ranked in Japan among the leading nanga (see BUNJINGA) artists. Chikuden was born in a small castle town called Taketa in Bungo Province (now Ōita Prefecture) in Kyūshū. After serving briefly in his inherited role as domain physician, he resigned and shortly thereafter was appointed to a commission that was to write a gazetteer of the domain for the Tokugawa shogunate. His duties necessitated traveling throughout the domain and provided him with his first chance to visit Ōsaka, Kyōto, and Edo (now Tōkyō). Chikuden finished the gazetteer in 1804 and subsequently became a scholar in the domain school in Taketa. However, he abruptly terminated his tenure as scholar in 1812 after his petitions to alleviate the sufferings of the local farmers had been repeatedly ignored. Although he maintained his home in Taketa for the rest of his life, Chikuden was continually traveling to various parts of Japan where he would visit such artists and scholars as RAI SAN'YŌ (1781–1832), AOKI MOKUBEI (1767–1833), URAGAMI GYOKUDŌ (1745–1820), and OKADA BEISANJIN (1744–1820). It was on one of these extended journeys that he became ill and died in a small village near Ōsaka.

Although familiar with the painting traditions of Japan and the contemporary Japanese nanga styles, Chikuden developed his own approach, based on his studies of Chinese painting of the Ming (1368–1644) and Qing (Ch'ing; 1644–1912) dynasties. His paintings, with their compositions carefully built with layers of delicate color and fine brushwork, possess a close relationship to Chinese literati painting. Through his disciples and associates Chikuden was one of the primary forces in the 19th-century reappraisal of Chinese painting by Japanese artists.

Paul BERRY

Tanomura Chokunyū (1814–1907)

Literati painter. Born in Bungo Province (now Ōita Prefecture) in Kyūshū. At age eight, he began studying literati painting (BUNJINGA) with TANOMURA CHIKUDEN, who adopted him two years later. He also studied Chinese literature with Tsunoda Kyūka (1784–1855) and poetry and calligraphy with Shinozaki Shōchiku (1781–1851). He was active in Kyūshū painting circles until 1868, when he established himself in Kyōto. The Kyōto Prefectural Painting School (Kyōto Fu Gagakkō), Japan's first painting school, opened in 1880, largely through his efforts. Tanomura served as a juror for the Domestic Expositions (Naikoku Kangyō Hakurankai) from their inception in 1877 and was instrumental in founding the Japan Literati Painting Association (Nihon Nanga Kyōkai) in 1897. In his later years he was known not only as a painter and a teacher but also as a scholar of Zen Buddhism, a calligrapher, and a poet. A competent and conservative artist, he conformed to the traditions of literati painting and concentrated on reinterpreting Chinese models. His best-known work is a pair of sixfold screens, Autumn View of the Takino River (1882). See also NIHONGA. Frederick BAEKELAND

tansen and tammai

(acreage coin and acreage rice). Incidental land tax levied upon peasant cultivators by the imperial court, the shogunate, military governors, and sometimes temples and shrines to cover the cost of special projects or important ceremonies during the Kamakura (1185–1333) and Muromachi (1333–1568) periods. It was in addition to the annual land tax (NENGU). The terms tansen and tammai derive from the practice of levying a certain amount of rice (mai) or an equivalent amount of money (sen) per tan (1 tan = about 0.10 hectare or 0.25 acre) of land. Tansen did not become an important instrument of taxation until the Muromachi period. It could be levied on a national or provincial basis and was collected by commissioners (tansen bugyō) dispatched from a central office in Kyōto. Military governors (SHUGO) were at first allowed to levy tansen only to cover their personal expenses; but by the 15th century, with the significant increase in their power, they were able to exact it without restriction. In the 16th century such daimyō as the HŌJŌ FAMILY of Odawara (now part of Kanagawa Prefecture) levied it regularly. See also MUNABETSUSEN.

Tan Taigi (1709–1771)

HAIKU poet. Born in Edo (now Tōkyō), he is known today chiefly as one of the forerunners of the late 18th century haiku revival. His early training was in the Edoza school of haiku established by TAKARAI KIKAKU. In 1751 he moved to Kyōto and became a priest in the

Tanuki

temple Daitokuji. He later established himself in the Shimabara pleasure quarter in the capacity of haiku master and mingled with its courtesans and their wealthy merchant clients. It was here that he met the haiku poet BUSON, whose close friendship stimulated his finest haiku, written in his final years. He culled material for his poems from everyday life and the activities of ordinary people; they display a human warmth and unaffected tone while manifesting a refinement of poetic technique. His principal haiku anthology is the *Taigi kusen* (1770).

tanuki

(raccoon dog). *Nyctereutes procyonoides;* often referred to in English as badger. A mammal of the family Canidae inhabiting East Asia. Its appearance resembles that of the North American raccoon, but it lacks the ring pattern on the tail. Its head and body measure about 60 centimeters (24 in) in length and the tail about 16 centimeters (6 in); it weighs about 5 kilograms (11 lb). It inhabits Hokkaidō, Honshū, Shikoku, and Kyūshū and frequents suburban gardens. It eats terrestrial snails and fruits and sometimes invades melon fields in summer. The *tanuki* nests in a natural hole as in a cave or tree hollow, and a litter of four or five is born in spring. It hibernates for a short time in cold districts such as Hokkaidō. Introduced to European Russia, the *tanuki's* habitat has been expanding over northern Europe. It is often confused with the badger *(anaguma)* with which it shares the alternate name *mujina*. IMAIZUMI Yoshiharu

The *tanuki* has long been compared with the fox in Japan as a crafty animal possessing supernatural powers, but unlike the latter it is considered to be amusing rather than fearsome. Since ancient times the Japanese have caught the *tanuki* for its meat and used its fur for brushes. It appears in many folk songs and tales, the most famous of which is probably the fairy tale BUMBUKU CHAGAMA, in which a *tanuki,* freed from a trap, repays his liberator's kindness. There are also many sayings involving the *tanuki,* such as *kitsune to tanuki no bakashi ai* (a fox and a *tanuki* outfoxing each other), referring to dealings between sly persons, and *tanuki oyaji* or *furudanuki,* referring to a crafty person. SANEYOSHI Tatsuo

Tanuma Okitsugu (1719–1788)

Official of the Tokugawa shogunate who gained prominence as a favorite of the ninth and tenth shōguns, TOKUGAWA IESHIGE and Tokugawa Ieharu (1737–86; r 1760–86). He was a controversial figure because of the unusual nature of his rise to political power and the unorthodox government policies with which he was associated. At a time when the Tokugawa officialdom allowed for little upward mobility, Tanuma stood out as one of the few men who attained the status of *daimyō* from very humble origins.

Tanuma entered shogunate service in 1734 as a page (KOSHŌ) in the entourage of the shōgun's heir, Ieshige. On his father's death he inherited an annual stipend of 600 *koku* (see KOKUDAKA). When Ieshige became shōgun in 1745, Tanuma remained in his service. He was named chamberlain (sobashū) in 1751 and acquired the status of daimyō in 1758, having received lands assessed at 10,000 *koku.* In

1760, a year before his death, Ieshige relinquished his position to his son Ieharu. Tanuma continued to enjoy the trust of the new shōgun. In 1767 he was appointed grand chamberlain (SOBAYŌNIN), and his domain was increased to 20,000 *koku.* (He was eventually to receive a total of 57,000 *koku.*) In 1772 Tanuma was named a senior councillor (RŌJŪ) concurrently with his post of grand chamberlain, a feat achieved only by him. Meanwhile his first son, Okitomo (1749–84), had entered shogunate service, becoming a junior councillor (WAKA-DOSHIYORI) in 1783. Father and son now combined the highest shogunate offices, while others related by marriage or identified as Tanuma followers assumed key positions in the shōgun's administration, especially in the office of the finance commissioner (KANJŌ BUGYŌ).

Despite his high status, however, Tanuma's position was precarious and rested heavily on the backing of the shōgun. When that support was lost, his fall was rapid. Ieharu died in 1786 and was succeeded by TOKUGAWA IENARI, then a minor. This circumstance permitted the Tokugawa senior collateral houses (GOSANKE) to intervene in shogunate affairs. Tanuma was quickly stripped of his offices and reduced in rank and income. His principal policies were reversed, and his followers expelled from government. Tanuma's memory was vilified by his successor as chief shogunal adviser, MATSUDAIRA SADANOBU, and by contemporary popular opinion. Historians, both in the Edo period (1600–1868) and in modern times, have held up Tanuma as a symbol of evil influence in Tokugawa government.

The period from roughly 1767 to 1786 during which Tanuma exerted his personal influence on shogunate policy is commonly referred to as the Tanuma period. It has been described as a time of governmental weakness brought on by the ascendancy of "inner" officials over a weak shōgun. This condition presumably contrasted with those periods when shōguns placed the affairs of state in the hands of their boards of senior councillors (rōjū), their "outer" officials. Tanuma was accused of gaining an unhealthy hold over the shōgun Ieharu and persuading him to accept ill-advised policies. Under his influence the shogunate is seen to have condoned corruption and luxurious living while neglecting the moral foundations of samurai government. Tanuma was held responsible for plunging the country into a period of economic dislocation, social unrest, and even natural disaster.

The Tanuma period did, in fact, witness a high incidence of peasant uprisings (HYAKUSHŌ IKKI) and acts of mob violence (UCHIKO-WASHI) in the cities. There was also an unusual number of natural disasters: the eruption of Mt. Asama in 1783 and severe famines in 1772 and 1786, followed by epidemic diseases. The people of Tokugawa Japan came to link Tanuma's influence with these calamities. Modern scholars have appeared ready to accept Tanuma as the symbol of the contradictions created by feudal government when faced by crisis.

More recent scholarship has arrived at a somewhat different assessment, viewing the policies associated with Tanuma not as his personal creation but as part of a growing effort of the finance commissioner's office to improve the shogunate's position within the country. This "shogunate-first" policy revealed an inherent conflict of interest between the shōgun and his primary administrators. A shōgun who wished to advance the shogunate-first policy would have to bypass the senior councillors and find his own mechanism for carrying it out. Tanuma provided such a mechanism. To this extent Tanuma may be considered symbolic of the effort to secure greater centralization of shogunal authority, and since this effort was generally opposed by the daimyō, who wished to protect their local autonomy, it provoked bitter attacks against him.

Generally speaking, the policies for which Tanuma was criticized were directed toward expanding the commercial economy of the shogunal domains and thereby increasing the tax income of the shogunate. Some policies were quite traditional, such as the attempt to increase farmland through reclamation of swamp areas like IMBA-NUMA. Others were more innovative: the licensing of commercial agents and monopoly associations (KABUNAKAMA) to extend shogunate control over important commodities like vegetable oil, silk, iron, ginseng, and lime and the expansion of foreign trade for profit through the production of exportable dried sea products *(tawara-mono).* Major changes were also attempted in the shogunate's fiscal structure. In an effort to increase the volume of circulating currency and to create a unified currency system that could be controlled by the shogunate, he ordered the minting of silver coins as an auxiliary to gold. A plan to set up a shogunate–managed revolving loan fund for the assistance of debt-ridden daimyō failed when merchants refused to contribute the initial capital.

Tanuma, as symbol, is best seen as representing both the desire of the shogunate to strengthen its position and the inability of the shōgun to gain legitimacy for such a policy. Tanuma's personal weaknesses, his lowly origin, and his openness to corruption were factors that complicated but did not create the bad repute of the policy with which he became associated.

■ —— John Whitney Hall, *Tanuma Okitsugu* (1955). Herman Ooms, *Charismatic Bureaucrat: A Political Biography of Matsudaira Sadanobu* (1975).   John W. HALL

Tan'yū → Kanō Tan'yū

Tanzawasan

Also called Tanzawayama. Mountain in northwestern Kanagawa Prefecture, central Honshū; a prominent peak in the Tanzawa Mountains and Tanzawa-Ōyama Quasi-National Park. Tanzawasan is noted for its sharp and rugged appearance and attracts many climbers and hikers. Height: 1,567 m (5,140 ft).

Taoka Reiun (1870–1912)

Literary critic and journalist; real name, Taoka Sayoji. Born in the Tosa domain (now Kōchi Prefecture), he graduated from Tōkyō University, where he studied the Chinese classics. He came under the influence of the FREEDOM AND PEOPLE'S RIGHTS MOVEMENT as a youth and was active in the local RISSHISHA organization. At the university he became known for his iconoclastic views, especially those against the KEN'YŪSHA, then a dominant literary coterie. In 1895 he started a magazine, *Seinembun* (Literature for Youth), through which he advocated a new literature based on social criticism. He also worked for the *Yorozu chōhō* and several other newspapers and traveled frequently to China, where he associated with Chinese revolutionaries. In his later writings Taoka became increasingly outspoken in his opposition to the government's commitment to capitalism, and many of his books were censored. His writings are collected in *Taoka Reiun zenshū*, 8 vols (Hōsei Daigaku Shuppan Kyoku 1969–).

Tappizaki

Cape on the northern Tsugaru Peninsula, northwestern Aomori Prefecture, northern Honshū. Separated from the cape Shirakamimisaki on Hokkaidō, 19 km (12 mi) away, by the Tsugaru Strait. Being the closest point on Honshū to Hokkaidō, it will serve as the southern exit for the Seikan (Aomori–Hakodate) Tunnel, a railway tunnel linking the islands which is expected to be completed in 1986. Famous for its varied coastal scenery with caves and grottos in cliffs along the shore and fantastically shaped rocks.

Taradake

Group of volcanoes, in the Aso Volcanic Zone, Saga and Nagasaki prefectures, Kyūshū. The main peaks are Kyōgadake (1,076 m; 3,529 ft) and Taradake (983 m; 3,224 ft). Deep valleys extend radially from the peak to the foot of the mountains. During heavy rains there are often landslides. Large tracts of azaleas and rhododendrons cover the slopes. The volcanoes are part of Taradake Prefectural Natural Park.

taranoki

(Japanese angelica tree). *Aralia elata*. A deciduous shrub of the ginseng family (Araliaceae) which grows wild in uncultivated fields and hills throughout Japan. It grows straight up usually to a height of about 4 meters (13 ft) and has spiny branches. The shrub has large leaves which are bipinnate compound in shape, and the ovate leaflets have serrated edges and whitish undersides. In August many small white flowers bloom in clusters (panicles). Each flower has five petals and bears a round black fruit. The young shoots of the *taranoki* are greatly appreciated for their taste and fragrance. Young shoots of the *udo* (*A. cordata*) of the same genus, which is a perennial herb 1–2 meters (3–6 ft) high, are appreciated as an early spring vegetable, and the plant is cultivated commercially.

MATSUDA Osamu

tariffs

(*kanzei*). Tariff policy in Japan, as in most nations, has been used to protect domestic industries from foreign competition. Tariff policies have changed with the development of the economy; in recent years, there has been a significant reduction in tariffs and nontariff barriers. However, changes in the exchange rate have tended to reduce the effect of efforts to liberalize trade.

Tariffs before World War II —— Japan gradually acquired tariff autonomy over the period from the 1890s to 1911. Tariff laws enacted at that time reflected an attempt to protect the processing industries and associated trade that had developed in the years after Japan established relations with the outside world in 1854. These early tariffs were marked by tax exemptions for industrial raw materials and foodstuffs and by a system of tariff escalation for manufactured products. (Tariff escalation is a system of graduated duty rates, which rise as the manufactured content of the imported product increases.)

As the Japanese economy embarked upon industrialization, tariffs continued to have a strongly protective function. Tariff reforms carried out in 1910 and 1926 were clearly aimed at fostering domestic industry by limiting imports of manufactured goods from developed countries while facilitating the import of raw materials. The goal of tariff policy during this period was to strengthen the international competitive position of Japanese industrial goods. By 1926 the tariffs had lost their revenue-producing function and were solely aimed at protection of domestic industry.

Tariffs after World War II —— During the immediate post–World War II period, Japanese trade came under strict control, and the protective function of tariffs was accomplished more directly through import restrictions and FOREIGN EXCHANGE CONTROL. The tariff system continued unchanged from prewar days until 1951, when it was completely overhauled. One important reform instituted at this time was a changeover from specific to *ad valorem* tariffs. The specific tariffs, which charged duties according to the quantity of the product imported, had become outmoded because of high inflation rates. The *ad valorem* tariffs, which assessed duties according to the value of the product, could fluctuate with changing price levels.

Tariff levels were also lowered in the early 1950s. This reduction did not indicate a move away from protectionism, but rather reflected Japanese negotiations to join in the GATT (General Agreement on Tariffs and Trade). Upon joining GATT in 1955, Japan was required to liberalize its trade policies significantly. Tariff concessions were made in a number of areas, including such newly developed industries as electronics and synthetic fibers. Liberalization of trade continued gradually in the early 1960s, and tariffs remained close to the center of attention. In tariff reforms in 1961, duties on farm produce, chemical products, metals, and machinery were raised, while those on industrial raw materials were lowered or removed altogether. Protectionism was also bolstered through the introduction of a number of new tariff systems, including mixed tariffs (a combination of specific and *ad valorem* tariffs, utilizing the higher of the two), tariff quotas (a method of keeping the tariff rate low but limiting imports once they exceed a certain level), and an emergency tariff. These measures allowed Japan to keep its basic tariff level low while at the same time discouraging imports.

Japan participated in the linear, across-the-board tariff reduction that was agreed to during the Kennedy Round talks in 1967. While at first reluctant to abandon its protective policies, it eventually agreed to relax its tariff barriers, partly in anticipation of the expanded export potential of its increasingly competitive industry. Tariffs were removed from 2,147 items in these negotiations; this amounted to 44 percent of the total value of imports at the time. During the same period in the late 1960s, Japan agreed to extend preferential duties to developing countries. In doing so, it exposed its small and medium enterprises and agricultural industry to international competition and gave a certain advantage to the directly competitive light industries of developing nations. Despite these risks, it went along with the general trend among developed nations and agreed to the preferential tariffs in 1967. Although Japan extended preferential tariffs to a greater number of countries than other developed nations did, the preferential duty system did not work satisfactorily. One reason was the quota and quality restrictions applied to mined and manufactured goods imported from these countries; another was the creation of ceilings whereby preferential duties would not be applied to a given beneficiary country if imports of specific goods passed 50 percent of an established quota.

These restrictions have since been relaxed in response to demands from the developing countries.

Tariffs were uniformly reduced by 20 percent in 1972 in an attempt to eliminate a surplus in the BALANCE OF PAYMENTS and to stabilize prices. This was a unilateral move which lowered tariffs on some 1,900 articles without demanding concessions from other countries. As a result of the agreements reached at the long-awaited Tōkyō Round of trade talks, it seemed likely in the late 1970s that there would be further reductions in tariffs. Through the step-by-step reductions, Japan's tariff rates were by then equal to or less than those of other advanced countries. See also FOREIGN TRADE; FOREIGN TRADE, GOVERNMENT POLICY ON. *Tsuchiya Rokurō*

tariki

(literally, "another's power"). A Buddhist term. Opposed to *jiriki* (literally, "one's own power"), *tariki* refers to the power of the Buddhas and bodhisattvas to save others, as well as to the process of approaching enlightenment through the power of Buddhas and bodhisattvas. *Jiriki*, on the other hand, refers to the process of attaining enlightenment through one's own resources and efforts, although it does not deny the need for the assistance of the Buddha. Thus there is no absolute *jiriki* or total self-reliance.

In the JŌDO SECT, *tariki* refers to the power of the vow made by the Buddha AMIDA to save all who invoke his name. People who place their trust in the power of this vow are born into paradise *(gokuraku),* also known as the Pure Land (Jōdo). There they achieve *satori* (enlightenment) and become Buddhas. The teachings of the JŌDO SHIN SECT are a more simplified and direct version of this same basic tenet. In their beliefs, any person who relies on the power of Amida is assured rebirth in paradise, and the practice of NEMBUTSU (reciting the name of the Buddha) is interpreted as an expression of thanks in return for this grace. See also BUDDHISM. *Matsunami Yoshihiro*

taru

Low, round, lidded vessel generally formed of wooden staves, with a wide-mouthed top, tapering sides, and bound with hoops. Originally used for storing and transporting liquids such as rice wine *(sake),* cooking oil, and soy sauce or nonliquids like bean paste (MISO) and pickles *(tsukemono).* The lids were called *kagami ita* ("mirror boards"). *Taru* were usually constructed of cryptomeria or willow and bound with bamboo-strip hoops. Some were lacquered or encased in rice-straw coverings. For convenience in storage, they were wider at the top than at the bottom and had no bulging sides. For temple or shrine offerings so-called *tsunodaru* were used. They were lacquered either red or black on the outside and red on the inside.

Taruhito, Prince → Arisugawa no Miya Taruhito

Tarui Tōkichi (1850–1922)

Politician and founder of the TŌYŌ SHAKAITŌ (Oriental Socialist Party). Born in what is now Nara Prefecture, he studied Confucianism and KOKUGAKU (National Learning) in Edo (now Tōkyō). Tarui was a supporter of Saigō Takamori during the SATSUMA REBELLION of 1877 and tried to raise troops for Saigō's cause in northern Japan. He joined the FREEDOM AND PEOPLE'S RIGHTS MOVEMENT and in May 1882, with Akamatsu Taisuke, he organized the Oriental Socialist Party in Shimabara, Nagasaki Prefecture. The party had as its objectives morality, social equality, and the happiness of the masses. It attracted about 3,000 local peasants who thought that Tarui's "socialism" would end tenancy and establish a system of equal distribution of wealth. Within a month of its formation the party was ordered by the government to dissolve, but Tarui continued to hold meetings until his arrest in 1883; he was sentenced to one month in jail. Thereafter he was implicated in the ŌSAKA INCIDENT and other schemes by radical members of the People's Rights Movement to increase Japanese influence in Asia. In 1892 he was elected as a representative from Nara Prefecture to the lower house of the Diet. He published several pamphlets advocating a union of East Asian nations under Japanese leadership, among them *Daitō gappō ron* (1893, On the Greater Asian Confederation).

taru kaisen → kaisen

Tarumaezan

Also called Tarumaesan. A triple volcano southeast of Lake Shikotsu, southwestern Hokkaidō, formed on the crater rim of the Lake Shikotsu caldera. It is part of Shikotsu-Tōya National Park. Height: 1,042 m (3,418 ft).

Tarumizu

City in Kagoshima Prefecture, Kyūshū, on the Ōsumi Peninsula, Kagoshima Bay. During the Edo period (1600–1868) Tarumizu was a castle town. Principal agricultural products are vegetables, mandarin oranges, and loquats; livestock are also raised. Marine catches include sardine and yellowtail. The Kaigata Hot Spring is known for its scenic surroundings. Pop: 24,178.

Tasaka Tomotaka (1902–1974)

Film director. Born in Hiroshima Prefecture. Began as a newspaper reporter after dropping out of school at an early age due to family financial difficulties. Joined NIKKATSU CORPORATION in 1924 and became a director in 1926. His films are noted for close attention to details of period and locale. Tasaka made masterpieces in two different genres in 1938. *Gonin no sekkōhei* (Five Scouts) virtually created the Japanese war-film genre, but it was by no means propagandistic. Rather, it was an extension of film realism to the events then taking place in China. That same year he also adapted *Robō no ishi* (A Pebble by the Wayside), a novel by YAMAMOTO YŪZŌ, as part of his continuing interest in the *jumbungaku* (pure literature) movement. It is considered one of the finest films ever made about the Meiji period (1868–1912). Tasaka suffered serious radiation poisoning from the bombing of Hiroshima in 1945 and was hospitalized until 1949. His work after the war did not match the quality of his prewar films, with one exception: *Jochūkko* (1955, The Maid's Kid) was a sensitive evocation of the struggles of a country girl and brought acclaim to actress HIDARI SACHIKO. *David Owens*

tashidaka

(literally, "added amount"). Supplementary stipend paid by the Tokugawa shogunate (1603–1867) to its promoted officials to make up any income gap between their hereditary stipends and those normally granted to holders of the particular posts to which they were appointed. The supplement was paid only so long as an official remained in a post above his hereditary rank. This form of payment, initiated by the eighth shōgun, TOKUGAWA YOSHIMUNE, in 1723 as part of the KYŌHŌ REFORMS, was intended to allow the shogunate more freedom to recruit new talent from the lower ranks of its retainers.

Tashiro Sanki (1465–1537)

Muromachi-period (1333–1568) physician. One of the founders of *goseihō,* the "latter-day school" of traditional Chinese medicine in Japan. A native of Musashi Province (now Tōkyō Prefecture, Saitama Prefecture, and part of Kanagawa Prefecture). Tashiro studied for 12 years in China, learning the Jin–Yuan (Chin–Yüan) school of medicine, the medicine practiced in China during the Jin (1125–1234) and Yuan (1279–1368) dynasties. Upon his return to Japan, he taught MANASE DŌSAN. Tashiro enjoyed the patronage of the KOGA KUBŌ, a branch of the powerful Ashikaga family in eastern Japan. See also MEDICINE: history of medicine. *Yamada Terutane*

Tashiro Shigeki (1890–   )

Businessman. Born in Fukuoka Prefecture. After graduating from Meiji Semmon Gakkō (now Kyūshū Institute of Technology), Tashiro joined Mitsui & Co in 1913 and served as manager of the New York and London branches. He later moved to Tōyō Rayon (now TŌRAY INDUSTRIES, INC), a subsidiary, in 1936 and became president in 1945. Purged by the Allied Occupation authorities after World War II but soon reinstated, Tashiro became the company chairman and started full-scale production of nylon by introducing Du Pont's technological innovations in 1951, a move that immensely improved Toray's business performance. *Kobayakawa Yōichi*

tasuki

Cloth band or cord used by workers and warriors dressed in traditional Japanese garb to tie up the wide sleeves of their KIMONO, giving the arms and hands unimpeded movement. The *tasuki* is usually tied together at the ends and twisted to form loops through which the arms are passed, the band or cord thus forming an X across the back between the shoulders. The donning of a *tasuki* along with a HACHIMAKI (headband) traditionally indicated the wearer's preparation for a ceremonial occasion or strenuous task. The earliest *tasuki,* seen on clay figures (HANIWA) of the prehistoric Kofun period (ca 300–710), are thought to have had a mostly decorative function. But in ancient times *tasuki* were clearly worn by both men and women as part of formal attire during festivals or rice-planting rituals, as well as for practical purposes. In later times, only the practical use survived, and the *tasuki* was removed on greeting visitors. With the predominance of Western clothing in Japan from the 20th century, the *tasuki* has almost disappeared. Its ceremonial function can still be observed, however, in the dress of festival participants or when candidates campaigning for election drape a single *tasuki* sash diagonally across the chest from shoulder to waist with their name inscribed in large characters.   *TSUCHIDA Mitsufumi*

tatami

A mat used as a flooring material in traditional Japanese-style rooms. The noun *tatami* is derived from the verb *tatamu,* meaning to fold or pile; this derivation is taken by some to be evidence that the earliest floor mats were thin and could be either folded up when not in use or used piled in layers.

In the Heian period (794–1185), *tatami* were used as isolated pieces and placed where necessary on top of wooden floors for sitting and sleeping. They came in various thicknesses, with the colors of the cloth borders *(herinuno)* signifying the householder's social rank. By the Muromachi period (1333–1568), the floors of some residences were covered completely with *tatami.* They were, however, used only infrequently in the houses of commoners until modern times.

Since the Muromachi period the *tatami* has been made of a thick base *(toko)* of straw covered with a soft surface *(omote)* of woven rush. Traditionally, *toko* were woven by hand, but since the Taishō period (1912–26), they have been produced by machines.

The size of *tatami* was gradually standardized within each region of Japan and today *tatami* continue to be used as a unit of measure for Japanese and sometimes even for Western-style rooms. A *tatami* generally measures 1.91 by 0.95 meters (6.3 by 3.1 ft) in the Kyōto area, 1.82 by 0.91 meters (6 by 3 ft) in the Nagoya area, and 1.76 by 0.88 meters (5.8 by 2.9 ft) in the Tōkyō area. The thickness is on the average 60 millimeters (2.4 in). A full-size *tatami* is called *muradatami;* a half mat is called a *hanjō,* and a mat of three-quarter size, which is used in tea-ceremony rooms, is called *daimedatami.* See also photograph at HOUSING, HISTORY OF.   *WATANABE Hiroshi*

tatara-buki

The traditional Japanese iron- or steel-making process. Blasts of air are blown from bellows into a clay furnace called *tatara,* raising the temperature inside to melt iron sand into iron or steel. Primitive forms of *tatara-buki* (*buki,* from *fuki,* means air blowing) were used before the Nara period (710–794), and variations of the process were widely used until the end of the 19th century. Kettles still used in the tea ceremony, Japanese swords, and other objects of great beauty, as well as farm implements and carpentry tools were made of *tatara* iron or steel.

Iron is usually refined from ore, but in Japan iron ore is scarce. Iron sand, however, is found in abundance, and *tatara-buki* was developed to make use of this resource. The idea of using hand bellows in iron making was brought from China via Korea. Use of the bellows was developed into *tatara-buki* in Izumo Province (now Shimane Prefecture). Every aspect of *tatara-buki* from the mining of the iron sand to furnace design underwent considerable development over the history of the process. Hand bellows were used at first, then simple foot bellows, and finally a kind of seesaw foot bellows that was operated by several men at once.

In the Edo period (1600–1868) the clay furnace used in the *tatara* process was typically 2.7 meters (8.9 ft) long, 90 centimeters (3 ft) wide, about 1 meter (3.3 ft) tall, and 9–15 centimeters (3.5–6 in) thick. A fire was built under the furnace from a bed of firewood or charcoal. The seesaw bellows would blow air into the furnace and

Tatami

A *tatami* maker outside a home replacing the woven-rush outer layer of a single *tatami* mat. He is sewing down one of the two cloth borders.

Tatara-buki

Air was forced through the pipes and nozzles into the furnace by men working the foot bellows inside the facing compartments. Slag could be tapped from the two apertures at the base of the furnace.

iron sand would periodically be charged into the furnace. Pig iron or slag would occasionally be tapped. After three or four days, firing would be stopped. The furnace would be broken up and the main mass of iron would be removed. Certain types of iron sand such as that found near the Sea of Japan would produce quantities of blister steel; other types such as that found by the Inland Sea would produce only pig or sponge iron.

Detailed manuals on *tatara-buki* practices were published during the Edo period. The classic eight-volume *Tetsuzan hitsuyō kiji* (1784, Essential Articles on Iron Mines), for example, describes every aspect of the processing of raw materials, construction of equipment, and management of workers.

In 1858 the first Western-style blast furnace was built in Japan, but *tatara-buki* remained the predominant iron-making method in Japan until the 1880s, after which it declined rapidly. During World War I an iron and steel shortage prompted a brief revival, but in the 1920s *tatara-buki* was abandoned for all practical purposes.
    Leonard LYNN

Tatebayashi

City in southeastern Gumma Prefecture, central Honshū, between the rivers Tonegawa and Watarasegawa. Tatebayashi developed as a castle town from the latter part of the 16th century. The city was formerly known for its silk (Yūki *tsumugi*). Principal industries include the manufacture of electrical machinery, metal goods, and chemicals. It also has flour, soy sauce, and silk yarn factories. Many of its residents commute to Tōkyō. Of note are the temple Morinji, familiar to many through the tale *(Bumbuku chagama)* about a "badger" (TANUKI) that is transformed into a teakettle, and the azaleas in Tsutsujigaoka Park. Pop: 70,246.

Tatebayashi Kagei (fl mid-18th century)

Artist of the RIMPA style; specialized in pines, plum blossoms, and flowering grasses. Real name Shirai Rittoku. Born in Kaga (now Ishikawa Prefecture), he lived in Edo (now Tōkyō) and painted in the style of KŌRIN with some influence from the KANŌ SCHOOL. Kagei is also said to have once studied with Kōrin's younger brother, KENZAN. His paintings often bear seal impressions similar to the ones used by Kōrin, to whom his works have sometimes been mistakenly attributed.   *Aya Louisa McDONALD*

Tatekawa Yoshitsugu (1880–1945)

Army general. Born in Niigata Prefecture, he graduated from the Army Academy and the Army Staff College. During the RUSSO-JAPANESE WAR (1904–05), Tatekawa distinguished himself by leading a commando unit behind enemy lines (his bravery was subsequently celebrated in a widely read book for children, *Tekichū ōdan sambyakuri* [1931, Seven Hundred Miles into Enemy Territory] by Yamanaka Minetarō [1885–1966]). After service as a military attaché in Britain and Germany, he was attached to the General Staff Office in Tōkyō. There he associated with the right-wing SAKURA-KAI and participated in the MARCH INCIDENT of 1931, an unsuccessful attempt to establish a military government. In September of that year he was sent to Manchuria to restrain Japanese GUANDONG (KWANTUNG) ARMY officers who were eager to seize Manchuria by force; but his sympathies lay with the young officers, and his tacit acceptance of their plans led directly to the MANCHURIAN INCIDENT and the takeover of Manchuria by the Guandong Army. It was thus ironic that he was sent the following year to the Geneva Disarmament Conference. He was placed in the reserves after the military insurrection of 1936 (FEBRUARY 26TH INCIDENT). As ambassador to the Soviet Union from 1940 to 1942 he helped to negotiate the Soviet-Japanese Neutrality Pact (April 1941).

tatemae and honne

Pair of words used to describe a situation in which a person's stated reason *(tatemae)* differs from his real intention or motive *(honne)*. It is analogous to the expressions *omote* and *ura* (front and back), which describe public character or behavior, as opposed to private interactions. Traditional Japanese social norms have greatly emphasized harmonious interpersonal relations and group solidarity. Self-assertion has been strongly discouraged, and the individual often finds that he must sacrifice personal needs and emotions so as to avoid confrontation in the group. Social norms are considered indispensable, and Japanese are taught from early on to follow their personal aims but not to defy *tatemae* openly. The result is that in certain social situations it becomes difficult to discern the person's real intentions. A host may offer hospitality to conform with the formalities of etiquette, yet hope that the guest will interpret the excessive cordiality as a sign to leave. The guest in turn is expected to make the appropriate response. For example, in Kyōto, when a host invites a guest who has overstayed to a bowl of rice with green tea *(ochazuke)* instead of to a proper lunch, he may actually be implying, "It is close to noon, so will you please leave!" The word *tatemae* alone can also refer to the etiquette of the TEA CEREMONY or the ceremony for erecting the framework of a house or building (see KENCHIKU GIREI). See also HAJI; GIRI AND NINJŌ.

📖 ——Takeo Doi, "Omote and Ura: Concepts Derived from the Japanese Twofold Structure of Consciousness," *Journal of Nervous and Mental Disease* 157.4 (1973).   *Hiroshi WAGATSUMA*

tateshakai → vertical society

Tateshina Kōgen

Highland in the foothills of Tateshinayama, central Nagano Prefecture, central Honshū. Covered mainly with dense birch and larch forests, it has several lakes, including Tateshinako and Shirakabako. Numerous hot spring resorts and camping grounds are located here. Elevation: 1,400–1,500 m (4,592–4,920 ft).

Tatewaki Sadayo (1904–   )

Labor activist. Born in Shimane Prefecture. After graduating from Matsue Higher School of Domestic Science, she went to work in Tōkyō in 1924; the following year she married Orimoto Toshi (1900–54), a member of Tōkyō University's SHINJINKAI political club who was later active in the NIHON RŌNŌTŌ (Japan Labor-Farmer Party). In 1927 she worked with Iwauchi Tomie (b 1898) to found the leftist Zenkoku Fujin Dōmei (All-Japan Women's League, a predecessor of the Musan Fujin Dōmei or Proletarian Women's League founded in 1929). Living near a textile factory in Kameido, Tōkyō, she held classes for the women workers there and began to write many articles and pamphlets on labor problems. For her activities, especially her part in organizing strikes, she was imprisoned from 1932 to 1934 and again in 1944. After World War II she continued writing on women's issues. Her works include *Nihon no fujin: Fujin undō no hatten o megutte* (1957, Japan's Women: The Growth of the Women's Movement) and *Josei no ikikata* (1973, How Women Should Live).

Tateyama

City in southern Chiba Prefecture, central Honshū, on the Bōsō Peninsula. Rice, vegetables, flowers, and fruit are grown. A part of Southern Bōsō Quasi-National Park, it is known for its fine beaches. Pop: 56,256.

Tateyama

A group of three mountains in eastern Toyama Prefecture, central Honshū, in the northern part of the Hida Mountains. The three peaks which are composed of granodiorite gneiss are Oyama, Ōnanjiyama, and Jōdosan. The mountainous area contains numerous snowy ravines, lava plateaus, such as Murodōdaira and Midagahara, a crater called Jigokudani (Hell's Valley), and abundant alpine flora. Yamasaki cirque is a natural monument. The Tateyama group is considered one of Japan's three holy mountains together with FUJI-SAN and HAKUSAN. Oyama Shrine is on the summit of Oyama. More than a million tourists and climbers have visited Tateyama annually since the 1971 opening of the Tateyama–Kurobe Alpine Route (a combination of train, bus, and ropeway) connecting Toyama and Nagano prefectures. The highest peak is Ōnanjiyama (3,015 m; 9,889 ft).

Tatsuno

City in southwestern Hyōgo Prefecture, western Honshū. Tatsuno developed as a castle town during the latter half of the 17th century, and several warrior residences have survived. It has long been known for its soy sauce and *sōmen* noodles. The city is the birthplace of the poet MIKI ROFŪ and the philosopher MIKI KIYOSHI. Pop: 40,941.

Tatsuno Kingo (1854–1919)

Pioneer modern architect of the late 19th and early 20th centuries. Born in Saga Prefecture. In 1879 he was among the first graduates of the building-engineering department of Kōbu College, a predecessor of Tōkyō University, where he was a student of the English architect Josiah CONDER. Upon graduating he went to England and trained under the noted Gothic revival architect William Burges. Returning to Japan in 1883, Tatsuno became professor and then dean of the school of engineering at Tōkyō University. He served as head of the Architectural Institute of Japan and was the most influential figure in Japanese architecture of his day. In 1902 he left the university and in 1903 opened his own firm. Among his many buildings are the BANK OF JAPAN BUILDING (1896) and Tōkyō Station (1914).
             WATANABE Hiroshi

Tatsutagawa

River in Nara Prefecture, central Honshū, flowing south through the lowlands east of the Ikoma Mountains. It is a tributary of the YAMATOGAWA. The upper reaches are called Ikomagawa, the middle reaches Hegurigawa, and Tatsutagawa refers to the lower reaches. Famous for its maple trees, the area along the river has long been a popular site for autumn foliage viewing. Length: 13.2 km (8.2 mi).

Tatsuta Shrine

(Tatsuta Taisha). Shintō shrine in Ikoma District, Nara Prefecture, dedicated to the deities Amenomihashira no Mikoto and Kuninomihashira no Mikoto. According to tradition, the shrine was built by the legendary emperor Sujin after he was informed through an oracle that only by building a shrine to these deities could the people end a series of natural disasters that had been destroying their crops. Associated with good harvests, the shrine was richly patronized by both the court and the common people. The shrine and its deities have long been celebrated for a supposed power over destructive winds, and it is often paired with the HIROSE SHRINE, which is believed to have the power of avoiding water-related disasters. In addition to the annual festival on 4 April, a well-known ceremony for warding off typhoons (Fūchinsai) is held on 4 July.

Stanley WEINSTEIN

tattoos

(irezumi). Also called horimono. Western experts agree that in Japan the ancient and worldwide practice of tattooing reached its highest level of artistic expression with bold, colorful, integrated pictorial designs based on traditional themes and skillfully "engraved" over large areas of the body. This singular preeminence in decorative design appeared suddenly and developed rapidly in urban areas during the mid–19th century.

Early records and origins. In describing Japan, the 3rd century Chinese chronicle WEI ZHI (Wei chih) mentions that "the men both great and small tattoo their faces and work designs upon their bodies." This would seem to indicate that in ancient Japan, as in other primitive societies, tattoos were associated with ritual and indicated status. More recent examples are the mouth markings once made (and still to be seen) on marriageable AINU women and the wrist markings of Okinawan female weavers observed by Langdon WARNER in 1904.

As a form of punishment. The first Japanese record of a tattoo appears in the NIHON SHOKI (720, Chronicle of Japan), in which the legendary emperor Richū is said to have commuted one Azumi no Muraji Hamako's death penalty to facial tattooing and, presumably, to social ostracism. Over the centuries, tattooing as a punishment followed a curious pattern of falling in and out of favor, its final official use being ordered in 1720 by the eighth Tokugawa shōgun, TOKUGAWA YOSHIMUNE. Markings varied by region and were applied to the arm as well as to the face, with designs allowing for additions for repeated offenses. In Ōsaka, at one time, criminals received marks on the forehead in such a way that four convictions produced the four-stroke character for "dog" (inu). During the Edo period (1600–1868) some criminals disguised their facial tattoos by altering them into small pictorial designs of a bat or Buddha figure. Others innocent of crime perversely went out of their way to have facial tattoos as a sign of manliness.

As a lover's pledge. In the Genroku era (1688–1704) it became a minor vogue among prostitutes of the gay quarters in Edo (now Tōkyō) and Ōsaka to have the name of a favored client tattooed on the upper arm or inner thigh. A more discreet affirmation could be made with a series of small dots numbering a lover's age or with a shared pattern on fingers and hands that was completed when the lovers' hands met. Called kishō-bori ("pledge marks") these love tattoos appear in woodblock prints illustrating the risqué literature of the period.

The Edo explosion. On the basis of such humble antecedents, it is not easy to explain the sudden and full-blown appearance of the uniquely Japanese "full body" tattoo in the 1820s and 1830s. Lacking further facts, the answer seems to lie in the theory of a sudden social explosion, which will be explained in a later paragraph. It is known that around the time of the MEIJI RESTORATION (1868) there was a significant demand among townsmen for tattoos that covered the entire back, most of the front, and often the upper arms and legs as well. To meet this demand, a distinct trade group had emerged. Its members were called horishi (tattooists); who possessed the techniques, tools, and skills to execute masterpieces on a grand scale with secondary design elements artfully integrated into a harmonious whole. Members of this select guild included street barbers who engraved tattoos as a side business to oblige occasional customers. Others came from the ranks of the artisans who carved the woodblocks used to print genre pictures (see UKIYO-E). Their customers were initially from the so-called naked trades—porters, palanquin bearers (who discovered that a good tattoo attracted fares), grooms,

and special delivery postal runners. Next came the artisans—carpenters, masons, gardeners—whose traditional, open-back work aprons (haragake) permitted more discreet, but still effective display. Volunteer firemen in particular became fervid tattoo fans. And the second sons of wealthy merchants soon discovered that a tattoo cut a fine swathe through the gay quarters. Geisha, too, occasionally sought their services. But samurai, it seems, seldom succumbed to the temptation; as the ruling class they did not have the same need as commoners to assert their independence and individuality.

Meiji suppression. As foreigners entered Japan after the Meiji Restoration, government officials became sensitive to the possibility of odious comparisons between Eastern "backwardness" and Western "enlightenment." Tattooing was banned as being barbaric. Tattoo parlors were raided by police, tools were confiscated, records and "pattern books" destroyed. Perplexingly (to officials), most foreigners found Japanese tattoos fascinating. They took pride in having the often-exposed bodies of their grooms and rickshaw men magnificently embellished, and not a few became participating patrons of the art. As a result, one or two establishments were unofficially allowed to stay open in Yokohama "for export only" as it were. To the most famous of these, Hori Chō's, came a young midshipman, the future King George V of England, to have a dragon tattooed on his forearm. He was followed by the tsarevich, later Nicholas II of Russia. A fine example of Hori Chō's work was carried as well to Boston, Massachusetts, on the back of Dr. Charles Goddard Weld, the famous Japanophile and benefactor of the Boston Museum of Fine Arts as well as the Peabody Museum of Salem. A photograph shows an enormous tiger and dragon locked in heroic combat.

Full body tattoo vogue. For an explanation of the sudden appearance of full body tattoos in the late Edo period, one must review the urban life of those times which was at once extremely sophisticated and politically repressed. Literacy was high, and as well as literature, there was a wealth of theater and art created expressly for the townsman's delight. Over the years bourgeois taste for daring colors and bold design had gradually combined with the Zen-influenced preference for restraint and understatement to produce what has been described as the heart of the Japanese aesthetic. Yet all this creativity and energy was stifled by the gradual stagnation of the impoverished warrior class which remained in complete control at the top. The resulting frustration produced a volatile and unstable society with an unhealthy appetite for escapist fantasy and a fascination with the grotesque. It was at this time, too, that in 1805, that Takizawa BAKIN began to publish his Shimpen suiko gaden, a translation of the Chinese picaresque novel known in Japanese as Suikoden (Ch: Shuihuzhuan or Shui-hu-chuan; The Water Margin; tr All Men Are Brothers), which deals with the adventures of daring outlaws of the Robin Hood type. It was about this time, too, that a hitherto unsuccessful artist named UTAGAWA KUNIYOSHI published the first five sheets of what was to become his most popular series, Tsūzoku suikoden gōketsu hyakuhachinin, "108 Heroes of the Suikoden." Both book and prints were immediate successes. Significantly, 17 of the heroes were dramatically tattooed, a fact odd in itself, since tattoos are almost unknown among the Chinese. Soon other contemporary artists—UTAGAWA TOYOKUNI and UTAGAWA KUNISADA—were producing prints of tattooed outlaws (always heroic) like Kumonryū Shishin and popular rascals from KABUKI plays like Benten Kozō. The tattoo boom had begun, in print and in person.

The question remains whether it was Kuniyoshi (along with Bakin) who created the vogue of the full-body tattoo or whether he was only the publicist, stimulating and giving direction to an existing trend. The answer might have been found in the tattooists' records destroyed by the Meiji police. But there is no question that it was Kuniyoshi who, with his bold colors and dramatic designs, set the canons of Japanese tattoo art.

The state of the art today. Tattooing is still done in Japan today, and the same themes are in demand. Taken from religion and popular mythology, they are chosen to help the bearer gain strength, health, wealth, wisdom, and various magical powers. They include such Buddhist deities as Fudō Myōō (Acalanātha; see MYŌO) with his attendants Kongara and Seitaka, Dainichi NYORAI (Skt: Mahāvairocana) meditating on a lotus, and the goddess of mercy, KANNON (Skt: Avalokiteśvara), riding on a golden carp. Folk heroes include Chōjun (a Suikoden character breaking from his underwater cell), Oniwakamaru (the childhood name of the legendary Japanese hero BENKEI) killing a giant carp, Ushiwakamaru (the childhood name of Benkei's master MINAMOTO NO YOSHITSUNE) fighting a karasutengu (see TENGU), and Tamatori Hime, the woman diver who stole the great treasure from the lord of the sea's underwater palace. Auspicious animals include dragons for wealth and protection from fire, carp for persistence, and *shishi* lions for courage and fortitude. Finally, there are peonies, chrysanthemums, and cherry blossoms as well as a gallery of assorted angels and rogues.

Tools have changed somewhat. American electric needles are used by some *horishi* to trace the initial *sumi* ink outline; for this black Nara ink, which turns blue under living skin, is favored. But other colors are filled in with traditional tools: clusters of steel needles—as many as 40 of them—bound to bone or ivory handles with silk thread. These and the unique Japanese technique of *hane-bari*, an up-and-down fluttering motion of the hand while piercing the epidermis, are what produce such remarkably delicate shadings of color.

Most changed perhaps are the customers. A fine, large-scale tattoo takes several months to complete and costs several thousand dollars. The people with the time and money and the greatest need for group identification are usually gangsters (see YAKUZA). But company presidents, bar hostesses, and college professors are patrons, too. And there is still the young dumptruck driver who, like his Edo artisan forebearer, spends all his free time and salary having a genuine work of art engraved upon his back.

■ ——George Burchett, *Memoirs of a Tattooist* (1958). Basil Hall Chamberlain, *Things Japanese* (1971). Gunji Masakatsu and Fukuda Kazuhiko, ed, *Genshoku ukiyo-e irezumi hanga* (1976). W. D. Hambly, H. F. Witherby, and G. Witherby, *History of Tattooing and Its Significance* (1925). Iizawa Tadasu and Fukushi Katsunari, ed, *Genshoku Nihon horimono taikan* (1973). Tamabayashi Haruo, *Bunshin hyakushi* (1936).   *John E.* THAYER III

Taue-zōshi

A late 16th century book of transplanting songs. A sequence of songs sung each year at the time of transplanting rice seedlings from nursery beds into the main fields. The work is done by women, who sing responsively with the director of the day's labor to the accompaniment of drums, flutes, and cymbals. There are many similar collections from a later period, but this one is generally regarded as the finest and most representative. It is preserved at Tōkyō University in the form of two tracings. Particulars about how and when it took its present shape are difficult to determine because its formation was in part an oral process.

This particular sequence is divided into four sets for the morning, two for noon, a set to be sung when *sake* is brought into the field, another after it has been drunk, followed by a third and a fourth set for noon and four sets for the evening. Two additional songs mark the conclusion of the day's labor. The first set for the morning is missing from the tracings but judging from related sequences it consisted of songs both of sexual love and of prayer to invoke the field god. This double ingredient suggests the nature of the larger series itself: secular songs were integrated into a whole sung at the time of this crucial agricultural, social, and religious event, in order to bring it to a successful conclusion. Some songs were originally extemporaneous; others were reworkings of what the contemporary body of popular song had to offer as suitable material for use in field labor.

■ ——Frank Hoff, "City and Country: Songs and the Performing Arts in Sixteenth-Century Japan," in George Elison and Bradwell Smith, ed, *Warlords, Artists, & Commoners: Japan in the Sixteenth Century* (1981). *Taue-zōshi*, tr Frank Hoff as *The Genial Seed: A Japanese Song Cycle* (1971). Manabe Masahiro, *Taue-zōshi kayō zenkōchū* (1974).   *Frank* HOFF

Taut, Bruno (1880–1938)

German expressionist architect who was influential in generating increased evaluation of traditional Japanese architecture. Born in Königsberg (now Kaliningrad) and a graduate from a local civil engineering college, Taut established himself as a progressive architect with his skillful use of glass and steel. He was active in Berlin as an apartment designer during the 1920s. In 1933, however, he moved to Japan to escape Nazism. In Japan he extolled the functionalism and rationalism of what he called "emperor art," as represented by the ISE SHRINE and KATSURA DETACHED PALACE, and condemned the decorative style of temples and the TŌSHŌGŪ, the Tokugawa family mausoleum at Nikkō, which he labeled "shōgun art." He thus contributed to a wider appreciation among the Japa-

nese for their own traditional culture. His writings on architecture include *Nippon* (1934). Taut left Japan in 1936 to teach in Istanbul where he died.   WATANABE *Hiroshi*

tawara

Large straw sacks of standardized size used for the storage or transport of rice, potatoes, charcoal, and so forth. Since rice taxes were delivered in *tawara* in ancient Japan, their size was presumably standardized quite early, at least regionally, and this led to the use of *hyō* (another reading of the Chinese character for *tawara*) as a unit for measuring rice. The circular straw cap at either end of the *tawara* (called *sandawara*) is used as a ritual object in some regions; for example, ceremonial red rice is sometimes offered to the deities known as DŌSOJIN on a *sandawara*.

Tawara Kuniichi (1872–1958)

Metallurgist known for his metallographical study of steel. Born in Shimane Prefecture, Tawara graduated from Tōkyō University in 1897 and immediately became assistant professor. He went to Germany in 1899 to study metallurgy and upon his return became full professor at Tōkyō University. He is also known for his analytical studies of traditional methods of refining iron sand and of making Japanese swords. He received the Order of Culture in 1946.

Tawara Sunao (1873–1952)

Pathologist and medical scientist. Discoverer, together with Ludwig Aschoff, of the Aschoff-Tawara node (the atrioventricular node). Born in Ōita Prefecture; graduate of Tōkyō University. Tawara studied in Germany from 1903 to 1906, and it was at Aschoff's laboratory at the University of Marburg that the two described the atrioventricular node, which is associated with the mechanism of the heartbeat in mammals. Tawara taught at Kyūshū University. He received the Imperial Prize of the Japan Academy in 1914.   ACHIWA *Gorō*

Tawarayama Hot Spring

(Tawarayama Onsen). Located in the city of Nagato, northwestern Yamaguchi Prefecture, western Honshū. A simple alkaline spring; water temperature around 40°C (104°F). This spa, located in a mountainous area, has a history of more than 1,000 years and has been designated as a National Health Resort Hot Spring.

Tawaraya Sōtatsu → Sōtatsu

Tawara Yoshizumi (1856–1935)

Pharmacologist. Born in Hizen Province (now Saga Prefecture and part of Nagasaki Prefecture). Graduate of Daigaku Nankō (now Tōkyō University). Tawara succeeded in extracting tetrodotoxin, a poisonous compound of medicinal value found in *fugu* (GLOBEFISHES). As head of the Tōkyō Institute of Hygienic Sciences of the Home Ministry for many years, he contributed greatly to the development of the domestic pharmaceutical industry.   SŌDA *Hajime*

tax accountants

(*zeirishi*). Professionally trained taxation specialists who operate under the provisions of the Tax Accountant Law (Zeirishi Hō). The tax accountant provides advice, prepares tax returns and petitions, and represents taxpayers in dealing with individual income, corporate income, inheritance, business, and property taxes. Persons desiring to become tax accountants are required to pass a national examination and have their names put on a national register. Attorneys at law and certified public accountants are also authorized to provide tax accounting services. In order to develop and improve the tax accounting practice, accountants form institutes in each regional tax administration area. Such institutes, in turn, form the Japan Association of Tax Accountants, a nationwide organization.   WAKASUGI *Akira*

tax accounting

(*zeimu kaikei*). In Japan, tax accounting (the calculation of taxable income for profit-making personal business ventures and corpora-

Taxes

Tax Revenues as Percentage of Gross Domestic Product, Selected Countries, 1976						
	Tax source					
	Individual income	Corporate income	Payroll	Goods and services[1]	Property	Wealth[2]	Total
Sweden	21.9	1.8	14.3	12.6	—[4]	0.3	50.9
Netherlands	12.5	3.2	17.5	12.0	0.6	0.4	46.2
Norway	16.9	1.9	8.3	18.1	0.2	0.7	46.2
Denmark	24.2	1.6	0.5	16.6	1.6	0.4	44.7
Belgium	13.2[3]	2.8[3]	13.2	12.3	—[4]	0.3	41.9
France	5.0[3]	2.3[3]	16.6	14.6	0.8	0.2	39.4
Austria	8.4	1.3	14.3	14.0	0.3	0.6	38.9
United Kingdom	14.0	1.7	7.1	9.7	3.9	0.3	36.7
West Germany	11.1	1.7	13.0	9.9	0.4	0.6	36.7
Italy	5.9	2.2	16.4	11.2	—[4]	0.1	35.8
Canada	11.4[3]	3.9[3]	3.6	10.8	2.8	0.3	32.9
United States	9.7	3.0	7.2	5.3	3.6	0.4	29.3
Japan	5.1	3.5	5.3	5.5	1.3	0.2	20.9

[1] Includes sales, value added, and excise taxes, taxes on imports, exports and transfers of property and other securities, and transactions taxes paid by enterprises.
[2] Includes annual net wealth taxes and death and gift taxes.
[3] Adjusted to include unallocable income taxes in proportion to individual and corporation income tax revenues.
[4] Less than 0.05 percent.
NOTE: Includes national and local taxes. Data are for calendar years except for United States (fiscal year begins 1 July) and Japan (fiscal year begins 1 April). Figures are rounded.
SOURCE: Organization for Economic Cooperation and Development, *Revenue Statistics of OECD Member Countries, 1965–76* (1978).

tions) is done in accordance with the Income Tax Law and Corporate Tax Law. Tax accounting takes as its basis the results of business accounting, computed in accordance with the Commercial Law and the Securities Exchange Law. Modifications are then made in order to comply with various regulations unique to the tax laws. Corporate business accounting follows a set of accounting postulates and observes various principles such as accrual basis, realization basis, matching costs with revenues, periodic allocation of costs, and cost basis. Corporate profits are calculated by deducting expenses from revenues. In tax accounting, however, taxable income is obtained by deducting expenses and losses from revenues and gains as defined in the Income Tax Law. Since revenues and expenses in business accounting are different from profits and losses in tax accounting, the net income of business accounts is adjusted under the tax law to produce taxable income. There are considerable differences in concepts and methods of calculation between tax accounting and business accounting, stemming from the different objectives of the two kinds of accounting. *WAKASUGI Akira*

taxes

The present tax system in Japan dates back to the early 1950s. Many of the characteristics of this system were designed by a commission headed by Carl S. Shoup, Professor of Economics at Columbia University, which was organized to reform the tax system and moderate the high tax rates that had remained as a legacy from World War II. Although several of its proposals were modified or not enacted, the SHOUP MISSION made a significant impact on Japanese tax policy and tax administration and helped in modernizing the tax system.

The Japanese tax system has remained fairly stable in the last 25 years. Major reliance has been placed on the individual and corporate income taxes, and the ratio of taxes to the national income has remained low by international standards (see table). In 1976 income taxes accounted for 41 percent of total tax revenues; taxes on commodities and services, 26 percent; payroll taxes, 26 percent; property tax, 6 percent; and death and gift taxes, 1 percent. This system resembles that of the United States more than those of the Western European countries, which raise a larger percentage of their revenues from payroll and consumption taxes.

Throughout the period of fast economic growth dating from the 1950s, the government has maintained tax revenues at about a fifth of the gross domestic product. A major issue in Japan is whether the tax system should be allowed to expand in order to provide more revenue for social welfare purposes.

Outline of the Tax System——The individual income tax is the mainstay of the Japanese tax system. Most types of income are aggregated and taxed at progressive rates, but some are taxed at flat rates (e.g., interest and dividends) or are not taxed at all (e.g., interest on small deposits and capital gains on the sale of securities). The combined national and local income tax rates range from 14 to 93 percent (with a maximum effective rate of 80 percent). Generous deductions are provided from employment income (as of 1982, 40 percent for the first ¥1.5 million wage income), and the income levels at which successive tax brackets begin are relatively high. The result is that the actual tax paid at various income levels is lower than in other developed countries.

The corporate income tax is a split rate system, with a higher rate applying to undistributed profits and the lower rate to distributed profits. In 1978 the tax rate ranged, according to size of firm, from about 39 percent to 59 percent on undistributed profits (including the taxes levied by local governments) and from 32 percent to 47 percent on distributed profits. The profits of small corporations are taxed at lower rates. There are generous allowances for depreciation and other investment tax subsidies, and these reduce the effective rates of tax actually paid by corporations to about 20 percent of gross profits (net profits plus capital consumption allowances).

The tax on transfers of wealth at death is a combination of inheritance and estate taxes. There is also a gift tax, which is levied on gifts accumulated for a period of only three years and is paid by the recipients. Tax rates on bequests and gifts range from 10 to 75 percent; but exemptions are high on bequests and valuations of property are low, so that only a small proportion of total wealth transferred between generations is actually subject to tax. Transfer taxes have not been a great impediment to the transfer of wealth.

There is no general consumption or sales tax in Japan, but selective excise taxes are levied on liquor, tobacco, gasoline, durable consumer goods, energy, and admissions. The tax rates are generally moderate (for example, the taxes on small automobiles and most household appliances are 15–20 percent). Payroll taxes are similar to those levied in Western Europe and the United States for social security and related programs. Most of the social insurance programs are financed by equal taxes paid by employers and employees on employees' earnings up to a prescribed maximum.

The property tax is used only by local governments. The prefectures levy a real estate transfer tax of 3 percent but have no annual real estate tax. At the municipal level, the standard real estate tax is 1.4 percent of assessed valuation, but it can be raised to a maximum of 2.1 percent. As in all countries, valuations for property tax purposes are gross understatements of true value.

Special Features of the Tax System —— The high rate of growth and moderate government expenditures that prevailed until the early 1970s permitted the Japanese government to adopt tax policies that were envied elsewhere. The tax system and the tax process illustrate the strong national bias toward consensus and gradualism, which have characterized national policies in Japan since the end of World War II. The Japanese have developed an elaborate process to formulate tax policy. A Tax Advisory Commission (Kokuzei Shinsakai) was established in 1955 to assist in the development of long-term tax policy, as well as to recommend year-to-year changes. The diversity of membership of the commission (there are 30 or so members in total) is designed so that the commission can act as arbiter among the interest groups that influence taxation. The commission's recommendations have played a vital role in tax policy ever since it was established.

In addition to the Tax Advisory Commission, the Tax Bureau (Shuzeikyoku) in the Ministry of Finance exercises an important influence. It consists of an unusually able group of career government officials who provide technical tax advice to the Tax Advisory Commission and to the cabinet and have managed to set the tone of tax policy and administration. Final tax decisions are made by the cabinet, but they rarely deviate much from the proposals of the Tax Bureau.

Annual tax reductions. Because its economy grew very fast between 1955 and 1973, Japan's tax revenues grew at very rapid rates, but the public sector did not grow in relation to the size of the economy. This circumstance provided the elbow room for the unique practice of annual tax reduction, which proved to be very popular with the Japanese people. The growth in revenues slowed considerably after the OIL CRISIS OF 1973, however, resulting in deficits in the national budget and making it impossible for the government to continue reducing taxes every year.

Special tax measures. The Japanese make active use of the tax system to promote economic growth. Numerous measures have been adopted to stimulate private investment and activities that have high economic or social priority, including special tax-free reserves, accelerated depreciation, tax credits, and the like. These measures are contained in the Tax Special Measures Law (Sozei Tokubetsu Sochi Hō), which includes most of the special provisions applying to individual and corporation income taxes. The annual budget usually contains some changes in the special tax measures, depending on shifts in national objectives.

The special tax measures erode the tax base and reduce the revenue potential of the income taxes. Studies of the impact of these measures on the economy are inconclusive, but the desirable effects have been purchased at the price of complexity and substantial inequities among taxpayers. The Tax Advisory Commission has urged that the special tax measures be curtailed and eventually abolished, but progress toward this goal has been slow.

Employee compensation, expense accounts, and retirement plans. Wage and salary workers are lightly taxed in Japan in comparison with the leading countries of the West. For the wage-earner, there are substantial deductions for employment expenses, and the value of subsidized housing is excluded from taxable income. For the business executive, there are tax-free expense accounts, company cars and chauffeurs, and either a large subsidized residence or subsidized loans to purchase residences (see COMPANY WELFARE SYSTEM). Of these features, the EXPENSE ACCOUNT is perhaps the most distinctive. Most executives spend several nights a week in town on business; the cost of an evening is usually high, and all of it is charged to the business firm. Firms are permitted to deduct only a small portion of such expenses in determining their taxable income, but they reimburse the full amount spent nevertheless.

Most Japanese firms do not have funded pension plans. Instead, they ordinarily make lump sum payments to their employees on retirement, commonly one or two months' wages in the last year of employment for every year of employment with the firm. Thus, if a worker has been employed for 35 years, he might be eligible for a retirement payment equal to three times his last annual wage. Half of retirement incomes are not subject to tax and there are generous exclusions for the remainder. Thus, most pensioners pay no tax, while those who are subject to tax pay very little. Retirement payments are usually not adequate for business executives, who often retire before age 60. To supplement their incomes, many executives continue to work for a subsidiary of the enterprise or obtain employment in other enterprises as advisers or active executives. See RETIREMENT.

Administrative practices. Japan's system of tax administration immediately following World War II was archaic. Because tax rates were high, taxpayer morale was at a low ebb and underreporting was rampant. To collect the taxes, tax officers were assigned collection quotas, which were often met by imposing arbitrary assessments on particular individuals. To improve taxpayer morale the Shoup mission recommended reduction of high marginal tax rates, elimination of quotas, simplification of tax returns for small taxpayers, public disclosure of high income tax returns, and the elimination of anonymous accounts. All these recommendations, except for the elimination of the anonymous accounts, were accepted, and the quality of administration improved almost immediately. Since then, Japan's tax system has been administered with a high degree of efficiency. The major remaining problem of tax administration is the continued use of anonymous accounts to conceal investment income. These accounts are commonplace in Japan and are apparently difficult to control. The government has attempted unsuccessfully to obtain legislation to prohibit the use of such accounts.

Wage-earners generally discharge their full income tax liability through the withholding system. Small amounts of property income are excluded from the tax base, while larger amounts are subject to separate flat taxes. As a result, the mass of wage and salary workers are not required to file returns. The advantage of this arrangement is that only a small minority of income recipients is required to file tax returns, but this is purchased at the cost of a system of deductions and exclusions that can hardly be justified on grounds of equity, even considering that a generous share of the deductions goes to wage incomes. Until the tax officials are persuaded that the masses of wage-earners can file tax returns, it will be difficult to improve the income tax system.

The Local Revenue System —— The operations of local governments are subject to much more supervision by the national government in Japan than they are in the United States. The Shoup mission recommended a substantial degree of local autonomy, but this advice was virtually disregarded. Practically all the revenue sources are controlled by the central government. (Local governments are permitted to change some tax rates, but within strict limits.) As in most countries, bond issues by local governments must be approved by the central government before they are floated.

More than half of all local tax revenues come from individual and corporate income taxes, which are patterned after the taxes levied by central government. The property tax, which is levied only by the municipal governments, accounts for about a sixth of local government revenues. Taxes on automobiles and tobacco, charges, fees, and other nontax revenues account for the rest.

Japan has a well-developed and efficient system of GOVERNMENT GRANTS-IN-AID, which accounts for almost half of local government receipts. The grants-in-aid consist of national subsidies and local allocations. The subsidies are categorical grants for particular purposes, while the allocations are general-purpose grants with no strings attached. The national subsidies are intended to maintain minimal standards for services provided by local government, the largest of them being payments of half the salaries of public school teachers and support for local public works. The local allocations program, a unique feature of intergovernmental relations in Japan, distributes funds for the regular activities of local governments and provides some equalization on the basis of need. See also FINANCE, LOCAL GOVERNMENT.

Conclusion —— Japan has an efficient tax system and tax rates that are low when compared with other countries. This fortunate circumstance can be explained by the absence of a defense program in the budget, but it also reflects reluctance on the part of the Japanese government to permit the public sector to expand in relation to the rest of the economy. With the rising demand for social services, Japan may find it difficult to maintain taxes at such low levels. The recession of the late 1970s increased the pressure on the tax system. Japan will have to seek other sources of revenue to supplement those that the present tax system yields. Part of this revenue will come from the individual income tax, which generates a great deal of revenue when the economy is growing fast. It is also possible to raise significant additional amounts of revenue from the income taxes by eliminating many of the eroding features of the tax law. Failing that, the Japanese may have to turn to a value added tax or a general sales

National and local taxes

Revenue Estimates by Tax Items, 1982
(in millions of US dollars)

National taxes	Amount	%	Local taxes	Amount	%
1. General account			1. Ordinary taxes		
Direct taxes			Prefectural taxes		
Income Tax	59,916	39.3	Prefectural In-habitants' Tax	9,682	12.7
Corporation Tax	47,804	31.3	Enterprise Tax	14,590	19.1
Inheritance Tax and Gift Tax	2,796	1.8	Real Property Acquisition Tax	1,342	1.8
Indirect taxes, etc			Prefectural Tobacco Consumption Tax	1,108	1.5
Liquor Tax	7,844	5.1			
Sugar Excise Tax	172	0.1	Local Entertain-ment Tax	337	0.4
Gasoline Tax	6,496	4.3	Tax on Consumption at Hotels and Restaurants	1,758	2.3
Liquefied Petro-leum Gas Tax	64	0.0			
Aviation Fuel Tax	216	0.1	Automobile Tax	3,342	4.4
Petroleum Tax	1,736	1.1	Mine-lot Tax	4	0.0
Commodity Tax	6,176	4.0	Hunters' License Tax	13	0.0
Playing-card Tax	4	0.0	Prefectural Prop-erty Tax	33	0.0
Bourse Tax	88	0.1	Municipal taxes		
Securities Trans-action Tax	1,848	1.2	Municipal In-habitants' Tax	20,996	27.5
Travel Tax	328	0.2	Municipal Prop-erty Tax [2]	13,124	17.2
Admission Tax	28	0.0	Light Vehicle Tax	186	0.2
Motor Vehicle Tonnage Tax	1,764	1.2	Municipal Tobacco Consumption Tax	1,947	2.5
Customs Duty	2,960	1.9			
Tonnage Due	40	0.0	Electricity Tax and Gas Tax	1,708	2.2
Stamp Revenue	6,216	4.1	Mineral Product Tax	16	0.0
Monopoly Profits	3,047	2.0	Timber Delivery Tax	12	0.0
2. Special accounts			Special Land-holding Tax	246	0.3
Local Road Tax [1]	1,168	0.8	2. Earmarked taxes		
Liquefied Petro-leum Gas Tax [1]	64	0.0	Prefectures [3]	3,020	4.0
Aviation Fuel Tax [1]	39	0.0	Cities, Towns, and Villages [4]	2,913	3.8
Motor Vehicle Tonnage Tax [1]	588	0.4	Total	76,377	100.0
Special Tonnage Duty [1]	50	0.0			
Customs Duty on Oil	580	0.4			
Promotion of Resources De-velopment Tax	574	0.4			
Total	152,606	100.0			

[1] Distributed to local governments.
[2] Includes charges on national assets and public corporations' assets.
[3] Among taxes earmarked for transfer to prefectural governments (including Tōkyō, Ōsaka, Kyōto, and Hokkaidō) are the Automobile Acquisition Tax and the Light Oil Delivery Tax.
[4] Includes Bathing Tax, Business Office Tax, City Planning Tax, and others.
NOTE: Original budget estimates, fiscal year 1982 (1 April 1982–31 March 1983). Converted into US dollars at the rate of ¥249.04 = $1.00. For further information on exchange rates, see YEN. Nomenclature in table is that of the Ministry of Finance and may differ from that used elsewhere in this encyclopedia.
SOURCE: Tax Bureau, Ministry of Finance, An Outline of Japanese Taxes (annual): 1982.

tax for the needed revenues, but this would introduce regressivity into the tax system.

The inequality of INCOME DISTRIBUTION before taxes is about the same in Japan as it is in other developed countries. Since the tax system is only mildly, if at all, progressive, it does not reduce income inequality to any significant degree. Nor do the death taxes prevent an increasing concentration of wealth and economic power as the nation grows. The effect of this policy is not yet an issue in Japan, but it may produce social and political strains if continued for long.

——Martin Bronfenbrenner and Kiichiro Kogiku, "The Aftermath of the Shoup Tax Reforms," National Tax Journal 10 (1957). Sei Fujita, "Tax Policy," in Ryūtarō Komiya, ed, Postwar Economic Growth in Japan (1966). Ryūtarō Komiya, "Japan," in National Bureau of Economic Research, ed, Foreign Tax Policies and Economic Growth (1966). Ministry of Finance, Tax Bureau, An Outline of Japanese Taxes (annual). Joseph A. Pechman and Keimei Kaizuka, "Taxation," in Hugh Patrick and Henry Rosovsky, ed, Asia's New Giant: How the Japanese Economy Works (1976).

Joseph A. PECHMAN

taxes, national and local

(kokuzei; chihōzei). The present tax system in Japan is based upon the SHOUP MISSION tax recommendations of 1949. It is characterized by the direct national taxation of personal and corporate in-come, and the replacement of the prewar local surtax with separate prefectural and municipal taxes.

The ratio of combined local and national tax revenue to national income was 19 percent in 1977 (12 percent national and 7 percent local taxes), placing Japan lowest in this regard among advanced industrial nations. Personal and corporate income taxes provided 70 percent of tax revenues in 1981. The revenue from the corporate income tax is about equal to that from the personal income tax; this unique phenomenon is not a result of a high rate of corporate taxation, but rather of the fact that even small enterprises are incorporated and that corporate profits occupy a high proportion of the national income. Indirect taxes include liquor and gasoline taxes, excise taxes, and customs duties. The gasoline tax is assigned to road construction. Neither value-added taxes nor general consumption taxes exist.

Prefectural taxes include the enterprise tax imposed on the profits of individual and corporate enterprises and a resident tax imposed on individual and corporate residents. Municipal taxes are a similar resident tax and a fixed asset tax on the owners of land, houses, and depreciable assets. Prefectural and municipal taxes provide only 30 percent of total local revenues, with the remainder coming largely from the national government. This has given rise to the phrase "30 percent local autonomy." See also FINANCE, LOCAL GOVERNMENT; TAX LAW; TAXES.

Udagawa Akihito

Tax law

	Income Tax Rates		
	Income (yen)		Tax rate (percent)
	¥ 600,000 or less		10
More than	600,000	but less than ¥ 1,200,000	12
"	1,200,000	" 1,800,000	14
"	1,800,000	" 2,400,000	16
"	2,400,000	" 3,000,000	18
"	3,000,000	" 4,000,000	21
"	4,000,000	" 5,000,000	24
"	5,000,000	" 6,000,000	27
"	6,000,000	" 7,000,000	30
"	7,000,000	" 8,000,000	34
"	8,000,000	" 10,000,000	38
"	10,000,000	" 12,000,000	42
"	12,000,000	" 15,000,000	46
"	15,000,000	" 20,000,000	50
"	20,000,000	" 30,000,000	55
"	30,000,000	" 40,000,000	60
"	40,000,000	" 60,000,000	65
"	60,000,000	" ¥80,000,000	70
over	¥80,000,000		75

NOTE: Individual income tax rates as specified in the Income Tax Law (Shotokuzei Hō) of 1965; unchanged as of 1982.
SOURCE: Ministry of Finance, Tax Bureau, *An Outline of Japanese Taxes* (annual): 1982.

tax law

The Japanese tax system is characterized by the following features: it places its major emphasis on direct rather than indirect taxation; it is administered in accordance with very detailed legislation and regulations that permit tax planning by nongovernment professionals; tax officials are highly trained and skilled in the performance of their duties; and the burden of local taxes as against national taxes is quite heavy in comparison with the pattern in many other developed countries in the world.

National tax and customs revenues for fiscal year 1978 (1 April 1978–31 March 1979) were a total of ¥23.2 trillion (US $11 billion). According to the Japanese government's distinction between direct and indirect taxes, 69.3 percent of the national tax revenues consisted of direct taxes and 30.7 percent indirect taxes.

Total taxes collected by the metropolis (*to;* i.e., Tōkyō To; sometimes called metropolitan prefecture), circuit (*dō;* i.e., Hokkaidō), urban prefectures (*fu;* i.e., Kyōto and Ōsaka), prefectures (*ken*), cities, towns, and villages were ¥13.2 trillion ($59.9 billion) in 1979. A significant portion of the local taxes is produced by the income taxes known as the inhabitants tax and the business activities tax (the latter levied only on business enterprises and professionals). Thus, of the total ¥11 trillion ($41 billion) local tax revenue in 1977, some ¥4 trillion ($15 billion) was collected as prefectural and municipal inhabitants tax and ¥1.9 trillion ($7.1 billion) as prefectural business activities tax in 1977; together these amounted to 54.4 percent of the total.

National Income Taxation —— The most significant tax by far is the national income tax, producing some 71.5 percent of national tax revenues in fiscal year 1978. This tax is imposed basically by two separate laws: (1) as an individual income tax, levied principally on individuals and, through a withholding tax in certain special circumstances, on corporations and other legal entities; and (2) as a corporate income tax imposed on all legal entities (known as HŌJIN or juridical persons [elsewhere in this encyclopedia called juristic persons]).

The individual income tax is technically called simply the income tax (*shotokuzei*), and it is levied in accordance with the Income Tax Law (Shotokuzei Hō, Law No. 33 of 1965, hereafter ITL), the Income Tax Law Enforcement Order (Shotokuzei Hō Shikō Rei, Cabinet Order No. 96 of 1965), and the Income Tax Law Enforcement Regulations (Shotokuzei Hō Shikō Kisoku, Ministry of Finance Order No.

11 of 1965). The corporate income tax is known as the juridical persons tax (*hōjinzei*), and it is dealt with in the Juridical Persons Tax Law (Hōjinzei Hō, Law No. 34 of 1965, hereafter JPTL), the Juridical Persons Tax Law Enforcement Order (Hōjinzei Hō Shikō Rei, Cabinet Order No. 97 of 1965), and the Juridical Persons Tax Law Enforcement Regulations (Hōjinzei Hō Shikō Kisoku, Ministry of Finance Order No. 12 of 1965). Certain special incentive measures affecting both the individual and corporate income taxes are contained in the Tax Special Measures Law (Sozei Tokubetsu Sochi Hō, Law No. 26 of 1957, hereafter TSML), the Tax Special Measures Law Enforcement Order (Sozei Tokubetsu Sochi Hō Shikō Rei, Cabinet Order No. 43 of 1957), and the Tax Special Measures Law Enforcement Regulations (Sozei Tokubetsu Sochi Hō Shikō Kisoku, Ministry of Finance Order No. 15 of 1957).

In principle, both the income and juridical persons taxes are imposed on net or taxable income, and this figure is arrived at in substantially the same manner by individuals and entities alike. The individual taxpayer begins by computing his "pecuniary amount of total income," "pecuniary amount of severance income," and "pecuniary amount of forestry income." This is done first by classifying all receipts, other than nonincome, nontaxable income, and exempt items, into one of ten enumerated categories and then making the expense deductions permitted under each category. The remainder is total income, except for severance and forestry income, which are left apart to be taxed separately. The next step calls for the subtraction of various special deductions, referred to as "deductions from income," from the amounts of total, forestry, and severance income in a prescribed order. The final results are the taxable total income, taxable forestry income, and taxable severance income, against which are applied the graduated rates contained in the Income Tax Law. The rates are shown in the table accompanying this article.

The different categories of individual income are (ITL art. 22): interest income, dividend income, income from immovables, business income, remuneration income, severance income, forestry income, assignment income (capital gain), occasional income, and miscellaneous income.

Interest income (rishi shotoku) does not comprise all interest in the economic sense but only interest that is most easily susceptible to withholding, namely, that produced principally by private saving, such as interest on deposits with financial institutions and public and company bonds (ITL art. 23[1]). *Dividend income (haitō shotoku)* covers dividends paid to shareholders and the gains of securities investment trusts investing principally in shares of stock (ITL art. 24[1]). *Income from immovables (fudōsan shotoku)* in Japan is income from the lease of immovable property and rights therein or from the lease of ships or aircraft (ITL art. 26[1]). *Business income (jigyō shotoku)* is not limited to income from commerce and industry; it is a broad concept also including income from agriculture, fishing, and the free professions such as medicine and law (ITL art. 27[1]). However, income from the assignment of fixed assets employed in a business, not being of a regular, recurring nature, is classified as assignment income (capital gain) and not business income. Basically, *remuneration income (kyūyo shotoku)* is compensation for rendering personal services under a contract of employment (ITL art. 28[1]), but it also encompasses pensions and annuities paid by one's prior employer following retirement. Moreover, annuities obtained after retirement from certain wage-earner-organized mutual aid societies specified by statute, annuity benefits received under the social insurance system, and annuities paid out of a pension fund established by a firm as prescribed by the law are deemed remuneration income. *Severance income (taishoku shotoku)* refers to a single lump-sum payment made to a wage-earner upon his leaving work or at retirement (ITL art. 30[1]). *Forestry income (sanrin shotoku)* is income from the cutting or assignment of timber provided that the income recipient has held the timber for more than five years (ITL art. 32[1–2]). *Assignment income (jōto shotoku)* is the Japanese term for capital gain, and, as a generalization, involves all income produced by the transfer of assets other than that of a regular, recurring character and other than that covered by *forestry income* (ITL art. 33[1]). *Occasional income (ichiji shotoku)* consists of casual or windfall gains such as gambling receipts and prize money, but it never includes consideration for services even if a one-time affair (ITL art. 34[1]). Finally, *miscellaneous income (zatsu shotoku)* is a catch-all category embracing all other sorts of income (ITL art. 35[1]).

Corporations and other entities are not faced with the need to classify. Instead they arrive at their income by deducting their outlays (*sonkin*) from their proceeds (*ekikin*), terms that essentially correspond to the accounting concepts of revenues and expenses. As no special deductions are available for juridical persons, the pecuniary amount of income and the taxable income are one and the same, this figure being subjected to the fixed tax rates specified by the Juridical Persons Tax Law and the modifications provided by the Tax Special Measures Law.

The tax rates for the ordinary income of an ordinary juridical person are as follows (JPTL art. 66; TSML art. 42[1, i–ii]): for a juridical person with more than ¥100 million in capital, 40 percent on undistributed income, and 30 percent on distributed income; for a juridical person with ¥100 million or less in capital, 28 percent on undistributed income of not over ¥7 million and 40 percent on undistributed income over ¥7 million, and 22 percent on distributed income of not over ¥7 million and 30 percent on distributed income over ¥7 million. There is also a special additional tax of 20 percent on the gain from certain assignments of land (TSML art. 63[1]) and a tax of 35 percent on liquidation income when a juridical person is dissolved (JPTL art. 99).

The Definition of Individual Income

Fundamentally, the Japanese individual income tax is a global or unitary tax, with the permanent segregation of severance and forestry income and temporary segregation of some forms of interest and dividend income regarded as exceptions dictated by special policy considerations that do not vitiate the general rule. Division of income into a number of categories is regarded today merely as a convenience to assist in the computation of income, and unlike the case of a schedular or classified tax, the all-inclusiveness of the final category—miscellaneous or other income—still theoretically necessitates a definition of just what is income. The problem is not new to interpreters of tax law, because the Income Tax Law has contained in one form or another, since its 19th-century inception, a vague reference to "other income." However, the Japanese courts, legislature, and administration have not attempted to render a definitive answer. Rather, they have limited themselves to the more pragmatic course of reducing the doubtful areas case by case through concrete decision, statutory amendment, and administrative circular. Thus, over the years there has been an ever-increasing body of specific items designated taxable or nontaxable in character.

The lack of a single integrated rule has left the field open for speculation by scholars, both jurists and economists, who have been strongly influenced by their German counterparts. Traditionally the question has been posed in terms of a conflict between the "net worth accretion" and "source" schools of thought. The net worth accretion theory (jun shisan zōka setsu) asserts that income is any increase in the value of the net assets held by a person over a given period of time, excluding—in the case of an individual—disbursements made as part of one's life as a consumer, such as personal or family expenditures, which are characterized as "disposition of income." In other words, the difference in a person's net worth at the beginning and end of a set period plus the total of expenditures in his or her consumption life during this period constitute his or her income. On the other hand, according to the source theory (gensen setsu), income is the regularly recurrent economic gain attributable to an individual from permanent income source types like interest, rent, and wages. Strictly speaking the theory of permanent sources can be separated from that of periodicity, which requires regularly recurrent receipts, but those people in Japan who deal with income taxation have tended to neglect this distinction. The differences between the two theories may be summarized as follows: (1) the source theory does not include fortuitous or casual receipts and capital gain (for example, inheritances, gifts, lottery prizes, and gain or loss from the sale of property other than stock in trade); (2) the net worth accretion theory takes into account interest paid on indebtedness, extraordinary living expenses, and losses from the damage or destruction of property; and (3) the net worth accretion theory considers as income the profit or loss resulting from a write-up or write-down in the valuation of assets.

The realistic approach of judges, legislators, and administrators has not meant that the theorists have been without their impact. Undeniably, throughout the history of the income tax at various stages, different theories have underlain the practical formulation. From its initial enactment until 1947, the Income Tax Law expressly excluded occasional income (here, by definition, including fortuitous or casual receipts and capital gain) from taxation, and as early as 1899, the statute began a detailed categorization of income for computation purposes. Not long after the turn of the century recommendations issued by the Japanese Tax Law Review Commission (Zeihō Shinsa Iinkai), a body composed of senior MINISTRY OF FI-

NANCE officials, and two bills proposed by the government to the Diet all clearly indicated that the tax administration regarded individual income as only receipts derived from assets (capital), labor, and both combined (business). In 1940 a major revision of the statute even went so far as to establish schedular taxation complimented by a unitary tax. Although a basic deduction for the taxpayer was first recognized in 1913, and special deductions for dependents, incapacitated persons, and life insurance premiums in 1920 and 1923, it was not until 1950 that, upon the suggestion of the SHOUP MISSION, Japan introduced a deduction for miscellaneous losses—permitting the subtraction of extraordinary losses that, despite their personal nature, result solely from disaster or theft—and a deduction for medical expenses. Accordingly, it seems quite clear that prior to the end of World War II the income tax was founded upon ideas of the sort expressed in the source theory.

How then is the concept of income in the present Income Tax Law to be characterized? Today, all fortuitous or casual receipts and capital gains (with the significant exception of transfers of stocks, bonds, and other valuable securities) are taxed, and capital losses are fully deductible. Remuneration paid in kind and, in principle, inheritances and gifts are regarded as income. However, in the latter case, only gifts from juridical persons are included for tax purposes, since separate inheritance and gift taxes are imposed on the heritable estates and gifts of individuals. Gain resulting from a cancellation of indebtedness is taxable if it can be included within one of the income categories, but for the reasons given above, it will be disregarded if it is a personal gift. Again, consumption of one's own farm products, with some de minimis exceptions, and one's own stock-in-trade constitutes income and is taxed. There are, however, limits to the inclusiveness of the conception. An individual, unlike a legal entity, may not write the value of his assets up or down and treat the change as profit or loss. Nor is the "imputed" rent of one's own home taxed, although in the first part of this century it was strongly recommended in many quarters in Japan. Some scholars described this structure as the source theory qualified by the net worth accretion theory, while others feel that the net worth accretion theory modified by the source theory governs. As a practical matter the difference between these two approaches seems to be solely one of emphasis. To the extent that a definite conclusion is called for, it is unquestionably true that within the Japanese government the net worth accretion theory, adjusted to the peculiar needs of the individual taxpayer and of practical tax administration, dominates all thinking about the problem.

The Definition of Juridical Persons' Income

The concept of income in the juridical persons' tax has been largely free of the controversy that has beset the individual income tax. It has long been assumed by both the tax administration and the courts in Japan that the net worth accretion theory applies. Thus, article 22(2) of the Juridical Persons Tax Law states that "The pecuniary amount to be included in the amount of proceeds of the said business year, in the computation of the amount of income of each business year of a domestic juridical person, is the amount of gain of the said business year pertaining to the sale of assets, the assignment of assets or provision of services for value or gratuitously, the acceptance of the gratuitous assignment of assets and other transactions, aside from capital transactions, etc, except where prescribed otherwise." This provision merely constitutes a restatement of the former Hōjinzei Kihon Tsūtatsu (Juridical Persons Tax Law Basic Circular, National Tax Agency Chokuhō 1-100, 25 September 1950, rev 1952), which provided that "'proceeds,' except where especially prescribed otherwise by a Law or Order, refers to all facts constituting a cause of increase in net assets other than a capital, etc, transaction" and, in the same vein, that "'outlays,' except where especially prescribed otherwise by a Law or Order, refers to all facts constituting a cause of reduction in net assets other than a capital, etc, transaction."

This language only echoes what has been accepted in the courts for many years. As early as 1917, the now defunct Japanese ADMINISTRATIVE COURT declared that "besides such things as the value of the increase in the balance of property owned, the value of the fruits derived from the assets, the value of the gain derived from the disposition of assets and the recurrent income appertaining to a profit-making business activity, occasional income not appertaining to a profit-making business activity is also included within the proceeds of a juridical person" (Sawano v Eitaibashi Zeimusho Chō, Administrative Court, 17 May 1917, 18 Gyōhan 409, 417). Again in 1922 and 1927, the same court said that "things which bring about an increase in a company's assets, other than payments into capital, should all be construed as constituting 'total proceeds'" (Inoue v Marugame

Zeimu Kantoku Kyoku Chō, Administrative Court, 15 May 1922, 33 *Gyōhan* 525, 530), and the "'total proceeds' and 'total outlays' of each business year do not mean the same as the receipts and disbursements within that year, but rather must be construed to include also an increase or reduction in property and the value of property within this business year" *(Kantō Suiryoku Denki Kabushiki Kaisha* v *Tōkyō Zeimu Kantoku Kyoku Chō,* Administrative Court, 16 July 1927, 38 *Gyōhan* 868, 876). Since the end of World War II, although the Japanese Supreme Court has not as yet seen fit to rule upon the question, there are a number of cases in which the Tōkyō High Court and other inferior Japanese courts have repeated the language of the circular issued by the National Tax Administration Agency (Kokuzeichō) with approval, while there are no reported cases disagreeing with this approach.

Therefore, in principle, proceeds include not only receipts from the sale of merchandise and manufactured goods, interest on loans, gifts, inheritances, prizes, capital gain (including that derived from the transfer of shares of stock and other valuable securities), and any other miscellaneous inflow that directly increases the assets (positive property) of the entity but also any fact that decreases its liabilities (negative property) such as the cancellation or extinctive prescription of indebtedness. It even includes unrealized gain resulting from a juridical person reappraising its assets in excess of acquisition value (cost) at current market value where permitted to do so by tax law and the COMMERCIAL CODE, but it does not go so far as to include the "imputed" or "psychic" rent of buildings owned and occupied by the entity. Of course, payments into capital are excluded.

Outlays occupy the opposite side of the coin. They cover such things as expenses and costs required for the sale of merchandise, manufacturing expenses, interest expense, and bad debts expense. Formerly, they also included almost any form of donation made by a legal entity. Japanese law now contains restrictions limiting deductible contributions to those within a formal framework. Here too, it is to be kept in mind that a return of capital or a disposition of profit, such as is involved in a dividend, is not taken into account.

There does remain, however, a theoretical problem that has plagued a number of scholars, although its practical significance is probably slight, namely, the degree to which the accounting doctrines of "property accounting" *(zaisan keisan)* and "profit-and-loss" *(son'eki keisan)* or "fruits accounting" *(seika keisan)* govern the determination of income. The conceptual basis is German in origin, but parallels may be found in certain aspects of American thought. In essence these ideas constitute two different approaches toward the purposes and functions of accounting. Property accounting places its emphasis on a correct representation of the present value of the assets of an enterprise at a given point in time, while profit-and-loss accounting seeks to give an accurate picture of the state of a concern's profits and losses without distortion over a specific accounting period.

In the former case, the normal procedure is to inventory all assets—fixed and current—and assign them a value dependent upon either their current replacement cost or current sale price. Then, these figures are entered on a balance sheet along with the amount of liabilities outstanding—the difference between the totals of the two constituting the enterprise's capital or deficit. Profits or losses during a period of time are determined by comparing the capital or deficit figures in two such balance sheets and arriving at the amount of variation. Thus, the balance sheet reigns supreme and the calculation of income is subordinate to it.

On the other hand, in profit-and-loss accounting just the reverse is true. The entire accounting process is dependent upon the manner in which entries are made in the income account. Assets are normally valued at cost, and adjusting entries are made for such things as depreciation and deferred assets. Each receivable or expenditure is analyzed as to its particular character in terms of its effect on profit and loss and then entered in the enterprise's books in accordance with the results of this analysis. The basic purpose of accounting is to render a fair account of profit and loss, and all operations are directed toward this end. The balance sheet does not attempt to state the current market value of the assets of the business, but rather presents figures founded upon accounting conventions concerned with the equitable allocation of costs, expenses, and revenues over a period of time. Consequently here the income statement is sovereign, and the balance sheet functions as the servant.

The property accounting doctrine is largely an outgrowth of continental European statutory principles seeking to protect the creditor. This line of legislation began with Louis XIV's Ordonnance de Commerce in 1673 requiring merchants to prepare and publish, at least

biannually, an inventory of their movables, immovables, claims, and debts—a rule subsequently incorporated, with slight changes in some cases, in the French Commercial Code of 1807, the German Commercial Codes of 1861 and 1897, and the Japanese Commercial Code. The record and balance sheets based thereon theoretically furnished creditors with an accurate account of the present actual value of the assets and liabilities of an enterprise, which they could use as a source of information to determine its state of solvency. Moreover, they formed the basis for the rules of law restricting the payment of dividends by an entity. Thus, overestimation of profits and excessive paying out of dividends were prevented by requiring distributable surplus to be measured in terms of a balance sheet test of the excess of net assets over stated capital and a legal reserve. However, toward the end of the 19th century it became readily apparent that the property accounting method was impractical for all but the smallest forms of enterprise, with the result that, although the provisions in the codes remained unchanged, business came to utilize profit-and-loss accounting in all cases except a few specialized situations requiring a single rather than a periodic determination, such as liquidation, merger, withdrawal of a member from a partnership, and rate-making by a public utility.

The tax significance of these two doctrines arose through the attempts of various scholars to connect them with the net worth accretion and source theories. It was contended that the net worth accretion view is the inevitable consequence of property accounting and the source view that of profit-and-loss accounting. Accordingly, certain Japanese scholars concluded that, since the profit-and-loss method governs modern business, the language of the Juridical Persons' Tax Law should be amended to incorporate the source approach, while others merely asserted that the net worth accretion and source theories must be construed in terms of property and profit-and-loss accounting. Japanese tax authorities have remained generally unimpressed. For them, "[T]he distinction between the theories of fruits accounting . . . and property accounting . . . , which from the standpoint of accounting theory are considered the principles of income computation, is not inevitably tied to the net worth accretion or income source theories. The latter deal with how the scope of taxable income should be regarded, while the former are founded upon a point of view directed toward the why and wherefore of the major purpose of business accounting and deal with what should be regarded as net profit of a period in periodic accounting and the amount of asset valuation at the end of a period. Both are not conceptions which can be set up in a common level relationship with each other" (Jun Shiozaki, ed, *Shinsen zeihō jiten,* 1958, pp. 225–226). Professor Chū Saichi of Chūō University, who for a time served as the director of the National Tax Administration Agency's former Tax Training Institute (now the College of Tax Affairs), even contends that the juridical persons' tax, despite its employment of the net worth accretion theory to determine income, presupposes profit-and-loss accounting in accounting matters. In support of this view he cites, in particular, the points that cost generally governs valuation (unrealized valuation gain being an exception to the rule) and that depreciation is determined against acquisition value (cost), with acquisition value minus depreciation constituting book value at the close of an accounting period. Another leading authority and former director of the Kanazawa National Tax Bureau, Ichimaru Kichizaemon, refuses, however, to go so far. Examining the historical development of the juridical persons' tax, he concludes that originally the concept of income therein was undoubtedly founded upon the former scheme of the Japanese Commercial Code, which in turn was structured to fit property accounting. The subsequent demands of adjusting tax accounting to standard business practices have brought about major modifications resulting in the dominant theme of the Juridical Persons' Tax Law, which had emerged as an amalgam of property and profit-and-loss accounting. See also ACCOUNTING AND AUDITING.

Income taxation in Japan is based on self-assessment rather than government assessment. Therefore, all corporate and other entity taxpayers must file a final juridical persons tax return with the TAX OFFICE *(zeimusho)* having jurisdiction over their head office within two months of the end of their business year (JPTL art. 74). However, most individual taxpayers need not file a tax return provided that they have received only remuneration income even if from more than one employer. They must report all of their total remuneration income to their principal employer, who will make a year-end adjustment either collecting additional tax or refunding tax to the taxpayer (ITL art. 190). Individual taxpayers with income other than remuneration income are required to file a final income tax return by 15 March of the year following the calendar year for which they are being taxed (ITL art. 120).

One other notable aspect of Japanese income taxation is the "blue return" (aoiro shinkoku) system, adopted during the Occupation after World War II on the recommendation of the 1949 and 1950 Shoup missions (see ITL art. 143; JPTL art. 121). This system has since become a model for other countries. It provides that individual businesses and all entity taxpayers which keep their books and records in accordance with certain standards prescribed by the Japanese tax authorities will be entitled to make use of certain deductions and other favorable tax measures not available to the general taxpayer. All taxpayers who are granted this privilege file their final return as a special blue return. The implementation of this system over some 30 years has resulted in bringing the keeping of business books and records for tax purposes in Japan to a high level of accomplishment.

Tax Legislation and Administration —— Something has already been said about the laws governing Japanese income taxation. Japan does not possess a general tax code. Rather a series of separate statutes, cabinet orders, and ministerial orders govern particular taxes and certain common general problems.

Among the most significant pieces of legislation besides the laws already mentioned are (1) the National Tax Common Provisions Law (Kokuzei Tsūsoku Hō, Law No. 66 of 1962), dealing with broad rules covering taxation as a whole and the National Tax Exceptions Tribunal (Kokuzei Fufuku Shimpanjo; see NATIONAL TAX TRIBUNAL), the Japanese tax court; (2) the Inheritance Tax Law (Sōzokuzei Hō, Law No. 73 of 1950), prescribing inheritance and gift taxes; (3) the Commodity Tax Law (Buppinzei Hō, Law No. 48 of 1962), dealing with the national excise tax; (4) the Local Tax Law (Chihōzei Hō, Law No. 226 of 1950), laying down all the standards for local taxes; (5) the National Tax Collection Law (Kokuzei Chōshū Hō, Law No. 147 of 1959); (6) the Customs Law (Kanzei Hō, Law No. 61 of 1954); and (7) the Customs Tariff Law (Kanzei Teiritsu Hō, Law No. 54 of 1910).

The national Japanese domestic tax system is administered by a semi-independent agency of the Ministry of Finance, known as the National Tax Administration Agency (Kokuzeichō) and headed by a director-general. This body oversees 11 regional national tax bureaus (kokuzeikyoku), in the Tōkyō, Kantō–Shin'etsu, Ōsaka, Sapporo, Sendai, Nagoya, Kanazawa, Hiroshima, Takamatsu, Fukuoka, and Kumamoto regions, an Okinawa National Tax Office (Okinawa Kokuzei Jimusho), and some 509 local tax offices (zeimusho) throughout the country. However, tax policy and the handling of all international tax negotiations, such as tax treaties, is in the hands of an internal bureau of the Ministry of Finance called the Tax Bureau (shūzei kyoku).

Customs matters come under the Customs and Tariff Bureau (Kanzeikyoku) of the Ministry of Finance, which oversees eight regional customhouses (zeikan), in Tōkyō, Yokohama, Kōbe, Ōsaka, Nagoya, Moji, Nagasaki, and Hakodate, and an Okinawa District Customhouse (Okinawa Chiku Zeikan).

Local tax matters are entirely in the hands of the local government imposing the tax. Nevertheless, a general framework is established by the Local Tax Law, which the Tax Affairs Bureau (Zeimukyoku) of the Ministry of Autonomy (officially, and elsewhere in this encyclopedia, called MINISTRY OF HOME AFFAIRS) oversees. See also LOCAL GOVERNMENT.

In the late 1970s, some 38,875 professionals had been registered as special tax attorneys (zeirishi; elsewhere in this encyclopedia called TAX ACCOUNTANTS) to give legal and accounting tax advice to the public. This figure contrasts with the much smaller number of 11,732 regular attorneys (bengoshi; see LAWYERS) admitted to the general practice of law in Japan.

Finally, it should be noted that a formal procedure exists for settling tax disputes with the government. Protests must first be filed with the chief of the tax office or the director of the national tax bureau responsible for the determination being questioned. If this process proves unsatisfactory, the taxpayer may claim review by the tax court called the National Tax Exceptions Tribunal, which, despite the fact that it is an administrative agency, functions in the same manner as a formal court. A ruling by the tax court may then be appealed to the regular judicial courts.

—— Martin Bronfenbrenner and Kiichiro Kogiku, "The Aftermath of the Shoup Tax Reforms," National Tax Journal 10 (1957). Chū Saichi, Kazei shotoku no gainen keisan ron (1980). Chū Saichi, Sozei hō no kihon ronri (1979). Rex Coleman, "Taxation of Capital Gains in Japan and Korea in Light of the Concept of Taxable Income," in J. Haley, ed, Current Legal Aspects of Doing Business in Japan and East Asia (1978). Rex Coleman and J. Haley, "Public Finance and Tax Law," in An Index to Japanese Law: A Bibliography of English Language Materials, 1867–1973 (1975). Ichimura Kichizaemon, Hōjinzei no riron to jitsumu (1959). Y. Komatsu, "The 1971 Income Tax Convention between Japan and the United States of America," Law in Japan: An Annual 7 (1974). Ministry of Finance Tax Bureau, Outline of Japanese Taxes (annual). Mutaguchi Minoru, Shotokuzei kaigi (1971). Ōkurashō Kanzei Kenkyūkai, Kanzei hōki seikai (1979). Saburō Shiomi, Japan's Finance and Taxation, 1940–1956 (1957). Morio Uematsu and Rex Coleman, "Computation of Income in Japanese Income Taxation: A Study of the Adjustment of Theory to Reality," in Arthur von Mehren, ed, Law in Japan: The Legal Order in a Changing Society (1963). Rex COLEMAN

tax office

(zeimusho). General name for local organs of the National Tax Administration Agency (Kokuzeichō). These public offices collect national taxes under the guidance and direction of the agency and the regional national tax bureaus (kokuzeikyoku). There are 11 of these regional offices, plus the Okinawa Regional Tax Administration Office (Okinawa Kokuzei Jimusho). Throughout Japan there are 509 district tax offices and 12 branch offices. Taxpayers with problems concerning national taxes are most likely to come into contact with the district tax office. These offices have the following functions: (1) National tax returns and requests for rectification are made to the heads of district tax offices; taxes are normally paid to the district tax offices or can also be paid to the Bank of Japan or the post office. (2) Rectifications and decrees regarding national taxes are performed by the heads of the district tax offices, and questions and examinations regarding rectifications and decrees are normally handled by the staffs of the district tax offices. (3) Delinquency dispositions and management of cases wherein taxpayers have failed to pay national taxes within the prescribed time limit are processed by the heads of the district tax offices. See NATIONAL TAX TRIBUNAL.

KANEKO Hiroshi

Tayama Katai (1872–1930)

Real name Tayama Rokuya. A prominent writer of the Japanese naturalist school; the author of over 400 short stories and full-length novels, as well as poetry and works of criticism and travel. His concern for strict realism, together with his vehement rejection of decorative writing, made him a genuine pioneer in modern Japanese fiction, as well as a major exponent of naturalism during its heyday in the final years of the Meiji period (1868–1912).

Katai was born in Tatebayashi, Gumma Prefecture, the son of a former low-ranking samurai. His father, who took his family to Tōkyō, died in the SATSUMA REBELLION in 1877. Thereafter Katai's family, experiencing great poverty, returned to Tatebayashi where they remained until 1886 when they went back to Tōkyō. His schooling was irregular, but even so he decided to pursue a literary career through self-study. For a time he studied traditional tanka (31-syllable WAKA) poetry and then immersed himself in the study of English and, through the medium of that language, Western literature in general.

In 1891 he visited the popular writer OZAKI KŌYŌ and, with the latter's help, began to publish his stories in literary magazines. While maintaining relations with Kōyō's conservative KEN'YŪSHA group, he became associated with a group of young writers, including KUNIKIDA DOPPO and Miyazaki Koshoshi (1864–1922), with whom he produced a collection of "new style" poetry entitled Jojōshi (1897, Lyric Poetry), his only venture in poetry. He remained an obscure writer, however, until about 1902 when he wrote "Jūemon no saigo" (The Death of Jūemon), an account of the life of a beastlike man. This work signaled his independence from the neoclassic Ken'yūsha style as well as his indebtedness to modern Western authors, especially the Russian novelist Turgenev and the French naturalist Zola.

In 1904 he published an important essay "Rokotsu naru byōsha" (Straightforward Description) in the magazine Taiyō, in which he set forth his ideas on a revolutionary writing style that would eschew all adornment. His experience as a correspondent in the Russo-Japanese War (1904–05) enabled him to write one of his most powerful naturalist stories "Ippeisotsu" (1908; tr "One Soldier," 1956), a portrayal of the lonely death of a soldier.

It was the story "Futon" (The Quilt) in the previous year, 1907, which truly launched him as a naturalist writer. Although he wrote in the third person, the work was a thinly veiled account of his own infatuation with a young girl student boarding at his home. It created a sensation upon publication and did much to establish the personal, confessional mode as a hallmark of the fledgling naturalist movement and indeed of much subsequent Japanese literature (see I-NOVEL).

Thereafter, he consolidated his position as a major naturalist author with many novels and works of criticism. The three novels, *Sei* (1908, Life), *Tsuma* (1908–09, Wives), and *En* (1910, Human Ties), which are usually considered a trilogy, represent a broadening of his concerns to the complexities and conflicts of the family system. Another novel, *Inaka kyōshi* (1909, Country Teacher) is often considered his best as well as his most representative work.

With the decline of the naturalist movement in the Taishō period (1912–1926), Katai moved away from his deep involvement with life's problems, attaining a contemplative state in his remarkable novel *Zansetsu* (1918, Lingering Snow). He continued to be active until his death, producing several historical novels in his later years, although throughout the 1920s he remained on the periphery of the literary world.

■——Tayama Katai, *Tayama Katai zenshū* (Katai Zenshū Kankōkai, 1936). Tayama Katai, "Ippeisotsu" (1908), tr G. W. Sargent as "One Soldier" (1956). Masamune Hakuchō, "Tayama Katai," in Masamune Hakuchō, *Sakkaron* (1942). Yoshida Seiichi, *Shizenshugi no kenkyū*, 2 vols (1955, 1958).　　　*Valdo H.* VIGLIELMO

Tayasu Munetake (1715–1771)

WAKA poet and KOKUGAKU (National Learning) scholar of the 18th century. The second son of the shōgun TOKUGAWA YOSHIMUNE. Born in Edo (now Tōkyō). He was a student of the poet and Kokugaku scholar KAMO NO MABUCHI, under whose influence he wrote over 300 excellent *waka* in the MAN'YŌSHŪ style. Main collection: *Amorigoto* (after 1771).

Tazaki Sōun (1815–1898)

Painter and book illustrator. Born in Edo (now Tōkyō) to a *samurai* family serving the *daimyō* of the Ashikaga domain (now part of Gumma Prefecture). He studied under several minor painters in the BUNJINGA (literati painting) style as well as with the literati master TANI BUNCHŌ. He also studied figure painting in the YAMATO-E tradition. His friendships with WATANABE KAZAN and TSUBAKI CHINZAN stimulated his interest in Chinese painting. In his youth he received training as a swordsman, and his associates included many distinguished swordsmen. Sōun began to teach painting in his home domain around 1860. On the eve of the Meiji Restoration (1868) he organized the militia group Seishintai to fight for the cause of the imperial restoration. In 1882, and again in 1884, he won silver medals at the first and second Domestic Painting Competitive Exhibitions (Naikoku Kaiga Kyōshinkai). He was a member of the conservative Japan Art Association (Nihon Bijutsu Kyōkai), and in 1890 he was one of the first four painters to be named artists for the imperial household *(teishitsu gigeiin)*. His landscape and BIRD-AND-FLOWER PAINTING were accomplished but were not innovative. His best-known pupil was Komuro Suiun (1874–1945). See also NIHONGA.　　　*Frederick* BAEKELAND

Tazawa, Lake

(Tazawako). Caldera lake, in eastern Akita Prefecture, northern Honshū. Deepest lake in Japan. Located in the Ōu Mountains, it is said to have been created when the Tazawa volcano caved in. Designated as a prefectural natural park. Area: 25.5 sq km (9.8 sq mi); circumference: 20 km (12 mi); depth: 423 m (1,387 ft); altitude: 249 m (817 ft).

Tazoe Tetsuji (1875–1908)

Socialist. Born in Kumamoto Prefecture. Tazoe was converted to Christianity while a student at a missionary school in Kumamoto and later, studying at the University of Chicago (1897–1900), became interested in socialism. Upon his return to Japan, he wrote articles on social problems from a Christian-socialist viewpoint for local newspapers. He then went to Tōkyō to work on a book, *Keizai shinkaron* (1904, Economic Evolutionism), in which he tried to apply the theories of social Darwinism to economics. He joined the Shakai Shugi Kyōkai, a socialist study group and successor to the SHAKAI SHUGI KENKYŪKAI, and helped to found the JAPAN SOCIALIST PARTY in 1906. At the annual convention of the party in 1907 Tazoe opposed KŌTOKU SHŪSUI, who advocated "direct action" or radical tactics to advance the socialist movement; Tazoe pleaded that they work through the Diet but was outvoted. Several days later the government banned the party.

TDK Corporation

(TDK; formerly called Tōkyō Denki Kagaku Kōgyō). Japan's largest producer of magnetic tapes, ferrite cores, and magnetic products. Established in 1935 to produce ferrite, the firm expanded with the development of the electronics industry after World War II. Recently emphasis has been placed on the mass production of videotapes. TDK's overseas manufacturing companies are located in the United States, Mexico, Brazil, South Korea, and Taiwan. Sales for the fiscal year ending November 1981 totaled ¥231.4 billion (US $1 billion), and the overseas sales ratio was 38 percent. In the same year the company was capitalized at ¥5.3 billion (US $23.7 million). Its head office is in Tōkyō.

tea

(cha). The dried, processed leaves of the tea plant, *Camellia sinensis,* from which a bitter, aromatic beverage containing caffeine and tannin is prepared by steeping the leaves in boiling water. Almost 1.9 million metric tons (2 million short tons) of tea were produced in the world in 1980. Production ratios for the three kinds of processed tea are: black (fermented) 80 percent; green (unfermented) 15 percent; and oolong (partially fermented) 5 percent. All tea produced in Japan—102,300 metric tons (112,530 short tons) in 1981—is green tea. In the same year, 4,143 metric tons (4,557 short tons) of green tea and 6,836 metric tons (7,519 short tons) of black tea were imported. Tea is produced in the warm climate regions of Japan, generally south of the 36th parallel. Half of all processed tea in Japan is produced in Shizuoka Prefecture. Recently, however, production has been increasing in Kyūshū.

Types——The various kinds of green tea produced in Japan differ according to cultivation practices and the method used in processing the leaves. In general, most of the planting is done in circular hedgerows, often on terraces or hillsides, the bushlike plants being set out in rows 60 to 90 centimeters (2–3 ft) apart. To facilitate plucking, the bushes are kept trimmed to an average height of 90 to 120 centimeters (3–4 ft). This in turn stimulates the plants to put forth more leaves to compensate for the interrupted growth in height. Crops of tender, young leaves are harvested by hand for processing every 40 days or so.

Sencha, which makes up 90 percent of all Japanese processed leaf tea, is made by first sterilizing the leaves with steam to stop fermentation (oxidation); this prevents the leaves from changing color. Next, the treated leaves are rolled to liberate juices and enzymes sealed within, and then dried with warm air, producing tiny, dark green, needle-shaped pieces ready for packaging. Brewed with hot (not boiling) water, *sencha* has a mildly astringent yet agreeable flavor.

Gyokuro is the top grade of leaf tea among Japan's green teas. It is made from the choicest, tenderest leaves of tea bushes kept covered by bamboo blinds during cultivation; processing methods are the same as for *sencha.* Its dark green leaves produce a light yellowish-green tea when brewed. Having a strongly aromatic flavor, *gyokuro* is less astringent than *sencha.*

Matcha is a powdered form of green tea used mainly in the Japanese TEA CEREMONY (chanoyu). Like *gyokuro,* it is made from the choicest tea leaves, which are steamed, dried, and then ground into powder instead of crushed into pieces. *Matcha* is not brewed by steeping; hot water is added to the powder and then rapidly beaten with a whisk. The tea is cloudy dark green in color and has a uniquely pleasing astringent flavor.

Kamairicha is produced in northern Kyūshū on a limited scale. It is made by roasting the leaves in a highly heated vat (200–300° C; about 390–570° F). The leaves are then dried by churning them in a slightly cooler vat (about 100° C; 212° F). *Kamairicha* is reddish brown in color and has a light savory, roasted flavor that lacks the leafy taste of *sencha.*

Bancha is low-grade, coarse green tea. It essentially is the same as *sencha* but made from older, brittle leaves. *Bancha* has a yellowish brown tint and a slightly astringent taste. *Hōjicha,* made from *sencha* and *bancha* heated at high temperature (150° C; about 300°

F) until the leaves turn brown, has a strong roasted flavor. It is a dark reddish brown color and has a strong robust flavor.

History ——— The use of tea is said to have originated in China. The oldest Chinese specialty book on tea is the *Chajing (Ch'a-ching,* 780) written by Lu Yu (Lu You) during the Tang (T'ang) dynasty. Many theories exist as to how tea was introduced into Japan. The names of numerous Japanese monks who visited China and supposedly returned with seeds are cited in early written accounts. The most widely accepted theory fixes the beginning of Japan's tea industry in the year 1191 when EISAI, a Buddhist monk, is thought to have planted seeds he brought from China on temple lands and then to have encouraged cultivation in other areas by extolling the benefits of the beverage. It was not until centuries later, toward the end of the 16th century, that SEN NO RIKYŪ perfected the tea ceremony.

For 500 years after its introduction to Japan, tea was used in the powdered *(matcha)* form. Prior to the Edo period (1600–1868), the consumption of tea was limited to the ruling class. It was not until the mid-18th century that the processing method for *sencha* was discovered. The special cultivation techniques for *gyokuro* were developed in the mid-19th century. Only after the beginning of the 20th century, with the mass production of tea made possible by mechanized technology, did tea become the national beverage of Japan. Today it is an integral part of the everyday life of the Japanese.

Brewing ——— The characteristic flavor of green tea is attributable to the fact that, like other teas, it contains three important chemical constituents: tea tannin, which has an astringent taste; caffeine, which is a stimulant; and amino acids, which have a sapid taste in contrast to the bitter taste of tea tannin. Of these three water-soluble ingredients, the amount of tannin that is dissolved when brewing tea depends on the temperature of the water; the two other constituents are not much affected by water temperature. Accordingly, the hotter the water, the stronger the astringent flavor.

In Japan, high-grade green teas like *gyokuro* and *sencha* are considered best brewed at a relatively low temperature (60–80° C; about 140–175° F); coarser teas like *bancha* and *hōjicha,* which are characterized mainly by their aromatic fragrance, are best brewed at a higher temperature (90–100° C; 190–210° F). Individual tastes vary of course, but in general two to three grams of loose tea are steeped for about one to two minutes in approximately 200 cubic centimeters (about 6.8 oz) of hot water to make an average cup of Japanese green tea. Tea should be steeped longer at a lower temperature or for a shorter period of time at higher temperatures.

◼ ——— Hayashi Eiichi, *Ocha no kikime* (1975). Kuwabara Yoshio and Sone Tomio, *Ryokucha yomihon* (1976). Narabayashi Tadao, *Sencha no sekai* (1971). *FURUYA KŌZŌ*

tea ceremony

(chanoyu, literally, "tea hot-water"; also called *chadō; sadō).* A highly structured method for preparing tea in the company of guests. Although its origins are in the tea ritual of Zen Buddhist temples in Tang (T'ang) dynasty (618–907) China, in its final form, the tea ceremony is a Japanese expression. Since the 16th century the manner of preparation in Japan has varied among masters who developed schools that promoted *chadō,* "the Way of tea" (also pronounced *sadō).* In its totality it also involves the preparation and service of food and the study and realization of architecture, gardening, ceramics, calligraphy, history, and religion. It is the culmination of a union of artistic creativity, sensitivity to nature, religious thought, and social interchange.

Origins in China ——— According to tradition, Bodhidharma, who left India and introduced Chan (Ch'an; J: Zen) Buddhism to China in 520, encouraged the custom of tea drinking for alertness during meditation. The Chinese regarded tea as an exceedingly beneficial medicine. In Tang Buddhist temples, a tea ritual was performed using a set of bronze utensils comprising a brazier with a wood fire, a kettle, a water jar, a waste-water bowl, a vaselike stand for a bamboo ladle and pair of tongs, and a cylindrical rest for the kettle lid. These objects were arranged on a baseboard, symbolic of earth *(jiita),* which supported an upper shelf, symbolic of heaven *(ten'ita).* The tea receptacle, whose original nature is not known, was placed on the upper shelf.

The tea was made by aging the tea leaves, fermenting them, and pressing them into a brick. This was pared with a knife and ground to a powder, which was put into a covered jar to be used in the rite. The powdered tea *(matcha)* was added to the hot water in the kettle and ladled into ceramic bowls. These bowls *(temmoku)* were of

Tea ceremony

The teahouse Yūin of the main branch of the Ura Senke school in Kyōto, as it appears to a guest approaching through the tea garden. Four-and-a-half *tatami* mats (2.73 m square) in size, it is considered an ideal *chashitsu.* Rebuilt in 1789 after fire destroyed the original of 1653.

conical form, glazed black to brown with spotted patterns or with flower or bird designs; the rims were frequently edged in silver. The bowl was rested on a lacquered wood stand *(dai)* composed of three parts: the cup-shaped holder, saucerlike wing, and flared foot. The bowl and stand are considered a single object.

Tea in Japan ——— During the Nara period (710–794) the influence of Chinese culture was great, and included the introduction of tea in conjunction with Buddhism, which had been introduced from the continent in the 6th century. At the ceremonies dedicating the temple TŌDAIJI in Nara, the emperor Shōmu (r 724–749) had tea served to 100 priests. But it was in the Heian period (794–1185), after the capital was moved to Heiankyō (now Kyōto), that tea became part of the general culture of Japan, distinct from the austere tea rites of the temples. Aristocrats, who collected the highly prized Chinese utensils, served tea in their pavilions. Eleventh-century records list tea utensils among temple objects, an indication that tea preparation remained widespread among priests.

Very early in the Kamakura period (1185–1333) the Japanese priest EISAI returned from Buddhist studies in China with seeds from the plant that was to become the source of much of the tea grown in Japan today. He also wrote an influential treatise on the benefits of tea drinking called *Kissa yōjō ki.* He gave these first tea seeds to the priest MYŌE, who planted them near his temple, KŌ-ZANJI, northwest of Kyōto. Although wild tea grew in Japan, it was considered inferior, and the tea grown from Eisai's seeds became known as "true tea" *(honcha).* Cuttings from these plants were cultivated at several locations, foremost of which was Uji, south of Kyōto, where the climate encouraged the growth of the finest-quality tea. See also TEA.

In the early part of the 13th century the priest DŌGEN brought the potter Tōshirō to China to study Song (Sung) dynasty (960–1279) ceramics; when Tōshirō returned to Japan he opened a kiln near Seto (now part of Aichi Prefecture), which remains a major center of ceramic production to this day. SETO WARE copies of Song jars were valued and collected along with their continental models. At around the same time, the priest EIZON was traveling around Japan preaching Zen and extolling the curative powers of tea. His mission made tea drinking a widespread custom and helped bring about a flowering of Zen.

The Muromachi period (1333–1568) saw the rise of tea tournaments, *tōcha,* contests in which the aristocracy attempted to discern "true tea" from other, more recently cultivated teas. Great prizes were awarded, a good deal of *sake* was consumed, and other excesses occurred. So riotous did the proceedings become that the government banned the revels.

Murata Shukō, Takeno Jōō, and Sen no Rikyū ——— Despite the ŌNIN WAR, which devastated Kyōto in the mid-15th century, and the hundred years of civil war that followed, the art of the tea ceremony continued to thrive. The practice of tea was maintained at the temples, and it was a priest, Murata Shukō (or Jukō; 1422–1502), who was the most notable tea man of his time. Shukō was a student of the priest IKKYŪ, who had been devoted to tea, and under Ikkyū's

Tea ceremony

Interior of the eight-mat (3.64 m square) tearoom Totsutotsusai, showing its *tokonoma* (alcove; right) with hanging scroll and flower arrangement. To the left can be seen the *ro*—a hearth sunk into the floor of the tearoom—and utensils for the preparation of tea. Ca 1854–60. Ura Senke, Kyōto.

influence he emphasized the spiritual aspect of tea, one expression of which might be displaying a scroll of Zen calligraphy in the tearoom. Shukō was a curator of Chinese art for the shōgun ASHIKAGA YOSHIMASA and was his tea master. At the shōgun's villa, which later was known as the Temple of the Silver Pavilion (GINKAKUJI), Shukō made tea using Chinese-style utensils in a room adjacent to a tearoom called Dōjinsai. The room in which the guests assembled was the size of four-and-a-half *tatami* mats (*yojōhan*; 2.73 m or 8.95 ft square), a size that would become standard for tearooms. The measurement is said to have come from the cell of the Indian Buddhist teacher Vimalakīrti (J: Yuima), who lived 100 years after the Buddha. The stand, *daisu*, for the tea utensils was large and outsized for the intimate scale of this room.

In the port city of Sakai (near present-day Ōsaka), wealthy merchants called *nayashū* were avid collectors of tea utensils. Out of this tradition emerged the master Takeno Jōō (1502–55), who had great influence, particularly as the teacher of SEN NO RIKYŪ (1522–91). Jōō taught the use of the *daisu* as it had been handed down from Shukō, a sensitive connoisseurship, and the aesthetic sensibility known as WABI, i.e., the contrast of refinement and rusticity.

His student Rikyū transformed the tea ceremony, perfecting the use of the *daisu*. In addition to costly, imported Chinese implements, Rikyū used plain, everyday Japanese-made objects, frequently employing folk items. Proportions and sizes were chosen to harmonize with the small interiors of the tearooms. Tea was no longer made in one room and served to guests in another, but rather was made in their midst, in emulation of Shukō making tea in the company of his followers and assistants. The use of Japanese objects for tea caused a tremendous surge of creativity in the arts and increased availability of utensils affordable by the common person. A multitude of people began to follow the Way of tea.

Rikyū became tea master to the hegemons ODA NOBUNAGA and TOYOTOMI HIDEYOSHI and brought the art of tea to unprecedented prominence. He and Hideyoshi were consummate antagonists in the matter of tea. Conflict between Rikyū's Way of tea and Hideyoshi's need for power ultimately resulted in Hideyoshi's demand for Rikyū to commit suicide. A similar fate befell Rikyū's successor, FURUTA ORIBE (1544–1615), who plotted against the first Tokugawa shōgun, TOKUGAWA IEYASU. Oribe introduced a decorative style and asymmetrical form that some considered superficial. Oribe's pupil KOBORI ENSHŪ continued the grand style, and was teacher to the Tokugawa shōguns, moving freely among the nobility, while also designing gardens and teahouses.

Schools of Tea——Many masters of tea coexisted, with heirs and followers who eventually gathered into schools that served either the aristocracy or the commoners. Rikyū's Way was passed to his grandson Sōtan (1578–1658), who was renowned for his humility and sensitivity. Sōtan was courted by the aristocracy but maintained his distance. Nevertheless, he was close to the dowager empress and was her teacher. Upon his retirement his three sons began schools of their own: Sōshitsu (1622–97) founded Ura Senke, Sōsa (1619–72)

Omote Senke, and Sōshu (1593–1675) Mushanokōji Senke. The first two are the leading schools in Japan today, with millions of students. Ura Senke is representative of the commoners' tea, Omote Senke of the aristocrats' tea. Oribe and Enshū founded their own schools, as did Yabunouchi Jōchi (or Shōchi, 1536–1627), a contemporary of Rikyū, who began a tradition for the nobility.

In spite of the differences among the many schools of tea, they share the same disciplined spirit. The styles of the buildings, tea gardens, and utensils, and the order and etiquette of the ceremony are products of the same urge to perfect one's existence without self-indulgence. To remind a tea follower of right direction, Zen Buddhism serves as a model of behavior, and each head of a school of tea (IEMOTO) is a diligent student of Zen.

Chaji: Service of Tea and Meal——The tea presentation and meal service here detailed is from the Ura Senke school. The word *chaji* is used for the fully developed tea ceremony: the presentation of tea and the accompanying meal. *Chaji* is the most complete expression of the spirit of the *chajin*, "tea person," requiring skill and concentrated energy to create an easy and congenial atmosphere. Primarily a social event, it is a formal occasion in which the guests are in a state of preparedness similar to that of the host. The host, *teishu*, having invited the guests, *kyaku*, prepares a meal, carefully balancing the flavors, serving utensils, and tea utensils. The *chaji* may be plain or in the elaborate, highly formal *daisu* style, the variety of utensils used being very different. The *chaji* may be presented at any time of the day throughout the year, taking into account the seasons and seasonal foods. The standard service begins around noon and is called *shōgo no chaji*, "noon tea"; it continues for about four hours. Variations are the *akatsuki no chaji* (dawn tea) at 4:00 AM in the coldest time of the year; *asa chaji* (morning tea) in summer at 6:00 AM; *yobanashi no chaji* (literally, "evening conversation tea") in winter at 6:00 PM; *hango no chaji* ("after-a-meal tea"); *atomi no chaji* ("following-look tea"), tea served to other guests after a *chaji;* and *rinji no chaji* (emergency tea), spontaneously assembled tea with a light meal, *tenshin*. The model described below is general and subject to many variations, depending on the occasion, the season, and the tea master. Attire is for the most part formal.

Roji: The Tea Garden——The guests arrive before the appointed hour and gather in the *machiai* (now also called *yoritsuki*), a room in which a hanging scroll may be displayed. They are served cups of hot water, *sayu*, so that they may sample the water to be used in making the tea and preparing the food. The water may be served by the host or by an assistant, *hantō*. When the guests finish, they proceed through the garden to a covered waiting bench, *koshikake machiai*.

The garden is called *roji* ("dew ground") and has a wooded appearance with evergreens and shrubs, ferns, and a moss ground cover. The guests, wearing sedge sandals or wooden clogs used only in the *roji*, tread on large stones set in the ground. The *roji* is divided into two parts by a small gate known as the *chūmon*: the outer garden *(soto roji)* of the waiting room and the inner garden *(uchi roji)* of the teahouse. The inner garden contains an arrangement of stones called *tsukubai* (literally "to squat"). In the central stone, the *chōzubachi*, is carved a basin containing water before which one crouches to rinse the hands and mouth. The surrounding stones support a lantern and a wooden bucket. In front of the basin is a stone on which the guest crouches. An area of small stones in the middle of the arrangement functions as a drain.

When the guests are seated on the waiting bench, the host exits from the teahouse carrying a bucket of water to refill the stone basin, then proceeds to ladle out half the water, taking some and rinsing the left hand and then the right; from the left hand the host sips some water and spits it on the ground. The rest of the water in the ladle is allowed to run down the handle and the remaining water in the basin is scattered around the area. The basin is refilled from the bucket and the ladle is rested across the basin rim. The host then goes to the gate and opens it, approaching the guests, who stand and bow in silence. The host returns to the teahouse and the guests, after returning to the bench, proceed one at a time to follow the host, stopping for purification at the stone basin.

Chashitsu: The Teahouse——Styles of teahouses vary dramatically, from tiny huts with tearooms large enough only for two mats (1.82 m or 5.97 ft square) to spacious, elegant pavilions of eight mats (3.64 m or 11.9 ft square) or more. Construction, however, is similar; wooden posts and floors raised off the ground; sand-finished, mortared walls over bamboo lattice; windows that may reveal the inner lattice; wooden sheet and bamboo ceilings; papered window panels, *shōji*; and sliding doors, *fusuma*. The roof may be thatched, shingled, or now occasionally tiled. Some rooms have normal-sized entrances with sliding-door panels; however, the ideal entrance is the *nijiriguchi*, only about 60–70 centimeters (23.6–27.5 in) wide by 70–80 centimeters (27.5–31.5 in) high, so that the guests have to crouch and crawl through. The sliding wooden door is shut and locked by the last guest, *tsume*.

The ideal tearoom has four-and-a-half mats and a *tokonoma*, alcove, on the north wall toward the east. In the *tokonoma* a hanging scroll, preferably a work of calligraphy by a Zen priest, may be displayed along with other objects. It consists of familiar phrases with only a few characters in a vertical line (*ichigyō-mono*). Scrolls with poems and paintings are also displayed, but much less frequently.

The *chaji* is divided into two parts: during the first, *shoiri* or *shoza*, the meal is served and a scroll is displayed in the *tokonoma*; during the second, *goiri* or *goza*, the tea is served and flowers are displayed. Flowers for tea, *chabana*, are placed simply in a container (*hanaire*), in a way in which they might appear in nature. Buds are preferred over full blooms. Camellias, clematis, rose of Sharon, bellflowers, and uncultivated grasses are preferred over flowers with strong scents, thorns, or large blossoms. Ideally, the flower is picked at dawn while it is a bud covered with dew, opens at noon, fades in the evening, and withers at night. This reflects a full year, a lifetime, reminding those who see it of mortality and evanescence. Flower containers are of bronze, porcelain (generally Chinese in origin), earthenware, bamboo, or basketwork. Some containers are designed to hang from a peg or from the ceiling. The scroll and flowers are sometimes displayed together.

The guest enters the tearoom and proceeds to the *tokonoma* to acknowledge the scroll and greet it as though the artist-author were present. Seated in front of the scroll, the guest places his small folding fan, *sensu*, horizontally before his knees as a gesture of appreciation. The fan is never used to create a breeze but acts either to separate or to join the guest to another person or object. (The fan is considered auspicious, since its inverted-V form is similar to the Chinese character for eight, the number symbolizing infinity.)

The guest, after examining the scroll, moves to the part of the room in which the tea is to be made and sits facing the kettle and brazier that heats the water for tea. In the cold half of the year the kettle may be placed over a *ro*, a hearth sunk into the floor of the tearoom, the larger fire providing added warmth. The *ro* is an adaptation of a farmhouse *irori*, a wide, shallow hearth. It was Rikyū who perfected the *ro* and established its size and use in the procedures for making tea. From May through October, however, the *furo*, a brazier, usually placed on a lacquer or ceramic base, is used.

The guests then take their places, usually along the east wall, and await the host's entrance. The first, principal guest, *shōkyaku*, acts as the others' representative and greets the host; the others follow. The principal guest thanks the host for the invitation and preparations and inquires about the various tea objects seen so far. The host serves the meal, which has been prepared in the *mizuya*, a pantry-like, adjacent room.

Kaiseki: The Tea Meal —— The meal should be light. The term *kaiseki* is derived from the ancient custom of Buddhist monks placing heated stones (*seki*) next to their stomachs in the front fold of their garment (*kai*) to stave off hunger pangs. To each guest the host hands a tray containing covered lacquered bowls of rice and *misoshiru* soup; a bowl containing fresh seafood, often vinegared (*mukōzuke*); and cedar chopsticks. The guests put down their trays and the host invites them to begin. Together they remove the lids and eat the rice and soup. *Sake*, served by the host, is poured from an iron pitcher, *kannabe*, and drunk from shallow saucers, *sakazuki*. The fish course then begins. Additional rice and soup are offered. The main course consists of seafood and vegetables cooked and served in broth (*nimono*) and presented in individual covered lacquered bowls. Grilled seafood, or another cooked dish, *yakimono*, is presented on a serving plate with a set of green bamboo chopsticks, and may be passed among the guests. The guests may eat by themselves, or if it has been prearranged, the host may be asked to join them, in which case the host brings in his fully prepared tray. When the serving dishes are removed, flavored hot water, *kosuimono* or *hashiarai*, is served in individual covered lacquered bowls; the chopsticks are rinsed, and the liquid is drunk.

The host then serves a course called *hassun* (literally, "eight *sun*," a reference to the length of the plain, square cedar tray used for this course, about 24.1 cm or 9.5 in), morsels of seafood and of vegetables, served with green bamboo chopsticks. This course, an adaptation of a Shintō offering, represents foods from the sea and

Tea ceremony

Tea utensils for the presentation of thick tea (*koicha-demae*). At center is a brazier containing a kettle. Ranged clockwise from the bamboo ladle (top) are a freshwater jar with a tea cloth on its lid, a tea whisk, a ceramic tea jar, a bamboo tea scoop, a teabowl, a waste-water bowl, and the kettle's lid.

from the land. *Sake* is served and sipped before eating this course, and the host may join in and be served *sake* by each individual guest. The final course consists of broth and salted browned rice. The rice is scraped from the cooker and served in a lacquered wooden pitcher, *yutō*. With a lacquered ladle, the rice is scooped into the rice bowls and the broth is poured into the soup bowls. Pickled vegetables, *kōnomono*, accompany the broth and are used to lightly scrub the bowls. The guests, left alone, finish the meal and wipe their bowls with papers (*kaishi*) that they have brought with them. The guests notify the host that they have finished by laying their chopsticks down flat on their trays. The guests individually hand their trays to the host for removal.

Sumi-demae: The Charcoal Ceremony —— *Shozumi: The first charcoal preparation.* A charcoal fire is built in the brazier called *furo*, made of bronze, iron or clay, to heat water for tea; a base fire of three pieces of burning charcoal, *shitabi*, will have already been started. The host brings into the room a basket containing five pieces of oak charcoal, *sumi*, of specific thicknesses and cut in specific lengths, together with three pieces of azalea-twig charcoal, *edazumi*; a feather brush, *habōki*; metal fire tongs, *hibashi*; metal rings to move the kettle, *kan*; and a lacquered covered box, *kōgō*, containing three chips of sandalwood incense, *byakudan*. In winter the *ro* requires a ceramic *kōgō* with kneaded incense (*nerikō*). Brought into the room next is an ash bowl, *haiki*, containing a small mound of white ash made from wisteria vines, *fujibai*, in which is supported a spoon, *haisaji*. The host carries a large packet of papers in the front of his *kimono*; used in former times for writing poems and various other purposes, it is here used to set the kettle on, and is called *kami kamashiki*. The guests carry smaller packets of papers, called *kaishi*.

After the host has moved the kettle out of the way, the brazier is dusted with the feather, the base fire is centered and the pieces of charcoal are added, and the brazier is dusted again. The face of the carefully laid bed of ash in the brazier is marred with the spoon making a crescent moon; this is to indicate that the ash was prepared for this occasion only. After a third dusting, two chips of incense are put into the fire. The principal guest asks to see the incense case. During the *ro* season the ash bowl contains damp ash which is sprinkled over the surface of the hearth ash, and the guests move close to the *ro* to watch the proceedings.

The kettle is replaced, the paper tucked into the host's kimono, and the rings are detached from the kettle and placed in the basket. The ash bowl is removed and the charcoal basket and utensils are taken away. The floor is swept with a large feather brush, *zabaki*. In the meantime, the guests examine the incense case and return it to the host's place. The host returns and wipes the lid of the kettle and the sides of a ceramic brazier with the *fukusa*, a doubled square of silk fabric. The host answers the guests' questions about the shape of the case, its maker, and the name of the blended incense.

Omogashi: The Principal Sweet —— *Nakadachi: the standing interval.* The host serves the principal sweet, such as *kinton*, which is made of *an*, sweetened, pureed beans, formed into egg-sized portions, the outside covered with *an* pressed through a sieve. Other typical sweets are *manjū* (a steamed pastry filled with *an*), *yōkan* (jellied *an*), *mochi* (rice pastry filled with *an*). These freshly made sweets are generally called *namagashi* and should ideally be made by the host. Fresh or dried fruit may be served as well. Originally, sweets for tea included deep-fried kelp, *kombu*, and dried fruits. Guests are served sweets in individual lacquered boxes that can be stacked up and covered with a single lid; the stack is called *fuchidaka*. Picks, *kuromoji*, one for each guest, made of spicebush wood with the bark left intact on the handle, are arranged on the lid. The guest takes the sweet with the pick, using the paper from his packet; the host asks the guests to leave the room after they have eaten the sweet, so that it may be prepared for the tea. As they do so, the host replenishes the stone basin and sprinkles the garden.

This recess is called *nakadachi*. During this period the guests may use the toilet facilities; traditionally there is a small chamber near the waiting bench with a sand-filled area called *suna setchin*, though this is now rarely used.

While the guests are relaxing, the host removes the scroll, covers the kettle, and sweeps the room. Flowers are placed in the *tokonoma*, the utensils for the preparation of tea are placed near the brazier, and the kettle lid is set ajar. The host rings a gong, *dora*, to signal that it is time for the guests to return. When they hear the gong, the guests crouch, listening intently in the manner of monks in Buddhist temples. They return, purifying their hands and mouth once again at the stone basin in the garden.

Koicha: The Thick Tea Ceremony——— *Goiri: The "second entering."* The proper preparation of thick tea and the proper use of the brazier is the foundation to understanding the Way of tea. The details given here are ideal standards, and countless variations exist.

The tea utensils, *chadōgu*, are placed on half of a full *tatami* mat; this area is called *dōgu tatami;* adjacent is the *temaeza*, presentation seat, where the host positions himself. Before the guests arrive in the tearoom, the brazier is centered on the left half of the *tatami*, 8 *sun* or 24 centimeters (9.4 in) from the imaginary line that divides the full mat into two squares: this line, demarcating the host's place, is called the knee line. The iron kettle, *kama*, contains approximately 20 ladles, or about 2.4 liters (2.5 qt) of water, just short of its capacity. The ceramic freshwater jar, *mizusashi*, is generally cylindrical and contains 20 ladles of water or nine-tenths of its capacity. It may have a lacquered wooden lid. The water jar is centered on the right half of the utensil mat, opposite the kettle on the brazier. These two objects create the primal balance of the forces of *yin* (J: *in*), represented by the water in the freshwater jar, and *yang* (J: *yō*), represented by the fire in the brazier. It is essential that the host sit on the axis of these two. The rough, unglazed water jar is placed directly on the floor, as are the buckets and other vessels made of wood. Vessels made of porcelain, Chinese wares as well as Japanese copies, are not placed directly on the floor but on a board; the baseboard of a small stand, *tana*, serves this purpose. The upper shelf is for the display of the container of tea powder for making thin tea. Other tea utensils may also rest on the upper shelf or shelves.

Tea powder is placed temporarily in a small ceramic jar, *chaire*, set in front of the water jar. The tea receptacle varies in size and form, but is large enough to contain the appropriate amount of tea powder to serve four or five guests. The tea jars are modeled after Chinese medicinal herb jars, and each has an ivory lid and a protective pouch, *shifuku*. While the jar may be ancient, the lid and the pouch may be new and made especially for the jar. The cloth for the pouch may also be old and rare, with designs copied from ancient Chinese and Persian fabrics (see MEIBUTSUGIRE); certain patterns are passed through generations of masters. The pouch has a silk drawstring tied in a bow.

Koicha-demae: The Presentation of Thick Tea——— After the guests have entered the tearoom, the host enters with a teabowl, *chawan*, which is used to carry the linen tea cloth, *chakin;* a tea whisk, *chasen;* and a bamboo tea scoop, *chashaku*. The tea jar is moved approximately 3.5 centimeters (about 1.4 in) to the right and the teabowl is set alongside it 7 centimeters (about 2.8 in) to the left.

The locations of the tea objects are exact and mathematically precise. Specific objects of standard sizes are employed as measuring devices, the most common being the *chū natsume*, an egg-shaped, lacquered, covered wooden receptacle for tea powder with a diameter of 1.8 *sun*, approximately 7 centimeters. This measurement is according to the large measuring stick, *kujirajaku*. In some cases, its counterpart, the *kanejaku* measuring stick, which is eight-tenths the length of the larger, is used. The concern for the numbers 10 and 8 may reflect a conscious effort to harmonize the differences

between the two measuring sticks, both of which are used in the construction of tea utensils. The space between objects, such as the space between the teabowl and the tea jar, is frequently the diameter of the *chū natsume*. The green bamboo lid rest is 1.8 *kanesun*, or 5.5 centimeters (2 in) high; Rikyū believed it was necessary to *wabi cha*, the Way of tea he perferred.

The host brings in the waste-water bowl, *kensui*, which contains the rest for the kettle lid, *futaoki*, made of freshly cut green bamboo, *hikikiri*, with a bamboo ladle, *hishaku*, resting across the rim of the bowl. The door to the room is shut, symbolically closing off the outside world. The host sits on the *tatami* facing the utensils, the knees at the so-called knee line. This position, called *imae* (or *temaeza*), is the one in which the host makes the tea. The waste-water bowl is placed on the floor to the host's left, the *hishaku* is taken up and held vertically in front of the host, who regards it as though it were a mirror reflecting the inner self; this gesture is called *kagamibishaku*. The lid rest is placed between the supporting lid of the brazier and the tape edge of the *tatami* mat, in front of the board. The ladle cup is placed on the top of the lid rest, the handle is dropped on the floor pointing toward the center of the knee line.

As the handle touches the floor all of the participants bow to begin the presentation. The waste-water jar is brought up to the knee line, centered between the knee and the tape edge of the *tatami*. The host pauses to concentrate energy. The teabowl is placed on the center line in front of the knees; the tea jar is placed on the center line between the bowl and knees; the tea jar is then removed from its pouch, which is laid on the floor between the brazier and water jar. The host takes the *fukusa* from his sash (OBI) and examines it while turning it clockwise one full revolution, relaxing and tensing each of the four sides. This is called *yohō sabaki*, four-side examination, and symbolizes the host's reflection on the four directions representing the physical world, and on deities, departed souls, family and friends, and the realm of spiritual relationships. The *fukusa* represents the host, just as the fan represents the guest.

The tea jar is wiped with the folded *fukusa* in a carefully prescribed manner: first the lid, then the jar turned clockwise three revolutions, with the cloth pressed to its side. The tea jar is placed in the previous location of the teabowl; the *fukusa* is refolded and used to wipe the tea scoop with three strokes; the scoop is placed on the lid of the tea jar, to the fire side of the knob, perpendicular to the knee line. The whisk is stood upright in the place of the tea jar. The bowl is centered between the knee line and the front edge of the board. The linen tea cloth is placed on the front half of the lid of the water jar; lacquered lids are wiped with the *fukusa* before placing the tea cloth. The ladle is raised upright; the lid of the kettle is removed and placed on the lid rest; the *fukusa* is not used by men to open the lid unless the knob is iron or silver. The *fukusa* is placed on the floor behind the waste-water bowl after use. A full ladle of hot water is poured into the bowl, and the ladle is rested across the kettle mouth, perpendicular to the knee line.

Chawan: The Teabowl——— The preferred teabowl is black-glazed RAKU WARE, a ceramic made first in the late 16th century by the Korean potter CHŌJIRŌ working from the designs and concepts of Sen no Rikyū. Rikyū changed the shape of the teabowls from the conical, Chinese *temmoku* bowls and Korean rice bowls, which were initially used for tea in Japan, to bowls with upright sides and slightly dished bottoms that accommodated the movement of the tea whisk. Black Raku is considered most appropriate for tea aesthetics. Other wares preferred for thick tea are HAGI WARE and KARATSU WARE, both originated by Korean potters. These wares require the use of *kobukusa*, a small square of doubled silk fabric that protects the hands from the heat of the bowl. The porous Raku-ware bowl does not need to be insulated. A teabowl has a capacity of approximately four ladles, but is never more than half filled.

The tea whisk is rinsed in hot water, which is used to warm the bowl, and examined for damaged tines. It is made from a single piece of aged bamboo approximately 11.4 centimeters (4.5 in) long and a thumb's diameter, split and pared into 90 to 120 tines, divided into an inner and outer ring separated by thread wound around the base of the tines. It is swished in the water, raised twice, and removed drawing the *hiragana* symbol *no*, signifying union.

The water is discarded and the bowl is dried with a damp linen cloth, linen being relatively lint-free. The cloth is then placed on the removed kettle lid. Three scoops of tea powder are spooned out of the tea jar in increasingly large amounts and put into the bowl. After the tea scoop is rested on the edge of the bowl, the tea jar is overturned, and the balance of the tea powder poured out. The tea jar is closed and placed again near the water jar; the tea scoop is used to level the tea powder, tapped on the edge of the bowl, and replaced on top of the tea jar. The lid of the water jar is removed and leaned against the brazier side of the water jar. A full ladle of cold water is taken and added to the kettle, replenishing that which was used to warm the teabowl. A full ladle of hot water is drawn, and four-fifths of it is poured onto the tea powder; the remaining fifth is returned to the kettle: it is inappropriate to empty the ladle into the teabowl, for that implies depletion. Another full ladle is drawn, and one-quarter of it is added to the teabowl. This is four-fifths of the total amount of hot water to be added to the tea powder. The ladle is rested on the kettle, and the handle is released with a flat hand gesture likened to releasing an arrow.

The tea is mixed with the whisk to break up any lumps; there should be no lumps or foam, according to Rikyū. A full ladle of hot water is drawn, and one-quarter of the water is added to the tea through the raised whisk to prevent splashing; the tea is blended. The remaining water is poured from the ladle back into the kettle, and the ladle is rested on the kettle. The bowl of tea is turned clockwise, the face turned away from the host. (Every object has a face or front, *shōmen*, which is directed toward the observer; it is essential to have an understanding of the nature of an object to determine its *shōmen*.) The bowl is offered to the guests and placed on the *tatami* adjacent to the host.

Itadakikata: Drinking the Tea——— The principal guest goes to the bowl, carries it back to his place, and, together with the other guests, bows in a gesture of sharing. The guest turns the bowl clockwise until the face is on the opposite side, and tastes the tea. After the first sip, the host asks the guest if the tea is adequate: *"Ofuku kagen wa,"* to which the guest responds that the tea is sufficient, *"Kekkō de gozaimasu,"* avoiding effusiveness. The host turns slightly toward the guest.

The first guest drinks one-quarter of the tea in three sips. The rim is wiped with the guest's own damp linen cloth; at this time the second guest apologizes for preceding the next guest: *"Osaki ni."* The bowl is turned counterclockwise and handed to the second guest, who raises the bowl in a gesture of acceptance while the first guest bows in apology for having gone first. After the first sip is taken by the second guest, the first guest asks the name and provenance of the tea, and inquires about the sweet eaten earlier, which the host himself probably made. The third and fourth guests drink. The last guest, *tsume*, wipes the bowl more carefully and passes it back so that it may be examined. When the guests have finished examining the bowl, it is returned to the host by the first guest.

While the guests are examining the bowl, the host replenishes the kettle with fresh water; resting the ladle on the kettle, he releases the handle with a gesture likened to drawing a bow, a reference to archery and Zen Buddhism. As the host takes the bowl, all bow in unison in an act of thanksgiving. A half-ladle of hot water is poured into the bowl and then discarded to rinse out the tea residue The host announces that the tea presentation is coming to a close: *"Oshimai ni itashimasu."*

A ladle of cold water is poured into the bowl and used to rinse the whisk; the water is discarded and the linen cloth is placed in the bowl. The scoop is taken up and the waste-water bowl is moved away from the center. The *fukusa* is folded and used to wipe the scoop in two strokes; the scoop is replaced on the bowl, and loose tea is brushed from the *fukusa* into the waste-water bowl. The *fukusa* is returned to the host's *obi*. The now-empty tea container and the bowl are placed in front of the water jar, as at the beginning. The kettle is replenished with a ladle of fresh water, and the lid is set slightly ajar to allow steam to escape. The ladle cup is rested on the lid rest and the water jar is closed. The first guest asks to examine the tea jar, scoop, and pouch. The ladle is laid across the waste-water bowl; the lid rest is put under the ladle handle next to the waste-water bowl; the bowl is placed near the wall next to the waste-water bowl.

Dōgu no Haiken: Examining the Utensils——— The tea jar is held by the host, who turns toward the guests; using the *fukusa* he wipes the jar and, removing the lid, wipes the rim. It is turned to face away from the host and is placed on the adjacent mat. The tea scoop is placed next to it, followed by the pouch. The host picks up the ladle and lid rest, turns toward the wall, and picks up the waste-water bowl; the host stands and turns away from the guests.

The first guest moves to take the jar, scoop, and pouch, and returns to admire them. The host removes the bowl, reenters the room, and takes away the water jar, closing the door to the tearoom; allowing the guests to be alone with the utensils shows the host's trust in the guests. The utensils are examined individually by the guests: the object is placed on the adjacent *tatami* and with the hands

Tea ceremony

The presentation of thin tea *(usucha temae)*. The host, seated before a kettle set in a sunken hearth, ladles hot water into a teabowl. To his left are ranged a tea whisk, a powdered tea container with a tea scoop placed on its lid, the freshwater jar, and, behind him, the waste-water bowl.

the observer lightly touches the *tatami* in front of the knees; this position is not a bow but a posture of respect. The lid of the tea jar is removed with the right hand, the jar itself is held with the left; the lid is examined with the elbows resting on the lap so that the forearms are immobilized and the object is held close to the floor for safety. Each object or part of an object is held with both hands, then passed on to the next guest, who returns them to the host's place. The host returns and answers questions about the shape and make of the tea jar, the maker and name of the tea scoop, and the name of the fabric and maker of the pouch. Tea scoops are often made by tea masters and Buddhist priests and given names from Buddhism or nature.

The utensils are taken from the room and placed outside the door. The host and guests bow in unison to complete the presentation. The charcoal fire may be rebuilt *(gozumi)* and the kettle replenished for making thin tea. Cushions may be provided, and, as a sign for relaxation, smoking paraphernalia on a tray *(tabakobon)* is offered to the guests. Smoking of slender bamboo pipes, *kiseru*, is rare, but a lighted piece of charcoal in a bowl of ash, *hiire*, and an ash receptacle of bamboo, *haifuki*, demonstrate the warmth of the host's spirit.

Higashi: Dry Sweets——— Dry sweets, *higashi*, are offered on a tray, which may be round, with a diameter of 8 *sun* (24.1 cm or 9.5 in), complimenting the square *hassun* tray of *kaiseki*. These sweets are of an endless variety of types and shapes; however, the most correct are of sugar and flour pressed into molds of various designs. Two kinds of sweets are served; the pressed-sugar sweets are arranged in the far-right quadrant, the other kind in the near left. This repeats the pattern of the seafood and vegetables that were served on a square tray during the *kaiseki* meal.

Usucha Temae: The Presentation of Thin Tea——— The thin tea service begins with a bow in unison, the host seated at the entrance to the tearoom. The host brings in the water jar, which is filled to eight-tenths of its capacity, and sets it to the right of the brazier-kettle. A lacquered, covered container for powdered tea, *chaki* or *natsume;* a teabowl with a linen cloth; a whisk; and a scoop are brought in and placed in front of the water jar. The waste-water bowl, lid rest, and ladle are then brought in. The door is left open. The tea jar and scoop are wiped with the *fukusa;* the bowl and whisk are cleaned with hot water, and the bowl is wiped with the linen cloth. The principal guest is asked to partake of the sweets, and does so after apologizing for going ahead of the others. Tea is made for the first guest; one-and-a-half scoops of tea are put into the warmed bowl.

The teabowl used here should complement the teabowl used earlier. A wide variety of wares and styles contributes to a seemingly endless array of teabowls; frequently preferred wares are Seto ware; MINO WARE (Shino, Oribe), and those made in Kyōto (see KYŌTO CERAMICS), including those created in the 17th century by KENZAN, some with his brother KŌRIN, and NONOMURA NINSEI. Bowls are copied faithfully generation after generation.

After the tea has been placed in the bowl, the fresh water jar is opened. A full ladle of hot water is then drawn; half of the ladle is poured into the bowl and the remainder poured back into the kettle. The tea is briskly whisked until a fine foam appears on the surface. The guest moves to get the bowl and moves back, apologizes for drinking before the others, and thanks the host for the tea: *"Otemae chōdai itashimasu."* The guest raises the bowl in acceptance, turns the *shōmen* away from himself, and drinks. After wiping the rim with the fingertips, the guest examines the bowl. The bowl is returned to the host and tea is made for the others individually. A guest may have another bowlful after everyone has been served. It is proper for the other guests to acknowledge sharing with the principal guest: *"Goshōban itashimasu."* As spokesman for all the guests, the principal guest asks the others if they have had enough: *"Mō ippuku ikaga desu ka,"* then asks the host to close the presentation: *"Dōzo oshimai o."* The host responds and ends the service.

The first guest asks to examine the thin-tea jar and the scoop after the host has finished cleaning the tea jar. The other utensils are taken from the room, and the guests begin to examine the tea jar and scoop. When they are finished, the host returns to answer questions about the shape of the container and the lacquerer who made it, and the maker and name of the scoop. The host takes the utensils and leaves the room, but stops outside the door and bows in unison with the others to end the presentation. The host returns to exchange final greetings. The guests leave and stand outside the door. The host appears in the door and all bow. The host watches as the guests leave through the garden. The guests should thank the host on the following day.

Sencha—— The etiquette for drinking *sencha,* "infused tea," is a modification of the tea ceremony that began in the 17th century. Green tea leaves of excellent quality are put into small ceramic pots *(kyūsu),* to which hot water is added. The water is heated in ceramic pots *(bōfura),* placed over a ceramic brazier *(ryōro)* containing a small charcoal fire. The hot water is cooled in a ceramic boat *(yuzamashi).* The steeped tea is poured into four or five small cups *(chawan)* which have been warmed with hot water and dried. They are served on small saucers *(chataku)* of wood, bamboo, or metal. Hot water is added to the tea leaves two more times; the tea is drunk after each steeping. The tea, enjoyed three times, is called sweet, bitter, and astringent. The water jar and bamboo trough *(sembai)* to dispense the leaves are highly prized. *Sencha* is quite similar to the tea drunk daily in Japan today.

At present, over 10 million people study the tea ceremony in Japan, over 90 percent of them women. More utensils are made for the tea ceremony than ever before in history, and many are of the highest technical quality. Several schools of tea have classes for foreigners, and a few have branches around the world to teach non-Japanese the tea ceremony. The tea ceremony is presented variously, daily in some homes, once or twice a year in others. It may be performed on any occasion and for no reason other than for itself, simply as tea for friends.

——Rand Castile, *The Way of Tea* (1971). Hayashiya Tatsusaburō, *Zuroku chadō shi* (1962). Horiguchi Sutemi, *Sōtei, tatemono to chanoyu no kenkyū* (1962). Kuwata Tadachika, *Chadō jiten* (1967). Tadachika Kuwata, *History of Chadō* (1967). Kakuzō Okakura, *The Book of Tea* (1906). Arthur J. Sadler, *Cha-no-yu: The Japanese Tea Ceremony* (1933). Sen Sōshitsu, *Asu e no chadō nyūmon* (1977). Sen Sōshitsu, *Chadō, ura no tomaya* (1930). *Chanoyu Quarterly* (Urasenke Foundation; monthly, 1970–). *Nagomi* (Tankōsha; monthly, 1980–). Shufu no Tomo Sha, ed, *Cha no kokoro to bi* (1976). Tōkyō National Museum, *Art of the Tea Ceremony* (1980).

Allan PALMER

teachers

As Japan entered the Meiji period (1868–1912) and public schools were established throughout the country, one of the first important tasks of the Ministry of Education was to determine how to gather and train teachers. Before World War II, teacher training was conducted at national NORMAL SCHOOLS *(shihan gakkō)* according to the policies of the government; during the post–World War II years, teacher training came to be conducted in four-year universities. The history of teacher training as well as teacher certification, in-service training, performance rating, and other related issues will be covered in this article.

Teacher Training—— There have been three major changes in the system of teacher training in Japan since the Meiji Restoration in 1868: the first was the establishment of normal schools in accordance with the EDUCATION ORDER OF 1872; the second was the issuance of the Normal School Order (1886); the third was the establishment of a new system and the abolition of normal schools in accordance with the educational reforms after World War II.

In 1872 the Ministry of Education established the Tōkyō Normal School (later Tōkyō University of Education; now Tsukuba University) in order to train teachers for elementary schools throughout the country. Marion McCarrell SCOTT, an American expert on teacher training, was invited to introduce modern teaching methods to these students who, upon graduation, were engaged by various prefectures, where they were themselves assigned to train elementary-school teachers. After 1873 national normal schools were established in Ōsaka, Miyagi, Aichi, Hiroshima, Nagasaki, and Niigata prefectures to furnish supervisory teachers for the teacher-training agencies of all prefectures. In 1874 the Tōkyō Women's Normal School (now Ochanomizu University) was founded for the training of women teachers; with the addition of a kindergarten and elementary school, it became the nucleus for women's education and for training kindergarten teachers in Japan. In 1875 a middle-school teachers' training department was created in the Tōkyō Normal School for the purpose of training teachers for middle school (the prewar equivalent of secondary school). This department later developed into the Tōkyō Higher Normal School (now Tōkyō University of Education), which sent out supervisory teachers to middle schools and normal schools in various parts of Japan. In 1880 normal schools were set up by law in each prefecture.

Normal schools, especially the Tōkyō Normal School under the guidance of Marion Scott, introduced the organization of classes according to grade level, uniform instruction, and modern textbooks. Methods of pedagogy taught by the Swiss educator Johann Heinrich Pestalozzi (1746–1827) were introduced by TAKAMINE HIDEO and became widespread.

The Normal School Order of 1886 systematically established normal schools. MORI ARINORI, who became the first minister of education when the cabinet system was initiated, felt that education should become the foundation of national development, and on this principle, embarked on an overall reform of the school educational system. He issued the Normal School Order as one part of the SCHOOL ORDERS.

There were two kinds of normal schools: a higher normal school to train middle-school teachers and primary normal schools to train primary-school teachers. The former was established in Tōkyō as a national school, and the latter were set up as public institutions in each prefecture. Students at these schools were exempted from paying tuition, but after graduation they were legally obligated to accept teaching positions. Because of the high social position of teachers and the fact that these schools offered free higher education, many superior students applied.

Mori thought that the first purpose of elementary schools should be to train devoted citizens united by the bonds of loyalty and patriotism, and that teachers in particular should personify these virtues. Accordingly, education was given in a rather military fashion in normal schools, which adopted the dormitory system and soon took on nationalistic overtones. As the level of the school system in general started to rise, that of normal schools also gradually approached that of a professional school or university.

Not all teachers were educated at normal schools. After 1886 for primary-school teachers, and 1884 for middle-school teachers, those who passed the certification exams could obtain a teacher's certificate. From 1900 certificates for teaching in middle schools were given without examination to university graduates who fulfilled the required conditions. Again, depending on the demand for teachers, teacher-training institutes were established from time to time on a temporary basis.

After World War II a drastic reform of the teacher-training system was instituted. The United States Education Mission to Japan of 1946 advised that: the curriculum for teacher training should comprise three areas—general education, course-related professional education, and professional education related to teaching; normal schools should be reorganized into four-year teachers' colleges; teacher-training programs could be carried on in regular universities. In 1949 liberal arts colleges were newly created and departments of arts and science and of education were established in the national universities in order to train teachers for the compulsory education grades. Moreover, a teacher's qualification could be acquired in other departments and at other universities. Teacher training became based on the certification law and was conducted at all universities.

Today, the training of teachers for primary schools and special schools (schools for the blind, deaf, and handicapped) is carried out primarily in education departments and national teachers' colleges, and that for middle and high schools primarily in regular universities. The training of kindergarten teachers is done in private junior colleges or training institutes designated by the Ministry of Education.

Teacher Qualification—— In 1949 the Educational Personnel Certification Law (Kyōiku Shokuin Menkyo Hō) was enacted, and, except for university instructors, it became necessary to obtain a teaching certificate in order to become a teacher. The fundamental intent of the law was to make the certification system thorough, to establish professionalism, and to make certification available to anyone who qualified. The authority of certification rested with the prefectures.

At present, certificates are divided into first and second class. For first-class certification, the basic requirement in the case of kindergarten, primary, and middle-school teachers is a bachelor's degree, and for high-school teachers, a master's degree. For second-class certification, kindergarten, primary-, and middle-school teachers must be graduates of junior college and high-school teachers must have a bachelor's degree. In addition to these, temporary certificates (of three-year duration) are given to high-school graduates who pass the certification examination given by the prefectural board of education. Through such means as in-service training, those who have fulfilled the required level can be promoted from temporary certification to second-class certification, or from second class to first class. Middle- and high-school certification varies according to the courses to be taught.

The Educational Personnel Certification Law sets the minimum units of credit to be taken in universities. These are divided into general education courses and specialized courses; the latter are further divided into courses related to subject areas and those related to teaching. Required courses related to teaching are principles of education, education psychology, education methods, studies in moral education, and practice teaching.

In-Service Training—— In order to improve the quality of public education, teachers are required to pursue their own research and training and to be provided with appropriate services. In-service training today is carried out in three general ways: study and training done individually, or in school, or with various organizations; in-service training in such organizations as education centers run by the Ministry of Education, boards of education, or by other public agencies; and in-service training at universities. Activities included under the first category are study meetings and open discussion sessions by one school or regional groups of schools, as well as regional and national meetings held by the Japan Teachers' Union (Nihon Kyō-shokuin Kumiai; NIKKYŌSO) for discussion of educational issues. Under the second are curriculum-study meetings conducted by the Ministry of Education, overseas teacher training and research, lectures and short training courses, and comparatively long-term training and observation tours outside the prefecture organized by the local boards of education. The third refers to the few cases where teachers reenter universities or graduate schools for further education. On the other hand, in order to ensure the opportunity for in-service training, teachers' colleges offering a graduate-level master's course have been recently established. Some private universities offer correspondence courses for those who want higher certification. In addition, schools that are affiliated with education departments of universities offer practice teaching and carry on various research and experiments. The public network NHK regularly broadcasts radio and television programs for teachers. Many monthly magazines and books are published for teachers.

Appointment, Dismissal, and Remuneration—— Teachers at national schools, such as schools affiliated with national universities, are appointed by the minister of education; teachers at public elementary and middle schools, by the prefectural board of education; and teachers at public high schools, by prefectural or city boards of education. There are four kinds of appointments: employment, promotion, demotions, and transfer. New teachers are selected from those who already possess teaching certificates and have passed the prefectural teacher employment examination. Promotion is given according to tests given by the prefectural boards of education. Transfers take place between schools within the same prefecture, and in order to avoid stagnation of personnel, transfers occur periodically. This is considered an important function of the board of education personnel administration. Assignment of university instructors is completely left up to the university faculty.

As government employees, public education personnel are required to maintain professional neutrality in politics and religion and, in comparison to other public officials, are regarded as having special responsibilities. For this reason, the following conditions are regulated by law: qualification certificates are necessary; assignments and promotion are by recommendation rather than by competitive

examinations; besides study and training by official directive, leaves-of-absence or time off are given for independent or long-term study and training. Also, a teacher is comparatively free to hold another job as long as it is related to education. Political activity is more strictly regulated than for ordinary public officials.

Performance ratings of teachers have been conducted since 1958 for public primary-, middle-, and high-school teachers. When it was first implemented, there was fierce opposition from Nikkyōso, the teachers' union, which saw it as a way of imposing control over education, as harmful to teacher solidarity, and as an encroachment on academic freedom. It also contended that because of the special nature of teaching it was difficult to assess teachers' performances. Criticism and opposition still continue.

Teachers' salaries are regulated according to a standardized scale and are better than those paid to government workers. Starting salaries are determined by educational background, type of certification, and experience. Salaries for public elementary- and middle-school teachers are provided by the prefecture. As for high-school teachers, either the prefecture or city—whichever established the school—is responsible for 50 percent of the salary, while the other 50 percent is paid from the national treasury.

Teaching Responsibility—— In primary schools a teacher generally teaches all subjects to a class of approximately 45 students in one grade level. Teaching hours average 45 minutes per class and 30 classes per week. In middle and high schools, teachers are assigned classes according to subject. Classes are 50 minutes in length and teaching loads average 20 classes per week in middle schools and 15 classes per week in high schools.

The teachers are completely responsible for guidance, club activities, student-council activities, and homeroom activities. In addition to performing various tasks related to guidance, student conferences, and PTA activities, they bear responsibility for some student activities outside the school. Teachers' working conditions and obligations are in general quite demanding.

Teachers' Unions—— In order to understand teachers and the school system in Japan, one cannot ignore the activities of teachers' groups, particularly the teachers' union, Nikkyōso. The first teachers' union was organized in 1919 by SHIMONAKA YASABURŌ. This union had a strong idealistic and humanitarian element. During the 1930s various education movements influenced by Marxism were established with a view toward proletarian education, but they were strongly suppressed. Nikkyōso was formed after World War II in 1947, and the Japan Upper Secondary School Teachers' Union (Nihon Kōtōgakkō Kyōshokuin Kumiai or Nikkōkyō) in 1956. They worked in unison and convened joint study meetings every year.

In 1952 Nikkyōso issued a code of ethics for teachers and clarified its stand on class struggles. In the same year it organized the Nihon Kyōshokuin Seiji Remmei (Political Federation for Teachers in Japan), later renamed the Nihon Minshu Kyōiku Seiji Remmei (Political Federation for Democratic Education in Japan), and endorsed Nikkyōso-nominated representatives for the Diet and prefectural assemblies. Nikkyōso has consistently regarded the educational policies of the Ministry of Education as reactionary and opposed them. It has also been active in political and economic struggles. Within Nikkyōso there is a split between the pro-Socialist Party main faction and the pro-Communist Party faction. As for the dispute on what constitutes teaching, the main faction regards teaching as work, while the opposition faction insists that it is both work and a sacred vocation. The two factions are also divided over the question of strategy.

Among teachers' organizations opposing the above-mentioned Nikkyōso and Nikkōkyō are the Nihon Kyōshokuin Remmei (Japan Federation of Teachers), the Nihon Kyōshokuin Kumiai Rengō (New Japanese Federation of Teachers Union), and several other national organizations. According to a survey conducted in 1980, 787,349 teachers (69.2 percent of the total) belonged to one of these organizations. The largest organization was Nikkyōso, with 52.0 percent of the teachers as members. Nikkyōso is an influential and active member of SŌHYŌ (General Council of Trade Unions of Japan). Membership and allegiance in the Nikkyōso vary greatly from prefecture to prefecture.

Composition of Teaching Personnel—— In 1980 the number of full-time teachers, as classified by kind of school, were as follows: elementary school, 467,931; middle school, 251,274; high school, 243,627; schools for the blind, 3,363; schools for the deaf, 4,756; schools for the handicapped, 25,347; kindergarten, 100,958. The percentage of women teachers in elementary schools is 56.6 percent; in middle schools, 32.0 percent; in high schools, 17.9 percent. Almost all kindergarten teachers are women. The student to full-time teacher ratios are: primary school, 25.3 to 1; middle school, 20.3 to 1; high school, 18.9 to 1; kindergarten, 23.8 to 1.

In 1980 there were 102,989 full-time university instructors. Student to full-time teacher ratios were as follows: national universities, 8.5 to 1; private universities, 27.9 to 1; national or public junior colleges, 13.1 to 1; private junior colleges, 24.4 to 1. In comparison to other nations (including England, the United States, France, West Germany, and the Soviet Union) the ratio of students to teachers in universities is high; this is especially noticeable in private universities.

As to composition of teachers by age, according to a 1980 survey the greatest percentage of kindergarten teachers were under 24 (35.6 percent); of elementary- and middle-school teachers, 50 percent were under 40. In private universities and junior colleges, a number of the instructors were over 70.

With regard to academic background, the same survey found that the percentage of teachers who were graduates of four-year universities increased as the grade level increased: kindergarten teachers, about 10 percent; primary-school teachers, about 40 percent; high-school teachers, about 80 percent. At the university level, 90 percent of the instructors are college graduates, and at junior colleges, 70 percent.

Problems Affecting the Teaching Profession —— There are some problems with the system of teacher training. Since it is easy to obtain a teaching certificate at universities, there has been a tendency for people to obtain certification just in case they cannot find other suitable employment. As a result, many people become teachers without motivation or ability. And in general, neither the staff nor the curriculum in university teacher-training departments can be considered particularly good. It is not possible to provide a period of practice teaching for all the teaching-certificate applicants. A reform of the teacher-training system and an amplification of the in-service training system are urgently needed.

Another problem concerns teachers' working conditions. In densely populated areas, classrooms are overcrowded. In isolated areas, there are too few students per class, resulting in multiple-grade classrooms, which increases the teacher's burden. In addition, in Japan there is a strong tendency to relegate all educational activities as well as various kinds of clerical work and record keeping to teachers.

Finally, because the educational system is nationally uniform, all schools and teachers have to teach in conformity to national standards, leaving little room for flexibility.

In addition to problems arising from the educational system, there is the issue of guidance. An increasing number of students remain in school beyond the compulsory nine years; some are "involuntary attendants" who lack motivation and ability and cannot adjust well to school; an increasing number of these become delinquents or resort to violence.

Under these circumstances, teachers must not only provide curriculum instruction, but must also be specialists in guiding their students' lives.

■ —— B. C. Duke, *Japan's Militant Teachers: A History of the Left Wing Teachers' Movement* (1973). Hosoya Tsuneo, *Kyōshi no shakaiteki chii* (1956). Japanese National Commission for UNESCO, *The Development of Modern Education and Teacher Training in Japan* (1970). Nihon Kyōiku Shakaigakukai, ed, *Nihon no kyōshi* (1973). SHIMBORI Michiya and ŌSHIMA Mitsuo

teaching methods

Classroom teaching began in Japan after the Meiji Restoration (1868) and has developed through successive stages of liberalization and reaction in the process of the modernization of education.

In the premodern Edo period (1600–1868), schools were of two main types: the TERAKOYA for the children of either *samurai* or commoners and the domain schools for children of the samurai class. At the *terakoya*, one teacher would instruct students of diverse ages and educational levels, and both teaching material and instruction were individualized. At the domain schools, emphasis was placed on the reading and interpretation of Chinese and Japanese classics, and the dominant teaching method was rote memorization. See also EDUCATION: Edo-period education.

With the inception of a national education system in the 1870s, teaching became centered in the classroom and the teacher assumed increased importance. Efforts were made to improve teaching methods in order to make education available to the greatest possible

number of people. The Meiji government hired the American Marion McCarrell SCOTT in 1871 to teach at the government-operated normal school in Tōkyō, and it was Scott who introduced American teaching methods over the following decade. Blackboards were installed in every classroom, which were also equipped with wall maps and textbooks. Manuals were published for teachers to introduce methods of teaching using questions and answers, and these methods remain at the core of Japanese teaching today.

The next method to be introduced was that of Johann Heinrich Pestalozzi (1746–1827), which was brought to Japan by TAKAMINE HIDEO who had studied it in the United States. This method stressed student participation and the pacing of education according to the interest and ability of the child. This method soon became little more than a formality, however, and the rigid question-and-answer method replaced student participation.

Government control over curriculum was increased in 1886, after which nationalistic German teaching methods were introduced. The government invited Emil HAUSKNECHT from Germany to teach Johann Friedrich Herbart's pedagogy. Herbart's method built on a child's knowledge and used the careful selection of materials to inculcate high moral values. The emphasis in Japan was placed on Herbart's technical methods, specifically the "five formal steps": preparation, presentation, comparison, generalization, and application. This method reached its widest dissemination between 1889 and 1897. It placed emphasis on the maintenance of strict order within the classroom. This fostered uniformity and formalization of teaching, which eventually led to the decline in popularity of this method.

With the development of capitalism in Japan and the spread of democratic ideas, the New Education Movement (SHIN KYŌIKU UNDŌ) emerged in opposition to the uniformity of Meiji-period education. Numerous Western educational theories, broadly referred to as the Progressive Education Movement, were introduced. Each of these advocated a student-centered teaching method. Ability groupings were developed within classrooms, and concrete experiences in learning were emphasized. The Dalton Plan, under which students and teachers concluded learning contracts based on interest and ability, was also utilized. Group study was also experimented with. Most of these efforts, however, were conducted at elementary schools attached to normal schools or at private schools operated by such progressive educators as SAWAYANAGI MASATARŌ and HANI MOTOKO (see also SEIKATSU TSUZURIKATA UNDŌ). The teaching methods of public elementary schools were not greatly affected by the new movements, and their methods were suppressed after the rise of militarism in the early Shōwa period (1926–).

During World War II, the objectives of education were tied to the war effort. Elementary schools were reorganized as KOKUMIN GAKKŌ (national people's schools), and children were taught to be loyal subjects of the emperor. Teaching included physical and military education and industrial projects as well as the traditional emphasis on hard facts.

Since the end of the war, increased emphasis has been placed on the interests of the student and the individual's stages of development. The use of audiovisual aids and discussion groups is now widespread. Nonetheless, schools continue to focus on the transmission of formal knowledge, and systematic methods of teaching have become more deeply entrenched with increasing government control of the curriculum since the mid-1950s. The entrance examination system, which tests the student's mastery of school subjects, and the multiple-choice method of testing have further reinforced traditional methods of teaching (see ENTRANCE EXAMINATIONS).

TAKAKUWA Yasuo

Teatoro

An important comprehensive theater journal originally established in 1934 and presently in its fourth revival. *Teatoro* is the Esperanto word for theater. Series one of the journal appeared from May 1934 to August 1940. Edited by Akita Ujaku (1883–1962), it was active in the promotion of leftist theater. From its inception *Teatoro* has focused on the introduction and development of Western dramatic theories and techniques, frequently serializing translations of foreign dramatic criticism and plays. For example, it carried essays on the Stanislavski method and plays by Clifford Odets and Sidney Kingsley. Revived after World War II, series two of *Teatoro* was published from October 1946 to July 1956. Under editors Hijikata Yoshi (1898–1959) and MURAYAMA TOMOYOSHI, it was smaller in size than series one but made a positive contribution to the development of postwar theater. Series three, revived by Akutagawa Hiroshi (1920–1981), KINOSHITA JUNJI, Senda Koreya (b 1904), and others, appeared from September 1956 to May 1964. It continued to be devoted to SHINGEKI ("new drama") and functioned as an organ of the progressive theater movement. After a reorganization of its editorial board, series four began publishing in June 1964 and continues to support actively all fields of the theatrical arts.

Theodore W. GOOSSEN

technical colleges

(kōtō semmon gakkō). Five-year institutions for professional and technical education, started in 1962 in order to train technicians. Graduation from middle school is a prerequisite for entrance. There are two types of technical colleges: industrial and merchant marine. Among the main courses are machinery, electricity, industrial chemistry, public works, and metalworking. In 1979 there were 62 technical colleges, of which 54 were national; there were approximately 46,000 students enrolled in these schools. Few universities accept graduates of technical colleges, and to meet the demand for further technical education two national universities have recently been opened: the Technological University of Nagaoka and Toyohashi University of Technology.

AMANO Ikuo

technological development

In an economy at any given time, many goods and services (output) are produced by combining the effort of people (labor input) and tools, machinery, equipment, and land (capital input). The production of output also utilizes technical knowledge. The store of technical knowledge employed in production is referred to as technology; it takes a multitude of forms, from the information contained in a farmers' almanac to a specific chemical reaction equation, from managerial skills and efficient organization of a large corporation to advances in electronic engineering. Advancement of the frontier of this store of knowledge is known as technological development.

Historical Path of Technological Development in Japan

Only slightly more than a century ago, Japan stood almost completely secluded from the rest of the world in an isolated corner of the northwest Pacific. Within decades of the MEIJI RESTORATION (1868) and the opening of relations with the West, the country had moved well down the path toward industrialization. Japan's industrial base had developed modern military capabilities by the turn of the century, and soon afterwards the country demanded recognition as a major international power. Since World War II, Japan's phenomenal growth has earned it a place among the world's great economic powers. The rapidity with which this once small and insignificant country achieved its transformation has come to be regarded as legendary in economic history. The legend remains largely intact, but the lessons from this piece of history have yet to be fully learned.

In his article titled "A Model of Economic Growth," Nicholas Kaldor wrote what seems now to be an accurate assessment of the source of Japan's successful growth performance: "The prime mover in the process of economic growth is the readiness to absorb technical changes combined with the willingness to invest capital in business ventures" (*Economic Journal*, December 1957, p 599). Japan, like other late-developing nations, found itself in the position to import technology originating in advanced Western countries. Differences in the productive environment and in the availability and the quality of productive input were obstacles for the technology importers, as was the premodern state of development of the social and political systems and institutions that supported the process of technological development. We shall trace below the history of modern technology in Japan, and how the nation prepared for, and enhanced its capacity to assimilate, imported technology for economic growth beyond these obstacles.

Since the 17th century the pattern of technological development in Japan has undergone two similar cycles, once from the 17th century to the 1930s, and again from the 1930s to the 1970s. This historical pattern consists of three sequential components: (1) a period of technological isolation; (2) a period of technological transformation; and (3) a period of technological absorption.

The periods of technological isolation were extended periods of time when a communication barrier between Japan and the rest of the world retarded the transfer of technological information. Most technological development during these periods can be characterized as indigenous, and the level of technology fell below that of the Western industrialized economies. The communication barrier was lowered after a time, and the periods of technological transformation arrived. As the economy was exposed to a store of technological knowledge previously unavailable, a process of selection and "translation" of new techniques adequate for adoption took place. During these periods, the indigenous technology was not immediately discarded, but used parallel to and in conjunction with the newly acquired technology. After this adjustment period, the economy continued to raise its level of technology toward the world level, and rapidly expanded its productive capacity. These were periods of technological absorption.

The critical point in this sequence of three historical phases is the time when the barrier to the flow of technological information is lowered. For the level of technology to advance, a set of prerequisites must be met during the period of technological isolation as well as the period of technological transformation. First, the economy must be ready for and receptive to technological progress. It must be endowed with a well-organized social system and some form of relatively stable and effective political process. The low level of technology and economic dormancy during the period of technological isolation are not necessarily accompanied by underdeveloped social and political systems. Second, the economy must be innovative during the period of technological transformation. Advanced technology usually requires greater amounts of capital input (structures, machinery, tools, and equipment) per person employed. Given the relative scarcity of capital input, this requires the economy to choose carefully the specific techniques that are to be adopted. It may also require some modification of the new techniques to suit the available resources for production. The need for more capital calls for investment in the nation's stock of capital input. The economy in transition requires innovative institutional changes that smooth the path for investment activities to continue through the period of technological transformation and into the period of technological absorption.

The 17th Century to the 1930s

In terms of technological development the years from the 17th century to the 1930s can be divided into three periods: (1) from the 17th century to 1868 (the Edo period); (2) from 1868 to 1905 (from the Meiji Restoration to the end of the RUSSO-JAPANESE WAR); and (3) from 1905 to the late 1930s. During the first period the NATIONAL SECLUSION (Sakoku) policy of the Tokugawa shogunate closed Japan's ports, with only minor exceptions, to the rest of the world and kept the country in a state of technological isolation for over two centuries (1639–1853). Under the rule of a highly centralized feudal government, the economy remained essentially agrarian and characterized by low per capita income, with more than three-fourths of the population employed in agriculture, forestry, and fishing. The governmental system that ruled this economically dormant country was stable, highly structured, and effective; it also bred a substantial stock of SAMURAI civil servants, who were well educated and able to take on the role of leadership when required. The social structure was advanced compared to other countries with equivalent per capita income. An important example can be observed in the standard of education: approximately one-half of the male population was exposed to some formal education by the end of this period.

Indigenous technology was labor intensive in its use of productive resources. Some specific techniques, however, were sophisticated and did withstand the test of time, such as the technology of construction and, in particular, the construction of large-scale structures. In sum, the prerequisites for progress in the level of technology had been met. By the time Commodore Matthew C. PERRY of the US Navy effected the OPENING OF JAPAN (1854), triggering a sequence of events that led to the Meiji Restoration of 1868, Japan was fully prepared to embark upon the course of technological advance and industrialization.

To young Meiji Japan and its new leaders, technological lag implied political vulnerability. It was not simply the observed efficiency of the new technology, but fear of losing sovereignty to the Western industrial powers that drove the new government hard at the task of technological transformation. Political urgency demanded a rapid rate of transformation and hence required the government to play a major role. The task of technological transformation could not be left in the hands of the private sector alone. Here lay the importance of the effective and stable government and of the ready supply of civil servants who were both highly educated and experienced in the management of state affairs.

The new government quickly stabilized its rule and dissolved the remains of the old feudal system. The feudal class structure was abolished and most feudal lords were pensioned off. Most importantly, a land reform, which gave the farmers title to the land they worked and created a new source of government revenue in a land tax, was successfully executed. Immediately after the establishment of its power, the government also set out to import new knowledge and technology. Many Western scholars, engineers, and other experts of technological know-how were invited by the government. Simultaneously, a continuous stream of Japanese were dispatched to Europe and the United States, some with no assignment other than to learn and absorb whatever they could, and others with specific assignments ranging from studying foreign government systems and constitutions to learning steam engine and railroad systems. Here lay the significance of a ready supply of well-educated men, some of whom had long studied foreign languages such as Dutch, German, and Portuguese. Advances in technology implied the need for an educated labor force that could be trained efficiently in the new skills required. Thus the government worked to raise the general level of education. In 1873 the rate of attendance for compulsory education was only 28 percent, but the figure rose to 53 percent by 1883, and 69 percent of the total population subject to compulsory education was actually in school by the end of the 19th century. The number of primary and secondary schools more than doubled during the period 1873–1900, from 12,643 to 27,186. The first national university was established in Tōkyō in 1877. These were some of the dimensions of the Meiji government's policy of SHOKUSAN KŌGYŌ ("Increase Production and Promote Industry"), which made it a national objective to attain technological progress, industrialization, and modernization as quickly as possible.

Under this policy, the government encouraged investment activities by the business sector, and invested its own resources heavily to facilitate industrialization and technological progress. It set up a series of pilot or model factories based on newly acquired technological knowledge. It also placed a high priority on modernizing the country's transportation system; it improved and extended roads, and began the construction of the national railroad system. It is not, however, the magnitude of these undertakings that was impressive but the manner in which they were planned and executed. From the outset, the utilization of new technology was carefully planned to meet existing domestic resource constraints. The first industries that received encouragement for growth were precisely those that required relatively less capital input and a relatively lower level of skill in the labor force, such as the TEXTILE INDUSTRY. Model factories were not always exact reproductions of those in the Western world, and there was already some evidence of the translation of new technologies to suit the domestic environment, such as a reduction in scale and a greater use of lumber than steel in new structures and equipment. Indigenous technology was not altogether abandoned, but was utilized to support the process of modernization. This was most evident in the construction of buildings, roads, and irrigation systems.

One of the most important contributions of the Meiji government to private business investment activities was the modernization of the country's financial institutions. Local coins had long been in circulation in Japan as a medium of exchange, and by the end of the Edo period, a very rudimentary form of commercial banking had emerged from the wealthy class of merchants, but the country's financial system was far too primitive to support the investment activities of an industrialized economy. The government attempted to establish a unified and convertible national currency system, beginning in the second year of the new government (1869) with the creation of the MINISTRY OF FINANCE and eight KAWASE KAISHA ("exchange," or commercial banks), followed by the Shinka Jōrei (New Currency Ordinance), officially establishing the gold standard (bimetalism in gold and sterling in practice) and setting standard units of account for the economy in 1871. After a series of trials and errors and brief returns to inconvertibility, the establishment of the central bank, the BANK OF JAPAN, finally set the economy on course for the sound development of a modern financial sector in 1882. The central banking system and the subsequent development of commercial banks stabilized the currency and credit systems, brought a continuous decline in interest rates, and triggered an investment spurt in the private business sector. Just before the creation of the Bank of Japan, the total number of business corporations was 1,803, of which a mere 78 were in manufacturing (1881). By the end of the period of technological transformation (1905), the number of corporations increased by approximately five times to a total of 9,006. Manufacturing in particular saw an astonishing increase by 31 times to a total of 2,449 companies.

While the Meiji government led the economy through the period of technological transformation under the shokusan kōgyō policy, it fought and won two wars (the SINO-JAPANESE WAR OF 1894–1895 and the Russo-Japanese War, 1904–05); faced periods of high inflation, particularly before the creation of the Bank of Japan; and suffered a severe recession, a major financial panic, and a near crash of its financial markets in 1890–91. The average annual growth rate of real gross national product (GNP) for the period 1880–1905 has been estimated to be at best about 3 percent. The path of technological transformation was by no means smooth, but it laid the necessary foundation for the economic growth and technological absorption to follow.

The period of technological absorption, from about 1905 to the late 1930s, was not a period of uninterrupted growth. The economy continued to be plagued by instability, particularly in its financial sector. Prior to the worldwide crash and depression that began in 1929, the Japanese economy underwent a series of four financial collapses and recessions in 1907–08, 1920, 1922–23, and 1927. In general, however, the period can be characterized as one of moderate economic growth, with the nation's real GNP rising at an average annual rate of 4 to 5 percent. For the first time in Japanese history, the output of the mining and manufacturing industries exceeded that of the agriculture, forestry, and fishing industries during World War I (1914–18), and heavy manufacturing industries began their growth during this period.

In contrast with the preceding period, the institutional innovations that promoted technological progress and business investment came from the private sector rather than the government. Two important developments were the shūshin koyō seido (the career-long or "lifetime" employment system) and the ZAIBATSU (financial and industrial combine). The exact origin of career-long employment and the so-called PATERNALISM of larger Japanese firms is a relatively controversial issue among scholars. It is generally agreed, however, that the system began to emerge slowly in the beginning of the 20th century within large-scale firms in order to reduce the costs attached to a high degree of labor mobility, turnover, and frequent recruitment. It has also been pointed out that part of the reason for this system was to combat rising labor unrest and the increasing power of the labor unions. Regardless of the managerial objectives, certain elements of Japanese culture such as traditional conformity to group norms provided a fertile ground for the growth of such a system (see EMPLOYMENT SYSTEM, MODERN). As the early 20th century also saw the rapid introduction of highly automated production-line technology, the career-long employment system, by providing workers with security and reducing their resistance to technological progress, enhanced the absorption of increasingly capital-intensive technology.

The contribution of the zaibatsu to technological progress during this period is immeasurable. The institution originated in the wealthy class of merchants of the Edo period and attained its prominence in the first two decades of the 20th century as various financial combines diversified their control over commerce, finance, mining, and manufacturing industries. With easy access to capital, they aggressively imported foreign technology, developed their own technology, exploited their economies of scale, developed many industries simultaneously, and cultivated a new class of elite business managers to match the able civil servants.

As industrialization and the growth of heavy industries proceeded under the aegis of the zaibatsu, the political environment of Japan led to a shift toward a military and war-oriented economy. Increasing military requirements and a set of conflicts between the military and the zaibatsu spawned a new generation of financial combines that specialized in heavy manufacturing industries catering to the military. At the beginning of the period of technological absorption, the real GNP (in 1934–36 prices) was ¥6.6 billion, and light industries dominated the manufacturing sector. In 1938 the output of heavy industries exceeded that of light manufacturing for the first time; and in 1939 the nation's real GNP (in 1934–36 prices) reached its prewar peak of ¥22 billion, a level which would not be regained for a decade-and-a-half. September 1939 marked the beginning of World War II, when Japan withdrew into another period of technological isolation.

World War II to the 1970s——The remainder of this history can be divided into three periods: (1) from World War II to the OCCUPATION; (2) from the Occupation to 1960; and (3) from 1960 to the 1970s. The war-induced second period of technological isolation was neither as long nor as complete as that of the Edo period. Nevertheless, the abnormal course of international relations slowed the flow of technology into Japan from the advanced countries. Indigenous technological development was active, particularly in the production of ordnance; this would later contribute to the growth of the peacetime economy after the defeat and the Allied Occupation (1945–1952). During the period of technological isolation, the rate of technological advance in the West was much faster than that of Japan's indigenous technology. At the end of the war, Japan found itself again in a position to import foreign technology while capital resources were scarce, this time because of the destruction of war.

During the Occupation, Japan's political, social, and economic systems were thoroughly overhauled. The sweeping changes, ranging from a new constitution to the ZAIBATSU DISSOLUTION program, from a new system of taxes to the reorganization of the commercial sector of the banking system, from antimonopoly laws to the new civil laws, were all aimed at the establishment of a stable, democratic Japan. Meanwhile, insufficient productive capacity due to wartime destruction forced the economy into a period of high inflation starting in 1946, despite efforts to suppress consumer demand. Although the Korean War stimulated the expansion of productive capacity from 1950 to 1953, the inflationary tendency and the resulting uncertainty of business expectations plagued the economy. The government of Prime Minister YOSHIDA SHIGERU introduced a deflationary budget in 1953 and succeeded in controlling inflation soon afterwards. The deflationary policy did not dampen business investment activities, and with regained confidence the private sector continued to add to the economy's productive capacity. The prewar peak of real GNP was matched in 1954, and it continued to grow throughout the decade despite brief but sharp fluctuations in the business cycle.

The economy in the process of technological transformation again required careful planning. The investment activities that brought about the transformation were closely overseen by the government, particularly the MINISTRY OF INTERNATIONAL TRADE AND INDUSTRY (MITI). Immediately after the assumption of its normal postwar functions, MITI began to survey the frontier of technological knowledge and kept itself fully informed of new technological advances. It set national priorities for technological progress by choosing certain industries to be encouraged for growth and others to be weeded out. In the implementation of technology policy, MITI's most effective tool was control of foreign trade. It controlled the allocation of foreign exchange needed for technology imports, and all licensing agreements and any other form of technology inflow required MITI's approval (see FOREIGN EXCHANGE CONTROL). A less obvious tool of policy implementation has been what is known as ADMINISTRATIVE GUIDANCE, informal agreements and arrangements between MITI and the private business sector that are without statutory foundation but nevertheless extremely effective. Thus the inflow of foreign technology was closely monitored through the period of technological transformation and into the period of technological absorption.

Indigenous wartime technology also helped to lay out the foundation for Japan's postwar technological progress. Producers of precision war equipment were transformed into peacetime precision equipment manufacturers, particularly in the optical field. Producers of military aircraft turned to the production of engines, automobiles, and other land transportation vehicles. Photographic films developed by the Imperial Japanese Navy were produced to capture peaceful snapshots, and battleships were replaced by supertankers at the shipyards.

As the Japanese economy rocked through the business cycles of the last half of the 1950s, a handful of government economists who began to understand Japan's potential for rapid economic growth emerged. Most prominent among them was Shimomura Osamu (b 1910), an economist and then a high-ranking bureaucrat at the Ministry of Finance. As early as 1955, he began to advocate an aggressive growth policy to stimulate technological progress via private business investment, thus increasing productivity and the economy's capacity to supply goods and services for intermediate and final demand. He became an informal adviser to IKEDA HAYATO in 1958, and is regarded as the chief architect of the Shotoku Baizō Keikaku (INCOME-DOUBLING PLAN), announced at the beginning of Prime Minister Ikeda's government in 1960. The plan envisaged the doubling of the Japanese national income within the decade at an average annual growth rate of 7.2 percent. Thus Japan stepped into the period of technological absorption and began its growth and technological progress at a historically unprecedented rate.

Japan and the United States Compared——In economic analysis, technology is conceived of as the technically feasible limits of production possibilities given a certain level of capital and labor

Technological development——Table 1

Average Annual Growth Rates of Output, Inputs, and Technology (in percent per year)				
	1952–1960		1960–1973	
	Japan	US	Japan	US
Output	8.4	2.9	10.5	4.3
Capital input	5.4	3.6	13.0	4.1
Labor input	5.0	0.7	2.0	2.2
Technology	3.3	1.0	3.9	1.3

SOURCE: Based on information contained in the article by Dale W. Jorgenson and Nishimizu Mieko, "U.S. and Japanese Economic Growth, 1952–1974: An International Comparison," *Economic Journal* (December 1978).

input. Technological development expands the frontier of production, bringing about an increase in productivity from the same level of production input. This advance in productivity can be measured in the aggregate for the national economy by comparing the rate of growth of input with growth in the national product. The result of these estimates for the United States and Japan for the periods 1952–60 and 1960–73 is presented in Table 1. (For a technical discussion of the methodology of the remainder of this article, readers are referred to D. W. Jorgenson and M. Nishimizu, "U.S. and Japanese Economic Growth, 1952–1974: An International Comparison," *Economic Journal*, December 1978.)

In both countries, the rate of economic growth increased substantially over the two periods. The average annual growth rate of output in the United States rose from 2.9 percent to 4.3 percent, and in Japan from 8.4 percent to 10.5 percent. The anatomy of this growth, however, differed greatly in the two countries. In Japan, it was accomplished by an astonishing increase in capital input, together with a substantial decline in the growth rate of labor input. In the United States, the acceleration in growth was associated with an increase in the growth rate of labor and a much more modest increase in the capital growth rate. Acceleration in the rate of technological progress is also observed in both countries. In both periods, however, Japan's technology advanced at a rate three times that of the United States.

These estimates lead to consideration of the magnitude of the gap in the level of technology between Japan and the United States during the postwar period. If the percent change in the level of technology in one country from one period to another can be measured, it should be possible to measure the percent difference in the level of technology between two countries at a given point in time. Analogous to the concept of technological progress, then, a technological gap can be captured as the percent difference in levels of output between countries given levels of labor and capital at a certain point in time. The technological gap is measured by combining the ratios of output and input between Japan and the United States. The resulting estimates are presented in Table 2.

In 1952 output in the United States was 12 times that of Japan. By 1960 the output ratio fell to 7.4; and by 1973 output in Japan was one-third that of the United States (column 1). A closer look at the results reveals one striking difference between the two countries: the narrowing of the output levels was accompanied in Japan by a rapid rise in the share of investment goods (goods produced for the business sector to add to its capital input) in total output (column 7), while no substantial change in the share was observed in the United States (column 6). In 1952 both countries were producing approximately one-third of total output as investment goods (column 7), and the quantity of investment goods output in the United States was more than 16 times that of Japan (column 2). In 1973 Japan was producing exactly one-half of its total output in investment goods, and the US–Japan ratio of investment-goods output fell to 2.2. With Japan's productive resources directed into investment-goods production, consumption goods lagged behind, and in 1973 the US output in consumption goods was 4.3 times that of Japan.

The dramatic role played by investment goods on the output side is consistent with the earlier finding of rapid growth in capital input. The quantity of capital input in the United States was more than 16 times that in Japan in 1952 and even higher in 1956, at 20 times. By

Technological development —— Table 2

| | Output and Input Ratios, and Technology Gap between the US and Japan | | | | | | | |
	1	2	3	4	5	6	7	8
1952	12.1	16.3	10.5	16.7	2.9	32.1	32.1	75.7
1953	11.6	17.0	9.8	18.2	2.8	31.7	29.2	76.2
1954	10.7	15.1	9.2	17.7	2.7	30.5	29.1	70.2
1955	10.5	15.0	8.9	18.4	2.6	33.7	30.9	65.7
1956	9.8	12.5	8.6	20.3	2.5	33.4	35.3	56.5
1957	9.2	10.1	8.6	18.9	2.4	32.6	40.1	56.4
1958	8.8	10.1	8.2	17.1	2.3	29.7	34.8	58.5
1959	8.3	9.4	7.8	16.8	2.3	31.8	37.3	51.7
1960	7.4	7.1	7.5	16.1	2.3	30.0	41.4	39.9
1961	6.5	5.3	7.3	15.2	2.2	29.4	48.1	26.4
1962	6.6	5.7	7.2	12.4	2.2	30.5	44.1	38.4
1963	6.1	5.2	6.6	11.3	2.2	30.9	44.6	32.1
1964	5.5	4.7	6.1	10.5	2.2	31.0	45.0	24.0
1965	5.5	5.0	5.8	9.7	2.2	31.7	42.0	26.3
1966	5.3	4.7	5.6	9.5	2.3	31.7	43.0	21.4
1967	4.9	3.7	5.7	9.0	2.3	30.4	46.0	16.5
1968	4.3	3.2	5.2	8.0	2.2	30.6	47.7	10.8
1969	4.0	2.9	4.9	7.5	2.2	30.3	48.1	6.1
1970	3.6	2.4	4.7	6.7	2.3	29.1	49.7	1.5
1971	3.4	2.3	4.4	5.6	2.2	29.6	47.9	4.7
1972	3.3	2.3	4.2	5.5	2.2	30.3	47.4	0.9
1973	3.3	2.2	4.3	5.9	2.3	30.6	50.0	−4.7

1. Total output ratio (US/Japan)
2. Investment goods output ratio (US/Japan)
3. Consumption goods output ratio (US/Japan)
4. Capital input ratio (US/Japan)
5. Labor input ratio (US/Japan)
6. Investment goods share in total output, US (in percentage)
7. Investment goods share in total output, Japan (in percentage)
8. Difference in technology (US less Japan, in percentage)

1973, however, this ratio was as low as 5.9 (column 4). As Japan increased its labor input during the period of technological transformation at a relatively higher rate, the labor input ratio between the United States and Japan fell from 2.9 to 2.2. After 1960, however, the ratio remained relatively constant, approaching the two countries' population ratio (column 5). A comparison of labor and capital input ratios gives the relative capital intensity in production between the two countries. In 1952 the capital intensity of US production was nearly 6 times that of Japan. Throughout the 1950s the United States continued to increase the intensity of capital input, while Japan's intensity remained at about the same level; and the relative capital intensity actually rose to 7.3 in 1959. Then the surging growth of capital in Japan began to narrow the difference. Although US capital intensity doubled Japan's in 1973, the reduction from sevenfold to twofold in slightly over a decade is indeed an astounding accomplishment.

By using the concepts and data discussed above, the annual percent difference between US and Japanese technology (the United States' less Japan's) for 1952–73 can be estimated (column 8). The results presented in Table 2 illustrate the remarkable closing of the technological gap between the two countries. In 1952 the Japanese level of technology was merely one-fourth of the US level. During the period 1952–59 the difference was reduced from 75.7 percent to 51.7 percent. Beginning in 1960, Japanese technology advanced rapidly, reaching nearly 90 percent of the US level by 1968. Japan had essentially caught up with US technology by the end of 1972, and stood slightly ahead in 1973.

A sustained gap still exists, however, between the two countries' GNP per capita. This difference is no longer due to Japan's technological lag; it is the result of the remaining difference in the capital intensity of production. A number of disturbances, since the OIL CRISIS OF 1973, have forced Japan into a new era of slower economic growth. Japan is in the process of adjusting to the new realities of

this era. Although the impact of the oil crisis and other international problems has overshadowed the significance of this accomplishment, Japan has achieved an economy-wide technological equivalence with the United States and entered an entirely new period of technological progress. See also TECHNOLOGY TRANSFER.

◾ ——Ezaki Mitsuo, *Nihon keizai no moderu bunseki* (1977). Dale W. Jorgenson and Nishimizu Mieko, "U.S. and Japanese Economic Growth, 1952–1974: An International Comparison," *Economic Journal* (December 1978). Allen C. Kelley and Jeffrey C. Williamson, *Lessons from Japanese Development* (1972). Lawrence Klein and Ohkawa Kazushi, ed, *Economic Growth: The Japanese Experience Since the Meiji Era* (1968). William W. Lockwood, ed, *The Economic Development of Japan* (1954). William W. Lockwood, ed, *The State and Economic Enterprise in Japan* (1965). James W. Morley, ed, *Dilemma of Growth in Prewar Japan* (1971). Nishimizu Mieko and Charles R. Hulten, "The Source of Japanese Economic Growth: 1955–1971," *The Review of Economics and Statistics* (August 1978). Ohkawa Kazushi and Hayami Yūjirō, ed, *Economic Growth: The Japanese Experience Since the Meiji Era* (1973). Ohkawa Kazushi and Henry Rosovsky, *Japanese Economic Growth: Trend Acceleration in the Twentieth Century* (1973). Ohkawa Kazushi and Henry Rosovsky, "The Indigenous Components in the Modern Japanese Economy," *Economic Development and Cultural Change* (April 1961). T. Ozawa, *Japan's Technological Challenge to the West: 1950–1974* (1974). Hugh Patrick, ed, *Japanese Industrialization and Its Social Consequences* (1976). Hugh Patrick and Henry Rosovsky, ed, *Asia's New Giant* (1976). Henry Rosovsky, *Capital Formation in Japan, 1868–1940* (1961). Henry Rosovsky, *Industrialization in Two Systems* (1966). Watanabe Tsunehiko, "Improvement of Labor Quality and Economic Growth—Japan's Postwar Experience," *Economic Development and Cultural Change* (October 1972).   NISHIMIZU Mieko

technological innovation

(gijutsu kakushin). As a late-developing nation, Japan has accomplished technological innovation primarily through the introduction of technology from the advanced nations, beginning in the mid-19th century. As a result, the rate of technological innovation in Japan has been faster than in other advanced industrial nations. Especially after 1960, Japanese economic growth was based on technological innovation.

Innovation after World War II was accelerated by economies of scale in the steel and shipbuilding industries and by the birth of new products in the petrochemical and electronics industries. In addition, the popularization of consumer durables, which first occurred in the 1930s in the United States, occurred in Japan at a rapid pace after World War II, resulting in the spectacular growth of the automobile and household electrical appliance industries. The structure of the postwar economy and society also helped speed technological innovation.

An Innovative Environment —— Among the factors conducive to technological innovation has been the Japanese love of novelty. In other countries, traditional customs, superstitions, and religious taboos often stood in the path of new technology. In addition, fear of technological displacement, such as that which sparked the famous Luddite resistance in England in 1779, has hampered innovation in many countries. Japan has experienced little resistance of this sort, in large part because of the people's disposition to face change without fear. The government reinforced this tendency during the MEIJI ENLIGHTENMENT with its policy of introducing Western civilization. This effort was vigorously pursued under the motto "Japanese spirit, Western learning" (WAKON YŌSAI).

A second factor has been the high level of growth and investment in the Japanese economy. Technological innovation, of course, can contribute to the economy only if it is utilized in the production process or a new product is manufactured and accepted in the market. Economic growth and large capital reserves have afforded ample opportunities to implement technological innovation. At the same time, strong competition between enterprises prevented technological monopolies from developing. For example, in the ammonium sulfate industry, five manufacturers started production almost simultaneously when the industry was inaugurated in the 1930s based on technology introduced from various foreign countries and supplemented by Japanese technology. In spite of duplicated investment in some cases, such strong competition helped accelerate technological innovation.

A third factor has been the high level of dependence on foreign technology. When the progress of science and technology results in innovation, utilization does not necessarily take place in the country where the invention or discovery was made. Japan ignited its industrialization by importing the technology of advanced nations. In the 1880s, for example, the Japanese learned silk reeling from the French, although silk was an indigenous product of Japan.

A fourth factor has been that Japan had a large market, especially for consumer durables. Technological innovation can produce excellent economic results only if the product produced by the new technology finds acceptance in the market. Japanese consumers had a strong desire for new consumer products. The popularization of consumer durables has been higher in Japan at lower income levels than in Western European countries. This has been instrumental in the promotion of technological innovation in the consumer goods industry (see CONSUMERS). The fact that Japanese society was suited to the economic patterns of advanced nations, namely, mass production, mass sales, and mass consumption, has been an important factor in promoting technological innovation.

Fruits of Technological Innovation —— Technological innovation in this context has made possible the unparalleled rapid growth of the Japanese economy. Before World War II the growth rate of the Japanese economy was higher than that of other countries, averaging an estimated 3.5 percent annually between 1880 and 1930. The average rate of growth in the first 30 years after the war was 11 percent per year, three times the average rate of countries in the Organization for Economic Cooperation and Development (OECD). Diligence, skillful administration of economic policy, and political stability can be cited as factors contributing to this growth, but most important was the high rate of technological progress. If the causal factors of economic growth are divided among capital, labor, and technological innovation and analyzed according to dynamic production-function equations, nearly half of the postwar growth can be explained by technological innovation. For example, of the average annual growth rate of 11.6 percent between 1965 and 1970, capital reserves accounted for 5.0 percent, the increase in labor supply accounted for 2.2 percent, and technological innovation accounted for the remaining 4.4 percent. Comparison of this production-function analysis with that of other advanced nations indicates that Japanese technological innovation was particularly high among the advanced nations.

A second consequence of technological innovation has been the rationalization of industry and the growth of the heavy chemical sector. Rationalization was spurred by what has been called condensed technological innovation; one result was that popularization of the washing machine, refrigerator, and television, which took 30 years in the United States, was accomplished in 15 years in Japan. The rapid growth of the automobile industry, and the expansion of the machine industry that accompanied it, contributed to the accelerated development of the Japanese heavy chemical industry. The industry has grown three times faster than its counterpart in the United States, and Japan achieved the world's highest rate of heavy chemical industrialization in the 1970s. See also INDUSTRIAL STRUCTURE.

Technological innovation has also brought about an information revolution. Japan stands second to the United States in the number of operating electronic computers, and the rate of Japanese popularization in such areas as on-line systems for banks and securities companies, computerization of production processes, and numerical production of machine tools matches that of the United States. The information revolution also has the power to change social behavior. The adoption of the on-line system in banks and the popularization of credit cards have relieved people to some extent of the necessity of carrying cash, and the widespread use of desk calculators has brought changes to the education system.

Prospects for the Future —— Japanese technological innovation was most intense in the 30 years after World War II, but since Japan attained the world's third largest gross national product (GNP) in 1970, the growth rate has dropped to around 5 percent per year, and the rate of technological progress is also expected to decrease in the future.

The first reason for this decrease is that technological innovation throughout the world appears to be slowing. The big wave of technological innovation that started in the 1950s was in atomic energy, electronics, computers, and polymer chemistry. Research in these fields is still producing new technology and new products, but seems to have passed the crest of the wave. Technological innovation is said to have a cycle of about 50 years, and the peak of the current wave was passed in the 1970s. The next major fields of technological innovation are expected to be in the life sciences and in new forms of energy. These innovations are likely to affect the economy only in the 21st century.

The second reason is that Japanese technology has already reached the levels of Western Europe and the United States. As described above, Japanese technological progress was brought about by introducing the technology of advanced nations. Japanese enterprises were so aggressive in doing this that by 1975 or thereabouts there remained little new technology and few products to be introduced. Some analyses indicate that by 1975 there was no technological gap between the United States and Japan.

The third reason is that the Japanese capacity for independent technological development is inferior to that of the United States and other countries. Japanese laboratories and technology experts were enthusiastic in learning technology from advanced nations, but little effort was made to produce creative technology of their own. Now that the Japanese have reached American technological levels, they may require fundamental reforms including reorganization of the research system. See RESEARCH AND DEVELOPMENT.

The fourth reason for a downturn in innovation is that Japanese economic, scientific, and technological policy has changed its stress from growth-orientation to stability and welfare. The 1977 *White Paper on Science and Technology* (issued by the SCIENCE AND TECHNOLOGY AGENCY) stated that the principal objective in the context of a steady-growth economy was to overcome restrictions in resources and to improve the quality of national life, goals corresponding to the "Small is beautiful" doctrine of E. F. Schumacher.

It is expected that Japanese technological innovation will change its course from imitation to creation, from growth to qualitative improvement, and from industry initiative to government initiative. See also TECHNOLOGY TRANSFER.   SHISHIDO Toshio

technology, modern

Japan developed an advanced modern technology in the three decades following World War II; although most of this technology was initially imported from abroad, Japan had in certain areas surpassed the technological level of the United States and other advanced nations by the late 1970s.

Historical Development —— Starting industrialization much later than most Western nations, Japan had to invest time and capital in laying the industrial, economic, and educational foundations for a technology that was already in practical use abroad. From the very beginning of the Meiji period (1868–1912) the national government promoted the development of industry and technology in Japan as part of its conscious policy of modernizing and militarily strengthening the nation. This policy was given particular emphasis by the Sino-Japanese War of 1894–95, and the Russo-Japanese War of 1904–05, and there was a systematic buildup of industry and technology following World War I. The Production Research Council, which was established in 1910 and reorganized as the Temporary Industrial Council in 1927 assisted certain designated industries. The INSTITUTE OF PHYSICAL AND CHEMICAL RESEARCH was organized in 1917 under the joint sponsorship of government and industry for the purpose of developing and applying creative technology. During the 1930s there was a rapid development of Japan's heavy and chemical industries. In this decade all industry and technology was mobilized for war (the Manchurian Incident of 1931, Japan's invasion of China in 1937, and its entry into World War II in 1941), and new developments were limited to military technology. Advances were made in shipbuilding, optics, and aircraft; however, because of the narrow application to military technology, Japan's overall productivity remained far below that of the United States.

Although most of Japan's technology was imported (of some 400 important discoveries and inventions in industrial technology from 1868 through the mid-1960s, only 70 were originally developed and produced in Japan), the following are some of the inventions made by the Japanese in the period before World War II: the production of Taka-diastase by TAKAMINE JŌKICHI in 1892, the invention of the Toyoda power loom by TOYODA SAKICHI in 1897, the extraction of adrenalin by Takamine Jōkichi in 1901, the invention of the seasoning Ajinomoto (L-monosodium glutamate; MSG) by IKEDA KIKUNAE (see AJINOMOTO CO, INC) in 1908, the invention of KS steel by HONDA KŌTARŌ in 1917, the development of a nitrogen fixation process for industrial use by the National Chemical Laboratory for Industry in 1920, and the invention of the Yagi antenna by YAGI HIDETSUGU in 1925.

After World War II technology once again broadened beyond military technology, and the national policy on science and technology was directed toward adapting imported technology to Japanese needs and standards. The SCIENCE AND TECHNOLOGY AGENCY was established in 1956 to unify policies for science and technology. The MINISTRY OF INTERNATIONAL TRADE AND INDUSTRY provided guidance to prevent excessive competition and the payment of unreasonably high licensing fees in importing technology. The ministry has assisted in introducing foreign technology while protecting and developing native industry. For example, in the case of thermoelectric power plants, the government approved the import of the first plant but enforced the use of domestically built plants thereafter.

Dependence on imported technology remained heavy in the postwar period. Important sectors of industry which emerged after the war, such as polymer chemistry, electronics, and atomic energy, have leaned heavily on imported technology. Technological rationalization and automation of production in more established industries, such as iron, steel, and machinery, have also been heavily dependent on foreign technology.

Payment of royalties for imported technology has increased remarkably. Even in 1977, when Japan caught up with American technological levels, $800 million was being paid in compensation. Since there has been little export of technology, the balance of international payments in technology has been unfavorable. However, export of technology has been increasing with the rise of the technological level in Japan. Royalties paid to Japan for technology amounted to only $300,000 in 1956, but this amount had increased to $150 million by 1976, and the ratio of payments received to payments made reached 17 percent. In the early 1980s Japan continued to pay out a large amount of foreign currency because of its heavy dependence on imported technology; however, it would have required several times as much time and money to develop the same technology independently.

Characteristics of Japanese Technology——The Japanese dependence on imported technology does not imply a simple imitation of imported technology. The Japanese have continuously endeavored not only to improve imported technology but to adapt it to fit new needs. For example, while all the fundamental technology for television, including television recording, has been based on foreign patents, Japanese engineers developed video recording for home use.

Japanese industry particularly stresses the development of applied technology, and the proportion of total research and development funds that is allocated to basic research is small. In 1974 it was only 6.3 percent, and most of this was, in actual fact, directed to the application and improvement of technology. See also RESEARCH AND DEVELOPMENT.

The major Japanese enterprises are in intense competition with each other and are anxious to introduce advanced technology from abroad ahead of others. The technology introduced by major enterprises is also speedily adopted by the small and medium enterprises that operate as subcontractors to the larger enterprises. The subcontracting enterprises obtain new technological information promptly from their parent companies and introduce new technology with the financial and technological aid of the latter.

Creativity. Japanese engineers, so gifted in their ability to find, import, and improve new technology from abroad, are, however, weak in developing new technology through their own efforts. Although there is no real way to measure creativity and the latent ability to develop technology, in a white paper on the world economy issued in 1969 by the Economic Planning Agency in Japan, an international comparison was made on the basis of the following eight indices: (1) the number of registered patents; (2) the ratio of payment to receipt in technological trade; (3) the ratio in total exports of technologically intensive industry; (4) the number of cases of successful industrialization of important new technology after 1945; (5) the total expenditure for research; (6) the number of persons engaged in research and development; (7) the number of graduates from schools of science and engineering; and (8) the number of computers installed. Combining these indices, the agency came up with a ratio for each country surveyed to the standard index (100) of the United States. According to this method, the rating of Japan at the end of the 1960s was 19, comparable to West Germany but far behind the United States.

Recent Trends——When environmental pollution came under severe attack in the 1970s, the government set up strict environmental standards, which resulted in the development of desulfurization technology ahead of the Western European countries. In particular,

the tightening of automobile emission standards has brought about the development of some of the cleanest automobile engines in the world (see LOW-POLLUTION ENGINES).

In the late 1970s and early 1980s new developments in the field of very large-scale integrated (VLSI) circuits were made in Japan. VLSI with 64 kilobits were completed in 1977 through the joint research of the Telegraph and Telephone Public Corporation, Nippon Electric Co, and Fujitsū, Ltd. Then, under the guidance of the Ministry of International Trade and Industry, the VLSI Technology Research Association (a research group composed of Tōshiba Corporation, Nippon Electric Co, Ltd, Hitachi, Fujitsū, Ltd, Mitsubishi Electric Corporation, and seven other companies) in 1980 completed an electron beam lithography system capable of drawing circuits with a width of 0.5 microns (5/10,000 millimeters). This technology has succeeded in increasing a hundredfold the capacity of semiconductors.

Japan caught up with the United States in labor productivity in the 1970s and has overtaken it in the technological level of certain production processes, as in the production of automobiles and television sets. Japan also has an advanced technology in such areas as the prevention of pollution and environmental science. There still exists, however, a substantial technological gap between the United States and Japan in such areas likely to be important in the future as atomic energy, aerospace, and oceanography. See also TECHNOLOGICAL DEVELOPMENT; TECHNOLOGICAL INNOVATION; TECHNOLOGY TRANSFER.

🕮——Ōshima Keiichi, "Science and Technology Policy in Japan's Economic Growth," *Proceedings of the Fourth Tsukuba International Symposium on the Role of the University in International Development* (1977). UNESCO, ed, *Technological Development in Japan* (1971). SHISHIDO Toshio

technology transfer

(gijutsu iten). The spread of commercially valuable knowledge and skills both within and across national borders. It is essentially an economic activity observable in the sequential process of invention (conception of technical feasibility), innovation (commercialization), and diffusion (widespread use following demonstration). Technology transfer occurs most frequently in the diffusion phase, after technology has been successfully developed, but the transfer of rudimentary research technology may also take place in the innovation stage. In the latter instance, adaptive research and development (R & D) is required for commercialization on the part of the technology recipient. The term "technology transfer" has only recently come into vogue as technology has been recognized as a significant determinant of economic growth. Technology has also emerged as an actively traded international resource for which demand, by developing countries in particular, is noticeably on the rise. Hence the term is usually used in an international context.

Ever since the MEIJI RESTORATION of 1868, Japan, as a buyer of advanced Western technologies, has been a beneficiary of this sort of economic transaction. In fact, it would not be wrong to describe Japan's phenomenal industrial expansion as basically a process of assimilating these technologies. Japan has experienced two long periods of continuous industrial growth: the first wave lasted over 70 years, from the Meiji Restoration until the outbreak of World War II; the second started after the end of that war and still continues. Each wave was initiated and given momentum by Japan's effort to catch up with the West in economic development through the importation of advanced industrial arts. In this endeavor Japanese industry itself has generated numerous improvements, developed its own innovations, and accumulated valuable skills. Particularly in the postwar period, Japan's original contributions to modern technology have been significant enough to make the country today a leading supplier of technology to the rest of the world.

Four basic modes of transfer can be identified, although they are often mutually complementary and inclusive: (1) transfer through human contact (mainly training) and technical literature; (2) transfer through machinery, equipment, and input materials; (3) transfer through licensing agreements (usually involving the use of patents, know-how, and trade names); and (4) transfer through direct foreign investment. The last mode entails more than technology transfer because it is the transplant of an entire production unit in which technology is "bundled" with capital and management, in contrast to other modes in which the supply of technology is "unbundled." The bundled way of supplying technology is controversial because it enables the technology supplier to retain ownership and to exercise managerial control over the foreign buyer of technology. Japan has intentionally kept the acquisition of bundled technology to a minimum for fear of foreign domination of its industry.

Cultural Borrowing in Early Japan —— Japan's first experience as the recipient of technology actually goes back to the 6th century, when the country began to model its social and political system on that of China. Not only was this undertaking encouraged by Prince SHŌTOKU in the early 7th century, but after the TAIKA REFORM of 645 the Yamato leaders launched a determined campaign to adopt much of the higher civilization of the Tang (T'ang) dynasty (618–907) in China. Cultural borrowing lasted, although with diminishing vigor, up to the mid-9th century, when a long period of isolationism from the continent began, and the Japanese became preoccupied with assimilating the culture they had borrowed.

Although significant industrial techniques in such fields as weaving, pottery, lacquer ware, mining, metallurgy, and farming were acquired, what had taken place was clearly more than an episode of technology transfer in the current meaning of the term. It was the religious, social, and political aspects of Tang China that the Yamato leaders were trying to incorporate into the existing Japanese society. In particular, they were interested in seeing Buddhism accepted as a national religion and in adopting a more effective means of government to consolidate and extend their rule over a nation still dominated by clans. Whatever higher forms of industrial arts were introduced from China were essentially incidental by-products of the broad scheme of upgrading Japan's native culture. Yet, as a result of more than two centuries of cultural borrowing, the country developed a tradition of assimilating superior alien culture, a tradition of being willing to learn from overseas. It was a national asset that proved valuable for Japan's modernization efforts in later periods.

After the Meiji Restoration —— It was the technological superiority displayed by Western military might in the form of the steam-powered KUROFUNE ("black ships") and their overpowering cannons in the mid-19th century that demonstrated to the Japanese how backward they were in technology and that compelled them to embark upon an all-out national effort to learn from abroad. Fearful of the Western colonialism then rampant, the Meiji government made a policy of not allowing the participation of foreign equity capital in either existing industries (such as coal and copper mines) or newly established ventures (such as railroads), despite the enormous need for capital funds. Even debt capital borrowing from abroad was kept to an absolute minimum.

The mode of transfer initially emphasized was a combination of human contact and the importation of machinery and equipment. The first of these took two routes: the employment of Western experts as on-site instructors to train Japanese technicians and the overseas study program for government officials and students. Through these routes the government concentrated on the training and development of indigenous technical manpower during the first 15 years of the Meiji period (1868–1912).

A large number of foreign experts were hired by the various ministries of the government and paid high salaries. These "hired teachers" were intended to train the Japanese in such key industrial activities as the construction and management of railroads, telegraphic communication, shipyards, the mint, spinning mills, iron works, Western-style office buildings, and other institutions then considered the essence of modernization. The top monthly salaries paid to foreigners reportedly reached ¥2,000 for a railroad manager and ¥1,250 for a chief construction engineer, while the Japanese prime minister's salary was only ¥800 a month. The salaries were so high that when employment of foreigners peaked in 1877, the Ministry of Industrial Affairs, for example, had to spend as much as two-thirds of its entire budget on its foreigners' payroll. This state of affairs prompted the Council of State in the following year to request that the ministry curtail its foreigners' payroll by expediting their resignations. The high cost of employing foreign experts was apparently a strong incentive for the government to train Japanese operatives as quickly as possible so that they could take over foreigners' positions. The Japanese proved to be quick learners. For example, a silk mill built by the government in Tomioka in 1872 with the help of a French company was able to dismiss its foreign experts in three years. See FOREIGN EMPLOYEES OF THE MEIJI PERIOD.

In addition to providing on-the-job training at home under foreign tutelage, the government sent a large number of officials and students to study in Europe and the United States. Upon their return home, the students trained overseas soon replaced foreigners at factories and in colleges. It was this determined emphasis on manpower development at the very outset of industrialization that eventually made it possible for Japan to continue to absorb and duplicate advanced technology autonomously, mainly through the acquisition of technical literature, machinery and equipment, and licenses—that is, in "unbundled" form.

Much later on, direct investment by foreign companies was also permitted as a vehicle for technology transfer in setting up the new growth industries that mushroomed in the early decades of the 20th century, industries such as electric machinery and apparatus, automobiles, tires and other rubber products, and glass products. For example, TŌSHIBA CORPORATION was originally set up in partnership with General Electric; MITSUBISHI ELECTRIC CORPORATION with Westinghouse; FUJI ELECTRIC CO, LTD, with Siemens; Nihon Victor with RCA Victor; SUMITOMO RUBBER INDUSTRIES, LTD, with Dunlop, and so forth. Up till the mid-1930s Japan's automobile industry was merely an assembly industry of parts imported by local subsidiaries of Ford and General Motors. But the government encouraged the "naturalization" of these enterprises as soon as the Japanese gained the necessary management and technical expertise, and foreign ownership subsequently declined or was completely withdrawn.

Postwar Experience —— On the eve of World War II the general level of Japan's industrial skills was still far below that of the West. Japan's isolation and defeat in the war, however, left the nation's industry out of touch with the pools of new scientific knowledge and technical skills rapidly accumulated by the Allied Western powers during and immediately after the war. Consequently, a huge technological gap had opened by the time the OCCUPATION formally ended in 1952.

To promote orderly inflows of foreign capital and technology under close supervision by the government, the Foreign Investment Law was passed in 1950, and the FOREIGN INVESTMENT COUNCIL, an administrative organ to screen technology imports, was set up in 1952. The law also specified that a list of desirable technologies be made public. The first such list, issued in 1950, covered only those technologies that were considered essential to improve the quality and efficiency of existing industries. But the second list, issued in 1959, reflected a further effort to introduce more sophisticated new industries such as jet aircraft and electronics products and to raise productivity through automated production processes. As a result of industry's nearly total dependence on advanced foreign technologies, the government was able to exercise effective guidance in directing industrial transformations by its regulatory authority over technology imports (see FOREIGN EXCHANGE CONTROL). Initially, Western manufacturers, notably American companies, did not show much interest in setting up plants in Japan's war-devastated economy, whose future looked so uncertain; their attention was focused much more on quickly recovering European economies and the Common Market that soon emerged. Thus, licensing agreements became the primary conduit for technology transfer in the postwar period.

Technology imports into Japan are officially classified into two types. Class A comprises those contracts that have an effective life of more than one year, with the payment of royalties guaranteed in foreign currency. Class B, on the other hand, covers those contracts that call for royalty payments in Japanese yen or that have an effective life of less than a year. The latter normally includes incidental arrangements such as an invitation to foreign engineers or the acquisiton of drawings. The use of a patent or a brand name or the transfer of major know-how necessitates a contract in class A because of the transaction's long-term nature. Over the first 28 years after the technology import program was introduced, Japan concluded more than 21,000 category-A contracts and 10,000 class-B contracts.

As was true after the Meiji Restoration, Japan has benefited throughout the postwar period from the liberal policies of the Western countries, particularly the United States, on technology outflow and trade. In the 1950s there was initially some resistance, notably among European manufacturers, to imparting technical knowledge to the Japanese for fear of potential competition. Yet the availability of alternative sources of technology and rapid technological progress in the United States made them realize the futility of such an attitude, so that eventually the Europeans, too, became willing suppliers. The United States is the major supplier of technology to Japan, accounting in recent years for about half the total number of technology contracts.

In contrast to the Meiji experience, in which the Japanese had to develop basic industrial knowledge from the ground level, in the postwar period they needed only minimum personal guidance from Western suppliers to adopt advanced technologies and to operate imported capital equipment. Their own wartime research efforts were no doubt helpful in this respect: they not only knew their technical deficiencies (and hence which technologies to import), but also were able to make the necessary adaptations. In most cases they simply bought the rights to use patented or unpatented techniques and acquired with them only a minimum of incidental know-how. The Japanese worked out details themselves in adapting techniques to profitable uses. In other words, they had a well-developed capacity to absorb foreign technologies in an "unbundled" manner.

Reminiscent of envoys to Tang China in early Japan and the envoys to the West in the Meiji period were the many study groups of businessmen and technical experts dispatched to the United States and Europe to gain firsthand information about the operations of modern plants and the markets which the Japanese strove to capture for their exports. The bulk of technologies the Japanese purchased was actually not in the diffusion stage of proven industrial techniques. Rather they were technologies about to be innovated or commercialized. For example, approximately 62 percent of imported technology during the period of 1950–68 was said to be still in uncommercialized stages of development and therefore required further adaptive R & D. In fact, one official survey made in 1962 showed that about one-third of the R & D expenditures of Japanese firms was devoted to "processing" imported technologies.

With the gradual liberalization of direct FOREIGN INVESTMENT IN JAPAN, a large number of foreign subsidiaries and joint ventures have been established. Yet the role of direct investment as a vehicle of technology transfer has been, on the whole, less important than that of licensing agreements. In the first place, the government lifted restrictions only gradually as particular domestic sectors attained international competitiveness; hence there was not much need for one-sided dependence on foreign technology. It is true, however, that in some instances, such as the case of IBM, direct investment was permitted as an exception because of the unwillingness of foreign firms to license the particular type of technology desired in Japan.

Both adaptive and original research activities led the Japanese to many improvements on imported technology, new technological breakthroughs, and their own innovations. Consequently Japan is now emerging as a leading exporter of technology, particularly to less developed countries. About 40 percent of the royalties and fees Japan receives from its technology exports is paid by Asian countries, 25 percent by Europe, and 15 percent by North America (mostly by the United States). The advanced West is the major customer of Japan's newest and most sophisticated technologies, sold mainly under licensing agreements (but also now increasingly "transplanted" through Japanese direct foreign investment), whereas the developing countries are the recipients of relatively standardized technologies transferred by way of manufacturing ventures.

So far as the balance on new technology contracts is concerned, Japan has been a net technology exporter since 1972, although the overall balance, if all existing old contracts are included, still makes Japan a country with a large deficit in technology trade. Even in this latter type of balance sheet, however, some industrial sectors, such as iron and steel, textiles, nonferrous metals, and construction, have recently become "surplus" sectors. See also RESEARCH AND DEVELOPMENT; TECHNOLOGICAL DEVELOPMENT; TENKAN NŌRYOKU; MINISTRY OF INTERNATIONAL TRADE AND INDUSTRY; MULTINATIONAL ENTERPRISES.

📖 ——Hugh Borton, *Japan's Modern Century* (1970). Koichi Emi, "Economic Development and Educational Investment in the Meiji Era," in UNESCO, *Readings in the Economics of Education* (1968). Jūkagaku Kōgyō Tsūshinsha, *Kaigai tōshi gijutsu yushutsu yōran* (1970).   OZAWA Terutomo

Tedorigawa

River in southern Ishikawa Prefecture, central Honshū; originating in Hakusan, the highest peak in the Hakusan National Park, and flowing north into the Sea of Japan. Numerous hot springs are located on its middle reaches. The water is utilized for irrigation and electric power. Length: 73 km (45 mi).

Teganuma

Marsh in the northwestern part of Chiba Prefecture, central Honshū. Located within Imba–Teganuma Prefectural Natural Park. This nar-row swamp running east to west was originally an inlet which later was obturated by deposits of the river Tonegawa. Land reclamation attempts were unsuccessful during the Edo period (1600–1868), but a large-scale government project initiated in 1946 was successfully completed in 1968. Famous for duck hunting, it is also a popular fishing spot with catches including carp and eels. Area before land reclamation: 10 sq km (3.9 sq mi); present area: 3.7 sq km (1.4 sq mi); depth: 2.9 m (9.5 ft).

Teigin Incident

(Teigin Jiken). Mass murder and robbery at a branch of the Teikoku Ginkō (Imperial Bank; abbreviated Teigin) in Tōkyō on 26 January 1948. A man posing as a public health official announced an outbreak of dysentery in the neighborhood and induced the bank's employees to drink an "antidote" containing cyanide. Twelve people died and about ¥160,000 was stolen. Seven months later, the police arrested Hirasawa Sadamichi (b 1892), an artist. On the strength of a confession, which he later repudiated, Hirasawa was convicted and sentenced to death in each of two lengthy trials; the sentence was upheld by the Supreme Court in 1955. The use of a confession as evidence in a capital case, however, stirred public criticism of obsolete criminal procedures and of capital punishment itself. Because of incessant appeals, Hirasawa, both mentally and physically ill, remains alive as of 1982.

Teijin Incident

(Teijin Jiken). Scandal of the 1930s involving the sale of shares in TEIJIN, LTD, a rayon manufacturer. Charges of official collusion and corruption caused the fall of the SAITŌ MAKOTO cabinet in 1934.

Upon declaring bankruptcy in 1927, the SUZUKI SHŌTEN trading company was obliged to give to its creditor, the Bank of Taiwan, more than 220,000 shares of stock in Teijin, Ltd. The bank was to sell the stock at intervals over the next 10 years to repay its own debts to the Bank of Japan. At one such sale, in June 1933, the Banchōkai, a group of young financiers including SHŌRIKI MATSUTARŌ and KOBAYASHI ATARU, purchased 100,000 shares of Teijin stock at ¥125 apiece. They had eyed with interest the promising prospects of rayon manufacture, they said, and wished to participate in Teijin's management. When by year's end the value of Teijin stock had risen to nearly ¥200 per share, the Banchōkai was widely suspected of having manipulated the stock market. Newspaper exposés and official reports called for the indictment of those involved. At that point, certain right-wing officials in the Ministry of Justice, hoping to replace the Saitō cabinet with a less moderate one under their former ministry head HIRANUMA KIICHIRŌ, claimed that cabinet ministers, high officials of the Ministry of Finance, and directors of the Bank of Taiwan had conspired to allow the Banchōkai to buy the Teijin shares at an artificially low price in return for Teijin shares and cash. In April and May 1934 the government arrested the vice-minister of finance, the president of Teijin, and a director of the Bank of Taiwan. Learning that certain cabinet ministers would soon be arrested as well, Saitō dissolved his cabinet on 3 July; he was replaced, however, not by Hiranuma but by another moderate, Admiral OKADA KEISUKE.

Eventually, 16 men were charged with corruption, including the former minister of commerce Nakajima Kumakichi (1873–1960) and the former minister of railways MITSUCHI CHŪZŌ. During the trial, 12 defendants who had admitted their guilt at the preliminary hearing retracted their statements, claiming that the public prosecutors had forced them to confess. Diet members decried this violation of the defendants' rights. In December 1937, after two and a half years of sessions, the court declared the stock transaction regular and the defendants blameless. However, since the government failed to prosecute the Justice Ministry officials who had brought the charges of malfeasance, the public was left with an impression of corruption in both the bureaucracy and financial circles.

📖 ——Aritake Shūji, *Shōwa ōkurashō gaishi*, vol 1 (1967). Wagatsuma Sakae et al, ed, *Nihon seiji saiban shi roku*, vol 4: Shōwa zen (1970).   MATSUO Takayoshi

Teijin, Ltd

A textile company manufacturing synthetic fibers, plastics, films, and pharmaceuticals, Teijin, Ltd, was established in 1918 as the Teikoku Jinzō Kenshi Co under the leadership of KANEKO NAOKICHI. It has the longest history in Japan as a synthetic fiber maker. It expanded its operations by constructing plants in Hiroshima in 1921, Iwakuni in 1927, and Mihara in 1935. It was Japan's leading rayon manufacturer for many years, but has stopped production of this textile for the present. In 1957 the company acquired technology on polyester fibers from the United Kingdom to consolidate its position as Japan's top manufacturer of this product. It has numerous overseas incorporated companies, and the volume of its investments abroad ranks at the top in the industry. It has 17 joint venture companies overseas with offices in New York, São Paulo, Düsseldorf, London, Singapore, Hong Kong, and Athens. Future plans call for the diversification of its lines of business, centering on films and pharmaceuticals. Sales for the fiscal year ending March 1982 totaled ¥460.9 billion (US $1.9 billion), with 56 percent derived from polyester fibers, 27 percent from chemicals, 13 percent from nylon, and 4 percent from other sources; the export ratio was 24 percent. The company was capitalized at ¥36.6 billion (US $152 million) in the same year. Corporate headquarters are located in Ōsaka and Tōkyō.

Teiki

(Record of the Emperors). A record of the imperial succession from the most ancient times; together with the KYŪJI, probably committed to writing sometime in the 6th century; now lost. The Teiki is said to have been a primary source for Japan's earliest histories, KOJIKI (712) and NIHON SHOKI (720), and for JŌGŪ SHŌTOKU HŌŌTEI SETSU, a biography of Prince SHŌTOKU. Its original form and scope are unknown, but it is thought to have included information on imperial genealogy, palaces, tombs, and the like. See also TENNŌKI AND KOKKI.

G. Cameron HURST III

Teikin ōrai

(Household-Precept Letter Writer). One of the best-known examples of a genre called ŌRAIMONO, i.e., collections of models for letter writing. Believed to have been written by GEN'E (1279–1350), a Buddhist priest of the TENDAI SECT. A letter and a reply are included for each month, from the first lunar month to the 12th, with one extra letter for the eighth intercalary month. The model letters deal with social affairs of the higher *samurai* class in the early years of the Muromachi period (1333–1568). The sentences are typical of SŌRŌBUN (the epistolary style). This book brought about the standardization of correspondence forms, and it was used for about 400 years to the end of the Edo period (1600–1868).

Gisaburō N. KIYOSE

Teikoku Gikai → Imperial Diet

Teikoku Nōkai

(Imperial Agricultural Association). Central organization for the agricultural associations (*nōkai*) that had been formed separately throughout the country from about 1880 onward for the purpose of improving agriculture; established in November 1910 with prefectural and county heads serving as regional officers, it provided guidance to individual agricultural associations, made recommendations to the government, conducted research and surveys in agriculture, and facilitated the sale of farm products. In September 1943, under the government's wartime agricultural control policy, it was absorbed by the Chūō Nōgyōkai (Central Agricultural Association).

Teikoku Oil Co, Ltd

(Teikoku Sekiyu). The largest domestic oil and gas producer in Japan. It was established as a public company in 1941 under the Teikoku Oil Company Law to provide a stable supply of oil under wartime conditions and also to explore oil fields and increase production. It took over the domestic oil wells and drilling equipment of Japan's private oil companies and carried out a unified development of domestic oil fields as well as oil fields in Southeast Asia. With the repeal of the law in 1950, it became a private company, engaged in the exploration and development of oil fields along the coast of the Sea of Japan as well as on continental shelf areas. Its oil drilling technology, which it developed on its own, is highly regarded. It has discovered large amounts of natural gas in Niigata Prefecture, and natural gas now constitutes its main line of business. The company is also active in the exploration of overseas oil fields. In 1964 it established a subsidiary in Malaysia and followed this

with exploration of oil fields in Zaire, Indonesia, Oman, Egypt, and elsewhere. It has a drilling area in the Sea of Japan measuring 350,000 square kilometers (135,000 sq mi), and is conducting exploratory drilling on continental shelf areas within Japan's territorial waters. It not only sells natural gas directly to enterprises but also provides city gas to gas companies. After refining, its crude oil is sold through KYŌDŌ OIL CO, LTD. Annual sales for 1981 totaled ¥45.5 billion (US $207.8 million), of which natural gas accounted for 49 percent, oil products 48 percent, and crude oil 3 percent. The company was capitalized at ¥10 billion (US $45.7 million) in the same year. Corporate headquarters are located in Tōkyō.

Teikokutō

(Imperial Party). Progovernment political party. Founded in July 1899 by former members of the KOKUMIN KYŌKAI, the Teikokutō provided support in the House of Representatives for programs, such as expanded armaments production, favored by the ruling oligarchy and bureaucracy. Led by Diet representatives from Kumamoto Prefecture, the party won the support of former independents and Yamaguchi Prefecture representatives, but it never held more than 20 seats. The defection of Motoda Hajime (1858–1938) and his faction to the RIKKEN SEIYŪKAI in 1900 ended all hope of expanding the Teikokutō, and in December 1905 it joined the Kōshin Kurabu and other groups to form the Daidō Kurabu. See also POLITICAL PARTIES.

Teikoku Zaigō Gunjinkai → Imperial Military Reservists' Association

teinensei

(age limit system). System of employment which designates ages for compulsory retirement. Promulgated from about the time of World War I, the age limit system now plays an important role in Japan's system of promotion through seniority.

The most common compulsory retirement age is 55. Many small- and medium-size enterprises, however, have either higher compulsory retirement ages or have no compulsory retirement regulations at all. Although no compulsory retirement regulations are set for public servants, they usually leave office when they reach the age of 60. At retirement, workers are paid allowances calculated from their basic monthly wages multiplied by the number of their years of service.

Because the Japanese average life expectancy was comparatively low before World War II, the compulsory retirement age of 55 was appropriate. Since World War II, however, the average life expectancy of the Japanese has increased significantly. As a result, retirees at the age of 55 now face a variety of serious postretirement problems. Finding new jobs is extremely difficult, except for those workers in administrative posts who are assured of other jobs in affiliated companies. In many cases, workers must accept lower wages in exchange for extensions of compulsory retirement ages. On their part, corporations are faced with the problem of sharply growing labor costs. The age limit system, along with the career-long employment system, has been changing gradually. See also RETIREMENT; EMPLOYMENT SYSTEM, MODERN; AMAKUDARI.

YAMADA Makiko

Teisan

Company producing oxygen, nitrogen, and other industrial gases. It was established in 1930. Among its other products are oxygen-welding equipment, low temperature equipment, deep-sea diving equipment, and rapid freezing systems for blood. It is also a major manufacturer of large-scale plants. It has an overseas incorporated company in South Korea. Annual sales for 1981 totaled ¥43.9 billion (US $200.5 million), and the company was capitalized at ¥3.5 billion (US $16 million) In the same year L'Air Liquide S.A. of France held 64 percent of its capital and also provided technical assistance. The head offices are in Tōkyō and Kōbe.

Tei Seikō → Zheng Chenggong (Cheng Ch'eng-kung)

Teito Rapid Transit Authority

(Teito Kōsokudo Kōtsū Eidan). A public enterprise established in 1941 with capital furnished by the Tōkyō Metropolitan Government and JAPANESE NATIONAL RAILWAYS to construct and operate subway lines in Tōkyō and adjacent areas. The first subway line in Tōkyō was opened in 1927 between Asakusa and Ueno. It was constructed by a subsidiary of the TŌBU RAILWAY CO, LTD. The second line, constructed by a subsidiary of the TŌKYŪ CORPORATION, was opened in 1939 between Shibuya and Shimbashi. The Edo Rapid Transit Authority began its operations by acquiring these two lines as well as the rights to operate the Keihin Subway Co. In 1981 the authority operated a total of seven lines—the Ginza, Marunouchi, Hibiya, Tōzai, Yūrakuchō, Chiyoda, and Hanzōmon lines, with a total length of 131.8 kilometers (82 mi). In January 1981 these lines carried an average of 4,562,000 passengers daily. Although the authority is a public enterprise, it differs from other public corporations in that its capital includes no national government funds, and it is treated legally as a private railway company. *HIRATA Masami*

Teizambori

Canal in central Miyagi Prefecture, northern Honshū. This landlocked canal runs parallel to the coast of Sendai Bay from the city of Shiogama to near the mouth of the river Abukumagawa. It is said to have been constructed in the beginning of the 17th century by order of Date Masamune, the lord of the Sendai domain, for transporting rice grown in the fief. It is no longer in use. Length: 36 km (22 mi).

Tejima Seiichi (1849–1918)

Educator who worked for the establishment of modern technical education in Japan. Born in the Numazu domain (now part of Shizuoka Prefecture). From 1870 to 1874 he studied educational practices throughout the United States and England. After returning to Japan he served as dean of students of the Tōkyō Kaisei Gakkō (a predecessor of Tōkyō University) and curator of the Tōkyō Kyōiku Hakubutsukan (now National Science Museum), devoting much effort to spreading science education in Japan. He later became president of Tōkyō Kōgyō Gakkō (now Tōkyō Institute of Technology) and experimented with practical training in technical education. He also promoted work-study programs, participated in the administration of both national and international expositions, and contributed to the promotion of industry and the development of social education. *KURAUCHI Shirō*

Tekijuku → Ogata Kōan

tekkō

Coverings for the back of the hand and wrist to protect them from injury, cold, and sunburn; traditionally used by peddlers and travelers, as well as by those who worked long hours outdoors. Today they are worn only by some farmers. They can be made of leather or cloth. The section covering the back of the hand is cut in a triangle or semi-circle and the part going over the wrist is square or cylindrical. *MIYAMOTO Mizuo*

telecommunications systems

(*tsūshin seido*). Telegraph and telephone services were established in Japan in the late 19th century. Relying initially on the advanced technology and equipment of Europe and the United States, Japan soon raised the level of its own technology and the size of its telecommunications networks. Telecommunications facilities deteriorated seriously during World War II, but their reconstruction was rapid after the war. The NIPPON TELEGRAPH AND TELEPHONE PUBLIC CORPORATION (NTT; Nihon Denshin Denwa Kōsha) carried out a series of five five-year plans, the first one starting in 1953, and achieved completion of a nationwide automatic telephone dialing system in 1978 and elimination of its backlog of telephone orders in 1977. International telecommunications, under the aegis of KOKUSAI DENSHIN DENWA CO, LTD (KDD), also increased. Since its inauguration NTT has actively promoted technological development in all fields of telecommunications, from telephone sets to switching equipment and transmission systems. Efforts are being made toward the development and introduction of nontelephone services in pursuit of digitalization of telecommunications networks, which can be combined in the future into a single integrated services digital network (ISDN).

History——Japan's age of modern telecommunications began in 1854 when Commodore Matthew PERRY, who had come to Japan seeking to conclude a treaty of friendship, presented the Tokugawa shogunate with a Morse telegraph apparatus. In 1868, the Meiji government leaders, who had come to power as a result of the MEIJI RESTORATION of that same year, quickly decided to make the establishment of telegraph service one of their top policy priorities. One year later a telegraph service between Tōkyō and Yokohama was already being provided to the general public. Subsequently, the telegraph service was rapidly expanded. In 1873 telegraph service was opened between Tōkyō and Nagasaki, and international service between Tōkyō and Europe was made possible by means of the submarine cable laid two years previously between Nagasaki and Shanghai. A nationwide telegraph network was completed by 1878.

The telephone was introduced into Japan in 1877, only one year after its invention in the United States. The first general public telephone service was provided in 1890. In that year services were inaugurated in both Tōkyō and Yokohama. It was some years before the public recognized the importance of having a telephone. With modernization of the economy, the demand for telephone service grew.

The TŌKYŌ EARTHQUAKE OF 1923, which registered 7.9 on the Richter scale, caused extensive damage to telephone and telegraph facilities in both Tōkyō and Yokohama. In reconstructing these facilities, the government introduced automatic switching equipment. It selected two types of step-by-step system: the Strowger type (A-type) automatic switching system (based on Anglo-American technology) was adopted for Tōkyō, and the Siemens Halske (H-type) automatic switching system (based on German technology) was adopted for Yokohama. The Siemens Halske type was later introduced in Ōsaka, Kōbe, Fukuoka, and Kita Kyūshū, and the Strowger type in all other parts of Japan. Telephone and telegraph services in Japan were established by importing advanced technology and equipment from Europe and the United States, but within a short time, Japan raised the level of its technology and the size of its telecommunications networks. Japan began to manufacture its own telephone sets and switching equipment and developed new systems, such as the nonloaded cable carrier transmission system (1937) and the VHF multichannel telephone system (1940). The number of telephone subscribers reached a peak of 1,080,000 at the end of fiscal 1943, but decreased sharply to less than 470,000 at the end of World War II as a result of war damage.

Up until the end of World War II, domestic telephone and telegraph services were operated entirely by the government. Both government and private enterprise were involved in international communication activities. The private Nippon Radio Telegraph Company, Ltd, was established in 1925 to construct and maintain international radiotelegraph facilities, and in 1932 the International Telephone Company, Ltd, was established to construct and maintain international telephone facilities. In 1938 the two companies were merged into the International Telecommunications Company, Ltd, in an attempt to improve the overall effectiveness of both organizations.

In 1948 General Douglas MACARTHUR, who was in command of the Occupation forces, ordered the Japanese government to separate the telephone and telegraph service from the postal services in order to promote the efficiency of each service. As a result, the Communications Ministry was abolished in 1949, and in its place two separate ministries were established, the Ministry of Telecommunications and the Ministry of Postal Service. This governmental reorganization led to the establishment of the Nippon Telegraph and Telephone Public Corporation in 1952. Because of the need to ensure service in the public interest and maintain the technological uniformity of the system and in recognition of the advantages of having such services rendered by a single organization, the government granted NTT the exclusive authority to provide domestic telecommunications services. Thus, a telecommunications organization was created that combined the efficiency of a private corporation with the concept of special management responsibility to the government and public to provide services in the public interest. In 1953 international service functions were separated from NTT, and the Kokusai Denshin Denwa Co, Ltd, was established as the organization with exclusive authority to provide international telecommunication services.

Beginning with its first five-year Telephone and Telegraph Expansion Program in 1953, NTT has planned and carried out a series of five such programs. The first five-year program was primarily designed to reconstruct war-damaged telecommunications facilities. The other programs have been designed primarily to attain NTT's two long-term goals: the elimination of its backlog of applications for new telephone installations and the completion of a 100 percent nationwide automatic dialing system. The former goal was achieved at the end of fiscal 1977 and the latter at the end of fiscal 1978.

Present Status of Services ——— Expenditures on telecommunications services in Japan for fiscal 1977 reached ¥3.4 trillion ($12.7 billion) or about 1.8 percent of the gross national product (GNP).

After the inauguration of NTT in 1952, the number of telephone subscriber lines increased at a high average annual growth rate of 13 to 14 percent. However, with the sustained period of high economic growth in Japan, demand for telephones increased rapidly, and the backlog of unfilled telephone applications reached 2,910,000 in 1970. Subsequently, this figure continued to decrease until it reached 130,000 at the end of fiscal 1978. This latter figure represents recent applications which are normally filled within a month. Today, the waiting period for telephone installation is only a few days in big cities. The number of telephone subscribers at the end of fiscal 1978 was 36,400,000, and the number of telephones was 51,070,000.

Since 1963 the number of telegrams sent has declined steadily. In 1977 the number of telegraphic messages per capita was about 0.3 per year. Today, most telegrams are sent to express congratulations or condolences.

Telex service was inaugurated in Japan in 1956. The number of telex subscriber lines increased from 188 at the time of inauguration to over 73,000 through the succeeding 20-year period. At present, Japan has the third largest number of telex subscribers in the world. The telex network was opened for on-line data communication in 1972, and telex station equipment now also functions as data communications terminal equipment. However, with the diversification of data communications terminal equipment and the diffusion of facsimile, the number of telex subscriber lines has begun to decrease.

With the increase in demand for international telecommunication services and the qualitative improvement and quantitative expansion of an international network to meet demand—which, in turn, has stimulated greater demand—international traffic has increased rapidly since the inauguration of KDD in 1953. This trend has been accompanied by growth in the number of international circuits, which rose from 51 at the end of 1953 to the 1,000 level at the end of 1969 and had topped 3,000 in fiscal 1977.

The Ministry of Construction, all police organizations, the Japan National Railways, electric power companies, and other organizations have their own private telecommunications facilities in Japan, for use in connection with their own activities. At the end of fiscal 1975, those private telecommunications facilities in the aggregate were made up of some 400,000 telephones, 140,000 radio terminals, 2,800 manual switchboards, 300,000 automatic switchboard terminals, 970,000 kilometers (602,370 mi) in total cable length, and 4,960,000 channel kilometers (3,080,160 mi) in fixed radio circuits.

There are two kinds of data communication system in Japan: one is the customer-provided data communication system where private corporations and other organizations install their own computers and terminal equipment, connected by telecommunications circuits leased from NTT, and the other is the NTT-provided data communication systems, where NTT provides computers and terminal equipment connected by telecommunications circuits to provide data communication services to customers. The latter system was formally included as a part of the public telecommunications activities of NTT through the revision of the Public Telecommunications Law in 1971 (prior to which it had been provided for three years on a trial basis). The total number of installations of data communication systems for fiscal 1966 was 20; this increased to 302 in 1969, to 1,168 in 1974 and to 2,749 in 1977.

Television program relay service connecting 99 NHK (Nippon Hōsō Kyōkai; Japan Broadcasting Corporation) stations and 116 commercial television stations is provided by NTT through a network of 64,000 system kilometers (39,744 mi) in total length, using a 4 GHz-band microwave system. To prevent errors caused by manual operation, computer-controlled program switching has been introduced.

With 51,070,000 telephones in use at the end of fiscal 1978, Japan ranked second in the world next to the United States (162,000,000 telephones at the end of 1977) in the number of telephones. Because of the small size of its land area (377,708 sq km; 145,800 sq mi), Japan ranks first in telephone density per unit area among countries having more than one million telephones.

Since most of the telecommunications facilities were constructed after World War II and particularly during the past 15 years, Japan's

modern telecommunications network fully incorporates the world's most up-to-date technologies. The percentage of total switching facilities for each of the three types of switching system—step-by-step system, crossbar system, and electronic switching system—are 10 percent, 80 percent, and 10 percent, respectively.

Since its inauguration, NTT has actively promoted technological development in all fields of telecommunication, from telephone sets to switching equipment and transmission systems. NTT possesses "state-of-the art" technologies in all these fields. Moreover, NTT has become one of the world leaders in the development of new transmission systems such as advanced microwave and coaxial cable systems.

In 1972 NTT introduced the analog C-60M system, which is capable of transmitting 10,800 voice channels per system by means of coaxial cable, and in 1978 NTT introduced the analog SF-E2 microwave system, which is capable of transmitting 3,600 channels per system by using a 5 GHz-band. NTT has also developed enhanced digital systems such as the 20L-P1 system (1976), which uses a 20 GHz-band, and the DC-400M system (1976), which uses coaxial cable. Both of these systems are capable of transmitting 5,760 channels.

Between 1965 and 1978, the number of problems reported per 100 subscriber lines per month sharply decreased from approximately 4 in 1965 to 0.6 in 1978. Such a remarkable improvement in reliability of telephone service owes much to the introduction of new equipment, such as the type-600 telephone set, a new type of set featuring better speech quality and higher reliability, and the adoption of color-coded polyethylene cable, whose sheath and insulator are both made of plastic.

To ensure communication during disasters, in addition to taking such measures as multirouting of major transmission routes and dispersion of long distance transit switches, NTT has prepared large-capacity transportable central office equipment and transportable microwave equipment. Since satellite communication is effective in maintaining communication in cases of large-scale disasters and also in communicating with the many remote islands of Japan, various experiments are now under way using Japan's experimental geostationary satellite, which was launched in 1977. A satellite for practical use is scheduled to be launched in fiscal 1982.

Various mobile radio communication services are provided to meet the public's needs to communicate anytime and anywhere.

Domestic maritime mobile radiotelephone service provides ship-to-shore communications on Japan's coastal waterways. The number of vessels equipped with radiotelephone equipment reached some 9,300 at the end of fiscal 1978 and is expected to increase in the future.

Public telephones are installed on trains of the New Tōkaidō-San'yō Line running from Tōkyō to Fukuoka, a distance of 1,200 kilometers. A passenger can call any point in the major cities along the line, or a passenger can be reached by telephone.

Radio paging service (Pocket Bell), using a 150 MHz-band was inaugurated in 1968 in Tōkyō. To meet rapidly increasing demand for this service, a new system was introduced in 1978. It uses a 250 MHz-band, and a compact, power efficient receiver provides for longer continuous use. This service is provided to some 820,000 subscribers in 53 districts.

An advanced fully automated mobile telephone service was introduced in late 1979, which features a mobile terminal unit possessing a 600-circuit frequency converting function. When a vehicle moves to a different radio zone, this function allows the mobile unit to be converted automatically to the frequency of the new telephone zone without interruption of the conversation. This system will make possible direct dial calls from a moving vehicle to any subscriber throughout the country or vice versa, including those in other moving vehicles.

Future of Telecommunications in Japan ——— The advent of computers has made it possible to process and store a tremendous amount of more complex information than could be handled by conventional means, resulting in what some analysts have called the "post-industrial society" or the "information society," in which the production of information itself plays a more important role than conventional industrial production. Nontelephone services such as data, facsimile, and video communication, are being developed and introduced for both domestic and international use.

In order to meet demands for data communication, leased digital circuits ranging from 50 b/s to 48 kb/s have been provided since 1978. They will be extended to major cities throughout the country within a few years.

For the purpose of realizing a more flexible and more advanced data communication network, a digital data switched (DDX) service was introduced in late 1979. A new rate structure suitable for data transmission has been adopted for DDX, and it is independent of that used for the telephone network. In addition, data communication network architecture is being developed which will allow for maximum compatibility among computers, networks, and terminals.

By adopting easy-to-use and inexpensive terminals and providing a variety of services such as multi-address communication, confidential communication, and communication between different kinds of equipment, a public facsimile communication network capable of storage conversion and redundancy suppression was initiated in 1981 in the Tōkyō (area code 03) and Ōsaka (area code 06) districts.

A one-year test period for the CAPTAIN (Character and Pattern Telephone Access Information Network) system, which permits subscribers to have access to various kinds of information stored in computers and display the desired information on their own home TV receivers in the form of words and charts, was conducted beginning in late 1979. In addition, experiments, which have been carried out for some years, are continuing on the development of the VRS (Video Response System), a more advanced video information system, capable of displaying motion pictures as well as still images.

The VENUS (Valuable and Efficient Network Utility Service) program is now under way, aiming at providing a high-speed and high-quality data and facsimile communication service by connecting domestic networks with data networks in every part of the world.

The present telecommunication networks are constituted on an analog basis and are designed mainly to provide telephone service. However, as a result of both the remarkable development of digital technology which came with the progress made in computer technology, and the rapid advances in semiconductor technology, it is foreseeable that telecommunications networks can be economically constituted on a digital basis. As the information industry develops, the transmission volume of information suitable for digital transmission, such as data communication and facsimile communication, is increasing. Accordingly, digitalization of telecommunications networks will be actively promoted.

For short-distance transmission lines, a 24-channel pulse-code-modulation (PCM) system using ordinary cables has been widely employed since 1965, and for long-distance transmission lines, the introduction of large-capacity PCM system using coaxial cables and microwave links is being promoted. In addition, digital transmission by means of optical fiber cables and domestic satellite communications is also being carefully investigated. Digital exchange systems have already been developed. They will first be applied in transit switches. Although the exact timing of the digitalization of local exchange systems will depend on such factors as the growth of non-telephone services and the circumstances of the existing analog electronic exchange systems, the full-scale introduction of digital exchange systems will probably be made around 1985. Subscriber lines and terminal equipment will be digitalized when broad-band or high-speed subscriber lines are required for video communication services and when optical fiber cables and CODEC (coding and decoding equipment) become more economical.

Individual digital networks, which are now being introduced in stages, will be steadily developed and finally combined into a single integrated services digital network (ISDN). Through the ISDN, an information network system will be completed in which all information can be transmitted, stored, converted and processed in a single network. Terminal connecting equipment is provided at the user's premises to interface between the network and terminals. Subscribers are linked with subscriber communication processing centers through broad-band, high-speed digital transmission paths utilizing optical fiber cables. Communication processing centers will be connected to each other by very-high-speed digital transmission links using optical fiber cables, as well as existing coaxial cables and microwave or communication satellites. Communication processing centers will be capable of sophisticated processing, such as protocol conversion and packeting, along with conventional switching. In addition to carrying out general transactions and time-sharing system (TSS) processing, information processing centers will also provide information services, such as information retrieval and information guide services by using the data banks or data bases which will be set up at the centers.

Because it incorporates every kind of service and has sophisticated network functions, the ISDN will make the exchange and processing of information more efficient for socioeconomic activities and will also permit a home telecommunications center (home terminal) to be installed in individual homes. This center will enable private citizens not only to receive information but also to use it for the purposes of entertainment, education, self-development, and for social activities. Thus the center will be able to meet all of the telecommunication needs of subscribers.

In the ISDN, the signals for different kinds of telephone and nontelephone services can be unified, permitting the amount of exchanged information to be consistently represented in terms of binary digits (bits). Thus, it can be foreseen that different kinds of telecommunication services, which have previously been provided separately under independent rate structures, will be combined in the ISDN by the use of the "bit" as the basic unit of information quantity, enabling the development of a uniform rate structure.

Furthermore, at this stage, as a result of the decrease shown in the proportion of the transmission cost to network cost, charges will become less dependent on distance; and it might even be possible to break away from the conventional rate structure, which is dependent on distance and time, not on the amount of information. Thus, future telecommunication services may overcome time and distance, and will include all functions as transmission, storage, and processing of information through on-line connections with computers. Telecommunications will soon be developed into an information network system, which will ultimately become the nucleus of the information society. See also TELEPHONES.

■ ———Kitahara Yasusada, "Nippon Telegraph and Telephone Public Corporation, 25 Years of Progress," *Japan Telecommunications Review* 20.3 (1978) and "New Telecommunications in the Information Society," *Japan Telecommunications Review* 22.1 (1980). Nihon Denshin Denwa Kōsha, ed, *Denshin denwa jigyō shi* (1962). Nihon Denshin Denwa Kōsha, ed, *Nihon denshin denwa kōsha nijū-gonen shi* (1978). Yūseishō, *Tsūshin hakusho* (annual).

KITAHARA Yasusada

telephones

The telephone was introduced into Japan in 1877, the year after its invention in the United States. It was successfully used in a telephonic communication experiment between the Ministry of Public Works and the Imperial Household Ministry. For some time it was used only for scientific research and by government agencies. The first commercial telephone service for use by the general public was a toll telephone service begun in 1889 between Tōkyō and Atami, and local telephone exchange operations began in 1890 in Tōkyō and Yokohama. These exchanges consisted of simple, manually operated, single-line switchboards and served 179 subscribers in Tōkyō and 45 in Yokohama.

Telephone operations in Japan were administered by the government from the beginning, with service originating in the big cities and expanding rapidly to smaller cities and towns. Early telephones utilized the magneto system in which the user turned a crank on the telephone set to call an operator. In a short time telephone exchanges with multiple switchboards which could handle approximately 2,000 subscribers on one exchange were developed. The common battery telephone, in which the user could signal an operator by lifting the receiver from its hook, was first introduced in Kyōto in 1903. Telephone switchboard systems in the big cities were converted to the common battery type, and exchanges capable of handling as many as 8,000 subscribers on one switching system were built. Toll telephone networks linking the cities were also developed, with long-distance telephone service being initiated between Tōkyō and Ōsaka in 1899; this was a magnetic system service in which users waited their turn in applying to make a call.

During the initial period after the introduction of new equipment systems early in the 20th century, Japan relied on imported telephone sets and switchboards. Gradually, however, its domestic production capability was built up, and original improvements were made so that almost all later expansion used domestically produced equipment. By about 1920 telephone switchboards had been installed in over 70 cities, and the number of subscribers had reached 320,000. If branch exchanges are included, over 3,000 localities were receiving telephone service.

Various types of automatic switchboard system had been put into commercial use in many other countries after their first practical demonstration in the United States in 1893, but they were not introduced into Japan until the reconstruction period following the TŌKYŌ EARTHQUAKE OF 1923. The first loaded circuits were opened to public use on a Tōkyō branch exchange in 1926 with the introduction of the step-by-step system. It was followed by the Strowger (A-type) and the Siemens Halske (H-type) switchboards, which were adopted for use in different regions. Full automation was accomplished first in the big cities. Domestic production of automatic equipment was increased, and production of the A-type switchboard was virtually perfected by 1930, and the H-type, by 1935.

In the early years after the introduction of the telephone in Japan, as in other foreign countries, telephone sets, switchboards, and the circuits linking the switchboards all used bare overhead wires. However, from around 1893 within the cities, and from around 1909 in suburban and rural areas, aerial cables were gradually replaced by underground cables outward from the cities. Multiplex communication technology for long-distance circuits was introduced quickly into Japan, and it advanced to bare wire transmission and loaded cable transmission. Japan took the initiative in 1932 in suggesting and putting into practical use the nonloaded carrier cable transmission system and put considerable effort into the expansion of a long-distance toll network.

The spread of telephone systems was rapid after the introduction of the automatic switchboard, and by 1940 the number of subscriber telephones reached over 1 million, with the installation of manual and automatic direct-distance dialing in the suburban districts of the large cities. The T-type automatic switchboard (the Communications Ministry type), originated in Japan, was put into practical use, and research began on an electron tube system automatic switchboard. However, Japan's city telephone facilities suffered serious damage during World War II.

Recovery of the telephone industry was rapid after the war. In 1952 the NIPPON TELEGRAPH AND TELEPHONE PUBLIC CORPORATION was founded and was soon followed by the KOKUSAI DENSHIN DENWA CO, LTD; these two entities continue to divide control and operation of domestic and international telephone communications. The postwar development of telephone systems has been outstanding. The number of subscribers at the time of the founding of the public telegraph and telephone corporation was 1.55 million. By 1968 it had surpassed 10 million and was over 40 million by 1982. The number of owners of telephones in Japan is second in the world, behind only the United States, and the rate of diffusion versus population places it seventh, with one telephone for every three people. The percentage of automatic telephones was 41 percent in 1952 but reached 100 percent at the beginning of 1979.

Networks —— The high density of subscription telephones—over 40 million as of 1982—is not found in any other country as small as Japan. As the volume of telephone usage has increased, automatic switching systems and direct dialing networks have been installed throughout the country, with complex transmission routes linking them together. In general, subscription exchange areas are formed corresponding to city, town, and village districts; calls made inside the same exchange and to certain other nearby exchanges are designated local calls and those between exchanges are toll calls. There are approximately 4,700 subscription areas throughout Japan; these, according to the demand within each area, are served by one or more local switching stations. In the case of multiple stations, a complex series of switches connects them together, and in larger cities relay stations are added to form a star-shaped network.

Long-distance telephone networks are arranged according to the zone system. The local switching station in a toll network is called the end office. Multiple adjacent exchanges are grouped together into local toll center areas. In like manner, these local toll center areas are grouped into districts and then into regions above that, with offices to oversee their respective operations. There are eight regional centers, such as those in Tōkyō and Ōsaka, throughout the country, and they are linked together by a complex system of circuits.

There are 78 district centers in prefectural capitals or equivalent medium-sized cities, and there are approximately 560 local toll centers. Circuits connecting the various regional centers to their branches, thereby maintaining an integrated relationship, are called nuclear circuits. By means of these interconnecting transmission routes, any combination of toll calls can be formed. However, this nuclear route is bypassed in the case of areas that have a high number of calls passing between them, and oblique circuits connecting them are installed at numerous different points. In addition, in Tōkyō, there is an international center above the regional center in order to handle international calls.

Switchboards. The unique Japanese crossbar system automatic switchboard is in wide use. There are many varieties of switch-

board, from small company-use models with up to 200 circuits, to models for large company use that can accommodate tens of thousands of circuits. There are two varieties of switchboard for exclusive relay use, those with two lines and those with four. In addition, an original electronic switchboard was introduced around 1971 and is already in use in over 200 offices. In this switchboard the control element, resembling a powerful computer, controls the large-scale electromagnetic communication switching network through its accumulated programs.

Transmission routes. Bare wires remain only in remote outlying areas. Multipair cables are in wide use in cities and suburban areas, with coaxial cables being used for long-distance circuits. The use of the latter expanded after the introduction of the 960 channel system in 1956. Following this Japan took the worldwide lead in introducing and putting into practical use the 12 MHz–2,700 channel system in 1960 and the 60 MHz–10,800 channel system in 1971. Since 1954 microwave circuits have also been in use between major population areas. First put into practical use in Japan, they include in addition to the 4 GHz (960 channel) and 6 GHz (1,800 channel) systems, systems with 2 G, 5 G, and 11 GHz bandwidths. Signal modulation systems have also undergone rapid development. In use now are such communication systems as the pulse-code-modulation (PCM) system using digitized and coded signals transmitted by multipair cables. Japan leads the world in practical application of PCM systems using semiextremely high or extremely high frequency signals. Progress has been made in developing methods of light ray communication by the use of optical fibers.

International calls. After 1934 international calls were handled by manual relay with operators at both ends using shortwave radios. The trans-Pacific coaxial cable was opened in 1964 and a semiautomatic system requiring an operator only at the point of origin of a call was adopted. In 1967 satellite circuits were inaugurated, and the following year circuits were placed in operation between Japan and Korea using signals bounced off the ionosphere. Today Japan has direct telephone circuits to over 30 countries, and general subscribers in the United States, England, and some other countries can dial direct to Japan. Installation of equipment making possible direct dialing abroad by general subscribers in Japan is proceeding steadily and is slated for completion by the mid-1980s.

Modern telephone services. The telephone is becoming an ever more convenient apparatus with the formation and diffusion of telephone networks. Some examples of optional services available to subscribers are: speed calling (whereby users can program their telephone to dial frequently called numbers using only one or two digit codes), call waiting, call forwarding, and answering services. Other types of service include pocket bell service and mobile and marine calls.

Other uses of telephone circuitry. Since telephone networks are widely established throughout the country, it has become possible to use lines mainly developed for telephone service for other purposes such as facsimile, television relay, or data transmission. Advances in the integration of communication networks with communication services other than telephone service can be expected in the future. As of 1980 service linking the general subscriber's telephone to a subscriber facsimile service has already begun, practical development of the television-telephone has been completed, and the development of a data switchboard is in an advanced stage. See also TELECOMMUNICATIONS SYSTEMS.

📖 ——Denshi Tsūshin Gakkai, ed, *Denshi tsūshin handobukku* (1978). Nihon Denshin Denwa Kōsha, ed, *Denshin denwa jigyō shi* (1962). Nihon Denshin Denwa Kōsha, ed, *Jidō denwa nijūgonen shi* (1953).

GANBE Eiichi

Television Tōkyō Channel 12, Ltd

(Terebi Tōkyō). A Tōkyō-based commercial television station serving the Kantō (eastern Honshū) area. A relatively new station, it was established in 1962. It began as a station devoted to special programs on technology and science backed by the Japan Science Foundation (Nihon Kagaku Gijutsu Shinkō Zaidan). Management difficulties led to its becoming a shareholding company in 1972. It later entered into a joint capital venture with the NIHON KEIZAI SHIMBUN, a major economic newspaper, and became a general programming station. Because of its relatively recent establishment and lack of network affiliation, broadcast operations are limited to the immediate Tōkyō area. Feature programs on the economy and developments in the financial world and television shows imported from the United States make up much of its broadcast programming.

SUDŌ Haruo

temari

(literally, "handball"). A small ball fashioned from cloth wound about with brightly colored thread. It is used in playing a kind of handball, a variant of KEMARI (kickball), which had been introduced from China around the 7th century. Originally used in a tossing game like *otedama* (see BEANBAG), from the 17th century on it was bounced against the hard surface of the floor. Rubber balls *(gomu mari)* appeared in the 1880s. Ball-bouncing games are usually played to the accompaniment of rhythmic songs known as *temari uta*.　　　　　　　　　　　　　　　　　　　SAITŌ Ryōsuke

tembimbō

(carrying poles). Wooden poles used to transport heavy loads, particularly liquids in pots or barrels, or salable goods. Loads of equal weight are suspended from the ends of a pole that is borne over one shoulder or across both shoulders and steadied with the hands. The poles are flat and flexible and normally measure 1.8 meters (5.9 ft) in length. They are rarely seen today.

tembu

(heavenly beings; Skt: *deva*). The fourth-ranking category in Japanese Buddhist iconography, after NYORAI (Buddha), *bosatsu* (BODHISATTVA), and MYŌŌ (kings of light or wisdom). The category of *tembu* comprises miscellaneous deities adopted from the Hindu pantheon into the Buddhist tradition. Some acquired indigenous features in China or in Japan; some are represented as explicitly feminine in contrast to the other iconographic categories (which transcend sex distinction); and some are animals deified. The best known types of *deva* images are as follows: (1) Bonten (Skt: Brahmā) and Taishakuten (Skt: Indra), examples of which are found in the Sangatsudō at the temple TŌDAIJI and the temples of TŌSHŌDAIJI and TŌJI; (2) Niō or Kongōrikishi (Skt: Vajrapāni), for example those at the *nandaimon* (great south gate) and Sangatsudō at Tōdaiji; (3) the Shitennō, or Four Heavenly Kings, i.e., Jikokuten (Skt: Dhṛtarāṣṭra), Zōchōten (Skt: Virūdhaka), Kōmokuten (Skt: Virūpākṣa), and Tamonten or Bishamonten (Skt: Vaiśravaṇa), for example those in the *kondō* at HŌRYŪJI, those at KŌFUKUJI, and those at Tōji; (4) the popular feminine deities Kisshōten or Kichijōten (Skt: Śrīmahādevī), Benzaiten or Benten (Skt: Sarasvatī), and KISHIBOJIN (Skt: Hārītī); and (5) Daikokuten (Skt: Mahākāla, i.e., Śiva), sometimes identified with the native Japanese deity ŌKUNINUSHI NO MIKOTO. Many of these deities have become objects of local cults, especially since the introduction of ESOTERIC BUDDHISM in the 9th century.
　　　　　　　　　　　　　　　　　　　TSUCHIDA Tomoaki

Temiya cave

(Temiya *dōkutsu*). A cave in Temiya Park, the city of Otaru, Hokkaidō, noted for its unusual prehistoric markings. Discovered in 1866, these markings, which cover an area of 1 by 2 meters (3.3 by 6.6 ft), were variously interpreted as Turkic runes or as ancient ideographs. The discovery in 1951 of similar markings in the nearby Fugoppe cave and subsequent surveys have led scholars to believe that the markings are abstract pictographs connected with hunting and fishing and that the cave was used for magical rites by preliterate peoples some 1,500 to 2,000 years ago.　　KITAMURA Bunji

temmangū

Also known as *temmagū*. General term for shrines dedicated to SUGAWARA NO MICHIZANE (845–903), a scholar-statesman who was exiled on false charges to Dazaifu in Kyūshū, where he died unpardoned. Kyōto, the capital, suffered repeated storms and earthquakes after his death. These were interpreted as acts perpetrated by the vengeful ghost (see GORYŌ) of Michizane, and he soon came to be associated with Tenjin, a god of heaven. The term *"temman"* literally means heaven-filling and was used in combination with Tenjin as an appellation for Michizane, who was now deified. His vengeful aspect was soon forgotten, and by the end of the Heian period (794–1185) he had come to be honored as the god of literature. Several centuries later he was also regarded as the god of calligraphy. *Temmangū* are found throughout the country. The head shrines are KITANO SHRINE in the city of Kyōto (constructed in 947) and DAZAIFU SHRINE in Fukuoka Prefecture (constructed in 919).

Temmei Famine

(Temmei no Kikin). A severe famine that affected nearly all of Japan from 1782 to 1787 (Temmei 2–7). Several hundred thousand (estimates vary from 200,000 to 900,000) people died as a result of the famine, which was one of the worst in the Edo period (1600–1868).

In 1782 unseasonable weather resulted in poor crops in northern Honshū, Shikoku, and Kyūshū. The following year Hokkaidō was added to the list of stricken areas when freezing rain in the spring was followed by severe flooding. Northern Honshū was particularly afflicted. The mountain Asamayama near Karuizawa erupted, burying 25 villages and covering a wide area with ash. In 1784, 30 domains in northern Honshū yielded no harvest at all, while more productive areas were producing 40 percent or less of normal yield. Cold winds from 1784 to 1786 continued to destroy crops; poor administration by the central and local governments compounded the difficulties. In many cases taxes already exceeded normal farm capacities, leaving the peasants no reserves of rice against such disasters or even for the next season's planting. Rice prices soared as speculators, often with the connivance of officials, hoarded the meager harvest. The Tokugawa shogunate attempted to meet the crisis by distributing relief food and money and setting up shelters, but these measures were largely ineffectual. The destitute were reduced to foraging for roots, to eating dogs and cats, and, in extreme cases, to cannibalism. Riots (HYAKUSHŌ IKKI; UCHIKOWASHI) broke out in unprecedented scale and numbers. The famine was one of several factors that led to the fall of TANUMA OKITSUGU from control of the shogunate government. See also KYŌHŌ FAMINE; TEMPŌ FAMINE.

Temmon Hokke Rebellion

(Temmon Hokke no Ran). A disturbance in August 1536 (Tembun 5.7; the name of this era can also be pronounced Temmon, hence the name of the disturbance) by adherents of the NICHIREN SECT (also known as the Hokke or Lotus sect), who held sway in Kyōto from 1532 to 1536 (the so-called Hokke Ikki). By the late 15th century about half the populace of Kyōto were followers of the Nichiren sect, which itself was becoming an armed power, with its Kyōto temples fortified against attacks by rival sects. The people of Kyōto, organized by townsmen (MACHISHŪ) for self-defense and other political activities, acted as the chief support of the military power of the sect. In 1532 the Hokke adherents, alarmed by rumors of an impending attack by supporters of the Ikkō or JŌDO SHIN SECT, enlisted the aid of the *daimyō* Hosokawa Harumoto (1514–63) and destroyed the Yamashina Honganji, the headquarters of the Ikkō sect. During the next four years the Hokke partisans asserted their virtual autonomy within Kyōto, refusing to pay rents and taxes. In 1536 a minor incident renewed the long-standing rivalry between the Hokke sect and the powerful Tendai establishment at Mt. Hiei (Hiezan) to the northeast of Kyōto; with the support of other sects as well as of the erstwhile allies of the Hokke group, the WARRIOR-MONKS of Mt. Hiei invaded Kyōto in force, destroying the 21 main temples of the Nichiren sect and totally destroying the commercial section of the city. The Nichiren adherents fled the city and established new headquarters in Sakai. Although they were allowed to return to rebuild their temples in 1542, they never regained their former political and military power.　　　　　　H. G. LAMONT

Temmu, Emperor (?–686)

The 40th sovereign *(tennō)* in the traditional count (which includes several nonhistorical emperors); reigned 672–686. His father was the 34th sovereign, Emperor Jomei (593–641; r 629–641), and his mother, Jomei's consort *(kōgō)*, twice assumed the throne after her husband's death, first as Empress Kōgyoku, then as Empress SAIMEI. His consort was a daughter of his elder brother, Emperor TENJI; she later reigned as Empress JITŌ. During the period of momentous changes that accompanied the TAIKA REFORM of 645, Prince Ōama, as Temmu was then known, remained in Tenji's shadow, although it is said that at one time he competed with his brother for the affections of NUKATA NO ŌKIMI. He emerged into political affairs after Japan's defeat in the Battle of HAKUSUKINOE in Korea in 663. He resented his brother's designation of Prince Ōtomo (Tenji's son) as his successor, and, following Ōtomo's enthronement as Emperor KŌBUN in 672, he rebelled (see JINSHIN DISTURBANCE). Within six months he gained a victory and thereupon established his capital at ASUKA KIYOMIHARA NO MIYA, where he ascended the throne. His formal enthronement was the following year (673).

Temmu furthered Tenji's administrative reforms, undermining the position of the powerful landed kin groups (UJI) in the provinces and establishing an efficient central bureaucracy. The system of ranks for imperial princes and other members of the court nobility was revised (see COURT RANKS), and the various important families were classified according to lineage and social status by means of eight honorific cognomens (postfixed to their family names) known as YAKUSA NO KABANE. To impress his subjects with the concept of "one emperor, supreme over all" (ikkun bammin), Temmu in 675 abolished the kakibe, groups of workers privately owned by certain wealthy families, and expropriated private lands held by officials and members of the imperial house. He also instituted the JŌRI SYSTEM of land division and the HANDEN SHŪJU SYSTEM of land allotment in order to rationalize land management and taxation, bringing to realization the system of "public lands and public workers" decreed in the Taika Reform.

In 681 Temmu ordered the systematic compilation of civil and penal laws known as the ASUKA KIYOMIHARA CODE, and he commissioned a national history. These undertakings were continued by his successors, the laws forming the basis of the TAIHŌ CODE (701) and the historiographical project producing the KOJIKI (712) and NI-HON SHOKI (720).

Emperor Temmu was the first sovereign who systematically attempted to make Chinese culture and administrative forms a living reality in Japan; he was also perhaps the first Japanese ruler who exercised real national leadership.   KITAMURA Bunji